About the Authors

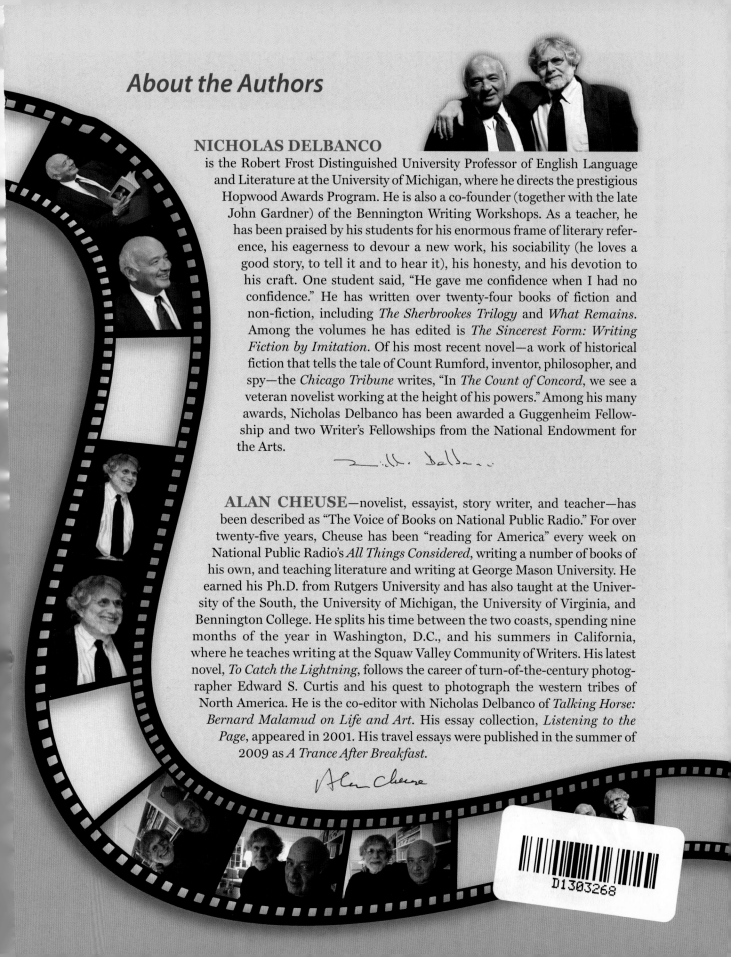

NICHOLAS DELBANCO
is the Robert Frost Distinguished University Professor of English Language and Literature at the University of Michigan, where he directs the prestigious Hopwood Awards Program. He is also a co-founder (together with the late John Gardner) of the Bennington Writing Workshops. As a teacher, he has been praised by his students for his enormous frame of literary reference, his eagerness to devour a new work, his sociability (he loves a good story, to tell it and to hear it), his honesty, and his devotion to his craft. One student said, "He gave me confidence when I had no confidence." He has written over twenty-four books of fiction and non-fiction, including *The Sherbrookes Trilogy* and *What Remains.* Among the volumes he has edited is *The Sincerest Form: Writing Fiction by Imitation.* Of his most recent novel—a work of historical fiction that tells the tale of Count Rumford, inventor, philosopher, and spy—the *Chicago Tribune* writes, "In *The Count of Concord*, we see a veteran novelist working at the height of his powers." Among his many awards, Nicholas Delbanco has been awarded a Guggenheim Fellowship and two Writer's Fellowships from the National Endowment for the Arts.

ALAN CHEUSE—novelist, essayist, story writer, and teacher—has been described as "The Voice of Books on National Public Radio." For over twenty-five years, Cheuse has been "reading for America" every week on National Public Radio's *All Things Considered*, writing a number of books of his own, and teaching literature and writing at George Mason University. He earned his Ph.D. from Rutgers University and has also taught at the University of the South, the University of Michigan, the University of Virginia, and Bennington College. He splits his time between the two coasts, spending nine months of the year in Washington, D.C., and his summers in California, where he teaches writing at the Squaw Valley Community of Writers. His latest novel, *To Catch the Lightning*, follows the career of turn-of-the-century photographer Edward S. Curtis and his quest to photograph the western tribes of North America. He is the co-editor with Nicholas Delbanco of *Talking Horse: Bernard Malamud on Life and Art.* His essay collection, *Listening to the Page*, appeared in 2001. His travel essays were published in the summer of 2009 as *A Trance After Breakfast.*

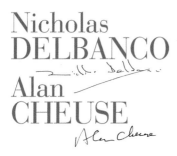
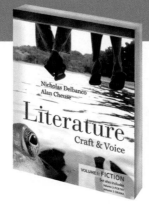
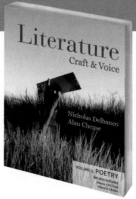
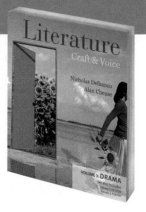

Conversations on Writing

Videos available online at http://www.mhhe.com/delbanco1e

Literature

Drama: Craft and Voice

Nicholas Delbanco
University of Michigan

Alan Cheuse
George Mason University

To Our Students

Mc Graw Hill | Higher Education

Published by McGraw-Hill, an imprint of The McGraw-Hill Companies, Inc., 1221 Avenue of the Americas, New York, NY 10020. Copyright © 2010. All rights reserved. No part of this publication may be reproduced or distributed in any form or by any means, or stored in a database or retrieval system, without the prior written consent of The McGraw-Hill Companies, Inc., including, but not limited to, in any network or other electronic storage or transmission, or broadcast for distance learning.

This book is printed on acid-free paper.

3 4 5 6 7 8 9 0 DOW/DOW 0 9

ISBN: 978-0-07-721422-7
MHID: 0-07-721422-6

Editor in Chief: *Michael Ryan*
Publisher: *Lisa Moore*
Executive Marketing Manager: *Allison Jones*
Editorial Coordinator: *Stephen Sachs*
Production Editor: *Jasmin Tokatlian*
Manuscript Editor: *Susan Norton*
Cover Designer: *Jeanne Schreiber*
Interior Designers: *Jeanne Schreiber and Linda Robertson*
Senior Photo Research Coordinator: *Nora Agbayani*
Lead Media Project Manager: *Ron Nelms*
Production Supervisor: *Louis Swaim*
Composition: *9.25/11.25 Miller Roman by Thompson Type*
Printing: *45# Influence Gloss, R. R. Donnelley & Sons/Willard, OH*

Cover: © (Red Door) Mark Lewis/Getty Images, (Field of Sunflowers) Herbert Kehrer/Zefa/Corbis, (Sunflower) Brand X Pictures/Punchstock, (Woman) Photo of Jasmin Tokatlian courtesy of Miroslav Wiesner.

Credits: The credits section for this book begins on page C-1 and is considered an extension of the copyright page.

Library of Congress Cataloging-in-Publication Data

Delbanco, Nicholas.
    Literature : craft and voice / Nicholas Delbanco, Alan Cheuse.—1st ed.
        p. cm.
    Includes index.
    3 vols. planned.
    ISBN-13: 978-0-07-721422-7 (v. 1 : acid-free paper)
    ISBN-10: 0-07-721422-6 (v. 1 : acid-free paper)   1. Literature.   I. Cheuse, Alan.   II. Title.
    PN45.D457 2009
    800—dc22

2008051003

The Internet addresses listed in the text were accurate at the time of publication. The inclusion of a Web site does not indicate an endorsement by the authors or McGraw-Hill, and McGraw-Hill does not guarantee the accuracy of the information presented at these sites.

Contents
DRAMA

Video interview with the authors available online at www.mhhe.com/delbancopreview

32 Writing about Drama 46

33 Ancient Greek Drama

34 William Shakespeare

35 Modern Drama 284

A HANDBOOK FOR WRITING FROM READING   H-1

1 Critical Approaches to Literature   H-3

It's like a miracle for me every time.

Q&A
A Conversation on Reading Drama
Marian Seldes

Every playwright awakens something in you you didn't know was there.

An Actor's View: Teaching Yourself to Read a Play

You can teach yourself how to read a play. . . . You just read the words the characters say, not worry[ing] too much about who's saying what. . . . When you've read it one way through, you'll have no difficulty in recognizing, Oh, that's the grandmother. Oh, that's . . . the doctor, of course. Oh, that's the beautiful woman . . . because no one else could speak that way.

Being Alone with a Script

When . . . someone sends you a script, you can pick it up whenever you want to, and part of the thrill is that you're alone with it. You're not sharing this experience with anybody else; it's yours. That frees your imagination. Even if the playwright gives a detailed description of where the play takes place or how the characters look, he can't control your mind, and you invent your play. For me, reading a script for the first time is one of the adventures of being in the theater.

Writing in the Margins

I think it's a good idea to write your thoughts down. . . . Write down what interests you. When I was young, you weren't allowed to write in the margin of a book. . . . I write things in the script, the acting script, the acting version of a play that I do. . . . Your opinions are as important as everybody else's—especially when you are in communion with a writer you care about: Write it down.

To see the entire interview with Marian Seldes, go to **www.mhhe.com/ delbanco1e.**

RESEARCH ASSIGNMENT   In her interview, Seldes talks about having a playwright at the staging of a play and indicates the answers to the questions she would ask are "all in the play." How does this influence her reading of a script?

Marian Seldes is one of America's foremost actors, having appeared on Broadway and off-Broadway in plays by Tennessee Williams and Edward Albee, among many others, as well as having played in numerous films and television productions. Her many honors include Obie, Drama Desk, and Tony awards in recognition of her achievements in live American theater as well as induction into the Theater Hall of Fame.

"I remember once being in a play, and it was the day we were going to open, and the director said to us, 'Try to remember what you felt when you first read this play.' And I thought that was such a wonderful thing to say. It wasn't, 'Use everything I've told you up until this moment,' and blah blah blah about the rehearsal. No. It was your reaction, your personal reaction to the play. So if you have a book full of plays, you are adding yourself to it."

Conversation with Marian Seldes, available on video at www.mhhe.com/delbanco1e

A FIRST READING

OF our three principal genres, drama is the one least studied and—in a way—least familiar. You have been exposed to poetry and fiction since you first heard nursery rhymes or fairy tales; you have no doubt read many more books than you've attended plays. But consider how many scripts you've watched enacted in movies and on television screens. The rules of this particular game have been with us since the dawn of Western culture, and there are those who argue—as did William Shakespeare—that "All the world's a stage, and all the men and women merely players." Theater is everywhere around us; we make an "exit" or an "entrance" each time we walk through a door. When you say, "That guy's a character" or "That girl's a prima donna," you're using the language of theater; when you decide what clothes to wear, you're dressing for a role. It's in the way we move and speak, the very air we breathe. When reading drama, you ask yourself many of the same basic questions you ask when watching a movie or TV show: What is all this about? Why is it happening to this person? What does it mean?

The first exposure to a play (as with poetry or fiction) is a crucial one. You will recognize if the play is funny or tragic—comedy and tragedy being two of the fundamental types of drama. Pay attention to your reaction to the story line, the themes that seem to be implied, the way the characters interact, and how you feel about the situation as you read along. A first reading of the script of *Trifles*, for example, reveals a problem—a mystery to be solved—and makes clear the basic elements of the plot. A man is dead; his wife is under suspicion. A neighbor recounts what he found in the Wright house. From his story we hear—secondhand—Mrs. Wright's statement about the circumstances of her husband's death. When reading for the first time, as Edwin Wilson says in another interview in this book, "Let yourself experience your own feelings as you go through . . . a play."

- Read with a pen or pencil in hand.
- Be forthright. Are you enjoying the play? What elements of the play make for enjoyment? Characters? Plot?
- Analyze the action and the motives of the characters. What are they seeking at the beginning of the play?
- Examine the relationship between the characters and the plot. How does what happens grow out of the characters' decisions and actions?
- What is the play's tone? How does the dialogue sound in your ear?

CONTINUED ON PAGE 13

30 Reading & Viewing a Play in its Elements

I DIDN'T hear or see anything; I knocked at the door, and still it was all quiet inside. I knew they must be up, it was past eight o'clock. So I knocked again, and I thought I heard somebody say, "Come in." I wasn't sure, I'm not sure yet, but I opened the door—this door and there in that rocker—sat Mrs. Wright.

—*from* Trifles *by Susan Glaspell*

Susan Glaspell (1876–1948)

Born in Davenport, Iowa, the daughter of a pioneer family, Susan Glaspell graduated from Drake University. She worked as a reporter until she decided to devote her time to fiction writing. Although she wrote nine novels (some of which were best sellers) and many short stories, she is best known for her contribution to American drama. She married George Cook, who encouraged Glaspell to write drama, and in 1916 they co-founded the Provincetown Players, a group of playwrights and actors that performed innovative drama. Glaspell's one-act plays were particularly well received. Among her contributions to the group was the way she encouraged the young Eugene O'Neill, who became one of the most important twentieth-century American dramatists. Glaspell's play *Alison's House* (1930), which is based on Emily Dickinson's life, won the Pulitzer Prize, but her early one-act *Trifles* (1916) is generally considered her finest achievement.

AS YOU READ Ask yourself how many kinds of investigations are under way in this brief play among the five people—the country attorney, the sheriff and his wife, and a neighboring farmer and his wife—who have come to investigate the scene of the death.

TIP

FOR INTERACTIVE READING . . . Note in the text any references to Mrs. Hale's regrets.

Trifles (1916)

CHARACTERS

GEORGE HENDERSON, *county attorney*

HENRY PETERS, *sheriff*

LEWIS HALE, *a neighboring farmer*

MRS. PETERS

MRS. HALE

SCENE: *The kitchen in the now abandoned farmhouse of John Wright, a gloomy kitchen, plainly left without having been put in order—unwashed pans under the sink, a loaf of bread outside the bread-box, a dish-towel on the table—other signs of incompleted work. Door opens rear and enter sheriff followed by* COUNTY ATTORNEY *and* HALE. *The* SHERIFF *and* HALE *are men in middle life, the* COUNTY ATTORNEY *is a young man; all are much bundled up and go at once to the stove. They are followed by the two women—the* SHERIFF's *wife first; she is a slight wiry woman, a thin nervous face.* MRS. HALE *is larger and would ordinarily be called more comfortable looking, but she is disturbed now and looks fearfully about as she enters. The women have come in slowly, and stand close together near the door.*

COUNTY ATTORNEY: *(Rubbing his hands)* This feels good. Come up to the fire, ladies.

MRS. PETERS: *(Takes a step forward and looks around)* I'm not—cold.

5 **SHERIFF:** *(Unbuttoning his overcoat and stepping away from the stove as if to mark the beginning of official business)* Now, Mr. Hale, before we move things about, you explain to Mr. Henderson just what you saw when you came here yesterday morning.

10 **COUNTY ATTORNEY:** By the way, has anything been moved? Are things just as you left them yesterday?

SHERIFF: *(Looking all about)* It's just the same. When it dropped below zero last night I thought I'd better send Frank out this morning to make a fire for us— 15 no use getting pneumonia with a big case on, but I told him not to touch anything except the stove—and you know Frank.

COUNTY ATTORNEY: Somebody should have been left here yesterday.

20 **SHERIFF:** Oh—yesterday. When I had to send Frank to Morris Center for that man who went crazy—I want you to know I had my hands full yesterday. I knew you could get back from Omaha by today and as long as I went over everything here myself—

25 **COUNTY ATTORNEY:** Well, Mr. Hale, tell just what happened when you came here yesterday morning.

HALE: Harry and I had started to town with a load of potatoes. We came along the road from my place and as I got here I said, "I'm going to see if I can't get 30 John Wright to go in with me on a party telephone." I spoke to Wright about it once before and he put me off, saying folks talked too much anyway, and all he asked was peace and quiet—I guess you know about how much he talked himself, but I thought maybe if I went to the house and talked about it before his wife, 35 though I said to Harry that I didn't know as what his wife wanted made much difference to John—

COUNTY ATTORNEY: Let's talk about that later, Mr. Hale. I do want to talk about that, but tell now just what happened when you got to the house. 40

HALE: I didn't hear or see anything; I knocked at the door, and still it was all quiet inside. I knew they must be up, it was past eight o'clock. So I knocked again, and I thought I heard somebody say, "Come in." I wasn't sure, I'm not sure yet, but I opened the 45 door—this door *(jerking a hand backward)* and there in that rocker—*(pointing to it)* sat Mrs. Wright. *(All look at the rocker)*

COUNTY ATTORNEY: What—was she doing?

HALE: She was rockin' back and forth. She had her 50 apron in her hand and was kind of—pleating it.

COUNTY ATTORNEY: And how did she—look?

HALE: Well, she looked queer.

COUNTY ATTORNEY: How do you mean—queer?

HALE: Well, as if she didn't know what she was going 55 to do next. And kind of done up.

COUNTY ATTORNEY: How did she seem to feel about your coming?

HALE: Why, I don't think she minded—one way or other. She didn't pay much attention. I said, "How 60 do, Mrs. Wright, it's cold, ain't it?" And she said, "Is it?"—and went on kind of pleating at her apron. Well, I was surprised; she didn't ask me to come up to the stove, or to set down, but just sat there, not even looking at me, so 65 I said, "I want to see John." And then she—laughed. I guess you would call it a laugh. I thought of Harry and the team outside, so I said a little sharp: "Can't 70 I see John?" "No," she says, kind o' dull like. "Ain't he home?" says I. "Yes," says she, "he's home." "Then why 75 can't I see him?" I asked her, out of patience. "'Cause he's dead," says 80

she. *"Dead?"* says I. She just nodded her head, not getting a bit excited, but rockin' back and forth. "Why—where is he?" says I, not knowing what to
85   say. She just pointed upstairs—like that *(himself pointing to the room above)*. I got up, with the idea of going up there. I walked from there to here—*(pointing)*—then I says, "Why,
90   what did he die of?" "He died of a rope round his neck," says she, and just went on pleatin' at her apron. Well, I went out and called Harry. I thought I might—need help. We went upstairs and there he was—lyin'—

95 **COUNTY ATTORNEY:** I think I'd rather have you go into that upstairs, where you can point it all out. Just go on now with the rest of the story.

  HALE: Well, my first thought was to get that rope off. It looked—*(stops, his face twitches)*—but Harry, he went
100   up to him, and he said, "No, he's dead all right, and we'd better not touch anything." So we went back down stairs. She was still sitting that same way. "Has anybody been notified?" I asked. "No," says she, unconcerned. "Who did this, Mrs. Wright?" said Harry.
105   He said it business-like—and she stopped pleatin' of her apron. "I don't know," she says. "You don't *know?*" says Harry. "No," says she. "Weren't you sleepin' in the bed with him?" says Harry. "Yes," says she, "but I was on the inside." "Somebody slipped a rope round
110   his neck and strangled him and you didn't wake up?" says Harry. "I didn't wake up," she said after him. We may have looked as if we didn't see how that could be, for after a minute she said, "I sleep sound." Harry was going to ask her more questions but I said
115   maybe we ought to let her tell her story first to the coroner, or the sheriff, so Harry went fast as he could to Rivers' place, where there's a telephone.

  COUNTY ATTORNEY: And what did Mrs. Wright do when she knew that you had gone for the coroner?

120 **HALE:** She moved from that chair to this one over here, *(pointing to a small chair in the corner)* and just sat there with her hands held together and looking down. I got a feeling that I ought to make some conversation, so I said I had come in to see if John wanted to
125   put in a telephone, and at that she started to laugh, and then she stopped and looked at me—scared. *(COUNTY ATTORNEY, who has had his notebook out, makes a note)* I dunno, maybe it wasn't scared. I wouldn't like to say it was. Soon Harry got back, and then
130   Dr. Lloyd came, and you, Mr. Peters, and so I guess that's all I know that you don't.

COUNTY ATTORNEY: *(Looking around)* I guess we'll go upstairs first—and then out to the barn and around there. *(To SHERIFF)* You're convinced that there was nothing important here—nothing that would point
135 to any motive?

SHERIFF: Nothing here but kitchen things.

COUNTY ATTORNEY: *(Opens the door of a cupboard closet. Gets up on a chair and looks on a shelf. Pulls his hand away, sticky)* Here's a nice mess. *(The women draw nearer)*
140

MRS. PETERS: Oh, her fruit; it did freeze. *(To COUNTY ATTORNEY)* She worried about that when it turned so cold. She said the fire'd go out and her jars would break.

SHERIFF: Well, can you beat the women! Held for
145 murder and worrying about her preserves.

COUNTY ATTORNEY: *(Setting his lips firmly)* I guess before we are through she may have something more serious than preserves to worry about.

HALE: Well, women are used to worrying over trifles.
150 *(The two women move a little closer together)*

COUNTY ATTORNEY: *(With the gallantry of a young politician)* And yet, for all their worries, what would we do without the ladies? *(The women do not unbend. He goes to the sink, takes a dipperful of water from pail and
155 pouring it into basin, washes his hands. Starts to wipe them on the roller towel, turns it for a cleaner place)* Dirty towels! *(Kicks his foot against pans under the sink)* Not much of a housekeeper, would you say, ladies?

MRS. HALE: *(Stiffly)* There's a great deal of work to be
160 done on a farm.

COUNTY ATTORNEY: *(With conciliation)* To be sure. And yet *(with a little bow to her)* I know there are some Dickson county farmhouses which do not have such roller towels. *(Gives it a pull to expose its full length again)*
165

MRS. HALE: Those towels get dirty awful quick. Men's hands aren't always as clean as they might be.

COUNTY ATTORNEY: Ah, loyal to your sex, I see. But you and Mrs. Wright were neighbors. I suppose you were friends, too.
170

MRS. HALE: *(Shaking her head)* I've not seen much of her of late years. I've not been in this house—it's more than a year.

COUNTY ATTORNEY: And why was that? You didn't like her?
175

MRS. HALE: I liked her all well enough. Farmer's wives have their hands full, Mr. Henderson. And then—

COUNTY ATTORNEY: Yes—?

180 **MRS. HALE:** *(Looking about)* It never seemed a very cheerful place.

COUNTY ATTORNEY: No—it's not cheerful. I shouldn't say she had the homemaking instinct.

MRS. HALE: Well, I don't know as Wright had, either.

185 **COUNTY ATTORNEY:** You mean that they didn't get on very well?

MRS. HALE: No, I don't mean anything. But I don't think a place'd be any cheerfuller for John Wright's being in it.

190 **COUNTY ATTORNEY:** I'd like to talk more of that a little later. I want to get the lay of things upstairs now. *(Moves to stair door, followed by the two men)*

SHERIFF: I suppose anything Mrs. Peters does'll be all right. She was to take in some clothes for her, you know, and a few little things. We left in such a hurry yesterday.

195 **COUNTY ATTORNEY:** Yes, but I would like to see what you take, Mrs. Peters, and keep an eye out for anything that might be of use to us.

MRS. PETERS: Yes, Mr. Henderson. *(The women listen to the men's steps on the stairs, then look about the kitchen)*

200 **MRS. HALE:** I'd hate to have men coming into my kitchen, snooping around and criticizing. *(Arranges pans under sink which the county attorney had shoved out of place)*

205 **MRS. PETERS:** Of course it's no more than their duty.

MRS. HALE: Duty's all right, but I guess that deputy sheriff that came out to make the fire might have got a little of this on. *(Gives roller towel a pull)* Wish I'd thought of that sooner. Seems mean to talk about her for not having things slicked up when she had to come away in such a hurry.

210 **MRS. PETERS:** *(Going to table at side, lifts one end of towel that covers a pan)* She had bread set. *(Stands still)*

215 **MRS. HALE:** *(Her eyes fixed on a loaf of bread outside breadbox. Moves slowly toward it)* She was going to put this in there. *(Picks up loaf, then abruptly drops it. In a manner of returning to familiar things)* It's a shame about her fruit. I wonder if it's all gone. *(Gets up on a chair and looks)* I think there's some here that is all right, Mrs. Peters. Yes—here; *(holding it toward the window)* this is cherries, too. *(Looking again)* I declare I believe that's the only one. *(Gets down, bottle in her hand. Goes to sink and wipes it off on the outside)* She'll feel awful bad after all her hard work in the hot weather. I remember the afternoon I put up my cherries last summer. *(Puts bottle on table. With a sigh starts to sit down in rocking-chair. Before she is seated realizes what chair it is; with a slow look at it, steps back. The chair which she has touched rocks back and forth)*

225

230 **MRS. PETERS:** Well, I must get those things from the front room closet. *(Starts to door left, looks into the other room, steps back)* You coming with me, Mrs. Hale? You could help me carry them. *(Both women go out; reappear, MRS. PETERS carrying a dress and skirt, MRS. HALE following with a pair of shoes)*

235

MRS. PETERS: My, it's cold in there. *(Puts clothes on table, goes up to stove)*

MRS. HALE: *(Holding up skirt and examining it)* Wright was close. I think maybe that's why she kept so much to herself. She didn't even belong to the Ladies Aid. I suppose she felt she couldn't do her part, and then you don't enjoy things when you feel shabby. She used to wear pretty clothes and be lively, when she was Minnie Foster, one of the town girls singing in the choir. But that was—oh, that was thirty years ago. This all you was to take in?

240

245

MRS. PETERS: She said she wanted an apron. Funny thing to want, for there isn't much to get you dirty in jail, goodness knows. But I suppose just to make her feel more natural. She said they was in the top drawer in this cupboard. Yes, here. And then her little shawl that always hung behind the door. *(Looks on stair door)* Yes, here it is.

250

MRS. HALE: *(Abruptly moving toward her)* Mrs. Peters?

MRS. PETERS: Yes, Mrs. Hale?

255

MRS. HALE: Do you think she did it?

MRS. PETERS: *(In a frightened voice)* Oh, I don't know.

MRS. HALE: Well, I don't think she did. Asking for an apron and her little shawl. Worrying about her fruit.

MRS. PETERS: *(Starts to speak, glances up, where footsteps are heard in the room above. In a low voice)* Mr. Peters says it looks bad for her. Mr. Henderson is awful sarcastic in a speech and he'll make fun of her sayin' she didn't wake up.

260

MRS. HALE: Well, I guess John Wright didn't wake when they was slipping that rope under his neck.

265

MRS. PETERS: No, it's strange. It must have been done awful crafty and still. They say it was such a—funny way to kill a man, rigging it all up like that.

270 **MRS. HALE:** That's just what Mr. Hale said. There was a gun in the house. He says that's what he can't understand.

MRS. PETERS: Mr. Henderson said coming out that what was needed for the case was a motive; some-
275 thing to show anger, or—sudden feeling.

MRS. HALE: *(Standing by table)* Well, I don't see any signs of anger around here, but *(puts hand on dish-towel in middle of table, stands looking at table, one half of which is clean, the other half messy)* It's wiped to here. *(Makes*
280 *a move as if to finish work, then turns and looks at loaf of bread beside the bread-box. Drops towel. In that voice of coming back to familiar things)* Wonder how they are finding things upstairs. I hope she had it a little more red-up up there. You know, it seems kind of *sneaking*. Lock-
285 ing her up in town and then coming out here and trying to get her own house to turn against her!

MRS. PETERS: But Mrs. Hale, the law is the law.

MRS. HALE: I spose't is. *(Unbuttoning her coat)* Better loosen up your things, Mrs. Peters. You won't feel
290 them when you go out.

MRS. PETERS: *(Taking off fur tippet, goes to hang it on hook at back of room, stands looking at the under part of the small table)* She was piecing a quilt. *(Brings large sewing basket to table front and they look at the bright pieces)*

295 **MRS. HALE:** It's log cabin pattern. Pretty, isn't it? I wonder if she was goin' to quilt it or just knot it? *(Footsteps have been heard coming down the stairs. The* SHERIFF *enters followed by* HALE *and* HENDERSON*)*

SHERIFF: They wonder if she was going to quilt it or just knot it. *(The men laugh, the women look abashed)*
300

COUNTY ATTORNEY: *(Rubbing his hands over the stove)* Frank's fire didn't do much up there, did it? Well, let's go out to the barn and get that cleared up. *(Exeunt men door rear)*

MRS. HALE: *(Resentfully)* I don't know as there's any-
305 thing so strange, our takin' up our time with little things while we're waiting for them to get the evidence. *(Sits down, smoothing out block with decision)* I don't see as it's anything to laugh about.

MRS. PETERS: *(Apologetically)* Of course they've got aw-
310 ful important things on their minds. *(Pulls up a chair and sits by the table)*

MRS. HALE: *(Examining another block)* Mrs. Peters, look at this one. Here, this is the one she was working on, and look at the sewing! All the rest of it has been
315 so nice and even. And look at this! It's all over the place! Why, it looks as if she didn't know what she was about! *(After she has said this they look at each other, then start to glance back at the door. After an instant* MRS. HALE *has pulled at a knot and ripped the sewing)*
320

MRS. PETERS: Oh, what are you doing, Mrs. Hale?

MRS. HALE: *(Mildly)* Just pulling out a stitch or two that's not sewed very good. *(Threading a needle)* Bad sewing always made me fidgety.

MRS. PETERS: *(Nervously)* I don't think we ought to
325 touch things.

MRS. HALE: I'll just finish up this end. *(Suddenly stopping and leaning forward)* Mrs. Peters?

MRS. PETERS: Yes, Mrs. Hale?

MRS. HALE: What do you suppose she was so nervous
330 about?

MRS. PETERS: Oh—I don't know. I don't know as she was nervous. I sometimes sew awful queer when I'm just tired. *(MRS. HALE starts to say something, looks at her, compresses her lips a little, goes on sewing)* Well,
335 I must get these things wrapped up. They may be through sooner than we think. *(Piling apron and other things up together)* I wonder where I can find a piece of paper, and string.

MRS. HALE: In that cupboard, maybe.
340

MRS. PETERS: *(Looking in cupboard)* Why, here's a birdcage. *(Holds it up)* Did she have a bird, Mrs. Hale?

MRS. HALE: Why, I don't know whether she did or not—I've not been here for so long. There was a man

345 around last year selling canaries cheap, but I don't
know as she took one; maybe she did. She used to
sing real pretty herself.

MRS. PETERS: *(Glancing around)* Seems funny to think
of a bird here. But she must have had one, or why
350 would she have a cage? I wonder what happened to it.

MRS. HALE: I s'pose maybe the cat got it.

MRS. PETERS: No, she didn't have a cat. She's got that
feeling some people have about cats—being afraid of
them. My cat got in her room and she was real upset
355 and asked me to take it out.

MRS. HALE: My sister Bessie was like that. Queer,
ain't it?

MRS. PETERS: *(Examining cage)* Why, look at this door.
It's broke. One hinge is pulled apart.

360 **MRS. HALE:** *(Looking too)* Looks as if someone must
have been rough with it.

MRS. PETERS: Why, yes. *(Puts cage on table)*

MRS. HALE: I wish if they're going to find any evidence
they'd be about it. I don't like this place.

365 **MRS. PETERS:** But I'm awful glad you came with me,
Mrs. Hale. It would be lonesome for me sitting here
alone.

MRS. HALE: It would, wouldn't it? *(Dropping sewing,
voice falling)* But I tell you what I do wish, Mrs. Pe-
370 ters. I wish I had come over sometimes when *she* was
here. I—*(looking around the room)*—wish I had.

MRS. PETERS: But of course you were awful busy, Mrs.
Hale—your house and your children.

MRS. HALE: I could've come. I stayed away because
375 it weren't cheerful—and that's why I ought to have
come. I—I've never liked this place. Maybe because
it's down in a hollow and you don't see the road. I
dunno what it is, but it's a lonesome place and always
was. I wish I had come over to see Minnie Foster
380 sometimes. I can see now— *(shakes her head)*

MRS. PETERS: Well, you mustn't reproach yourself,
Mrs. Hale. Somehow we just don't see how it is with
other folks until—something comes up.

MRS. HALE: Not having children makes less work—
385 but it makes a quiet house, and Wright out to work
all day, and no company when he did come in. Did
you know John Wright, Mrs. Peters?

MRS. PETERS: Not to know him; I've seen him in
town. They say he was a good man.

MRS. HALE: Yes—good; he didn't drink, and kept his
390 word as well as most, I guess, and paid his debts. But
he was a hard man, Mrs. Peters. Just to pass the time
of day with him—*(shivers)* Like a raw wind that gets
to the bone. *(Pauses, her eye falling on the cage)* I should
think she would 'a wanted a bird. But what do you
395 suppose went with it?

MRS. PETERS: I don't know, unless it got sick and
died. *(She reaches over and swings the broken door, swings
it again, both women watch it)*

MRS. HALE: You weren't raised round here, were you?
400 *(MRS. PETERS shakes her head)* You didn't know—her?

MRS. PETERS: Not till they brought her yesterday.

MRS. HALE: She—come to think of it, she was kind of
like a bird herself—real sweet and pretty, but kind
of timid and—fluttery. How—she—did—change.
405 *(Silence; then as if struck by a happy thought and relieved to
get back to everyday things)* Tell you what, Mrs. Peters,
why don't you take the quilt in with you? It might
take up her mind.

MRS. PETERS: Why, I think that's a real nice idea,
410 Mrs. Hale. There couldn't possibly be any objection
to it, could there? Now, just what would I take? I
wonder if her patches are in here—and her things.
(Both look in sewing basket)

MRS. HALE: Here's some red. I expect this has got
415 sewing things in it. *(Brings out a fancy box)* What a
pretty box. Looks like something somebody would
give you. Maybe her scissors are in here. *(Opens box.
Suddenly puts her hand to her nose)* Why—(MRS. PETERS
bends nearer, then turns her face away)* There's some-
420 thing wrapped up in this piece of silk.

MRS. PETERS: Why, this isn't her scissors.

MRS. HALE: *(Lifting the silk)* Oh, Mrs. Peters—it's
(MRS. PETERS *bends closer)*

425   **MRS. PETERS:**   It's the bird.

MRS. HALE: *(Jumping up)* But, Mrs. Peters—look at it! Its neck! Look at its neck! It's all—other side *to*.

MRS. PETERS: Somebody—wrung—its—neck. *(Their eyes meet. A look of growing comprehension, of horror. Steps*
430   *are heard outside.* MRS. HALE *slips box under quilt pieces, and sinks into her chair. Enter* SHERIFF *and* COUNTY ATTORNEY. MRS. PETERS *rises)*

COUNTY ATTORNEY: *(As one turning from serious things to little pleasantries)* Well, ladies, have you decided
435   whether she was going to quilt it or knot it?

MRS. PETERS: We think she was going to—knot it.

COUNTY ATTORNEY: Well, that's interesting, I am sure. *(Looking at bird-cage)* Has the bird flown?

MRS. HALE: *(Piling more quilt pieces over the box)* We
440   think the—cat got it.

COUNTY ATTORNEY: *(Preoccupied)* Is there a cat? *(*MRS. HALE *glances in a quick covert way at* MRS. PETERS*)*

MRS. PETERS: Well, not *now*. They're superstitious, you know. They leave.

445   **COUNTY ATTORNEY:**   *(To* PETERS, *in the manner of continuing an interrupted conversation)* No sign at all of anyone having come from the outside. Their own rope. Now let's go up again and go over it piece by piece. *(They start upstairs)* It would have to have been
450   someone who knew just the—*(*MRS. PETERS *sinks into her chair. The two women sit there not looking at one another, but as if peering into something and at the same time holding back. When they talk now it is in the manner of feeling their way over strange ground, as if afraid of what they*
455   *are saying, but as if they can not help saying it)*

MRS. HALE: She liked the bird. She was going to bury it in that pretty box.

MRS. PETERS: *(In a whisper)* When I was a girl—my kitten—there was a boy took a hatchet, and before my eyes—and before I could get there—*(covers her face*
460   *an instant)* If they hadn't held me back I would have—*(catches herself, looks upstairs where steps are heard, falters weakly)*—hurt him.

MRS. HALE: *(With a slow look around her)* I wonder
465   how it would seem never to have had any children around. *(Pause)* No, Wright wouldn't like the bird—a thing that sang. She used to sing. He killed that, too.

MRS. PETERS: *(Moving uneasily)* We don't know who killed the bird.

470   **MRS. HALE:**   I knew John Wright.

MRS. PETERS: It was an awful thing was done in this house that night, Mrs. Hale. Killing a man while he slept, slipping a rope around his neck that choked the life out of him.

MRS. HALE: His neck. Choked the life out of him. *(Her* 475 *hand goes out and rests on the bird-cage)*

MRS. PETERS: *(With rising voice)* We don't know who killed him. We don't *know*.

MRS. HALE: *(Her own feeling not interrupted)* If there'd been years and years of nothing, then a bird to sing 480 to you, it would be awful—still, after the bird was still.

MRS. PETERS: *(Something within her speaking)* I know what stillness is. When we homesteaded in Dakota, and my first baby died—after he was two years old, 485 and me with no other then—

MRS. HALE: *(Moving)* How soon do you suppose they'll be through, looking for the evidence?

MRS. PETERS: I know what stillness is. *(Pulling herself back)* The law has got to punish crime, Mrs. Hale. 490

MRS. HALE: *(Not as if answering that)* I wish you'd seen Minnie Foster when she wore a white dress with blue ribbons and stood up there in the choir and sang. *(Suddenly looking around the room)* Oh, I *wish* I'd come over here once in a while! That was a crime! That 495 was a crime! Who's going to punish that?

MRS. PETERS: *(Looking upstairs)* We mustn't—take on.

MRS. HALE: I might have known she needed help! I know how things can be—for women. I tell you, it's queer, Mrs. Peters. We live close together and we 500 live far apart. We all go through the same things—it's all just a different kind of the same thing— *(Brushes her eyes, then seeing the bottle of fruit, reaches out for it)* If I was you I wouldn't tell her her fruit was gone. Tell her it *ain't*. Tell her it's all right. Take this in to prove 505 it to her. She—she may never know whether it was broke or not.

MRS. PETERS: *(Picks up the bottle, looks about for something to wrap it in; takes petticoat from clothes brought from front room, very nervously begins winding that around it. In a false voice)* My, it's a good thing the men couldn't 510 *In a false voice)* My, it's a good thing the men couldn't hear us. Wouldn't they just laugh! Getting all stirred up over a little thing like a—dead canary. As if that could have anything to do with—with—wouldn't they *laugh!* *(The men are heard coming down stairs)* 515

MRS. HALE: *(Muttering)* Maybe they would—maybe they wouldn't.

COUNTY ATTORNEY: No, Peters, it's all perfectly clear except a reason for doing it. But you know juries when it comes to women. If there was some definite thing. Something to show—something to make a story about—a thing that would connect up with this strange way of doing it—(*The women's eyes meet for an instant. Enter* HALE *from outer door*)

HALE: Well, I've got the team around. Pretty cold out there.

COUNTY ATTORNEY: I'm going to stay here a while by myself. (*To* SHERIFF) You can send Frank out for me, can't you? I want to go over everything. I'm not satisfied that we can't do better.

SHERIFF: Do you want to see what Mrs. Peters is going to take in?

COUNTY ATTORNEY: (*Goes to the table. Picks up apron, laughs*) Oh, I guess they're not very dangerous things the ladies have picked out. (*Moves a few things about, disturbing the quilt pieces which cover the box. Steps back*) No, Mrs. Peters doesn't need supervising. For that matter, a sheriff's wife is married to the law. Ever think of it that way, Mrs. Peters?

MRS. PETERS: Not—just that way.

SHERIFF: (*Chuckling*) Married to the law. (*Moves toward front room*) I just want you to come in here a minute, George. We ought to take a look at these windows.

COUNTY ATTORNEY: Oh, windows!

SHERIFF: We'll be right out, Mr. Hale. (*Exit* HALE *door rear.* SHERIFF *follows the* COUNTY ATTORNEY *through door left. The two women's eyes follow them out.* MRS. HALE *rises, hands tightly together, looking intensely at* MRS. PETERS, *whose eyes make a slow turn, finally meeting* MRS. HALE's. *A moment* MRS. HALE *holds her, then her own eyes point the way to the spot where the box is concealed. Suddenly* MRS. PETERS *throws back quilt pieces and tries to put box in the bag she is wearing. It is too big. She opens box, starts to take bird out, cannot touch it, goes to pieces, stands there helpless. Sound of a knob turning in the other room.* MRS. HALE *snatches box and puts it in the pocket of her big coat. Enter* COUNTY ATTORNEY *and* SHERIFF.)

COUNTY ATTORNEY: (*Facetiously*) Well, Henry, at least we found out that she was not going to quilt it. She was going to—what is it you call it, ladies?

MRS. HALE: (*Hand against her pocket*) We call it—knot it, Mr. Henderson.

Writing from Reading

Summarize

1 Scan the script for references to Mrs. Wright's life. What do you know about her before and after her marriage?

2 List the "trifles" in this play. What do they have in common?

3 Who is the central character in the play? Who stands in opposition to this character?

Analyze Craft

4 What is the significance of setting the play during winter?

5 What is the significance of the kitchen as a setting for this play?

Analyze Voice

6 Identify an exchange of dialogue that you found particularly powerful and explain why. How does it promote or portray the conflict and theme of the play?

Synthesize Summary and Analysis

7 Compare the themes of "Trifles" to those of Kate Chopin's "The Story of an Hour" (in Fiction). How do Glaspell and Chopin, writing in the same country and at roughly the same time, approach the issues of the thwarted housewife?

Interpret the Play

8 What is the attitude of the women toward the men, the men toward the women?

9 What is the relationship between Mrs. Hale's regrets and her instinct to protect Mrs. Wright?

10 Which character goes through the most dramatic change in the course of the play? What is the change, and how does it come about?

11 How are power and powerlessness represented in the play?

CONTINUED FROM PAGE 3

A CLOSER LOOK

The term **drama** comes from the Greek word for *performing an action* or *doing*—and playwrights almost always intend their work to be brought to life on a stage by actors (except in the case of **closet dramas,** which are plays written to be read aloud rather than performed). Even the term we use to refer to the author of a dramatic work—**playwright** (not play-*write*)—reflects the three-dimensionality of a play: a *wright* is a medieval term for one skilled in manufacturing three-dimensional items, such as a shipwright or a wheelwright. The word suggests "maker," or "craftsman"; a carefully built thing has been well *wrought.*

"A play exists on the page completely as an artwork if it is an artwork, but for anybody to really involve themselves in it . . . it has to be performed." Conversation with Edward Albee

In fact, much of the world's great theater—from Sophocles (chapter 33) to Shakespeare (chapter 34)—had no life on the page *before* or *separate from* enactment on the stage. The playwright did not print out notes for actors or the audience to read. Thus, the original staging had nothing to do with words on a page. Drama had everything to do with how the play worked in performance. Dramas can occur on a **proscenium stage,** a raised platform with a missing fourth wall through which we as audience watch the action (see chapter 34 on Shakespeare). In other cases, the play may be presented **in the round,** where the audience surrounds the actors, or in an **amphitheater,** where the audience looks down on the drama (see chapter 33 on Greek drama). When the philosopher Aristotle asserted that much of the physical action of Greek drama must take place offstage, this was in part a function of necessity. The ancient

Proscenium stage

Theater in the round

Amphitheater

Greeks could not mount battle or death scenes persuasively in their amphitheaters—and so the audience learned of such events after the fact. No contemporary director would miss a chance to stage a combat or a love scene, but Glaspell apparently chose to keep the second-floor rooms of the farm offstage because it simplifies the issues of production. First, the production needs only one set—which allows for economy. Second, when the men go offstage and upstairs, they're gone; the women can pursue their inquiries alone. Even the simplest of dramas is multidimensional in conception.

THE ORIGINS OF DRAMA

Drama grew in part out of pre-classical Greek religious ceremonies and the public performances of poetry, Homer's *Iliad* and *Odyssey* in particular. These were not put into written form until after the Homeric epics were copied down in the sixth century B.C.E.; thanks to the collectors and librarians of the early Arab world, scrolls of papyrus with the texts of poems and the play scripts remained safe in libraries across the Mediterranean long after the decline of Greek civilization.

Elements of Drama

Trifles is a one-act play, a small miracle of compression that occurs in a single location and in one continuous action. A full-length play generally has three to five **acts,** and these divisions function in ways similar to fiction, as though they were chapters in a book that shift to a new location, mood, time, or configuration of characters. Acts, in turn, are divided into **scenes,** smaller segments of dramatic action. Here are one student's notes on how scenes work even in this one-act play.

Student Note on Scenes in *Trifles*

The action comes in waves, one associated with the male characters, the other with the female.

"There's something in there that's very sensitive to who you are, and things that are important to you. Attach yourself to that person and own that. So when you're reading, that's you. We've all been there. So find yourself in the play. Get inside the play, don't stay outside the play." Conversation with Ruben Santiago-Hudson

As you read through a play the first time, get to know the **characters.** The list of characters is found at the beginning of the play. (In the classical period of Greek theater, discussed in chapter 33, this list would be called **Dramatis Personae,** or "people of the play.") Just as in fiction, you will find a **protagonist,** who is the central character (the lead actor in the play), and an **antagonist,** who is a character or force that opposes the protagonist. A student's notes on characters in *Trifles* follow:

Student Notes on Characters in *Trifles*

*Men are rational: The men—the county attorney, the sheriff, and their witness, the farmer— are rational investigators, trying to establish a motive for the crime.

*Women are emotional: The women feel their way toward understanding, sorting through memories. The women are, in the words of the neighboring farmer, "worrying over trifles."

Irony: While the men go elsewhere in the house to search for clues, the women find the truth, the essence, of what has happened here.

A playwright must use the characters to move forward the play's **plot**—the important events in the story. The central incident in *Trifles*—the death of Mr. Wright—occurs before the onstage action begins, and is therefore introduced by means of **exposition,** a literary technique by which a character presents necessary background information. In addition to exposition, the plot unfolds in **dialogue,** the conversations

> "Don't just try to figure out the character. If you don't put the character in the plot, you'll never figure out the character. Character and plot are supposed to be organically interwoven."
>
> Conversation with Gregory Nagy

that occur between the characters. When you read a play, notice how the complications the characters face crystallize in a **conflict,** leading to **rising action,** an intensification of the predicament. The moment of greatest tension is the play's **climax** or turning point. Frequently, the climax causes a character to change in some way or at least to gain new understanding as a result of the conflict or crisis. The conclusion of the play, or the resolution of conflicts that follows the climax, is referred to as the **denouement,** a French word that literally means "untying." In the denouement, the knots of the story are untied and conflicts are further resolved. A longer play than *Trifles* might also include a **subplot** or two—secondary stories that involve characters other than the central figure in the play.

The play's **setting**—the location of the action—as depicted onstage is called the **set.** Glaspell describes the set she envisions down to a loaf of bread beside the bread-box and a dish towel on the table. The playwright's instructions on how actors are to move and position themselves onstage, as well as how they are to deliver certain lines—the **stage directions**—usually appear in parentheses and in italics in the **script,** which consists mainly of dialogue and staging instructions. At various points in *Trifles,* Glaspell instructs actors to unbutton a coat, point, look at the rocker, twitch, or speak stiffly.

Student Notes on the Staging in *Trifles*

The kitchen is cluttered, ill-tended. In the mess of things, of "trifles," the women do find evidence:

- the frenzied stitches in the farm wife's quilting,

- the empty birdcage, and then

- the dead songbird with a twisted neck, an emblem of the crime and a clear if metaphorical

  motive. The wife—like the bird—has been caged and strangled.

Susan Glaspell's stage directions clarify that the women know what they have found: "<u>Their eyes</u>

<u>meet. A look of growing comprehension, of horror. Steps are heard outside.</u>"

Finally, consider the theme of the play, the **dramatic** or **central question** that drives the story of the play. For *Trifles* you have to ask yourself what kind of woman, under what sort of pressure, would commit murder? The desperation of the housewife's act is anything but a "trifle"; her situation was profound enough to yield lethal results.

Sample Student Response to *Trifles*

James Ness

Professor Crane

ENGL 1202

October 22, 2008

Trifles: Song and Stillness

At first sight, Susan Glaspell's *Trifles* is a play about a wife suffering at the hands of a coldhearted and arrogant husband. At the end of her rope, she finally goes mad and kills him. But the play also explores what happens in a marriage when one partner fails to communicate with another or care about her happiness. Even more importantly, it reveals the differences between the way men and women view themselves and each other, and it tells a lot about the way these views affect marriage.

Early on, Mr. Hale reveals a lot about the way Wright treated his wife: he "didn't know as what his [Wright's] wife wanted made much difference" (6) to him. Clearly, her needs and desires in life didn't matter much to him. Perhaps he was just selfish. Later on, Mrs. Hale reveals more about the Wrights' marriage when, after finding the broken bird cage, she describes the house in which they lived as a "lonesome place" (10). It "weren't cheerful," she says, and she compares Mr. Wright to "raw wind that gets to the bone" (10). Mrs. Hale also says that Minnie Foster "was kind of like a bird herself" (10) before she married Wright. It is at this point that Mrs. Hale and Mrs. Peters find the bloody, dead canary which Mr. Wright killed and which his wife wrapped up in silk and placed in an expensive box.

The finding of the broken bird cage and the dead canary is also important because they are symbols of the Wrights' marriage. In fact, the canary might very well refer to Mrs. Wright, who, as Mrs. Hale tells us, "used to wear pretty

Ness 2

clothes and be lively, when she was Minnie Foster, one of the town girls singing in the choir" (11). The cage symbolizes the cheerless house in which Mr. Wright kept her. This idea is reinforced later in the play when Mrs. Hale says "Wright wouldn't like the bird—a thing that sang. She used to sing. He killed that, too" (11). There's a good chance that Wright objected to his wife's singing, made her quit the choir, and kept her from socializing with her neighbors.

The fact that Wright killed the bird completes the picture of his character as a coldhearted, arrogant, and violent person. But it also reveals an even more important aspect of the play's theme. Remember that the women come upon the dead bird after searching for some quilt patches to take to Mrs. Wright, who has been arrested. Their motive is to cheer her up while she is in jail. Of course, these are the kinds of female actions and thoughts that Mr. Hale refers to earlier in the play when he claims that "women are used to worrying over trifles" (11). This was said in reaction to hearing that Mrs. Wright was worried that her house had gotten cold and that her preserve jars would freeze and crack. However, the women's natural instinct to comfort someone in pain—what the men in this play might call a trifle—reveals the murder's motive, a motive that the men in the play have no success in finding no matter how hard they search.

Work Cited

Glaspell, Susan. *Trifles. Literature: Craft & Voice.* Eds. Nicholas Delbanco and Alan Cheuse. New York: McGraw-Hill, 2009. Print.

Types of Drama

To read drama critically, you need in addition to the literary elements of plot and character, a basic vocabulary of theatrical forms and conventions. The two most common dramatic forms are tragedy and comedy, and both date at least as far back as the drama of ancient Greece (chapter 33).

- In **tragedy,** characters face serious and important challenges that end in disastrous failure or defeat for the protagonist.
- In **comedy,** life usually turns out well for the main character, and the primary purpose of the play is to amuse the audience.

"What we try to do is illuminate something so that people can make up their own minds based upon the reality of the situation rather than the mythology. And if one can do that, it's enough."

Conversation with Arthur Miller

Within these two large groupings there are a number of variations and blendings, such as **tragicomedies** (where the protagonist isn't defeated but there is a downturn in his or her situation), **melodramas** (where the forces of good and evil are in absolute and often violent opposition), and **problem plays** (which explore social issues, such as *Trifles'* exploration of a woman's place and power (or powerlessness) in the home.

Tragedy

The structure of Greek tragedy shapes tragic drama even today (a fuller discussion of Greek tragedy can be found in chapter 33). Tragedy in real life might be brought on by a natural disaster or wartime or personal heartache, but tragedy in drama begins and ends with the qualities found in the main character: the **hero.** A hero is more than just the protagonist, or lead character, in a play. The hero's nature must be such that in some way the audience feels admiration for his or her qualities (wisdom, generosity, bravery, and love of family) and must feel compassion and fear when the character falls. The audience finds the hero at least in some degree sympathetic.

In a tragedy, the hero stands in conflict with forces larger than himself. These might be an unjust society (as in many modern plays, see chapter 35) or it might be another human being, a villain (as in the conflict between Othello and Iago in Shakespeare's *Othello*, chapter 34). Often the adversary might consist of fate itself, as in

"The heart of drama . . . has been . . . really since it began . . . character types and the conflict and the encounter with character types. And I don't care whether you go back to . . . the Greek theater . . . you have . . . this conflict of characters."

Conversation with Edwin Wilson

Sophocles' *Oedipus the King*, about whose hero it was prophesied that he would kill his father and marry his mother (chapter 33). However, *external* forces don't turn the hero into a **tragic hero.** Rather, from the beginning there is something about the hero's character that undermines what the audience finds sympathetic, and this **tragic flaw**—be it arrogance or jealousy or stubbornness—speeds along the hero's downfall.

Sophocles' *Oedipus the King* is the very prototype of the tragic mode of drama, from the five-act structure to the noble position of the central figure and the inevitable trajectory of decline. The proximity to power is a significant attribute of the hero. Even today we can see the voyeuristic fascination with the fall from grace of a politician because of a sex scandal or a celebrity because of drug abuse or violence. In classical tragic drama, however, the hero proves his or her heroic stature by accepting the justice of the punishment for mortal flaws. Several tragedies and the many faces of the tragic hero will be more fully studied in chapters and casebooks on ancient Greek drama, Shakespeare, and modern drama that appear later in this volume.

Comedy

Comedy stands as the countervailing force to tragedy. Laughter illuminates the human condition just as effectively as tears. As in tragedy, the main characters will possess weaknesses, though unlike tragic figures, the main characters fall short of heroism and do not appear to be the larger-than-life people who show what our best selves can be. These characters are much more likely to prick our pride with the revelation that we are no more heroic than is the frog who requires the princess's kiss. To be sure, we can find comic characters written into a tragedy for **comic relief,** but a comedy in general is a play that makes us laugh at our flaws and ultimately forgive ourselves for our foibles.

Satyr plays—named for the half horse/half man mythological characters full of mischief and vulgar sexuality—employed excess, unrestrained sexuality, and outlandish characters. They might well be akin to the exaggerated presentation of modern-day **burlesque,** with its sexual innuendo, striptease, and **slapstick** or **farce.** A man who slips on a banana peel, or a character with a three-foot nose, belongs to the broad comic mode of burlesque. Satyr plays were part of Greek festivals, and out of these grew Aristophanes' great comedies of invective, ridicule, and political satire, the most famous of which is *Lysistrata,* in which the wives of soldiers withhold sex from their husbands until the men are willing to end the war. Some **satiric comedies** can be violent, crude, and nasty—biting commentaries on the human condition without any guarantee that good will prevail.

Other forms of comedies evolved from this early Greek theater, such as the **comedy of manners,** which shines an indulgent light on the hypocrisy of the social elite, and, much later, **restoration drama**—bawdy plays of fallen virtue and infidelity, which played to sold-out houses in London after the Puritans were displaced from power. Today we're familiar with **romantic comedy,** where two would-be/should-be lovers find

"When you are reading a . . . comedy, it helps to know something about the history of the time in which it was written. Because what was making the public laugh, not when they were in the theater? Who was the king at that time? Who was the queen? Who were the serfs? Who were the slaves? Who were the masters? What was the situation politically? And so on. If you have that in your head, or if you . . . look it up, I think it makes all plays more interesting."

Conversation with Marian Seldes

each other after a series of misunderstandings and false starts. A play such as this gently pokes fun at the difficulties of finding love and of keeping one's dignity in the search for it. Whether a play uses **high comedy**—wordplay and wit—or **low comedy**—gags and pratfalls—its storyline contains the unexpected; the French philosopher Henri Bergson argued that this unexpectedness was a crucial part of the comedic mode. Further, the one all-embracing definition of comedy, separating this mode from tragedy, is that it is a kind of play that ends happily—or, in any case, with its main players still alive.

In that vein, we offer you *The Wedding Story* by Julianne Homokay, a satiric one-act comedy about romantic relationships. Look at this modern parable about marriage—in both its ideal and its actual state—and compare Homokay's attitude toward gender relations to those in *Trifles,* a play first performed in 1916. When Glaspell wrote her play, women were not allowed to serve on juries, so if Mrs. Wright were to go on trial, she would not have been judged by a "jury of her peers." In fact, as the play makes clear, the men who judge her would have little understanding of her motives or her life. We look at such relationships through a different kind of lens in *The Wedding*. Compare how the storyteller in *The Wedding Story* conjures up his characters, making creatures of his imagination who take on the flesh-and-blood guise of "Bride" and "Groom," and then start to answer back.

Julianne Homokay (b. 1966)

Julianne Homokay holds an M.F.A. in playwriting from the University of Nevada, Las Vegas and has put it to use writing plays such as *Judy Gray, Living Roanoke,* and *Cottonmouth.* She also collaborated on a musical version of *Around the World in 80 Days* that debuted at the Fulton Opera House in Lancaster, Pennsylvania. She has taught at the Fulton Opera House and currently teaches at Pasadena City College. Her many honors include a grant from the Nevada Arts Council and a term as playwright-in-residence at Franklin and Marshall College. She lives in Los Angeles.

AS YOU READ Look for evidence of role reversal, both on the storyteller's and on the characters' part.

The Wedding Story (2000)

CHARACTERS

STORYTELLER

BRIDE

GROOM

SETTING: *A land where grass is always green, the sun is always shining, and fences are always white picket.*

TIME: *A sunny day in sunny June, the height of the perfect wedding season. In Vermont.*

[Lights up on the STORYTELLER *reading from a leatherbound volume with gilded pages.]*

STORYTELLER: *(closing the volume)* The End. Good night, sleep tight, don't let the bedbugs bite. What? You want to hear another one? But it's a school night. Okay, okay, just this once. I'm such a pushover. What
5 type of story shall we hear?
[ad lib if the audience yells out suggestions]
How about a fairy tale for our times? A field of dreams fenced in by white picket, a story of the young man and woman we all hope to be someday? Too bad, that's what you're getting.
[The STORYTELLER *opens the volume back up. Lights up on* BRIDE *and* GROOM *in traditional garb standing on top of a wedding cake.]*
10 Once upon a time there was a young woman, pretty as a day in June.
[The BRIDE *does the royal wave.]*
A young man stood by her side, smart as a whip and handsome as a polo horse.
[The GROOM *salutes.]*
They met in high school and fell in love on a merry
15 day in May.
[The BRIDE *and* GROOM *whisper to each other.]*
Before long, the young man dropped to his knee, pulled a diamond from his pocket, and won the young woman's hand in marriage.

BRIDE: Uh, excuse us, Mr. Storyteller?
[The STORYTELLER *looks back at them, confused. The* BRIDE *and* GROOM *smile and wave. The* STORYTELLER *waves back.]*

20 **STORYTELLER:** Moving right along. With the blessings of their compatible—

BRIDE: Mr. Storyteller!

STORYTELLER: Excuse me a moment. *(to* BRIDE*)* Yes, what is it?

25 **BRIDE:** We didn't exactly meet in high school.

STORYTELLER: Yes you did, it says so right here.

BRIDE: We met in a bar.

GROOM: And we dated on and off for five years while she experimented with foreigners.

30 **STORYTELLER:** How nice. Well. For our purposes, let's say you met in high school, shall we?
[back to the kids]
So. With the blessings of their compatible families, the young man and woman were to be Bride and Groom.

35 **BRIDE:** *(to* GROOM*)* Wait a minute. As I recall, you kept breaking it off.

GROOM: What?

BRIDE: Yeah. Then you'd want me back the minute I had a new boyfriend.

40 **GROOM:** You certainly didn't waste any time running into the arms of the first guy who had an accent.

STORYTELLER: *(to* BRIDE *and* GROOM*)* Sssssh. Let's don't argue in front of the impressionable youngsters. *(to children)* The bride soon set in on the wed-
45 ding preparations.

BRIDE: *(to* GROOM*)* I never realized you were a racist.

GROOM: I'm not, I was fine with the fact you'd slept with black men.

BRIDE: You're assuming that "racism" automatically refers to African-Americans. Isn't that a form of rac-
50 ism itself?

STORYTELLER: Excuse me, ma'am, sir, firmie those bouches so I can return to the story thank you.

GROOM: By all means. Don't let anything silly like our issues get in your way.
55

STORYTELLER: Look, will you play along? The children will have ample opportunity to be disillusioned later, let's just have a nice bedtime story, okay? Okay.
[to the children]
AS I WAS SAYING, the preparations. They were to be married in a beautiful church—
60

GROOM: *(under his breath)* Drive-thru chapel in Vegas.

STORYTELLER: —followed by an elegant reception at an old inn in Vermont.

BRIDE: *(under her breath)* Back room at the Star Dust Lounge.
65

STORYTELLER: The bride put Martha Stewart to shame as she had the evening designed to the last detail—

GROOM: *(to* BRIDE*)* Ha! That really sounds like you.

STORYTELLER: —from the linen
70 napkins to the centerpieces of purple freesia and Italian ruscus.

BRIDE: *(to* GROOM*)* I think he was invited to someone else's
75 wedding.

GROOM: And why is he assuming the bride always has the taste? Does it never occur to anyone that the groom might want to
80

participate? I worked my way though law school as a floral designer, that's how I know freesia is all wrong for a centerpiece, except maybe as an accent flower.

BRIDE: You were a floral designer?

85 **GROOM:** You need to base your arrangement on a more substantial bloom, like a lily or an orchid.

BRIDE: Brad, is there something you want to tell me?

STORYTELLER: Actually, there is something I want to tell these youngsters so they can get to bed at a de-
90 cent hour. THE STORY.

BRIDE: Well huffy huff huff.

STORYTELLER: SO, they had their flawless reception for 300 guests at a turn-of-the-century inn in Vermont—

95 **BRIDE:** You know, we're not from Vermont. We've never even been to Vermont.

STORYTELLER: —at which all had a delightful time.

GROOM: *(to BRIDE)* What do you mean is there something I want to tell you?

100 **STORYTELLER:** Immediately following the splendid reception—

BRIDE: I mean, is there something you haven't been honest with me about? With yourself about?

GROOM: Like what?

105 **STORYTELLER:** The bride, at the tender age of 24—
  [The GROOM laughs out loud.]
  WHAT? WHAT'S SO FUNNY?

GROOM: She's not even close to 24.

STORYTELLER: Now just wait a minute here, Buster Brown, whose story is this?

110 **BRIDE/GROOM:** Ours.

STORYTELLER: Wrong. This is a fairy tale, I'm going for prototypes.

BRIDE: But I'm 35.

STORYTELLER: In this story, you're 24. The average
115 American woman gets married at 24.

BRIDE: How old's that make him?

STORYTELLER: 27. Why, how old is he really?

GROOM: I'm the one that's 24.

STORYTELLER: Isn't that a little young to be getting
120 married?

BRIDE: How come 24's okay for me but not for him?

STORYTELLER: You're the woman. You're supposed to be younger.

BRIDE: Jesus.   125

STORYTELLER: Now, before I was inter-
rupted for the umpteenth time, boys and girls, I was saying that after the reception, the 24-year-old bride was whisked away in a horse-drawn carriage   130
by her 27-year-old Prince Charming.

BRIDE: Whisked away where?

STORYTELLER: I don't know. To . . . the . . . airport.

BRIDE: Which one?

STORYTELLER: The Airport of . . . Vermont.   135

BRIDE: There's one in Burlington and one in Montpelier.

GROOM: How did you know that?

BRIDE: I majored in geography.

GROOM: You did?

BRIDE: *(to STORYTELLER)* So Mr. Fancy Pants, which   140
one was it?

STORYTELLER: The one where you caught your flight to Hawaii for your honeymoon.

BRIDE: This whole fairy tale is completely out of hand. Anyone knows there's no flights from Vermont to   145
Hawaii. You have to fly through Logan or LAX. Or both. And anyway, I highly doubt they'd let the horses in the terminal.

STORYTELLER: Oh, for God's sake, what's the big deal in telling the children a nice little story?   150

BRIDE: No one's life turns out like that. How many of those kids will live up to your version of the story? None! They can't, it's too much pressure. It's like why Catholic women are all messed up, you can't be a virgin AND be a mother. And Brad, I probably   155
shouldn't have married you to begin with.

GROOM: Shayna, how can you say that?

BRIDE: You're probably gay.

GROOM: What?

BRIDE: Oh c'mon, how many straight male floral de-   160
signers do you know?

GROOM: That's what you thought I needed to be honest about?

BRIDE: You didn't even know I majored in Geography! Listen, if we're talking averages here, most people don't get married in Vermont. They get married in their one-horse hometowns that have WalMarts and bad zoning.

STORYTELLER: What's wrong with that?

BRIDE: NOTHING. THAT'S MY POINT. MOST people do get married in their hometowns. MOST people cheat on their spouses or end up in counseling or sell everything they own to get into a lousy nursing home. Put that in your fairy tale and smoke it.

STORYTELLER: No one's smoking anything. There are children present.

BRIDE: And God forbid we tell them what life is really like.

GROOM: She's got a point there. You're opening yourself up for multiple class-action suits, Mister.

STORYTELLER: Fine. I've had it. You want the truth, the whole truth, and nothing but the truth, the whole enchilada, the proverbial hook, line, and sinker? Well far be it from me to give these little souls something to which to aspire.

BRIDE/GROOM: Do it! Do it! *(ad lib)*

STORYTELLER: I'm warning you, it won't be pretty.

BRIDE/GROOM: We stand warned.

STORYTELLER: I'm such a pushover.
[opens the volume back up]
Once upon a time in a trailer park not so far away, there lived a woman approaching middle age who drank a lot of bourbon, smoked a pack a day, hung out in places where they throw peanut shells on the floor—

BRIDE: All right already.

STORYTELLER: —and a young, slightly effeminate man who took it up the ass once from a fellow Eagle Scout, but since it only happened once when he was 17 and drunk on Kahlua, he still considered himself straight.

GROOM: Hey hey hey.

STORYTELLER: The woman and the man met in a bar one night where they got drunk and slept together afterwards at her place. Since the woman felt guilty about the one-night stand, she felt she needed to make a legitimate relationship out of the encounter to justify the sex, even though she really prefers black men. To stay deep in the dark closet, the man pro-

posed to the woman, and since she's 35 and, let's face it, not getting any younger, she accepted his pathetic offer because it was a real ego boost to have snagged a hot stud eleven years younger than she, even if he does have the occasional problem getting a stiffy with her because he's really gay. Although the man offered to plan the entire wedding with his best friend Steve, the woman insisted they hire a horse-drawn carriage to drop them off at the Airport of Vermont, from which they took six connecting flights to Las Vegas to get married by an Elvis impersonator. To celebrate, they showed up at the Star Dust Lounge, at which they bought all the bar patrons cheeseballs and Budweiser. When they arrived back home in Weehawken, New Jersey, the Groom, unable to suppress his inner self for a moment longer, took up with a drag queen from SoHo, and the Bride, realizing she'd never be a mother, consoled herself with vodka and Xanax and died of a somewhat accidental overdose three years later. The Groom, now 27, took up wearing cowboy hats and chaps, and made the unfortunate mistake of traveling to Wyoming on business where he was dragged to his death behind a 4x4 by a bunch of homophobic rednecks. The drag queen wrote a show about the three of them in which he played all the parts, won a Genius Grant, and landed his own talk show on New York City cable access.
[shuts book, exits]
I bid you good night and sweet dreams, children. The End.

BRIDE/GROOM: *(ad lib, following the* STORYTELLER *off)* Uh, Mr. Storyteller, wait, it's okay, you can tell the other version, etc. . . .

Writing from Reading

Summarize

1 What is the story the storyteller wants to tell? What story gets told?

Analyze Craft

2 What is the effect of the encounters between the bride and groom and the storyteller? How do these interactions create humor?

3 The play speaks to contemporary social arrangements involving love and social life. How would you describe the tone of the play? What is accomplished by this particular tone?

Analyze Voice

4 The back-and-forth between the couple and the storyteller—and between themselves—makes for three distinct voices. Describe each. Does any one seem dominant at first? Does that condition last for the entire play?

5 Does the first speech the storyteller offers depend on a response to his question—"How about? . . ." When he says "Too bad, that's what you're getting," he's addressing both his invisible onstage audience of children and the audience in the hall. How does this strategy implicate the listener/viewer in the tale as told?

Synthesize Summary and Analysis

6 Does the presentation about the perfect wedding made by the storyteller to the bride and groom seem closer to fantasy or reality, and why?

7 In this play, a realistic bedtime story about love and the beginning of marriage veers toward the comical. What is inherently comic about the situation? Might the storyteller have told about the meeting, courtship, and marriage in another way?

8 What effect does the storyteller create by insisting on his version of reality? How does the difference between the storyteller's first and second story and the story "play" out?

9 How well suited to the stage are the themes of "illusion" and "reality" here?

Interpret the Play

10 What does the use of the bedtime fairy tale tell us about the story the playwright wants to tell?

Suggestions for Writing

1. Both *Trifles* and *The Wedding Story* deal with the institution of marriage, its expectations and disappointments. The older play does so in an essentially tragic mode, the contemporary one in an essentially comic vein. Give examples of each, focusing on tone.

2. Imagine turning a poem (Robert Browning's "My Last Duchess," for example) or a story (like Anton Chekhov's "Rapture") into a play. What are the issues you will face in terms of physical (re)presentation?

3. Speculate on the role of theater in today's society. Is it important to have traditional staged theater? Has theater been sidelined by movies, TV, the Internet, and YouTube? Speculate on the theatrical aspects of all of these, using specific examples.

31 Going Further with Reading

Reading for the Stage

A DIRECTOR might push an actor trying to find a connection to his or her character in exactly this fashion: Go deeper! After reading an entire play and beginning to explore the story line and how the characters make sense to you, you are ready to go deeper into the matter of understanding a play in all its elements and writing about it with an audience in mind. Reading a play allows you to be, as actress Marian Seldes says in her interview, "alone with it. . . . That frees your imagination." As you go deeper, imagine yourself as the actors, the director, and the audience.

- As the actor you're onstage delivering lines to the other actors and responding to an audience

- As the director you're trying to draw the audience into the play as a whole through lighting, costumes, setting, and characters

- As the audience you're seeing actors on a stage and responding to how you are drawn into the play

I HOPED . . . and I don't really know why I expected the dog to understand anything, much less my motivations. . . . I hoped that the dog would understand. (PETER *seems to be hypnotized*) It's just . . . it's just that . . . (JERRY *is abnormally tense, now*) . . . it's just that if you can't deal with people, you have to make a start somewhere. WITH ANIMALS ! (*Much faster now, and like a conspirator*) Don't you see? A person has to have some way of dealing with SOMETHING. If not with people . . . SOMETHING.

—*from* The Zoo Story *by Edward Albee*

When you read the play in the context of the stage, try to hear the voices of the actors. Decide if the words I love you, for example, are spoken as if for the first time by a younger romantic or as if for the thousandth time by an old seducer. See the characters' movements across the stage, the clothes they wear, the spotlights on them, and the objects they hold. Considering these extra dimensions, you are staging the play in what the critic Francis Fergusson called "the theater of the mind."

CONTINUED ON PAGE 44

"No two people see the same play. No two performances of the same production are identical. And there's more than one way to skin a cat. Why, I don't know, but there is."

Conversation with Edward Albee

Art changes people if they wish to be changed

Entertainment is misunderstood.

A Conversation on Writing

Edward Albee

The Zoo Story and the Writing Life

Well, I wrote poetry from the age of eight to twenty-eight when I quit because I was getting better but not better enough, and I wrote two terrible novels in my teens, really very bad novels . . . and since I decided I was a creative writer, which meant I didn't have to be able to think coherently in a straight line . . . essays were beyond me too . . . so I started writing plays. . . . When *The Zoo Story* opened in German in Berlin and got good reviews and it opened in New York in English and got good reviews, I guess it encouraged me to think maybe . . . [I] should go on with this.

Entertainment

I think a playwright's obligation is to be coherent, to not waste people's time, to do something onstage that makes people think, makes them perhaps reconsider some of their values—accept change, not accept change—to have something in which they are participating, not just some kind of escapist entertainment that will just slide right off the mind. . . . Entertainment is misunderstood. Entertainment seems these days to mean something at which you do not have to think, at which you don't have any troubling experiences. But if art isn't engaging or troubling in some sense, it is a total waste of time.

The Experience in the Text

The intention is there in the text. The intention is the experience of the play that I had while I was writing it. Because when I write a play . . . I see it, I hear it as a play being performed in front of me, and that's what I want to see on the stage—the same experience that I had while writing it.

This interview with Edward Albee was conducted by Jesse Green for the *Times Talks* program sponsored by *The New York Times* on the occasion of Albee's eightieth birthday.

A STUDENT'S INITIAL REACTION TO *THE ZOO STORY*

When I look at this, I imagine from the title that animals are likely to play a role. Two men are sitting on a park bench. The playwright gives some guidance in stage directions in italics. If I imagine acting out the two parts, how would I draw the audience into the play?

An Interactive Reading from Edward Albee's *The Zoo Story*

The role of questioner gives Jerry more power, almost like a detective. I would cast someone with a bigger presence for his role than for Peter's.

Drinking beer and calling the bathroom "john" gives clues that his character is "low brow," perhaps; Peter isn't—foils to each other?

The first animal mentioned in "Zoo Story" is not a zoo animal at all! I think of guinea pigs as docile household pets, kept in a cage.

I wonder why Jerry is so interested in Peter's pets. Their dialogue seems to say that having cats makes Peter less "manly."

Birds are another caged pet. Parakeets especially are common household birds (it would be different if he owned cardinals or toucans, say).

The interaction of animals becomes disturbing when Jerry puts it this way. Why would he say this? And why would he imagine Peter's pets are diseased in the first place?

If these two are foils, how might I represent that on stage?

We know from clues early on that this is New York's Central Park. There are lots of ways I can imagine staging this—just two benches on a stage, or a more elaborate park backdrop. But I think it would be interesting to do it outside.

Cues for very expressive gestures. Peter shows how he feels without saying it.

Cue for clearing throat and the amount of ellipses make it seem like he says this hesitantly.

Peter reacts hesitantly to Jerry's jab. I think I'd play them as a kind of boxing match with Jerry dancing around Peter throwing punches that Peter politely dodges

JERRY: Do you mind if I ask you questions?

PETER: Oh, not really.

JERRY: I'll tell you why I do it; I don't talk to many people—except to say like: give me a beer, or where's the john, or what time does the feature go on, or keep your hands to yourself, buddy. You know—things like that.

PETER: I must say I don't . . .

JERRY: But every once in a while I like to talk to somebody, really *talk;* like to get to know somebody, know all about him.

PETER: *(Lightly laughing, still a little uncomfortable)* And am I the guinea pig for today?

JERRY: On a sun-drenched Sunday afternoon like this? Who better than a nice married man with two daughters and . . . uh . . . a dog? *(PETER shakes his head)* No? Two dogs. *(PETER shakes his head again)* Hm. No dogs? *(PETER shakes his head, sadly)* Oh, that's a shame. But you look like an animal man. CATS? *(PETER nods his head, ruefully)* Cats! But, that can't be your idea. No, sir. Your wife and daughters? *(PETER nods his head)* Is there anything else I should know?

PETER: *(He has to clear his throat)* There are . . . there are two parakeets. One . . . uh . . . one for each of my daughters.

JERRY: Birds.

PETER: My daughters keep them in a cage in their bedroom.

JERRY: Do they carry disease? The birds.

PETER: I don't believe so.

JERRY: That's too bad. If they did you could set them loose in the house and the cats could eat them and die, maybe. *(PETER looks blank for a moment, then laughs)* And what else? What do you do to support your enormous household?

PETER: I . . . uh . . . I have an executive position with a . . . a small publishing house. We . . . uh . . . we publish textbooks.

JERRY: That sounds nice; very nice.

Edward Albee (b. 1928)

Edward Albee was adopted as an infant into a wealthy New York family. His privileged upbringing included limousine rides to see Broadway productions and access to his parents' library, even though the young Albee got in trouble for actually reading the books that his parents maintained for looks only. After expulsion from three prep schools and Trinity College in Connecticut, he had a falling out with his parents that caused a twenty-year estrangement. Living on his own, Albee worked odd jobs until he wrote his first play, *The Zoo Story,* as a thirtieth birthday present to himself. Its debut in America brought the freshest approach to drama on the American stage since Eugene O'Neill and Thornton Wilder. Financially supported to begin with by stipends from his grandparents, Albee made a successful career of writing, and in his long productive life as playwright has garnered three Pulitzer Prizes. He might have received a fourth had not the recommendation of the committee to award the Pulitzer Prize to arguably his best and most important play, *Who's Afraid of Virginia Woolf?* (1962), been overturned because of the play's controversial sexual content. In 1966 the play was made into a movie starring Elizabeth Taylor and Richard Burton. Although Albee's plays have met with varying levels of success, *The Zoo Story* has remained significant to American drama, and some credit it as one of the biggest influence on off-Broadway works. In 2005 Albee was awarded the Special Tony Award for Lifetime Achievement.

AS YOU READ Ask yourself what the play's title conveys, and why Albee might have wished to call his play a "story." Make notes about how you would move the actors around on the set if you were directing this play.

The Zoo Story (1958)

—for William Flanagan

CHARACTERS

PETER *A man in his early forties, neither fat nor gaunt, neither handsome nor homely. He wears tweeds, smokes a pipe, carries horn-rimmed glasses. Although he is moving into middle age, his dress and his manner would suggest a man younger.*

JERRY *A man in his late thirties, not poorly dressed, but carelessly. What was once a trim and lightly muscled body has begun to go to fat; and while he is no longer handsome, it is evident that he once was. His fall from physical grace should not suggest debauchery; he has, to come closest to it, a great weariness.*

THE SCENE *It is Central Park; a Sunday afternoon in summer; the present. There are two park benches, one toward either side of the stage; they both face the audience. Behind them: foliage, trees, sky. At the beginning, Peter is seated on one of the benches.*

(As the curtain rises, PETER *is seated on the bench stage-right. He is reading a book. He stops reading, cleans his glasses, goes back to reading.* JERRY *enters.)*

JERRY: I've been to the zoo. *(*PETER *doesn't notice)* I said, I've been to the zoo. MISTER, I'VE BEEN TO THE ZOO!

PETER: Hm? . . . What? . . . I'm sorry, were you talking
5 to me?

JERRY: I went to the zoo, and then I walked until I came here. Have I been walking north?

PETER: *(Puzzled)* North? Why . . . I . . . I think so. Let me see.

10 **JERRY:** *(Pointing past the audience)* Is that Fifth Avenue?

PETER: Why yes; yes, it is.

JERRY: And what is that cross street there; that one, to the right?

PETER: That? Oh, that's Seventy-fourth Street.

15 **JERRY:** And the zoo is around Sixty-fifth Street; so, I've been walking north.

PETER: *(Anxious to get back to his reading)* Yes; it would seem so.

JERRY: Good old north.

20 **PETER:** *(Lightly, by reflex)* Ha, ha.

JERRY: *(After a slight pause)* But not due north.

PETER: I . . . well, no, not due north; but, we . . . call it north. It's northerly.

JERRY: *(Watches as* PETER, *anxious to dismiss him, prepares*
25 *his pipe)* Well, boy; *you're* not going to get lung cancer, are you?

PETER: *(Looks up, a little annoyed, then smiles)* No, sir. Not from this.

JERRY: No, sir. What you'll probably get is cancer of
30 the mouth, and then you'll have to wear one of those things Freud wore after they took one whole side of his jaw away. What do they call those things?

PETER: *(Uncomfortable)* A prosthesis?

JERRY: The very thing! A prosthesis. You're an edu-
35 cated man, aren't you? Are you a doctor?

PETER: Oh, no; no. I read about it somewhere; *Time* magazine, I think. *(He turns to his book)*

JERRY: Well, *Time* magazine isn't for blockheads.

PETER: No, I suppose not.

Peter sits reading before Jerry's arrival, in this 2006 production starring Paul Christophe and Pitt Simon.

JERRY: *(After a pause)* Boy, I'm glad that's Fifth Avenue 40 there.

PETER: *(Vaguely)* Yes.

JERRY: I don't like the west side of the park much.

PETER: Oh? *(Then, slightly wary, but interested)* Why?

JERRY: *(Offhand)* I don't know. 45

PETER: Oh. *(He returns to his book)*

JERRY: *(He stands for a few seconds, looking at* PETER, *who finally looks up again, puzzled)* Do you mind if we talk?

PETER: *(Obviously minding)* Why . . . no, no.

JERRY: Yes you do; you do. 50

PETER: *(Puts his book down, his pipe out and away, smiling)* No, really; I don't mind.

JERRY: Yes you do.

PETER: *(Finally decided)* No; I don't mind at all, really.

JERRY: It's . . . it's a nice day. 55

PETER: *(Stares unnecessarily at the sky)* Yes. Yes, it is; lovely.

JERRY: I've been to the zoo.

PETER: Yes, I think you said so . . . didn't you?

JERRY: I bet you've got TV, huh? 60

PETER: Why yes, we have two; one for the children.

JERRY: You're married!

PETER: *(With pleased emphasis)* Why, certainly.

JERRY: It isn't a law, for God's sake.

65 **PETER:** No . . . no, of course not.

JERRY: And you have a wife.

PETER: *(Bewildered by the seeming lack of communication)* Yes!

JERRY: And you have children.

70 **PETER:** Yes; two.

JERRY: Boys?

PETER: No, girls . . . both girls.

JERRY: But you wanted boys.

PETER: Well . . . naturally, every man wants a son, 75 but . . .

JERRY: *(Lightly mocking)* But that's the way the cookie crumbles?

PETER: *(Annoyed)* I wasn't going to say that.

JERRY: And you're not going to have any more kids, 80 are you?

PETER: *(A bit distantly)* No. No more. *(Then back, and irksome)* Why did you say that? How would you know about that?

JERRY: The way you cross your legs, perhaps; some-85 thing in the voice. Or maybe I'm just guessing. Is it your wife?

PETER: *(Furious)* That's none of your business! *(A silence)* Do you understand? *(JERRY nods. PETER is quiet now)* Well, you're right. We'll have no more children.

90 **JERRY:** *(Softly)* That *is* the way the cookie crumbles.

PETER: *(Forgiving)* Yes . . . I guess so.

JERRY: Do you mind if I ask you questions?

PETER: Oh, not really.

JERRY: I'll tell you why I do it; I don't talk to many 95 people—except to say like: give me a beer, or where's the john, or what time does the feature go on, or keep your hands to yourself, buddy. You know— things like that.

PETER: I must say I don't . . .

100 **JERRY:** But every once in a while I like to talk to some-body, really *talk;* like to get to know somebody, know all about him.

PETER: *(Lightly laughing, still a little uncomfortable)* And am I the guinea pig for today?

105 **JERRY:** On a sun-drenched Sunday afternoon like this? Who better than a nice married man with two

daughters and . . . uh . . . a dog? *(PETER shakes his head)* No? Two dogs. *(PETER shakes his head again)* Hm. No dogs? *(PETER shakes his head, sadly)* Oh, that's a shame. But you look like an animal man. CATS? 110 *(PETER nods his head, ruefully)* Cats! But, that can't be your idea. No, sir. Your wife and daughters? *(PETER nods his head)* Is there anything else I should know?

PETER: *(He has to clear his throat)* There are . . . there are two parakeets. One . . . uh . . . one for each of my 115 daughters.

JERRY: Birds.

PETER: My daughters keep them in a cage in their bedroom.

JERRY: Do they carry disease? The birds. 120

PETER: I don't believe so.

JERRY: That's too bad. If they did you could set them loose in the house and the cats could eat them and die, maybe. *(PETER looks blank for a moment, then laughs)* And what else? What do you do to support 125 your enormous household?

PETER: I . . . uh . . . I have an executive position with a . . . a small publishing house. We . . . uh . . . we publish textbooks.

JERRY: That sounds nice; very nice. What do you make? 130

PETER: *(Still cheerful)* Now look here!

JERRY: Oh, come on.

PETER: Well, I make around two hundred thousand a year, but I don't carry more than forty dollars at any one time . . . in case you're a . . . a holdup man . . . ha, 135 ha, ha.

JERRY: *(Ignoring the above)* Where do you live? *(PETER is reluctant)* Oh, look; I'm not going to rob you, and I'm not going to kidnap your parakeets, your cats, or your daughters. 140

PETER: *(Too loud)* I live between Lexington and Third Avenue, on Seventy-fourth Street.

JERRY: That wasn't so hard, was it?

PETER: I didn't mean to seem . . . ah . . . it's that you don't really carry on a conversation; you just ask 145 questions. And I'm . . . I'm normally . . . uh . . . reti-cent. Why do you just stand there?

JERRY: Say, what's the dividing line between upper-middle-middle-class and lower-upper-middle-class?

PETER: My dear fellow, I . . . 150

JERRY: Don't my dear fellow me.

Jerry and Peter begin their conversation.

PETER: *(Unhappily)* Was I patronizing? I believe I was; I'm sorry. But, you see your question about the classes bewildered me.

155 **JERRY:** And when you're bewildered you become patronizing?

PETER: I . . . I don't express myself too well, sometimes. *(He attempts a joke on himself)* I'm in publishing, not writing.

160 **JERRY:** *(Amused, but not at the humor)* So be it. The truth *is: I* was being patronizing.

PETER: Oh, now; you needn't say that.
    (It is at this point that JERRY *may begin to move about the stage with slowly increasing determination and authority, but pacing himself, so that the long speech about the dog comes at the high point of the arc)*

JERRY: All right. Who are your favorite writers? Baudelaire and Stephen King?

165 **PETER:** *(Wary)* Well, I like a great many writers; I have a considerable catholicity of taste, if I may say so. Those two men are fine, each in his way. *(Warming up)* Baudelaire, of course . . . uh . . . is by far the finer of the two, but Stephen King has a place . . .
170 in our . . . uh . . . national . . .

JERRY: Skip it.

PETER: I . . . sorry.

JERRY: Do you know what I did before I went to the zoo today? I walked all the way up Fifth Avenue
175 from Washington Square; all the way.

PETER: Oh; you live in Greenwich Village! *(This seems to enlighten* PETER*)*

JERRY: No, I don't. I took the subway down to the Village so I could walk all the way up Fifth Avenue
180 to the zoo. It's one of those things a person has to do; sometimes a person has to go a very long distance out of his way to come back a short distance correctly.

PETER: *(Almost pouting)* Oh, I thought you lived in Greenwich Village.

JERRY: What were you trying to do? Make sense 185 out of things? Bring order? The old pigeonhole bit? Well, that's easy; I'll tell you. I live in a four-story brownstone roominghouse on the Upper West Side between Columbus Avenue and Central Park West. I live on the top floor; rear; west. It's a laughably 190 small room, and one of my walls is made of beaverboard; this beaverboard separates my room from another laughably small room, so I assume that the two rooms were once one room, a small room, but not necessarily laughable. The room beyond my 195 beaverboard wall is occupied by a colored queen who always keeps his door open; well, not always but *always* when he's plucking his eyebrows, which he does with Buddhist concentration. This colored queen has rotten teeth, which is rare, and he has a Japanese 200 kimono, which is also pretty rare; and he wears this kimono to and from the john in the hall, which is pretty frequent. I mean, he goes to the john a lot. He never bothers me, and he never brings anyone up to his room. All he does is pluck his eyebrows, wear his 205 kimono and go to the john. Now, the two front rooms on my floor are a little larger, I guess; but they're pretty small, too. There's a Puerto Rican family in one of them, a husband, a wife, and some kids; I don't know how many. These people entertain a lot. 210 And in the other front room, there's somebody living there, but I don't know who it is. I've never seen who it is. Never. Never ever.

PETER: *(Embarrassed)* Why . . . why do you live there?

JERRY: *(From a distance again)* I don't know. 215

PETER: It doesn't sound like a very nice place . . . where you live.

JERRY: Well, no; it isn't an apartment in the East Seventies. But, then again, I don't have one wife, two daughters, two cats and two parakeets. What I do 220 have, I have toilet articles, a few clothes, a hot plate that I'm not supposed to have, a can opener, one that works with a key, you know; a knife, two forks, and two spoons, one small, one large; three plates, a cup, a saucer, a drinking glass, two picture frames, both 225 empty, eight or nine books, a pack of pornographic playing cards, regular deck, an old Western Union typewriter that prints nothing but capital letters, and a small strongbox without a lock which has in it . . . what? Rocks! Some rocks . . . sea-rounded 230 rocks I picked up on the beach when I was a kid. Under which . . . weighed down . . . are some letters . . . please letters . . . please why don't you do this, and please when will you do that letters. And when letters, too. When will you write? When will 235

Jerry talks about his apartment.

you come? When? These letters are from more recent years.

PETER: *(Stares glumly at his shoes, then)* About those two
empty picture frames . . . ?

240 **JERRY:** I don't see why they need any explanation at
all. Isn't it clear? I don't have pictures of anyone to
put in them.

PETER: Your parents . . . perhaps . . . a girl friend . . .

JERRY: You're a very sweet man, and you're possessed
245 of a truly enviable innocence. But good old Mom
and good old Pop are dead . . . you know? . . . I'm
broken up about it, too . . . I mean really. BUT. That
particular vaudeville act is playing the cloud circuit
now, so I don't see how I can look at them, all neat
250 and framed. Besides, or, rather, to be pointed about
it, good old Mom walked out on good old Pop when
I was ten and a half years old; she embarked on an
adulterous turn of our southern states . . . a journey
of a year's duration . . . and her most constant com-
255 panion . . . among others, among many others . . .
was a Mr. Barleycorn. At least, that's what good old
Pop told me after he went down . . . came back . . .
brought her body north. We'd received the news between Christmas and New Year's, you see, that good
260 old Mom had parted with the ghost in some dump
in Alabama. And, without the ghost . . . she was less
welcome. I mean, what was she? A stiff . . . a northern stiff. At any rate, good old Pop celebrated the
New Year for an even two weeks and then slapped
265 into the front of a somewhat moving city omnibus,
which sort of cleaned things out family-wise. Well
no; then there was Mom's sister, who was given neither to sin nor the consolations of the bottle. I moved
in on her, and my memory of her is slight excepting I

remember still that she did all things dourly: sleep- 270
ing, eating, working, praying. She dropped dead on
the stairs to her apartment, my apartment then, too,
on the afternoon of my high school graduation. A
terribly middle-European joke, if you ask me.

PETER: Oh, my; oh, my. 275

JERRY: Oh, your what? But that was a long time ago,
and I have no feeling about any of it that I care to
admit to myself. Perhaps you can see, though, why
good old Mom and good old Pop are frameless.
What's your name? Your first name? 280

PETER: I'm Peter.

JERRY: I'd forgotten to ask you. I'm Jerry.

PETER: *(With a slight, nervous laugh)* Hello, Jerry.

JERRY: *(Nods his hello)* And let's see now; what's the
point of having a girl's picture, especially in two 285
frames? I have two picture frames, you remember. I
never see the pretty little ladies more than once, and
most of them wouldn't be caught in the same room
with a camera. It's odd, and I wonder if it's sad.

PETER: The girls? 290

JERRY: No. I wonder if it's sad that I never see the little
ladies more than once. I've never been able to have
sex with, or, how is it put? . . . make love to anybody
more than once. Once; that's it. . . . Oh, wait; for a
week and a half, when I was fifteen and I hang my 295
head in shame that puberty was late . . . I was a
h-o-m-o-s-e-x-u-a-l. I mean, I was queer . . . *(Very
fast)* . . . queer, queer, queer . . . with bells ringing,
banners snapping in the wind. And for those eleven
days, I met at least twice a day with the park super- 300
intendent's son . . . a Greek boy, whose birthday was
the same as mine, except he was a year older. I think
I was very much in love . . . maybe just with sex. But
that was the jazz of a very special hotel, wasn't it?
And now; oh, do I love the little ladies; really, I love 305
them. For about an hour.

PETER: Well, it seems perfectly simple to me . . .

JERRY: *(Angry)* Look! Are you going to tell me to get
married and have parakeets?

PETER: *(Angry himself)* Forget the parakeets! And stay 310
single if you want to. It's no business of mine. I didn't
start this conversation in the . . .

JERRY: All right, all right. I'm sorry. All right? You're
not angry?

PETER: *(Laughing)* No, I'm not angry. 315

JERRY: (*Relieved*) Good. (*Now back to his previous tone*) Interesting that you asked me about the picture frames. I would have thought that you would have asked me about the pornographic playing cards.

320 **PETER:** (*With a knowing smile*) Oh, I've seen those cards.

JERRY: That's not the point. (*Laughs*) I suppose when you were a kid you and your pals passed them around, or you had a pack of your own.

PETER: Well, I guess a lot of us did.

325 **JERRY:** And you threw them away just before you got married.

PETER: Oh, now; look here. I didn't *need* anything like that when I got older.

JERRY: No?

330 **PETER:** (*Embarrassed*) I'd rather not talk about these things.

JERRY: So? Don't. Besides, I wasn't trying to plumb your post-adolescent sexual life and hard times; what I wanted to get at is the value difference be-
335 tween pornographic playing cards when you're a kid, and pornographic playing cards when you're older. It's that when you're a kid you use the cards as a substitute for a real experience, and when you're older you use real experience as a substitute for the
340 fantasy. But I imagine you'd rather hear about what happened at the zoo.

PETER: (*Enthusiastic*) Oh, yes; the zoo. (*Then, awkward*) That is . . . if you . . .

JERRY: Let me tell you about why I went . . . well,
345 let me tell you some things. I've told you about the fourth floor of the roominghouse where I live. I think the rooms are better as you go down, floor by floor. I guess they are; I don't know. I don't know any of the people on the third and second floors. Oh, wait!
350 I do know that there's a lady living on the third floor, in the front. I know because she cries all the time. Whenever I go out or come back in, whenever I pass her door, I always hear her crying, muffled, but . . . very determined. Very determined indeed. But the
355 one I'm getting to, and all about the dog, is the land-lady. I don't like to use words that are too harsh in describing people. I don't like to. But the landlady is a fat, ugly, mean, stupid, unwashed, misanthropic, cheap, drunken bag of garbage. And you may have
360 noticed that I very seldom use profanity, so I can't describe her as well as I might.

PETER: You describe her . . . vividly.

JERRY: Well, thanks. Anyway, she has a dog, and I will tell you about the dog, and she and her dog are the gatekeepers of my dwelling. The woman is bad 365 enough; she leans around in the entrance hall, spying to see that I don't bring in things or people, and when she's had her mid-afternoon pint of lemon-flavored gin she always stops me in the hall, and grabs ahold of my coat or my arm, and she presses 370 her disgusting body up against me to keep me in a corner so she can talk to me. The smell of her body and her breath . . . you can't imagine it . . . and some-where, somewhere in the back of that pea-sized brain of hers, an organ developed just enough to let 375 her eat, drink, and emit, she has some foul parody of sexual desire. And I, Peter, I am the object of her sweaty lust.

PETER: That's disgusting. That's . . . horrible.

JERRY: But I have found a way to keep her off. When 380 she talks to me, when she presses herself to my body and mumbles about her room and how I should come there, I merely say: but, Love; wasn't yester-day enough for you, and the day before? Then she puzzles, she makes slits of her tiny eyes, she sways 385 a little, and then, Peter . . . and it is at this moment that I think I might be doing some good in that tor-mented house . . . a simple-minded smile begins to form on her unthinkable face, and she giggles and groans as she thinks about yesterday and the day 390 before; as she believes and relives what never hap-pened. Then, she motions to that black monster of a dog she has, and she goes back to her room. And I am safe until our next meeting.

PETER: It's so . . . unthinkable. I find it hard to believe 395 that people such as that really *are*.

JERRY: (*Lightly mocking*) It's for reading about, isn't it?

PETER: (*Seriously*) Yes.

JERRY: And fact is better left to fiction. You're right, Peter. Well, what I have been meaning to tell you 400 about is the dog; I shall, now.

PETER: (*Nervously*) Oh, yes; the dog.

JERRY: Don't go. You're not thinking of going, are you?

PETER: Well . . . no, I don't think so.

JERRY: (*As if to a child*) Because after I tell you about the 405 dog, do you know what then? Then . . . then I'll tell you about what happened at the zoo.

PETER: (*Laughing faintly*) You're . . . you're full of stories, aren't you?

410   **JERRY:**   You don't *have* to listen. Nobody is holding you here; remember that. Keep that in your mind.

         PETER: *(Irritably)* I know that.

         JERRY: You do? Good.

         (The following long speech, it seems to me, should be done with a great deal of action, to achieve a hypnotic effect on PETER, *and on the audience, too. Some specific actions have been suggested, but the director and the actor playing* JERRY *might best work it out for themselves)*

415   ALL RIGHT. *(As if reading from a huge billboard)* THE STORY OF JERRY AND THE DOG! *(Natural again)* What I am going to tell you has something to do with how sometimes it's necessary to go a long distance out of the way in order to come back a short

420   distance correctly; or, maybe I only think that it has something to do with that. But, it's why I went to the zoo today, and why I walked north . . . northerly, rather . . . until I came here. All right. The dog, I think I told you, is a black monster of a beast: an

425   oversized head, tiny, tiny ears, and eyes . . . bloodshot, infected, maybe; and a body you can see the ribs through the skin. The dog is black, all black; all black except for the bloodshot eyes, and . . . yes . . . and an open sore on its . . . *right* forepaw; that is red, too. And, oh yes; the poor monster, and I do

430   believe it's an old dog . . . it's certainly a misused one . . . almost always has an erection . . . of sorts. That's red, too. And . . . what else? . . . oh, yes; there's a gray-yellow-white color, too, when he bares his fangs. Like this: Grrrrrrr! Which is what he did

435   when he saw me for the first time . . . the day I moved in. I worried about that animal the very first minute I met him. Now, animals don't take to me like Saint Francis had birds hanging off him all the time. What I mean is: Animals are indifferent to me . . . like

440   people *(He smiles slightly)* . . . most of the time. But this dog wasn't indifferent. From the very beginning he'd snarl and then go for me, to get one of my legs. Not like he was rabid, you know; he was sort of a stumbly dog, but he wasn't half-assed, either. It was a good,

445   stumbly run; but I always got away. He got a piece of my trouser leg, look, you can see right here, where it's mended; he got that the second day I lived there; but, I kicked free and got upstairs fast, so that was that. *(Puzzles)* I still don't know to this day how the

450   other roomers manage it, but you know what I *think:* I think it had to do only with me. Cozy. So. Anyway, this went on for over a week, whenever I came in; but never when I went out. That's funny. Or, it *was* funny. I could pack up and live in the street for all

455   the dog cared. Well, I thought about it up in my room one day, one of the times after I'd bolted upstairs, and I made up my mind. I decided: First, I'll kill the

dog with kindness, and if that doesn't work . . . I'll just kill him. *(PETER winces)* Don't react, Peter; just listen. So, the next day I went out and bought a bag 460 of hamburgers, medium rare, no catsup, no onion; and on the way home I threw away all the rolls and kept just the meat.

     (Action for the following, perhaps)

When I got back to the roominghouse the dog was waiting for me. I half opened the door that led into 465 the entrance hall, and there he was; waiting for me. It figured. I went in, very cautiously, and I had the hamburgers, you remember; I opened the bag, and I set the meat down about twelve feet from where the dog was snarling at me. Like so! He snarled; 470 stopped snarling; sniffed; moved slowly; then faster; then faster toward the meat. Well, when he got to it he stopped, and he looked at me. I smiled; but tentatively, you understand. He turned his face back to the hamburgers, smelled, sniffed some more, and 475 then . . . RRRAAAAGGGGGHHHH, like that . . . he tore into them. It was as if he had never eaten anything in his life before, except like garbage. Which might very well have been the truth. I don't think the landlady ever eats anything but garbage. But. He 480 ate all the hamburgers, almost all at once, making sounds in his throat like a woman. *Then*, when he'd finished the meat, the hamburger, and tried to eat the paper, too, he sat down and smiled. I think he smiled; I know cats do. It was a very gratifying few 485 moments. Then, BAM, he snarled and made for me again. He didn't get me this time, either. So, I got upstairs, and I lay down on my bed and started to think about the dog again. To be truthful, I was offended, and I was damn mad, too. It was six perfectly good 490 hamburgers with not enough pork in them to make it disgusting. I was offended. But, after a while, I decided to try it for a few more days. If you think about it, this dog had what amounted to an antipathy toward me; really. And, I wondered if I mightn't 495 overcome this antipathy. So, I tried it for five more days, but it was always the same: snarl, sniff, move; faster; stare; gobble; RAAGGGHHH; smile; snarl; BAM. Well, now; by this time Columbus Avenue was strewn with hamburger rolls and I was less offended 500 than disgusted. So, I decided to kill the dog.

     (PETER raises a hand in protest)

Oh, don't be so alarmed, Peter; I didn't succeed. The day I tried to kill the dog I bought only one hamburger and what I thought was a murderous portion of rat poison. When I bought the hamburger I asked 505 the man not to bother with the roll, all I wanted was the meat. I expected some reaction from him, like: we don't sell no hamburgers without rolls; or,

Jerry tells Peter about his neighbor's dog.

wha' d'ya wanna do, eat it out'a ya han's? But no;
he smiled benignly, wrapped up the hamburger
in waxed paper, and said: A bite for ya pussy-cat?
I wanted to say: No, not really; it's part of a plan
to poison a dog I know. But, you can't say "a dog I
know" without sounding funny; so I said, a little too
loud, I'm afraid, and too formally: YES, A BITE FOR
MY PUSSY-CAT. People looked up. It always happens when I try to simplify things; people look up.
But that's neither hither nor thither. So. On my way
back to the roominghouse, I kneaded the hamburger
and the rat poison together between my hands, at
that point feeling as much sadness as disgust. I
opened the door to the entrance hall, and there the
monster was, waiting to take the offering and then
jump me. Poor bastard; he never learned that the
moment he took to smile before he went for me gave
me time enough to get out of range. BUT, there he
was; malevolence with an erection, waiting. I put
the poison patty down, moved toward the stairs and
watched. The poor animal gobbled the food down
as usual, smiled, which made me almost sick, and
then, BAM. But, I sprinted up the stairs, as usual,
and the dog didn't get me, as usual. AND IT CAME
TO PASS THAT THE BEAST WAS DEATHLY ILL.
I knew this because he no longer attended me, and
because the landlady sobered up. She stopped me in
the hall the same evening of the attempted murder
and confided the information that God had stuck
her puppy-dog a surely fatal blow. She had forgotten
her bewildered lust, and her eyes were wide open for
the first time. They looked like the dog's eyes. She
sniveled and implored me to pray for the animal. I
wanted to say to her: Madam, I have myself to pray
for, the colored queen, the Puerto Rican family, the
person in the front room whom I've never seen, the
woman who cries deliberately behind her closed
door, and the rest of the people in all roominghouses,
everywhere; besides, Madam, I don't understand
how to pray. But . . . to simplify things . . . I told her I
would pray. She looked up. She said that I was a liar,
and that I probably wanted the dog to die. I told her,
and there was so much truth here, that I didn't want
the dog to die. I didn't, and not just because I'd poi-

soned him. I'm afraid that I must tell you I wanted
the dog to live so that I could see what our new relationship might come to.   555
    (PETER *indicates his increasing displeasure
    and slowly growing antagonism*)
Please understand, Peter; that sort of thing is important. You must believe me; it *is* important. We have
to know the effect of our actions. (*Another deep sigh*)
Well, anyway; the dog recovered. I have no idea
why, unless he was a descendant of the puppy that   560
guarded the gates of hell or some such resort. I'm
not up on my mythology. (*He pronounces the word
myth*-o-logy) Are you?
    (PETER *sets to thinking, but* JERRY *goes on*)
At any rate, and you've missed the eight-thousand-
dollar question, Peter; at any rate, the dog recovered   565
his health and the landlady recovered her thirst,
in no way altered by the bow-wow's deliverance.
When I came home from a movie that was playing
on Forty-second Street, a movie I'd seen, or one that
was very much like one or several I'd seen, after the   570
landlady told me puppykins was better, I was so hoping for the dog to be waiting for me. I was . . . well,
how would you put it . . . enticed? . . . fascinated? . . .
no, I don't think so . . . heart-shatteringly anxious,
that's it; I was heart-shatteringly anxious to confront   575
my friend again.
    (PETER *reacts scoffingly*)
Yes, Peter; friend. That's the only word for it. I was
heart-shatteringly et cetera to confront my doggy
friend again. I came in the door and advanced,
unafraid, to the center of the entrance hall. The   580
beast was there . . . looking at me. And, you know,
he looked better for his scrape with the nevermind.
I stopped; I looked at him; he looked at me. I think
. . . I think we stayed a long time that way . . . still,
stone-statue . . . just looking at one another. I looked   585
more into his face than he looked into mine. I mean,
I can concentrate longer at looking into a dog's face
than a dog can concentrate at looking into mine, or
into anybody else's face, for that matter. But during
that twenty seconds or two hours that we looked   590
into each other's face, we made contact. Now, here is
what I had wanted to happen: I loved the dog now,
and I wanted him to love me. I had tried to love, and
I had tried to kill, and both had been unsuccessful
by themselves. I hoped . . . and I don't really know   595
why I expected the dog to understand anything,
much less my motivations . . . I hoped that the dog
would understand.
    (PETER *seems to be hypnotized*)
It's just . . . it's just that . . . (JERRY *is abnormally tense,
now*) . . . it's just that if you can't deal with people,   600

you have to make a start somewhere. WITH ANI-
MALS! *(Much faster now, and like a conspirator)* Don't
you see? A person has to have some way of dealing
with SOMETHING. If not with people . . . if not with
605 people . . . SOMETHING. With a bed, with a cockroach, with a mirror . . . no, that's too hard, that's one
of the last steps. With a cockroach, with a . . . with
a . . . with a carpet, a roll of toilet paper . . . no, not
that, either . . . that's a mirror, too; always check
610 bleeding. You see how hard it is to find things?
With a street corner, and too many lights, all colors
reflecting on the oily-wet streets . . . with a wisp of
smoke, a wisp . . . of smoke . . . with . . . with pornographic playing cards, with a strongbox . . . WITH-
615 OUT A LOCK . . . with love, with vomiting, with
crying, with fury because the pretty little ladies
aren't pretty little ladies, with making money with
your body which is an act of love and I could prove it,
with howling because you're alive; with God. How
620 about that? WITH GOD WHO IS A COLORED
QUEEN WHO WEARS A KIMONO AND PLUCKS
HIS EYEBROWS, WHO IS A WOMAN WHO
CRIES WITH DETERMINATION BEHIND HER
CLOSED DOOR . . . with God who, I'm told, turned
625 his back on the whole thing some time ago . . . with
. . . someday, with people. *(JERRY sighs the next word
heavily)* People. With an idea; a concept. And where
better, where ever better in this humiliating excuse
for a jail, where better to communicate one single,
630 simple-minded idea than in an entrance hall?
Where? It would be A START! Where better to make
a beginning . . . to understand and just possibly be
understood . . . a beginning of an understanding,
than with . . .
(Here JERRY seems to fall into almost grotesque fatigue)
635 than with A DOG. Just that; a dog.
*(Here there is a silence that might be prolonged for a
moment or so; then JERRY wearily finishes his story)*
A dog. It seemed like a perfectly sensible idea. Man
is a dog's best friend, remember. So: the dog and I
looked at each other. I longer than the dog. And what
I saw then has been the same ever since. Whenever
640 the dog and I see each other we both stop where we
are. We regard each other with a mixture of sadness
and suspicion, and then we feign indifference. We
walk past each other safely; we have an understanding. It's very sad, but you'll have to admit that it is
645 an understanding. We had made many attempts at
contact, and we had failed. The dog has returned to
garbage, and I to solitary but free passage. I have not
returned. I mean to say, I have *gained* solitary free
passage, if that much further loss can be said to be
650 gain. I have learned that neither kindness nor cruelty
by themselves, independent of each other, creates any

effect beyond themselves; and I have learned that
the two combined, together, at the same time, are the
teaching emotion. And what is gained is loss. And
what has been the result: the dog and I have attained 655
a compromise; more of a bargain, really. We neither
love nor hurt because we do not try to reach each
other. And, *was* trying to feed the dog an act of love?
And, perhaps, was the dog's attempt to bite me *not*
an act of love? If we can so misunderstand, well then, 660
why have we invented the word love in the first place?
*(There is silence. JERRY moves to PETER's bench
and sits down beside him. This is the first time
that JERRY has sat down during the play.)*
The Story of Jerry and the Dog: the end.
(PETER is silent)
Well, Peter? *(JERRY is suddenly cheerful)* Well, Peter?
Do you think I could sell that story to the *Reader's
Digest* and make a couple of hundred bucks for *The* 665
Most Unforgettable Character I've Ever Met? Huh?
(JERRY is animated, but PETER is disturbed)
Oh, come on now, Peter; tell me what you think.

PETER: *(Numb)* I . . . I don't understand what . . . I don't
think I . . . *(Now, almost tearfully)* Why did you tell me
all of this? 670

JERRY: Why not?

PETER: I DON'T UNDERSTAND!

JERRY: *(Furious, but whispering)* That's a lie.

PETER: No. No, it's not.

JERRY: *(Quietly)* I tried to explain it to you as I went 675
along. I went slowly; it all has to do with . . .

PETER: I DON'T WANT TO HEAR ANY MORE. I
don't understand you, or your landlady, or her dog . . .

JERRY: *Her* dog! I thought it was my . . . No. No, you're
right. It *is* her dog. *(Looks at PETER intently, shaking* 680
his head) I don't know what I was thinking about; of
course you don't understand. *(In a monotone, wearily)* I
don't live in your block I'm not married to two parakeets, or whatever your setup is. I am a *permanent
transient*, and my home is the sickening rooming- 685
houses on the West Side of New York City, which is
the greatest city in the world. Amen.

PETER: I'm . . . I'm sorry; I didn't mean to . . .

JERRY: Forget it. I suppose you don't quite know what
to make of me, eh? 690

PETER: *(A joke)* We get all kinds in publishing. *(Chuckles)*

JERRY: You're a funny man. *(He forces a laugh)* You know
that? You're a very . . . a richly comic person.

PETER: *(Modestly, but amused)* Oh, now, not really. *(Still chuckling)* 695

JERRY: Peter, do I annoy you, or confuse you?

PETER: *(Lightly)* Well, I must confess that this wasn't the kind of afternoon I'd anticipated.

JERRY: You mean, I'm not the gentleman you were expecting. 700

PETER: I wasn't expecting anybody.

JERRY: No, I don't imagine you were. But I'm here, and I'm not leaving.

PETER: *(Consulting his watch)* Well, you may not be, but I must be getting home now. 705

JERRY: Oh, come on; stay a while longer.

PETER: I really should get home; you see . . .

JERRY: *(Tickles PETER's ribs with his fingers)* Oh, come on.

PETER: *(He is very ticklish; as JERRY continues to tickle him his voice becomes falsetto)* No, I . . . OHHHHH! Don't do that. Stop, stop. Ohhh, no, no. 710

JERRY: Oh, come on.

PETER: *(As JERRY tickles)* Oh, hee, hee, hee. I must go. I . . . hee, hee, hee. After all, stop, stop, hee, hee, hee, after all, the parakeets will be getting dinner ready soon. Hee, hee. And the cats are setting the table. Stop, stop, and, and . . . *(PETER is beside himself now)* and we're having . . . hee, hee . . . uh . . . ho, ho, ho. 715
(JERRY stops tickling PETER, but the combination of the tickling and his own mad whimsy has PETER laughing almost hysterically. As his laughter continues, then subsides, JERRY watches him, with a curious fixed smile.)

JERRY: Peter?

PETER: Oh, ha, ha, ha, ha, ha. What? What?

JERRY: Listen, now. 720

PETER: Oh, ho, ho. What . . . what is it, Jerry? Oh, my.

JERRY: *(Mysteriously)* Peter, do you want to know what happened at the zoo?

PETER: Ah, ha, ha. The what? Oh, yes; the zoo. Oh, ho, ho. Well, I had my own zoo there for a moment with . . . hee, hee, the parakeets getting dinner ready, and the . . . ha, ha, whatever it was, the . . . 725

JERRY: *(Calmly)* Yes, that was very funny, Peter. I wouldn't have expected it. But do you want to hear about what happened at the zoo, or not? 730

PETER: Yes. Yes, by all means; tell me what happened at the zoo. Oh, my. I don't know what happened to me.

JERRY: Now I'll let you in on what happened at the zoo; but first, I should tell you why I went to the zoo. I went to the zoo to find out more about the way people exist with animals, and the way animals exist with each other, and with people too. It probably wasn't a fair test, what with everyone separated by bars from everyone else, the animals for the most part from each other, and always the people from the animals. But, if it's a zoo, that's the way it is. *(He pokes PETER on the arm)* Move over. 735 740

PETER: *(Friendly)* I'm sorry, haven't you enough room? *(He shifts a little)*

JERRY: *(Smiling slightly)* Well, all the animals are there, and all the people are there, and it's Sunday and all the children are there. *(He pokes PETER again)* Move over. 745

PETER: *(Patiently, still friendly)* All right.
(He moves some more, and JERRY has all the room he might need)

JERRY: And it's a hot day, so all the stench is there, too, and all the balloon sellers, and all the ice cream sellers, and all the seals are barking, and all the birds are screaming. *(Pokes PETER harder)* Move over! 750

PETER: *(Beginning to be annoyed)* Look here, you have more than enough room! *(But he moves more, and is now fairly cramped at one end of the bench)* 755

JERRY: And I am there, and it's feeding time at the lions' house, and the lion keeper comes into the lion cage, one of the lion cages, to feed one of the lions. *(Punches PETER on the arm, hard)* MOVE OVER! 760

Peter begins to lose his patience.

PETER: (*Very annoyed*) I can't move over any more, and stop hitting me. What's the matter with you?

JERRY: Do you want to hear the story? (*Punches* PETER's *arm again*)

765 **PETER:** (*Flabbergasted*) I'm not so sure! I certainly don't want to be punched in the arm.

JERRY: (*Punches* PETER's *arm again*) Like that?

PETER: Stop it! What's the matter with you?

JERRY: I'm crazy, you bastard.

770 **PETER:** That isn't funny.

JERRY: Listen to me, Peter. I want this bench. You go sit on the bench over there, and if you're good I'll tell you the rest of the story.

775 **PETER:** (*Flustered*) But . . . whatever for? What *is* the matter with you? Besides, I see no reason why I should give up this bench. I sit on this bench almost every Sunday afternoon, in good weather. It's se- cluded here; there's never anyone sitting here, so I have it all to myself.

780 **JERRY:** (*Softly*) Get off this bench, Peter; I want it.

PETER: (*Almost whining*) No.

JERRY: I said I want this bench, and I'm going to have it. Now get over there.

PETER: People can't have everything they want. You
785 should know that; it's a rule; people can have some of the things they want, but they can't have everything.

JERRY: (*Laughs*) Imbecile! You're slow-witted!

PETER: Stop that!

JERRY: You're a vegetable! Go lie down on the ground.

790 **PETER:** Now *you* listen to me. I've put up with you all afternoon.

JERRY: Not really.

PETER: LONG ENOUGH. I've put up with you long enough. I've listened to you because you seemed
795 . . . well, because I thought you wanted to talk to somebody.

JERRY: You put things well; economically, and, yet . . . oh, what is the word I want to put justice to your . . . JESUS, you make me sick . . . get off here and give
800 me my bench.

PETER: MY BENCH!

JERRY: (*Pushes* PETER *almost, but not quite, off the bench*) Get out of my sight.

PETER: (*Regaining his position*) God da . . . mn you.
That's enough! I've had enough of you. I will not give 805
up this bench; you can't have it, and that's that. Now, go away.
    (JERRY *snorts but does not move*)
Go away, I said.
    (JERRY *does not move*)
Get away from here. If you don't move on . . . you're a bum . . . that's what you are. . . . If you don't move on, 810
I'll get a policeman here and make you go.
    (JERRY *laughs, stays*)
I warn you, I'll call a policeman.

JERRY: (*Softly*) You won't find a policeman around here; they're all over on the west side of the park chasing fairies down from trees or out of the bushes. That's 815
all they do. That's their function. So scream your head off; it won't do you any good.

PETER: POLICE! I warn you, I'll have you arrested. POLICE! (*Pause*) I said POLICE! (*Pause*) I feel ridiculous. 820

JERRY: You look ridiculous: a grown man screaming for the police on a bright Sunday afternoon in the park with nobody harming you. If a policeman *did* fill his quota and come sludging over this way he'd probably take you in as a nut. 825

PETER: (*With disgust and impotence*) Great God, I just came here to read, and now you want me to give up the bench. You're mad.

JERRY: Hey, I got news for you, as they say. I'm on your precious bench, and you're never going to have it for 830
yourself again.

PETER: (*Furious*) Look, you; get off my bench. I don't care if it makes any sense or not. I want this bench to myself; I want you OFF IT!

JERRY: (*Mocking*) Aw . . . look who's mad. 835

PETER: GET OUT!

JERRY: No.

PETER: I WARN YOU!

JERRY: Do you know how ridiculous you look *now?*

PETER: (*His fury and self-consciousness have possessed him*) 840
It doesn't matter. (*He is almost crying*) GET AWAY FROM MY BENCH!

JERRY: Why? You have everything in the world you want; you've told me about your home, and your family, and *your own* little zoo. You have everything, 845
and now you want this bench. Are these the things men fight for? Tell me, Peter, is this bench, this iron

850 and this wood, is this your honor? Is this the thing in the world you'd fight for? Can you think of anything more absurd?

PETER: Absurd? Look, I'm not going to talk to you about honor, or even try to explain it to you. Besides, it isn't a question of honor; but even if it were, you wouldn't understand.

855 JERRY: *(Contemptuously)* You don't even know what you're saying, do you? This is probably the first time in your life you've had anything more trying to face than changing your cats' toilet box. Stupid! Don't you have any idea, not even the slightest, what other 860 people *need?*

PETER: Oh, boy, listen to you; well, you don't need this bench. That's for sure.

JERRY: Yes; yes, I do.

PETER: *(Quivering)* I've come here for years; I have 865 hours of great pleasure, great satisfaction, right here. And that's important to a man. I'm a responsible person, and I'm a GROWNUP. This is my bench, and you have no right to take it away from me.

JERRY: Fight for it, then. Defend yourself; defend your 870 bench.

PETER: You've *pushed* me to it. Get up and fight.

JERRY: Like a man?

PETER: *(Still angry)* Yes, like a man, if you insist on mocking me even further.

875 JERRY: I'll have to give you credit for one thing; you *are* a vegetable, and a slightly nearsighted one, I think . . .

PETER: THAT'S ENOUGH. . . .

JERRY: . . . but, you know, as they say on TV all the 880 time—you know—and I mean this, Peter, you have a certain dignity; it surprises me . . .

PETER: STOP!

JERRY: *(Rises lazily)* Very well, Peter, we'll battle for the bench, but we're not evenly matched.
(He takes out and clicks open an ugly-looking knife)

PETER: *(Suddenly awakening to the reality of the situation)* 885 You *are* mad! You're stark raving mad! YOU'RE GOING TO KILL ME!
(But before PETER has time to think what to do, JERRY tosses the knife at PETER's feet)

JERRY: There you go. Pick it up. You have the knife and we'll be more evenly matched.

Peter brandishes Jerry's knife.

PETER: *(Horrified)* No!

JERRY: *(Rushes over to PETER, grabs him by the collar; PETER rises; their faces almost touch)*
Now you pick up that knife and you fight with me. 890 You fight for your self-respect; you fight for that god-damned bench.

PETER: *(Struggling)* No! Let . . . let go of me! He . . . Help!

JERRY: *(Slaps PETER on each "fight")* You fight, you miserable bastard; fight for that bench; fight for your man- 895 hood, you pathetic little vegetable. *(Spits in PETER's face)* You couldn't even get your wife with a male child.

PETER: *(Breaks away, enraged)* It's a matter of genetics, not manhood, you . . . you monster.
(He darts down, picks up the knife and backs off a little; he is breathing heavily)
I'll give you one last chance; get out of here and leave 900 me alone!
(He holds the knife with a firm arm, but far in front of him, not to attack, but to defend)

JERRY: *(Sighs heavily)* So be it!
(With a rush he charges PETER and impales himself on the knife. Tableau: For just a moment, complete silence, JERRY impaled on the knife at the end of PE-TER's still firm arm. Then PETER screams, pulls away, leaving the knife in JERRY. JERRY is motionless, on point. Then he, too, screams, and it must be the sound of an infuriated and fatally wounded animal. With the knife in him, he stumbles back to the bench that PETER had vacated. He crumbles there, sitting, fac-ing PETER, his eyes wide in agony, his mouth open)

PETER: *(Whispering)* Oh my God, oh my God, oh my God. . . .
(He repeats these words many times, very rapidly)

JERRY: *(JERRY is dying; but now his expression seems to change. His features relax, and while his voice varies, sometimes wrenched with pain, for the most part he seems removed from his dying. He smiles)*

905   Peter, thank you, Peter. I mean that now; thank you very much.

(PETER's mouth drops open. He cannot move; he is transfixed)

I came unto you *(He laughs, so faintly)* and you have comforted me. Dear Peter.

PETER: *(Almost fainting)* Oh my God!

910   **JERRY:** You'd better go now. Somebody might come by, and you don't want to be here when anyone comes.

PETER: *(Does not move, but begins to weep)* Oh my God, oh my God.

JERRY: And Peter, I'll tell you something now; you're not really a vegetable; it's all right, you're an animal.
915   You're an animal, too. But you'd better hurry now, Peter. Hurry, you'd better go . . . see?

(JERRY takes a handkerchief and with great effort and pain wipes the knife handle clean of fingerprints)

Hurry away, Peter.

(PETER begins to stagger away)

Wait . . . wait, Peter. Take your book . . . book. Right here . . . beside me . . . on your bench . . . my bench,
920   rather. Come . . . take your book.

(PETER starts for the book, but retreats)

Hurry . . . Peter.

(PETER rushes to the bench, grabs the book, retreats)

Jerry lies dead on the park bench.

Very good, Peter . . . very good. Now . . . hurry away.

(PETER hesitates for a moment, then flees, stage-left)

Hurry away. . . . *(His eyes are closed now)* Hurry away, your parakeets are making the dinner . . . the cats . . . are setting the table . . .   925

PETER: *(Offstage)* *(A pitiful howl)* OH MY GOD!

JERRY: *(His eyes still closed, he shakes his head and speaks; a combination of scornful mimicry and supplication)* Oh . . . my . . . God.

(He is dead)

Writing from Reading

Summarize

1 Two men meet in a park in an incident that leads to a disastrous end. Did you have any sense when first reading the play of the conclusion to come?

Analyze Craft

2 The setting is spare, there are only two actors, and their dialogue seems low-key, offhand. How does the playwright create suspense and then heighten it by means of their speech?

Analyze Voice

3 How would you characterize the diction—the vocabulary and word choice—of the two actors? Use examples from the dialogue to show the difference between the social standing of the establishment figure, Peter, and the outcast, Jerry. Is Jerry's long monologue realistic?

Synthesize Summary and Analysis

4 This play focuses partly on isolation and its perils. How does its staging emphasize this condition?

Interpret the Play

5 In what ways does the play lead us to see the animal in all of us?

CONTINUED FROM PAGE 27

Anyone who's ever sat quietly in a dark room facing forward while another person under a spotlight speaks has had the experience of the theater. In addition to creating characters and dialogue and plot, a playwright must make the play come alive on the stage. In his interview, Edward Albee says everything you need to know about how to stage a play can be found in reading the text itself:

> *The intention is there in the text. The intention is the experience of the play that I had while I was writing it. Because when I write a play . . . I see it, I hear it as a play being performed in front of me, and that's what I want to see on the stage—the same experience that I had while writing it.*

He directs his actors back to the text when they have a question about how to perform a work. The experience of the play can begin with the text, but its success or failure is on the stage, where a lot of its energy and—at its best—its electric feel comes from the vitality of the immediate interaction of live actors with a live audience.

If you are fortunate enough to be able to see a play performed, then you can look at how those elements come alive onstage. It's not perhaps an accident that there are fewer classic works of drama than of poetry or prose; the additional dimension of stagecraft makes the genre all the more demanding and complex. In a short story or poem, a good deal of the action transpires in the reader's mind; in drama, however, it must be played out. You have to get your characters on and off the stage, you have to hear what they're thinking in the form of uttered speech. Dialogue is crucial (though there's a subset of theater called **mime,** in which silence is the rule), and gestures must be clear. Even the simplest of dramas is multidimensional when performed; stage "business" is a major—indeed an inescapable—component of the whole.

"I don't think that the theater is, necessarily, only about entertainment. I think it's entertainment that reaches the soul."

Conversation with Arthur Miller

Your experience of yourself as one person among many in the audience when the curtain goes up is different even from your experience of viewing a movie, where performances don't alter night by night and the actors interact with a camera lens rather than an audience. But even with the movies, your reaction as the audience can depend on whether you watch it at home alone or at a crowded cineplex. Once you've imagined yourself as the director, the actors, and the audience, you can evaluate the director's approach, the actor's efforts and energy, and the attention of the audience as the plot unfolds. Following is part of a *New York Times* review of the first production in America of Edward Albee's first play, *The Zoo Story*. Note how the reviewer comments on the staging, the acting, and the plot.

"Why, when people can play any rock star they want to on a CD, do they flock to a concert in huge numbers? Why, when they can see a political figure on television . . . do they go to a political rally? The reason is for the experience of being with other people, having a communal experience, and being able to share that with other people. The reason theater has withstood the challenges . . . is the experience of going to a live performance." Conversation with Ed Wilson

Brooks Atkinson's *New York Times* January 15, 1960, review of the opening in America of Edward Albee's *The Zoo Story*

After the banalities of Broadway it tones the muscles and freshens the system to examine the squalor of Off Broadway. . . . [Two actors] sufficed for the short play put on at the Provincetown Playhouse last evening [of] Edward Albee's "The Zoo Story."

The Cast
Jerry . . . . George Maharis
Peter . . . . William Daniels

"The Zoo Story" is a dialogue . . . interesting and well acted by intelligent professionals. Nothing of enduring value is said . . . but [the play] captures some part of the dismal mood that infects many writers today.

Mr. Albee's "The Zoo Story" does not have so much literary distinction. . . . Mr Albee is more the reporter. There are two characters and two benches in his play set in Central Park. A cultivated, complacent publisher is reading a book. An intense, aggressive young man in shabby dress strikes up a conversation with him.

Or, to be exact, a monologue. For the intruder wants to unburden his mind of his private miseries and resentments, and they pour out of him in a flow of wild, scabrous, psychotic details. Since Mr. Albee is an excellent writer and the designer of dialogue and since he apparently knows the city, "The Zoo Story" is consistently interesting and illuminating—odd and pithy. It ends melodramatically as if Mr. Albee had lost control of his material. Although the conclusion is theatrical, it lacks the sense of improvisation that characterizes the main body of the play.

Milton Katselas has staged "The Zoo Story" admirably; and Mr. Maharis' overwrought yet searching intruder, and Mr. Daniels' perplexed publisher are first-rate pieces of acting.

Although the Provincetown bill is hardly glamorous, it has a point of view. Mr. Albee write[s] on the assumption that the human condition is stupid and ludicrous.

Suggestions for Writing

1. Why does Brooks Atkinson write that the ending is "theatrical," and is that intended as a compliment? Is the rest of the play theatrical? How would you characterize a theater style that is not theatrical?

2. Go to the crime page of your daily or weekly newspaper or your Internet source for news and single out a crime report. Try to reimagine it as a one-act play.

3. Compare your reaction to that of the reviewer. Brooks Atkinson was an important force in American theater of the day and a major factor in the question of whether or not a play would succeed. Find several other articles about this play and compare the current opinion of the importance of *The Zoo Story*, which is still being performed nearly fifty years after its opening night.

"Writing is a way of thinking. It's a way of thinking about what you have read or what you have seen. It is your mirror to that, your reaction to that, and you have to be sure you're able to say exactly how it was this . . . affected you. . . . So what you are trying to do is not only understand how you felt about something . . . but you want then to communicate that to somebody else. . . . If you are muddy about it, or if you are too repetitious, or whatever the case might be, you have to find that out when you reread it and then you rewrite it."

Conversation with Edwin Wilson, available online at www.mhhe.com/delbanco1e

32 Writing

FROM READING TO WRITING

WHEN you write about what you read, first think about the title of the work. (What does The Zoo Story say to you?) Find out something about the author. (Edward Albee is a living playwright. He's still writing plays today. In his interview he says that "entertainment is misunderstood," and he wants to write plays that make people think. His plays were influential as "experimental theater.") Then think about the context in which the play was written. (Albee wrote the play in the 1950s and set it in the same time period. In a sense it's a tragedy, since someone dies in the play.) Annotate the work and record your general impressions of the play. (As one student writes, "The surprise ending was really upsetting. I thought the guy was going to try to kill Peter till the end. I was left with a really uneasy feeling about why Jerry would do that.") Your annotations of the play will help you think about how the play works and what it means to you.

Aside from a constant demand that you apply your understanding of what you read to the creation of a good paper about a work of literature, writing about drama requires a slight change in the way you prepare to write your essay. Its form is performance. It comes alive on the stage, not the page. Of the three principal literary modes (fiction, poetry, drama), drama relies most on voice. The actors must enter into the spirit and style of a role; a director should be able to communicate his or her interpretation of a play. To convey that attitude and interpretation, the director and actor establish a focal point of performance—a way of staging (and sometimes improvising on) a text. To write about drama, we do much the same; we imagine the text we are reading as if it were being performed.

about Drama

Q & A
A Conversation on Writing
Edwin Wilson

Writing As a Reporter

One [way to write about a play is] to simply report what happens in the play. This is what this play is about. Here are the characters. Here's what happens in the action. Here's where it takes place in terms of the setting. It takes place in the seventeenth century, the eighteenth century, or in modern times, World War II or the Vietnam War or the war in Iraq. It takes place in a certain time in a certain place with certain characters. And you are in effect being a reporter.

Experiencing a Play

Maybe you can say to yourself, "I don't really know what's going on in this play." That's a personal reaction. . . . Usually people do decide they like certain kinds of plays and don't like others, which is fine because it's a very individual sort of thing. So another way of writing about a play, and these are not mutually exclusive, but another way of writing about a play is to say how you feel about it. . . . You kind of analyze your feelings too as you go through the play because you shouldn't be locked into just one position. You should let yourself experience your own feelings as you go through reading a play.

Writing and Revising

There's an old saying . . . that plays are not written, they're rewritten. And what that means is the first time a play is written, it's almost never the finished product. Almost never. . . . Writing is really a process.

If you would like to view the entire interview with Edwin Wilson, go to **www.mhhe.com./delbanco1e.**

RESEARCH ASSIGNMENT   After viewing the entire video, describe what Edwin Wilson believes to be the special role played by the audience in the theater.

Edwin Wilson was the theater critic for *The Wall Street Journal* for twenty-two years and is the author of *The Theater Experience* as well as coauthor, with Alvin Goldfarb, of *Living Theater: A History* and *Theater: The Lively Art*. He has produced plays on and off-Broadway and the feature film *The Nashville Sound*. Wilson is also the author of two original plays, *The Bettinger Prize* and *Waterfall*.

TIP

Writing about Drama

- Ask yourself which elements (plot, character, setting) will have the biggest impact on the audience.
- Mark where scenes begin and end and show how the action unfolds.
- Note which character in the play changes the most and your own personal reaction to these changes.
- Use act and scene numbers when you quote lines from a play. Also use line numbers if the play is written in verse. For one-act plays, cite by page number.

A SAMPLE STUDENT ESSAY IN PROGRESS

Analyze the Assignment

When you write, are you doing an analysis or a review? These are common responses to a play. Make sure you know which you've been asked to write. A review is an argument. If you are asked to write a review (see Brooks Atkinson's review in chapter 31), you will need to include your opinion along with a summary of the work. List the actors, the director (or stage designer and costume designer, if these aspects are included as important points in your review), and the theater where the work is being performed. Then you will need to persuade your reader that your evaluation of the work is worthwhile. Provide your opinion of the work based on how effectively the script engaged you, how effectively the actors drew you in with their performances, and how effectively the director (or stage designer, costume designer, producer) interpreted the play for the stage. If the play is staged often (such as with Shakespeare), you may be able to use a point of comparison in your discussion of the performance you have reviewed.

If you are asked to compare, explain, or analyze, your paper will go beyond a summary of what happened in the play and will require an interpretation. That interpretation in drama will depend on recording how the play works. In the sections that follow you can chart the progress of our student Jim Hanks as he works through his considered response to this assignment:

> Assignment: Expand the close reading you completed of Edward Albee's *The Zoo Story* into a 4- to 5-page essay in which you analyze the unfolding of the dramatic action and what it suggests about contemporary life.

Jim thinks he has a kernel of an idea of what "*the unfolding of the dramatic action*" means, beginning with a sense of how to relate the beginning of the play to the unfolding middle and to the shocking conclusion. He also believes he can find his way from what he sees on the stage that the page conjures up in his imagination to "*what it suggests about contemporary life*." The vague sense he developed as he read the play that drama can serve as a lens through which we better understand our relationship to life and the world has grown for him into a clear idea. He has never been to Central Park in New York City and has never suffered Jerry's problems, or Peter's complacencies, but he can see aspects of his life in new and surprising ways.

One Student Begins

As Jim Hanks prepares to write about *The Zoo Story* by contemporary playwright Edward Albee, he wonders what he is supposed to focus on and how he will work up the material for his initial draft.

How do different elements affect the audience?   First, Jim builds his analysis on some practical understanding of the elements and techniques the play employs. He figures out which of the several elements of drama, such as dialogue, character, and setting, seem to have the most impact on the audience.

"To fully get a play, not just this one, but any play, you need to also imagine the impact on a crowd because it means that you are both specific as a person and part of an anonymous group that is responding. And the actors are responding to the audience. The play is not complete until the audience completes it."

Conversation with Arthur Kopit

Does the play's historical context help provide insight into the play?   After looking at what elements might have the most impact on the audience, Jim assesses the importance of the social and historical context of the play by noting when it was written and whether the piece is written about its own time.

"[I gather] my research, and then I start dealing with relationships. Change comes from what you absorbed from your relationships."

Conversation with Ruben Santiago-Hudson

What genre of play is it?   Jim feels his way into the tradition and conventions of the play's genre. For example, though a modern play, *The Zoo Story* can in a limited and technical sense also be described as a tragedy (see the discussion of tragedy and comedy in chapter 30), since it entails the death of a protagonist.

But, as your reading will show, there's also much real humor here, and you shouldn't overlook the comic aspects of the text. The term *tragicomedy* might be applied, though Albee would probably resist such a label; tragicomedy is the way another great modern playwright, Samuel Beckett (whom Albee praises in his interview), described his groundbreaking *Waiting for Godot* (a play in which the two characters spend the entire drama awaiting the arrival of a figure called Godot who never arrives and whose mysterious absence is sometimes considered a metaphor for God). Not even a hyphen divides the tragic and the comic mode: *tragicomedy* combines the two in one word.

A HISTORY OF COMEDY IN TRAGEDY

Greeks appended a satyr play—one of those down-and-dirty comic afterthoughts—to a trilogy of tragedies that were submitted for competition to be performed in their great drama festivals. This ironic mix of high seriousness and low humor—the "comic relief"—is also found in even the darkest plays of William Shakespeare. Although tragicomedies are found as early as Shakespeare as tragic plays with happy endings, modern tragicomedies are a complex blend of serious and light tones that yields dark or satiric results.

"It's a temptation of course to look at [a play] as if it were a short story or a novel, because there are a lot of similarities on the printed page. . . . It's an encounter just between you and what's on the page. . . . You have to begin to visualize . . . in effect, as you begin to read the play, you set the stage . . . then the play begins to unfold." Conversation with Edwin Wilson

Initial Response

Jim's annotations indicated that he felt surprised and confused by the play's ending. (In this regard he's not so very different from the reviewer for *The New York Times*, Brooks Atkinson, who also questioned the final action.) Jim records his feelings in a short initial response that might later help him see where his interest lies.

> Well, that was an unexpected conclusion. Not what I initially expected from a play called *The Zoo Story*. Jerry and Peter were both interesting characters. Strange, even though Jerry does most of the talking, I feel like I know Peter better. The details of his life are clearer in my mind than Jerry's, maybe because they're closer to my own. I can picture the black dog because it was described so much. Why is the anecdote about the dog such a focal point of the play? I mean, Jerry goes on and on about it, but it's not clear what a dog has to do with a "zoo story."

Explore Your Ideas

As Jim reviews his annotations, he imagines what he might see if he were to watch this play staged. In the "theater" of his mind, he sees two characters and a park setting. He decides to focus first on the characters, trying to figure out his response to them. Then he looks at the setting, comparing the zoo motif to the freedom of the park where the action takes place. He wonders about the mystery of the zoo and what has happened there. How does this relate to the meaning of the action? Jerry's death confuses him. He decides to put down his thoughts in a **freewriting** exercise.

Freewriting

> What happened at the zoo?! I can't decide if that was frustrating or confusing. Jerry made me uncomfortable. I can't decide how I would react if I was Peter on that bench. I think it would be easier to understand his reaction over the bench if

you saw this acted out. You could see the tension building more, the way Jerry forces him off the bench. I wonder what the zoo has to do with this. There were no animals and only two people. The setting is strange too: a wide open park. What animals were there? Cats and birds, and that detailed description of the dog. Were there any cages? Maybe there's a metaphor for a zoo here. I'd like to consider what Jerry and Peter might represent

Next, Jim takes his freewriting responses to a higher level of questioning—and comprehension—by writing a slightly more formal **journal entry.** Here he tries to expand the ideas in his freewriting and organize them into paragraphs.

"It's said to writers, write about what you know. I always like to turn that on its head and say write about what you didn't know you knew." Conversation with Arthur Kopit

Journaling

The first thing I noticed when I started *The Zoo Story* was that it was set in a park instead of a zoo. I was surprised because a park is a wide open place, but a zoo is full of cages. When I read more of the play I realized that *The Zoo Story* referred to Jerry's story about his trip to the zoo rather than the events of the play.

But now that I think about it, there are a lot of animal references in this story. Peter says he has cats and birds and Jerry keeps bringing it back up, even at the last line. And Jerry tells the whole long story about trying to bond with his landlady's dog. But cats and birds and dogs aren't really "zoo animals." Maybe there's some meaning in that—a "zoo story" about house pets?

I had trouble understanding the ending of the play because I never really sympathized with Jerry. I felt bad for him mostly, but I couldn't relate to him. It was weird to have a play with only two characters, and then one you can't relate to at all. That might be an interpretation: Peter as the house pet that you get along with, and Jerry as the dog you try to get along with but never can. So what does Jerry's "suicide" mean?

Jim feels like he has hit upon a good idea in the last paragraph of his journal entry. He decides to explore it further. Clarity begins to emerge when he organizes the animal references in the play by listing them under the character most closely associated with the animal. His **brainstorming** session leads him to find a pattern: The domestic animals belong to Peter; the wild animals he associates with Jerry.

> "When my writing is not working for me, then I start listening: listening to music, listening to other writers, listening to other actors, listening to my soul. And then I start writing. And I build, build, build. Then I start learning how to chisel, chisel, chisel down . . . beginning, middle, and end of something that's not only entertaining but [also] educating, and enlightening, and hopefully an experience that will leave you in some way or another changed. And that's how I approach my writing."

Conversation with Ruben Santiago-Hudson

Brainstorming

PETER	JERRY
• Domestic	• Wild
• Cats and parakeets	• Landlady's black dog
• Guinea pig	• Zoo as wild place
• Caged	• Unable to connect
• Holds the knife	• Dies
• Conventional	• Nonconformist

Develop a Working Thesis

Jim used his brainstorming notes to sharpen his topic and focus his **thesis.** He decided to use the first draft as a "working thesis" and refined it as he revised his paper.

First-draft thesis

Edward Albee reveals a lot about the characters by associating them with different animals.

Second-draft thesis

A close reading of *The Zoo Story* reveals an argument about ways to live based on the association of the characters with specific references to animals, wild and caged and free.

Final thesis

A close reading of *The Zoo Story* reveals that Albee, using animals as metaphors, has dramatized an argument about two ways to live in the modern world.

Create a Plan

Jim's brainstorming exercise led him to create the following brief **outline.** His method of working is slightly different from that of the other students we saw in the fiction and poetry sections; he prefers to add to his thesis and support progressively, with each draft, rather than figure out all the details before writing. He will use a comparison/contrast structure to organize his paper.

    I.   Introduction
   II.   Peter—Domestic
       A.   Cats
       B.   Parakeets—caged!
  III.   Jerry—Wild
       A.   Interest in zoo
       B.   Landlady's dog
  IV.   Compare the two men: Domestic vs. Wild
   V.   Conclusion: A way to understand Jerry's death

Generate a First Draft

Sitting in front of his blank screen, fingers hovering over the keyboard, Jim takes the leap from reviewing his notes to composing the opening lines of a draft. "Animals are very important to the play . . ." he writes. The point of a first draft is to get ideas onto paper. Then everything can be revisited, reorganized, and refined. The draft allows you to think about your own feelings and experiences in reading or observing a play. You may find it easier to draft the introduction and the conclusion at the end. These sections should answer each other. The introduction introduces the thesis, and the conclusion relates the thesis to a larger issue that explains why the thesis is significant. The paragraphs in the body allow you to use the text to support your thesis.

"Writing . . . is a very mysterious process. . . . It's so easy to panic, and even in rewriting, look at what the material is. What are you trying to do? You go back to basics. What's this piece about? What do I think it's about? . . . What does this piece want to be?" Conversation with Arthur Kopit

FIRST DRAFT

Hanks 1

Jim Hanks

Professor Hernandez

English 1102

February 16, 2009

Animals in *The Zoo Story*

Animals are very important to the play *The Zoo Story*. They factor into a lot of conversations, and it is interesting to see which character talks about which animal. Edward Albee reveals a lot about the characters by associating them with different animals.

Peter talks about his pets because Jerry asks him to. He says he has a cat and two parakeets, which his daughters keep in a cage. The image of caged birds is a strong one—it suggests that a bird who would otherwise fly freely is restrained.

Jerry begins the play by talking about the zoo. The zoo also has cages, but when you think about a zoo, you see that there are wild animals, very unlike cats and parakeets. In a way, then, Jerry aligns himself with wild animals by talking so much about the zoo. But Jerry also talks about his landlady's dog, which he calls "a black monster of a beast" (36). This does not sound like a friendly house dog like the ones we associated with Peter. Yet this is the animal Jerry tries to connect with, and it is significant that Jerry chooses a wild beast with which to establish a relationship (even though his attempt fails).

Hanks 2

Since Peter prefers domestic animals and Jerry prefers wild animals, we can understand something about their characters: Peter is himself domesticated in a 9-to-5 job, while Jerry remains wild and outside of that type of stability. Peter, then, is unable to understand the zoo in the way that Jerry can. Jerry sees the zoo not just as a place for wild animals, but as a place where those animals are separated by bars and cages. Like these animals, Jerry seems unable to connect with those around him.

In the end, then, it is significant that Peter holds the knife that kills Jerry. It seems to mean on a symbolic level that a domesticated life wins out over people who are outside of it. In this way, we can understand Jerry's death as a statement that Albee is making against conventional society.

Work Cited

Albee, Edward. *The Zoo Story. Literature: Craft & Voice*. Eds. Nicholas Delbanco and Alan Cheuse. Vol. 3. New York: McGraw-Hill, 2009. Print.

Revise Your Draft

Jim was pleased with his first draft in that his ideas about Peter, Jerry, and the animals aligned with them seemed to come together in a logical way. However, after reviewing his notes, he realized that he had not used much from the text to support his claim. He returned to his annotations and reread the sections that had to do with animals. He also highlighted the quotations that would best support his argument.

By rereading and selecting quotations, Jim came to a more nuanced understanding of the play. He realized he could add an additional paragraph analyzing Peter's and Jerry's different understandings of the zoo. Although the kernel of that idea was present in his first draft, he fully expands it in his second draft.

"What you read on the page looks like it's been there forever, but believe me, it hasn't. It's always a struggle to find what you are looking for." Conversation with Arthur Miller

Jim thus makes several major improvements in his second draft. He includes support for his argument from the text itself. He also expands his discussion of quotes from the text, allowing him to more thoroughly analyze the specific language the play uses. Finally, after writing the second draft, Jim rereads his paper and adds annotations. These annotations show him where to refine his language and where to add proper MLA citations when he writes his final draft (see the Handbook for Writing from Reading at the end of this book for information on MLA citation).

SECOND DRAFT

Hanks 1

Jim Hanks

Professor Hernandez

English 1102

February 20, 2009

Caged or Free?

Animals As Metaphor in Edward Albee's *The Zoo Story*

From the title of Edward Albee's play *The Zoo Story*, the reader is presented with the idea of animals. The meeting between Jerry and Peter is difficult to understand and leaves the reader with many questions. A close reading of *The Zoo Story* reveals an argument about ways to live based on the association of the characters with specific references to animals, wild and caged and free.

Throughout the play, Peter is closely aligned with domesticated animals. After learning that Peter has a wife and two daughters, Jerry is eager to know what type of pets Peter owns. The animals he guesses are typical pets you would have around the house, like dogs and cats. Peter says that his family owns a cat and two parakeets that his daughters keep in a cage in their bedroom. He also calls himself a guinea pig: When Jerry says he likes to talk to people and learn about them, Peter says, "And am I the guinea pig for today?" (36). In conversation Peter is simply using a popular turn of phrase. But in the context of the larger play, Peter's word choice is extremely significant, because a guinea pig is a passive subject, just like Peter is a passive subject in Jerry's dialogue experiment until Jerry provokes him physically. The first line of the play has Jerry declaring loudly several times that he has just come from the zoo, associating him with wild animals. The zoo, of course, is filled with wild animals, and even though they are caged they are vastly different from house pets like Peter's cat and birds. The speech where Jerry describes his

---

Margin annotations:

Better way to start than a preposition?

Such as?—why the detailed description of the dog, Jerry's suicide . . .

"you" too familiar?

Direct quote from play . . . put in quotes and cite!

Discuss significance of birds more?

Break this sentence up to make the point clearer. Mention Peter's conventional life?

Reword sentence to focus on Jerry.

Hanks 2

relationship with the landlady's dog is most significant. Jerry says the dog is "a black monster of a beast" (27). The words "monster" and "beast" tell us that this is not a typical house dog, but one that is practically feral. Jerry also notes the dog's constant erection, which represents an unfulfilled desire. Similarly, Jerry's unfulfilled desire to connect with others is made apparent when he tries to connect with the dog. At best, he and the dog achieve a status of mutual indifference. But it is significant that Jerry chose this wild beast as the object with which to make a start at "dealing" with the world.

Seeing Peter as a domesticated guinea pig and Jerry as a feral dog clarifies their approach to life: Peter is happy to be caged in fulfilling society's expectations through a conventional home, family, and job, but Jerry can't function in such a setting. The closest Peter comes to breaking out of his neat, ordered life is when he mistakenly says he must get home because the parakeets and the cat will be preparing dinner. This slipup makes Peter say, "I had my own zoo there for a moment." Peter has a very shallow understanding of the zoo. He sees it only in the sense of a wild place, with all kinds of animals mixed up together. Jerry's understanding of the zoo is deeper: He describes it as a place where everyone is separated by bars, with all the animals separated from the other animals, and all the people separated from the animals. "But, if it's a zoo, that's the way it is," he says (36). Since Peter and Jerry are domesticated and wild animals, this quote shows that Jerry— the wild animal—views convention not as something that brings comforting order, but as the bars that are divisive and that keep people from connecting to one another.

Everyone knows that the wild animals that populate the zoo are not free to be wild. In the same way, Jerry is not free to be himself in a world of conventions. And just like a wild animal can't flourish in captivity, Jerry can't survive in our oppressive society. Thus, an exploration into the connection between animals and characters

---

Marginal annotations:

Include more quote to support "erection" discussion.

"us" too familiar

Better paragraph conclusion: So what??

Break into two sentences, emphasize thesis.

More info: How do we know that?

Quote from play? Need to cite!

Confusing sentence . . . just quote Jerry's actual words.

awkward wording.

Assuming too much? Too familiar to the reader?

Need to watch out for these— too familiar for formal paper.

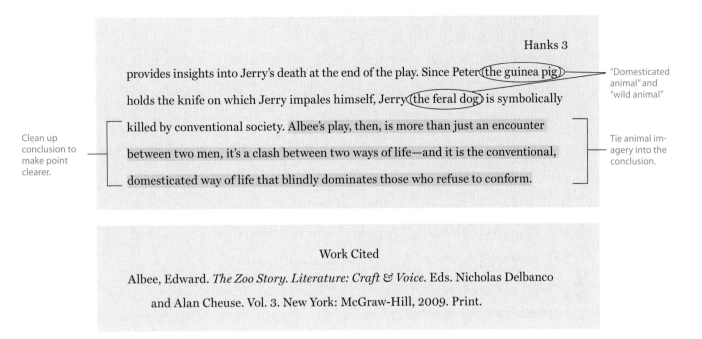

Hanks 3

provides insights into Jerry's death at the end of the play. Since Peter (the guinea pig)

holds the knife on which Jerry impales himself, Jerry (the feral dog) is symbolically

killed by conventional society. Albee's play, then, is more than just an encounter

between two men, it's a clash between two ways of life—and it is the conventional,

domesticated way of life that blindly dominates those who refuse to conform.

Clean up conclusion to make point clearer.

"Domesticated animal" and "wild animal"

Tie animal imagery into the conclusion.

Work Cited

Albee, Edward. *The Zoo Story. Literature: Craft & Voice.* Eds. Nicholas Delbanco and Alan Cheuse. Vol. 3. New York: McGraw-Hill, 2009. Print.

Edit Your Sentences, Proofread, and Format Your Paper

Jim uses the annotations on his second draft to develop his final draft, in which he fleshes out his character analysis and examines each sentence for clarity. For the final draft, he checks his spelling, word choice, and transitions. He also makes sure he has provided ample evidence from the play itself with quotations and checks to make sure these quotations are correctly formatted in-text references, which correspond to a Work Cited page at the end of his paper (see chapters 3–6 in the Handbook for Writing from Reading). Jim's progress shows his interaction with the story as he continually revises his interpretation.

FINAL DRAFT

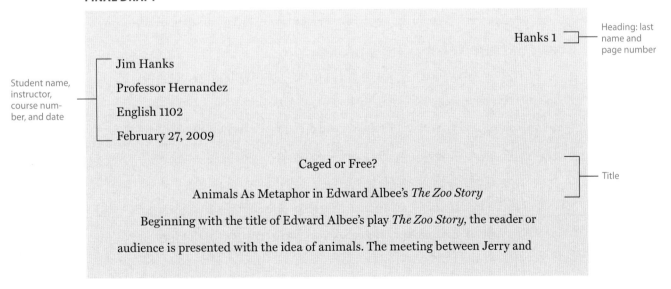

Hanks 1

Heading: last name and page number

Jim Hanks

Professor Hernandez

English 1102

February 27, 2009

Student name, instructor, course number, and date

Caged or Free?

Animals As Metaphor in Edward Albee's *The Zoo Story*

Title

Beginning with the title of Edward Albee's play *The Zoo Story*, the reader or audience is presented with the idea of animals. The meeting between Jerry and

Peter is difficult to understand and leaves the reader with many questions, such as why Jerry tells about his landlady's dog in such detail, and why he ultimately kills himself. A close reading of *The Zoo Story* reveals that Albee, using animals as metaphors, has dramatized an argument about two ways to live in the modern world. — Thesis

Throughout the play, Peter is closely aligned with domesticated animals. After learning that Peter has a wife and two daughters, Jerry is eager to know what type of pets Peter owns. The animals he guesses are typical house pets: dogs and cats. Peter reveals that his family owns a cat and two parakeets, which Peter says his daughters "keep in a cage in their bedroom" (32). The image of caged birds is powerful, as it highlights unnatural captivity; birds were meant to fly, but here they are kept from one of their most basic activities by the cage imposed on them. In fact, all the animals associated with Peter are domesticated. Peter even calls himself a guinea pig: When Jerry says he likes to talk to people and learn about them, Peter says, "And am I the guinea pig for today?" (32). In conversation, Peter is simply using a popular turn of phrase. But in the context of the larger play, Peter's word choice is extremely significant. A guinea pig brings to mind a harmless, large rodent who passes its life in a cage, a passive subject in any experiment. Likewise, Peter is a passive subject in Jerry's dialogue experiment until Jerry provokes him physically. Furthermore, Peter seems caged in, wholly domesticated, by his conventional family life and publishing job.

evidence from the play

evidence from the play

Textual analysis of Peter's character as domestic

Jerry is associated with wild animals from the start. The first line of the play has him declaring loudly several times that he has just come from the zoo. The zoo, of course, is filled with wild animals, and even though they are caged, they are vastly different from house pets like Peter's. Perhaps the most significant speech in the play is Jerry's account of his relationship with the landlady's dog. In it, Jerry describes the dog as "a black monster of a beast: an oversized head, tiny, tiny ears, and eyes . . . bloodshot, infected, maybe; and a body you can see the ribs through

evidence from the play

Textual analysis of Jerry's character as wild

the skin. [. . .] and an open sore on its . . . *right* forepaw; that is red, too. And, oh yes; the poor monster [. . .] almost always has an erection . . . of sorts. That's red, too" (36). The words "monster" and "beast" tell us that this is not a typical house dog, but one that is practically feral. The attention to the dog's constant erection suggests that he represents unfulfilled desire. As the story unfolds, Jerry, too, has a desire to connect with others, which ultimately goes unfulfilled. His first attempt to connect is with the dog, but he fails. At best, he and the dog achieve a status of mutual in-difference. But it is significant that Jerry chooses this wild beast as the object with which to make a start at dealing with the world, for it suggests that he must make peace with what is unconventional before he can deal with the rest of the conven-tional world.

Seeing Peter as a domesticated guinea pig and Jerry as a feral dog clarifies their approaches to life. While Peter is happy to be caged in fulfilling society's expecta-tions through a conventional home, family, and job, Jerry cannot function in such a setting. The closest Peter comes to breaking out of his neatly ordered life is when he mistakenly says that he must get home because the parakeets and the cat will be preparing dinner. This disruption of conventional order leads Peter to say, "I had my own zoo there for a moment" (39). This quote highlights that Peter, blind to his own captivity in society, has a very shallow understanding of the zoo. He sees it only in the sense of a wild place, with all kinds of animals mixed up together. Jerry, however, shows a deeper understanding when he describes the zoo as a place where "everyone [is] separated by bars from everyone else, the animals for the most part from each other, and always the people from the animals. But, if it's a zoo, that's the way it is" (39). Since metaphorically Peter and Jerry are domesticated and wild animals, this quote shows that Jerry—the untamed one—views convention not as something that brings comforting order, but as divisive bars that keep people from connecting with one another.

Synthesis of analysis to develop argument

Textual support

Textual support

Hanks 4

Conclusion summarizes preceding analysis

The zoo is a place where wild animals that populate it are not free to be wild. Likewise, Jerry is not free to be himself in a world where convention imposes its rules. And just as a wild animal cannot flourish in captivity, neither can Jerry survive in an oppressive society. Thus, an exploration of the connection between animals and the characters provides insight into why Jerry kills himself at the end of the play. Since Peter (the domesticated man) holds the knife on which Jerry impales himself, Jerry (the feral being) is symbolically killed by conventional society. Albee's play, then, is more than just an encounter between two men; it is a clash between two ways of life. By associating the conflicting characters with animal imagery, he illustrates how ultimately it is the conventional, domesticated way of life that blindly dominates those who refuse to conform.

Concluding statement restates and reinforces thesis

Work Cited

Albee, Edward. *The Zoo Story. Literature: Craft & Voice*. Eds. Nicholas Delbanco and Alan Cheuse. Vol. 3. New York: McGraw-Hill, 2009. Print.

Suggestions for Writing

1. What is the relationship of plot to character in *The Zoo Story*? How do these elements of drama depend on each other in this play?

2. Compare the role of setting in *Trifles* and *The Zoo Story*. Consider how, for example, *Trifles* would change if it were staged at the prison, or how *The Zoo Story* would change if Peter and Jerry ran into one another at a coffee shop.

3. Dialogue drives the action in *The Zoo Story*, but the play was written to be performed. Choose one of the longer monologues (for instance, Jerry's on page 36) and write stage directions for the character not speaking. Cite specific lines that require certain reactions or gestures. How would your directions enhance the audience's experience of the monologue?

4. Focus on an episode of your favorite television drama, if you have one, or a recent movie you enjoyed, and compare it in relation to character and plot to any of these plays. Do television plays and movies stress the same element as these theater pieces? If they differ, how would you describe the differences?

33 Ancient Greek Drama

A Case Study on Sophocles

PICTURE this: The hillside theater is dark except for the stars above the pillars that form the set. A figure—the king—limps forward and speaks.

My children, generations of the living
In the line of Kadmos, nursed at his ancient hearth:
Why have you strewn yourselves before these altars
In supplication, with your boughs and garlands? . . .

A second figure—a priest—speaks:

Great Oedipus, O powerful King of Thebes!
You see how all the ages of our people
Cling to your altar steps. . . .

Disaster has struck the land and its people, and the leader hopes to set things right. At the moment the play begins, chaos threatens to destroy life within the city walls. The people have come to hear what the king has to say—much the way children caught up in misery and illness go to their father for help and relief.

These speeches mark the opening of the ancient Greek play *Oedipus the King*. They are among the first words of stage dialogue ever heard by a Western audience, and they reverberate today. The story starts with Oedipus, the main character, who limps onto the stage. The name *Oedipus* in Greek means "lame" or "club-footed," but the limp is more than literal. It's an outward sign of a wound in the hero's character—which we will come to recognize as the full story unfolds.

The Greeks called this play *Oedipus Tyrannos* (Oedipus the Tyrant—which signifies, in Greek, an illegitimate king); it was known to the Romans as *Oedipus Rex,* or as we know it today, *Oedipus the King*. It is a highly formal and stylized work of theater. Yet the presence of a live human being—an actor—standing in a place marked off from ordinary space—the stage—compels our attention. As you approach this play, picture the design of the set, an open-air stage with its spare setting: a few columns, steps, and the sky above—that's it.

Pathos *is emotion.*

Q & A

We're really the participants of drama.

A Conversation on Sophocles

Gregory Nagy

Drama As Spiritual and Governmental Requirement

In Athens, the classical period, the Golden Age of Greek civilization, all Athenians have to be theatergoers because it's a civic obligation to go to theater. . . . It's not just political . . . it's a religious duty—in fact, festivals and religion go together. . . . It's very important when we look at theater in the fifth century, or even before . . . [that] when the Athenian[s], twenty thousand, thirty thousand of them, go to Athenian state theater, they're going . . . to participate . . . and in this . . . what is achieved is a purification of the body politic, a renewal. . . . We might . . . call it . . . a sacred narrative . . . of . . . heroic values.

Pathos and *Catharsis*

Imagine looking down at a sea of faces, twenty thousand pairs of eyes are weeping simultaneously, twenty thousand people have their hair stand on end in terror. . . . The *pathos*—of the hero, who is . . . larger than life, let's say Oedipus . . . this chemistry brings about *catharsis*. . . . It's a Greek word that means . . . "purification."

Sophocles As Public Figure

Artists in the ancient world . . . and Sophocles was no exception . . . [were] public figures . . . Sophocles was not only a master dramaturge, he was a master poet, a master composer of music, a master musician. . . . He was everything to the Athenians. When he died in his late eighties . . . there was such an outpouring of emotion that there are many anecdotes about how Sophocles became not only . . . the national poet of the Athenians, but . . . was actually worshipped as a cult hero.

To watch the entire interview online, go to **www.mhhe.com/delbanco1e**.

RESEARCH ASSIGNMENT After watching the interview with Nagy, explain how epic poetry and tragic drama were influenced by each other. How would you describe the influence on Sophocles of the tradition of epic poetry in Greece?

Gregory Nagy [Nahzh] is Director of the Center for Hellenic Studies in Washington, D.C., and the Francis Jones Professor of Classical Greek Literature and Professor of Comparative Literature at Harvard University.

"Pathos *is emotion. . . . That's how we get the borrowing in English.* Pathos. Pathetic. *That shows you the everyday meaning of* pathos. *But, when Oedipus experiences* pathos, *it's not everyday, it's larger than life, it's heroic, it goes back to the heroic world. This is that. That's what happens in theater, that's how the process of* catharsis *happens, that's how the* pathos, *which is the larger-than-life experience of Oedipus, can become part of your life, your emotional life, as you are drawn into this larger-than-life character.*"

Conversation with Gregory Nagy, available on video at www.mhhe.com/delbanco1e

THE OEDIPUS STORY

Versions of the Oedipus story were part of an oral tradition hundreds of years before Sophocles enacted it as drama. It has its roots in myth, that of the house (or kingdom) of Atreus—a complicated tapestry of guilt and revenge, generational conflict, loss, and gain. The story would have been well known to the Athenian audience; what matters here is not *suspense* (we all know "who done it" already) but *how* the tale is told. Old Thebes, where the action of the play takes place, is ruled by high-minded Oedipus, who appeared one day after the death of the previous king, Laïos. Thebes has been an outpost of civilization in an otherwise wild countryside where bandits reign, terrors lurk, and odd events take place. The city traditionally stands for order, the countryside for chaos, yet Sophocles reverses this—chaos has entered in.

The playwright takes the material of the Oedipus myth, folds and manipulates the time span, and molds it into one of the central texts of our culture, a play whose subject is the essence of human character, the relation of character to destiny or fate, and the links between the middle world of human life and the upper world of the gods. As the play unfolds, the great king discovers that he himself is the cause of the troubles. This truth reveals itself gradually, brought to him in pieces by various characters. At some points, he refuses to believe what he is told; at others, he begs to be told what others prefer not to tell him. Toward the end, Oedipus discovers the truth about himself, and this leads to a desperate act of self-mutilation—which, ironically, turns his vision dark and allows him to "see" for the first time the enormity of his sin.

Sophocles (496?–406/5 B.C.)

The greatest playwright of the Golden Age of Greek drama, Sophocles, the son of a successful Athenian armorer, attained extraordinary mastery of the dramatic art. He also participated fully in the political life of his city. Early in his life as a creator of plays, he was influenced by the work of his predecessor Aeschylus but went on to stamp his own productions with the particular mark of great character, diction, and dramatic irony that we recognize today. He wrote over a hundred plays, only seven of which have survived in their entirety. Of these *Oedipus The King* remains the pinnacle of Western drama and is the subject of the *Poetics,* the Greek philosopher Aristotle's treatise on the nature of drama. Sophocles' plays were performed at public festivals and employed Athenian citizens as well as trained actors and musicians. Along with those of William Shakespeare, they stand as the most important dramas in the life of Western culture.

▶ The Oedipus Myth

Laïos, King of Thebes, is warned in a prophecy that his son will murder him and marry Laïos's wife Iocaste, the Queen of Thebes.

To prevent that prophecy from coming true, Laïos orders a herdsman to take his firstborn son into the country and murder him there.

The herdsman pities the baby. Instead of killing him, he pierces his feet and gives him to another herdsman to keep. The baby is named Oedipus, which means "swollen foot."

The second herdsman takes the baby Oedipus to his master, the King of Corinth, who adopts him and raises him as a prince.

Oedipus, now a young man, receives a prophecy that he will kill his father and marry his mother.

Assuming the "father" and "mother" of the prophecy are the king and queen of Corinth, Oedipus flees that city for the countryside.

AS YOU READ   Picture the design of the amphitheater, with its spare setting of columns and bright air. Read through the play once, and you find that it takes place in this single location, with no change of scene. Only the entrances and exits of the various characters mark the rhythmic development of the action here.

Oedipus the King (c. 430 B.C.)

—translated by Dudley Fitts and Robert Fitzgerald

CHARACTERS:

OEDIPUS

A PRIEST

CREON

TEIRESIAS

IOCASTE

MESSENGER

SHEPHERD OF LAÏOS

SECOND MESSENGER

CHORUS OF THEBAN ELDERS

In his travels, Oedipus comes to a crossroads and gets into an argument. His temper gets the better of him, and he murders his opponents, who, unbeknownst to him, include Laïos, Oedipus's true father.

Oedipus comes to Thebes, which is threatened by the Sphinx who guards the gate of the city and devours all who cannot answer her riddle.

Oedipus solves the Sphinx's riddle. Its riddle solved, the Sphinx throws itself off a cliff and dies.

Thankful to Oedipus, and recently having lost its king, the city of Thebes awards him the crown and the Queen, Oedipus's mother Iocaste, as a bride.

The prophecies conveyed to Laïos and Oedipus have now come true.

Some time later, Thebes suffers plague as a result of "sin" and King Oedipus painfully discovers that he is the sinner.

THE SCENE. *Before the palace of Oedipus, King of Thebes. A central door and two lateral doors open onto a platform which runs the length of the façade. On the platform, right and left, are altars; and three steps lead down into the "orchestra," or chorus-ground. At the beginning of the action these steps are crowded by suppliants who have brought branches and chaplets of olive leaves and who lie in various attitudes of despair.* OEDIPUS *enters.*

PROLOGUE

OEDIPUS: My children, generations of the living
In the line of Kadmos, nursed at his ancient hearth:
Why have you strewn yourselves before these altars
In supplication, with your boughs and garlands?
5   The breath of incense rises from the city
With a sound of prayer and lamentation
                       Children,
I would not have you speak through messengers,
And therefore I have come myself to hear you—
I, Oedipus, who bear the famous name.
     [To a PRIEST:
10   You, there, since you are eldest in the company,
Speak for them all, tell me what preys upon you,
Whether you come in dread, or crave some blessing:

Tell me, and never doubt that I will help you
In every way I can; I should be heartless
Were I not moved to find you suppliant here.   15

PRIEST: Great Oedipus, O powerful King of Thebes!
You see how all the ages of our people
Cling to your altar steps: here are boys
Who can barely stand alone, and here are priests
By weight of age, as I am a priest of God,   20
And young men chosen from those yet unmarried;
As for the others, all that multitude,
They wait with olive chaplets in the squares,
At the two shrines of Pallas, and where Apollo
Speaks in the glowing embers.
                    Your own eyes   25
Must tell you: Thebes is tossed on a murdering sea
And can not lift her head from the death surge.
A rust consumes the buds and fruits of the earth;
The herds are sick; children die unborn,
And labor is vain. The god of plague and pyre   30
Raids like detestable lightning through the city,
And all the house of Kadmos is laid waste,
All emptied, and all darkened: Death alone
Battens upon the misery of Thebes.
You are not one of the immortal gods, we know;   35
Yet we have come to you to make our prayer

The old priest (Eric House) beseeches Oedipus (Douglas Campbell) to find a cure for the plague in *Oedipus Rex* (1957).

As to the man surest in mortal ways
And wisest in the ways of God. You saved us
From the Sphinx, that flinty singer, and the tribute
40   We paid to her so long; yet you were never
Better informed than we, nor could we teach you:
It was some god breathed in you to set us free.

Therefore, O mighty King, we turn to you:
Find us our safety, find us a remedy,
45   Whether by counsel of the gods or men.
A king of wisdom tested in the past
Can act in a time of troubles, and act well.
Noblest of men, restore
Life to your city! Think how all men call you
50   Liberator for your triumph long ago;
Ah, when your years of kingship are remembered,
Let them not say *We rose, but later fell*—
Keep the State from going down in the storm!
Once, years ago, with happy augury,
55   You brought us fortune; be the same again!
No man questions your power to rule the land:
But rule over men, not over a dead city!
Ships are only hulls, citadels are nothing,
When no life moves in the empty passageways.

60   OEDIPUS: Poor children! You may be sure I know
All that you longed for in your coming here.
I know that you are deathly sick; and yet,
Sick as you are, not one is as sick as I.
Each of you suffers in himself alone
65   His anguish, not another's; but my spirit
Groans for the city, for myself, for you.
I was not sleeping, you are not waking me.
No, I have been in tears for a long while
And in my restless thought walked many ways.
70   In all my search, I found one helpful course,
And that I have taken: I have sent Creon,
Son of Menoikeus, brother of the Queen,

To Delphi, Apollo's place of revelation,
To learn there, if he can,
What act or pledge of mine may save the city.   75
I have counted the days, and now, this very day,
I am troubled, for he has overstayed his time.
What is he doing? He has been gone too long.
Yet whenever he comes back, I should do ill
To scant whatever duty God reveals.   80

PRIEST: It is a timely promise. At this instant
They tell me Creon is here.

OEDIPUS: O Lord Apollo!
May his news be fair as his face is radiant!

PRIEST: It could not be otherwise: he is crowned
    with bay,
The chaplet is thick with berries.

OEDIPUS: We shall soon know;   85
  He is near enough to hear us now.
    [Enter CREON
                      O Prince:
Brother: son of Menoikeus:
What answer do you bring us from the god?

CREON: A strong one. I can tell you, great afflictions
Will turn out well, if they are taken well.   90

OEDIPUS: What was the oracle? These vague words
Leave me still hanging between hope and fear.

CREON: Is it your pleasure to hear me with all these
Gathered around us? I am prepared to speak,
But should we not go in?

OEDIPUS: Let them all hear it.   95
It is for them I suffer, more than for myself.

CREON: Then I will tell you what I heard at Delphi.

In plain words
The god commands us to expel from the land of
    Thebes
An old defilement we are sheltering.   100
It is a deathly thing, beyond cure;
We must not let it feed upon us longer.

OEDIPUS: What defilement? How shall we rid
    ourselves of it?

CREON: By exile or death, blood for blood. It was
Murder that brought the plague-wind on the city.   105

OEDIPUS: Murder of whom? Surely the god has
    named him?

CREON: My lord: long ago Laïos was our king,
Before you came to govern us.

OEDIPUS: I know;
I learned of him from others; I never saw him.

110 CREON: He was murdered; and Apollo commands
us now
To take revenge upon whoever killed him.

OEDIPUS: Upon whom? Where are they? Where shall
we find a clue
To solve that crime, after so many years?

CREON: Here in this land, he said.
                                     If we make enquiry,
115 We may touch things that otherwise escape us.

OEDIPUS: Tell me: Was Laïos murdered in his house,
Or in the fields, or in some foreign country?

CREON: He said he planned to make a pilgrimage.
He did not come home again.

OEDIPUS: And was there no one,
120 No witness, no companion, to tell what happened?

CREON: They were all killed but one, and he got away
So frightened that he could remember one thing
only.

OEDIPUS: What was that one thing? One may be
the key
To everything, if we resolve to use it.

125 CREON: He said that a band of highwaymen attacked
them,
Outnumbered them, and overwhelmed the King.

OEDIPUS: Strange, that a highwayman should be so
daring—
Unless some faction here bribed him to do it.

CREON: We thought of that. But after Laïos' death
130 New troubles arose and we had no avenger.

OEDIPUS: What troubles could prevent your hunting
down the killers?

CREON: The riddling Sphinx's song
Made us deaf to all mysteries but her own.

OEDIPUS: Then once more I must bring what is dark
to light.
135 It is most fitting that Apollo shows,
As you do, this compunction for the dead.
You shall see how I stand by you, as I should,
To avenge the city and the city's god,
And not as though it were for some distant friend,
140 But for my own sake, to be rid of evil.

Whoever killed King Laïos might— who knows?—
Decide at any moment to kill me as well.
By avenging the murdered king I protect myself.

Come, then, my children: leave the altar steps,
Lift up your olive boughs!
                                     One of you go   145
And summon the people of Kadmos to gather here.
I will do all that I can; you may tell them that.
    [*Exit a* PAGE
So, with the help of God,
We shall be saved—or else indeed we are lost.

PRIEST: Let us rise, children. It was for this we came,   150
And now the King has promised it himself.
Phoibos has sent us an oracle; may he descend
Himself to save us and drive out the plague.
    [*Exeunt* OEDIPUS *and* CREON *into the palace
    by the central door. The* PRIEST *and the*
    SUPPLIANTS *disperse R and L. After a short
    pause the* CHORUS *enters the orchestra.*

Oedipus (Philip Langridge) addresses the people of Thebes in *Oedipus Rex* (1993).

PÁRODOS

CHORUS: [STROPHE 1
What is God singing in his profound
Delphi of gold and shadow?
What oracle for Thebes, the sunwhipped city?

Fear unjoints me, the roots of my heart tremble.

Now I remember, O Healer, your power, and wonder: 5
Will you send doom like a sudden cloud, or weave it
Like nightfall of the past?

Speak, speak to us, issue of holy sound:
Dearest to our expectancy: be tender!

The chorus in *Oedipus Rex* (1993).

Send the besieger plunging from our homes
Into the vast sea-room of the Atlantic
Or into the waves that foam eastward to Thrace—

For the day ravages what the night spares—

Destroy our enemy, lord of the thunder!   40
Let him be riven by lightning from heaven!

                          [ANTISTROPHE 3
Phoibos Apollo, stretch the sun's bowstring,
That golden cord, until it sing for us,
Flashing arrows in heaven!
                    Artemis, Huntress,
Race with flaring lights upon our mountains!   45

O scarlet god, O golden-banded brow,
O Theban Bacchos in a storm of Maenads,
    [Enter OEDIPUS, *C*
Whirl upon Death, that all the Undying hate!
Come with blinding torches, come in joy!

SCENE I

OEDIPUS: Is this your prayer? It may be answered.
    Come,
    Listen to me, act as the crisis demands,
    And you shall have relief from all these evils.

    Until now I was a stranger to this tale,
    As I had been a stranger to the crime.   5
    Could I track down the murderer without a clue?
    But now, friends,
    As one who became a citizen after the murder,
    I make this proclamation to all Thebans:
    If any man knows by whose hand Laïos, son of   10
        Labdakos,
    Met his death, I direct that man to tell me
        everything,
    No matter what he fears for having so long
        withheld it.
    Let it stand as promised that no further trouble
    Will come to him, but he may leave the land in
        safety.

    Moreover: If anyone knows the murderer to be   15
        foreign,
    Let him not keep silent: he shall have his reward
        from me.
    However, if he does conceal it; if any man
    Fearing for his friend or for himself disobeys this
        edict,
    Hear what I propose to do:

                  [ANTISTROPHE 1
10   Let me pray to Athenê, the immortal daughter of
        Zeus,
    And to Artemis her sister
    Who keeps her famous throne in the market ring,
    And to Apollo, bowman at the far butts of heaven—

    O gods, descend! Like three streams leap against
15   The fires of our grief, the fires of darkness;
    Be swift to bring us rest!

    As in the old time from the brilliant house
    Of air you stepped to save us, come again!

    Now our afflictions have no end,   [STROPHE 2
20   Now all our stricken host lies down
    And no man fights off death with his mind;

    The noble plowland bears no grain,
    And groaning mothers can not bear—

    See, how our lives like birds take wing,
25   Like sparks that fly when a fire soars,
    To the shore of the god of evening.

    The plague burns on, it is pitiless,   [ANTISTROPHE 2
    Though pallid children laden with death
    Lie unwept in the stony ways,

30   And old gray women by every path
    Flock to the strand about the altars

    There to strike their breasts and cry
    Worship of Phoibos in wailing prayers:
    Be kind, God's golden child!

                     [STROPHE 3
    There are no swords in this attack by fire,
35   No shields, but we are ringed with cries.

20 I solemnly forbid the people of this country,
    Where power and throne are mine, ever to receive
        that man
    Or speak to him, no matter who he is, or let him
    Join in sacrifice, lustration, or in prayer.
    I decree that he be driven from every house,
25 Being, as he is, corruption itself to us: the Delphic
    Voice of Zeus has pronounced this revelation.
    Thus I associate myself with the oracle
    And take the side of the murdered king.

    As for the criminal, I pray to God—
30 Whether it be a lurking thief, or one of a number—
    I pray that that man's life be consumed in evil and
        wretchedness.
    And as for me, this curse applies no less
    If it should turn out that the culprit is my guest here,
    Sharing my hearth.
                        You have heard the penalty.
35 I lay it on you now to attend to this
    For my sake, for Apollo's, for the sick
    Sterile city that heaven has abandoned.
    Suppose the oracle had given you no command:
    Should this defilement go uncleansed for ever?
40 You should have found the murderer: your king,
    A noble king, had been destroyed!
                            Now I,
    Having the power that he held before me,
    Having his bed, begetting children there
    Upon his wife, as he would have, had he lived—
45 Their son would have been my children's brother,
    If Laïos had had luck in fatherhood!
    (But surely ill luck rushed upon his reign)—
    I say I take the son's part, just as though
    I were his son, to press the fight for him
50 And see it won! I'll find the hand that brought
    Death to Labdakos' and Polydoros' child,
    Heir of Kadmos' and Agenor's line.

And as for those who fail me,
May the gods deny them the fruit of the earth,
Fruit of the womb, and may they rot utterly!   55
Let them be wretched as we are wretched, and
    worse!

For you, for loyal Thebans, and for all
Who find my actions right, I pray the favor
Of justice, and of all the immortal gods.

CHORAGOS: Since I am under oath, my lord, I swear   60
    I did not do the murder, I can not name
    The murderer. Might not the oracle
    That has ordained the search tell where to find him?

OEDIPUS: An honest question. But no man in the
    world
    Can make the gods do more than the gods will.   65

CHORAGOS: There is one last expedient—

OEDIPUS: Tell me what it is.
    Though it seem slight, you must not hold it back.

CHORAGOS: A lord clairvoyant to the lord Apollo,
    As we all know, is the skilled Teiresias.
    One might learn much about this from him,   70
        Oedipus.

OEDIPUS: I am not wasting time:
    Creon spoke of this, and I have sent for him—
    Twice, in fact; it is strange that he is not here.

CHORAGOS: The other matter—that old report—
    seems useless.

OEDIPUS: Tell me. I am interested in all reports.   75

CHORAGOS: The King was said to have been killed by
    highwaymen.

OEDIPUS: I know. But we have no witnesses to that.

CHORAGOS: If the killer can feel a particle of dread,
    Your curse will bring him out of hiding!

OEDIPUS: No.
    The man who dared that act will fear no curse.   80
        [Enter the blind seer TEIRESIAS, led by a PAGE

CHORAGOS: But there is one man who may detect
        the criminal.
    This is Teiresias, this is the holy prophet
    In whom, alone of all men, truth was born.

OEDIPUS: Teiresias: seer: student of mysteries,
    Of all that's taught and all that no man tells,   85
    Secrets of Heaven and secrets of the earth:

Oedipus vows to find King Laïos's murderer in *Oedipus Rex* (1957).

Blind though you are, you know the city lies
Sick with plague; and from this plague, my lord,
We find that you alone can guard or save us.
90 Possibly you did not hear the messengers?
Apollo, when we sent to him,
Sent us back word that this great pestilence
Would lift, but only if we established clearly
The identity of those who murdered Laïos.
95 They must be killed or exiled.
                            Can you use
Birdflight or any art of divination
To purify yourself, and Thebes, and me
From this contagion? We are in your hands.
There is no fairer duty
100 Than that of helping others in distress.

TEIRESIAS: How dreadful knowledge of the truth can be
When there's no help in truth! I knew this well,
But made myself forget. I should not have come.

OEDIPUS: What is troubling you? Why are your eyes
so cold?

105 **TEIRESIAS:** Let me go home. Bear your own fate, and I'll
Bear mine. It is better so: trust what I say.

OEDIPUS: What you say is ungracious and unhelpful
To your native country. Do not refuse to speak.

TEIRESIAS: When it comes to speech, your own is
neither temperate
110 Nor opportune. I wish to be more prudent.

OEDIPUS: In God's name, we all beg you—

TEIRESIAS: You are all ignorant.
No; I will never tell you what I know.
Now it is my misery; then, it would be yours.

OEDIPUS: What! You do know something, and will not
tell us?
You would betray us all and wreck the State? 115

TEIRESIAS: I do not intend to torture myself, or you.
Why persist in asking? You will not persuade me.

OEDIPUS: What a wicked old man you are! You'd try a
stone's
Patience! Out with it! Have you no feeling at all?

TEIRESIAS: You call me unfeeling. If you could only 120
see
The nature of your own feelings . . .

OEDIPUS: Why,
Who would not feel as I do? Who could endure
Your arrogance toward the city?

TEIRESIAS: What does it matter!
Whether I speak or not, it is bound to come.

OEDIPUS: Then, if "it" is bound to come, you are bound 125
to tell me.

TEIRESIAS: No, I will not go on. Rage as you please.

OEDIPUS: Rage? Why not!
                And I'll tell you what I think:
You planned it, you had it done, you all but
Killed him with your own hands: if you had eyes, 130
I'd say the crime was yours, and yours alone.

TEIRESIAS: So? I charge you, then,
Abide by the proclamation you have made:
From this day forth
Never speak again to these men or to me; 135
You yourself are the pollution of this country.

OEDIPUS: You dare say that! Can you possibly think
you have
Some way of going free, after such insolence?

TEIRESIAS: I have gone free. It is the truth
sustains me.

OEDIPUS: Who taught you shamelessness? It was not 140
your craft.

TEIRESIAS: You did. You made me speak. I did not
want to.

OEDIPUS: Speak what? Let me hear it again more
clearly.

TEIRESIAS: Was it not clear before? Are you
tempting me?

OEDIPUS: I did not understand it. Say it again.

Teiresias (Harry Peeters) tells Oedipus he is the source of the plague in
Oedipus Rex (1993).

145   TEIRESIAS: I say that you are the murderer whom
       you seek.

OEDIPUS: Now twice you have spat out infamy. You'll
       pay for it!

TEIRESIAS: Would you care for more? Do you wish to
       be really angry?

OEDIPUS: Say what you will. Whatever you say is
       worthless.

TEIRESIAS: I say you live in hideous shame with those
150   Most dear to you. You can not see the evil.

OEDIPUS: It seems you can go on mouthing like this
       for ever.

TEIRESIAS: I can, if there is power in truth.

OEDIPUS: There is:
       But not for you, not for you,
       You sightless, witless, senseless, mad old man!

155   TEIRESIAS: You are the madman. There is no one here
       Who will not curse you soon, as you curse me.

OEDIPUS: You child of endless night! You can not
       hurt me
       Or any other man who sees the sun.

TEIRESIAS: True: it is not from me your fate will
       come.
160   That lies within Apollo's competence,
       As it is his concern.

OEDIPUS: Tell me:
       Are you speaking for Creon, or for yourself?

TEIRESIAS: Creon is no threat. You weave your own
       doom.

OEDIPUS: Wealth, power, craft of statesmanship!
165   Kingly position, everywhere admired!
       What savage envy is stored up against these,
       If Creon, whom I trusted, Creon my friend,
       For this great office which the city once
       Put in my hands unsought—if for this power
170   Creon desires in secret to destroy me!

He has bought this decrepit fortune-teller, this
       Collector of dirty pennies, this prophet fraud—
       Why, he is no more clairvoyant than I am!
                               Tell us:
       Has your mystic mummery ever approached the
       truth?
175   When that hellcat the Sphinx was performing here,
       What help were you to these people?
       Her magic was not for the first man who came along:

Teiresias (Donald Davis) prophesies Oedipus's downfall in *Oedipus Rex* (1957).

It demanded a real exorcist. Your birds—
What good were they? or the gods, for the matter
       of that?
But I came by,   180
Oedipus, the simple man, who knows nothing—
I thought it out for myself, no birds helped me!
And this is the man you think you can destroy,
That you may be close to Creon when he's king!
Well, you and your friend Creon, it seems to me,   185
Will suffer most. If you were not an old man,
You would have paid already for your plot.

CHORAGOS: We can not see that his words or yours
Have been spoken except in anger, Oedipus,
And of anger we have no need. How can God's will   190
Be accomplished best? That is what most
       concerns us.

TEIRESIAS: You are a king. But where argument's
       concerned
I am your man, as much a king as you.
I am not your servant, but Apollo's.
I have no need of Creon to speak for me.   195

Listen to me. You mock my blindness, do you?
But I say that you, with both your eyes, are blind:
You can not see the wretchedness of your life,
Nor in whose house you live, no, nor with whom.
Who are your father and mother? Can you tell me?   200
You do not even know the blind wrongs
That you have done them, on earth and in the world
       below.
But the double lash of your parents' curse will
       whip you
Out of this land some day, with only night
Upon your precious eyes.   205
Your cries then—where will they not be heard?
What fastness of Kithairon will not echo them?

And that bridal-descant of yours—you'll know
    it then,
The song they sang when you came here to Thebes
210   And found your misguided berthing.
All this, and more, that you can not guess at now,
Will bring you to yourself among your children.

Be angry, then. Curse Creon. Curse my words.
I tell you, no man that walks upon the earth
215   Shall be rooted out more horribly than you.

OEDIPUS: Am I to bear this from him?—Damnation
Take you! Out of this place! Out of my sight!

TEIRESIAS: I would not have come at all if you had not
    asked me.

OEDIPUS: Could I have told that you'd talk nonsense,
    that
220   You'd come here to make a fool of yourself, and
    of me?

TEIRESIAS: A fool? Your parents thought me sane
    enough.

OEDIPUS: My parents again!—Wait: who were my
    parents?

TEIRESIAS: This day will give you a father, and break
    your heart.

OEDIPUS: Your infantile riddles! Your damned
    abracadabra!

225   **TEIRESIAS:**   You were a great man once at solving
    riddles.

OEDIPUS: Mock me with that if you like; you will find
    it true.

TEIRESIAS: It was true enough. It brought about
    your ruin.

OEDIPUS: But if it saved this town?

TEIRESIAS: *[To the* PAGE:
                Boy, give me your hand.

OEDIPUS: Yes, boy; lead him away.
                —While you are here
230   We can do nothing. Go; leave us in peace.

TEIRESIAS: I will go when I have said what I have
    to say.
How can you hurt me? And I tell you again:
The man you have been looking for all this time,
The damned man, the murderer of Laïos,
235   The man is in Thebes. To your mind he is foreign-
    born,

But it will soon be shown that he is a Theban,
A revelation that will fail to please.
                      A blind man,
Who has his eyes now; a penniless man, who is
    rich now;
And he will go tapping the strange earth with
    his staff.
To the children with whom he lives now he will be   240
Brother and father—the very same; to her
Who bore him, son and husband—the very same
Who came to his father's bed, wet with his father's
    blood.

Enough. Go think that over.
If later you find error in what I have said,   245
You may say that I have no skill in prophecy.
    [Exit TEIRESIAS, *led by his* PAGE.
    OEDIPUS *goes into the palace.*

ODE I

CHORUS: The Delphic stone of prophecies   [STROPHE 1
Remembers ancient regicide
And a still bloody hand.
That killer's hour of flight has come.
He must be stronger than riderless   5
Courses of untiring wind,
For the son of Zeus armed with his father's thunder
Leaps in lightning after him;
And the Furies follow him, the sad Furies.

Holy Parnassos' peak of snow   [ANTISTROPHE 1 10
Flashes and blinds that secret man,
That all shall hunt him down:
Though he may roam the forest shade
Like a bull gone wild from pasture
To rage through glooms of stone.   15
Doom comes down on him; flight will not avail him;
For the world's heart calls him desolate,
And the immortal Furies follow, for ever follow.

But now a wilder thing is heard   [STROPHE 2
From the old man skilled at hearing Fate in the   20
    wingbeat of a bird.
Bewildered as a blown bird, my soul hovers and can
    not find
Foothold in this debate, or any reason or rest of
    mind.
But no man ever brought—none can bring
Proof of strife between Thebes' royal house,
Labdakos' line, and the son Polybos;   25
And never until now has any man brought word
Of Laïos' dark death staining Oedipus the King.

Divine Zeus and Apollo hold   [ANTISTROPHE 2
Perfect intelligence alone of all tales ever told;
30 And well though this diviner works, he works in his
    own night;
No man can judge that rough unknown or trust in
    second sight,
For wisdom changes hands among the wise.
Shall I believe my great lord criminal
At a raging word that a blind old man let fall?
35 I saw him, when the carrion woman faced him
    of old,
Prove his heroic mind! These evil words are lies.

SCENE II

CREON: Men of Thebes:
I am told that heavy accusations
Have been brought against me by King Oedipus.

I am not the kind of man to bear this tamely.

5 If in these present difficulties
He holds me accountable for any harm to him
Through anything I have said or done—why, then,
I do not value life in this dishonor.
It is not as though this rumor touched upon
10 Some private indiscretion. The matter is grave.
The fact is that I am being called disloyal
To the State, to my fellow citizens, to my friends.

CHORAGOS: He may have spoken in anger, not from
    his mind.

CREON: But did you not hear him say I was the one
15 Who seduced the old prophet into lying?

CHORAGOS: The thing was said; I do not know how
    seriously.

Creon (Douglas Rain) and Oedipus quarrel in *Oedipus Rex* (1957).

CREON: But you were watching him! Were his eyes
    steady?
Did he look like a man in his right mind?

CHORAGOS: I do not know.
I can not judge the behavior of great men.
But here is the King himself.
    [Enter OEDIPUS

OEDIPUS: So you dared come back. 20
Why? How brazen of you to come to my house,
You murderer!
         Do you think I do not know
That you plotted to kill me, plotted to steal my
    throne?
Tell me, in God's name: am I coward, a fool,
That you should dream you could accomplish this? 25
A fool who could not see your slippery game?
A coward, not to fight back when I saw it?
You are the fool, Creon, are you not? hoping
Without support or friends to get a throne?
Thrones may be won or bought: you could do 30
    neither.

CREON: Now listen to me. You have talked; let me
    talk, too.
You can not judge unless you know the facts.

OEDIPUS: You speak well: there is one fact; but I find
    it hard
To learn from the deadliest enemy I have.

CREON: That above all I must dispute with you. 35

OEDIPUS: That above all I will not hear you deny.

CREON: If you think there is anything good in being
    stubborn
Against all reason, then I say you are wrong.

OEDIPUS: If you think a man can sin against his
    own kind
And not be punished for it, I say you are mad. 40

CREON: I agree. But tell me: what have I done to you?

OEDIPUS: You advised me to send for that wizard, did
    you not?

CREON: I did. I should do it again.

OEDIPUS: Very well. Now tell me:
How long has it been since Laïos—

CREON: What of Laïos—

OEDIPUS: Since he vanished in that onset by the 45
    road?

CREON: It was long ago, a long time.

OEDIPUS: And this prophet,
 Was he practicing here then?

CREON: He was; and with honor, as now.

OEDIPUS: Did he speak of me that time?

CREON: He never did;
 At least, not when I was present.

OEDIPUS: But . . . the enquiry?
50   I suppose you held one?

CREON: We did, but we learned nothing.

OEDIPUS: Why did the prophet not speak against
 me then?

CREON: I do not know; and I am the kind of man
 Who holds his tongue when he has no facts to go on.

OEDIPUS: There's one fact that you know, and you
 could tell it.

55   **CREON:**   What fact is that? If I know it, you shall
 have it.

OEDIPUS: If he were not involved with you, he could
 not say
 That it was I who murdered Laïos.

CREON: If he says that, you are the one that knows it!—
 But now it is my turn to question you.

60   **OEDIPUS:**   Put your questions. I am no murderer.

CREON: First, then: You married my sister?

OEDIPUS: I married your sister.

CREON: And you rule the kingdom equally with her?

OEDIPUS: Everything that she wants she has from me.

CREON: And I am the third, equal to both of you?

65   **OEDIPUS:**   That is why I call you a bad friend.

CREON: No. Reason it out, as I have done.
 Think of this first: Would any sane man prefer
 Power, with all a king's anxieties,
 To that same power and the grace of sleep?
70   Certainly not I.
 I have never longed for the king's power—only his
 rights.
 Would any wise man differ from me in this?
 As matters stand, I have my way in everything
 With your consent, and no responsibilities.
75   If I were king, I should be a slave to policy.

How could I desire a scepter more
Than what is now mine—untroubled influence?
No, I have not gone mad; I need no honors,
Except those with the perquisites I have now.
I am welcome everywhere; every man salutes me,   80
And those who want your favor seek my ear,
Since I know how to manage what they ask.
Should I exchange this ease for that anxiety?
Besides, no sober mind is treasonable.
I hate anarchy   85
And never would deal with any man who likes it.
Test what I have said. Go to the priestess
At Delphi, ask if I quoted her correctly.
And as for this other thing: if I am found
Guilty of treason with Teiresias,   90
Then sentence me to death! You have my word
It is a sentence I should cast my vote for—
But not without evidence!
                          You do wrong
When you take good men for bad, bad men for good.
A true friend thrown aside—why, life itself   95
Is not more precious!
                          In time you will know this well:
For time, and time alone, will show the just man,
Though scoundrels are discovered in a day.

CHORAGOS: This is well said, and a prudent man
          would ponder it.
Judgments too quickly formed are dangerous.   100

OEDIPUS: But is he not quick in his duplicity?
And shall I not be quick to parry him?
Would you have me stand still, hold my peace,
          and let
This man win everything, through my inaction?

CREON: And you want—what is it, then? To   105
          banish me?

OEDIPUS: No, not exile. It is your death I want,
So that all the world may see what treason means.

CREON: You will persist, then? You will not believe me?

OEDIPUS: How can I believe you?

CREON: Then you are a fool.

OEDIPUS: To save myself?

CREON: In justice, think of me.   110

OEDIPUS: You are evil incarnate.

CREON: But suppose that you are wrong?

OEDIPUS: Still I must rule.

CREON: But not if you rule badly.

OEDIPUS: O city, city!

CREON: It is my city, too!

CHORAGOS: Now, my lords, be still. I see the Queen,
115   Iocastê, coming from her palace chambers;
And it is time she came, for the sake of you both.
This dreadful quarrel can be resolved through her.
    [Enter IOCASTE

IOCASTE: Poor foolish men, what wicked din is this?
With Thebes sick to death, is it not shameful
120   That you should rake some private quarrel up?
    [To OEDIPUS:
Come into the house.
    —And you, Creon, go now:
Let us have no more of this tumult over nothing.

CREON: Nothing? No, sister: what your husband plans
    for me
Is one of two great evils: exile or death.

125 **OEDIPUS:** He is right.
    Why, woman I have caught him squarely
Plotting against my life.

CREON: No! Let me die
Accurst if ever I have wished you harm!

IOCASTE: Ah, believe it, Oedipus!
In the name of the gods, respect this oath of his
130   For my sake, for the sake of these people here!

CHORAGOS: [STROPHE 1
Open your mind to her, my lord. Be ruled by her, I
    beg you!

OEDIPUS: What would you have me do?

CHORAGOS: Respect Creon's word. He has never
    spoken like a fool,
And now he has sworn an oath.

OEDIPUS: You know what you ask?

CHORAGOS: I do.

OEDIPUS: Speak on, then.

135 **CHORAGOS:** A friend so sworn should not be baited so,
In blind malice, and without final proof.

OEDIPUS: You are aware, I hope, that what you say
Means death for me, or exile at the least.

CHORAGOS: [STROPHE 2
No, I swear by Helios, first in Heaven!
    May I die friendless and accurst, 140
The worst of deaths, if ever I meant that!
    It is the withering fields
      That hurt my sick heart:
      Must we bear all these ills,
        And now your bad blood as well? 145

OEDIPUS: Then let him go. And let me die, if I must,
Or be driven by him in shame from the land of
    Thebes.
It is your unhappiness, and not his talk,
That touches me.
    As for him—
Wherever he goes, hatred will follow him. 150

CREON: Ugly in yielding, as you were ugly in rage!
Natures like yours chiefly torment themselves.

OEDIPUS: Can you not go? Can you not leave me?

CREON: I can.
You do not know me; but the city knows me,
And in its eyes I am just, if not in yours. 155
    [Exit CREON

CHORAGOS: [ANTISTROPHE 1
Lady Iocastê, did you not ask the King to go to his
    chambers?

IOCASTE: First tell me what has happened.

CHORAGOS: There was suspicion without evidence;
    yet it rankled
As even false charges will.

IOCASTE: On both sides?

CHORAGOS: On both.

IOCASTE: But what was said?

CHORAGOS: Oh let it rest, let it be done with! 160
Have we not suffered enough?

OEDIPUS: You see to what your decency has brought
    you:
You have made difficulties where my heart saw none.

CHORAGOS: [ANTISTROPHE 2
Oedipus, it is not once only I have told you—
    You must know I should count myself unwise 165
To the point of madness, should I now forsake you—
    You, under whose hand,
      In the storm of another time,
      Our dear land sailed out free.
      But now stand fast at the helm! 170

IOCASTE: In God's name, Oedipus, inform your wife
        as well:
    Why are you so set in this hard anger?

OEDIPUS: I will tell you, for none of these men
        deserves
    My confidence as you do. It is Creon's work,
175   His treachery, his plotting against me.

IOCASTE: Go on, if you can make this clear to me.

OEDIPUS: He charges me with the murder of Laïos.

IOCASTE: Has he some knowledge? Or does he speak
    from hearsay?

OEDIPUS: He would not commit himself to such a
        charge,
180   But he has brought in that damnable soothsayer
    To tell his story.

IOCASTE: Set your mind at rest.
    If it is a question of soothsayers, I tell you
    That you will find no man whose craft gives
        knowledge
    Of the unknowable.

               Here is my proof:

185   An oracle was reported to Laïos once
    (I will not say from Phoibos himself, but from
    His appointed ministers, at any rate)
    That his doom would be death at the hands of his
        own son—
    His son, born of his flesh and of mine!

190   Now, you remember the story: Laïos was killed
    By marauding strangers where three highways meet:
    But his child had not been three days in this world
    Before the King had pierced the baby's ankles
    And left him to die on a lonely mountainside.

195   Thus, Apollo never caused that child
    To kill his father, and it was not Laïos' fate
    To die at the hands of his son, as he had feared.
    This is what prophets and prophecies are worth!
    Have no dread of them.
              It is God himself
200   Who can show us what he wills, in his own way.

OEDIPUS: How strange a shadowy memory crossed
        my mind,
    Just now while you were speaking; it chilled my
        heart.

IOCASTE: What do you mean? What memory do you
    speak of?

Iocaste (Eleanor Stuart) comforts her husband Oedipus in *Oedipus Rex* (1957).

OEDIPUS: If I understand you, Laïos was killed
    At a place where three roads meet.

IOCASTE: So it was said;   205
    We have no later story.

OEDIPUS: Where did it happen?

IOCASTE: Phokis, it is called: at a place where the
        Theban Way
    Divides into the roads toward Delphi and Daulia.

OEDIPUS: When?

IOCASTE: We had the news not long before you came 210
    And proved the right to your succession here.

OEDIPUS: Ah, what net has God been weaving for me?

IOCASTE: Oedipus! Why does this trouble you?

OEDIPUS: Do not ask me yet.
    First, tell me how Laïos looked, and tell me
    How old he was.

IOCASTE: He was tall, his hair just touched 215
    With white; his form was not unlike your own.

OEDIPUS: I think that I myself may be accurst
    By my own ignorant edict.

IOCASTE: You speak strangely.
    It makes me tremble to look at you, my King.

OEDIPUS: I am not sure that the blind man can 220
        not see.
    But I should know better if you were to tell me—

IOCASTE: Anything—though I dread to hear you ask it.

OEDIPUS: Was the King lightly escorted, or did he ride
    With a large company, as a ruler should?

225 IOCASTE: There were five men with him in all: one was
          a herald,
          And a single chariot, which he was driving.

OEDIPUS: Alas, that makes it plain enough!
                                        But who—
          Who told you how it happened?

IOCASTE: A household servant,
          The only one to escape.

OEDIPUS: And is he still
230   A servant of ours?

IOCASTE: No; for when he came back at last
          And found you enthroned in the place of the dead
            king,
          He came to me, touched my hand with his, and
            begged
          That I would send him away to the frontier district
          Where only the shepherds go—
235   As far away from the city as I could send him.
          I granted his prayer; for although the man was
            a slave,
          He had earned more than this favor at my hands.

OEDIPUS: Can he be called back quickly?

IOCASTE: Easily.
          But why?

OEDIPUS: I have taken too much upon myself
240   Without enquiry; therefore I wish to consult him.

IOCASTE: Then he shall come.
                            But am I not one also
          To whom you might confide these fears of yours?

OEDIPUS: That is your right; it will not be denied you,
          Now least of all; for I have reached a pitch
245   Of wild foreboding. Is there anyone
          To whom I should sooner speak?

          Polybos of Corinth is my father.
          My mother is a Dorian: Meropê.
          I grew up chief among the men of Corinth
250   Until a strange thing happened—
          Not worth my passion, it may be, but strange.

          At a feast, a drunken man maundering in his cups
          Cries out that I am not my father's son!

          I contained myself that night, though I felt anger
255   And a sinking heart. The next day I visited
          My father and mother, and questioned them. They
            stormed,
          Calling it all the slanderous rant of a fool;
          And this relieved me. Yet the suspicion

Iocaste (Jessye Norman) talks with her husband Oedipus in *Oedipus Rex* (1993).

Remained always aching in my mind;
I knew there was talk; I could not rest;   260
And finally, saying nothing to my parents,
I went to the shrine at Delphi.
The god dismissed my question without reply;
He spoke of other things.
                        Some were clear,
Full of wretchedness, dreadful, unbearable: 265
As, that I should lie with my own mother, breed
Children from whom all men would turn their eyes;
And that I should be my father's murderer.

I heard all this, and fled. And from that day
Corinth to me was only in the stars   270
Descending in that quarter of the sky,
As I wandered farther and farther on my way
To a land where I should never see the evil
Sung by the oracle. And I came to this country
Where, so you say, King Laïos was killed.   275

I will tell you all that happened there, my lady.

There were three highways
Coming together at a place I passed;
And there a herald came towards me, and a chariot
Drawn by horses, with a man such as you describe   280
Seated in it. The groom leading the horses
Forced me off the road at his lord's command;
But as this charioteer lurched over towards me
I struck him in my rage. The old man saw me
And brought his double goad down upon my head   285
As I came abreast.
                    He was paid back, and more!
Swinging my club in this right hand I knocked him
Out of his car, and he rolled on the ground.
                            I killed him.

I killed them all.
290 Now if that stranger and Laïos were—kin,
Where is a man more miserable than I?
More hated by the gods? Citizen and alien alike
Must never shelter me or speak to me—
I must be shunned by all.
                                    And I myself
295 Pronounced this malediction upon myself!

Think of it: I have touched you with these hands,
These hands that killed your husband. What
        defilement!

Am I all evil, then? It must be so,
Since I must flee from Thebes, yet never again
300 See my own countrymen, my own country,
For fear of joining my mother in marriage
And killing Polybos, my father.
                                    Ah,
If I was created so, born to this fate,
Who could deny the savagery of God?

305 O holy majesty of heavenly powers!
May I never see that day! Never!
Rather let me vanish from the race of men
Than know the abomination destined me!

CHORAGOS: We too, my lord, have felt dismay at this.
310 But there is hope: you have yet to hear the shepherd.

OEDIPUS: Indeed, I fear no other hope is left me.

IOCASTE: What do you hope from him when he
        comes?

OEDIPUS: This much:
If his account of the murder tallies with yours,
Then I am cleared.

IOCASTE: What was it that I said
315 Of such importance?

OEDIPUS: Why, "marauders," you said,
Killed the King, according to this man's story.
If he maintains that still, if there were several,
Clearly the guilt is not mine: I was alone.
But if he says one man, singlehanded, did it,
Then the evidence all points to me.   320

IOCASTE: You may be sure that he said there were
        several;
And can he call back that story now? He can not.
The whole city heard it as plainly as I.
But suppose he alters some detail of it:
He can not ever show that Laïos' death   325
Fulfilled the oracle: for Apollo said
My child was doomed to kill him; and my child—
Poor baby!—it was my child that died first.

No. From now on, where oracles are concerned,
I would not waste a second thought on any.   330

OEDIPUS: You may be right.
                                    But come: let someone go
For the shepherd at once. This matter must be
        settled.

IOCASTE: I will send for him.
I would not wish to cross you in anything,
And surely not in this.—Let us go in.   335
        [Exeunt into the palace

ODE II

CHORUS: [STROPHE 1
Let me be reverent in the ways of right,
Lowly the paths I journey on;
Let all my words and actions keep
The laws of the pure universe
From highest Heaven handed down.   5
For Heaven is their bright nurse,
Those generations of the realms of light;
Ah, never of mortal kind were they begot,
Nor are they slaves of memory, lost in sleep:
Their Father is greater than Time, and ages not.   10

The tyrant is a child of Pride   [ANTISTROPHE 1
Who drinks from his great sickening cup
Recklessness and vanity,
Until from his high crest headlong
He plummets to the dust of hope.   15
That strong man is not strong.
But let no fair ambition be denied;
May God protect the wrestler for the State
In government, in comely policy,
Who will fear God, and on His ordinance wait.   20

Iocaste promises Oedipus she will send for the shepherd in *Oedipus Rex* (1957).

[STROPHE 2

Haughtiness and the high hand of disdain
Tempt and outrage God's holy law;
And any mortal who dares hold
No immortal Power in awe
25   Will be caught up in a net of pain:
The price for which his levity is sold.
Let each man take due earnings, then,
And keep his hands from holy things,
And from blasphemy stand apart—
30   Else the crackling blast of heaven
Blows on his head, and on his desperate heart;
Though fools will honor impious men,
In their cities no tragic poet sings.

[ANTISTROPHE 2

Shall we lose faith in Delphi's obscurities,
35   We who have heard the world's core
Discredited, and the sacred wood
Of Zeus at Elis praised no more?
The deeds and the strange prophecies
Must make a pattern yet to be understood.
40   Zeus, if indeed you are lord of all,
Throned in light over night and day,
Mirror this in your endless mind:
Our masters call the oracle
Words on the wind, and the Delphic vision blind!
45   Their hearts no longer know Apollo,
And reverence for the gods has died away.

SCENE III

[Enter IOCASTE

IOCASTE: Princes of Thebes, it has occurred to me
To visit the altars of the gods, bearing
These branches as a suppliant, and this incense.
Our King is not himself: his noble soul
5   Is overwrought with fantasies of dread,
Else he would consider
The new prophecies in the light of the old.
He will listen to any voice that speaks disaster,
And my advice goes for nothing.
[She approaches the altar, R.
                      To you, then, Apollo,
10   Lycean lord, since you are nearest, I turn in prayer.
Receive these offerings, and grant us deliverance
From defilement. Our hearts are heavy with fear
When we see our leader distracted, as helpless
    sailors
Are terrified by the confusion of their helmsman.
[Enter MESSENGER

The messenger from Corinth (Tony Van Bridge) delivers his message to Oedipus in *Oedipus Rex* (1957).

MESSENGER: Friends, no doubt you can direct me: 15
Where shall I find the house of Oedipus,
Or, better still, where is the King himself?

CHORAGOS: It is this very place, stranger; he is inside.
This is his wife and mother of his children.

MESSENGER: I wish her happiness in a happy house,   20
Blest in all the fulfillment of her marriage.

IOCASTE: I wish as much for you: your courtesy
Deserves a like good fortune. But now, tell me:
Why have you come? What have you to say to us?

MESSENGER: Good news, my lady, for your house and   25
    your husband.

IOCASTE: What news? Who sent you here?

MESSENGER: I am from Corinth.
The news I bring ought to mean joy for you,
Though it may be you will find some grief in it.

IOCASTE: What is it? How can it touch us in both
    ways?

MESSENGER: The word is that the people of the   30
    Isthmus
Intend to call Oedipus to be their king.

IOCASTE: But old King Polybos—is he not reigning
    still?

MESSENGER: No. Death holds him in his sepulchre.

IOCASTE: What are you saying? Polybos is dead?

MESSENGER: If I am not telling the truth, may I die   35
    myself.

IOCASTE: [To a MAIDSERVANT:
Go in, go quickly; tell this to your master.

O riddlers of God's will, where are you now!
This was the man whom Oedipus, long ago,
Feared so, fled so, in dread of destroying him—
40 But it was another fate by which he died.

      [Enter OEPIDUS, *C*

OEDIPUS: Dearest Iocastê, why have you sent for me?

IOCASTE: Listen to what this man says, and then
    tell me
What has become of the solemn prophecies.

OEDIPUS: Who is this man? What is his news for me?

45 **IOCASTE:** He has come from Corinth to announce your
    father's death!

OEDIPUS: Is it true, stranger? Tell me in your own
    words.

MESSENGER: I can not say it more clearly: the King
    is dead.

OEDIPUS: Was it by treason? Or by an attack of
    illness?

MESSENGER: A little thing brings old men to
    their rest.

50 **OEDIPUS:** It was sickness, then?

MESSENGER: Yes, and his many years.

OEDIPUS: Ah!
Why should a man respect the Pythian hearth, or
Give heed to the birds that jangle above his head?
They prophesied that I should kill Polybos,
55 Kill my own father; but he is dead and buried,
And I am here—I never touched him, never,
Unless he died of grief for my departure,
And thus, in a sense, through me. No. Polybos
Has packed the oracles off with him underground.
60 They are empty words.

IOCASTE: Had I not told you so?

OEDIPUS: You had; it was my faint heart that
    betrayed me.

IOCASTE: From now on never think of those things
    again.

OEDIPUS: And yet—must I not fear my mother's bed?

IOCASTE: Why should anyone in this world be afraid,
65 Since Fate rules us and nothing can be foreseen?
A man should live only for the present day.

Have no more fear of sleeping with your mother:
How many men, in dreams, have lain with their
    mothers!
No reasonable man is troubled by such things.

OEDIPUS: That is true; only—   70
If only my mother were not still alive!
But she is alive. I can not help my dread.

IOCASTE: Yet this news of your father's death is
    wonderful.

OEDIPUS: Wonderful. But I fear the living woman.

MESSENGER: Tell me, who is this woman that you   75
    fear?

OEDIPUS: It is Meropê, man; the wife of King Polybos.

MESSENGER: Meropê? Why should you be afraid
    of her?

OEDIPUS: An oracle of the gods, a dreadful saying.

MESSENGER: Can you tell me about it or are you
    sworn to silence?

OEDIPUS: I can tell you, and I will.   80
Apollo said through his prophet that I was the man
Who should marry his own mother, shed his father's
    blood
With his own hands. And so, for all these years
I have kept clear of Corinth, and no harm has
    come—
Though it would have been sweet to see my parents   85
    again

MESSENGER: And is this the fear that drove you out
    of Corinth?

OEDIPUS: Would you have me kill my father?

MESSENGER: As for that
You must be reassured by the news I gave you.

OEDIPUS: If you could reassure me, I would
    reward you.

MESSENGER: I had that in mind, I will confess: I   90
    thought
I could count on you when you returned to Corinth.

OEDIPUS: No. I will never go near my parents again.

MESSENGER: Ah, son, you still do not know what you
    are doing—

OEDIPUS: What do you mean? In the name of God
    tell me!

The messenger from Corinth (Michio Tatara) delivers his message to Oedipus in *Oedipus Rex* (1993).

95 **MESSENGER:**   —If these are your reasons for not going home.

OEDIPUS: I tell you, I fear the oracle may come true.

MESSENGER: And guilt may come upon you through your parents?

OEDIPUS: That is the dread that is always in my heart.

MESSENGER: Can you not see that all your fears are groundless?

100 **OEDIPUS:**   How can you say that? They are my parents, surely?

MESSENGER: Polybos was not your father.

OEDIPUS: Not my father?

MESSENGER: No more your father than the man speaking to you.

OEDIPUS: But you are nothing to me!

MESSENGER: Neither was he.

OEDIPUS: Then why did he call me son?

MESSENGER: I will tell you:
105   Long ago he had you from my hands, as a gift.

OEDIPUS: Then how could he love me so, if I was not his?

MESSENGER: He had no children, and his heart turned to you.

OEDIPUS: What of you? Did you buy me? Did you find me by chance?

MESSENGER: I came upon you in the crooked pass of Kithairon.

OEDIPUS: And what were you doing there?

MESSENGER: Tending my flocks.   110

OEDIPUS: A wandering shepherd?

MESSENGER: But your savior, son, that day.

OEDIPUS: From what did you save me?

MESSENGER: Your ankles should tell you that.

OEDIPUS: Ah, stranger, why do you speak of that childhood pain?

MESSENGER: I cut the bonds that tied your ankles together.

OEDIPUS: I have had the mark as long as I can   115
remember.

MESSENGER: That was why you were given the name you bear.

OEDIPUS: God! Was it my father or my mother who did it?
Tell me!

MESSENGER: I do not know. The man who gave you to me
Can tell you better than I.   120

OEDIPUS: It was not you that found me, but another?

MESSENGER: It was another shepherd gave you to me.

OEDIPUS: Who was he? Can you tell me who he was?

MESSENGER: I think he was said to be one of Laïos' people.

OEDIPUS: You mean the Laïos who was king here   125
years ago?

MESSENGER: Yes; King Laïos; and the man was one of his herdsmen.

OEDIPUS: Is he still alive? Can I see him?

MESSENGER: These men here
Know best about such things.

OEDIPUS: Does anyone here
Know this shepherd that he is talking about?
Have you seen him in the fields, or in the town?   130
If you have, tell me. It is time things were made plain.

CHORAGOS: I think the man he means is that same shepherd
You have already asked to see. Iocastê perhaps
Could tell you something.

OEDIPUS: Do you know anything
135 About him, Lady? Is he the man we have
summoned?
Is that the man this shepherd means?

IOCASTE: Why think of him?
Forget this herdsman. Forget it all.
This talk is a waste of time.

OEDIPUS: How can you say that,
When the clues to my true birth are in my hands?

140 IOCASTE: For God's love, let us have no more
questioning!
Is your life nothing to you?
My own is pain enough for me to bear.

OEDIPUS: You need not worry. Suppose my mother
a slave,
And born of slaves: no baseness can touch you.

145 IOCASTE: Listen to me, I beg you: do not do this thing!

OEDIPUS: I will not listen; the truth must be made
known.

IOCASTE: Everything that I say is for your own good!

OEDIPUS: My own good
Snaps my patience, then; I want none of it.

IOCASTE: You are fatally wrong! May you never learn
who you are!

150 OEDIPUS: Go, one of you, and bring the shepherd here.
Let us leave this woman to brag of her royal name.

IOCASTE: Ah, miserable!
That is the only word I have for you now.
That is the only word I can ever have.
[Exit into the palace

155 CHORAGOS: Why has she left us, Oedipus? Why has
she gone
In such a passion of sorrow? I fear this silence:
Something dreadful may come of it.

OEDIPUS: Let it come!
However base my birth, I must know about it.
The Queen, like a woman, is perhaps ashamed
160 To think of my low origin. But I
Am a child of Luck; I can not be dishonored.

Luck is my mother; the passing months, my brothers,
Have seen me rich and poor.
If this is so,
How could I wish that I were someone else?
How could I not be glad to know my birth? 165

ODE III

CHORUS: [STROPHE
If ever the coming time were known
To my heart's pondering,
Kithairon, now by Heaven I see the torches
At the festival of the next full moon,
And see the dance, and hear the choir sing 5
A grace to your gentle shade:
Mountain where Oedipus was found,
O mountain guard of a noble race!
May the god who heals us lend his aid,
And let that glory come to pass 10
For our king's cradling-ground.

[ANTISTROPHE
Of the nymphs that flower beyond the years,
Who bore you, royal child,
To Pan of the hills or the timberline Apollo,
Cold in delight where the upland clears, 15
Or Hermês for whom Kyllenê's heights are piled?
Or flushed as evening cloud,
Great Dionysos, roamer of mountains,
He—was it he who found you there,
And caught you up in his own proud 20
Arms from the sweet god-ravisher
Who laughed by the Muses' fountains?

SCENE IV

OEDIPUS: Sirs: though I do not know the man,
I think I see him coming, this shepherd we want:
He is old, like our friend here, and the men
Bringing him seem to be servants of my house.
But you can tell, if you have ever seen him. 5
[Enter SHEPHERD escorted by servants

CHORAGOS: I know him, he was Laïos' man. You can
trust him.

OEDIPUS: Tell me first, you from Corinth: is this the
shepherd
We were discussing?

MESSENGER: This is the very man.

OEDIPUS: [*To* SHEPHERD
     Come here. No, look at me. You must answer
10   Everything I ask.—You belonged to Laïos?

SHEPHERD: Yes: born his slave, brought up in his
     house.

OEDIPUS: Tell me: what kind of work did you do
     for him?

SHEPHERD: I was a shepherd of his, most of my life.

OEDIPUS: Where mainly did you go for pasturage?

15 **SHEPHERD:**   Sometimes Kithairon, sometimes the
     hills near-by.

OEDIPUS: Do you remember ever seeing this man out
     there?

SHEPHERD: What would he be doing there? This
     man?

OEDIPUS: This man standing here. Have you ever seen
     him before?

SHEPHERD: No. At least, not to my recollection.

20 **MESSENGER:**   And that is not strange, my lord. But I'll
     refresh
     His memory: he must remember when we two
     Spent three whole seasons together, March to
        September,
     On Kithairon or thereabouts. He had two flocks;
     I had one. Each autumn I'd drive mine home
25   And he would go back with his to Laïos' sheepfold.—
     Is this not true, just as I have described it?

SHEPHERD: True, yes; but it was all so long ago.

MESSENGER: Well, then: do you remember, back in
        those days,
     That you gave me a baby boy to bring up as my own?

30 **SHEPHERD:**   What if I did? What are you trying to say?

MESSENGER: King Oedipus was once that little child.

SHEPHERD: Damn you, hold your tongue!

OEDIPUS: No more of that!
     It is your tongue needs watching, not this man's.

SHEPHERD: My King, my Master, what is it I have
     done wrong?

35 **OEDIPUS:**   You have not answered his question about
     the boy.

SHEPHERD: He does not know . . . He is only making
     trouble . . .

OEDIPUS: Come, speak plainly, or it will go hard
     with you.

SHEPHERD: In God's name, do not torture an old
     man!

OEDIPUS: Come here, one of you; bind his arms
     behind him.

SHEPHERD: Unhappy king! What more do you wish   40
     to learn?

OEDIPUS: Did you give this man the child he
     speaks of?

SHEPHERD: I did.
     And I would to God I had died that very day.

OEDIPUS: You will die now unless you speak the truth.

SHEPHERD: Yet if I speak the truth, I am worse than
     dead.

OEDIPUS: Very well; since you insist upon delaying—   45

SHEPHERD: No! I have told you already that I gave
     him the boy.

OEDIPUS: Where did you get him? From your house?
     From somewhere else?

SHEPHERD: Not from mine, no. A man gave him
     to me.

OEDIPUS: Is that man here? Do you know whose slave
     he was?

SHEPHERD: For God's love, my King, do not ask me   50
     any more!

Oedipus interrogates the shepherd (Eric House) in *Oedipus Rex* (1957).

OEDIPUS: You are a dead man if I have to ask you again.

SHEPHERD: Then . . . Then the child was from the palace of Laïos.

OEDIPUS: A slave child? or a child of his own line?

SHEPHERD: Ah, I am on the brink of dreadful speech!

55 **OEDIPUS:** And I of dreadful hearing. Yet I must hear.

SHEPHERD: If you must be told, then . . .
They said it was Laïos' child;
But it is your wife who can tell you about that.

OEDIPUS: My wife!—Did she give it to you?

SHEPHERD: My lord, she did.

OEDIPUS: Do you know why?

SHEPHERD: I was told to get rid of it.

60 **OEDIPUS:** An unspeakable mother!

SHEPHERD: There had been prophecies . . .

OEDIPUS: Tell me.

SHEPHERD: It was said that the boy would kill his own father.

OEDIPUS: Then why did you give him over to this old man?

SHEPHERD: I pitied the baby, my King,
65 And I thought that this man would take him far away
To his own country.
He saved him—but for what a fate!
For if you are what this man says you are,
No man living is more wretched than Oedipus.

OEDIPUS: Ah God!
70 It was true!
All the prophecies!
—Now,
O Light, may I look on you for the last time!
I, Oedipus,
Oedipus, damned in his birth, in his marriage damned,
Damned in the blood he shed with his own hand!
[He rushes into the palace

The chorus in *Oedipus Rex* (1957).

ODE IV

CHORUS: Alas for the seed of men. [STROPHE 1

What measure shall I give these generations
That breathe on the void and are void
And exist and do not exist?

Who bears more weight of joy 5
Than mass of sunlight shifting in images,
Or who shall make his thought stay on
That down time drifts away?

Your splendor is all fallen.

O naked brow of wrath and tears, 10
O change of Oedipus!
I who saw your days call no man blest—
Your great days like ghósts góne.

That mind was a strong bow. [ANTISTROPHE 1

Deep, how deep you drew it then, hard archer, 15
At a dim fearful range,
And brought dear glory down!

You overcame the stranger—
The virgin with her hooking lion claws—
And though death sang, stood like a tower 20
To make pale Thebes take heart.

Fortress against our sorrow!

True king, giver of laws,
Majestic Oedipus!
No prince in Thebes had ever such renown, 25
No prince won such grace of power.

And now of all men ever known [STROPHE 2
Most pitiful is this man's story:
His fortunes are most changed, his state
Fallen to a low slave's 30
Ground under bitter fate.

O Oedipus, most royal one!
The great door that expelled you to the light
Gave at night—ah, gave night to your glory:
35   As to the father, to the fathering son.

All understood too late.

How could that queen whom Laïos won,
The garden that he harrowed at his height,
Be silent when that act was done?

40   But all eyes fail before time's eye,   [ANTISTROPHE 2
All actions come to justice there.
Though never willed, though far down the deep past,
Your bed, your dread sirings,
Are brought to book at last.

45   Child by Laïos doomed to die,
Then doomed to lose that fortunate little death,
Would God you never took breath in this air
That with my wailing lips I take to cry:

For I weep the world's outcast.

50   I was blind, and now I can tell why:
Asleep, for you had given ease of breath
To Thebes, while the false years went by.

ÉXODOS

[Enter, from the palace, SECOND MESSENGER

SECOND MESSENGER: Elders of Thebes, most
        honored in this land,
What horrors are yours to see and hear, what weight
Of sorrow to be endured, if, true to your birth,
You venerate the line of Labdakos!
5   I think neither Istros nor Phasis, those great rivers,
Could purify this place of the corruption
It shelters now, or soon must bring to light—
Evil not done unconsciously, but willed.

The greatest griefs are those we cause ourselves.

10   **CHORAGOS:**   Surely, friend, we have grief enough
        already;
What new sorrow do you mean?

SECOND MESSENGER: The Queen is dead.

CHORAGOS: Iocastê? Dead? But at whose hand?

SECOND MESSENGER: Her own.
The full horror of what happened you can not know,
For you did not see it; but I, who did, will tell you
15   As clearly as I can how she met her death.

When she had left us,
In passionate silence, passing through the court,
She ran to her apartment in the house,
Her hair clutched by the fingers of both hands.
She closed the doors behind her; then, by that bed   20
Where long ago the fatal son was conceived—
That son who should bring about his father's death—
We heard her call upon Laïos, dead so many years,
And heard her wail for the double fruit of her
        marriage,
A husband by her husband, children by her child.   25

Exactly how she died I do not know:
For Oedipus burst in moaning and would not let us
Keep vigil to the end: it was by him
As he stormed about the room that our eyes were
        caught.
From one to another of us he went, begging a sword,   30
Cursing the wife who was not his wife, the mother
Whose womb had carried his own children and
        himself.
I do not know: it was none of us aided him,
But surely one of the gods was in control!
For with a dreadful cry   35
He hurled his weight, as though wrenched out of
        himself,
At the twin doors: the bolts gave, and he rushed in.
And there we saw her hanging, her body swaying
From the cruel cord she had noosed about her neck.
A great sob broke from him, heartbreaking to hear,   40
As he loosed the rope and lowered her to the ground.

I would blot out from my mind what happened next!
For the King ripped from her gown the golden
        brooches
That were her ornament, and raised them, and
        plunged them down

The second messenger comes to announce his bad news in *Oedipus Rex* (1957).

45 Straight into his own eyeballs, crying, "No more,
No more shall you look on the misery about me,
The horrors of my own doing! Too long you have
known
The faces of those whom I should never have seen,
Too long been blind to those for whom I was
searching!

50 From this hour, go in darkness!" And as he spoke,
He struck at his eyes—not once, but many times;
And the blood spattered his beard,
Bursting from his ruined sockets like red hail.

So from the unhappiness of two this evil has sprung.
55 A curse on the man and woman alike. The old
Happiness of the house of Labdakos
Was happiness enough: where is it today?
It is all wailing and ruin, disgrace, death—all
The misery of mankind that has a name—
60 And it is wholly and for ever theirs.

CHORAGOS: Is he in agony still? Is there no rest
for him?

SECOND MESSENGER: He is calling for someone to
lead him to the gates
So that all the children of Kadmos may look upon
His father's murderer, his mother's—no,
65 I can not say it!
And then he will leave Thebes,
Self-exiled, in order that the curse
Which he himself pronounced may depart from the
house.
He is weak, and there is none to lead him,
So terrible is his suffering.
But you will see:
70 Look, the doors are opening; in a moment
You will see a thing that would crush a heart of
stone.
[The central door is opened; OE-
DIPUS, *blinded, is led in*

CHORAGOS: Dreadful indeed for men to see.
Never have my own eyes
Looked on a sight so full of fear.

75 Oedipus!
What madness came upon you, what daemon
Leaped on your life with heavier
Punishment than a mortal man can bear?
No: I can not even
80 Look at you, poor ruined one.
And I would speak, question, ponder,
If I were able. No.
You make me shudder.

The blinded Oedipus addresses his people in *Oedipus Rex* (1957).

OEDIPUS: God.   God.
Is there a sorrow greater?   85
Where shall I find harbor in this world?
My voice is hurled far on a dark wind.
What has God done to me?

CHORAGOS: Too terrible to think of, or to see.

OEDIPUS: O cloud of night,   [STROPHE 1 90
Never to be turned away: night coming on,
I can not tell how: night like a shroud!

My fair winds brought me here.
O God. Again
The pain of the spikes where I had sight,
The flooding pain   95
Of memory, never to be gouged out.

CHORAGOS: This is not strange.
You suffer it all twice over, remorse in pain,
Pain in remorse.

OEDIPUS: Ah dear friend   [ANTISTROPHE 1 100
Are you faithful even yet, you alone?
Are you still standing near me, will you stay here,
Patient, to care for the blind?
The blind man!
Yet even blind I know who it is attends me,
By the voice's tone—   105
Though my new darkness hide the comforter.

CHORAGOS: Oh fearful act!
What god was it drove you to rake black
Night across your eyes?

OEDIPUS: Apollo. Apollo. Dear   [STROPHE 2 110
Children, the god was Apollo.
He brought my sick, sick fate upon me.
But the blinding hand was my own!
How could I bear to see
When all my sight was horror everywhere?   115

CHORAGOS: Everywhere; that is true.

OEDIPUS: And now what is left?
Images? Love? A greeting even,
Sweet to the senses? Is there anything?
120 Ah, no, friends: lead me away.
Lead me away from Thebes.
                                Lead the great wreck
And hell of Oedipus, whom the gods hate.

CHORAGOS: Your fate is clear, you are not blind
      to that.
Would God you had never found it out!

OEDIPUS: [ANTISTROPHE 2
125 Death take the man who unbound
My feet on that hillside
And delivered me from death to life! What life?
If only I had died,
This weight of monstrous doom
130 Could not have dragged me and my darlings down.

CHORAGOS: I would have wished the same.

OEDIPUS: Oh never to have come here
With my father's blood upon me! Never
To have been the man they call his mother's
      husband!
135 Oh accurst! Oh child of evil,
To have entered that wretched bed—
                              the selfsame one!
More primal than sin itself, this fell to me.

CHORAGOS: I do not know how I can answer you.
You were better dead than alive and blind.

140 OEDIPUS: Do not counsel me any more. This
      punishment
That I have laid upon myself is just.
If I had eyes,
I do not know how I could bear the sight
Of my father, when I came to the house of Death,
145 Or my mother: for I have sinned against them both
So vilely that I could not make my peace
By strangling my own life.
                        Or do you think my children,
Born as they were born, would be sweet to my eyes?
Ah never, never! Nor this town with its high walls,
150 Nor the holy images of the gods.
                  For I,
Thrice miserable!—Oedipus, noblest of all the line
Of Kadmos, have condemned myself to enjoy
These things no more, by my own malediction

Expelling that man whom the gods declared
To be a defilement in the house of Laïos.   155
After exposing the rankness of my own guilt,
How could I look men frankly in the eyes?
No, I swear it,
If I could have stifled my hearing at its source,
I would have done it and made all this body   160
A tight cell of misery, blank to light and sound:
So I should have been safe in a dark agony
Beyond all recollection.
                  Ah Kithairon!
Why did you shelter me? When I was cast upon you,
Why did I not die? Then I should never   165
Have shown the world my execrable birth.

Ah Polybos! Corinth, city that I believed
The ancient seat of my ancestors: how fair
I seemed, your child! And all the while this evil
Was cancerous within me!
                        For I am sick   170
In my daily life, sick in my origin.

O three roads, dark ravine, woodland and way
Where three roads met: you, drinking my father's
      blood,
My own blood, spilled by my own hand: can you
      remember
The unspeakable things I did there, and the things 175
I went on from there to do?
                        O marriage, marriage!
The act that engendered me, and again the act
Performed by the son in the same bed—
                              Ah, the net
Of incest, mingling fathers, brothers, sons,
With brides, wives, mothers: the last evil   180
That can be known by men: no tongue can say
How evil!
            No. For the love of God, conceal me
Somewhere far from Thebes; or kill me; or hurl me
Into the sea, away from men's eyes for ever.

Come, lead me. You need not fear to touch me.   185
Of all men, I alone can bear this guilt.
      [Enter CREON

CHORAGOS: We are not the ones to decide; but
      Creon here
May fitly judge of what you ask. He only
Is left to protect the city in your place.

OEDIPUS: Alas, how can I speak to him? What right   190
      have I
To beg his courtesy whom I have deeply wronged?

CREON: I have not come to mock you, Oedipus,
Or to reproach you, either.
     [*To* ATTENDANTS:

                 —You, standing there:
If you have lost all respect for man's dignity,
195   At least respect the flame of Lord Helios:
Do not allow this pollution to show itself
Openly here, an affront to the earth
And Heaven's rain and the light of day. No, take him
Into the house as quickly as you can.
200   For it is proper
That only the close kindred see his grief.

OEDIPUS: I pray you in God's name, since your
     courtesy
Ignores my dark expectation, visiting
With mercy this man of all men most execrable:
205   Give me what I ask—for your good, not for mine.

CREON: And what is it that you would have me do?

OEDIPUS: Drive me out of this country as quickly as
     may be
To a place where no human voice can ever greet me.

CREON: I should have done that before now—only,
210   God's will had not been wholly revealed to me.

OEDIPUS: But his command is plain: the parricide
Must be destroyed. I am that evil man.

CREON: That is the sense of it, yes; but as things are,
We had best discover clearly what is to be done.

215 **OEDIPUS:** You would learn more about a man like me?

CREON: You are ready now to listen to the god.

OEDIPUS: I will listen. But it is to you
That I must turn for help. I beg you, hear me.

The woman in there—
220   Give her whatever funeral you think proper:
She is your sister.
          —But let me go, Creon!
Let me purge my father's Thebes of the pollution
Of my living here, and go out to the wild hills,
To Kithairon, that has won such fame with me,
225   The tomb my mother and father appointed for me,
And let me die there, as they willed I should.
And yet I know
Death will not ever come to me through sickness
Or in any natural way: I have been preserved
230   For some unthinkable fate. But let that be.

The blinded Oedipus speaks to Creon in *Oedipus Rex* (1957).

As for my sons, you need not care for them.
They are men, they will find some way to live.
But my poor daughters, who have shared my table,
Who never before have been parted from their
    father—
Take care of them, Creon; do this for me.   235
And will you let me touch them with my hands
A last time, and let us weep together?
Be kind, my lord,
Great prince, be kind!
             Could I but touch them,
They would be mine again, as when I had my eyes. 240
    [*Enter* ANTIGONE *and* ISMENE, *attended*
Ah, God!
It is my dearest children I hear weeping?
Has Creon pitied me and sent my daughters?

CREON: Yes, Oedipus: I knew that they were dear
     to you
In the old days, and know you must love them still. 245

OEDIPUS: May God bless you for this—and be a
     friendlier
Guardian to you than he has been to me!

Children, where are you?
Come quickly to my hands: they are your brother's—
Hands that have brought your father's once clear 250
    eyes
To this way of seeing—
            Ah dearest ones,
I had neither sight nor knowledge then, your father
By the woman who was the source of his own life!
And I weep for you—having no strength to see you—,
I weep for you when I think of the bitterness 255
That men will visit upon you all your lives.
What homes, what festivals can you attend
Without being forced to depart again in tears?

And when you come to marriageable age,
260 Where is the man, my daughters, who would dare
Risk the bane that lies on all my children?
Is there any evil wanting? Your father killed
His father; sowed the womb of her who bore him;
Engendered you at the fount of his own existence!
265 That is what they will say of you.

                      Then, whom
Can you ever marry? There are no bridegrooms
   for you,
And your lives must wither away in sterile dreaming.

O Creon, son of Menoikeus!
You are the only father my daughters have,
270 Since we, their parents, are both of us gone for ever.
They are your own blood: you will not let them
Fall into beggary and loneliness;
You will keep them from the miseries that are mine!
Take pity on them; see, they are only children,
275 Friendless except for you. Promise me this,
Great Prince, and give me your hand in token of it.

     [CREON *clasps his right hand*

Children:
I would say much, if you could understand me,
But as it is, I have only this prayer for you:
280 Live where you can, be as happy as you can—
Happier, please God, than God has made your
   father!

CREON: Enough. You have wept enough. Now go
   within.

OEDIPUS: I must; but it is hard.

CREON: Time eases all things.

OEDIPUS: But you must promise—

CREON: Say what you desire.

OEDIPUS: Send me from Thebes!   285

CREON: God grant that I may!

OEDIPUS: But since God hates me . . .

CREON: No, he will grant your wish.

OEDIPUS: You promise?

CREON: I can not speak beyond my knowledge.

OEDIPUS: Then lead me in.

CREON: Come now, and leave your children.

OEDIPUS: No! Do not take them from me!

CREON: Think no longer
That you are in command here, but rather think   290
How, when you were, you served your own
   destruction.

     [Exeunt into the house all but the CHORUS;
     CHORAGOS *chants directly to the audience:*

CHORAGOS: Men of Thebes: look upon Oedipus.

This is the king who solved the famous riddle
And towered up, most powerful of men.
No mortal eyes but looked on him with envy,   295
Yet in the end ruin swept over him.

Let every man in mankind's frailty
Consider his last day; and let none
Presume on his good fortune until he find
Life, at his death, a memory without pain.   300

Oedipus, blinded, faces his fate in *Oedipus Rex* (1993).

Writing from Reading

Summarize

1 Write an outline of the story behind the plot. What is the first incident in the dramatized story of the rise and fall of King Oedipus? The second?

Analyze Craft

2 Given what you know about the story of the myth, you can see that the play opens when the story is quite far along in its unfolding. Why does the playwright, having the entire story to work with, choose to begin where he does? Would the play have the same effect if it began in Oedipus's infancy? Or with the story of the shepherd? Or with an opening at the death of Iocaste and then flashing back to the moment when the messenger returns from the oracle?

3 How many actors does the play have? Imagine the visual effect of King Oedipus wearing the mask. What if the actor wore no mask? How might that affect the way you view the scene in your mind? How does Iocaste's action contribute to the deepening of the drama and its forward motion? What is the role of the shepherd? What is the role of the chorus?

4 A series of ironic revelations—or "reversals"—helps propel the play forward. Identify at least two and discuss.

Analyze Voice

5 Dialogue in a play such as this reveals character at the same time that it advances the story. How does Oedipus's first exchange of dialogue with Iocaste create a certain false mood of calm? Contrast it with their round of dialogue after the shepherd has made his speech.

6 How does the collective voice of the chorus differ from the speech of the individual actors? How might Sophocles have choreographed the citizen chorus? What moves would they make? How would a contemporary chorus move? What music and moves would you use if you were staging a contemporary version of the play?

Synthesize Summary and Analysis

7 The playwright has chosen to dramatize a major Greek myth, but in such a way as to maximize its impact on the audience. His presentation of the Oedipus story establishes the template for all future drama in the West and sets forward a series of dramatic techniques that playwrights will find invaluable. How might you imagine a major American playwright dramatizing the story of George Washington or Abraham Lincoln or Martin Luther King.

Interpret the Play

8 The largest questions—those of fate and human destiny—come to the surface here. In *Oedipus the King,* we have a thoughtful concerned leader—a good man—who fulfills a tragic prophecy. What role do his actions have in his fulfillment of this prophecy? What does his reaction to the knowledge that he has fulfilled this dreadful prophecy tell us about Oedipus's character? What is the play's answer to the human dilemma of how to live a good life?

Ancient Greek Drama

Western culture today owes a very great deal to the Greeks. Our sense of narrative was born on the lips of Greek poets reciting heroic tales of their ancestors; plays such as *Oedipus* were part of seasonal daylong competitions staged in open-air amphitheaters with seats built into the sides of hills, creating an atmosphere that somewhat resembles that of "March Madness" or the Super Bowl in our contemporary sports arenas. (A better analogy might be to a political rally, where a famous entertainer warms up the waiting crowd.) In the golden period of Greek culture, these plays, which the Athenians considered the highest creations of their best artists, became a central part of civic life. They simultaneously portrayed the honored past and the difficulties of life in the moment and projected a future in which human life coexisted with that of the gods. Everyone in democratic Athens participated, either as part of the play or as part of the audience.

"The Greeks came in the daytime to a huge amphitheater . . . perhaps they brought some food; they probably brought their families with them . . . and spent the whole day there. And when the night came, the night would come in the play too."
Conversation with Marian Seldes

The plays honored the history of Athens, and—as Athens was in a protracted war with Sparta—also honored the power of the gods and goddesses who might be prevailed upon for protection. What we today call patriotism comingled with religious ritual as Athenians fulfilled their obligation as good citizens to attend the festivals. In his interview, Gregory Nagy discusses how Athenian citizens in the tens of thousands were required to attend the annual theatrical festivals of tragedy and comedy. He describes the way all free Athenians would share simultaneously in the emotion of the play's hero; this participation made even more powerful the connection they felt with their heroic past.

> **WAR AND *OEDIPUS THE KING***
>
> The first historian, Herodotus, in his history of the Greco-Persian War, now and then offers genealogies that link kings and heroes of the Greeks' immediate past in a long line of kinship to heroes out of mythology. (Thucydides, the second great Greek historian, focused more on politics and tactics in his *History of the Peloponnesian War,* his narrative about the war between Athens and Sparta.) However, the difference between genealogy and chronology and the shaped and remade element of time in a work of art shows itself clearly in the presentation of mythological stories in classic Greek tragic theater. We get the essence of the myth, in all its depth and breadth, without watching the entire history in sequential detail.

What were the forces in Greek life that gave rise to the theatrical spectacles of ancient Greece? We have to look to Greek religion for an answer, because drama, in its original form, was inseparable from ritual observance and collective worship. The system of faith, as best we can tell from scattered references throughout Greek drama and later commentaries, was grounded in the pantheon of gods and goddesses from Homeric times. Dramatic theater evolved out of ceremonies celebrating Dionysus, the god of change and transformation.

"Theater . . . was taken so seriously that we might as well call it . . . a sacred narrative. . . . It's as real as what history might be to us." Conversation with Gregory Nagy

In *The Birth of Tragedy,* nineteenth-century German philosopher Friedrich Nietzsche argues that a priest would lead the Dionysian ceremonies surrounding the planting of the grain; over time, he became the first actor, speaking through a mask. Later, as this art form evolved, a second actor appeared, challenging the statements of the first, and dramatic conflict was born. We can't say exactly how much time passed between the early ceremonies of Dionysus—ceremonies presided over by priests wearing sacred masks—and the first appearance of a play (with actors wearing masks), a work of art that was steeped in the old religion but no longer a part of it. However long the period between early religious ceremonies and the great theatrical festivals of Athens might have been, the Greeks would have considered these myths to be true stories of the origins of their present culture. Sophocles' play is, therefore, a sacred story transformed into a work of art.

"Sophocles . . . occupies a special place . . . as having . . . 'the most comprehensive soul.'" Conversation with Ralph Williams

The United States is a diverse culture. But in order to try and imagine the relation of Greek drama to Greek culture allow yourself to picture an America in which no one held any religious view other than Christianity—no Jews, no Muslims, no Buddhists, and certainly no atheists—and several times a year greatly gifted playwrights tried out in competition full-length (three- to five-act) plays on various aspects of Christian belief, from the Christmas story to the Easter story and everything in between, and everyone in every city came either to work in the productions or to sit as part of the audience.

Conventions of Greek Drama

Sophocles is not, of course, the only playwright of consequence from the classic period. Others include Aeschylus, the author of a trilogy of plays about another doomed dynasty (*Agamemnon*, *The Libation Bearers* or *Electra*, and *Eumenides* or *The Furies*), and Euripides, among whose surviving works are *Alcestis*, *The Phoenician Women*, and *The Bacchae*. Routinely, three such plays would be presented in succession at a festival—followed by a fourth, or **satyr** play, which provided a kind of comic relief (for more information on satyr plays, see chapter 30). The great Greek comic playwright Aristophanes is the author of such texts as *Lysistrata* and *The Frogs*, and the comic mask is just as central to the idea of Greek theater as the tragic one. So some fourth performance would likely have followed Sophocles' trilogy, which includes the story of Oedipus's children's fate (*Antigone*) and the old king's death (*Oedipus at Colonus*).

"Greek plays . . . are thrilling and almost more modern than any other plays I can think of, including plays that are being written now. They're clean. There's no extra word in them. And there are no stage directions—there don't need to be." Conversation with Marian Seldes

In his interview, Gregory Nagy tells us that in addition to being poets, playwrights were musical composers—and in the case of Sophocles, both a musician and a singer. He put this talent to work in the creation of one of the major elements in his drama, the singing-chanting-dancing **chorus.** Here amateurs honored to be included in the play worked side by side with trained actors to portray a group of representative citizens with worries and questions, expressed in poetry and music and dance movement. The presence of the chorus immediately puts us in a special state of awareness; it's almost as if we witness the life of their emotions as well as the music of their fears.

The all-male casts wore **masks,** enabling one actor to appear onstage as many different characters, and elevated shoes (*cothurni*). The mask also served as an amplification device so that members of the audience seated at some distance could hear the actor's words. Imagine what it would be like to see this frozen face and hear a

"Actors do perform with masks. . . . These performances are . . . dialogues, it's a form of verse. . . . Technically, when actors have a dialogue with each other, representing heroes and the heroic world . . . it is, shall we say, modified song . . . there is a melodic contour to it, but it's not full-blown singing. By contrast, when the chorus sings, that is full-blown music, that's singing and dancing." Conversation with Gregory Nagy

solemn voice speaking through the mouth hole, a voice that you, as spectator, identify as coming from a god or goddess. The shoes would have made the actors taller, larger than life. This formality may, on first reading, make these ancient dramas seem overly regulated or ritualistic for modern tastes. However, when you consider the material that the play puts forward—murder, incest, child abuse, and a madness that questions language that comes directly from the gods—you can see how the playwright achieves a certain stability with all of this potentially frenzied subject matter by grounding the intense emotions in such a formal fashion.

The **amphitheater** was outdoors and unroofed, with seats built into the side of a hill. In acoustical terms, the amphitheater is an almost perfect amplifying structure; in this way—thousands of years before the microphone—a single voice could make its way up to the most distant rows. The seats came partway around the **orchestra,** which was the area in front of the *skene* (or stage), where the chorus sang and danced. The actors played several roles and changed in a building behind the *skene* that could be designed as part of the setting for the play. Sometimes actors played gods who, when lowered from the roof of the building with a chariot-like machine (***deus ex machina***), could physically rescue a character from danger when the action in the play itself didn't provide an escape. The backdrop for *Oedipus the King* would have been spare, those few columns providing a single setting for the entire play, with all eyes on Oedipus from his first entrance to his final moments onstage.

By convention, each play was composed of five parts and arranged in what is sometimes called the Apollonian mode, after the Greek god Apollo. In the early Greek religion, Dionysus was the god of change and transformation and Apollo the god of form and stability. This tension between the stability of form and the frenzy of the content dramatizes an ancient polarity in Greek culture, and in all Western culture that grows from it: the struggle between the so-called Dionysian mode and the Apollonian mode. After a reading of this play, you can see how the mad chaotic energy and devastating content of the play itself is balanced by the orderliness of a sculpted Apollonian five-part structure.

The first part is the **prologue,** in which the audience learns of the problem of the play—the complication that the characters, and especially the hero or protagonist, must face.

> **The *prologue* in *Oedipus the King.*** *As the Oedipus story begins, in the prologue we learn that the kingdom is suffering from a plague, and the king is seeking a cure. He has consulted the oracle in hope of a message from the gods that might rid the city of its sickness. His duty demands that he rid the city of the murderer whose presence has brought the plague to Thebes.*

Following the prologue is the ***parados,*** the chorus's first **ode**—the song and dance of the chorus. Like an ancient version of the football stadium wave, the members of the chorus weave and bend; they dance and chant their reaction to the problem presented in the prologue.

> **The *parados* in *Oedipus the King.*** *Turning one way ("strophe") and then another ("antistrophe") and using their voices as well as movement, the chorus members declare their worry and confusion about the situation that has overtaken the city they love. What does the oracle say? We're afraid. How will it affect us? Let us pray to Athena for help. The fields are barren, so are the women, the plague continues to ravage us. The chorus calls on the gods to come to the aid of the tortured city.*

Next comes a series of ***episodia,*** or scenes. Each scene is followed by another choral ode, or ***stasimon,*** the chorus's interpretation of and response to the action of the preceding scene, including the final choral poem—dubbed the ***paean***—before the last scene of the play.

> **The *episodia* in *Oedipus the King.*** *In the first of four scenes, Oedipus and Iocaste learn more and more about the problem with the plague, until what they take to be the truth becomes completely reversed. Irony is the great driving engine of the plot. Each action Oedipus takes produces the opposite of the result he seeks. The audience knows exactly how things will turn out and watches the great man writhing in the web of his own destiny. To reiterate, as the play unfolds, the great king discovers that he himself is the cause of the troubles. This truth reveals itself gradually, brought to him in pieces by these various characters. At some points, he refuses to believe what he is told; at others, he begs to be told what others prefer not to tell him. Oedipus struggles against his own nature and against the fate constructed for him by the gods.*

Last, we have the **exodos,** the concluding scene, followed by the final lines from the chorus. The king speaks, and the chorus reflects out loud in its specially choreographed fashion on what he means, questioning, chanting, swaying, bending.

> **The *exodos* in *Oedipus the King*.** *Toward the end, the truth Oedipus discovers about his role in the death of the old king and his marriage to Iocaste leads him to a desperate act of violent self-mutilation. Paradoxically, however, once blind he truly "sees." The graceful exodos serves as a sculpted, stabile vehicle for the destructive energy of his mad recognition. The final words of the chorus provide a caution that no matter how powerful and well situated someone may appear at the beginning, those who offend the gods will pay for the offense and be brought low. The chorus assures us that no one is off the hook until he or she is dead.*
>
> > *Let every man in mankind's frailty*
> > *Consider his last day; and let none*
> > *Presume on his good fortune until he find*
> > *Life, at his death, a memory without pain.*

Greek Tragedy

We usually talk about Greek tragedy as a style in itself, a particular art form that treats characters and life in a certain fashion, that is to say, presents its stories as illustrative of the lives of "high" figures. These are kings, mainly, who because of a **tragic flaw** in their character—in the case of Oedipus, his inability to contain his anger mixed with a nearly uncontrollable sense of pride, or arrogance (**hubris**)—fall into death or misery or disrepute. The Greek concept of **hamartia,** defined as a mistake or error in judgment, is the essential element in tragedy. In other words, the offense to the gods may be committed in ignorance, as was the case with Oedipus, but it will not go unpunished. His misfortune is brought about not by villainy but rather by circumstances and errors of understanding and goes beyond the notion of a single tragic flaw.

> "If the exaltation of tragic action were truly a property of the high-bred character alone, it is inconceivable that the mass of mankind should cherish tragedy above all other forms, let alone be capable of understanding it." Conversation with Arthur Miller

Dramatic or **tragic irony** sums up the relation between the play and its contemporary audience, the citizens of classical Athens, and gives birth to a particular relation between all art and the audience in modern times. The hero cannot know his fate, may not even be aware of his offense, but the audience does know. Strutting across the stage, our hero is unaware of what his past action propels him toward. **Peripeteia,** or *reversal of circumstances,* is an element of Greek tragedy meaning that an action has the opposite result of what was intended. The classical hero's change of fortune may be surprising and unpredictable to him, the opposite of what he might naturally expect to happen based on his action. Nonetheless, the result of the hero's action appears inevitable to an audience steeped in the myth that gave rise to the play and serves as a continually troubling reminder of the fragility of human life and action. If you take Oedipus as a model, you can see that the Greeks viewed all life as transient, an existence built out of a series of ironic reversals.

Aristotle, one of the most significant philosophers of ancient Greece, made his assessment of the play *Oedipus the King* in his *Poetics,* a collection of lectures his students put together from their notes; it has survived as one of the major documents of classic Greek culture. He describes how tragedy is founded on the playwright's successful yoking of favored myths and an intuitive awareness of what one of Aristotle's later devotees, the twentieth-century literary critic Kenneth Burke, describes as the "tragic rhythm of action." That tragic rhythm consists of a movement from, as Burke puts it, *purpose* to *passion* to *perception.* **Anagnorisis,** or *recognition* (the original Greek way of describing what Burke calls "perception"), is "a change from ignorance to knowledge, producing love or hate between the persons destined by the poet for good or bad fortune"; it is the apparent wisdom that comes out of all the reversals and suffering.

"Oedipus learns . . . to have more humility as he goes through the play. . . . And . . . as the character learns, we learn."

Conversation with Edwin Wilson

In his interview, Gregory Nagy describes the audience as participants in the dramatic experience of tragedy. The audience can see what the outcome will be, but the characters cannot. Those who witness have an advantage over the characters in the play but also a feeling of apprehension or, in some cases, sorrow. This combination of pity—*look what happened to that poor character*—and fear—*there but for the grace of God go I*—is commonly defined as *catharsis.* It is a complicated mix of emotions and central to the experience of theater. By invoking and purging the emotions of pity and fear in the audience, the play ideally creates a *catharsis* (purgation), or emotional renewal, in the spectators, and with this a vision of wholeness. A well-intentioned man, a hero, goes down, and his goodness, greatness even, allows him to see the justice in his demise; his acceptance of his fate makes the tragedy complete. For us in the modern world, such a play as *Oedipus* produces a recognition of our own roles in life, of how we are all strutting across the stage without being fully aware of what our past actions might mean. The impact of the tragic form of drama is probably greater than that of any other ancient creation.

Reading Greek Tragedy

When reading or viewing Greek tragedy, it's useful to keep in mind the vocabulary of the theater.

Basic performance conventions and stage techniques of Greek tragedy:	<ul><li>**Dramatic poems:** Poems meant to be performed with a particular meter and design.</li><li>**Chorus:** Amateur and professional actors who represent the citizens in a Greek tragedy.</li><li>*Personae* (masks) and *cothurni* (elevated shoes): Devices to amplify an actor's voice and appearance, both to make him larger than life and to project the performance to the back rows of the amphitheater.</li><li>*Deus ex machina:* A practical reference to a "god" (*deus*) who was lowered by machine (*ex machina*) onto the stage to physically rescue characters from harm. The language is Latin, but the device itself originated with the Greeks.</li></ul>

Five-part structure of most Greek tragedies:	• **Prologue:** The introduction of the play, in which the audience learns the conflict that the protagonist must face. • *Parados:* The Chorus's first *ode* (song), offering an interpretation of the conflict learned in the Prologue. • *Episodia:* A series of scenes, usually debates between characters, in which the action and events of the play are presented. • *Stasimon:* The Chorus's interpretation and response to the preceding scene. • *Exodos:* The concluding scene, including the final lines from the Chorus.

Literary conventions of Greek tragedy that shape the audience's reaction to plot events:	• **Tragic hero:** A "high" figure—typically a king—who, because of some character flaw or inevitable mistake, falls into death, misery, or disrepute.
	• **Dramatic irony:** The audience's recognition of the hero's errors or fate before that of the hero.
	• **Tragic flaw:** The personality trait or fated mistake that leads to a tragic hero's downfall.
	  • **Hubris:** The sin of pride. A common tragic flaw characterized by arrogance and quick temper.
	  • *Hamartia:* An error or mistake in judgment. Although a mistake may be committed out of good intention or ignorance, it will not go unpunished.
	  • *Peripeteia:* An action that has a result opposite to the intention.
	  • *Anagnorisis:* The wisdom that results from reversals (*peripeteia*) and suffering.
	• **Catharsis:** The emotional renewal created by an audience's feelings of pity and terror for a tragic hero, resulting in the recognition that the hero's tragic fate was just and that his acceptance of that fate makes the tragedy complete.

Getting Started: A Research Project

Research is a skill that will carry you through your college career. To help acquaint you with the research process, the materials you need for this project are made available on our website (*www.mhhe.com/delbanco1e*). Other ideas for research projects and sources appear at the end of this chapter.

Chances are you have heard of the Oedipus complex, a term that surfaces now and again in popular culture. But you may not know that the Oedipus complex was first identified by the seminal psychoanalyst Sigmund Freud, who based his idea of the complex on Sophocles' play *Oedipus the King*. Since Freud identified the Oedipus complex in his *Interpretation of Dreams*, his theory has shaped psychoanalysis both as it relates to the study of human psychology and as it relates to the theory of psychoanalysis as a form of literary criticism.

Our website will provide you with several articles that will help you understand the Oedipus complex and its potential applications. First, read the excerpt of Freud's *Interpretation of Dreams* in which he defines the Oedipus complex. Then, read the interview with scholar Jean-Pierre Vernant on the enduring value of tragedy and its relationship to Freud's theories. Refer to Haven McClure's introduction to his book *The Modern Reader's Hamlet* to get an idea of how the Oedipus complex is evident in other works of literature—in this case, Shakespeare's *Hamlet*. And finally, read Sarah Boxer's *New York Times* article to see the many challenges to Freud's theory over time.

After consulting these sources, choose one of the prompts below to get you started on writing a research paper.

1. Write a paper in which you define the Oedipus complex based on Freud's description of it. Then, describe challenges to Freud's theory, from the interview with Jean-Pierre Vernant, from Sarah Boxer's article, and from your own ideas. Conclude your paper with your own evaluation of Freud's theory, based on your reading of *Oedipus the King* and your responses to the articles you have researched.

2. Choose one literary work—whether a short story, novel, or play—in which you see the Oedipus complex, or a version of it, at work. Write a paper in which you examine how the Oedipus complex appears in that work, even if it doesn't literally align with the circumstances of *Oedipus the King*. (You might, for example, choose to examine the parent/child conflict in works like Willa Cather's "Paul's Case" or the budding sexuality of a character like the narrator of James Joyce's "Araby" in our *Fiction* volume. Or, you might offer your own reading of the Oedipus complex in the next chapter on *Hamlet*.)

Further Suggestions for Writing and Research

1. A distinctive feature of Greek theater—and one that has survived—is the chorus. Visit *www.mhhe.com/delbanco1e* to listen to the entire interview with Gregory Nagy, taking notes on what he says about the Greek chorus. Using one of the sources below, you may wish to do some more research into the original function of the chorus. Then, locate a copy of *A Chorus Line*, the hit Broadway musical that was made into a 1985 film directed by Richard Attenborough and starring Michael Douglas and Alyson Reed. Write an essay in which you compare the use of the Greek chorus in *Oedipus* with the use of the choric effect in *A Chorus Line*. Support your ideas with specific examples from your reading of *Oedipus*, your understanding of Nagy's interview, and any other source you consult in learning about the Greek chorus.

   - Ley, Graham. "Chorus." *A Short Introduction to the Ancient Greek Theater*. Chicago: University of Chicago Press, 2006. 30–33. Print.

   - Weiner, Albert. "The Function of the Tragic Greek Chorus." *Theatre Journal* 32.2 (May 1980): 205–212. Print.

   - Zarifi, Yana. "Chorus and Dance in the Ancient World." *The Cambridge Companion to Greek and Roman Theatre*. Ed. Marianne McDonald and J. Michael Walton. New York: Cambridge University Press, 2007. 227–246. Print.

2. If it weren't for translation, *Oedipus the King* would be known only to the few people who could read ancient Greek. Fortunately, many translators have created versions of *Oedipus the King* in English—like the one printed in this chapter. To understand a few of the characteristics of Sophocles' Greek, read Robert Fitzgerald's notes to his translation of *Oedipus the King*, as listed in the sources below. You can use the additional resources to learn more about the problems and challenges of translation.

Find a passage of *Oedipus the King* that you particularly enjoyed or found memorable. Then, find another translation of the same play. Write a paper in which you compare the two translators' choices, drawing upon your research to help you analyze the translators' work.

- Sophocles. *The Oedipus Cycle.* Trans. Dudley Fitts and Robert Fitzgerald. New York: Harvest Books, 2002. Print. See especially pp. 181–185, Robert Fitzgerald's commentary on his translation.
- Venuti, Lawrence, ed. *The Translation Studies Reader.* 2nd ed. New York: Routledge, 2004. Print.
- Walton, J. Michael. "Sophocles' *Oedipus Tyrannus:* Words and Concepts." *Found in Translation: Greek Drama in English.* New York: Cambridge University Press, 2006. 85–105. Print.

Some Sources for Research

Aristotle. *Poetics.* New York: Penguin, 1997. Print.

Bloom, Harold, ed. *Sophocles.* Philadelphia: Chelsea House, 2003. Print.

Burton, Reginald William Boteler. *The Chorus in Sophocles' Tragedies.* New York: Oxford University Press, 1980. Print.

Dodds, E. R. "On Misunderstanding the *Oedipus Rex.*" *Greece & Rome* 13.1 (April 1966): 37–49. Print.

Frosh, Stephen. "Oedipus Complex." *Key Concepts in Psychoanalysis.* New York: New York University Press, 2003. pp. 62–73. Print.

Haigh, A. E. *The Tragic Drama of the Greeks.* Oxford: Clarendon Press, 1946. Print.

Knox, Bernard. *The Heroic Temper: Studies in Sophoclean Tragedy.* Berkeley: University of California Press, 1983. Print.

———. *Word and Action: Essays on the Ancient Theater.* Baltimore: Johns Hopkins University Press, 1979. Print.

Ley, Graham. *A Short Introduction to the Ancient Greek Theater.* Chicago: University of Chicago Press, 2006. Print.

McDonald, Marianne, and Michael J. Walton, eds. *The Cambridge Companion to Greek and Roman Theatre.* New York: Cambridge University Press, 2007. Print.

Webster, T. B. L. *An Introduction to Sophocles.* London: Methuen, 1969. Print.

For examples of student papers, see chapter 3, Common Writing Assignments, and chapter 5, Writing the Research Paper, in the Handbook for Writing from Reading.

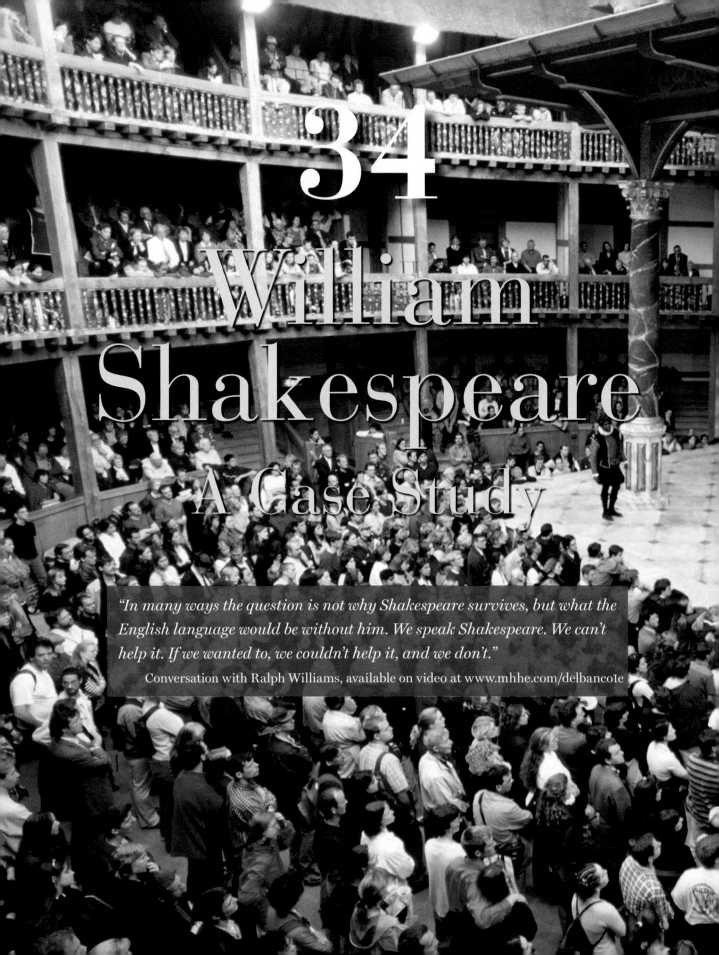

34

William Shakespeare

A Case Study

"In many ways the question is not why Shakespeare survives, but what the English language would be without him. We speak Shakespeare. We can't help it. If we wanted to, we couldn't help it, and we don't."

Conversation with Ralph Williams, available on video at www.mhhe.com/delbanco1e

IMAGINE yourself in the open air of an Elizabethan public theater on a sunny afternoon. You're standing elbow to elbow in a throng of commoners—drinkers and brawlers, pickpockets and prostitutes. The curtain opens and Hamlet enters with three players, the traveling actors who will perform the play the mad prince has written to confront his treacherous uncle. The occasion is of utmost importance, and the players have only a few hours to memorize their parts. Dire and passionate, Hamlet instructs them in Act III, Scene II:

HAMLET: Speak the speech, I pray you, as I pronounced it to you, trippingly on the tongue. But if you mouth it, as many of our players do, I had as lief the town crier spoke my lines. Nor do not saw the air too much with your hand, thus, but use all gently; for in the very torrent, tempest, and, as I may say, whirlwind of your passion, you must acquire and beget a temperance that may give it smoothness.

Notice what he demands: natural speech, gentle gestures, an even temper. Contrast these pointers with the demands of the Greek theater: booming delivery to reach the thousands of gathered citizens of Athens, large gestures that can be seen from the back row of an amphitheater, tall shoes, padded garb, and a mask that makes natural expression impossible. In the Elizabethan theater, acting was not a stylized civic performance; rather, as Hamlet reminds his actors, "the purpose of playing, whose end, both at the first and now, was and is to hold, as 't were, the mirror up to nature."

Whereas the previous chapter presented a tragedy that depicts nobility and civic responsibility, this chapter presents three plays whose subjects are the passions of humanity. *Hamlet* is a play rich in plot and subplot, full of mirrors and doubling tales. The complications of Prince Hamlet himself, as well as his charm and intelligence, demand agility in performance; his quicksilver wit and self-awareness make for a nearly irresistible combination, and a *modern* one. By the time we first encounter him, however, he's steeped in sadness, brooding. He's the dark prince. What Hamlet mourns is understandable: his father's death. Understandably, also, he's upset by the "hot haste" with which his mother has married her husband's (Hamlet's father's) brother.

(CONTINUED ON PAGE 177)

As you begin to read the play, you set the stage.

O&A
A Conversation on Shakespeare

We speak Shakespeare. We can't help it.

Ralph Williams

Why Does Shakespeare Endure?

There are a number of reasons, I think, that Shakespeare endures. . . . He's the rain forest of our language . . . in fact . . . the first user of thousands of words . . . and he is one of the great creators of beauty. . . . You can't solve . . . the pain of life. But you can set beauty against it and maybe endure it. . . . "When we're born, we cry that we are come to this great stage of fools." Of youth . . . "Come kiss me, sweet and twenty, youth's the stuff will not endure." As we reach times of despair . . . "Out out, brief candle, life's but a walking shadow, a poor player that struts and frets his hour upon the stage and then is heard no more." The phrases, the lines, are the vocabulary of our lives really. . . . He lasts for that reason.

Shakespeare's Moral Imagination

Shakespeare imagined a Richard III . . . who in defense of his claim to the throne orders the two young children of his elder brother, the one who had been king, killed. . . . Then in speaking with the man who oversaw the murder, says to him, "But come to me after dinner and I will hear the process of their deaths." This is evil at a depth which rings absolutely true of a sociopath, a psychopathic murderer. . . . On the other end he can imagine a . . . Desdemona [from *Othello*]. . . . It's that range of moral imagination . . . that makes Shakespeare such an astonishing companion and voice for us all in our human journeys.

To watch this entire interview, go to **www.mhhe.com/delbanco1e.**

RESEARCH ASSIGNMENT   After you have watched his interview, describe how Ralph Williams sees the categories of comedy and tragedy affecting Shakespeare's plays. Do you agree with Williams's assessment of Shakespeare's bravura?

Ralph Williams is the Arthur F. Thurnau Professor in the Department of English Language and Literature and Adjunct Lecturer in Near Eastern Studies, College of Literature, Science, and the Arts at the University of Michigan. Since 2000 he has collaborated with the Royal Shakespeare Company on its Residency Program.

William Shakespeare (1564–1616)

Although the speaker here is praising Cleopatra, queen of Egypt, these lines from *Antony and Cleopatra* seem an apt description of Shakespeare the playwright himself:

> Age cannot wither her, nor custom stale
> Her infinite variety. Other women cloy
> The appetites they feed, but she makes hungry
> Where most she satisfies.

The "infinite variety" of William Shakespeare's talent has raised many questions as to his actual identity. Some argue that he must have been a nobleman, citing his knowledge of courtly behavior; others insist he was a commoner because of his detailed knowledge of country matters. Scholars have suggested aristocrats such as the Earl of Oxford or Sir Phillip Sidney used the name "Shakespeare" as a pseudonym. Others propose the translator John Florio or Shakespeare's dead rival Christopher Marlowe. But, time and again, the name seems to fit no one so well as the glove maker's son from the small British town of Stratford-on-Avon.

The truth is, we actually know more about the historical figure called William Shakespeare, born in April 1564, than about most other men or women of the period. His father was a successful merchant of the town who later fell on hard times; he attended local schools, where he learned some Latin and a little Greek. Anne Hathaway was twenty-six, eight years older than William Shakespeare, when they obtained a marriage license in November 1582; she bore him a daughter six months later and, in 1585, a pair of twins. In 1597, the playwright purchased New Place, a fine house in Stratford-on-Avon—a sign that he had prospered in his own chosen career.

William Shakespeare spent most of his working life in the city of London, as one of a troupe of players called the Lord Chamberlain's Men. He was an actor in the group as well as its principal playwright. This was the troupe that in 1599 built the great Globe Theater, which stood on the south bank of the Thames outside city regulations and housed the performances of a number of Shakespeare's plays. Under the patronage of King James I (king of England from 1603 to 1625, following the death of Elizabeth I), the company became known as the King's Men. A bare-bones summary of his life leaves out, of course, the crucial thing: the work itself. It exists in two separate genres: poetry and plays. His poetry, which we have looked at elsewhere, includes long narrative poems such as "Venus and Adonis" and "The Rape of Lucrece" and the 154 sonnets (see chapter 16 on reading further in poetry and chapter 25 on song and spoken word poetry). By most counts he also composed some 37 plays. A few fragments of disputed authorship survive, but Shakespeare's pre-eminence as playwright is based on the work produced between 1591 and 1611—twenty years of unmatched productivity and enduring art. A collection of 35 plays appeared posthumously in 1623, published by two other members of the King's Men, John Heminge and Henry Condell.

Shakespeare retired to New Place, most likely in 1611, and died on April 23, 1616. Contemporaries wrote often about him—competitively, at first, then respectfully, and after his death, in terms of extravagant praise.

TIPS FOR READING SHAKESPEARE

- *Take it slow.* The characters in Shakespeare's plays speak often in poetry and seldom in language intended to imitate everyday speech. Read lines carefully and take note of annotations where they occur. If language seems especially lofty, or especially straightforward, ask yourself why that is appropriate to the lines being delivered or to the character speaking.
- *Read out loud.* Shakespeare intended his plays not to be read but to be performed. If you are hung up on a line, don't hesitate to give it a voice. Unfamiliar words and phrases can become clearer in meaning when you hear them aloud.
- *Imagine the experience.* The theaters of Elizabethan England did not have elaborate sets, and plays were staged outdoors on sunny afternoons. Thus, playwrights had to work the physical situation into their characters' speech. Notice cues that the moon is in the sky, the ocean is nearby, or snow is falling outside, and use them to construct a mental picture of the action taking place.
- *Become the audience.* The commoners in Shakespeare's audience would have experienced many of the same challenges you do interpreting Shakespeare's poetic, sometimes invented, language. To some extent you must let language, familiar and unfamiliar, carry itself forward. You will want to perform deeper analysis on certain lines when crafting a paper, but for your first reading you should focus less on dissecting the language and more on appreciating the action of the play.
- *Consider watching a staged or filmed production* of the play *after* your first reading. This can lend clarity to difficult portions of the play and also help identify aspects of the play worthy of critical analysis. Ask yourself about the differences and similarities between the way you envisioned the play and the way it is performed. Why have certain aspects been interpreted differently? What qualities of Shakespeare's language contribute to similarities across interpretations?

Hamlet, Prince of Denmark (c. 1600)

—edited by David Bevington

CHARACTERS

GHOST *of Hamlet, the former King of Denmark*

CLAUDIUS, *King of Denmark, the former King's brother*

GERTRUDE, *Queen of Denmark, widow of the former King and now wife of Claudius*

HAMLET, *Prince of Denmark, son of the late King and of Gertrude*

POLONIUS, *councillor to the King*

LAERTES, *his son*

OPHELIA, *his daughter*

REYNALDO, *his servant*

HORATIO, *Hamlet's friend and fellow student*

VOLTIMAND,
CORNELIUS,
ROSENCRANTZ,
GUILDENSTERN, } *members of the Danish court*
OSRIC,
A GENTLEMAN,
A LORD,

BERNARDO,
FRANCISCO, } *officers and soldiers on watch*
MARCELLUS,

FORTINBRAS, *Prince of Norway*

CAPTAIN *in his army*

Three or Four **PLAYERS,** *taking the roles of* **PROLOGUE, PLAYER KING, PLAYER QUEEN,** *and* **LUCIANUS**

Two **MESSENGERS**

FIRST SAILOR

Two **CLOWNS,** *a gravedigger and his companion*

PRIEST

FIRST AMBASSADOR *from England*

Lords, Soldiers, Attendants, Guards, other Players, Followers of Laertes, other Sailors, another Ambassador or Ambassadors from England

SCENE: *Denmark]*

1.1   *Enter* BERNARDO *and* FRANCISCO, *two sentinels,*
[meeting].

BERNARDO: Who's there?

FRANCISCO: Nay, answer me. Stand and unfold
yourself.

BERNARDO: Long live the King!

FRANCISCO: Bernardo?

5 **BERNARDO:** He.

FRANCISCO: You come most carefully upon your hour.

BERNARDO: 'Tis now struck twelve. Get thee to bed,
Francisco.

FRANCISCO: For this relief much thanks. 'Tis
bitter cold,
And I am sick at heart.

10 **BERNARDO:** Have you had quiet guard?

FRANCISCO: Not a mouse stirring.

BERNARDO: Well, good night.
If you do meet Horatio and Marcellus,
The rivals of my watch, bid them make haste.

          Enter HORATIO *and* MARCELLUS.

15 **FRANCISCO:** I think I hear them.—Stand, ho! Who
is there?

HORATIO: Friends to this ground.

MARCELLUS: And liegemen to the Dane.

FRANCISCO: Give you good night.

MARCELLUS: O, farewell, honest soldier. Who hath
relieved you?

20 **FRANCISCO:** Bernardo hath my place. Give you good
night.

          Exit FRANCISCO.

MARCELLUS: Holla! Bernardo!

BERNARDO: Say, what, is Horatio there?

HORATIO: A piece of him.

Horatio (Nicholas Farrell), Marcellus (Jack Lemmon), and Bernardo (Ian McElhinney) gape at the ghost of the dead king in the 1996 film directed by Kenneth Branagh.

BERNARDO: Welcome, Horatio. Welcome, good
Marcellus.

HORATIO: What, has this thing appeared again
tonight?   25

BERNARDO: I have seen nothing.

MARCELLUS: Horatio says 'tis but our fantasy,
And will not let belief take hold of him
Touching this dreaded sight twice seen of us.
Therefore I have entreated him along   30
With us to watch the minutes of this night,
That if again this apparition come
He may approve our eyes and speak to it.

HORATIO: Tush, tush, 'twill not appear.

BERNARDO: Sit down awhile,
And let us once again assail your ears,   35
That are so fortified against our story,
What we have two nights seen.

HORATIO: Well, sit we down,
And let us hear Bernardo speak of this.

BERNARDO: Last night of all,
When yond same star that's westward from the pole 40
Had made his course t' illume that part of heaven
Where now it burns, Marcellus and myself,
The bell then beating one—

          Enter GHOST.

MARCELLUS: Peace, break thee off! Look where it
comes again!

1.1 Location: Elsinore castle. A guard platform.
2 me (Francisco emphasizes that *he* is the sentry currently on watch.) **unfold yourself** reveal your identity **14 rivals** partners **16 ground** country, land **17 liegemen to the Dane** men sworn to serve the Danish king **18 Give** i.e., may God give

27 fantasy imagination **30 along** to come along **31 watch** keep watch during **33 approve** corroborate **37 What** with what **39 Last . . . all** i.e., this *very* last night. (Emphatic.) **40 pole** polestar, north star **41 his** its. **illume** illuminate

The ghost of King Hamlet (Brian Blessed) approaches.

45 **BERNARDO:**   In the same figure like the King that's dead.

MARCELLUS: Thou art a scholar. Speak to it, Horatio.

BERNARDO: Looks 'a not like the King? Mark it, Horatio.

HORATIO: Most like. It harrows me with fear and wonder.

BERNARDO: It would be spoke to.

MARCELLUS: Speak to it, Horatio.

50 **HORATIO:**   What are thou that usurp'st this time of night,
Together with that fair and warlike form
In which the majesty of buried Denmark
Did sometime march? By heaven, I charge thee, speak!

MARCELLUS: It is offended.

BERNARDO: See, it stalks away.

55 **HORATIO:**   Stay! Speak, speak! I charge thee, speak!
Exit GHOST.

MARCELLUS: 'Tis gone and will not answer.

BERNARDO: How now, Horatio? You tremble and look pale.
Is not this something more than fantasy?
What think you on 't?

HORATIO: Before my God, I might not this believe   60
Without the sensible and true avouch
Of mine own eyes.

MARCELLUS: Is it not like the King?

HORATIO: As thou art to thyself.
Such was the very armor he had on
When he the ambitious Norway combated.   65
So frowned he once when, in an angry parle,
He smote the sledded Polacks on the ice.
'Tis strange.

MARCELLUS: Thus twice before, and jump at this dead hour,
With martial stalk hath he gone by our watch.   70

HORATIO: In what particular thought to work I know not,
But in the gross and scope of mine opinion
This bodes some strange eruption to our state.

MARCELLUS: Good now, sit down, and tell me, he that knows,
Why this same strict and most observant watch   75
So nightly toils the subject of the land,
And why such daily cast of brazen cannon
And foreign mart for implements of war,
Why such impress of shipwrights, whose sore task
Does not divide the Sunday from the week.   80
What might be toward, that this sweaty haste
Doth make the night joint-laborer with the day?
Who is 't that can inform me?

HORATIO: That can I;
At least, the whisper goes so. Our last king,
Whose image even but now appeared to us,   85
Was, as you know, by Fortinbras of Norway,
Thereto pricked on by a most emulate pride,
Dared to the combat; in which our valiant Hamlet—
For so this side of our known world esteemed him—
Did slay this Fortinbras; who by a sealed compact   90
Well ratified by and law and heraldry
Did forfeit, with his life, all those his lands
Which he stood seized of, to the conqueror;

---

46 **scholar** one learned enough to know how to question a ghost properly   47 **'a** he   49 **It . . . to** (It was commonly believed that a ghost could not speak until spoken to.)   50 **usurp'st** wrongfully takes over   52 **buried Denmark** the buried King of Denmark   53 **sometime** formerly   59 **on 't** of it

61 **sensible** confirmed by the senses.   **avouch** warrant, evidence   65 **Norway** King of Norway   66 **parle** parley   67 **sledded** traveling on sleds.   **Polacks** Poles   69 **jump** exactly   70 **stalk** stride   71 **to work** i.e., to collect my thoughts and try to understand this   72 **gross and scope** general drift   74 **Good now** (An expression denoting entreaty or expostulation.)   76 **toils** causes to toil.   **subject** subjects   77 **cast** casting   78 **mart** buying and selling   79 **impress** impressment, conscription   81 **toward** in preparation   87 **Thereto . . . pride** (Refers to old Fortinbras, not the Danish King.)   **pricked on** incited.   **emulate** emulous, ambitious   89 **this . . . world** i.e., all Europe, the Western world   90 **sealed** certified, confirmed   93 **seized** possessed

95
96
97

100

105

110

Against the which a moiety competent
Was gagèd by our king, which had returned
To the inheritance of Fortinbras
Had he been vanquisher, as, by the same cov'nant
And carriage of the article designed,
His fell to Hamlet. Now, sir, young Fortinbras,
Of unimprovèd mettle hot and full,
Hath in the skirts of Norway here and there
Sharked up a list of lawless resolutes
For food and diet to some enterprise
That hath a stomach in 't, which is no other—
As it doth well appear unto our state—
But to recover of us, by strong hand
And terms compulsatory, those foresaid lands
So by his father lost. And this, I take it,
Is the main motive of our preparations,
The source of this our watch, and the chief head
Of this posthaste and rummage in the land.

BERNARDO: I think it be no other but e'en so.
Well may it sort that this portentous figure
Comes armèd through our watch so like the King
That was and is the question of these wars.

115

HORATIO: A mote it is to trouble the mind's eye.
In the most high and palmy state of Rome,
A little ere the mightiest Julius fell,
The graves stood tenantless, and the sheeted dead
Did squeak and gibber in the Roman streets;
As stars with trains of fire and dews of blood,
Disasters in the sun; and the moist star
Upon whose influence Neptune's empire stands
Was sick almost to doomsday with eclipse.
And even the like precurse of feared events,
As harbingers preceding still the fates
And prologue to the omen coming on,

120

125

Have heaven and earth together demonstrated
Unto our climatures and countrymen.

Enter GHOST.

But soft, behold! Lo, where it comes again!   130
I'll cross it, though it blast me.   (*It spreads his arms.*)
    Stay, illusion!
If thou hast any sound or use of voice,
Speak to me!
If there be any good thing to be done
That may to thee do ease and grace to me,   135
Speak to me!
If thou art privy to thy country's fate,
Which, happily, foreknowing may avoid,
O, speak!
Or if thou has uphoarded in thy life   140
Extorted treasure in the womb of earth,
For which, they say, you spirits oft walk in death,
Speak of it! (*The cock crows.*) Stay and speak!—Stop it,
    Marcellus.

MARCELLUS: Shall I strike at it with my partisan?

HORATIO: Do, if it will not stand.   [*They strike at it.*]   145

BERNARDO: 'Tis here!

HORATIO: 'Tis here!   [*Exit* GHOST.]

MARCELLUS: 'Tis gone.
We do it wrong, being so majestical,
To offer it the show of violence,   150
For it is as the air invulnerable,
And our vain blows malicious mockery.

BERNARDO: It was about to speak when the cock crew.

HORATIO: And then it started like a guilty thing
Upon a fearful summons. I have heard   155
The cock, that is the trumpet to the morn,
Doth with his lofty and shrill-sounding throat
Awake the god of day, and at his warning,
Whether in sea or fire, in earth or air,
Th' extravagant and erring spirit hies   160
To his confine; and of the truth herein
This present object made probation.

MARCELLUS: It faded on the crowing of the cock.
Some say that ever 'gainst that season comes
Wherein our Savior's birth is celebrated,   165

---

94 Against the in return for. **moiety competent** corresponding portion **95 gagèd** engaged, pledged. **had returned** would have passed **96 inheritance** possession **97 cov'nant** i.e., the *sealed compact* of line 90 **98 carriage . . . designed** carrying out of the article or clause drawn up to cover the point **100 unimprovèd mettle** untried, undisciplined spirits **101 skirts** outlying regions, outskirts **102 Sharked up** gathered up, as a shark takes fish. **list** i.e., troop. **resolutes** desperadoes **103 For food and diet** i.e., they are to serve as *food,* or "means," *to some enterprise;* also they serve in return for the rations they get **104 stomach** (1) a spirit of daring (2) an appetite that is fed by the *lawless resolutes* **110 head** source **111 rummage** bustle, commotion **113 sort** suit **115 question** focus of contention **116 mote** speck of dust **117 palmy** flourishing **119 sheeted** shrouded **121 As** (This abrupt transition suggests that matter is possibly omitted between lines 120 and 121.) **trains** trails **122 Disasters** unfavorable signs or aspects. **moist star** i.e., moon, governing tides **123 Neptune** god of the sea. **stands** depends **124 sick . . . doomsday** (See Matthew 24:29 and Revelation 6:12.) **125 precurse** heralding, foreshadowing **126 harbingers** forerunners. **still** continually **127 omen** calamitous event

---

129 climatures regions **130 soft** i.e., enough, break off **131 cross** stand in its path, confront. **blast** wither, strike with a curse. **s.d. his** its **137 privy to** in on the secret of **138 happily** haply, perchance **144 partisan** long-handled spear **156 trumpet** trumpeter **160 extravagant and erring** wandering beyond bounds. (The words have similar meaning.) **hies** hastens **162 probation** proof **164 'gainst** just before

This bird of dawning singeth all night long,
And then, they say, no spirit dare stir abroad;
The nights are wholesome, then no planets strike,
No fairy takes, nor witch hath power to charm,
170   So hallowed and so gracious is that time.

HORATIO: So have I heard and do in part believe it.
But, look, the morn in russet mantle clad
Walks o'er the dew of yon high eastward hill.
Break we our watch up, and by my advice
175   Let us impart what we have seen tonight
Unto young Hamlet; for upon my life,
This spirit, dumb to us, will speak to him.
Do you consent we shall acquaint him with it,
As needful in our loves, fitting our duty?

180 **MARCELLUS:**   Let's do 't, I pray, and I this morning
          know
Where we shall find him most conveniently.

                                                        Exeunt.

1.2   *Flourish. Enter* CLAUDIUS, *King of Denmark,*
          GERTRUDE *the Queen, [the] Council, as* POLONIUS
          and his son LAERTES, HAMLET, *cum aliis [including*
          VOLTIMAND *and* CORNELIUS].

KING: Though yet of Hamlet our dear brother's death
The memory be green, and that it us befitted
To bear our hearts in grief and our whole kingdom
To be contracted in one brow of woe,
5   Yet so far hath discretion fought with nature
That we with wisest sorrow think on him
Together with remembrance of ourselves.
Therefore our sometime sister, now our queen,
Th' imperial jointress to this warlike state,
10   Have we, as 'twere with a defeated joy—
With an auspicious and a dropping eye,
With mirth in funeral and with dirge in marriage,
In equal scale weighing delight and dole—
Taken to wife. Nor have we herein barred
15   Your better wisdoms, which have freely gone
With this affair along. For all, our thanks.
Now follows that you know young Fortinbras,
Holding a weak supposal of our worth,

Claudius (Basil Sydney) and Gertrude (Eileen Herlie) greet the court in the 1948 film directed by Laurence Olivier.

Or thinking by our late dear brother's death
Our state to be disjoint and out of frame,   20
Co-leaguèd with this dream of his advantage,
He hath not failed to pester us with message
Importing the surrender of those lands
Lost by his father, with all bonds of law,
To our most valiant brother. So much for him.   25
Now for ourself and for this time of meeting.
Thus much the business is: we have here writ
To Norway, uncle of young Fortinbras—
Who, impotent and bed-rid, scarcely hears
Of this his nephew's purpose—to suppress   30
His further gait herein, in that the levies,
The lists, and full proportions are all made
Out of his subject; and we here dispatch
You, good Cornelius, and you, Voltimand,
For bearers of this greeting to old Norway,   35
Giving to you no further personal power
To business with the King more than the scope
Of these dilated articles allow.   *[He gives a paper.]*
Farewell, and let your haste commend your duty.

CORNELIUS, VOLTIMAND: In that, and all things,
          will we show our duty.   40

KING: We doubt it nothing. Heartily farewell.
                            [Exeunt VOLTIMAND *and* CORNELIUS.]

---

168 strike destroy by evil influence   **169 takes** bewitches
170 gracious full of grace

1.2. Location: The castle.
s.d. as i.e., such as, including.   **cum aliis** with others   **1 our** my.
(The royal "we"; also in the following lines.)   **8 sometime** former
9 jointress woman possessing property with her husband   **11
With . . . eye** with one eye smiling and the other weeping   **13 dole**
grief   **17 that you know** what you know already, that; or, that you
be informed as follows   **18 weak supposal** low estimate

---

21 Co-leaguèd with joined to, allied with.   **dream . . . advantage** illusory hope of having the advantage. (His only ally is this
hope.)   **23 Importing** pertaining to   **24 bonds** contracts
29 impotent helpless   **31 His** i.e., Fortinbras'.   **gait** proceeding   **31–33 in that . . . subject** since the levying of troops and supplies is drawn entirely from the King of Norway's own subjects
38 dilated set out at length   **39 let . . . duty** let your swift obeying
of orders, rather than mere words, express your dutifulness
41 nothing not at all

And now, Laertes, what's the news with you?
You told us of some suit; what is 't, Laertes?
You cannot speak of reason to the Dane
45 And lose your voice. What wouldst thou beg, Laertes,
That shall not be my offer, not thy asking?
The head is not more native to the heart,
The hand more instrumental to the mouth,
Than is the throne of Denmark to thy father.
50 What wouldst thou have, Laertes?

LAERTES: My dread lord,
Your leave and favor to return to France,
From whence though willingly I came to Denmark
To show my duty in your coronation,
Yet now I must confess, that duty done,
55 My thoughts and wishes bend again toward France
And bow them to your gracious leave and pardon.

KING: Have you your father's leave? What says Polonius?

POLONIUS: H'ath, my lord, wrung from me my slow
leave
By laborsome petition, and at last
60 Upon his will I sealed my hard consent.
I do beseech you, give him leave to go.

KING: Take thy fair hour, Laertes. Time be thine,
And thy best graces spend it at thy will!
But now, my cousin Hamlet, and my son—

65 **HAMLET:** A little more than kin, and less than kind.

KING: How is it that the clouds still hang on you?

HAMLET: Not so, my lord. I am too much in the sun.

QUEEN: Good Hamlet, cast thy nighted color off,
And let thine eye look like a friend on Denmark.
70 Do not forever with thy vailèd lids

Seek for thy noble father in the dust.
Thou know'st 'tis common, all that lives must die,
Passing through nature to eternity.

HAMLET: Ay, madam, it is common.

QUEEN: If it be,
Why seems it so particular with thee? 75

HAMLET: Seems, madam? Nay, it is. I know not
"seems."
'Tis not alone my inky cloak, good Mother,
Nor customary suits of solemn black,
Nor windy suspiration of forced breath,
No, nor the fruitful river in the eye, 80
Nor the dejected havior of the visage,
Together with all forms, moods, shapes of grief,
That can denote me truly. These indeed seem,
For they are actions that a man might play.
But I have that within which passes show; 85
These but the trappings and the suits of woe.

KING: 'Tis sweet and commendable in your nature,
Hamlet,
To give these mourning duties to your father.
But you must know your father lost a father,
That father lost, lost his, and the survivor bound 90
In filial obligation for some term
To do obsequious sorrow. But to persever
In obstinate condolement is a course
Of impious stubbornness. 'Tis unmanly grief.
It shows a will most incorrect to heaven, 95
A heart unfortified, a mind impatient,
An understanding simple and unschooled.
For what we know must be and is as common
As any the most vulgar thing to sense,
Why should we in our peevish opposition 100
Take it to heart? Fie, 'tis a fault to heaven,
A fault against the dead, a fault to nature,
To reason most absurd, whose common theme
Is death of fathers, and who still hath cried,
From the first corpse till he that died today, 105
"This must be so." We pray you, throw to earth
This unprevailing woe and think of us
As of a father; for let the world take note,

---

44 **the Dane** the Danish king   45 **lose your voice** waste your
speech   47 **native** closely connected, related   48 **instrumental**
serviceable   51 **leave and favor** kind permission   56 **bow . . .
pardon** entreatingly make a deep bow, asking your permission to
depart   58 **H'ath** he has   60 **sealed** (as if sealing a legal document).   **hard** reluctant   62 **Take thy fair hour** enjoy your time
of youth   63 **And . . . will** and may your finest qualities guide the
way you choose to spend your time   64 **cousin** any kin not of the
immediate family   65 **A little . . . kind** i.e., closer than an ordinary
nephew (since I am stepson), and yet more separated in natural
feeling (with pun on *kind* meaning "affectionate" and "natural,"
"lawful." This line is often read as an aside, but it need not be. The
King chooses perhaps not to respond to Hamlet's cryptic and bitter remark.)   67 **the sun** i.e., the sunshine of the King's royal favor
(with pun on *son*)   68 **nighted color** (1) mourning garments of
black (2) dark melancholy   69 **Denmark** the King of Denmark
70 **vailèd lids** lowered eyes

---

72 **common** of universal occurrence. (But Hamlet plays on the
sense of "vulgar" in line 74.)   75 **particular** personal   78 **customary** (1) socially conventional (2) habitual with me   79 **suspiration** sighing   80 **fruitful** abundant   81 **havior** expression   82
moods outward expression of feeling   92 **obsequious** suited to
obsequies or funerals.   **persever** persevere   93 **condolement** sor-
rowing   96 **unfortified** i.e., against adversity   97 **simple** ignorant   99 **As . . . sense** as the most ordinary experience   104 **still**
always   105 **the first corpse** (Abel's)   107 **unprevailing** unavailing, useless

You are the most immediate to our throne,
110 And with no less nobility of love
Than that which dearest father bears his son
Do I impart toward you. For your intent
In going back to school in Wittenberg,
It is most retrograde to our desire,
115 And we beseech you bend you to remain
Here in the cheer and comfort of our eye,
Our chiefest courtier, cousin, and our son.

QUEEN: Let not thy mother lose her prayers, Hamlet.
I pray thee, stay with us, go not to Wittenberg.

120 **HAMLET:** I shall in all my best obey you, madam.

KING: Why, 'tis a loving and a fair reply.
Be as ourself in Denmark. Madam, come.
This gentle and unforced accord of Hamlet
Sits smiling to my heart, in grace whereof
125 No jocund health that Denmark drinks today
But the great cannon to the clouds shall tell,
And the King's rouse the heaven shall bruit again,
Respeaking earthly thunder. Come away.

Flourish. Exeunt all but HAMLET.

HAMLET: O, that this too sullied flesh would melt,
130 Thaw, and resolve itself into a dew!
Or that the Everlasting had not fixed
His canon 'gainst self-slaughter! O God, God,
How weary, stale, flat, and unprofitable
Seem to me all the uses of this world!
135 Fie on 't, ah fie! 'Tis an unweeded garden
That grows to seed. Things rank and gross in nature
Possess it merely. That it should come to this!
But two months dead—nay, not so much, not two.
So excellent a king, that was to this
140 Hyperion to a satyr, so loving to my mother
That he might not beteem the winds of heaven
Visit her face too roughly. Heaven and earth,
Must I remember? Why, she would hang on him
As if increase of appetite had grown
145 By what it fed on, and yet within a month—

Let me not think on 't; frailty, thy name is woman!—
A little month, or ere those shoes were old
With which she followed my poor father's body,
Like Niobe, all tears, why she, even she—
O God, a beast, that wants discourse of reason, 150
Would have mourned longer—married with my
uncle,
My father's brother, but no more like my father
Than I to Hercules. Within a month,
Ere yet the salt of most unrighteous tears
Had left the flushing in her gallèd eyes, 155
She married. O, most wicked speed, to post
With such dexterity to incestuous sheets!
It is not, nor it cannot come to good.
But break, my heart, for I must hold my tongue.

Enter HORATIO, MARCELLUS, *and* BERNARDO.

HORATIO: Hail to your lordship!

HAMLET: I am glad to see you well. 160
Horatio!—or I do forget myself.

HORATIO: The same, my lord, and your poor servant
ever.

HAMLET: Sir, my good friend; I'll change that name
with you.
And what make you from Wittenberg, Horatio?
Marcellus. 165

MARCELLUS: My good lord.

HAMLET: I am very glad to see you. *[To* BERNARDO.*]*
Good even, sir.—
But what in faith make you from Wittenberg?

HORATIO: A truant disposition, good my lord.

HAMLET: I would not hear your enemy say so, 170
Nor shall you do my ear that violence
To make it truster of your own report
Against yourself. I know you are no truant.
But what is your affair in Elsinore?
We'll teach you to drink deep ere you depart. 175

---

109 most immediate next in succession **112 impart toward**
i.e., bestow my affection on. **For** as for **113 to school** i.e., to
your studies. **Wittenberg** famous German university founded
in 1502 **114 retrograde** contrary **115 bend you** incline yourself **120 in all my best** to the best of my ability **124 to** i.e., at.
grace thanksgiving **125 jocund** merry **127 rouse** drinking
of a draft of liquor. **bruit again** loudly echo **128 thunder** i.e.,
of trumpet and kettledrum, sounded when the King drinks; see
1.4.8–12 **129 sullied** defiled. (The early quartos read *sallied;* the
Folio, *solid.*) **132 canon** law **134 all the uses** the whole routine
137 merely completely **139 to** in comparison to **140 Hyperion**
Titan sun-god, father of Helios. **satyr** a lecherous creature of classical mythology, half-human but with a goat's legs, tail, ears, and
horns **141 beteem** allow

---

147 or ere even before **149 Niobe** Tantalus' daughter, Queen of
Thebes, who boasted that she had more sons and daughters than
Leto; for this, Apollo and Artemis, children of Leto, slew her fourteen children. She was turned by Zeus into a stone that continually
dropped tears. **150 wants . . . reason** lacks the faculty of reason
155 gallèd irritated, inflamed **156 post** hasten **157 incestuous**
(In Shakespeare's day, the marriage of a man like Claudius to his
deceased brother's wife was considered incestuous.) **163 change
that name** i.e., give and receive reciprocally the name of "friend"
(rather than talk of "servant") **164 make you from** are you doing
away from

HORATIO: My lord, I came to see your father's funeral.

HAMLET: I prithee, do not mock me, fellow student;
I think it was to see my mother's wedding.

HORATIO: Indeed, my lord, it followed hard upon.

180 **HAMLET:** Thrift, thrift, Horatio! The funeral baked
meats
Did coldly furnish forth the marriage tables.
Would I had met my dearest foe in heaven
Or ever I had seen that day, Horatio!
My father!—Methinks I see my father.

185 **HORATIO:** Where, my lord?

HAMLET: In my mind's eye, Horatio.

HORATIO: I saw him once. 'A was a goodly king.

HAMLET: 'A was a man. Take him for all in all,
I shall not look upon his like again.

HORATIO: My lord, I think I saw him yesternight.

190 **HAMLET:** Saw? Who?

HORATIO: My lord, the King your father.

HAMLET: The King my father?

HORATIO: Season your admiration for a while
With an attent ear till I may deliver,
195 Upon the witness of these gentlemen,
This marvel to you.

HAMLET: For God's love, let me hear!

HORATIO: Two nights together had these gentlemen,
Marcellus and Bernardo, on their watch,
In the dead waste and middle of the night,
200 Been thus encountered. A figure like your father,
Armèd at point exactly, cap-à-pie,
Appears before them, and with solemn march
Goes slow and stately by them. Thrice he walked
By their oppressed and fear-surprisèd eyes
205 Within his truncheon's length, whilst they, distilled
Almost to jelly with the act of fear,
Stand dumb and speak not to him. This to me
In dreadful secrecy impart they did,
And I with them the third night kept the watch,
210 Where, as they had delivered, both in time,
Form of the thing, each word made true and good,

Hamlet (Kevin Kline) addresses Horatio (Peter Francis James) in the 1990 film directed by Kevin Kline.

The apparition comes. I knew your father;
These hands are not more like.

HAMLET: But where was this?

MARCELLUS: My lord, upon the platform where we
watch.

HAMLET: Did you not speak to it?

HORATIO: My lord, I did, 215
But answer made it none. Yet once methought
It lifted up its head and did address
Itself to motion, like as it would speak;
But even then the morning cock crew loud,
And at the sound it shrunk in haste away 220
And vanished from our sight.

HAMLET: 'Tis very strange.

HORATIO: As I do live, my honored lord, 'tis true,
And we did think it writ down in our duty
To let you know of it.

HAMLET: Indeed, indeed, sirs. But this troubles me. 225
Hold you the watch tonight?

ALL: We do, my lord.

HAMLET: Armed, say you?

ALL: Armed, my lord.

HAMLET: From top to toe?

ALL: My lord, from head to foot. 230

HAMLET: Then saw you not his face?

---

179 **hard** close   180 **baked meats** meat pies   181 **coldly** i.e., as cold leftovers   182 **dearest** closest (and therefore deadliest)   183 **Or ever** before   186 **'A** he   193 **Season your admiration** restrain your astonishment   194 **attent** attentive   199 **dead waste** desolate stillness   201 **at point** correctly in every detail.   **cap-à-pie** from head to foot   205 **truncheon** officer's staff.   **distilled** dissolved   206 **act** action, operation   208 **dreadful** full of dread

217–218 **did . . . speak** began to move as though it were about to speak   219 **even then** at that very instant

HORATIO: O, yes, my lord, he wore his beaver up.

HAMLET: What looked he, frowningly?

HORATIO: A countenance more in sorrow than in anger.

235 **HAMLET:** Pale or red?

HORATIO: Nay, very pale.

HAMLET: And fixed his eyes upon you?

HORATIO: Most constantly.

HAMLET: I would I had been there.

240 **HORATIO:** It would have much amazed you.

HAMLET: Very like, very like. Stayed it long?

HORATIO: While one with moderate haste might tell a hundred.

MARCELLUS, BERNARDO: Longer, longer.

HORATIO: Not when I saw 't.

245 **HAMLET:** His beard was grizzled—no?

HORATIO: It was, as I have seen it in his life, A sable silvered.

HAMLET: I will watch tonight. Perchance 'twill walk again.

HORATIO: I warrant it will.

HAMLET: If it assume my noble father's person,
250 I'll speak to it though hell itself should gape
And bid me hold my peace. I pray you all,
If you have hitherto concealed this sight,
Let it be tenable in your silence still,
And whatsoever else shall hap tonight,
255 Give it an understanding but no tongue.
I will requite your loves. So, fare you well.
Upon the platform twixt eleven and twelve
I'll visit you.

ALL: Our duty to your honor.

HAMLET: Your loves, as mine to you. Farewell.

Exeunt [all but HAMLET].

260 My father's spirit in arms! All is not well.
I doubt some foul play. Would the night were come!
Till then sit still, my soul. Foul deeds will rise,
Though all the earth o'erwhelm them, to men's eyes.

Exit.

---

232 **beaver** visor on the helmet   233 **What** how   242 **tell** count
245 **grizzled** gray   247 **sable silvered** black mixed with white
248 **warrant** assure you   253 **tenable** held   261 **doubt** suspect

Laertes (Nathaniel Parker) warns Ophelia (Helena Bonham Carter) to be careful of Hamlet in the 1990 film directed by Franco Zeffirelli.

1.3 *Enter* LAERTES *and* OPHELIA, *his sister.*

LAERTES: My necessaries are embarked. Farewell.
And, sister, as the winds give benefit
And convoy is assistant, do not sleep
But let me hear from you.

OPHELIA: Do you doubt that?

LAERTES: For Hamlet, and the trifling of his favor,   5
Hold it a fashion and a toy in blood,
A violet in the youth of primy nature
Forward, not permanent, sweet, not lasting,
The perfume and suppliance of a minute—
No more.

OPHELIA: No more but so?

LAERTES: Think it no more.   10
For nature crescent does not grow alone
In thews and bulk, but as this temple waxes
The inward service of the mind and soul
Grows wide withal. Perhaps he loves you now,
And now no soil nor cautel doth besmirch   15
The virtue of his will; but you must fear,
His greatness weighed, his will is not his own.
For he himself is subject to his birth.
He may not, as unvalued persons do,
Carve for himself, for on his choice depends   20
The safety and health of this whole state,

1.3. Location: Polonius' chambers.
3 **convoy is assistant** means of conveyance are available   6 **toy in
blood** passing amorous fancy   7 **primy** in its prime, springtime
8 **Forward** precocious   9 **suppliance** supply, filler   11 **crescent**
growing, waxing   12 **thews** bodily strength.   **temple** i.e., body
14 **Grows wide withal** grows along with it   15 **soil** blemish.
cautel deceit   16 **will** desire   17 **His greatness weighed** if you
take into account his high position   20 **Carve** i.e., choose

And therefore must his choice be circumscribed
Unto the voice and yielding of that body
Whereof he is the head. Then if he says he loves you,
25 It fits your wisdom so far to believe it
As he in his particular act and place
May give his saying deed, which is no further
Than the main voice of Denmark goes withal.
Then weigh what loss your honor may sustain
30 If with too credent ear you list his songs,
Or lose your heart, or your chaste treasure open
To his unmastered importunity.
Fear it, Ophelia, fear it, my dear sister,
And keep you in the rear of your affection,
35 Out of the shot and danger of desire.
The chariest maid is prodigal enough
If she unmask her beauty to the moon.
Virtue itself scapes not calumnious strokes.
The canker galls the infants of the spring
40 Too oft before their buttons be disclosed,
And in the morn and liquid dew of youth
Contagious blastments are most imminent.
Be wary then; best safety lies in fear.
Youth to itself rebels, though none else near.

45 **OPHELIA:** I shall the effect of this good lesson keep
As watchman to my heart. But, good my brother,
Do not, as some ungracious pastors do,
Show me the steep and thorny way to heaven,
Whiles like a puffed and reckless libertine
50 Himself the primrose path of dalliance treads,
And recks not his own rede.

Enter POLONIUS.

LAERTES: O, fear me not.
I stay too long. But here my father comes.
A double blessing is a double grace;
Occasion smiles upon a second leave.

---

23 **voice and yielding** assent, approval 26 **in . . . place** in his particular restricted circumstances 28 **main voice** general assent. **withal** along with 30 **credent** credulous. **list** listen to 34 **keep . . . affection** don't advance as far as your affection might lead you. (A military metaphor.) 36 **chariest** most scrupulously modest 37 **If she unmask** if she does no more than show her beauty. **moon** (Symbol of chastity.) 39 **canker galls** cankerworm destroys 40 **buttons** buds. **disclosed** opened 41 **liquid dew** i.e., time when dew is fresh and bright 42 **blastments** blights 44 **Youth . . . rebels** youth is inherently rebellious 47 **ungracious** ungodly 49 **puffed** bloated, or swollen with pride 51 **recks** heeds. **rede** counsel. **fear me not** don't worry on my account 53 **double** (Laertes has already bid his father good-bye.) 54 **Occasion . . . leave** happy is the circumstance that provides a second leave-taking. (The goddess Occasion, or Opportunity, smiles.)

POLONIUS: Yet here, Laertes? Aboard, aboard, for
shame!   55
The wind sits in the shoulder of your sail,
And you are stayed for. There—my blessing with
thee!
And these few precepts in thy memory
Look thou character. Give thy thoughts no tongue,
Nor any unproportioned thought his act.   60
Be thou familiar, but by no means vulgar.
Those friends thou hast, and their adoption tried,
Grapple them unto thy soul with hoops of steel,
But do not dull thy palm with entertainment
Of each new-hatched, unfledged courage. Beware   65
Of entrance to a quarrel, but being in,
Bear 't that th' opposèd may beware of thee.
Give every man thy ear, but few thy voice;
Take each man's censure, but reserve thy judgment.
Costly thy habit as thy purse can buy,   70
But not expressed in fancy; rich, not gaudy,
For the apparel oft proclaims the man,
And they in France of the best rank and station
Are of a most select and generous chief in that.
Neither a borrower nor a lender be,   75
For loan oft loses both itself and friend,
And borrowing dulleth edge of husbandry.
This above all: to thine own self be true,
And it must follow, as the night the day,
Thou canst not then be false to any man.   80
Farewell. My blessing season this in thee!

LAERTES: Most humbly do I take my leave, my lord.

POLONIUS: The time invests you. Go, your servants
tend.

LAERTES: Farewell, Ophelia, and remember well
What I have said to you.   85

OPHELIA: 'Tis in my memory locked,
And you yourself shall keep the key of it.

LAERTES: Farewell.   *Exit* LAERTES.

POLONIUS: What is 't, Ophelia, he hath said to you?

---

59 **Look** be sure that. **character** inscribe 60 **unproportioned** badly calculated, intemperate. **his** its 61 **familiar** sociable. **vulgar** common 62 **and their adoption tried** and also their suitability for adoption as friends having been tested 64 **dull thy palm** i.e., shake hands so often as to make the gesture meaningless 65 **courage** young man of spirit 67 **Bear 't that** manage it so that 69 **censure** opinion, judgment 70 **habit** clothing 71 **fancy** excessive ornament, decadent fashion 74 **Are . . . that** are of a most refined and well-bred preeminence in choosing what to wear 77 **husbandry** thrift 81 **season** mature 83 **invests** besieges, presses upon

90   **OPHELIA:**   So please you, something touching the Lord
      Hamlet.

  POLONIUS: Marry, well bethought.
    'Tis told me he hath very oft of late
    Given private time to you, and you yourself
    Have of your audience been most free and
      bounteous.
95   If it be so—as so 'tis put on me,
    And that in way of caution—I must tell you
    You do not understand yourself so clearly
    As it behooves my daughter and your honor.
    What is between you? Give me up the truth.

100   **OPHELIA:**   He hath, my lord, of late made many
      tenders
    Of his affection to me.

  POLONIUS: Affection? Pooh! You speak like a green
      girl,
    Unsifted in such perilous circumstance.
    Do you believe his tenders, as you call them?

105   **OPHELIA:**   I do not know, my lord, what I should think.

  POLONIUS: Marry, I will teach you. Think yourself a
      baby
    That you have ta'en these tenders for true pay
    Which are not sterling. Tender yourself more dearly,
    Or—not to crack the wind of the poor phrase,
110   Running it thus—you'll tender me a fool.

  OPHELIA: My lord, he hath importuned me with love
    In honorable fashion.

  POLONIUS: Ay, fashion you may call it. Go to, go to.

  OPHELIA: And hath given countenance to his speech,
      my lord,
115   With almost all the holy vows of heaven.

  POLONIUS: Ay, springes to catch woodcocks. I do
      know,
    When the blood burns, how prodigal the soul
    Lends the tongue vows. These blazes, daughter,
    Giving more light than heat, extinct in both

    Even in their promise as it is a-making,   120
    You must not take for fire. From this time
    Be something scanter of your maiden presence.
    Set your entreatments at a higher rate
    Than a command to parle. For Lord Hamlet,
    Believe so much in him that he is young,   125
    And with a larger tether may he walk
    Than may be given you. In few, Ophelia,
    Do not believe his vows, for they are brokers,
    Not of that dye which their investments show,
    But mere implorators of unholy suits,   130
    Breathing like sanctified and pious bawds,
    The better to beguile. This is for all:
    I would not, in plain terms, from this time forth
    Have you so slander any moment leisure
    As to give words or talk with the Lord Hamlet.   135
    Look to 't, I charge you. Come your ways.

  OPHELIA: I shall obey, my lord.   *Exeunt.*

1.4   *Enter* HAMLET, HORATIO, *and* MARCELLUS

HAMLET: The air bites shrewdly; it is very cold.

HORATIO: It is a nipping and an eager air.

HAMLET: What hour now?

HORATIO: I think it lacks of twelve.

MARCELLUS: No, it is struck.

HORATIO: Indeed? I heard it not.
    It then draws near the season   5
    Wherein the spirit held his wont to walk.
      A flourish of trumpets, and two pieces go off [within].
    What does this mean, my lord?

HAMLET: The King doth wake tonight and takes his
      rouse,
    Keeps wassail, and the swaggering upspring reels;

---

91 Marry i.e., by the Virgin Mary. (A mild oath.)   **95 put on** impressed on, told to   **98 behooves** befits   **100 tenders** offers **103 Unsifted** i.e., untried   **108 sterling** legal currency.   **Tender** hold, look after, offer   **109 crack the wind** i.e., run it until it is broken-winded   **110 tender me a fool** (1) show yourself to me as a fool (2) show me up as a fool (3) present me with a grandchild. (*Fool* was a term of endearment for a child.)   **113 fashion** mere form, pretense.   **Go to** (An expression of impatience.)   **114 countenance** credit, confirmation   **116 springes** snares.   **woodcocks** birds easily caught; here used to connote gullibility   **117 prodigal** prodigally

120 it i.e., the promise   **122 something** somewhat   **123 entreatments** negotiations for surrender. (A military term.)   **124 parle** discuss terms with the enemy. (Polonius urges his daughter, in the metaphor of military language, not to meet with Hamlet and consider giving in to him merely because he requests an interview.) **125 so . . . him** this much concerning him   **127 In few** briefly   **128 brokers** go-betweens, procurers   **129 dye** color or sort.   **investments** clothes. (The vows are not what they seem.)   **130 mere implorators** out-and-out solicitors   **131 Breathing** speaking   **132 for all** once for all, in sum   **134 slander** abuse, misuse.   **moment** moment's   **136 Come your ways** come along

1.4. Location: The guard platform.
1 shrewdly keenly, sharply   **2 eager** biting   **3 lacks of** is just short of   **5 season** time   **6 held his wont** was accustomed   **s.d. pieces** i.e., of ordnance, cannon   **8 wake** stay awake and hold revel.   **takes his rouse** carouses   **9 wassail** carousal.   **upspring** wild German dance.   **reels** dances

10 And as he drains his drafts of Rhenish down,
The kettledrum and trumpet thus bray out
The triumph of his pledge.

HORATIO: Is it a custom?

HAMLET: Ay, marry, is 't,
But to my mind, though I am native here
15 And to the manner born, it is a custom
More honored in the breach than the observance.
This heavy-headed revel east and west
Makes us traduced and taxed of other nations.
They clepe us drunkards, and with swinish phrase
20 Soil our addition; and indeed it takes
From our achievements, though performed at height,
The pith and marrow of our attribute.
So, oft it chances in particular men,
That for some vicious mole of nature in them,
25 As in their birth—wherein they are not guilty,
Since nature cannot choose his origin—
By their o'ergrowth of some complexion,
Oft breaking down the pales and forts of reason,
Or by some habit that too much o'erleavens
30 The form of plausive manners, that these men
Carrying, I say, the stamp of one defect,
Being nature's livery or fortune's star,
His virtues else, be they as pure as grace,
As infinite as man may undergo,
35 Shall in the general censure take corruption
From that particular fault. The dram of evil
Doth all the noble substance often dout
To his own scandal.

Enter GHOST.

HORATIO: Look, my lord, it comes!

Hamlet (Kenneth Branagh) goes with Marcellus and Horatio to confront the ghost.

HAMLET: Angels and ministers of grace defend us!
Be thou a spirit of health or goblin damned,   40
Bring with thee airs from heaven or blasts from hell,
Be thy intents wicked or charitable,
Thou com'st in such a questionable shape
That I will speak to thee. I'll call thee Hamlet,
King, father, royal Dane. O, answer me!   45
Let me not burst in ignorance, but tell
Why thy canonized bones, hearsèd in death,
Have burst their cerements; why the sepulcher
Wherein we saw thee quietly inurned
Hath oped his ponderous and marble jaws   50
To cast thee up again. What may this mean,
That thou, dead corpse, again in complete steel,
Revisits thus the glimpses of the moon,
Making night hideous, and we fools of nature
So horridly to shake our disposition   55
With thoughts beyond the reaches of our souls?
Say, why is this? Wherefore? What should we do?
[The GHOST*] beckons [*HAMLET*].*

HORATIO: It beckons you to go away with it,
As if it some impartment did desire
To you alone.

MARCELLUS: Look with what courteous action   60
It wafts you to a more removèd ground.
But do not go with it.

---

10 Rhenish Rhine wine   **12 The triumph . . . pledge** i.e., his feat
in draining the wine in a single draft   **15 manner** custom (of
drinking)   **16 More . . . observance** better neglected than followed
17 east and west i.e., everywhere   **18 taxed of** censured by   **19
clepe** call.   **with swinish phrase** i.e., by calling us swine   **20
addition** reputation   **21 at height** outstandingly   **22 The pith . . .
attribute** the essence of the reputation that others attribute to us
24 for on account of.   **mole of nature** natural blemish in one's
constitution   **26 his** its   **27 their o'ergrowth . . . complexion** the
excessive growth in individuals of some natural trait   **28 pales** pal-
ings, fences (as of a fortification)   **29 o'erleavens** induces a change
throughout (as yeast works in dough)   **30 plausive** pleasing   **32
nature's livery** sign of one's servitude to nature.   **fortune's star**
the destiny that chance brings   **33 His virtues else** i.e., the other
qualities of *these men* (line 30)   **34 may undergo** can sustain
35 general censure general opinion that people have of him
36–38 The dram . . . scandal i.e., the small drop of evil blots out
or works against the noble substance of the whole and brings it into
disrepute. To *dout* is to blot out. (A famous crux.)

---

39 ministers of grace messengers of God   **40 Be thou** whether
you are.   **spirit of health** good angel   **41 Bring** whether you bring
42 Be thy intents whether your intentions are   **43 questionable**
inviting question   **47 canonized** buried according to the canons of
the church.   **hearsèd** coffined   **48 cerements** grave clothes   **49
inurned** entombed   **52 complete steel** full armor   **53 glimpses
of the moon** pale and uncertain moonlight   **54 fools of nature**
mere men, limited to natural knowledge and subject to nature
55 So . . . disposition to distress our mental composure so violently
59 impartment communication

HORATIO: No, by no means.

HAMLET: It will not speak. Then I will follow it.

HORATIO: Do not, my lord!

HAMLET: Why, what should be the fear?
65 I do not set my life at a pin's fee,
And for my soul, what can it do to that,
Being a thing immortal as itself?
It waves me forth again. I'll follow it.

HORATIO: What if it tempt you toward the flood,
     my lord,
70 Or to the dreadful summit of the cliff
That beetles o'er his base into the sea,
And there assume some other horrible form
Which might deprive your sovereignty of reason
And draw you into madness? Think of it.
75 The very place puts toys of desperation,
Without more motive, into every brain
That looks so many fathoms to the sea
And hears it roar beneath.

HAMLET: It wafts me still.—Go on, I'll follow thee.

80 **MARCELLUS:**   You shall not go, my lord.
                              [They try to stop him.]

HAMLET: Hold off your hands!

HORATIO: Be ruled. You shall not go.

HAMLET: My fate cries out,
And makes each petty artery in this body
As hardy as the Nemean lion's nerve.
Still am I called. Unhand me, gentlemen.
85 By heaven, I'll make a ghost of him that lets me!
I say, away!—Go on, I'll follow thee.
                              Exeunt GHOST *and* HAMLET.

HORATIO: He waxes desperate with imagination.

MARCELLUS: Let's follow. 'Tis not fit thus to obey him.

HORATIO: Have after. To what issue will this come?

90 **MARCELLUS:**   Something is rotten in the state of
     Denmark.

---

65 **fee** value   69 **flood** sea   71 **beetles o'er** overhangs threateningly (like bushy eyebrows).   **his** its   73 **deprive . . . reason** take
away the rule of reason over your mind   75 **toys of desperation**
fancies of desperate acts, i.e., suicide   81 **My fate cries out** my
destiny summons me   82 **petty** weak.   **artery** (through which the
vital spirits were thought to have been conveyed)   83 **Nemean lion**
one of the monsters slain by Hercules in his twelve labors.   **nerve**
sinew   85 **lets** hinders   89 **Have after** let's go after him.   **issue**
outcome

HORATIO: Heaven will direct it.

MARCELLUS: Nay, let's follow him.
                              Exeunt.

1.5   *Enter* GHOST *and* HAMLET.

HAMLET: Whither wilt thou lead me? Speak. I'll go no
     further.

GHOST: Mark me.

HAMLET: I will.

GHOST: My hour is almost come,
When I to sulfurous and tormenting flames
Must render up myself.

HAMLET: Alas, poor ghost!

GHOST: Pity me not, but lend thy serious hearing   5
To what I shall unfold.

HAMLET: Speak, I am bound to hear.

GHOST: So art thou to revenge, when thou shalt hear.

HAMLET: What?

GHOST: I am thy father's spirit,   10
Doomed for a certain term to walk the night,
And for the day confined to fast in fires,
Till the foul crimes done in my days of nature
Are burnt and purged away. But that I am forbid
To tell the secrets of my prison house,   15
I could a tale unfold whose lightest word
Would harrow up thy soul, freeze thy young blood,
Make thy two eyes like stars start from their spheres,
Thy knotted and combinèd locks to part,
And each particular hair to stand on end   20
Like quills upon the fretful porcupine.
But this eternal blazon must not be
To ears of flesh and blood. List, list, O, list!
If thou didst ever thy dear father love—

HAMLET: O God!   25

GHOST: Revenge his foul and most unnatural murder.

---

91 **it** i.e., the outcome

1.5. Location: The battlements of the castle.
7 **bound** (1) ready (2) obligated by duty and fate. (The Ghost, in
line 8, answers in the second sense.)   12 **fast** do penance by fasting   13 **crimes** sins.   **of nature** as a mortal   14 **But that** were it
not that   17 **harrow up** lacerate, tear   18 **spheres** i.e., eye-sockets,
here compared to the orbits or transparent revolving spheres in
which, according to Ptolemaic astronomy, the heavenly bodies were
fixed   19 **knotted . . . locks** hair neatly arranged and confined
22 **eternal blazon** revelation of the secrets of eternity

The ghost (Paul Scofield) tells Hamlet of Claudius's betrayal.

HAMLET: Murder?

GHOST: Murder most foul, as in the best it is,
But this most foul, strange, and unnatural.

30 **HAMLET:**   Haste me to know 't, that I, with wings as
          swift
     As meditation or the thoughts of love,
     May sweep to my revenge.

GHOST: I find thee apt;
     And duller shouldst thou be than the fat weed
35   That roots itself in ease on Lethe wharf,
     Wouldst thou not stir in this. Now, Hamlet, hear.
     'Tis given out that, sleeping in my orchard,
     A serpent stung me. So the whole ear of Denmark
     Is by a forgèd process of my death
40   Rankly abused. But know, thou noble youth,
     The serpent that did sting thy father's life
     Now wears his crown.

HAMLET: O, my prophetic soul! My uncle!

GHOST: Ay, that incestuous, that adulterate beast,
     With witchcraft of his wit, with traitorous gifts—
45   O wicked wit and gifts, that have the power
     So to seduce!—won to his shameful lust
     The will of my most seeming-virtuous queen.
     O Hamlet, what a falling off was there!
     From me, whose love was of that dignity
50   That it went hand in hand even with the vow
     I made to her in marriage, and to decline
     Upon a wretch whose natural gifts were poor
     To those of mine!

But virtue, as it never will be moved,
Though lewdness court it in a shape of heaven,   55
So lust, though to a radiant angel linked,
Will sate itself in a celestial bed
And prey on garbage.
But soft, methinks I scent the morning air.
Brief let me be. Sleeping within my orchard,   60
My custom always of the afternoon,
Upon my secure hour thy uncle stole,
With juice of cursèd hebona in a vial,
And in the porches of my ears did pour
The leprous distillment, whose effect   65
Holds such an enmity with blood of man
That swift as quicksilver it courses through
The natural gates and alleys of the body,
And with a sudden vigor it doth posset
And curd, like eager droppings into milk,   70
The thin and wholesome blood. So did it mine,
And a most instant tetter barked about,
Most lazar-like, with vile and loathsome crust,
All my smooth body.
Thus was I, sleeping, by a brother's hand   75
Of life, of crown, of queen at once dispatched,
Cut off even in the blossoms of my sin,
Unhouseled, disappointed, unaneled,
No reckoning made, but sent to my account
With all my imperfections on my head.   80
O, horrible! O, horrible, most horrible!
If thou hast nature in thee, bear it not.
Let not the royal bed of Denmark be
A couch for luxury and damnèd incest.
But, howsoever thou pursues this act,   85
Taint not thy mind nor let thy soul contrive
Against thy mother aught. Leave her to heaven
And to those thorns that in her bosom lodge,
To prick and sting her. Fare thee well at once.
The glowworm shows the matin to be near,   90
And 'gins to pale his uneffectual fire.
Adieu, adieu, adieu! Remember me.   *[Exit.]*

---

28 in the best even at best **33 shouldst thou be** you would have to be. **fat** torpid, lethargic **34 Lethe** the river of forgetfulness in Hades **36 orchard** garden **38 forgèd process** falsified account **39 abused** deceived **43 adulterate** adulterous **44 gifts** (1) talents (2) presents **50 even with the vow** with the very vow **53 To** compared to

54 virtue, as it as virtue **55 shape of heaven** heavenly form **57 sate . . . bed** cease to find sexual pleasure in a virtuously lawful marriage **62 secure** confident, unsuspicious **63 hebona** a poison. (The word seems to be a form of *ebony*, though it is thought perhaps to be related to *henbane*, a poison, or to *ebenus*, "yew.") **64 porches of my ears** ears as a porch or entrance of the body **65 leprous distillment** distillation causing leprosylike disfigurement **69 posset** coagulate, curdle **70 eager** sour, acid **72 tetter** eruption of scabs. **barked** covered with a rough covering, like bark on a tree **73 lazar-like** leperlike **76 dispatched** suddenly deprived **78 Unhouseled** without having received the Sacrament. **disappointed** unready (spiritually) for the last journey. **unaneled** without having received extreme unction **79 reckoning** settling of accounts **82 nature** i.e., the promptings of a son **84 luxury** lechery **90 matin** morning **91 his** its

HAMLET: O all you host of heaven! O earth! What else?
And shall I couple hell? O, fie! Hold, hold, my heart,
95   And you, my sinews, grow not instant old,
But bear me stiffly up. Remember thee?
Ay, thou poor ghost, whiles memory holds a seat
In this distracted globe. Remember thee?
Yea, from the table of my memory
100   I'll wipe away all trivial fond records,
All saws of books, all forms, all pressures past
That youth and observation copied there,
And thy commandment all alone shall live
Within the book and volume of my brain,
105   Unmixed with baser matter. Yes, by heaven!
O most pernicious woman!
O villain, villain, smiling, damnèd villain!
My tables—meet it is I set it down
That one may smile, and smile, and be a villain.
110   At least I am sure it may be so in Denmark.

[Writing.]

So, uncle, there you are. Now to my word:
It is "Adieu, adieu! Remember me."
I have sworn 't.

Enter HORATIO *and* MARCELLUS.

HORATIO: My lord, my lord!

115 **MARCELLUS:** Lord Hamlet!

HORATIO: Heavens secure him!

HAMLET: So be it.

MARCELLUS: Hilo, ho, ho, my lord!

HAMLET: Hillo, ho, ho, boy! Come, bird, come.

120 **MARCELLUS:** How is 't, my noble lord?

HORATIO: What news, my lord?

HAMLET: O, wonderful!

HORATIO: Good my lord, tell it.

HAMLET: No, you will reveal it.

125 **HORATIO:** Not I, my lord, by heaven.

MARCELLUS: Nor I, my lord.

Hamlet (Mel Gibson) swears his companions to secrecy.

HAMLET: How say you, then, would heart of man once
think it?
But you'll be secret?

HORATIO, MARCELLUS: Ay, by heaven, my lord.

HAMLET: There's never a villain dwelling in all
Denmark
But he's an arrant knave.   130

HORATIO: There needs no ghost, my lord, come from
the grave
To tell us this.

HAMLET: Why, right, you are in the right.
And so, without more circumstance at all,
I hold it fit that we shake hands and part,
You as your business and desire shall point you— 135
For every man hath business and desire,
Such as it is—and for my own poor part,
Look you, I'll go pray.

HORATIO: These are but wild and whirling words,
my lord.

HAMLET: I am sorry they offend you, heartily; 140
Yes, faith, heartily.

HORATIO: There's no offense, my lord.

HAMLET: Yes, by Saint Patrick, but there is, Horatio,
And much offense too. Touching this vision here,
It is an honest ghost, that let me tell you.

---

94 couple add. **Hold** hold together **95 instant** instantly **98 globe** (1) head (2) world **99 table** tablet, slate **100 fond** foolish **101 saws** wise sayings. **forms** shapes or images copied onto the slate; general ideas. **pressures** impressions stamped **108 tables** writing tablets. **meet it is** it is fitting **111 there you are** i.e., there, I've written that down against you **116 secure him** keep him safe **119 Hillo . . . come** (A falconer's call to a hawk in air. Hamlet mocks the hallooing as though it were a part of hawking.)

---

127 once ever **130 arrant** thoroughgoing **133 circumstance** ceremony, elaboration **142 Saint Patrick** (The keeper of Purgatory and patron saint of all blunders and confusion.) **143 offense** (Hamlet deliberately changes Horatio's "no offense taken" to "an offense against all decency.") **144 an honest ghost** i.e., a real ghost and not an evil spirit

145 For your desire to know what is between us,
O'ermaster 't as you may. And now, good friends,
As you are friends, scholars, and soldiers,
Give me one poor request.

HORATIO: What is 't, my lord? We will.

150 **HAMLET:** Never make known what you have seen
tonight.

HORATIO, MARCELLUS: My lord, we will not.

HAMLET: Nay, but swear 't.

HORATIO: In faith, my lord, not I.

MARCELLUS: Nor I, my lord, in faith.

155 **HAMLET:** Upon my sword.   *[He holds out his sword.]*

MARCELLUS: We have sworn, my lord, already.

HAMLET: Indeed, upon my sword, indeed.

GHOST *(cries under the stage)*: Swear.

HAMLET: Ha, ha, boy, sayst thou so? Art thou there,
truepenny?
160 Come on, you hear this fellow in the cellarage.
Consent to swear.

HORATIO: Propose the oath, my lord.

HAMLET: Never to speak of this that you have seen,
Swear by my sword.

GHOST *[beneath]*: Swear.   *[They swear.]*

165 **HAMLET:** *Hic et ubique?* Then we'll shift our ground.
          [He moves to another spot.]
Come hither, gentlemen,
And lay your hands again upon my sword.
Swear by my sword
Never to speak of this that you have heard.

170 **GHOST** *[beneath]*: Swear by his sword.   *[They swear.]*

HAMLET: Well said, old mole. Canst work i' th' earth
so fast?
A worthy pioner!—Once more remove, good friends.
          [He moves again.]

HORATIO: O day and night, but this is wondrous
strange!

HAMLET: And therefore as a stranger give it welcome.
There are more things in heaven and earth, Horatio, 175
Than are dreamt of in your philosophy.
But come;
Here, as before, never, so help you mercy,
How strange or odd soe'er I bear myself—
As I perchance hereafter shall think meet 180
To put an antic disposition on—
That you, at such times seeing me, never shall,
With arms encumbered thus, or this headshake,
Or by pronouncing of some doubtful phrase
As "Well, we know," or "We could, an if we would," 185
Or "If we list to speak," or "There be, an if they might,"
Or such ambiguous giving out, to note
That you know aught of me—this do swear,
So grace and mercy at your most need help you.

GHOST *[beneath]*: Swear.   *[They swear.]* 190

HAMLET: Rest, rest, perturbèd spirit! So, gentlemen,
With all my love I do commend me to you;
And what so poor a man as Hamlet is
May do t' express his love and friending to you,
God willing, shall not lack. Let us go in together, 195
And still your fingers on your lips, I pray.
The time is out of joint. O cursèd spite
That ever I was born to set it right!
          [They wait for him to leave first.]
Nay, come, let's go together.   *Exeunt.*

2.1 *Enter old* POLONIUS *with his man [*REYNALDO*].*

POLONIUS: Give him this money and these notes,
Reynaldo.
          [He gives money and papers.]

REYNALDO: I will, my lord.

---

153 In faith . . . I i.e., I swear not to tell what I have seen. (Horatio is not refusing to swear.) **155 sword** i.e., the hilt in the form of a cross **156 We . . . already** i.e., we swore *in faith* **159 truepenny** honest old fellow **164 s.d. They swear** (Seemingly they swear here, and at lines 170 and 190, as they lay their hands on Hamlet's sword. Tripled oaths would have particular force; these three oaths deal with what they have seen, what they have heard, and what they promise about Hamlet's *antic disposition*.) **165 Hic et ubique** here and everywhere (Latin.) **172 pioner** foot soldier assigned to dig tunnels and excavations

174 as a stranger i.e., needing your hospitality **176 your philosophy** this subject called "natural philosophy" or "science" that people talk about **178 so help you mercy** as you hope for God's mercy when you are judged **181 antic** fantastic **183 encumbered** folded **185 an if** if **186 list** wished. **There . . . might** i.e., there are people here (we, in fact) who could tell news if we were at liberty to do so **187 giving out** intimation. **note** draw attention to the fact **188 aught** i.e., something secret **192 do . . . you** entrust myself to you **194 friending** friendliness **195 lack** be lacking **196 still** always **197 The time** the state of affairs. **spite** i.e., the spite of Fortune **199 let's go together** (Probably they wait for him to leave first, but he refuses this ceremoniousness.)

2.1. Location: Polonius' chambers.

POLONIUS: You shall do marvelous wisely, good
    Reynaldo,
    Before you visit him, to make inquire
5   Of his behavior.

REYNALDO: My lord, I did intend it.

POLONIUS: Marry, well said, very well said. Look
    you, sir,
    Inquire me first what Danskers are in Paris,
    And how, and who, what means, and where they
      keep,
    What company, at what expense; and finding
10   By this encompassment and drift of question
    That they do know my son, come you more nearer
    Than your particular demands will touch it.
    Take you, as 'twere, some distant knowledge of him,
    As thus, "I know his father and his friends,
15   And in part him." Do you mark this, Reynaldo?

REYNALDO: Ay, very well, my lord.

POLONIUS: "And in part him, but," you may say,
    "not well.
    But if 't be he I mean, he's very wild,
    Addicted so and so," and there put on him
20   What forgeries you please—marry, none so rank
    As may dishonor him, take heed of that,
    But, sir, such wanton, wild, and usual slips
    As are companions noted and most known
    To youth and liberty.

25 **REYNALDO:** As gaming, my lord.

POLONIUS: Ay, or drinking, fencing, swearing,
    Quarreling, drabbing—you may go so far.

REYNALDO: My lord, that would dishonor him.

POLONIUS: Faith, no, as you may season it in the
    charge.
30   You must not put another scandal on him
    That he is open to incontinency;
    That's not my meaning. But breathe his faults so
    quaintly
    That they may seem the taints of liberty,

    The flash and outbreak of a fiery mind,
    A savageness in unreclaimèd blood,   35
    Of general assault.

REYNALDO: But, my good lord—

POLONIUS: Wherefore should you do this?

REYNALDO: Ay, my lord, I would know that.

POLONIUS: Marry, sir, here's my drift,   40
    And I believe it is a fetch of warrant.
    You laying these slight sullies on my son,
    As 'twere a thing a little soiled wi' the working,
    Mark you,
    Your party in converse, him you would sound,   45
    Having ever seen in the prenominate crimes
    The youth you breathe of guilty, be assured
    He closes with you in this consequence:
    "Good sir," or so, or "friend," or "gentleman,"
    According to the phrase or the addition   50
    Of man and country.

REYNALDO: Very good, my lord.

POLONIUS: And then, sir, does 'a this—'a does—what
    was I about to say? By the Mass, I was about to say
    something. Where did I leave?

REYNALDO: At "closes in the consequence."   55

POLONIUS: At "closes in the consequence," ay, marry.
    He closes thus: "I know the gentleman,
    I saw him yesterday," or "th' other day,"
    Or then, or then, with such or such, "and as you say,
    There was 'a gaming," "there o'ertook in 's rouse,"   60
    "There falling out at tennis," or perchance
    "I saw him enter such a house of sale,"
    Videlicet a brothel, or so forth. See you now,
    Your bait of falsehood takes this carp of truth;
    And thus do we of wisdom and of reach,   65
    With windlasses and with assays of bias,

---

3 marvelous marvelously **4 inquire** inquiry **7 Danskers**
Danes **8 what means** what wealth (they have). **keep** dwell **10
encompassment** roundabout talking. **drift** gradual approach
or course **11–12 come . . . it** you will find out more this way than
by asking pointed questions (*particular demands*) **13 Take you**
assume, pretend **19 put on** impute to **20 forgeries** invented
tales. **rank** gross **22 wanton** sportive, unrestrained **27 drab-
bing** whoring **29 season** temper, soften **31 incontinency** habitual sexual excess **32 quaintly** artfully, subtly **33 taints of
liberty** faults resulting from free living

35–36 A savageness . . . assault a wildness in untamed youth that
assails all indiscriminately **41 fetch of warrant** legitimate trick
43 soiled wi' the working soiled by handling while it is being
made, i.e., by involvement in the ways of the world **45 converse**
conversation. **sound** i.e., sound out **46 Having ever** if he has
ever. **prenominate crimes** before-mentioned offenses **47 breathe**
speak **48 closes . . . consequence** takes you into his confidence
in some fashion, as follows **50 addition** title **60 o'ertook in 's
rouse** overcome by drink **61 falling out** quarreling **63 Videlicet**
namely **64 carp** a fish **65 reach** capacity, ability **66 wind-
lasses** i.e., circuitous paths. (Literally, circuits made to head off
the game in hunting.) **assays of bias** attempts through indirec-
tion (like the curving path of the bowling ball, which is biased or
weighted to one side)

By indirections find directions out.
So by my former lecture and advice
Shall you my son. You have me, have you not?

70 **REYNALDO:**   My lord, I have.

POLONIUS: God b' wi' ye; fare ye well.

REYNALDO: Good my lord.

POLONIUS: Observe his inclination in yourself.

REYNALDO: I shall, my lord.

POLONIUS: And let him ply his music.

75 **REYNALDO:**   Well, my lord.

POLONIUS: Farewell.   *Exit* REYNALDO.

                                             Enter OPHELIA.

                 How now, Ophelia, what's the matter?

OPHELIA: O my lord, my lord, I have been so
      affrighted!

POLONIUS: With what, i' the name of God?

OPHELIA: My lord, as I was sewing in my closet,
80   Lord Hamlet, with his doublet all unbraced,
      Not hat upon his head, his stockings fouled,
      Ungartered, and down-gyvèd to his ankle,
      Pale as his shirt, his knees knocking each other,
      And with a look so piteous in purport
85   As if he had been loosèd out of hell
      To speak of horrors—he comes before me.

POLONIUS: Mad for thy love?

OPHELIA: My lord, I do not know,
      But truly I do fear it.

POLONIUS: What said he?

OPHELIA: He took me by the wrist and held me hard.
90   Then goes he to the length of all his arm,
      And, with his other hand thus o'er his brow
      He falls to such perusal of my face
      As 'a would draw it. Long stayed he so.
      At last, a little shaking of mine arm
95   And thrice his head thus waving up and down,
      He raised a sigh so piteous and profound
      As it did seem to shatter all his bulk

Ophelia (Kate Winslet) tells Polonius (Richard Briers) of her encounter with Hamlet.

      And end his being. That done, he lets me go,
      And with his head over his shoulder turned
      He seemed to find his way without his eyes,   100
      For out o' doors he went without their helps,
      And to the last bended their light on me.

POLONIUS: Come, go with me, I will go seek the King.
      This is the very ecstasy of love,
      Whose violent property fordoes itself   105
      And leads the will to desperate undertakings
      As oft as any passion under heaven
      That does afflict our natures. I am sorry.
      What, have you given him any hard words of late?

OPHELIA: No, my good lord, but as you did command   110
      I did repel his letter and denied
      His access to me.

POLONIUS: That hath made him mad.
      I am sorry that with better heed and judgment
      I had not quoted him. I feared he did but trifle
      And meant to wrack thee. But beshrew my jealousy!   115
      By heaven, it is as proper to our age
      To cast beyond ourselves in our opinions
      As it is common for the younger sort
      To lack discretion. Come, go we to the King.
      This must be known, which, being kept close, might
         move   120
      More grief to hide than hate to utter love.
      Come.   *Exeunt.*

---

67 directions i.e., the way things really are   **69 have** understand
70 b' wi' be with   **72 in yourself** in your own person (as well as
by asking questions)   **79 closet** private chamber   **80 doublet**
close-fitting jacket. **unbraced** unfastened   **82 down-gyvèd**
fallen to the ankles (like gyves or fetters)   **84 in purport** in what
is expressed   **93 As** as if (also in line 97)   **97 bulk** body

104 ecstasy madness   **105 property** nature. **fordoes** destroys
114 quoted observed   **115 wrack** ruin, seduce. **beshrew my
jealousy** a plague upon my suspicious nature   **116 proper . . . age**
characteristic of us (old) men   **117 cast beyond** overshoot, miscal-
culate. (A metaphor from hunting.)   **120 known** made known (to
the King). **close** secret   **120–121 might . . . love** i.e., might cause
more grief (because of what Hamlet might do) by hiding the knowledge of Hamlet's strange behavior to Ophelia than unpleasantness
by telling it

2.2 *Flourish. Enter* KING *and* QUEEN, ROSENCRANTZ, *and* GUILDENSTERN *[with others].*

KING: Welcome, dear Rosencrantz and Guildenstern.
Moreover that we much did long to see you,
The need we have to use you did provoke
Our hasty sending. Something have you heard
Of Hamlet's tranformation—so call it, 5
Sith nor th' exterior nor the inward man
Resembles that it was. What it should be,
More than his father's death, that thus hath put him
So much from th' understanding of himself,
I cannot dream of. I entreat you both 10
That, being of so young days brought up with him,
And sith so neighbored to his youth and havior,
That you vouchsafe your rest here in our court
Some little time, so by your companies
To draw him on to pleasures, and to gather 15
So much as from occasion you may glean,
Whether aught to us unknown afflicts him thus
That, opened, lies within our remedy.

QUEEN: Good gentlemen, he hath much talked of you,
And sure I am two men there is not living 20
To whom he more adheres. If it will please you
To show us so much gentry and good will
As to expend your time with us awhile
For the supply and profit of our hope,
Your visitation shall receive such thanks 25
As fits a king's remembrance.

ROSENCRANTZ: Both Your Majesties
Might, by the sovereign power you have of us,
Put your dread pleasures more into command
Than to entreaty.

GUILDENSTERN: But we both obey,
And here give up ourselves in the full bent 30
To lay our service freely at your feet,
To be commanded.

KING: Thanks, Rosencrantz and gentle Guildenstern.

QUEEN: Thanks, Guildenstern and gentle Rosencrantz.
And I beseech you instantly to visit 35
My too much changèd son. Go, some of you,
And bring these gentlemen where Hamlet is.

GUILDENSTERN: Heavens make our presence and our practices
Pleasant and helpful to him!

QUEEN: Ay, amen!
Exeunt ROSENCRANTZ *and* GUILDENSTERN
[with some attendants].

Enter POLONIUS

POLONIUS: Th' ambassadors from Norway, my good lord,
Are joyfully returned. 40

KING: Thou still hast been the father of good news.

POLONIUS: Have I, my lord? I assure my good liege
I hold my duty, as I hold my soul,
Both to my God and to my gracious king;
And I do think, or else this brain of mine 45
Hunts not the trail of policy so sure
As it hath used to do, that I have found
The very cause of Hamlet's lunacy.

KING: O, speak of that! That do I long to hear. 50

POLONIUS: Give first admittance to th' ambassadors.
My news shall be the fruit to that great feast.

KING: Thyself do grace to them and bring them in.
[Exit POLONIUS.*]*
He tells me, my dear Gertrude, he hath found
The head and source of all your son's distemper. 55

QUEEN: I doubt it is no other but the main,
His father's death and our o'erhasty marriage.

Enter AMBASSADORS *[* VOLTIMAND *and*
CORNELIUS, *with* POLONIUS*].*

KING: Well, we shall sift him.—Welcome my good friends!
Say, Voltimand, what from our brother Norway?

VOLTIMAND: Most fair return of greetings and desires. 60
Upon our first, he sent out to suppress
His nephew's levies, which to him appeared

2.2. Location: The castle.
2 Moreover that besides the fact that **6 Sith nor** since neither
7 that what **11 of . . . days** from such early youth **12 And sith so
neighbored to** and since you are (or, and since that time you are)
intimately acquainted with. **havior** demeanor **13 vouchsafe
your rest** please to stay **16 occasion** opportunity **18 opened**
being revealed **22 gentry** courtesy **24 supply . . . hope** aid and
furtherance of what we hope for **26 As fits . . . remembrance** as
would be a fitting gift of a king who rewards true service **27 of**
over **28 dread** inspiring awe **30 in . . . bent** to the utmost degree
of our capacity. (An archery metaphor.)

---

38 practices doings **42 still** always **44 hold** maintain. **as** as
firmly as **47 policy** sagacity **52 fruit** dessert **53 grace** honor
(punning on *grace* said before a *feast*, line 52) **56 doubt** fear,
suspect. **main** chief point, principal concern **58 sift him** question Polonius closely **59 brother** fellow king **60 desires** good
wishes **61 Upon our first** at our first words on the business

Polonius (Ian Holm) discusses Hamlet with Claudius (Alan Bates) and Gertrude (Glenn Close).

To be a preparation 'gainst the Polack,
But, better looked into, he truly found
65   It was against Your Highness. Whereat grieved
That so his sickness, age, and impotence
Was falsely borne in hand, sends out arrests
On Fortinbras, which he, in brief, obeys,
Receives rebuke from Norway, and in fine
70   Makes vow before his uncle never more
To give th' assay of arms against Your Majesty.
Whereon old Norway, overcome with joy,
Gives him three thousand crowns in annual fee
And his commission to employ those soldiers,
75   So levied as before, against the Polack,
With an entreaty, herein further shown,
                              [giving a paper]
That it might please you to give quiet pass
Through your dominions for this enterprise
On such regards of safety and allowance
80   As therein are set down.

KING: It likes us well,
And at our more considered time we'll read,
Answer, and think upon this business.
Meantime we thank you for your well-took labor.
Go to your rest; at night we'll feast together.
85   Most welcome home!   *Exeunt* AMBASSADORS.

POLONIUS: This business is well ended.
My liege, and madam, to expostulate
What majesty should be, what duty is,

Why day is day, night night, and time is time,
Were nothing but to waste night, day, and time.
Therefore, since brevity is the soul of wit,   90
And tediousness the limbs and outward flourishes,
I will be brief. Your noble son is mad.
Mad call I it, for, to define true madness,
What is 't but to be nothing else but mad?
But let that go.

QUEEN: More matter, with less art.   95

POLONIUS: Madam, I swear I use no art at all.
That he's mad, 'tis true; 'tis true 'tis pity,
And pity 'tis 'tis true—a foolish figure,
But farewell it, for I will use no art.
Mad let us grant him, then, and now remains   100
That we find out the cause of this effect,
Or rather say, the cause of this defect,
For this effect defective comes by cause.
Thus it remains, and the remainder thus.
Perpend.   105
I have a daughter—have while she is mine—
Who, in her duty and obedience, mark,
Hath given me this. Now gather and surmise.
[He reads the letter.] "To the celestial and my soul's
idol, the most beautified Ophelia"—   110
That's an ill phrase, a vile phrase; "beautified" is a
vile phrase. But you shall hear. Thus: *[He reads.]*
"In her excellent white bosom, these, etc."

QUEEN: Came this from Hamlet to her?

POLONIUS: Good madam, stay awhile, I will be
faithful.   *[He reads.]*   115
"Doubt thou the stars are fire,
    Doubt that the sun doth move,
Doubt truth to be a liar,
    But never doubt I love.
O dear Ophelia, I am ill at these numbers. I have not 120
art to reckon my groans. But that I love thee best, O
most best, believe it. Adieu.
        Thine evermore, most dear lady, whilst this
                machine is to him, Hamlet."
This in obedience hath my daughter shown me,   125
And, more above, hath his solicitings,

---

66 **impotence** helplessness   67 **borne in hand** deluded, taken advantage of.   **arrests** orders to desist   69 **in fine** in conclusion   71 **give th' assay** make trial of strength, challenge   79 **On . . . allowance** i.e., with such considerations for the safety of Denmark and permission for Fortinbras   80 **likes** pleases   81 **considered** suitable for deliberation   86 **expostulate** expound, inquire into

90 **wit** sense or judgment   98 **figure** figure of speech   103 **For . . . cause** i.e., for this defective behavior, this madness, has a cause   105 **Perpend** consider   108 **gather and surmise** draw your own conclusions   113 **In . . . bosom** (The letter is poetically addressed to her heart.)   **these** i.e., the letter   115 **stay** wait.   **faithful** i.e., in reading the letter accurately   118 **Doubt** suspect   120 **ill . . . numbers** unskilled at writing verses   121 **reckon** (1) count (2) number metrically, scan   124 **machine** i.e., body   126 **more above** moreover

Gertrude (Julie Christie), Claudius (Derek Jacobi), and Polonius discuss Hamlet.

As they fell out by time, by means, and place,
All given to mine ear.

KING: But how hath she
Received his love?

POLONIUS: What do you think of me?

130 **KING:**   As of a man faithful and honorable.

POLONIUS: I would fain prove so. But what might
    you think,
When I had seen this hot love on the wing—
As I perceived it, I must tell you that,
Before my daughter told me—what might you,
135 Or my dear Majesty your queen here, think,
If I had played the desk or table book,
Or given my heart a winking, mute and dumb,
Or looked upon this love with idle sight?
What might you think? No, I went round to work,
140 And my young mistress thus I did bespeak:
"Lord Hamlet is a prince out of thy star;
This must not be." And then I prescripts gave her,
That she should lock herself from his resort,
Admit no messengers, receive no tokens.
145 Which done, she took the fruits of my advice;
And he, repellèd—a short take to make—
Fell into a sadness, then into a fast,
Thence to a watch, thence into a weakness,

Thence to a lightness, and by this declension
Into the madness wherein now he raves,   150
And all we mourn for.

KING *[to the* QUEEN*]:*   Do you think 'tis this?

QUEEN: It may be, very like.

POLONIUS: Hath there been such a time—I would fain
    know that—
That I have positively said "'Tis so,"
When it proved otherwise?

KING: Not that I know.   155

POLONIUS: Take this from this, if this be otherwise.
If circumstances lead me, I will find
Where truth is hid, though it were hid indeed
Within the center.

KING: How may we try it further?

POLONIUS: You know sometimes he walks four hours
    together   160
Here in the lobby.

QUEEN: So he does indeed.

POLONIUS: At such a time I'll loose my daughter to
    him.
Be you and I behind an arras then.
Mark the encounter. If he love her not
And be not from his reason fall'n thereon,   165
Let me be no assistant for a state,
But keep a farm and carters.

KING: We will try it.

Enter HAMLET *[reading on a book].*

QUEEN: But look where sadly the poor wretch comes
    reading.

POLONIUS: Away, I do beseech you both, away.
I'll board him presently. O, give me leave.   170
        Exeunt KING *and* QUEEN *[with attendants].*
How does my good Lord Hamlet?

---

127 fell out occurred.   **by** according to   **128 given . . . ear** i.e., told me about   **131 fain** gladly   **136 played . . . table book** i.e., remained shut up, concealing the information   **137 given . . . winking** closed the eyes of my heart to this   **138 with idle sight** complacently or incomprehendingly   **139 round** roundly, plainly   **140 bespeak** address   **141 out of thy star** above your sphere, position   **142 prescripts** orders   **143 his resort** his visits   **148 watch** state of sleeplessness

149 lightness lightheadedness.   **declension** decline, deterioration (with a pun on the grammatical sense)   **151 all we** all of us, or, into everything that we   **156 Take this from this** (The actor probably gestures, indicating that he means his head from his shoulders, or his staff or office or chain from his hands or neck, or something similar.)   **159 center** middle point of the earth (which is also the center of the Ptolemaic universe).   **try** test, judge   **162 loose** (as one might release an animal that is being mated)   **163 arras** hanging, tapestry   **165 thereon** on that account   **167 carters** wagon drivers   **168 sadly** seriously   **170 board** accost.   **presently** at once.   **give me leave** i.e., excuse me, leave me alone. (Said to those he hurries offstage, including the King and Queen.)

HAMLET: Well, God-a-mercy.

POLONIUS: Do you know me, my lord?

HAMLET: Excellent well. You are a fishmonger.

175 **POLONIUS:** Not I, my lord.

HAMLET: Then I would you were so honest a man.

POLONIUS: Honest, my lord?

HAMLET: Ay, sir. To be honest, as this world goes, is to be one man picked out of ten thousand.

180 **POLONIUS:** That's very true, my lord.

HAMLET: For if the sun breed maggots in a dead dog, being a good kissing carrion—Have you a daughter?

POLONIUS: I have, my lord.

HAMLET: Let her not walk i' the sun. Conception is a
185 blessing, but as your daughter may conceive, friend, look to 't.

POLONIUS [aside]: How say you by that? Still harping on my daughter. Yet he knew me not at first; 'a said I was a fishmonger. 'A is far gone. And truly in my
190 youth I suffered much extremity for love, very near this. I'll speak to him again.—What do you read, my lord?

HAMLET: Words, words, words.

POLONIUS: What is the matter, my lord?

195 **HAMLET:** Between who?

POLONIUS: I mean, the matter that you read, my lord.

HAMLET: Slanders, sir; for the satirical rogue says here that old men have gray beards, that their faces are wrinkled, their eyes purging thick amber and
200 plum-tree gum, and that they have a plentiful lack of wit, together with most weak hams. All which, sir, though I most powerfully and potently believe, yet I hold it not honesty to have it thus set down, for your-self, sir, shall grow old as I am, if like a crab you
205 could go backward.

POLONIUS [aside]: Though this be madness, yet there is method in 't.—Will you walk out of the air, my lord?

HAMLET: Into my grave.

POLONIUS: Indeed, that's out of the air. [Aside.] How
pregnant sometimes his replies are! A happiness 210
that often madness hits on, which reason and sanity
could not so prosperously be delivered of. I will leave
him and suddenly contrive the means of meeting
between him and my daughter.—My honorable lord,
I will most humbly take my leave of you. 215

HAMLET: You cannot, sir, take from me anything that I will more willingly part withal—except my life, except my life, except my life.

Enter GUILDENSTERN *and* ROSENCRANTZ.

POLONIUS: Fare you well, my lord.

HAMLET: These tedious old fools! 220

POLONIUS: You go to seek the Lord Hamlet. There he is.

ROSENCRANTZ [to POLONIUS]: God save you, sir!
[Exit POLONIUS.]

GUILDENSTERN: My honored lord!

ROSENCRANTZ: My most dear lord!

HAMLET: My excellent good friends! How dost thou, 225
Guildenstern? Ah, Rosencrantz! Good lads, how do
you both?

ROSENCRANTZ: As the indifferent children of the earth.

GUILDENSTERN: Happy in that we are not overhappy.
On Fortune's cap we are not the very button. 230

HAMLET: Nor the soles of her shoe?

ROSENCRANTZ: Neither, my lord.

HAMLET: Then you live about her waist, or in the middle of her favors?

GUILDENSTERN: Faith, her privates we. 235

---

172 **God-a-mercy** God have mercy, i.e., thank you   174 **fish-monger** fish merchant   182 **a good kissing carrion** i.e., a good piece of flesh for kissing, or for the sun to kiss   184 **i' the sun** in public (with additional implication of the sunshine of princely favors).   **Conception** (1) understanding (2) pregnancy   188 **'a** he   194 **matter** substance (But Hamlet plays on the sense of "basis for a dispute.")   199 **purging** discharging.   **amber** i.e., resin, like the resinous *plum-tree gum*   201 **wit** understanding   203 **hon-esty** decency, decorum   204 **old** as old

---

207 **out of the air** (The open air was considered dangerous for sick people.)   210 **pregnant** quick-witted, full of meaning.   **happi-ness** felicity of expression   212 **prosperously** successfully   213 **suddenly** immediately   217 **withal** with   220 **old fools** i.e., old men like Polonius   228 **indifferent** ordinary, at neither extreme of fortune or misfortune   234 **favors** i.e., sexual favors   235 **her privates we** i.e., (1) we are sexually intimate with Fortune, the fickle goddess who bestows her favors indiscriminately (2) we are her private citizens

HAMLET: In the secret parts of Fortune? O, most true, she is a strumpet. What news?

ROSENCRANTZ: None, my lord, but the world's grown honest.

240 **HAMLET:** Then is doomsday near. But your news is not true. Let me question more in particular. What have you, my good friends, deserved at the hands of Fortune that she sends you to prison hither?

GUILDENSTERN: Prison, my lord?

245 **HAMLET:** Denmark's a prison.

ROSENCRANTZ: Then is the world one.

HAMLET: A goodly one, in which there are many confines, wards, and dungeons, Denmark being one o' the worst.

250 **ROSENCRANTZ:** We think not so, my lord.

HAMLET: Why then 'tis none to you, for there is nothing either good or bad but thinking makes it so. To me it is a prison.

ROSENCRANTZ: Why then, your ambition makes it 255 one. 'Tis too narrow for your mind.

HAMLET: O God, I could be bounded in a nutshell and count myself a king of infinite space, were it not that I have bad dreams.

GUILDENSTERN: Which dreams indeed are ambition, 260 for the very substance of the ambitious is merely the shadow of a dream.

HAMLET: A dream itself is but a shadow.

ROSENCRANTZ: Truly, and I hold ambition of so airy and light a quality that it is but a shadow's shadow.

265 **HAMLET:** Then are our beggars bodies, and our monarchs and outstretched heroes the beggars' shadows. Shall we to the court? For, by my fay, I cannot reason.

ROSENCRANTZ, GUILDENSTERN: We'll wait upon you.

Hamlet (Kevin Kline) talks with Rosencrantz (Philip Goodwin) and Guildenstern (Reg E. Cathey) in the 1990 film directed by Kevin Kline.

HAMLET: No such matter. I will not sort you with the rest of my servants, for, to speak to you like an honest man, I am most dreadfully attended. But, in the beaten way of friendship, what make you at Elsinore? 270

ROSENCRANTZ: To visit you, my lord, no other occasion.

HAMLET: Beggar that I am, I am even poor in thanks; but I thank you, and sure, dear friends, my thanks are too dear a halfpenny. Were you not sent for? Is it your own inclining? Is it a free visitation? Come, come, deal justly with me. Come, come. Nay, speak. 275

GUILDENSTERN: What should we say, my lord?

HAMLET: Anything but to the purpose. You were sent for, and there is a kind of confession in your looks which your modesties have not craft enough to color. I know the good King and Queen have sent for you. 280

ROSENCRANTZ: To what end, my lord?

HAMLET: That you must teach me. But let me conjure you, by the rights of our fellowship, by the consonancy of our youth, by the obligation of our ever-preserved love, and by what more dear a better proposer could charge you withal, be even and direct with me whether you were sent for or no. 285 290

---

237 **strumpet** prostitute (A common epithet for indiscriminate Fortune; see line 493.) 248 **confines** places of confinement. **wards** cells 260 **the very . . . ambitious** that seemingly very substantial thing that the ambitious pursue 265 **bodies** i.e., solid substances rather than shadows (since beggars are not ambitious) 266 **outstretched** (1) far-reaching in their ambition (2) elongated as shadows 267 **fay** faith 268 **wait upon** accompany, attend. (But Hamlet uses the phrase in the sense of providing menial service.)

269 **sort** class, categorize 271 **dreadfully attended** waited upon in slovenly fashion 272 **beaten way** familiar path, tried-and-true course. **make** do 276 **too dear a halfpenny** (1) too expensive at even a halfpenny, i.e., of little worth (2) too expensive *by* a halfpenny in return for worthless kindness 277 **free** voluntary 280 **Anything but to the purpose** anything except a straightforward answer. (Said ironically.) 282 **modesties** sense of shame. **color** disguise 285 **conjure** adjure, entreat 286–287 **the consonancy of our youth** our closeness in our younger days 288 **better** more skillful 289 **charge** urge. **even** straight, honest

ROSENCRANTZ *[aside to* GUILDENSTERN*]*:   What say you?

HAMLET *[aside]*:   Nay, then, I have an eye of you.—If you love me, hold not off.

GUILDENSTERN: My lord, we were sent for.

295 **HAMLET:**   I will tell you why; so shall my anticipation prevent your discovery, and your secrecy to the King and Queen molt no feather. I have of late—but wherefore I know not—lost all my mirth, forgone all custom of exercises; and indeed it goes so heavily with my dis-
300 position that this goodly frame, the earth, seems to me a sterile promontory; this most excellent canopy, the air, look you, this brave o'erhanging firmament, this majestical roof fretted with golden fire, why, it appeareth nothing to me but a foul and pestilent congre-
305 gation of vapors. What a piece of work is a man! How noble in reason, how infinite in faculties, in form and moving how express and admirable, in action how like an angel, in apprehension how like a god! The beauty of the world, the paragon of animals! And yet,
310 to me, what is this quintessence of dust? Man delights not me—no, nor woman neither, though by your smiling you seem to say so.

ROSENCRANTZ: My lord, there was no such stuff in my thoughts.

315 **HAMLET:**   Why did you laugh, then, when I said man delights not me?

ROSENCRANTZ: To think, my lord, if you delight not in man, what Lenten entertainment the players shall receive from you. We coted them on the way, and
320 hither are they coming to offer you service.

HAMLET: He that plays the king shall be welcome; His Majesty shall have tribute of me. The adventurous knight shall use his foil and target, the lover shall not sigh gratis, the humorous man shall end his part
325 in peace, the clown shall make those laugh whose

lungs are tickle o' the sear, and the lady shall say her mind freely, or the blank verse shall halt for 't. What players are they?

ROSENCRANTZ: Even those you were wont to take such delight in, the tragedians of the city.   330

HAMLET: How chances it they travel? Their residence, both in reputation and profit, was better both ways.

ROSENCRANTZ: I think their inhibition comes by the means of the late innovation.

HAMLET: Do they hold the same estimation they did   335 when I was in the city? Are they so followed?

ROSENCRANTZ: No, indeed are they not.

HAMLET: How comes it? Do they grow rusty?

ROSENCRANTZ: Nay, their endeavor keeps in the wonted pace. But there is, sir, an aerie of children,   340 little eyases, that cry out on the top of question and are most tyrannically clapped for 't. These are now the fashion, and so berattle the common stages—so they call them—that many wearing rapiers are afraid of goose quills and dare scarce come thither.   345

HAMLET: What, are they children? Who maintains 'em? How are they escoted? Will they pursue the quality no longer than they can sing? Will they not say afterwards, if they should grow themselves to common players—as it is most like, if their means   350 are no better—their writers do them wrong to make them exclaim against their own succession?

---

326 tickle o' the sear easy on the trigger, ready to laugh easily. (A *sear* is part of a gunlock.)   **327 halt** limp   **330 tragedians** actors   **331 residence** remaining in their usual place, i.e., in the city   **333 inhibition** formal prohibition (from acting plays in the city)   **334 late** recent.   **innovation** i.e., the new fashion in satirical plays performed by boy actors in the "private" theaters; or possibly a political uprising; or the strict limitations set on the theaters in London in 1600   **338–363 How . . . load too** (The passage, omitted from the early quartos, alludes to the so-called War of the Theaters, 1599–1602, the rivalry between the children's companies and the adult actors.)   **339 keeps** continues.   **340 wonted** usual   **aerie** nest   **341 eyases** young hawks.   **cry . . . question** speak shrilly, dominating the controversy (in decrying the public theaters)   **342 tyrannically** outrageously   **343 berattle** berate, clamor against.   **common stages** public theaters   **344 many wearing rapiers** i.e., many men of fashion, afraid to patronize the common players for fear of being satirized by the poets writing for the boy actors   **345 goose quills** i.e., pens of satirists   **347 escoted** maintained   **348 quality** (acting) profession.   **no longer . . . sing** i.e., only until their voices change   **350 common** regular, adult.   **like** likely   **350–351 if . . . better** if they find no better way to support themselves   **352 succession** i.e., future careers

---

292 of on   **293 hold not off** don't hold back   **295–296 so . . . discovery** in that way my saying it first will spare you from revealing the truth   **297 molt no feather** i.e., not diminish in the least   **302 brave** splendid   **303 fretted** adorned (with fretwork, as in a vaulted ceiling)   **304–305 congregation** mass   **305 piece of work** masterpiece   **307 express** well-framed, exact, expressive   **308 apprehension** power of comprehending   **310 quintessence** the fifth essence of ancient philosophy, beyond earth, water, air, and fire, supposed to be the substance of the heavenly bodies and to be latent in all things   **318 Lenten entertainment** meager reception (appropriate to Lent)   **319 coted** overtook and passed by   **322 tribute** (1) applause (2) homage paid in money.   **of** from   **323 foil and target** sword and shield   **324 gratis** for nothing.   **humorous man** eccentric character, dominated by one trait or "humor"   **325 in peace** i.e., with full license

ROSENCRANTZ: Faith, there has been much to-do on both sides, and the nation holds it no sin to tar them to controversy. There was for a while no money bid for argument unless the poet and the player went to cuffs in the question.

HAMLET: Is 't possible?

GUILDENSTERN: O, there has been much throwing about of brains.

HAMLET: Do the boys carry it away?

ROSENCRANTZ: Ay, that they do, my lord—Hercules and his load too.

HAMLET: It is not very strange; for my uncle is King of Denmark, and those that would make mouths at him while my father lived give twenty, forty, fifty, a hundred ducats apiece for his picture in little. 'Sblood, there is something in this more than natural, if philosophy could find it out.

A flourish [of trumpets within].

GUILDENSTERN: There are the players.

HAMLET: Gentlemen, you are welcome to Elsinore. Your hands, come then. Th' appurtenance of welcome is fashion and ceremony. Let me comply with you in this garb, lest my extent to the players, which, I tell you, must show fairly outwards, should more appear like entertainment than yours. You are welcome. But my uncle-father and aunt-mother are deceived.

GUILDENSTERN: In what, my dear lord?

HAMLET: I am but mad north-north-west. When the wind is southerly I know a hawk from a handsaw.

Enter POLONIUS.

POLONIUS: Well be with you, gentlemen!

HAMLET: Hark you, Guildenstern, and you too; at each ear a hearer. That great baby you see there is not yet out of his swaddling clouts.

ROSENCRANTZ: Haply he is the second time come to them, for they say an old man is twice a child.

HAMLET: I will prophesy he comes to tell me of the players. Mark it.—You say right, sir, o' Monday morning, 'twas then indeed.

POLONIUS: My lord, I have news to tell you.

HAMLET: My lord, I have news to tell you. When Roscius was an actor in Rome—

POLONIUS: The actors are come hither, my lord.

HAMLET: Buzz, buzz!

POLONIUS: Upon my honor—

HAMLET: Then came each actor on his ass.

POLONIUS: The best actors in the world, either for tragedy, comedy, history, pastoral, pastoral-comical, historical-pastoral, tragical-historical, tragical-comical-historical-pastoral, scene individable, or poem unlimited. Seneca cannot be too heavy, nor Plautus too light. For the law of writ and the liberty, these are the only men.

HAMLET: O Jephthah, judge of Israel, what a treasure hadst thou!

POLONIUS: What a treasure had he, my lord?

HAMLET: Why,
"One fair daughter, and no more,
The which he lovèd passing well."

POLONIUS [*aside*]: Still on my daughter.

HAMLET: Am I not i' the right, old Jephthah?

---

353 **to-do** ado   354 **tar** set on (as dogs)   355–357 **There . . . question** i.e., for a while, no money was offered by the acting companies to playwrights for the plot to a play unless the satirical poets who wrote for the boys and the adult actors came to blows in the play itself   361 **carry it away** i.e., win the day   362–363 **Hercules . . . load** (Thought to be an allusion to the sign of the Globe Theatre, which was Hercules bearing the world on his shoulders.)   365 **mouths** faces   367 **ducats** gold coins.   **in little** in miniature.   **'Sblood** by God's (Christ's) blood   368–369 **philosophy** i.e., scientific inquiry   372 **appurtenance** proper accompaniment   373 **comply** observe the formalities of courtesy   374 **garb** i.e., manner.   **my extent** that which I extend, i.e., my polite behavior   375 **show fairly outwards** show every evidence of cordiality   376 **entertainment** a (warm) reception   379 **north-north-west** just off true north, only party   380 **hawk, handsaw** i.e., two very different things; though also perhaps meaning a mattock (or *hack*) and a carpenter's cutting tool, respectively; also birds, with a play on *hernshaw*, or heron

384 **swaddling clouts** cloths in which to wrap a newborn baby   385 **Haply** perhaps   392 **Roscius** a famous Roman actor who died in 62 B.C.   394 **Buzz** (An interjection used to denote stale news.)   400 **scene individable** a play observing the unity of place; or perhaps one that is unclassifiable, or performed without intermission   401 **poem unlimited** a play disregarding the unities of time and place; one that is all-inclusive.   **Seneca** writer of Latin tragedies.   402 **Plautus** writer of Latin comedy.   **law . . . liberty** dramatic composition both according to the rules and disregarding the rules   403 **these** i.e., the actors   404 **Jephthah . . . Israel** (Jephthah had to sacrifice his daughter; see Judges 11. Hamlet goes on to quote from a ballad on the theme.)   409 **passing** surpassingly

POLONIUS: If you call me Jephthah, my lord, I have a daughter that I love passing well.

HAMLET: Nay, that follows not.

415 **POLONIUS:** What follows then, my lord?

HAMLET: Why,
   "As by lot, God wot,"
and then, you know,
   "It came to pass, as most like it was"—
420 the first row of the pious chanson will show you more,
for look where my abridgement comes.

Enter the PLAYERS.

You are welcome, masters; welcome, all. I am glad to see thee well. Welcome, good friends. O, old friend! Why, thy face is valanced since I saw thee last.
425 Com'st thou to beard me in Denmark? What, my young lady and mistress! By 'r Lady, your ladyship is nearer to heaven than when I saw you last, by the altitude of a chopine. Pray God your voice, like a piece of uncurrent gold, be not cracked within the ring.
430 Masters, you are all welcome. We'll e'en to 't like French falconers, fly at anything we see. We'll have a speech straight. Come, give us a taste of your quality. Come, a passionate speech.

FIRST PLAYER: What speech, my good lord?

435 **HAMLET:** I heard thee speak me a speech once, but it was never acted, or if it was, not above once, for the play, I remember, pleased not the million; 'twas caviar to the general. But it was—as I received it, and others, whose judgments in such matters cried in the
440 top of mine—an excellent play, well digested in the scenes, set down with as much modesty as cunning. I remember one said there were no sallets in the

Hamlet (Kenneth Branagh) talks with the players.

lines to make the matter savory, nor no matter in the phrase that might indict the author of affectation, but called it an honest method, as wholesome as 445 sweet, and by very much more handsome than fine. One speech in 't I chiefly loved: 'twas Aeneas' tale to Dido, and thereabout of it especially when he speaks of Priam's slaughter. If it live in your memory, begin at this line: let me see, let me see— 450
   "The rugged Pyrrhus, like th' Hyrcanian beast"—
'Tis not so. It begins with Pyrrhus:
   "The rugged Pyrrhus, he whose sable arms,
   Black as his purpose, did the night resemble
   When he lay couchèd in the ominous horse, 455
   Hath now this dread and black complexion smeared
   With heraldry more dismal. Head to foot
   Now is he total gules, horridly tricked
   With blood of fathers, mothers, daughters, sons,
   Baked and impasted with the parching streets, 460
   That lend a tyrannous and a damnèd light
   To their lord's murder. Roasted in wrath and fire,

---

417 lot chance. **wot** knows **419 like** likely, probable **420 row** stanza. **chanson** ballad, song **421 my abridgement** something that cuts short my conversation; also, a diversion **424 valanced** fringed (with a beard) **425 beard** confront, challenge (with obvious pun) **426 young lady** i.e., boy playing women's parts. **By 'r Lady** by Our Lady **428 chopine** thick-soled shoe of Italian fashion **429 uncurrent** not passable as lawful coinage. **cracked . . . ring** i.e., changed from adolescent to male voice, no longer suitable for women's roles. (Coins featured rings enclosing the sovereign's head; if the coin was cracked within this ring, it was unfit for currency.) **430 e'en to 't** go at it **432 straight** at once. **quality** professional skill **438 caviar to the general** caviar to the multitude, i.e., a choice dish too elegant for coarse tastes **439–440 cried in the top of** i.e., spoke with greater authority than **440 digested** arranged, ordered **441 modesty** moderation, restraint. **cunning** skill **442 sallets** i.e., something savory, spicy improprieties

444 indict convict **446 handsome** well-proportioned. **fine** elaborately ornamented, showy **449 Priam's slaughter** the slaying of the ruler of Troy, when the Greeks finally took the city **451 Pyrrhus** a Greek hero in the Trojan War, also known as Neoptolemus, son of Achilles—another avenging son. **Hyrcanian beast** i.e., tiger. (On the death of Priam, see Virgil, *Aeneid*, 2.506 ff.; compare the whole speech with Marlowe's *Dido Queen of Carthage*, 2.1.214 ff. On the *Hyrcanian* tiger, see *Aeneid*, 4.366–367. Hyrcania is on the Caspian Sea.) **453 rugged** shaggy, savage. **sable** black (for reasons of camouflage during the episode of the Trojan horse) **455 couchèd** concealed. **ominous horse** fateful Trojan horse, by which the Greeks gained access to Troy **457 dismal** ill-omened **458 total gules** entirely red. (A heraldic term.) **tricked** spotted and smeared. (Heraldic.) **460 impasted** crusted, like a thick paste. **with . . . streets** by the parching heat of the streets (because of the fires everywhere) **461 tyrannous** cruel **462 their lord's** i.e., Priam's

And thus o'ersizèd with coagulate gore,
With eyes like carbuncles, the hellish Pyrrhus
465 Old grandsire Priam seeks."
So proceed you.

POLONIUS: 'Fore God, my lord, well spoken, with good accent and good discretion.

FIRST PLAYER: "Anon he finds him
Striking too short at Greeks. His antique sword,
470 Rebellious to his arm, lies where it falls,
Repugnant to command. Unequal matched,
Pyrrhus at Priam drives, in rage strikes wide,
But with the whiff and wind of his fell sword
Th' unnervèd father falls. Then senseless Ilium,
475 Seeming to feel this blow, with flaming top
Stoops to his base, and with a hideous crash
Takes prisoner Pyrrhus' ear. For, lo! His sword,
Which was declining on the milky head
Of reverend Priam, seemed i' th' air to stick.
480 So as a painted tyrant Pyrrhus stood,
And, like a neutral to his will and matter,
Did nothing.
But as we often see against some storm
A silence in the heavens, the rack stand still,
485 The bold winds speechless, and the orb below
As hush as death, anon the dreadful thunder
Doth rend the region, so, after Pyrrhus' pause,
A rousèd vengeance sets him new a-work,
And never did the Cyclops' hammers fall
490 On Mars's armor forged for proof eterne
With less remorse than Pyrrhus' bleeding sword
Now falls on Priam.
Out, out, thou strumpet Fortune! All you gods
In general synod take away her power!
495 Break all the spokes and fellies from her wheel,
And bowl the round nave down the hill of heaven
As low as to the fiends!"

POLONIUS: This is too long.

---

463 **o'ersizèd** covered as with size or glue   464 **carbuncles** large fiery-red precious stones thought to emit their own light   469 **antique** ancient, long-used   471 **Repugnant** disobedient, resistant   473 **fell** cruel   474 **unnervèd** strengthless.   **senseless Ilium** inanimate citadel of Troy   476 **his** its   478 **declining** descending.   **milky** white-haired   480 **painted** i.e., painted in a picture   481 **like . . . matter** i.e., as though suspended between his intention and its fulfillment   483 **against** just before   484 **rack** mass of clouds   485 **orb** globe, earth   487 **region** sky   489 **Cyclops** giant armor makers in the smithy of Vulcan   490 **proof eterne** eternal resistance to assault   491 **remorse** pity   494 **synod** assembly   495 **fellies** pieces of wood forming the rim of a wheel   496 **nave** hub.   **hill of heaven** Mount Olympus

Hamlet and Polonius discuss the play with the players.

HAMLET: It shall to the barber's with your beard.—
Prithee, say on. He's for a jig or a tale of bawdry, or
500 he sleeps. Say on; come to Hecuba.

FIRST PLAYER: "But who, ah woe! had seen the moblèd queen"—

HAMLET: "The moblèd queen"?

POLONIUS: That's good. "Moblèd queen" is good.

FIRST PLAYER: "Run barefoot up and down,
                    threat'ning the flames   505
With bisson rheum, a clout upon that head
Where late the diadem stood, and, for a robe,
About her lank and all o'erteemèd loins
A blanket, in the alarm of fear caught up—
Who this had seen, with tongue in venom steeped, 510
'Gainst Fortune's state would treason have
                    pronounced.
But if the gods themselves did see her then
When she saw Pyrrhus make malicious sport
In mincing with his sword her husband's limbs,
The instant burst of clamor that she made,   515
Unless things mortal move them not at all,
Would have made milch the burning eyes of heaven,
And passion in the gods."

POLONIUS: Look whe'er he has not turned his color
and has tears in 's eyes. Prithee, no more.   520

---

500 **jig** comic song and dance often given at the end of a play   501 **Hecuba** wife of Priam   502 **who . . . had** anyone who had (also in line 510).   **moblèd** muffled   505 **threat'ning the flames** i.e., weeping hard enough to dampen the flames   506 **bisson rheum** blinding tears.   **clout** cloth   507 **late** lately   508 **all o'erteemèd** utterly worn out with bearing children   511 **state** rule, managing.   **pronounced** proclaimed   517 **milch** milky, moist with tears.   **burning eyes of heaven** i.e., heavenly bodies   518 **passion** overpowering emotion   519 **whe'er** whether

HAMLET: 'Tis well; I'll have thee speak out the rest of this soon.—Good my lord, will you see the players well bestowed? Do you hear, let them be well used, for they are the abstract and brief chronicles of the time. After your death you were better have a bad epitaph than their ill report while you live.

POLONIUS: My lord, I will use them according to their desert.

HAMLET: God's bodikin, man, much better. Use every man after his desert, and who shall scape whipping? Use them after your own honor and dignity. The less they deserve, the more merit is in your bounty. Take them in.

POLONIUS: Come, sirs. *[Exit.]*

HAMLET: Follow him, friends. We'll hear a play tomorrow. *[As they start to leave,* HAMLET *detains the* FIRST PLAYER.*]* Dost thou hear me, old friend? Can you play *The Murder of Gonzago?*

FIRST PLAYER: Ay, my lord.

HAMLET: We'll ha 't tomorrow night. You could, for a need, study a speech of some dozen or sixteen lines which I would set down and insert in 't, could you not?

FIRST PLAYER: Ay, my lord.

HAMLET: Very well. Follow that lord, and look you mock him not. *(Exeunt* PLAYERS.*)* My good friends, I'll leave you till night. You are welcome to Elsinore.

ROSENCRANTZ: Good my lord!

*Exeunt [*ROSENCRANTZ *and* GUILDENSTERN*].*

HAMLET: Ay, so, goodbye to you.—Now I am alone.
O, what a rogue and peasant slave am I!
Is it not monstrous that this player here,
But in a fiction, in a dream of passion,
Could force his soul so to his own conceit
That from her working all this visage wanned,
Tears in his eyes, distraction in his aspect,
A broken voice, and his whole function suiting
With forms to his conceit? And all for nothing!
For Hecuba!

What's Hecuba to him, or he to Hecuba,
That he should weep for her? What would he do
Had he the motive and the cue for passion
That I have? He would drown the stage with tears
And cleave the general ear with horrid speech,
Made mad the guilty and appall the free,
Confound the ignorant, and amaze indeed
The very faculties of eyes and ears. Yet I,
A dull and muddy-mettled rascal, peak
Like John-a-dreams, unpregnant of my cause,
And can say nothing—no, not for a king
Upon whose property and most dear life
A damned defeat was made. Am I a coward?
Who calls me villain? Breaks my pate across?
Plucks off my beard and blows it in my face?
Tweaks me by the nose? Gives me the lie i' the throat
As deep as to the lungs? Who does me this?
Ha, 'swounds, I should take it; for it cannot be
But I am pigeon-livered and lack gall
To make oppression bitter, or ere this
I should ha' fatted all the region kites
With this slave's offal. Bloody, bawdy villain!
Remorseless, treacherous, lecherous, kindless villain!
O, vengeance!
Why, what an ass am I! This is most brave,
That I, the son of a dear father murdered,
Prompted to my revenge by heaven and hell,
Must like a whore unpack my heart with words
And fall a-cursing, like a very drab,
A scullion! Fie upon 't, foh! About, my brains!
Hum, I have heard
That guilty creatures sitting at a play
Have by the very cunning of the scene
Been struck so to the soul that presently
They have proclaimed their malefactions;
For murder, though it have no tongue, will speak

---

523 **bestowed** lodged   524 **abstract** summary account   529 **God's bodikin** by God's (Christ's) little body, *bodykin*. (Not to be confused with *bodkin*, "dagger.")   531 **after** according to   540 **ha 't** have it   541 **study** memorize   552 **But** merely   553 **force . . . conceit** bring his innermost being so entirely into accord with his conception (of the role)   554 **from her working** as a result of, or in response to, his soul's activity.   **wanned** grew pale   555 **aspect** look, glance   556–557 **his whole . . . conceit** all his bodily powers responding with actions to suit his thought

563 **the general ear** everyone's ear.   **horrid** horrible   564 **appall** (Literally, make pale.)   **free** innocent   565 **Confound the ignorant** i.e., dumbfound those who know nothing of the crime that has been committed.   **amaze** stun   567 **muddy-mettled** dull-spirited.   **peak** mope, pine   568 **John-a-dreams** a sleepy, dreaming idler.   **unpregnant of** not quickened by   570 **property** i.e., the crown; also character, quality   571 **damned defeat** damnable act of destruction   572 **pate** head   574 **Gives . . . throat** calls me an out-and-out liar   576 **'swounds** by his (Christ's) wounds   577 **pigeon-livered** (The pigeon or dove was popularly supposed to be mild because it secreted no gall.)   578 **bitter** i.e., bitter to me   579 **region kites** kites (birds of prey) of the air   580 **offal** entrails   581 **Remorseless** pitiless.   **kindless** unnatural   583 **brave** fine, admirable. (Said ironically.)   587 **drab** whore   588 **scullion** menial kitchen servant (apt to be foul-mouthed).   **About** about it, to work   591 **cunning** art, skill.   **scene** dramatic presentation   592 **presently** at once

595 With most miraculous organ. I'll have these players
Play something like the murder of my father
Before mine uncle. I'll observe his looks;
I'll tent him to the quick. If 'a do blench,
I know my course. The spirit that I have seen
600 May be the devil, and the devil hath power
T' assume a pleasing shape; yea, and perhaps,
Out of my weakness and my melancholy,
As he is very potent with such spirits,
Abuses me to damn me. I'll have grounds
605 More relative than this. The play's the thing
Wherein I'll catch the conscience of the King.　　*Exit.*

3.1　*Enter* KING, QUEEN, POLONIUS, OPHELIA,
　　　　ROSENCRANTZ, GUILDENSTERN, *lords.*

KING:　And can you by no drift of conference
Get from him why he puts on this confusion,
Grating so harshly all his days of quiet
With turbulent and dangerous lunacy?

5 **ROSENCRANTZ:**　He does confess he feels himself
　　　distracted,
But from what cause 'a will by no means speak.

GUILDENSTERN:　Nor do we find him forward to be
　　　sounded,
But with a crafty madness keeps aloof
When we would bring him on to some confession
10　　Of his true state.

QUEEN:　　　　　Did he receive you well?

ROSENCRANTZ:　Most like a gentleman.

GUILDENSTERN:　But with much forcing of his
　　　disposition.

ROSENCRANTZ:　Niggard of question, but of our
　　　demands
Most free in his reply.

QUEEN:　　　　　Did you assay him
15　　To any pastime?

ROSENCRANTZ:　Madam, it so fell out that certain
　　　players
We o'erraught on the way. Of these we told him,
And there did seem in him a kind of joy

To hear of it. They are here about the court,
And, as I think, they have already order　　20
This night to play before him.

POLONIUS:　　　　　'Tis most true,
And he beseeched me to entreat Your Majesties
To hear and see the matter.

KING:　With all my heart, and it doth much content me
To hear him so inclined.　　25
Good gentlemen, give him a further edge
And drive his purpose into these delights.

ROSENCRANTZ:　We shall, my lord.
　　　　　Exeunt ROSENCRANTZ *and* GUILDENSTERN.

KING:　　　　　Sweet Gertrude, leave us too,
For we have closely sent for Hamlet hither,
That he, as 'twere by accident, may here　　30
Affront Ophelia.
Her father and myself, lawful espials,
Will so bestow ourselves that seeing, unseen,
We may of their encounter frankly judge,
And gather by him, as he is behaved,　　35
If 't be th' affliction of his love or no
That thus he suffers for.

QUEEN:　　　　　I shall obey you.
And for your part, Ophelia, I do wish
That your good beauties be the happy cause
Of Hamlet's wildness. So shall I hope your virtues　　40
Will bring him to his wonted way again,
To both your honors.

OPHELIA:　　　　　Madam, I wish it may.
　　　　　[Exit QUEEN.*]*

POLONIUS:　Ophelia, walk you here.—Gracious, so
　　　please you,
We will bestow ourselves. *[To* OPHELIA.*]* Read on
　　　this book,　　*[giving her a book]*
That show of such an exercise may color　　45
Your loneliness. We are oft to blame in this—
'Tis too much proved—that with devotion's visage
And pious action we do sugar o'er
The devil himself.

KING *[aside]*:　O, 'tis too true!　　50
How smart a lash that speech doth give my
　　　conscience!
The harlot's cheek, beautied with plastering art,

---

598 tent probe.　**the quick** the tender part of a wound, the core.
blench quail, flinch　**603 spirits** humors (of melancholy)　**604
Abuses** deludes　**605 relative** cogent, pertinent

3.1. Location: The castle.
1 drift of conference directing of conversation　**7 forward** willing.　**sounded** questioned　**12 disposition** inclination　**13 Niggard** stingy.　**question** conversation　**14 assay** try to win　**17
o'erraught** overtook

---

26 edge incitement　**29 closely** privately　**31 Affront** confront,
meet　**32 espials** spies　**41 wonted** accustomed　**43 Gracious**
Your Grace (i.e., the King)　**44 bestow** conceal　**45 exercise**
religious exercise. (The book she reads is one of devotion.)　**color**
give a plausible appearance to　**46 loneliness** being alone　**47 too
much proved** too often shown to be true, too often practiced

Is not more ugly to the thing that helps it
Than is my deed to my most painted word.
55 O heavy burden!

POLONIUS: I hear him coming. Let's withdraw, my
lord.

[The KING *and* POLONIUS *withdraw.]*

Enter HAMLET. *[*OPHELIA *pretends to read a book.]*

HAMLET: To be, or not to be, that is the question:
Whether 'tis nobler in the mind to suffer
The slings and arrows of outrageous fortune,
60 Or to take arms against a sea of troubles
And by opposing end them. To die, to sleep—
No more—and by a sleep to say we end
The heartache and the thousand natural shocks
That flesh is heir to. 'Tis a consummation
65 Devoutly to be wished. To die, to sleep;
To sleep, perchance to dream. Ay, there's the rub,
For in that sleep of death what dreams may come,
When we have shuffled off this mortal coil,
Must give us pause. There's the respect
70 That makes calamity of so long life.
For who would bear the whips and scorns of time,
Th' oppressor's wrong, the proud man's contumely,
The pangs of disprized love, the law's delay,
The insolence of office, and the spurns
75 That patient merit of th' unworthy takes,
When he himself might his quietus make
With a bare bodkin? Who would fardels bear,
To grunt and sweat under a weary life,
But that the dread of something after death,
80 The undiscovered country from whose bourn
No traveler returns, puzzles the will,
And makes us rather bear those ills we have
Than fly to others that we know not of?
Thus conscience does make cowards of us all;
85 And thus the native hue of resolution
Is sicklied o'er with the pale cast of thought,
And enterprises of great pitch and moment

Hamlet (Laurence Olivier) talks with Ophelia (Jean Simmons).

With this regard their currents turn awry
And lose the name of action.—Soft you now,
The fair Ophelia. Nymph, in thy orisons 90
Be all my sins remembered.

OPHELIA: Good my lord,
How does your honor for this many a day?

HAMLET: I humbly thank you; well, well, well.

OPHELIA: My lord, I have remembrances of yours,
That I have longèd long to redeliver. 95
I pray you, now receive them. *[She offers tokens.]*

HAMLET: No, not I, I never gave you aught.

OPHELIA: My honored lord, you know right well you
did,
And with them words of so sweet breath composed
As made the things more rich. Their perfume lost, 100
Take these again, for to the noble mind
Rich gifts wax poor when givers prove unkind.
There, my lord. *[She gives tokens.]*

HAMLET: Ha, ha! Are you honest?

OPHELIA: My lord? 105

HAMLET: Are you fair?

OPHELIA: What means your lordship?

HAMLET: That if you be honest and fair, your honesty
should admit no discourse to your beauty.

---

53 to compared to. **the thing** i.e., the cosmetic **56 s.d. withdraw** (The King and Polonius may retire behind an arras. The stage directions specify that they "enter" again near the end of the scene.) **59 slings** missiles **66 rub** (Literally, an obstacle in the game of bowls.) **68 shuffled** sloughed, cast. **coil** turmoil **69 respect** consideration **70 of . . . life** so long-lived, something we willingly endure for so long (also suggesting that long life is itself a calamity) **72 contumely** insolent abuse **73 disprized** unvalued **74 office** officialdom. **spurns** insults **75 of . . . takes** receives from unworthy persons **76 quietus** acquaintance; here, death **77 a bare bodkin** a mere dagger, unsheathed. **fardels** burdens **80 bourn** frontier, boundary **85 native hue** natural color, complexion **86 cast** tinge, shade of color **87 pitch** height (as of a falcon's flight). **moment** importance

---

88 regard respect, consideration. **currents** courses **89 Soft you** i.e., wait a minute, gently **90 orisons** prayers **104 honest** (1) truthful (2) chaste **106 fair** (1) beautiful (2) just, honorable **108 your honesty** your chastity **109 discourse to** familiar dealings with

110 **OPHELIA:** Could beauty, my lord, have better commerce than with honesty?

HAMLET: Ay, truly, for the power of beauty will sooner transform honesty from what it is to a bawd than the force of honesty can translate beauty into his like-
115 ness. This was sometime a paradox, but now the time gives it proof. I did love you once.

OPHELIA: Indeed, my lord, you made me believe so.

HAMLET: You should not have believed me, for virtue cannot so inoculate our old stock but we shall relish
120 of it. I loved you not.

OPHELIA: I was the more deceived.

HAMLET: Get thee to a nunnery. Why wouldst thou be a breeder of sinners? I am myself indifferent honest, but yet I could accuse me of such things that it
125 were better my mother had not borne me: I am very proud, revengeful, ambitious, with more offenses at my beck than I have thoughts to put them in, imagination to give them shape, or time to act them in. What should such fellows as I do crawling between
130 earth and heaven? We are arrant knaves all; believe none of us. Go thy ways to a nunnery. Where's your father?

OPHELIA: At home, my lord.

HAMLET: Let the doors be shut upon him, that he may
135 play the fool nowhere but in 's own house. Farewell.

OPHELIA: O, help him, you sweet heavens!

HAMLET: If thou dost marry, I'll give thee this plague for thy dowry: be thou as chaste as ice, as pure as snow, thou shalt not escape calumny. Get thee to
140 a nunnery, farewell. Or, if thou wilt needs marry, marry a fool, for wise men know well enough what monsters you make of them. To a nunnery, go, and quickly too. Farewell.

OPHELIA: Heavenly powers, restore him!

145 **HAMLET:** I have heard of your paintings too, well enough. God hath given you one face, and you make

Hamlet (Mel Gibson) raves at Ophelia.

yourselves another. You jig, you amble, and you lisp, you nickname God's creatures, and make your wantonness your ignorance. Go to, I'll no more on 't; it hath made me mad. I say we will have no more 150 marriage. Those that are married already—all but one—shall live. The rest shall keep as they are. To a nunnery, go. *Exit.*

OPHELIA: O, what a noble mind is here o'erthrown! The courtier's, soldier's, scholar's, eye, tongue, sword, 155 Th' expectancy and rose of the fair state, The glass of fashion and the mold of form, Th' observed of all observers, quite, quite down! And I, of ladies most deject and wretched, That sucked the honey of his music vows, 160 Now see that noble and most sovereign reason Like sweet bells jangled out of tune and harsh, That unmatched form and feature of blown youth Blasted with ecstasy. O, woe is me, T' have seen what I have seen, see what I see! 165

Enter KING *and* POLONIUS.

KING: Love? His affections do not that way tend; Nor what he spake, though it lacked form a little, Was not like madness. There's something in his soul O'er which his melancholy sits on brood, And I do doubt the hatch and the disclose 170

110–111 **commerce** dealings, intercourse 114 **his** its 115 **sometime** formerly. **a paradox** a view opposite to commonly held opinion. **the time** the present age 119 **inoculate** graft, be engrafted to 119–120 **but . . . it** that we do not still have about us a taste of the old stock, i.e., retain our sinfulness 122 **nunnery** convent (with possibly an awareness that the word was also used derisively to denote a brothel) 123–124 **indifferent honest** reasonably virtuous 127 **beck** command 142 **monsters** (An allusion to the horns of a cuckold.) **you** i.e., you women

147 **jig** dance. **amble** move coyly 148 **you nickname . . . creatures** i.e., you give trendy names to things in place of their God-given names 148–149 **make . . . ignorance** i.e., excuse your affectation on the grounds of pretended ignorance 149 **on 't** of it 156 **expectancy** hope. **rose** ornament 157 **The glass . . . form** the mirror of true self-fashioning and the pattern of courtly behavior 158 **Th' observed . . . observers** i.e., the center of attention and honor in the court 160 **music** musical, sweetly uttered 163 **blown** blooming 164 **Blasted** withered. **ecstasy** madness 166 **affections** emotions, feelings 169 **sits on brood** sits like a bird on a nest, about to *hatch* mischief (line 170) 170 **doubt** fear. **disclose** disclosure, hatching

Will be some danger; which for to prevent,
I have in quick determination
Thus set it down: he shall with speed to England
For the demand of our neglected tribute.
175 Haply the seas and countries different
With variable objects shall expel
This something-settled matter in his heart,
Whereon his brains still beating puts him thus
From fashion of himself. What think you on 't?

180 **POLONIUS:** It shall do well. But yet do I believe
The origin and commencement of his grief
Sprung from neglected love.—How now, Ophelia?
You need not tell us what Lord Hamlet said;
We heard it all.—My lord, do as you please,
185 But, if you hold it fit, after the play
Let his queen-mother all alone entreat him
To show his grief. Let her be round with him;
And I'll be placed, so please you, in the ear
Of all their conference. If she find him not,
190 To England send him, or confine him where
Your wisdom best shall think.

KING: It shall be so.
Madness in great ones must not unwatched go.

Exeunt.

3.2 *Enter* HAMLET *and three of the* PLAYERS.

HAMLET: Speak the speech, I pray you, as I pronounced it to you, trippingly on the tongue. But if you
mouth it, as many of our players do, I had as lief the
town crier spoke my lines. Nor do not saw the air too
5 much with your hand, thus, but use all gently; for in
the very torrent, tempest, and, as I may say, whirlwind of your passion, you must acquire and beget a
temperance that may give it smoothness. O, it offends
me to the soul to hear a robustious periwig-pated
10 fellow tear a passion to tatters, to very rags, to split
the ears of the groundlings, who for the most part
are capable of nothing but inexplicable dumb shows

and noise. I would have such a fellow whipped for
o'erdoing Termagant. It out-Herods Herod. Pray you,
avoid it. 15

FIRST PLAYER: I warrant your honor.

HAMLET: Be not too tame neither, but let your own
discretion be your tutor. Suit the action to the word,
the word to the action, with this special observance,
that you o'erstep not the modesty of nature. For 20
anything so o'erdone is from the purpose of playing,
whose end, both at the first and now, was and is to
hold as 't were the mirror up to nature, to show virtue her feature, scorn her own image, and the very
age and body of the time his form and pressure. Now 25
this overdone or come tardy off, though it makes
the unskillful laugh, cannot but make the judicious
grieve, the censure of the which one must in your allowance o'erweigh a whole theater of others. O,
there be players that I have seen play, and heard oth- 30
ers praise, and that highly, not to speak it profanely,
that, neither having th' accent of Christians nor the
gait of Christian, pagan, nor man, have so strutted
and bellowed that I have thought some of nature's
journeymen had made men and not made them well, 35
they imitated humanity so abominably.

FIRST PLAYER: I hope we have reformed that indifferently with us, sir.

HAMLET: O, reform it altogether. And let those that
play your clowns speak no more than is set down for 40
them; for there be of them that will themselves laugh,
to set on some quantity of barren spectators to laugh
too, though in the meantime some necessary question
of the play be then to be considered. That's villainous,

---

173 **set it down** resolved   174 **For . . . of** to demand   176 **variable
objects** various sights and surroundings to divert him   177 **This
something . . . heart** the strange matter settled in his heart   178
still continually   179 **From . . . himself** out of his natural manner
186 **queen-mother** queen and mother   187 **round** blunt   189
find him not fails to discover what is troubling him

3.2. Location: The castle.
3 **our players** players nowadays.   **I had as lief** I would just as soon
9 **robustious** violent, boisterous.   **periwig-pated** wearing a wig
11 **groundlings** spectators who paid least and stood in the yard
of the theater   12 **capable of** able to understand.   **dumb shows**
mimed performances, often used before Shakespeare's time to
precede a play or each act

---

14 **Termagant** a supposed deity of the Mohammedans, not found
in any English medieval play but elsewhere portrayed as violent
and blustering   14 **Herod** Herod of Jewry. (A character in *The
Slaughter of the Innocents* and other cycle plays. The part was
played with great noise and fury.)   20 **modesty** restraint, moderation   21 **from** contrary to   24 **scorn** i.e., something foolish and
deserving of scorn   24–25 **the very . . . time** i.e., the present state
of affairs   25 **his** its.   **pressure** stamp, impressed character   26
come tardy off inadequately done   27 **the unskillful** those lacking
in judgment   28 **the censure . . . one** the judgment of even one of
whom   28–29 **your allowance** your scale of values   31 **not . . .
profanely** (Hamlet anticipates his idea in lines 34–35 that some
men were not made by God at all.)   32 **Christians** i.e., ordinary
decent folk   33 **nor man** i.e., nor any human being at all   35
journeymen laborers who are not yet masters in their trade   36
abominably (Shakespeare's usual spelling, *abhominably*, suggests
a literal though etymologically incorrect meaning, "removed from
human nature.")   37–38 **indifferently** tolerably   41 **of them** some
among them   42 **barren** i.e., of wit

Hamlet coaches the First Player (Ben Thom).

45 and shows a most pitiful ambition in the fool that uses
it. Go make you ready.   *[Exeunt* PLAYERS.*]*

Enter POLONIUS, GUILDENSTERN, *and* ROSENCRANTZ.

How now, my lord, will the King hear this piece of
work?

POLONIUS: And the Queen too, and that presently.

HAMLET: Bid the players make haste. *[Exit* POLONIUS.*]*
50 Will you two help to hasten them?

ROSENCRANTZ: Ay, my lord.   *[Exeunt they two.]*

HAMLET: What ho, Horatio!

Enter HORATIO.

HORATIO: Here, sweet lord, at your service.

HAMLET: Horatio, thou art e'en as just a man
As e'er my conversation coped withal.

55 **HORATIO:**   O, my dear lord—

HAMLET: Nay, do not think I flatter,
For what advancement may I hope from thee
That no revenue hast but thy good spirits
To feed and clothe thee? Why should the poor be
flattered?
No, let the candied tongue lick absurd pomp,
60 And crook the pregnant hinges of the knee
Where thrift may follow fawning. Dost thou hear?
Since my dear soul was mistress of her choice
And could of men distinguish her election,
Sh' hath sealed thee for herself, for thou hast been
65 As one, in suffering all, that suffers nothing,

A man that Fortune's buffets and rewards
Hast ta'en with equal thanks; and blest are those
Whose blood and judgment are so well commeddled
That they are not a pipe for Fortune's finger
To sound what stop she please. Give me that man   70
That is not passion's slave, and I will wear him
In my heart's core, ay, in my heart of heart,
As I do thee.—Something too much of this.—
There is a play tonight before the King.
One scene of it comes near the circumstance   75
Which I have told thee of my father's death.
I prithee, when thou seest that act afoot,
Even with the very comment of thy soul
Observe my uncle. If his occulted guilt
Do not itself unkennel in one speech,   80
It is a damnèd ghost that we have seen,
And my imaginations are as foul
As Vulcan's stithy. Give him heedful note,
For mine eyes will rivet to his face,
And after we will both our judgments join   85
In censure of his seeming.

HORATIO: Well, my lord.
If 'a steal aught the whilst this play is playing
And scape detecting, I will pay the theft.

[Flourish.] Enter trumpets and kettledrums,
KING, QUEEN, POLONIUS, OPHELIA,
*[*ROSENCRANTZ, GUILDENSTERN, *and*
other lords, with guards carrying torches].

HAMLET: They are coming to the play. I must be idle.
Get you a place.   *[The* KING, QUEEN, *and courtiers sit.]*   90

KING: How fares our cousin Hamlet?

HAMLET: Excellent i' faith, of the chameleon's dish: I eat
the air, promise-crammed. You cannot feed capons so.

KING: I have nothing with this answer, Hamlet. These
words are not mine.   95

---

68 **blood** passion.   **commeddled** commingled   70 **stop** hole in a
wind instrument for controlling the sound   78 **very . . . soul** your
most penetrating observation and consideration   79 **occulted**
hidden   80 **unkennel** (As one would say of a fox driven from its
lair.)   81 **damnèd** in league with Satan   83 **stithy** smithy, place
of stiths (anvils)   86 **censure of his seeming** judgment of his
appearance or behavior   87 **If 'a steal aught** if he gets away with
anything   89 **idle** (1) unoccupied (2) mad   91 **cousin** i.e., close
relative   92 **chameleon's dish** (Chameleons were supposed to feed
on air. Hamlet deliberately misinterprets the King's *fares* as "feeds."
By his phrase *eat the air* he also plays on the idea of feeding himself with the promise of succession, of being the *heir*.)   93 **capons**
roosters castrated and *crammed* with feed to make them succulent
94 **have . . . with** make nothing of, or gain nothing from   95 **are
not mine** do not respond to what I asked

---

48 **presently** at once   54 **my . . . withal** my dealings encountered
59 **candied** sugared, flattering   60 **pregnant** compliant   61 **thrift**
profit   63 **could . . . election** could make distinguishing choices
among persons   64 **sealed thee** (Literally, as one would seal a legal
document to mark possession.)

HAMLET: No, nor mine now. *[To* POLONIUS.*]* My lord, you played once i' th' university, you say?

POLONIUS: That did I, my lord, and was accounted a good actor.

100 **HAMLET:** What did you enact?

POLONIUS: I did enact Julius Caesar. I was killed i' the Capitol; Brutus killed me.

HAMLET: It was a brute part of him to kill so capital a calf there.—Be the players ready?

105 **ROSENCRANTZ:** Ay, my lord. They stay upon your patience.

QUEEN: Come hither, my dear Hamlet, sit by me.

HAMLET: No, good Mother, here's metal more attractive.

POLONIUS *[to the* KING*]*: O, ho, do you mark that?

110 **HAMLET:** Lady, shall I lie in your lap?

[Lying down at OPHELIA's *feet.]*

OPHELIA: No, my lord.

HAMLET: I mean, my head upon your lap?

OPHELIA: Ay, my lord.

HAMLET: Do you think I meant country matters?

115 **OPHELIA:** I think nothing, my lord.

HAMLET: That's a fair thought to lie between maids' legs.

OPHELIA: What is, my lord?

HAMLET: Nothing.

120 **OPHELIA:** You are merry, my lord.

HAMLET: Who, I?

OPHELIA: Ay, my lord.

HAMLET: O God, your only jig maker. What should a man do but be merry? For look you how cheerfully my mother looks, and my father died within 's two hours. 125

OPHELIA: Nay, 'tis twice two months, my lord.

HAMLET: So long? Nay then, let the devil wear black, for I'll have a suit of sables. O heavens! Die two months ago, and not forgotten yet? Then there's hope a great man's memory may outlive his life half a year. But, by 130 'r Lady, 'a must build churches, then, or else shall 'a suffer not thinking on, with the hobbyhorse, whose epitaph is "For O, for O, the hobbyhorse is forgot."

The trumpets sound. Dumb show follows.

Enter a KING *and a* QUEEN *[very lovingly]; the* QUEEN *embracing him, and he her. [She kneels, and makes show of protestation unto him.] He takes her up, and declines his head upon her neck. He lies him down upon a bank of flowers. She, seeing him asleep, leaves him. Anon comes in another man, takes off his crown, kisses it, pours poison in the sleeper's ears, and leaves him. The* QUEEN *returns, finds the* KING *dead, makes passionate action. The Poisoner with some three or four come in again, seem to condole with her. The dead body is carried away. The Poisoner woos the* QUEEN *with gifts; she seems harsh awhile, but in the end accepts love. [Exeunt* PLAYERS.*]*

OPHELIA: What means this, my lord?

HAMLET: Marry, this' miching mallico; it means 135 mischief.

OPHELIA: Belike this show imports the argument of the play.

Enter PROLOGUE.

HAMLET: We shall know by this fellow. The players cannot keep counsel; they'll tell all. 140

OPHELIA: Will 'a tell us what this show meant?

---

96 nor mine now (Once spoken, words are proverbially no longer the speaker's own—and hence should be uttered warily.) **103 brute** (The Latin meaning of *brutus*, "stupid," was often used punningly with the name Brutus.) **part** (1) deed (2) role **104 calf** fool **105 stay upon** await **108 metal** substance that is *attractive*, i.e., magnetic, but with suggestion also of *mettle*, "disposition" **114 country matters** sexual intercourse (making a bawdy pun on the first syllable of *country*) **119 Nothing** the figure zero or naught, suggesting the female sexual anatomy. (*Thing* not infrequently has a bawdy connotation of male or female anatomy, and the reference here could be male.)

---

123 only jig maker very best composer of jigs, i.e., pointless merriment. (Hamlet replies sardonically to Ophelia's observation that he is merry by saying, "If you're looking for someone who is really merry, you've come to the right person.") **125 within 's** within this (i.e., these) **128 suit of sables** garments trimmed with the fur of the sable and hence suited for a wealthy person, not a mourner (but with a pun on *sable*, "black," ironically suggesting mourning once again) **132 suffer . . . on** undergo oblivion **133 For . . . forgot** (Verse of a song occurring also in *Love's Labor's Lost*, 3.1.27–28. The hobbyhorse was a character made up to resemble a horse and rider, appearing in the morris dance and such May-game sports. This song laments the disappearance of such customs under pressure from the Puritans.) **135 this' miching mallico** this is sneaking mischief **137 Belike** probably. **argument** plot **140 counsel** secret

HAMLET: Ay, or any show that you will show him. Be not you ashamed to show, he'll not shame to tell you what it means.

145 **OPHELIA:**   You are naught, you are naught. I'll mark the play.

PROLOGUE: For us, and for our tragedy,
Here stooping to your clemency,
We beg your hearing patiently.   [*Exit.*]

150 **HAMLET:**   Is this a prologue, or the posy of a ring?

OPHELIA: 'Tis brief, my lord.

HAMLET: As woman's love.

Enter [two PLAYERS *as]* KING *and* QUEEN.

PLAYER KING: Full thirty times hath Phoebus' cart gone round
Neptune's salt wash and Tellus' orbèd ground,
155 And thirty dozen moons with borrowed sheen
About the world have times twelve thirties been,
Since love our hearts and Hymen did our hands
Unite commutual in most sacred bands.

PLAYER QUEEN: So many journeys may the sun and moon
160 Make us again count o'er ere love be done!
But, woe is me, you are so sick of late,
So far from cheer and from your former state,
That I distrust you. Yet, though I distrust,
Discomfort you, my lord, it nothing must.
165 For women's fear and love hold quantity;
In neither aught, or in extremity.
Now, what my love is, proof hath made you know,
And as my love is sized, my fear is so.
Where love is great, the littlest doubts are fear;
170 Where little fears grow great, great love grows there.

PLAYER KING: Faith, I must leave thee, love, and shortly too;
My operant powers their functions leave to do.

And thou shalt live in this fair world behind,
Honored, beloved; and haply one as kind
For husband shalt thou—

PLAYER QUEEN: O, confound the rest!   175
Such love must needs be treason in my breast.
In second husband let me be accurst!
None wed the second but who killed the first.

HAMLET: Wormwood, wormwood.

PLAYER QUEEN: The instances that second marriage   180
move
Are base respects of thrift, but none of love.
A second time I kill my husband dead
When second husband kisses me in bed.

PLAYER KING: I do believe you think what now you speak,
But what we do determine oft we break.   185
Purpose is but the slave to memory,
Of violent birth, but poor validity,
Which now, like fruit unripe, sticks on the tree,
But fall unshaken when they mellow be.
Most necessary 'tis that we forget   190
To pay ourselves what to ourselves is debt.
What to ourselves in passion we propose,
The passion ending, doth the purpose lose.
The violence of either grief or joy
Their own enactures with themselves destroy.   195
Where joy most revels, grief doth most lament;
Grief joys, joy grieves, on slender accident.
This world is not for aye, nor 'tis not strange
That even our loves should with our fortunes change;
For 'tis a question left us yet to prove,   200
Whether love lead fortune, or else fortune love.
The great man down, you mark his favorite flies;
The poor advanced makes friends of enemies.
And hitherto doth love on fortune tend;

142–143 **Be not you** provided you are not   145 **naught** indecent. (Ophelia is reacting to Hamlet's pointed remarks about not being ashamed to show all.)   148 **stooping** bowing   150 **posy . . . ring** brief motto in verse inscribed in a ring   153 **Phoebus' cart** the sun-god's chariot, making its yearly cycle   154 **salt wash** the sea.   **Tellus** goddess of the earth, of the *orbèd ground*   155 **borrowed** i.e., reflected   157 **Hymen** god of matrimony   158 **commutual** mutually.   **bands** bonds   163 **distrust** am anxious about   164 **Discomfort** distress.   **nothing** not at all   165 **hold quantity** keep proportion with one another   166 **In . . . extremity** i.e., women fear and love either too little or too much, but the two, fear and love, are equal in either case   167 **proof** experience   168 **sized** in size   172 **operant powers** vital functions.   **leave to do** cease to perform

---

173 **behind** after I have gone   178 **None** i.e., let no woman.   **but who** except the one who   179 **Wormwood** i.e., how bitter. (Literally, a bitter-tasting plant.)   180 **instances** motives.   **move** motivate   181 **base . . . thrift** ignoble considerations of material prosperity   186 **Purpose . . . memory** our good intentions are subject to forgetfulness   187 **validity** strength, durability   188 **Which** i.e., purpose   190–191 **Most . . . debt** it's inevitable that in time we forget the obligations we have imposed on ourselves   195 **enactures** fulfillments   196–197 **Where . . . accident** the capacity for extreme joy and grief go together, and often one extreme is instantly changed into its opposite on the slightest provocation   198 **aye** ever   202 **down** fallen in fortune   203 **The poor . . . enemies** when one of humble station is promoted, you see his enemies suddenly becoming his friends   204 **hitherto** up to this point in the argument, or, to this extent.   **tend** attend

The players perform Hamlet's play.

205   For who not needs shall never lack a friend,
    And who in want a hollow friend doth try
    Directly seasons him his enemy.
    But, orderly to end where I begun,
    Our wills and fates do so contrary run
210   That our devices still are overthrown;
    Our thoughts are ours, their ends none of our own.
    So think thou wilt no second husband wed,
    But die thy thoughts when thy first lord is dead.

PLAYER QUEEN: Nor earth to me give food, nor
      heaven light,
215   Sport and repose lock from me day and night,
    To desperation turn my trust and hope,
    An anchor's cheer in prison be my scope!
    Each opposite that blanks the face of joy
    Meet what I would have well and it destroy!
220   Both here and hence pursue me lasting strife
    If, once a widow, ever I be wife!

HAMLET: If she should break it now!

PLAYER KING: 'Tis deeply sworn. Sweet, leave me
      here awhile;
    My spirits grow dull, and fain I would beguile
225   The tedious day with sleep.

PLAYER QUEEN: Sleep rock thy brain,
    And never come mischance between us twain!
                [He sleeps.] Exit [PLAYER QUEEN].

---

205 who not needs he who is not in need (of wealth) **206 who in want** he who, being in need. **try** test (his generosity) **207 seasons him** ripens him into **209 Our . . . run** what we want and what we get go so contrarily **210 devices still** intentions continually **211 ends** results **214 Nor** let neither **215 Sport . . . night** may day deny me its pastimes and night its repose **217 anchor's cheer** anchorite's or hermit's fare. **my scope** the extent of my happiness **218–219 Each . . . destroy** may every adverse thing that causes the face of joy to turn pale meet and destroy everything that I desire to see prosper. **blanks** causes to blanch or grow pale **220 hence** in the life hereafter **224 spirits** vital spirits

HAMLET: Madam, how like you this play?

QUEEN: The lady doth protest too much, methinks.

HAMLET: O, but she'll keep her word.

KING: Have you heard the argument? Is there no   230
    offense in 't?

HAMLET: No, no, they do but jest, poison in jest. No
    offense i' the world.

KING: What do you call the play?

HAMLET: *The Mousetrap.* Marry, how? Tropically.   235
    This play is the image of a murder done in Vienna.
    Gonzago is the Duke's name, his wife, Baptista. You
    shall see anon. 'Tis a knavish piece of work, but what
    of that? Your Majesty, and we that have free souls, it
    touches us not. Let the galled jade wince, our with-   240
    ers are unwrung.

                      Enter LUCIANUS.

    This is one Lucianus, nephew to the King.

OPHELIA: You are as good as a chorus, my lord.

HAMLET: I could interpret between you and your love,
    if I could see the puppets dallying.   245

OPHELIA: You are keen, my lord, you are keen.

HAMLET: It would cost you a groaning to take off mine
    edge.

OPHELIA: Still better, and worse.

HAMLET: So you mis-take your husbands. Begin, mur-   250
    derer; leave thy damnable faces and begin. Come,
    the croaking raven doth bellow for revenge.

---

228 doth . . . much makes too many promises and protestations **230 argument** plot **231–233 offense . . . offense** cause for objection . . . actual injury, crime **232 jest** make believe **235 Tropically** figuratively. (The First Quarto reading, *trapically,* suggests a pun on *trap* in *Mousetrap.*) **237 Duke's** i.e., King's. (A slip that may be due to Shakespeare's possible source, the alleged murder of the Duke of Urbino by Luigi Gonzaga in 1538.) **239 free** guiltless **240 galled jade** horse whose hide is rubbed by saddle or harness **240–241 withers** the part between the horse's shoulder blades **241 unwrung** not rubbed sore **243 chorus** (In many Elizabethan plays, the forthcoming action was explained by an actor known as the "chorus"; at a puppet show, the actor who spoke the dialogue was known as an "interpreter," as indicated by the lines following.) **244 interpret** (1) ventriloquize the dialogue, as in a puppet show (2) act as pander **245 puppets dallying** (With suggestion of sexual play, continued in *keen,* "sexually aroused," *groaning,* "moaning in pregnancy," and *edge,* "sexual desire" or "impetuosity.") **246 keen** sharp, bitter **249 Still . . . worse** more keen, always *bettering* what other people say with witty wordplay, but at the same time more offensive **250 So** even thus (in marriage). **mis-take** take falseheartedly and cheat on. (The marriage vows say "for better, for worse.")

LUCIANUS: Thoughts black, hands apt, drugs fit, and
time agreeing,
Confederate season, else no creature seeing,
255 Thou mixture rank, of midnight weeds collected,
With Hecate's ban thrice blasted, thrice infected,
Thy natural magic and dire property
On wholesome life usurp immediately.

[He pours the poison into the sleeper's ear.]

HAMLET: 'A poisons him i' the garden for his estate.
260 His name's Gonzago. The story is extant, and written in very choice Italian. You shall see anon how the
murderer gets the love of Gonzago's wife.

[CLAUDIUS rises.]

OPHELIA: The King rises.

HAMLET: What, frighted with false fire?

265 **QUEEN:** How fares my lord?

POLONIUS: Give o'er the play.

KING: Give me some light. Away!

POLONIUS: Lights, lights, lights!

Exeunt all but HAMLET *and* HORATIO.

HAMLET:
"Why, let the stricken deer go weep,
270 The hart ungallèd play.
For some must watch, while some must sleep;
Thus runs the world away."
Would not this, sir, and a forest of feathers—if the
rest of my fortunes turn Turk with me—with two
275 Provincial roses on my razed shoes, get me a fellowship in a cry of players?

HORATIO: Half a share.

Hamlet and Horatio (Stephen Dillane) discuss the result of their scheme.

HAMLET: A whole one, I.
"For thou dost know, O Damon dear,
This realm dismantled was 280
Of Jove himself, and now reigns here
A very, very—pajock."

HORATIO: You might have rhymed.

HAMLET: O good Horatio, I'll take the ghost's word for
a thousand pound. Didst perceive? 285

HORATIO: Very well, my lord.

HAMLET: Upon the talk of the poisoning?

HORATIO: I did very well note him.

Enter ROSENCRANTZ *and* GUILDENSTERN.

HAMLET: Aha! Come, some music! Come, the
recorders. 290
"For if the King like not the comedy,
Why then, belike, he likes it not, perdy."
Come, some music.

GUILDENSTERN: Good my lord, vouchsafe me a word
with you. 295

HAMLET: Sir, a whole history.

GUILDENSTERN: The King, sir—

---

254 **Confederate season** the time and occasion conspiring (to
assist the murderer). **else** otherwise. **seeing** seeing me 256
Hecate's ban the curse of Hecate, the goddess of witchcraft 257
dire property baleful quality 259 **estate** i.e., the kingship 260
His i.e., the King's 264 **false fire** the blank discharge of a gun
loaded with powder but no shot 269–272 **Why . . . away** (Probably from an old ballad, with allusion to the popular belief that a
wounded deer retires to weep and die; compare with *As You Like
It*, 2.1.33–66.) 270 **ungallèd** unaffected 271 **watch** remain
awake 272 **Thus . . . away** thus the world goes 273 **this** i.e., the
play. **feathers** (Allusion to the plumes that Elizabethan actors
were fond of wearing.) 274 **turn Turk with** turn renegade against,
go back on 275 **Provincial roses** rosettes of ribbon, named for
roses grown in a part of France. **razed** with ornamental slash-
ing 275–276 **fellowship . . . players** partnership in a theatrical
company 276 **cry** pack (of hounds)

---

279 **Damon** the friend of Pythias, as Horatio is friend of Hamlet;
or, a traditional pastoral name 280–282 **This realm . . . pajock**
i.e., Jove, representing divine authority and justice, has abandoned
this realm to its own devices, leaving in his stead only a peacock or
vain pretender to virtue (though the rhyme-word expected in place
of *pajock* or "peacock" suggests that the realm is now ruled over by
an "ass"). 280 **dismantled** stripped, divested 290 **recorders**
wind instruments of the flute kind 292 **perdy** (A corruption of the
French *par dieu*, "by God.")

HAMLET: Ay, sir, what of him?

GUILDENSTERN: Is in his retirement marvelous
300 distempered.

HAMLET: With drink, sir?

GUILDENSTERN: No, my lord, with choler.

HAMLET: Your wisdom should show itself more richer
to signify this to the doctor, for for me to put him to
305 his purgation would perhaps plunge him into more
choler.

GUILDENSTERN: Good my lord, put your discourse into
some frame and start not so wildly from my affair.

HAMLET: I am tame, sir. Pronounce.

310 **GUILDENSTERN:** The Queen, your mother, in most
great affliction of spirit, hath sent me to you.

HAMLET: You are welcome.

GUILDENSTERN: Nay, good my lord, this courtesy is
not of the right breed. If it shall please you to make
315 me a wholesome answer, I will do your mother's
commandment; if not, your pardon and my return
shall be the end of my business.

HAMLET: Sir, I cannot.

ROSENCRANTZ: What, my lord?

320 **HAMLET:** Make you a wholesome answer; my wit's diseased. But, sir, such answer as I can make, you shall
command, or rather, as you say, my mother. Therefore no more, but to the matter. My mother, you say—

ROSENCRANTZ: Then thus she says: your behavior
325 hath struck her into amazement and admiration.

HAMLET: O wonderful son, that can so stonish a
mother! But is there no sequel at the heels of this
mother's admiration? Impart.

ROSENCRANTZ: She desires to speak with you in her
330 closet ere you go to bed.

HAMLET: We shall obey, were she ten times our
mother. Have you any further trade with us?

ROSENCRANTZ: My lord, you once did love me.

HAMLET: And do still, by these pickers and stealers.

ROSENCRANTZ: Good my lord, what is your cause   335
of distemper? You do surely bar the door upon your
own liberty if you deny your griefs to your friend.

HAMLET: Sir, I lack advancement.

ROSENCRANTZ: How can that be, when you have
the voice of the King himself for your succession in   340
Denmark?

HAMLET: Ay, sir, but "While the grass grows"—the
proverb is something musty.

Enter the PLAYERS *with recorders.*

O, the recorders. Let me see one. *[He takes a recorder.]*
To withdraw with you: why do you go about to recover   345
the wind of me, as if you would drive me into a toil?

GUILDENSTERN: O, my lord, if my duty be too bold,
my love is too unmannerly.

HAMLET: I do not well understand that. Will you play
upon this pipe?   350

GUILDENSTERN: My lord, I cannot.

HAMLET: I pray you.

GUILDENSTERN: Believe me, I cannot.

HAMLET: I do beseech you.

GUILDENSTERN: I know no touch of it, my lord.   355

HAMLET: It is as easy as lying. Govern these ventages
with your fingers and thumb, give it breath with your
mouth, and it will discourse most eloquent music.
Look you, these are the stops.

---

299 retirement withdrawal to his chambers **300 distempered**
out of humor. (But Hamlet deliberately plays on the wider application to any illness of mind or body, as in lines 335–336, especially
to drunkenness.) **302 choler** anger. (But Hamlet takes the word
in its more basic humoral sense of "bilious disorder.") **305 purgation** (Hamlet hints at something going beyond medical treatment
to blood-letting and the extraction of confession.) **308 frame**
order. **start** shy or jump away (like a horse; the opposite of *tame*
in line 309) **314 breed** (1) kind (2) breeding, manners **316 pardon** permission to depart **325 admiration** bewilderment **330
closet** private chamber

334 pickers and stealers i.e., hands. (So called from the catechism,
"to keep my hands from picking and stealing.") **337 liberty** i.e., being freed from *distemper* (line 336); but perhaps with a veiled threat
as well. **deny** refuse to share **342 While . . . grows** (The rest of
the proverb is "the silly horse starves"; Hamlet may not live long
enough to succeed to the kingdom.) **343 something** somewhat.
s.d. Players actors **345 withdraw** speak privately **345–346
recover the wind** get to the windward side (thus driving the game
into the *toil*, or "net") **346 toil** snare **347–348 if . . . unmannerly**
if I am using an unmannerly boldness, it is my love that occasions
it **349 I . . . that** i.e., I don't understand how genuine love can be
unmannerly **356 ventages** finger-holes or *stops* (line 359) of the
recorder

360 **GUILDENSTERN:** But these cannot I command to any utterance of harmony. I have not the skill.

HAMLET: Why, look you now, how unworthy a thing you make of me! You would play upon me, you would seem to know my stops, you would pluck out the
365 heart of my mystery, you would sound me from my lowest note to the top of my compass, and there is much music, excellent voice, in this little organ, yet cannot you make it speak. 'Sblood, do you think I am easier to be played on than a pipe? Call me what
370 instrument you will, though you can fret me, you cannot play upon me.

Enter POLONIUS.

God bless you, sir!

POLONIUS: My lord, the Queen would speak with you, and presently.

375 **HAMLET:** Do you see yonder cloud that's almost in shape of a camel?

POLONIUS: By the Mass and 'tis, like a camel indeed.

HAMLET: Methinks it is like a weasel.

POLONIUS: It is backed like a weasel.

380 **HAMLET:** Or like a whale.

POLONIUS: Very like a whale.

HAMLET: Then I will come to my mother by and by. *[Aside.]* They fool me to the top of my bent.—I will come by and by.

385 **POLONIUS :** I will say so. *[Exit.]*

HAMLET: "By and by" is easily said. Leave me, friends.
[Exeunt all but HAMLET.*]*
'Tis now the very witching time of night,
When churchyards yawn and hell itself breathes out
Contagion to this world. Now could I drink hot blood
390 And do such bitter business as the day
Would quake to look on. Soft, now to my mother.
O heart, lose not thy nature! Let not ever
The soul of Nero enter this firm bosom.

Let me be cruel, not unnatural;
I will speak daggers to her, but use none. 395
My tongue and soul in this be hypocrites:
How in my words soever she be shent,
To give them seals never my soul consent! *Exit.*

3.3 *Enter* KING, ROSENCRANTZ, *and* GUILDENSTERN.

KING: I like him not, nor stands it safe with us
To let his madness range. Therefore prepare you.
I your commission will forthwith dispatch,
And he to England shall along with you.
The terms of our estate may not endure 5
Hazard so near 's as doth hourly grow
Out of his brows.

GUILDENSTERN: We will ourselves provide.
Most holy and religious fear it is
To keep those many many bodies safe
That live and feed upon Your Majesty. 10

ROSENCRANTZ: The single and peculiar life is bound
With all the strength and armor of the mind
To keep itself from noyance, but much more
That spirit upon whose weal depends and rests
The lives of many. The cess of majesty 15
Dies not alone, but like a gulf doth draw
What's near it with it; or it is a massy wheel
Fixed on the summit of the highest mount,
To whose huge spokes ten thousand lesser things
Are mortised and adjoined, which, when it falls, 20
Each small annexment, petty consequence,
Attends the boisterous ruin. Never alone
Did the King sigh, but with a general groan.

KING: Arm you, I pray you, to this speedy voyage,
For we will fetters put about this fear, 25
Which now goes too free-footed.

ROSENCRANTZ: We will haste us.
*Exeunt gentlemen [*ROSENCRANTZ *and* GUILDENSTERN*].*

Enter POLONIUS.

---

397 **How . . . soever** however much by my words.   **shent** rebuked
398 **give them seals** i.e., confirm them with deeds

3.3. Location: The castle.
1 **him** i.e., his behavior   3 **dispatch** prepare, cause to be drawn up
5 **terms of our estate** circumstances of my royal position   7 **Out of his brows** i.e., from his brain, in the form of plots and threats
8 **religious fear** sacred concern   11 **single and peculiar** individual and private   13 **noyance** harm   15 **cess** decease, cessation   16 **gulf** whirlpool   17 **massy** massive   20 **mortised** fastened (as with a fitted joint).   **when it falls** i.e., when it descends, like the wheel of Fortune, bringing a king down with it   21 **Each . . . consequence** i.e., every hanger-on and unimportant person or thing connected with the King   22 **Attends** participates in   24 **Arm** prepare

---

365 **sound** (1) fathom (2) produce sound in   366 **compass** range (of voice)   367 **organ** musical instrument   370 **fret** irritate (with a quibble on *fret*, meaning the piece of wood, gut, or metal that regulates the fingering on an instrument)   374 **presently** at once   382 **by and by** quite soon   383 **fool me** trifle with me, humor my fooling.   **top of my bent** limit of my ability or endurance. (Literally, the extent to which a bow may be bent.)   387 **witching time** time when spells are cast and evil is abroad   392 **nature** natural feeling   393 **Nero** murderer of his mother, Agrippina

POLONIUS: My lord, he's going to his mother's closet.
    Behind the arras I'll convey myself
    To hear the process. I'll warrant she'll tax him home,
30   And, as you said—and wisely was it said—
    'Tis meet that some more audience than a mother,
    Since nature makes them partial, should o'erhear
    The speech, of vantage. Fare you well, my liege.
    I'll call upon you ere you go to bed
35   And tell you what I know.

KING: Thanks, dear my lord.

                           Exit [POLONIUS].
    O, my offense is rank! It smells to heaven.
    It hath the primal eldest curse upon 't,
    A brother's murder. Pray can I not,
    Though inclination be as sharp as will;
40   My stronger guilt defeats my strong intent,
    And like a man to double business bound
    I stand in pause where I shall first begin,
    And both neglect. What if this cursèd hand
    Were thicker than itself with brother's blood,
45   Is there not rain enough in the sweet heavens
    To wash it white as snow? Whereto serves mercy
    But to confront the visage of offense?
    And what's in prayer but this twofold force,
    To be forestallèd ere we come to fall,
50   Or pardoned being down? Then I'll look up.
    My fault is past. But O, what form of prayer
    Can serve my turn? "Forgive me my foul murder"?
    That cannot be, since I am still possessed
    Of those effects for which I did the murder:
55   My crown, mine own ambition, and my queen.
    May one be pardoned and retain th' offense?
    In the corrupted currents of this world
    Offense's gilded hand may shove by justice,
    And oft 'tis seen the wicked prize itself
60   Buys out the law. But 'tis not so above.
    There is no shuffling, there the action lies

Hamlet sits armed in the confessional. Claudius prays, but he hesitates.

    In his true nature, and we ourselves compelled,
    Even to the teeth and forehead of our faults,
    To give in evidence. What then? What rests?
    Try what repentance can. What can it not?   65
    Yet what can it, when one cannot repent?
    O wretched state, O bosom black as death,
    O limèd soul that, struggling to be free,
    Art more engaged! Help, angels! Make assay.
    Bow, stubborn knees, and heart with strings of steel,   70
    Be soft as sinews of the newborn babe!
    All may be well.   *[He kneels.]*

                          Enter HAMLET.

HAMLET: Now might I do it pat, now 'a is a-praying;
    And now I'll do 't. *[He draws his sword.]* And so 'a goes
       to heaven,
    And so am I revenged. That would be scanned: 75
    A villain kills my father, and for that,
    I, his sole son, do this same villain send
    To heaven.
    Why, this is hire and salary, not revenge.
    'A took my father grossly, full of bread,   80
    With all his crimes broad blown, as flush as May;
    And how his audit stands who knows save heaven?
    But in our circumstance and course of thought
    'Tis heavy with him. And am I then revenged,

---

28 arras screen of tapestry placed around the walls of household apartments. (On the Elizabethan stage, the arras was presumably over a door or discovery space in the tiring-house facade.) **29 process** proceedings. **tax him home** reprove him severely **31 meet** fitting **33 of vantage** from an advantageous place, or, in addition **37 the primal eldest curse** the curse of Cain, the first murderer; he killed his brother Abel **39 Though . . . will** though my desire is as strong as my determination **41 bound** (1) destined (2) obliged. (The King wants to repent and still enjoy what he has gained.) **46–47 Whereto . . . offense** what function does mercy serve other than to meet sin face to face? **49 forestallèd** prevented (from sinning) **56 th' offense** the thing for which one offended **57 currents** courses **58 gilded hand** hand offering gold as a bribe. **shove by** thrust aside **59 wicked prize** prize won by wickedness **61 There** i.e., in heaven. **shuffling** escape by trickery. **the action lies** the accusation is made manifest. (A legal metaphor.)

---

62 his its **63 to the teeth and forehead** face to face, concealing nothing **64 give in** provide. **rests** remains **68 limèd** caught as with birdlime, a sticky substance used to ensnare birds **69 engaged** entangled. **assay** trial. (Said to himself.) **73 pat** opportunely **75 would be scanned** needs to be looked into, or, would be interpreted as follows **80 grossly, full of bread** i.e., enjoying his worldly pleasures rather than fasting. (See Ezekiel 16:49.) **81 crimes broad blown** sins in full bloom. **flush** vigorous **82 audit** account. **save** except for **83 in . . . thought** as we see it from our mortal perspective

85　To take him in the purging of his soul,
　　When he is fit and seasoned for his passage?
　　No!
　　Up, sword, and know thou a more horrid hent.

[He puts up his sword.]

　　When he is drunk asleep, or in his rage,
90　Or in th' incestuous pleasure of his bed,
　　At game, a-swearing, or about some act
　　That has no relish of salvation in 't—
　　Then trip him, that his heels may kick at heaven,
　　And that his soul may be as damned and black
95　As hell, whereto it goes. My mother stays.
　　This physic but prolongs thy sickly days.　　*Exit.*

KING:　My words fly up, my thoughts remain below.
　　Words without thoughts never to heaven go.　　*Exit.*

3.4　*Enter* [QUEEN] GERTRUDE *and* POLONIUS.

POLONIUS:　'A will come straight. Look you lay home
　　　　to him.
　　Tell him his pranks have been too broad to bear
　　　　with,
　　And that Your Grace hath screened and stood
　　　　between
　　Much heat and him. I'll shroud me even here.
5　Pray you be round with him.

HAMLET *(within)*:　Mother, Mother, Mother!

QUEEN:　I'll warrant you, fear me not.
　　Withdraw, I hear him coming.

[POLONIUS hides behind the arras.]

Enter HAMLET.

HAMLET:　Now, Mother, what's the matter?

10　**QUEEN:**　Hamlet, thou hast thy father much offended.

HAMLET:　Mother, you have my father much offended.

QUEEN:　Come, come, you answer with an idle tongue.

---

86 **seasoned** matured, readied　88 **know . . . hent** await to be grasped by me on a more horrid occasion.　**hent** act of seizing　89 **drunk . . . rage** dead drunk, or in a fit of sexual passion　91 **game** gambling　92 **relish** trace, savor　95 **stays** awaits (me)　96 **physic** purging (by prayer), or, Hamlet's postponement of the killing

3.4. Location: The Queen's private chamber.
1 **lay home** thrust to the heart, reprove him soundly　2 **broad** unrestrained　4 **Much heat** i.e., the King's anger.　**shroud** conceal (with ironic fitness to Polonius' imminent death. The word is only in the First Quarto; the Second Quarto and the Folio read "silence.")　5 **round** blunt　10 **thy father** i.e., your stepfather, Claudius　12 **idle** foolish

---

HAMLET:　Go, go, you question with a wicked tongue.

QUEEN:　Why, how now, Hamlet?

HAMLET:　　　　　　　What's the matter now?

QUEEN:　Have you forgot me?　　　　　　　15

HAMLET:　　　　　　　No, by the rood, not so:
　　You are the Queen, your husband's brother's wife,
　　And—would it were not so!—you are my mother.

QUEEN:　Nay, then, I'll set those to you that can speak.

HAMLET:　Come, come, and sit you down; you shall not
　　　　budge.
　　You go not till I set you up a glass　　　　20
　　Where you may see the inmost part of you.

QUEEN:　What wilt thou do? Thou wilt not murder me?
　　Help, ho!

POLONIUS *[behind the arras]*:　What ho! Help!

HAMLET *[drawing]*:　How now? A rat? Dead for a ducat,
　　　　dead!　　　　25

[He thrusts his rapier through the arras.]

POLONIUS *[behind the arras]*:　O, I am slain!

[He falls and dies.]

QUEEN:　　　　　　　O me, what hast thou done?

HAMLET:　Nay, I know not. Is it the King?

QUEEN:　O, what a rash and bloody deed is this!

HAMLET:　A bloody deed—almost as bad, good Mother,
　　As kill a king, and marry with his brother.　　30

QUEEN:　As kill a king!

HAMLET:　　　　　　　Ay, lady, it was my word.

[He parts the arras and discovers POLONIUS.]

　　Thou wretched, rash, intruding fool, farewell!
　　I took thee for thy better. Take thy fortune.
　　Thou find'st to be too busy is some danger.—
　　Leave wringing of your hands. Peace, sit you down,　35
　　And let me wring your heart, for so I shall,
　　If it be made of penetrable stuff,
　　If damnèd custom have not brazed it so
　　That it be proof and bulwark against sense.

QUEEN:　What have I done, that thou dar'st wag thy
　　　　tongue　　　　40
　　In noise so rude against me?

---

15 **forgot me** i.e., forgotten that I am your mother.　**rood** cross of Christ　18 **speak** i.e., to someone so rude　25 **Dead for a ducat** i.e., I bet a ducat he's dead; or, a ducat is his life's fee　34 **busy** nosey　38 **damnèd custom** habitual wickedness.　**brazed** brazened, hardened　39 **proof** armor.　**sense** feeling

Hamlet confides in Gertrude.

HAMLET: Such an act
   That blurs the grace and blush of modesty,
   Calls virtue hypocrite, takes off the rose
   From the fair forehead of an innocent love
45 And sets a blister there, makes marriage vows
   As false as dicers' oaths. O, such a deed
   As from the body of contraction plucks
   The very soul, and sweet religion makes
   A rhapsody of words. Heaven's face does glow
50 O'er this solidity and compound mass
   With tristful visage, as against the doom,
   Is thought-sick at the act.

QUEEN: Ay me, what act,
   That roars so loud and thunders in the index?

HAMLET [*showing her two likenesses*]:   Look here upon
       this picture, and on this,
55 The counterfeit presentment of two brothers.
   See what a grace was seated on this brow:
   Hyperion's curls, the front of Jove himself,
   An eye like Mars to threaten and command,
   A station like the herald Mercury
60 New-lighted on a heaven-kissing hill—
   A combination and a form indeed
   Where every god did seem to set his seal
   To give the world assurance of a man.
   This was your husband. Look you now what follows:
65 Here is your husband, like a mildewed ear,

Blasting his wholesome brother. Have you eyes?
Could you on this fair mountain leave to feed
And batten on this moor? Ha, have you eyes?
You cannot call it love, for at your age
The heyday in the blood is tame, it's humble, 70
And waits upon the judgment, and what judgment
Would step from this to this? Sense, sure, you have,
Else could you not have motion, but sure that sense
Is apoplexed, for madness would not err,
Nor sense to ecstasy was ne'er so thralled, 75
But it reserved some quantity of choice
To serve in such a difference. What devil was 't
That thus hath cozened you at hoodman-blind?
Eyes without feeling, feeling without sight,
Ears without hands or eyes, smelling sans all, 80
Or but a sickly part of one true sense
Could not so mope. O shame, where is thy blush?
Rebellious hell,
If thou canst mutine in a matron's bones,
To flaming youth let virtue be as wax 85
And melt in her own fire. Proclaim no shame
When the compulsive ardor gives the charge,
Since frost itself as actively doth burn,
And reason panders will.

QUEEN: O Hamlet, speak no more! 90
   Thou turn'st mine eyes into my very soul,
   And there I see such black and grainèd spots
   As will not leave their tinct.

HAMLET: Nay, but to live
   In the rank sweat of an enseamèd bed,
   Stewed in corruption, honeying and making love 95
   Over the nasty sty!

---

45 sets a blister i.e., brands as a harlot   **47 contraction** the marriage contract   **48 sweet religion makes** i.e., makes marriage vows   **49 rhapsody** senseless string   **49–52 Heaven's . . . act** heaven's face blushes at this solid world compounded of the various elements, with sorrowful face as though the day of doom were near, and is sick with horror at the deed (i.e., Gertrude's marriage)   **53 index** table of contents, prelude or preface   **55 counterfeit presentment** portrayed representation   **57 Hyperion's** the sun-god's.   **front** brow   **58 Mars** god of war   **59 station** manner of standing.   **Mercury** winged messenger of the gods   **60 New-lighted** newly alighted   **62 set his seal** i.e., affix his approval   **65 ear** i.e., of grain

66 Blasting blighting   **67 leave** cease   **68 batten** gorge.   **moor** barren or marshy ground (suggesting also "dark-skinned")   **70 heyday** state of excitement.   **blood** passion   **72 Sense** perception through the five senses (the functions of the middle or sensible soul)   **74 apoplexed** paralyzed. (Hamlet goes on to explain that, without such a paralysis of will, mere madness would not so err, nor would the five senses so enthrall themselves to *ecstasy* or lunacy; even such deranged states of mind would be able to make the obvious choice between Hamlet Senior and Claudius.)   **err** so err   **76 But** but that   **77 To . . . difference** to help in making a choice between two such men   **78 cozened** cheated.   **hoodman-blind** blindman's bluff. (In this game, says Hamlet, the devil must have pushed Claudius toward Gertrude while she was blindfolded.)   **80 sans** without   **82 mope** be dazed, act aimlessly   **84 mutine** incite mutiny   **85–86 be as wax . . . fire** melt like a candle or stick of sealing wax held over the candle flame   **86–89 Proclaim . . . will** call it no shameful business when the compelling ardor of youth delivers the attack, i.e, commits lechery, since the *frost* of advanced age burns with as active a fire of lust and reason perverts itself by fomenting lust rather than restraining it   **92 grainèd** dyed in grain, indelible   **93 leave their tinct** surrender their color   **94 enseamèd** saturated in the grease and filth of passionate lovemaking   **95 Stewed** soaked, bathed (with a suggestion of "stew," brothel)

Hamlet kneels by Polonius's (Brian Murray) dead body.

QUEEN: O, speak to me no more!
These words like daggers enter in my ears.
No more, sweet Hamlet!

HAMLET: A murderer and a villain,
100 A slave that is not twentieth part the tithe
Of your precedent lord, a vice of kings,
A cutpurse of the empire and the rule,
That from a shelf the precious diadem stole
And put it in his pocket!

105 **QUEEN:** No more!

Enter GHOST *[in his nightgown].*

HAMLET: A king of shreds and patches—
Save me, and hover o'er me with your wings,
You heavenly guards! What would your gracious
figure?

QUEEN: Alas, he's mad!

110 **HAMLET:** Do you not come your tardy son to chide,
That, lapsed in time and passion, lets go by
Th' important acting of your dread command?
O, say!

GHOST: Do not forget. This visitation
115 Is but to whet thy almost blunted purpose.
But look, amazement on thy mother sits.
O, step between her and her fighting soul!

---

100 **tithe** tenth part   101 **precedent lord** former husband.   **vice**
buffoon. (A reference to the Vice of the morality plays.)   106
shreds and patches i.e., motley, the traditional costume of the
clown or fool   111 **lapsed** delaying   112 **important** importunate,
urgent   116 **amazement** distraction

Conceit in weakest bodies strongest works.
Speak to her, Hamlet.

HAMLET: How is it with you, lady?

QUEEN: Alas, how is 't with you,   120
That you do bend your eye on vacancy,
And with th' incorporal air do hold discourse?
Forth at your eyes your spirits wildly peep,
And, as the sleeping soldiers in th' alarm,
Your bedded hair, like life in excrements,   125
Start up and stand on end. O gentle son,
Upon the heat and flame of thy distemper
Sprinkle cool patience. Whereon do you look?

HAMLET: On him, on him! Look you how pale he
glares!
His form and cause conjoined, preaching to stones,   130
Would make them capable.—Do not look upon me,
Lest with this piteous action you convert
My stern effects. Then what I have to do
Will want true color—tears perchance for blood.

QUEEN: To whom do you speak this?   135

HAMLET: Do you see nothing there?

QUEEN: Nothing at all, yet all that is I see.

HAMLET: Nor did you nothing hear?

QUEEN: No, nothing but ourselves.

HAMLET: Why, look you there, look how it steals away!   140
My father, in his habit as he lived!
Look where he goes even now out at the portal!

Exit GHOST.

QUEEN: This is the very coinage of your brain.
This bodiless creation ecstasy
Is very cunning in.   145

HAMLET: Ecstasy?
My pulse as yours doth temperately keep time,
And makes as healthful music. It is not madness
That I have uttered. Bring me to the test,

---

118 **Conceit** imagination   122 **incorporal** immaterial   124 **as . . .**
alarm like soldiers called out of sleep by an alarum   125 **bedded**
laid flat.   **like life in excrements** i.e., as though hair, an outgrowth
of the body, had a life of its own. (Hair was thought to be lifeless
because it lacks sensation, and so its standing on end would be unnatural and ominous.)   127 **distemper** disorder   130 **His . . .**
conjoined his appearance joined to his cause for speaking   131
capable receptive   132–133 **convert . . . effects** divert me from my
stern duty   134 **want . . . blood** lack plausibility so that (with a play
on the normal sense of *color*) I shall shed colorless tears instead of
blood   141 **habit** clothes.   **as** as when   143 **very** mere   144–145
This . . . in madness is skillful in creating this kind of hallucination

150　　And I the matter will reword, which madness
　　　Would gambol from. Mother, for love of grace,
　　　Lay not that flattering unction to your soul
　　　That not your trespass but my madness speaks.
　　　It will but skin and film the ulcerous place,
155　　Whiles rank corruption, mining all within,
　　　Infects unseen. Confess yourself to heaven,
　　　Repent what's past, avoid what is to come,
　　　And do not spread the compost on the weeds
　　　To make them ranker. Forgive me this my virtue;
160　　For in the fatness of these pursy times
　　　Virtue itself of vice must pardon beg,
　　　Yea, curb and woo for leave to do him good.

QUEEN: O Hamlet, thou hast cleft my heart in twain.

HAMLET: O, throw away the worser part of it,
165　　And live the purer with the other half.
　　　Good night. But go not to my uncle's bed;
　　　Assume a virtue, if you have it not.
　　　That monster, custom, who all sense doth eat,
　　　Of habits devil, is angel yet in this,
170　　That to the use of actions fair and good
　　　He likewise gives a frock or livery
　　　That aptly is put on. Refrain tonight,
　　　And that shall lend a kind of easiness
　　　To the next abstinence; the next more easy;
175　　For use almost can change the stamp of nature,
　　　And either . . . the devil, or throw him out
　　　With wondrous potency. Once more, good night;
　　　And when you are desirous to be blest,
　　　I'll blessing beg of you. For this same lord,

[pointing to POLONIUS*]*

180　　I do repent; but heaven hath pleased it so
　　　To punish me with this, and this with me,
　　　That I must be their scourge and minister.

I will bestow him, and will answer well
The death I gave him. So, again, good night.
I must be cruel only to be kind. 185
This bad begins, and worse remains behind.
One word more, good lady.

QUEEN:　　　　　　　　　　What shall I do?

HAMLET: Not this by no means that I bid you do:
Let the bloat king tempt you again in bed,
Pinch wanton on your cheek, call you his mouse, 190
And let him, for a pair of reechy kisses,
Or paddling in your neck with his damned fingers,
Make you to ravel all this matter out
That I essentially am not in madness,
But mad in craft. 'Twere good you let him know, 195
For who that's but a queen, fair, sober, wise,
Would from a paddock, from a bat, a gib,
Such dear concernings hide? Who would do so?
No, in despite of sense and secrecy,
Unpeg the basket on the house's top, 200
Let the birds fly, and like the famous ape,
To try conclusions, in the basket creep
And break your own neck down.

QUEEN: Be thou assured, if words be made of breath,
And breath of life, I have no life to breathe 205
What thou hast said to me.

HAMLET: I must to England. You know that?

QUEEN:　　　　　　　　　　　　Alack,
I had forgot. 'Tis so concluded on.

HAMLET: There's letters sealed, and my two
　　schoolfellows,
Whom I will trust as I will adders fanged, 210
They bear the mandate; they must sweep my way
And marshal me to knavery. Let it work.
For 'tis the sport to have the enginer

---

150 reword repeat word for word　**151 gambol** skip away　**152 unction** ointment　**154 skin** grow a skin for　**155 mining** working under the surface　**158 compost** manure　**159 this my virtue** my virtuous talk in reproving you　**160 fatness** grossness. **pursy** flabby, out of shape　**162 curb** bow, bend the knee. **leave** permission　**168 who . . . eat** which consumes all proper or natural feeling, all sensibility　**169 Of habits devil** devil-like in prompting evil habits　**171 livery** an outer appearance, a customary garb (and hence a predisposition easily assumed in time of stress)　**172 aptly** readily　**175 use** habit. **the stamp of nature** our inborn traits　**176 And either** (A defective line, usually emended by inserting the word *master* after *either,* following the Fourth Quarto and early editors.)　**178–179 when . . . you** i.e., when you are ready to be penitent and seek God's blessing, I will ask your blessing as a dutiful son should　**182 their scourge and minister** i.e., agent of heavenly retribution. (By *scourge,* Hamlet also suggests that he himself will eventually suffer punishment in the process of fulfilling heaven's will.)

---

183 bestow stow, dispose of. **answer** account or pay for　**186 This** i.e., the killing of Polonius. **behind** to come　**189 bloat** bloated　**190 Pinch wanton** i.e., leave his love pinches on your cheeks, branding you as wanton　**191 reechy** dirty, filthy　**192 paddling** fingering amorously　**193 ravel . . . out** unravel, disclose　**195 in craft** by cunning. **good** (Said sarcastically; also the following eight lines.)　**197 paddock** toad. **gib** tomcat　**198 dear concernings** important affairs　**199 sense and secrecy** secrecy that common sense requires　**200 Unpeg the basket** open the cage, i.e., let out the secret　**201 famous ape** (In a story now lost.)　**202 try conclusions** test the outcome (in which the ape apparently enters a cage from which birds have been released and then tries to fly out of the cage as they have done, falling to its death)　**203 down** in the fall; utterly　**211–212 sweep . . . knavery** sweep a path before me and conduct me to some *knavery* or treachery prepared for me　**212 work** proceed　**213 enginer** maker of military contrivances

Hoist with his own petard, and 't shall go hard
215 But I will delve one yard below their mines
And blow them at the moon. O, 'tis most sweet
When in one line two crafts directly meet.
This man shall set me packing.
I'll lug the guts into the neighbor room.
220 Mother, good night indeed. This counselor
Is now most still, most secret, and most grave,
Who was in life a foolish prating knave.—
Come, sir, to draw toward an end with you.—
Good night, Mother.

Exeunt [separately, HAMLET *dragging in* POLONIUS].

4.1 *Enter* KING *and* QUEEN, *with* ROSENCRANTZ *and* GUILDENSTERN.

KING: There's matter in these sighs, these profound heaves.
You must translate; 'tis fit we understand them.
Where is your son?

QUEEN: Bestow this place on us a little while.
[Exeunt ROSENCRANTZ *and* GUILDENSTERN.]
5 Ah, mine own lord, what have I seen tonight!

KING: What, Gertrude? How does Hamlet?

QUEEN: Mad as the sea and wind when both contend
Which is the mightier. In his lawless fit,
Behind the arras hearing something stir,
10 Whips out his rapier, cries, "A rat, a rat!"
And in this brainish apprehension kills
The unseen good old man.

KING: O heavy deed!
It had been so with us, had we been there.
His liberty is full of threats to all—

To you yourself, to us, to everyone. 15
Alas, how shall this bloody deed be answered?
It will be laid to us, whose providence
Should have kept short, restrained, and out of haunt
This mad young man. But so much was our love,
We would not understand what was most fit, 20
But, like the owner of a foul disease,
To keep it from divulging, let it feed
Even on the pith of life. Where is he gone?

QUEEN: To draw apart the body he hath killed,
O'er whom his very madness, like some ore 25
Among a mineral of metals base,
Shows itself pure: 'a weeps for what is done.

KING: O Gertrude, come away!
The sun no sooner shall the mountains touch
But we will ship him hence, and this vile deed 30
We must with all our majesty and skill
Both countenance and excuse.—Ho, Guildenstern!

Enter ROSENCRANTZ *and* GUILDENSTERN.

Friends both, go join you with some further aid.
Hamlet in madness hath Polonius slain,
And from his mother's closet hath he dragged him. 35
Go seek him out, speak fair, and bring the body
Into the chapel. I pray you, haste in this.
[Exeunt ROSENCRANTZ *and* GUILDENSTERN.]
Come, Gertrude, we'll call up our wisest friends
And let them know both what we mean to do
And what's untimely done 40
Whose whisper o'er the world's diameter,
As level as the cannon to his blank,
Transports his poisoned shot, may miss our name
And hit the woundless air. O, come away!
My soul is full of discord and dismay. *Exeunt.* 45

4.2 *Enter* HAMLET.

HAMLET: Safely stowed.

ROSENCRANTZ, GUILDENSTERN (*within*): Hamlet!
Lord Hamlet!

---

214 Hoist with blown up by.   **petard** an explosive used to blow in a door or make a breach   **214–215 't shall . . . will** unless luck is against me, I will   **215 mines** tunnels used in warfare to undermine the enemy's emplacements; Hamlet will countermine by going under their mines   **217 in one line** i.e., mines and countermines on a collision course, or the countermines directly below the mines. **crafts** acts of guile, plots   **218 set me packing** set me to making schemes, and set me to lugging (him), and, also, send me off in a hurry   **223 draw . . . end** finish up (with a pun on *draw,* "pull")

4.1. Location: The castle.
s.d. Enter . . . Queen (Some editors argue that Gertrude never exits in 3.4 and that the scene is continuous here, as suggested in the Folio, but the Second Quarto marks an entrance for her and at line 35 Claudius speaks of Gertrude's *closet* as though it were elsewhere. A short time has elapsed, during which the King has become aware of her highly wrought emotional state.)   **1 matter** significance.   **heaves** heavy sighs   **11 brainish apprehension** headstrong conception   **12 heavy** grievous   **13 us** i.e., me. (The royal "we"; also in line 15.)

16 answered explained   **17 providence** foresight   **18 short** i.e., on a short tether.   **out of haunt** secluded   **22 divulging** becoming evident   **25 ore** vein of gold   **26 mineral** mine   **32 countenance** put the best face on   **40 And . . . done** (A defective line; conjectures as to the missing words include *So, haply, slander* [Capell and others]; *For, haply, slander* [Theobald and others]; and *So envious slander* [Jenkins].)   **41 diameter** extent from side to side   **42 As level** with as direct aim.   **his blank** its target at point-blank range   **44 woundless** invulnerable

4.2. Location: The castle.

Rosencrantz and Guildenstern question Hamlet about Polonius's body.

HAMLET: But soft, what noise? Who calls on Hamlet?
5   O, here they come.

Enter ROSENCRANTZ *and* GUILDENSTERN.

ROSENCRANTZ: What have you done, my lord, with
the dead body?

HAMLET: Compounded it with dust, whereto 'tis kin.

ROSENCRANTZ: Tell us where 'tis, that we may take it
thence
And bear it to the chapel.

10 **HAMLET:** Do not believe it.

ROSENCRANTZ: Believe what?

HAMLET: That I can keep your counsel and not mine
own. Besides, to be demanded of a sponge, what
replication should be made by the son of a king?

15 **ROSENCRANTZ:** Take you me for a sponge, my lord?

HAMLET: Ay, sir, that soaks up the King's countenance, his rewards, his authorities. But such officers
do the King best service in the end. He keeps them,
like an ape, an apple, in the corner of his jaw,
20   first mouthed to be last swallowed. When he needs
what you have gleaned, it is but squeezing you, and,
sponge, you shall be dry again.

ROSENCRANTZ: I understand you not, my lord.

HAMLET: I am glad of it. A knavish speech sleeps in a
25   foolish ear.

ROSENCRANTZ: My lord, you must tell us where the
body is and go with us to the King.

12–13 That . . . own i.e., that I can follow your advice (by telling
where the body is) and still keep my own secret   **13 demanded of**
questioned by   **14 replication** reply   **16–17 countenance** favor
17 authorities delegated power, influence   **24 sleeps in** has no
meaning to

HAMLET: The body is with the King, but the King is
not with the body. The King is a thing—

GUILDENSTERN: A thing, my lord?   30

HAMLET: Of nothing. Bring me to him. Hide fox,
and all after!   *Exeunt [running].*

4.3   *Enter* KING, *and two or three.*

KING: I have sent to seek him, and to find the body.
How dangerous is it that this man goes loose!
Yet must not we put the strong law on him.
He's loved of the distracted multitude,
Who like not in their judgment, but their eyes,   5
And where 'tis so, th' offender's scourge is weighed,
But never the offense. To bear all smooth and even,
This sudden sending him away must seem
Deliberate pause. Diseases desperate grown
By desperate appliance are relieved,   10
Or not at all.

Enter ROSENCRANTZ, *[GUILDENSTERN,]*
and all the rest.

How now, what hath befall'n?

ROSENCRANTZ: Where the dead body is bestowed,
my lord,
We cannot get from him.

KING: But where is he?

ROSENCRANTZ: Without, my lord; guarded, to know
your pleasure.

KING: Bring him before us.

ROSENCRANTZ: Ho! Bring in the lord.   15

They enter [with HAMLET*].*

28–29 The . . . body (Perhaps alludes to the legal commonplace
of "the king's two bodies," which drew a distinction between the
sacred office of kingship and the particular mortal who possessed
it at any given time. Hence, although Claudius' body is necessarily a
part of him, true kingship is not contained in it. Similarly, Claudius
will have Polonius' body when it is found, but there is no kingship in
this business either.)   **31 Of nothing** (1) of no account (2) lacking
the essence of kingship, as in lines 28–29 and note   **31–32 Hide . . .**
after (An old signal cry in the game of hide-and-seek, suggesting
that Hamlet now runs away from them.)

4.3. Location: The castle.
4 of by.   **distracted** fickle, unstable   **5 Who . . . eyes** who choose
not by judgment but by appearance   **6 scourge** punishment. (Literally, blow with a whip.)   **weighed** sympathetically considered
7 To . . . even to manage the business in an unprovocative way
9 Deliberate pause carefully considered action   **10 appliance**
remedies

Claudius asks Hamlet about Polonius.

KING: Now, Hamlet, where's Polonius?

HAMLET: At supper.

KING: At supper? Where?

HAMLET: Not where he eats, but where 'a is eaten.
20 A certain convocation of politic worms are e'en at
him. Your worm is your only emperor for diet. We
fat all creatures else to fat us, and we fat ourselves
for maggots. Your fat king and your lean beggar is
but variable service—two dishes, but to one table.
25 That's the end.

KING: Alas, alas!

HAMLET: A man may fish with the worm that hath
eat of a king, and eat of the fish that hath fed of that
worm.

30 **KING:** What dost thou mean by this?

HAMLET: Nothing but to show you how a king may go
a progress through the guts of a beggar.

KING: Where is Polonius?

HAMLET: In heaven. Send thither to see. If your mes-
35 senger find him not there, seek him i' th' other place
yourself. But if indeed you find him not within this
month, you shall nose him as you go up the stairs
into the lobby.

KING [to some attendants]: Go seek him there.

40 **HAMLET:** 'A will stay till you come. [Exeunt attendants.]

KING: Hamlet, this deed, for thine especial safety—
Which we do tender, as we dearly grieve
For that which thou hast done—must send thee
hence
With fiery quickness. Therefore prepare thyself.
The bark is ready, and the wind at help, 45
Th' associates tend, and everything is bent
For England.

HAMLET: For England!

KING: Ay, Hamlet.

HAMLET: Good. 50

KING: So is it, if thou knew'st our purposes.

HAMLET: I see a cherub that sees them. But come, for
England! Farewell, dear mother.

KING: Thy loving father, Hamlet.

HAMLET: My mother. Father and mother is man and 55
wife, man and wife is one flesh, and so, my mother.
Come, for England! *Exit.*

KING: Follow him at foot; tempt him with speed
aboard.
Delay it not. I'll have him hence tonight.
Away! For everything is sealed and done 60
That else leans on th' affair. Pray you, make haste.
[*Exeunt all but the* KING.]
And, England, if my love thou hold'st at aught—
As my great power thereof may give thee sense,
Since yet thy cicatrice looks raw and red
After the Danish sword, and thy free awe 65
Pays homage to us—thou mayst not coldly set
Our sovereign process, which imports at full,
By letters conjuring to that effect,
The present death of Hamlet. Do it, England,
For like the hectic in my blood he rages, 70
And thou must cure me. Till I know 'tis done,
Howe'er my haps, my joys were ne'er begun *Exit.*

---

20 **politic worms** crafty worms (suited to a master spy like Polonius). **e'en** even now 21 **Your worm** your average worm. (Compare *your fat king and your lean beggar* in line 23.) **diet** food,
eating (with a punning reference to the Diet of Worms, a famous
convocation held in 1521) 24 **variable service** different courses of
a single meal 28 **eat** eaten (Pronounced *et.*) 32 **progress** royal
journey of state

42 **tender** regard, hold dear. **dearly** intensely 45 **bark** sailing
vessel 46 **tend** wait. **bent** in readiness 52 **cherub** (Cherubim
are angels of knowledge. Hamlet hints that both he and heaven are
onto Claudius' tricks.) 58 **at foot** close behind, at heel 61 **leans
on** bears upon, is related to 62 **England** i.e., King of England.
at aught at any value 63 **As . . . sense** for so my great power
may give you a just appreciation of the importance of valuing
my love 64 **cicatrice** scar 65 **free awe** voluntary show of
respect 66 **coldly set** regard with indifference 67 **process**
command. **imports at full** conveys specific directions for 68
conjuring agreeing 69 **present** immediate 70 **hectic** persistent
fever 72 **haps** fortunes

4.4   *Enter* FORTINBRAS *with his army over the stage.*

FORTINBRAS: Go, Captain, from me greet the Danish
      king.
    Tell him that by his license Fortinbras
    Craves the conveyance of a promised march
    Over his kingdom. You know the rendezvous.
5   If that His Majesty would aught with us,
    We shall express our duty in his eye;
    And let him know so.

CAPTAIN: I will do 't, my lord

FORTINBRAS: Go softly on.

          [Exeunt all but the CAPTAIN.*]*

       Enter HAMLET, ROSENCRANTZ,
       *[*GUILDENSTERN,*] etc.*

10 **HAMLET:**   Good sir, whose powers are these?

CAPTAIN: They are of Norway, sir.

HAMLET: How purposed, sir, I pray you?

CAPTAIN: Against some part of Poland.

HAMLET: Who commands them, sir?

15 **CAPTAIN:**   The nephew to old Norway, Fortinbras.

HAMLET: Goes it against the main of Poland, sir,
    Or for some frontier?

CAPTAIN: Truly to speak, and with no addition,
    We go to gain a little patch of ground
20   That hath in it no profit but the name.
    To pay five ducats, five, I would not farm it;
    Nor will it yield to Norway or the Pole
    A ranker rate, should it be sold in fee.

HAMLET: Why, then the Polack never will defend it.

25 **CAPTAIN:**   Yes, it is already garrisoned.

HAMLET: Two thousand souls and twenty thousand
      ducats
    Will not debate the question of this straw.
    This is th' impostume of much wealth and peace,
    That inward breaks, and shows no cause without
30   Why the man dies. I humbly thank you, sir.

CAPTAIN: God b' wi' you, sir.   *[Exit.]*

ROSENCRANTZ: Will 't please you go, my lord?

HAMLET: I'll be with you straight. Go a little before.
          [Exeunt all except HAMLET.*]*
    How all occasions do inform against me
    And spur my dull revenge! What is a man,
    If his chief good and market of his time   35
    Be but to sleep and feed? A beast, no more.
    Sure he that made us with such large discourse,
    Looking before and after, gave us not
    That capability and godlike reason
    To fust in us unused. Now, whether it be   40
    Bestial oblivion, or some craven scruple
    Of thinking too precisely on th' event—
    A thought which, quartered, hath but one part
      wisdom
    And ever three parts coward—I do not know
    Why yet I live to say "This thing's to do,"   45
    Sith I have cause, and will, and strength, and means
    To do 't. Examples gross as earth exhort me:
    Witness this army of such mass and charge,
    Led by a delicate and tender prince,
    Whose spirit with divine ambition puffed   50
    Makes mouths at the invisible event,
    Exposing what is mortal and unsure
    To all that fortune, death, and danger dare,
    Even for an eggshell. Rightly to be great
    Is not to stir without great argument,   55
    But greatly to find quarrel in a straw
    When honor's at the stake. How stand I, then,
    That have a father killed, a mother stained,
    Excitements of my reason and my blood,
    And let all sleep, while to my shame I see   60
    The imminent death of twenty thousand men
    That for a fantasy and trick of fame
    Go to their graves like beds, fight for a plot

4.4. Location: The coast of Denmark.
2 license permission   **3 the conveyance of** escort during   **6 duty** respect.   **eye** presence   **9 softly** slowly, circumspectly   **10 powers** forces   **16 main** main part   **18 addition** exaggeration   **21 To pay** i.e., for a yearly rental of.   **farm it** take a lease of it   **23 ranker** higher.   **in fee** fee simple, outright   **27 debate . . . straw** settle this trifling matter   **28 impostume** abscess

---

33 inform against denounce, betray; take shape against   **35 market of** profit of, compensation for   **37 discourse** power of reasoning   **38 Looking before and after** able to review past events and anticipate the future   **40 fust** grow moldy   **41 oblivion** forgetfulness.   **craven** cowardly   **42 precisely** scrupulously.   **event** outcome   **46 Sith** since   **47 gross** obvious   **48 charge** expense   **49 delicate and tender** of fine and youthful qualities   **51 Makes mouths** makes scornful faces.   **invisible event** unforeseeable outcome   **53 dare** could do (to him)   **54–57 Rightly . . . stake** true greatness does not normally consist of rushing into action over some trivial provocation; however, when one's honor is involved, even a trifling insult requires that one respond greatly (?)   **57 at the stake** (A metaphor from gambling or bear-baiting.)   **59 Excitements of** promptings by   **62 fantasy** fanciful caprice, illusion.   **trick** trifle, deceit   **63 plot** plot of ground

Whereon the numbers cannot try the cause,
65   Which is not tomb enough and continent
To hide the slain? O, from this time forth
My thoughts be bloody or be nothing worth!   *Exit.*

4.5   *Enter* HORATIO, [QUEEN] GERTRUDE, *and a*
GENTLEMAN.

QUEEN: I will not speak with her.

GENTLEMAN: She is importunate,
Indeed distract. Her mood will needs be pitied.

QUEEN: What would she have?

GENTLEMAN: She speaks much of her father, says she
hears
5   There's tricks i' the world, and hems, and beats her
heart,
Spurns enviously at straws, speaks things in doubt
That carry but half sense. Her speech is nothing,
Yet the unshapèd use of it doth move
The hearers to collection; they yawn at it,
10   And botch the words up fit to their own thoughts,
Which, as her winks and nods and gestures yield
them,
Indeed would make one think there might be
thought,
Though nothing sure, yet much unhappily.

HORATIO: 'Twere good she were spoken with, for she
may strew
15   Dangerous conjectures in ill-breeding minds.

QUEEN: Let her come in.   *[Exit* GENTLEMAN.*]*
[Aside.] To my sick soul, as sin's true nature is,
Each toy seems prologue to some great amiss.
So full of artless jealousy is guilt,
20   It spills itself in fearing to be spilt.

Enter OPHELIA *[distracted].*

---

64 **Whereon . . . cause** on which there is insufficient room for the
soldiers needed to engage in a military contest   65 **continent**
receptacle, container

4.5. Location: The castle.
2 **distract** distracted   5 **tricks** deceptions.   **hems** makes "hmm"
sounds.   **heart** i.e., breast   6 **Spurns . . . straws** kicks spitefully,
takes offense at trifles.   **in doubt** obscurely   8 **unshapèd use**
incoherent manner   9 **collection** inference, a guess at some sort of
meaning.   **yawn** gape, wonder; grasp. (The Folio reading, *aim*, is
possible.)   10 **botch** patch   11 **Which** which words.   **yield** deliver,
represent   12 **thought** intended   13 **unhappily** unpleasantly near
the truth, shrewdly   15 **ill-breeding** prone to suspect the worst
and to make mischief   18 **toy** trifle.   **amiss** calamity   19–20 **So
. . . spilt** guilt is so full of suspicion that it unskillfully betrays itself
in fearing betrayal   20 s.d. **Enter Ophelia** (In the First Quarto,
Ophelia enters, "playing on a lute, and her hair down, singing.")

OPHELIA: Where is the beauteous majesty of
Denmark?

QUEEN: How now, Ophelia?

OPHELIA *(she sings)*:
"How should I your true love know
From another one?
By his cockle hat and staff,   25
And his sandal shoon."

QUEEN: Alas, sweet lady, what imports this song?

OPHELIA: Say you? Nay, pray you, mark.
"He is dead and gone, lady,   *(Song.)*
He is dead and gone;   30
At his head a grass-green turf,
At his heels a stone."
O, ho!

QUEEN: Nay, but Ophelia—

OPHELIA: Pray you, mark.   35
[Sings.] "White his shroud as the mountain snow"—

Enter KING.

QUEEN: Alas, look here, my lord.

OPHELIA: "Larded with sweet flowers;   *(Song.)*
Which bewept to the ground did not go
With true-love showers."   40

KING: How do you, pretty lady?

OPHELIA: Well, God 'ild you! They say the owl was a
baker's daughter. Lord, we know what we are, but
know not what we may be. God be at your table!

KING: Conceit upon her father.   45

OPHELIA: Pray let's have no words of this; but when
they ask you what it means, say you this:
"Tomorrow is Saint Valentine's day,   *(Song.)*
All in the morning betime,
And I a maid at your window,   50
To be your Valentine.
Then up he rose, and donned his clothes,
And dupped the chamber door,
Let in the maid, that out a maid
Never departed more."   55

---

25 **cockle hat** hat with cockleshell stuck in it as a sign that the
wearer had been a pilgrim to the shrine of Saint James of Com-
postela in Spain   26 **shoon** shoes   38 **Larded** decorated   40
showers i.e., tears   42 **God 'ild** God yield or reward.   **owl** (Refers
to a legend about a baker's daughter who was turned into an owl for
being ungenerous when Jesus begged a loaf of bread.)   45 **Conceit**
brooding   49 **betime** early   53 **dupped** did up, opened

Ophelia (Diane Venora), having gone mad, speaks to the king and queen.

KING: Pretty Ophelia—

OPHELIA: Indeed, la, without an oath, I'll make an
end on 't:
    [Sings.] "By Gis and by Saint Charity,
60   Alack, and fie for shame!
    You men will do 't, if they come to 't;
        By Cock, they are to blame.
    Quoth she, 'Before you tumbled me,
        You promised me to wed.'"
65 He answers:
    "'So would I ha' done, by yonder sun,
    An thou hadst not come to my bed.'"

KING: How long hath she been thus?

OPHELIA: I hope all will be well. We must be patient,
70 but I cannot choose but weep to think they would lay
him i' the cold ground. My brother shall know of it.
And so I thank you for your good counsel. Come, my
coach! Good night, ladies, good night, sweet ladies,
good night, good night.   *[Exit.]*

75 **KING** *[to* HORATIO*]:*   Follow her close. Give her good
watch, I pray you.
                      [Exit HORATIO.*]*
O, this is the poison of deep grief; it springs
All from her father's death—and now behold!
O Gertrude, Gertrude,
When sorrows come, they come not single spies,
80 But in battalions. First, her father slain;
Next, your son gone, and he most violent author

Of his own just remove; the people muddied,
Thick and unwholesome in their thoughts and
    whispers
For good Polonius' death—and we have done but
    greenly,
In hugger-mugger to inter him; poor Ophelia   85
Divided from herself and her fair judgment,
Without the which we are pictures or mere beasts;
Last, and as much containing as all these,
Her brother is in secret come from France,
Feeds on this wonder, keeps himself in clouds,   90
And wants not buzzers to infect his ear
With pestilent speeches of his father's death,
Wherein necessity, of matter beggared,
Will nothing stick our person to arraign
In ear and ear. O my dear Gertrude, this,   95
Like to a murdering piece, in many places
Gives me superfluous death.   *A noise within.*

QUEEN: Alack, what noise is this?

KING: Attend!
Where is my Switzers? Let them guard the door.   100
                Enter a MESSENGER.
What is the matter?

MESSENGER: Save yourself, my lord!
The ocean, overpeering of his list,
Eats not the flats with more impetuous haste
Than young Laertes, in a riotous head,
O'erbears your officers. The rabble call him lord,   105
And, as the world were now but to begin,
Antiquity forgot, custom not known,
The ratifiers and props of every word,
They cry, "Choose we! Laertes shall be king!"
Caps, hands, and tongues applaud it to the clouds,   110
"Laertes shall be king, Laertes king!"

---

59 **Gis** Jesus   62 **Cock** (A perversion of "God" in oaths; here also
with a quibble on the slang word for penis.)   67 **An** if   79 **spies**
scouts sent in advance of the main force

---

82 **remove** removal. **muddied** stirred up, confused   84 **greenly**
in an inexperienced way, foolishly   85 **hugger-mugger** secret
haste   88 **as much containing** as full of serious matter   90 **Feeds
. . . clouds** feeds his resentment or shocked grievance, holds himself inscrutable and aloof amid all this rumor   91 **wants** lacks.
buzzers gossipers, informers   93 **necessity** i.e., the need to invent
some plausible explanation. **of matter beggared** unprovided
with facts   94–95 **Will . . . ear** will not hesitate to accuse my
(royal) person in everybody's ears   96 **murdering piece** cannon
loaded so as to scatter its shot   97 **Gives . . . death** kills me over
and over   99 **Attend** i.e., guard me   100 **Switzers** Swiss guards,
mercenaries   102 **overpeering of his list** overflowing its shore,
boundary   103 **flats** i.e., flatlands near shore. **impetuous** violent
(perhaps also with the meaning of *impiteous* [*impitious*, Q2], "pitiless")   104 **head** insurrection   106 **as** as if   108 **The ratifiers . . .
word** i.e., *antiquity* (or tradition) and *custom* ought to confirm
(*ratify*) and underprop our every word or promise   110 **Caps** (The
caps are thrown in the air.)

QUEEN: How cheerfully on the false trail they cry!

A noise within.

O, this is counter, you false Danish dogs!

Enter LAERTES *with others.*

KING: The doors are broke.

115   **LAERTES:**   Where is this King?—Sirs, stand you all
without.

ALL: No, let's come in.

LAERTES: I pray you, give me leave.

ALL: We will, we will.

LAERTES: I thank you. Keep the door. *[Exeunt
followers.]* O thou vile king,

120   Give me my father!

QUEEN *[restraining him]*:   Calmly, good Laertes.

LAERTES: That drop of blood that's calm proclaims
me bastard,
Cries cuckold to my father, brands the harlot
Even here, between the chaste unsmirchèd brow
Of my true mother.

KING: What is the cause, Laertes,

125   That thy rebellion looks so giantlike?
Let him go, Gertrude. Do not fear our person.
There's such divinity doth hedge a king
That treason can but peep to what it would,
Acts little of his will. Tell me, Laertes,

130   Why thou art thus incensed. Let him go, Gertrude.
Speak, man.

LAERTES: Where is my father?

KING: Dead.

QUEEN: But not by him.

KING: Let him demand his fill.

LAERTES: How came he dead? I'll not be juggled with.
To hell, allegiance! Vows, to the blackest devil!

135   Conscience and grace, to the profoundest pit!
I dare damnation. To this point I stand,

Ophelia, driven mad, approaches the king and queen.

That both the worlds I give to negligence,
Let come what comes, only I'll be revenged
Most throughly for my father.

KING: Who shall stay you?   140

LAERTES: My will, not all the world's.
And for my means, I'll husband them so well
They shall go far with little.

KING: Good Laertes,
If you desire to know the certainty
Of your dear father, is 't writ in your revenge   145
That, swoopstake, you will draw both friend and foe,
Winner and loser?

LAERTES: None but his enemies.

KING: Will you know them, then?

LAERTES: To his good friends thus wide I'll ope my
arms,   150
And like the kind life-rendering pelican
Repast them with my blood.

KING: Why, now you speak
Like a good child and a true gentleman.
That I am guiltless of your father's death,
And am most sensibly in grief for it,   155
It shall as level to your judgment 'pear
As day does to your eye.   *A noise within.*

LAERTES: How now, what noise is that?

---

113 counter (A hunting term, meaning to follow the trail in a direction opposite to that which the game has taken.)   **123 between** in the middle of   **126 fear our** fear for my   **127 hedge** protect, as with a surrounding barrier   **128 can . . . would** can only peep furtively, as through a barrier, at what it would intend   **129 Acts . . . will** (but) performs little of what it intends   **133 juggled with** cheated, deceived   **136 To . . . stand** I am resolved in this

---

137 both . . . negligence i.e., both this world and the next are of no consequence to me   **139 throughly** thoroughly   **141 My will . . . world's** I'll stop (*stay*) when my will is accomplished, not for anyone else's   **142 for** as for   **146 swoopstake** i.e., indiscriminately. (Literally, taking all stakes on the gambling table at once. *Draw* is also a gambling term, meaning "take from.")   **151 pelican** (Refers to the belief that the female pelican fed its young with its own blood.)   **152 Repast** feed   **155 sensibly** feelingly   **156 level** plain

Enter OPHELIA.

KING: Let her come in.

LAERTES: O heat, dry up my brains! Tears seven times salt
160 Burn out the sense and virtue of mine eye!
By heaven, thy madness shall be paid with weight
Till our scale turn the beam. O rose of May!
Dear maid, kind sister, sweet Ophelia!
O heavens, is 't possible a young maid's wits
165 Should be as mortal as an old man's life?
Nature is fine in love, and where 'tis fine
It sends some precious instance of itself
After the thing it loves.

OPHELIA: "They bore him barefaced on the bier, *(Song.)*
170 Hey non nonny, nonny, hey nonny,
And in his grave rained many a tear—"
Fare you well, my dove!

LAERTES: Hadst thou thy wits and didst persuade revenge,
It could not move thus.

175 **OPHELIA:** You must sing "A-down a-down," and you
"call him a-down-a." O, how the wheel becomes it! It
is the false steward that stole his master's daughter.

LAERTES: This nothing's more than matter.

OPHELIA: There's rosemary, that's for remembrance;
180 pray you, love, remember. And there is pansies; that's
for thoughts.

LAERTES: A document in madness, thoughts and
remembrance fitted.

OPHELIA: There's fennel for you, and columbines.
185 There's rue for you, and here's some for me; we may
call it herb of grace o' Sundays. You must wear your

rue with a difference. There's a daisy. I would give
you some violets, but they withered all when my
father died. They say 'a made a good end— *[Sings.]*
"For bonny sweet Robin is all my joy." 190

LAERTES: Thought and affliction, passion, hell itself,
She turns to favor and to prettiness.

OPHELIA: "And will 'a not come again? *(Song.)*
And will 'a not come again?
No, no, he is head. 195
Go to thy deathbed,
He never will come again.

"His beard was as white as snow,
All flaxen was his poll.
He is gone, he is gone, 200
And we cast away moan.
God ha' mercy on his soul!"
And of all Christian souls, I pray God. God b' wi' you.
[Exit, followed by GERTRUDE.*]*

LAERTES: Do you see this, O God?

KING: Laertes, I must commune with your grief, 205
Or you deny me right. Go but apart,
Make choice of whom your wisest friends you will,
And they shall hear and judge twixt you and me.
If by direct or by collateral hand
They find us touched, we will our kingdom give, 210
Our crown, our life, and all that we call ours
To you in satisfaction; but if not,
Be you content to lend your patience to us,
And we shall jointly labor with your soul
To give it due content.

LAERTES: Let this be so. 215
His means of death, his obscure funeral—
No trophy, sword, nor hatchment o'er his bones,
No noble rite, nor formal ostentation—
Cry to be heard, as 'twere from heaven to earth,
That I must call 't in question. 220

160 virtue faculty, power **161 paid with weight** repaid, avenged equally or more **162 beam** crossbar of a balance **166 fine in** refined by **167 instance** token **168 After . . . loves** i.e., into the grave, along with Polonius **173 persuade** argue cogently for **175–176 You . . . a-down-a** (Ophelia assigns the singing of refrains, like her own "Hey non nonny," to others present.) **176 wheel** spinning wheel as accompaniment to the song, or refrain **177 false steward** (The story is unknown.) **178 This . . . matter** this seeming nonsense is more eloquent than sane utterance **179 rosemary** (Used as a symbol of remembrance both at weddings and at funerals.) **180 pansies** (Emblems of love and courtship; perhaps from French *pensées*, "thoughts.") **182 document** instruction, lesson **184 fennel** (Emblem of flattery.) **columbines** (Emblems of unchastity or ingratitude.) **185 rue** (Emblem of repentance—a signification that is evident in its popular name, *herb of grace*.)

187 with a difference (A device used in heraldry to distinguish one family from another on the coat of arms, here suggesting that Ophelia and the others have different causes of sorrow and repentance; perhaps with a play on *rue* in the sense of "ruth," "pity.") **daisy** (Emblem of dissembling, faithlessness.) **188 violets** (Emblems of faithfulness.) **191 Thought** melancholy. **passion** suffering **192 favor** grace, beauty **199 poll** head **207 whom** whichever of **209 collateral hand** indirect agency **210 us touched** me implicated **217 trophy** memorial. **hatchment** tablet displaying the armorial bearings of a deceased person **218 ostentation** ceremony **220 That** so that. **call 't in question** demand an explanation

KING: So you shall,
And where th' offense is, let the great ax fall.
I pray you, go with me.   *Exeunt.*

4.6   *Enter* HORATIO *and others.*

HORATIO: What are they that would speak with me?

GENTLEMAN: Seafaring men, sir. They say they have
letters for you.

HORATIO: Let them come in.   *[Exit* GENTLEMAN.*]*
5   I do not know from what part of the world
I should be greeted, if not from Lord Hamlet.

Enter SAILORS.

FIRST SAILOR: God bless you, sir.

HORATIO: Let him bless thee too.

FIRST SAILOR: 'A shall, sir, an 't please him. There's a
10   letter for you, sir—it came from th' ambassador that
was bound for England—if your name be Horatio, as
I am let to know it is.   *[He gives a letter.]*

HORATIO *[reads]:*   "Horatio, when thou shalt have overlooked this, give these fellows some means to
15   the King; they have letters for him. Ere we were two
days old at sea, a pirate of very warlike appointment
gave us chase. Finding ourselves too slow of sail,
we put on a compelled valor, and in the grapple I
boarded them. On the instant they got clear of our
20   ship, so I alone became their prisoner. They have
dealt with me like thieves of mercy, but they knew
what they did: I am to do a good turn for them. Let
the King have the letters I have sent, and repair thou
to me with as much speed as thou wouldest fly death.
25   I have words to speak in thine ear will make thee
dumb, yet are they much too light for the bore of the
matter. These good fellows will bring thee where I
am. Rosencrantz and Guildenstern hold their course
for England. Of them I have much to tell thee.
30   Farewell.

He that thou knowest thine, Hamlet."
Come, I will give you way for these your letters,
And do 't the speedier that you may direct me
To him from whom you brought them.   *Exeunt.*

4.6. Location: The castle.
9 an 't if it   **10 th' ambassador** (Evidently Hamlet. The sailor is
being circumspect.)   **13–14 overlooked** looked over   **14 means**
means of access   **16 appointment** equipage   **21 thieves of mercy**
merciful thieves   **23 repair** come   **26 bore** caliber, i.e., importance   **31 way** means of access

4.7   *Enter* KING *and* LAERTES.

KING: Now must your conscience my acquittance seal,
And you must put me in your heart for friend,
Sith you have heard, and with a knowing ear,
That he which hath your noble father slain
Pursued my life.

LAERTES: It well appears. But tell me   5
Why you proceeded not against these feats
So crimeful and so capital in nature,
As by your safety, greatness, wisdom, all things else,
You mainly were stirred up.

KING: O, for two special reasons,   10
Which may to you perhaps seem much unsinewed,
But yet to me they're strong. The Queen his mother
Lives almost by his looks, and for myself—
My virtue or my plague, be it either which—
She is so conjunctive to my life and soul   15
That, as the star moves not but in his sphere,
I could not but by her. The other motive
Why to a public count I might not go
Is the great love the general gender bear him,
Who, dipping all his faults in their affection,   20
Work like the spring that turneth wood to stone,
Convert his gyves to graces, so that my arrows,
Too slightly timbered for so loud a wind,
Would have reverted to my bow again
But not where I had aimed them.   25

LAERTES: And so have I a noble father lost,
A sister driven into desperate terms,
Whose worth, if praises may go back again,
Stood challenger on mount of all the age
For her perfections. But my revenge will come.   30

KING: Break not your sleeps for that. You must not
think
That we are made of stuff so flat and dull
That we can let our beard be shook with danger
And think it pastime. You shortly shall hear more.

4.7. Location: The castle.
1 my acquittance seal confirm or acknowledge my innocence   **3
Sith** since   **6 feats** acts   **7 capital** punishable by death   **9 mainly**
greatly   **11 unsinewed** weak   **15 conjunctive** closely united. (An
astronomical metaphor.)   **16 his** its.   **sphere** one of the hollow
spheres in which, according to Ptolemaic astronomy, the planets
were supposed to move   **18 count** account, reckoning, indictment
19 general gender common people   **21 Work** operate, act.
spring i.e., a spring with such a concentration of lime that it coats
a piece of wood with limestone, in effect gilding and petrifying it
22 gyves fetters (which, gilded by the people's praise, would look
like badges of honor)   **23 slightly timbered** light.   **loud** (suggesting public outcry on Hamlet's behalf)   **24 reverted** returned
27 terms state, condition   **28 go back** i.e., recall what she was
29 on mount set up on high

35 I loved your father, and we love ourself;
And that, I hope, will teach you to imagine—

Enter a MESSENGER *with letters.*

How now? What news?

MESSENGER: Letters, my lord, from Hamlet:
This to Your Majesty, this to the Queen.

[He gives letters.]

KING: From Hamlet? Who brought them?

40 **MESSENGER:** Sailors, my lord, they say. I saw them not.
They were given me by Claudio. He received them
Of him that brought them.

KING: Laertes, you shall hear them.—
Leave us. *[Exit MESSENGER.]*
[He reads.] "High and mighty, you shall know I am set
45 naked on your kingdom. Tomorrow shall I beg leave
to see your kingly eyes, when I shall, first asking your
pardon, thereunto recount the occasion of my sudden and more strange return. Hamlet."
What should this mean? Are all the rest come back?
50 Or is it some abuse, and no such thing?

LAERTES: Know you the hand?

KING: 'Tis Hamlet's character. "Naked"!
And in a postscript here he says "alone."
Can you devise me?

LAERTES: I am lost in it, my lord. But let him come.
55 It warms the very sickness in my heart
That I shall live and tell him to this teeth,
"Thus didst thou."

KING: If it be so, Laertes—
As how should it be so? How otherwise?—
Will you be ruled by me?

LAERTES: Ay, my lord,
60 So you will not o'errule me to a peace.

KING: To thine own peace. If he be now returned,
As checking at his voyage, and that he means
No more to undertake it, I will work him
To an exploit, now ripe in my device,
65 Under the which he shall not choose but fall;
And for his death no wind of blame shall breathe,

Claudius and Laertes (Michael Cumpsty) read Hamlet's letters.

But even his mother shall uncharge the practice
And call it accident.

LAERTES: My lord, I will be ruled,
The rather if you could devise it so
That I might be the organ.

KING: It falls right. 70
You have been talked of since your travel much,
And that in Hamlet's hearing, for a quality
Wherein they say you shine. Your sum of parts
Did not together pluck such envy from him
As did that one, and that, in my regard, 75
Of the unworthiest siege.

LAERTES: What part is that, my lord?

KING: A very ribbon in the cap of youth,
Yet needful too, for youth no less becomes
The light and careless livery that it wears 80
Than settled age his sables and his weeds
Importing health and graveness. Two months since
Here was a gentleman of Normandy.
I have seen myself, and served against, the French,
And they can well on horseback, but this gallant 85
Had witchcraft in 't; he grew unto his seat,
And to such wondrous doing brought his horse
As had he been incorpsed and demi-natured

---

45 naked destitute, unarmed, without following **47 pardon** permission **50 abuse** deceit. **no such thing** not what it appears **51 character** handwriting **53 devise** explain to **57 Thus didst thou** i.e., here's for what you did to my father **58 As . . . otherwise** how can this (Hamlet's return) be true? Yet how otherwise than true (since we have the evidence of his letter)? **60 So** provided that **62 checking at** i.e., turning aside from (like a falcon leaving the quarry to fly at a chance bird). **that** if **64 device** devising, invention

---

67 uncharge the practice acquit the stratagem of being a plot **70 organ** agent, instrument **73 Your . . . parts** i.e., all your other virtues **76 unworthiest siege** least important rank **79 no less becomes** is no less suited by **81 his sables** its rich robes furred with sable. **weeds** garments **82 Importing . . . graveness** signifying a concern for health and dignified prosperity; also, giving an impression of comfortable prosperity **85 can well** are skilled **88 As . . . demi-natured** as if he had been of one body and nearly of one nature (like the centaur)

Claudius persuades Laertes to his plans.

With the brass beast. So far he topped my thought
90 That I in forgery of shapes and tricks
Come short of what he did.

LAERTES: A Norman was 't?

KING: A Norman.

LAERTES: Upon my life, Lamord.

KING: The very same.

LAERTES: I know him well. He is the brooch indeed
95 And gem of all the nation.

KING: He made confession of you,
And gave you such a masterly report
For art and exercise in your defense,
And for your rapier most especial,
100 That he cried out 'twould be a sight indeed
If one could match you. Th' escrimers of their nation,
He swore, had neither motion, guard, nor eye
If you opposed them. Sir, this report of his
Did Hamlet so envenom with his envy
105 That he could nothing do but wish and beg
Your sudden coming o'er, to play with you.
Now, out of this—

LAERTES: What out of this, my lord?

KING: Laertes, was your father dear to you?
Or are you like the painting of a sorrow,
110 A face without a heart?

LAERTES: Why ask you this?

KING: Not that I think you did not love your father,
But that I know love is begun by time,
And that I see, in passages of proof,
Time qualifies the spark and fire of it.
115 There lives within the very flame of love
A kind of wick or snuff that will abate it,
And nothing is at a like goodness still,
For goodness, growing to a pleurisy,
Dies in his own too much. That we would do,
120 We should do when we would; for this "would" changes
And hath abatements and delays as many
As there are tongues, are hands, are accidents,
And then this "should" is like a spendthrift sigh,
That hurts by easing. But, to the quick o' th' ulcer:
125 Hamlet comes back. What would you undertake
To show yourself in deed your father's son
More than in words?

LAERTES: To cut his throat i' the church.

KING: No place, indeed, should murder sanctuarize;
Revenge should have no bounds. But good Laertes,
130 Will you do this, keep close within your chamber.
Hamlet returned shall know you are come home.
We'll put on those shall praise your excellence
And set a double varnish on the fame
The Frenchman gave you, bring you in fine together,
135 And wager on your heads. He, being remiss,
Most generous, and free from all contriving,
Will not peruse the foils, so that with ease,
Or with a little shuffling, you may choose
A sword unbated, and in a pass of practice
Requite him for your father.

LAERTES: I will do 't,
140 And for that purpose I'll anoint my sword.

---

89 topped surpassed   90 forgery imagining   94 brooch ornament
96 confession testimonial, admission of superiority   98 For . . .
defense with respect to your skill and practice with your weapon
101 escrimers fencers   106 sudden immediate.   play fence

112 begun by time i.e., created by the right circumstance and
hence subject to change   113 passages of proof actual instances
that prove it   114 qualifies weakens, moderates   116 snuff
the charred part of a candlewick   117 nothing . . . still nothing
remains at a constant level of perfection   118 pleurisy excess,
plethora. (Literally, a chest inflammation.)   119 in . . . much of its
own excess.   That that which   121 abatements diminutions   122
As . . . accidents as there are tongues to dissuade, hands to prevent,
and chance events to intervene   123 spendthrift sigh (An allusion
to the belief that sighs draw blood from the heart.)   124 hurts by
easing i.e., costs the heart blood and wastes precious opportunity
even while it affords emotional relief.   quick o' th' ulcer i.e., heart
of the matter   128 sanctuarize protect from punishment. (Alludes
to the right of sanctuary with which certain religious places were
invested.)   130 Will you do this if you wish to do this   132 put on
those shall arrange for some to   134 in fine finally   135 remiss
negligently unsuspicious   136 generous noble-minded   139 unbated not blunted, having no button.   pass of practice treacherous
thrust

I bought an unction of a mountebank
So mortal that, but dip a knife in it,
Where it draws blood no cataplasm so rare,
145 Collected from all simples that have virtue
Under the moon, can save the thing from death
That is but scratched withal. I'll touch my point
With this contagion, that if I gall him slightly,
It may be death.

KING: Let's further think of this,
150 Weigh what convenience both of time and means
May fit us to our shape. If this should fail,
And that our drift look through our bad
        performance,
'Twere better not assayed. Therefore this project
Should have a back or second, that might hold
155 If this did blast in proof. Soft, let me see.
We'll make a solemn wager on your cunnings—
I ha 't!
When in your motion you are hot and dry—
As make your bouts more violent to that end—
160 And that he calls for drink, I'll have prepared him
A chalice for the nonce, whereon but sipping,
If he by chance escape your venomed stuck,
Our purpose may hold there. *[A cry within.]* But stay,
        what noise?

                                        Enter QUEEN.

QUEEN: One woe doth tread upon another's heel,
165   So fast they follow. Your's sister's drowned, Laertes.

LAERTES: Drowned! O, where?

QUEEN: There is a willow grows askant the brook,
That shows his hoar leaves in the glassy stream;
Therewith fantastic garlands did she make
170 Of crowflowers, nettles, daisies, and long purples,
That liberal shepherds give a grosser name,
But our cold maids do dead men's fingers call them.
There on the pendent boughs her crownet weeds

Clamb'ring to hang, an envious sliver broke,
When down her weedy trophies and herself   175
Fell in the weeping brook. Her clothes spread wide,
And mermaidlike awhile they bore her up,
Which time she chanted snatches of old lauds,
As one incapable of her own distress,
Or like a creature native and endued   180
Unto that element. But long it could not be
Till that her garments, heavy with their drink,
Pulled the poor wretch from her melodious lay
To muddy death.

LAERTES: Alas, then she is drowned?

QUEEN: Drowned, drowned.   185

LAERTES: Too much of water hast thou, poor Ophelia,
And therefore I forbid my tears. But yet
It is our trick; nature her custom holds,
Let shame say what it will. *[He weeps.]* When these
        are gone,
The woman will be out. Adieu, my lord.   190
I have a speech of fire that fain would blaze,
But that this folly douts it.   *Exit.*

KING: Let's follow, Gertrude.
How much I had to do to calm his rage!
Now fear I this will give it start again;
Therefore let's follow.   *Exeunt.*   195

5.1   *Enter two* CLOWNS *[with spades and mattocks].*

FIRST CLOWN: Is she to be buried in Christian burial,
    when she willfully seeks her own salvation?

SECOND CLOWN: I tell thee she is; therefore make
    her grave straight. The crowner hath sat on her, and
    finds it Christian burial.   5

FIRST CLOWN: How can that be, unless she drowned
    herself in her own defense?

---

142 unction ointment.   **mountebank** quack doctor   **144 cataplasm** plaster or poultice   **145 simples** herbs.   **virtue** potency
146 Under the moon i.e., anywhere (with reference perhaps to the belief that herbs gathered at night had a special power)   **148 gall** graze, wound   **151 shape** part we propose to act   **152 drift . . . performance** intention should be made visible by our bungling
155 blast in proof burst in the test (like a cannon)   **156 cunnings** respective skills   **159 As** i.e., and you should   **161 nonce** occasion
162 stuck thrust. (From *stoccado*, a fencing term.)   **167 askant** aslant   **168 hoar leaves** white or gray undersides of the leaves
170 long purples early purple orchids   **171 liberal** free-spoken.
a grosser name (The testicle-resembling tubers of the orchid, which also in some cases resemble *dead men's fingers*, have earned various slang names like "dogstones" and "cullions.")   **172 cold** chaste   **173 pendent** overhanging.   **crownet** made into a chaplet or coronet

---

174 envious sliver malicious branch   **175 weedy** i.e., of plants
178 lauds hymns   **179 incapable of** lacking capacity to apprehend   **180 endued** adapted by nature   **188 It is our trick** i.e., weeping is our natural way (when sad)   **189–190 When . . . out** when my tears are all shed, the woman in me will be expended, satisfied   **192 douts** extinguishes. (The Second Quarto reads "drowns.")

5.1. Location: A churchyard.
s.d. Clowns rustics   **2 salvation** (A blunder for "damnation," or perhaps a suggestion that Ophelia was taking her own shortcut to heaven.)   **4 straight** straightway, immediately. (But with a pun on *strait*, "narrow.")   **crowner** coroner.   **sat on her** conducted an inquest on her case   **5 finds it** gives his official verdict that her means of death was consistent with

SECOND CLOWN: Why, 'tis found so.

FIRST CLOWN: It must be *se offendendo*, it cannot
10   be else. For here lies the point: if I drown myself
  wittingly, it argues an act, and an act hath three
  branches—it is to act, to do, and to perform. Argal,
  she drowned herself wittingly.

SECOND CLOWN: Nay, but hear you, goodman delver—

15 **FIRST CLOWN:** Give me leave. Here lies the water;
  good. Here stands the man; good. If the man go to
  this water and drown himself, it is, will he, nill he, he
  goes, mark you that. But if the water come to him and
  drown him, he drowns not himself. Argal, he that is
20   not guilty of his own death shortens not his own life.

SECOND CLOWN: But is this law?

FIRST CLOWN: Ay, marry, is 't—crowner's quest law.

SECOND CLOWN: Will you ha' the truth on 't? If this
  had not been a gentlewoman, she should have been
25   buried out o' Christian burial.

FIRST CLOWN: Why, there thou sayst. And the more
  pity that great folk should have countenance in this
  world to drown or hang themselves, more than their
  even-Christian. Come, my spade. There is no ancient
30   gentlemen but gardeners, ditchers, and grave makers. They hold up Adam's profession.

SECOND CLOWN: Was he a gentleman?

FIRST CLOWN: 'A was the first that ever bore arms.

SECOND CLOWN: Why, he had none.

35 **FIRST CLOWN:** What, art a heathen? How dost thou
  understand the Scripture? The Scripture says Adam
  digged. Could he dig without arms? I'll put another
  question to thee. If thou answerest me not to the
  purpose, confess thyself—

SECOND CLOWN: Go to.   40

FIRST CLOWN: What is he that builds stronger than
  either the mason, the shipwright, or the carpenter?

SECOND CLOWN: The gallows maker, for that frame
  outlives a thousand tenants.

FIRST CLOWN: I like thy wit well, in good faith. The   45
  gallows does well. But how does it well? It does well
  to those that do ill. Now thou dost ill to say the gallows is built stronger than the church. Argal, the gallows may do well to thee. To 't again, come.

SECOND CLOWN: "Who builds stronger than a mason,   50
  a shipwright, or a carpenter?"

FIRST CLOWN: Ay, tell me that, and unyoke.

SECOND CLOWN: Marry, now I can tell.

FIRST CLOWN: To 't.

SECOND CLOWN: Mass, I cannot tell.   55

Enter HAMLET *and* HORATIO *[at a distance].*

FIRST CLOWN: Cudgel thy brains no more about it, for
  your dull ass will not mend his pace with beating;
  and when you are asked this question next, say "a
  grave maker." The houses he makes lasts till doomsday. Go get thee in and fetch me a stoup of liquor.   60
  [Exit SECOND CLOWN. FIRST CLOWN *digs.]*
  Song.

  "In youth, when I did love, did love,
    Methought it was very sweet,
  To contract—O—the time for—a—my behove,
    O, methought there—a—was nothing—a—
    meet."

HAMLET: Has this fellow no feeling of his business, 'a   65
  sings in grave-making?

HORATIO: Custom hath made it in him a property of
  easiness

HAMLET: 'Tis e'en so. The hand of little employment
  hath the daintier sense.   70

---

8 found so determined so in the coroner's verdict   **9 se offendendo** (A comic mistake for *se defendendo*, a term used in verdicts
of justifiable homicide.)   **12 Argal** (Corruption of *ergo*, "therefore.")
14 goodman (An honorific title often used with the name of a profession or craft.)   **17 will he, nill he** whether he will or no, willy-
nilly   **22 quest** inquest   **26 there thou sayst** i.e., that's right   **27
countenance** privilege   **29 even-Christian** fellow Christians.
ancient going back to ancient times   **31 hold up** maintain   **33
bore arms** (To be entitled to bear a coat of arms would make Adam
a gentleman, but as one who bore a spade, our common ancestor
was an ordinary delver in the earth.)   **37 arms** i.e., the arms of the
body   **39 confess thyself** (The saying continues, "and be hanged.")

43 frame (1) gallows (2) structure   **46 does well** (1) is an apt
answer (2) does a good turn   **52 unyoke** i.e., after this great effort, you may unharness the team of your wits   **55 Mass** by the
Mass   **60 stoup** two-quart measure   **61 In . . . love** (This and the
two following stanzas, with nonsensical variations, are from a poem
attributed to Lord Vaux and printed in *Tottel's Miscellany*, 1557.
The *O* and *a* [for "ah"] seemingly are the grunts of the digger.)
63 To contract . . . behove i.e., to shorten the time for my own
advantage. (Perhaps he means to *prolong* it.)   **64 meet** suitable,
i.e., more suitable   **65 'a** that he   **67–68 property of easiness**
something he can do easily and indifferently   **70 daintier sense**
more delicate sense of feeling

FIRST CLOWN: *Song.*
> "But age with his stealing steps
>   Hath clawed me in his clutch,
> And hath shipped me into the land,
>   As if I had never been such."
>   *[He throws up a skull.]*

75 **HAMLET:** That skull had a tongue in it and could sing once. How the knave jowls it to the ground, as if 'twere Cain's jawbone, that did the first murder! This might be the pate of a politician, which this ass now o'erreaches, one that would circumvent God, might 80 it not?

HORATIO: It might, my lord.

HAMLET: Or of a courtier, which could say, "Good morrow, sweet lord! How dost thou, sweet lord?" This might be my Lord Such-a-one, that praised my 85 Lord Such-a-one's horse when 'a meant to beg it, might it not?

HORATIO: Ay, my lord.

HAMLET: Why, e'en so, and now my Lady Worm's, chapless, and knocked about the mazard with a 90 sexton's spade. Here's fine revolution, an we had the trick to see 't. Did these bones cost no more the breeding but to play at loggets with them? Mine ache to think on 't.

FIRST CLOWN: *Song.*
> "A pickax and a spade, a spade,
95 >   For and a shrouding sheet;
> O, a pit of clay for to be made
>   For such a guest is meet."
>   *[He throws up another skull.]*

HAMLET: There's another. Why may not that be the skull of a lawyer? Where be his quiddities now, his 100 quillities, his cases, his tenures, and his tricks? Why does he suffer this mad knave now to knock him about the sconce with a dirty shovel, and will not tell

The First Clown (Billy Crystal) shows off a skull.

him of his action of battery? Hum, this fellow might be in 's time a great buyer of land, with his statutes, his recognizances, his fines, his double vouchers, 105 his recoveries. Is this the fine of his fines and the recovery of his recoveries, to have his fine pate full of fine dirt? Will his vouchers vouch him no more of his purchases, and double ones too, than the length and breadth of a pair of indentures? The very con- 110 veyances of his lands will scarcely lie in this box, and must th' inheritor himself have no more, ha?

HORATIO: Not a jot more, my lord.

HAMLET: Is not parchment made of sheepskins?

HORATIO: Ay, my lord, and of calves' skins too. 115

HAMLET: They are sheep and calves which seek out assurance in that. I will speak to this fellow.—Whose grave's this, sirrah?

FIRST CLOWN: Mine, sir.
> *[Sings.]* "O, pit of clay for to be made 120
>   For such a guest is meet."

HAMLET: I think it be thine, indeed, for thou liest in 't.

FIRST CLOWN: You lie out on 't, sir, and therefore 'tis not yours. For my part, I do not lie in 't, yet it is mine.

---

73 into the land i.e., toward my grave (?) (But note the lack of rhyme in *steps, land.*) **76 jowls** dashes (with a pun on *jowl,* "jawbone") **78 politician** schemer, plotter **79 o'erreaches** circumvents, gets the better of (with a quibble on the literal sense) **89 chapless** having no lower jaw. **mazard** i.e., head. (Literally, a drinking vessel.) **90 revolution** turn of Fortune's wheel, change. **an if** **91 trick to see** knack of seeing **91–92 cost . . . but** involve so little expense and care in upbringing that we may **92 loggets** a game in which pieces of hard wood shaped like Indian clubs or bowling pins are thrown to lie as near as possible to a stake **95 For and** and moreover **99 quiddities** subtleties, quibbles. (From Latin *quid,* "a thing.") **100 quillities** verbal niceties, subtle distinctions. (Variation of *quiddities.*) **tenures** the holding of a piece of property or office, or the conditions or period of such holding **102 sconce** head

103 action of battery lawsuit about physical assault **104–105 statutes, recognizances** legal documents guaranteeing a debt by attaching land and property **105–106 fines, recoveries** ways of converting entailed estates into "fee simple" or freehold **105 double** signed by two signatories. **vouchers** guarantees of the legality of a title to real estate **106–108 fine of his fines . . . fine pate . . . fine dirt** end of his legal maneuvers . . . elegant head . . . minutely sifted dirt **110 pair of indentures** legal document drawn up in duplicate on a single sheet and then cut apart on a zigzag line so that each pair was uniquely matched. (Hamlet may refer to two rows of teeth or dentures.) **110–111 conveyances** deeds **111 box** (1) deed box (2) coffin. ("Skull" has been suggested.) **112 inheritor** possessor, owner **117 assurance in that** safety in legal parchments **118 sirrah** (A term of address to inferiors.)

125 **HAMLET:** Thou dost lie in 't, to be in 't and say it is thine. 'Tis for the dead, not for the quick; therefore thou liest.

FIRST CLOWN: 'Tis a quick lie, sir; 'twill away again from me to you.

130 **HAMLET:** What man dost thou dig it for?

FIRST CLOWN: For no man, sir.

HAMLET: What woman, then?

FIRST CLOWN: For none, neither.

HAMLET: Who is to be buried in 't?

135 **FIRST CLOWN:** One that was a woman, sir, but, rest her soul, she's dead.

HAMLET: How absolute the knave is! We must speak by the card, or equivocation will undo us. By the Lord, Horatio, this three years I have took note of it: 140 the age is grown so picked that the toe of the peasant comes so near the heel of the courtier, he galls his kibe.—How long hast thou been grave maker?

FIRST CLOWN: Of all the days i' the year, I came to 't that day that our last king Hamlet overcame Fortinbras.

145 **HAMLET:** How long is that since?

FIRST CLOWN: Cannot you tell that? Every fool can tell that. It was that very day that young Hamlet was born—he that is mad and sent into England.

HAMLET: Ay, marry, why was he sent into England?

150 **FIRST CLOWN:** Why, because 'a was mad. 'A shall recover his wits there, or if 'a do not, 'tis no great matter there.

HAMLET: Why?

FIRST CLOWN: 'Twill not be seen in him there. There 155 the men are as mad as he.

HAMLET: How came he mad?

FIRST CLOWN: Very strangely, they say.

HAMLET: How strangely?

FIRST CLOWN: Faith, e'en with losing his wits.

HAMLET: Upon what ground? 160

FIRST CLOWN: Why, here in Denmark. I have been sexton here, man and boy, thirty years.

HAMLET: How long will a man lie i' th' earth ere he rot?

FIRST CLOWN: Faith, if 'a be not rotten before 'a die— as we have many pocky corpses nowadays, that will 165 scarce hold the laying in—'a will last you some eight year or nine year. A tanner will last you nine year.

HAMLET: Why he more than another?

FIRST CLOWN: Why, sir, his hide is so tanned with his trade that 'a will keep out water a great while, and 170 your water is a sore decayer of your whoreson dead body *[He picks up a skull.]* Here's a skull now hath lien you i' th' earth three-and-twenty years.

HAMLET: Whose was it?

FIRST CLOWN: A whoreson mad fellow's it was. 175 Whose do you think it was?

HAMLET: Nay, I know not.

FIRST CLOWN: A pestilence on him for a mad rogue! 'A poured a flagon of Rhenish on my head once. This same skull, sir, was, sir, Yorick's skull, the King's jester. 180

HAMLET: This?

FIRST CLOWN: E'en that.

HAMLET: Let me see. *[He takes the skull.]* Alas, poor Yorick! I knew him, Horatio, a fellow of infinite jest, of most excellent fancy. He hath bore me on 185 his back a thousand times, and now how abhorred in my imagination it is! My gorge rises at it. Here hung those lips that I have kissed I know not how oft. Where be your gibes now? Your gambols, your songs, your flashes of merriment that were wont to 190 set the table on a roar? Not one now, to mock your own grinning? Quite chopfallen? Now get you to my lady's chamber and tell her, let her paint an inch

---

126 **quick** living 137 **absolute** strict, precise 138 **by the card** i.e., with precision. (Literally, by the mariner's compass-card, on which the points of the compass were marked.) **equivocation** ambiguity in the use of terms 139 **took** taken 140 **picked** refined, fastidious 141–142 **galls his kibe** chafes the courtier's chilblain

160 **ground** cause. (But, in the next line, the gravedigger takes the word in the sense of "land," "country.") 165 **pocky** rotten, diseased. (Literally, with the pox, or syphilis.) 166 **hold the laying in** hold together long enough to be interred. **last you** last. (*You* is used colloquially here and in the following lines.) 171 **sore** i.e., terrible, great. **whoreson** i.e., vile, scurvy 172–173 **lien you** lain. (See the note at line 166.) 179 **Rhenish** Rhine wine 185 **bore** borne 187 **My gorge rises** i.e., I feel nauseated 190 **were wont** used 191–192 **mock your own grinning** mock at the way your skull seems to be grinning (just as you used to mock at yourself and those who grinned at you) 192 **chopfallen** (1) lacking the lower jaw (2) dejected

Hamlet speaks to the skull tossed to him by the First Clown.

thick, to this favor she must come. Make her laugh at
that. Prithee, Horatio, tell me one thing. 195

HORATIO: What's that, my lord?

HAMLET: Dost thou think Alexander looked o' this
fashion i' th' earth?

HORATIO: E'en so.

HAMLET: And smelt so? Pah! *[He throws down the skull.]* 200

HORATIO: E'en so, my lord.

HAMLET: To what base uses we may return, Horatio!
Why may not imagination trace the noble dust of
Alexander till 'a find it stopping a bunghole?

HORATIO: 'Twere to consider too curiously to
consider so. 205

HAMLET: No, faith, not a jot, but to follow him thither
with modesty enough, and likelihood to lead it. As
thus: Alexander died, Alexander was buried, Alexander returneth to dust, the dust is earth, of earth
we make loam, and why of that loam whereto he 210
was converted might they not stop a beer barrel?
Imperious Caesar, dead and turned to clay,
Might stop a hole to keep the wind away.
O, that that earth which kept the world in awe
Should patch a wall t' expel the winter's flaw! 215

*Enter KING, QUEEN, LAERTES, and the corpse [of
OPHELIA, in procession, with PRIEST, lords, etc.]*

But soft, but soft awhile! Here comes the King,
The Queen, the courtiers. Who is this they follow?

And with such maimèd rites? This doth betoken
The corpse they follow did with desperate hand 220
Fordo its own life. 'Twas of some estate.
Couch we awhile and mark.

> *[He and HORATIO conceal themselves.
> OPHELIA's body is taken to the grave.]*

LAERTES: What ceremony else?

HAMLET *[to HORATIO]:* That is Laertes, a very noble
youth. Mark.

LAERTES: What ceremony else? 225

PRIEST: Her obsequies have been as far enlarged
As we have warranty. Her death was doubtful,
And but that great command o'ersways the order
She should in ground unsanctified been lodged
Till the last trumpet. For charitable prayers, 230
Shards, flints, and pebbles should be thrown on her.
Yet here she is allowed her virgin crants,
Her maiden strewments, and the bringing home
Of bell and burial.

LAERTES: Must there no more be done?

PRIEST: No more be done. 235
We should profane the service of the dead
To sing a requiem and such rest to her
As to peace-parted souls.

LAERTES: Lay her i' th' earth,
And from her fair and unpolluted flesh
May violets spring! I tell thee, churlish priest, 240
A ministering angel shall my sister be
When thou liest howling.

HAMLET *[to HORATIO]:* What, the fair Ophelia!

QUEEN *[scattering flowers]:* Sweets to the sweet!
Farewell.
I hoped thou shouldst have been my Hamlet's wife.
I thought thy bride-bed to have decked, sweet maid, 245
And not t' have strewed thy grave.

LAERTES: O, treble woe
Fall ten times treble on that cursèd head

---

194 **favor** aspect, appearance   204 **bunghole** hole for filling or
emptying a cask   205 **curiously** minutely   208 **modesty** plausible
moderation   211 **loam** mortar consisting chiefly of moistened clay
and straw   213 **Imperious** imperial   216 **flaw** gust of wind
217 **soft** i.e., wait, be careful

---

219 **maimèd** mutilated, incomplete   221 **Fordo** destroy.   **estate**
rank   222 **Couch we** let's hide, lie low   227 **warranty** i.e., eccle-
siastical authority   228 **great . . . order** orders from on high
overrule the prescribed procedures   229 **She should . . . lodged**
she should have been buried in unsanctified ground   230 **For** in
place of   231 **Shards** broken bits of pottery   232 **crants** garlands
betokening maidenhood   233 **strewments** flowers strewn on a
coffin   233–234 **bringing . . . burial** laying the body to rest, to
the sound of the bell   237 **such rest** i.e., to pray for such rest   238
peace-parted souls those who have died at peace with God   240
violets (See 4.5.188 and note.)   242 **howling** i.e., in hell

Ophelia is put to rest.

Whose wicked deed thy most ingenious sense
Deprived thee of! Hold off the earth awhile,
250   Till I have caught her once more in mine arms.
       [He leaps into the grave and embraces OPHELIA.*]*
Now pile your dust upon the quick and dead,
Till of this flat a mountain you have made
T' o'ertop old Pelion or the skyish head
Of blue Olympus.

HAMLET *[coming forward]:*   What is he whose grief
255   Bears such an emphasis, whose phrase of sorrow
Conjures the wandering stars and makes them stand
Like wonder-wounded hearers? This is I,
Hamlet the Dane.

LAERTES *[grappling with him]:*   The devil take thy soul!

260   **HAMLET:**   Thou pray'st not well.
I prithee, take thy fingers from my throat,
For though I am not splenitive and rash,
Yet have I in me something dangerous,
Which let thy wisdom fear. Hold off thy hand.

265   **KING:**   Pluck them asunder.

QUEEN: Hamlet, Hamlet!

ALL: Gentlemen!

---

248 ingenious sense a mind that is quick, alert, of fine qualities   **253–254 Pelion, Olympus** sacred mountains in the north
of Thessaly; see also *Ossa*, below, at line 286   **255 emphasis** i.e.,
rhetorical and florid emphasis. (*Phrase* has a similar rhetorical connotation.)   **256 wandering stars** planets   **257 wonder-wounded**
struck with amazement   **258 the Dane** (This title normally signifies the King; see 1.1.17 and note.)   **259 s.d. grappling with him**
The testimony of the First Quarto that *"Hamlet leaps in after
Laertes"* and the "Elegy on Burbage" ("Oft have I seen him leap into
the grave") seem to indicate one way in which this fight was staged;
however, the difficulty of fitting two contenders and Ophelia's body
into a confined space (probably the trapdoor) suggests to many
editors the alternative, that Laertes jumps out of the grave to attack
Hamlet.)   **262 splenitive** quick-tempered

HORATIO: Good my lord, be quiet.
       *[*HAMLET *and* LAERTES *are parted.]*

HAMLET: Why, I will fight with him upon this theme
Until my eyelids will no longer wag.   270

QUEEN: O my son, what theme?

HAMLET: I loved Ophelia. Forty thousand brothers
Could not with all their quantity of love
Make up my sum. What wilt thou do for her?

KING: O, he is mad, Laertes.   275

QUEEN: For love of God, forbear him.

HAMLET: 'Swounds, show me what thou'lt do.
Woo't weep? Woo't fight? Woo't fast? Woo't tear
     thyself?
Woo't drink up eisel? Eat a crocodile?
I'll do 't. Dost come here to whine?   280
To outface me with leaping in her grave?
Be buried quick with her, and so will I.
And if thou prate of mountains, let them throw
Millions of acres on us, till our ground,
Singeing his pate against the burning zone,   285
Make Ossa like a wart! Nay, an thou'lt mouth,
I'll rant as well as thou.

QUEEN: This is mere madness,
And thus awhile the fit will work on him;
Anon, as patient as the female dove
When that her golden couplets are disclosed,   290
His silence will sit drooping.

HAMLET: Hear you, sir.
What is the reason that you use me thus?
I loved you ever. But it is no matter.
Let Hercules himself do what he may,
The cat will mew, and dog will have his day.   295
                         Exit HAMLET.

---

270 wag move (A fluttering eyelid is a conventional sign that
life has not yet gone.)   **276 forbear him** leave him alone   **277
'Swounds** by His (Christ's) wounds   **278 Woo't** wilt thou   **279
drink up** drink deeply. **eisel** vinegar. **crocodile** (Crocodiles
were tough and dangerous, and were supposed to shed hypocritical
tears.)   **282 quick** alive   **285 his pate** his head, i.e., top. **burning zone** zone in the celestial sphere containing the sun's orbit,
between the tropics of Cancer and Capricorn   **286 Ossa** another
mountain in Thessaly. (In their war against the Olympian gods,
the giants attempted to heap Ossa on Pelion to scale Olympus.)
an if. **mouth** i.e., rant   **287 mere** utter   **290 golden couplets**
two baby pigeons, covered with yellow down. **disclosed** hatched
294–295 Let . . . day i.e., (1) even Hercules couldn't stop Laertes'
theatrical rant (2) I, too, will have my turn; i.e., despite any blustering attempts at interference, every person will sooner or later do
what he or she must do

KING: I pray thee, good Horatio, wait upon him.

[Exit] HORATIO.

[To LAERTES.*]* Strengthen your patience in our last
    night's speech;
We'll put the matter to the present push.—
Good Gertrude, set some watch over your son.—
300 This grave shall have a living monument.
An hour of quiet shortly shall we see;
Till then, in patience our proceeding be.   *Exeunt.*

5.2   *Enter* HAMLET *and* HORATIO.

HAMLET: So much for this, sir; now shall you see the
    other.
You do remember all the circumstance?

HORATIO: Remember it, my lord!

HAMLET: Sir, in my heart there was a kind of fighting
5 That would not let me sleep. Methought I lay
Worse than the mutines in the bilboes. Rashly,
And praised by rashness for it—let us know
Our indiscretion sometimes serves us well
When our deep plots do pall, and that should learn us
10 There's a divinity that shapes our ends,
Rough-hew them how we will—

HORATIO: That is most certain.

HAMLET: Up from my cabin,
My sea-gown scarfed about me, in the dark
Groped I to find out them, had my desire,
15 Fingered their packet, and in fine withdrew
To mine own room again, making so bold,
My fears forgetting manners, to unseal
Their grand commission; where I found, Horatio—
Ah, royal knavery!—an exact command,
20 Larded with many several sorts of reasons
Importing Denmark's health and England's too,
With, ho! such bugs and goblins in my life,

That on the supervise, no leisure bated,
No, not to stay the grinding of the ax,
My head should be struck off.

HORATIO: Is 't possible?   25

HAMLET *[giving a document]*: Here's the commission.
    Read it at more leisure.
But wilt thou hear now how I did proceed?

HORATIO: I beseech you.

HAMLET: Being thus benetted round with villainies—
Ere I could make a prologue to my brains,   30
They had begun the play—I sat me down,
Devised a new commission, wrote it fair.
I once did hold it, as our statists do,
A baseness to write fair, and labored much
How to forget that learning, but, sir, now   35
It did me yeoman's service. Wilt thou know
Th' effect of what I wrote?

HORATIO: Ay, good my lord.

HAMLET: An earnest conjuration from the King,
As England was his faithful tributary,
As love between them like the palm might flourish,   40
As peace should still her wheaten garland wear
And stand a comma 'tween their amities,
And many suchlike "as"es of great charge,
That on the view and knowing of these contents,
Without debatement further more or less,   45
He should those bearers put to sudden death,
Not shriving time allowed.

HORATIO: How was this sealed?

HAMLET: Why, even in that was heaven ordinant.
I had my father's signet in my purse,
Which was the model of that Danish seal;   50
Folded the writ up in the form of th' other,
Subscribed it, gave 't th' impression, placed it safety,
The changeling never known. Now, the next day

---

297 in i.e., by recalling   **298 present push** immediate test   **300 living** lasting. (For Laertes' private understanding, Claudius also hints that Hamlet's death will serve as such a monument.)   **301 hour of quiet** time free of conflict

5.2. Location: The castle.
1 see the other hear the other news   **6 mutines** mutineers. **bilboes** shackles.   **Rashly** on impulse. (This adverb goes with lines 12 ff.)   **7 know** acknowledge   **8 indiscretion** lack of foresight and judgment (not an indiscreet act)   **9 pall** fail, falter, go stale.   **learn** teach   **11 Rough-hew** shape roughly   **13 sea-gown** seaman's coat.   **scarfed** loosely wrapped   **14 them** i.e. Rosencrantz and Guildenstern   **15 Fingered** pilfered, pinched.   **in fine** finally, in conclusion   **20 Larded** garnished.   **several** different   **21 Importing** relating to   **22 bugs, goblins** bugbears, hobgoblins.   **in my life** i.e., to be feared if I were allowed to live

23 supervise reading.   **leisure bated** delay allowed   **24 stay** await   **30–31 Ere . . . play** before I could consciously turn my brain to the matter, it had started working on a plan   **32 fair** in a clear hand   **33 statists** statesmen   **34 baseness** i.e., lower-class trait   **36 yeoman's** i.e., substantial, faithful, loyal   **37 effect** purport   **38 conjuration** entreaty   **40 palm** (An image of health; see Psalms 92:12.)   **41 still** always.   **wheaten garland** (Symbolic of fruitful agriculture, of peace and plenty.)   **42 comma** (Indicating continuity, link.)   **43 "as"es** (1) the "whereases" of a formal document (2) asses.   **charge** (1) import (2) burden (appropriate to asses)   **47 shriving time** time for confession and absolution   **48 ordinant** directing   **49 signet** small seal   **50 model** replica   **51 writ** writing   **52 Subscribed** signed (with forged signature).   **impression** i.e., with a wax seal   **53 changeling** i.e., substituted letter. (Literally, a fairy child substituted for a human one.)

Was our sea fight, and what to this was sequent
55　　Thou knowest already.

HORATIO:　So Guildenstern and Rosencrantz go to 't.

HAMLET:　Why, man, they did make love to this
　　employment.
They are not near my conscience. Their defeat
Does by their own insinuation grow.
60　'Tis dangerous when the baser nature comes
Between the pass and fell incensèd points
Of mighty opposites.

HORATIO:　　　　　　　Why, what a king is this!

HAMLET:　Does it not, think thee, stand me now upon—
He that hath killed my king and whored my mother,
65　Popped in between th' election and my hopes,
Thrown out his angle for my proper life,
And with such cozenage—is 't not perfect conscience
To quit him with this arm? And is 't not to be
　　damned
To let this canker of our nature come
70　In further evil?

HORATIO:　It must be shortly known to him from
　　England
What is the issue of the business there.

HAMLET:　It will be short. The interim is mine,
And a man's life no more than to say "one."
75　But I am very sorry, good Horatio,
That to Laertes I forgot myself,
For by the image of my cause I see
The portraiture of his. I'll court his favors.
But, sure, the bravery of his grief did put me
80　Into a tow'ring passion.

HORATIO:　　　　　　Peace, who comes here?

Enter a Courtier [OSRIC].

OSRIC:　Your lordship is right welcome back to Denmark.

HAMLET:　I humbly thank you, sir. *[To* HORATIO.*]* Dost
know this water fly?

HORATIO:　No, my good lord.

HAMLET:　Thy state is the more gracious, for 'tis a vice　85
to know him. He hath much land, and fertile. Let a
beast be lord of beasts, and his crib shall stand at the
King's mess. 'Tis a chuff, but, as I say, spacious in the
possession of dirt.

OSRIC:　Sweet lord, if your lordship were at leisure, I　90
should impart a thing to you from His Majesty.

HAMLET:　I will receive it, sir, with diligence of spirit.
Put your bonnet to his right use; 'tis for the head.

OSRIC:　I thank you lordship, it is very hot.

HAMLET:　No, believe me, 'tis very cold. The wind is　95
northerly.

OSRIC:　It is indifferent cold, my lord, indeed.

HAMLET:　But yet methinks it is very sultry and hot for
my complexion.

OSRIC:　Exceedingly, my lord. It is very sultry, as　100
'twere—I cannot tell how. My lord, His Majesty bade
me signify to you that 'a has laid a great wager on
your head. Sir, this is the matter—

HAMLET:　I beseech you, remember:
　　　　[HAMLET moves him to put on his hat.]

OSRIC:　Nay, good my lord; for my ease, in good faith.　105
Sir, here is newly come to court Laertes—believe me,
an absolute gentleman, full of most excellent differences, of very soft society and great showing. Indeed,
to speak feelingly of him, he is the card or calendar
of gentry, for you shall find in him the continent of　110
what part a gentleman would see.

HAMLET:　Sir, his definement suffers no perdition
in you, though I know to divide him inventorially

---

54 was sequent followed　**58 defeat** destruction　**59 insinuation** intrusive intervention, sticking their noses in my business
60 baser of lower social station　**61 pass** thrust.　**fell** fierce
62 opposites antagonists　**63 stand me now upon** become incum-
bent on me now　**65 election** (The Danish monarch was "elected"
by a small number of high-ranking electors.)　**66 angle** fishhook.
proper very　**67 cozenage** trickery　**68 quit** requite, pay back
69 canker ulcer　**69–70 come In** grow into　**74 a man's . . . "one"**
one's whole life occupies such a short time, only as long as it takes to
count to 1　**79 bravery** bravado

86–88 Let . . . mess i.e., if a man, no matter how beastlike, is as
rich in livestock and possessions as Osric, he may eat at the King's
table　**87 crib** manger　**88 chuff** boor, churl. (The Second Quarto
spelling, *chough*, is a variant spelling that also suggests the meaning here of "chattering jackdaw.")　**93 bonnet** any kind of cap or
hat.　**his** its　**97 indifferent** somewhat　**99 complexion** temperament　**105 for my ease** (A conventional reply declining the
invitation to put his hat back on.)　**107 absolute** perfect　**107–108
differences** special qualities　**108 soft society** agreeable manners.
great showing distinguished appearance　**109 feelingly** with just
perception.　**card** chart, map.　**calendar** guide　**110 gentry** good
breeding　**110–111 the continent . . . see** one who contains in him
all the qualities a gentleman would like to see. (A *continent* is that
which contains.)　**112 definement** definition. (Hamlet proceeds to
mock Osric by throwing his lofty diction back at him.)　**perdition**
loss, diminution　**113 you** your description.　**divide him inventorially** enumerate his graces

Osric (Robin Williams) tells Hamlet of the duel.

would dozy th' arithmetic of memory, and yet but
115 yaw neither in respect of his quick sail. But, in the
verity of extolment, I take him to be a soul of great
article, and his infusion of such dearth and rareness
as, to make true diction of him, his semblable is his
mirror and who else would trace him his umbrage,
120 nothing more.

OSRIC: Your lordship speaks most infallibly of him.

HAMLET: The concernancy, sir? Why do we wrap the
gentleman in our more rawer breath?

OSRIC: Sir?

125 HORATIO: Is 't not possible to understand in another
tongue? You will do 't, sir, really.

HAMLET: What imports the nomination of this
gentleman?

OSRIC: Of Laertes?

130 HORATIO [to HAMLET]:   His purse is empty already;
all 's golden words are spent.

HAMLET: Of him, sir.

OSRIC: I know you are not ignorant—

HAMLET: I would you did, sir. Yet in faith if you did, it
would not much approve me. Well, sir?   135

OSRIC: You are not ignorant of what excellence Laertes
is—

HAMLET: I dare not confess that, lest I should compare with him in excellence. But to know a man well
were to know himself.   140

OSRIC: I mean, sir, for his weapon; but in the imputation laid on him by them, in his meed he's unfellowed.

HAMLET: What's his weapon?

OSRIC: Rapier and dagger.

HAMLET: That's two of his weapons—but well.   145

OSRIC: The King, sir, hath wagered with him six Barbary horses, against the which he has impawned, as
I take it, six French rapiers and poniards, with their
assigns, as girdle, hangers, and so. Three of the carriages, in faith, are very dear to fancy, very respon-   150
sive to the hilts, most delicate carriages, and of very
liberal conceit.

HAMLET: What call you the carriages?

HORATIO [to HAMLET]:   I knew you must be edified by
the margent ere you had done.   155

OSRIC: The carriages, sir, are the hangers.

HAMLET: The phrase would be more germane to the
matter if we could carry a cannon by our sides; I
would it might be hangers till then. But, on: six
Barbary horses against six French swords, their as-   160
signs, and three liberal-conceited carriages; that's
the French bet against the Danish. Why is this impawned, as you call it?

---

114 dozy dizzy.   **115 yaw** swing unsteadily off course. (Said of a
ship.)   **neither** for all that.   **in respect of** in comparison with
115–116 in . . . extolment in true praise (of him)   **116–117 of great
article** one with many articles in his inventory   **117 infusion**
essence, character infused into him by nature.   **dearth and
rareness** rarity   **118 make true diction** speak truly   **118–119
semblable** only true likeness   **119 who . . . trace** any other person
who would wish to follow.   **umbrage** shadow   **122 concernancy**
import, relevance   **123 rawer breath** unrefined speech that can
only come short in praising him   **125–126 to understand . . .
tongue** i.e., for you, Osric, to understand when someone else speaks
your language. (Horatio twits Osric for not being able to understand the kind of flowery speech he himself uses, when Hamlet
speaks in such a vein. Alternatively, all this could be said to Hamlet.)   **126 You will do 't** i.e., you can if you try, or, you may well
have to try (to speak plainly)   **127 nomination** naming

135 approve commend   **138–140 I dare . . . himself** I dare not
boast of knowing Laertes' excellence lest I seem to imply a comparable excellence in myself. Certainly, to know another person well,
one must know oneself.   **141 for** i.e., with   **141–142 imputation
. . . them** reputation given him by others   **142 meed** merit.   **unfellowed** unmatched   **145 but well** but never mind   **147 he** i.e.,
Laertes.   **impawned** staked, wagered   **148 poniards** daggers
149 assigns appurtenances.   **hangers** straps on the sword belt
(*girdle*), from which the sword hung.   **and so** and so on   **149–150
carriages** (An affected way of saying *hangers*; literally, gun carriages.)   **150 dear to fancy** delightful to the fancy   **150–151
responsive** corresponding closely, matching or well adjusted   **151
delicate** (i.e., in workmanship)   **152 liberal conceit** elaborate
design   **155 margent** margin of a book, place for explanatory notes

OSRIC: The King, sir, hath laid, sir, that in a dozen
165   passes between yourself and him, he shall not exceed
you three hits. He hath laid on twelve for nine, and
it would come to immediate trial, if your lordship
would vouchsafe the answer.

HAMLET: How if I answer no?

170 OSRIC: I mean, my lord, the opposition of your person
in trial.

HAMLET: Sir, I will walk here in the hall. If it please His
Majesty, it is the breathing time of day with me. Let the
foils be brought, the gentleman willing, and the King
175   hold his purpose, I will win for him an I can; if not,
I will gain nothing but my shame and the odd hits.

OSRIC: Shall I deliver you so?

HAMLET: To this effect, sir—after what flourish your
nature will.

180 OSRIC: I commend my duty to your lordship.

HAMLET: Yours, yours. *[Exit* OSRIC.*]* 'A does well to
commend it himself; there are no tongues else for
's turn.

HORATIO: This lapwing runs away with the shell on
185   his head.

HAMLET: 'A did comply with his dug before 'a sucked it.
Thus has he—and many more of the same breed that
I know the drossy age dotes on—only got the tune of
the time and, out of an habit of encounter, a kind of
190   yeasty collection, which carries them through and
through the most fanned and winnowed opinions;

---

164 laid wagered   **165 passes** bouts. (The odds of the betting are
hard to explain. Possibly the King bets that Hamlet will win at least
five out of twelve, at which point Laertes raises the odds against
himself by betting he will win nine.)   **168 vouchsafe the answer**
be so good as to accept the challenge. (Hamlet deliberately takes the
phrase in its literal sense of replying.)   **173 breathing time** exercise
period.   **Let** i.e., if   **177 deliver you** report what you say   **180 commend** commit to your favor. (A conventional salutation, but Hamlet
wryly uses a more literal meaning, "recommend," "praise," in line
182.)   **182–183 for 's turn** for his purposes, i.e., to do it for him   **184
lapwing** (A proverbial type of youthful forwardness. Also, a bird that
draws intruders away from its nest and was thought to run about
with its head in the shell when newly hatched; a seeming reference
to Osric's hat.)   **186 comply . . . dug** observe ceremonious formality
toward his nurse's or mother's teat   **188 drossy** laden with scum and
impurities, frivolous   **tune** temper, mood, manner of speech.   **189
an habit of encounter** a demeanor in conversing (with courtiers
of his own kind)   **190 yeasty** frothy.   **collection** i.e., of current
phrases   **190–191 carries . . . opinions** sustains them right through
the scrutiny of persons whose opinions are select and refined. (Literally, like grain separated from its chaff. Osric is both the chaff and
the bubbly froth on the surface of the liquor that is soon blown away.)

and do but blow them to their trial, the bubbles
are out.

Enter a LORD.

LORD: My lord, His Majesty commended him to you by
young Osric, who brings back to him that you attend   195
him in the hall. He sends to know if your pleasure
hold to play with Laertes, or that you will take longer
time.

HAMLET: I am constant to my purposes; they follow the
King's pleasure. If his fitness speaks, mine is ready;   200
now or whensoever, provided I be so able as now.

LORD: The King and Queen and all are coming down.

HAMLET: In happy time.

LORD: The Queen desires you to use some gentle entertainment to Laertes before you fall to play.   205

HAMLET: She well instructs me.   *[Exit* LORD.*]*

HORATIO: You will lose, my lord.

HAMLET: I do not think so. Since he went into France,
I have been in continual practice; I shall win at the
odds. But thou wouldst not think how ill all's here   210
about my heart; but it is no matter.

HORATIO: Nay, good my lord—

HAMLET: It is but foolery, but it is such a kind of gaingiving as would perhaps trouble a woman.

HORATIO: If your mind dislike anything, obey it. I will   215
forestall their repair hither and say you are not fit.

HAMLET: Not a whit, we defy augury. There is special
providence in the fall of a sparrow. If it be now, 'tis
not to come; if it be not to come, it will be now; if
it be not now; yet it will come. The readiness is all.   220
Since no man of aught he leaves knows, what is 't to
leave betimes? Let be.

A table prepared. [Enter] trumpets, drums,
and officers with cushions; KING, QUEEN,
*[*OSRIC,*] and all the state; foils, daggers,*
[and wine borne in;] and LAERTES.

---

192 and do yet do   **192–193 blow . . . out** test them by merely
blowing on them, and their bubbles burst   **197 that** if   **200 If
. . . ready** if he declares his readiness, my convenience waits on
his   **203 In happy time** (A phrase of courtesy indicating that the
time is convenient.)   **204–205 entertainment** greeting   **213–214
gaingiving** misgiving   **216 repair** coming   **221–222 Since . . .
Let be** since no one has knowledge of what he is leaving behind,
what does an early death matter after all? Enough; don't struggle
against it.

KING: Come, Hamlet, come and take this hand from me.
[*The* KING *puts* LAERTES' *hand into* HAMLET'*s.*]

HAMLET [*to* LAERTES]: Give me your pardon, sir. I have
done you wrong,
225   But pardon 't as you are a gentleman.
This presence knows,
And you must needs have heard, how I am punished
With a sore distraction. What I have done
That might your nature, honor, and exception
230   Roughly awake, I here proclaim was madness.
Was 't Hamlet wronged Laertes? Never Hamlet.
If Hamlet from himself be ta'en away,
And when he's not himself does wrong Laertes,
Then Hamlet does it not, Hamlet denies it.
235   Who does it, then? His madness. If 't be so,
Hamlet is of the faction that is wronged;
His madness is poor Hamlet's enemy.
Sir, in this audience
Let my disclaiming from a purposed evil
240   Free me so far in your most generous thoughts
That I have shot my arrow o'er the house
And hurt my brother.

LAERTES: I am satisfied in nature,
Whose motive in this case should stir me most
To my revenge. But in my terms of honor
245   I stand aloof, and will no reconcilement
Till by some elder masters of known honor
I have a voice and precedent of peace
To keep my name ungored. But till that time
I do receive your offered love like love,
250   And will not wrong it.

HAMLET: I embrace it freely,
And will this brothers' wager frankly play.—
Give us the foils. Come on.

LAERTES: Come, one for me.

HAMLET: I'll be your foil, Laertes. In mine ignorance
Your skill shall, like a star i' the darkest night,
255   Stick fiery off indeed.

LAERTES: You mock me, sir.

HAMLET: No, by this hand.

Laertes (Michael Maloney) and Hamlet duel.

KING: Give them the foils, young Osric. Cousin Hamlet,
You know the wager?

HAMLET: Very well, my lord.
Your Grace has laid the odds o' the weaker side.

KING: I do not fear it; I have seen you both.   260
But since he is bettered, we have therefore odds.

LAERTES: This is too heavy. Let me see another.
[*He exchanges his foil for another.*]

HAMLET: This likes me well. These foils have all a
length?
[*They prepare to play.*]

OSRIC: Ay, my good lord.

KING: Set me the stoups of wine upon that table.   265
If Hamlet give the first or second hit,
Or quit in answer of the third exchange,
Let all the battlements their ordnance fire.
The King shall drink to Hamlet's better breath,
And in the cup an union shall he throw   270
Richer than that which four successive kings
In Denmark's crown have worn. Give me the cups,
And let the kettle to the trumpet speak,
The trumpet to the cannoneer without,
The cannons to the heavens, the heaven to earth,   275
"Now the King drinks to Hamlet." Come, begin.
Trumpets the while.
And you, the judges, bear a wary eye.

HAMLET: Come on, sir.

---

226 presence royal assembly **227 punished** afflicted **229
exception** disapproval **236 faction** party **241 That I have** as if
I had **242 in nature** i.e., as to my personal feelings **243 motive**
prompting **247 voice** authoritative pronouncement. **of peace** for
reconciliation **248 name ungored** reputation unwounded **251
frankly** without ill feeling or the burden of rancor **253 foil** thin
metal background that sets a jewel off (with pun on the blunted
rapier for fencing) **255 Stick fiery off** stand out brilliantly

---

259 laid the odds o' bet on, backed **261 is bettered** has improved; is the odds-on favorite. (Laertes' handicap is the "three
hits" specified in line 166.) **263 likes me** pleases me **267 Or . . .
exchange** i.e., or requites Laertes in the third bout for having won
the first two **269 better breath** improved vigor **270 union**
pearl. (So called, according to Pliny's *Natural History,* 9, because
pearls are *unique,* never identical.) **273 kettle** kettledrum

LAERTES: Come, my lord. *[They play.* HAMLET *scores a hit.]*

280 HAMLET: One.

LAERTES: No.

HAMLET: Judgment.

OSRIC: A hit, a very palpable hit.
Drum, trumpets, and shot. Flourish.
A piece goes off.

LAERTES: Well, again.

KING: Stay, give me drink. Hamlet, this pearl is thine.
[He drinks, and throws a pearl
in HAMLET's *cup.]*

285 Here's to thy health. Give him the cup.

HAMLET: I'll play this bout first. Set it by awhile.
Come. *[They play.]* Another hit; what say you?

LAERTES: A touch, a touch, I do confess 't.

KING: Our son shall win.

QUEEN: He's fat and scant of breath.
290 Here, Hamlet, take my napkin, rub thy brows.
The Queen carouses to thy fortune, Hamlet.

HAMLET: Good madam!

KING: Gertrude, do not drink.

QUEEN: I will, my lord, I pray you pardon me.
[She drinks.]

295 KING *[aside]*: It is the poisoned cup. It is too late.

HAMLET: I dare not drink yet, madam; by and by.

QUEEN: Come, let me wipe thy face.

LAERTES *[to* KING*]*: My lord, I'll hit him now.

KING: I do not think 't.

LAERTES *[aside]*: And yet it is almost against my conscience.

300 HAMLET: Come, for the third, Laertes. You do but dally.
I pray you, pass with your best violence;
I am afeard you make a wanton of me.

LAERTES: Say you so? Come on. *[They play.]*

OSRIC: Nothing neither way.

LAERTES: Have at you now! 305
*[*LAERTES *wounds* HAMLET; *then, in scuffling, they change rapiers, and* HAMLET *wounds* LAERTES.*]*

KING: Part them! They are incensed.

HAMLET: Nay, come, again. *[The* QUEEN *falls.]*

OSRIC: Look to the Queen there, ho!

HORATIO: They bleed on both sides. How is it, my lord?

OSRIC: How is 't, Laertes?

LAERTES: Why, as a woodcock to mine own springe, Osric;
I am justly killed with mine own treachery. 310

HAMLET: How does the Queen?

KING: She swoons to see them bleed.

QUEEN: No, no, the drink, the drink—O my dear Hamlet—
The drink, the drink! I am poisoned. *[She dies.]*

HAMLET: O villainy! Ho, let the door be locked!
Treachery! Seek it out. *[*LAERTES *falls. Exit* OSRIC.*]* 315

LAERTES: It is here, Hamlet. Hamlet, thou art slain.
No med'cine in the world can do thee good;
In thee there is not half an hour's life.
The treacherous instrument is in thy hand,
Unbated and envenomed. The foul practice 320
Hath turned itself on me. Lo, here I lie,
Never to rise again. Thy mother's poisoned.
I can no more. The King, the King's to blame.

HAMLET: The point envenomed too? Then, venom, to thy work. *[He stabs the* KING.*]*

ALL: Treason! Treason! 325

KING: O, yet defend me, friends! I am but hurt.

HAMLET *[forcing the* KING *to drink]*: Here, thou incestuous, murderous, damnèd Dane,
Drink off this potion. Is thy union here?
Follow my mother. *[The* KING *dies.]*

---

289 **fat** not physically fit, out of training   290 **napkin** handkerchief   291 **carouses** drinks a toast   301 **pass** thrust   302 **make . . . me** i.e., treat me like a spoiled child, trifle with me

305 **s.d. in scuffling, they change rapiers** (This stage direction occurs in the Folio. According to a widespread stage tradition, Hamlet receives a scratch, realizes that Laertes' sword is unbated, and accordingly forces an exchange.)   309 **woodcock** a bird, a type of stupidity or as a decoy. **springe** trap, snare   320 **Unbated** not blunted with a button. **practice** plot   328 **union** pearl. (See line 270; with grim puns on the word's other meanings: marriage, shared death.)

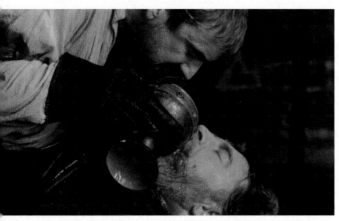

Hamlet forces Claudius to drink the poisoned wine.

LAERTES: He is justly served.
330   It is a poison tempered by himself.
        Exchange forgiveness with me, noble Hamlet.
        Mine and my father's death come not upon thee,
        Nor thine on me!   *[He dies]*

HAMLET: Heaven make thee free of it! I follow thee.
335   I am dead, Horatio. Wretched Queen, adieu!
        You that look pale and tremble at this chance,
        That are but mutes or audience to this act,
        Had I but time—as this fell sergeant, Death,
        Is strict in his arrest—O, I could tell you—
340   But let it be. Horatio, I am dead;
        Thou livest. Report me and my cause aright
        To the unsatisfied.

HORATIO: Never believe it.
        I am more an antique Roman than a Dane.
        Here's yet some liquor left.

            [He attempts to drink from the poisoned
            cup. HAMLET *prevents him.]*

HAMLET: As thou'rt a man,
345   Give me the cup! Let go! By heaven, I'll ha 't.
        O God, Horatio, what a wounded name,
        Things standing thus unknown, shall I leave behind
            me!
        If thou didst ever hold me in thy heart,
        Absent thee from felicity awhile,
350   And in this harsh world draw thy breath in pain
        To tell my story.   *A march afar off [and a volley within].*
            What warlike noise is this?

---

330 tempered mixed   **336 chance** mischance   **337 mutes** silent observers. (Literally, actors with nonspeaking parts.)   **338 fell** cruel.   **sergeant** sheriff's officer   **339 strict** (1) severely just (2) unavoidable.   **arrest** (1) taking into custody (2) stopping my speech   **343 Roman** (Suicide was an honorable choice for many Romans as an alternative to a dishonorable life.)

                    Enter OSRIC.

OSRIC: Young Fortinbras, with conquest come from
            Poland,
        To th' ambassadors of England gives
        This warlike volley.

HAMLET: O, I die, Horatio!
        The potent poison quite o'ercrows my spirit.   355
        I cannot live to hear the news from England,
        But I do prophesy th' election lights
        On Fortinbras. He has my dying voice.
        So tell him, with th' occurrents more and less
        Which have solicited—the rest is silence.   *[He dies.]*   360

HORATIO: Now cracks a noble heart. Good night,
            sweet prince,
        And flights of angels sing thee to thy rest!
                            [March within.]
        Why does the drum come hither?

        Enter FORTINBRAS, *with the [English]* AMBAS-
        SADORS *[with drum, colors, and attendants].*

FORTINBRAS: Where is this sight?

HORATIO: What is it you would see?
        If aught of woe or wonder, cease your search.   365

FORTINBRAS: This quarry cries on havoc. O proud
            Death,
        What feast is toward in thine eternal cell,
        That thou so many princes at a shot
        So bloodily hast struck?

FIRST AMBASSADOR: The sight is dismal,
        And our affairs from England come too late.   370
        The ears are senseless that should give us hearing,
        To tell him his commandment is fulfilled,
        That Rosencrantz and Guildenstern are dead.
        Where should we have our thanks?

HORATIO: Not from his mouth,
        Had it th' ability of life to thank you.   375
        He never gave commandment for their death.
        But since, so jump upon his bloody question,
        You from the Polack wars, and you from England,
        Are here arrived, give order that these bodies

---

355 o'ercrows triumphs over (like the winner in a cockfight)
358 voice vote   **359 occurrents** events, incidents   **360 solicited** moved, urged. (Hamlet doesn't finish saying what the events have prompted—presumably, his acts of vengeance, or his reporting of those events to Fortinbras.)   **366 quarry** heap of dead.   **cries on havoc** proclaims a general slaughter   **367 feast** i.e., Death feasting on those who have fallen.   **toward** in preparation   **374 his** i.e., Claudius'   **377 jump** precisely, immediately.   **question** dispute, affair

380 High on a stage be placèd to the view,
And let me speak to th' yet unknowing world
How these things came about. So shall you hear
Of carnal, bloody, and unnatural acts,
Of accidental judgments, casual slaughters,
385 Of deaths put on by cunning and forced cause,
And, in this upshot, purposes mistook
Fall'n on th' inventors' heads. All this can I
Truly deliver.

FORTINBRAS: Let us haste to hear it,
And call the noblest to the audience.
390 For me, with sorrow I embrace my fortune.
I have some rights of memory in this kingdom,
Which now to claim my vantage doth invite me.

HORATIO: Of that I shall have also cause to speak,
And from his mouth whose voice will draw on more.
395 But let this same be presently performed,
Even while men's minds are wild, lest more
mischance
On plots and errors happen.

---

380 **stage** platform   384 **judgments** retributions.   **casual** occurring by chance   385 **put on** instigated.   **forced cause** contrivance   391 **of memory** traditional, remembered, unforgotten   392 **vantage** favorable opportunity   394 **voice . . . more** vote will influence still others   395 **presently** immediately   397 **On** on the basis of; on top of

Hamlet is laid to rest.

FORTINBRAS: Let four captains
Bear Hamlet, like a soldier, to the stage,
For he was likely, had he been put on,
To have proved most royal; and for his passage,   400
The soldiers' music and the rite of war
Speak loudly for him.
Take up the bodies. Such a sight as this
Becomes the field, but here shows much amiss.
Go bid the soldiers shoot.   405

*Exeunt [marching, bearing off the dead
bodies; a peal of ordnance is shot off].*

---

399 **put on** i.e., invested in royal office and so put to the test   400 **passage** i.e., from life to death   402 **Speak** (let them) speak   404 **Becomes the field** suits the field of battle

Writing from Reading

Summarize

1 Think of this play as a revenge tragedy, a story of justice played out. Describe how Hamlet chooses to avenge his father's murder and the result of his choice. During the course of the play, what wrongs are righted? In what ways do innocent people suffer or succeed?

2 This is a complex play with many subplots that mirror the main plot of Hamlet's revenge. Consider, for instance, that Laertes also loves Ophelia, is also of noble birth and travels abroad. He is an excellent fencer, and also has a father who has been killed. How does his story amplify that of the prince?

3 What is the plot of the play within the play? Does the play have the effect Hamlet hopes for?

Analyze Craft

4 How would you describe Hamlet's character? How does indecision help the tragedy unfold?

5 How would you describe Ophelia's character: her history, her education and upbringing, her feelings for her father and brother and lover? What causes Ophelia to go mad (is it a single event, or a combination of causes that makes her drown herself?), and what effect does her suicide have on the play?

6 How do you imagine Claudius and Gertrude? How old are they? In what sort of physical health? What attitude do they have? What in the play makes you imagine them this way?

7 Laertes is a kind of shadow twin to Hamlet. As suggested in question 2, he too is noble and a fine fencer, and his father has also been killed. What differences in character make him, in effect, the king's pawn and the unwitting agent of Prince Hamlet's death?

8 How do the secondary characters—the gravedigger, Fortinbras, Horatio, etc.—advance the action? What perspectives and what commentary do they offer?

Analyze Voice

9 How do the speeches and high formal tone of the royal characters contrast with the speech of the low characters? Give examples.

10 Do you have any sympathy for the character Claudius when he admits, "Oh, my offence is rank"? What about *rank* in the court? Find other examples of Shakespeare's use of double meaning and puns (as, for example, when Hamlet flirts with and teases Ophelia before the play's performance).

11 Do "these few precepts" that Polonius offers to his son make sense? What of the advice he gives his daughter? Given the solemn nature of this advice, what in his character makes Hamlet thinks him a "rash, intruding fool"? What does the difference between what seems like wise advice and Polonius's character allow us to discover in the play?

12 Focus on the humor in the text. Study the gravediggers' scene and try to play it for laughs.

Synthesize Summary and Analysis

13 Why would Shakespeare set this play in Denmark and the somewhat distant past? It is, after all, a story about regicide (the killing of a king). What risks would he have taken if he set the tale in England instead?

14 Why did Shakespeare mount a play within the play, and what kind of commentary does it offer on the larger text? How is this similar to or different from the play staged within Hamlet's *A Midsummer Night's Dream* (also in this chapter)?

Interpret the Play

15 Is Hamlet's story tragic? If so, what makes his story tragic?

16 Does Hamlet choose the most efficient path to avenge his father's murder? At play's end, is everything redeemed?

CONTINUED FROM PAGE 105

THE ORIGINS OF THE HAMLET STORY

The particular source of this play derives from an old Norse legend in which we first hear of a character called Amlothi, whose name has been translated as "desperate in battle" and is recorded in *Historica Danica* of Saxo Grammaticus (a book printed in 1514). The seed story of Hamlet is used by the French writer Belleforest in his *Histoires Tragiques* (1576), and scholars show Shakespeare did read it. Indeed, the playwright rarely made up his stories out of whole cloth. He was familiar with Plutarch and Holinshed (historians of the classical and medieval world respectively); he adapted histories and voyage accounts and other authors' narratives for most of his career. The father's murder and the sweetheart's madness (sometimes the Ophelia figure is a courtesan, sometimes a princess) and the duel with an exchange of swords all figure in previous sources—but the character of Hamlet is something Shakespeare filled out on his own.

THE ELIZABETHAN THEATER

From time to time—in periods of plague, for instance, or when the authorities found the crowd's behavior too unruly—the theaters were closed down. To avoid the complications stemming from these unpredictable gaps in business, Shakespeare's troupe,

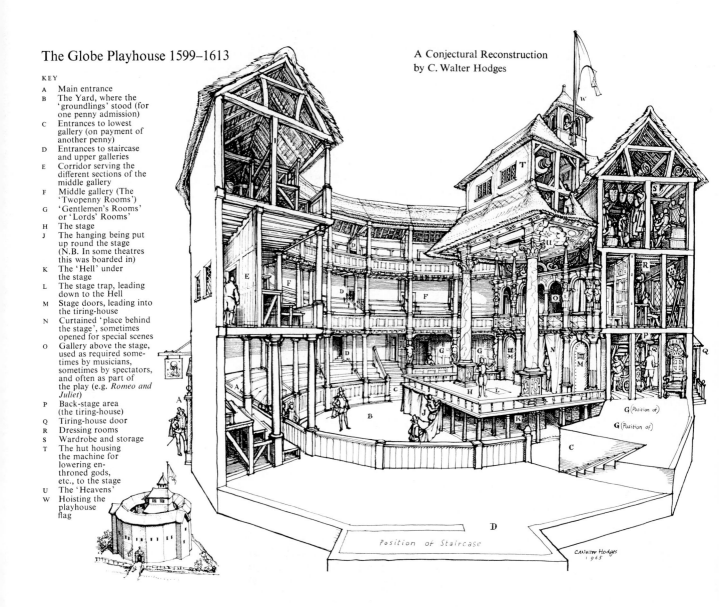

The Globe Playhouse 1599–1613

A Conjectural Reconstruction
by C. Walter Hodges

KEY

A Main entrance
B The Yard, where the 'groundlings' stood (for one penny admission)
C Entrances to lowest gallery (on payment of another penny)
D Entrances to staircase and upper galleries
E Corridor serving the different sections of the middle gallery
F Middle gallery (The 'Twopenny Rooms')
G 'Gentlemen's Rooms' or 'Lords' Rooms'
H The stage
J The hanging being put up round the stage (N.B. In some theatres this was boarded in)
K The 'Hell' under the stage
L The stage trap, leading down to the Hell
M Stage doors, leading into the tiring-house
N Curtained 'place behind the stage', sometimes opened for special scenes
O Gallery above the stage, used as required sometimes by musicians, sometimes by spectators, and often as part of the play (e.g. *Romeo and Juliet*)
P Back-stage area (the tiring-house)
Q Tiring-house door
R Dressing rooms
S Wardrobe and storage
T The hut housing the machine for lowering enthroned gods, etc., to the stage
U The 'Heavens'
W Hoisting the playhouse flag

the Lord Chamberlain's Men, decided to build its own space in 1599. The **Globe Theater,** constructed on the model of a tavern, stood on the south bank of the Thames River, beyond the city limits and the close watch of the law; it could accommodate—by some estimates—as many as three thousand.

Before the construction of the Globe Theater, the central stage was often a courtyard of taverns or inns. Today, an audience at a boxing match or football game is probably more similar to the Elizabethan clientele than is the well-heeled, well-behaved audience at a Broadway show. Like Greek theater, these stages made for sparse sets. There was only a **tiring house** hidden by a curtain behind the **arena stage**—in essence, a platform—that allowed quick costume changes between scenes. The stage was open to the sky to take advantage of natural light. Similar to the Greek amphithe-

"I have always felt that the . . . works that last . . . address the condition of mankind at any one time. They're not simply private emotional works. . . . They're reflecting the larger reality of the time. And I think that's true with Shakespeare. . . . The original purpose or color of creative art was always the community." Conversation with Arthur Miller

ater, surrounded on three sides, the Elizabethan theater would have been three stories high, each story with a gallery from which patrons could watch; those who paid an additional penny could be seated and look down.

Not since the fall of Rome had theater played such a role in public life, bringing in a boisterous and broad mix of society, from nobles, including Queen Elizabeth herself, to **groundlings,** who paid a penny to stand on the ground surrounding the stage. Puritans decried theaters as brothels, and Queen Elizabeth censored plays closely due to their enormous influence. Shakespeare himself wrote only of royalty that was long gone, since predicting the future or commenting on royalty of the day could have had dire consequences. The theater was a highly competitive place that vied for public support as well as for patrons, sponsoring aristocrats who might order a private performance or commission a celebratory work.

Traveling **players**—hired men and boys who spoke their lines for pay—acted out the plays of the day, and it is just such a group of actors Prince Hamlet is hiring in Act III, Scene II, when he decides to get his message of revenge to the murderous king. Players were always males, with boys usually playing women's roles. The costumes worn by players were generally very elaborate—brightly colored and visually appealing. Acting companies owned a wide variety of costumes for players to wear, some of which held certain conventions and connotations—such as a robe that represented invisibility. And since these costumes were expensive and not readily replaced, the playwright had to "tailor" his lines accordingly. In the beginning of another Shakespeare

"You don't want to lose faith in the plays you love. I can separate the written word from a performance . . . I've seen poor performances of Shakespeare. Particularly the comedies, which are more difficult to do than the tragedies. And I think, Oh don't spoil this play for me! I still love it, I'm still faithful to it, I love this play." Conversation with Marian Seldes

play, *The Tempest,* there's a storm conjured up by Prospero, the great magician, and his servant Ariel. Shakespeare describes how the shipwrecked crew washes up upon the island, writing "On their sustaining garments not a blemish / But fresher than before." In the movies nowadays we'd no doubt show the sailors wet and bedraggled, their "sustaining garments" torn—but in Elizabethan England the costumes would need to stay dry and "fresher than before."

LANGUAGE ONSTAGE

When the character Jacques in Shakespeare's *As You Like It* famously pronounces that "All the world's a stage, and all the men and women merely players," he may well have been describing the great Globe Theater itself. Though it contained no elaborate scenery, the size of the stage and the structure of the building offered occasions for action; when Orlando, in the same play, hangs his love letters to Rosalind on trees of the Forest of Arden, he almost surely did so from the columns of the Globe. Props and furniture could be employed, and elaborate costumes worn, but "the willing suspension of disbelief"—which Samuel Taylor Coleridge argued "constitutes poetic faith"—was necessary, always, for those theatergoers who came to listen and look. The prologue to *Henry V* admits as much—indeed, is close to apologetic when the speaker asks:

> *Can this cockpit hold*
> *The vasty fields of France? Or may we cram*
> *Within this wooden O the very casques*
> *That did affright the air at Agincourt?*

Mostly the answer was yes. Scene after scene in Shakespeare is introduced by vivid description, a speech about a battlefield or palace, a lyric evocation of a forest or the stars. In Act V, Scene 1, of *The Merchant of Venice,* one character observes,

> *How sweet the moonlight sits upon this bank!*
> *Here will we sit and let the sounds of music*
> *Creep in our ears. Soft stillness and the night*
> *Become the touches of sweet harmony.*
> *Sit, Jessica. Look how the floor of heaven*
> *Is thick inlaid with patens of bright gold . . .*

There's no need for stage directions once the scene has been set in such elegant style. Lorenzo, the speaker, is wooing his heart's darling—Jessica, the daughter of Shylock, the Merchant of Venice—looking up while, no doubt, music plays. The opening phrase

"[Shakespeare's] plays are capable of an endless number of good productions. . . . There are no stage directions, so they're endlessly fertile as performance." Conversation with Ralph Williams

of this courtship scene is "The moon shines bright," and though the play was first presented on a London afternoon, we're transported, via the artist's verbal prowess, to the Venetian night.

The configuration of this arena theater gave rise to a convention of drama called the **aside**—a speech directed to the audience only, that the other actors onstage do not appear to hear. The aside can deliver background information to the audience, without the actors having to act it out or act upon it. More importantly, it is used to create a connection between the actor and the audience, to make them partners or co-conspirators. In this way, the audience gains access to secrets and ironies, and to inner thoughts that are withheld from other characters. Another dramatic convention that arose in this era was the **soliloquy,** a monologue delivered by a character standing alone onstage. A soliloquy gives the audience deep access to a character's inner world, as it does in *Hamlet,* when the troubled prince reveals the extent of his dilemmas.

THE ORIGINS OF DRAMA IN THE CHRISTIAN CHURCH

Around the tenth century, drama, which had been suppressed by the Church as a pagan ritual, became part of the Christian Mass. These dramas were anonymous works intended less as entertainments than as a form of religious instruction. In other words, those who could not read the Bible could watch it being acted out and profit from the "show." **Miracle plays,** one type of drama in this tradition, enacted the lives of the saints. **Mystery plays,** a second type, brought to life stories of the Bible—such as the Creation or the Crucifixion. *The Second Shepherd's Play* (c. 1400), for example, told the story of Christ's birth. Allegory (see chapter 20 in the poetry volume for more on allegory) enters into theatrical productions of the third type—**morality plays.** In this form of drama, the figures onstage taught right and proper behavior—morality—to those who watched. In one well-known morality play, *Everyman,* the titular character is called before God to make his reckoning. Other characters in this play have names such as Kindred, Knowledge, and Beauty. In the end, however, none of those other figures cares enough about Everyman's plight to accompany him and help him plead his case in heaven. Only Good Deeds is up to that task—thus, the moral lesson that good deeds are what matter in life.

SHAKESPEARE'S CONFOUNDING DIVERSITY

No matter how useful we find it to be, the business of categorization began only after Shakespeare's death. Critics tend to divide the playwright's compositions for theater into four categories.

- **Histories** focus on the reign of kings from the past, from Julius Caesar to Henry V. Because histories naturally contain very astute and sometimes troubling political commentaries, playwrights had to limit their subjects to rulers of the distant past.

- **Comedies** are plays for entertainment and as a convention end in the marriage of two main characters. A comedic plot generally begins with a complication or misunderstanding between two lovers, which is complicated by further scheming and misunderstandings until finally a resolution is attained and the two are wed.

- **Tragedies** are darker plays, with more complex characters and more dire consequences. Tragedies commonly feature murder and as a convention end in a funeral—usually the death of the main character himself.

- **Romances** (from the French *roman,* which means an "extended narrative") involve lovers whose potential happiness is complicated by misunderstandings, mistaken identities, and any number of other difficulties. Although similar in plot to a comedy, a romance play does not guarantee a happy ending.

These categories are loose and overlapping units, and as Ralph Williams discusses in his interview, Shakespeare may have taken a bravura delight in confounding definitions, which in any case are more a matter of critical convenience than of theatrical

"One of the most frightening and thrilling aspects of Shakespeare's plays is the constant reminder of how tentative a thing it is that life turns out to be tragedy or comedy, or some mixture of the two." Conversation with Ralph Williams

form. Even the darkest of Shakespeare's plays have some comedic component, called **comic relief**—such as the banter between Hamlet and his bewildered old friends Rosencrantz and Guildenstern—which gives the audience a breather from the tension and can also serve to emphasize the tragic elements of the play.

Many plays belong to more than one category. *Macbeth* and *King Lear,* for example, take place in the distant "historical" past but belong to the group called *tragedies. Romeo and Juliet* is a story of complicated love, but it has a famously tragic ending. Plays such as *Measure for Measure* and *The Merchant of Venice*—which don't fit obviously into these four categories—are often referred to as **problem plays.**

A MIDSUMMER NIGHT'S DREAM

This particular comedy was written and performed roughly five years earlier than *Hamlet,* and its style is very different, its purpose to amuse. The "dream" announced in the title is crucial to the play. Often hallucinatory and sometimes edging up to nightmare, dream is the operative mode here. There are three sets of players:

- Athenians of noble rank
- A group of "rude mechanicals" (by which Shakespeare means tradesmen who work at such crafts as tailoring, carpentry, weaving)
- The King and Queen of the Fairies along with their court

The first group (Theseus and Hippolyta and their attendants) is supremely rational and a little dull; the second and third set of players are susceptible to dreaming and a good deal more fun. The King and Queen of the Fairies are as much alive, as physical and needy, as the humans portrayed here; Oberon and Titania may have supernatural powers, but their marriage, with its jealousies and passions, is portrayed in "natural" terms.

> "In comic plays, the playwright so often is referring to what is happening in his world, in the real world, at the moment . . . and . . . making fun." Conversation with Marian Seldes

The events of the play begin with the imminent wedding of Theseus, the Duke of Athens, and his Amazonian queen Hippolyta. Eager for his daughter to marry at the same wedding, a nobleman named Egeus orders Hermia to marry her suitor Demetrius. Hermia refuses because she is in love with another man named Lysander, with whom she makes plans to elope in the forest. Hermia makes the mistake of confiding in her friend Helena, who herself has eyes for Demetrius. Thus, when Hermia and Lysander flee to the forest to marry, they are pursued by Helena and Demetrius, who have been informed of their scheme.

Meanwhile, the fairies in the third group of players listed above are up to their own antics. Oberon, King of the Fairies, and his Queen Titania have arrived in the woods to celebrate the wedding of Theseus and Hippolyta; however, the King and Queen are estranged because Titania will not give over her Indian love child, a "changeling" she keeps by her side. Following a very human argument between husband and wife, Oberon orders his servant Puck to enchant Titania with a flower so she will fall in love with the next person she sees (who ends up being the player Bottom, whose head has recently been transformed by Puck into that of an ass). The events of the play unfold from these confusions, with plenty of enchanting and magically induced love. Ultimately all get what they want, or at least what they deserve, and not without some help from the lingering effects of Puck's mischievous magic.

"Shakespeare's plays are society-driven in a lot of ways, but also class-driven. There are regular people, the common man, and then you have the hierarchy . . . the warriors, the soldiers, the clowns." Conversation with Ruben Santiago-Hudson

Of the three groups of players involved in this web of comedy, the most surprising and original are Bottom and his friends; their performance in the final act of "A tedious brief scene of young Pyramis / and his love Thisbe; very tragical mirth" is a triumph of comic invention. "How shall we find the concord of this discord?" Theseus asks, and when he and members of his court—along with us as audience—view the foolishness within the play, they laugh at happy length. The low humor of Quince, Bottom, Flute, Snout, Snug, and Starveling stands in contrast to the high seriousness of the nobles and their intended nuptials: In musical terms they serve as counterpoint or variation on the theme. That's the point, after all, of "tragical mirth"; they're just as strange bedfellows as are the Queen of the Fairies and a man with the head of an ass. The "rude mechanicals" may not *intend* to be funny, may think themselves serious "players," but Shakespeare stacks the comic deck.

How he does so is in part by *incongruity*. There's pretension and lack of self-knowledge in the way the workers mount their play; the "bumpkin" who believes himself a hero is a comic figure. Shakespeare's making jokes, as well, about his own profession; when Bottom "struts his stuff," he's doing what bad actors do (and what

"Bottom and Snout and the group have the most hilarious imaginings of what it might be to act. . . . And Shakespeare here is hilariously . . . parodying . . . the infelicities of the theater of the time." Conversation with Ralph Williams

Hamlet had cautioned the players against). The idea of Pyramis and Thisbe making love through a make-believe wall is full of **satiric** excess and the gestures of **burlesque**; this scene is often staged in **broad** and **slapstick** terms. (See chapter 31 for more on comedy and its variations.) Lines like these are hard to take seriously, easy to find foolish (and the watching royals cue us that it's all right to laugh):

> *But stay, O spite!*
> *But mark, poor knight,*
> *What dreadful dole is here!*
> *Eyes, do you see?*
> *How can it be?*
> *O dainty duck! O dear!*

The first and final point, and the one that's worth repeating, is that reading William Shakespeare and hearing him and watching him, especially in a play like this, should be *fun*. As Puck, or Robin Goodfellow, says at the close of the performance: "Give me your hands, if we be friends / And Robin shall restore amends." He's asking for applause, approval; the promised result is that the several sets of lovers will live "happily ever after." The first lines of Puck's final speech capture the tone of the whole:

> *If we shadows have offended,*
> *Think but this, and all is mended,*
> *That you have but slumbered here*
> *While these visions did appear.*

AS YOU READ Pay special attention to Puck's role in the events of the play. To what extent is he a "director" of this play? When he says, "Lord, what fools these mortals be," does he refer to the actors or the audience or both?

A Midsummer Night's Dream (c. 1595)

CHARACTERS

THESEUS, *Duke of Athens*

HIPPOLYTA, *Queen of the Amazons, betrothed to Theseus*

PHILOSTRATE, *Master of the Revels*

EGEUS, *father of Hermia*

HERMIA, *daughter of Egeus, in love with Lysander*

LYSANDER, *in love with Hermia*

DEMETRIUS, *in love with Hermia and favored by Egeus*

HELENA, *in love with Demetrius*

OBERON, *King of the Fairies*

TITANIA, *Queen of the Fairies*

PUCK, *or* **ROBIN GOODFELLOW**

PEASEBLOSSOM,

COBWEB,

MOTE,

MUSTARDSEED,

} *fairies attending Titania*

Other **FAIRIES** *attending*

PETER QUINCE, *a carpenter,*		**PROLOGUE**
NICK BOTTOM, *a weaver,*		**PYRAMUS**
FRANCIS FLUTE, *a bellows mender*	*repre-senting*	**THISBE**
TOM SNOUT, *a tinker,*		**WALL**
SNUG, *a joiner,*		**LION**
ROBIN STARVELING, *a tailor,*		**MOONSHINE**

Lords and Attendants on Theseus and Hippolyta

SCENE: *Athens, and a wood near it]*

1.1 *Enter* THESEUS, HIPPOLYTA, *[and* PHILOSTRATE,*]*
with others.

THESEUS: Now, fair Hippolyta, our nuptial hour
Draws on apace. Four happy days bring in
Another moon; but, O, methinks, how slow
This old moon wanes! She lingers my desires,
5   Like to a stepdame or a dowager
Long withering out a young man's revenue.

HIPPOLYTA: Four days will quickly steep themselves
    in night;
Four nights will quickly dream away the time;
And then the moon, like to a silver bow
10   New bent in heaven, shall behold the night
Of our solemnities.

THESEUS: Go, Philostrate,
Stir up the Athenian youth to merriments.
Awake the pert and nimble spirit of mirth.
Turn melancholy forth to funerals;
15   The pale companion is not for our pomp.
                    [Exit PHILOSTRATE.*]*
Hippolyta, I wooed thee with my sword
And won thy love doing thee injuries;
But I will wed thee in another key,
With pomp, with triumph, and with reveling.

        Enter EGEUS *and his daughter* HERMIA,
        and LYSANDER, *and* DEMETRIUS.

20 **EGEUS:** Happy be Theseus, our renownèd duke!

THESEUS: Thanks, good Egeus. What's the news with
    thee?

EGEUS: Full vexation come I, with complaint
Against my child, my daughter Hermia.—
Stand forth, Demetrius.—My noble lord,
25   This man hath my consent to marry her.—
Stand forth, Lysander.—And, my gracious Duke,
This man hath bewitched the bosom of my child.
Thou, thou Lysander, thou hast given her rhymes

Egeus (Nicholas Selby) brings his daughter Hermia (Helen Mirren) before the duke in the 1968 film directed by Peter Hall.

And interchanged love tokens with my child.
30   Thou hast by moonlight at her window sung
With feigning voice verses of feigning love,
And stol'n the impression of her fantasy
With bracelets of thy hair, rings, gauds, conceits,
Knacks, trifles, nosegays, sweetmeats—messengers
35   Of strong prevailment in unhardened youth.
With cunning hast thou filched my daughter's heart,
Turned her obedience, which is due to me,
To stubborn harshness. And, my gracious Duke,
Be it so she will not here before Your Grace
40   Consent to marry with Demetrius,
I beg the ancient privilege of Athens:
As she is mine, I may dispose of her,
Which shall be either to this gentleman
Or to her death, according to our law
45   Immediately provided in that case.

THESEUS: What say you, Hermia? Be advised, fair
    maid.
To you your father should be as a god—
One that composed your beauties, yea, and one
To whom you are but as a form in wax
50   By him imprinted, and within his power
To leave the figure or disfigure it.
Demetrius is a worthy gentleman.

1.1. Location: Athens. Theseus' court.
4 lingers postpones, delays the fulfillment of   **5 stepdame** stepmother.   **a dowager** i.e., a widow (whose right of inheritance from her dead husband is eating into her son's estate)   **6 withering out** causing to dwindle   **7 steep themselves** saturate themselves, be absorbed in   **11 solemnities** festive ceremonies of marriage   **15 companion** fellow. **pomp** ceremonial magnificence   **16 with my sword** i.e., in a military engagement against the Amazons, when Hippolyta was taken captive   **19 triumph** public festivity

---

31 feigning (1) counterfeiting (2) faining, desirous   **32 And . . . fantasy** and made her fall in love with you (imprinting your image on her imagination) by stealthy and dishonest means   **33 gauds** playthings. **conceits** fanciful trifles   **34 Knacks** knickknacks   **35 prevailment in** influence on   **39 Be it so** if   **45 Immediately** directly, with nothing intervening   **51 leave** i.e., leave unaltered. **disfigure** obliterate

HERMIA: So is Lysander.

THESEUS: In himself he is;
But in this kind, wanting your father's voice,
55 The other must be held the worthier.

HERMIA: I would my father looked but with my eyes.

THESEUS: Rather your eyes must with his judgment
look.

HERMIA: I do entreat Your Grace to pardon me.
I know not by what power I am made bold,
60 Nor how it may concern my modesty
In such a presence here to plead my thoughts;
But I beseech Your Grace that I may know
The worst that may befall me in this case
If I refuse to wed Demetrius.

65 **THESEUS:**   Either to die the death or to abjure
Forever the society of men.
Therefore, fair Hermia, question your desires,
Know of your youth, examine well your blood,
Whether, if you yield not to your father's choice,
70 You can endure the livery of a nun,
For aye to be in shady cloister mewed,
To live a barren sister all your life,
Chanting faint hymns to the cold fruitless moon.
Thrice blessèd they that master so their blood
75 To undergo such maiden pilgrimage;
But earthlier happy is the rose distilled
Than that which, withering on the virgin thorn,
Grows, lives, and dies in single blessedness.

HERMIA: So will I grow, so live, so die, my lord,
80 Ere I will yield my virgin patent up
Unto his lordship, whose unwishèd yoke
My soul consents not to give sovereignty.

THESEUS: Take time to pause, and by the next new
moon—
The sealing day betwixt my love and me
85 For everlasting bond of fellowship—
Upon that day either prepare to die
For disobedience to your father's will,
Or else to wed Demetrius, as he would,
Or on Diana's altar to protest
90 For aye austerity and single life.

DEMETRIUS: Relent, sweet Hermia, and, Lysander,
yield
Thy crazèd title to my certain right.

LYSANDER: You have her father's love, Demetrius;
Let me have Hermia's. Do you marry him.

EGEUS: Scornful Lysander! True, he hath my love,   95
And what is mine my love shall render him.
And she is mine, and all my right of her
I do estate unto Demetrius.

LYSANDER: I am, my lord, as well derived as he,
As well possessed; my love is more than his;   100
My fortunes every way as fairly ranked,
If not with vantage, as Demetrius';
And, which is more than all these boasts can be,
I am beloved of beauteous Hermia.
Why should not I then prosecute my right?   105
Demetrius, I'll avouch it to his head,
Made love to Nedar's daughter, Helena,
And won her soul; and she, sweet lady, dotes,
Devoutly dotes, dotes in idolatry
Upon this spotted and inconstant man.   110

THESEUS: I must confess that I have heard so much,
And with Demetrius thought to have spoke thereof;
But, being overfull of self-affairs,
My mind did lose it. But, Demetrius, come,
And come, Egeus, you shall go with me;   115
I have some private schooling for you both.
For you, fair Hermia, look you arm yourself
To fit your fancies to your father's will,
Or else the law of Athens yields you up—
Which by no means we may extenuate—   120
To death or to a vow of single life.
Come, my Hippolyta. What cheer, my love?
Demetrius and Egeus, go along.
I must employ you in some business
Against our nuptial, and confer with you   125
Of something nearly that concerns yourselves.

EGEUS: With duty and desire we follow you.
                    Exeunt [all but LYSANDER *and* HERMIA*].*

LYSANDER: How now, my love, why is your cheek
so pale?
How chance the roses there do fade so fast?

---

54 kind respect. **wanting** lacking. **voice** approval   **60 concern** befit   **65 die the death** be executed by legal process   **68 blood** passions   **70 livery** habit, costume   **71 aye** ever.   **mewed** shut in. (Said of a hawk, poultry, etc.)   **76 earthlier happy** happier as respects this world.   **distilled** i.e., to make perfume   **80 patent** privilege   **88 Or** either   **89 protest** vow

92 crazèd cracked, unsound   **98 estate unto** settle or bestow upon   **99 as well derived** as well born and descended   **100 possessed** endowed with wealth   **101 fairly** handsomely   **102 vantage** superiority   **106 head** i.e., face   **110 spotted** i.e., morally stained   **113 self-affairs** my own concerns   **116 schooling** admonition   **117 look you arm** take care you prepare   **118 fancies** likings, thoughts of love   **120 extenuate** mitigate, relax   **123 go** i.e., come   **125 Against** in preparation for   **126 nearly that** that closely

A MIDSUMMER NIGHT'S DREAM **187**

Hermia and Lysander (David Warner) plan their marriage.

130 **HERMIA:** Belike for want of rain, which I could well
Beteem them from the tempest of my eyes.

LYSANDER: Ay me! For aught that I could ever read,
Could ever hear by tale or history,
The course of true love never did run smooth;
135 But either it was different in blood—

HERMIA: O cross! Too high to be enthralled to low.

LYSANDER: Or else misgrafted in respect of years—

HERMIA: O spite! Too old to be engaged to young.

LYSANDER: Or else it stood upon the choice of
friends—

140 **HERMIA:** O hell, to choose love by another's eyes!

LYSANDER: Or if there were a sympathy in choice,
War, death, or sickness did lay siege to it,
Making it momentany as a sound,
Swift as a shadow, short as any dream,
145 Brief as the lightning in the collied night
That in a spleen unfolds both heaven and earth,
And ere a man hath power to say "Behold!"
The jaws of darkness do devour it up.
So quick bright things come to confusion.

150 **HERMIA:** If then true lovers have been ever crossed,
It stands as an edict in destiny.

Then let us teach our trial patience,
Because it is a customary cross,
As due to love as thoughts, and dreams, and sighs,
Wishes, and tears, poor fancy's followers.   155

LYSANDER: A good persuasion. Therefore, hear me,
Hermia:
I have a widow aunt, a dowager
Of great revenue, and she hath no child.
From Athens is her house remote seven leagues;
And she respects me as her only son.   160
There, gentle Hermia, may I marry thee,
And to that place the sharp Athenian law
Cannot pursue us. If thou lovest me, then,
Steal forth thy father's house tomorrow night;
And in the wood, a league without the town,   165
Where I did meet thee once with Helena
To do observance to a morn of May,
There will I stay for thee.

HERMIA: My good Lysander!
I swear to thee, by Cupid's strongest bow,
By his best arrow with the golden head,   170
By the simplicity of Venus' doves,
By that which knitteth souls and prospers loves,
And by that fire which burned the Carthage queen
When the false Trojan under sail was seen,
By all the vows that ever men have broke,   175
In number more than ever women spoke,
In that same place thou hast appointed me
Tomorrow truly will I meet with thee.

LYSANDER: Keep promise, love. Look, here comes
Helena.

Enter HELENA.

HERMIA: God speed, fair Helena! Whither away?   180

HELENA: Call you me fair? That "fair" again unsay.
Demetrius loves your fair. O happy fair!
Your eyes are lodestars, and your tongue's sweet air
More tunable than lark to shepherd's ear

---

130 Belike very likely   **131 Beteem** grant, afford   **135 blood**
hereditary station   **136 cross** vexation   **137 misgrafted** ill
grafted, badly matched   **139 friends** relatives   **141 sympathy**
agreement   **143 momentany** lasting but a moment   **145 collied**
blackened (as with coal dust), darkened   **146 in a spleen** in a swift
impulse, in a violent flash.   **unfolds** reveals   **149 quick** quickly;
also, living, alive.   **confusion** ruin   **150 ever crossed** always
thwarted

152 teach . . . patience i.e., teach ourselves patience in this trial
155 fancy's amorous passion's   **156 persuasion** doctrine   **160 respects** regards   **165 without** outside   **167 do . . . May** perform the
ceremonies of May Day   **170 best arrow** (Cupid's best gold-pointed
arrows were supposed to induce love; his blunt leaden arrows, aver-
sion.)   **171 simplicity** innocence.   **doves** i.e., those that drew Venus' chariot   **173, 174 Carthage queen, false Trojan** (Dido, Queen
of Carthage, immolated herself on a funeral pyre after having been
deserted by the Trojan hero Aeneas.)   **180 fair** fair-complexioned
(generally regarded by the Elizabethans as more beautiful than a
dark complexion)   **182 your fair** your beauty (even though Hermia
is dark complexioned).   **happy fair** lucky fair one   **183 lodestars**
guiding stars.   **air** music   **184 tunable** tuneful, melodious

185 When wheat is green, when hawthorn buds appear.
Sickness is catching. O, were favor so,
Yours would I catch, fair Hermia, ere I go;
My ear should catch your voice, my eye your eye,
My tongue should catch your tongue's sweet melody.
190 Were the world mine, Demetrius being bated,
The rest I'd give to be to you translated.
O, teach me how you look and with what art
You sway the motion of Demetrius' heart.

HERMIA: I frown upon him, yet he loves me still.

195 **HELENA:** O, that your frowns would teach my smiles
such skill!

HERMIA: I give him curses, yet he gives me love.

HELENA: O, that my prayers could such affection
move!

HERMIA: The more I hate, the more he follows me.

HELENA: The more I love, the more he hateth me.

200 **HERMIA:** His folly, Helena, is no fault of mine.

HELENA: None, but your beauty. Would that fault were
mine!

HERMIA: Take comfort. He no more shall see my face.
Lysander and myself will fly this place.
Before the time I did Lysander see
205 Seemed Athens as a paradise to me.
O, then, what graces in my love do dwell,
That he hath turned a heaven unto a hell?

LYSANDER: Helen, to you our minds we will unfold.
Tomorrow night, when Phoebe doth behold
210 Her silver visage in the watery glass,
Decking with liquid pearl the bladed grass,
A time that lovers' flights doth still conceal,
Through Athens' gates have we devised to steal.

HERMIA: And in the wood, where often you and I
215 Upon faint primrose beds were wont to lie,
Emptying our bosoms of their counsel sweet,
There my Lysander and myself shall meet,
And thence from Athens turn away our eyes
To seek new friends and stranger companies.
220 Farewell, sweet playfellow. Pray thou for us,
And good luck grant thee thy Demetrius!

Keep word, Lysander. We must starve our sight
From lovers' food till morrow deep midnight.

LYSANDER: I will, my Hermia. (*Exit* HERMIA.) Helena,
adieu.
As you on him, Demetrius dote on you! 225
Exit LYSANDER.

HELENA: How happy some o'er other some can be!
Through Athens I am thought as fair as she.
But what of that? Demetrius thinks not so;
He will not know what all but he do know.
And as he errs, doting on Hermia's eyes, 230
So I, admiring of his qualities.
Things base and vile, holding no quantity,
Love can transpose to form and dignity.
Love looks not with the eyes, but with the mind,
And therefore is winged Cupid painted blind. 235
Nor hath Love's mind of any judgment taste;
Wings and no eyes figure unheedy haste.
And therefore is Love said to be a child,
Because in choice he is so oft beguiled.
As waggish boys in game themselves forswear, 240
So the boy Love is perjured everywhere.
For ere Demetrius looked on Hermia's eyne,
He hailed down oaths that he was only mine;
And when this hail some heat from Hermia felt,
So he dissolved, and showers of oaths did melt. 245
I will go tell him of fair Hermia's flight.
Then to the wood will he tomorrow night
Pursue her; and for this intelligence
If I have thanks, it is a dear expense.
But herein mean I to enrich my pain, 250
To have his sight thither and back again. *Exit.*

1.2 *Enter* QUINCE *the carpenter, and* SNUG *the joiner, and*
BOTTOM *the weaver, and* FLUTE *the bellows mender,*
and SNOUT *the tinker, and* STARVELING *the tailor.*

QUINCE: Is all our company here?

BOTTOM: You were best to call them generally, man by
man, according to the scrip.

---

186 **favor** appearance, looks   190 **bated** excepted   191 **translated**
transformed   193 **sway** control.   **motion** impulse   197 **affec-**
tion passion.   **move** arouse   204–205 **Before . . . to me** (Hermia
seemingly means that love has led to complications and jealousies,
making Athens hell for her.)   209 **Phoebe** Diana, the moon   210
glass mirror   212 **still** always   215 **faint** pale   216 **counsel** secret thought   219 **stranger companies** the company of strangers

226 **o'er . . . can be** can be in comparison to some others   231
admiring of wondering at   232 **holding no quantity** i.e., unsub-
stantial, unshapely   236 **Nor . . . taste** i.e., nor has Love, which
dwells in the fancy or imagination, any *taste* or least bit of judgment
or reason   237 **figure** are a symbol of   239 **in choice** in choosing.
beguiled self-deluded, making unaccountable choices   240 **wag-**
gish playful, mischievous.   **game** sport, jest   242 **eyne** eyes. (Old
form of plural.)   248 **intelligence** information   249 **a dear ex-**
pense i.e., a trouble worth taking on my part, or a begrudging effort
on his part.   **dear** costly

1.2 Location: Athens.
2 **generally** (Bottom's blunder for "individually.")   3 **scrip** scrap.
(Bottom's error for "script.")

5 **QUINCE:** Here is the scroll of every man's name which is thought fit, through all Athens, to play in our interlude before the Duke and the Duchess on his wedding day at night.

BOTTOM: First, good Peter Quince, say what the play treats on, then read the names of the actors, and so 10 grow to a point.

QUINCE: Marry, our play is "The most lamentable comedy and most cruel death of Pyramus and Thisbe."

BOTTOM: A very good piece of work, I assure you, and a merry. Now, good Peter Quince, call forth your ac- 15 tors by the scroll. Masters, spread yourselves.

QUINCE: Answer as I call you. Nick Bottom, the weaver.

BOTTOM: Ready. Name what part I am for, and proceed.

QUINCE: You, Nick Bottom, are set down for Pyramus.

BOTTOM: What is Pyramus? A lover or a tyrant?

20 **QUINCE:** A lover, that kills himself most gallant for love.

BOTTOM: That will ask some tears in the true performing of it. If I do it, let the audience look to their eyes. I will move storms; I will condole in some measure. To the rest—yet my chief humor is for a tyrant. I could play 25 Ercles rarely, or a part to tear a cat in, to make all split.
　　"The raging rocks
　　And shivering shocks
　　Shall break the locks
　　　　Of prison gates;
30 　　And Phibbus' car
　　Shall shine from far
　　And make and mar
　　　　The foolish Fates."
This was lofty! Now name the rest of the players. This 35 is Ercles' vein, a tyrant's vein. A lover is more condoling.

QUINCE: Francis Flute, the bellows mender.

FLUTE: Here, Peter Quince.

QUINCE: Flute, you must take Thisbe on you.

FLUTE: What is Thisbe? A wandering knight?

40 **QUINCE:** It is the lady that Pyramus must love.

Quince (Sebastian Shaw) persuades Bottom (Paul Rogers) to play Pyramus.

FLUTE: Nay, faith, let not me play a woman. I have a beard coming.

QUINCE: That's all one. You shall play it in a mask, and you may speak as small as you will.

BOTTOM: An I may hide my face, let me play Thisbe 45 too. I'll speak in a monstrous little voice: "Thisne, Thisne!" "Ah, Pyramus, my lover dear! Thy Thisbe dear, and lady dear!"

QUINCE: No, no, you must play Pyramus, and Flute, you Thisbe. 50

BOTTOM: Well, proceed.

QUINCE: Robin Starveling, the tailor.

STARVELING: Here, Peter Quince.

QUINCE: Robin Starveling, you must play Thisbe's mother. Tom Snout, the tinker. 55

SNOUT: Here, Peter Quince.

QUINCE: You, Pyramus' father; myself, Thisbe's father; Snug, the joiner, you, the lion's part; and I hope here is a play fitted.

SNUG: Have you the lion's part written? Pray you, if it 60 be, give it me, for I am slow of study.

QUINCE: You may do it extempore, for it is nothing but roaring.

5–6 **interlude** play　10 **grow to** come to　11 **Marry** (A mild oath; originally the name of the Virgin Mary.)　16 **Bottom** (As a weaver's term, a *bottom* was an object around which thread was wound.)　23 **condole** lament, arouse pity　24 **humor** inclination, whim　25 **Ercles** Hercules. (The tradition of ranting came from Seneca's *Hercules Furens*.)　**tear a cat** i.e., rant.　**make all split** i.e., cause a stir, bring the house down　30 **Phibbus' car** Phoebus', the sun god's, chariot

---

43 **That's all one** it makes no difference　44 **small** high-pitched　45 **An** if. (Also at line 68.)

BOTTOM: Let me play the lion too. I will roar that I
will do any man's heart good to hear me. I will roar
that I will make the Duke say, "Let him roar again,
let him roar again."

QUINCE: An you should do it too terribly, you would
fright the Duchess and the ladies, that they would
shriek; and that were enough to hang us all.

ALL: That would hang us, every mother's son.

BOTTOM: I grant you, friends, if you should fright the
ladies out of their wits, they would have no more discretion but to hang us; but I will aggravate my voice
so that I will roar you as gently as any sucking dove;
I will roar you an 'twere any nightingale.

QUINCE: You can play no part but Pyramus; for Pyramus is a sweet-faced man, a proper man as one shall
see in a summer's day, a most lovely gentlemanlike
man. Therefore you must needs play Pyramus.

BOTTOM: Well, I will undertake it What beard were I
best to play it in?

QUINCE: Why, what you will.

BOTTOM: I will discharge it in either your straw-color
beard, your orange-tawny beard, your purple-in-
grain beard, or your French-crown-color beard, your
perfect yellow.

QUINCE: Some of your French crowns have no hair at
all, and then you will play barefaced. But, masters,
here are your parts. *[He distributes parts.]* And I am
to entreat you, request you, and desire you to con
them by tomorrow night, and meet me in the palace
wood, a mile without the town, by moonlight. There
will we rehearse; for if we meet in the city, we shall
be dogged with company, and our devices known. In
the meantime I will draw a bill of properties, such as
our play wants. I pray you, fail me not.

BOTTOM: We will meet, and there we may rehearse
most obscenely and courageously. Take pains, be
perfect. Adieu.

Oberon (Rupert Everett) sits in his fairy court in the 1999 film directed by Michael Hoffman.

QUINCE: At the Duke's oak we meet.

BOTTOM: Enough. Hold, or cut bowstrings. *Exeunt.*

2.1 *Enter a* FAIRY *at one door, and* ROBIN GOODFELLOW *[PUCK] at another.*

PUCK: How now, spirit, whither wander you?

FAIRY:
> Over hill, over dale,
>> Thorough bush, thorough brier,
> Over park, over pale,
>> Thorough flood, thorough fire,
> I do wander everywhere,
> Swifter than the moon's sphere;
> And I serve the Fairy Queen,
> To dew her orbs upon the green.
> The cowslips tall her pensioners be.
> In their gold coats spots you see;
> Those be rubies, fairy favors;
> In those freckles live their savors.
> I must go seek some dewdrops here
> And hang a pearl in every cowslip's ear.
> Farewell, thou lob of spirits; I'll be gone.
> Our Queen and all her elves come here anon.

PUCK: The King doth keep his revels here tonight.
Take heed the Queen come not within his sight.
For Oberon is passing fell and wrath,

---

74 aggravate (Bottom's blunder for "moderate.") **75 roar you** i.e.,
roar for you. **sucking dove** (Bottom conflates *sitting dove* and
sucking lamb, two proverbial images of innocence.) **76 an 'twere**
as if it were **78 proper** handsome **84 discharge** perform **your**
i.e., you know the kind I mean **85–86 purple-in-grain** dyed a very
deep red. (From *grain,* the name applied to the dried insect used
to make the dye.) **86 French-crown-color** i.e., color of a French
crown, a gold coin **88 crowns** heads bald from syphilis, the "French
disease" **91 con** learn by heart **95 devices** plans **96 draw a bill**
draw up a list **99 obscenely** (An unintentionally funny blunder,
whatever Bottom meant to say.) **100 perfect** i.e., letter-perfect in
memorizing your parts

102 Hold . . . bowstrings (An archers' expression, not definitely
explained, but probably meaning here "keep your promises, or give
up the play.")

2.1 Location: A wood near Athens.
3 Thorough through **4 pale** enclosure **7 sphere** orbit **9 dew**
sprinkle with dew. **orbs** circles, i.e., fairy rings (circular bands
of grass, darker than the surrounding area, caused by fungi en-
riching the soil) **10 pensioners** retainers, members of the royal
bodyguard **12 favors** love tokens **13 savors** sweet smells **16 lob**
country bumpkin **17 anon** at once **20 passing fell** exceedingly
angry. **wrath** wrathful

Because that she as her attendant hath
A lovely boy, stolen from an Indian king;
She never had so sweet a changeling.
And jealous Oberon would have the child
25 Knight of his train, to trace the forests wild.
But she perforce withholds the lovèd boy,
Crowns him with flowers, and makes him all her joy.
And now they never meet in grove or green,
By fountain clear, or spangled starlight sheen,
30 But they do square, that all their elves for fear
Creep into acorn cups and hide them there.

FAIRY: Either I mistake your shape and making quite,
Or else you are that shrewd and knavish sprite
Called Robin Goodfellow. Are not you he
35 That frights the maidens of the villagery,
Skim milk, and sometimes labor in the quern,
And bootless make the breathless huswife churn,
And sometimes make the drink to bear no barm,
Mislead night wanderers, laughing at their harm?
40 Those that "Hobgoblin" call you, and "Sweet Puck,"
You do their work, and they shall have good luck.
Are you not he?

PUCK: Thou speakest aright;
I am that merry wanderer of the night.
I jest to Oberon and make him smile
45 When I a fat and bean-fed horse beguile,
Neighing in likeness of a filly foal;
And sometimes lurk I in a gossip's bowl
In very likeness of a roasted crab,
And when she drinks, against her lips I bob
50 And on her withered dewlap pour the ale.
The wisest aunt, telling the saddest tale,
Sometimes for three-foot stool mistaketh me;
Then slip I from her bum, down topples she,
And "Tailor" cries, and falls into a cough;
55 And then the whole choir hold their hips and laugh,

And waxen in their mirth, and neeze, and swear
A merrier hour was never wasted there.
But, room, fairy! Here comes Oberon.

FAIRY: And here my mistress. Would that he were gone!

*Enter [OBERON] the King of Fairies at
one door, with his train, and [TITANIA]
the Queen at another, with hers.*

OBERON: Ill met by moonlight, proud Titania.   60

TITANIA: What, jealous Oberon? Fairies, skip hence.
I have forsworn his bed and company.

OBERON: Tarry, rash wanton. Am not I thy lord?

TITANIA: Then I must be thy lady; but I know
When thou hast stolen away from Fairyland   65
And in the shape of Corin sat all day,
Playing on pipes of corn and versing love
To amorous Phillida. Why art thou here
Come from the farthest step of India,
But that, forsooth, the bouncing Amazon,   70
Your buskined mistress and your warrior love,
To Theseus must be wedded, and you come
To give their bed joy and prosperity.

OBERON: How canst thou thus for shame, Titania,
Glance at my credit with Hippolyta,   75
Knowing I know thy love to Theseus?
Didst not thou lead him through the glimmering
        night
From Perigenia, whom he ravishèd?
And make him with fair Aegles break his faith,
With Ariadne and Antiopa?   80

TITANIA: These are the forgeries of jealousy;
And never, since the middle summer's spring,
Met we on hill, in dale, forest, or mead,

---

23 changeling child exchanged for another by the fairies **25 trace** range through **26 perforce** forcibly **29 fountain** spring. **starlight sheen** shining starlight **30 square** quarrel **33 shrewd** mischievous. **sprite** spirit **35 villagery** village population **36 Skim milk** i.e., steal the cream. **quern** hand mill (where Puck presumably hampers the grinding of grain) **37 bootless** in vain. (Puck prevents the cream from turning to butter.) **huswife** housewife **38 barm** head on the ale. (Puck prevents the barm or yeast from producing fermentation.) **39 Mislead night wanderers** i.e., mislead with false fire those who walk abroad at night (hence earning Puck his other names of Jack o' Lantern and Will o' the Wisp) **40 Those . . . Puck** i.e., those who call you by the names you favor rather than those denoting the mischief you do **45 bean-fed** well fed on field beans **47 gossip's** old woman's **48 crab** crab apple **50 dewlap** loose skin on neck **51 aunt** old woman. **saddest** most serious **54 Tailor** (possibly because she ends up sitting cross-legged on the floor, looking like a tailor, or else referring to the *tail* or buttocks) **55 choir** company

56 waxen increase. **neeze** sneeze **57 wasted** spent **58 room** stand aside, make room **63 wanton** headstrong creature **66, 68 Corin, Phillida** (Conventional names of pastoral lovers.) **67 corn** (Here, oat stalks.) **69 step** farthest limit of travel, or, perhaps, *steep*, "mountain range" **71 buskined** wearing half-boots called buskins **75 Glance . . . Hippolyta** make insinuations about my favored relationship with Hippolyta **78 Perigenia** i.e., Perigouna, one of Theseus' conquests. (This and the following women are named in Thomas North's translation of Plutarch's "Life of Theseus.") **79 Aegles** i.e., Aegle, for whom Theseus deserted Ariadne according to some accounts **80 Ariadne** the daughter of Minos, King of Crete, who helped Theseus to escape the labyrinth after killing the Minotaur; later she was abandoned by Theseus. **Antiopa** Queen of the Amazons and wife of Theseus; elsewhere identified with Hippolyta but here thought of as a separate woman **82 middle summer's spring** beginning of midsummer **83 mead** meadow

Titania (Michelle Pfeiffer) argues with Oberon.

By pavèd fountain or by rushy brook,
85   Or in the beachèd margent of the sea,
To dance our ringlets to the whistling wind,
But with thy brawls thou hast disturbed our sport.
Therefore the winds, piping to us in vain,
As in revenge, have sucked up from the sea
90   Contagious fogs which, falling in the land,
Hath every pelting river made so proud
That they have overborne their continents.
The ox hath therefore stretched his yoke in vain,
The plowman lost his sweat, and the green corn
95   Hath rotted ere his youth attained a beard;
The fold stands empty in the drownèd field,
And crows are fatted with the murrain flock;
The nine-men's morris is filled up with mud,
And the quaint mazes in the wanton green
100   For lack of tread are undistinguishable.
The human mortals want their winter here;
No night is now with hymn or carol blessed.
Therefore the moon, the governess of floods,
Pale in her anger, washes all the air,
105   That rheumatic diseases do abound.
And thorough this distemperature we see
The seasons alter: hoary-headed frosts

Fall in the fresh lap of the crimson rose,
And on old Hiems' thin and icy crown
An odorous chaplet of sweet summer buds   110
Is, as in mockery, set. The spring, the summer,
The childing autumn, angry winter, change
Their wonted liveries, and the mazèd world
By their increase now knows not which is which.
And this same progeny of evils comes   115
From our debate, from our dissension.
We are their parents and original.

OBERON: Do you amend it, then. It lies in you.
Why should Titania cross her Oberon?
I do but beg a little changeling boy   120
To be my henchman.

TITANIA: Set your heart at rest.
The fairy land buys not the child of me.
His mother was a vot'ress of my order,
And in the spicèd Indian air by night
Full often hath she gossiped by my side   125
And sat with me on Neptune's yellow sands,
Marking th' embarkèd traders on the flood,
When we have laughed to see the sails conceive
And grow big-bellied with the wanton wind;
Which she, with pretty and with swimming gait,   130
Following—her womb then rich with my young
          squire—
Would imitate, and sail upon the land
To fetch me trifles, and return again
As from a voyage, rich with merchandise.
But she, being mortal, of that boy did die;   135
And for her sake do I rear up her boy,
And for her sake I will not part with him.

OBERON: How long within this wood intend you stay?

TITANIA: Perchance till after Theseus' wedding day.
If you will patiently dance in our round   140
And see our moonlight revels, go with us;
If not, shun me, and I will spare your haunts.

OBERON: Give me that boy, and I will go with thee.

TITANIA: Not for thy fairy kingdom. Fairies, away!
We shall chide downright, if I longer stay.   145
          *Exeunt [*TITANIA *with her train].*

---

84 **pavèd** with pebbled bottom.   **rushy** bordered with rushes   85
in on.   **margent** edge, border   86 **ringlets** dances in a ring. (See
orbs in line 9.)   **to** to the sound of   90 **Contagious** noxious   91
pelting paltry   92 **continents** banks that contain them   93
stretched his yoke i.e., pulled at his yoke in plowing   94 **corn**
grain of any kind   96 **fold** pen for sheep or cattle   97 **murrain**
having died of the plague   98 **nine-men's morris** i.e., portion of
the village green marked out in a square for a game played with
nine pebbles or pegs   99 **quaint mazes** i.e., intricate paths marked
out on the village green to be followed rapidly on foot as a kind of
contest.   **wanton** luxuriant   101 **want** lack.   **winter** i.e., regular
winter season; or, proper observances of winter, such as the *hymn*
or *carol* in the next line (?)   103 **Therefore** i.e., as a result of our
quarrel   104 **washes** saturates with moisture   105 **rheumatic**
diseases colds, flu, and other respiratory infections   106 **distem-**
perature disturbance in nature

---

109 **Hiems'** the winter god's   112 **childing** fruitful, pregnant   113
wonted liveries usual apparel.   **mazèd** bewildered   114 **their**
increase their yield, what they produce   116 **debate** quarrel   117
original origin   121 **henchman** attendant, page   123 **was . . .**
order had taken a vow to serve me   127 **traders** trading vessels.
flood flood tide   129 **wanton** (1) playful (2) amorous   130 **swim-**
ming smooth, gliding   140 **round** circular dance   142 **spare** shun

OBERON: Well, go thy way. Thou shalt not from this
    grove
    Till I torment thee for this injury.
    My gentle Puck, come hither. Thou rememb'rest
    Since once I sat upon a promontory,
150   And heard a mermaid on a dolphin's back
    Uttering such dulcet and harmonious breath
    That the rude sea grew civil at her song,
    And certain stars shot madly from their spheres
    To hear the sea-maid's music?

PUCK: I remember.

155 **OBERON:** That very time I saw, but thou couldst not,
    Flying between the cold moon and the earth
    Cupid, all armed. A certain aim he took
    At a fair vestal thronèd by the west,
    And loosed his love shaft smartly from his bow
160   As it should pierce a hundred thousand hearts;
    But I might see young Cupid's fiery shaft
    Quenched in the chaste beams of the watery moon,
    And the imperial vot'ress passèd on,
    In maiden meditation, fancy-free.
165   Yet marked I where the bolt of Cupid fell:
    It fell upon a little western flower,
    Before milk-white, now purple with love's wound,
    And maidens call it love-in-idleness.
    Fetch me that flower; the herb I showed thee once.
170   The juice of it on sleeping eyelids laid
    Will make or man or woman madly dote
    Upon the next live creature that it sees.
    Fetch me this herb, and be thou here again
    Ere the leviathan can swim a league.

175 **PUCK:** I'll put a girdle round about the earth
    In forty minutes.   *[Exit.]*

OBERON: Having once this juice,
    I'll watch Titania when she is asleep
    And drop the liquor of it in her eyes.
    The next thing then she waking looks upon,
180   Be it on lion, bear, or wolf, or bull,
    On meddling monkey, or on busy ape,
    She shall pursue it with the soul of love.
    And ere I take this charm from off her sight,

As I can take it with another herb,
I'll make her render up her page to me.   185
But who comes here? I am invisible,
And I will overhear their conference.

Enter DEMETRIUS, HELENA *following him.*

DEMETRIUS: I love thee not; therefore pursue me not.
    Where is Lysander and fair Hermia?
    The one I'll slay; the other slayeth me.   190
    Thou toldst me they were stol'n unto this wood;
    And here am I, and wood within this wood
    Because I cannot meet my Hermia.
    Hence, get thee gone, and follow me no more.

HELENA: You draw me, you hardhearted adamant!   195
    But yet you draw not iron, for my heart
    Is true as steel. Leave you your power to draw,
    And I shall have no power to follow you.

DEMETRIUS: Do I entice you? Do I speak you fair?
    Or rather do I not in plainest truth   200
    Tell you I do not nor I cannot love you?

HELENA: And even for that do I love you the more.
    I am your spaniel; and, Demetrius,
    The more you beat me I will fawn on you.
    Use me but as your spaniel, spurn me, strike me,   205
    Neglect me, lose me; only give me leave,
    Unworthy as I am, to follow you.
    What worser place can I beg in your love—
    And yet a place of high respect with me—
    Than to be usèd as you use your dog?   210

DEMETRIUS: Tempt not too much the hatred of my
    spirit,
    For I am sick when I do look on thee.

HELENA: And I am sick when I look not on you.

DEMETRIUS: You do impeach your modesty too much
    To leave the city and commit yourself   215
    Into the hands of one that loves you not,
    To trust the opportunity of night
    And the ill counsel of a desert place
    With the rich worth of your virginity.

HELENA: Your virtue is my privilege. For that   220
    It is not night when I do see your face,

---

146 **from** go from 149 **Since** when 151 **dulcet** sweet. **breath**
voice, song 152 **rude** rough 157 **all** fully. **certain** sure 158
vestal vestal virgin. (Contains a complimentary allusion to Queen
Elizabeth as a votaress of Diana and probably refers to an actual
entertainment in her honor at Elvetham in 1591.) **by** in the region
of 159 **loosed** released 160 **As** as if 161 **might** could 164
fancy-free free of love's spell 165 **bolt** arrow 168 **love-in-idleness**
pansy, heartsease 171 **or . . . or** either . . . or 174 **leviathan** sea
monster, whale 176 **forty** (Used indefinitely.)

---

192 **and wood** and mad, frantic (with an obvious wordplay on
wood, meaning "woods") 195 **adamant** lodestone, magnet (with
pun on *hardhearted*, since adamant was also thought to be the
hardest of all stones and was confused with the diamond) 197
Leave you give up 199 **speak you fair** speak courteously to
you 214 **impeach** call into question 215 **To leave** by leaving
218 **desert** deserted 220 **virtue** goodness or power to attract.
privilege safeguard, warrant. **For that** because

Therefore I think I am not in the night;
Nor doth this wood lack worlds of company,
For you, in my respect, are all the world.
225 Then how can it be said I am alone
When all the world is here to look on me?

DEMETRIUS: I'll run from thee and hide me in the brakes,
And leave thee to the mercy of wild beasts.

HELENA: The wildest hath not such a heart as you.
230 Run when you will. The story shall be changed:
Apollo flies and Daphne holds the chase,
The dove pursues the griffin, the mild hind
Makes speed to catch the tiger—bootless speed,
When cowardice pursues and valor flies!

235 **DEMETRIUS:**   I will not stay thy questions. Let me go!
Or if thou follow me, do not believe
But I shall do thee mischief in the wood.

HELENA: Ay, in the temple, in the town, the field,
You do me mischief. Fie, Demetrius!
240 Your wrongs do set a scandal on my sex.
We cannot fight for love, as men may do;
We should be wooed and were not made to woo.
[Exit DEMETRIUS.]
I'll follow thee and make a heaven of hell,
To die upon the hand I love so well.   *[Exit.]*

245 **OBERON:**   Fare thee well, nymph. Ere he do leave this grove
Thou shalt fly him, and he shall seek thy love.
Enter PUCK.
Hast thou the flower there? Welcome, wanderer.

PUCK: Ay, there it is.   *[He offers the flower.]*

OBERON: I pray thee, give it me.
I know a bank where the wild thyme blows,
250 Where oxlips and the nodding violet grows,
Quite overcanopied with luscious woodbine,

Puck (Stanley Tucci) shows the magic flower to Oberon.

With sweet muskroses and with eglantine.
There sleeps Titania sometime of the night,
Lulled in these flowers with dances and delight;
And there the snake throws her enameled skin,   255
Weed wide enough to wrap a fairy in.
And with the juice of this I'll streak her eyes
And make her full of hateful fantasies.
Take thou some of it, and seek through this grove.
[He gives some love juice.]
A sweet Athenian lady is in love   260
With a disdainful youth. Anoint his eyes,
But do it when the next thing he espies
May be the lady. Thou shalt know the man
By the Athenian garments he hath on.
Effect it with some care, that he may prove   265
More fond on her than she upon her love;
And look thou meet me ere the first cock crow.

PUCK: Fear not, my lord, your servant shall do so.
Exeunt [separately].

2.2   *Enter TITANIA, Queen of Fairies, with her train.*

TITANIA: Come, now a roundel and a fairy song;
Then, for the third part of a minute, hence—
Some to kill cankers in the muskrose buds,
Some war with reremice for their leathern wings
To make my small elves coats, and some keep back   5
The clamorous owl, that nightly hoots and wonders
At our quaint spirits. Sing me now asleep.
Then to your offices, and let me rest.

---

224 in my respect as far as I am concerned, in my esteem   **227 brakes** thickets   **231 Apollo . . . chase** (In the ancient myth, Daphne fled from Apollo and was saved from rape by being transformed into a laurel tree; here it is the female who *holds the chase*, or pursues, instead of the male.)   **232 griffin** a fabulous monster with the head and wings of an eagle and the body of a lion.   **hind** female deer   **233 bootless** fruitless   **235 stay** wait for, put up with.   **questions** talk or argument   **240 Your . . . sex** i.e., the wrongs that you do me cause me to act in a manner that disgraces my sex   **244 upon** by   **249 blows** blooms   **250 oxlips** flowers resembling cowslip and primrose   **251 woodbine** honeysuckle

---

252 muskroses a kind of large, sweet-scented rose.   **eglantine** sweetbrier, another kind of rose   **253 sometime of** for part of   **255 throws** sloughs off, sheds   **256 Weed** garment   **257 streak** anoint, touch gently   **266 fond on** doting on

2.2 Location: The wood.
1 roundel dance in a ring   **2 the third . . . minute** (Indicative of the fairies' quickness.)   **3 cankers** cankerworms (i.e., caterpillars or grubs)   **4 reremice** bats   **7 quaint** dainty

FAIRIES *sing.*

FIRST FAIRY:
> You spotted snakes with double tongue,
> 10   Thorny hedgehogs, be not seen;
> Newts and blindworms, do no wrong;
> Come not near our Fairy Queen.

CHORUS *[dancing]:*
> Philomel, with melody
> Sing in our sweet lullaby;
> 15   Lulla, lulla, lullaby, lulla, lulla, lullaby.
> Never harm
> Nor spell nor charm
> Come our lovely lady nigh.
> So good night, with lullaby.

FIRST FAIRY:
> 20   Weaving spiders, come not here;
> Hence, you long-legged spinners, hence!
> Beetles black, approach not near;
> Worm nor snail, do no offense.

CHORUS *[dancing]:*
> Philomel, with melody
> 25   Sing in our sweet lullaby;
> Lulla, lulla, lullaby, lulla, lulla, lullaby.
> Never harm
> Nor spell nor charm
> Come our lovely lady nigh.
> 30   So good night, with lullaby.

[TITANIA sleeps.]

SECOND FAIRY:
> Hence, away! Now all is well.
> One aloof stand sentinel.

[Exeunt FAIRIES, leaving one sentinel.]

*Enter OBERON [and squeezes the
flower on TITANIA's eyelids].*

OBERON:
> What thou seest when thou dost wake,
> Do it for thy true love take;
> 35   Love and languish for his sake.
> Be it ounce, or cat, or bear,
> Pard, or boar with bristled hair,
> In thy eye that shall appear
> When thou wak'st, it is thy dear.
> 40   Wake when some vile thing is near.   *[Exit.]*

---

9 double forked   **11 Newts** water lizards (considered poisonous, as were *blindworms* —small snakes with tiny eyes—and spiders)   **13 Philomel** the nightingale. (Philomela, daughter of King Pandion, was transformed into a nightingale, according to Ovid's *Metamorphoses* 6, after she had been raped by her sister Procne's husband, Tereus.)   **23 offense** harm   **32 sentinel** (Presumably Oberon is able to outwit or intimidate this guard.)   **36 ounce** lynx   **37 Pard** leopard

Enter LYSANDER and HERMIA.

LYSANDER: Fair love, you faint with wandering in
> the wood;
> And to speak truth, I have forgot our way.
> We'll rest us, Hermia, if you think it good,
> And tarry for the comfort of the day.

HERMIA: Be it so, Lysander. Find you out a bed,   45
> For I upon this bank will rest my head.

LYSANDER: One turf shall serve as pillow for us both;
> One heart, one bed, two bosoms, and one troth.

HERMIA: Nay, good Lysander, for my sake, my dear,
> Lie further off yet. Do not lie so near.   50

LYSANDER: O, take the sense, sweet, of my innocence!
> Love takes the meaning in love's conference.
> I mean that my heart unto yours is knit,
> So that but one heart we can make of it;
> Two bosoms interchainèd with an oath—   55
> So then two bosoms and a single troth.
> Then by your side no bed-room me deny,
> For lying so, Hermia, I do not lie.

HERMIA: Lysander riddles very prettily.
> Now much beshrew my manners and my pride   60
> If Hermia meant to say Lysander lied.
> But, gentle friend, for love and courtesy
> Lie further off, in human modesty.
> Such separation as may well be said
> Becomes a virtuous bachelor and a maid,   65
> So far be distant; and, good night, sweet friend.
> Thy love ne'er alter till thy sweet life end!

LYSANDER: Amen, amen, to that fair prayer, say I,
> And then end life when I end loyalty!
> Here is my bed. Sleep give thee all his rest!   70

HERMIA: With half that wish the wisher's eyes be
> pressed!

[They sleep, separated by a short distance.]

Enter PUCK.

PUCK: Through the forest have I gone,
> But Athenian found I none

---

48 troth faith, trothplight   **51 take ... innocence** i.e., interpret my intention as innocent   **52 Love ... conference** i.e., when lovers confer, love teaches each lover to interpret the other's meaning lovingly   **58 lie** tell a falsehood (with a riddling pun on *lie*, "recline")   **60 beshrew** curse. (But mildly meant.)   **63 human** courteous (and perhaps suggesting "humane," the Quarto spelling)   **71 With ... pressed** i.e., may we share your wish, so that your eyes too are *pressed*, closed, in sleep

75 On whose eyes I might approve
This flower's force in stirring love.
Night and silence.—Who is here?
Weeds of Athens he doth wear.
This is he, my master said,
Despisèd the Athenian maid;
80 And here the maiden, sleeping sound,
On the dank and dirty ground.
Pretty soul, she durst not lie
Near this lack-love, this kill-courtesy.
Churl, upon thy eyes I throw
85 All the power this charm doth owe.

[He applies the love juice.]

When thou wak'st, let love forbid
Sleep his seat on thy eyelid.
So awake when I am gone,
For I must now to Oberon. *Exit.*

Enter DEMETRIUS *and* HELENA, *running.*

90 **HELENA:** Stay, though thou kill me, sweet Demetrius!

DEMETRIUS: I charge thee, hence, and do not haunt
me thus.

HELENA: O, wilt thou darkling leave me? Do not so.

DEMETRIUS: Stay, on thy peril! I alone will go. *[Exit.]*

HELENA: O, I am out of breath in this fond chase!
95 The more my prayer, the lesser is my grace.
Happy is Hermia, wheresoe'er she lies,
For she hath blessèd and attractive eyes.
How came her eyes so bright? Not with salt tears;
If so, my eyes are oftener washed than hers.
100 No, no, I am as ugly as a bear,
For beasts that meet me run away for fear.
Therefore no marvel though Demetrius
Do, as a monster, fly my presence thus.
What wicked and dissembling glass of mine
105 Made me compare with Hermia's sphery eyne?
But who is here? Lysander, on the ground?
Dead, or asleep? I see no blood, no wound.
Lysander, if you live, good sir, awake.

LYSANDER *[awaking]*: And run through fire I will for
thy sweet sake.
110 Transparent Helena! Nature shows art,

That through thy bosom makes me see thy heart.
Where is Demetrius? O, how fit a word
Is that vile name to perish on my sword!

HELENA: Do not say so, Lysander; say not so.
What though he love your Hermia? Lord, what
though? 115
Yet Hermia still loves you. Then be content.

LYSANDER: Content with Hermia? No! I do repent
The tedious minutes I with her have spent.
Not Hermia but Helena I love.
Who will not change a raven for a dove? 120
The will of man is by his reason swayed,
And reason says you are the worthier maid.
Things growing are not ripe until their season;
So I, being young, till now ripe not to reason.
And, touching now the point of human skill, 125
Reason becomes the marshal to my will
And leads me to your eyes, where I o'erlook
Love's stories written in love's richest book.

HELENA: Wherefore was I to this keen mockery born?
When at your hands did I deserve this scorn? 130
Is 't not enough, is 't not enough, young man,
That I did never—no, nor never can—
Deserve a sweet look from Demetrius' eye,
But you must flout my insufficiency?
Good troth, you do me wrong, good sooth, you do, 135
In such disdainful manner me to woo.
But fare you well. Perforce I must confess
I thought you lord of more true gentleness.
O, that a lady, of one man refused,
Should of another therefore be abused! *Exit.* 140

LYSANDER: She sees not Hermia. Hermia, sleep thou
there,
And never mayst thou come Lysander near!
For as a surfeit of the sweetest things
The deepest loathing to the stomach brings,
Or as the heresies that men do leave 145
Are hated most of those they did deceive,
So thou, my surfeit and my heresy,
Of all be hated, but the most of me!
And, all my powers, address your love and might
To honor Helen and to be her knight! *Exit.* 150

---

74 approve test **85 owe** own **92 darkling** in the dark **93 on
thy peril** i.e., on pain of danger to you if you don't obey me and stay
94 fond doting **95 my grace** the favor I obtain **96 lies** dwells
102–103 no marvel . . . thus i.e., no wonder that Demetrius flies
from me as from a monster **105 compare** vie. **sphery eyne** eyes
as bright as stars in their spheres **110 Transparent** (1) radiant
(2) able to be seen through, lacking in deceit. **art** skill, magic power

121 will desire **124 ripe not** (am) not ripened **125 touching**
reaching. **point** summit. **skill** judgment **127 o'erlook** read
129 Wherefore why **135 Good troth, good sooth** i.e., indeed,
truly **138 lord of** i.e., possessor of. **gentleness** courtesy **139 of**
by **140 abused** ill treated **145–146 as . . . deceive** as renounced
heresies are hated most by those persons who formerly were deceived by them **148 Of . . . of** by . . . by **149 address** direct, apply

Lysander (Dominic West) tells the sleeping Hermia (Anna Friel) to stay away from him.

HERMIA [*awaking*]:   Help me, Lysander, help me! Do
    thy best
    To pluck this crawling serpent from my breast!
    Ay me, for pity! What a dream was here!
    Lysander, look how I do quake with fear.
155   Methought a serpent ate my heart away,
    And you sat smiling at his cruel prey.
    Lysander! What, removed? Lysander! Lord!
    What, out of hearing? Gone? No sound, no word?
    Alack, where are you? Speak, an if you hear;
160   Speak, of all loves! I swoon almost with fear.
    No? Then I well perceive you are not nigh.
    Either death, or you, I'll find immediately.

             Exit. [*The sleeping* TITANIA *remains.*]

3.1   *Enter the clowns* [QUINCE, SNUG, BOTTOM, FLUTE,
      SNOUT, *and* STARVELING].

BOTTOM: Are we all met?

QUINCE: Pat, pat; and here's a marvelous convenient
    place for our rehearsal. This green plot shall be our
    stage, this hawthorn brake our tiring-house, and we
5   will do it in action as we will do it before the Duke.

BOTTOM: Peter Quince?

QUINCE: What sayest thou, bully Bottom?

BOTTOM: There are things in this comedy of Pyramus
    and Thisbe that will never please. First, Pyramus
10   must draw a sword to kill himself, which the ladies
    cannot abide. How answer you that?

SNOUT: By 'r lakin, a parlous fear.

STARVELING: I believe we must leave the killing out,
    when all is done.

BOTTOM: Not a whit. I have a device to make all well.   15
    Write me a prologue, and let the prologue seem to
    say, we will do no harm with our swords, and that
    Pyramus is not killed indeed; and for the more better
    assurance, tell them that I, Pyramus, am not Pyramus
    but Bottom the weaver. This will put them out of fear.   20

QUINCE: Well, we will have such a prologue, and it
    shall be written in eight and six.

BOTTOM: No, make it two more: let it be written in
    eight and eight.

SNOUT: Will not the ladies be afeard of the lion?   25

STARVELING: I fear it, I promise you.

BOTTOM: Masters, you ought to consider with your-
    self, to bring in—God shield us!—a lion among ladies
    is a most dreadful thing. For there is not a more fear-
    ful wildfowl than your lion living, and we ought to   30
    look to 't.

SNOUT: Therefore another prologue must tell he is not
    a lion.

BOTTOM: Nay, you must name his name, and half his
    face must be seen through the lion's neck, and he   35
    himself must speak through, saying thus or to the
    same defect: "Ladies," or "Fair ladies, I would wish
    you," or "I would request you," or "I would entreat
    you, not to fear, not to tremble; my life for yours.
    If you think I come hither as a lion, it were pity of   40
    my life. No, I am no such thing; I am a man as other
    men are." And there indeed let him name his name,
    and tell them plainly he is Snug the joiner.

QUINCE: Well, it shall be so. But there is two hard things:
    that is, to bring the moonlight into a chamber; for,   45
    you know, Pyramus and Thisbe meet by moonlight.

---

156 prey act of preying   **159 an if** if   **160 of all loves** for love's
sake

3.1. Location: The action is continuous.
s.d. clowns rustics
2 Pat on the dot, punctually   **4 brake** thicket.   **tiring-house** attir-
ing area, hence backstage   **7 bully** i.e., worthy, jolly, fine fellow

---

12 By 'r lakin by our ladykin, i.e., the Virgin Mary.   **parlous**
perilous, alarming   **14 when all is done** i.e., when all is said and
done   **16 Write me** i.e., write at my suggestion. (*Me* is used colloquially.)   **22 eight and six** alternate lines of eight and six syllables,
a common ballad measure   **28 lion among ladies** (A contemporary pamphlet tells how, at the christening in 1594 of Prince Henry,
eldest son of King James VI of Scotland, later James I of England,
a "blackamoor" instead of a lion drew the triumphal chariot, since
the lion's presence might have "brought some fear to the nearest.")   **29–30 fearful** fear-inspiring   **37 defect** (Bottom's blunder
for "effect.")   **39 my life for yours** i.e., I pledge my life to make
your lives safe   **40–41 it were . . . life** i.e., I should be sorry, by my
life; or, my life would be endangered

Bottom (Kevin Kline) and the players meet to discuss their performance.

SNOUT: Doth the moon shine that night we play our play?

50 **BOTTOM:** A calendar, a calendar! Look in the almanac. Find out moonshine, find out moonshine.

[They consult an almanac.]

QUINCE: Yes, it doth shine that night.

BOTTOM: Why then may you leave a casement of the great chamber window where we play open, and the moon may shine in at the casement.

55 **QUINCE:** Ay; or else one must come in with a bush of thorns and a lantern and say he comes to disfigure, or to present, the person of Moonshine. Then there is another thing: we must have a wall in the great chamber; for Pyramus and Thisbe, says the story, did 60 talk through the chink of a wall.

SNOUT: You can never bring in a wall. What say you, Bottom?

BOTTOM: Some man or other must present Wall. And let him have some plaster, or some loam, or some 65 roughcast about him, to signify wall; or let him hold his fingers thus, and through that cranny shall Pyramus and Thisbe whisper.

QUINCE: If that may be, then all is well. Come, sit down, every mother's son, and rehearse your parts. Pyramus, 70 you begin. When you have spoken your speech, enter into that brake, and so everyone according to his cue.

Enter ROBIN [PUCK].

PUCK *[aside]:* What hempen homespuns have we swaggering here
So near the cradle of the Fairy Queen?
What, a play toward? I'll be an auditor;
An actor, too, perhaps, if I see cause.   75

QUINCE: Speak, Pyramus. Thisbe, stand forth.

BOTTOM *[as PYRAMUS]:* "Thisbe, the flowers of odious savors sweet—"

QUINCE: Odors, odors.

BOTTOM: "—Odors savors sweet;
So hath thy breath, my dearest Thisbe dear.   80
But hark, a voice! Stay thou but here awhile,
And by and by I will to thee appear."   *Exit.*

PUCK: A stranger Pyramus than e'er played here.   *[Exit.]*

FLUTE: Must I speak now?

QUINCE: Ay, marry, must you; for you must under-   85
stand he goes but to see a noise that he heard, and is to come again.

FLUTE *[as THISBE]:* "Most radiant Pyramus, most lily-white of hue,
Of color like the red rose on triumphant brier,
Most brisky juvenal and eke most lovely Jew,   90
As true as truest horse that yet would never tire.
I'll meet thee, Pyramus, at Ninny's tomb."

QUINCE: "Ninus' tomb," man. Why, you must not speak that yet. That you answer to Pyramus. You speak all your part at once, cues and all. Pyramus, enter. Your   95
cue is past; it is "never tire."

FLUTE: O—"As true as truest horse, that yet would never tire."

[Enter PUCK, and BOTTOM as PYRAMUS with the ass head.]

BOTTOM: "If I were fair, Thisbe, I were only thine."

55–56 **bush of thorns** bundle of thornbush fagots (part of the accoutrements of the man in the moon, according to the popular notions of the time, along with his lantern and his dog)   56 **disfigure** (Quince's blunder for "figure.")   57 **present** represent   64–65 **roughcast** a mixture of lime and gravel used to plaster the outside of buildings

72 **hempen homespuns** i.e., rustics dressed in clothes woven of coarse, homespun fabric made from hemp   73 **cradle** i.e., Titania's bower   74 **toward** about to take place   83 **A stranger . . . here** (Either Puck refers to an earlier dramatic version played in the same theater, or he has conceived of a plan to present a "stranger" Pyramus than ever seen before.)   89 **triumphant** magnificent   90 **brisky juvenal** lively youth.   **eke** also.   **Jew** (An absurd repetition of the first syllable of *juvenal* and an indication of how desperately Quince searches for his rhymes.)   93 **Ninus** mythical founder of Nineveh (whose wife, Semiramis, was supposed to have built the walls of Babylon where the story of Pyramus and Thisbe takes place)   95 **part** (An actor's *part* was a script consisting only of his speeches and their cues.)   97 **s.d. with the ass head** (This stage direction, taken from the Folio, presumably refers to a standard stage property.)   98 **fair** handsome.   **were** would be

QUINCE: O, monstrous! O, strange! We are haunted.
100   Pray, masters! Fly, masters! Help!
                    [Exeunt QUINCE, SNUG, FLUTE,
                        SNOUT, and STARVELING.]

PUCK: I'll follow you, I'll lead you about a round,
        Thorough bog, thorough bush, thorough brake,
            thorough brier.
        Sometimes a horse I'll be, sometimes a hound,
        A hog, a headless bear, sometimes a fire;
105   And neigh, and bark, and grunt, and roar, and burn,
        Like horse, hound, hog, bear, fire, at every turn.   *Exit.*

BOTTOM: Why do they run away? This is a knavery of
        them to make me afeard.

                            Enter SNOUT.

SNOUT: O Bottom, thou art changed! What do I see
110   on thee?

BOTTOM: What do you see? You see an ass head of
        your own, do you?   *[Exit SNOUT.]*

                            Enter QUINCE.

QUINCE: Bless thee, Bottom, bless thee! Thou art
        translated.   *Exit.*

115 BOTTOM: I see their knavery. This is to make an ass
        of me, to fright me, if they could. But I will not stir
        from this place, do what they can. I will walk up and
        down here, and will sing, that they shall hear I am
        not afraid.   *[He sings.]*
120   The ouzel cock so black of hue,
                With orange-tawny bill,
            The throstle with his note so true,
                The wren with little quill—

TITANIA *[awaking]*:   What angel wakes me from my
        flowery bed?

BOTTOM: *[sings]*
125   The finch, the sparrow, and the lark,
                The plainsong cuckoo gray,
            Whose note full many a man doth mark,
                And dares not answer nay—
        For indeed, who would set his wit to so foolish a
130   bird? Who would give a bird the lie, though he cry
        "cuckoo" never so?

---

101 **about a round** roundabout   104 **fire** will-o'-the-wisp   114
translated transformed   120 **ouzel cock** male blackbird   122
throstle song thrush   123 **quill** (Literally, a reed pipe; hence,
the bird's piping song.)   126 **plainsong** singing a melody without
variations   128 **dares . . . nay** i.e., cannot deny that he is a cuckold
129 **set his wit to** to employ his intelligence to answer   130 **give . . .
lie** call the bird a liar   131 **never so** ever so much

TITANIA: I pray thee, gentle mortal, sing again.
        Mine ear is much enamored of thy note;
        So is mine eye enthrallèd to thy shape;
        And thy fair virtue's force perforce doth move me   135
        On the first view to say, to swear, I love thee.

BOTTOM: Methinks, mistress, you should have little
        reason for that. And yet, to say the truth, reason and
        love keep little company together nowadays—the
        more the pity that some honest neighbors will not   140
        make them friends. Nay, I can gleek upon occasion.

TITANIA: Thou art as wise as thou art beautiful.

BOTTOM: Not so, neither. But if I had wit enough to
        get out of this wood, I have enough to serve mine
        own turn.   145

TITANIA: Out of this wood do not desire to go.
        Thou shalt remain here, whether thou wilt or no.
        I am a spirit of no common rate.
        The summer still doth tend upon my state,
        And I do love thee. Therefore, go with me.   150
        I'll give thee fairies to attend on thee,
        And they shall fetch thee jewels from the deep,
        And sing while thou on pressèd flowers dost sleep.
        And I will purge thy mortal grossness so
        That thou shalt like an airy spirit go.   155
        Peaseblossom, Cobweb, Mote, and Mustardseed!

                Enter four FAIRIES [PEASEBLOSSOM,
                    COBWEB, MOTE, and MUSTARDSEED].

PEASEBLOSSOM: Ready.

COBWEB: And I.

MOTE: And I.

MUSTARDSEED: And I.

ALL: Where shall we go?

TITANIA: Be kind and courteous to this gentleman.
        Hop in his walks and gambol in his eyes;   160
        Feed him with apricots and dewberries,
        With purple grapes, green figs, and mulberries;
        The honey bags steal from the humble-bees,

---

135 **thy . . . force** the power of your unblemished excellence   141
gleek jest   144–145 **serve . . . turn** answer my purpose   148 **rate**
rank, value   149 **still . . . state** always waits upon me as a part
of my royal retinue   154 **mortal grossness** materiality (i.e., the
corporal nature of a mortal being)   156 **Mote** i.e., speck. (The two
words *moth* and *mote* were pronounced alike, and both meanings
may be present.)   160 **in his eyes** in his sight (i.e., before him)
161 **dewberries** blackberries

And for night tapers crop their waxen thighs
165 And light them at the fiery glowworms' eyes,
To have my love to bed and to arise;
And pluck the wings from painted butterflies
To fan the moonbeams from his sleeping eyes.
Nod to him, elves, and do him courtesies.

170 **PEASEBLOSSOM:** Hail, mortal!

COBWEB: Hail!

MOTE: Hail!

MUSTARDSEED: Hail!

BOTTOM: I cry your worship's mercy, heartily. I be-
175 seech your worship's name.

COBWEB: Cobweb.

BOTTOM: I shall desire you of more acquaintance,
good Master Cobweb. If I cut my finger, I shall make
bold with you.—Your name, honest gentleman?

180 **PEASEBLOSSOM:** Peaseblossom.

BOTTOM: I pray you, commend me to Mistress Squash,
your mother, and to Master Peascod, your father.
Good Master Peaseblossom, I shall desire you of more
acquaintance too.—Your name, I beseech you, sir?

185 **MUSTARDSEED:** Mustardseed.

BOTTOM: Good Master Mustardseed, I know your
patience well. That same cowardly, giantlike ox-beef
hath devoured many a gentleman of your house. I
promise you, your kindred hath made my eyes water
190 ere now. I desire you of more acquaintance, good
Master Mustardseed.

TITANIA: Come wait upon him; lead him to my bower.
The moon methinks looks with a watery eye;
And when she weeps, weeps every little flower,
195 Lamenting some enforcèd chastity.
Tie up my lover's tongue; bring him silently.

Exeunt.

Titania (Judi Dench), enchanted, kisses the transformed Bottom.

3.2 *Enter [OBERON,] King of Fairies.*

OBERON: I wonder if Titania be awaked;
Then, what it was that next came in her eye,
Which she must dote on in extremity.

[Enter] ROBIN GOODFELLOW [PUCK].

Here comes my messenger. How now, mad spirit?
What night-rule now about this haunted grove? 5

PUCK: My mistress with a monster is in love.
Near to her close and consecrated bower,
While she was in her dull and sleeping hour,
A crew of patches, rude mechanicals,
That work for bread upon Athenian stalls, 10
Were met together to rehearse a play
Intended for great Theseus' nuptial day.
The shallowest thickskin of that barren sort,
Who Pyramus presented, in their sport
Forsook his scene and entered in a brake. 15
When I did him at this advantage take,
An ass's noll I fixèd on his head.
Anon his Thisbe must be answerèd,
And forth my mimic comes. When they him spy,
As wild geese that the creeping fowler eye, 20
Or russet-pated choughs, many in sort,

174 **I cry ... mercy** I beg pardon of your worships (for presuming to ask a question) 177 **I ... acquaintance** I crave to be better acquainted with you 178–179 **If ... you** (Cobwebs were used to stanch bleeding.) 181 **Squash** unripe pea pod 182 **Peascod** ripe pea pod 186–187 **your patience** what you have endured. (Mustard is eaten with beef.) 189 **water** (1) weep for sympathy (2) smart, sting 194 **she weeps** i.e., she causes dew 195 **enforcèd** forced, violated; or, possibly, constrained (since Titania at this moment is hardly concerned about chastity) 196 **Tie ... tongue** (Presumably Bottom is braying like an ass.)

3.2 **Location: The wood.**
5 **night-rule** diversion or misrule for the night. **haunted** much frequented 7 **close** secret, private 8 **dull** drowsy 9 **patches** clowns, fools. **rude mechanicals** ignorant artisans 10 **stalls** market booths 13 **barren sort** stupid company or crew 14 **presented** acted 15 **scene** playing area 17 **noll** noddle, head 19 **mimic** burlesque actor 20 **fowler** hunter of game birds 21 **russet-pated choughs** reddish brown or gray-headed jackdaws. **in sort** in a flock

Rising and cawing at the gun's report,
Sever themselves and madly sweep the sky,
So, at his sight, away his fellow fly;
25 And, at our stamp, here o'er and o'er one falls;
He "Murder!" cries and help from Athens calls.
Their sense thus weak, lost with their fears thus
strong,
Made senseless things begin to do them wrong,
For briers and thorns at their apparel snatch;
30 Some, sleeves—some, hats; from yielders all things
catch.
I led them on in this distracted fear
And left sweet Pyramus translated there,
When in that moment, so it came to pass,
Titania waked and straightway loved an ass.

35 **OBERON:** This falls out better than I could devise.
But has thou yet latched the Athenian's eyes
With the love juice, as I did bid thee do?

PUCK: I took him sleeping—that is finished too—
And the Athenian woman by his side,
40 That, when he waked, of force she must be eyed.

Enter DEMETRIUS *and* HERMIA.

OBERON: Stand close. This is the same Athenian.

PUCK: This is the woman, but not this the man.
[They stand aside.]

DEMETRIUS: O, why rebuke you him that loves
you so?
Lay breath so bitter on your bitter foe.

45 **HERMIA:** Now I but chide; but I should use thee worse,
For thou, I fear, hast given me cause to curse.
If thou hast slain Lysander in his sleep,
Being o'er shoes in blood, plunge in the deep,
And kill me too.
50 The sun was not so true unto the day
As he to me. Would he have stolen away
From sleeping Hermia? I'll believe as soon
This whole earth may be bored, and that the moon
May through the center creep, and so displease
55 Her brother's noontide with th' Antipodes.
It cannot be but thou hast murdered him;
So should a murder look, so dead, so grim.

DEMETRIUS: So should the murdered look, and so
should I,
Pierced through the heart with your stern cruelty.
Yet you, the murderer, look as bright, as clear   60
As yonder Venus in her glimmering sphere.

HERMIA: What's this to my Lysander? Where is he?
Ah, good Demetrius, wilt thou give him me?

DEMETRIUS: I had rather give his carcass to my
hounds.

HERMIA: Out, dog! Out, cur! Thou driv'st me past the
bounds   65
Of maiden's patience. Hast thou slain him, then?
Henceforth be never numbered among men.
O, once tell true, tell true, even for my sake:
Durst thou have looked upon him being awake?
And hast thou killed him sleeping? O brave touch!   70
Could not a worm, an adder, do so much?
An adder did it; for with doubler tongue
Than thine, thou serpent, never adder stung.

DEMETRIUS: You spend your passion on a misprised
mood.
I am not guilty of Lysander's blood,   75
Nor is he dead, for aught that I can tell.

HERMIA: I pray thee, tell me then that he is well.

DEMETRIUS: And if I could, what should I get therefor?

HERMIA: A privilege never to see me more.
And from thy hated presence part I so.   80
See me no more, whether he be dead or no.   *Exit.*

DEMETRIUS: There is no following her in this fierce
vein.
Here therefore for a while I will remain.
So sorrow's heaviness doth heavier grow
For debt that bankrupt sleep doth sorrow owe,   85
Which now in some slight measure it will pay,
If for his tender here I make some stay.
[He] lie[s] down [and sleeps].

OBERON: What hast thou done? Thou hast mistaken
quite
And laid the love juice on some true love's sight.

---

23 **Sever** i.e., scatter 30 **from . . . catch** i.e., everything preys on
those who yield to fear 36 **latched** fastened, snared 40 **of force**
perforce 48 **Being o'er shoes** having waded in so far 53 **whole**
solid 55 **Her brother's** i.e., the sun's. **th' Antipodes** the people
on the opposite side of the earth (where the moon is imagined
bringing night to noontime) 57 **dead** deadly, or deathly pale

---

62 **to** to do with 68 **once** once and for all 70 **brave touch!** fine
stroke! (Said ironically.) 71 **worm** serpent 72 **doubler** (1) more
forked (2) more deceitful 74 **passion** violent feelings. **misprised
mood** anger based on misconception 78 **therefor** in return for
that 84 **heavier** (1) harder to bear (2) more drowsy 85 **bankrupt** (Demetrius is saying that his sleepiness adds to the weariness
caused by sorrow.) 86–87 **Which . . . stay** i.e., to a small extent,
I will be able to "pay back" and hence find some relief from sorrow,
if I pause here awhile (*make some stay*) while sleep "tenders," or
offers, itself by way of paying the debt owed to sorrow

90 Of thy misprision must perforce ensue
  Some true loved turned, and not a false turned true.

PUCK: Then fate o'errules, that, one man holding troth,
  A million fail, confounding oath on oath.

OBERON: About the wood go swifter than the wind,
95 And Helena of Athens look thou find.
  All fancy-sick she is and pale of cheer
  With sighs of love, that cost the fresh blood dear.
  By some illusion see thou bring her here.
  I'll charm his eyes against she do appear.

100 PUCK: I go, I go, look how I go,
  Swifter than arrow from the Tartar's bow. *[Exit.]*

OBERON *[applying love juice to* DEMETRIUS' *eyes]*:
  Flower of this purple dye,
  Hit with Cupid archery,
  Sink in apple of his eye.
105 When his love he doth espy,
  Let her shine as gloriously
  As the Venus of the sky.
  When thou wak'st, if she be by,
  Beg of her for remedy.

       Enter PUCK.

110 PUCK: Captain of our fairy band,
  Helena is here at hand,
  And the youth, mistook by me,
  Pleading for a lover's fee.
  Shall we their fond pageant see?
115 Lord, what fools these mortals be!

OBERON: Stand aside. The noise they make
  Will cause Demetrius to awake.

PUCK: Then will two at once woo one;
  That must needs be sport alone.
120 And those things do best please me
  That befall preposterously.

      [They stand aside.]

    Enter LYSANDER *and* HELENA.

LYSANDER: Why should you think that I should woo
  in scorn?

  Scorn and derision never come in tears.
  Look when I vow, I weep; and vows so born,
  In their nativity all truth appears. 125
  How can these things in me seem scorn to you,
  Bearing the badge of faith to prove them true?

HELENA: You do advance your cunning more and more.
  When truth kills truth, O, devilish-holy fray!
  These vows are Hermia's. Will you give her o'er? 130
  Weigh oath with oath, and you will nothing
   weigh.
  Your vows to her and me, put in two scales,
  Will even weigh, and both as light as tales.

LYSANDER: I had no judgment when to her I swore.

HELENA: Nor none, in my mind, now you give her o'er. 135

LYSANDER: Demetrius loves her, and he loves not you.

DEMETRIUS *[awaking]*: O Helen, goddess, nymph,
  perfect, divine!
  To what, my love, shall I compare thine eyne?
  Crystal is muddy. O, how ripe in show
  Thy lips, those kissing cherries, tempting grow! 140
  That pure congealèd white, high Taurus' snow,
  Fanned with the eastern wind, turns to a crow
  When thou hold'st up thy hand. O, let me kiss
  This princess of pure white, this seal of bliss!

HELENA: O spite! O hell! I see you all are bent 145
  To set against me for your merriment.
  If you were civil and knew courtesy,
  You would not do me thus much injury.
  Can you not hate me, as I know you do,
  But you must join in souls to mock me too? 150
  If you were men, as men you are in show,
  You would not use a gentle lady so—
  To vow, and swear, and superpraise my parts,
  When I am sure you hate me with your hearts.
  You both are rivals, and love Hermia, 155
  And now both rivals to mock Helena.
  A trim exploit, a many enterprise,
  To conjure tears up in a poor maid's eyes

---

90 **misprision** mistake 92 **that . . . troth** in that, for each man keeping true faith in love 93 **confounding . . . oath** i.e., breaking oath after oath 95 **look** i.e., be sure 96 **fancy-sick** lovesick. **cheer** face 97 **sighs . . . blood** (An allusion to the physiological theory that each sigh costs the heart a drop of blood.) 99 **against . . . appear** in anticipation of her coming 101 **Tartar's bow** (Tartars were famed for their skill with the bow.) 104 **apple** pupil 113 **fee** privilege, reward 114 **fond pageant** foolish spectacle 119 **alone** unequaled 121 **preposterously** out of the natural order

124 **Look when** whenever 124–125 **vows . . . appears** i.e., vows made by one who is weeping give evidence thereby of their sincerity 127 **badge** identifying device such as that worn on servants' livery (here, his tears) 128 **advance** carry forward, display 129 **truth kills truth** i.e., one of Lysander's vows must invalidate the other 133 **tales** lies 139 **show** appearance 141 **Taurus** a lofty mountain range in Asia Minor 142 **turns to a crow** i.e., seems black by contrast 144 **seal** pledge 146 **set against** attack 150 **in souls** i.e., heart and soul 153 **superpraise** overpraise. **parts** qualities 157 **trim** pretty, fine. (Said ironically.)

160 With your derision! None of noble sort
Would so offend a virgin and extort
A poor soul's patience, all to make you sport.

LYSANDER: You are unkind, Demetrius. Be not so.
For you love Hermia; this you know I know.
And here, with all good will, with all my heart,
165 In Hermia's love I yield you up my part;
And yours of Helena to me bequeath,
Whom I do love, and will do till my death.

HELENA: Never did mockers waste more idle breath.

DEMETRIUS: Lysander, keep thy Hermia; I will none.
170 If e'er I loved her, all that love is gone.
My heart to her but as guestwise sojourned,
And now to Helen is it home returned,
There to remain.

LYSANDER: Helen, it is not so.

DEMETRIUS: Disparage not the faith thou dost not
know,
175 Lest, to thy peril, thou aby it dear.
Look where thy love comes; yonder is thy dear.

Enter HERMIA.

HERMIA: Dark night, that from the eye his function
takes,
The ear more quick of apprehension makes;
Wherein it doth impair the seeing sense,
180 It pays the hearing double recompense.
Thou art not by mine eye, Lysander, found;
Mine ear, I thank it, brought me to thy sound.
But why unkindly didst thou leave me so?

LYSANDER: Why should he stay, whom love doth press
to go?

185 **HERMIA:** What love could press Lysander from my
side?

LYSANDER: Lysander's love that would not let him
bide—
Fair Helena, who more engilds the night
Than all yon fiery oes and eyes of light.
Why seek'st thou me? Could not this make thee
know
190 The hate I bear thee made me leave thee so?

HERMIA: You speak not as you think. It cannot be.

Hermia bemoans Lysander's betrayal to Demetrius (Christian Bale).

HELENA: Lo, she is one of this confederacy!
Now I perceive they have conjoined all three
To fashion this false sport, in spite of me.
Injurious Hermia, most ungrateful maid! 195
Have you conspired, have you with these contrived
To bait me with this foul derision?
Is all the counsel that we two have shared—
The sisters' vows, the hours that we have spent
When we have chid the hasty-footed time 200
For parting us—O, is all forgot?
All schooldays' friendship, childhood innocence?
We, Hermia, like two artificial gods
Have with our needles created both one flower,
Both on one sampler, sitting on one cushion, 205
Both warbling of one song, both in one key,
As if our hands, our sides, voices, and minds
Had been incorporate. So we grew together,
Like to a double cherry, seeming parted,
But yet an union in partition, 210
Two lovely berries molded on one stem;
So, with two seeming bodies but one heart,
Two of the first, like coats in heraldry,
Due but to one and crownèd with one crest.
And will you rend our ancient love asunder, 215
To join with men in scorning your poor friend?
It is not friendly, 'tis not maidenly.
Our sex, as well as I, may chide you for it,
Though I alone do feel the injury.

HERMIA: I am amazèd at your passionate words. 220
I scorn you not. It seems that you scorn me.

---

159 **sort** character, quality   160 **extort** twist, torture   169 **will none** i.e., want no part of her   171 **to . . . sojourned** only visited with her   175 **aby** pay for   177 **his** its   187 **engilds** gilds, brightens with a golden light   188 **oes** spangles (here, stars)

194 **in spite of me** to vex me   196 **contrived** plotted   197 **bait** torment, as one sets on dogs to bait a bear   198 **counsel** confidential talk   203 **artificial** skilled in art or creation   208 **incorporate** of one body   211 **lovely** loving   213–214 **Two . . . crest** i.e., we have two separate bodies, just as a coat of arms in heraldry can be represented twice on a shield but surmounted by a single crest

HELENA: Have you not set Lysander, as in scorn,
To follow me and praise my eyes and face?
And made your other love, Demetrius,
225   Who even but now did spurn me with his foot,
To call me goddess, nymph, divine, and rare,
Precious, celestial? Wherefore speaks he this
To her he hates? And wherefore doth Lysander
Deny your love, so rich within his soul,
230   And tender me, forsooth, affection,
But by your setting on, by your consent?
What though I be not so in grace as you,
So hung upon with love, so fortunate,
But miserable most, to love unloved?
235   This you should pity rather than despise.

HERMIA: I understand not what you mean by this.

HELENA: Ay, do! Persever, counterfeit sad looks,
Make mouths upon me when I turn my back,
Wink each at other, hold the sweet jest up.
240   This sport, well carried, shall be chronicled.
If you have any pity, grace, or manners,
You would not make me such an argument.
But fare ye well. 'Tis partly my own fault,
Which death, or absence, soon shall remedy.

245   **LYSANDER:**   Stay, gentle Helena; hear my excuse,
My love, my life, my soul, fair Helena!

HELENA: O excellent!

HERMIA *[to* LYSANDER*]*:   Sweet, do not scorn her so.

DEMETRIUS *[to* LYSANDER*]*:   If she cannot entreat, I
can compel.

LYSANDER: Thou canst compel no more than she
entreat.
250   Thy threats have no more strength than her weak
prayers.
Helen, I love thee, by my life, I do!
I swear by that which I will lose for thee,
To prove him false that says I love thee not.

DEMETRIUS *[to* HERMIA*]*:   I say I love thee more than
he can do.

255   **LYSANDER:**   If thou say so, withdraw, and prove it too.

DEMETRIUS: Quick, come!

HERMIA: Lysander, whereto tends all this?

LYSANDER: Away, you Ethiope!
                    [He tries to break away from HERMIA.*]*

DEMETRIUS: No, no; he'll
Seem to break loose; take on as you would follow,
But yet come not. You are a tame man. Go!

LYSANDER *[to* HERMIA*]*:   Hang off, thou cat, thou burr!   260
Vile thing, let loose,
Or I will shake thee from me like a serpent!

HERMIA: Why are you grown so rude? What change
is this,
Sweet love?

LYSANDER: Thy love? Out, tawny Tartar, out!
Out, loathèd med'cine! O hated potion, hence!

HERMIA: Do you not jest?

HELENA: Yes, sooth, and so do you.   265

LYSANDER: Demetrius, I will keep my word with thee.

DEMETRIUS: I would I had your bond, for I perceive
A weak bond holds you. I'll not trust your word.

LYSANDER: What, should I hurt her, strike her, kill
her dead?
Although I hate her, I'll not harm her so.   270

HERMIA: What, can you do me greater harm than
hate?
Hate me? Wherefore? O me, what news, my love?
Am not I Hermia? Are you not Lysander?
I am as fair now as I was erewhile.
Since night you loved me; yet since night you left me.   275
Why, then you left me—O, the gods forbid!—
In earnest, shall I say?

LYSANDER: Ay, by my life!
And never did desire to see thee more.
Therefore be out of hope, of question, of doubt;
Be certain, nothing truer. 'Tis no jest   280
That I do hate thee and love Helena.

HERMIA *[to* HELENA*]*:   O me! You juggler! You
cankerblossom!
You thief of love! What, have you come by night
And stol'n my love's heart from him?

HELENA: Fine, i' faith!
Have you no modesty, no maiden shame,   285

---

230 **tender** offer   232 **grace** favor   237 **sad** grave, serious   238
mouths i.e., mows, faces, grimaces.   **upon** at   239 **hold . . . up**
keep up the joke   240 **carried** managed   242 **argument** subject
for a jest   248 **entreat** i.e., succeed by entreaty   255 **withdraw . . .
too** i.e., withdraw with me and prove your claim in a duel. (The two
gentlemen are armed.)

---

257 **Ethiope** (Referring to Hermia's relatively dark hair and complexion; see also *tawny Tartar* six lines later.)   258 **take on as** act
as if, make a fuss as if   260 **Hang off** let go   264 **med'cine** i.e.,
poison   265 **sooth** truly   268 **weak bond** i.e., Hermia's arm (with
a pun on *bond,* "oath," in the previous line)   272 **what news** what
is the matter   274 **erewhile** just now   282 **cankerblossom** worm
that destroys the flower bud, or wild rose

Helena (Diana Rigg) hides from Hermia between Lysander and Demetrius (Michael Jayston).

No touch of bashfulness? What, will you tear
Impatient answers from my gentle tongue?
Fie, fie! You counterfeit, you puppet, you!

HERMIA: "Puppet"? Why, so! Ay, that way goes the
game.
290 Now I perceive that she hath made compare
Between our statures; she hath urged her height,
And with her personage, her tall personage,
Her height, forsooth, she hath prevailed with him.
And are you grown so high in his esteem
295 Because I am so dwarfish and so low?
How low am I, thou painted maypole? Speak!
How low am I? I am not yet so low
But that my nails can reach unto thine eyes.
                    [*She flails at* HELENA *but is restrained.*]

HELENA: I pray you, though you mock me, gentlemen,
300 Let her not hurt me. I was never curst;
I have no gift at all in shrewishness;
I am a right maid for my cowardice.
Let her not strike me. You perhaps may think,
Because she is something lower than myself,
305 That I can match her.

HERMIA: Lower? Hark, again!

HELENA: Good Hermia, do not be so bitter with me.
I evermore did love you, Hermia,
Did ever keep your counsels, never wronged you,
Save that, in love unto Demetrius,

I told him of your stealth unto this wood.   310
He followed you; for love I followed him.
But he hath chid me hence and threatened me
To strike me, spurn me, nay, to kill me too.
And now, so you will let me quiet go,
To Athens will I bear my folly back   315
And follow you no further. Let me go.
You see how simple and how fond I am.

HERMIA: Why, get you gone. Who is 't that hinders
you?

HELENA: A foolish heart, that I leave here behind.

HERMIA: What, with Lysander?

HELENA: With Demetrius.   320

LYSANDER: Be not afraid; she shall not harm thee,
Helena.

DEMETRIUS: No, sir, she shall not, though you take
her part.

HELENA: O, when she is angry, she is keen and shrewd.
She was a vixen when she went to school;
And though she be but little, she is fierce.   325

HERMIA: "Little" again? Nothing but "low" and "little"?
Why will you suffer her to flout me thus?
Let me come to her.

LYSANDER: Get you gone, you dwarf!
You minimus, of hindering knotgrass made!
You bean, you acorn!

DEMETRIUS: You are too officious   330
In her behalf that scorns your services.
Let her alone. Speak not of Helena;
Take not her part. For, if thou dost intend
Never so little show of love to her,
Thou shalt aby it.

LYSANDER: Now she holds me not.   335
Now follow, if thou dar'st, to try whose right,
Of thine or mine, is most in Helena   [*Exit.*]

DEMETRIUS: Follow? Nay, I'll go with the, cheek
by jowl.
                    [*Exit, following* LYSANDER.]

---

288 **puppet** (1) counterfeit (2) dwarfish woman (in reference to Hermia's smaller stature)   289 **Why, so** i.e., Oh, so that's how it is   300 **curst** shrewish   302 **right** true   304 **something** somewhat

310 **stealth** stealing away   312 **chid me hence** driven me away with his scolding   314 **so** if only   317 **fond** foolish   323 **keen** fierce, cruel.   **shrewd** shrewish   329 **minimus** diminutive creature.   **knotgrass** a weed, an infusion of which was thought to stunt the growth   333 **intend** give sign of   335 **aby** pay for   338 **cheek by jowl** i.e., side by side

HERMIA: You, mistress, all this coil is 'long of you.
340   Nay, go not back.

HELENA: I will not trust you, I,
Nor longer stay in your curst company.
Your hands than mine are quicker for a fray;
My legs are longer, though, to run away.   *[Exit.]*

HERMIA: I am amazed and know not what to say.   *Exit.*

          [OBERON and PUCK come forward.]

345 **OBERON:** This is thy negligence. Still thou mistak'st,
Or else committ'st thy knaveries willfully.

PUCK: Believe me, king of shadows, I mistook.
Did not you tell me I should know the man
By the Athenian garments he had on?
350   And so far blameless proves my enterprise
That I have 'nointed an Athenian's eyes;
And so far am I glad it so did sort,
As this their jangling I esteem a sport.

OBERON: Thou seest these lovers seek a place to fight.
355   Hie therefore, Robin, overcast the night;
The starry welkin cover thou anon
With drooping fog as black as Acheron,
And lead these testy rivals so astray
As one come not within another's way.
360   Like to Lysander sometimes frame thy tongue,
Then stir Demetrius up with bitter wrong;
And sometimes rail thou like Demetrius.
And from each other look thou lead them thus,
Till o'er their brows death-counterfeiting sleep
365   With leaden legs and batty wings doth creep.
Then crush this herb into Lysander's eye,
          [giving herb]
Whose liquor hath this virtuous property,
To take from thence all error with his might
And make his eyeballs roll with wonted sight.
370   When they next wake, all this derision
Shall seem a dream and fruitless vision,
And back to Athens shall the lovers wend
With league whose date till death shall never end.
Whiles I in this affair do thee employ,
375   I'll to my queen and beg her Indian boy;
And then I will her charmèd eye release
From monster's view, and all things shall be peace.

PUCK: My fairy lord, this must be done with haste,
For night's swift dragons cut the clouds full fast,
And yonder shines Aurora's harbinger,   380
At whose approach ghosts, wand'ring here and there,
Troop home to churchyards. Damnèd spirits all,
That in crossways and floods have burial,
Already to their wormy beds are gone.
For fear lest day should look their shames upon,   385
They willfully themselves exile from light
And must for aye consort with black-browed night.

OBERON: But we are spirits of another sort.
I with the Morning's love have oft made sport,
And, like a forester, the groves may tread   390
Even till the eastern gate, all fiery red,
Opening on Neptune with fair blessèd beams,
Turns into yellow gold his salt green streams.
But notwithstanding, haste, make no delay.
We may effect this business yet ere day.   *[Exit.]* 395

PUCK: Up and down, up and down,
      I will lead them up and down.
      I am feared in field and town.
      Goblin, lead them up and down.
Here comes one.   400

          Enter LYSANDER.

LYSANDER: Where art thou, proud Demetrius? Speak
thou now.

PUCK *[mimicking DEMETRIUS]*: Here, villain, drawn and
ready. Where art thou?

LYSANDER: I will be with thee straight.

PUCK: Follow me, then,
To plainer ground.
    [LYSANDER wanders about, following the voice.]

          Enter DEMETRIUS.

---

339 coil turmoil, dissension. **'long of** on account of **340 go not back** i.e., don't retreat. (Hermia is again proposing a fight.) **352 so far** at least to this extent. **sort** turn out **353 As** in that **355 Hie** hasten **356 welkin** sky **357 Acheron** river of Hades (here representing Hades itself) **359 As** that **361 wrong** insults **365 batty** batlike **366 this herb** i.e., the antidote (mentioned in 2.1.184) to love-in-idleness **367 virtuous** efficacious **368 his** its **369 wonted** accustomed **370 derision** laughable business **373 date** term of existence

379 dragons (Supposed by Shakespeare to be yoked to the car of the goddess of night or the moon.) **380 Aurora's harbinger** the morning star, precursor of dawn **383 crossways . . . burial** (Those who had committed suicide were buried at crossways, with a stake driven through them; those who intentionally or accidentally drowned (in *floods* or deep water) would be condemned to wander disconsolately for lack of burial rites.) **387 for aye** forever **389 the Morning's love** Cephalus, a beautiful youth beloved by Aurora; or perhaps the goddess of the dawn herself **390 forester** keeper of a royal forest **399 Goblin** Hobgoblin. (Puck refers to himself.) **402 drawn** with drawn sword **403 straight** immediately **404 plainer** more open. **s.d. Lysander wanders about** (Lysander may exit here, but perhaps not; neither exit nor reentrance is indicated in the early texts.)

DEMETRIUS: Lysander! Speak again!
405   Thou runaway, thou coward, art thou fled?
        Speak! In some bush? Where dost thou hide thy
            head?

PUCK *[mimicking* LYSANDER*]:*   Thou coward, art thou
            bragging to the stars,
        Telling the bushes that thou look'st for wars,
        And wilt not come? Come, recreant; come, thou
            child,
410   I'll whip thee with a rod. He is defiled
        That draws a sword on thee.

DEMETRIUS: Yea, art thou there?

PUCK: Follow my voice. We'll try no manhood here.
                                    Exeunt.

                        *[*LYSANDER *returns.]*

LYSANDER: He goes before me and still dares me on.
        When I come where he calls, then he is gone.
415   The villain is much lighter-heeled than I.
        I followed fast, but faster he did fly,
        That fallen am I in dark uneven way,
        And here will rest me. *[He lies down.]* Come, thou
            gentle day!
        For if but once thou show me thy gray light,
420   I'll find Demetrius and revenge this spite. *[He sleeps.]*

                [Enter] ROBIN *[*PUCK*] and* DEMETRIUS.

PUCK: Ho, ho, ho! Coward, why com'st thou not?

DEMETRIUS: Abide me, if thou dar'st; for well I wot
        Thou runn'st before me, shifting every place,
        And dar'st not stand nor look me in the face.
425   Where art thou now?

PUCK: Come hither. I am here.

DEMETRIUS: Nay, then, thou mock'st me. Thou shalt
            buy this dear,
        If ever I thy face by daylight see.
        Now go thy way. Faintness constraineth me
        To measure out my length on this cold bed.
430   By day's approach look to be visited.
                        [He lies down and sleeps.]

                        Enter HELENA.

HELENA: O weary night, O long and tedious night,
        Abate thy hours! Shine comforts from the east,
        That I may back to Athens by daylight
        From these that my poor company detest;

Puck, invisible, taunts the bewildered Demetrius (Christian Bale).

        And sleep, that sometimes shuts up sorrow's eye,   435
        Steal me awhile from mine own company.
                        [She lies down and] sleep[s].

PUCK: Yet but three? Come one more;
            Two of both kinds makes up four.
            Here she comes, curst and sad.
            Cupid is a knavish lad,   440
            Thus to make poor females mad.

                        [Enter HERMIA.*]*

HERMIA: Never so weary, never so in woe,
        Bedabbled with the dew and torn with briers,
        I can no further crawl, no further go;
        My legs can keep no pace with my desires.   445
        Here will I rest me till the break of day.
        Heavens shield Lysander, if they mean a fray!
                        [She lies down and sleeps.]

PUCK: On the ground
                Sleep sound.
                I'll apply   450
                To your eye,
            Gentle lover, remedy.
                [He squeezes the juice on LYSANDER*'s eyes.]*
                When thou wak'st,
                Thou tak'st
                True delight   455
                In the sight
            Of thy former lady's eye;
            And the country proverb known,
            That every man should take his own,
            In your waking shall be shown: 460
                Jack shall have Jill;
                Naught shall go ill;
            The man shall have his mare again, and all shall
                be well. *[Exit. The four sleeping lovers remain.]*

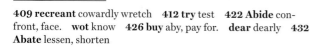

409 recreant cowardly wretch   **412 try** test   **422 Abide** confront, face. **wot** know   **426 buy** aby, pay for. **dear** dearly **432 Abate** lessen, shorten

439 curst ill-tempered   **461 Jack shall have Jill** (Proverbial for "boy gets girl.")

4.1 *Enter [*TITANIA,*] Queen of Fairies, and [*BOTTOM *the]*
clown, and FAIRIES; *and [*OBERON,*] the King, behind*
them.

TITANIA: Come, sit thee down upon this flowery bed,
 While I thy amiable cheeks do coy,
And stick muskroses in thy sleek smooth head,
 And kiss thy fair large ears, my gentle joy.

[They recline.]

5   **BOTTOM:** Where's Peaseblossom?

PEASEBLOSSOM: Ready.

BOTTOM: Scratch my head, Peaseblossom. Where's
Monsieur Cobweb?

COBWEB: Ready.

10   **BOTTOM:** Monsieur Cobweb, good monsieur, get you
your weapons in your hand, and kill me a red-hipped
humble-bee on the top of a thistle; and, good monsieur, bring me the honey bag. Do not fret yourself too
much in the action, monsieur; and, good monsieur,
15   have a care the honey bag break not. I would be loath
to have you overflown with a honey bag, signor. *[Exit*
COBWEB.*]* Where's Monsieur Mustardseed?

MUSTARDSEED: Ready.

BOTTOM: Give me your neaf, Monsieur Mustardseed.
20   Pray you, leave your courtesy, good monsieur.

MUSTARDSEED: What's your will?

BOTTOM: Nothing, good monsieur, but to help Cavalery Cobweb to scratch. I must to the barber's, monsieur, for methinks I am marvelous hairy about
25   the face; and I am such a tender ass, if my hair do
but tickle me I must scratch.

TITANIA: What, wilt thou hear some music, my sweet
love?

BOTTOM: I have a reasonable good ear in music. Let's
have the tongs and the bones.

[Music: tongs, rural music.]

Bottom is entertained by Titania.

TITANIA: Or say, sweet love, what thou desirest to eat.   30

BOTTOM: Truly, a peck of provender. I could munch
your good dry oats. Methinks I have a great desire to
a bottle of hay. Good hay, sweet hay, hath no fellow.

TITANIA: I have a venturous fairy that shall seek
The squirrel's hoard, and fetch thee new nuts.   35

BOTTOM: I had rather have a handful or two of dried
peas. But, I pray you, let none of your people stir me.
I have an exposition of sleep come upon me.

TITANIA: Sleep thou, and I will wind thee in my arms.
Fairies, begone, and be all ways away.   40

[Exeunt FAIRIES.*]*
So doth the woodbine the sweet honeysuckle
Gently entwist; the female ivy so
Enrings the barky fingers of the elm.
O, how I love thee! How I dote on thee!

[They sleep.]

Enter ROBIN GOODFELLOW *[*PUCK*].*

OBERON *[coming forward]:* Welcome, good Robin. Seest
thou this sweet sight?   45
Her dotage now I do begin to pity.
For, meeting her of late behind the wood
Seeking sweet favors for this hateful fool,
I did upbraid her and fall out with her.
For she his hairy temples then had rounded   50
With coronet of fresh and fragrant flowers;
And that same dew, which sometime on the buds
Was wont to swell like round and orient pearls,

**4.1 Location: The action is continuous. The four lovers are still
asleep onstage. (Compare with the Folio stage direction: "They
sleep all the act.")**
2 amiable lovely.   **coy** caress   **19 neaf** fist   **20 leave your courtesy** i.e., stop bowing, or put on your hat   **22–23 Cavalery** cavalier.
(Form of address for a gentleman.)   **23 Cobweb** (Seemingly an error, since Cobweb has been sent to bring honey, while Peaseblossom
has been asked to scratch.)   **29 tongs . . . bones** instruments for
rustic music. (The tongs were played like a triangle, whereas the
bones were held between the fingers and used as clappers.)   **s.d.
Music . . . music** (This stage direction is added from the Folio.)

31 peck of provender one-quarter bushel of grain   **33 bottle**
bundle.   **fellow** equal   **37 stir** disturb   **38 exposition of** (Bottom's phrase for "disposition to.")   **40 all ways** in all directions
41 woodbine bindweed, a climbing plant that twines in the opposite direction from that of honeysuckle   **48 favors** i.e., gifts of
flowers   **52 sometime** formerly   **53 orient pearls** i.e., the most
beautiful of all pearls, those coming from the Orient

55 Stood now within the pretty flowerets' eyes
Like tears that did their own disgrace bewail.
When I had at my pleasure taunted her,
And she in mild terms begged my patience,
I then did ask of her her changeling child,
Which straight she gave me, and her fairy sent
60 To bear him to my bower in Fairyland.
And, now I have the boy, I will undo
This hateful imperfection of her eyes.
And, gentle Puck, take this transformèd scalp
From off the head of this Athenian swain,
65 That he, awaking when the other do,
May all to Athens back again repair,
And think no more of this night's accidents
But as the fierce vexation of a dream.
But first I will release the Fairy Queen.

[He squeezes an herb on her eyes.]

70 Be as thou wast wont to be;
See as thou wast wont to see.
Dian's bud o'er Cupid's flower
Hath such force and blessèd power.
Now, my Titania, wake you, my sweet queen.

75 **TITANIA** *[awaking]*:   My Oberon! What visions have I
seen!
Methought I was enamored of an ass.

OBERON: There lies your love.

TITANIA: How came these things to pass?
O, how mine eyes do loathe his visage now!

OBERON: Silence awhile. Robin, take off his head.
80 Titania, music call, and strike more dead
Than common sleep of all these five the sense.

TITANIA: Music, ho! Music, such as charmeth sleep!

[Music.]

PUCK *[removing the ass head]*:   Now, when thou wak'st,
with thine own fool's eyes peep.

OBERON: Sound, music! Come, my queen, take hands
with me,
85 And rock the ground whereon these sleepers be.

[They dance.]

Now thou and I are new in amity,
And will tomorrow midnight solemnly

Dance in Duke Theseus' house triumphantly,
And bless it to all fair prosperity.
90 There shall the pairs of faithful lovers be
Wedded, with Theseus, all in jollity.

PUCK: Fairy King, attend, and mark:
I do hear the morning lark.

OBERON: Then, my queen, in silence sad,
95 Trip we after night's shade.
We the globe can compass soon,
Swifter than the wandering moon.

TITANIA: Come, my lord, and in our flight
Tell me how it came this night
100 That I sleeping here was found
With these mortals on the ground.

Exeunt [OBERON, TITANIA, and PUCK].
Wind horn [within].

Enter THESEUS and all his train;
[HIPPOLYTA, EGEUS].

THESEUS: Go, one of you, find out the forester,
For now our observation is performed;
And since we have the vaward of the day,
105 My love shall hear the music of my hounds.
Uncouple in the western valley; let them go.
Dispatch, I say, and find the forester.

[Exit an ATTENDANT.]

We will, fair queen, up to the mountain's top
And mark the musical confusion
110 Of hounds and echo in conjunction.

HIPPOLYTA: I was with Hercules and Cadmus once
When in a wood of Crete they bayed the bear
With hounds of Sparta. Never did I hear
Such gallant chiding; for, besides the groves,
115 The skies, the fountains, every region near
Seemed all one mutual cry. I never heard
So musical a discord, such sweet thunder.

THESEUS: My hounds are bred out of the Spartan kind,
So flewed, so sanded; and their heads are hung
120 With ears that sweep away the morning dew;
Crook-kneed, and dewlapped like Thessalian bulls;

---

65 other others   **66 repair** return   **72 Dian's bud** (Perhaps the flower of the *agnus castus*, or chaste-tree, supposed to preserve chastity; or perhaps referring simply to Oberon's herb by which he can undo the effects of "Cupid's flower," the love-in-idleness of 2.1.166–168.)   **81 these five** i.e., the four lovers and Bottom   **82 charmeth** brings about, as though by a charm   **87 solemnly** ceremoniously

94 sad sober   **103 observation** i.e., observance to a morn of May (1.1.167)   **104 vaward** vanguard, i.e., earliest part   **106 Uncouple** set free for the hunt   **111 Cadmus** mythical founder of Thebes. (This story about him is unknown.)   **112 bayed** brought to bay   **113 hounds of Sparta** (A breed famous in antiquity for its hunting skill.)   **114 chiding** i.e., yelping   **118 kind** strain, breed   **119 So flewed** similarly having large hanging chaps or fleshy covering of the jaw.   **sanded** of sandy color   **121 dewlapped** having pendulous folds of skin under the neck

The lovers, Helena (Calista Flockhart), Demetrius, Lysander, and Hermia, are discovered.

Slow in pursuit, but matched in mouth like bells,
Each under each. A cry more tunable
Was never holloed to nor cheered with horn
125   In Crete, in Sparta, nor in Thessaly.
Judge when you hear. *[He sees the sleepers.]* But soft!
   What nymphs are these?

EGEUS: My lord, this is my daughter here asleep,
And this Lysander; this Demetrius is;
This Helena, old Nedar's Helena.
130   I wonder of their being here together.

THESEUS: No doubt they rose up early to observe
The rite of May, and hearing our intent,
Came here in grace of our solemnity.
But speak, Egeus. Is not this the day
135   That Hermia should give answer of her choice?

EGEUS: It is, my lord.

THESEUS: Go bid the huntsmen wake them with their
   horns.
                                        [Exit an ATTENDANT.*]*

   Shout within. Wind horns. They all start up.

Good morrow, friends. Saint Valentine is past.
Begin these woodbirds but to couple now?

140   LYSANDER: Pardon, my lord.   *[They kneel.]*

THESEUS: I pray you all, stand up.
                                        [They stand.]
I know you two are rival enemies;
How comes this gentle concord in the world,

That hatred is so far from jealousy
To sleep by hate and fear no enmity?

LYSANDER: My lord, I shall reply amazedly,   145
Half sleep, half waking; but as yet, I swear,
I cannot truly say how I came here.
But, as I think—for truly would I speak,
And now I do bethink me, so it is—
I came with Hermia hither. Our intent   150
Was to be gone from Athens, where we might,
Without the peril of the Athenian law—

EGEUS: Enough, enough, my lord; you have enough.
I beg the law, the law, upon his head.
They would have stol'n away; they would, Demetrius,   155
Thereby to have defeated you and me,
You of your wife and me of my consent,
Of my consent that she should be your wife.

DEMETRIUS: My lord, fair Helen told me of their
   stealth,
Of this their purpose hither to this wood,   160
And I in fury hither followed them,
Fair Helena in fancy following me.
But, my good lord, I wot not by what power—
But by some power it is—my love to Hermia,
Melted as the snow, seems to me now   165
As the remembrance of an idle gaud
Which in my childhood I did dote upon;
And all the faith, the virtue of my heart,
The object and the pleasure of mine eye,
Is only Helena. To her, my lord,   170
Was I betrothed ere I saw Hermia,
But like a sickness did I loathe this food;
But, as in health, come to my natural taste,
Now I do wish it, love it, long for it,
And will forevermore be true to it.   175

THESEUS: Fair lovers, you are fortunately met.
Of this discourse we more will hear anon.
Egeus, I will overbear your will;
For in the temple, by and by, with us
These couples shall eternally be knit.   180
And, for the morning now is something worn,
Our purposed hunting shall be set aside.
Away with us to Athens. Three and three,
We'll hold a feast in great solemnity.
Come, Hippolyta.   185
                [Exeunt THESEUS, HIPPOLYTA, EGEUS, *and train.]*

122–123 **matched . . . each** i.e., harmoniously matched in their various cries like a set of bells, from treble down to bass   123 **cry** pack of hounds.   **tunable** well tuned, melodious   124 **cheered** encouraged   126 **soft** i.e., gently, wait a minute   130 **wonder of** wonder at   133 **in . . . solemnity** in honor of our wedding ceremony   138 **Saint Valentine** (Birds were supposed to choose their mates on Saint Valentine's Day.)

143 **jealousy** suspicion   151 **where** wherever; or, to where   152 **Without** outside of, beyond   156 **defeated** defrauded   160 **hither** in coming hither   162 **in fancy** driven by love   166 **idle gaud** worthless trinket   181 **for** since.   **something** somewhat   184 **in great solemnity** with great ceremony

DEMETRIUS: These things seem small and
    undistinguishable,
Like far-off mountains turnèd into clouds.

HERMIA: Methinks I see these things with parted eye,
When everything seems double.

HELENA: So methinks;
190   And I have found Demetrius like a jewel,
Mine own, and not mine own.

DEMETRIUS: Are you sure
That we are awake? It seems to me
That yet we sleep, we dream. Do not you think
The Duke was here, and bid us follow him?

195 **HERMIA:** Yea, and my father.

HELENA: And Hippolyta.

LYSANDER: And he did bid us follow to the temple.

DEMETRIUS: Why, then, we are awake. Let's follow
    him,
And by the way let us recount our dreams.
                      [Exeunt the lovers.]

BOTTOM *[awaking]:* When my cue comes, call me,
200   and I will answer. My next is "Most fair Pyramus."
Heigh-ho! Peter Quince! Flute, the bellows mender!
Snout, the tinker! Starveling! God's my life, stolen
hence and left me asleep! I have had a most rare vision. I have had a dream, past the wit of man to say
205 what dream it was. Man is but an ass if he go about
to expound this dream. Methought I was—there is
no man can tell what. Methought I was—and methought I had—but man is but a patched fool if he
will offer to say what methought I had. The eye of
210 man hath not heard, the ear of man hath not seen,
man's hand is not able to taste, his tongue to conceive, nor his heart to report, what my dream was. I
will get Peter Quince to write a ballad of this dream.
It shall be called "Bottom's Dream," because it hath
215 no bottom; and I will sing it in the latter end of a
play, before the Duke. Peradventure, to make it the
more gracious, I shall sing it at her death.   *[Exit.]*

4.2   *Enter* QUINCE, FLUTE, *[*SNOUT, *and* STARVELING*].*

QUINCE: Have you sent to Bottom's house? Is he come
home yet?

STARVELING: He cannot be heard of. Out of doubt he
is transported.

FLUTE: If he come not, then the play is marred. It goes 5
not forward. Doth it?

QUINCE: It is not possible. You have not a man in all
Athens able to discharge Pyramus but he.

FLUTE: No, he hath simply the best wit of any handi-
craft man in Athens. 10

QUINCE: Yea, and the best person too, and he is a very
paramour for a sweet voice.

FLUTE: You must say "paragon." A paramour is, God
bless us, a thing of naught.

                        Enter SNUG *the joiner.*

SNUG: Masters, the Duke is coming from the temple, 15
and there is two or three lords and ladies more married. If our sport had gone forward, we had all been
made men.

FLUTE: O sweet bully Bottom! Thus hath he lost sixpence a day during his life; he could not have scaped 20
sixpence a day. An the Duke had not given him sixpence a day for playing Pyramus, I'll be hanged. He
would have deserved it. Sixpence a day in Pyramus,
or nothing.

                        Enter BOTTOM.

BOTTOM: Where are these lads? Where are these hearts? 25

QUINCE: Bottom! O most courageous day! O most
happy hour!

BOTTOM: Masters, I am to discourse wonders. But ask
me not what; for if I tell you, I am no true Athenian.
I will tell you everything, right as it fell out. 30

QUINCE: Let us hear, sweet Bottom.

---

188 parted i.e., improperly focused   **190–191 like ... mine own**
i.e., like a jewel that one finds by chance and therefore possesses but
cannot certainly consider one's own property   **202 God's** may God
save   **205 go about** attempt   **208 patched** wearing motley, i.e.,
a dress of various colors   **209 offer** venture   **209–212 The eye
... report** (Bottom garbles the terms of 1 Corinthians 2:9.)   **213
ballad** (The proper medium for relating sensational stories and
preposterous events.)   **214–215 hath no bottom** is unfathomable
217 her Thisbe's (?)

4.2 Location: Athens.
4 transported carried off by fairies; or, possibly, transformed   **8
discharge** perform   **9 wit** intellect   **11 person** appearance   **14
a ... naught** a shameful thing   **17–18 we ... men** i.e., we would
have had our fortunes made   **19–20 sixpence a day** i.e., as a royal
pension   **25 hearts** good fellows   **28 am ... wonders** have wonders to relate

BOTTOM: Not a word of me. All that I will tell you is that the Duke hath dined. Get your apparel together, good strings to your beards, new ribbons to your
35   pumps; meet presently at the palace; every man look o'er his part; for the short and the long is, our play is preferred. In any case, let Thisbe have clean linen; and let not him that plays the lion pare his nails, for they shall hang out for the lion's claws. And, most dear
40   actors, eat no onions nor garlic, for we are to utter sweet breath; and I do not doubt but to hear them say it is a sweet comedy. No more words. Away! Go, away!

[Exeunt.]

5.1   *Enter* THESEUS, HIPPOLYTA, *and* PHILOSTRATE,
[lords, and attendants].

HIPPOLYTA: 'Tis strange, my Theseus, that these lovers speak of.

THESEUS: More strange than true. I never may believe
These antique fables nor these fairy toys.
Lovers and madmen have such seething brains,
5   Such shaping fantasies, that apprehend
More than cool reason ever comprehends.
The lunatic, the lover, and the poet
Are of imagination all compact.
One sees more devils than vast hell can hold;
10   That is the madman. The lover, all as frantic,
Sees Helen's beauty in a brow of Egypt.
The poet's eye, in a fine frenzy rolling,
Doth glance from heaven to earth, from earth to heaven;
And as imagination bodies forth
15   The forms of things unknown, the poet's pen
Turns them to shapes and gives to airy nothing
A local habitation and a name.
Such tricks hath strong imagination
That, if it would but apprehend some joy,
20   It comprehends some bringer of that joy;
Or in the night, imagining some fear,
How easy is a bush supposed a bear!

HIPPOLYTA: But all the story of the night told over,
And all their minds transfigured so together,
More witnesseth than fancy's images   25
And grows to something of great constancy;
But, howsoever, strange and admirable.

Enter lovers: LYSANDER, DEMETRIUS,
HERMIA, *and* HELENA.

THESEUS: Here come the lovers, full of joy and mirth.
Joy, gentle friends! Joy and fresh days of love
Accompany your hearts!

LYSANDER: More than to us   30
Wait in your royal walks, your board, your bed!

THESEUS: Come now, what masques, what dances shall we have,
To wear away this long age of three hours
Between our after-supper and bedtime?
Where is our usual manager of mirth?   35
What revels are in hand? Is there no play
To ease the anguish of a torturing hour?
Call Philostrate.

PHILOSTRATE: Here, mighty Theseus.

THESEUS: Say, what abridgment have you for this evening?
What masque? What music? How shall we beguile   40
The lazy time, if not with some delight?

PHILOSTRATE *[giving him a paper]*:   There is a brief
how many sports are ripe.
Make choice of which Your Highness will see first.

THESEUS *[reads]*: "The battle with the Centaurs,
to be sung
By an Athenian eunuch to the harp"?   45
We'll none of that. That have I told my love,
In glory of my kinsman Hercules.
[He reads.] "The riot of the tipsy Bacchanals,
Tearing the Thracian singer in their rage"?
That is an old device; and it was played   50

---

32 of out of   **34 strings** (to attach the beards)   **35 pumps** light shoes or slippers.   **presently** immediately   **37 preferred** selected for consideration

5.1 Location: Athens. The palace of Theseus.
1 that that which   **2 may** can   **3 antique** old-fashioned (punning, too, on *antic*, "strange," "grotesque").   **fairy toys** trifling stories about fairies   **5 fantasies** imaginations.   **apprehend** conceive, imagine   **6 comprehends** understands   **8 compact** formed, composed   **11 Helen's** i.e., of Helen of Troy, pattern of beauty.   **brow of Egypt** i.e., face of a gypsy   **20 bringer** i.e., source   **21 fear** object of fear

---

25 More . . . images testifies to something more substantial than mere imaginings   **26 constancy** certainty   **27 howsoever** in any case.   **admirable** a source of wonder   **32 masques** courtly entertainments   **39 abridgment** pastime (to abridge or shorten the evening)   **42 brief** short written statement, summary   **44 battle . . . Centaurs** (Probably refers to the battle of the Centaurs and the Lapithae, when the Centaurs attempted to carry off Hippodamia, bride of Theseus' friend Pirothous. The story is told in Ovid's *Metamorphoses* 12.)   **47 kinsman** (Plutarch's "Life of Theseus" states that Hercules and Theseus were near kinsmen. Theseus is referring to a version of the battle of the Centaurs in which Hercules was said to be present.)   **48–49 The riot . . . rage** (This was the story of the death of Orpheus, as told in *Metamorphoses* 11.)   **50 device** show, performance

When I from Thebes came last a conqueror.
[He reads.] "The thrice three Muses mourning for the death
Of Learning, late deceased in beggary"?
That is some satire, keen and critical,
55   Not sorting with a nuptial ceremony.
[He reads.] "A tedious brief scene of young Pyramus
And his love Thisbe; very tragical mirth"?
Merry and tragical? Tedious and brief?
That is, hot ice and wondrous strange snow.
60   How shall we find the concord of this discord?

PHILOSTRATE: A play there is, my lord, some ten words long,
Which is as brief as I have known a play;
But by ten words, my lord, it is too long,
Which makes it tedious. For in all the play
65   There is not one word apt, one player fitted.
And tragical, my noble lord, it is,
For Pyramus therein doth kill himself.
Which, when I saw rehearsed, I must confess,
Made mine eyes water; but more merry tears
70   The passion of loud laughter never shed.

THESEUS: What are they that do play it?

PHILOSTRATE: Hardhanded men that work in Athens here,
Which never labored in their minds till now,
And now have toiled their unbreathed memories
75   With this same play, against your nuptial.

THESEUS: And we will hear it.

PHILOSTRATE: No, my noble lord,
It is not for you. I have heard it over,
And it is nothing, nothing in the world;
Unless you can find sport in their intents,
80   Extremely stretched and conned with cruel pain
To do you service.

THESEUS: I will hear that play;
For never anything can be a miss
When simpleness and duty tender it.
Go, bring them in; and take your places, ladies.

[PHILOSTRATE goes to summon the players.]

Duke Theseus (Derek Godfrey), seated beside his wife Hippolyta (Barbara Jefford), bids the players approach.

HIPPOLYTA: I love not to see wretchedness o'ercharged,   85
And duty in his service perishing.

THESEUS: Why, gentle sweet, you shall see no such thing.

HIPPOLYTA: He says they can do nothing in this kind.

THESEUS: The kinder we, to give them thanks for nothing.
Our sport shall be to take what they mistake;   90
And what poor duty cannot do, noble respect
Takes it in might, not merit.
Where I have come, great clerks have purposèd
To greet me with premeditated welcomes;
Where I have seen them shiver and look pale,   95
Make periods in the midst of sentences,
Throttle their practiced accent in their fears,
And in conclusion dumbly have broke off,
Not paying me a welcome. Trust me, sweet,
Out of this silence yet I picked a welcome;   100
And in the modesty of fearful duty
I read as much as from the rattling tongue
Of saucy and audacious eloquence.
Love, therefore, and tongue-tied simplicity
In least speak most, to my capacity.   105

[PHILOSTRATE returns.]

52–53 **The thrice . . . beggary** (Possibly an allusion to Spenser's *Teares of the Muses*, 1591, though "satires" deploring the neglect of learning and the creative arts were commonplace.) 55 **sorting with** befitting 59 **strange** (Sometimes emended to an adjective that would contrast with *snow*, just as *hot* contrasts with *ice*.) 74 **toiled** taxed. **unbreathed** unexercised 75 **against** in preparation for 80 **stretched** strained. **conned** memorized 83 **simpleness** simplicity

---

85 **wretchedness o'ercharged** social or intellectual inferiors overburdened 86 **his service** its attempt to serve 88 **kind** kind of thing 91 **respect** evaluation, consideration 92 **Takes . . . merit** values it for the effort made rather than for the excellence achieved 93 **clerks** learned men 97 **practiced accent** i.e., rehearsed speech; or, usual way of speaking 105 **least** i.e., saying least. **to my capacity** in my judgment and understanding

PHILOSTRATE: So please Your Grace, the Prologue is addressed.

THESEUS: Let him approach. *[A flourish of trumpets.]*

Enter the PROLOGUE *[QUINCE].*

PROLOGUE: If we offend, it is with our good will.
    That you should think, we come not to offend,
110 But with good will. To show our simple skill,
    That is the true beginning of our end.
    Consider, then, we come but in despite.
        We do not come, as minding to content you,
    Our true intent is. All for your delight
115   We are not here. That you should here repent
            you,
    The actors are at hand; and, by their show,
    You shall know all that you are like to know.

THESEUS: This fellow doth not stand upon points.

LYSANDER: He hath rid his prologue like a rough colt;
120 he knows not the stop. A good moral, my lord: it is
not enough to speak, but to speak true.

HIPPOLYTA: Indeed, he hath played on his prologue like
a child on a recorder: a sound, but not in government.

THESEUS: His speech was like a tangled chain: noth-
125 ing impaired, but all disordered. Who is next?

Enter PYRAMUS *[BOTTOM], and* THISBE *[FLUTE],
and* WALL *[SNOUT], and* MOONSHINE
[STARVELING], and LION *[SNUG].*

PROLOGUE: Gentles, perchance you wonder at this
            show;
    But wonder on, till truth make all things plain.
    This man is Pyramus, if you would know;
    This beauteous lady Thisbe is, certain.
130 This man with lime and roughcast doth present
        Wall, that vile wall which did these lovers sunder;
    And through Wall's chink, poor souls, they are
            content
        To whisper. At the which let no man wonder.
    This man, with lantern, dog, and bush of thorn,
135   Presenteth Moonshine; for, if you will know,
    By moonshine did these lovers think no scorn
        To meet at Ninus' tomb, there, there to woo.

This grisly beast, which Lion hight by name,
The trusty Thisbe coming first by night
Did scare away, or rather did affright;   140
And as she fled, her mantle she did fall,
    Which Lion vile with bloody mouth did stain.
Anon comes Pyramus, sweet youth and tall,
    And finds his trusty Thisbe's mantle slain;
Whereat, with blade, with bloody, blameful blade,   145
    He bravely broached his boiling bloody breast.
And Thisbe, tarrying in mulberry shade,
    His dagger drew, and died. For all the rest,
Let Lion, Moonshine, Wall, and lovers twain
At large discourse, while here they do remain.   150

Exeunt LION, THISBE, *and* MOONSHINE.

THESEUS: I wonder if the lion be to speak.

DEMETRIUS: No wonder, my lord. One lion may, when
many asses do.

WALL: In this same interlude it doth befall
    That I, one Snout by name, present a wall;   155
    And such a wall as I would have you think
    That had in it a crannied hole or chink,
    Through which the lovers, Pyramus and Thisbe,
    Did whisper often, very secretly.
    This loam, this roughcast, and this stone doth show   160
    That I am that same wall; the truth is so.
    And this the cranny is, right and sinister,
    Through which the fearful lovers are to whisper.

THESEUS: Would you desire lime and hair to speak
better?   165

DEMETRIUS: It is the wittiest partition that ever I
heard discourse, my lord.

[PYRAMUS comes forward.]

THESEUS: Pyramus draws near the wall. Silence!

PYRAMUS: O grim-looked night! O night with hue
            so black!
        O night, which ever art when day is not!   170
    O night, O night! alack, alack, alack,
        I fear my Thisbe's promise is forgot.
    And thou, O wall, O sweet, O lovely wall,
        That stand'st between her father's ground and
            mine,

---

106 **Prologue** speaker of the prologue. **addressed** ready 113 **minding** intending 118 **stand upon points** (1) heed niceties or small points (2) pay attention to punctuation in his reading. (The humor of Quince's speech is in the blunders of its punctuation.) 119 **rid** ridden. **rough** unbroken 120 **stop** (1) stopping of a colt by reining it in (2) punctuation mark 123 **recorder** wind instrument like a flute. **government** control 124–125 **nothing** not at all 136 **think no scorn** think it no disgraceful matter

---

138 **hight** is called 141 **fall** let fall 143 **tall** courageous 146 **broached** stabbed 150 **At large** in full, at length 154 **interlude** play 162 **right and sinister** i.e., the right side of it and the left; or, running from right to left, horizontally 166 **partition** (1) wall (2) section of a learned treatise or oration 169 **grim-looked** grim-looking

Thisbe (Sam Rockwell) and Pyramus speak through the wall.

175 Thou wall, O wall, O sweet and lovely wall,
    Show me thy chink, to blink through with mine
        eyne.   *[WALL makes a chink with his fingers.]*
    Thanks, courteous wall. Jove shield thee well for
        this.
    But what see I? No Thisbe do I see.
    O wicked wall, through whom I see no bliss!
180   Cursed be thy stones for thus deceiving me!

THESEUS: The wall, methinks, being sensible, should
    curse again.

PYRAMUS: No, in truth, sir, he should not. "Deceiving
    me" is Thisbe's cue: she is to enter now, and I am to
185   spy her through the wall. You shall see, it will fall pat
    as I told you. Yonder she comes.

                              Enter THISBE.

THISBE: O wall, full often hast thou heard my moans
    For parting my fair Pyramus and me.
    My cherry lips have often kissed thy stones,
190   Thy stones with lime and hair knit up in thee.

PYRAMUS: I see a voice. Now will I to the chink,
    To spy an I can hear my Thisbe's face.
    Thisbe!

THISBE: My love! Thou art my love, I think.

PYRAMUS:
    Think what thou wilt, I am thy lover's grace,
195   And like Limander am I trusty still.

THISBE: And I like Helen, till the Fates me kill.

PYRAMUS: Not Shafalus to Procrus was so true.

THISBE: As Shafalus to Procrus, I to you.

PYRAMUS: O, kiss me through the hole of this vile
    wall!

THISBE: I kiss the wall's hole, not your lips at all.   200

PYRAMUS: Wilt thou at Ninny's tomb meet me
    straightaway?

THISBE: 'Tide life, 'tide death, I come without delay.
                    [Exeunt PYRAMUS *and* THISBE.*]*

WALL: Thus have I, Wall, my part dischargèd so;
    And, being done, thus Wall away doth go.   *[Exit.]*

THESEUS: Now is the mural down between the two   205
    neighbors.

DEMETRIUS: No remedy, my lord, when walls are so
    willful to hear without warning.

HIPPOLYTA: This is the silliest stuff that ever I heard.

THESEUS: The best in this kind are but shadows; and   210
    the worst are no worse, if imagination amend them.

HIPPOLYTA: It must be your imagination then, and
    not theirs.

THESEUS: If we imagine no worse of them than they
    of themselves, they may pass for excellent men. Here   215
    come two noble beasts in, a man and a lion.

                    Enter LION *and* MOONSHINE.

LION: You, ladies, you, whose gentle hearts do fear
    The smallest monstrous mouse that creeps
        on floor,
    May now perchance both quake and tremble here,
        When lion rough in wildest rage doth roar.   220
    Then know that I, as Snug the joiner, am
    A lion fell, nor else no lion's dam;
    For, if I should as lion come in strife
    Into this place, 'twere pity on my life.

THESEUS: A very gentle beast, and of a good conscience.   225

DEMETRIUS: The very best at a beast, my lord, that
    e'er I saw.

LYSANDER: This lion is a very fox for his valor.

THESEUS: True; and a goose for his discretion.

DEMETRIUS: Not so, my lord, for his valor cannot   230
    carry his discretion, and the fox carries the goose.

---

181 sensible capable of feeling **182 again** in return **185 pat** exactly **192 an** if **194 lover's grace** i.e., gracious lover **195, 196 Limander, Helen** (Blunders for "Leander" and "Hero.") **197 Shafalus, Procrus** (Blunders for "Cephalus" and "Procris," also famous lovers.)

202 'Tide betide, come **208 willful** willing. **without warning** i.e., without warning the parents. (Demetrius makes a joke on the proverb "Walls have ears.") **210 in this kind** of this sort. **shadows** likenesses, representations **222 lion fell** fierce lion (with a play on the idea of "lion skin") **228 is . . . valor** i.e., his valor consists of craftiness and discretion **229 a goose . . . discretion** i.e., as discreet as a goose, that is, more foolish than discreet

THESEUS: His discretion, I am sure, cannot carry his valor; for the goose carries not the fox. It is well. Leave it to his discretion, and let us listen to the moon.

235 **MOON:** This lanthorn doth the hornèd moon present—

DEMETRIUS: He should have worn the horns on his head.

THESEUS: He is no crescent, and his horns are invisible within the circumference.

240 **MOON:** This lanthorn doth the hornèd moon present;
Myself the man i' the moon do seem to be.

THESEUS: This is the greatest error of all the rest. The man should be put into the lanthorn. How is it else the man i' the moon?

245 **DEMETRIUS:** He dares not come there for the candle, for you see it is already in snuff.

HIPPOLYTA: I am aweary of this moon. Would he would change!

THESEUS: It appears, by his small light of discretion,
250 that he is in the wane; but yet, in courtesy, in all reason, we must stay the time.

LYSANDER: Proceed, Moon.

MOON: All that I have to say is to tell you that the lanthorn is the moon, I, the man i' the moon, this thorn-
255 bush my thornbush, and this dog my dog.

DEMETRIUS: Why, all these should be in the lanthorn, for all these are in the moon. But silence! Here comes Thisbe.

Enter THISBE.

THISBE: This is old Ninny's tomb. Where is my love?

260 **LION** [*roaring*]: O!

DEMETRIUS: Well roared, Lion.

[THISBE *runs off, dropping her mantle.*]

THESEUS: Well run, Thisbe.

HIPPOLYTA: Well shone, Moon. Truly, the moon shines with a good grace.

[*The* LION *worries* THISBE's *mantle.*]

THESEUS: Well moused, Lion.   265

[*Enter* PYRAMUS; *exit* LION.]

DEMETRIUS: And then came Pyramus.

LYSANDER: And so the lion vanished.

PYRAMUS: Sweet Moon, I thank thee for thy sunny beams;
I thank thee, Moon, for shining now so bright;
For, by thy gracious, golden, glittering gleams,   270
I trust to take of truest Thisbe sight.
But stay, O spite!
But mark, poor knight,
What dreadful dole is here?
Eyes, do you see?   275
How can it be?
O dainty duck! O dear!
Thy mantle good,
What, stained with blood?
Approach, ye Furies fell!   280
O Fates, come, come,
Cut thread and thrum;
Quail, crush, conclude, and quell!

THESEUS: This passion, and the death of a dear friend, would go near to make a man look sad.   285

HIPPOLYTA: Beshrew my heart, but I pity the man.

PYRAMUS: O, wherefore, Nature, didst thou lions frame?
Since lion vile hath here deflowered my dear,
Which is—no, no, which was—the fairest dame
That lived, that loved, that liked, that looked with cheer.   290
Come, tears, confound,
Out, sword, and wound
The pap of Pyramus;
Ay, that left pap,
Where heart doth hop.   [*He stabs himself.*]   295
Thus die I, thus, thus, thus.
Now am I dead,
Now am I fled;
My soul is in the sky.
Tongue, lose thy light;   300
Moon, take thy flight.   [*Exit* MOONSHINE.]
Now die, die, die, die, die.   [PYRAMUS *dies.*]

---

235 **lanthorn** (This original spelling, *lanthorn*, may suggest a play on the *horn* of which lanterns were made and also on a cuckold's horns; however, the spelling *lanthorn* is not used consistently for comic effect in this play or elsewhere. At 5.1.134, for example, the word is *lantern* in the original.) 236–237 **on his head** (as a sign of cuckoldry) 238 **crescent** a waxing moon 245 **for** because of, for fear of 246 **in snuff** (1) offended (2) in need of snuffing or trimming

265 **moused** shaken, torn, bitten 274 **dole** grievous event 280 **Furies** avenging goddesses of Greek myth **fell** fierce 281 **Fates** the three goddesses (Clotho, Lachesis, Atropos) of Greek myth who spun, drew, and cut the thread of human life 282 **thread and thrum** i.e., everything—the good and bad alike; literally, the warp in weaving and the loose end of the warp 283 **Quail** overpower. **quell** kill, destroy 284–285 **This . . . sad** i.e., if one had other reason to grieve, one might be sad, but not from this absurd portrayal of passion 290 **cheer** countenance 293 **pap** breast

DEMETRIUS: No die, but an ace, for him; for he is but one.

305 **LYSANDER:**   Less than an ace, man; for he is dead, he is nothing.

THESEUS: With the help of a surgeon he might yet recover, and yet prove an ass.

HIPPOLYTA: How chance Moonshine is gone before
310   Thisbe comes back and finds her lover?

THESEUS: She will find him by starlight.

[Enter THISBE.]

Here she comes; and her passion ends the play.

HIPPOLYTA: Methinks she should not use a long one for such a Pyramus. I hope she will be brief.

315 **DEMETRIUS:**   A mote will turn the balance, which Pyramus, which Thisbe, is the better: he for a man, God warrant us; she for a woman, God bless us.

LYSANDER: She hath spied him already with those sweet eyes.

320 **DEMETRIUS:**   And thus she means, videlicet:

THISBE: Asleep, my love?
          What, dead, my dove?
        O Pyramus, arise!
          Speak, speak. Quite dumb?
325   Dead, dead? A tomb
        Must cover thy sweet eyes.
          These lily lips,
          This cherry nose,
        These yellow cowslip cheeks,
330   Are gone, are gone!
          Lovers, make moan.
        His eyes were green as leeks.
          O Sisters Three,
          Come, come to me,
335   With hands as pale as milk;
          Lay them in gore,
          Since you have shore

---

303 ace the side of the die featuring the single pip, or spot. (The pun is on *die* as a singular of *dice;* Bottom's performance is not worth a whole *die* but rather one single face of it, one small portion.)   **304 one** (1) an individual person (2) unique   **308 ass** (with a pun on *ace*)   **315 mote** small particle   **315–316 which . . . which** whether . . . or   **320 means** moans, laments (with a pun on the meaning, "lodge a formal complaint").   **videlicet** to wit   **333 Sisters Three** the Fates   **337 shore** shorn

Thisbe mourns the dead Pyramus.

        With shears his thread of silk.
          Tongue, not a word.
          Come, trusty sword,
340   Come, blade, my breast imbrue!

[She stabs herself.]

          And farewell, friends.
          Thus Thisbe ends.
        Adieu, adieu, adieu.   *[She dies.]*

THESEUS: Moonshine and Lion are left to bury the dead.   345

DEMETRIUS: Ay, and Wall too.

BOTTOM *[starting up, as FLUTE does also]*:   No, I assure you, the wall is down that parted their fathers. Will it please you to see the epilogue, or to hear a Bergomask dance between two of our company?   350

[The other players enter.]

THESEUS: No epilogue, I pray you; for your play needs no excuse. Never excuse; for when the players are all dead, there need none to be blamed. Marry, if he that writ it had played Pyramus and hanged himself in Thisbe's garter, it would have been a fine tragedy; and 355 so it is, truly, and very notably discharged. But, come, your Bergomask. Let your epilogue alone.   *[A dance.]*
The iron tongue of midnight hath told twelve.
Lovers, to bed, 'tis almost fairy time.
I fear we shall outsleep the coming morn   360
As much as we this night have overwatched.
This palpable-gross play hath well beguiled
The heavy gait of night. Sweet friends, to bed.
A fortnight hold we this solemnity,
In nightly revels and new jollity.   *Exeunt.* 365

---

341 imbrue stain with blood   **349–350 Bergomask dance** a rustic dance named for Bergamo, a province in the state of Venice   **358 iron tongue** i.e., of a bell.   **told** counted, struck ("tolled")   **361 overwatched** stayed up too late   **362 palpable-gross** palpably gross, obviously crude   **363 heavy** drowsy, dull

Enter PUCK *[carrying a broom].*

PUCK:
Now the hungry lion roars,
    And the wolf behowls the moon,
Whilst the heavy plowman snores,
    All with weary task fordone.
370 Now the wasted brands do glow,
    Whilst the screech owl, screeching loud,
Puts the wretch that lies in woe
    In remembrance of a shroud.
Now it is the time of night
375   That the graves, all gaping wide,
Every one lets forth his sprite,
    In the church-way paths to glide.
And we fairies, that do run
    By the triple Hecate's team.
380 From the presence of the sun,
    Following darkness like a dream,
Now are frolic. Not a mouse
    Shall disturb this hallowed house.
I am sent with broom before,
385 To sweep the dust behind the door.

*Enter [*OBERON *and* TITANIA,*] King and*
Queen of Fairies, with all their train.

OBERON:
Through the house give glimmering light,
    By the dead and drowsy fire;
Every elf and fairy sprite
    Hop as light as bird from brier;
390 And this ditty, after me,
    Sing, and dance it trippingly.

TITANIA:
First, rehearse your song by rote,
To each word a warbling note.
Hand in hand, with fairy grace,
395 Will we sing, and bless this place.

[Song and dance.]

OBERON:
Now, until the break of day,
Through this house each fairy stray.
To the best bride-bed will we,
Which by us shall blessèd be;
400 And the issue there create
Ever shall be fortunate.
So shall all the couples three
Ever true in loving be;
And the blots of Nature's hand

Puck (Ian Holm) delivers his final monologue.

Shall not in their issue stand;   405
Never mole, harelip, nor scar,
Nor mark prodigious, such as are
Despisèd in nativity,
Shall upon their children be.
With this field dew consecrate,   410
Every fairy take his gait,
And each several chamber bless,
Though this palace, with sweet peace;
And the owner of it blest
Ever shall in safety rest.   415
Trip away; make no stay;
Meet me all by break of day.

*Exeunt [*OBERON, TITANIA, *and train].*

PUCK *[to the audience]:*
If we shadows have offended,
Think but this, and all is mended,
That you have but slumbered here   420
While these visions did appear.
And this weak and idle theme,
No more yielding but a dream,
Gentles, do not reprehend.
If you pardon, we will mend.   425
And, as I am an honest Puck,
If we have unearnèd luck
Now to scape the serpent's tongue,
We will make amends ere long;
Else the Puck a liar call.   430
So, good night unto you all.
Give me your hands, if we be friends,
And Robin shall restore amends.   *[Exit.]*

---

368 heavy tired   **369 fordone** exhausted   **370 wasted brands**
burned-out logs   **376 Every . . . sprite** every grave lets forth its
ghost   **379 triple Hecate's** (Hecate ruled in three capacities: as
Luna or Cynthia in heaven, as Diana on earth, and as Proserpina
in hell.)   **382 frolic** merry   **385 behind** from behind, or else
like sweeping the dirt under the carpet. (Robin Goodfellow was a
household spirit who helped good housemaids and punished lazy
ones, but he could, of course, be mischievous.)   **392 rehearse**
recite   **400 create** created

---

407 prodigious monstrous, unnatural   **410 consecrate** consecrated   **411 take his gait** go his way   **412 several** separate   **420**
That . . . here i.e., that it is a "midsummer night's dream"   **423 No**
. . . but yielding no more than   **425 mend** improve   **428 serpent's**
tongue i.e., hissing   **432 Give . . . hands** applaud   **433 restore**
amends give satisfaction in return

Writing from Reading

Summarize

1 A series of clearly established scenes adds up to a struggle between illusion and reality. Describe the unfolding of the struggle in plain language.

Analyze Craft

2 Some scholars have suggested that the play itself was commissioned to celebrate a royal wedding or betrothal. As a wedding play, what does this suggest about the condition of marriage? How do Oberon and Titania mirror their mortal counterparts? What does the play's title suggest?

3 What do these "rude mechanicals" tell us about the nature of love?

4 What is the symbolic function of the marriage between Theseus and Hippolyta?

5 Characterize the four young lovers—the two mismatched and then matched pairs. How individual do they seem, or are they interchangeable, and if the latter, is that part of the playwright's point?

Analyze Voice

6 Why is Bottom so unforgettably comic; what about his behavior reflects on members of the court? When Titania grows passionate about him, is her love truly blind? Look at her protestations of devotion and give examples of what's serious and what's foolish in her speech.

7 This play is a comedy, but in *A Midsummer Night's Dream,* there is danger and the risk of madness or at least delusion. How could this "dream" have been transformed to "nightmare," the comedy to tragedy? The Latin word for "moon"—*luna*—is at the root of "lunatic," and the behavior of the lovers seems more than a little bit crazy when enacted onstage. Analyze the playwright's tone.

Synthesize Summary and Analysis

8 The play is set in ancient Athens, but the woods are those of Elizabethan England. How easy or uneasy is the fit between the two?

9 How do the fairies help bridge the gap between aristocrat and worker?

10 What do the women have in common here? The men?

11 Compare and contrast the "play within the play," in *A Midsummer Night's Dream* with the one in *Hamlet.*

Interpret the Play

12 The almost literal lunacy of all this moonlit madness—amorous coupling in the dark, the change of sexual partners, the loss of recognizable identity—evokes a far more pagan set of behaviors than those otherwise permitted to the royal entourage. Are Demetrius, Lysander, Hermia, and Helena very different when "lost" in the woods from when found in court?

13 The themes of marriage and fertility are scarcely new to Shakespeare, but the intersections of society and the primitive world provide his focus now. There are three levels of society here—the kingly, the aristocratic, and the working poor. How do they reflect upon one another, or are they a study in contrasts and the distinctions of class?

OTHELLO

In his celebration of Shakespeare, the poet Matthew Arnold (see chapter 18) wrote:

> *"Others abide our question. Thou art free. . . ."*

He means by this that, though it's possible to understand or at least imagine the creative processes of authors, Shakespeare outstrips understanding. In his hands, such universal matters as the conflict between good and evil, love and suspicion, nobility and "base" ambition become specific and embodied; figures like those you will encounter in this tragedy—Iago, Desdemona, and Othello—have come to represent evil, trust,

"Shakespeare used the phrase 'holding a mirror up to nature.' It's a mirror in which we can reflect, we can contemplate, we can feel, we can understand. And really the arts do this in a way that nothing else can. They are really the most human of all expressions, the most humane and most human of all enterprises. You can talk about philosophy, you can talk about all kinds of things; but nothing taps in to who we are, who we might be, who we're afraid of, we might become if we don't have the right human qualities— there is something about the arts that touches the wellspring, the really deepest parts of who we are, and makes us more human."

Conversation with Edwin Wilson

and jealousy both in the old allegorical mode (see chapter 20 in Poetry) and in modern terms. *Othello* was most probably composed in 1601, and we know it was performed by 1604; it is, then, the tragedy that follows *Hamlet*—yet with a wholly separate set of characters and problems. The original situation derives from a sixteenth-century tale by Giraldi Cinthio, which portrays the tragedy that ensues when an unnamed Moor in Venice falls in love with the woman Desdemona. But as he had done with the old Norse legend that was the inspiration for *Hamlet*, in *Othello* Shakespeare deepened and changed the sixteenth-century story in important ways.

Two of the most obvious and crucial changes Shakespeare made was to flesh out the main characters of the tragedy and to add new ones. In Othello we see a brand of tortured soul altogether different from that of Hamlet. Indeed, Othello struggles not with vengeance or abandonment but with self-doubt and too much faith in the honesty of those around him. Near the end of the play, Othello says:

> When you shall these unlucky deeds relate,
> Speak of me as I am; nothing extenuate,
> Nor set down aught in malice. Then must you speak
> Of one that loved not wisely but too well;
> Of one not easily jealous but, being wrought
> Perplexed in the extreme. . . .

As you read, decide whether Shakespeare's depiction is the telling or the retelling. Is Othello's story being related with "nothing extenuate," or are we receiving an embellished tale secondhand? Consider the Greek qualities of this tragedy: the nobility of Othello, his fatally short temper, the inevitability of his demise. In what ways is the downfall of Othello larger than life, and in what ways is it poignantly real?

"A mark of the very greatest artists, in my view, is honesty . . . [Shakespeare] allows people to see to the depths of their moral imagination." Conversation with Ralph Williams

RECONSTRUCTING SHAKESPEARE

The written texts we have of Shakespeare's plays do not always or exactly match what the actors said. Troupes competed for new stories, and playwrights had no copyright protection, so the managers of the King's Men did not want their pages distributed and used by others. Much of what we have, therefore, was reconstructed afterward, from an actor's or a theatergoer's memory; often the written versions differ. All this by way of saying that versions may contain different spellings—from "sullied" to "solid" to the now generally accepted "sallied"—of a single word.

Pronunciation has also changed in the course of 400 years, and the way the language *sounded* must be deduced; obviously no tape recordings exist. It's a pretty good guess, for example, that the words "love" and "move" were rhyming words—as in Hamlet's poem, "Doubt that the stars are fire / Doubt that the sun doth move / Doubt truth to be a liar / But never doubt I love."

AS YOU READ Keep track of the shifts in Othello's attitude and moods—from glad devotion to murderous jealousy and, in the end, a self-destructive self-awareness. Is he deluded or noble, or both?

Othello, the Moor of Venice (c. 1601)

CHARACTERS

OTHELLO, *the Moor*

BRABANTIO, *[a senator,] father to Desdemona*

CASSIO, *an honorable lieutenant [to Othello]*

IAGO, *[Othello's ancient,] a villain*

RODERIGO, *a gulled gentleman*

DUKE OF VENICE

SENATORS *[of Venice]*

MONTANO, *Governor of Cyprus*

GENTLEMEN *of Cyprus*

LODOVICO AND GRATIANO, *[kinsmen to Brabantio,] two noble Venetians*

SAILORS

CLOWN

DESDEMONA, *[daughter to Brabantio and] wife to Othello*

EMILIA, *wife to Iago*

BIANCA, *a courtesan [and mistress to Cassio]*

[A MESSENGER

A HERALD

A MUSICIAN

Servants, Attendants, Officers, Senators, Musicians, Gentlemen

SCENE: *Venice; a seaport in Cyprus]*

1.1 *Enter* RODERIGO *and* IAGO.

RODERIGO: Tush, never tell me! I take it much unkindly
That thou, Iago, who hast had my purse
As if the strings were thine, shouldst know of this.

IAGO: 'Sblood, but you'll not hear me.
5   If ever I did dream of such a matter,
Abhor me.

RODERIGO: Thou toldst me thou didst hold him in thy hate.

IAGO: Despise me
If I do not. Three great ones of the city,
10   In personal suit to make me his lieutenant,
Off-capped to him; and by the faith of man,
I know my price, I am worth no worse a place.
But he, as loving his own pride and purposes,
Evades them with a bombast circumstance
15   Horribly stuffed with epithets of war,
And, in conclusion,
Nonsuits my mediators. For, "Certes," says he,
"I have already chose my officer."
And what was he?
20   Forsooth, a great arithmetician,
One Michael Cassio, a Florentine,
A fellow almost damned in a fair wife,
That never set a squadron in the field
Nor the division of a battle knows
25   More than a spinster—unless the bookish theoric,
Wherein the togaed consuls can propose
As masterly as he. Mere prattle without practice
Is all his soldiership. But he, sir, had th' election;
And I, of whom his eyes had seen the proof
30   At Rhodes, at Cyprus, and on other grounds
Christened and heathen, must be beleed and calmed

By debitor and creditor. This countercaster,
He, in good time, must his lieutenant be,
And I—God bless the mark!—his Moorship's ancient.

RODERIGO: By heaven, I rather would have been his hangman.   35

IAGO: Why, there's no remedy. 'Tis the curse of service;
Preferment goes by letter and affection,
And not by old gradation, where each second
Stood heir to th' first. Now, sir, be judge yourself,
Whether I in any just term am affined   40
To love the Moor.

RODERIGO: I would not follow him then.

IAGO: O, sir, content you.
I follow him to serve my turn upon him.
We cannot all be masters, nor all masters   45
Cannot be truly followed. You shall mark
Many a duteous and knee-crooking knave
That, doting on his own obsequious bondage,
Wears out his time, much like his master's ass,
For naught but provender, and when he's old, cashiered.   50
Whip me such honest knaves. Others there are
Who, trimmed in forms and visages of duty,
Keep yet their hearts attending on themselves,
And, throwing but shows of service on their lords,
Do well thrive by them, and when they have lined their coats,   55
Do themselves homage. These fellows have some soul,
And such a one do I profess myself. For, sir,
It is as sure as you are Roderigo,
Were I the Moor I would not be Iago.
In following him, I follow but myself—   60
Heaven is my judge, not I for love and duty,

1.1 Location: Venice. A street.
1 never tell me (An expression of incredulity, like "tell me another one.")   **3 this** i.e., Desdemona's elopement   **4 'Sblood** by His (Christ's) blood   **11 him** i.e., Othello   **14 bombast circumstance** wordy evasion. (*Bombast* is cotton padding.)   **15 epithets of war** military expressions   **17 Nonsuits** rejects the petition of.   **Certes** certainly   **20 arithmetician** i.e., a man whose military knowledge is merely theoretical, based on books of tactics   **22 A . . . wife** (Cassio does not seem to be married, but his counterpart in Shakespeare's source does have a woman in his house. See also 4.1.131.)   **24 division of a battle** disposition of a military unit   **25 a spinster** i.e., a housewife, one whose regular occupation is spinning.   **theoric** theory   **26 togaed** wearing the toga.   **consuls** counselors, senators.   **propose** discuss   **29 his** i.e., Othello's   **31 Christened** Christian.   **beleed and calmed** left to leeward without wind, becalmed. (A sailing metaphor.)

32 debitor and creditor (A name for a system of bookkeeping, here used as a contemptuous nickname for Cassio.)   **countercaster** i.e., bookkeeper, one who tallies with *counters,* or "metal disks." (Said contemptuously.)   **33 in good time** opportunely, i.e., forsooth   **34 God bless the mark** (Perhaps originally a formula to ward off evil; here an expression of impatience.)   **ancient** standard-bearer, ensign   **35 his hangman** the executioner of him   **37 Preferment** promotion.   **letter and affection** personal influence and favoritism   **38 old gradation** step-by-step seniority, the traditional way   **40 term** respect.   **affined** bound   **43 content you** don't you worry about that   **46 truly** faithfully   **50 cashiered** dismissed from service   **51 Whip me** whip, as far as I'm concerned   **52 trimmed . . . duty** dressed up in the mere form and show of dutifulness   **55 lined their coats** i.e., stuffed their purses   **56 Do themselves homage** i.e., attend to self-interest solely   **59 Were . . . Iago** i.e., if I were able to assume command, I certainly would not choose to remain a subordinate, or, I would keep a suspicious eye on a flattering subordinate

Iago (Tim McInnerny) tells Roderigo (Sam Crane) his plans in the 2007 production directed by Wilson Milam.

But seeming so for my peculiar end.
For when my outward action doth demonstrate
The native act and figure of my heart
65 In compliment extern, 'tis not long after
But I will wear my heart upon my sleeve
For daws to peck at. I am not what I am.

RODERIGO: What a full fortune does the thick-lips owe
If he can carry 't thus!

IAGO: Call up her father.
70 Rouse him, make after him, poison his delight,
Proclaim him in the streets; incense her kinsmen,
And, though he in a fertile climate dwell,
Plague him with flies. Though that his joy be joy,
Yet throw such changes of vexation on 't
75 As it may lose some color.

RODERIGO: Here is her father's house. I'll call aloud.

IAGO: Do, with like timorous accent and dire yell
As when, by night and negligence, the fire
Is spied in populous cities.

RODERIGO: What ho, Brabantio! Signor Brabantio, ho!   80

IAGO: Awake! What, ho, Brabantio! Thieves, thieves,
thieves!
Look to your house, your daughter, and your bags!
Thieves, thieves!

BRABANTIO *[enters] above [at a window].*

BRABANTIO: What is the reason of this terrible
summons?
What is the matter there?   85

RODERIGO: Signor, is all your family within?

IAGO: Are your doors locked?

BRABANTIO: Why, wherefore ask you this?

IAGO: Zounds, sir, you're robbed! For shame, put on
your gown!
Your heart is burst; you have lost half your soul.
Even now, now, very now, an old black ram   90
Is tupping your white ewe. Arise, arise!
Awake the snorting citizens with the bell,
Or else the devil will make a grandsire of you.
Arise, I say!

BRABANTIO: What, have you lost your wits?

RODERIGO: Most reverend signor, do you know my
voice?   95

BRABANTIO: Not I. What are you?

RODERIGO: My name is Roderigo.

BRABANTIO: The worser welcome.
I have charged thee not to haunt about my doors.
In honest plainness thou hast heard me say   100
My daughter is not for thee; and now, in madness,
Being full of supper and distempering drafts,
Upon malicious bravery dost thou come
To start my quiet.

RODERIGO: Sir, sir, sir—

BRABANTIO: But thou must needs be sure   105
My spirits and my place have in their power
To make this bitter to thee.

---

62 **peculiar** particular, personal   64 **native** innate.   **figure** shape, intent   65 **compliment extern** outward show (conforming in this case to the inner workings and intention of the heart)   67 **daws** small crowlike birds, proverbially stupid and avaricious. **I am not what I am** i.e., I am not one who wears his heart on his sleeve   68 **full** swelling.   **thick-lips** (Elizabethans often applied the term "Moor" to Negroes.)   **owe** own   69 **carry 't thus** carry this off   72–73 **though . . . flies** though he seems prosperous and happy now, vex him with misery   73 **Though . . . be joy** although he seems fortunate and happy. (Repeats the idea of line 72.)   74 **changes of vexation** vexing changes   75 **As it may** that may cause it to.   **some color** some of its fresh gloss   77 **timorous** frightening   78 **and negligence** i.e., by negligence

---

83 **s.d. at a window** (This stage direction, from the Quarto, probably calls for an appearance on the gallery above and rearstage.)   85 **the matter** your business   88 **Zounds** by His (Christ's) wounds   91 **tupping** covering, copulating with. (Said of sheep.)   92 **snorting** snoring   93 **the devil** (The devil was conventionally pictured as black.)   102 **distempering** intoxicating   103 **Upon malicious bravery** with hostile intent to defy me   104 **start** startle, disrupt   106 **My spirits and my place** my temperament and my authority of office.   **have in** have it in

RODERIGO: Patience, good sir.

BRABANTIO: What tell'st thou me of robbing? This is Venice;
  My house is not a grange.

RODERIGO: Most grave Brabantio,
110 In simple and pure soul I come to you.

IAGO: Zounds, sir, you are one of those that will not
  serve God if the devil bid you. Because we come to do
  you service and you think we are ruffians, you'll have
  your daughter covered with a Barbary horse; you'll
115 have your nephews neigh to you; you'll have coursers
  for cousins and jennets for germans.

BRABANTIO: What profane wretch art thou?

IAGO: I am one, sir, that comes to tell you your daughter and the Moor are now making the beast with two
120 backs.

BRABANTIO: Thou art a villain.

IAGO: You are—a senator.

BRABANTIO: This thou shalt answer. I know thee,
  Roderigo.

RODERIGO: Sir, I will answer anything. But I beseech
  you,
  If 't be your pleasure and most wise consent—
125 As partly I find it is—that your fair daughter,
  At this odd-even and dull watch o' the night,
  Transported with no worse nor better guard
  But with a knave of common hire, a gondolier,
  To the gross clasps of a lascivious Moor—
130 If this be known to you and your allowance
  We then have done you bold and saucy wrongs.
  But if you know not this, my manners tell me
  We have your wrong rebuke. Do not believe
  That, from the sense of all civility,
135 I thus would play and trifle with your reverence.
  Your daughter, if you have not given her leave,

Brabantio (Pierre Vaneck) hears the news of his daughter's betrayal in the 1995 film directed by Oliver Parker.

  I say again, hath made a gross revolt,
  Tying her duty, beauty, wit, and fortunes
  In an extravagant and wheeling stranger
  Of here and everywhere. Straight satisfy yourself. 140
  If she be in her chamber or your house,
  Let loose on me the justice of the state
  For thus deluding you.

BRABANTIO: Strike on the tinder, ho!
  Give me a taper! Call up all my people! 145
  This accident is not unlike my dream.
  Belief of it oppresses me already.
  Light, I say, light! *Exit [above.]*

IAGO: Farewell, for I must leave you.
  It seems not meet nor wholesome to my place
  To be produced—as, if I stay, I shall— 150
  Against the Moor. For I do know the state,
  However this may gall him with some check,
  Cannot with safety cast him, for he's embarked
  With such loud reason to the Cyprus wars,
  Which even now stands in act, that, for their souls, 155
  Another of his fathom they have none
  To lead their business; in which regard,
  Though I do hate him as I do hell pains,

---

109 grange isolated country house **110 simple** sincere **114 Barbary** from northern Africa (and hence associated with Othello)
115 nephews i.e., grandsons. **coursers** powerful horses **116 cousins** kinsmen. **jennets** small Spanish horses. **germans** near relatives **121 a senator** (Said with mock politeness, as though the word itself were an insult.) **122 answer** be held accountable for
124 wise well-informed **126 odd-even** between one day and the next, i.e., about midnight **127 with** by **128 But with a knave** than by a low fellow, a servant **130 allowance** permission **131 saucy** insolent **134 from** contrary to. **civility** good manners, decency **135 your reverence** the respect due to you

---

138 wit intelligence **139 extravagant** expatriate, wandering far from home. **wheeling** roving about, vagabond. **stranger** foreigner **140 Straight** straightway **144 tinder,** charred linen ignited by a spark from flint and steel, used to light torches or *tapers* (lines 145, 170) **146 accident** occurrence, event **149 meet** fitting. **place** position (as ensign) **150 produced** produced (as a witness) **152 gall** rub; oppress. **check** rebuke **153 cast** dismiss. **embarked** engaged **154 loud reason** unanimous shout of confirmation (in the Senate) **155 stands in act** are going on. **for their souls** to save themselves **156 fathom** i.e., ability, depth of experience **157 in which regard** out of regard for which

Yet for necessity of present life

160 I must show out a flag and sign of love,
Which is indeed but sign. That you shall surely find
him,
Lead to the Sagittary that raisèd search,
And there will I be with him. So farewell.   *Exit.*

Enter [below] BRABANTIO *[in his
nightgown] with servants and torches.*

BRABANTIO: It is too true an evil. Gone she is;

165 And what's to come of my despisèd time
Is naught but bitterness. Now, Roderigo,
Where didst thou see her?—O unhappy girl!—
With the Moor, say'st thou?—Who would be a
father?—
How didst thou know 'twas she?—O, she deceives me

170 Past thought!—What said she to you?—Get more
tapers.
Raise all my kindred.—Are they married, think you?

RODERIGO: Truly, I think they are.

BRABANTIO: O heaven! How got she out? O treason of
the blood!
Fathers, from hence trust not your daughters' minds

175 By what you see them act. Is there not charms
By which the property of youth and maidhood
May be abused? Have you not read, Roderigo,
Of some such thing?

RODERIGO: Yes, sir, I have indeed.

BRABANTIO: Call up my brother.—O, would you had
had her!—

180 Some one way, some another.—Do you know
Where we may apprehend her and the Moor?

RODERIGO: I think I can discover him, if you please
To get good guard and go along with me.

BRABANTIO: Pray you, lead on. At every house
I'll call;

185 I may command at most.—Get weapons, ho!
And raise some special officers of night.—
On, good Roderigo. I will deserve your pains.

Exeunt.

---

159 **life** livelihood   162 **Sagittary** (An inn or house where Othello
and Desdemona are staying, named for its sign of Sagittarius, or
Centaur.)   **raisèd search** search party roused out of sleep   163
s.d. nightgown dressing gown. (This costuming is specified in the
Quarto text.)   165 **time** i.e., remainder of life   175 **charms** spells
176 **property** special quality, nature   177 **abused** deceived   182
discover reveal, uncover   185 **command** demand assistance   187
deserve show gratitude for

1.2   *Enter* OTHELLO, IAGO, *attendants with torches.*

IAGO: Though in the trade of war I have slain men,
Yet do I hold it very stuff o' the conscience
To do no contrived murder. I lack iniquity
Sometimes to do me service. Nine or ten times

5 I had thought t' have yerked him here under the ribs.

OTHELLO: 'Tis better as it is.

IAGO: Nay, but he prated,
And spoke such scurvy and provoking terms
Against your honor
That, with the little godliness I have,

10 I did full hard forbear him. But, I pray you, sir,
Are you fast married? Be assured of this,
That the magnifico is much beloved,
And hath in his effect a voice potential
As double as the Duke's. He will divorce you,

15 Or put upon you what restraint or grievance
The law, with all his might to enforce it on,
Will give him cable.

OTHELLO: Let him do his spite.
My services which I have done the seigniory
Shall out-tongue his complaints. 'Tis yet to know—

20 Which, when I know that boasting is an honor,
I shall promulgate—I fetch my life and being
From men of royal siege, and my demerits
May speak unbonneted to as proud a fortune
As this that I have reached. For know, Iago,

25 But that I love the gentle Desdemona,
I would not my unhousèd free condition
Put into circumscription and confine
For the sea's worth. But look, what lights come yond?

Enter CASSIO *[and certain officers]
with torches.*

1.2 Location: Venice. Another street, before Othello's lodgings.
2 **very stuff** essence, basic material (continuing the metaphor of
trade from line 1)   3 **contrived** premeditated   5 **yerked** stabbed.
him i.e., Roderigo   10 **. . . him** I restrained myself with great difficulty from assaulting him   12 **magnifico** Venetian grandee, i.e.,
Brabantio   13 **in his effect** at his command.   **potential** powerful   17 **cable** i.e., scope   18 **seigniory** Venetian government   19
yet to know not yet widely known   22 **siege** i.e., rank. (Literally,
a seat used by a person of distinction.)   **demerits** deserts   23
unbonneted without removing the hat, i.e., on equal terms (? Or
"with hat off," "in all due modesty.")   26 **unhousèd** unconfined,
undomesticated   27 **circumscription and confine** restriction and
confinement   28 **the sea's worth** all the riches at the bottom of the
sea.   **s.d. officers** (The Quarto text calls for "Cassio with lights,
officers with torches.")

IAGO   Those are the raisèd father and his friends.
30   You were best go in.

OTHELLO: Not I. I must be found.
My parts, my title, and my perfect soul
Shall manifest me rightly. Is it they?

IAGO: By Janus, I think no.

OTHELLO: The servants of the Duke? And my
                    lieutenant?
35   The goodness of the night upon you, friends!
What is the news?

CASSIO: The Duke does greet you, General,
And he requires your haste-post-haste appearance
Even on the instant.

OTHELLO: What is the matter, think you?

CASSIO: Something from Cyprus, as I may divine.
40   It is a business of some heat. The galleys
Have sent a dozen sequent messengers
This very night at one another's heels,
And many of the consuls, raised and met,
Are at the Duke's already. You have been hotly called
        for;
45   When, being not at your lodging to be found,
The Senate hath sent about three several quests
To search you out.

OTHELLO: 'Tis well I am found by you.
I will but spend a word here in the house
And go with you.   *[Exit.]*

CASSIO: Ancient, what makes he here?

50   **IAGO:**   Faith, he tonight hath boarded a land carrack.
If it prove lawful prize, he's made forever.

CASSIO: I do not understand.

IAGO: He's married.

CASSIO: To who?

                                    [Enter OTHELLO.]

IAGO: Marry, to—Come, Captain, will you go?

OTHELLO: Have with you.

CASSIO: Here comes another troop to seek for you.   55

        Enter BRABANTIO, RODERIGO, *with officers and torches.*

IAGO: It is Brabantio. General, be advised.
He comes to bad intent.

OTHELLO: Holla! Stand there!

RODERIGO: Signor, it is the Moor.

BRABANTIO: Down with him, thief!
                    [They draw on both sides.]

IAGO: You, Roderigo! Come, sir, I am for you.

OTHELLO: Keep up your bright swords, for the dew
    will rust them.   60
Good signor, you shall more command with years
Than with your weapons.

BRABANTIO: O thou foul thief, where hast thou
        stowed my daughter?
Damned as thou art, thou hast enchanted her!
For I'll refer me to all things of sense,   65
If she in chains of magic were not bound
Whether a maid so tender, fair, and happy,
So opposite to marriage that she shunned
The wealthy curlèd darlings of our nation,
Would ever have, t' incur a general mock,   70
Run from her guardage to the sooty bosom
Of such a thing as thou—to fear, not to delight.
Judge me the world if 'tis not gross in sense
That thou hast practiced on her with foul charms,
Abused her delicate youth with drugs or minerals   75
That weakens motion. I'll have 't disputed on;
'Tis probable and palpable to thinking.
I therefore apprehend and do attach thee
For an abuser of the world, a practicer
Of arts inhibited and out of warrant.—   80
Lay hold upon him! If he do resist,
Subdue him at his peril.

OTHELLO: Hold your hands,
Both you of my inclining and the rest.
Were it my cue to fight, I should have known it
Without a prompter.—Whither will you that I go   85
To answer this your charge?

---

31 My . . . soul my natural gifts, my position or reputation, and my unflawed conscience **33 Janus** Roman two-faced god of beginnings **38 matter** business **39 divine** guess **40 heat** urgency **41 sequent** successive **43 consuls** senators **46 about** all over the city. **several** separate **49 makes** does **50 boarded** gone aboard and seized as an act of piracy (with sexual suggestion). **carrack** large merchant ship **51 prize** booty **53 Marry** (An oath, originally "by the Virgin Mary"; here used with wordplay on *married*.) **54 Have with you** i.e., let's go

---

55 s.d. officers and torches (The Quarto text calls for "others with lights and weapons.") **56 be advised** be on your guard **60 Keep up** keep in the sheath **65 refer me** submit my case. **things of sense** commonsense understandings, or, creatures possessing common sense **71 her guardage** my guardianship of her **73 gross in sense** obvious **75 minerals** i.e., poisons **76 weakens motion** impair the vital faculties. **disputed on** argued in court by professional counsel, debated by experts **78 attach** arrest **80 arts inhibited** prohibited arts, black magic. **out of warrant** illegal **83 inclining** following, party

BRABANTIO: To prison, till fit time
Of law and course of direct session
Call thee to answer.

OTHELLO: What if I do obey?
90 How may the Duke be therewith satisfied,
Whose messengers are here about my side
Upon some present business of the state
To bring me to him?

OFFICER: 'Tis true, most worthy signor.
The Duke's in council, and your noble self,
95 I am sure, is sent for.

BRABANTIO: How? The Duke in council?
In this time of the night? Bring him away.
Mine's not an idle cause. The Duke himself,
Or any of my brothers of the state,
Cannot but feel this wrong as 'twere their own;
100 For if such actions may have passage free,
Bondslaves and pagans shall our statesmen be.

Exeunt.

1.3   _Enter_ DUKE _[and]_ SENATORS _[and sit at a table, with
lights], and officers. [The_ DUKE _and_ SENATORS _are
reading dispatches.]_

DUKE: There is no composition in these news
That gives them credit.

FIRST SENATOR: Indeed, they are disproportioned.
My letters say a hundred and seven galleys.

5   **DUKE:**   And mine, a hundred forty.

SECOND SENATOR: And mine, two hundred.
But though they jump not on a just account—
As in these cases, where the aim reports
'Tis oft with difference—yet do they all confirm
A Turkish fleet, and bearing up to Cyprus.

10   **DUKE:**   Nay, it is possible enough to judgment.
I do not so secure me in the error
But the main article I do approve
In fearful sense.

The Duke, senators, and officers sit to hear Othello's claims.

SAILOR (_within_):   What ho, what ho, what ho!

Enter SAILOR.

OFFICER: A messenger from the galleys.

DUKE: Now, what's the business?   15

SAILOR: The Turkish preparation makes for Rhodes.
So was I bid report here to the state
By Signor Angelo.

DUKE: How say you by this change?

FIRST SENATOR: This cannot be
By no assay of reason. 'Tis a pageant   20
To keep us in false gaze. When we consider
Th' importancy of Cyprus to the Turk,
And let ourselves again but understand
That, as it more concerns the Turk than Rhodes,
So may he with more facile question bear it,   25
For that it stands not in such warlike brace,
But altogether lacks th' abilities
That Rhodes is dressed in—if we make thought of
this,
We must not think the Turk is so unskillful
To leave that latest which concerns him first,   30
Neglecting an attempt of ease and gain
To wake and wage a danger profitless.

---

88 course of direct session regular or specially convened legal
proceedings   **96 away** right along   **97 idle** trifling   **100 have
passage free** are allowed to go unchecked

1.3. Location: Venice. A council chamber.
s.d. Enter . . . Officers (The Quarto text calls for the Duke and
senators to "sit at a table with lights and attendants.")   **1 composition** consistency   **3 disproportioned** inconsistent   **6 jump** agree.
just exact   **7 the aim** conjecture   **11–12 I do not . . . approve** I
do not take such (false) comfort in the discrepancies that I fail to
perceive the main point, i.e., that the Turkish fleet is threatening

---

16 preparation fleet prepared for battle   **19 by** about   **20 assay**
test.   **pageant** mere show   **21 in false gaze** looking the wrong
way   **25 So may . . . it** so also he (the Turk) can more easily capture
it (Cyprus)   **26 For that** since.   **brace** state of defense   **27 abilities** means of self-defense   **28 dressed in** equipped with   **29
unskillful** deficient in judgment   **30 latest** last   **32 wake** stir up.
wage risk

DUKE: Nay, in all confidence, he's not for Rhodes.

OFFICER: Here is more news.

Enter a MESSENGER.

35 **MESSENGER:** The Ottomites, reverend and gracious,
Steering with due course toward the isle of Rhodes,
Have there injointed them with an after fleet.

FIRST SENATOR: Ay, so I thought. How many, as you guess?

MESSENGER: Of thirty sail; and now they do restem
40 Their backward course, bearing with frank appearance
Their purposes toward Cyprus. Signor Montano,
Your trusty and most valiant servitor,
With his free duty recommends you thus,
And prays you to believe him.

45 **DUKE:** 'Tis certain then for Cyprus.
Marcus Luccicos, is not he in town?

FIRST SENATOR: He's now in Florence.

DUKE: Write from us to him, post-post-haste. Dispatch.

FIRST SENATOR: Here comes Brabantio and the valiant Moor.

Enter BRABANTIO, OTHELLO, CASSIO,
IAGO, RODERIGO, *and officers.*

50 **DUKE:** Valiant Othello, we must straight employ you
Against the general enemy Ottoman.
[To BRABANTIO.*]* I did not see you; welcome, gentle signor.
We lacked your counsel and your help tonight.

BRABANTIO: So did I yours. Good Your Grace, pardon me;
55 Neither my place nor aught I heard of business
Hath raised me from my bed, nor doth the general care
Take hold on me, for my particular grief
Is of so floodgate and o'erbearing nature
That it engluts and swallows other sorrows
60 And it is still itself.

DUKE: Why, what's the matter?

BRABANTIO: My daughter! O, my daughter!

DUKE AND SENATORS: Dead?

BRABANTIO: Ay, to me.
She is abused, stol'n from me, and corrupted
By spells and medicines bought of mountebanks;
For nature so preposterously to err,
Being not deficient, blind, or lame of sense,   65
Sans witchcraft could not.

DUKE: Whoe'er he be that in this foul proceeding
Hath thus beguiled your daughter of herself,
And you of her, the bloody book of law
You shall yourself read in the bitter letter   70
After your own sense—yea, though our proper son
Stood in your action.

BRABANTIO: Humbly I thank Your Grace.
Here is the man, this Moor, whom now it seems
Your special mandate for the state affairs
Hath hither brought.

ALL: We are very sorry for 't.   75

DUKE *[To* OTHELLO*]*: What, in your own part, can you say to this?

BRABANTIO: Nothing, but this is so.

OTHELLO: Most potent, grave, and reverend signors,
My very noble and approved good masters:
That I have ta'en away this old man's daughter,   80
It is most true; true, I have married her.
The very head and front of my offending
Hath this extent, no more. Rude am I in my speech,
And little blessed with the soft phrase of peace;
For since these arms of mine had seven years' pith,   85
Till now some nine moons wasted, they have used
Their dearest action in the tented field;
And little of this great world can I speak
More than pertains to feats of broils and battle,
And therefore little shall I grace my cause   90
In speaking for myself. Yet, by your gracious patience,
I will a round unvarnished tale deliver
Of my whole course of love—what drugs, what charms,

---

37 **injointed them** joined themselves. **after** second, following
39–40 **restem . . . course** retrace their original course 40 **frank
appearance** undisguised intent 42 **servitor** officer under your
command 43 **free duty** freely given and loyal service. **recommends** commends himself and reports to 50 **straight** straightway 51 **general enemy** universal enemy to all Christendom 52
gentle noble 55 **place** official position 57 **particular** personal
58 **floodgate** i.e., overwhelming (as when floodgates are opened)
59 **engluts** engulfs 60 **is still itself** remains undiminished

62 **abused** deceived 65 **deficient** defective. **lame of sense** deficient in sensory perception 66 **Sans** without 71 **After . . . sense**
according to your own interpretation. **our proper** my own
72 **Stood . . . action** were under your accusation 79 **approved**
proved, esteemed 82 **head and front** height and breadth, entire
extent 83 **Rude** unpolished 85 **since . . . pith** i.e., since I was
seven. **pith** strength, vigor 86 **Till . . . wasted** until some nine
months ago (since when Othello has evidently been not on active
duty but in Venice) 87 **dearest** most valuable 92 **round** plain

Othello (Laurence Fishburne) and Cassio (Nathaniel Parker) stand in defense before the Duke.

What conjuration, and what mighty magic,
95　For such proceeding I am charged withal,
　　I won his daughter.

BRABANTIO:　　　A maiden never bold;
　　Of spirit so still and quiet that her motion
　　Blushed at herself; and she, in spite of nature,
　　Of years, of country, credit, everything,
100　To fall in love with what she feared to look on!
　　It is a judgment maimed and most imperfect
　　That will confess perfection so could err
　　Against all rules of nature, and must be driven
　　To find out practices of cunning hell
105　Why this should be. I therefore vouch again
　　That with some mixtures powerful o'er the blood,
　　Or with some dram conjured to this effect,
　　He wrought upon her.

DUKE:　　　　To vouch this is no proof,
　　Without more wider and more overt test
110　Than these thin habits and poor likelihoods
　　Of modern seeming do prefer against him.

FIRST SENATOR:　But Othello, speak.
　　Did you by indirect and forcèd courses

Subdue and poison this young maid's affections?
Or came it by request and such fair question　115
As soul to soul affordeth?

OTHELLO:　　　　　I do beseech you,
　　Send for the lady to the Sagittary
　　And let her speak of me before her father.
　　If you do find me foul in her report,
　　The trust, the office I do hold of you　120
　　Not only take away, but let your sentence
　　Even fall upon my life.

DUKE:　　　　　Fetch Desdemona hither.

OTHELLO:　Ancient, conduct them. You best know
　　the place.
　　　　　　　　[Exeunt IAGO *and attendants.]*
　　And, till she come, as truly as to heaven
　　I do confess the vices of my blood,　125
　　So justly to your grave ears I'll present
　　How I did thrive in this fair lady's love,
　　And she in mine.

DUKE:　Say it, Othello.

OTHELLO:　Her father loved me, oft invited me,　130
　　Still questioned me the story of my life
　　From year to year—the battles, sieges, fortunes
　　That I have passed.
　　I ran it through, even from my boyish days
　　To th' very moment that he bade me tell it,　135
　　Wherein I spoke of most disastrous chances,
　　Of moving accidents by flood and field,
　　Of hairbreadth scapes i' th' imminent deadly breach,
　　Of being taken by the insolent foe
　　And sold to slavery, of my redemption thence,　140
　　And portance in my travel's history,
　　Wherein of antres vast and deserts idle,
　　Rough quarries, rocks, and hills whose heads touch
　　　heaven,
　　It was my hint to speak—such was my process—
　　And of the Cannibals that each other eat,　145
　　The Anthropophagi, and men whose heads
　　Do grow beneath their shoulders. These things to
　　　hear
　　Would Desdemona seriously incline;
　　But still the house affairs would draw her thence,
　　Which ever as she could with haste dispatch　150

---

95 withal with　**97–98 her . . . herself** i.e., she blushed easily at herself. (*Motion* can suggest the impulse of the soul or of the emotions, or physical movement.)　**99 years** i.e., difference in age. **credit** virtuous reputation　**102 confess** concede (that)　**104 practices** plots　**105 vouch** assert　**106 blood** passions　**107 dram . . . effect** dose made by magical spells to have this effect　**109 more wider** fuller.　**test** testimony　**110 habits** garments, i.e., appearances.　**poor likelihoods** weak inferences　**111 modern seeming** commonplace assumption.　**prefer** bring forth　**113 forcèd courses** means used against her will

---

115 question conversation　**125 blood** passions, human nature **126 justly** truthfully, accurately　**131 Still** continually　**137 moving accidents** stirring happenings　**138 imminent . . . breach** death-threatening gaps made in a fortification　**141 portance** conduct　**142 antres** caverns.　**idle** barren, desolate　**143 Rough quarries** rugged rock formations　**144 hint** occasion, opportunity **146 Anthropophagi** man-eaters. (A term from Pliny's *Natural History*).

She'd come again, and with a greedy ear
Devour up my discourse. Which I, observing,
Took once a pliant hour, and found good means
To draw from her a prayer of earnest heart
155 That I would all my pilgrimage dilate,
Whereof by parcels she had something heard,
But not intentively. I did consent,
And often did beguile her of her tears,
When I did speak of some distressful stroke
160 That my youth suffered. My story being done,
She gave me for my pains a world of sighs.
She swore, in faith, 'twas strange, 'twas passing
strange,
'Twas pitiful, 'twas wondrous pitiful.
She wished she had not heard it, yet she wished
165 That heaven had made her such a man. She thanked
me,
And bade me, if I had a friend that loved her,
I should but teach him how to tell my story,
And that would woo her. Upon this hint I spake.
She loved me for the dangers I had passed,
170 And I loved her that she did pity them.
This only is the witchcraft I have used.
Here comes the lady. Let her witness it.

Enter DESDEMONA, IAGO, *[and] attendants.*

DUKE: I think this tale would win my daughter too.
Good Brabantio,
175 Take up this mangled matter at the best.
Men do their broken weapons rather use
Than their bare hands.

BRABANTIO: I pray you, hear her speak.
If she confess that she was half the wooer,
Destruction on my head if my bad blame
180 Light on the man!—Come hither, gentle mistress.
Do you perceive in all this noble company
Where most you owe obedience?

DESDEMONA: My noble Father,
I do perceive here a divided duty.
To you I am bound for life and education;
185 My life and education both do learn me
How to respect you. You are the lord of duty;
I am hitherto your daughter. But here's my husband,
And so much duty as my mother showed
To you, preferring you before her father,

Brabantio (Pierre Vaneck) bids Desdemona speak.

So much I challenge that I may profess   190
Due to the Moor my lord.

BRABANTIO: God be with you! I have done.
Please it Your Grace, on to the state affairs.
I had rather to adopt a child than get it.
Come hither, Moor.   *[He joins the hands of* OTHELLO   195
and DESDEMONA.*]*
I here do give thee that with all my heart
Which, but thou hast already, with all my heart
I would keep from thee.—For your sake, jewel,
I am glad at soul I have no other child,
For thy escape would teach me tyranny,   200
To hang clogs on them.—I have done, my lord.

DUKE: Let me speak like yourself, and lay a sentence
Which, as a grece or step, may help these lovers
Into your favor.
When remedies are past, the griefs are ended   205
By seeing the worst, which late on hopes depended.
To mourn a mischief that is past and gone
Is the next way to draw new mischief on.
What cannot be preserved when fortune takes,
Patience her injury a mockery makes.   210
The robbed that smiles steals something from the
thief;
He robs himself that spends a bootless grief.

---

153 **pliant** well-suiting   155 **dilate** relate in detail   156 **by parcels**
piecemeal   157 **intentively** with full attention, continuously   162
passing exceedingly   165 **made her** created her to be   168 **hint**
opportunity. (Othello does not mean that she was dropping hints.)
175 **Take . . . best** make the best of a bad bargain   184 **education**
upbringing   185 **learn** teach   186 **of duty** to whom duty is due

190 **challenge** claim   194 **get** beget   196 **with all my heart**
wherein my whole affection has been engaged   197 **with all my
heart** willingly, gladly   198 **For your sake** on your account   200
escape elopement   201 **clogs** (Literally, blocks of wood fastened to
the legs of criminals or convicts to inhibit escape.)   202 **like yourself** i.e., as you would, in your proper temper.   **lay a sentence** apply
a maxim   203 **grece** step   205 **remedies** hopes of remedy   206
which . . . depended which griefs were sustained until recently
by hopeful anticipation   207 **mischief** misfortune, injury   208
next nearest   209 **What** whatever   210 **Patience . . . makes**
patience laughs at the injury inflicted by fortune (and thus eases the
pain)   212 **spends a bootless grief** indulges in unavailing grief

BRABANTIO: So let the Turk of Cyprus us beguile,
We lose it not, so long as we can smile.
215 He bears the sentence well that nothing bears
But the free comfort which from thence he hears,
But he bears both the sentence and the sorrow
That, to pay grief, must of poor patience borrow.
These sentences, to sugar or to gall,
220 Being strong on both sides, are equivocal.
But words are words. I never yet did hear
That the bruisèd heart was piercèd through the ear.
I humbly beseech you, proceed to th' affairs of state.

DUKE: The Turk with a most mighty preparation
225 makes for Cyprus. Othello, the fortitude of the place
is best known to you; and though we have there a
substitute of most allowed sufficiency, yet opinion,
a sovereign mistress of effects, throws a more safer
voice on you. You must therefore be content to
230 slubber the gloss of your new fortunes with this
more stubborn and boisterous expedition.

OTHELLO: The tyrant custom, most grave senators,
Hath made the flinty and steel couch of war
My thrice-driven bed of down. I do agnize
235 A natural and prompt alacrity
I find in hardness, and do undertake
These present wars against the Ottomites.
Most humbly therefore bending to your state,
I crave fit disposition for my wife,
240 Due reference of place, and exhibition,
With such accommodation and besort
As levels with her breeding.

DUKE: Why, at her father's.

BRABANTIO: I will not have it so.

OTHELLO: Nor I.

DESDEMONA: Nor I. I would not there reside,
To put my father in impatient thoughts   245
By being in his eye. Most gracious Duke,
To my unfolding lend your prosperous ear,
And let me find a charter in your voice,
T' assist my simpleness.

DUKE: What would you, Desdemona?   250

DESDEMONA: That I did love the Moor to live with
him,
My downright violence and storm of fortunes
May trumpet to the world. My heart's subdued
Even to the very quality of my lord.
I saw Othello's visage in his mind,   255
And to his honors and his valiant parts
Did I my soul and fortunes consecrate.
So that, dear lords, if I be left behind,
A moth of peace, and he go to the war,
The rites for why I love him are bereft me,   260
And I a heavy interim shall support
By his dear absence. Let me go with him.

OTHELLO: Let her have your voice.
Vouch with me, heaven, I therefor beg it not
To please the palate of my appetite,   265
Nor to comply with heat—the young affects
In me defunct—and proper satisfaction,
But to be free and bounteous to her mind.
And heaven defend your good souls that you think
I will your serious and great business scant   270
When she is with me. No, when light-winged toys
Of feathered Cupid seel with wanton dullness
My speculative and officed instruments,
That my disports corrupt and taint my business,
Let huswives make a skillet of my helm,   275
And all indign and base adversities
Make head against my estimation!

215–218 **He bears ... borrow** a person well bears out your maxim who can enjoy its platitudinous comfort, free of all genuine sorrow, but anyone whose grief bankrupts his poor patience is left with your saying and his sorrow, too. (*Bears the sentence* also plays on the meaning "receives judicial sentence.") 219–220 **These ... equivocal** these fine maxims are equivocal, either sweet or bitter in their application 222 **piercèd ... ear** i.e., surgically lanced and cured by mere words of advice 225 **fortitude** strength 227 **substitute** deputy 227 **allowed** acknowledged 227–229 **opinion ... on you** general opinion, an important determiner of affairs, chooses you as the best man 230 **slubber** soil, sully 231 **stubborn** harsh, rough 234 **thrice-driven** thrice sifted, winnowed. **agnize** know in myself, acknowledge 236 **hardness** hardship 238 **bending ... state** bowing or kneeling to your authority 240 **reference ... exhibition** provision of appropriate place to live and allowance of money 241 **accommodation** suitable provision. **besort** attendance 242 **levels** equals, suits. **breeding** social position, upbringing

---

247 **unfolding** explanation, proposal. **prosperous** propitious 248 **charter** privilege, authorization 252 **My ... fortunes** my plain and total breach of social custom, taking my future by storm and disrupting my whole life. 253–254 **My heart's ... lord** my heart is brought wholly into accord with Othello's virtues; I love him for his virtues 256 **parts** qualities 259 **moth** i.e., one who consumes merely 260 **rites** rites of love (with a suggestion, too, of "rights," sharing) 262 **dear** (1) heartfelt (2) costly 263 **voice** consent 266 **heat** sexual passion. **young affects** passions of youth, desires 267 **proper** personal 268 **free** generous 269 **defend** forbid. **think** should think 272 **seel** i.e., make blind (as in falconry, by sewing up the eyes of the hawk during training) 273 **speculative ... instruments** eyes and other faculties used in the performance of duty 274 **That** so that. **disports** sexual pastimes. **taint** impair 276 **indign** unworthy, shameful 277 **Make head** raise an army. **estimation** reputation

DUKE: Be it as you shall privately determine,
Either for her stay or going. Th' affair cries haste,
280 And speed must answer it.

A SENATOR: You must away tonight.

DESDEMONA: Tonight, my lord?

DUKE: This night.

OTHELLO: With all my heart.

DUKE: At nine i' the morning here we'll meet again.
Othello, leave some officer behind,
And he shall our commission bring to you,
285 With such things else of quality and respect
As doth import you.

OTHELLO: So please Your grace, my ancient;
A man he is of honesty and trust.
To his conveyance I assign my wife,
With what else needful Your Good Grace shall think
290 To be sent after me.

DUKE: Let it be so.
Good night to everyone. [*To* BRABANTIO.] And, noble
signor,
If virtue no delighted beauty lack,
Your son-in-law is far more fair than black.

FIRST SENATOR: Adieu, brave Moor. Use Desdemona
well.

295 **BRABANTIO:** Look to her, Moor, if thou hast eyes
to see.
She has deceived her father, and may thee.
*Exeunt [*DUKE, BRABANTIO,
CASSIO, SENATORS, *and officers*].

OTHELLO: My life upon her faith! Honest Iago,
My Desdemona must I leave to thee.
I prithee, let thy wife attend on her,
300 And bring them after in the best advantage.
Come, Desdemona. I have but an hour
Of love, of worldly matters and direction,
To spend with thee. We must obey the time.
Exit [with DESDEMONA].

RODERIGO: Iago—

305 **IAGO:** What sayst thou, noble heart?

RODERIGO: What will I do, think'st thou?

IAGO: Why, go to bed and sleep.

RODERIGO: I will incontinently drown myself.

IAGO: If thou dost, I shall never love thee after. Why,
thou silly gentleman?   310

RODERIGO: It is silliness to live when to live is torment; and then have we a prescription to die when
death is our physician.

IAGO: O villainous! I have looked upon the world for
four times seven years, and, since I could distinguish 315
betwixt a benefit and an injury, I never found man
that knew how to love himself. Ere I would say I
would drown myself for the love of a guinea hen, I
would change my humanity with a baboon.

RODERIGO: What should I do? I confess it is my shame 320
to be so fond, but it is not in my virtue to amend it.

IAGO: Virtue? A fig! 'Tis in ourselves that we are thus
or thus. Our bodies are our gardens, to the which our
wills are gardeners; so that if we will plant nettles or
sow lettuce, set hyssop and weed up thyme, supply it 325
with one gender of herbs or distract it with many, either to have it sterile with idleness or manured with
industry—why, the power and corrigible authority of
this lies in our wills. If the beam of our lives had not
one scale of reason to poise another of sensuality, the 330
blood and baseness of our natures would conduct us
to most preposterous conclusions. But we have reason to cool our raging motions, our carnal stings, our
unbitted lusts, whereof I take this that you call love
to be a sect or scion.   335

RODERIGO: It cannot be.

IAGO: It is merely a lust of the blood and a permission
of the will. Come, be a man. Drown thyself? Drown
cats and blind puppies. I have professed me thy
friend, and I confess me knit to thy deserving with   340
cables of perdurable toughness. I could never better
stead thee than now. Put money in thy purse. Fol-

---

285 of quality and respect of importance and relevance **286 import** concern **292 delighted** capable of delighting **300 in . . . advantage** at the most favorable opportunity **302 direction** instructions **303 the time** the urgency of the present crisis

308 incontinently immediately, without self-restraint **312 prescription** (1) right based on long-established custom (2) doctor's prescription **314 villainous** i.e., what perfect nonsense **318 guinea hen** (A slang term for a prostitute.) **321 fond** infatuated. **virtue** strength, nature **322 fig** (To give a fig is to thrust the thumb between the first and second fingers in a vulgar and insulting gesture.) **325 hyssop** a herb of the mint family **326 gender** kind. **distract it with** divide it among **327 idleness** want of cultivation **328 corrigible authority** power to correct **329 beam** balance **330 poise** counterbalance **331 blood** natural passions **333 motions** appetites **334 unbitted** unbridled, uncontrolled **335 sect or scion** cutting or offshoot **341 perdurable** very durable **342 stead** assist

low thou the wars; defeat thy favor with an usurped
beard. I say, put money in thy purse. It cannot be
345   long that Desdemona should continue her love to the
Moor—put money in thy purse—nor he his to her. It
was a violent commencement in her, and thou shalt
see an answerable sequestration—put but money in
thy purse. These Moors are changeable in their wills—
350   fill thy purse with money. The food that to him now is
as luscious as locusts shall be to him shortly as bitter
as coloquintida. She must change for youth; when she
is sated with his body, she will find the error of her
choice. She must have change, she must. Therefore
355   put money in thy purse. If thou wilt needs damn thyself, do it a more delicate way than drowning. Make
all the money thou canst. If sanctimony and a frail
vow betwixt an erring barbarian and a supersubtle
Venetian be not too hard for my wits and all the tribe
360   of hell, thou shalt enjoy her. Therefore make money.
A pox of drowning thyself! It is clean out of the way.
Seek thou rather to be hanged in compassing thy joy 380
than to be drowned and go without her.

RODERIGO: Wilt thou be fast to my hopes if I depend
365   on the issue?

IAGO: Thou art sure of me. Go, make money. I have told
thee often, and I retell thee again and again, I hate
the Moor. My cause is hearted; thine hath no less reason. Let us be conjunctive in our revenge against him.
370   If thou canst cuckold him, thou dost thyself a pleasure,
me a sport. There are many events in the womb of
time which will be delivered. Traverse, go, provide thy
money. We will have more of this tomorrow. Adieu.

RODERIGO: Where shall we meet i' the morning?

375   **IAGO:**   At my lodging.

RODERIGO: I'll be with thee betimes. *[He starts to leave.]*

IAGO: Go to, farewell.—Do you hear, Roderigo?

RODERIGO: What say you?

IAGO: No more of drowning, do you hear?

Iago (Kenneth Branagh) and Roderigo (Michael Maloney) discuss how to deal with Othello.

RODERIGO: I am changed

IAGO: Go to, farewell. Put money enough in your
purse.

RODERIGO: I'll sell all my land.   *Exit.*

IAGO: Thus do I ever make my fool my purse;
For I mine own gained knowledge should profane   385
If I would time expend with such a snipe
But for my sport and profit. I hate the Moor;
And it is thought abroad that twixt my sheets
He's done my office. I know not if 't be true;
But I, for mere suspicion in that kind,   390
Will do as if for surety. He holds me well;
The better shall my purpose work on him.
Cassio's a proper man. Let me see now:
To get his place and to plume up my will
In double knavery—How, how?—Let's see: 395
After some time, to abuse Othello's ear
That he is too familiar with his wife.
He hath a person and a smooth dispose
To be suspected, framed to make women false.
The Moor is of a free and open nature,   400
That thinks men honest that but seem to be so,
And will as tenderly be led by the nose
As asses are.

---

343 defeat thy favor disguise your face.   **usurped** (The suggestion
is that Roderigo is not man enough to have a beard of his own.)
348 an answerable sequestration a corresponding separation or
estrangement   **349 wills** carnal appetites   **351 locusts** fruit of the
carob tree (see Matthew 3:4), or perhaps honeysuckle   **352 coloquintida** colocynth or bitter apple, a purgative   **356 Make** raise,
collect   **357 sanctimony** sacred ceremony   **358 erring** wandering, vagabond, unsteady   **361 clean . . . way** entirely unsuitable as
a course of action   **362 compassing** encompassing, embracing
364 fast true   **365 issue** (successful) outcome   **368 hearted** fixed
in the heart, heartfelt   **369 conjunctive** united   **372 Traverse** (A
military marching term.)   **376 betimes** early

---

386 snipe woodcock, i.e., fool   **388 it is thought abroad** it is rumored   **389 my office** i.e., my sexual function as husband   **391 do
. . . surety** act as if on certain knowledge.   **holds me well** regards
me favorably   **393 proper** handsome   **394 plume up** put a feather
in the cap of, i.e., glorify, gratify   **396 abuse** deceive   **397 he** i.e.,
Cassio   **398 dispose** disposition   **400 free** frank, generous
open unsuspicious   **402 tenderly** readily

I have 't. It is engendered. Hell and night
405 Must bring this monstrous birth to the world's light.

[Exit.]

2.1 *Enter* MONTANO *and two* GENTLEMEN.

MONTANO: What from the cape can you discern at sea?

FIRST GENTLEMAN: Nothing at all. It is a high-
wrought flood.
I cannot, twixt the heaven and the main,
Descry a sail.

5 **MONTANO:** Methinks the wind hath spoke aloud at
land;
A fuller blast ne'er shook our battlements.
If it hath ruffianed so upon the sea,
What ribs of oak, when mountains melt on them,
Can hold the mortise? What shall we hear of this?

10 **SECOND GENTLEMAN:** A segregation of the Turkish
fleet.
For do but stand upon the foaming shore,
The chidden billow seems to pelt the clouds;
The wind-shaked surge, with high and monstrous
mane,
Seems to cast water on the burning Bear
15 And quench the guards of th' ever-fixèd pole.
I never did like molestation view
On the enchafèd flood.

MONTANO: If that the Turkish fleet
Be not ensheltered and embayed, they are drowned;
20 It is impossible to bear it out.

Enter a [THIRD] GENTLEMAN.

THIRD GENTLEMAN: News, lads! Our wars are done.
The desperate tempest hath so banged the Turks
That their designment halts. A noble ship of Venice

The men return home from overseas.

Hath seen a grievous wreck and sufferance
On most part of their fleet. 25

MONTANO: How? Is this true?

THIRD GENTLEMAN: The ship is here put in,
A Veronesa; Michael Cassio,
Lieutenant to the warlike Moor Othello,
Is come on shore; the Moor himself at sea, 30
And is in full commission here for Cyprus.

MONTANO: I am glad on 't. 'Tis a worthy governor.

THIRD GENTLEMAN: But this same Cassio, though he
speak of comfort
Touching the Turkish loss, yet he looks sadly
And prays the Moor be safe, for they were parted 35
With foul and violent tempest.

MONTANO: Pray heaven he be,
For I have served him, and the man commands
Like a full soldier. Let's to the seaside, ho!
As well to see the vessel that's come in
As to throw out our eyes for brave Othello, 40
Even till we make the main and th' aerial blue
An indistinct regard.

THIRD GENTLEMAN: Come, let's do so,
For every minute is expectancy
Of more arrivance.

2.1. Location: A seaport in Cyprus. An open place near the quay.
2 high-wrought flood very agitated sea   **3 main** ocean (also at line
41)   **7 ruffianed** raged   **8 mountains** i.e., of water   **9 hold the
mortise** hold their joints together. (A *mortise* is the socket hollowed
out in fitting timbers.)   **10 segregation** dispersal   **12 chidden**
i.e., rebuked, repelled (by the shore), and thus shot into the air   **13
monstrous mane** (The surf is like the mane of a wild beast.)   **14
the burning Bear** i.e., the constellation Ursa Minor or the Little
Bear, which includes the polestar (and hence regarded as the *guards
of th' ever-fixèd pole* in the next line; sometimes the term *guards* is
applied to the two "pointers" of the Big Bear or Dipper, which may be
intended here.)   **16 like molestation** comparable disturbance   **17
enchafèd** angry   **18 If that** if   **19 embayed** sheltered by a bay   **20
bear it out** survive, weather the storm   **23 designment** design,
enterprise.   **halts** is lame

24 wreck shipwreck.   **sufferance** damage, disaster   **28 Veronesa**
i.e., fitted out in Verona for Venetian service, or possibly *Verennessa*
(the Folio spelling), i.e., *verrinessa*, a cutter (from *verrinare*, "to
cut through")   **34 sadly** gravely   **38 full** perfect   **41 the main . . .
blue** the sea and the sky   **42 An indistinct regard** indistinguish-
able in our view   **43 is expectancy** gives expectation   **44 arrivance** arrival

Enter CASSIO.

45 **CASSIO:** Thanks, you the valiant of the warlike isle,
That so approve the Moor! O, let the heavens
Give him defense against the elements,
For I have lost him on a dangerous sea.

MONTANO: Is he well shipped?

50 **CASSIO:** His bark is stoutly timbered, and his pilot
Of very expert and approved allowance;
Therefore my hopes, not surfeited to death,
Stand in bold cure.

[A cry] within: "A sail, a sail, a sail!"

CASSIO: What noise?

55 **A GENTLEMAN:** The town is empty. On the brow o' the
sea
Stand ranks of people, and they cry, "A sail!"

CASSIO: My hopes do shape him for the governor.

[A shot within.]

SECOND GENTLEMAN: They do discharge their shot
of courtesy;
Our friends at least.

CASSIO: I pray you, sir, go forth,
60 And give us truth who 'tis that is arrived.

SECOND GENTLEMAN: I shall. *Exit.*

MONTANO: But, good Lieutenant, is your general
wived?

CASSIO: Most fortunately. He hath achieved a maid
That paragons description and wild fame,
65 One that excels the quirks of blazoning pens,
And in th' essential vesture of creation
Does tire the enginer.

Enter [SECOND] GENTLEMAN.

How now? Who has put in?

SECOND GENTLEMAN: 'Tis one Iago, ancient to the
General.

CASSIO: He's had most favorable and happy speed.
Tempests themselves, high seas, and howling winds, 70
The guttered rocks and congregated sands—
Traitors ensteeped to clog the guiltless keel—
As having sense of beauty, do omit
Their mortal natures, letting go safely by
The divine Desdemona.

MONTANO: What is she? 75

CASSIO: She that I spake of, our great captain's
captain,
Left in the conduct of the bold Iago,
Whose footing here anticipates our thoughts
A sennight's speed. Great Jove, Othello guard,
And swell his sail with thine own powerful breath, 80
That he may bless this bay with his tall ship,
Make love's quick pants in Desdemona's arms,
Give renewed fire to our extinct spirits,
And bring all Cyprus comfort!

Enter DESDEMONA, IAGO, RODERIGO, *and* EMILIA.

O, behold!
The riches of the ship is come on shore! 85
You men of Cyprus, let her have your knees.

[The GENTLEMEN *make curtsy to* DESDEMONA.]
Hail to thee, lady! And the grace of heaven
Before, behind thee, and on every hand
Enwheel thee round!

DESDEMONA: I thank you, valiant Cassio.
What tidings can you tell me of my lord? 90

CASSIO: He is not yet arrived, nor know I aught
But that he's well and will be shortly here.

DESDEMONA: O, but I fear—How lost you company?

CASSIO: The great contention of sea and skies
Parted our fellowship.
(Within) "A sail, a sail!" *[A shot.]*
But hark. A sail! 95

SECOND GENTLEMAN: They give their greeting to
the citadel.
This likewise is a friend.

CASSIO: See for the news.
[Exit SECOND GENTLEMAN.]

46 approve admire, honor **51 approved allowance** tested reputation **52 surfeited to death** i.e., overextended, worn thin through repeated application or delayed fulfillment **53 in bold cure** in strong hopes of fulfillment **55 brow o' the sea** cliff-edge **57 My . . . for** I hope it is **58 discharge . . . courtesy** fire a salute in token of respect and courtesy **64 paragons** surpasses. **wild fame** extravagant report **65 quirks** witty conceits. **blazoning** setting forth as though in heraldic language **66–67 in . . . enginer** in her real, God-given, beauty, (she) defeats any attempt to praise her. **enginer** engineer, i.e., poet, one who devises. **s.d. Second Gentleman** (So identified in the Quarto text here and in lines 58, 61, 68, and 96; the Folio calls him a gentleman.) **67 put in** i.e., to harbor

71 guttered jagged, trenched **72 ensteeped** lying under water **73 As** as if. **omit** forbear to exercise **74 mortal** deadly **78 footing** landing **79 sennight's** week's **81 tall** splendid, gallant

Good Ancient, you are welcome. [*Kissing* EMILIA.]
Welcome, mistress.
Let it not gall your patience, good Iago,
100 That I extend my manners; 'tis my breeding
That gives me this bold show of courtesy.

IAGO: Sir, would she give you so much of her lips
As of her tongue she oft bestows on me,
You would have enough.

105 DESDEMONA: Alas, she has no speech!

IAGO: In faith, too much.
I find it still, when I have list to sleep.
Marry, before your ladyship, I grant,
She puts her tongue a little in her heart
110 And chides with thinking.

EMILIA: You have little cause to say so.

IAGO: Come on, come on. You are pictures out of doors,
Bells in your parlors, wildcats in your kitchens,
Saints in your injuries, devils being offended,
Players in your huswifery, and huswives in your
beds.

115 DESDEMONA: O, fie upon thee, slanderer!

IAGO: Nay, it is true, or else I am a Turk.
You rise to play, and go to bed to work.

EMILIA: You shall not write my praise.

IAGO: No, let me not.

DESDEMONA: What wouldst write of me, if thou
shouldst praise me?

120 IAGO: O gentle lady, do not put me to 't,
For I am nothing if not critical.

DESDEMONA: Come on, essay.—There's one gone to
the harbor?

IAGO: Ay, madam.

DESDEMONA: I am not merry, but I do beguile
125 The thing I am by seeming otherwise.
Come, how wouldst thou praise me?

IAGO: I am about it, but indeed my invention
Comes from my pate as birdlime does from frieze—
It plucks out brains and all. But my Muse labors,
And thus she is delivered: 130
If she be fair and wise, fairness and wit,
The one's for use, the other useth it.

DESDEMONA: Well praised! How if she be black and
witty?

IAGO: If she be black, and thereto have a wit,
She'll find a white that shall her blackness fit. 135

DESDEMONA: Worse and worse.

EMILIA: How if fair and foolish?

IAGO: She never yet was foolish that was fair,
For even her folly helped her to an heir.

DESDEMONA: Those are old fond paradoxes to make
fools laugh i' th' alehouse. What miserable praise 140
hast thou for her that's foul and foolish?

IAGO: There's none so foul and foolish thereunto,
But does foul pranks which fair and wise ones do.

DESDEMONA: O heavy ignorance! Thou praisest the
worst best. But what praise couldst thou bestow on 145
a deserving woman indeed, one that, in the authority of her merit, did justly put on the vouch of very
malice itself?

IAGO: She that was ever fair, and never proud,
Had tongue at will, and yet was never loud, 150
Never lacked gold and yet went never gay,
Fled from her wish, and yet said, "Now I may,"
She that being angered, her revenge being nigh,
Bade her wrong stay and her displeasure fly,
She that in wisdom never was so frail 155
To change the cod's head for the salmon's tail,
She that could think and ne'er disclose her mind,
See suitors following and not look behind,
She was a wight, if ever such wight were—

---

100 **extend** give scope to. **breeding** training in the niceties of etiquette   105 **she has no speech** i.e., she's not a chatterbox, as you allege   107 **still** always   **list** desire   110 **with thinking** i.e., in her thoughts only   111 **pictures out of doors** i.e., silent and well-behaved in public   112 **Bells** i.e., jangling, noisy, and brazen. **in your kitchens** i.e., in domestic affairs. (Ladies would not do the cooking.)   113 **Saints** martyrs   114 **Players** idlers, triflers, or deceivers.   **huswifery** housekeeping.   **huswives** hussies (i.e., women are "busy" in bed, or unduly thrifty in dispensing sexual favors)   116 **a Turk** an infidel, not to be believed   121 **critical** censorious   122 **essay** try   125 **The thing I am** i.e., my anxious self

128 **birdlime** sticky substance used to catch small birds.   **frieze** coarse woolen cloth   129 **labors** (1) exerts herself (2) prepares to deliver a child (with a following pun on *delivered* in line 130)   132 **The one's . . . it** i.e., her cleverness will make use of her beauty   133 **black** dark-complexioned, brunette   135 **a white** a fair person (with wordplay on "wight," a person).   **fit** (with sexual suggestion of mating)   138 **folly** (with added meaning of "lechery, wantonness").   **to an heir** i.e., to bear a child   139 **fond** foolish   141 **foul** ugly   142 **thereunto** in addition   143 **foul** sluttish   147 **put . . . vouch** compel the approval   151 **gay** extravagantly clothed   152 **Fled . . . may** avoided temptation where the choice was hers   154 **Bade . . . stay** i.e., resolved to put up with her injury patiently   156 **To . . . tail** i.e., to exchange a lackluster husband for a sexy lover (?) (*Cod's head* is slang for "penis," and *tail* for "pudendum.")

160 DESDEMONA: To do what?

IAGO: To suckle fools and chronicle small beer.

DESDEMONA: O most lame and impotent conclusion! Do not learn of him, Emilia, though he be thy husband. How say you, Cassio? Is he not a most profane **165** and liberal counselor?

CASSIO: He speaks home, madam. You may relish him more in the soldier than in the scholar.

[CASSIO and DESDEMONA stand together, conversing intimately.]

IAGO *[aside]*: He takes her by the palm. Ay, well said, whisper. With as little a web as this will I ensnare as **170** great a fly as Cassio. Ay, smile upon her, do; I will gyve thee in thine own courtship. You say true; 'tis so, indeed. If such tricks as these strip you out of your lieutenantry, it had been better you had not kissed your three fingers so oft, which now again you are most apt **175** to play the sir in. Very good; well kissed! An excellent courtesy! 'Tis so, indeed. Yet again your fingers to your lips? Would they were clyster pipes for your sake! *[Trumpet within.]* The Moor! I know his trumpet.

CASSIO: 'Tis truly so.

DESDEMONA: Let's meet him and receive him.

180 CASSIO: Lo, where he comes!

Enter OTHELLO and attendants.

OTHELLO: O my fair warrior!

DESDEMONA: My dear Othello!

OTHELLO: It gives me wonder great as my content To see you here before me. O my soul's joy, If after every tempest come such calms, **185** May the winds blow till they have wakened death, And let the laboring bark climb hills of seas Olympus-high, and duck again as low As hell's from heaven! If it were now to die, 'Twere now to be most happy, for I fear **190** My soul hath her content so absolute That not another comfort like to this Succeeds in unknown fate.

Othello greets his bride, Desdemona (Irène Jacob).

DESDEMONA: The heavens forbid But that our loves and comforts should increase Even as our days do grow!

OTHELLO: Amen to that, sweet powers! **195** I cannot speak enough of this content. It stops me here; it is too much of joy. And this, and this, the greatest discords be

[They kiss.]

That e'er our hearts shall make!

IAGO *[aside]*: O, you are well tuned now! **200** But I'll set down the pegs that make this music, As honest as I am.

OTHELLO: Come, let us to the castle. News, friends! Our wars are done, the Turks are drowned. How does my old acquaintance of this isle?— **205** Honey, you shall be well desired in Cyprus; I have found great love amongst them. O my sweet, I prattle out of fashion, and I dote In mine own comforts.—I prithee, good Iago, Go to the bay and disembark my coffers. **210** Bring thou the master to the citadel; He is a good one, and his worthiness Does challenge much respect.—Come, Desdemona.— Once more, well met at Cyprus!

Exeunt OTHELLO and DESDEMONA [and all but IAGO and RODERIGO].

---

161 suckle fools breastfeed babies. **chronicle small beer** i.e., keep petty household accounts, keep track of trivial matters **164 profane** irreverent, ribald **165 liberal** licentious, free-spoken **166 home** right to the target. (A term from fencing.) **relish** appreciate **167 in** in the character of **168 well said** well done **170 gyve** fetter, shackle **171 courtship** courtesy, show of courtly manners. **You say true** i.e., that's right, go ahead **175 the sir** i.e., the fine gentleman **177 clyster pipes** tubes used for enemas and douches **192 Succeeds . . . fate** i.e., can follow in the unknown future

---

198 s.d. They kiss (The direction is from the Quarto.) **201 set down** loosen (and hence untune the instrument) **202 As . . . I am** for all my supposed honesty **206 desired** welcomed **208 out of fashion** irrelevantly, incoherently (?) **210 coffers** chests, baggage **211 master** ship's captain **213 challenge** lay claim to, deserve

Iago watches from a distance as Othello makes his triumphant entry.

215 **IAGO** *[to an attendant]*:   Do thou meet me presently at
the harbor. *[To* RODERIGO.*]* Come hither. If thou be'st
valiant—as, they say, base men being in love have
then a nobility in their natures more than is native to
them—list me. The Lieutenant tonight watches on the
220 court of guard. First, I must tell thee this: Desdemona
is directly in love with him.

RODERIGO: With him? Why, 'tis not possible.

IAGO: Lay thy finger thus, and let thy soul be instructed. Mark me with what violence she first loved
225 the Moor, but for bragging and telling her fantastical
lies. To love him still for prating? Let not thy discreet
heart think it. Her eye must be fed; and what delight
shall she have to look on the devil? When the blood
is made dull with the act of sport, there should be,
230 again to inflame it and to give satiety a fresh appetite, loveliness in favor, sympathy in years, manners,
and beauties—all which the Moor is defective in.
Now, for want of these required conveniences, her
delicate tenderness will find itself abused, begin to
235 heave the gorge, disrelish and abhor the Moor. Very
nature will instruct her in it and compel her to some
second choice. Now, sir, this granted—as it is a most
pregnant and unforced position—who stands so emi-
nent in the degree of this fortune as Cassio does? A

knave very voluble, no further conscionable than in   240
putting on the mere form of civil and humane seeming for the better compassing of his salt and most
hidden loose affection. Why, none, why, none. A slipper and subtle knave, a finder out of occasions, that
has an eye can stamp and counterfeit advantages,   245
though true advantage never present itself; a devilish
knave. Besides, the knave is handsome, young, and
hath all those requisites in him that folly and green
minds look after. A pestilent complete knave, and
the woman hath found him already.   250

RODERIGO: I cannot believe that in her. She's full of
most blessed condition.

IAGO: Blessed fig's end! The wine she drinks is made
of grapes. If she had been blessed, she would never
have loved the Moor. Blessed pudding! Didst thou   255
not see her paddle with the palm of his hand? Didst
not mark that?

RODERIGO: Yes, that I did; but that was but courtesy.

IAGO: Lechery, by this hand. An index and obscure
prologue to the history of lust and foul thoughts.   260
They met so near with their lips that their breaths
embraced together. Villainous thoughts, Roderigo!
When these mutualities so marshal the way, hard at
hand comes the master and main exercise, th' incorporate conclusion. Pish! But, sir, be you ruled by me.   265
I have brought you from Venice. Watch you tonight;
for the command, I'll lay 't upon you. Cassio knows
you not. I'll not be far from you. Do you find some occasion to anger Cassio, either by speaking too loud, or
tainting his discipline, or from what other course you   270
please, which the time shall more favorably minister.

RODERIGO: Well.

IAGO: Sir, he's rash and very sudden in choler, and
haply may strike at you. Provoke him that he may,
for even out of that will I cause these of Cyprus to   275

---

217 base men even lowly born men   **219 list** listen to   **220 court
of guard** guardhouse. (Cassio is in charge of the watch.)   **223 thus**
i.e., on your lips   **225 but** only   **229 the act of sport** sex   **231
favor** appearance.   **sympathy** correspondence, similarity   **233
required conveniences** things conducive to sexual compatibil-
ity   **234 abused** cheated, revolted.   **235 heave the gorge** experience nausea   **235–236 Very nature** her very instincts   **238
pregnant** evident, cogent   **239 in . . . of** as next in line for

240 voluble facile, glib.   **conscionable** conscientious, conscience-
bound   **241 humane** polite, courteous   **242 salt** licentious   **243
affection** passion   **243–244 slipper** slippery   **245 an eye can
stamp** an eye that can coin, create.   **advantages** favorable oppor-
tunities   **248 folly** wantonness.   **green** immature   **250 found
him** sized him up, perceived his intent   **252 condition** disposition   **253 fig's end** (See 1.3.322 for the vulgar gesture of the fig.)
255 pudding sausage   **259 index** table of contents.   **obsure** (i.e.,
the *lust and foul thoughts,* line 260, are secret, hidden from view)
263 mutualities exchanges, intimacies   **263–264 hard at hand**
closely following.   **264–265 incorporate** carnal   **266 Watch you**
stand watch   **267 for the command . . . you** I'll arrange for you to
be appointed, given orders   **270 tainting** disparaging   **271 minister** provide   **273 choler** wrath   **274 haply** perhaps

mutiny, whose qualification shall come into no true taste again but by the displanting of Cassio. So shall you have a shorter journey to your desires by the means I shall then have to prefer them, and the impediment most profitably removed, without the which there were no expectation of our prosperity.

RODERIGO: I will do this, if you can bring it to any opportunity.

IAGO: I warrant thee. Meet me by and by at the citadel. I must fetch his necessaries ashore. Farewell.

RODERIGO: Adieu. *Exit.*

IAGO: That Cassio loves her, I do well believe 't;
That she loves him, 'tis apt and of great credit.
The Moor, howbeit that I endure him not,
Is of a constant, loving, noble nature,
And I dare think he'll prove to Desdemona
A most dear husband. Now, I do love her too,
Not out of absolute lust—though peradventure
I stand accountant for as great a sin—
But partly led to diet my revenge
For that I do suspect the lusty Moor
Hath leaped into my seat, the thought whereof
Doth, like a poisonous mineral, gnaw my innards;
And nothing can or shall content my soul
Till I am evened with him, wife for wife,
Or failing so, yet that I put the Moor
At least into a jealousy so strong
That judgment cannot cure. Which thing to do,
If this poor trash of Venice, whom I trace
For his quick hunting, stand the putting on,
I'll have our Michael Cassio on the hip,
Abuse him to the Moor in the rank garb—
For I fear Cassio with my nightcap too—
Make the Moor thank me, love me, and reward me
For making him egregiously an ass
And practicing upon his peace and quiet
Even to madness. 'Tis here, but yet confused.
Knavery's plain face is never seen till used. *Exit.*

280

285

290

295

300

305

310

---

276 **mutiny** riot. **qualification** appeasement 276–277 **true taste** i.e., acceptable state 279 **prefer** advance 284 **warrant** assure. **by and by** immediately 288 **apt** probable. **credit** credibility 294 **accountant** accountable 295 **diet** feed 304 **trace** i.e., train, or follow (?), or perhaps *trash*, a hunting term, meaning to put weights on a hunting dog in order to slow him down 305 **For** to make more eager. **stand . . . on** respond properly when I incite him to quarrel 306 **on the hip** at my mercy, where I can throw him. (A wrestling term.) 307 **Abuse** slander. **rank garb** coarse manner, gross fashion 308 **with my nightcap** i.e., as a rival in my bed, as one who gives me cuckold's horns 311 **practicing upon** plotting against

---

2.2 *Enter* OTHELLO's HERALD *with a proclamation.*

HERALD: It is Othello's pleasure, our noble and valiant general, that, upon certain tidings now arrived, importing the mere perdition of the Turkish fleet, every man put himself into triumph: some to dance, some to make bonfires, each man to what sport and revels his addiction leads him. For, besides these beneficial news, it is the celebration of his nuptial. So much was his pleasure should be proclaimed. All offices are open, and there is full liberty of feasting from this present hour of five till the bell have told eleven. Heaven bless the isle of Cyprus and our noble general Othello!

5

10

Exit.

2.3 *Enter* OTHELLO, DESDEMONA, CASSIO, *and attendants.*

OTHELLO: Good Michael, look you to the guard tonight.
Let's teach ourselves that honorable stop
Not to outsport discretion.

CASSIO: Iago hath direction what to do,
But notwithstanding, with my personal eye
Will I look to 't.

OTHELLO: Iago is most honest.
Michael, good night. Tomorrow with your earliest
Let me have speech with you. *[To* DESDEMONA.*]*
Come, my dear love,
The purchase made, the fruits are to ensue;
That profit's yet to come 'tween me and you.—
Good night.

5

10

*Exit [*OTHELLO, *with* DESDEMONA *and attendants].*

Enter IAGO.

CASSIO: Welcome, Iago. We must to the watch.

IAGO: Not this hour, Lieutenant; 'tis not yet ten o' the clock. Our general cast us thus early for the love of his Desdemona; who let us not therefore blame. He hath not yet made wanton the night with her, and she is sport for Jove.

15

2.2. Location: Cyprus. A street.
3 **mere perdition** complete destruction 4 **triumph** public celebration 6 **addiction** inclination 8 **offices** rooms where food and drink are kept

2.3. Location: Cyprus. The citadel.
2 **stop** restraint 3 **outsport** celebrate beyond the bounds of 7 **with your earliest** at your earliest convenience 9–10 **The purchase . . . you** i.e., though married, we haven't yet consummated our love 13 **Not this hour** not for an hour yet 14 **cast** dismissed 15 **who** i.e., Othello

CASSIO: She's a most exquisite lady.

IAGO: And, I'll warrant her, full of game.

20 **CASSIO:** Indeed, she's a most fresh and delicate creature.

IAGO: What an eye she has! Methinks it sounds a parley to provocation.

CASSIO: An inviting eye, and yet methinks right modest.

IAGO: And when she speaks, is it not an alarum to love?

25 **CASSIO:** She is indeed perfection.

IAGO: Well, happiness to their sheets! Come, Lieutenant, I have a stoup of wine, and here without are a brace of Cyprus gallants that would fain have a measure to the health of black Othello.

30 **CASSIO:** Not tonight, good Iago. I have very poor and unhappy brains for drinking. I could well wish courtesy would invent some other custom of entertainment.

IAGO: O, they are our friends. But one cup! I'll drink
35 for you.

CASSIO: I have drunk but one cup tonight, and that was craftily qualified too, and behold what innovation it makes here. I am unfortunate in the infirmity and dare not task my weakness with any more.

40 **IAGO:** What, man? 'Tis a night of revels. The gallants desire it.

CASSIO: Where are they?

IAGO: Here at the door. I pray you, call them in.

CASSIO: I'll do 't, but it dislikes me. _Exit._

45 **IAGO:** If I can fasten but one cup upon him,
With that which he hath drunk tonight already,
He'll be as full of quarrel and offense
As my young mistress' dog. Now, my sick fool
    Roderigo,
Whom love hath turned almost the wrong side out,

To Desdemona hath tonight caroused 50
Potations pottle-deep; and he's to watch.
Three lads of Cyprus—noble swelling spirits,
That hold their honors in a wary distance,
The very elements of this warlike isle—
Have I tonight flustered with flowing cups, 55
And they watch too. Now, 'mongst this flock of
    drunkards
Am I to put our Cassio in some action
That may offend the isle.—But here they come.

Enter CASSIO, MONTANO, _and_ GENTLE-
MEN; _[servants following with wine]._

If consequence do but approve my dream,
My boat sails freely both with wind and stream. 60

CASSIO: 'Fore God, they have given me a rouse already.

MONTANO: Good faith, a little one; not past a pint, as I am a soldier.

IAGO: Some wine, ho!

[He sings.] "And let me the cannikin clink, clink, 65
    And let me the cannikin clink.
        A soldier's a man,
        O, man's life's but a span;
    Why, then, let a soldier drink."

Some wine, boys! 70

CASSIO: 'Fore God, an excellent song.

IAGO: I learned it in England, where indeed they are most potent in potting. Your Dane, your German, and your swag-bellied Hollander—drink, ho!—are nothing to your English. 75

CASSIO: Is your Englishman so exquisite in his drinking?

IAGO: Why, he drinks you, with facility, your Dane dead drunk; he sweats not to overthrow your Almain; he gives your Hollander a vomit ere the next pottle can be filled. 80

---

21 **sounds a parley** calls for a conference, issues an invitation 24 **alarum** signal calling men to arms (continuing the military metaphor of _parley,_ line 21) 27 **stoup** measure of liquor, two quarts. **without** outside. **brace** pair 28–29 **fain have a measure** gladly drink a toast 35 **for you** in your place. (Iago will do the steady drinking to keep the gallants company while Cassio has only one cup.) 37 **qualified** diluted. 37–38 **innovation** disturbance, insurrection 38 **here** i.e., in my head 44 **it dislikes me** i.e., I'm reluctant 47 **offense** readiness to take offense

50 **caroused** drunk off 51 **pottle-deep** to the bottom of the tankard. **watch** stand watch 52 **swelling** proud 53 **hold . . . distance** i.e., are extremely sensitive of their honor 54 **very elements** typical sort 56 **watch** are members of the guard 59 **If . . . dream** if subsequent events will only substantiate my scheme 60 **stream** current 61 **rouse** full draft of liquor 65 **cannikin** small drinking vessel 68 **span** brief span of time. (Compare Psalms 39:5 as rendered in the Book of Common Prayer: "Thou hast made my days as it were a span long.") 73 **potting** drinking 77 **drinks you** drinks. **your Dane** your typical Dane 78 **sweats not** i.e., need not exert himself. **Almain** German

Iago deludes the drunken Cassio.

CASSIO: To the health of our general!

MONTANO: I am for it, Lieutenant, and I'll do you
justice.

IAGO: O sweet England! *[He sings.]*

"King Stephen was and-a worthy peer,
    His breeches cost him but a crown;
85   He held them sixpence all too dear,
    With that he called the tailor lown.

He was a wight of high renown,
    And thou art but of low degree.
90   'Tis pride that pulls the country down;
    Then take thy auld cloak about thee."

Some wine, ho!

CASSIO: 'Fore God, this is a more exquisite song than
the other.

95 **IAGO:** Will you hear 't again?

CASSIO: No, for I hold him to be unworthy of his place
that does those things. Well, God's above all; and
there be souls must be saved, and there be souls
must not be saved.

100 **IAGO:** It's true, good Lieutenant.

CASSIO: For mine own part—no offense to the General, nor any man of quality—I hope to be saved.

IAGO: And so do I too, Lieutenant.

---

82 **I'll . . . justice** i.e., I'll drink as much as you   87 **lown** lout, rascal
90 **pride** i.e., extravagance in dress.   91 **auld** old   102 **quality** rank

---

CASSIO: Ay, but, by your leave, not before me; the lieutenant is to be saved before the ancient. Let's have no   105
more of this; let's to our affairs.—God forgive us our
sins!—Gentlemen, let's look to our business. Do not
think, gentlemen, I am drunk. This is my ancient; this
is my right hand, and this is my left. I am not drunk
now. I can stand well enough, and speak well enough.   110

GENTLEMEN: Excellent well.

CASSIO: Why, very well then; you must not think then
that I am drunk. *Exit.*

MONTANO: To th' platform, masters. Come, let's set
the watch.

[Exeunt GENTLEMEN.*]*

IAGO: You see this fellow that is gone before.   115
He's a soldier fit to stand by Caesar
And give direction; and do but see his vice.
'Tis to his virtue a just equinox,
The one as long as th' other. 'Tis pity of him.
I fear the trust Othello puts him in,   120
On some odd time of his infirmity,
Will shake this island.

MONTANO: But is he often thus?

IAGO: 'Tis evermore the prologue to his sleep.
He'll watch the horologe a double set,
If drink rock not his cradle.

MONTANO: It were well   125
The General were put in mind of it.
Perhaps he sees it not, or his good nature
Prizes the virtue that appears in Cassio
And looks not on his evils. Is not this true?

Enter RODERIGO.

IAGO *[aside to him]:* How now, Roderigo?   130
I pray you, after the Lieutenant; go. *[Exit* RODERIGO.*]*

MONTANO: And 'tis great pity that the noble Moor
Should hazard such a place as his own second
With one of an engraffed infirmity.
It were an honest action to say so   135
To the Moor.

IAGO: Not I, for this fair island.
I do love Cassio well and would do much
To cure him of this evil. *[Cry within:* "Help! Help!"*]*
        But, hark! What noise?

---

114 **set the watch** mount the guard   118 **just equinox** exact counterpart. (*Equinox* is an equal length of days and nights.)   124
watch . . . set stay awake twice around the clock or *horologe*   133–
134 **hazard . . . With** risk giving such an important position as his
second in command to   134 **engraffed** engrafted, inveterate

Enter CASSIO, *pursuing* RODERIGO.

CASSIO: Zounds, you rogue! You rascal!

140 **MONTANO:** What's the matter, Lieutenant?

CASSIO: A knave teach me my duty? I'll beat the knave into a twiggen bottle.

RODERIGO: Beat me?

CASSIO: Dost thou prate, rogue? *[He strikes* RODERIGO.*]*

145 **MONTANO:** Nay, good Lieutenant. *[Restraining him.]* I pray you, sir, hold your hand.

CASSIO: Let me go, sir, or I'll knock you o'er the mazzard.

MONTANO: Come, come, you're drunk.

150 **CASSIO:** Drunk? *[They fight.]*

IAGO: *[aside to* RODERIGO*]:* Away, I say. Go out and cry a mutiny.
[Exit RODERIGO.*]*
Nay, good Lieutenant.—God's will, gentlemen—
Help, ho!—Lieutenant—sir—Montano—sir—
Help, masters!—Here's a goodly watch indeed!
[A bell rings.]
155 Who's that which rings the bell?—Diablo, ho!
The town will rise. God's will, Lieutenant, hold!
You'll be ashamed forever.

Enter OTHELLO *and attendants [with weapons].*

OTHELLO: What is the matter here?

MONTANO: Zounds, I bleed still.
I am hurt to th' death. He dies! *[He thrusts at* CASSIO.*]*

OTHELLO: Hold, for your lives!

160 **IAGO:** Hold, ho! Lieutenant—sir—Montano—
gentlemen—
Have you forgot all sense of place and duty?
Hold! The General speaks to you. Hold, for shame!

OTHELLO: Why, how now, ho? From whence ariseth this?
Are we turned Turks, and to ourselves do that
165 Which heaven hath forbid the Ottomites?

Othello hears from Cassio after the scuffle.

For Christian shame, put by this barbarous brawl!
He that stirs next to carve for his own rage
Holds his soul light; he dies upon his motion.
Silence that dreadful bell. It frights the isle
From her propriety. What is the matter, masters? 170
Honest Iago, that looks dead with grieving,
Speak. Who began this? On thy love, I charge thee.

IAGO: I do not know. Friends all but now, even now,
In quarter and in terms like bride and groom
Devesting them for bed; and then, but now— 175
As if some planet had unwitted men—
Swords out, and tilting one at others' breasts
In opposition bloody. I cannot speak
Any beginning to this peevish odds;
And would in action glorious I had lost 180
Those legs that brought me to a part of it!

OTHELLO: How comes it, Michael, you are thus forgot?

CASSIO: I pray you, pardon me. I cannot speak.

OTHELLO: Worthy Montano, you were wont be civil;
Thy gravity and stillness of your youth 185
The world hath noted, and your name is great
In mouths of wisest censure. What's the matter
That you unlace your reputation thus
And spend your rich opinion for the name
Of a night-brawler? Give me answer to it. 190

---

138 s.d. **pursuing** (The Quarto text reads "driving in.")   142 **twiggen** wicker-covered. (Cassio vows to assail Roderigo until his skin resembles wickerwork or until he has driven Roderigo through the holes in a wickerwork.)   148 **mazard** i.e., head. (Literally, a drinking vessel.)   151 **mutiny** riot   154 **masters** sirs.   **s.d. A bell rings** (This direction is from the Quarto, as are *Exit Roderigo* at line 131, *They fight* at line 150, and *with weapons* at line 157.)   155 **Diablo** the devil   156 **rise** grow riotous   164–165 **to ourselves . . . Ottomites** inflict on ourselves the harm that heaven has prevented the Turks from doing (by destroying their fleet)

167 **carve for** i.e., indulge, satisfy with his sword   168 **Holds . . . light** i.e., places little value on his life.   **upon his motion** if he moves   170 **propriety** proper state or condition   174 **In quarter** in friendly conduct, within bounds.   **in terms** on good terms   175 **Devesting them** undressing themselves   178 **speak** explain   179 **peevish odds** childish quarrel   182 **are thus forgot** have forgotten yourself thus   184 **wont be** accustomed to be   185 **stillness** sobriety   187 **censure** judgment   188 **unlace** undo, lay open (as one might loose the strings of a purse containing reputation)   189 **opinion** reputation

MONTANO: Worthy Othello, I am hurt to danger.
Your officer, Iago, can inform you—
While I spare speech, which something now offends
       me—
Of all that I do know; nor know I aught
195 By me that's said or done amiss this night,
Unless self-charity be sometimes a vice,
And to defend ourselves it be a sin
When violence assails us.

OTHELLO: Now, by heaven,
My blood begins my safer guides to rule,
200 And passion, having my best judgment collied,
Essays to lead the way. Zounds, if I stir,
Or do but lift this arm, the best of you
Shall sink in my rebuke. Give me to know
How this foul rout began, who set it on;
205 And he that is approved in this offense,
Though he had twinned with me, both at a birth,
Shall lose me. What? In a town of war
Yet wild, the people's hearts brim full of fear,
To manage private and domestic quarrel?
210 In night, and on the court and guard of safety?
'Tis monstrous. Iago, who began 't?

MONTANO *[to* IAGO*]:*   If partially affined, or leagued in
       office,
Thou dost deliver more or less than truth,
Thou art no soldier.

IAGO: Touch me not so near.
215 I had rather have this tongue cut from my mouth
Than it should do offense to Michael Cassio;
Yet, I persuade myself, to speak the truth
Shall nothing wrong him. This it is, General.
Montano and myself being in speech,
220 There comes a fellow crying out for help,
And Cassio following him with determined sword
To execute upon him. Sir, this gentleman
                              [indicating MONTANO*]*
Steps in to Cassio and entreats his pause.
Myself the crying fellow did pursue,
225 Lest by his clamor—as it so fell out—
The town might fall in fright. He, swift of foot,
Outran my purpose, and I returned, the rather
For that I heard the clink and fall of swords
And Cassio high in oath, which till tonight

I ne'er might say before. When I came back—   230
For this was brief—I found them close together
At blow and thrust, even as again they were
When you yourself did part them.
More of this matter cannot I report.
But men are men; the best sometimes forget.   235
Though Cassio did some little wrong to him,
As men in rage strike those that wish them best,
Yet surely Cassio, I believe, received
From him that fled some strange indignity,
Which patience could not pass.

OTHELLO: I know, Iago,   240
Thy honesty and love doth mince this matter,
Making it light to Cassio. Cassio, I love thee,
But nevermore be officer of mine.

                         Enter DESDEMONA, *attended.*

Look if my gentle love be not raised up.
I'll make thee an example.   245

DESDEMONA: What is the matter, dear?

OTHELLO: All's well now, sweeting;
Come away to bed. *[To* MONTANO.*]* Sir, for your hurts,
Myself will be your surgeon.—Lead him off.
                         *[*MONTANO *is led off.]*
Iago, look with care about the town
And silence those whom this vile brawl distracted.   250
Come, Desdemona. 'Tis the soldiers' life
To have their balmy slumbers waked with strife.
                         Exit [with all but IAGO *and* CASSIO*].*

IAGO: What, are you hurt, Lieutenant?

CASSIO: Ay, past all surgery.

IAGO: Marry, God forbid!   255

CASSIO: Reputation, reputation, reputation! O, I have
lost my reputation! I have lost the immortal part of
myself, and what remains is bestial. My reputation,
Iago, my reputation!

IAGO: As I am an honest man, I thought you had re-   260
ceived some bodily wound; there is more sense in
that than in reputation. Reputation is an idle and
most false imposition, oft got without merit and lost
without deserving. You have lost no reputation at all,
unless you repute yourself such a loser. What, man,   265
there are more ways to recover the General again.
You are but now cast in his mood—a punishment

---

193 **something** somewhat.   **offends** pains   199 **blood** passion (of anger).   **guides** i.e., reason   200 **collied** darkened   201 **Essays** undertakes   204 **rout** riot   205 **approved in** found guilty of   207 **town of** town garrisoned for   209 **manage** undertake   210 **on . . . safety** at the main guardhouse or headquarters and on watch   212 **partially affined** made partial by some personal relationship.   **leagued in office** in league as fellow officers   222 **execute** give effect to (his anger)   223 **his pause** him to stop   227 **rather** sooner

---

235 **forget** forget themselves   237 **those . . . best** i.e., even those who are well disposed   240 **pass** pass over, overlook   248 **be your surgeon** i.e., make sure you receive medical attention   263 **false imposition** thing artificially imposed and of no real value   266 **recover** regain favor with   267 **cast in his mood** dismissed in a moment of anger

Iago cleverly advises Cassio (Nick Barber).

more in policy than in malice, even so as one would
beat his offenseless dog to affright an imperious lion.
270   Sue to him again and he's yours.

CASSIO: I will rather sue to be despised than to deceive
so good a commander with so slight, so drunken,
and so indiscreet an officer. Drunk? And speak parrot? And squabble? Swagger? Swear? And discourse
275   fustian with one's own shadow? O thou invisible
spirit of wine, if thou hast no name to be known by,
let us call thee devil!

IAGO: What was he that you followed with your sword?
What had he done to you?

280   CASSIO: I know not.

IAGO: Is 't possible?

CASSIO: I remember a mass of things, but nothing
distinctly; a quarrel, but nothing wherefore. O God,
that men should put an enemy in their mouths to
285   steal away their brains! That we should, with joy,
pleasance, revel, and applause transform ourselves
into beasts!

IAGO: Why, but you are now well enough. How came
you thus recovered?

290   CASSIO: It hath pleased the devil drunkenness to give
place to the devil wrath. One unperfectness shows
me another, to make me frankly despise myself.

IAGO: Come, you are too severe a moraler. As the time,
the place, and the condition of this country stands, I
could heartily wish this had not befallen; but since it   295
is as it is, mend it for your own good.

CASSIO: I will ask him for my place again; he shall
tell me I am a drunkard. Had I as many mouths as
Hydra, such an answer would stop them all. To be
now a sensible man, by and by a fool, and presently a   300
beast! O, strange! Every inordinate cup is unblessed,
and the ingredient is a devil.

IAGO: Come, come, good wine is a good familiar creature, if it be well used. Exclaim no more against it.
And, good Lieutenant, I think you think I love you.   305

CASSIO: I have well approved it, sir. I drunk!

IAGO: You or any man living may be drunk at a time,
man. I'll tell you what you shall do. Our general's
wife is now the general—I may say so in this respect,
for that he hath devoted and given up himself to the   310
contemplation, mark, and denotement of her parts
and graces. Confess yourself freely to her; importune
her help to put you in your place again. She is of so
free, so kind, so apt, so blessed a disposition, she
holds it a vice in her goodness not to do more than   315
she is requested. This broken joint between you and
her husband entreat her to splinter; and, my fortunes
against any lay worth naming, this crack of your love
shall grow stronger than it was before.

CASSIO: You advise me well.   320

IAGO: I protest, in the sincerity of love and honest
kindness.

CASSIO: I think it freely; and betimes in the morning I
will beseech the virtuous Desdemona to undertake
for me. I am desperate of my fortunes if they check   325
me here.

IAGO: You are in the right. Good night, Lieutenant. I
must to the watch.

CASSIO: Good night, honest Iago.   *Exit* CASSIO.

---

268 **in policy** done for expediency's sake and as a public gesture
268–269 **would . . . lion** i.e., would make an example of a minor
offender in order to deter more important and dangerous offenders
269 **Sue** petition   272 **slight** worthless   273–274 **speak parrot**
talk nonsense, rant. (*Discourse fustian*, lines 274–275, has much
the same meaning.)   283 **wherefore** why   286 **applause** desire
for applause

293 **moraler** moralizer   299 **Hydra** the Lernaean Hydra, a monster with many heads and the ability to grow two heads when one
was cut off, slain by Hercules as the second of his twelve labors
306 **approved** proved   307 **at a time** at one time or another
309–310 **in . . . that** in view of this fact, that   311 **mark, and denotement** (Both words mean "observation.")   **parts** qualities
314 **free** generous   317 **splinter** bind with splints   318 **lay** stake,
wager   321 **protest** insist, declare   323 **freely** unreservedly
325 **check** repulse

330 IAGO: And what's he then that says I play the villain,
When this advice is free I give, and honest,
Probal to thinking, and indeed the course
To win the Moor again? For 'tis most easy
Th' inclining Desdemona to subdue
335 In any honest suit; she's framed as fruitful
As the free elements. And then for her
To win the Moor—were 't to renounce his baptism,
All seals and symbols of redeemèd sin—
His soul is so enfettered to her love
340 That she may make, unmake, do what she list,
Even as her appetite shall play the god
With his weak function. How am I then a villain,
To counsel Cassio to this parallel course
Directly to his good? Divinity of hell!
345 When devils will the blackest sins put on,
They do suggest at first with heavenly shows,
As I do now. For whiles this honest fool
Plies Desdemona to repair his fortune,
And she for him pleads strongly to the Moor,
350 I'll pour this pestilence into his ear,
That she repeals him for her body's lust;
And by how much she strives to do him good,
She shall undo her credit with the Moor.
So will I turn her virtue into pitch,
355 And out of her own goodness make the net
That shall enmesh them all.

Enter RODERIGO.

How now, Roderigo?

RODERIGO: I do follow here in the chase, not like a
hound that hunts, but one that fills up the cry. My
money is almost spent; I have been tonight exceed-
360 ingly well cudgeled; and I think the issue will be I
shall have so much experience for my pains, and so,
with no money at all and a little more wit, return
again to Venice.

IAGO: How poor are they that have not patience!
365 What wound did ever heal but by degrees?

Thou know'st we work by wit, and not by witchcraft,
And wit depends on dilatory time.
Does 't not go well? Cassio hath beaten thee,
And thou, by that small hurt, hast cashiered Cassio.
Though other things grow fair against the sun, 370
Yet fruits that blossom first will first be ripe.
Content thyself awhile. By the Mass, 'tis morning!
Pleasure and action make the hours seem short.
Retire thee; go where thou art billeted.
Away, I say! Thou shalt know more hereafter. 375
Nay, get thee gone. *Exit* RODERIGO.
Two things are to be done.
My wife must move for Cassio to her mistress;
I'll set her on;
Myself the while to draw the Moor apart
And bring him jump when he may Cassio find 380
Soliciting his wife. Ay, that's the way.
Dull not device by coldness and delay. *Exit.*

3.1 *Enter* CASSIO *[and]* MUSICIANS.

CASSIO: Masters, play here—I will content your pains—
Something that's brief, and bid "Good morrow,
General." *[They play.]*

[Enter] CLOWN.

CLOWN: Why, masters, have your instruments been in
Naples, that they speak i' the nose thus?

A MUSICIAN: How, sir, how? 5

CLOWN: Are these, I pray you, wind instruments?

A MUSICIAN: Ay, marry, are they, sir.

CLOWN: O, thereby hangs a tail.

A MUSICIAN: Whereby hangs a tale, sir?

CLOWN: Marry, sir, by many a wind instrument that 10
I know. But, masters, here's money for you. *[He gives money.]* And the General so likes your music that he
desires you, for love's sake, to make no more noise
with it.

---

331 free (1) free from guile (2) freely given   **332 Probal** probable, reasonable   **334 inclining** favorably disposed.   **subdue** persuade   **335 framed as fruitful** created as generous   **336 free elements** i.e., earth, air, fire, and water, unrestrained and spontaneous   **341 her appetite** her desire, or, perhaps, his desire for her   **342 function** exercise of faculties (weakened by his fondness for her)   **343 parallel** corresponding to these facts and to his best interests   **344 Divinity of hell** inverted theology of hell (which seduces the soul to its damnation)   **345 put on** further, instigate   **346 suggest** tempt   **351 repeals him** attempts to get him restored   **354 pitch** i.e., (1) foul blackness (2) a snaring substance   **358 fills up the cry** merely takes part as one of the pack   **361 so much** just so much and no more

---

369 cashiered dismissed from service   **370–371 Though . . . ripe** i.e., plans that are well prepared and set expeditiously in motion will soonest ripen into success   **377 move** plead   **380 jump** precisely   **382 device** plot.   **coldness** lack of zeal

3.1. Location: Before the chamber of Othello and Desdemona. 1 content your pains reward your efforts   **4 speak i' the nose** (1) sound nasal (2) sound like one whose nose has been attacked by syphilis. (Naples was popularly supposed to have a high incidence of venereal disease.)   **10 wind instrument** (With a joke on flatulence. The *tail*, line 8, that hangs nearby the *wind instrument* suggests the penis.)   **13 for love's sake** (1) out of friendship and affection (2) for the sake of lovemaking in Othello's marriage

15 A MUSICIAN: Well, sir, we will not.

CLOWN: If you have any music that may not be heard, to 't again; but, as they say, to hear music the General does not greatly care.

A MUSICIAN: We have none such, sir.

20 CLOWN: Then put up your pipes in your bag, for I'll away. Go, vanish into air, away! *Exeunt* MUSICIANS.

CASSIO: Dost thou hear, mine honest friend?

CLOWN: No, I hear not your honest friend; I hear you.

CASSIO: Prithee, keep up thy quillets. There's a poor
25   piece of gold for thee. *[He gives money.]* If the gentle-woman that attends the General's wife be stirring, tell her there's one Cassio entreats her a little favor of speech. Wilt thou do this?

CLOWN: She is stirring, sir. If she will stir hither, I
30   shall seem to notify unto her.

CASSIO: Do, good my friend. *Exit* CLOWN.

Enter IAGO.

In happy time, Iago.

IAGO: You have not been abed, then?

CASSIO: Why, no. The day had broke
Before we parted. I have made bold, Iago,
35   To send in to your wife. My suit to her
Is that she will to virtuous Desdemona
Procure me some access.

IAGO: I'll send her to you presently;
And I'll devise a means to draw the Moor
40   Out of the way, that your converse and business
May be more free.

CASSIO: I humbly thank you for 't. *Exit* [IAGO.]
                    I never knew
A Florentine more kind and honest.

Enter EMILIA.

EMILIA: Good morrow, good Lieutenant. I am sorry
45   For your displeasure; but all will sure be well.
The General and his wife are talking of it,
And she speaks for you stoutly. The Moor replies

That he you hurt is of great fame in Cyprus
And great affinity, and that in wholesome wisdom
He might not but refuse you; but he protests he loves
     you   50
And needs no other suitor but his likings
To take the safest occasion by the front
To bring you in again.

CASSIO: Yet I beseech you,
If you think fit, or that it may be done,
Give me advantage of some brief discourse   55
With Desdemona alone.

EMILIA: Pray you, come in.
I will bestow you where you shall have time
To speak your bosom freely.

CASSIO: I am much bound to you. *[Exeunt.]*

3.2 *Enter* OTHELLO, IAGO, *and* GENTLEMEN.

OTHELLO *[giving letters]*: These letters give, Iago,
     to the pilot,
And by him do my duties to the Senate.
That done, I will be walking on the works;
Repair there to me.

IAGO: Well, my good lord, I'll do 't.

OTHELLO: This fortification, gentlemen, shall we see 't?   5

GENTLEMEN: We'll wait upon your lordship. *Exeunt.*

3.3 *Enter* DESDEMONA, CASSIO, *and* EMILIA.

DESDEMONA: Be thou assured, good Cassio, I will do
All my abilities in thy behalf.

EMILIA: Good madam, do. I warrant it grieves my
     husband
As if the cause were his.

DESDEMONA: O, that's an honest fellow. Do not doubt,
     Cassio,   5
But I will have my lord and you again
As friendly as you were.

CASSIO: Bounteous madam,
Whatever shall become of Michael Cassio,
He's never anything but your true servant.

16 may not cannot   **20–21 I'll away** (Possibly a misprint, or a snatch of song?)   **24 keep up** do not bring out, do not use.   **quillets** quibbles, puns   **27–28 a little . . . speech** the favor of a brief talk   **29 stir** bestir herself (with a play on *stirring,* "rousing herself from rest")   **30 seem** deem it good, think fit   **31 In happy time** i.e., well met   **43 Florentine** i.e., even a fellow Florentine (Iago is a Venetian; Cassio is a Florentine.)   **45 displeasure** fall from favor   **47 stoutly** spiritedly

48 fame reputation, importance   **49 affinity** kindred, family connection   **50 protests** insists   **52 occasion . . . front** opportunity by the forelock   **58 bosom** inmost thoughts

3.2. Location: The citadel.
2 do my duties convey my respects   **3 works** breastworks, fortifications   **4 Repair** return, come   **6 wait upon** attend

3.3. Location: The garden of the citadel.

10 **DESDEMONA:**   I know 't. I thank you. You do love my lord;
You have known him long, and be you well assured
He shall in strangeness stand no farther off
Than in a politic distance.

CASSIO: Ay, but, lady,
That policy may either last so long,
15 Or feed upon such nice and waterish diet,
Or breed itself so out of circumstance,
That, I being absent and my place supplied,
My general will forget my love and service.

DESDEMONA: Do not doubt that. Before Emilia here
20 I give thee warrant of thy place. Assure thee,
If I do vow a friendship I'll perform it
To the last article. My lord shall never rest.
I'll watch him tame and talk him out of patience;
His bed shall seem a school, his board a shrift;
25 I'll intermingle everything he does
With Cassio's suit. Therefore be merry, Cassio,
For thy solicitor shall rather die
Than give thy cause away.

Enter OTHELLO *and* IAGO *[at a distance].*

EMILIA: Madam, here comes my lord.

30 **CASSIO:**   Madam, I'll take my leave.

DESDEMONA: Why, stay, and hear me speak.

CASSIO: Madam, not now. I am very ill at ease,
Unfit for mine own purposes.

DESDEMONA: Well, do your discretion.   *Exit* CASSIO.

35 **IAGO:**   Ha? I like not that.

OTHELLO: What dost thou say?

IAGO: Nothing, my lord; or if—I know not what.

OTHELLO: Was not that Cassio parted from my wife?

IAGO: Cassio, my lord? No, sure, I cannot think it,
40 That he would steal away so guiltylike,
Seeing you coming.

OTHELLO: I do believe 'twas he.

Desdemona (Zoë Tapper) asks Othello (Eamonn Walker) to pardon Cassio.

DESDEMONA: How now, my lord?
I have been talking with a suitor here,
A man that languishes in your displeasure.   45

OTHELLO: Who is 't you mean?

DESDEMONA: Why, your lieutenant, Cassio. Good my lord,
If I have any grace or power to move you,
His present reconciliation take;
For if he be not one that truly loves you,   50
That errs in ignorance and not in cunning,
I have no judgment in an honest face.
I prithee, call him back.

OTHELLO: Went he hence now?

DESDEMONA: Yes, faith, so humbled   55
That he hath left part of his grief with me
To suffer with him. Good love, call him back.

OTHELLO: Not now, sweet Desdemon. Some other time.

DESDEMONA: But shall 't be shortly?

OTHELLO: The sooner, sweet, for you.   60

DESDEMONA: Shall 't be tonight at supper?

OTHELLO: No, not tonight.

DESDEMONA: Tomorrow dinner, then?

OTHELLO: I shall not dine at home.
I meet the captains at the citadel.   65

---

12 strangeness aloofness   **13 politic** required by wise policy   **15 Or . . . diet** or sustain itself at length upon such trivial and meager technicalities   **16 breed . . . circumstance** continually renew itself so out of chance events, or yield so few chances for my being pardoned   **17 supplied** filled by another person   **19 doubt** fear   **20 warrant** guarantee   **23 watch him tame** tame him by keeping him from sleeping. (A term from falconry.)   **out of patience** past his endurance   **24 board** dining table.   **shrift** confessional   **27 solicitor** advocate   **28 away** up   **34 do your discretion** act according to your own discretion

---

49 His . . . take let him be reconciled to you right away   **51 in cunning** wittingly   **63 dinner** (The noontime meal.)

DESDEMONA: Why, then, tomorrow night, or Tuesday morn,
On Tuesday noon, or night, on Wednesday morn.
I prithee, name the time, but let it not
Exceed three days. In faith, he's penitent;
70 And yet his trespass, in our common reason—
Save that, they say, the wars must make example
Out of her best—is not almost a fault
T' incur a private check. When shall he come?
Tell me, Othello. I wonder in my soul
75 What you would ask me that I should deny,
Or stand so mammering on. What? Michael Cassio,
That came a-wooing with you, and so many a time,
When I have spoke of you dispraisingly,
Hath ta'en your part—to have so much to do
80 To bring him in! By 'r Lady, I could do much—

OTHELLO: Prithee, no more. Let him come when he will;
I will deny thee nothing.

DESDEMONA: Why, this is not a boon.
'Tis as I should entreat you wear your gloves,
85 Or feed on nourishing dishes, or keep you warm,
Or sue to you to do a peculiar profit
To your own person. Nay, when I have a suit
Wherein I mean to touch your love indeed,
It shall be full of poise and difficult weight,
90 And fearful to be granted.

OTHELLO: I will deny thee nothing.
Whereon, I do beseech thee, grant me this,
To leave me but a little to myself.

DESDEMONA: Shall I deny you? No. Farewell, my lord.

95 **OTHELLO:**   Farewell, my Desdemona. I'll come to thee straight.

DESDEMONA: Emilia, come.—Be as your fancies teach you;
Whate'er you be, I am obedient.   *Exit [with* EMILIA*].*

---

70 common reason everyday judgments   **71–72 Save . . . best** were it not that, as the saying goes, military discipline requires making an example of the very best men. (*Her* refers to *wars* as a singular concept.)   **72 not almost** scarcely   **73 a private check** even a private reprimand   **76 mammering on** wavering about   **80 bring him in** restore him to favor   **86 peculiar** particular, personal   **88 touch** test   **89 poise** weight, heaviness; or equipoise, delicate balance involving hard choice   **92 Whereon** in return for which   **95 straight** straightway   **96 fancies** inclinations

OTHELLO: Excellent wretch! Perdition catch my soul
But I do love thee! And when I love thee not,
Chaos is come again.   100

IAGO: My noble lord—

OTHELLO: What dost thou say, Iago?

IAGO: Did Michael Cassio, when you wooed my lady,
Know of your love?

OTHELLO: He did, from first to last. Why dost thou ask?   105

IAGO: But for a satisfaction of my thought;
No further harm.

OTHELLO: Why of thy thought, Iago?

IAGO: I did not think he had been acquainted with her.

OTHELLO: O, yes, and went between us very oft.

IAGO: Indeed?   110

OTHELLO: Indeed? Ay, indeed. Discern'st thou aught in that?
Is he not honest?

IAGO: Honest, my lord?

OTHELLO: Honest. Ay, honest.

IAGO: My lord, for aught I know.   115

OTHELLO: What dost thou think?

IAGO: Think, my lord?

OTHELLO: "Think, my lord?" By heaven, thou echo'st me,
As if there were some monster in thy thought
Too hideous to be shown. Thou dost mean something.   120
I heard thee say even now, thou lik'st not that,
When Cassio left my wife. What didst not like?
And when I told thee he was of my counsel
In my whole course of wooing, thou criedst "Indeed?"
And didst contract and purse thy brow together   125
As if thou then hadst shut up in thy brain
Some horrible conceit. If thou dost love me,
Show me thy thought.

IAGO: My lord, you know I love you.

---

98 wretch (A term of affectionate endearment.)   **99–100 And . . . again** i.e., my love for you will last forever, until the end of time when chaos will return. (But with an unconscious, ironic suggestion that, if anything should induce Othello to cease loving Desdemona, the result would be chaos.)   **123 of my counsel** in my confidence   **125 purse** knit   **127 conceit** fancy

Sometimes intrude not? Who has that breast so pure
But some uncleanly apprehensions
Keep leets and law days, and in sessions sit
With meditations lawful?

OTHELLO: Thou dost conspire against thy friend, Iago,   155
If thou but think'st him wronged and mak'st his ear
A stranger to thy thoughts.

IAGO: I do beseech you,
Though I perchance am vicious in my guess—
As I confess it is my nature's plague
To spy into abuses, and oft my jealousy   160
Shapes faults that are not—that your wisdom then,
From one that so imperfectly conceits,
Would take no notice, nor build yourself a trouble
Out of his scattering and unsure observance.
It were not for your quiet nor your good,   165
Nor for my manhood, honesty, and wisdom,
To let you know my thoughts.

OTHELLO: What dost thou mean?

IAGO: Good name in man and woman, dear my lord,
Is the immediate jewel of their souls.
Who steals my purse steals trash; 'tis something, nothing;   170
'Twas mine, 'tis his, and has been slave to thousands;
But he that filches from me my good name
Robs me of that which not enriches him
And makes me poor indeed.

OTHELLO: By heaven, I'll know thy thoughts.   175

IAGO: You cannot, if my heart were in your hand,
Nor shall not, whilst 'tis in my custody.

OTHELLO: Ha?

IAGO: O, beware, my lord, of jealousy.
It is the green-eyed monster which doth mock
The meat it feeds on. That cuckold lives in bliss   180
Who, certain of his fate, loves not his wronger;

---

153 **Keep leets and law days** i.e., hold court, set up their authority in one's heart. (*Leets* are a kind of manor court; *law days* are the days courts sit in session, or those sessions.) 154 **With** along with. **lawful** innocent 155 **thy friend** i.e., Othello 158 **vicious** wrong 160 **jealousy** suspicious nature 161 **then** on that account 162 **one** i.e., myself, Iago. **conceits** judges, conjectures 164 **scattering** random 169 **immediate** essential, most precious 176 **if** even if 179–180 **doth mock . . . on** mocks and torments the heart of its victim, the man who suffers jealousy 181 **his wronger** i.e., his faithless wife. (The unsuspecting cuckold is spared the misery of loving his wife only to discover she is cheating on him.)

Othello, jealous of Cassio, is beguiled by Iago.

130 **OTHELLO:** I think thou dost;
And, for I know thou'rt full of love and honesty,
And weigh'st thy words before thou giv'st them breath,
Therefore these stops of thine fright me the more;
For such things in a false disloyal knave
135 Are tricks of custom, but in a man that's just
They're close dilations, working from the heart
That passion cannot rule.

IAGO: For Michael Cassio,
I dare be sworn I think that he is honest.

OTHELLO: I think so too.

IAGO: Men should be what they seem;
140 Or those that be not, would they might seem none!

OTHELLO: Certain, men should be what they seem.

IAGO: Why, then, I think Cassio's an honest man.

OTHELLO: Nay, yet there's more in this.
I prithee, speak to me as to thy thinkings,
145 As thou dost ruminate, and give thy worst of thoughts
The worst of words.

IAGO: Good my lord, pardon me.
Though I am bound to every act of duty,
I am not bound to that all slaves are free to.
Utter my thoughts? Why, say they are vile and false,
150 As where's that palace whereinto foul things

---

131 **for** because 133 **stops** pauses 135 **of custom** customary 136 **close dilations** secret or involuntary expressions or delays 137 **That passion cannot rule** i.e., that are too passionately strong to be restrained (referring to the workings), or, that cannot rule its own passions (referring to the heart). **For** as for 140 **none** i.e., not to be men, or not seem to be honest 148 **that** that which. **free to** free with respect to

Othello is deceived by Iago.

But O, what damnèd minutes tells he o'er
Who dotes, yet doubts, suspects, yet fondly loves!

OTHELLO: O misery!

185   IAGO: Poor and content is rich, and rich enough,
But riches fineless is as poor as winter
To him that ever fears he shall be poor.
Good God, the souls of all my tribe defend
From jealousy!

190   OTHELLO: Why, why is this?
Think'st thou I'd make a life of jealousy,
To follow still the changes of the moon
With fresh suspicions? No! To be once in doubt
Is once to be resolved. Exchange me for a goat
195   When I shall turn the business of my soul
To such exsufflicate and blown surmises
Matching thy inference. 'Tis not to make me jealous
To say my wife is fair, feeds well, loves company,
Is free of speech, sings, plays, and dances well;
200   Where virtue is, these are more virtuous.
Nor from mine own weak merits will I draw
The smallest fear or doubt of her revolt,
For she had eyes, and chose me. No, Iago,
I'll see before I doubt; when I doubt, prove;
205   And on the proof, there is no more but this—
Away at once with love or jealousy.

IAGO: I am glad of this, for now I shall have reason
To show the love and duty that I bear you
With franker spirit. Therefore, as I am bound,
Receive it from me. I speak not yet of proof.   210
Look to your wife; observe her well with Cassio.
Wear your eyes thus, not jealous nor secure.
I would not have your free and noble nature,
Out of self-bounty, be abused. Look to 't.
I know our country disposition well;   215
In Venice they do let God see the pranks
They dare not show their husbands; their best
    conscience
Is not to leave 't undone, but keep 't unknown.

OTHELLO: Dost thou say so?

IAGO: She did deceive her father, marrying you;   220
And when she seemed to shake and fear your looks,
She loved them most.

OTHELLO: And so she did.

IAGO: Why, go to, then!
She that, so young, could give out such a seeming,
To seel her father's eyes up close as oak,
He thought 'twas witchcraft! But I am much to blame.   225
I humbly do beseech you of your pardon
For too much loving you.

OTHELLO: I am bound to thee forever.

IAGO: I see this hath a little dashed your spirits.

OTHELLO: Not a jot, not a jot.

IAGO: I' faith, I fear it has.   230
I hope you will consider what is spoke
Comes from my love. But I do see you're moved.
I am to pray you not to strain my speech
To grosser issues nor to larger reach
Than to suspicion.   235

OTHELLO: I will not.

IAGO: Should you do so, my lord,
My speech should fall into such vile success
Which my thoughts aimed not. Cassio's my worthy
    friend.
My lord, I see you're moved.   240

---

182 tells counts   **185 Poor . . . enough** to be content with what little one has is the greatest wealth of all. (Proverbial.)   **186 fineless** boundless   **192–193 To follow . . . suspicions** to be constantly imagining new causes for suspicion, changing incessantly like the moon   **194 once** once and for all.   **resolved** free of doubt, having settled the matter   **196 exsufflicate and blown** inflated and blown up, rumored about, or, spat out and flyblown, hence, loathsome, disgusting   **197 inference** description or allegation   **202 doubt . . . revolt** fear or her unfaithfulness

212 not neither.   **secure** free from uncertainty   **214 self-bounty** inherent or natural goodness and generosity.   **abused** deceived   **222 go to** (An expression of impatience.)   **223 seeming** false appearance   **224 seel** blind. (A term from falconry.)   **oak** (A close-grained wood.)   **228 bound** indebted (but perhaps with ironic sense of "tied")   **234 issues** significances.   **reach** meaning, scope   **238 success** effect, result

OTHELLO: No, not much moved.
I do not think but Desdemona's honest.

IAGO: Long live she so! And long live you to think so!

OTHELLO: And yet, how nature erring from itself—

IAGO: Ay, there's the point! As—to be bold with you—
245   Not to affect many proposèd matches
Of her own clime, complexion, and degree,
Whereto we see in all things nature tends—
Foh! One may smell in such a will most rank,
Foul disproportion, thoughts unnatural.
250   But, pardon me. I do not in position
Distinctly speak of her, though I may fear
Her will, recoiling to her better judgment,
May fall to match you with her country forms
And happily repent.

OTHELLO: Farewell, farewell!
255   If more thou dost perceive, let me know more.
Set on thy wife to observe. Leave me, Iago.

IAGO *[going]:*   My lord, I take my leave.

OTHELLO: Why did I marry? This honest creature doubtless
Sees and knows more, much more, than he unfolds.

260   **IAGO** *[returning]:*   My lord, I would I might entreat your honor
To scan this thing no farther. Leave it to time.
Although 'tis fit that Cassio have his place—
For, sure, he fills it up with great ability—
Yet, if you please to hold him off awhile,
265   You shall by that perceive him and his means.
Note if your lady strain his entertainment
With any strong or vehement importunity;
Much will be seen in that. In the meantime,
Let me be thought too busy in my fears—
270   As worthy cause I have to fear I am—
And hold her free, I do beseech your honor.

OTHELLO: Fear not my government.

IAGO: I once more take my leave.   *Exit.*

---

241 **honest** chaste   245 **affect** prefer, desire   246 **clime . . . degree** country, color, and social position   248 **will** sensuality, appetite   249 **disproportion** abnormality   250 **position** argument, proposition   252 **recoiling** reverting.   **better** i.e., more natural and reconsidered   253 **fall . . . forms** undertake to compare you with Venetian norms of handsomeness   254 **happily repent** haply repent her marriage   261 **scan** scrutinize   265 **his means** the method he uses (to regain his post)   266 **strain his entertainment** urge his reinstatement   269 **busy** interfering   271 **hold her free** regard her as innocent   272 **government** self-control, conduct

OTHELLO: This fellow's of exceeding honesty,
And knows all qualities, with a learnèd spirit,   275
Of human dealings. If I do prove her haggard,
Though that her jesses were my dear heartstrings,
I'd whistle her off and let her down the wind
To prey at fortune. Haply, for I am black
And have not those soft parts of conversation   280
That chamberers have, or for I am declined
Into the vale of years—yet that's not much—
She's gone. I am abused, and my relief
Must be to loathe her. O curse of marriage,
That we can call these delicate creatures ours   285
And not their appetites! I had rather be a toad
And live upon the vapor of a dungeon
Than keep a corner in the thing I love
For others' uses. Yet, 'tis the plague to great ones;
Prerogatived are they less than the base.   290
'Tis destiny unshunnable, like death.
Even then this forkèd plague is fated to us
When we do quicken. Look where she comes.

Enter DESDEMONA *and* EMILIA.

If she be false, O, then heaven mocks itself!
I'll not believe 't.   295

DESDEMONA: How now, my dear Othello?
Your dinner, and the generous islanders
By you invited, do attend your presence.

OTHELLO: I am to blame.

DESDEMONA: Why do you speak so faintly?
Are you not well?

OTHELLO: I have a pain upon my forehead here.   300

DESDEMONA: Faith, that's with watching. 'Twill away again.

[She offers her handkerchief.]
Let me but bind it hard, within this hour
It will be well.

---

275 **qualities** natures, types   276 **haggard** wild (like a wild female hawk)   277 **jesses** straps fastened around the legs of a trained hawk   278 **I'd . . . wind** i.e., I'd let her go forever. (To release a hawk downwind was to invite it not to return.)   279 **prey at fortune** fend for herself in the wild.   **Haply, for** perhaps because   280 **soft . . . conversation** pleasing graces of social behavior   281 **chamberers** gallants   283 **abused** deceived   290 **Prerogatived** privileged (to have honest wives).   **the base** ordinary citizens. (Socially prominent men are especially prone to the unavoidable destiny of being cuckolded and to the public shame that goes with it.)   292 **forkèd** (An allusion to the horns of the cuckold.)   293 **quicken** receive life. (*Quicken* may also mean to swarm with maggots as the body festers, as in 4.2.69, in which case lines 292–293 suggest that *even then*, in death, we are cuckolded by *forkèd* worms.)   296 **generous** noble   297 **attend** await   301 **watching** too little sleep

OTHELLO: Your napkin is too little.
Let it alone. Come, I'll go in with you.
[He puts the handkerchief from him, and it drops.]

305 **DESDEMONA:**   I am very sorry that you are not well.
Exit [with OTHELLO*].*

EMILIA *[picking up the handkerchief]*:   I am glad I have
found this napkin.
This was her first remembrance from the Moor.
My wayward husband hath a hundred times
Wooed me to steal it, but she so loves the token—
310 For he conjured her she should ever keep it—
That she reserves it evermore about her
To kiss and talk to. I'll have the work ta'en out,
And give 't Iago. What he will do with it
Heaven knows, not I;
315 I nothing but to please his fantasy.

Enter IAGO.

IAGO: How now? What do you here alone?

EMILIA: Do not you chide. I have a thing for you.

IAGO: You have a thing for me? It is a common thing—

EMILIA: Ha?

320 **IAGO:**   To have a foolish wife.

EMILIA: O, is that all? What will you give me now
For that same handkerchief?

IAGO: What handkerchief?

EMILIA: What handkerchief?
325 Why, that the Moor first gave to Desdemona;
That which so often you did bid me steal.

IAGO: Hast stolen it from her?

EMILIA: No, faith. She let it drop by negligence,
And to th' advantage I, being here, took 't up.
330 Look, here 'tis.

IAGO: A good wench! Give it me.

EMILIA: What will you do with 't, that you have been
so earnest
To have me filch it?

IAGO *[snatching it]*:   Why, what is that to you?

Emilia (Anna Patrick) brings Iago Desdemona's handkerchief.

EMILIA: If it be not for some purpose of import,
Give 't me again. Poor lady, she'll run mad
When she shall lack it.

IAGO: Be not acknown on 't.   335
I have use for it. Go, leave me.   *Exit* EMILIA.
I will in Cassio's lodging lose this napkin
And let him find it. Trifles light as air
Are to the jealous confirmations strong
As proofs of Holy Writ. This may do something.   340
The Moor already changes with my poison.
Dangerous conceits are in their natures poisons,
Which at the first are scarce found to distaste,
But with a little act upon the blood
Burn like the mines of sulfur.

Enter OTHELLO.

             I did say so.   345
Look where he comes! Not poppy nor mandragora
Nor all the drowsy syrups of the world
Shall ever medicine thee to that sweet sleep
Which thou owedst yesterday.

OTHELLO: Ha, ha, false to me?

IAGO: Why, how now, General? No more of that.   350

OTHELLO: Avaunt! Begone! Thou hast set me on the
rack.
I swear 'tis better to be much abused
Than but to know 't a little.

IAGO: How now, my lord?

OTHELLO: What sense had I of her stolen hours of lust?
I saw 't not, thought it not, it harmed not me.   355

---

303 napkin handkerchief **304 Let it alone** i.e., never mind **308
wayward** capricious **312 work ta'en out** design of the embroidery
copied **315 fantasy** whim **318 common thing** (With bawdy suggestion; *common* suggests coarseness and availability to all comers,
and *thing* is a slang term for the pudendum.) **329 to th' advantage** taking the opportunity

---

335 lack miss. **Be . . . on 't** do not confess knowledge of it **337
lose** (The Folio spelling, *loose*, is a normal spelling for "lose," but
it may also contain the idea of "let go," "release.") **342 conceits**
fancies, ideas **343 distaste** be distasteful **344 act** action, working **346 mandragora** an opiate made of the mandrake root **349
thou owedst** you did own

I slept the next night well, fed well, was free and
   merry;
I found not Cassio's kisses on her lips.
He that is robbed, not wanting what is stolen,
Let him not know 't and he's not robbed at all.

360 **IAGO:** I am sorry to hear this.

OTHELLO: I had been happy if the general camp,
Pioners and all, had tasted her sweet body,
So I had nothing known. O, now, forever
Farewell the tranquil mind! Farewell content!
365 Farewell the plumèd troops and the big wars
That makes ambition virtue! O, farewell!
Farewell the neighing steed and the shrill trump,
The spirit-stirring drum, th' ear-piercing fife,
The royal banner, and all quality,
370 Pride, pomp, and circumstance of glorious war!
And O, you mortal engines, whose rude throats
Th' immortal Jove's dread clamors counterfeit,
Farewell! Othello's occupation's gone.

IAGO: Is 't possible, my lord?

375 **OTHELLO:** Villain, be sure thou prove my love a
   whore!
Be sure of it. Give me the ocular proof,
Or, by the worth of mine eternal soul,
Thou hadst been better have been born a dog
Than answer my waked wrath!

IAGO: Is 't come to this?

380 **OTHELLO:** Make me to see 't, or at the least so prove it
That the probation bear no hinge nor loop
To hang a doubt on, or woe upon thy life!

IAGO: My noble lord—

OTHELLO: If thou dost slander her and torture me,
385 Never pray more; abandon all remorse;
On horror's head horrors accumulate;
Do deeds to make heaven weep, all earth amazed;
For nothing canst thou to damnation add
Greater than that.

IAGO: O grace! O heaven forgive me!
390 Are you a man? Have you a soul or sense?

God b' wi' you; take mine office. O wretched fool,
That lov'st to make thine honesty a vice!
O monstrous world! Take note, take note, O world,
To be direct and honest is not safe.
I thank you for this profit, and from hence   395
I'll love no friend, sith love breeds such offense.

OTHELLO: Nay, stay. Thou shouldst be honest.

IAGO: I should be wise, for honesty's a fool
And loses that it works for.

OTHELLO: By the world,
I think my wife be honest and think she is not;   400
I think that thou art just and think thou art not.
I'll have some proof. My name, that was as fresh
As Dian's visage, is now begrimed and black
As mine own face. If there be cords, or knives,
Poison, or fire, or suffocating streams,   405
I'll not endure it. Would I were satisfied!

IAGO: I see, sir, you are eaten up with passion.
I do repent me that I put it to you.
You would be satisfied?

OTHELLO: Would? Nay, and I will.

IAGO: And may; but how? How satisfied, my lord?   410
Would you, the supervisor, grossly gape on?
Behold her topped?

OTHELLO: Death and damnation! O!

IAGO: It were a tedious difficulty, I think,
To bring them to that prospect. Damn them then,
If ever mortal eyes do see them bolster   415
More than their own. What then? How then?
What shall I say? Where's satisfaction?
It is impossible you should see this,
Were they as prime as goats, as hot as monkeys,
As salt as wolves in pride, and fools as gross   420
As ignorance made drunk. But yet I say,
If imputation and strong circumstances
Which lead directly to the door of truth
Will give you satisfaction, you might have 't.

---

391 O wretched fool (Iago addresses himself as a fool for having carried honesty too far.) **392 vice** failing, something overdone **395 profit** profitable instruction. **hence** henceforth **396 sith** since. **offense** i.e., harm to the one who offers help and friendship **397 Thou shouldst be** it appears that you are. (But Iago replies in the sense of "ought to be.") **399 that** what **403 Dian** Diana, goddess of the moon and of chastity **411 supervisor** onlooker **414 Damn them then** i.e., they would have to be really incorrigible **415 bolster** go to bed together, share a bolster **416 More** other. **own** own eyes **419 prime** lustful **420 salt** wanton, sensual. **pride** heat **422 imputation . . . circumstances** strong circumstantial evidence

---

356 free carefree **358 wanting** missing **362 Pioners** diggers of mines, the lowest grade of soldiers **363 So** provided **365 big** stately **369 quality** character, essential nature **370 Pride** rich display. **circumstance** pageantry **371 mortal engines** i.e., cannon. (*Mortal* means "deadly.") **372 Jove's dread clamors** i.e., thunder **381 probation** proof **385 remorse** pity, penitent hope for salvation **386 horrors accumulate** add still more horrors **387 amazed** confounded with horror

Othello, enraged by jealousy, seeks Iago's counsel.

425 **OTHELLO:** Give me a living reason she's disloyal.

IAGO: I do not like the office.
But sith I am entered in this cause so far,
Pricked to 't by foolish honesty and love,
I will go on. I lay with Cassio lately,
430 And being troubled with a raging tooth
I could not sleep. There are a kind of men
So loose of soul that in their sleeps will mutter
Their affairs. One of this kind is Cassio.
In sleep I heard him say, "Sweet Desdemona,
435 Let us be wary, let us hide our loves!"
And then, sir, would he grip and wring my hand,
Cry "O sweet creature!", then kiss me hard,
As if he plucked up kisses by the roots
That grew upon my lips; then laid his leg
440 Over my thigh, and sighed, and kissed, and then
Cried, "Cursèd fate that gave thee to the Moor!"

OTHELLO: O monstrous! Monstrous!

IAGO: Nay, this was but his dream.

OTHELLO: But this denoted a foregone conclusion.
'Tis a shrewd doubt, though it be but a dream.

445 **IAGO:** And this may help to thicken other proofs
That do demonstrate thinly.

OTHELLO: I'll tear her all to pieces.

IAGO: Nay, but be wise. Yet we see nothing done;
She may be honest yet. Tell me but this:
Have you not sometimes seen a handkerchief
450 Spotted with strawberries in your wife's hand?

---

427 **sith** since   428 **Pricked** spurred   443 **foregone conclusion** concluded experience or action   444 **shrewd doubt** suspicious circumstance   450 **Spotted with strawberries** embroidered with a strawberry pattern

OTHELLO: I gave her such a one. 'Twas my first gift.

IAGO: I know not that; but such a handkerchief—
I am sure it was your wife's—did I today
See Cassio wipe his beard with.

OTHELLO: If it be that—

IAGO: If it be that, or any that was hers, 455
It speaks against her with the other proofs.

OTHELLO: O, that the slave had forty thousand lives!
One is too poor, too weak for my revenge.
Now do I see 'tis true. Look here, Iago,
All my fond love thus do I blow to heaven. 460
'Tis gone.
Arise, black vengeance, from the hollow hell!
Yield up, O love, thy crown and hearted throne
To tyrannous hate! Swell, bosom, with thy freight,
For 'tis of aspics' tongues! 465

IAGO: Yet be content.

OTHELLO: O, blood, blood, blood!

IAGO: Patience, I say. Your mind perhaps may change.

OTHELLO: Never, Iago. Like to the Pontic Sea,
Whose icy current and compulsive course 470
Ne'er feels retiring ebb, but keeps due on
To the Propontic and the Hellespont,
Even so my bloody thoughts with violent pace
Shall ne'er look back, ne'er ebb to humble love,
Till that a capable and wide revenge 475
Swallow them up. Now, by yond marble heaven,
[Kneeling] In the due reverence of a sacred vow
I here engage my words.

IAGO: Do not rise yet.
[He kneels.] Witness, you ever-burning lights above,
You elements that clip us round about, 480
Witness that here Iago doth give up
The execution of his wit, hands, heart,
To wronged Othello's service. Let him command,
And to obey shall be in me remorse,
What bloody business ever. *[They rise.]* 485

---

457 **the slave** i.e., Cassio   460 **fond** foolish (but also suggesting "affectionate")   463 **hearted** fixed in the heart   464 **freight** burden   465 **aspics'** venomous serpents'   466 **content** calm   469 **Pontic Sea** Black Sea   472 **Propontic** Sea of Marmora, between the Black Sea and the Aegean.   **Hellespont** Dardanelles, straits where the Sea of Marmora joins with the Aegean   475 **capable** ample, comprehensive   476 **marble** i.e., gleaming like marble and unrelenting   479 **s.d. He kneels** (In the Quarto text, Iago kneels here after Othello has knelt at line 477.)   480 **clip** encompass   482 **execution** exercise, action.   **wit** mind   484 **remorse** pity (for Othello's wrongs)   485 **ever** soever

OTHELLO: I greet thy love,
Not with vain thanks, but with acceptance
bounteous,
And will upon the instant put thee to 't.
Within these three days let me hear thee say
That Cassio's not alive.

IAGO: My friend is dead;
490 'Tis done at your request. But let her live.

OTHELLO: Damn her, lewd minx! O, damn her,
damn her!
Come, go with me apart. I will withdraw
To furnish me with some swift means of death
For the fair devil. Now art thou my lieutenant.

495 **IAGO:** I am your own forever. *Exeunt.*

3.4 *Enter* DESDEMONA, EMILIA, *and* CLOWN.

DESDEMONA: Do you know, sirrah, where Lieutenant
Cassio lies?

CLOWN: I dare not say he lies anywhere.

DESDEMONA: Why, man?

5 **CLOWN:** He's a soldier, and for me to say a soldier lies,
'tis stabbing.

DESDEMONA: Go to. Where lodges he?

CLOWN: To tell you where he lodges is to tell you where
I lie.

10 **DESDEMONA:** Can anything be made of this?

CLOWN: I know not where he lodges, and for me to
devise a lodging and say he lies here, or he lies there,
were to lie in mine own throat.

DESDEMONA: Can you inquire him out, and be edified
15 by report?

CLOWN: I will catechize the world for him; that is,
make questions, and by them answer.

DESDEMONA: Seek him, bid him come hither. Tell him
I have moved my lord on his behalf and hope all will
20 be well

CLOWN: To do this is within the compass of man's wit,
and therefore I will attempt the doing it. *Exit* CLOWN.

---

487 **to 't** to the proof   491 **minx** wanton

3.4 Location: Before the citadel.
1 **sirrah** (A form of address to an inferior.)   2 **lies** lodges. (But the
Clown makes the obvious pun.)   13 **lie . . . throat** (1) lie egregiously
and deliberately (2) use the windpipe to speak a lie   19 **moved**
petitioned

DESDEMONA: Where should I lose that handkerchief,
Emilia?

EMILIA: I know not, madam.

DESDEMONA: Believe me, I had rather have lost my
purse   25
Full of crusadoes; and but my noble Moor
Is true of mind and made of no such baseness
As jealous creatures are, it were enough
To put him to ill thinking.

EMILIA: Is he not jealous?

DESDEMONA: Who, he? I think the sun where he
was born   30
Drew all such humors from him.

EMILIA Look where he comes.

Enter OTHELLO.

DESDEMONA: I will not leave him now till Cassio
Be called to him.—How is 't with you, my lord?

OTHELLO: Well, my good lady. *[Aside.]* O, hardness to
dissemble!—
How do you, Desdemona?

DESDEMONA: Well, my good lord.   35

OTHELLO: Give me your hand. *[She gives her hand.]* This
hand is moist, my lady.

DESDEMONA: It yet hath felt no age nor known no
sorrow.

OTHELLO: This argues fruitfulness and liberal heart.
Hot, hot, and moist. This hand of yours requires
A sequester from liberty, fasting and prayer,   40
Much castigation, exercise devout;
For here's a young and sweating devil here
That commonly rebels. 'Tis a good hand,
A frank one.

DESDEMONA: You may indeed say so,
For 'twas that hand that gave away my heart.   45

OTHELLO: A liberal hand. The hearts of old gave hands,
But our new heraldry is hands, not hearts.

---

26 **crusadoes** Portuguese gold coins   31 **humors** (Refers to the
four bodily fluids thought to determine temperament.)   38 **argues**
gives evidence of.   **fruitfulness** generosity, amorousness, and fe-
cundity.   **liberal** generous and sexually free   40 **sequester** separation, sequestration   41 **castigation** corrective discipline.
exercise devout i.e., prayer, religious meditation, etc.   44 **frank**
generous, open (with sexual suggestion)   46 **The hearts . . . hands**
i.e., in former times, people would give their hearts when they gave
their hands to something   47 **But . . . hearts** i.e., in our decadent
times, the joining of hands is no longer a badge to signify the giving
of hearts

DESDEMONA: I cannot speak of this. Come now, your
promise.

OTHELLO: What promise, chuck?

50 **DESDEMONA:** I have sent to bid Cassio come speak
with you.

OTHELLO: I have a salt and sorry rheum offends me;
Lend me thy handkerchief.

DESDEMONA: Here, my lord. *[She offers a handkerchief.]*

OTHELLO: That which I gave you.

DESDEMONA: I have it not about me.

55 **OTHELLO:** Not?

DESDEMONA: No, faith, my lord.

OTHELLO: That's a fault. That handkerchief
Did an Egyptian to my mother give.
She was a charmer, and could almost read
60 The thoughts of people. She told her, while she
kept it
'Twould make her amiable and subdue my father
Entirely to her love, but if she lost it
Or made a gift of it, my father's eye
Should hold her loathèd and his spirits should hunt
65 After new fancies. She, dying, gave it me,
And bid me, when my fate would have me wived,
To give it her. I did so; and take heed on 't;
Make it a darling like your precious eye.
To lose 't or give 't away were such perdition
70 As nothing else could match.

DESDEMONA: Is 't possible?

OTHELLO: 'Tis true. There's magic in the web of it.
A sibyl, that had numbered in the world
The sun to course two hundred compasses,
In her prophetic fury sewed the work;
75 The worms were hallowed that did breed the silk,
And it was dyed in mummy which the skillful
Conserved of maidens' hearts.

DESDEMONA: I' faith! Is 't true?

OTHELLO: Most veritable. Therefore look to 't well.

DESDEMONA: Then would to God that I had never
seen 't!

OTHELLO: Ha? Wherefore? 80

DESDEMONA: Why do you speak so startingly and
rash?

OTHELLO: Is 't lost? Is 't gone? Speak, is 't out o' the
way?

DESDEMONA: Heaven bless us!

OTHELLO: Say you?

DESDEMONA: It is not lost; but what an if it were? 85

OTHELLO: How?

DESDEMONA: I say it is not lost.

OTHELLO: Fetch 't, let me see 't.

DESDEMONA: Why, so I can, sir, but I will not now.
This is a trick to put me from my suit.
Pray you, let Cassio be received again. 90

OTHELLO: Fetch me the handkerchief! My mind
misgives.

DESDEMONA: Come, come,
You'll never meet a more sufficient man.

OTHELLO: The handkerchief!

DESDEMONA: I pray, talk me of Cassio.

OTHELLO: The handkerchief!

DESDEMONA: A man that all his time 95
Hath founded his good fortunes on your love,
Shared dangers with you—

OTHELLO: The handkerchief!

DESDEMONA: I' faith, you are to blame.

OTHELLO: Zounds! *Exit* OTHELLO. 100

EMILIA: Is not this man jealous?

DESDEMONA: I ne'er saw this before.
Sure, there's some wonder in this handkerchief.
I am most unhappy in the loss of it.

EMILIA: 'Tis not a year or two shows us a man. 105
They are all but stomachs, and we all but food;

---

49 **chuck** (A term of endearment.) 51 **salt . . . rheum** distressful
head cold or watering of the eyes 59 **charmer** sorceress 61 **amiable** desirable 65 **fancies** loves 67 **her** i.e., to my wife 69 **perdition** loss 71 **web** fabric, weaving 73 **compasses** annual circlings.
(The *sibyl*, or prophetess, was two hundred years old.) 74 **prophetic fury** frenzy of prophetic inspiration. **work** embroidered pattern 76 **mummy** medicinal or magical preparation drained from
mummified bodies 77 **Conserved of** prepared or preserved out of

---

81 **startingly and rash** disjointedly and impetuously, excitedly
82 **out of the way** lost, misplaced 85 **an if** if 93 **sufficient** able,
complete 94 **talk** talk to 95 **all his time** throughout his career
105 **'Tis . . . man** i.e., you can't really know a man even in a year or
two of experience (?), or, real men come along seldom (?) 106 **but**
nothing but

Othello asks Desdemona for the handkerchief he gave her.

They eat us hungerly, and when they are full
They belch us.

Enter IAGO *and* CASSIO.

Look you, Cassio and my husband.

IAGO [*to* CASSIO]:   There is no other way; 'tis she must
do 't.
110   And, lo, the happiness! Go and importune her.

DESDEMONA: How now, good Cassio? What's the
news with you?

CASSIO: Madam, my former suit. I do beseech you
That by your virtuous means I may again
Exist and be a member of his love
115   Whom I, with all the office of my heart,
Entirely honor. I would not be delayed.
If my offense be of such mortal kind
That nor my service past, nor present sorrows,
Nor purposed merit in futurity
120   Can ransom me into his love again,
But to know so must be my benefit;
So shall I clothe me in a forced content,
And shut myself up in some other course,
To fortune's alms.

DESDEMONA: Alas, thrice-gentle Cassio,
125   My advocation is not now in tune.
My lord is not my lord; nor should I know him,
Were he in favor as in humor altered.
So help me every spirit sanctified

As I have spoken for you all my best
And stood within the blank of his displeasure   130
For my free speech! You must awhile be patient.
What I can do I will, and more I will
Than for myself I dare. Let that suffice you.

IAGO: Is my lord angry?

EMILIA: He went hence but now,
And certainly in strange unquietness.   135

IAGO: Can he be angry? I have seen the cannon
When it hath blown his ranks into the air,
And like the devil from his very arm
Puffed his own brother—and is he angry?
Something of moment then. I will go meet him.   140
There's matter in 't indeed, if he be angry.

DESDEMONA: I prithee, do so.   *Exit* [IAGO].
                Something, sure, of state,
Either from Venice, or some unhatched practice
Made demonstrable here in Cyprus to him,
Hath puddled his clear spirit; and in such cases   145
Men's natures wrangle with inferior things,
Though great ones are their object. 'Tis even so;
For let our finger ache, and it indues
Our other, healthful members even to a sense
Of pain. Nay, we must think men are not gods,   150
Nor of them look for such observancy
As fits the bridal. Beshrew me much, Emilia,
I was, unhandsome warrior as I am,
Arraigning his unkindness with my soul;
But now I find I had suborned the witness,   155
And he's indicted falsely.

EMILIA: Pray heaven it be
State matters, as you think, and no conception
Nor no jealous toy concerning you.

DESDEMONA: Alas the day! I never gave him cause.

EMILIA: But jealous souls will not be answered so;   160
They are not ever jealous for the cause,
But jealous for they're jealous. It is a monster
Begot upon itself, born on itself.

---

107 hungerly hungrily   **110 the happiness** in happy time, fortunately met   **113 virtuous** efficacious   **115 office** loyal service   **117 mortal** fatal   **118 nor . . . nor** neither . . . nor   **121 But . . . benefit** merely to know that my case is hopeless will have to content me (and will be better than uncertainty)   **123 shut . . . in** confine myself to   **124 To fortune's alms** throwing myself on the mercy of fortune   **125 advocation** advocacy   **127 favor** appearance. **humor** mood

---

130 within the blank within point-blank range. (The *blank* is the center of the target.)   **140 of moment** of immediate importance, momentous   **142 of state** concerning state affairs   **143 unhatched practice** as yet unexecuted or undiscovered plot   **145 puddled** muddied   **148 indues** brings to the same condition   **151 observancy** attentiveness   **152 bridal** wedding (when a bridegroom is newly attentive to his bride). **Beshrew me** (A mild oath.)   **153 unhandsome** insufficient, unskillful   **154 with** before the bar of   **155 suborned the witness** induced the witness to give false testimony   **158 toy** fancy   **162 for** because   **163 Begot upon itself** generated solely from itself

DESDEMONA: Heaven keep that monster from Othello's mind!

165 **EMILIA:** Lady, amen.

DESDEMONA: I will go seek him. Cassio, walk hereabout.
If I do find him fit, I'll move your suit
And seek to effect it to my uttermost.

CASSIO: I humbly thank your ladyship.

*Exit [*DESDEMONA *with* EMILIA*].*

Enter BIANCA.

170 **BIANCA:** Save you, friend Cassio!

CASSIO: What make you from home?
How is 't with you, my most fair Bianca?
I' faith, sweet love, I was coming to your house.

BIANCA: And I was going to your lodging, Cassio.
What, keep a week away? Seven days and nights?
175 Eightscore-eight hours? And lovers' absent hours
More tedious than the dial eightscore times?
O weary reckoning!

CASSIO: Pardon me, Bianca.
I have this while with leaden thoughts been pressed;
But I shall, in a more continuate time,
180 Strike off this score of absence. Sweet Bianca,

[giving her DESDEMONA's *handkerchief]*

Take me this work out.

BIANCA: O Cassio, whence came this?
This is some token from a newer friend.
To the felt absence now I feel a cause.
Is 't come to this? Well, well.

CASSIO: Go to, woman!
185 Throw your vile guesses in the devil's teeth,
From whence you have them. You are jealous now
That this is from some mistress, some remembrance.
No, by my faith, Bianca.

BIANCA: Why, whose is it?

CASSIO: I know not, neither. I found it in my chamber.
190 I like the work well. Ere it be demanded—
As like enough it will—I would have it copied.
Take it and do 't, and leave me for this time.

Cassio gives Bianca (Zawe Ashton) the handkerchief he found in his room.

BIANCA: Leave you? Wherefore?

CASSIO: I do attend here on the General,
And think it no addition, nor my wish,   195
To have him see me womaned.

BIANCA: Why, I pray you?

CASSIO: Not that I love you not.

BIANCA: But that you do not love me.
I pray you, bring me on the way a little,   200
And say if I shall see you soon at night.

CASSIO: 'Tis but a little way that I can bring you,
For I attend here; but I'll see you soon.

BIANCA: 'Tis very good. I must be circumstanced.

Exeunt omnes.

4.1 *Enter* OTHELLO *and* IAGO.

IAGO: Will you think so?

OTHELLO: Think so, Iago?

IAGO: What,
To kiss in private?

OTHELLO: An unauthorized kiss!

IAGO: Or to be naked with her friend in bed
An hour or more, not meaning any harm?

---

170 **Save** God save. **make** do   175 **Eightscore-eight** one hundred sixty-eight, the number of hours in a week   176 **the dial** a complete revolution of the clock   179 **continuate** uninterrupted   180 **Strike . . . score** settle this account   181 **Take . . . out** copy this embroidery for me   182 **friend** mistress   190 **demanded** inquired for   191 **like** likely

195 **addition** i.e., addition to my reputation   200 **bring** accompany   204 **be circumstanced** be governed by circumstance, yield to your conditions

4.1 Location: Before the citadel.

5   **OTHELLO:**   Naked in bed, Iago, and not mean harm?
     It is hypocrisy against the devil.
     They that mean virtuously and yet do so,
     The devil their virtue tempts, and they tempt
     heaven.

    IAGO: If they do nothing, 'tis a venial slip.
10   But if I give my wife a handkerchief—

    OTHELLO: What then?

    IAGO: Why then, 'tis hers, my lord, and being hers,
    She may, I think, bestow 't on any man.

    OTHELLO: She is protectress of her honor too.
15   May she give that?

    IAGO: Her honor is an essence that's not seen;
    They have it very oft that have it not.
    But, for the handkerchief—

    OTHELLO: By heaven, I would most gladly have
     forgot it.
20   Thou saidst—O, it comes o'er my memory
    As doth the raven o'er the infectious house,
    Boding to all—he had my handkerchief.

    IAGO: Ay, what of that?

    OTHELLO: That's not so good now.

    IAGO: What
    If I had said I had seen him do you wrong?
25   Or heard him say—as knaves be such abroad,
    Who having, by their own importunate suit,
    Or voluntary dotage of some mistress,
    Convincèd or supplied them, cannot choose
    But they must blab—

    OTHELLO: Hath he said anything?

30 **IAGO:**   He hath, my lord; but, be you well assured,
    No more than he'll unswear.

    OTHELLO: What hath he said?

    IAGO: Faith, that he did—I know not what he did.

    OTHELLO: What? What?

    IAGO: Lie—

    OTHELLO: With her?

    IAGO: With her, on her; what you will.

OTHELLO: Lie with her? Lie on her? We say "lie on 35
her" when they belie her. Lie with her? Zounds, that's
fulsome.—Handkerchief—confessions—handkerchief!—To confess and be hanged for his labor—first
to be hanged and then to confess.—I tremble at it.
Nature would not invest herself in such shadowing 40
passion without some instruction. It is not words
that shakes me thus. Pish! Noses, ears, and lips.—
Is 't possible?—Confess—handkerchief!—O devil!

                  Falls in a trance.

IAGO: Work on,
    My medicine, work! Thus credulous fools are caught, 45
    And many worthy and chaste dames even thus,
    All guiltless, meet reproach.—What, ho! My lord!
    My lord, I say! Othello!

              Enter CASSIO.

      How now, Cassio?

CASSIO: What's the matter?

IAGO: My lord is fall'n into an epilepsy. 50
    This is his second fit. He had one yesterday.

CASSIO: Rub him about the temples.

IAGO: No, forbear.
    The lethargy must have his quiet course.
    If not, he foams at mouth, and by and by
    Breaks out to savage madness. Look, he stirs. 55
    Do you withdraw yourself a little while.
    He will recover straight. When he is gone,
    I would on great occasion speak with you.

             [Exit CASSIO.]
    How is it, General? Have you not hurt your head?

OTHELLO: Dost thou mock me?

IAGO: I mock you not, by heaven. 60
    Would you would bear your fortune like a man!

OTHELLO: A hornèd man's a monster and a beast.

IAGO: There's many a beast then in a populous city,
    And many a civil monster.

---

9 venial pardonable   **17 They have it** i.e., they enjoy a reputation for it   **21 raven . . . house** (Allusion to the belief that the raven hovered over a house of sickness or infection, such as one visited by the plague.)   **25 abroad** around about   **27 voluntary dotage** willing infatuation   **28 Convincèd or supplied** seduced or sexually gratified

36 belie slander   **37 fulsome** foul   **38–39 first . . . to confess** (Othello reverses the proverbial *confess and be hanged;* Cassio is to be given no time to confess before he dies.)   **40–41 Nature . . . instruction** i.e., without some foundation in fact, nature would not have dressed herself in such an overwhelming passion that comes over me now and fills my mind with images, or in such a lifelike fantasy as Cassio had in his dreams of lying with Desdemona   **41 words** mere words   **53 lethargy** coma.   **his** its   **58 on great occasion** on a matter of great importance   **60 mock me** (Othello takes Iago's question about hurting his head to be a mocking reference to the cuckold's horns.)   **64 civil** i.e., dwelling in a city

65 **OTHELLO:** Did he confess it?

IAGO: Good sir, be a man.
Think every bearded fellow that's but yoked
May draw with you. There's millions now alive
That nightly lie in those unproper beds
70 Which they dare swear peculiar. Your case is better.
O, 'tis the spite of hell, the fiend's arch-mock,
To lip a wanton in a secure couch
And to suppose her chaste! No, let me know,
And knowing what I am, I know what she shall be.

75 **OTHELLO:** O, thou art wise. 'Tis certain.

IAGO: Stand you awhile apart;
Confine yourself but in a patient list.
Whilst you were here o'erwhelmèd with your grief—
A passion most unsuiting such a man—
80 Cassio came hither. I shifted him away,
And laid good 'scuse upon your ecstasy,
Bade him anon return and here speak with me,
The which he promised. Do but encave yourself
And mark the fleers, the gibes, and notable scorns
85 That dwell in every region of his face;
For I will make him tell the tale anew,
Where, how, how oft, how long ago, and when
He hath and is again to cope your wife.
I say, but mark his gesture. Marry, patience!
90 Or I shall say you're all-in-all in spleen,
And nothing of a man.

OTHELLO: Dost thou hear, Iago?
I will be found most cunning in my patience;
But—dost thou hear?—most bloody.

IAGO: That's not amiss;
But yet keep time in all. Will you withdraw?
[OTHELLO stands apart.]
95 Now will I question Cassio of Bianca,
A huswife that by selling her desires
Buys herself bread and clothes. It is a creature
That dotes on Cassio—as 'tis the strumpet's plague
To beguile many and be beguiled by one.

---

67 yoked (1) married (2) put into the yoke of infamy and cuckoldry
68 draw with you pull as you do, like oxen who are yoked, i.e.,
share your fate as cuckold   **69 unproper** not exclusively their own
70 peculiar private, their own.   **better** i.e., because you know
the truth   **72 lip** kiss.   **secure** free from suspicion   **74 what
I am** i.e., a cuckold.   **she shall be** will happen to her   **77 in . . .
list** within the bounds of patience   **80 shifted him away** used a
dodge to get rid of him   **81 ecstasy** trance   **83 encave** conceal
84 fleers sneers.   **notable** obvious   **88 cope** encounter with, have
sex with   **90 all-in-all in spleen** utterly governed by passionate
impulses   **94 keep time** keep yourself steady (as in music)
96 huswife hussy

He, when he hears of her, cannot restrain 100
From the excess of laughter. Here he comes.

Enter CASSIO.

As he shall smile, Othello shall go mad;
And his unbookish jealousy must conster
Poor Cassio's smiles, gestures, and light behaviors
Quite in the wrong.—How do you now, Lieutenant? 105

CASSIO: The worser that you give me the addition
Whose want even kills me.

IAGO: Ply Desdemona well and you are sure on 't.
[Speaking lower.] Now, if this suit lay in Bianca's
power,
How quickly should you speed! 110

CASSIO *[laughing]:* Alas, poor caitiff!

OTHELLO *[aside]:* Look how he laughs already!

IAGO: I never knew a woman love man so.

CASSIO: Alas, poor rogue! I think, i' faith, she loves me.

OTHELLO: Now he denies it faintly, and laughs it out. 115

IAGO: Do you hear, Cassio?

OTHELLO: Now he importunes him
To tell it o'er. Go to! Well said, well said.

IAGO: She gives it out that you shall marry her.
Do you intend it?

CASSIO: Ha, ha, ha! 120

OTHELLO: Do you triumph, Roman? Do you triumph?

CASSIO: I marry her? What? A customer? Prithee, bear
some charity to my wit; do not think it so unwholesome. Ha, ha, ha!

OTHELLO: So, so, so, so! They laugh that win. 125

IAGO: Faith, the cry goes that you shall marry her.

CASSIO: Prithee, say true.

IAGO: I am a very villain else.

OTHELLO: Have you scored me? Well.

---

100 restrain refrain   **103 unbookish** uninstructed.   **conster**
construe   **106 addition** title   **107 Whose want** the lack of which
111 caitiff wretch   **117 Go to** (An expression of remonstrance.)
Well said well done   **121 Roman** (The Romans were noted for
their *triumphs* or triumphal processions.)   **122 customer** i.e.,
prostitute   **122–123 bear . . . wit** be more charitable to my judgment   **125 They . . . win** i.e., they that laugh last laugh best   **126
cry** rumor   **128 I . . . else** call me a complete rogue if I'm not telling
the truth   **129 scored me** scored off me, beaten me, made up my
reckoning, branded me

130 **CASSIO:** This is the monkey's own giving out. She is persuaded I will marry her out of her own love and flattery, not out of my promise.

OTHELLO: Iago beckons me. Now he begins the story.

CASSIO: She was here even now; she haunts me in every
135 place. I was the other day talking on the seabank with certain Venetians, and thither comes the bauble, and, by this hand, she falls me thus about my neck—
[He embraces IAGO.]

OTHELLO: Crying, "O dear Cassio!" as it were; his gesture imports it.

140 **CASSIO:** So hangs and lolls and weeps upon me, so shakes and pulls me. Ha, ha, ha!

OTHELLO: Now he tells how she plucked him to my chamber. O, I see that nose of yours, but not that dog I shall throw it to.

145 **CASSIO:** Well, I must leave her company.

IAGO: Before me, look where she comes.

Enter BIANCA [with OTHELLO's handkerchief].

CASSIO: 'Tis such another fitchew! Marry, a perfumed one.—What do you mean by this haunting of me?

BIANCA: Let the devil and his dam haunt you! What
150 did you mean by that same handkerchief you gave me even now? I was a fine fool to take it. I must take out the work? A likely piece of work, that you should find it in your chamber and know not who left it there! This is some minx's token, and I must take out
155 the work? There, give it your hobbyhorse. *[She gives him the handkerchief.]* Wheresoever you had it, I'll take out no work on 't.

CASSIO: How now, my sweet Bianca? How now? How now?

OTHELLO: By heaven, that should be my handkerchief!

160 **BIANCA:** If you'll come to supper tonight, you may; if you will not, come when you are next prepared for.
Exit.

---

132 **flattery** self-flattery, self-deception   133 **beckons** signals
135 **seabank** seashore   136 **bauble** plaything   137 **by this hand**
I make my vow   143–144 **not . . . to** (Othello imagines himself
cutting off Cassio's nose and throwing it to a dog.)   146 **Before me**
i.e., on my soul   147 **'Tis . . . fitchew** what a polecat she is! Just like
all the others.   **fitchew** (Polecats were often compared with prostitutes because of their rank smell and presumed lechery.)   149
dam mother   152 **A likely . . . work** a fine story   155 **hobbyhorse**
harlot   159 **should be** must be   161 **when . . . for** when I'm ready
for you (i.e., never)

Bianca enters with the handkerchief.

IAGO: After her, after her.

CASSIO: Faith, I must. She'll rail in the streets else.

IAGO: Will you sup there?

CASSIO: Faith, I intend so. 165

IAGO: Well, I may chance to see you, for I would very fain speak with you.

CASSIO: Prithee, come. Will you?

IAGO: Go to. Say no more. *[Exit CASSIO.]*

OTHELLO *[advancing]*: How shall I murder him, Iago? 170

IAGO: Did you perceive how he laughed at his vice?

OTHELLO: O, Iago!

IAGO: And did you see the handkerchief?

OTHELLO: Was that mine?

IAGO: Yours, by this hand. And to see how he prizes 175
the foolish woman your wife! She gave it him, and he
hath given it his whore.

OTHELLO: I would have him nine years a-killing. A
fine woman! A fair woman! A sweet woman!

IAGO: Nay, you must forget that. 180

OTHELLO: Ay, let her rot and perish, and be damned
tonight, for she shall not live. No, my heart is turned
to stone; I strike it, and it hurts my hand. O, the
world hath not a sweeter creature! She might lie by
an emperor's side and command him tasks. 185

---

169 **Go to** (An expression of remonstrance.)

IAGO: Nay, that's not your way.

OTHELLO: Hang her! I do but say what she is. So delicate with her needle! An admirable musician! O, she will sing the savageness out of a bear. Of so high and plenteous wit and invention!

190

IAGO: She's the worse for all this.

OTHELLO: O, a thousand, a thousand times! And then, of so gentle a condition!

OTHELLO: Ay, too gentle.

195 **OTHELLO:** Nay, that's certain. But yet the pity of it, Iago! O, Iago, the pity of it, Iago!

IAGO: If you are so fond over her iniquity, give her patent to offend, for if it touch not you it comes near nobody.

OTHELLO: I will chop her into messes. Cuckold me?

200 **IAGO:** O, 'tis foul in her.

OTHELLO: With mine officer?

IAGO: That's fouler.

OTHELLO: Get me some poison, Iago, this night. I'll not expostulate with her, lest her body and beauty unprovide my mind again. This night, Iago.

205

IAGO: Do it not with poison. Strangle her in her bed, even the bed she hath contaminated.

OTHELLO: Good, good! The justice of it pleases. Very good.

IAGO: And for Cassio, let me be his undertaker. You shall hear more by midnight.

210

OTHELLO: Excellent good. *[A trumpet within.]* What trumpet is that same?

IAGO: I warrant, something from Venice.

Enter LODOVICO, DESDEMONA, and attendants.

'Tis Lodovico. This comes from the Duke.
See, your wife's with him.

215 **LODOVICO:** God save you, worthy General!

OTHELLO: With all my heart, sir.

LODOVICO *[giving him a letter]*: The Duke and the senators of Venice greet you.

OTHELLO: I kiss the instrument of their pleasures.
[He opens the letter, and reads.]

DESDEMONA: And what's the news, good cousin Lodovico?

IAGO: I am very glad to see you, signor. Welcome to Cyprus. 220

LODOVICO: I thank you. How does Lieutenant Cassio?

IAGO: Lives, sir.

DESDEMONA: Cousin, there's fall'n between him and my lord
An unkind breach; but you shall make all well.

OTHELLO: Are you sure of that? 225

DESDEMONA: My lord?

OTHELLO *[reads]*: "This fail you not to do, as you will—"

LODOVICO: He did not call; he's busy in the paper.
Is there division twixt my lord and Cassio?

DESDEMONA: A most unhappy one. I would do much 230
T' atone them, for the love I bear to Cassio.

OTHELLO: Fire and brimstone!

DESDEMONA: My lord?

OTHELLO: Are you wise?

DESDEMONA: What, is he angry?

LODOVICO: Maybe the letter moved him; 235
For, as I think, they do command him home,
Deputing Cassio in his government.

DESDEMONA: By my troth, I am glad on 't.

OTHELLO: Indeed?

DESDEMONA: My lord? 240

OTHELLO: I am glad to see you mad.

DESDEMONA: Why, sweet Othello—

OTHELLO *[striking her]*: Devil!

DESDEMONA: I have not deserved this.

---

186 your way i.e., the way you should think of her   **190 invention** imagination   **193 gentle a condition** wellborn and well-bred   **194 gentle** generous, yielding (to other men)   **197 fond** foolish. **patent** license   **199 messes** portions of meat, i.e., bits   **205 unprovide** weaken, render unfit   **209 be his undertaker** undertake to dispatch him   **215 With all my heart** i.e., I thank you most heartily

224 unkind unnatural, contrary to their natures; hurtful   **231 atone** reconcile   **237 government** office   **238 on 't** of it   **241 I am . . . mad** i.e., I am glad to see that you are insane enough to rejoice in Cassio's promotion (? Othello bitterly plays on Desdemona's *I am glad.*)

245 **LODOVICO:** My lord, this would not be believed in
Venice,
Though I should swear I saw 't. 'Tis very much.
Make her amends; she weeps.

OTHELLO: O devil, devil!
If that the earth could teem with woman's tears,
Each drop she falls would prove a crocodile.
250 Out of my sight!

DESDEMONA: I will not stay to offend you. *[Going.]*

LODOVICO: Truly, an obedient lady.
I do beseech your lordship, call her back.

OTHELLO: Mistress!

DESDEMONA *[returning]*: My lord?

255 **OTHELLO:** What would you with her, sir?

LODOVICO: Who, I, my lord?

OTHELLO: Ay, you did wish that I would make her
turn.
Sir, she can turn, and turn, and yet go on
And turn again; and she can weep, sir, weep;
260 And she's obedient, as you say, obedient,
Very obedient.—Proceed you in your tears.—
Concerning this, sir—O well-painted passion!—
I am commanded home.—Get you away;
I'll send for you anon.—Sir, I obey the mandate
265 And will return to Venice.—Hence, avaunt!
[Exit DESDEMONA.]
Cassio shall have my place. And, sir, tonight
I do entreat that we may sup together.
You are welcome, sir, to Cyprus.—Goats and
monkeys! *Exit.*

LODOVICO: Is this the noble Moor whom our full
Senate
270 Call all in all sufficient? Is this the nature
Whom passion could not shake? Whose solid virtue
The shot of accident nor dart of chance
Could neither graze nor pierce?

IAGO: He is much changed.

LODOVICO: Are his wits safe? Is he not light of brain?

Othello pumps Emilia (Lorraine Burroughs) for information regarding Desdemona's affair.

IAGO: He's that he is. I may not breathe my censure 275
What he might be. If what he might he is not,
I would to heaven he were!

LODOVICO: What, strike his wife?

IAGO: Faith, that was not so well; yet would I knew
That stroke would prove the worst!

LODOVICO: Is it his use?
Or did the letters work upon his blood 280
And new-create his fault?

IAGO: Alas, alas!
It is not honesty in me to speak
What I have seen and known. You shall observe him,
And his own courses will denote him so
That I may save my speech. Do but go after, 285
And mark how he continues.

LODOVICO: I am sorry that I am deceived in him.
Exeunt.

4.2 *Enter OTHELLO and EMILIA.*

OTHELLO: You have seen nothing then?

EMILIA: Nor ever heard, nor ever did suspect.

OTHELLO: Yes, you have seen Cassio and she together.

EMILIA: But then I saw no harm, and then I heard
Each syllable that breath made up between them. 5

---

246 **very much** too much, outrageous   248 **teem** breed, be impregnated   249 **falls** lets fall.   **crocodile** (Crocodiles were supposed to weep hypocritical tears for their victims.)   255 **What . . . sir** (Othello implies that Desdemona is pliant and will do a *turn*, lines 257–259, for any man.)   260 **obedient** (With much the same sexual connotation as *turn* in lines 257–259.)   262 **passion** i.e., grief   268 **Goats and monkeys** (See 3.3.419.)

275–277 **I may . . . were** i.e., I dare not venture an opinion as to whether he's of unsound mind, as you suggest, but, if he isn't, then it might be better to wish he were in fact insane, since only that could excuse his wild behavior   279 **use** custom   280 **blood** passions   284 **courses will denote** actions will reveal

4.2. Location: The citadel.

OTHELLO: What, did they never whisper?

EMILIA: Never, my lord.

OTHELLO: Nor send you out o' the way?

EMILIA: Never.

10 **OTHELLO:** To fetch her fan, her gloves, her mask, nor nothing?

EMILIA: Never, my lord.

OTHELLO: That's strange.

EMILIA: I durst, my lord, to wager she is honest,
Lay down my soul at stake. If you think other,
15 Remove your thought; it doth abuse your bosom.
If any wretch have put this in your head,
Let heaven requite it with the serpent's curse!
For if she be not honest, chaste, and true,
There's no man happy; the purest of their wives
20 Is foul as slander.

OTHELLO: Bid her come hither. Go.
Exit EMILIA.
She says enough; yet she's a simple bawd
That cannot say as much. This is a subtle whore,
A closet lock and key of villainous secrets.
And yet she'll kneel and pray; I have seen her do 't.

Enter DESDEMONA *and* EMILIA.

25 **DESDEMONA:** My lord, what is your will?

OTHELLO: Pray you, chuck, come hither.

DESDEMONA: What is your pleasure?

OTHELLO: Let me see your eyes.
Look in my face.

DESDEMONA: What horrible fancy's this?

OTHELLO *[to* EMILIA*]:* Some of your function, mistress.
30 Leave procreants alone and shut the door;
Cough or cry "hem" if anybody come.
Your mystery, your mystery! Nay, dispatch.
Exit EMILIA.

---

14 **at stake** as the wager 15 **abuse your bosom** deceive you 17 **the serpent's curse** the curse pronounced by God on the serpent for deceiving Eve, just as some man has done to Othello and Desdemona. (See Genesis 3:14.) 21–22 **she's . . . much** i.e., any procuress or go-between who couldn't make up as plausible a story as Emilia's would have to be pretty stupid 22 **This** i.e., Desdemona 23 **closet lock and key** i.e., concealer 29 **Some . . . function** i.e., practice your chosen profession, that of bawd (by guarding the door) 30 **procreants** mating couples 32 **mystery** trade, occupation

---

DESDEMONA *[kneeling]:* Upon my knees, what doth your speech import?
I understand a fury in your words,
But not the words. 35

OTHELLO: Why, what art thou?

DESDEMONA: Your wife, my lord, your true
And loyal wife.

OTHELLO: Come, swear it, damn thyself,
Lest, being like one of heaven, the devils themselves
Should fear to seize thee. Therefore be double damned:
Swear thou art honest.

DESDEMONA: Heaven doth truly know it. 40

OTHELLO: Heaven truly knows that thou art false as hell.

DESDEMONA: To whom, my lord? With whom? How am I false?

OTHELLO *[weeping]:* Ah, Desdemon! Away, away, away!

DESDEMONA: Alas the heavy day! Why do you weep?
Am I the motive of these tears, my lord? 45
If haply you my father do suspect
An instrument of this your calling back,
Lay not your blame on me. If you have lost him,
I have lost him too.

OTHELLO: Had it pleased heaven
To try me with affliction, had they rained 50
All kinds of sores and shames on my bare head,
Steeped me in poverty to the very lips,
Given to captivity me and my utmost hopes,
I should have found in some place of my soul
A drop of patience. But, alas, to make me 55
A fixèd figure for the time of scorn
To point his slow and moving finger at!
Yet could I bear that too, well, very well.
But there where I have garnered up my heart,
Where either I must live or bear no life, 60
The fountain from the which my current runs
Or else dries up—to be discarded thence!
Or keep it as a cistern for foul toads
To knot and gender in! Turn they complexion there,

---

38 **being . . . heaven** looking like an angel 45 **motive** cause 50 **they** i.e., heavenly powers 56 **time of scorn** i.e., scornful world 57 **his** its. **slow and moving finger** i.e., hour hand of the clock, moving so slowly it seems hardly to move at all. (Othello envisions himself as being eternally pointed at by the scornful world as the numbers on a clock are pointed at by the hour hand.) 59 **garnered** stored 61 **fountain** spring 63 **cistern** cesspool 64 **knot** couple. **gender** engender. **Turn . . . there** change your color, grow pale, at such a sight

Othello accuses Desdemona of being false.

65 Patience, thou young and rose-lipped cherubin—
Ay, there look grim as hell!

DESDEMONA: I hope my noble lord esteems me honest.

OTHELLO: O, ay, as summer flies are in the shambles,
That quicken even with blowing. O thou weed,
70 Who art so lovely fair and smell'st so sweet
That the sense aches at thee, would thou hadst ne'er
been born!

DESDEMONA: Alas, what ignorant sin have I
committed?

OTHELLO: Was this fair paper, this most goodly book,
Made to write "whore" upon? What committed?
75 Committed? O thou public commoner!
I should make very forges of my cheeks,
That would to cinders burn up modesty,
Did I but speak thy deeds. What committed?
Heaven stops the nose at it and the moon winks;
80 The bawdy wind, that kisses all it meets,
Is hushed within the hollow mine of earth
And will not hear 't. What committed?
Impudent strumpet!

DESDEMONA: By heaven, you do me wrong.

OTHELLO: Are not you a strumpet?

DESDEMONA: No, as I am a Christian.   85
If to preserve this vessel for my lord
From any other foul unlawful touch
Be not to be a strumpet, I am none.

OTHELLO: What, not a whore?

DESDEMONA: No, as I shall be saved.   90

OTHELLO: Is 't possible?

DESDEMONA: O, heaven forgive us!

OTHELLO: I cry you mercy, then.
I took you for that cunning whore of Venice
That married with Othello. *[Calling out.]* You, mistress,
That have the office opposite to Saint Peter   95
And keep the gate of hell!

Enter EMILIA.

You, you, ay, you!
We have done our course. There's money for your
pains.   *[He gives money.]*
I pray you, turn the key and keep our counsel. *Exit.*

EMILIA: Alas, what does this gentleman conceive?
How do you, madam? How do you, my good lady?   100

DESDEMONA: Faith, half asleep.

EMILIA: Good madam, what's the matter with my
lord?

DESDEMONA: With who?

EMILIA: Why, with my lord, madam.

DESDEMONA: Who is thy lord?

EMILIA: He that is yours, sweet lady. 105

DESDEMONA: I have none. Do not talk to me, Emilia.
I cannot weep, nor answers have I none
But what should go by water. Prithee, tonight
Lay on my bed my wedding sheets, remember;
And call thy husband hither.   110

EMILIA: Here's a change indeed!   *Exit.*

DESDEMONA: 'Tis meet I should be used so, very meet.
How have I been behaved, that he might stick
The small'st opinion on my least misuse?

Enter IAGO *and* EMILIA.

IAGO: What is your pleasure, madam? How is 't with
you?   115

65–66 Patience . . . hell (Even Patience, that rose-lipped cherub, will look grim and pale at this spectacle.) **67 honest** chaste **68 shambles** slaughterhouse **69 quicken** come to life. **with blowing** i.e., with the puffing up of something rotten in which maggots are breeding **72 ignorant sin** sin in ignorance **75 commoner** prostitute **79 winks** closes her eyes. (The moon symbolizes chastity.) **80 bawdy** kissing one and all **81 mine** cave (where the winds were thought to dwell)

86 vessel body **92 cry you mercy** beg your pardon **97 course** business (with an indecent suggestion of "trick," turn at sex) **99 conceive** suppose, think **101 half asleep** i.e., dazed **108 go by water** be expressed by tears **112 meet** fitting **113 stick** attach **114 opinion** censure. **least misuse** slightest misconduct

Desdemona seeks the advice of Iago and Emilia regarding Othello's accusations.

DESDEMONA: I cannot tell. Those that do teach young babes
Do it with gentle means and easy tasks.
He might have chid me so, for, in good faith,
I am a child to chiding.

120 **IAGO:**   What is the matter, lady?

EMILIA: Alas, Iago, my lord hath so bewhored her,
Thrown such despite and heavy terms upon her,
That true hearts cannot bear it.

DESDEMONA: Am I that name, Iago?

125 **IAGO:**   What name, fair lady?

DESDEMONA: Such as she said my lord did say I was.

EMILIA: He called her whore. A beggar in his drink
Could not have laid such terms upon his callet.

IAGO: Why did he so?

130 **DESDEMONA** *[weeping]*:   I do not know. I am sure I am none such.

IAGO: Do not weep, do not weep. Alas the day!

EMILIA: Hath she forsook so many noble matches,
Her father and her country and her friends,
To be called whore? Would it not make one weep?

135 **DESDEMONA:**   It is my wretched fortune.

IAGO: Beshrew him for 't!
How comes this trick upon him?

DESDEMONA: Nay, heaven doth know.

---

128 **callet** whore   135 **Beshrew** curse   136 **trick** strange behavior, delusion

EMILIA: I will be hanged if some eternal villain,
Some busy and insinuating rogue,
Some cogging, cozening slave, to get some office,
Have not devised this slander. I will be hanged else.   140

IAGO: Fie, there is no such man. It is impossible.

DESDEMONA: If any such there be, heaven pardon him!

EMILIA: A halter pardon him! And hell gnaw his bones!
Why should he call her whore? Who keeps her company?
What place? What time? What form? What likelihood?   145
The Moor's abused by some most villainous knave,
Some base notorious knave, some scurvy fellow.
O heaven, that such companions thou'dst unfold,
And put in every honest hand a whip
To lash the rascals naked through the world   150
Even from the east to th' west!

IAGO: Speak within door.

EMILIA: O, fie upon them! Some such squire he was
That turned your wit the seamy side without
And made you to suspect me with the Moor.

IAGO: You are a fool. Go to.

DESDEMONA: Alas, Iago,   155
What shall I do to win my lord again?
Good friend, go to him; for, by this light of heaven,
I know not how I lost him. Here I kneel.   *[She kneels.]*
If e'er my will did trespass 'gainst his love,
Either in discourse of thought or actual deed,   160
Or that mine eyes, mine ears, or any sense
Delighted them in any other form;
Or that I do not yet, and ever did,
And ever will—though he do shake me off
To beggarly divorcement—love him dearly,   165
Comfort forswear me! Unkindness may do much,
And his unkindness may defeat my life,
But never taint my love. I cannot say "whore."
It does abhor me now I speak the word;

---

137 **eternal** inveterate   138 **insinuating** ingratiating, fawning, wheedling   139 **cogging** cheating.   **cozening** defrauding   143 **halter** hangman's noose   145 **form** appearance, circumstance   148 **that** would that.   **companions** fellows.   **unfold** expose   151 **within door** i.e., not so loud   152 **squire** fellow   153 **seamy side without** wrong side out   155 **Go to** i.e., that's enough   160 **discourse of thought** process of thinking   161 **that** if. (Also in line 163.)   162 **Delighted them** took delight   163 **yet** still   166 **Comfort forswear** may heavenly comfort forsake   167 **defeat** destroy   169 **abhor** (1) fill me with abhorrence (2) make me whorelike

170 To do the act that might the addition earn
Not the world's mass of vanity could make me.

[She rises.]

IAGO: I pray you, be content. 'Tis but his humor.
The business of the state does him offense,
And he does chide with you.

175 DESDEMONA: If 'twere no other—

IAGO: It is but so, I warrant.   *[Trumpets within.]*
Hark, how these instruments summon you to
    supper!
The messengers of Venice stays the meat.
Go in, and weep not. All things shall be well.

Exeunt DESDEMONA *and* EMILIA.

Enter RODERIGO.

180 How now, Roderigo?

RODERIGO: I do not find that thou deal'st justly with
me.

IAGO: What in the contrary?

RODERIGO: Every day thou daff'st me with some device, Iago, and rather, as it seems to me now, keep'st
185 from me all conveniency than suppliest me with
the least advantage of hope. I will indeed no longer
endure it, nor am I yet persuaded to put up in peace
what already I have foolishly suffered.

IAGO: Will you hear me, Roderigo?

190 RODERIGO: Faith, I have heard too much, for your
words and performances are no kin together.

IAGO: You charge me most unjustly.

RODERIGO: With naught but truth. I have wasted myself out of my means. The jewels you have had from
195 me to deliver Desdemona would half have corrupted
a votarist. You have told me she hath received them
and returned me expectations and comforts of sudden respect and acquaintance, but I find none.

IAGO: Well, go to, very well.

200 RODERIGO: "Very well"! "Go to"! I cannot go to, man,
nor 'tis not very well. By this hand, I think it is scurvy,
and begin to find myself fopped in it.

IAGO: Very well.

RODERIGO: I tell you 'tis not very well. I will make
myself known to Desdemona. If she will return me   205
my jewels, I will give over my suit and repent my unlawful solicitation; if not, assure yourself I will seek
satisfaction of you.

IAGO: You have said now?

RODERIGO: Ay, and said nothing but what I protest   210
intendment of doing.

IAGO: Why, now I see there's mettle in thee, and even
from this instant do build on thee a better opinion
than ever before. Give me thy hand, Roderigo. Thou
hast taken against me a most just exception; but yet   215
I protest I have dealt most directly in thy affair.

RODERIGO: It hath not appeared.

IAGO: I grant indeed it hath not appeared, and your
suspicion is not without wit and judgment. But,
Roderigo, if thou hast that in thee indeed which   220
I have greater reason to believe now than ever—I
mean purpose, courage, and valor—this night show
it. If thou the next night following enjoy not Desdemona, take me from this world with treachery and
devise engines for my life.   225

RODERIGO: Well, what is it? Is it within reason and
compass?

IAGO: Sir, there is especial commission come from
Venice to depute Cassio in Othello's place.

RODERIGO: Is that true? Why, then Othello and Des-   230
demona return again to Venice.

IAGO: O, no; he goes into Mauritania and takes away
with him the fair Desdemona, unless his abode be
lingered here by some accident; wherein none can be
so determinate as the removing of Cassio.   235

RODERIGO: How do you mean, removing of him?

IAGO: Why, by making him uncapable of Othello's
place—knocking out his brains.

RODERIGO: And that you would have me to do?

IAGO: Ay, if you dare do yourself a profit and a right.   240
He sups tonight with a harlotry, and thither will I go
to him. He knows not yet of his honorable fortune. If

---

170 addition title   **171 vanity** showy splendor   **172 humor** mood
178 stays the meat are waiting to dine   **183 thou daff'st me** you
put me off   **183–184 device** excuse, trick   **185 conveniency**
advantage, opportunity   **186 advantage** increase   **187 put up**
submit to, tolerate   **195 deliver** deliver to   **196 votarist** nun
197–198 sudden respect immediate consideration   **200 I cannot
go to** (Roderigo changes Iago's *go to*, an expression urging patience,
to *I cannot go to*, "I have no opportunity for success in wooing.")
202 fopped fooled, duped

---

204 not very well (Roderigo changes Iago's *very well*, "all right,
then," to *not very well*, "not at all good.")   **207 satisfaction** repay-
ment. (The term normally means settling of accounts in a duel.)
209 You . . . now have you finished?   **211 intendment** intention
225 engines for plots against   **235 determinate** conclusive
241 harlotry slut

you will watch his going thence, which I will fashion
to fall out between twelve and one, you may take
him at your pleasure. I will be near to second your
attempt, and he shall fall between us. Come, stand
not amazed at it, but go along with me. I will show
you such a necessity in his death that you shall
think yourself bound to put it on him. It is now high
suppertime, and the night grows to waste. About it.

RODERIGO: I will hear further reason for this.

IAGO: And you shall be satisfied. *Exeunt.*

4.3 *Enter* OTHELLO, LODOVICO, DESDEMONA, EMILIA, *and attendants.*

LODOVICO: I do beseech you, sir, trouble yourself no
further.

OTHELLO: O, pardon me; 'twill do me good to walk.

LODOVICO: Madam, good night. I humbly thank your
ladyship.

DESDEMONA: Your honor is most welcome.

OTHELLO: Will you walk, sir?
O, Desdemona!

DESDEMONA: My lord?

OTHELLO: Get you to bed on th' instant. I will be
returned forthwith. Dismiss your attendant there.
Look 't be done.

DESDEMONA: I will, my lord.
Exit [OTHELLO, with LODOVICO and attendants].

EMILIA: How goes it now? He looks gentler than
he did.

DESDEMONA: He says he will return incontinent,
And hath commanded me to go to bed,
And bid me to dismiss you.

EMILIA: Dismiss me?

DESDEMONA: It was his bidding. Therefore, good
Emilia,
Give me my nightly wearing, and adieu.
We must not now displease him.

EMILIA: I would you had never seen him!

DESDEMONA: So would not I. My love doth so approve
him
That even his stubbornness, his checks, his frowns—
Prithee, unpin me—have grace and favor in them.
[EMILIA prepares DESDEMONA for bed.]

EMILIA: I have laid those sheets you bade me on the
bed.

DESDEMONA: All's one. Good faith, how foolish are
our minds!
If I do die before thee, prithee shroud me
In one of these same sheets.

EMILIA: Come, come, you talk.

DESDEMONA: My mother had a maid called Barbary.
She was in love, and he she loved proved mad
And did forsake her. She had a song of "Willow."
An old thing 'twas, but it expressed her fortune,
And she died singing it. That song tonight
Will not go from my mind; I have much to do
But to go hang my head all at one side
And sing it like poor Barbary. Prithee, dispatch.

EMILIA: Shall I go fetch your nightgown?

DESDEMONA: No, unpin me here.
This Lodovico is a proper man.

EMILIA: A very handsome man.

DESDEMONA: He speaks well.

EMILIA: I know a lady in Venice would have walked
barefoot to Palestine for a touch of his nether lip.

DESDEMONA *[singing]:*
"The poor soul sat sighing by a sycamore tree,
Sing all a green willow;
Her hand on her bosom, her head on her knee,
Sing willow, willow, willow.
The fresh streams ran by her and murmured
her moans;
Sing willow, willow, willow;
Her salt tears fell from her, and softened the
stones—"
Lay by these.
[Singing.] "Sing willow, willow, willow—"
Prithee, hie thee. He'll come anon.
[Singing.] "Sing all a green willow must be my garland.
Let nobody blame him; his scorn I approve—"
Nay, that's not next.—Hark! Who is 't that knocks?

---

244 **fall out** occur   249 **high** fully   250 **grows to waste** wastes away

4.3. Location: The citadel.
12 **incontinent** immediately

---

21 **stubbornness** roughness.   **checks** rebukes   25 **All's one** all right. It doesn't really matter   27 **talk** i.e., prattle   29 **mad** wild, i.e., faithless   33–34 **I . . . hang** I can scarcely keep myself from hanging   36 **nightgown** dressing gown   38 **proper** handsome   44 **willow** (A conventional emblem of disappointed love.)   52 **hie thee** hurry.   **anon** right away

for a joint ring, nor for measures of lawn, nor for
gowns, petticoats, nor caps, nor any petty exhibition.
But for all the whole world! Uds pity, who would not
make her husband a cuckold to make him a mon-
arch? I should venture purgatory for 't.   80

DESDEMONA: Beshrew me if I would do such a wrong
For the whole world.

EMILIA: Why, the wrong is but a wrong i' the world,
and having the world for your labor, 'tis a wrong in
your own world, and you might quickly make it right.   85

DESDEMONA: I do not think there is any such woman.

EMILIA: Yes, a dozen, and as many
To th' vantage as would store the world they played
for.
But I do think it is their husbands' faults
If wives do fall. Say that they slack their duties   90
And pour our treasures into foreign laps,
Or else break out in peevish jealousies,
Throwing restraint upon us? Or say they strike us,
Or scant our former having in despite?
Why, we have galls, and though we have some grace,   95
Yet have we some revenge. Let husbands know
Their wives have sense like them. They see, and smell,
And have their palates both for sweet and sour,
As husbands have. What is it that they do
When they change us for others? Is it sport?   100
I think it is. And doth affection breed it?
I think it doth. Is 't frailty that thus errs?
It is so, too. And have not we affections,
Desires for sport, and frailty, as men have?
Then let them use us well; else let them know,   105
The ills we do, their ills instruct us so.

DESDEMONA: Good night, good night. God me such
uses send
Not to pick bad from bad, but by bad mend!

Exeunt.

Emilia helps Desdemona prepare for bed as she sings.

EMILIA: It's the wind.

DESDEMONA *[singing]*:
"I called my love false love; but what said he then?
Sing willow, willow, willow;
If I court more women, you'll couch with more
men."
60   So, get thee gone. Good night. Mine eyes do itch;
Doth that bode weeping?

EMILIA: 'Tis neither here nor there.

DESDEMONA: I have heard it said so. O, these men,
these men!
Dost thou in conscience think—tell me, Emilia—
That there be women do abuse their husbands
65   In such gross kind?

EMILIA: There be some such, no question.

DESDEMONA: Wouldst thou do such a deed for all the
world?

EMILIA: Why, would not you?

DESDEMONA: No, by this heavenly light!

EMILIA: Nor I neither by this heavenly light;
I might do 't as well i' the dark.

70   DESDEMONA: Wouldst thou do such a deed for all the
world?

EMILIA: The world's a huge thing. It is a great price
For a small vice.

DESDEMONA: Good troth, I think thou wouldst not.

EMILIA: By my troth, I think I should, and undo 't
75   when I had done. Marry, I would not do such a thing

64 **abuse** deceive

76 **joint ring** a ring made in separate halves. **lawn** fine linen 77
exhibition gift 78 **Uds** God's 88 **To th' vantage** in addition, to
boot. **store** populate. **played** (1) gambled (2) sported sexually
90 **duties** marital duties 91 **pour . . . laps** i.e., are unfaithful, give
what is rightfully ours (semen) to other women 93 **Throwing . . .
us** i.e., jealousy restricting our freedom to see other men 94
scant . . . despite reduce our allowance to spite us 95 **have galls**
i.e., are capable of resenting injury and insult 97 **sense** physical
sense 100 **sport** sexual pastime 101 **affection** passion 107
uses habit, practice 108 **Not . . . mend** i.e., not to learn bad conduct from others' badness (as Emilia has suggested women learn
from men), but to mend my ways by perceiving what badness is,
making spiritual benefit out of evil and adversity

Cassio mortally wounds Roderigo.

5.1 *Enter* IAGO *and* RODERIGO.

IAGO: Here stand behind this bulk. Straight will he
    come.
  Wear thy good rapier bare, and put it home.
  Quick, quick! Fear nothing. I'll be at thy elbow.
  It makes us or it mars us. Think on that,
5 And fix most firm thy resolution.

RODERIGO: Be near at hand. I may miscarry in 't.

IAGO: Here, at thy hand. Be bold, and take thy stand.
    *[*IAGO *stands aside.* RODERIGO *conceals himself.]*

RODERIGO: I have no great devotion to the deed;
  And yet he hath given me satisfying reasons.
10 'Tis but a man gone. Forth, my sword! He dies.
                         [He draws.]

IAGO: I have rubbed this young quat almost to the
    sense,
  And he grows angry. Now, whether he kill Cassio
  Or Cassio him, or each do kill the other,
  Every way makes my gain. Live Roderigo,
15 He calls me to a restitution large
  Of gold and jewels that I bobbled from him
  As gifts to Desdemona.
  It must not be. If Cassio do remain,
  He hath a daily beauty in his life
20 That makes me ugly; and besides, the Moor
  May unfold me to him; there stand I in much peril.
  No, he must die. Be 't so. I hear him coming.

5.1. Location: A street in Cyprus.
1 bulk framework projecting from the front of a shop **2 bare** unsheathed **11 quat** pimple, pustule. **to the sense** to the quick **14 Live Roderigo** if Roderigo lives **16 bobbled** swindled **21 unfold** expose

---

Enter CASSIO.

RODERIGO *[coming forth]*:   I know his gait, 'tis he.—
  Villain, thou diest!
                       [He attacks CASSIO.]*

CASSIO: That thrust had been mine enemy indeed,
  But that my coat is better than thou know'st.   25
  I will make proof of thine.
          [He draws, and wounds RODERIGO.]*

RODERIGO: O, I am slain!   *[He falls.]*

  *[*IAGO, *from behind, wounds* CASSIO *in the leg, and exit.]*

CASSIO: I am maimed forever. Help, ho! Murder!
  Murder!

                      Enter OTHELLO.

OTHELLO: The voice of Cassio! Iago keeps his word.

RODERIGO: O, villain that I am!

OTHELLO: It is even so.   30

CASSIO: O, help, ho! Light! A surgeon!

OTHELLO: 'Tis he. O brave Iago, honest and just,
  That hast such noble sense of thy friend's wrong!
  Thou teachest me. Minion, your dear lies dead,
  And your unblest fate hies. Strumpet, I come.   35
  Forth of my heart those charms, thine eyes, are
    blotted;
  Thy bed, lust-stained, shall with lust's blood be
    spotted.   *Exit* OTHELLO.

              Enter LODOVICO *and* GRATIANO.

CASSIO: What ho! No watch? No passage? Murder!
  Murder!

GRATIANO: 'Tis some mischance. The voice is very
  direful.

CASSIO: O, help!   40

LODOVICO: Hark!

RODERIGO: O wretched villain!

LODOVICO: Two or three groan. 'Tis heavy night;
  These may be counterfeits. Let's think 't unsafe
  To come in to the cry without more help.   45
                [They remain near the entrance.]

---

25 coat (Possibly a garment of mail under the outer clothing, or simply a tougher coat than Roderigo expected.) **26 proof** a test **34 Minion** hussy (i.e., Desdemona) **35 hies** hastens on **36 Forth of** from out **38 passage** people passing by **43 heavy** thick, dark **45 come in to** approach

RODERIGO: Nobody come? Then shall I bleed to death.

Enter IAGO *[in his shirtsleeves, with a light].*

LODOVICO: Hark!

GRATIANO: Here's one comes in his shirt, with light
and weapons.

IAGO: Who's there? Whose noise is this that cries on
murder?

50 **LODOVICO:** We do not know.

IAGO: Did not you hear a cry?

CASSIO: Here, here! For heaven's sake, help me!

IAGO: What's the matter?
[He moves toward CASSIO.*]*

GRATIANO *[to* LODOVICO*]:* This is Othello's ancient, as
I take it.

LODOVICO *[to* GRATIANO*]:* The same indeed, a very
valiant fellow.

IAGO *[to* CASSIO*]:* What are you here that cry so
grievously?

55 **CASSIO:** Iago? O, I am spoiled, undone by villains!
Give me some help.

IAGO: O me, Lieutenant! What villains have done this?

CASSIO: I think that one of them is hereabout,
And cannot make away.

IAGO: O treacherous villains!
60 *[To* LODOVICO *and* GRATIANO.*]* What are you there?
Come in, and give some help. *[They advance.]*

RODERIGO: O, help me there!

CASSIO: That's one of them.

IAGO: O murderous slave! O villain!
[He stabs RODERIGO.*]*

RODERIGO: O damned Iago! O inhuman dog!

IAGO: Kill men i' the dark?—Where be these bloody
thieves?—
65 How silent is this town!—Ho! Murder, murder!—
[To LODOVICO *and* GRATIANO.*]* What may you be?
Are you of good or evil?

LODOVICO: As you shall prove us, praise us.

---

49 cries on cries out **54 What** who (also at lines 60 and 66) **55 spoiled** ruined, done for **59 make** get **67 praise** appraise

IAGO: Signor Lodovico?

LODOVICO: He, sir.

IAGO: I cry you mercy. Here's Cassio hurt by villains. 70

GRATIANO: Cassio?

IAGO: How is 't, brother?

CASSIO: My leg is cut in two.

IAGO: Marry, heaven forbid!
Light, gentlemen! I'll bind it with my shirt. 75
[He hands them the light, and tends to
CASSIO's *wound.]*

Enter BIANCA.

BIANCA: What is the matter, ho? Who is 't that cried?

IAGO: Who is 't that cried?

BIANCA: O my dear Cassio!
My sweet Cassio! O Cassio, Cassio, Cassio!

IAGO: O notable strumpet! Cassio, may you suspect
Who they should be that have thus mangled you? 80

CASSIO: No.

GRATIANO: I am sorry to find you thus. I have been to
seek you.

IAGO: Lend me a garter. *[He applies a tourniquet.]* So.—
O, for a chair,
To bear him easily hence!

BIANCA: Alas, he faints! O Cassio, Cassio, Cassio! 85

IAGO: Gentlemen all, I do suspect this trash
To be a party in this injury.—
Patience awhile, good Cassio.—Come, come;
Lend me a light. *[He shines the light on* RODERIGO.*]*
Know we this face or no?
Alas, my friend and my dear countryman 90
Roderigo! No.—Yes, sure.—O heaven! Roderigo!

GRATIANO: What, of Venice?

IAGO: Even he, sir. Did you know him?

GRATIANO: Know him? Ay.

IAGO: Signor Gratiano? I cry your gentle pardon. 95
These bloods accidents must excuse my manners
That so neglected you.

GRATIANO: I am glad to see you.

---

70 I cry you mercy I beg your pardon **83 chair** litter **95 gentle** noble **96 accidents** sudden events

IAGO: How do you, Cassio? O, a chair, a chair!

GRATIANO: Roderigo!

100 **IAGO:**   He, he, 'tis he. *[A litter is brought in.]* O, that's
well said; the chair.
Some good man bear him carefully from hence;
I'll fetch the General's surgeon. *[To* BIANCA.*]* For you,
mistress,
Save you your labor.—He that lies slain here, Cassio,
Was my dear friend. What malice was between you?

105 **CASSIO:**   None in the world, nor do I know the man.

IAGO *[to* BIANCA*]***:**   What, look you pale?—O, bear him
out o' th' air.

[CASSIO and RODERIGO *are borne off.]*

Stay you, good gentlemen.—Look you pale,
mistress?—
Do you perceive the gastness of here eye?—
Nay, if you stare, we shall hear more anon.—
110 Behold her well; I pray you, look upon her.
Do you see, gentlemen? Nay, guiltiness
Will speak, though tongues were out of use.

[Enter EMILIA.*]*

EMILIA: 'Las, what's the matter? What's the matter,
husband?

IAGO: Cassio hath here been set on in the dark
115 By Roderigo and fellows that are scaped.
He's almost slain, and Roderigo dead.

EMILIA: Alas, good gentleman! Alas, good Cassio!

IAGO: This is the fruits of whoring. Prithee, Emilia,
Go know of Cassio where he supped tonight.
120 *[To* BIANCA.*]* What, do you shake at that?

BIANCA: He supped at my house, but I therefore shake
not.

IAGO: O, did he so? I charge you go with me.

EMILIA: O, fie upon thee, strumpet!

BIANCA: I am no strumpet, but of life as honest
125 As you that thus abuse me.

EMILIA: As I? Faugh! Fie upon thee!

---

100 **well said** well done   103 **Save . . . labor** i.e., never you mind
tending Cassio   104 **malice** enmity   106 **bear . . . air** (Fresh
air was thought to be dangerous for a wound.)   107 **Stay you**
(Lodovico and Gratiano are evidently about to leave.)   108 **gastness** terror   109 **stare** (Iago pretends to interpret Bianca's wild
looks as an involuntary confession of guilt.)   119 **know** learn   124
honest chaste

IAGO: Kind gentlemen, let's go see poor Cassio
dressed.—
Come, mistress, you must tell 's another tale.
Emilia, run you to the citadel
And tell my lord and lady what hath happed.—   130
Will you go on afore? *[Aside.]* This is the night
That either makes me or fordoes me quite.   *Exeunt.*

5.2   *Enter* OTHELLO *[with a light], and* DESDEMONA *in
her bed.*

OTHELLO: It is the cause, it is the cause, my soul.
Let me not name it to you, you chaste stars!
It is the cause. Yet I'll not shed her blood,
Nor scar that whiter skin of hers than snow,
And smooth as monumental alabaster.   5
Yet she must die, else she'll betray more men.
Put out the light, and then put out the light.
If I quench thee, thou flaming minister,
I can again thy former light restore,
Should I repent me; but once put out thy light,   10
Thou cunning'st pattern of excelling nature,
I know not where is that Promethean heat
That can thy light relume. When I have plucked thy
rose,
I cannot give it vital growth again;
It needs must wither. I'll smell thee on the tree.   15

[He kisses her.]

O balmy breath, that dost almost persuade
Justice to break her sword! One more, one more.
Be thus when thou art dead, and I will kill thee,
And love thee after. One more, and that's the last.

[He kisses her.]

So sweet was ne'er so fatal. I must weep,   20
But they are cruel tears. This sorrow's heavenly;
It strikes where it doth love. She wakes.

DESDEMONA: Who's there? Othello?

OTHELLO: Ay, Desdemona.

---

127 **Cassio dressed** Cassio's wounds dressed   132 **fordoes** undoes,
ruins

5.2. Location: A bedchamber in the citadel.
s.d. in her bed (Either the curtains are drawn back to reveal the
bed in a recessed area backstage, or the bed is "thrust out" onstage
as the scene begins.)   1 **cause** i.e., cause of justice, the offense itself,
which Othello must correct as an agent of justice   5 **monumental**
i.e., used in making tombs and funeral monuments   7 **the light . . .
light** the torch or lamp . . . Desdemona's life   8 **flaming minister**
torch or lamp that serves me   10 **repent me** change my mind   11
Thou . . . pattern you skillfully wrought perfect example   12 **Promethean heat** divine fire. (Alluding to the theft of fire from heaven
by Prometheus.)   13 **relume** rekindle   21 **cruel** unrelenting   22
It . . . love (Compare Hebrews 12:6: "For whom the Lord loveth he
chasteneth.")

25 DESDEMONA: Will you come to bed, my lord?

OTHELLO: Have you prayed tonight, Desdemon?

DESDEMONA: Ay, my lord.

OTHELLO: If you bethink yourself of any crime
Unreconciled as yet to heaven and grace,
30 Solicit for it straight.

DESDEMONA: Alack, my lord, what may you mean by
that?

OTHELLO: Well, do it, and be brief. I will walk by.
I would not kill thy unprepared spirit.
No, heaven forfend! I would not kill thy soul.

35 DESDEMONA: Talk you of killing?

OTHELLO: Ay, I do.

DESDEMONA: Then heaven
Have mercy on me!

OTHELLO: Amen, with all my heart!

DESDEMONA: If you say so, I hope you will not kill me.

OTHELLO: Humh!

DESDEMONA: And yet I fear you; for you're fatal then
40 When your eyes roll so. Why I should fear I know not,
Since guiltiness I know not; but yet I feel I fear.

OTHELLO: Think on thy sins.

DESDEMONA: They are loves I bear to you.

OTHELLO: Ay, and for that thou diest.

DESDEMONA: That death's unnatural that kills for
loving.
45 Alas, why gnaw you so your nether lip?
Some bloody passion shakes your very frame.
These are portents; but yet I hope, I hope,
They do not point on me.

OTHELLO: Peace, and be still!

50 DESDEMONA: I will so. What's the matter?

OTHELLO: That handkerchief which I so loved and
gave thee
Thou gav'st to Cassio.

DESDEMONA: No, by my life and soul!
Send for the man and ask him.

Othello dispatches Desdemona.

OTHELLO: Sweet soul, take heed, take heed of perjury.
Thou art on thy deathbed. 55

DESDEMONA: Ay, but not yet to die.

OTHELLO: Yes, presently.
Therefore confess thee freely of thy sin;
For to deny each article with oath
Cannot remove nor choke the strong conception
That I do groan withal. Thou art to die. 60

DESDEMONA: Then Lord have mercy on me!

OTHELLO: I say, amen.

DESDEMONA: And have you mercy too! I never did
Offend you in my life; never loved Cassio
But with such general warranty of heaven
As I might love. I never gave him token. 65

OTHELLO: By heaven, I saw my handkerchief in 's hand.
O perjured woman! Thou dost stone my heart,
And makes me call what I intend to do
A murder, which I thought a sacrifice.
I saw the handkerchief.

DESDEMONA: He found it, then. 70
I never gave it him. Send for him hither;
Let him confess a truth.

OTHELLO: He hath confessed.

DESDEMONA: What, my lord?

OTHELLO: That he hath used thee.

DESDEMONA: How? Unlawfully?

OTHELLO: Ay.

---

28 **crime** sin   30 **Solicit** petition, pray.   **straight** immediately
34 **forfend** forbid   42 **They are . . . you** i.e., if I sinned, it was in
loving you more than my father or more than God   48 **point on**
point at, predict what is to happen to

---

56 **presently** immediately   59 **conception** (1) belief in your guilt
(2) plan in my mind   60 **groan withal** (1) groan at in sorrow (2)
as in giving birth   63 **Offend** wrong   64 **warranty** sanction   67
stone turn to stone, harden

75 **DESDEMONA:** He will not say so.

OTHELLO: No, his mouth is stopped;
  Honest Iago hath ta'en order for 't.

DESDEMONA: O, my fear interprets. What, is he dead?

OTHELLO: Had all his hairs been lives, my great
    revenge
  Had stomach for them all.

80 **DESDEMONA:** Alas, he is betrayed and I undone!

                                   [She weeps.]

OTHELLO: Out, strumpet! Weep'st thou for him to my
    face?

DESDEMONA: O, banish me, my lord, but kill me not!

OTHELLO: Down, strumpet!

DESDEMONA: Kill me tomorrow; let me live tonight!

85 **OTHELLO:** Nay, if you strive—

DESDEMONA: But half an hour!

OTHELLO: Being done, there is no pause.

DESDEMONA: But while I say one prayer!

OTHELLO: It is too late.

                                   Smothers her.

EMILIA *(at the door):* My lord, my lord! What, ho! My
    lord, my lord!

OTHELLO: What noise is this? Not dead? Not yet quite
    dead?
90 I that am cruel am yet merciful;
  I would not have thee linger in thy pain.

                                   [He dispatches her.]
  So, so.

EMILIA *(within):* What, ho! My lord, my lord!

OTHELLO: Who's there?

EMILIA *[within]:* O, good my lord, I would speak a word
    with you!

OTHELLO: Yes, 'tis Emilia.—By and by.—She's dead.
95 'Tis like she comes to speak of Cassio's death.—
  The noise was here. Ha! No more moving?
  Still as the grave. Shall she come in? Were 't good?—
  I think she stirs again. No. What's best to do?
  If she come in, she'll sure speak to my wife.

My wife! My wife! What wife? I have no wife. 100
O, insupportable! O heavy hour!
Methinks it should be now a huge eclipse
Of sun and moon, and that th' affrighted globe
Should yawn at alteration.

EMILIA *[within]:*   I do beseech you
That I may speak with you, O, good my lord! 105

OTHELLO: I had forgot thee. O, come in, Emilia.—
  Soft, by and by. Let me the curtains draw.—
          [He closes the bed-curtains and opens the door.]
Where art thou?

                                   Enter EMILIA.

          What's the matter with thee now?

EMILIA: O, my good lord, yonder's foul murders done!

OTHELLO: What, now? 110

EMILIA: But now, my lord.

OTHELLO: It is the very error of the moon;
  She comes more nearer earth than she was wont,
  And makes men mad.

EMILIA: Cassio, my lord, hath killed a young Venetian 115
  Called Roderigo.

OTHELLO: Roderigo killed?
  And Cassio killed?

EMILIA: No, Cassio is not killed.

OTHELLO: Not Cassio killed? Then murder's out of
    tune,
  And sweet revenge grows harsh.

DESDEMONA: O, falsely, falsely murdered! 120

EMILIA: O Lord, what cry is that?

OTHELLO: That? What?

EMILIA: Out and alas, that was my lady's voice.
                          [She opens the bed-curtains.]
  Help, help, ho, help! O lady, speak again!
  Sweet Desdemona! O sweet mistress, speak! 125

DESDEMONA: A guiltless death I die.

EMILIA: O, who hath done this deed?

DESDEMONA: Nobody; I myself. Farewell.
  Commend me to my kind lord. O, farewell! *[She dies.]*

---

76 **ta'en order** taken measures   86 **Being done** i.e., since justice has begun its relentless course   95 **like** likely that   96 **here** (The Folio's *high* is possible, suggesting that the commotion of the attack on Cassio was loud.)

104 **yawn** gape in amazement, i.e., move in an earthquake. (According to Pliny, earthquakes often happen during eclipses.)   **at alteration** at these cataclysmic events in nature, well suited to express the horror of Desdemona's death   107 **Soft** wait a minute   112 **error** aberration, irregularity   123 **Out** (A cry of dismay, intensifying *alas.*)

130   **OTHELLO:**   Why, how should she be murdered?

EMILIA: Alas, who knows?

OTHELLO: You heard her say herself it was not I.

EMILIA: She said so. I must needs report the truth.

OTHELLO: She's like a liar gone to burning hell!
    'Twas I that killed her.

EMILIA: O, the more angel she,
135   And you the blacker devil!

OTHELLO: She turned to folly, and she was a whore.

EMILIA: Thou dost belie her, and thou art a devil.

OTHELLO: She was false as water.

EMILIA: Thou art rash as fire to say
140   That she was false. O, she was heavenly true!

OTHELLO: Cassio did top her. Ask thy husband else.
    O, I were damned beneath all depth in hell
    But that I did proceed upon just grounds
    To this extremity. Thy husband knew it all.

145   **EMILIA:**   My husband?

OTHELLO: Thy husband.

EMILIA: That she was false to wedlock?

OTHELLO: Ay, with Cassio. Nay, had she been true,
    If heaven would make me such another world
150   Of one entire and perfect chrysolite,
    I'd not have sold her for it.

EMILIA: My husband?

OTHELLO: Ay, 'twas he that told me on her first.
    An honest man he is, and hates the slime
155   That sticks on filthy deeds.

EMILIA: My husband?

OTHELLO: What needs this iterance, woman? I say thy
    husband.

EMILIA: O mistress, villainy hath made mocks with
    love!
    My husband say she was false?

OTHELLO: He, woman;
160   I say thy husband. Dost understand the word?
    My friend, thy husband, honest, honest Iago.

---

136 **folly** i.e., wantonness, fleshly sin   137 **belie** slander   141 **else** i.e., if you don't believe me   150 **chrysolite** precious topaz   157 **iterance** iteration, repetition   158 **made mocks with** derided, made sport of

Montano (Nicholas Farrell) and Gratiano (André Oumansky) enter with swords drawn.

EMILIA: If he say so, may his pernicious soul
    Rot half a grain a day! He lies to th' heart.
    She was too fond of her most filthy bargain.

OTHELLO: Ha?   *[He draws.]*   165

EMILIA: Do thy worst!
    This deed of thine is no more worthy heaven
    Than thou wast worthy her.

OTHELLO: Peace, you were best.

EMILIA: Thou hast not half that power to do me harm
    As I have to be hurt. O gull! O dolt!   170
    As ignorant as dirt! Thou hast done a deed—
    I care not for thy sword; I'll make thee known,
    Though I lost twenty lives.—Help! Help, ho, help!
    The Moor hath killed my mistress! Murder, murder!

Enter MONTANO, GRATIANO, *and* IAGO.

MONTANO: What is the matter? How now, General?   175

EMILIA: O, are you come, Iago? You have done well,
    That men must lay their murders on your neck.

GRATIANO: What is the matter?

EMILIA *[to* IAGO*]*:   Disprove this villain, if thou be'st
    a man.
    He says thou toldst him that his wife was false.   180
    I know thou didst not; thou'rt not such a villain.
    Speak, for my heart is full.

IAGO: I told him what I thought, and told no more
    Than what he found himself was apt and true.

---

168 **you were best** it would be best for you   170 **to be hurt** i.e., to endure hurt.   **gull** dupe   184 **apt** plausible

Othello confronts Iago.

185 **EMILIA:**   But did you ever tell him she was false?

IAGO: I did.

EMILIA: You told a lie, an odious, damnèd lie!
   Upon my soul, a lie, a wicked lie.
   She false with Cassio? Did you say with Cassio?

190 **IAGO:**   With Cassio, mistress. Go to, charm your tongue.

EMILIA: I will not charm my tongue; I am bound to
      speak.
   My mistress here lies murdered in her bed—

ALL   O heavens forfend!

EMILIA: And your reports have set the murder on.

195 **OTHELLO:**   Nay, stare not, masters. It is true indeed.

GRATIANO: 'Tis a strange truth.

MONTANO: O monstrous act!

EMILIA: Villainy, villainy, villainy!
   I think upon 't—I think I smell 't! O villainy!
   I thought so then—I'll kill myself for grief—
200   O villainy, villainy!

IAGO: What, are you mad? I charge you, get you home.

EMILIA: Good gentlemen, let me have leave to speak.
   'Tis proper I obey him, but not now.
   Perchance, Iago, I will ne'er go home.

205 **OTHELLO:**   O! O! O!   [OTHELLO *falls on the bed.*]

---

190 **charm** keep silent (as though by a magic spell)   199 **then**
(Perhaps at 3.3.331–332 and 4.2.137–154.)   205 **s.d. Othello . . .
bed** (This direction is from the Quarto, as also *He kisses her* at line
19 and *She dies* at line 129.)

EMILIA: Nay, lay thee down and roar,
   For thou hast killed the sweetest innocent
   That e'er did lift up eye.

OTHELLO [*rising*]:   O, she was foul!
   I scarce did know you, uncle. There lies your niece,
   Whose breath indeed these hands have newly
      stopped.
   I know this act shows horrible and grim.   210

GRATIANO: Poor Desdemon! I am glad thy father's
      dead.
   Thy match was mortal to him, and pure grief
   Shore his old thread in twain. Did he live now,
   This sight would make him do a desperate turn,
   Yea, curse his better angel from his side,   215
   And fall to reprobance.

OTHELLO: 'Tis pitiful. But yet Iago knows
   That she with Cassio hath the act of shame
   A thousand times committed. Cassio confessed it;
   And she did gratify his amorous works   220
   With that recognizance and pledge of love
   Which I first gave her. I saw it in his hand;
   It was a handkerchief, an antique token
   My father gave my mother.

EMILIA: O God! O heavenly God!   225

IAGO: Zounds, hold your peace.

EMILIA: 'Twill out, 'twill out! I peace?
   No, I will speak as liberal as the north.
   Let heaven and men and devils, let them all,
   All, all, cry shame against me, yet I'll speak.

IAGO: Be wise, and get you home.

EMILIA: I will not.
                    [*IAGO threatens* EMILIA.]

GRATIANO: Fie,   230
   Your sword upon a woman?

EMILIA: O thou dull Moor! That handkerchief thou
      speak'st of
   I found by fortune and did give my husband;
   For often, with a solemn earnestness,
   More than indeed belonged to such a trifle,   235
   He begged of me to steal 't.

IAGO: Villainous whore!

---

207 **lift up eye** i.e., lift her eyes to heaven   210 **shows** looks   213
Shore . . . thread sheared the thread of his old age (as Atropos,
one of the three Fates, was thought to do)   214 **turn** deed   216
reprobance damnation, i.e., suicide   220 **gratify** reward   221
recognizance token   227 **liberal as the north** freely as the north
wind (blows)   235 **belonged** was appropriate

EMILIA: She give it Cassio? No, alas! I found it,
And I did give 't my husband.

IAGO: Filth, thou liest!

EMILIA: By heaven, I do not, I do not, gentlemen.
240 O murderous coxcomb! What should such a fool
Do with so good a wife?

OTHELLO: Are there no stones in heaven
But what serves for the thunder?—Precious villain!
[He runs at IAGO; MONTANO disarms OTHELLO.
IAGO, from behind, stabs EMILIA.]

GRATIANO: The woman falls! Sure he hath killed his
wife.

245 **EMILIA:** Ay, ay. O, lay me by my mistress' side.
[Exit IAGO.]

GRATIANO: He's gone, but his wife's killed.

MONTANO: 'Tis a notorious villain. Take you this
weapon,
Which I have here recovered from the Moor.
Come, guard the door without. Let him not pass,
250 But kill him rather. I'll after that same villain,
For 'tis a damnèd slave.
Exit [with all but OTHELLO and EMILIA, who
has been laid by DESDEMONA's side].

OTHELLO: I am not valiant neither,
But every puny whipster gets my sword.
But why should honor outlive honesty?
255 Let it go all.

EMILIA: What did thy song bode, lady?
Hark, canst thou hear me? I will play the swan,
And die in music. *[She sings.]* "Willow, willow, willow."
Moor, she was chaste. She loved thee, cruel Moor.
So come my soul to bliss as I speak true.
260 So speaking as I think, alas, I die.   *[She dies.]*

OTHELLO: I have another weapon in this chamber;
It was a sword of Spain, the ice-brook's temper—
O, here it is. *[He finds a sword.]* Uncle, I must come
forth.

GRATIANO *[within]:* If thou attempt it, it will cost thee
dear.
265 Thou hast no weapon, and perforce must suffer.

OTHELLO: Look in upon me then and speak with me,
Or, naked as I am, I will assault thee.
[Enter GRATIANO.]

GRATIANO: What is the matter?

OTHELLO: Behold, I have a weapon;
A better never did itself sustain
Upon a soldier's thigh. I have seen the day   270
That, with this little arm and this good sword,
I have made my way through more impediments
Than twenty times your stop. But O, vain boast!
Who can control his fate? 'Tis not so now.
Be not afraid, though you do see me weaponed;   275
Here is my journey's end, here is my butt
And very seamark of my utmost sail.
[GRATIANO steps back.]
Do you go back dismayed? 'Tis a lost fear;
Man but a rush against Othello's breast
And he retires. Where should Othello go?   280
[He turns to DESDEMONA.]
Now, how dost thou look now? O ill-starred wench!
Pale as thy smock! When we shall meet at compt,
This look of thine will hurl my soul from heaven,
And fiends will snatch at it. Cold, cold, my girl?
Even like thy chastity. O cursèd, cursèd slave!   285
Whip me, ye devils,
From the possession of this heavenly sight!
Blow me about in winds! Roast me in sulfur!
Wash me in steep-down gulfs of liquid fire!
O Desdemon! Dead, Desdemon! Dead! O! O!   290

Enter LODOVICO, CASSIO [carried in a litter],
MONTANO, and IAGO [prisoner], with officers.

LODOVICO: Where is this rash and most unfortunate
man?

OTHELLO: That's he that was Othello. Here I am.

LODOVICO: Where is that viper? Bring the villain
forth.
[IAGO is led forward.]

OTHELLO: I look down towards his feet; but that's a
fable.
If that thou be'st a devil, I cannot kill thee.   295
[He wounds IAGO.]

240 **coxcomb** fool. (Addressed to Othello.) 242 **stones** bolts, such as those used for thunderbolts 243 **Precious** i.e., arrant, utter. **s.d. He . . . Emilia** (The Quarto text reads "The Moor runs at Iago. Iago kills his wife." The Quarto also specifies the exit of Iago at line 245 and the death of Emilia at line 260.) 253 **whipster** contemptible fellow (one who is always ready to whip out his sword) 254 **honor** i.e., the bravery for which one enjoys a soldier's reputation. **honesty** true integrity 262 **the icebrook's temper** tempered in ice-cold water

267 **naked** unarmed 273 **stop** power (to stop) 276 **butt** goal, limit. (An archery term.) 277 **seamark** beacon (marking his destination or limit) 278 **lost** wasted, unneeded 279 **Man . . . rush** wield no more than a reed 282 **compt** account, judgment day 285 **slave** i.e., Othello himself 290 **s.d. in a litter** (The Quarto specifies that Cassio is "in a chair.") 294 **towards his feet** i.e., to see if they are cloven, as the devil's are fabled to be

LODOVICO: Wrench his sword from him.

[OTHELLO is disarmed.]

IAGO: I bleed, sir, but not killed.

OTHELLO: I am not sorry neither. I'd have thee live,
For in my sense 'tis happiness to die.

LODOVICO: O thou Othello, that was once so good,
300   Fall'n in the practice of a cursèd slave,
What shall be said to thee?

OTHELLO: Why, anything,
An honorable murderer, if you will,
For naught I did in hate, but all in honor.

LODOVICO: This wretch hath part confessed his
villainy.
305   Did you and he consent in Cassio's death?

OTHELLO: Ay.

CASSIO: Dear General, I never gave you cause.

OTHELLO: I do believe it, and I ask your pardon.
Will you, I pray, demand that demi-devil
310   Why he hath thus ensnared my soul and body?

IAGO: Demand me nothing. What you know, you know.
From this time forth I never will speak word.

LODOVICO: What, not to pray?

GRATIANO: Torments will ope your lips.

315   **OTHELLO:** Well, thou dost best.

LODOVICO: Sir, you shall understand what hath
befall'n,
Which, as I think, you know not. Here is a letter
Found in the pocket of the slain Roderigo;
And here another. *[He produces letters.]* The one of
them imports
320   The death of Cassio, to be undertook
By Roderigo.

OTHELLO: O villain!

CASSIO: Most heathenish and most gross!

Othello delivers his final words.

LODOVICO *[showing another paper]***:** Now here's another
discontented paper
Found in his pocket too. And this, it seems,
Roderigo meant t' have sent this damnèd villain;   325
But that belike Iago in the interim
Came in and satisfied him.

OTHELLO: O thou pernicious caitiff!—
How came you, Cassio, by that handkerchief
That was my wife's?

CASSIO: I found it in my chamber;   330
And he himself confessed but even now
That there he dropped it for a special purpose
Which wrought to his desire.

OTHELLO: O fool, fool, fool!

CASSIO: There is besides in Roderigo's letter
How he upbraids Iago, that he made him   335
Brave me upon the watch, whereon it came
That I was cast; and even but now he spake,
After long seeming dead, Iago hurt him,
Iago set him on.

LODOVICO *[to OTHELLO]***:** You must forsake this room
and go with us.   340

---

298 in my sense to one who feels as I do   **300 in the practice**
through the plotting, into the snare.   **slave** villain   **305 consent**
agree   **314 Torments** torture   **322 gross** monstrous

323 discontented full of discontent   **326 belike** most likely   **327
Came . . . him** interposed and gave him satisfactory explanation   **333 wrought . . . desire** worked out as he wished, fitted in
with his plan   **336 Brave** defy.   **whereon it came** whereof it came
about   **337 cast** dismissed

Your power and your command is taken off,
And Cassio rules in Cyprus. For this slave,
If there be any cunning cruelty
That can torment him much and hold him long,
345   It shall be his. You shall close prisoner rest
Till that the nature of your fault be known
To the Venetian state.—Come, bring away.

OTHELLO: Soft you; a word or two before you go.
I have done the state some service, and they know 't.
350   No more of that. I pray you, in your letters,
When you shall these unlucky deeds relate,
Speak of me as I am; nothing extenuate,
Nor set down aught in malice. Then must you speak
Of one that loved not wisely but too well;
355   Of one not easily jealous but, being wrought,
Perplexed in the extreme; of one whose hand,
Like the base Indian, threw a pearl away
Richer than all his tribe; of one whose subdued eyes,
Albeit unusèd to the melting mood,
360   Drops tears as fast as the Arabian trees
Their medicinable gum. Set you down this;
And say besides that in Aleppo once,
Where a malignant and a turbaned Turk
Beat a Venetian and traduced the state,
365   I took by th' throat the circumcisèd dog
And smote him, thus   *[He stabs himself.]*

LODOVICO: O bloody period!

GRATIANO: All that is spoke is marred.

OTHELLO: I kissed thee ere I killed thee. No way but
    this,
370   Killing myself, to die upon a kiss.
                [He kisses DESDEMONA and] dies.

Othello lies dead beside his murdered wife, her maid Emilia, and their betrayer, Iago.

CASSIO: This did I fear, but thought he had no weapon;
For he was great of heart.

LODOVICO *[to IAGO]:*   O Spartan dog,
More fell than anguish, hunger, or the sea!
Look on the tragic loading of this bed.
This is thy work. The object poisons sight;   375
Let it be hid. Gratiano, keep the house,
              [The bed-curtains are drawn]
And seize upon the fortunes of the Moor,
For they succeed on you. *[To CASSIO.]* To you, Lord
    Governor,
Remains the censure of this hellish villain,
The time, the place, the torture. O, enforce it!   380
Myself will straight aboard, and to the state
This heavy act with heavy heart relate.   *Exeunt.*

---

341 taken off taken away   **344 hold him long** keep him alive a long time (during his torture)   **345 rest** remain   **348 Soft you** one moment   **351 unlucky** unfortunate   **355 wrought** worked upon, worked into a frenzy   **356 Perplexed** distraught   **357 Indian** (This reading from the Quarto pictures an ignorant savage who cannot recognize the value of a precious jewel. The Folio reading, *Iudean* or *Judean*, i.e., infidel or disbeliever, may refer to Herod, who slew Miriamne in a fit of jealousy, or to Judas Iscariot, the betrayer of Christ.)   **358 subdued** i.e., overcome by grief   **361 gum** i.e., myrrh   **366 s.d. He stabs himself** (This direction is in the Quarto text.)   **367 period** termination, conclusion

372 Spartan dog (Spartan dogs were noted for their savagery and silence.)   **373 fell** cruel   **376 Let it be hid** i.e., draw the bed-curtains. (No stage direction specifies that the dead are to be carried offstage at the end of the play.)   **keep** remain in   **377 seize upon** take legal possession of   **378 succeed on** pass as though by inheritance to   **379 censure** sentencing

Writing from Reading

Summarize

1 The play opens, in effect, with a summary of action previous to the action we witness; it closes with another kind of summary, and one in which Othello demonstrates self-awareness (a quality largely absent in him earlier). At the end of the play (and this is quite similar to Hamlet's request of Horatio), Othello asks that those who survive him will tell his story truly:

"No more of that. I pray you, in your letters,
When you shall these unlucky deeds relate,
Speak of me as I am; nothing extenuate,
Nor set down aught in malice. Then must you speak
Of one that loved not wisely but too well. . . ."

How would you tell his story?

2 If Desdemona were to write letters home to her father and friends, how would she explain herself and her situation?

Analyze Craft

3 What makes Othello a hero, in the Greek sense of one whose fate is intertwined with those of his people and who discovers that his tragic flaw has led to his demise? What makes his growth through suffering and coming to understand himself sufficient to move us to terror and pity (*catharsis*)? How do you interpret the line in which he says of himself that he "loved not wisely but too well"?

4 Iago has been described as a creature of "motiveless malignity." What motives does he offer for his behavior? What sense do they make? And when he says, at the close of Act 5, "From this time forth I never will speak word," what does his silence suggest?

5 The timeline of the play does not in fact provide an opportunity for Desdemona to betray her husband. Shakespeare must have known this. Why does he compress the action so as to make infidelity improbable if not impossible?

Analyze Voice

6 Can you distinguish a difference in tone between this play and *Hamlet*? Describe. Pick a soliloquy by Hamlet and Othello and compare them.

7 Othello says about his courtship of Desdemona:

"She loved me for the dangers I had passed,
And I loved her that she did pity them."

What does this suggest about Othello's character? In what ways is this representation accurate or inaccurate?

Synthesize Summary and Analysis

8 The tale starts out in seeming bliss and ends in total misery. Is that a definition of the tragic mode? And if, as we have seen, Shakespeare mixes low comedy together with high seriousness, what if any comic elements do you find in the play?

9 How closely related is character to plot? How can so great a general be so easily deluded and so completely fooled? Is Othello sane? Give examples to support your answer.

10 To what degree is this a play about empire and armed conflict; how do the domestic wars mirror those between the characters onstage?

Interpret the Play

11 Is this primarily a play about jealousy—Othello's for Cassio, Iago's for Othello? Is Iago jealous of Othello in ways that mirror or distort the ways the husband grows jealous of his wife?

12 Othello is a well-positioned outcast in society. In what ways is this a play about race relations or class conflict or about power and control?

13 Is this a play about the psychology of insecurity and delusion or, rather, about good and evil in the religious sense?

Getting Started: A Research Project

Research is a skill that will carry you through your college career. To help acquaint you with the research process, the materials you need for this project are made available on our website (www.mhhe.com/delbanco1e). Other ideas for research projects and sources appear at the end of this chapter.

"Shakespeare has had the status of a secular Bible for the last two centuries," writes critic Harold Bloom in *Shakespeare: The Invention of the Human.* "Textual scholarship on the plays approaches biblical commentary in scope and intensiveness, while the quantity of literary criticism devoted to Shakespeare rivals theological interpretation of the Holy Scripture."

As Bloom points out, the body of critical work on Shakespeare is vast. In part, this is because serious Shakespearean criticism has been growing for more than three centuries! This research assignment will help you chart some of the major views of

Shakespeare throughout the last three centuries by asking you to read two prominent views of Shakespeare: that of Samuel Johnson, the great eighteenth-century critic; and that of Samuel Taylor Coleridge, the nineteenth-century Romantic poet.

Excerpts are available on our website. After reading each of the critics, choose one of the prompts below to get you started on writing a research paper.

1. Read Johnson's and Coleridge's ideas on Shakespeare. Then write a summary of each critic's view. Based on your summaries, evaluate which you find most accurate given your reading of Shakespeare. Then, using one of Shakespeare's plays from this chapter, show how you see the critic's view playing out in the drama.

2. After reading Johnson's and Coleridge's critical perspectives,

choose an idea or topic from one of them that you find interesting; for example, you might choose Johnson's idea that Shakespeare holds a mirror to the world, or Coleridge's observation of unity in Shakespeare's plays. Then write a compare/contrast paper in which you examine how each critic develops, complicates, or is silent on that particular idea. As you write, you may want to draw support from not just the critics but also a Shakespeare play you have read.

3. After reading these critics, write your own general statement about Shakespeare based on observations from your reading of Shakespearean drama. In other words, use the three critics as a model for how to write your own critical statement on one or more Shakespearean plays.

Further Suggestions for Writing and Research

1. Ophelia, in *Hamlet,* is one of Shakespeare's most recognizable female characters. However, critics throughout the centuries—and up through contemporary feminist criticism—have disagreed on how we can best understand her role and herself as a female character. After reviewing Ophelia's lines in *Hamlet,* read the Ophelia research resources that appear on our website at www.mhhe.com/delbanco1e. You will find a nineteenth-century critic, Anna Murphy Jameson, whose *Shakespeare's Heroines,* published in 1832, became one of the earliest works by a female critic to deal directly with Shakespeare's female characters. You can compare her view with that of a contemporary feminist critic, Elaine Showalter, who explains Ophelia's place in feminist criticism. And finally, you can follow our link to a popular painting of Ophelia by nineteenth-century artist John Everett Millais.

Based on your research, write an essay in which you argue for or against a particular interpretation of Ophelia, being sure to support your argument with quotes from the critics and the text itself.

- Jameson, Anna Murphy. *Shakespeare's Heroines.* Ed. Cheri L. Larsen Hoeckley. Ontario: Broadview, 2005. See esp. pp. 177–185.
- Showalter, Elaine. "Representing Ophelia: Women, Madness, and the Responsibilities of Feminist Criticism." *Shakespeare and the Question of Theory.* Ed. Geoffrey Hartman and Patricia Parker. New York: Methuen, 1985. See esp. pp. 77–80.
- John Everett Millais's *Ophelia* at the Tate Gallery. www.tate.org.uk/ophelia/

2. As you have learned from this chapter, Shakespeare's plays are classified as tragedies, comedies, or histories. Using the resources listed below, or others you might find on your own, research Shakespearean comedy and the conventions of the genre, with a particular focus on *A Midsummer Night's Dream.* Write a paper in which you use your research on comedy to show how *A Midsummer Night's Dream* follows, varies from, or complicates the conventions of comedy.

- Dillon, Janette. "Shakespeare and the Traditions of English Stage Comedy." *A Companion to Shakespeare's Works: Comedies.* Vol. 3. Ed. Richard Dutton and Jean E. Howard. Malden, MA: Blackwell, 2003. pp. 4–22.
- Snyder, Susan. "The Genres of Shakespeare's Plays." *The Cambridge Companion to Shakespeare.* Ed. Margreta de Grazia and Stanley Wells. New York: Cambridge, 2001. pp. 83–98.
- Greenblatt, Stephen. "Wooing, Wedding, and Repenting." *Will in the World.* New York: W. W. Norton, 2004. See esp. pp. 133–140.

Some Sources for Research

Online Sources

1. Beckman, Katherine, Rebecca Scott, David Covington, Rachel Clark, Aisha Fikes, Anisa Haidary, Caryn Lazzuri, Ginger Simpson, Jane Pisano, Liz Pohland, Teri Cross Davis, Kindra Mizell, Carol Kelly, Niki Jacobsen, Mimi Godfrey, Donnajean Ward, and Sara Weiner, eds. *Folger Shakespeare Library.* Amherst College, 2005. Web. 30 April 2009. <http://www.folger.edu>.

2. Gray, Terry A., ed. *Shakespeare and the Internet.* Terry Gray, 28 April 2009. Web. 30 April 2009. <http://www.Shakespeare.palomar.edu>.

3. "History of the Monarchy." *The Official Website of the British Monarchy.* The Royal Household, 2009. Web. 30 April 2009. <http://www.royal.gov.uk/HistoryoftheMonarchy/HistoryoftheMonarchy.aspx>.

4. Johnson, Samuel. "Preface to Shakespeare." *The Works of Samuel Johnson.* Ed. F. P. Walesby. London: Oxford University Press, 1985. 103–154. Google. Web. 30 April 2009. <http://www.books.google.com/books?id=azsCAAAAQAAJ&pg=PA103&dg="samuel+johnson"+"preface+to+shakespeare"&lr=>.

5. Larque, Thomas, ed. *Shakespeare and his Critics.* N.p., n.d. Web. 30 April 2009. <http://www.shakespearean.org.uk>.

6. *Shakespeare's Globe.* The Shakespeare Globe Trust, 2009. Web. 30 April 2009. <http://www.shakespeares-globe.org>.

Print Sources

1. Auden, W. H. "The Joker in the Pack." *Shakespeare's Middle Tragedies: A Collection of Critical Essays.* Ed. David Young. Englewood Cliffs, NJ: Prentice Hall, 1993. 75–90. Print.

2. Bloom, Harold. *Shakespeare: The Invention of the Human.* New York: Riverhead, 1998. Print.

3. Bradley, A. C. *Shakespearean Tragedy: Lectures on Hamlet, Othello, King Lear, Macbeth.* New York: Palgrave Macmillan, 2007. Print.

4. Charney, Maurice. "Shakespeare's Villains." *How to Read Shakespeare.* New York: McGraw-Hill, 1971. Print.

5. De Grazia, Margreta and Stanley Wells, eds. *The Cambridge Companion to Shakespeare.* New York: Cambridge, 2001. Print.

6. Dutton, Richard, and Jean E. Howard, eds. *A Companion to Shakespeare's Works.* 3 vols. Malden, MA; Blackwell, 2003. Print.

7. Empson, William. "Honest in Othello." *The Structure of Complex Words.* Cambridge: Harvard University Press, 1989. 218–249. Print.

8. Knight, George Wilson. "On the Principles of Shakespeare Interpretation." *The Wheel of Fire: Interpretations of Shakespearian Tragedy.* New York: Routledge, 2001. 1–16. Print.

9. Mack, Maynard. "'The Readiness Is All': Hamlet." *Everybody's Shakespeare.* Lincoln: University of Nebraska Press, 1993. 107–128. Print.

10. Poole, Adrian. "Hamlet and Oedipus." *Tragedy: Shakespeare and the Greek Example.* New York: Blackwell, 1987. Print.

11. Zgang, Siyang, and Mason Y. H. Wang. "Hamlet's Melancholy." *Shakespeare and the Triple Play.* Lewisburg, PA: Bucknell University Press, 1988. Print.

For examples of student papers, see chapter 3, Common Writing Assignments, and chapter 5, Writing the Research Paper, in the Handbook for Writing from Reading.

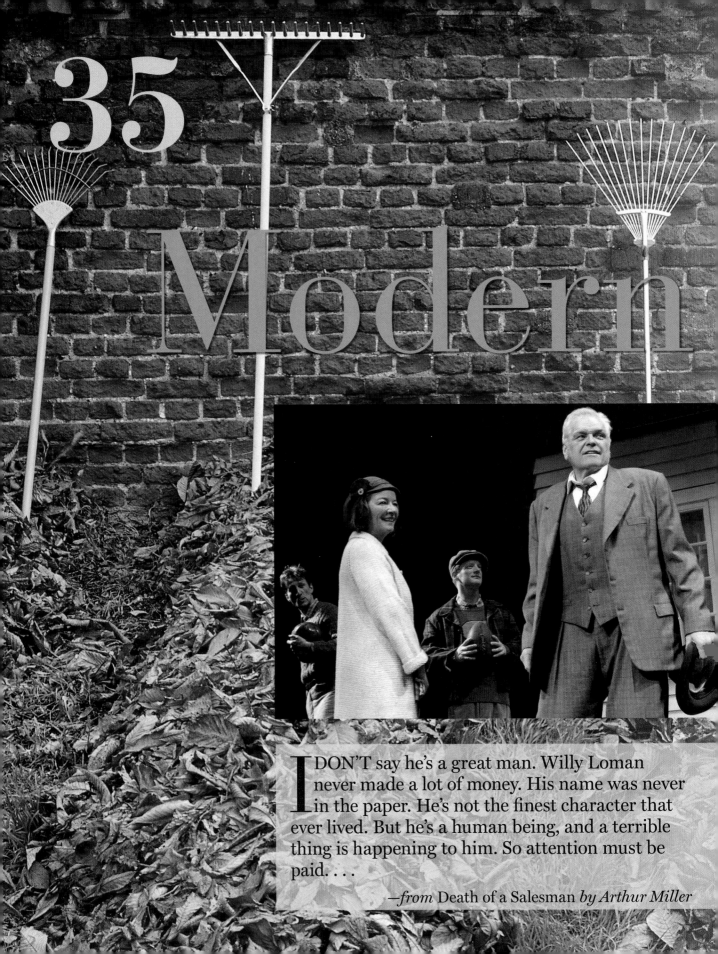

35

Modern

I DON'T say he's a great man. Willy Loman never made a lot of money. His name was never in the paper. He's not the finest character that ever lived. But he's a human being, and a terrible thing is happening to him. So attention must be paid. . . .

—*from* Death of a Salesman *by Arthur Miller*

> *"In this age few tragedies are written. It has often been held that the lack is due to a paucity of heroes among us, or else that modern man has had the blood drawn out of his organs of belief by the skepticism of science. . . . For one reason or another, we are often held to be below tragedy—or tragedy above us. The inevitable conclusion is, of course, that the tragic mode is archaic, fit only for the very highly placed, the kings or the kingly. . . . I believe that the common man is as apt a subject for tragedy in its highest sense as kings were."*
>
> —from "Tragedy and the Common Man" by Arthur Miller; video of his interview conducted in 1998 at the University of Michigan available online at www.mhhe.com/delbanco1e

Drama

FOR Sophocles and Shakespeare, the open stage was furnished largely by the imagination of the audience; today, we can expect the stage to have tables and chairs and paintings and grandfather clocks and carpets and glasses and bottles on display. The convention, or the agreed upon "reality" of the modern play, assumes that we're watching the action as if the **fourth wall** of the room has been removed so that we can look in on the private lives of a family. A scene with language and physical gestures, enacted by characters we find familiar, in a setting that resembles space we occupy offstage: that is the essence of the style we call **realism.**

As straightforward and simple as these attributes may seem, it took many centuries for this particular style to evolve. The Greek playwrights portrayed gods and heroes. Shakespeare wrote of monarchs and generals. Theatrical talk consisted of poetry or highly stylized speech. The focus of modern theater altered everything: characters grew recognizable, not exalted or debased, and their very human failings became the stuff of drama, redefining the conditions of tragedy. A tragic hero like Oedipus or Hamlet had to be of elevated rank in society, so that his fate and the fate of the common people can be intertwined. His collapse and fall have consequences for the people of his court and the community at large. His moment of realization provides him with a kind of wisdom that replaces power, and by play's end, the blind Oedipus is truly visionary; when we witness this reversal experience, or so the conventional wisdom about tragic theater would have it, we feel paired emotions of pity and fear, since a hero's death *matters* to us all.

The democratic ideal of the modern world, however, suggests that every man or woman can be a kind of hero. You need not be aristocratic or from an imperial family to have a tale worth telling or a fate that matters to others. *Death of a Salesman* deals with the exigencies of family life, and in unsparing terms. When Willy Loman's wife insists "attention must be finally paid to such a person," she's declaring, in effect, that every single character has his own important history and an aging, ill salesman down on his luck is also in some sense as important as a king.

(CONTINUED ON PAGE 340)

Q&A

A Conversation on Writing

Arthur Miller

Radical Drama and Becoming a Playwright

In the '30s the theater in New York was exploding. For the first time probably in its history, it was beginning to reflect real life, which was the Depression. These small radical groups of actors were putting on plays in storefronts and garages, and places like that. . . . Prose seemed to be remote and distant in comparison.

On His Writing Process

I generally work because I am struck by something somebody has said. Usually playwriting is an aural art. It's not an art of the writer expecting to be read. It's the writer expecting to be heard. So I think that if I hear a character speaking, either one I have invented or one I've confronted, it can start a process of creating.

Casting *Death of a Salesman*

I remember Lee Cobb, who was the original [Willy Loman]. . . . I imagined the character to be a little guy full of ginger, one of those little salesmen who [look] more or less like a squirrel. Here is Lee looking like a big beef. . . . My son Bobby was a little boy playing to the floor, and at one point Lee looked down—Bobby had done something funny—and he laughed. In that laugh—it was a real hearty laugh— you wanted to just burst out crying because it was so filled with sadness. He was very funny. He could be very funny. But while he was being funny he was dying in front of you. And I knew that was Willy.

To watch the entire interview with Arthur Miller, go to **www.mhhe.com/ delbanco1e**

RESEARCH ASSIGNMENT   After reading Arthur Miller's interview, how would you describe his ideas on the importance of "making it big" in theater? Do you agree with his position?

This interview was taped at the University of Michigan in April 1998, when the playwright was in Ann Arbor to celebrate the opening of the Arthur Miller Theater at his alma mater.

Arthur Miller (1915–2005)

Arthur Miller was born in New York City on October 17, 1915; he died at his home in Roxbury, Connecticut, on February 10, 2005. He worked as a playwright for all his long life and was among the most influential artists of his time. The son of Jewish immigrants living on the edge of poverty (his father had a garment manufacturing business that failed in the Depression), he never lost the social awareness or moral alertness that are hallmarks of his work. Though world-famous and much photographed—particularly during his brief marriage to film icon Marilyn Monroe—he remained a spokesman for and champion of the "common man."

In 1934, Miller enrolled at the University of Michigan—and, while a student there, won a Hopwood Award for playwriting. As he records in his autobiography, *Timebends: A Life* (1989), this ratified his sense of a career: "The magical force of making marks on a piece of paper and reaching into another human being, making him see what I had seen and feel my feelings—I had made a new shadow on the earth." His first play, however, *The Man Who Had All the Luck,* opened to negative reviews in 1944, and it was not until *All My Sons* in 1947 that he had a Broadway success. A tragedy about a manufacturer who sells faulty parts to the military in order to save his business, this play deals with many of the themes that characterize Miller's writing: the prospect of commercial failure, the intricacies of family life, the hard moral choices every person must face. Two years thereafter, he produced his most successful play, *Death of a Salesman*—which won both a Pulitzer Prize and a Drama Critics Circle Award. It ran for 700 performances after its first opening, and it's probably safe to say that no week now passes without a production of *Death of a Salesman* somewhere in the world.

Overwhelmed by postwar paranoia and intolerance, Miller wrote the third of his major plays, *The Crucible,* which had its Broadway premiere in 1953. Set in Salem during the witch hunts of the late seventeenth century, this story reports on extraordinary tragedy in ordinary lives. Within three years, Miller was called before the House Un-American Activities Committee and convicted of contempt of Congress for not cooperating in the more modern version of a witch hunt for Communists in the entertainment industry. His steady output continued, however, and his bibliography includes *After the Fall* (1963), *Incident at Vichy* (1964), *The Ride Down Mount Morgan* (1991), and *The Last Yankee* (1993). By his death, he had written essays, stories, a novel, *Focus* (1945), an autobiography, and the dozens of plays for which he remains most celebrated and from which continues to emerge his magisterial voice.

AS YOU READ   Compare the main character, Willy Loman, with Oedipus the King. How are they similar and how are they different?

"What you read on the page looks like it's been there forever, but believe me, it hasn't. It's always a struggle to find what you are looking for. Certainly the play is as much rewritten as it is written." Conversation with Arthur Miller

Death of a Salesman (1949)

Certain Private Conversations in Two Acts and a Requiem

CHARACTERS

WILLY LOMAN

LINDA

BIFF

HAPPY

BERNARD

THE WOMAN

CHARLEY

UNCLE BEN

HOWARD WAGNER

JENNY

STANLEY

MISS FORSYTHE

LETTA

SCENE: *The action takes place in* WILLY LOMAN'S *house and yard and in various places he visits in the New York and Boston of today.*

 Throughout the play, in the stage directions, left and right mean stage left and stage right.

ACT I

A melody is heard, played upon a flute. It is small and fine, telling of grass and trees and the horizon. The curtain rises.

 Before us is the Salesman's house. We are aware of towering, angular shapes behind it, surrounding it on all sides. Only the blue light of the sky falls upon the house and forestage; the surrounding area shows an angry glow of orange. As more light appears, we see a solid vault of apartment houses around the small, fragile-seeming home. An air of the dream clings to the place, a dream rising out of reality. The kitchen at center seems actual enough, for there is a kitchen table with three chairs, and a refrigerator. But no other fixtures are seen. At the back of the kitchen there is a draped entrance, which leads to the living-room. To the right of the kitchen, on a level raised two feet, is a bedroom furnished only with a brass bedstead and a straight chair. On a shelf over the bed a silver athletic trophy stands. A window opens onto the apartment house at the side.

 Behind the kitchen, on a level raised six and a half feet, is the boys' bedroom, at present barely visible. Two beds are dimly seen, and at the back of the room a dormer window. (This bedroom is above the unseen living-room.) At the left a stairway curves up to it from the kitchen.

 The entire setting is wholly or, in some places, partially transparent. The roof-line of the house is one-dimensional; under and over it we see the apartment buildings. Before the house lies an apron, curving beyond the forestage into the orchestra. This forward area serves as the back yard as well as the locale of all WILLY'S *imaginings and of his city scenes. Whenever the action is in the present the actors observe the imaginary wall-lines, entering the house only through its door at the left. But in the scenes of the past these boundaries are broken, and characters enter or leave a room by stepping "through" a wall onto the forestage.*

From the right, WILLY LOMAN, *the Salesman, enters, carrying two large sample cases. The flute plays on. He hears but is not aware of it. He is past sixty years of age, dressed quietly. Even as he crosses the stage to the doorway of the house, his exhaustion is apparent. He unlocks the door, comes into the kitchen, and thankfully lets his burden down, feeling the soreness of his palms. A word-sigh escapes his lips—it might be "Oh, boy, oh, boy." He closes the door, then carries his cases out into the living-room, through the draped kitchen doorway.*

LINDA, *his wife, has stirred in her bed at the right. She gets out and puts on a robe, listening. Most often jovial, she has developed an iron repression of her exceptions to* WILLY'S *behavior—she more than loves him, she admires him, as though his mercurial nature, his temper, his massive dreams and little cruelties, served her only as sharp reminders of the turbulent longings within him, longings which she shares but lacks the temperament to utter and follow to their end.*

LINDA: *(hearing* WILLY *outside the bedroom, calls with some trepidation)* Willy!

WILLY: It's all right. I came back.

LINDA: Why? What happened? *(Slight pause.)* Did something happen, Willy?

WILLY: No, nothing happened.

LINDA: You didn't smash the car, did you?

WILLY: *(with casual irritation)* I said nothing happened. Didn't you hear me?

LINDA: Don't you feel well?

WILLY: I'm tired to the death. *(The flute has faded away. He sits on the bed beside her, a little numb.)* I couldn't make it. I just couldn't make it, Linda.

LINDA: *(very carefully, delicately)* Where were you all day? You look terrible.

WILLY: I got as far as a little above Yonkers. I stopped for a cup of coffee. Maybe it was the coffee.

LINDA: What?

WILLY: *(after a pause)* I suddenly couldn't drive any more. The car kept going off onto the shoulder, y'know?

LINDA: *(helpfully)* Oh. Maybe it was the steering again. I don't think Angelo knows the Studebaker.

WILLY: No, it's me, it's me. Suddenly I realize I'm goin' sixty miles an hour and I don't remember the last five minutes. I'm—I can't seem to—keep my mind to it.

Willy Loman (Dustin Hoffman) talks with his wife, Linda (Kate Reid), in the 1985 film directed by Volker Schlöndorff.

LINDA: Maybe it's your glasses. You never went for your new glasses.

WILLY: No, I see everything. I came back ten miles an hour. It took me nearly four hours from Yonkers.

LINDA: *(resigned)* Well, you'll just have to take a rest, Willy, you can't continue this way.

WILLY: I just got back from Florida.

LINDA: But you didn't rest your mind. Your mind is overactive, and the mind is what counts, dear.

WILLY: I'll start out in the morning. Maybe I'll feel better in the morning. *(She is taking off his shoes.)* These goddam arch supports are killing me.

LINDA: Take an aspirin. Should I get you an aspirin? It'll soothe you.

WILLY: *(with wonder)* I was driving along, you understand? And I was fine. I was even observing the scenery. You can imagine, me looking at scenery, on the road every week of my life. But it's so beautiful up there, Linda, the trees are so thick, and the sun is warm. I opened the windshield and just let the warm air bathe over me. And then all of a sudden I'm goin' off the road! I'm tellin' ya, I absolutely forgot I was driving. If I'd've gone the other way over the white line I might've killed somebody. So I went on again—and five minutes later I'm dreamin' again, and I nearly—*(He presses two fingers against his eyes.)* I have such thoughts, I have such strange thoughts.

LINDA: Willy, dear. Talk to them again. There's no reason why you can't work in New York.

55 **WILLY:**   They don't need me in New York. I'm the New England man. I'm vital in New England.

LINDA: But you're sixty years old. They can't expect you to keep traveling every week.

WILLY: I'll have to send a wire to Portland. I'm sup-
60 posed to see Brown and Morrison tomorrow morning at ten o'clock to show the line. Goddammit, I could sell them! *(He starts putting on his jacket.)*

LINDA: *(taking the jacket from him)*   Why don't you go down to the place tomorrow and tell Howard you've
65 simply got to work in New York? You're too accommodating, dear.

WILLY: If old man Wagner was alive I'd a been in charge of New York now! That man was a prince, he was a masterful man. But that boy of his, that How-
70 ard, he don't appreciate. When I went north the first time, the Wagner Company didn't know where New England was!

LINDA: Why don't you tell those things to Howard, dear?

75 **WILLY:** *(encouraged)*   I will, I definitely will. Is there any cheese?

LINDA: I'll make you a sandwich.

WILLY: No, go to sleep. I'll take some milk. I'll be up right away. The boys in?

80 **LINDA:**   They're sleeping. Happy took Biff on a date tonight.

WILLY: *(interested)*   That so?

Willy (Lee J. Cobb) talks with his wife, Linda (Mildred Dunnock), in the 1966 film directed by Alex Segal.

LINDA: It was so nice to see them shaving together, one behind the other, in the bathroom. And going out together. You notice? The whole house smells of shaving lotion. 85

WILLY: Figure it out. Work a lifetime to pay off a house. You finally own it, and there's nobody to live in it.

LINDA: Well, dear, life is a casting off. It's always that way. 90

WILLY: No, no, some people—some people accomplish something. Did Biff say anything after I went this morning?

LINDA: You shouldn't have criticized him, Willy, especially after he just got off the train. You mustn't lose 95 your temper with him.

WILLY: When the hell did I lose my temper? I simply asked him if he was making any money. Is that a criticism?

LINDA: But, dear, how could he make any money? 100

WILLY: *(worried and angered)*   There's such an undercurrent in him. He became a moody man. Did he apologize when I left this morning?

LINDA: He was crestfallen, Willy. You know how he admires you. I think if he finds himself, then you'll 105 both be happier and not fight any more.

WILLY: How can he find himself on a farm? Is that a life? A farmhand? In the beginning, when he was young, I thought, well, a young man, it's good for him to tramp around, take a lot of different jobs. But 110 it's more than ten years now and he has yet to make thirty-five dollars a week!

LINDA: He's finding himself, Willy.

WILLY: Not finding yourself at the age of thirty-four is a disgrace! 115

LINDA: Shh!

WILLY: The trouble is he's lazy, goddammit!

LINDA: Willy, please!

WILLY: Biff is a lazy bum!

LINDA: They're sleeping. Get something to eat. Go on 120 down.

WILLY: Why did he come home? I would like to know what brought him home.

LINDA: I don't know. I think he's still lost, Willy. I think he's very lost. 125

WILLY: Biff Loman is lost. In the greatest country in the world a young man with such—personal attractiveness, gets lost. And such a hard worker. There's one thing about Biff—he's not lazy.

130 **LINDA:** Never.

WILLY: (with pity and resolve) I'll see him in the morning; I'll have a nice talk with him. I'll get him a job selling. He could be big in no time. My God! Remember how they used to follow him around in high 135 school? When he smiled at one of them their faces lit up. When he walked down the street . . . (He loses himself in reminiscences.)

LINDA: (trying to bring him out of it) Willy, dear, I got a new kind of American-type cheese today. It's 140 whipped.

WILLY: Why do you get American when I like Swiss?

LINDA: I just thought you'd like a change—

WILLY: I don't want a change! I want Swiss cheese. Why am I always being contradicted?

145 **LINDA:** (with a covering laugh) I thought it would be a surprise.

WILLY: Why don't you open a window in here, for God's sake?

LINDA: (with infinite patience) They're all open, dear.

150 **WILLY:** The way they boxed us in here. Bricks and windows, windows and bricks.

LINDA: We should've bought the land next door.

WILLY: The street is lined with cars. There's not a breath of fresh air in the neighborhood. The grass 155 don't grow any more, you can't raise a carrot in the back yard. They should've had a law against apartment houses. Remember those two beautiful elm trees out there? When I and Biff hung the swing between them?

160 **LINDA:** Yeah, like being a million miles from the city.

WILLY: They should've arrested the builder for cutting those down. They massacred the neighborhood. (Lost.) More and more I think of those days, Linda. This time of year it was lilac and wisteria. And then 165 the peonies would come out, and the daffodils. What fragrance in this room!

LINDA: Well, after all, people had to move somewhere.

WILLY: No, there's more people now.

LINDA: I don't think there's more people. I think—

WILLY: There's more people! That's what's ruining this 170 country! Population is getting out of control. The competition is maddening! Smell the stink from that apartment house! And another one on the other side . . . How can they whip cheese?

On WILLY's *last line,* BIFF *and* HAPPY *raise themselves up in their beds, listening.*

LINDA: Go down, try it. And be quiet. 175

WILLY: (turning to LINDA, guiltily) You're not worried about me, are you, sweetheart?

BIFF: What's the matter?

HAPPY: Listen!

LINDA: You've got too much on the ball to worry about. 180

WILLY: You're my foundation and my support, Linda.

LINDA: Just try to relax, dear. You make mountains out of molehills.

WILLY: I won't fight with him any more. If he wants to go back to Texas, let him go. 185

LINDA: He'll find his way.

WILLY: Sure. Certain men just don't get started till later in life. Like Thomas Edison, I think. Or B. F. Goodrich. One of them was deaf. (He starts for the bedroom doorway.) I'll put my money on Biff. 190

LINDA: And Willy—if it's warm Sunday we'll drive in the country. And we'll open the windshield, and take lunch.

WILLY: No, the windshields don't open on the new cars.

LINDA: But you opened it today. 195

WILLY: Me? I didn't. (He stops.) Now isn't that peculiar! Isn't that a remarkable—(He breaks off in amazement and fright as the flute is heard distantly.)

LINDA: What, darling?

WILLY: That is the most remarkable thing. 200

LINDA: What, dear?

WILLY: I was thinking of the Chevy. (Slight pause.) Nineteen twenty-eight . . . when I had that red Chevy—(Breaks off.) That funny? I coulda sworn I was driving that Chevy today. 205

LINDA: Well, that's nothing. Something must've reminded you.

WILLY: Remarkable. Ts. Remember those days? The way Biff used to simonize that car? The dealer

210   refused to believe there was eighty thousand miles on it. (*He shakes his head.*) Heh! (*To* LINDA.) Close your eyes, I'll be right up. (*He walks out of the bedroom.*)

215   **HAPPY:** (*to* BIFF)   Jesus, maybe he smashed up the car again!

LINDA: (*calling after* WILLY)   Be careful on the stairs, dear! The cheese is on the middle shelf! (*She turns, goes over to the bed, takes his jacket, and goes out of the bedroom.*)

Light has risen on the boys' room. Unseen, WILLY *is heard talking to himself, "Eighty thousand miles," and a little laugh.* BIFF *gets out of bed, comes downstage a bit, and stands attentively.* BIFF *is two years older than his brother* HAPPY, *well built, but in these days bears a worn air and seems less self-assured. He has succeeded less, and his dreams are stronger and less acceptable than* HAPPY's. HAPPY *is tall, powerfully made. Sexuality is like a visible color on him, or a scent that many women have discovered. He, like his brother, is lost, but in a different way, for he has never allowed himself to turn his face toward defeat and is thus more confused and hard-skinned, although seemingly more content.*

220   **HAPPY:** (*getting out of bed*)   He's going to get his license taken away if he keeps that up. I'm getting nervous about him, y'know, Biff?

BIFF: His eyes are going.

225   **HAPPY:**   No, I've driven with him. He sees all right. He just doesn't keep his mind on it. I drove into the city with him last week. He stops at a green light and then it turns red and he goes. (*He laughs.*)

BIFF: Maybe he's color-blind.

230   **HAPPY:**   Pop? Why he's got the finest eye for color in the business. You know that.

BIFF: (*sitting down on his bed*)   I'm going to sleep.

HAPPY: You're not still sour on Dad, are you, Biff?

BIFF: He's all right, I guess.

235   **WILLY:** (*underneath them, in the living-room*)   Yes, sir, eighty thousand miles—eighty-two thousand!

BIFF: You smoking?

HAPPY: (*holding out a pack of cigarettes*)   Want one?

BIFF: (*taking a cigarette*)   I can never sleep when I smell it.

WILLY: What a simonizing job, heh!

240   **HAPPY:** (*with deep sentiment*)   Funny, Biff, y'know? Us sleeping in here again? The old beds. (*He pats his bed affectionately.*) All the talk that went across those two beds, huh? Our whole lives.

BIFF: Yeah. Lotta dreams and plans.

245   **HAPPY:** (*with a deep and masculine laugh*)   About five hundred women would like to know what was said in this room.

They share a soft laugh.

BIFF: Remember that big Betsy something—what the hell was her name—over on Bushwick Avenue?

250   **HAPPY:** (*combing his hair*)   With the collie dog!

BIFF: That's the one. I got you in there, remember?

HAPPY: Yeah, that was my first time—I think. Boy, there was a pig! (*They laugh, almost crudely.*) You taught me everything I know about women. Don't forget that.

255

BIFF: I bet you forgot how bashful you used to be. Especially with girls.

HAPPY: Oh, I still am, Biff.

BIFF: Oh, go on.

260   **HAPPY:**   I just control it, that's all. I think I got less bashful and you got more so. What happened, Biff? Where's the old humor, the old confidence? (*He shakes* BIFF's *knee.* BIFF *gets up and moves restlessly about the room.*) What's the matter?

265   **BIFF:**   Why does Dad mock me all the time?

HAPPY: He's not mocking you, he—

BIFF: Everything I say there's a twist of mockery on his face. I can't get near him.

270   **HAPPY:**   He just wants you to make good, that's all. I wanted to talk to you about Dad for a long time, Biff. Something's—happening to him. He—talks to himself.

BIFF: I noticed that this morning. But he always mumbled.

275   **HAPPY:**   But not so noticeable. It got so embarrassing I sent him to Florida. And you know something? Most of the time he's talking to you.

BIFF: What's he say about me?

HAPPY: I can't make it out.

280   **BIFF:**   What's he say about me?

Biff (John Malkovich) and Happy (Stephen Lang) talk about their plans.

HAPPY: I think the fact that you're not settled, that you're still kind of up in the air . . .

BIFF: There's one or two other things depressing him, Happy.

285 **HAPPY:** What do you mean?

BIFF: Never mind. Just don't lay it all to me.

HAPPY: But I think if you just got started—I mean—is there any future for you out there?

BIFF: I tell ya, Hap, I don't know what the future is. I
290 don't know—what I'm supposed to want.

HAPPY: What do you mean?

BIFF: Well, I spent six or seven years after high school trying to work myself up. Shipping clerk, salesman, business of one kind or another. And it's a measly
295 manner of existence. To get on that subway on the hot mornings in summer. To devote your whole life to keeping stock, or making phone calls, or selling or buying. To suffer fifty weeks of the year for the sake of a two-week vacation, when all you really desire
300 is to be outdoors, with your shirt off. And always to have to get ahead of the next fella. And still—that's how you build a future.

HAPPY: Well, you really enjoy it on a farm? Are you content out there?

305 **BIFF:** *(with rising agitation)* Hap, I've had twenty or thirty different kinds of jobs since I left home before the war, and it always turns out the same. I just realized it lately. In Nebraska when I herded cattle, and the Dakotas, and Arizona, and now in Texas. It's
310 why I came home now, I guess, because I realized it. This farm I work on, it's spring there now, see? And

they've got about fifteen new colts. There's nothing more inspiring or—beautiful than the sight of a mare and a new colt. And it's cool there now, see? Texas is cool now, and it's spring. And whenever spring comes 315 to where I am, I suddenly get the feeling, my God, I'm not gettin' anywhere! What the hell am I doing, playing around with horses, twenty-eight dollars a week! I'm thirty-four years old, I oughta be makin' 320 my future. That's when I come running home. And now, I get here, and I don't know what to do with myself. *(After a pause.)* I've always made a point of not wasting my life, and everytime I come back here I know that all I've done is to waste my life. 325

HAPPY: You're a poet, you know that, Biff? You're a— you're an idealist!

BIFF: No, I'm mixed up very bad. Maybe I oughta get married. Maybe I oughta get stuck into something. Maybe that's my trouble. I'm like a boy. I'm not mar- 330 ried. I'm not in business, I just—I'm like a boy. Are you content, Hap? You're a success, aren't you? Are you content?

HAPPY: Hell, no!

BIFF: Why? You're making money, aren't you? 335

HAPPY: *(moving about with energy, expressiveness)* All I can do now is wait for the merchandise manager to die. And suppose I get to be merchandise manager? He's a good friend of mine, and he just built a terrific estate on Long Island. And he lived there about two 340 months and sold it, and now he's building another one. He can't enjoy it once it's finished. And I know that's just what I would do. I don't know what the hell I'm workin' for. Sometimes I sit in my apart- ment—all alone. And I think of the rent I'm paying. 345 And it's crazy. But then, it's what I always wanted. My own apartment, a car, and plenty of women. And still, goddammit, I'm lonely.

BIFF: *(with enthusiasm)* Listen, why don't you come out West with me? 350

HAPPY: You and I, heh?

BIFF: Sure, maybe we could buy a ranch. Raise cattle, use our muscles. Men built like we are should be working out in the open.

HAPPY: *(avidly)* The Loman Brothers, heh? 355

BIFF: *(with vast affection)* Sure, we'd be known all over the counties!

HAPPY: *(enthralled)* That's what I dream about, Biff. Sometimes I want to just rip my clothes off in the

360 middle of the store and outbox that goddam merchandise manager. I mean I can outbox, outrun,
and outlift anybody in that store, and I have to take
orders from those common, petty sons-of-bitches till
I can't stand it any more.

365 **BIFF:** I'm tellin' you, kid, if you were with me I'd be
happy out there.

HAPPY: (*enthused*) See, Biff, everybody around me is so
false that I'm constantly lowering my ideals . . .

BIFF: Baby, together we'd stand up for one another,
370 we'd have someone to trust.

HAPPY: If I were around you—

BIFF: Hap, the trouble is we weren't brought up to grub
for money. I don't know how to do it.

HAPPY: Neither can I!

375 **BIFF:** Then let's go!

HAPPY: The only thing is—what can you make out
there?

BIFF: But look at your friend. Builds an estate and then
hasn't the peace of mind to live in it.

380 **HAPPY:** Yeah, but when he walks into the store the
waves part in front of him. That's fifty-two thousand
dollars a year coming through the revolving door,
and I got more in my pinky finger than he's got in his
head.

385 **BIFF:** Yeah, but you just said—

HAPPY: I gotta show some of those pompous, self-
important executives over there that Hap Loman
can make the grade. I want to walk into the store
the way he walks in. Then I'll go with you, Biff. We'll
390 be together yet, I swear. But take those two we had
tonight. Now weren't they gorgeous creatures?

BIFF: Yeah, yeah, most gorgeous I've had in years.

HAPPY: I get that any time I want, Biff. Whenever I
feel disgusted. The trouble is, it gets like bowling
395 or something. I just keep knockin' them over and it
doesn't mean anything. You still run around a lot?

BIFF: Naa. I'd like to find a girl—steady, somebody with
substance.

HAPPY: That's what I long for.

400 **BIFF:** Go on! You'd never come home.

HAPPY: I would! Somebody with character, with resistance! Like Mom, y'know? You're gonna call me a
bastard when I tell you this. That girl Charlotte

I was with tonight is engaged to be married in five
weeks. (*He tries on his new hat.*) 405

BIFF: No kiddin'!

HAPPY: Sure, the guy's in line for the vice-presidency
of the store. I don't know what gets into me, maybe
I just have an overdeveloped sense of competition
or something, but I went and ruined her, and fur- 410
thermore I can't get rid of her. And he's the third
executive I've done that to. Isn't that a crummy characteristic? And to top it all, I go to their weddings!
(*Indignantly, but laughing.*) Like I'm not supposed to
take bribes. Manufacturers offer me a hundred- 415
dollar bill now and then to throw an order their way.
You know how honest I am, but it's like this girl, see.
I hate myself for it. Because I don't want the girl,
and, still, I take it and—I love it!

BIFF: Let's go to sleep. 420

HAPPY: I guess we didn't settle anything, heh?

BIFF: I just got one idea that I think I'm going to try.

HAPPY: What's that?

BIFF: Remember Bill Oliver?

HAPPY: Sure, Oliver is very big now. You want to work 425
for him again?

BIFF: No, but when I quit he said something to me. He
put his arm on my shoulder, and he said, "Biff, if you
ever need anything, come to me."

HAPPY: I remember that. That sounds good. 430

BIFF: I think I'll go to see him. If I could get ten thousand or even seven or eight thousand dollars I could
buy a beautiful ranch.

HAPPY: I bet he'd back you. 'Cause he thought highly of
you, Biff. I mean, they all do. You're well liked, Biff. 435
That's why I say to come back here, and we both have
the apartment. And I'm tellin' you, Biff, any babe you
want . . .

BIFF: No, with a ranch I could do the work I like and
still be something. I just wonder though. I wonder if 440
Oliver still thinks I stole that carton of basketballs.

HAPPY: Oh, he probably forgot that long ago. It's almost ten years. You're too sensitive. Anyway, he
didn't really fire you.

BIFF: Well, I think he was going to. I think that's why 445
I quit. I was never sure whether he knew or not. I
know he thought the world of me, though. I was the
only one he'd let lock up the place.

WILLY: (*below*) You gonna wash the engine, Biff?

450 **HAPPY:** Shh!

BIFF looks at HAPPY, who is gazing down, listening. WILLY is mumbling in the parlor.

HAPPY: You hear that?

They listen. WILLY laughs warmly.

BIFF: *(growing angry)* Doesn't he know Mom can hear that?

WILLY: Don't get your sweater dirty, Biff!

A look of pain crosses BIFF's face.

455 **HAPPY:** Isn't that terrible? Don't leave again, will you? You'll find a job here. You gotta stick around. I don't know what to do about him, it's getting embarrassing.

WILLY: What a simonizing job!

460 **BIFF:** Mom's hearing that!

WILLY: No kiddin', Biff, you got a date? Wonderful!

HAPPY: Go on to sleep. But talk to him in the morning, will you?

BIFF: *(reluctantly getting into bed)* With her in the house.
465 Brother!

HAPPY: *(getting into bed)* I wish you'd have a good talk with him.

The light on their room begins to fade.

BIFF: *(to himself in bed)* That selfish, stupid . . .

HAPPY: Sh . . . Sleep, Biff.

Their light is out. Well before they have finished speaking, WILLY's form is dimly seen below in the darkened kitchen. He opens the refrigerator, searches in there, and takes out a bottle of milk. The apartment houses are fading out, and the entire house and surroundings become covered with leaves. Music insinuates itself as the leaves appear.

470 **WILLY:** Just wanna be careful with those girls, Biff, that's all. Don't make any promises. No promises of any kind. Because a girl, y'know, they always believe what you tell 'em, and you're very young, Biff, you're too young to be talking seriously to girls.

Light rises on the kitchen. WILLY, talking, shuts the refrigerator door and comes downstage to the kitchen table. He pours milk into a glass. He is totally immersed in himself, smiling faintly.

475 **WILLY:** Too young entirely, Biff. You want to watch your schooling first. Then when you're all set, there'll be plenty of girls for a boy like you. *(He smiles broadly at a kitchen chair.)* That so? The girls pay for you? *(He laughs.)* Boy, you must really be makin' a hit.

WILLY is gradually addressing—physically—a point offstage, speaking through the wall of the kitchen, and his voice has been rising in volume to that of a normal conversation.

WILLY: I been wondering why you polish the car so 480 careful. Ha! Don't leave the hubcaps, boys. Get the chamois to the hubcaps. Happy, use newspaper on the windows, it's the easiest thing. Show him how to do it, Biff! You see, Happy? Pad it up, use it like a pad. That's it, that's it, good work. You're doin' all 485 right, Hap. *(He pauses, then nods in approbation for a few seconds, then looks upward.)* Biff, first thing we gotta do when we get time is clip that big branch over the house. Afraid it's gonna fall in a storm and hit the roof. Tell you what. We get a rope and sling her 490 around, and then we climb up there with a couple of saws and take her down. Soon as you finish the car, boys, I wanna see ya. I got a surprise for you, boys.

BIFF: *(offstage)* Whatta ya got, Dad?

WILLY: No, you finish first. Never leave a job till you're 495 finished—remember that. *(Looking toward the "big trees.")* Biff, up in Albany I saw a beautiful hammock. I think I'll buy it next trip, and we'll hang it right between those two elms. Wouldn't that be something? Just swingin' there under those branches. Boy, that 500 would be . . .

Young BIFF and Young HAPPY appear from the direction WILLY was addressing. HAPPY carries rags and a pail of water. BIFF, wearing a sweater with a block "S," carries a football.

Willy drinks his milk as he addresses a point offstage.

BIFF: *(pointing in the direction of the car offstage)* How's that, Pop, professional?

WILLY: Terrific. Terrific job, boys. Good work, Biff.

505 **HAPPY:** Where's the surprise, Pop?

WILLY: In the back seat of the car.

HAPPY: Boy! *(He runs off.)*

BIFF: What is it, Dad? Tell me, what'd you buy?

WILLY: *(laughing, cuffs him)* Never mind, something I
510 want you to have.

BIFF: *(turns and starts off)* What is it, Hap?

HAPPY: *(offstage)* It's a punching bag!

BIFF: Oh, Pop!

WILLY: It's got Gene Tunney's signature on it!

HAPPY *runs onstage with a punching bag.*

515 **BIFF:** Gee, how'd you know we wanted a punching bag?

WILLY: Well, it's the finest thing for the timing.

HAPPY: *(lies down on his back and pedals with his feet)* I'm
losing weight, you notice, Pop?

WILLY: *(to HAPPY)* Jumping rope is good too.

520 **BIFF:** Did you see the new football I got?

WILLY: *(examining the ball)* Where'd you get a new ball?

BIFF: The coach told me to practice my passing.

WILLY: That so? And he gave you the ball, heh?

BIFF: Well, I borrowed it from the locker room. *(He*
525 *laughs confidentially.)*

WILLY: *(laughing with him at the theft)* I want you to return that.

HAPPY: I told you he wouldn't like it!

BIFF: *(angrily)* Well, I'm bringing it back!

530 **WILLY:** *(stopping the incipient argument, to HAPPY)* Sure,
he's gotta practice with a regulation ball, doesn't he?
(To BIFF.) Coach'll probably congratulate you on your
initiative!

BIFF: Oh, he keeps congratulating my initiative all the
535 time, Pop.

WILLY: That's because he likes you. If somebody else
took that ball there'd be an uproar. So what's the
report, boys, what's the report?

Willy and his boys, in happier times, discuss the future.

BIFF: Where'd you go this time, Dad? Gee we were
lonesome for you. 540

WILLY: *(pleased, puts an arm around each boy and they come
down to the apron)* Lonesome, heh?

BIFF: Missed you every minute.

WILLY: Don't say? Tell you a secret, boys. Don't breathe
it to a soul. Someday I'll have my own business, and 545
I'll never have to leave home any more.

HAPPY: Like Uncle Charley, heh?

WILLY: Bigger than Uncle Charley! Because Charley is
not—liked. He's liked, but he's not—well liked.

BIFF: Where'd you go this time, Dad? 550

WILLY: Well, I got on the road, and I went north to
Providence. Met the Mayor.

BIFF: The Mayor of Providence!

WILLY: He was sitting in the hotel lobby.

BIFF: What'd he say? 555

WILLY: He said, "Morning!" And I said, "You got a fine
city here, Mayor." And then he had coffee with me.
And then I went to Waterbury. Waterbury is a fine
city. Big clock city, the famous Waterbury clock. Sold
a nice bill there. And then Boston—Boston is the 560
cradle of the Revolution. A fine city. And a couple of
other towns in Mass., and on to Portland and Bangor
and straight home!

BIFF: Gee, I'd love to go with you sometime, Dad.

WILLY: Soon as summer comes. 565

HAPPY: Promise?

WILLY: You and Hap and I, and I'll show you all the
towns. America is full of beautiful towns and fine,

WILLY: upstanding people. And they know me, boys, they know me up and down New England. The finest people. And when I bring you fellas up, there'll be open sesame for all of us, 'cause one thing, boys: I have friends. I can park my car in any street in New England, and the cops protect it like their own. This summer, heh?

BIFF AND HAPPY: *(together)* Yeah! You bet!

WILLY: We'll take our bathing suits.

HAPPY: We'll carry your bags, Pop!

WILLY: Oh, won't that be something! Me comin' into the Boston stores with you boys carryin' my bags. What a sensation!

BIFF is prancing around, practicing passing the ball.

WILLY: You nervous, Biff, about the game?

BIFF: Not if you're gonna be there.

WILLY: What do they say about you in school, now that they made you captain?

HAPPY: There's a crowd of girls behind him everytime the classes change.

BIFF: *(taking WILLY's hand)* This Saturday, Pop, this Saturday—just for you, I'm going to break through for a touchdown.

HAPPY: You're supposed to pass.

BIFF: I'm takin' one play for Pop. You watch me, Pop, and when I take off my helmet, that means I'm breakin' out. Then you watch me crash through that line!

WILLY: *(kisses BIFF)* Oh, wait'll I tell this in Boston!

BERNARD enters in knickers. He is younger than BIFF, earnest and loyal, a worried boy.

BERNARD: Biff, where are you? You're supposed to study with me today.

WILLY: Hey, looka Bernard. What're you lookin' so anemic about, Bernard?

BERNARD: He's gotta study, Uncle Willy. He's got Regents next week.

HAPPY: *(tauntingly, spinning BERNARD around)* Let's box, Bernard!

BERNARD: Biff! *(He gets away from HAPPY.)* Listen, Biff, I heard Mr. Birnbaum say that if you don't start studyin' math, he's gonna flunk you, and you won't graduate. I heard him!

WILLY: You better study with him, Biff. Go ahead now.

BERNARD: I heard him!

BIFF: Oh, Pop, you didn't see my sneakers! *(He holds up a foot for WILLY to look at.)*

WILLY: Hey, that's a beautiful job of printing!

BERNARD: *(wiping his glasses)* Just because he printed University of Virginia on his sneakers doesn't mean they've got to graduate him, Uncle Willy!

WILLY: *(angrily)* What're you talking about? With scholarships to three universities they're gonna flunk him?

BERNARD: But I heard Mr. Birnbaum say—

WILLY: Don't be a pest, Bernard! *(To his boys.)* What an anemic!

BERNARD: Okay, I'm waiting for you in my house, Biff.

BERNARD goes off. The Lomans laugh.

WILLY: Bernard is not well liked, is he?

BIFF: He's liked, but he's not well liked.

HAPPY: That's right, Pop.

WILLY: That's just what I mean. Bernard can get the best marks in school, y'understand, but when he gets out in the business world, y'understand, you are going to be five times ahead of him. That's why I thank Almighty God you're both built like Adonises. Because the man who makes an appearance in the business world, the man who creates personal interest, is the man who gets ahead. Be liked and you will never want. You take me, for instance. I never have to wait in line to see a buyer. "Willy Loman is here!" That's all they have to know, and I go right through.

BIFF: Did you knock them dead, Pop?

WILLY: Knocked 'em cold in Providence, slaughtered 'em in Boston.

HAPPY: *(on his back, pedaling again)* I'm losing weight, you notice, Pop?

LINDA enters, as of old, a ribbon in her hair, carrying a basket of washing.

LINDA: *(with youthful energy)* Hello, dear!

WILLY: Sweetheart!

LINDA: How'd the Chevy run?

WILLY: Chevrolet, Linda, is the greatest car ever built. *(To the boys.)* Since when do you let your mother carry wash up the stairs?

Willy, Happy (James Farentino), and Biff (George Segal) scoff at Bernard's (Gene Wilder) attitude toward education.

BIFF: Grab hold there, boy!

HAPPY: Where to, Mom?

650 **LINDA:** Hang them up on the line. And you better go down to your friends, Biff. The cellar is full of boys. They don't know what to do with themselves.

BIFF: Ah, when Pop comes home they can wait!

WILLY: *(laughs appreciatively)* You better go down and
655 tell them what to do, Biff.

BIFF: I think I'll have them sweep out the furnace room.

WILLY: Good work, Biff.

BIFF: *(goes through wall-line of kitchen to doorway at back and calls down)* Fellas! Everybody sweep out the fur-
660 nace room! I'll be right down!

VOICES: All right! Okay, Biff.

BIFF: George and Sam and Frank, come out back! We're hangin' up the wash! Come on, Hap, on the double! *(He and HAPPY carry out the basket.)*

665 **LINDA:** The way they obey him!

WILLY: Well, that's training, the training. I'm tellin' you, I was sellin' thousands and thousands, but I had to come home.

LINDA: Oh, the whole block'll be at that game. Did you
670 sell anything?

WILLY: I did five hundred gross in Providence and seven hundred gross in Boston.

LINDA: No! Wait a minute, I've got a pencil. *(She pulls pencil and paper out of her apron pocket.)* That makes

your commission . . . Two hundred—my God! Two 675 hundred and twelve dollars!

WILLY: Well, I didn't figure it yet, but . . .

LINDA: How much did you do?

WILLY: Well, I—I did—about a hundred and eighty gross in Providence. Well, no—it came to—roughly 680 two hundred gross on the whole trip.

LINDA: *(without hesitation)* Two hundred gross. That's . . . *(She figures.)*

WILLY: The trouble was that three of the stores were half closed for inventory in Boston. Otherwise I 685 woulda broke records.

LINDA: Well, it makes seventy dollars and some pennies. That's very good.

WILLY: What do we owe?

LINDA: Well, on the first there's sixteen dollars on the 690 refrigerator—

WILLY: Why sixteen?

LINDA: Well, the fan belt broke, so it was a dollar eighty.

WILLY: But it's brand new.

LINDA: Well, the man said that's the way it is. Till they 695 work themselves in, y'know.

They move through the wall-line into the kitchen.

WILLY: I hope we didn't get stuck on that machine.

LINDA: They got the biggest ads of any of them!

WILLY: I know, it's a fine machine. What else?

LINDA: Well, there's nine-sixty for the washing ma- 700 chine. And for the vacuum cleaner there's three and a half due on the fifteenth. Then the roof, you got twenty-one dollars remaining.

WILLY: It don't leak, does it?

LINDA: No, they did a wonderful job. Then you owe 705 Frank for the carburetor.

WILLY: I'm not going to pay that man! That goddam Chevrolet, they ought to prohibit the manufacture of that car!

LINDA: Well, you owe him three and a half. And odds 710 and ends, comes to around a hundred and twenty dollars by the fifteenth.

WILLY: A hundred and twenty dollars! My God, if business don't pick up I don't know what I'm gonna do!

715 **LINDA:** Well, next week you'll do better.

WILLY: Oh, I'll knock 'em dead next week. I'll go to Hartford. I'm very well liked in Hartford. You know, the trouble is, Linda, people don't seem to take to me.

They move onto the forestage.

LINDA: Oh, don't be foolish.

720 **WILLY:** I know it when I walk in. They seem to laugh at me.

LINDA: Why? Why would they laugh at you? Don't talk that way, Willy.

WILLY moves to the edge of the stage. LINDA goes into the kitchen and starts to darn stockings.

WILLY: I don't know the reason for it, but they just
725 pass me by. I'm not noticed.

LINDA: But you're doing wonderful, dear. You're making seventy to a hundred dollars a week.

WILLY: But I gotta be at it ten, twelve hours a day. Other men—I don't know—they do it easier. I don't
730 know why—I can't stop myself—I talk too much. A man oughta come in with a few words. One thing about Charley. He's a man of few words, and they respect him.

LINDA: You don't talk too much, you're just lively.

735 **WILLY:** *(smiling)* Well, I figure, what the hell, life is short, a couple of jokes. *(To himself.)* I joke too much! *(The smile goes.)*

LINDA: Why? You're—

WILLY: I'm fat. I'm very—foolish to look at, Linda. I
740 didn't tell you, but Christmas time I happened to be calling on F. H. Stewarts, and a salesman I know, as I was going in to see the buyer I heard him say something about—walrus. And I—I cracked him right across the face. I won't take that. I simply will not
745 take that. But they do laugh at me. I know that.

LINDA: Darling . . .

WILLY: I gotta overcome it. I know I gotta overcome it. I'm not dressing to advantage, maybe.

LINDA: Willy, darling, you're the handsomest man in
750 the world—

WILLY: Oh, no, Linda.

LINDA: To me you are. *(Slight pause.)* The handsomest.

From the darkness is heard the laughter of a woman. WILLY doesn't turn to it, but it continues through LINDA's lines.

LINDA: And the boys, Willy. Few men are idolized by their children the way you are.

Music is heard as behind a scrim, to the left of the house, THE WOMAN, dimly seen, is dressing.

WILLY: *(with great feeling)* You're the best there is, Linda, 755 you're a pal, you know that? On the road—on the road I want to grab you sometimes and just kiss the life outa you.

The laughter is loud now, and he moves into a brightening area at the left, where THE WOMAN has come from behind the scrim and is standing, putting on her hat, looking into a "mirror" and laughing.

WILLY: 'Cause I get so lonely—especially when business is bad and there's nobody to talk to. I get the 760 feeling that I'll never sell anything again, that I won't make a living for you, or a business, a business for the boys. *(He talks through THE WOMAN's subsiding laughter; THE WOMAN primps at the "mirror.")* There's so much I want to make for— 765

THE WOMAN: Me? You didn't make me, Willy. I picked you.

WILLY: *(pleased)* You picked me?

THE WOMAN: *(who is quite proper-looking, WILLY's age)* I did. I've been sitting at that desk watching all the 770 salesmen go by, day in, day out. But you've got such a sense of humor, and we do have such a good time together, don't we?

WILLY: Sure, sure. *(He takes her in his arms.)* Why do you have to go now? 775

THE WOMAN: It's two o'clock . . .

WILLY: No, come on in! *(He pulls her.)*

THE WOMAN: . . . my sisters'll be scandalized. When'll you be back?

WILLY: Oh, two weeks about. Will you come up again? 780

THE WOMAN: Sure thing. You do make me laugh. It's good for me. *(She squeezes his arm, kisses him.)* And I think you're a wonderful man.

WILLY: You picked me, heh?

THE WOMAN: Sure. Because you're so sweet. And such 785 a kidder.

WILLY: Well, I'll see you next time I'm in Boston.

THE WOMAN: I'll put you right through to the buyers.

WILLY: *(slapping her bottom)* Right. Well, bottoms up!

790 **THE WOMAN:** *(slaps him gently and laughs)* You just kill me, Willy. *(He suddenly grabs her and kisses her roughly.)* You kill me. And thanks for the stockings. I love a lot of stockings. Well, good night.

WILLY: Good night. And keep your pores open!

795 **THE WOMAN:** Oh, Willy!

> THE WOMAN *bursts out laughing, and* LINDA's *laughter blends in.* THE WOMAN *disappears into the dark. Now the area at the kitchen table brightens.* LINDA *is sitting where she was at the kitchen table, but now is mending a pair of her silk stockings.*

LINDA: You are, Willy. The handsomest man. You've got no reason to feel that—

WILLY: *(coming out of* THE WOMAN's *dimming area and going over to* LINDA*)* I'll make it all up to you, Linda, I'll—

800 **LINDA:** There's nothing to make up, dear. You're doing fine, better than—

WILLY: *(noticing her mending)* What's that?

LINDA: Just mending my stockings. They're so expensive—

805 **WILLY:** *(angrily, taking them from her)* I won't have you mending stockings in this house! Now throw them out!

> LINDA *puts the stockings in her pocket.*

BERNARD: *(entering on the run)* Where is he? If he doesn't study!

810 **WILLY:** *(moving to the forestage, with great agitation)* You'll give him the answers!

BERNARD: I do, but I can't on a Regents! That's a state exam! They're liable to arrest me!

WILLY: Where is he? I'll whip him, I'll whip him!

815 **LINDA:** And he'd better give back that football, Willy, it's not nice.

WILLY: Biff! Where is he? Why is he taking everything?

LINDA: He's too rough with the girls, Willy. All the mothers are afraid of him!

820 **WILLY:** I'll whip him!

BERNARD: He's driving the car without a license!

> THE WOMAN's *laugh is heard.*

WILLY: Shut up!

LINDA: All the mothers—

Willy and The Woman (Kathy Rossetter) say good-bye in their hotel room.

WILLY: Shut up!

BERNARD: *(backing quietly away and out)* Mr. Birnbaum 825 says he's stuck up.

WILLY: Get outa here!

BERNARD: If he doesn't buckle down he'll flunk math! *(He goes off.)*

LINDA: He's right, Willy, you've gotta— 830

WILLY: *(exploding at her)* There's nothing the matter with him! You want him to be a worm like Bernard? He's got spirit, personality . . .

> As he speaks, LINDA, *almost in tears, exits into the living-room.* WILLY *is alone in the kitchen, wilting and staring. The leaves are gone. It is night again, and the apartment houses look down from behind.*

WILLY: Loaded with it. Loaded! What is he stealing? He's giving it back, isn't he? Why is he stealing? 835 What did I tell him? I never in my life told him anything but decent things.

> HAPPY *in pajamas has come down the stairs;* WILLY *suddenly becomes aware of* HAPPY's *presence.*

HAPPY: Let's go now, come on.

WILLY: *(sitting down at the kitchen table)* Huh! Why did she have to wax the floors herself? Everytime she 840 waxes the floors she keels over. She knows that!

HAPPY: Shh! Take it easy. What brought you back tonight?

WILLY: I got an awful scare. Nearly hit a kid in Yonkers. God! Why didn't I go to Alaska with my 845 brother Ben that time! Ben! That man was a genius, that man was success incarnate! What a mistake! He begged me to go.

HAPPY: Well, there's no use in—

850 **WILLY:** You guys! There was a man started with the clothes on his back and ended up with diamond mines!

HAPPY: Boy, someday I'd like to know how he did it.

855 **WILLY:** What's the mystery? The man knew what he wanted and went out and got it! Walked into a jungle, and comes out, the age of twenty-one, and he's rich! The world is an oyster, but you don't crack it open on a mattress!

HAPPY: Pop, I told you I'm gonna retire you for life.

860 **WILLY:** You'll retire me for life on seventy goddam dollars a week? And your women and your car and your apartment, and you'll retire me for life! Christ's sake, I couldn't get past Yonkers today! Where are you guys, where are you? The woods are burning! I can't
865 drive a car!

CHARLEY has appeared in the doorway. He is a large man, slow of speech, laconic, immovable. In all he says, despite what he says, there is pity, and, now, trepidation. He has a robe over pajamas, slippers on his feet. He enters the kitchen.

CHARLEY: Everything all right?

HAPPY: Yeah, Charley, everything's . . .

WILLY: What's the matter?

CHARLEY: I heard some noise. I thought something
870 happened. Can't we do something about the walls? You sneeze in here, and in my house hats blow off.

HAPPY: Let's go to bed, Dad. Come on.

CHARLEY signals to HAPPY to go.

WILLY: You go ahead, I'm not tired at the moment.

HAPPY: *(to WILLY)* Take it easy, huh? *(He exits.)*

875 **WILLY:** What're you doin' up?

CHARLEY: *(sitting down at the kitchen table opposite WILLY)* Couldn't sleep good. I had a heartburn.

WILLY: Well, you don't know how to eat.

CHARLEY: I eat with my mouth.

880 **WILLY:** No, you're ignorant. You gotta know about vitamins and things like that.

CHARLEY: Come on, let's shoot. Tire you out a little.

WILLY: *(hesitantly)* All right. You got cards?

CHARLEY: *(taking a deck from his pocket)* Yeah, I got them. Someplace. What is it with those vitamins? 885

WILLY: *(dealing)* They build up your bones. Chemistry.

CHARLEY: Yeah, but there's no bones in a heartburn.

WILLY: What are you talkin' about? Do you know the first thing about it?

CHARLEY: Don't get insulted. 890

WILLY: Don't talk about something you don't know anything about.

They are playing. Pause.

CHARLEY: What're you doin' home?

WILLY: A little trouble with the car.

CHARLEY: Oh. *(Pause.)* I'd like to take a trip to 895 California.

WILLY: Don't say.

CHARLEY: You want a job?

WILLY: I got a job, I told you that. *(After a slight pause.)* What the hell are you offering me a job for? 900

CHARLEY: Don't get insulted.

WILLY: Don't insult me.

CHARLEY: I don't see no sense in it. You don't have to go on this way.

WILLY: I got a good job. *(Slight pause.)* What do you 905 keep comin' in here for?

CHARLEY: You want me to go?

WILLY: *(after a pause, withering)* I can't understand it. He's going back to Texas again. What the hell is that?

CHARLEY: Let him go. 910

WILLY: I got nothin' to give him, Charley, I'm clean, I'm clean.

CHARLEY: He won't starve. None a them starve. Forget about him.

WILLY: Then what have I got to remember? 915

CHARLEY: You take it too hard. To hell with it. When a deposit bottle is broken you don't get your nickel back.

WILLY: That's easy enough for you to say.

CHARLEY: That ain't easy for me to say. 920

WILLY: Did you see the ceiling I put up in the living-room?

CHARLEY: Yeah, that's a piece of work. To put up a ceiling is a mystery to me. How do you do it?

925 **WILLY:** What's the difference?

CHARLEY: Well, talk about it.

WILLY: You gonna put up a ceiling?

CHARLEY: How could I put up a ceiling?

WILLY: Then what the hell are you bothering me for?

930 **CHARLEY:** You're insulted again.

WILLY: A man who can't handle tools is not a man. You're disgusting.

CHARLEY: Don't call me disgusting, Willy.

Uncle BEN, *carrying a valise and an umbrella, enters the forestage from around the right corner of the house. He is a stolid man, in his sixties, with a mustache and an authoritative air. He is utterly certain of his destiny, and there is an aura of far places about him. He enters exactly as* WILLY *speaks.*

WILLY: I'm getting awfully tired, Ben.

BEN's *music is heard.* BEN *looks around at everything.*

935 **CHARLEY:** Good, keep playing; you'll sleep better. Did you call me Ben?

BEN *looks at his watch.*

WILLY: That's funny. For a second there you reminded me of my brother Ben.

BEN: I only have a few minutes. *(He strolls, inspecting the* 940 *place.* WILLY *and* CHARLEY *continue playing.)*

CHARLEY: You never heard from him again, heh? Since that time?

WILLY: Didn't Linda tell you? Couple of weeks ago we got a letter from his wife in Africa. He died.

945 **CHARLEY:** That so.

BEN: *(chuckling)* So this is Brooklyn, eh?

CHARLEY: Maybe you're in for some of his money.

WILLY: Naa, he had seven sons. There's just one opportunity I had with that man . . .

950 **BEN:** I must make a train, William. There are several properties I'm looking at in Alaska.

WILLY: Sure, sure! If I'd gone with him to Alaska that time, everything would've been totally different.

CHARLEY: Go on, you'd froze to death up there.

WILLY: What're you talking about? 955

BEN: Opportunity is tremendous in Alaska, William. Surprised you're not up there.

WILLY: Sure, tremendous.

CHARLEY: Heh?

WILLY: There was the only man I ever met who knew 960 the answers.

CHARLEY: Who?

BEN: How are you all?

WILLY: *(taking a pot, smiling)* Fine, fine.

CHARLEY: Pretty sharp tonight. 965

BEN: Is Mother living with you?

WILLY: No, she died a long time ago.

CHARLEY: Who?

BEN: That's too bad. Fine specimen of a lady, Mother.

WILLY: *(to* CHARLEY*)* Heh? 970

BEN: I'd hoped to see the old girl.

CHARLEY: Who died?

BEN: Heard anything from Father, have you?

WILLY: *(unnerved)* What do you mean, who died?

CHARLEY: *(taking a pot)* What're you talkin' about? 975

BEN: *(looking at his watch)* William, it's half-past eight!

WILLY: *(as though to dispel his confusion he angrily stops* CHARLEY's *hand)* That's my build!

CHARLEY: I put the ace—

WILLY: If you don't know how to play the game I'm not 980 gonna throw my money away on you!

CHARLEY: *(rising)* It was my ace, for God's sake!

WILLY: I'm through, I'm through!

BEN: When did Mother die?

WILLY: Long ago. Since the beginning you never knew 985 how to play cards.

CHARLEY: *(picks up the cards and goes to the door)* All right! Next time I'll bring a deck with five aces.

WILLY: I don't play that kind of game!

CHARLEY: *(turning to him)* You ought to be ashamed of 990 yourself!

Willy and Charley (Edward Andrews) play a game of cards as Ben (Albert Dekker) appears.

WILLY: Yeah?

CHARLEY: Yeah! *(He goes out.)*

WILLY: *(slamming the door after him)* Ignoramus!

BEN: *(as* WILLY *comes toward him through the wall-line of the kitchen)* So you're William.

WILLY: *(shaking Ben's hand)* Ben! I've been waiting for you so long! What's the answer? How did you do it?

BEN: Oh, there's a story in that.

LINDA *enters the forestage, as of old, carrying the wash basket.*

LINDA: Is this Ben?

BEN: *(gallantly)* How do you do, my dear.

LINDA: Where've you been all these years? Willy's always wondered why you—

WILLY: *(pulling Ben away from her impatiently)* Where is Dad? Didn't you follow him? How did you get started?

BEN: Well, I don't know how much you remember.

WILLY: Well, I was just a baby, of course, only three or four years old—

BEN: Three years and eleven months.

WILLY: What a memory, Ben!

BEN: I have many enterprises, William, and I have never kept books.

WILLY: I remember I was sitting under the wagon in—was it Nebraska?

BEN: It was South Dakota, and I gave you a bunch of wild flowers.

WILLY: I remember you walking away down some open road.

BEN: *(laughing)* I was going to find Father in Alaska.

WILLY: Where is he?

BEN: At that age I had a very faulty view of geography, William. I discovered after a few days that I was heading due south, so instead of Alaska, I ended up in Africa.

LINDA: Africa!

WILLY: The Gold Coast!

BEN: Principally diamond mines.

LINDA: Diamond mines!

BEN: Yes, my dear. But I've only a few minutes—

WILLY: No! Boys! Boys! *(Young* BIFF *and* HAPPY *appear.)* Listen to this. This is your Uncle Ben, a great man! Tell my boys, Ben!

BEN: Why, boys, when I was seventeen I walked into the jungle, and when I was twenty-one I walked out. *(He laughs.)* And by God I was rich.

WILLY: *(to the boys)* You see what I been talking about? The greatest things can happen!

BEN: *(glancing at his watch)* I have an appointment in Ketchikan Tuesday next week.

WILLY: No, Ben! Please tell about Dad. I want my boys to hear. I want them to know the kind of stock they spring from. All I remember is a man with a big beard, and I was in Mamma's lap, sitting around a fire, and some kind of high music.

BEN: His flute. He played the flute.

WILLY: Sure, the flute, that's right!

New music is heard, a high, rollicking tune.

BEN: Father was a very great and a very wild-hearted man. We would start in Boston, and he'd toss the whole family into the wagon, and then he'd drive the team right across the country; through Ohio, and Indiana, Michigan, Illinois, and all the Western states. And we'd stop in the towns and sell the flutes that he'd made on the way. Great inventor, Father. With one gadget he made more in a week than a man like you could make in a lifetime.

WILLY: That's just the way I'm bringing them up, Ben—rugged, well liked, all-around.

BEN: Yeah? *(To* BIFF.*)* Hit that, boy—hard as you can. *(He pounds his stomach.)*

1060 **BIFF:** Oh, no, sir!

BEN: *(taking boxing stance)* Come on, get to me. *(He laughs.)*

WILLY: Go to it, Biff! Go ahead, show him!

BIFF: Okay! *(He cocks his fists and starts in.)*

LINDA: *(to* WILLY*)* Why must he fight, dear?

1065 **BEN:** *(sparring with* BIFF*)* Good boy! Good boy!

WILLY: How's that, Ben, heh?

HAPPY: Give him the left, Biff!

LINDA: Why are you fighting?

BEN: Good boy! *(Suddenly comes in, trips* BIFF, *and stands*
1070 *over him, the point of his umbrella poised over* BIFF's *eye.)*

LINDA: Look out, Biff!

BIFF: Gee!

BEN: *(patting* BIFF's *knee)* Never fight fair with a stranger, boy. You'll never get out of the jungle that way. *(Tak-*
1075 *ing* LINDA's *hand and bowing):* It was an honor and a pleasure to meet you, Linda.

LINDA: *(withdrawing her hand coldly, frightened)* Have a nice—trip.

BEN: *(to* WILLY*)* And good luck with your—what do
1080 you do?

WILLY: Selling.

BEN: Yes. Well . . . *(He raises his hand in farewell to all.)*

Willy and Ben have a laugh at Charley.

WILLY: No, Ben, I don't want you to think . . . *(He takes Ben's arm to show him.)* It's Brooklyn, I know, but we hunt too. 108

BEN: Really, now.

WILLY: Oh, sure, there's snakes and rabbits and—that's why I moved out here. Why, Biff can fell any one of these trees in no time! Boys! Go right over to where they're building the apartment house and get some 109 sand. We're gonna rebuild the entire front stoop now! Watch this, Ben!

BIFF: Yes, sir! On the double, Hap!

HAPPY: *(as he and* BIFF *run off)* I lost weight, Pop, you notice? 109

CHARLEY *enters in knickers, even before the boys are gone.*

CHARLEY: Listen, if they steal any more from that building the watchman'll put the cops on them!

LINDA: *(to* WILLY*)* Don't let Biff . . .

BEN *laughs lustily.*

WILLY: You shoulda seen the lumber they brought home last week. At least a dozen six-by-tens worth 110 all kinds a money.

CHARLEY: Listen, if that watchman—

WILLY: I gave them hell, understand. But I got a couple of fearless characters there.

CHARLEY: Willy, the jails are full of fearless characters. 110

BEN: *(clapping* WILLY *on the back, with a laugh at* CHARLEY*)* And the stock exchange, friend!

WILLY: *(joining in Ben's laughter)* Where are the rest of your pants?

CHARLEY: My wife bought them. 111

WILLY: Now all you need is a golf club and you can go upstairs and go to sleep. *(To Ben).* Great athlete! Between him and his son Bernard they can't hammer a nail!

BERNARD: *(rushing in)* The watchman's chasing Biff! 111

WILLY: *(angrily)* Shut up! He's not stealing anything!

LINDA: *(alarmed, hurrying off left)* Where is he? Biff, dear! *(She exits.)*

WILLY: *(moving toward the left, away from Ben)* There's nothing wrong. What's the matter with you? 112

BEN: Nervy boy. Good!

WILLY: *(laughing)* Oh, nerves of iron, that Biff!

CHARLEY: Don't know what it is. My New England man comes back and he's bleedin', they murdered 1125 him up there.

WILLY: It's contacts, Charley, I got important contacts!

CHARLEY: *(sarcastically)* Glad to hear it, Willy. Come in later, we'll shoot a little casino. I'll take some of your Portland money. *(He laughs at* WILLY *and exits.)*

1130 **WILLY:** *(turning to Ben)* Business is bad, it's murderous. But not for me, of course.

BEN: I'll stop by on my way back to Africa.

WILLY: *(longingly)* Can't you stay a few days? You're just what I need, Ben, because I—I have a fine position 1135 here, but I—well, Dad left when I was such a baby and I never had a chance to talk to him and I still feel—kind of temporary about myself.

BEN: I'll be late for my train.

They are at opposite ends of the stage.

WILLY: Ben, my boys—can't we talk? They'd go into 1140 the jaws of hell for me, see, but I—

BEN: William, you're being first-rate with your boys. Outstanding, manly chaps!

WILLY: *(hanging on to his words)* Oh, Ben, that's good to hear! Because sometimes I'm afraid that I'm not 1145 teaching them the right kind of—Ben, how should I teach them?

BEN: *(giving great weight to each word, and with a certain vicious audacity)* William, when I walked into the jungle, I was seventeen. When I walked out I was 1150 twenty-one. And, by God, I was rich! *(He goes off into darkness around the right corner of the house.)*

WILLY: . . . was rich! That's just the spirit I want to imbue them with! To walk into a jungle! I was right! I was right! I was right!

BEN is gone, but WILLY *is still speaking to him as* LINDA, *in nightgown and robe, enters the kitchen, glances around for* WILLY, *then goes to the door of the house, looks out, and sees him. Comes down to his left. He looks at her.*

1155 **LINDA:** Willy, dear? Willy?

WILLY: I was right!

LINDA: Did you have some cheese? *(He can't answer.)* It's very late, darling. Come to bed, heh?

WILLY: *(looking straight up)* Gotta break your neck to 1160 see a star in this yard.

LINDA: You coming in?

WILLY: Whatever happened to that diamond watch fob? Remember? When Ben came from Africa that time? Didn't he give me a watch fob with a diamond in it? 1165

LINDA: You pawned it, dear. Twelve, thirteen years ago. For Biff's radio correspondence course.

WILLY: Gee, that was a beautiful thing. I'll take a walk.

LINDA: But you're in your slippers.

WILLY: *(starting to go around the house at the left)* I was 1170 right! I was! *(Half to* LINDA, *as he goes, shaking his head.)* What a man! There was a man worth talking to. I was right!

LINDA: *(calling after* WILLY*)* But in your slippers, Willy!

WILLY *is almost gone when* BIFF, *in his pajamas, comes down the stairs and enters the kitchen.*

BIFF: What is he doing out there? 1175

LINDA: Sh!

BIFF: God Almighty, Mom, how long has he been doing this?

LINDA: Don't, he'll hear you.

BIFF: What the hell is the matter with him? 1180

LINDA: It'll pass by morning.

BIFF: Shouldn't we do anything?

LINDA: Oh, my dear, you should do a lot of things, but there's nothing to do, so go to sleep.

HAPPY *comes down the stairs and sits on the steps.*

HAPPY: I never heard him so loud, Mom. 1185

LINDA: Well, come around more often; you'll hear him. *(She sits down at the table and mends the lining of* WILLY's *jacket.)*

BIFF: Why didn't you ever write me about this, Mom?

LINDA: How would I write to you? For over three 1190 months you had no address.

BIFF: I was on the move. But you know I thought of you all the time. You know that, don't you, pal?

LINDA: I know, dear, I know. But he likes to have a letter. Just to know that there's still a possibility for 1195 better things.

BIFF: He's not like this all the time, is he?

LINDA: It's when you come home he's always the worst.

BIFF: When I come home?

1200 **LINDA:**   When you write you're coming, he's all smiles, and talks about the future, and—he's just wonderful. And then the closer you seem to come, the more shaky he gets, and then, by the time you get here, he's arguing, and he seems angry at you. I think it's
1205 just that maybe he can't bring himself to—to open up to you. Why are you so hateful to each other? Why is that?

BIFF: *(evasively)*   I'm not hateful, Mom.

LINDA: But you no sooner come in the door than you're
1210 fighting!

BIFF: I don't know why. I mean to change. I'm tryin', Mom, you understand?

LINDA: Are you home to stay now?

BIFF: I don't know. I want to look around, see what's
1215 doin'.

LINDA: Biff, you can't look around all your life, can you?

BIFF: I just can't take hold, Mom. I can't take hold of some kind of a life.

LINDA: Biff, a man is not a bird, to come and go with
1220 the springtime.

BIFF: Your hair . . . *(He touches her hair.)* Your hair got so gray.

LINDA: Oh, it's been gray since you were in high school. I just stopped dyeing it, that's all.

1225 **BIFF:**   Dye it again, will ya? I don't want my pal looking old. *(He smiles.)*

LINDA: You're such a boy! You think you can go away for a year and . . . You've got to get it into your head now that one day you'll knock on this door and
1230 there'll be strange people here—

BIFF: What are you talking about? You're not even sixty, Mom.

LINDA: But what about your father?

BIFF: *(lamely)*   Well, I meant him too.

1235 **HAPPY:**   He admires Pop.

LINDA: Biff, dear, if you don't have any feeling for him, then you can't have any feeling for me.

BIFF: Sure I can, Mom.

LINDA: No. You can't just come to see me, because I
1240 love him. *(With a threat, but only a threat, of tears.)* He's

The Lomans argue about Willy.

the dearest man in the world to me, and I won't have anyone making him feel unwanted and low and blue. You've got to make up your mind now, darling, there's no leeway any more. Either he's your father and you pay him that respect, or else you're not to   1245 come here. I know he's not easy to get along with—nobody knows that better than me—but . . .

WILLY: *(from the left, with a laugh)*   Hey, hey, Biffo!

BIFF: *(starting to go out after* WILLY*)*   What the hell is the matter with him? (HAPPY *stops him.)*   1250

LINDA: Don't—don't go near him!

BIFF: Stop making excuses for him! He always, always wiped the floor with you. Never had an ounce of respect for you.

HAPPY: He's always had respect for—   1255

BIFF: What the hell do you know about it?

HAPPY: *(surlily)*   Just don't call him crazy!

BIFF: He's got no character—Charley wouldn't do this. Not in his own house—spewing out that vomit from his mind.   1260

HAPPY: Charley never had to cope with what he's got to.

BIFF: People are worse off than Willy Loman. Believe me, I've seen them!

LINDA: Then make Charley your father, Biff. You can't do that, can you? I don't say he's a great man. Willy   1265 Loman never made a lot of money. His name was never in the paper. He's not the finest character that ever lived. But he's a human being, and a terrible thing is happening to him. So attention must be

1270 paid. He's not to be allowed to fall into his grave like an old dog. Attention, attention must be finally paid to such a person. You called him crazy—

BIFF: I didn't mean—

1275 **LINDA:** No, a lot of people think he's lost his—balance. But you don't have to be very smart to know what his trouble is. The man is exhausted.

HAPPY: Sure!

LINDA: A small man can be just as exhausted as a great man. He works for a company thirty-six years 1280 this March, opens up unheard-of territories to their trademark, and now in his old age they take his salary away.

HAPPY: *(indignantly)* I didn't know that, Mom.

LINDA: You never asked, my dear! Now that you get 1285 your spending money someplace else you don't trouble your mind with him.

HAPPY: But I gave you money last—

LINDA: Christmas time, fifty dollars! To fix the hot water it cost ninety-seven fifty! For five weeks he's 1290 been on straight commission, like a beginner, an unknown!

BIFF: Those ungrateful bastards!

LINDA: Are they any worse than his sons? When he brought them business, when he was young, they 1295 were glad to see him. But now his old friends, the old buyers that loved him so and always found some order to hand him in a pinch—they're all dead, retired. He used to be able to make six, seven calls a day in Boston. Now he takes his valises out of the car 1300 and puts them back and takes them out again and he's exhausted. Instead of walking he talks now. He drives seven hundred miles, and when he gets there no one knows him any more, no one welcomes him. And what goes through a man's mind, driving seven 1305 hundred miles home without having earned a cent? Why shouldn't he talk to himself? Why? When he has to go to Charley and borrow fifty dollars a week and pretend to me that it's his pay? How long can that go on? How long? You see what I'm sitting here 1310 and waiting for? And you tell me he has no character? The man who never worked a day but for your benefit? When does he get the medal for that? Is this his reward—to turn around at the age of sixty-three and find his sons, who he loved better than his life, 1315 one a philandering bum—

HAPPY: Mom!

LINDA: That's all you are, my baby! *(To BIFF.)* And you! What happened to the love you had for him? You were such pals! How you used to talk to him on the phone every night! How lonely he was till he could 1320 come home to you!

BIFF: All right, Mom. I'll live here in my room, and I'll get a job. I'll keep away from him, that's all.

LINDA: No, Biff. You can't stay here and fight all the time. 1325

BIFF: He threw me out of this house, remember that.

LINDA: Why did he do that? I never knew why.

BIFF: Because I know he's a fake and he doesn't like anybody around who knows!

LINDA: Why a fake? In what way? What do you mean? 1330

BIFF: Just don't lay it all at my feet. It's between me and him—that's all I have to say. I'll chip in from now on. He'll settle for half my pay check. He'll be all right. I'm going to bed. *(He starts for the stairs.)*

LINDA: He won't be all right. 1335

BIFF: *(turning on the stairs, furiously)* I hate this city and I'll stay here. Now what do you want?

LINDA: He's dying, Biff.

HAPPY *turns quickly to her, shocked.*

BIFF: *(after a pause)* Why is he dying?

LINDA: He's been trying to kill himself. 1340

BIFF: *(with great horror)* How?

LINDA: I live from day to day.

BIFF: What're you talking about?

LINDA: Remember I wrote you that he smashed up the car again? In February? 1345

BIFF: Well?

LINDA: The insurance inspector came. He said that they have evidence. That all these accidents in the last year—weren't—weren't—accidents.

HAPPY: How can they tell that? That's a lie. 1350

LINDA: It seems there's a woman . . . *(She takes a breath as):*
   BIFF *(sharply but contained):* What woman?
   LINDA *(simultaneously):* . . . and this woman . . .

LINDA: What?

BIFF: Nothing. Go ahead. 1355

LINDA: What did you say?

BIFF: Nothing. I just said what woman?

HAPPY: What about her?

LINDA: Well, it seems she was walking down the road
1360 and saw his car. She says that he wasn't driving fast
at all, and that he didn't skid. She says he came to
that little bridge, and then deliberately smashed into
the railing, and it was only the shallowness of the
water that saved him.

1365 **BIFF:** Oh, no, he probably just fell asleep again.

LINDA: I don't think he fell asleep.

BIFF: Why not?

LINDA: Last month . . . (*With great difficulty.*) Oh, boys,
it's so hard to say a thing like this! He's just a big
1370 stupid man to you, but I tell you there's more good
in him than in many other people. (*She chokes, wipes
her eyes.*) I was looking for a fuse. The lights blew out,
and I went down the cellar. And behind the fuse
box—it happened to fall out—was a length of rubber
1375 pipe—just short.

HAPPY: No kidding?

LINDA: There's a little attachment on the end of it. I
knew right away. And sure enough, on the bottom
of the water heater there's a new little nipple on the
1380 gas pipe.

HAPPY: (*angrily*) That—jerk.

BIFF: Did you have it taken off?

LINDA: I'm—I'm ashamed to. How can I mention it to
him? Every day I go down and take away that little
1385 rubber pipe. But, when he comes home, I put it back
where it was. How can I insult him that way? I don't
know what to do. I live from day to day, boys. I tell
you, I know every thought in his mind. It sounds so
old-fashioned and silly, but I tell you he put his whole
1390 life into you and you've turned your backs on him.
(*She is bent over in chair, weeping, her face in her hands.*)
Biff, I swear to God! Biff, his life is in your hands!

HAPPY: (*to* BIFF) How do you like that damned fool!

BIFF: (*kissing her*) All right, pal, all right. It's all settled
1395 now. I've been remiss. I know that, Mom. But now
I'll stay, and I swear to you, I'll apply myself. (*Kneeling in front of her, in a fever of self-reproach.*) It's just—you
see, Mom, I don't fit in business. Not that I won't try.
I'll try, and I'll make good.

1400 **HAPPY:** Sure you will. The trouble with you in business
was you never tried to please people.

BIFF: I know, I—

HAPPY: Like when you worked for Harrison's. Bob
Harrison said you were tops, and then you go and do
some damn fool thing like whistling whole songs in 1405
the elevator like a comedian.

BIFF: (*against* HAPPY) So what? I like to whistle
sometimes.

HAPPY: You don't raise a guy to a responsible job who
whistles in the elevator! 1410

LINDA: Well, don't argue about it now.

HAPPY: Like when you'd go off and swim in the middle
of the day instead of taking the line around.

BIFF: (*his resentment rising*) Well, don't you run off? You
take off sometimes, don't you? On a nice summer day? 1415

HAPPY: Yeah, but I cover myself!

LINDA: Boys!

HAPPY: If I'm going to take a fade the boss can call any
number where I'm supposed to be and they'll swear
to him that I just left. I'll tell you something that I 1420
hate to say, Biff, but in the business world some of
them think you're crazy.

BIFF: (*angered*) Screw the business world!

HAPPY: All right, screw it! Great, but cover yourself!

LINDA: Hap, Hap! 1425

BIFF: I don't care what they think! They've laughed at
Dad for years, and you know why? Because we don't
belong in this nuthouse of a city! We should be mixing cement on some open plain, or—or carpenters. A
carpenter is allowed to whistle! 1430

WILLY *walks in from the entrance of the house, at left.*

WILLY: Even your grandfather was better than a carpenter. (*Pause. They watch him.*) You never grew up.
Bernard does not whistle in the elevator, I assure you.

BIFF: (*as though to laugh* WILLY *out of it*) Yeah, but you do,
Pop. 1435

WILLY: I never in my life whistled in an elevator! And
who in the business world thinks I'm crazy?

BIFF: I didn't mean it like that, Pop. Now don't make a
whole thing out of it, will ya?

WILLY: Go back to the West! Be a carpenter, a cowboy, 1440
enjoy yourself!

LINDA: Willy, he was just saying—

WILLY: I heard what he said!

HAPPY: *(trying to quiet* WILLY) Hey, Pop, come on now . . .

1445 **WILLY:** *(continuing over* HAPPY's *line)* They laugh at me, heh? Go to Filene's, go to the Hub, go to Slattery's, Boston. Call out the name Willy Loman and see what happens! Big shot!

BIFF: All right, Pop.

1450 **WILLY:** Big!

BIFF: All right!

WILLY: Why do you always insult me?

BIFF: I didn't say a word. *(To* LINDA.) Did I say a word?

LINDA: He didn't say anything, Willy.

1455 **WILLY:** *(going to the doorway of the living-room)* All right, good night, good night.

LINDA: Willy, dear, he just decided . . .

WILLY: *(to* BIFF) If you get tired hanging around tomorrow, paint the ceiling I put up in the living-room.

1460 **BIFF:** I'm leaving early tomorrow.

HAPPY: He's going to see Bill Oliver, Pop.

WILLY: *(interestedly)* Oliver? For what?

BIFF: *(with reserve, but trying, trying)* He always said he'd stake me. I'd like to go into business, so maybe I can 1465 take him up on it.

LINDA: Isn't that wonderful?

WILLY: Don't interrupt. What's wonderful about it? There's fifty men in the City of New York who'd stake him. *(To* BIFF.) Sporting goods?

Willy and the boys discuss their million-dollar ideas.

BIFF: I guess so. I know something about it and— 1470

WILLY: He knows something about it! You know sporting goods better than Spalding, for God's sake! How much is he giving you?

BIFF: I don't know, I didn't even see him yet, but—

WILLY: Then what're you talkin' about? 1475

BIFF: *(getting angry)* Well, all I said was I'm gonna see him, that's all!

WILLY: *(turning away)* Ah, you're counting your chickens again.

BIFF: *(starting left for the stairs)* Oh, Jesus, I'm going to 1480 sleep!

WILLY: *(calling after him)* Don't curse in this house!

BIFF: *(turning)* Since when did you get so clean?

HAPPY: *(trying to stop them)* Wait a . . .

WILLY: Don't use that language to me! I won't have it! 1485

HAPPY: *(grabbing* BIFF, *shouts)* Wait a minute! I got an idea. I got a feasible idea. Come here, Biff, let's talk this over now, let's talk some sense here. When I was down in Florida last time, I thought of a great idea to sell sporting goods. It just came back to me. You 1490 and I, Biff—we have a line, the Loman Line. We train a couple of weeks, and put on a couple of exhibitions, see?

WILLY: That's an idea!

HAPPY: Wait! We form two basketball teams, see? Two 1495 water-polo teams. We play each other. It's a million dollars' worth of publicity. Two brothers, see? The Loman Brothers. Displays in the Royal Palms—all the hotels. And banners over the ring and the basketball court: "Loman Brothers." Baby, we could sell 1500 sporting goods!

WILLY: That is a one-million-dollar idea!

LINDA: Marvelous!

BIFF: I'm in great shape as far as that's concerned.

HAPPY: And the beauty of it is, Biff, it wouldn't be like 1505 a business. We'd be out playin' ball again . . .

BIFF: *(enthused)* Yeah, that's . . .

WILLY: Million-dollar . . .

HAPPY: And you wouldn't get fed up with it, Biff. It'd be the family again. There'd be the old honor, and 1510 comradeship, and if you wanted to go off for a swim or somethin'—well, you'd do it! Without some smart cooky gettin' up ahead of you!

WILLY: Lick the world! You guys together could absolutely lick the civilized world.

BIFF: I'll see Oliver tomorrow. Hap, if we could work that out . . .

LINDA: Maybe things are beginning to—

WILLY: (*wildly enthused, to* LINDA) Stop interrupting! (*To* BIFF.) But don't wear sport jacket and slacks when you see Oliver.

BIFF: No, I'll—

WILLY: A business suit, and talk as little as possible, and don't crack any jokes.

BIFF: He did like me. Always liked me.

LINDA: He loved you!

WILLY: (*to* LINDA) Will you stop! (*To* BIFF.) Walk in very serious. You are not applying for a boy's job. Money is to pass. Be quiet, fine, and serious. Everybody likes a kidder, but nobody lends him money.

HAPPY: I'll try to get some myself, Biff. I'm sure I can.

WILLY: I see great things for you kids, I think your troubles are over. But remember, start big and you'll end big. Ask for fifteen. How much you gonna ask for?

BIFF: Gee, I don't know—

WILLY: And don't say "Gee." "Gee" is a boy's word. A man walking in for fifteen thousand dollars does not say "Gee!"

BIFF: Ten, I think, would be top though.

WILLY: Don't be so modest. You always started too low. Walk in with a big laugh. Don't look worried. Start off with a couple of your good stories to lighten things up. It's not what you say, it's how you say it—because personality always wins the day.

LINDA: Oliver always thought the highest of him—

WILLY: Will you let me talk?

BIFF: Don't yell at her, Pop, will ya?

WILLY: (*angrily*) I was talking, wasn't I?

BIFF: I don't like you yelling at her all the time, and I'm tellin' you, that's all.

WILLY: What're you, takin' over this house?

LINDA: Willy—

WILLY: (*turning on her*) Don't take his side all the time, goddammit!

BIFF: (*furiously*) Stop yelling at her!

WILLY: (*suddenly pulling on his cheek, beaten down, guilt ridden*) Give my best to Bill Oliver—he may remember me. (*He exits through the living-room doorway.*)

LINDA: (*her voice subdued*) What'd you have to start that for? (BIFF *turns away.*) You see how sweet he was as soon as you talked hopefully? (*She goes over to* BIFF.) Come up and say good night to him. Don't let him go to bed that way.

HAPPY: Come on, Biff, let's buck him up.

LINDA: Please, dear. Just say good night. It takes so little to make him happy. Come. (*She goes through the living-room doorway, calling upstairs from within the living-room.*) Your pajamas are hanging in the bathroom, Willy!

HAPPY: (*looking toward where* LINDA *went out*) What a woman! They broke the mold when they made her. You know that, Biff?

BIFF: He's off salary. My God, working on commission!

HAPPY: Well, let's face it: he's no hot-shot selling man. Except that sometimes, you have to admit, he's a sweet personality.

BIFF: (*deciding*) Lend me ten bucks, will ya? I want to buy some new ties.

HAPPY: I'll take you to a place I know. Beautiful stuff. Wear one of my striped shirts tomorrow.

BIFF: She got gray. Mom got awful old. Gee, I'm gonna go in to Oliver tomorrow and knock him for a—

HAPPY: Come on up. Tell that to Dad. Let's give him a whirl. Come on.

BIFF: (*steamed up*) You know, with ten thousand bucks, boy!

HAPPY: (*as they go into the living-room*) That's the talk, Biff, that's the first time I've heard the old confidence out of you! (*From within the living-room, fading off.*) You're gonna live with me, kid, and any babe you want just say the word . . . (*The last lines are hardly heard. They are mounting the stairs to their parents' bedroom.*)

LINDA: (*entering her bedroom and addressing* WILLY, *who is in the bathroom. She is straightening the bed for him*) Can you do anything about the shower? It drips.

WILLY: (*from the bathroom*) All of a sudden everything falls to pieces! Goddam plumbing, oughta be sued, those people. I hardly finished putting it in and the thing . . . (*His words rumble off.*)

600 **LINDA:** I'm just wondering if Oliver will remember him. You think he might?

WILLY: (*coming out of the bathroom in his pajamas*) Remember him? What's the matter with you, you crazy? If he'd've stayed with Oliver he'd be on top

605 by now! Wait'll Oliver gets a look at him. You don't know the average caliber any more. The average young man today—(*he is getting into bed*)—is got a caliber of zero. Greatest thing in the world for him was to bum around.

BIFF and HAPPY enter the bedroom. Slight pause.

610 **WILLY:** (*stops short, looking at BIFF*) Glad to hear it, boy.

HAPPY: He wanted to say good night to you, sport.

WILLY: (*to BIFF*) Yeah. Knock him dead, boy. What'd you want to tell me?

BIFF: Just take it easy, Pop. Good night. (*He turns to go.*)

615 **WILLY:** (*unable to resist*) And if anything falls off the desk while you're talking to him—like a package or something—don't you pick it up. They have office boys for that.

LINDA: I'll make a big breakfast—

620 **WILLY:** Will you let me finish? (*To BIFF.*) Tell him you were in the business in the West. Not farm work.

BIFF: All right, Dad.

LINDA: I think everything—

WILLY: (*going right through her speech*) And don't under-

625 sell yourself. No less than fifteen thousand dollars.

BIFF: (*unable to bear him*) Okay. Good night, Mom. (*He starts moving.*)

WILLY: Because you got a greatness in you, Biff, remember that. You got all kinds a greatness . . . (*He lies*

630 *back, exhausted. BIFF walks out.*)

LINDA: (*calling after BIFF*) Sleep well, darling!

HAPPY: I'm gonna get married, Mom. I wanted to tell you.

LINDA: Go to sleep, dear.

635 **HAPPY:** (*going*) I just wanted to tell you.

WILLY: Keep up the good work. (*HAPPY exits.*) God . . . remember that Ebbets Field game? The championship of the city?

LINDA: Just rest. Should I sing to you?

WILLY: Yeah. Sing to me. (*LINDA hums a soft lullaby.*) 1640 When that team came out—he was the tallest, remember?

LINDA: Oh, yes. And in gold.

BIFF enters the darkened kitchen, takes a cigarette, and leaves the house. He comes downstage into a golden pool of light. He smokes, staring at the night.

WILLY: Like a young god. Hercules—something like that. And the sun, the sun all around him. Remem- 1645 ber how he waved to me? Right up from the field, with the representatives of three colleges standing by? And the buyers I brought, and the cheers when he came out—Loman, Loman, Loman! God Almighty, he'll be great yet. A star like that, magnifi- 1650 cent, can never really fade away!

The light on WILLY is fading. The gas heater begins to glow through the kitchen wall, near the stairs, a blue flame beneath red coils.

LINDA: (*timidly*) Willy, dear, what has he got against you?

WILLY: I'm so tired. Don't talk any more.

BIFF slowly returns to the kitchen. He stops, stares toward the heater.

LINDA: Will you ask Howard to let you work in New 1655 York?

WILLY: First thing in the morning. Everything'll be all right.

Linda hums as Willy reminisces.

BIFF *reaches behind the heater and draws out a length of rubber tubing. He is horrified and turns his head toward* WILLY's *room, still dimly lit, from which the strains of* LINDA's *desperate but monotonous humming rise.*

WILLY: (*staring through the window into the moonlight*) Gee, look at the moon moving between the buildings!

1660

BIFF *wraps the tubing around his hand and quickly goes up the stairs.*

Curtain.

ACT II

Music is heard, gay and bright. The curtain rises as the music fades away. WILLY, *in shirt sleeves, is sitting at the kitchen table, sipping coffee, his hat in his lap.* LINDA *is filling his cup when she can.*

WILLY: Wonderful coffee. Meal in itself.

LINDA: Can I make you some eggs?

WILLY: No. Take a breath.

LINDA: You look so rested, dear.

5 **WILLY:** I slept like a dead one. First time in months. Imagine, sleeping till ten on a Tuesday morning. Boys left nice and early, heh?

LINDA: They were out of here by eight o'clock.

WILLY: Good work!

10 **LINDA:** It was so thrilling to see them leaving together. I can't get over the shaving lotion in this house!

WILLY: (*smiling*) Mmm—

LINDA: Biff was very changed this morning. His whole attitude seemed to be hopeful. He couldn't wait to get downtown to see Oliver.

15

WILLY: He's heading for a change. There's no question, there simply are certain men that take longer to get—solidified. How did he dress?

LINDA: His blue suit. He's so handsome in that suit. He could be a—anything in that suit!

20

WILLY *gets up from the table.* LINDA *holds his jacket for him.*

WILLY: There's no question, no question at all. Gee, on the way home tonight I'd like to buy some seeds.

LINDA: (*laughing*) That'd be wonderful. But not enough sun gets back there. Nothing'll grow any more.

25 **WILLY:** You wait, kid, before it's all over we're gonna get a little place out in the country, and I'll raise some vegetables, a couple of chickens . . .

LINDA: You'll do it yet, dear.

WILLY *walks out of his jacket.* LINDA *follows him.*

WILLY: And they'll get married, and come for a weekend. I'd build a little guest house. 'Cause I got so many fine tools, all I'd need would be a little lumber and some peace of mind.

30

LINDA: (*joyfully*) I sewed the lining . . .

WILLY: I could build two guest houses, so they'd both come. Did he decide how much he's going to ask Oliver for?

35

LINDA: (*getting him into the jacket*) He didn't mention it, but I imagine ten or fifteen thousand. You going to talk to Howard today?

WILLY: Yeah. I'll put it to him straight and simple. He'll just have to take me off the road.

40

LINDA: And Willy, don't forget to ask for a little advance, because we've got the insurance premium. It's the grace period now.

WILLY: That's a hundred . . . ?

45

LINDA: A hundred and eight, sixty-eight. Because we're a little short again.

WILLY: Why are we short?

LINDA: Well, you had the motor job on the car . . .

WILLY: That goddam Studebaker!

50

LINDA: And you got one more payment on the refrigerator . . .

Linda helps Willy into his coat.

WILLY: But it just broke again!

LINDA: Well, it's old, dear.

55 **WILLY:** I told you we should've bought a well-advertised machine. Charley bought a General Electric and it's twenty years old and it's still good, that son-of-a-bitch.

LINDA: But, Willy—

WILLY: Whoever heard of a Hastings refrigerator?
60 Once in my life I would like to own something out-right before it's broken! I'm always in a race with the junkyard! I just finished paying for the car and it's on its last legs. The refrigerator consumes belts like a goddam maniac. They time those things. They
65 time them so when you finally paid for them, they're used up.

LINDA: *(buttoning up his jacket as he unbuttons it)* All told, about two hundred dollars would carry us, dear. But that includes the last payment on the mortgage.
70 After this payment, Willy, the house belongs to us.

WILLY: It's twenty-five years!

LINDA: Biff was nine years old when we bought it.

WILLY: Well, that's a great thing. To weather a twenty-five year mortgage is—

75 **LINDA:** It's an accomplishment.

WILLY: All the cement, the lumber, the reconstruction I put in this house! There ain't a crack to be found in it any more.

LINDA: Well, it served its purpose.

80 **WILLY:** What purpose? Some stranger'll come along, move in, and that's that. If only Biff would take this house, and raise a family . . . *(He starts to go.)* Good-by, I'm late.

LINDA: *(suddenly remembering)* Oh, I forgot! You're sup-
85 posed to meet them for dinner.

WILLY: Me?

LINDA: At Frank's Chop House on Forty-eighth near Sixth Avenue.

WILLY: Is that so! How about you?

90 **LINDA:** No, just the three of you. They're gonna blow you to a big meal!

WILLY: Don't say! Who thought of that?

LINDA: Biff came to me this morning, Willy, and he said, "Tell Dad, we want to blow him to a big meal."

Be there six o'clock. You and your two boys are going 95
to have dinner.

WILLY: Gee whiz! That's really somethin'. I'm gonna knock Howard for a loop, kid. I'll get an advance, and I'll come home with a New York job. Goddam-mit, now I'm gonna do it! 100

LINDA: Oh, that's the spirit, Willy!

WILLY: I will never get behind a wheel the rest of my life!

LINDA: It's changing, Willy, I can feel it changing!

WILLY: Beyond a question. G'by, I'm late. *(He starts to go* 105
again.)

LINDA: *(calling after him as she runs to the kitchen table for a handkerchief)* You got your glasses?

WILLY: *(feels for them, then comes back in)* Yeah, yeah, got my glasses. 110

LINDA: *(giving him the handkerchief)* And a handkerchief.

WILLY: Yeah, handkerchief.

LINDA: And your saccharine?

WILLY: Yeah, my saccharine.

LINDA: Be careful on the subway stairs. 115

She kisses him, and a silk stocking is seen hanging from her hand. WILLY *notices it.*

WILLY: Will you stop mending stockings? At least while I'm in the house. It gets me nervous. I can't tell you. Please.

LINDA hides the stocking in her hand as she follows WILLY *across the forestage in front of the house.*

LINDA: Remember, Frank's Chop House.

WILLY: *(passing the apron)* Maybe beets would grow out 120
there.

LINDA *: (laughing)* But you tried so many times.

WILLY: Yeah. Well, don't work hard today. *(He disap-pears around the right corner of the house.)*

LINDA: Be careful! 125

As WILLY *vanishes,* LINDA *waves to him. Suddenly the phone rings. She runs across the stage and into the kitchen and lifts it.*

LINDA: Hello? Oh, Biff! I'm so glad you called, I just . . .
Yes, sure, I just told him. Yes, he'll be there for din-ner at six o'clock, I didn't forget. Listen, I was just

Willy notices the stocking that Linda is mending.

130   dying to tell you. You know that little rubber pipe I told you about? That he connected to the gas heater? I finally decided to go down the cellar this morning and take it away and destroy it. But it's gone! Imag-ine? He took it away himself, it isn't there! *(She lis-*

135   *tens.)* When? Oh, then you took it. Oh—nothing, it's just that I'd hoped he'd taken it away himself. Oh, I'm not worried, darling, because this morning he left in such high spirits, it was like the old days! I'm not afraid any more. Did Mr. Oliver see you? . . . Well,

140   you wait there then. And make a nice impression on him, darling. Just don't perspire too much before you see him. And have a nice time with Dad. He may have big news too! . . . That's right, a New York job. And be sweet to him tonight, dear. Be loving to

145   him. Because he's only a little boat looking for a harbor. *(She is trembling with sorrow and joy.)* Oh, that's wonderful, Biff, you'll save his life. Thanks, darling. Just put your arm around him when he comes into the restaurant. Give him a smile. That's the boy . . .

150   Good-by, dear. . . . You got your comb? . . . That's fine. Good-by, Biff dear.

In the middle of her speech, HOWARD WAGNER, *thirty-six, wheels in a small typewriter table on which is a wire-recording machine and proceeds to plug it in. This is on the left forestage. Light slowly fades on* LINDA *as it rises on* HOWARD. HOWARD *is intent on threading the machine and only glances over his shoulder as* WILLY *appears.*

WILLY: Pst! Pst!

HOWARD: Hello, Willy, come in.

WILLY: Like to have a little talk with you, Howard.

HOWARD: Sorry to keep you waiting. I'll be with you
155   in a minute.

WILLY: What's that, Howard?

HOWARD: Didn't you ever see one of these? Wire recorder.

WILLY: Oh. Can we talk a minute?

160   HOWARD: Records things. Just got delivery yesterday. Been driving me crazy, the most terrific machine I ever saw in my life. I was up all night with it.

WILLY: What do you do with it?

165   HOWARD: I bought it for dictation, but you can do anything with it. Listen to this. I had it home last night. Listen to what I picked up. The first one is my daughter. Get this. *(He flicks the switch and "Roll Out the Barrel" is heard being whistled.)* Listen to that kid whistle.

170   WILLY: That is lifelike, isn't it?

HOWARD: Seven years old. Get that tone.

WILLY: Ts, ts. Like to ask a little favor if you . . .

The whistling breaks off, and the voice of HOWARD's *daughter is heard.*

HIS DAUGHTER: "Now you, Daddy."

175   HOWARD: She's crazy for me! *(Again the same song is whistled.)* That's me! Ha! *(He winks.)*

WILLY: You're very good!

The whistling breaks off again. The machine runs silent for a moment.

HOWARD: Sh! Get this now, this is my son.

180   HIS SON: "The capital of Alabama is Montgomery; the capital of Arizona is Phoenix; the capital of Arkan-sas is Little Rock; the capital of California is Sacra-mento . . ." *(and on, and on.)*

HOWARD: *(holding up five fingers)*   Five years old, Willy!

WILLY: He'll make an announcer some day!

HIS SON: *(continuing)*   "The capital . . ."

185   HOWARD: Get that—alphabetical order! *(The machine breaks off suddenly.)* Wait a minute. The maid kicked the plug out.

WILLY: It certainly is a—

HOWARD: Sh, for God's sake!

190   HIS SON: "It's nine o'clock, Bulova watch time. So I have to go to sleep."

WILLY: That really is—

HOWARD: Wait a minute! The next is my wife.

They wait.

HOWARD'S VOICE: "Go on, say something." *(Pause.)*
195   "Well, you gonna talk?"

HIS WIFE: "I can't think of anything."

HOWARD'S VOICE: "Well, talk—it's turning."

HIS WIFE: *(shyly, beaten)*   "Hello." *(Silence.)* "Oh, Howard, I can't talk into this . . ."

200   **HOWARD:** *(snapping the machine off)*   That was my wife.

WILLY: That is a wonderful machine. Can we—

HOWARD: I tell you, Willy, I'm gonna take my camera, and my bandsaw, and all my hobbies, and out they go. This is the most fascinating relaxation I ever found.

205   **WILLY:**   I think I'll get one myself.

HOWARD: Sure, they're only a hundred and a half. You can't do without it. Supposing you wanna hear Jack Benny, see? But you can't be at home at that hour. So you tell the maid to turn the radio on when Jack
210   Benny comes on, and this automatically goes on with the radio . . .

WILLY: And when you come home you . . .

HOWARD: You can come home twelve o'clock, one o'clock, any time you like, and you get yourself a Coke and sit yourself down, throw the switch, and there's
215   Jack Benny's program in the middle of the night!

WILLY: I'm definitely going to get one. Because lots of time I'm on the road, and I think to myself, what I must be missing on the radio!

220   **HOWARD:**   Don't you have a radio in the car?

WILLY: Well, yeah, but who ever thinks of turning it on?

HOWARD: Say, aren't you supposed to be in Boston?

WILLY: That's what I want to talk to you about, Howard. You got a minute? *(He draws a chair in from the wing.)*

225   **HOWARD:**   What happened? What're you doing here?

WILLY: Well . . .

HOWARD: You didn't crack up again, did you?

WILLY: Oh, no. No . . .

HOWARD: Geez, you had me worried there for a min-
230   ute. What's the trouble?

WILLY: Well, tell you the truth, Howard. I've come to the decision that I'd rather not travel any more.

HOWARD: Not travel! Well, what'll you do?

WILLY: Remember, Christmas time, when you had the party here? You said you'd try to think of some spot   235
for me here in town.

HOWARD: With us?

WILLY: Well, sure.

HOWARD: Oh, yeah, yeah. I remember. Well, I couldn't think of anything for you, Willy.   240

WILLY: I tell ya, Howard. The kids are all grown up, y'know. I don't need much any more. If I could take home—well, sixty-five dollars a week. I could swing it.

HOWARD: Yeah, but Willy, see I—

WILLY: I tell ya why, Howard. Speaking frankly and   245
between the two of us, y'know—I'm just a little tired.

HOWARD: Oh, I could understand that, Willy. But you're a road man, Willy, and we do a road business. We've only got a half-dozen salesmen on the floor
here.   250

WILLY: God knows, Howard, I never asked a favor of any man. But I was with the firm when your father used to carry you in here in his arms.

HOWARD: I know that, Willy, but—

WILLY: Your father came to me the day you were born   255
and asked me what I thought of the name of How-
ard, may he rest in peace.

HOWARD: I appreciate that, Willy, but there just is no spot here for you. If I had a spot I'd slam you right in, but I just don't have a single solitary spot.   260

He looks for his lighter. WILLY *has picked it up and gives it to him. Pause.*

WILLY: *(with increasing anger)*   Howard, all I need to set my table is fifty dollars a week.

HOWARD: But where am I going to put you, kid?

WILLY: Look, it isn't a question of whether I can sell merchandise, is it?   265

HOWARD: No, but it's a business, kid, and everybody's gotta pull his own weight.

WILLY: *(desperately)*   Just let me tell you a story, Howard—

HOWARD: 'Cause you gotta admit, business is   270
business.

WILLY: *(angrily)*   Business is definitely business, but just listen for a minute. You don't understand this. When

275 I was a boy—eighteen, nineteen—I was already on the road. And there was a question in my mind as to whether selling had a future for me. Because in those days I had a yearning to go to Alaska. See, there were three gold strikes in one month in Alaska, and I felt like going out. Just for the ride, you might say.

280 HOWARD: *(barely interested)* Don't say.

WILLY: Oh, yeah, my father lived many years in Alaska. He was an adventurous man. We've got quite a little streak of self-reliance in our family. I thought I'd go out with my older brother and try to locate him, and

285 maybe settle in the North with the old man. And I was almost decided to go, when I met a salesman in the Parker House. His name was Dave Singleman. And he was eighty-four years old, and he'd drummed merchandise in thirty-one states. And old Dave, he'd

290 go up to his room, y'understand, put on his green velvet slippers—I'll never forget—and pick up his phone and call the buyers, and without ever leaving his room, at the age of eighty-four, he made his living. And when I saw that, I realized that selling was the

295 greatest career a man could want. 'Cause what could be more satisfying than to be able to go, at the age of eighty-four, into twenty or thirty different cities, and pick up a phone, and be remembered and loved and helped by so many different people? Do you know?

300 When he died—and by the way he died the death of a salesman, in his green velvet slippers in the smoker of the New York, New Haven, and Hartford, going into Boston—when he died, hundreds of salesmen and buyers were at his funeral. Things were sad on a lotta

305 trains for months after that. *(He stands up. HOWARD has not looked at him.)* In those days there was personality in it, Howard. There was respect, and comradeship, and gratitude in it. Today, it's all cut and dried, and there's no chance for bringing friendship to

310 bear—or personality. You see what I mean? They don't know me any more.

HOWARD: *(moving away, to the right)* That's just the thing, Willy.

WILLY: If I had forty dollars a week—that's all I'd need.
315 Forty dollars, Howard.

HOWARD: Kid, I can't take blood from a stone, I—

WILLY: *(desperation is on him now)* Howard, the year Al Smith was nominated, your father came to me and—

320 HOWARD: *(starting to go off)* I've got to see some people, kid.

WILLY: *(stopping him)* I'm talking about your father! There were promises made across this desk! You mustn't tell me you've got people to see—I put thirty-four years into this firm, Howard, and now I can't
325 pay my insurance! You can't eat the orange and throw the peel away—a man is not a piece of fruit! *(After a pause.)* Now pay attention. Your father—in 1928 I had a big year. I averaged a hundred and seventy dollars a week in commissions.
330

HOWARD: *(impatiently)* Now, Willy, you never averaged—

WILLY: *(banging his hand on the desk)* I averaged a hundred and seventy dollars a week in the year of 1928! And your father came to me—or rather, I was in the
335 office here—it was right over this desk—and he put his hand on my shoulder—

HOWARD: *(getting up)* You'll have to excuse me, Willy, I gotta see some people. Pull yourself together. *(Going out.)* I'll be back in a little while.
340

On HOWARD's exit, the light on his chair grows very bright and strange.

WILLY: Pull myself together! What the hell did I say to him? My God, I was yelling at him! How could I? *(WILLY breaks off, staring at the light, which occupies the chair, animating it. He approaches this chair, standing across the desk from it.)* Frank, Frank, don't you
345 remember what you told me that time? How you put your hand on my shoulder, and Frank . . . *(He leans on the desk and as he speaks the dead man's name he accidentally switches on the recorder, and instantly:)*

HOWARD'S SON: ". . . of New York is Albany. The capi-
350 tal of Ohio is Cincinnati, the capital of Rhode Island is . . ." *(The recitation continues.)*

WILLY: *(leaping away with fright, shouting)* Ha! Howard! Howard! Howard!

HOWARD: *(rushing in)* What happened?
355

WILLY: *(pointing at the machine, which continues nasally, childishly, with the capital cities)* Shut it off! Shut it off!

HOWARD: *(pulling the plug out)* Look, Willy . . .

WILLY: *(pressing his hands to his eyes)* I gotta get myself some coffee. I'll get some coffee . . .
360

WILLY starts to walk out. HOWARD stops him.

HOWARD: *(rolling up the cord)* Willy, look . . .

WILLY: I'll go to Boston.

Howard (Jon Polito) talks to Willy about his job performance.

HOWARD: Willy, you can't go to Boston for us.

WILLY: Why can't I go?

365 **HOWARD:** I don't want you to represent us. I've been meaning to tell you for a long time now.

WILLY: Howard, are you firing me?

HOWARD: I think you need a good long rest, Willy.

WILLY: Howard—

370 **HOWARD:** And when you feel better, come back, and we'll see if we can work something out.

WILLY: But I gotta earn money, Howard. I'm in no position to—

HOWARD: Where are your sons? Why don't your sons
375 give you a hand?

WILLY: They're working on a very big deal.

HOWARD: This is no time for false pride, Willy. You go to your sons and you tell them that you're tired. You've got two great boys haven't you?

380 **WILLY:** Oh, no question, no question, but in the meantime . . .

HOWARD: Then that's that, heh?

WILLY: All right, I'll go to Boston tomorrow.

HOWARD: No, no.

385 **WILLY:** I can't throw myself on my sons. I'm not a cripple!

HOWARD: Look, kid, I'm busy this morning.

WILLY: (grasping HOWARD's arm) Howard, you've got to let me go to Boston!

HOWARD: (hard, keeping himself under control) I've got 390 a line of people to see this morning. Sit down, take five minutes, and pull yourself together, and then go home, will ya? I need the office, Willy. (He starts to go, turns, remembering the recorder, starts to push off the table holding the recorder.) Oh, yeah. Whenever you can this 395 week, stop by and drop off the samples. You'll feel better, Willy, and then come back and we'll talk. Pull yourself together, kid, there's people outside.

HOWARD exits, pushing the table off left. WILLY stares into space, exhausted. Now the music is heard—BEN's music— first distantly, then closer, closer. As WILLY speaks, BEN enters from the right. He carries valise and umbrella.

WILLY: Oh, Ben, how did you do it? What is the answer? Did you wind up the Alaska deal already? 400

BEN: Doesn't take much time if you know what you're doing. Just a short business trip. Boarding ship in an hour. Wanted to say good-by.

WILLY: Ben, I've got to talk to you.

BEN: (glancing at his watch) Haven't the time, William. 405

WILLY: (crossing the apron to BEN) Ben, nothing's working out. I don't know what to do.

BEN: Now, look here, William. I've bought timberland in Alaska and I need a man to look after things for me.

WILLY: God, timberland! Me and my boys in those 410 grand outdoors!

BEN: You've a new continent at your doorstep, William. Get out of these cities, they're full of talk and time payments and courts of law. Screw on your fists and you can fight for a fortune up there. 415

WILLY: Yes, yes! Linda, Linda!

LINDA enters as of old, with the wash.

LINDA: Oh, you're back?

BEN: I haven't much time.

WILLY: No, wait! Linda, he's got a proposition for me in Alaska. 420

LINDA: But you've got—(To BEN.) He's got a beautiful job here.

WILLY: But in Alaska, kid, I could—

LINDA: You're doing well enough, Willy!

BEN: (to LINDA) Enough for what, my dear? 425

LINDA: *(frightened of* BEN *and angry at him)* Don't say those things to him! Enough to be Happy right here, right now. *(To* WILLY, *while* BEN *laughs.)* Why must everybody conquer the world? You're well liked, and the boys love you, and someday—*(to* BEN*)*—why, old man Wagner told him just the other day that if he keeps it up he'll be a member of the firm, didn't he, Willy?

430

WILLY: Sure, sure. I am building something with this firm, Ben, and if a man is building something he must be on the right track, mustn't he?

435

BEN: What are you building? Lay your hand on it. Where is it?

WILLY: *(hesitantly)* That's true, Linda, there's nothing.

LINDA: Why? *(To* BEN.*)* There's a man eighty-four years old—

440

WILLY: That's right, Ben, that's right. When I look at that man I say, what is there to worry about?

BEN: Bah!

WILLY: It's true, Ben. All he has to do is go into any city, pick up the phone, and he's making his living and you know why?

445

BEN: *(picking up his valise)* I've got to go.

WILLY: *(holding* BEN *back)* Look at this boy!

BIFF, *in his high school sweater, enters carrying suitcase.* HAPPY *carries* BIFF's *shoulder guards, gold helmet, and football pants.*

WILLY: Without a penny to his name, three great universities are begging for him, and from there the sky's

450

Willy and Linda react to Ben's Alaska proposition.

the limit, because it's not what you do, Ben. It's who you know and the smile on your face! It's contacts, Ben, contacts! The whole wealth of Alaska passes over the lunch table at the Commodore Hotel, and that's the wonder, the wonder of this country, that a man can end with diamonds here on the basis of being liked! *(He turns to* BIFF.*)* And that's why when you get out on that field today it's important. Because thousands of people will be rooting for you and loving you. *(To* BEN, *who has again begun to leave.)* And Ben! when he walks into a business office his name will sound out like a bell and all the doors will open to him! I've seen it, Ben, I've seen it a thousand times! You can't feel it with your hand like timber, but it's there!

455

460

465

BEN: Good-by, William.

WILLY: Ben, am I right? Don't you think I'm right? I value your advice.

BEN: There's a new continent at your doorstep, William. You could walk out rich. Rich! *(He is gone.)*

470

WILLY: We'll do it here, Ben! You hear me? We're gonna do it here!

Young BERNARD *rushes in. The gay music of the Boys is heard.*

BERNARD: Oh, gee, I was afraid you left already!

WILLY: Why? What time is it?

475

BERNARD: It's half-past one!

WILLY: Well, come on, everybody! Ebbets Field next stop! Where's the pennants? *(He rushes through the wall-line of the kitchen and out into the living-room.)*

LINDA: *(to* BIFF*)* Did you pack fresh underwear?

480

BIFF: *(who has been limbering up)* I want to go!

BERNARD: Biff, I'm carrying your helmet, ain't I?

HAPPY: I'm carrying the helmet.

BERNARD: How am I going to get in the locker room?

LINDA: Let him carry the shoulder guards. *(She puts her coat and hat on in the kitchen.)*

485

BERNARD: Can I, Biff? 'Cause I told everybody I'm going to be in the locker room.

HAPPY: In Ebbets Field it's the clubhouse.

BERNARD: I meant the clubhouse. Biff!

490

HAPPY: Biff!

BIFF: (*grandly, after a slight pause*) Let him carry the shoulder guards.

HAPPY: (*as he gives* BERNARD *the shoulder guards*) Stay
495   close to us now.

    WILLY *rushes in with the pennants.*

WILLY: (*handing them out*) Everybody wave when Biff comes out on the field. (HAPPY *and* BERNARD *run off.*) You set now, boy?

    The music has died away.

BIFF: Ready to go, Pop. Every muscle is ready.

500 **WILLY:** (*at the edge of the apron*) You realize what this means?

BIFF: That's right, Pop.

WILLY: (*feeling* BIFF's *muscles*) You're comin' home this afternoon captain of the All-Scholastic Champion-
505   ship Team of the City of New York.

BIFF: I got it, Pop. And remember, pal, when I take off my helmet, that touchdown is for you.

WILLY: Let's go! (*He is starting out, with his arm around* BIFF, *when* CHARLEY *enters, as of old, in knickers.*) I got
510   no room for you, Charley.

CHARLEY: Room? For what?

WILLY: In the car.

CHARLEY: You goin' for a ride? I wanted to shoot some casino.

515 **WILLY:** (*furiously*) Casino! (*Incredulously.*) Don't you realize what today is?

LINDA: Oh, he knows, Willy. He's just kidding you.

WILLY: That's nothing to kid about!

CHARLEY: No, Linda, what's goin' on?

520 **LINDA:** He's playing in Ebbets Field.

CHARLEY: Baseball in this weather?

WILLY: Don't talk to him. Come on, come on! (*He is pushing them out.*)

CHARLEY: Wait a minute, didn't you hear the news?

525 **WILLY:** What?

CHARLEY: Don't you listen to the radio? Ebbets Field just blew up.

WILLY: You go to hell! (CHARLEY *laughs. Pushing them out.*) Come on, come on! We're late.

CHARLEY: (*as they go*) Knock a homer, Biff, knock a   530
homer!

WILLY: (*the last to leave, turning to* CHARLEY) I don't think that was funny, Charley. This is the greatest day of his life.

CHARLEY: Willy, when are you going to grow up?   535

WILLY: Yeah, heh? When this game is over, Charley, you'll be laughing out of the other side of your face. They'll be calling him another Red Grange. Twenty-five thousand a year.

CHARLEY: (*kidding*) Is that so?   540

WILLY: Yeah, that's so.

CHARLEY: Well, then, I'm sorry, Willy. But tell me something.

WILLY: What?

CHARLEY: Who is Red Grange?   545

WILLY: Put up your hands. Goddam you, put up your hands!

    CHARLEY, *chuckling, shakes his head and walks away, around the left corner of the stage.* WILLY *follows him. The music rises to a mocking frenzy.*

WILLY: Who the hell do you think you are, better than everybody else? You don't know everything, you big, ignorant, stupid . . . Put up your hands!   550

    Light rises, on the right side of the forestage, on a small table in the reception room of CHARLEY's *office. Traffic sounds are heard.* BERNARD, *now mature, sits whistling to himself. A pair of tennis rackets and an overnight bag are on the floor beside him.*

WILLY: (*offstage*) What are you walking away for? Don't walk away! If you're going to say something say it to my face! I know you laugh at me behind my back. You'll laugh out of the other side of your goddam face after this game. Touchdown! Touchdown! Eighty   555
thousand people! Touchdown! Right between the goal posts.

    BERNARD *is a quiet, earnest, but self-assured young man.* WILLY's *voice is coming from right upstage now.* BERNARD *lowers his feet off the table and listens.* JENNY, *his father's secretary, enters.*

JENNY: (*distressed*) Say, Bernard, will you go out in the hall?

BERNARD: What is that noise? Who is it?   560

JENNY: Mr. Loman. He just got off the elevator.

BERNARD: (getting up) Who's he arguing with?

JENNY: Nobody. There's nobody with him. I can't deal
with him any more, and your father gets all upset
everytime he comes. I've got a lot of typing to do, and
your father's waiting to sign it. Will you see him?

WILLY: (entering) Touchdown! Touch—(He sees Jenny.)
Jenny, Jenny, good to see you. How're ya? Workin'?
Or still honest?

JENNY: Fine. How've you been feeling?

WILLY: Not much any more, Jenny. Ha, ha! (He is surprised to see the rackets.)

BERNARD: Hello, Uncle Willy.

WILLY: (almost shocked) Bernard! Well, look who's here!
(He comes quickly, guiltily, to BERNARD and warmly
shakes his hand.)

BERNARD: How are you? Good to see you.

WILLY: What are you doing here?

BERNARD: Oh, just stopped by to see Pop. Get off my
feet till my train leaves. I'm going to Washington in a
few minutes.

WILLY: Is he in?

BERNARD: Yes, he's in his office with the accountant.
Sit down.

WILLY: (sitting down) What're you going to do in
Washington?

BERNARD: Oh, just a case I've got there, Willy.

WILLY: That so? (Indicating the rackets.) You going to
play tennis there?

BERNARD: I'm staying with a friend who's got a court.

WILLY: Don't say. His own tennis court. Must be fine
people, I bet.

BERNARD: They are, very nice. Dad tells me Biff's in
town.

WILLY: (with a big smile) Yeah, Biff's in. Working on a
very big deal, Bernard.

BERNARD: What's Biff doing?

WILLY: Well, he's been doing very big things in the West.
But he decided to establish himself here. Very big.
We're having dinner. Did I hear your wife had a boy?

BERNARD: That's right. Our second.

WILLY: Two boys! What do you know!

BERNARD: What kind of a deal has Biff got?

WILLY: Well, Bill Oliver—very big sporting-goods
man—he wants Biff very badly. Called him in from
the West. Long distance, carte blanche, special de-
liveries. Your friends have their own private tennis
court?

BERNARD: You still with the old firm, Willy?

WILLY: (after a pause) I'm—I'm overjoyed to see how
you made the grade, Bernard, overjoyed. It's an en-
couraging thing to see a young man really—really—
Looks very good for Biff—very—(He breaks off, then.)
Bernard—(He is so full of emotion, he breaks off again.)

BERNARD: What is it, Willy?

WILLY: (small and alone) What—what's the secret?

BERNARD: What secret?

WILLY: How—how did you? Why didn't he ever
catch on?

BERNARD: I wouldn't know that, Willy.

WILLY: (confidentially, desperately) You were his friend,
his boyhood friend. There's something I don't understand about it. His life ended after that Ebbets Field
game. From the age of seventeen nothing good ever
happened to him.

BERNARD: He never trained himself for anything.

WILLY: But he did, he did. After high school he took
so many correspondence courses. Radio mechanics;
television; God knows what, and never made the
slightest mark.

BERNARD: (taking off his glasses) Willy, do you want to
talk candidly?

WILLY: (rising, faces BERNARD) I regard you as a very
brilliant man, Bernard. I value your advice.

BERNARD: Oh, the hell with the advice, Willy. I couldn't
advise you. There's just one thing I've always wanted
to ask you. When he was supposed to graduate, and
the math teacher flunked him—

WILLY: Oh, that son-of-a-bitch ruined his life.

BERNARD: Yeah, but, Willy, all he had to do was go to
summer school and make up that subject.

WILLY: That's right, that's right.

BERNARD: Did you tell him not to go to summer
school?

645   **WILLY:**   Me? I begged him to go. I ordered him to go!

BERNARD: Then why wouldn't he go?

WILLY: Why? Why! Bernard, that question has been trailing me like a ghost for the last fifteen years. He flunked the subject, and laid down and died like a

650   hammer hit him!

BERNARD: Take it easy, kid.

WILLY: Let me talk to you—I got nobody to talk to. Bernard, Bernard, was it my fault? Y'see? It keeps going around in my mind, maybe I did something

655   to him. I got nothing to give him.

BERNARD: Don't take it so hard.

WILLY: Why did he lay down? What is the story there? You were his friend!

BERNARD: Willy, I remember, it was June, and our

660   grades came out. And he'd flunked math.

WILLY: That son-of-a-bitch!

BERNARD: No, it wasn't right then. Biff just got very angry, I remember, and he was ready to enroll in summer school.

665   **WILLY:**   (*surprised*)   He was?

BERNARD: He wasn't beaten by it at all. But then, Willy, he disappeared from the block for almost a month. And I got the idea that he'd gone up to New England to see you. Did he have a talk with you then?

       WILLY *stares in silence.*

670   **BERNARD:**   Willy?

WILLY: (*with a strong edge of resentment in his voice*)   Yeah, he came to Boston. What about it?

BERNARD: Well, just that when he came back—I'll never forget this, it always mystifies me. Because

675   I'd thought so well of Biff, even though he'd always taken advantage of me. I loved him, Willy, y'know? And he came back after that month and took his sneakers—remember those sneakers with "University of Virginia" printed on them? He was so proud of

680   those, wore them every day. And he took them down in the cellar, and burned them up in the furnace. We had a fist fight. It lasted at least half an hour. Just the two of us, punching each other down the cellar, and crying right through it. I've often thought of

685   how strange it was that I knew he'd given up his life. What happened in Boston, Willy?

       WILLY *looks at him as at an intruder.*

Willy and Bernard puzzle over Biff's decline.

BERNARD: I just bring it up because you asked me.

WILLY: (*angrily*)   Nothing. What do you mean, "What happened?" What's that got to do with anything?

BERNARD: Well, don't get sore.   690

WILLY: What are you trying to do, blame it on me? If a boy lays down is that my fault?

BERNARD: Now, Willy, don't get—

WILLY: Well, don't—don't talk to me that way! What does that mean, "What happened?"   695

       CHARLEY *enters. He is in his vest, and he carries a bottle of bourbon.*

CHARLEY: Hey, you're going to miss that train. (*He waves the bottle.*)

BERNARD: Yeah, I'm going. (*He takes the bottle.*) Thanks, Pop. (*He picks up his rackets and bag.*) Good-by, Willy, and don't worry about it. You know. "If at first you   700 don't succeed . . ."

WILLY: Yes, I believe in that.

BERNARD: But sometimes, Willy, it's better for a man just to walk away.

WILLY: Walk away?   705

BERNARD: That's right.

WILLY: But if you can't walk away?

BERNARD: (*after a slight pause*)   I guess that's when it's tough. (*Extending his hand.*) Good-by, Willy.

WILLY: (*shaking* BERNARD's *hand*)   Good-by, boy.   710

CHARLEY: (*an arm on* BERNARD's *shoulder*)   How do you like this kid? Gonna argue a case in front of the Supreme Court.

BERNARD: (*protesting*)   Pop!

715 **WILLY:** (*genuinely shocked, pained, and happy*)   No! The Supreme Court!

BERNARD: I gotta run. 'By, Dad!

CHARLEY: Knock 'em dead, Bernard!

> BERNARD *goes off.*

WILLY: (*as* CHARLEY *takes out his wallet*)   The Supreme
720 Court! And he didn't even mention it!

CHARLEY: (*counting out money on the desk*)   He don't have to—he's gonna do it.

WILLY: And you never told him what to do, did you? You never took any interest in him.

725 **CHARLEY:**   My salvation is that I never took any interest in anything. There's some money—fifty dollars. I got an accountant inside.

WILLY: Charley, look . . . (*With difficulty.*) I got my insurance to pay. If you can manage it—I need a hundred
730 and ten dollars.

> CHARLEY *doesn't reply for a moment; merely stops moving.*

WILLY: I'd draw it from my bank but Linda would know, and I . . .

CHARLEY: Sit down, Willy.

WILLY: (*moving toward the chair*)   I'm keeping an account
735 of everything, remember. I'll pay every penny back. (*He sits.*)

CHARLEY: Now listen to me, Willy.

WILLY: I want you to know I appreciate . . .

CHARLEY: (*sitting down on the table*)   Willy, what're you
740 doin'? What the hell is goin' on in your head?

WILLY: Why? I'm simply . . .

CHARLEY: I offered you a job. You can make fifty dollars a week. And I won't send you on the road.

WILLY: I've got a job.

745 **CHARLEY:**   Without pay? What kind of a job is a job without pay? (*He rises.*) Now, look, kid, enough is enough. I'm no genius but I know when I'm being insulted.

WILLY: Insulted!

CHARLEY: Why don't you want to work for me?   750

WILLY: What's the matter with you? I've got a job.

CHARLEY: Then what're you walkin' in here every week for?

WILLY: (*getting up*)   Well, if you don't want me to walk in here—   755

CHARLEY: I am offering you a job.

WILLY: I don't want your goddam job!

CHARLEY: When the hell are you going to grow up?

WILLY: (*furiously*)   You big ignoramus, if you say that to me again I'll rap you one! I don't care how big you   760 are! (*He's ready to fight.*)

> Pause.

CHARLEY: (*kindly, going to him*)   How much do you need, Willy?

WILLY: Charley, I'm strapped. I'm strapped. I don't know what to do. I was just fired.   765

CHARLEY: Howard fired you?

WILLY: That snotnose. Imagine that? I named him. I named him Howard.

CHARLEY: Willy, when're you gonna realize that them things don't mean anything? You named him How-   770 ard, but you can't sell that. The only thing you got in this world is what you can sell. And the funny thing is that you're a salesman, and you don't know that.

WILLY: I've always tried to think otherwise, I guess. I always felt that if a man was impressive, and well   775 liked, that nothing—

CHARLEY: Why must everybody like you? Who liked J. P. Morgan? Was he impressive? In a Turkish bath he'd look like a butcher. But with his pockets on he was very well liked. Now listen, Willy, I know you   780 don't like me, and nobody can say I'm in love with you, but I'll give you a job because—just for the hell of it, put it that way. Now what do you say?

WILLY: I—I just can't work for you, Charley.

CHARLEY: What're you, jealous of me?   785

WILLY: I can't work for you, that's all, don't ask me why.

CHARLEY: (*angered, takes out more bills*)   You been jealous of me all your life, you damned fool! Here, pay your insurance. (*He puts the money in* WILLY's *hand.*)

WILLY: I'm keeping strict accounts.   790

Charley puts money in Willy's hand.

CHARLEY: I've got some work to do. Take care of yourself. And pay your insurance.

795 **WILLY:** (*moving to the right*) Funny, y'know? After all the highways, and the trains, and the appointments, and the years, you end up worth more dead than alive.

CHARLEY: Willy, nobody's worth nothin' dead. (*After a slight pause.*) Did you hear what I said?

WILLY *stands still, dreaming.*

CHARLEY: Willy!

800 **WILLY:** Apologize to Bernard for me when you see him. I didn't mean to argue with him. He's a fine boy. They're all fine boys, and they'll end up big—all of them. Someday they'll all play tennis together. Wish me luck, Charley. He saw Bill Oliver today.

CHARLEY: Good luck.

805 **WILLY:** (*on the verge of tears*) Charley, you're the only friend I got. Isn't that a remarkable thing? (*He goes out.*)

CHARLEY: Jesus!

CHARLEY *stares after him a moment and follows. All light blacks out. Suddenly raucous music is heard, and a red glow rises behind the screen at right.* STANLEY, *a young waiter, appears, carrying a table, followed by* HAPPY, *who is carrying two chairs.*

810 **STANLEY:** (*putting the table down*) That's all right, Mr. Loman, I can handle it myself. (*He turns and takes the chairs from* HAPPY *and places them at the table.*)

HAPPY: (*glancing around*) Oh, this is better.

STANLEY: Sure, in the front there you're in the middle of all kinds a noise. Whenever you got a party, Mr. Loman, you just tell me and I'll put you back here. 815 Y'know, there's a lotta people they don't like it private, because when they go out they like to see a lotta action around them because they're sick and tired to stay in the house by theirself. But I know you, you ain't from Hackensack. You know what I mean? 820

HAPPY: (*sitting down*) So how's it coming, Stanley?

STANLEY: Ah, it's a dog's life. I only wish during the war they'd a took me in the Army. I coulda been dead by now.

HAPPY: My brother's back, Stanley. 825

STANLEY: Oh, he come back, heh? From the Far West.

HAPPY: Yeah, big cattle man, my brother, so treat him right. And my father's coming too.

STANLEY: Oh, your father too!

HAPPY: You got a couple of nice lobsters? 830

STANLEY: Hundred per cent, big.

HAPPY: I want them with the claws.

STANLEY: Don't worry, I don't give you no mice. (HAPPY *laughs.*) How about some wine? It'll put a head on the meal. 835

HAPPY: No. You remember, Stanley, that recipe I brought you from overseas? With the champagne in it?

STANLEY: Oh, yeah, sure. I still got it tacked up yet in the kitchen. But that'll have to cost a buck apiece 840 anyways.

HAPPY: That's all right.

STANLEY: What'd you, hit a number or somethin'?

HAPPY: No, it's a little celebration. My brother is—I think he pulled off a big deal today. I think we're go- 845 ing into business together.

STANLEY: Great! That's the best for you. Because a family business, you know what I mean?—that's the best.

HAPPY: That's what I think. 850

STANLEY: 'Cause what's the difference? Somebody steals? It's in the family. Know what I mean? (*Sotto voce.*) Like this bartender here. The boss is goin'

855 crazy what kinda leak he's got in the cash register. You put it in but it don't come out.

HAPPY: (*raising his head*) Sh!

STANLEY: What?

HAPPY: You notice I wasn't lookin' right or left, was I?

STANLEY: No.

860 **HAPPY:** And my eyes are closed.

STANLEY: So what's the—?

HAPPY: Strudel's comin'.

STANLEY: (*catching on, looks around*) Ah, no, there's no—

> He breaks off as a furred, lavishly dressed GIRL enters and sits at the next table. Both follow her with their eyes.

STANLEY: Geez, how'd ya know?

865 **HAPPY:** I got radar or something. (*Staring directly at her profile.*) Oooooooo . . . Stanley.

STANLEY: I think that's for you, Mr. Loman.

HAPPY: Look at that mouth. Oh, God. And the binoculars.

870 **STANLEY:** Geez, you got a life, Mr. Loman.

HAPPY: Wait on her.

STANLEY: (*going to the GIRL's table*) Would you like a menu, ma'am?

GIRL: I'm expecting someone, but I'd like a—

875 **HAPPY:** Why don't you bring her—excuse me, miss, do you mind? I sell champagne, and I'd like you to try my brand. Bring her a champagne, Stanley.

GIRL: That's awfully nice of you.

HAPPY: Don't mention it. It's all company money. (*He laughs.*)

880

GIRL: That's a charming product to be selling, isn't it?

HAPPY: Oh, gets to be like everything else. Selling is selling, y'know.

GIRL: I suppose.

885 **HAPPY:** You don't happen to sell, do you?

GIRL: No, I don't sell.

HAPPY: Would you object to a compliment from a stranger? You ought to be on a magazine cover.

GIRL: (*looking at him a little archly*) I have been.

> STANLEY comes in with a glass of champagne.

HAPPY: What'd I say before, Stanley? You see? She's a cover girl. 890

STANLEY: Oh, I could see, I could see.

HAPPY: (*to the GIRL*) What magazine?

GIRL: Oh, a lot of them. (*She takes the drink.*) Thank you.

HAPPY: You know what they say in France, don't you? "Champagne is the drink of the complexion"—Hya, Biff! 895

> BIFF has entered and sits with HAPPY.

BIFF: Hello, kid. Sorry I'm late.

HAPPY: I just got here. Uh, Miss—?

GIRL: Forsythe. 900

HAPPY: Miss Forsythe, this is my brother.

BIFF: Is Dad here?

HAPPY: His name is Biff. You might've heard of him. Great football player.

GIRL: Really? What team? 905

HAPPY: Are you familiar with football?

GIRL: No, I'm afraid I'm not.

HAPPY: Biff is quarterback with the New York Giants.

GIRL: Well, that is nice, isn't it? (*She drinks.*)

HAPPY: Good health. 910

GIRL: I'm happy to meet you.

HAPPY: That's my name. Hap. It's really Harold, but at West Point they called me Happy.

GIRL: (*now really impressed*) Oh, I see. How do you do? (*She turns her profile.*) 915

BIFF: Isn't Dad coming?

HAPPY: You want her?

BIFF: Oh, I could never make that.

HAPPY: I remember the time that idea would never come into your head. Where's the old confidence, Biff? 920

BIFF: I just saw Oliver—

HAPPY: Wait a minute. I've got to see that old confidence again. Do you want her? She's on call.

BIFF: Oh, no. (*He turns to look at the GIRL.*) 925

HAPPY: I'm telling you. Watch this. (*Turning to the* GIRL.) Honey? (*She turns to him.*) Are you busy?

GIRL: Well, I am . . . but I could make a phone call.

HAPPY: Do that, will you, honey? And see if you can get a friend. We'll be here for a while. Biff is one of the greatest football players in the country. `930`

GIRL: (*standing up*) Well, I'm certainly happy to meet you.

HAPPY: Come back soon.

GIRL: I'll try.

HAPPY: Don't try, honey, try hard. `935`

> The GIRL *exits.* STANLEY *follows, shaking his head in bewildered admiration.*

HAPPY: Isn't that a shame now? A beautiful girl like that? That's why I can't get married. There's not a good woman in a thousand. New York is loaded with them, kid!

BIFF: Hap, look— `940`

HAPPY: I told you she was on call!

BIFF: (*strangely unnerved*) Cut it out, will ya? I want to say something to you.

HAPPY: Did you see Oliver?

BIFF: I saw him all right. Now look, I want to tell Dad a couple of things and I want you to help me. `945`

HAPPY: What? Is he going to back you?

BIFF: Are you crazy? You're out of your goddam head, you know that?

HAPPY: Why? What happened? `950`

BIFF: (*breathlessly*) I did a terrible thing today, Hap. It's been the strangest day I ever went through. I'm all numb, I swear.

HAPPY: You mean he wouldn't see you?

BIFF: Well, I waited six hours for him, see? All day. Kept sending my name in. Even tried to date his secretary so she'd get me to him, but no soap. `955`

HAPPY: Because you're not showin' the old confidence, Biff. He remembered you, didn't he?

BIFF: (*stopping* HAPPY *with a gesture*) Finally, about five o'clock, he comes out. Didn't remember who I was or anything. I felt like such an idiot, Hap. `960`

HAPPY: Did you tell him my Florida idea?

BIFF: He walked away. I saw him for one minute. I got so mad I could've torn the walls down! How the hell did I ever get the idea I was a salesman there? I even believed myself that I'd been a salesman for him! And then he gave me one look and—I realized what a ridiculous lie my whole life has been! We've been talking in a dream for fifteen years. I was a shipping clerk. `965` `970`

HAPPY: What'd you do?

BIFF: (*with great tension and wonder*) Well, he left, see. And the secretary went out. I was all alone in the waiting-room. I don't know what came over me, Hap. The next thing I know I'm in his office—paneled walls, everything. I can't explain it. I—Hap, I took his fountain pen. `975`

HAPPY: Geez, did he catch you?

BIFF: I ran out. I ran down all eleven flights. I ran and ran and ran. `980`

HAPPY: That was an awful dumb—what'd you do that for?

BIFF: (*agonized*) I don't know, I just—wanted to take something, I don't know. You gotta help me, Hap, I'm gonna tell Pop. `985`

HAPPY: You crazy? What for?

BIFF: Hap, he's got to understand that I'm not the man somebody lends that kind of money to. He thinks I've been spiting him all these years and it's eating him up. `990`

HAPPY: That's just it. You tell him something nice.

Willy and Happy celebrate at Stanley's (Tom Signorelli) restaurant.

BIFF: I can't.

HAPPY: Say you got a lunch date with Oliver tomorrow.

995 **BIFF:** So what do I do tomorrow?

HAPPY: You leave the house tomorrow and come back at night and say Oliver is thinking it over. And he thinks it over for a couple of weeks, and gradually it fades away and nobody's the worse.

1000 **BIFF:** But it'll go on forever!

HAPPY: Dad is never so happy as when he's looking forward to something!

WILLY *enters.*

HAPPY: Hello, scout!

WILLY: Gee, I haven't been here in years!

STANLEY *has followed* WILLY *in and sets a chair for him.* STANLEY *starts off but* HAPPY *stops him.*

1005 **HAPPY:** Stanley!

STANLEY *stands by, waiting for an order.*

BIFF: *(going to* WILLY *with guilt, as to an invalid)* Sit down, Pop. You want a drink?

WILLY: Sure, I don't mind.

BIFF: Let's get a load on.

1010 **WILLY:** You look worried.

BIFF: N-no. *(To* STANLEY.*)* Scotch all around. Make it doubles.

STANLEY: Doubles, right. *(He goes.)*

WILLY: You had a couple already, didn't you?

1015 **BIFF:** Just a couple, yeah.

WILLY: Well, what happened, boy? *(Nodding affirmatively, with a smile.)* Everything go all right?

BIFF: *(takes a breath, then reaches out and grasps* WILLY's *hand)* Pal . . . *(He is smiling bravely, and* WILLY *is*
1020 *smiling too.)* I had an experience today.

HAPPY: Terrific, Pop.

WILLY: That so? What happened?

BIFF: *(high, slightly alcoholic, above the earth)* I'm going to tell you everything from first to last. It's been a
1025 strange day. *(Silence. He looks around, composes himself as best he can, but his breath keeps breaking the rhythm of his voice.)* I had to wait quite a while for him, and—

WILLY: Oliver.

Willy and Biff argue about the meeting with Oliver.

BIFF: Yeah, Oliver. All day, as a matter of cold fact. And a lot of—instances—facts, Pop, facts about my life 1030 came back to me. Who was it, Pop? Who ever said I was a salesman with Oliver?

WILLY: Well, you were.

BIFF: No, Dad, I was a shipping clerk.

WILLY: But you were practically— 1035

BIFF: *(with determination)* Dad, I don't know who said it first, but I was never a salesman for Bill Oliver.

WILLY: What're you talking about?

BIFF: Let's hold on to the facts tonight, Pop. We're not going to get anywhere bullin' around. I was a ship- 1040 ping clerk.

WILLY: *(angrily)* All right, now listen to me—

BIFF: Why don't you let me finish?

WILLY: I'm not interested in stories about the past or any crap of that kind because the woods are burning, 1045 boys, you understand? There's a big blaze going on all around. I was fired today.

BIFF: *(shocked)* How could you be?

WILLY: I was fired, and I'm looking for a little good news to tell your mother, because the woman has 1050 waited and the woman has suffered. The gist of it is that I haven't got a story left in my head, Biff. So don't give me a lecture about facts and aspects. I am not interested. Now what've you got to say to me?

STANLEY *enters with three drinks. They wait until he leaves.*

WILLY: Did you see Oliver? 1055

BIFF: Jesus, Dad!

WILLY: You mean you didn't go up there?

HAPPY: Sure he went up there.

BIFF: I did. I—saw him. How could they fire you?

1060 **WILLY:** *(on the edge of his chair)* What kind of a welcome did he give you?

BIFF: He won't even let you work on commission?

WILLY: I'm out! *(Driving.)* So tell me, he gave you a warm welcome?

1065 **HAPPY:** Sure, Pop, sure!

BIFF: *(driven)* Well, it was kind of—

WILLY: I was wondering if he'd remember you. *(To* HAPPY.*)* Imagine, man doesn't see him for ten, twelve years and gives him that kind of a welcome!

1070 **HAPPY:** Damn right!

BIFF: *(trying to return to the offensive)* Pop, look—

WILLY: You know why he remembered you, don't you? Because you impressed him in those days.

BIFF: Let's talk quietly and get this down to the facts, 1075 huh?

WILLY: *(as though* BIFF *had been interrupting)* Well, what happened? It's great news, Biff. Did he take you into his office or'd you talk in the waiting-room?

BIFF: Well, he came in, see, and—

1080 **WILLY:** *(with a big smile)* What'd he say? Betcha he threw his arm around you.

BIFF: Well, he kinda—

WILLY: He's a fine man. *(To* HAPPY.*)* Very hard man to see, y'know.

1085 **HAPPY:** *(agreeing)* Oh, I know.

WILLY: *(to* BIFF*)* Is that where you had the drinks?

BIFF: Yeah, he gave me a couple of—no, no!

HAPPY: *(cutting in)* He told him my Florida idea.

WILLY: Don't interrupt. *(To* BIFF.*)* How'd he react to the 1090 Florida idea?

BIFF: Dad, will you give me a minute to explain?

WILLY: I've been waiting for you to explain since I sat down here! What happened? He took you into his office and what?

BIFF: Well—I talked. And—and he listened, see. 1095

WILLY: Famous for the way he listens, y'know. What was his answer?

BIFF: His answer was—*(He breaks off, suddenly angry.)* Dad, you're not letting me tell you what I want to tell you! 1100

WILLY: *(accusing, angered)* You didn't see him, did you?

BIFF: I did see him!

WILLY: What'd you insult him or something? You insulted him, didn't you? 1105

BIFF: Listen, will you let me out of it, will you just let me out of it!

HAPPY: What the hell!

WILLY: Tell me what happened!

BIFF: *(to* HAPPY*)* I can't talk to him! 1110

A single trumpet note jars the ear. The light of green leaves stains the house, which holds the air of night and a dream. Young BERNARD *enters and knocks on the door of the house.*

YOUNG BERNARD: *(frantically)* Mrs. Loman, Mrs. Loman!

HAPPY: Tell him what happened!

BIFF: *(to* HAPPY*)* Shut up and leave me alone!

WILLY: No, no! You had to go and flunk math! 1115

BIFF: What math? What're you talking about?

YOUNG BERNARD: Mrs. Loman, Mrs. Loman!

LINDA *appears in the house, as of old.*

WILLY: *(wildly)* Math, math, math!

BIFF: Take it easy, Pop!

YOUNG BERNARD: Mrs. Loman! 1120

WILLY: *(furiously)* If you hadn't flunked you'd've been set by now!

BIFF: Now, look, I'm gonna tell you what happened, and you're going to listen to me.

YOUNG BERNARD: Mrs. Loman! 1125

BIFF: I waited six hours—

HAPPY: What the hell are you saying?

BIFF: I kept sending in my name but he wouldn't see me. So finally he . . . *(He continues unheard as light fades low on the restaurant.)* 1130

Willy remembers receiving the news of Biff's flunking math.

YOUNG BERNARD: Biff flunked math!

LINDA: No!

YOUNG BERNARD: Birnbaum flunked him! They won't graduate him!

1135 **LINDA:**   But they have to. He's gotta go to the university. Where is he? Biff! Biff!

YOUNG BERNARD: No, he left. He went to Grand Central.

LINDA: Grand—You mean he went to Boston!

1140 **YOUNG BERNARD:**   Is Uncle Willy in Boston?

LINDA: Oh, maybe Willy can talk to the teacher. Oh, the poor, poor boy!

Light on house area snaps out.

BIFF: *(at the table, now audible, holding up a gold fountain pen)*   . . . so I'm washed up with Oliver, you under-
1145   stand? Are you listening to me?

WILLY: *(at a loss)*   Yeah, sure. If you hadn't flunked—

BIFF: Flunked what? What're you talking about?

WILLY: Don't blame everything on me! I didn't flunk math—you did! What pen?

1150 **HAPPY:**   That was awful dumb, Biff, a pen like that is worth—

WILLY: *(seeing the pen for the first time)*   You took Oliver's pen?

BIFF: *(weakening)*   Dad, I just explained it to you.

1155 **WILLY:**   You stole Bill Oliver's fountain pen!

BIFF: I didn't exactly steal it! That's just what I've been explaining to you!

HAPPY: He had it in his hand and just then Oliver walked in, so he got nervous and stuck it in his pocket!   1160

WILLY: My God, Biff!

BIFF: I never intended to do it, Dad!

OPERATOR'S VOICE: Standish Arms, good evening!

WILLY: *(shouting)*   I'm not in my room!

BIFF: *(frightened)*   Dad, what's the matter? *(He and* HAPPY   1165
stand up.)

OPERATOR: Ringing Mr. Loman for you!

WILLY: I'm not there, stop it!

BIFF: *(horrified, gets down on one knee before* WILLY*)*   Dad, I'll make good, I'll make good. *(*WILLY *tries to get to his*   1170
feet. BIFF *holds him down.)* Sit down now.

WILLY: No, you're no good, you're no good for anything.

BIFF: I am, Dad, I'll find something else, you under-stand? Now don't worry about anything. *(He holds up* WILLY's *face.)* Talk to me, Dad.   1175

OPERATOR: Mr. Loman does not answer. Shall I page him?

WILLY: *(attempting to stand, as though to rush and silence the* OPERATOR*)*   No, no, no!

HAPPY: He'll strike something, Pop.   1180

WILLY: No, no . . .

BIFF: *(desperately, standing over* WILLY*)*   Pop, listen! Listen to me! I'm telling you something good. Oliver talked to his partner about the Florida idea. You listening? He—he talked to his partner, and he came to me . . .   1185
I'm going to be all right, you hear? Dad, listen to me, he said it was just a question of the amount!

WILLY: Then you . . . got it?

HAPPY: He's gonna be terrific, Pop!

WILLY: *(trying to stand)*   Then you got it, haven't you?   1190
You got it! You got it!

BIFF: *(agonized, holds* WILLY *down)*   No, no. Look, Pop. I'm supposed to have lunch with them tomorrow. I'm just telling you this so you'll know that I can still make an impression, Pop. And I'll make good some-   1195
where, but I can't go tomorrow, see?

WILLY: Why not? You simply—

BIFF: But the pen, Pop!

WILLY: You give it to him and tell him it was an
1200　oversight!

HAPPY: Sure, have lunch tomorrow!

BIFF: I can't say that—

WILLY: You were doing a crossword puzzle and accidentally used his pen!

1205　**BIFF:** Listen, kid, I took those balls years ago, now I
walk in with his fountain pen? That clinches it, don't
you see? I can't face him like that! I'll try elsewhere.

PAGE'S VOICE: Paging Mr. Loman!

WILLY: Don't you want to be anything?

1210　**BIFF:** Pop, how can I go back?

WILLY: You don't want to be anything, is that what's
behind it?

BIFF: (now angry at WILLY for not crediting his sympathy)
Don't take it that way! You think it was easy walking
1215　into that office after what I'd done to him? A team of
horses couldn't have dragged me back to Bill Oliver!

WILLY: Then why'd you go?

BIFF: Why did I go? Why did I go! Look at you! Look at
what's become of you!

Off left, THE WOMAN *laughs.*

1220　**WILLY:** Biff, you're going to go to that lunch tomorrow, or—

BIFF: I can't go. I've got no appointment!

HAPPY: Biff, for . . . !

WILLY: Are you spiting me?

1225　**BIFF:** Don't take it that way! Goddammit!

WILLY: (strikes BIFF and falters away from the table) You
rotten little louse! Are you spiting me?

THE WOMAN: Someone's at the door, Willy!

BIFF: I'm no good, can't you see what I am?

1230　**HAPPY:** (separating them) Hey, you're in a restaurant!
Now cut it out, both of you! (The girls enter.) Hello,
girls, sit down.

THE WOMAN *laughs, off left.*

MISS FORSYTHE: I guess we might as well. This is
Letta.

1235　**THE WOMAN:** Willy, are you going to wake up?

BIFF: (ignoring WILLY) How're ya, miss, sit down. What
do you drink?

MISS FORSYTHE: Letta might not be able to stay long.

LETTA: I gotta get up very early tomorrow. I got jury
duty. I'm so excited! Were you fellows ever on a jury?　1240

BIFF: No, but I been in front of them! (The girls laugh.)
This is my father.

LETTA: Isn't he cute? Sit down with us, Pop.

HAPPY: Sit him down, Biff!

BIFF: (going to him) Come on, slugger, drink us under　1245
the table. To hell with it! Come on, sit down, pal.

On BIFF's *last insistence,* WILLY *is about to sit.*

THE WOMAN: (now urgently) Willy, are you going to
answer the door!

THE WOMAN's *call pulls* WILLY *back. He starts right,
befuddled.*

BIFF: Hey, where are you going?

WILLY: Open the door.　1250

BIFF: The door?

WILLY: The washroom . . . the door . . . where's the door?

BIFF: (leading WILLY to the left) Just go straight down.

WILLY *moves left.*

THE WOMAN: Willy, Willy, are you going to get up, get
up, get up, get up?　1255

WILLY *exits left.*

LETTA: I think it's sweet you bring your daddy along.

MISS FORSYTHE: Oh, he isn't really your father!

BIFF: (at left, turning to her resentfully) Miss Forsythe,
you've just seen a prince walk by. A fine, troubled
prince. A hard-working, unappreciated prince. A　1260
pal, you understand? A good companion. Always
for his boys.

LETTA: That's so sweet.

HAPPY: Well, girls, what's the program? We're wasting
time. Come on, Biff. Gather round. Where would you　1265
like to go?

BIFF: Why don't you do something for him?

HAPPY: Me!

BIFF: Don't you give a damn for him, Hap?

1270 **HAPPY:** What're you talking about? I'm the one who—

BIFF: I sense it, you don't give a good goddam about him. (*He takes the rolled-up hose from his pocket and puts it on the table in front of* HAPPY.) Look what I found in the cellar, for Christ's sake. How can you bear to let

1275 it go on?

HAPPY: Me? Who goes away? Who runs off and—

BIFF: Yeah, but he doesn't mean anything to you. You could help him—I can't! Don't you understand what I'm talking about? He's going to kill himself, don't

1280 you know that?

HAPPY: Don't I know it! Me!

BIFF: Hap, help him! Jesus . . . help him . . . Help me, help me, I can't bear to look at his face! (*Ready to weep, he hurries out, up right.*)

1285 **HAPPY:** (*starting after him*) Where are you going?

MISS FORSYTHE: What's he so mad about?

HAPPY: Come on, girls, we'll catch up with him.

MISS FORSYTHE: (*as* HAPPY *pushes her out*) Say, I don't like that temper of his!

1290 **HAPPY:** He's just a little overstrung, he'll be all right!

WILLY: (*off left, as* THE WOMAN *laughs*) Don't answer! Don't answer!

LETTA: Don't you want to tell your father—

HAPPY: No, that's not my father. He's just a guy. Come

1295 on, we'll catch Biff, and, honey, we're going to paint this town! Stanley, where's the check! Hey, Stanley!

They exit. STANLEY *looks toward left.*

STANLEY: (*calling to* HAPPY *indignantly*) Mr. Loman! Mr. Loman!

STANLEY picks up a chair and follows them off. Knocking is heard off left. THE WOMAN *enters, laughing.* WILLY *follows her. She is in a black slip; he is buttoning his shirt. Raw, sensuous music accompanies their speech.*

WILLY: Will you stop laughing? Will you stop?

1300 **THE WOMAN:** Aren't you going to answer the door? He'll wake the whole hotel.

WILLY: I'm not expecting anybody.

THE WOMAN: Whyn't you have another drink, honey, and stop being so damn self-centered?

1305 **WILLY:** I'm so lonely.

THE WOMAN: You know you ruined me, Willy? From now on, whenever you come to the office, I'll see that you go right through to the buyers. No waiting at my desk any more, Willy. You ruined me.

WILLY: That's nice of you to say that. 1310

THE WOMAN: Gee, you are self-centered! Why so sad? You are the saddest, self-centeredest soul I ever did see-saw. (*She laughs. He kisses her.*) Come on inside, drummer boy. It's silly to be dressing in the middle of the night. (*As knocking is heard.*) Aren't you going to 1315 answer the door?

WILLY: They're knocking on the wrong door.

THE WOMAN: But I felt the knocking. And he heard us talking in here. Maybe the hotel's on fire!

WILLY: (*his terror rising*) It's a mistake. 1320

THE WOMAN: Then tell him to go away!

WILLY: There's nobody there.

THE WOMAN: It's getting on my nerves, Willy. There's somebody standing out there and it's getting on my nerves! 1325

WILLY: (*pushing her away from him*) All right, stay in the bathroom here, and don't come out. I think there's a law in Massachusetts about it, so don't come out. It may be that new room clerk. He looked very mean. So don't come out. It's a mistake, there's no fire. 1330

The knocking is heard again. He takes a few steps away from her, and she vanishes into the wing. The light follows him, and now he is facing Young BIFF, *who carries a suitcase.* BIFF *steps toward him. The music is gone.*

BIFF: Why didn't you answer?

WILLY: Biff! What are you doing in Boston?

BIFF: Why didn't you answer? I've been knocking for five minutes, I called you on the phone—

WILLY: I just heard you. I was in the bathroom and 1335 had the door shut. Did anything happen home?

BIFF: Dad—I let you down.

WILLY: What do you mean?

BIFF: Dad . . .

WILLY: Biffo, what's this about? (*Putting his arm around* 1340 BIFF.) Come on, let's go downstairs and get you a malted.

BIFF: Dad, I flunked math.

WILLY: Not for the term?

1345 **BIFF:** The term. I haven't got enough credits to graduate.

WILLY: You mean to say Bernard wouldn't give you the answers?

BIFF: He did, he tried, but I only got a sixty-one.

WILLY: And they wouldn't give you four points?

1350 **BIFF:** Birnbaum refused absolutely. I begged him, Pop, but he won't give me those points. You gotta talk to him before they close the school. Because if he saw the kind of man you are, and you just talked to him in your way, I'm sure he'd come through for me. The
1355 class came right before practice, see, and I didn't go enough. Would you talk to him? He'd like you, Pop. You know the way you could talk.

WILLY: You're on. We'll drive right back.

BIFF: Oh, Dad, good work! I'm sure he'll change it
1360 for you!

WILLY: Go downstairs and tell the clerk I'm checkin' out. Go right down.

BIFF: Yes, sir! See, the reason he hates me, Pop—one day he was late for class so I got up at the blackboard
1365 and imitated him. I crossed my eyes and talked with a lithp.

WILLY: (*laughing*) You did? The kids like it?

BIFF: They nearly died laughing!

WILLY: Yeah? What'd you do?

1370 **BIFF:** The thquare root of thixthy twee is . . . (WILLY *bursts out laughing;* BIFF *joins him.*) And in the middle of it he walked in!

WILLY *laughs and* THE WOMAN *joins in offstage.*

WILLY: (*without hesitation*) Hurry downstairs and—

BIFF: Somebody in there?

1375 **WILLY:** No, that was next door.

THE WOMAN *laughs offstage.*

BIFF: Somebody got in your bathroom!

WILLY: No, it's the next room, there's a party—

THE WOMAN: (*enters, laughing. She lisps this*) Can I come in? There's something in the bathtub, Willy, and it's
1380 moving!

WILLY *looks at* BIFF, *who is staring open-mouthed and horrified at* THE WOMAN.

WILLY: Ah—you better go back to your room. They must be finished painting by now. They're painting her room so I let her take a shower here. Go back, go back . . . (*He pushes her.*)

THE WOMAN: (*resisting*) But I've got to get dressed, 1385 Willy, I can't—

WILLY: Get out of here! Go back, go back . . . (*Suddenly striving for the ordinary*): This is Miss Francis, Biff, she's a buyer. They're painting her room. Go back, Miss Francis, go back . . . 1390

THE WOMAN: But my clothes, I can't go out naked in the hall!

WILLY: (*pushing her offstage*) Get outa here! Go back, go back!

BIFF *slowly sits down on his suitcase as the argument continues offstage.*

THE WOMAN: Where's my stockings? You promised 1395 me stockings, Willy!

WILLY: I have no stockings here!

THE WOMAN: You had two boxes of size nine sheers for me, and I want them!

WILLY: Here, for God's sake, will you get outa here! 1400

THE WOMAN: (*enters holding a box of stockings*) I just hope there's nobody in the hall. That's all I hope. (*To* BIFF.) Are you football or baseball?

BIFF: Football.

THE WOMAN: (*angry, humiliated*) That's me too. G'night. 1405 (*She snatches her clothes from* WILLY, *and walks out.*)

Humiliated, The Woman encounters Biff inside the hotel room.

WILLY: *(after a pause)* Well, better get going. I want to get to the school first thing in the morning. Get my suits out of the closet. I'll get my valise. (BIFF *doesn't move.*) What's the matter? (BIFF *remains motionless, tears falling.*) She's a buyer. Buys for J. H. Simmons. She lives down the hall—they're painting. You don't imagine—(*He breaks off. After a pause.*) Now listen, pal, she's just a buyer. She sees merchandise in her room and they have to keep it looking just so . . . *(Pause. Assuming command.)* All right, get my suits. (BIFF *doesn't move.*) Now stop crying and do as I say. I gave you an order. Biff, I gave you an order! Is that what you do when I give you an order? How dare you cry! *(Putting his arm around* BIFF.) Now look, Biff, when you grow up you'll understand about these things. You mustn't—you mustn't overemphasize a thing like this. I'll see Birnbaum first thing in the morning.

BIFF: Never mind.

WILLY: *(getting down beside* BIFF) Never mind! He's going to give you those points. I'll see to it.

BIFF: He wouldn't listen to you.

WILLY: He certainly will listen to me. You need those points for the U. of Virginia.

BIFF: I'm not going there.

WILLY: Heh? If I can't get him to change that mark you'll make it up in summer school. You've got all summer to—

BIFF: *(his weeping breaking from him)* Dad . . .

WILLY: *(infected by it)* Oh, my boy . . .

BIFF: Dad . . .

WILLY: She's nothing to me, Biff. I was lonely, I was terribly lonely.

BIFF: You—you gave her Mama's stockings! *(His tears break through and he rises to go.)*

WILLY: *(grabbing for* BIFF) I gave you an order!

BIFF: Don't touch me, you—liar!

WILLY: Apologize for that!

BIFF: You fake! You phony little fake! You fake! *(Overcome, he turns quickly and weeping fully goes out with his suitcase.* WILLY *is left on the floor on his knees.)*

WILLY: I gave you an order! Biff, come back here or I'll beat you! Come back here! I'll whip you!

STANLEY *comes quickly in from the right and stands in front of* WILLY.

WILLY: *(shouts at* STANLEY) I gave you an order . . .

STANLEY: Hey, let's pick it up, pick it up, Mr. Loman. *(He helps* WILLY *to his feet.)* Your boys left with the chippies. They said they'll see you at home.

A second waiter watches some distance away.

WILLY: But we were supposed to have dinner together.

Music is heard, WILLY's theme.

STANLEY: Can you make it?

WILLY: I'll—sure, I can make it. *(Suddenly concerned about his clothes.)* Do I—I look all right?

STANLEY: Sure, you look all right. *(He flicks a speck off* WILLY's lapel.)

WILLY: Here—here's a dollar.

STANLEY: Oh, your son paid me. It's all right.

WILLY: *(putting it in* STANLEY's hand) No, take it. You're a good boy.

STANLEY: Oh, no, you don't have to . . .

WILLY: Here—here's some more, I don't need it any more. *(After a slight pause.)* Tell me—is there a seed store in the neighborhood?

STANLEY: Seeds? You mean like to plant?

As WILLY turns, STANLEY slips the money back into his jacket pocket.

WILLY: Yes. Carrots, peas . . .

STANLEY: Well, there's hardware stores on Sixth Avenue, but it may be too late now.

WILLY: *(anxiously)* Oh, I'd better hurry. I've got to get some seeds. *(He starts off to the right.)* I've got to get some seeds, right away. Nothing's planted. I don't have a thing in the ground.

WILLY *hurries out as the light goes down.* STANLEY *moves over to the right after him, watches him off. The other waiter has been staring at* WILLY.

STANLEY: *(to the waiter)* Well, whatta you looking at?

The waiter picks up the chairs and moves off right. STANLEY *takes the table and follows him. The light fades on this area. There is a long pause, the sound of the flute coming over. The light gradually rises on the kitchen, which is empty.* HAPPY *appears at the door of the house, followed by* BIFF. HAPPY *is carrying a large bunch of long-stemmed roses. He enters the kitchen, looks around for* LINDA. *Not seeing her, he turns to* BIFF, *who is just outside the house*

Linda scolds her sons for leaving Willy alone at dinner.

door, and makes a gesture with his hands, indicating "Not here, I guess." He looks into the living-room and freezes. Inside, LINDA, *unseen, is seated,* WILLY's *coat on her lap. She rises ominously and quietly and moves toward* HAPPY, *who backs up into the kitchen, afraid.*

HAPPY: Hey, what're you doing up? (LINDA *says nothing but moves toward him implacably.*) Where's Pop? (*He keeps backing to the right, and now* LINDA *is in full view in the doorway to the living-room.*) Is he sleeping?

1480 **LINDA:** Where were you?

HAPPY: (*trying to laugh it off*) We met two girls, Mom, very fine types. Here, we brought you some flowers. (*Offering them to her.*) Put them in your room, Ma.

She knocks them to the floor at BIFF's *feet. He has now come inside and closed the door behind him. She stares at* BIFF, *silent.*

HAPPY: Now what'd you do that for? Mom, I want you
1485 to have some flowers—

LINDA: (*cutting* HAPPY *off, violently to* BIFF) Don't you care whether he lives or dies?

HAPPY: (*going to the stairs*) Come upstairs, Biff.

BIFF: (*with a flare of disgust, to* HAPPY) Go away from me!
1490 (*To* LINDA.) What do you mean, lives or dies? No-body's dying around here, pal.

LINDA: Get out of my sight! Get out of here!

BIFF: I wanna see the boss.

LINDA: You're not going near him!

1495 **BIFF:** Where is he? (*He moves into the living-room and* LINDA *follows.*)

LINDA: (*shouting after* BIFF) You invite him for dinner. He looks forward to it all day—(BIFF *appears in his parents'*

bedroom, looks around, and exits.)—and then you desert him there. There's no stranger you'd do that to!   1500

HAPPY: Why? He had a swell time with us. Listen, when I—(LINDA *comes back into the kitchen*)—desert him I hope I don't outlive the day!

LINDA: Get out of here!

HAPPY: Now look, Mom . . .   1505

LINDA: Did you have to go to women tonight? You and your lousy rotten whores!

BIFF *re-enters the kitchen.*

HAPPY: Mom, all we did was follow Biff around try-ing to cheer him up! (*To* BIFF.) Boy, what a night you gave me!   1510

LINDA: Get out of here, both of you, and don't come back! I don't want you tormenting him any more. Go on now, get your things together! (*To* BIFF.) You can sleep in his apartment. (*She starts to pick up the flowers and stops herself.*) Pick up this stuff, I'm not your maid   1515
any more. Pick it up, you bum, you!

HAPPY *turns his back to her in refusal.* BIFF *slowly moves over and gets down on his knees, picking up the flowers.*

LINDA: You're a pair of animals! Not one, not another living soul would have had the cruelty to walk out on that man in a restaurant!

BIFF: (*not looking at her*) Is that what he said?   1520

LINDA: He didn't have to say anything. He was so hu-miliated he nearly limped when he came in.

HAPPY: But, Mom, he had a great time with us—

BIFF: (*cutting him off violently*) Shut up!

Without another word, HAPPY *goes upstairs.*

LINDA: You! You didn't even go in to see if he was all   1525
right!

BIFF: (*still on the floor in front of* LINDA, *the flowers in his hand; with self-loathing*) No. Didn't. Didn't do a damned thing. How do you like that, heh? Left him babbling in a toilet.   1530

LINDA: You louse. You . . .

BIFF: Now you hit it on the nose! (*He gets up, throws the flowers in the wastebasket.*) The scum of the earth, and you're looking at him!

LINDA: Get out of here!   1535

BIFF: I gotta talk to the boss, Mom. Where is he?

LINDA: You're not going near him. Get out of this house!

BIFF: *(with absolute assurance, determination)* No. We're gonna have an abrupt conversation, him and me.

1540 LINDA: You're not talking to him!

Hammering is heard from outside the house, off right. BIFF *turns toward the noise.*

LINDA: *(suddenly pleading)* Will you please leave him alone?

BIFF: What's he doing out there?

LINDA: He's planting the garden!

1545 BIFF: *(quietly)* Now? Oh, my God!

BIFF moves outside, LINDA *following. The light dies down on them and comes up on the center of the apron as* WILLY *walks into it. He is carrying a flashlight, a hoe, and handful of seed packets. He raps the top of the hoe sharply to fix it firmly, and then moves to the left, measuring off the distance with his foot. He holds the flashlight to look at the seed packets, reading off the instructions. He is in the blue of night.*

WILLY: Carrots . . . quarter-inch apart. Rows . . . one-foot rows. *(He measures it off.)* One foot. *(He puts down a package and measures off.)* Beets. *(He puts down another package and measures again.)* Lettuce. *(He reads the package, puts it down.)* One foot— *(He breaks off as* BEN *appears at the right and moves slowly down to him.)* What a proposition, ts, ts. Terrific, terrific. 'Cause she's suffered, Ben, the woman has suffered. You understand me? A man can't go out the way he came in, Ben, a man has got to add up to something. You can't, you can't— *(*BEN *moves toward him as though to interrupt.)* You gotta consider, now. Don't answer so quick. Remember, it's a guaranteed twenty-thousand-dollar proposition. Now look, Ben, I want you to go through the ins and outs of this thing with me. I've got nobody to talk to, Ben, and the woman has suffered, you hear me?

BEN: *(standing still, considering)* What's the proposition?

WILLY: It's twenty thousand dollars on the barrelhead. Guaranteed, gilt-edged, you understand?

1565 BEN: You don't want to make a fool of yourself. They might not honor the policy.

WILLY: How can they dare refuse? Didn't I work like a coolie to meet every premium on the nose? And now they don't pay off? Impossible!

1570 BEN: It's called a cowardly thing, William.

WILLY: Why? Does it take more guts to stand here the rest of my life ringing up a zero?

BEN: *(yielding)* That's a point, William. *(He moves, thinking, turns.)* And twenty thousand—that *is* something one can feel with the hand, it is there. 1575

WILLY: *(now assured, with rising power)* Oh, Ben, that's the whole beauty of it! I see it like a diamond, shining in the dark, hard and rough, that I can pick up and touch in my hand. Not like—like an appointment! This would not be another damned-fool appointment, Ben, and it changes all the aspects. Because he thinks I'm nothing, see, and so he spites me. But the funeral—*(Straightening up.)* Ben, that funeral will be massive! They'll come from Maine, Massachusetts, Vermont, New Hampshire! All the old-timers with the strange license plates—that boy will be thunder-struck, Ben, because he never realized—I am known! Rhode Island, New York, New Jersey—I am known, Ben, and he'll see it with his eyes once and for all. He'll see what I am, Ben! He's in for a shock, that boy! 1580 1585 1590

BEN: *(coming down to the edge of the garden)* He'll call you a coward.

WILLY: *(suddenly fearful)* No, that would be terrible.

BEN: Yes. And a damned fool. 1595

WILLY: No, no, he mustn't, I won't have that! *(He is broken and desperate.)*

BEN: He'll hate you, William.

The gay music of the Boys is heard.

WILLY: Oh, Ben, how do we get back to all the great times? Used to be so full of light, and comradeship, 1600

Willy discusses his business proposition with Ben.

the sleigh-riding in winter, and the ruddiness on his cheeks. And always some kind of good news coming up, always something nice coming up ahead. And never even let me carry the valises in the house, and simonizing, simonizing that little red car! Why, why can't I give him something and not have him hate me?

BEN: Let me think about it. (*He glances at his watch.*) I still have a little time. Remarkable proposition, but you've got to be sure you're not making a fool of yourself.

BEN drifts off upstage and goes out of sight. BIFF comes down from the left.

WILLY: (*suddenly conscious of BIFF, turns and looks up at him, then begins picking up the packages of seeds in confusion*) Where the hell is that seed? (*Indignantly.*) You can't see nothing out here! They boxed in the whole god-damn neighborhood!

BIFF: There are people all around here. Don't you realize that?

WILLY: I'm busy. Don't bother me.

BIFF: (*taking the hoe from WILLY*) I'm saying good-by to you, Pop. (*WILLY looks at him, silent, unable to move.*) I'm not coming back any more.

WILLY: You're not going to see Oliver tomorrow?

BIFF: I've got no appointment, Dad.

WILLY: He put his arm around you, and you've got no appointment?

BIFF: Pop, get this now, will you? Everytime I've left it's been a fight that sent me out of here. Today I realized something about myself and I tried to explain it to you and I—I think I'm just not smart enough to make any sense out of it for you. To hell with whose fault it is or anything like that. (*He takes WILLY's arm.*) Let's just wrap it up, heh? Come on in, we'll tell Mom. (*He gently tries to pull WILLY to left.*)

WILLY: (*frozen, immobile, with guilt in his voice*) No, I don't want to see her.

BIFF: Come on! (*He pulls again, and WILLY tries to pull away.*)

WILLY: (*highly nervous*) No, no, I don't want to see her.

BIFF: (*tries to look into WILLY's face, as if to find the answer there*) Why don't you want to see her?

WILLY: (*more harshly now*) Don't bother me, will you?

BIFF: What do you mean, you don't want to see her? You don't want them calling you yellow, do you? This

isn't your fault; it's me, I'm a bum. Now come inside! (*WILLY strains to get away.*) Did you hear what I said to you?

WILLY pulls away and quickly goes by himself into the house. BIFF follows.

LINDA: (*to WILLY*) Did you plant, dear?

BIFF: (*at the door, to LINDA*) All right, we had it out. I'm going and I'm not writing any more.

LINDA: (*going to WILLY in the kitchen*) I think that's the best way, dear. 'Cause there's no use drawing it out, you'll just never get along.

WILLY doesn't respond.

BIFF: People ask where I am and what I'm doing, you don't know, and you don't care. That way it'll be off your mind and you can start brightening up again. All right? That clears it, doesn't it? (*WILLY is silent, and BIFF goes to him.*) You gonna wish me luck, scout? (*He extends his hand.*) What do you say?

LINDA: Shake his hand, Willy.

WILLY: (*turning to her, seething with hurt*) There's no necessity to mention the pen at all, y'know.

BIFF: (*gently*) I've got no appointment, Dad.

WILLY: (*erupting fiercely*) He put his arm around . . . ?

BIFF: Dad, you're never going to see what I am, so what's the use of arguing? If I strike oil I'll send you a check. Meantime forget I'm alive.

WILLY: (*to LINDA*) Spite, see?

BIFF: Shake hands, Dad.

WILLY: Not my hand.

BIFF: I was hoping not to go this way.

WILLY: Well, this is the way you're going. Good-by.

BIFF looks at him a moment, then turns sharply and goes to the stairs.

WILLY: (*stops him with*) May you rot in hell if you leave this house!

BIFF: (*turning*) Exactly what is it that you want from me?

WILLY: I want you to know, on the train, in the mountains, in the valleys, wherever you go, that you cut down your life for spite!

BIFF: No, no.

WILLY: Spite, spite, is the word of your undoing! And when you're down and out, remember what did it. When you're rotting somewhere beside the railroad tracks, remember, and don't you dare blame it on me!

1680

BIFF: I'm not blaming it on you!

WILLY: I won't take the rap for this, you hear?

HAPPY comes down the stairs and stands on the bottom step, watching.

1685 BIFF: That's just what I'm telling you!

WILLY: *(sinking into a chair at the table, with full accusation)* You're trying to put a knife in me—don't think I don't know what you're doing!

BIFF: All right, phony! Then let's lay it on the line. *(He whips the rubber tube out of his pocket and puts it on the table.)*

1690

HAPPY: You crazy—

LINDA: Biff! *(She moves to grab the hose, but BIFF holds it down with his hand.)*

1695 BIFF: Leave it there! Don't move it!

WILLY: *(not looking at it)* What is that?

BIFF: You know goddam well what that is.

WILLY: *(caged, wanting to escape)* I never saw that.

BIFF: You saw it. The mice didn't bring it into the cellar! What is this supposed to do, make a hero out of you? This supposed to make me sorry for you?

1700

WILLY: Never heard of it.

BIFF: There'll be no pity for you, you hear it? No pity!

WILLY: *(to LINDA)* You hear the spite!

1705 BIFF: No, you're going to hear the truth—what you are and what I am!

LINDA: Stop it!

WILLY: Spite!

HAPPY: *(coming down toward BIFF)* You cut it now!

1710 BIFF: *(to HAPPY)* The man don't know who we are! The man is gonna know! *(To WILLY.)* We never told the truth for ten minutes in this house!

HAPPY: We always told the truth!

BIFF: *(turning on him)* You big blow, are you the assistant buyer? You're one of the two assistants to the assistant, aren't you?

1715

HAPPY: Well, I'm practically—

BIFF: You're practically full of it! We all are! And I'm through with it. *(To WILLY.)* Now hear this, Willy, this is me.

1720

WILLY: I know you!

BIFF: You know why I had no address for three months? I stole a suit in Kansas City and I was in jail. *(To LINDA, who is sobbing.)* Stop crying. I'm through with it.

LINDA turns away from them, her hands covering her face.

WILLY: I suppose that's my fault!

1725

BIFF: I stole myself out of every good job since high school!

WILLY: And whose fault is that?

BIFF: And I never got anywhere because you blew me so full of hot air I could never stand taking orders from anybody! That's whose fault it is!

1730

WILLY: I hear that!

LINDA: Don't, Biff!

BIFF: It's goddam time you heard that! I had to be boss big shot in two weeks, and I'm through with it!

1735

WILLY: Then hang yourself! For spite, hang yourself!

BIFF: No! Nobody's hanging himself, Willy! I ran down eleven flights with a pen in my hand today. And suddenly I stopped, you hear me? And in the middle of that office building, do you hear this? I stopped in the middle of that building and I saw—the sky. I saw the things that I love in this world. The work and the food and time to sit and smoke. And I looked at the pen and said to myself, what the hell am I grabbing this for? Why am I trying to become what I don't want to be? What am I doing in an office, making a contemptuous, begging fool of myself, when all I want is out there, waiting for me the minute I say I know who I am! Why can't I say that, Willy? *(He tries to make WILLY face him, but WILLY pulls away and moves to the left.)*

1740

1745

1750

WILLY: *(with hatred, threateningly)* The door of your life is wide open!

BIFF: Pop! I'm a dime a dozen, and so are you!

WILLY: *(turning on him now in an uncontrolled outburst)* I am not a dime a dozen! I am Willy Loman, and you are Biff Loman!

1755

BIFF starts for WILLY, but is blocked by HAPPY. In his fury, BIFF seems on the verge of attacking his father.

BIFF: I am not a leader of men, Willy, and neither are you. You were never anything but a hard-working drummer who landed in the ash can like all the rest of them! I'm one dollar an hour, Willy! I tried seven states and couldn't raise it. A buck an hour! Do you gather my meaning? I'm not bringing home any prizes any more, and you're going to stop waiting for me to bring them home!

WILLY: *(directly to BIFF)* You vengeful, spiteful mutt!

BIFF breaks from HAPPY. WILLY, in fright, starts up the stairs. BIFF grabs him.

BIFF: *(at the peak of his fury)* Pop, I'm nothing! I'm nothing, Pop. Can't you understand that? There's no spite in it any more. I'm just what I am, that's all.

BIFF's fury has spent itself, and he breaks down, sobbing, holding on to WILLY, who dumbly fumbles for BIFF's face.

WILLY: *(astonished)* What're you doing? What're you doing? *(To LINDA.)* Why is he crying?

BIFF: *(crying, broken)* Will you let me go, for Christ's sake? Will you take that phony dream and burn it before something happens? *(Struggling to contain himself, he pulls away and moves to the stairs.)* I'll go in the morning. Put him—put him to bed. *(Exhausted, BIFF moves up the stairs to his room.)*

WILLY: *(after a long pause, astonished, elevated)* Isn't that—isn't that remarkable? Biff—he likes me!

LINDA: He loves you, Willy!

HAPPY: *(deeply moved)* Always did, Pop.

Biff curses Willy for lying.

WILLY: Oh, Biff! *(Staring wildly.)* He cried! Cried to me. *(He is choking with his love, and now cries out his promise.)* That boy—that boy is going to be magnificent!

BEN appears in the light just outside the kitchen.

BEN: Yes, outstanding, with twenty thousand behind him.

LINDA: *(sensing the racing of his mind, fearfully, carefully)* Now come to bed, Willy. It's all settled now.

WILLY: *(finding it difficult not to rush out of the house)* Yes, we'll sleep. Come on. Go to sleep, Hap.

BEN: And it does take a great kind of a man to crack the jungle.

In accents of dread, BEN's idyllic music starts up.

HAPPY: *(his arm around LINDA)* I'm getting married, Pop, don't forget it. I'm changing everything. I'm gonna run that department before the year is up. You'll see, Mom. *(He kisses her.)*

BEN: The jungle is dark but full of diamonds, Willy.

WILLY turns, moves, listening to BEN.

LINDA: Be good. You're both good boys, just act that way, that's all.

HAPPY: 'Night, Pop. *(He goes upstairs.)*

LINDA: *(to WILLY)* Come, dear.

BEN: *(with greater force)* One must go in to fetch a diamond out.

WILLY: *(to LINDA, as he moves slowly along the edge of the kitchen, toward the door)* I just want to get settled down, Linda. Let me sit alone for a little.

LINDA: *(almost uttering her fear)* I want you upstairs.

WILLY: *(taking her in his arms)* In a few minutes, Linda. I couldn't sleep right now. Go on, you look awful tired. *(He kisses her.)*

BEN: Not like an appointment at all. A diamond is rough and hard to the touch.

WILLY: Go on now. I'll be right up.

LINDA: I think this is the only way, Willy.

WILLY: Sure, it's the best thing.

BEN: Best thing!

WILLY: The only way. Everything is gonna be—go on, kid, get to bed. You look so tired.

LINDA: Come right up.

1820 **WILLY:** Two minutes.

LINDA goes into the living-room, then reappears in her bedroom. WILLY moves just outside the kitchen door.

WILLY: Loves me. *(Wonderingly.)* Always loved me. Isn't that a remarkable thing? Ben, he'll worship me for it!

BEN: *(with promise)* It's dark there, but full of diamonds.

1825 **WILLY:** Can you imagine that magnificence with twenty thousand dollars in his pocket?

LINDA: *(calling from her room)* Willy! Come up!

WILLY: *(calling into the kitchen)* Yes! Yes. Coming! It's very smart, you realize that, don't you, sweetheart? Even Ben sees it. I gotta go, baby. 'By! 'By! *(Going over to BEN, almost dancing.)* Imagine? When the mail comes he'll be ahead of Bernard again!

1830

BEN: A perfect proposition all around.

WILLY: Did you see how he cried to me? Oh, if I could kiss him, Ben!

1835 **BEN:** Time, William, time!

WILLY: Oh, Ben, I always knew one way or another we were gonna make it, Biff and I!

BEN: *(looking at his watch)* The boat. We'll be late. *(He moves slowly off into the darkness.)*

1840 **WILLY:** *(elegiacally, turning to the house)* Now when you kick off, boy, I want a seventy-yard boot, and get right down the field under the ball, and when you hit, hit low and hit hard, because it's important, boy. *(He swings around and faces the audience.)* There's all kinds of important people in the stands, and the first thing you know . . . *(Suddenly realizing he is alone.)* Ben! Ben, where do I . . . ? *(He makes a sudden movement of search.)* Ben, how do I . . . ?

1845

LINDA: *(calling)* Willy, you coming up?

1850 **WILLY:** *(uttering a gasp of fear, whirling about as if to quiet her)* Sh! *(He turns around as if to find his way; sounds, faces, voices, seem to be swarming in upon him and he flicks at them, crying.)* Sh! Sh! *(Suddenly music, faint and high, stops him. It rises in intensity, almost to an unbearable scream. He goes up and down on his toes, and rushes off around the house.)* Shhh!

1855

LINDA: Willy?

There is no answer. LINDA waits. BIFF gets up off his bed. He is still in his clothes. HAPPY sits up. BIFF stands listening.

Willy climbs into the car.

LINDA: *(with real fear)* Willy, answer me! Willy!

There is the sound of a car starting and moving away at full speed.

LINDA: No!

BIFF: *(rushing down the stairs)* Pop!   1860

As the car speeds off, the music crashes down in a frenzy of sound, which becomes the soft pulsation of a single cello string. BIFF slowly returns to his bedroom. He and HAPPY gravely don their jackets. LINDA slowly walks out of her room. The music has developed into a dead march. The leaves of day are appearing over everything. CHARLEY and BERNARD, somberly dressed, appear and knock on the kitchen door. BIFF and HAPPY slowly descend the stairs to the kitchen as CHARLEY and BERNARD enter. All stop a moment when LINDA, in clothes of mourning, bearing a little bunch of roses, comes through the draped doorway into the kitchen. She goes to CHARLEY and takes his arm. Now all move toward the audience, through the wall-line of the kitchen. At the limit of the apron, LINDA lays down the flowers, kneels, and sits back on her heels. All stare down at the grave.

REQUIEM

CHARLEY: It's getting dark, Linda.

LINDA doesn't react. She stares at the grave.

BIFF: How about it, Mom? Better get some rest, heh? They'll be closing the gate soon.

LINDA makes no move. Pause.

HAPPY: *(deeply angered)* He had no right to do that. There was no necessity for it. We would've helped him.   5

CHARLEY: *(grunting)* Hmmm.

BIFF: Come along, Mom.

LINDA: Why didn't anybody come?

CHARLEY: It was a very nice funeral.

10 **LINDA:** But where are all the people he knew? Maybe they blame him.

CHARLEY: Naa. It's a rough world, Linda. They wouldn't blame him.

LINDA: I can't understand it. At this time especially.
15 First time in thirty-five years we were just about free and clear. He only needed a little salary. He was even finished with the dentist.

CHARLEY: No man only needs a little salary.

LINDA: I can't understand it.

20 **BIFF:** There were a lot of nice days. When he'd come home from a trip; or on Sundays, making the stoop; finishing the cellar; putting on the new porch; when he built the extra bathroom; and put up the garage. You know something, Charley, there's more of him in
25 that front stoop than in all the sales he ever made.

CHARLEY: Yeah. He was a happy man with a batch of cement.

LINDA: He was so wonderful with his hands.

BIFF: He had the wrong dreams. All, all, wrong.

30 **HAPPY:** *(almost ready to fight BIFF)* Don't say that!

BIFF: He never knew who he was.

CHARLEY: *(stopping HAPPY's movement and reply. To BIFF)* Nobody dast blame this man. You don't understand: Willy was a salesman. And for a salesman, there is

no rock bottom to the life. He don't put a bolt to a 35
nut, he don't tell you the law or give you medicine.
He's a man way out there in the blue, riding on a
smile and a shoeshine. And when they start not
smiling back—that's an earthquake. And then you
get yourself a couple of spots on your hat, and you're 40
finished. Nobody dast blame this man. A salesman is
got to dream, boy. It comes with the territory.

BIFF: Charley, the man didn't know who he was.

HAPPY: *(infuriated)* Don't say that!

BIFF: Why don't you come with me, Happy? 45

HAPPY: I'm not licked that easily. I'm staying right in
this city, and I'm gonna beat this racket! *(He looks at
BIFF, his chin set.)* The Loman Brothers!

BIFF: I know who I am, kid.

HAPPY: All right, boy. I'm gonna show you and every- 50
body else that Willy Loman did not die in vain.
He had a good dream. It's the only dream you can
have—to come out number-one man. He fought it
out here, and this is where I'm gonna win it for him.

BIFF: *(with a hopeless glance at HAPPY, bends toward his* 55
mother) Let's go, Mom.

LINDA: I'll be with you in a minute. Go on, Charley. *(He
hesitates.)* I want to, just for a minute. I never had a
chance to say good-by.

CHARLEY *moves away, followed by* HAPPY. BIFF *remains
a slight distance up and left of* LINDA. *She sits there, sum-
moning herself. The flute begins, not far away, playing
behind her speech.*

LINDA: Forgive me, dear. I can't cry. I don't know what 60
it is, but I can't cry. I don't understand it. Why did
you ever do that? Help me, Willy, I can't cry. It seems
to me that you're just on another trip. I keep expecting you. Willy, dear, I can't cry. Why did you do it?
I search and search and I search, and I can't under- 65
stand it, Willy. I made the last payment on the house
today. Today, dear. And there'll be nobody home. *(A
sob rises in her throat.)* We're free and clear. *(Sobbing
more fully, released.)* We're free. *(BIFF comes slowly toward her.)* We're free . . . We're free . . . 70

BIFF *lifts her to her feet and moves out up right with her in
his arms.* LINDA *sobs quietly.* BERNARD *and* CHARLEY
come together and follow them, followed by HAPPY. *Only the
music of the flute is left on the darkening stage as over the
house the hard towers of the apartment buildings rise into
sharp focus, and*

The Curtain Falls.

The family stands over Willy's grave.

Writing from Reading

Summarize

1 How would you condense the plot into a few lines, to the size of something you might write, say, on the back of a postcard?

2 Explain how the title *Life of a Salesman* compares with the current title? What other titles might describe the play? Which do you prefer and why?

Analyze Craft

3 Aspects of this play are highly stylized and theatrical—the salesman's hallucinations, for example, and the fade-in and fade-out of characters from his past. How do these imagined conversations alter the concept of realism? Why do they feel appropriate to Willy Loman's collapse?

4 Certain expenses in this play (the price of a drink, the cost of a mortgage) have increased since 1949; others have not. To what extent does this text seem timeless, and what would be the effect of inflating the cost of commodities so as to make them more contemporary?

5 How much of the family dynamic here, in terms of both the siblings and their relation to their parents, grows out of Willy's main desire to sell himself? To what degree does it seem true to your understanding of how families function?

6 Why does Willy feel like a failure? In what ways—as salesman, husband, father—does he succeed? What does his love of gardening suggest?

Analyze Voice

7 What does Arthur Miller mean when he writes in "Tragedy and the Common Man" (1949) "that the plays we revere, century after century, are the tragedies. In them, and in them alone, lies the belief—optimistic, if you will—in the perfectibility of man. It is time, I think, that we who are without kings, took up this bright thread of our history and followed it to the only place it can possibly lead in our time—the heart and spirit of the average man"?

8 Miller in his lifetime was famous as a voice of conscience, protesting against totalitarianism wherever he found it—and refusing to answer questions from the House Un-American Activities Committee when it subpoenaed him to testify against his "communist" friends. Indeed, one of his crucial plays, *The Crucible,* dealt with the mass hysteria of the Salem witch trials in seventeenth-century America and, by extension, with the hysteria engendered by Joseph McCarthy, junior senator from Wisconsin. In what ways is *Death of a Salesman* a play of social protest, and what are Willy's ideals?

Synthesize Summary and Analysis

9 To what extent is Willy Loman like the character of Oedipus? Or, more plausibly, to what extent does he remind you of *Hamlet's* Polonius? Loman, however, can be considered as a tragic character; Polonius cannot. Why?

10 The entire action of the play seems to come together in the statement by Linda Loman in which she says of her husband "Attention must be paid." Why does she forgive what her sons resent so much—his infidelities, his drunkenness? What did she know about his life as a traveling salesman and his missed financial chances? What does she want from and for him now?

Interpret the Play

11 Willy dreams the American dream. In what way does it become a nightmare for him—or does he die content?

(CONTINUED FROM PAGE 285)

FROM THE PALACE TO THE LIVING ROOM, OR, THE ORIGINS OF MODERN THEATER

As you know from your encounters with Greek tragedy and Shakespeare's plays, theater in the West did not begin by depicting ordinary people. In early forms of theater, it was permissible to show ordinary folk as comic and to make fun of the human condition—its pitfalls and pratfalls—in the low or middle class. There was satiric fun to be had at the expense of the common man. The tragic mode was previously reserved, as we have discussed, for elevated members of the society. Middle-class revolutions across Europe brought to power a social class—made up primarily of lawyers, bankers, and landowners—that had served royalty but never before played a dominant role. The fall of monarchies, and the emergence of middle-class democracies driven by industry and finance, gave rise to another sort of audience and another form of theater in western Europe.

> "So whether it's in a play from 1919, or whether it's a play from 1942, or 2010, I approach them all the same: from the truth of that character. . . . Where am I? Who am I? What am I? Why am I here? . . . You always play the truth."
>
> Conversation with Ruben Santiago-Hudson

While kings and queens ruled in Europe, playwrights wrote in a style and took on subjects that catered, at least in part, to the aristocratic audience. With the rise of democratic parliaments, playwrights made a theater for the middle class these legislators represented. In this way marriage and family and various other sorts of everyday social relations replaced the staged deliberations and decisions of kings. Theatergoers wished to see their *own* situations reflected, their *own* society described. In place of the old systems of belief we find a new variety of thought—and therefore a new kind of play. At the start of this chapter we suggested that the movement from palace to living room was a function of the shift in power from monarchy to democracy—and that the possibility of realistic theater was born out of such a shift.

Today it may be difficult to recognize the importance of this distinction in styles, or how much it means even as we witness it. Actors perform the Oedipus play wearing stylized masks that emphasize the difference between the royal family and the audience and the difference between the royals and the gods who rule their lives. Issues of marriage and family in Elizabethan theater are more closely related to matters of kingdom and empire than to domestic relations. Shakespeare's scenes when staged with flair and intelligence remind us of the difference between performers on the stage and our ordinary selves in the audience. Great poetry that it is, the language alone can make us hear—and, by simply hearing, see—the distance between the playwright's characters of high and low station. Here the importance of staging comes, again, to bear. This kind of realistic stage or set design, a **proscenium** stage, forces the playwright to consider the mechanics of staging actors in relation to the audience and to quick, easy, and inexpensive set changes to keep from changing the scenery every time the action shifts.

Death of a Salesman, Arthur Miller's most influential work, lies squarely within the tradition of realistic or **naturalistic** theater, theater that shines a light on painful realities. In the course of his lengthy productive career, Miller tried his hand at other modes of representation—writing short experimental plays or ones with an historical context or dabbling in surrealism—but it is his realistic plays that brought his work into the mainstream of American drama. In *Death of a Salesman*, Miller takes his protagonist, a modern-day tragic hero (or **antihero** in that he is not elevated socially or morally), a step further: He is an Everyman in a modern **morality play** (see chapter 34 for more on the medieval morality play).

"America is happiest with a naturalistic play or play that gives the illusion of being naturalistic. . . . We all know that in theater there is no such thing as absolute naturalism. People do not talk the way they do in real life, thank heavens. On stage they talk coherently. . . . We call something naturalistic if it is not highly stylized."

Conversation with Edward Albee

In some ways the American playwright Arthur Miller is the direct inheritor of the playwright who defined the practice of realism onstage: Henrik Ibsen. The nineteenth-century Norwegian Ibsen is the writer who more than any other brought the realistic strategy to the Western stage. Ibsen takes on the difficult and piercing social issues of his period and, to a certain extent, our own. In *A Doll's House* we witness the dramatization of problems that touch on the lives of ordinary middle-class people—the role of women in modern marriage, a struggle about money and employment, the effort to keep up appearances for the outside world. Ibsen highlights the problems of family life, of married life within society—subjects not addressed in any detail in early forms of drama. In his theater we meet people we can legitimately call modern, people mostly like ourselves in recognizable and often unpleasant situations. What made it possible for a playwright to create this sort of play and what makes it possible for an audience to respond to it?

METHOD ACTING—REALISM ONSTAGE

An entirely new style of performance—first propounded by the Russian Konstantin Stanislavski and practiced in America most famously by such graduates of the Actors Studio as Marilyn Monroe and Marlon Brando—made a method out of naturalism onstage. An actor and his or her character should merge so that the role becomes *inhabited* by the person cast in it; the facial tics or accent of a *method* actor were not acquired in the dressing room ten minutes before curtain time but were built into rehearsal and the interpretative process. This notion of identity between the player and the part played is based, of course, on the assumption that behavior must be internalized and is best copied when most natural. Gone were the highly polished performances and perfectly articulated speech of characters in period dress; instead, as some disgruntled reviewers complained, the actors scratched themselves and mumbled and turned their backs on the audience in order to seem *real*.

In nineteenth-century France, the **well-made play** became the norm. Popularized by such playwrights as Eugène Scribe (1791–1861) and Victorien Sardou (1831–1908), this three-act sequence *posed* a problem, *complicated* it, and then *resolved* it; usually that resolution came when a character's past was revealed. The first act offers *exposition*, the second a *situation*, the third an unraveling or *completion*. Meticulous plotting and suspense were components of this mode of theater. Ibsen—who had directed a number of Scribe's well-made plays in Norway—deeply understood how to adapt those cause-and-effect plot arrangements for his own use. Cowardice, hypocrisy, complacency within the expectation of conventional behavior, and a kind of stifled yearning are the problems Ibsen brings to center stage in his drama.

Here's one reason that *A Doll's House* is a **problem play;** it's hard to *read* the central figure and decide if she's a spoiled child or a brave pioneer or some combination of both. Indeed, there have been various interpretations of the role: Nora has been played as everything from victim to victimizer, self-indulgent society matron to selfless ingenue. Nora desires what we desire. The protagonist Nora yearns to become a fully aware human being rather than live as the subservient creature known to soci-

> "Every playwright awakens something in you you didn't know was there. . . . Ibsen, for example, . . . had such a tremendous influence. . . . His women were as startling and as modern as any woman I've ever worked on. . . . The ideas in Ibsen are so brave and so bold." Conversation with Marian Seldes

ety as Torvald's wife. She struggles with confusion as we struggle with confusion. She achieves a breakthrough in her understanding that mirrors our own recognition; her fear of causing embarrassment to and dishonor for her husband feels in many respects contemporary. The way she wrestles with the problem of family duty as opposed to her own individual freedom should seem familiar as well. In any case her progress toward independence feels modern and quite up-to-date. As one of our culture's first great feminist characters, she embodies—in terms of her growth from first to final act—a form of liberation surprising, even shocking, at the time. Here's a portrait of a woman and a family that resonates today.

Henrik Ibsen (1828–1906)

Henrik Ibsen, known today as the father of modern drama, was born near Oslo, Norway. Initially wealthy, the Ibsens were left in poverty when their family business failed; Henrik was six years old at the time. As a teenager, he was apprenticed to a pharmacist, but by 1851, he held the position of stage manager and playwright at the Norwegian The-ater in Bergen, and after that he worked as a theater director in Norway's capital. Ibsen later lived abroad in Germany and Italy, remaining away from Norway for a twenty-seven-year period because he felt he could better write Norwegian drama from a distance. Supported by stipends from the government, Ibsen devoted himself to writing plays. His work moved theater away from popular nineteenth-century melodramas and into the realm of realism, which allowed him to examine his characters' psychological lives and the individual's conflict with convention and society. Plays such as *A Doll's House* (1879), *Ghosts* (1881), and *Hedda Gabler* (1890) established Ibsen's dramaturgical prowess. In 1891, Ibsen returned to Oslo, where he remained for the rest of his life.

A Doll's House (1879)

—translated by B. Farquharson Sharp

CHARACTERS

TORVALD HELMER.

NORA, HIS WIFE.

DOCTOR RANK.

MRS. LINDE.

NILS KROGSTAD.

HELMERS' THREE YOUNG CHILDREN.

ANNE, THEIR NURSE.

A HOUSEMAID.

A PORTER.

(The action takes place in Helmer's house.)

ACT I

SCENE: —*A room furnished comfortably and tastefully, but not extravagantly. At the back, a door to the right leads to the entrance-hall, another to the left leads to Helmer's study. Between the doors stands a piano. In the middle of the left-hand wall is a door, and beyond it a window. Near the window are a round table, arm-chairs and a small sofa. In the right-hand wall, at the farther end, another door; and on the same side, nearer the footlights, a stove, two easy chairs and a rocking-chair; between the stove and the door, a small table. Engravings on the walls; a cabinet with china and other small objects; a small book-case with well-bound books. The floors are carpeted, and a fire burns in the stove. It is winter.*

A bell rings in the hall; shortly afterwards the door is heard to open. Enter NORA, *humming a tune and in high spirits. She is in out-door dress and carries a number of parcels; these she lays on the table to the right. She leaves the outer door open after her, and through it is seen a* PORTER *who is carrying a Christmas Tree and a basket, which he gives to the* MAID *who has opened the door.*

NORA: Hide the Christmas Tree carefully, Helen. Be sure the children do not see it till this evening, when it is dressed. *(To the* PORTER, *taking out her purse.)* How much?

PORTER: Sixpence. 5

NORA: There is a shilling. No, keep the change. *(The* PORTER *thanks her, and goes out.* NORA *shuts the door. She is laughing to herself, as she takes off her hat and coat. She takes a packet of macaroons from her pocket and eats one or two; then goes cautiously to her husband's door and* 10 *listens.)* Yes, he is in. *(Still humming, she goes to the table on the right.)*

HELMER: *(calls out from his room)* Is that my little lark twittering out there?

NORA: *(busy opening some of the parcels)* Yes, it is! 15

HELMER: Is it my little squirrel bustling about?

NORA: Yes!

HELMER: When did my squirrel come home?

NORA: Just now. *(Puts the bag of macaroons into her pocket and wipes her mouth.)* Come in here, Torvald, and see 20 what I have bought.

HELMER: Don't disturb me. (*A little later, he opens the door and looks into the room, pen in hand.*) Bought, did you say? All these things? Has my little spendthrift
25 been wasting money again?

NORA: Yes but, Torvald, this year we really can let ourselves go a little. This is the first Christmas that we have not needed to economise.

HELMER: Still, you know, we can't spend money
30 recklessly.

NORA: Yes, Torvald, we may be a wee bit more reckless now, mayn't we? Just a tiny wee bit! You are going to have a big salary and earn lots and lots of money.

HELMER: Yes, after the New Year; but then it will be a
35 whole quarter before the salary is due.

NORA: Pooh! we can borrow till then.

HELMER: Nora! (*Goes up to her and takes her playfully by the ear.*) The same little featherhead! Suppose, now, that I borrowed fifty pounds to-day, and you spent
40 it all in the Christmas week, and then on New Year's Eve a slate fell on my head and killed me, and—

NORA: (*putting her hands over his mouth*) Oh! don't say such horrid things!

HELMER: Still, suppose that happened,—what then?

45 **NORA:** If that were to happen, I don't suppose I should care whether I owed money or not.

HELMER: Yes, but what about the people who had lent it?

NORA: They? Who would bother about them? I should
50 not know who they were.

HELMER: That is like a woman! But seriously, Nora, you know what I think about that. No debt, no borrowing. There can be no freedom or beauty about a home life that depends on borrowing and debt. We
55 two have kept bravely on the straight road so far, and we will go on the same way for the short time longer that there need be any struggle.

NORA: (*moving towards the stove*) As you please, Torvald.

HELMER: (*following her*) Come, come, my little skylark
60 must not droop her wings. What is this! Is my little squirrel out of temper? (*Taking out his purse.*) Nora, what do you think I have got here?

NORA: (*turning round quickly*) Money!

HELMER: There you are. (*Gives her some money.*) Do you
65 think I don't know what a lot is wanted for housekeeping at Christmas-time?

Nora (Claire Bloom) and Torvald (Anthony Hopkins) Helmer discuss their Christmas plans in the 1973 film directed by Patrick Garland.

NORA: (*counting*) Ten shillings—a pound—two pounds! Thank you, thank you, Torvald; that will keep me going for a long time.

HELMER: Indeed it must.   70

NORA: Yes, yes, it will. But come here and let me show you what I have bought. And all so cheap! Look, here is a new suit for Ivar, and a sword; and a horse and a trumpet for Bob; and a doll and dolly's bedstead for Emmy,—they are very plain, but anyway she   75 will soon break them in pieces. And here are dresslengths and handkerchiefs for the maids; old Anne ought really to have something better.

HELMER: And what is in this parcel?

NORA: (*crying out*) No, no! you mustn't see that till this   80 evening.

HELMER: Very well. But now tell me, you extravagant little person, what would you like for yourself?

NORA: For myself? Oh, I am sure I don't want anything.

HELMER: Yes, but you must. Tell me something rea-   85 sonable that you would particularly like to have.

NORA: No, I really can't think of anything—unless, Torvald—

HELMER: Well?

NORA: (*playing with his coat buttons, and without raising her   90 eyes to his*) If you really want to give me something, you might—you might—

HELMER: Well, out with it!

NORA: (*speaking quickly*) You might give me money, Torvald. Only just as much as you can afford; and   95 then one of these days I will buy something with it.

Nora tells Torvald what she would like for Christmas.

HELMER: But Nora—

NORA: Oh, do! dear Torvald; please, please do! Then I will wrap it up in beautiful gilt paper and hang it on the Christmas Tree. Wouldn't that be fun?

HELMER: What are little people called that are always wasting money?

NORA: Spendthrifts—I know. Let us do as you suggest, Torvald, and then I shall have time to think what I am most in want of. That is a very sensible plan, isn't it?

HELMER: *(smiling)* Indeed it is—that is to say, if you were really to save out of the money I give you, and then really buy something for yourself. But if you spend it all on the housekeeping and any number of unnecessary things, then I merely have to pay up again.

NORA: Oh but, Torvald—

HELMER: You can't deny it, my dear little Nora. *(Puts his arm around her waist.)* It's a sweet little spendthrift, but she uses up a deal of money. One would hardly believe how expensive such little persons are!

NORA: It's a shame to say that. I do really save all I can.

HELMER: *(laughing)* That's very true,—all you can. But you can't save anything!

NORA: *(smiling quietly and happily)* You haven't any idea how many expenses we skylarks and squirrels have, Torvald.

HELMER: You are an odd little soul. Very like your father. You always find some new way of wheedling money out of me, and, as soon as you have got it, it seems to melt in your hands. You never know where it has gone. Still, one must take you as you are. It is in the blood; for indeed it is true that you can inherit these things, Nora.

NORA: Ah, I wish I had inherited many of papa's qualities.

HELMER: And I would not wish you to be anything but just what you are, my sweet little skylark. But, do you know, it strikes me that you are looking rather— what shall I say—rather uneasy to-day?

NORA: Do I?

HELMER: You do, really. Look straight at me.

NORA: *(looks at him)* Well?

HELMER: *(wagging his finger at her)* Hasn't Miss Sweet-Tooth been breaking rules in town to-day?

NORA: No; what makes you think that?

HELMER: Hasn't she paid a visit to the confectioner's?

NORA: No, I assure you, Torvald—

HELMER: Not been nibbling sweets?

NORA: No, certainly not.

HELMER: Not even taken a bite at a macaroon or two?

NORA: No, Torvald, I assure you really—

HELMER: There, there, of course I was only joking.

NORA: *(going to the table on the right)* I should not think of going against your wishes.

HELMER: No, I am sure of that; besides, you gave me your word—*(Going up to her.)* Keep your little Christmas secrets to yourself, my darling. They will all be revealed to-night when the Christmas Tree is lit, no doubt.

NORA: Did you remember to invite Doctor Rank?

HELMER: No. But there is no need; as a matter of course he will come to dinner with us. However, I will ask him when he comes in this morning. I have ordered some good wine. Nora, you can't think how I am looking forward to this evening.

NORA: So am I! And how the children will enjoy themselves, Torvald!

HELMER: It is splendid to feel that one has a perfectly safe appointment, and a big enough income. It's delightful to think of, isn't it?

NORA: It's wonderful!

HELMER: Do you remember last Christmas? For a full three weeks beforehand you shut yourself up every evening till long after midnight, making ornaments for the Christmas Tree, and all the other fine things that were to be a surprise to us. It was the dullest three weeks I ever spent!

NORA: I didn't find it dull.

HELMER: (*smiling*) But there was precious little result, Nora.

NORA: Oh, you shouldn't tease me about that again. How could I help the cat's going in and tearing everything to pieces?

HELMER: Of course you couldn't, poor little girl. You had the best of intentions to please us all, and that's the main thing. But it is a good thing that our hard times are over.

NORA: Yes, it is really wonderful.

HELMER: This time I needn't sit here and be dull all alone, and you needn't ruin your dear eyes and your pretty little hands—

NORA: (*clapping her hands*) No, Torvald, I needn't any longer, need I! It's wonderfully lovely to hear you say so! (*Taking his arm.*) Now I will tell you how I have been thinking we ought to arrange things, Torvald. As soon as Christmas is over—(*A bell rings in the hall.*) There's the bell. (*She tidies the room a little.*) There's some one at the door. What a nuisance!

HELMER: If it is a caller, remember I am not at home.

MAID: (*in the doorway*) A lady to see you, ma'am,—a stranger.

NORA: Ask her to come in.

MAID: (*to* HELMER) The doctor came at the same time, sir.

HELMER: Did he go straight into my room?

MAID: Yes, sir.

(HELMER *goes into his room. The* MAID *ushers in* MRS. LINDE, *who is in travelling dress, and shuts the door.*)

MRS. LINDE: (*in a dejected and timid voice*) How do you do, Nora?

NORA: (*doubtfully*) How do you do—

MRS. LINDE: You don't recognise me, I suppose.

NORA: No, I don't know—yes, to be sure, I seem to— (*Suddenly.*) Yes! Christine! Is it really you?

MRS. LINDE: Yes, it is I.

NORA: Christine! To think of my not recognising you! And yet how could I— (*In a gentle voice.*) How you have altered, Christine!

MRS. LINDE: Yes, I have indeed. In nine, ten long years—

NORA: Is it so long since we met? I suppose it is. The last eight years have been a happy time for me, I can tell you. And so now you have come into the town, and have taken this long journey in winter—that was plucky of you.

MRS. LINDE: I arrived by steamer this morning.

NORA: To have some fun at Christmas-time, of course. How delightful! We will have such fun together! But take off your things. You're not cold, I hope. (*Helps her.*) Now we will sit down by the stove, and be cosy. No, take this arm-chair; I will sit here in the rocking-chair. (*Takes her hands.*) Now you look like your old self again; it was only the first moment—You are a little paler, Christine, and perhaps a little thinner.

MRS. LINDE: And much, much older, Nora.

NORA: Perhaps a little older; very, very little; certainly not much. (*Stops suddenly and speaks seriously.*) What a thoughtless creature I am, chattering away like this. My poor, dear Christine, do forgive me.

MRS. LINDE: What do you mean, Nora?

NORA: (*gently*) Poor Christine, you are a widow.

MRS. LINDE: Yes; it is three years ago now.

NORA: Yes, I knew; I saw it in the papers. I assure you, Christine, I meant ever so often to write to you at the time, but I always put it off and something always prevented me.

MRS. LINDE: I quite understand, dear.

NORA: It was very bad of me, Christine. Poor thing, how you must have suffered. And he left you nothing?

MRS. LINDE: No.

NORA: And no children?

MRS. LINDE: No.

NORA: Nothing at all, then.

MRS. LINDE: Not even any sorrow or grief to live upon.

NORA: (*looking incredulously at her*) But Christine, is that possible?

MRS. LINDE: (*smiles sadly and strokes her hair*) It sometimes happens, Nora.

255 **NORA:** So you are quite alone. How dreadfully sad that must be. I have three lovely children. You can't see them just now, for they are out with their nurse. But now you must tell me all about it.

MRS. LINDE: No, no; I want to hear about you.

260 **NORA:** No, you must begin. I mustn't be selfish to-day; to-day I must only think of your affairs. But there is one thing I must tell you. Do you know we have just had a great piece of good luck?

MRS. LINDE: No, what is it?

265 **NORA:** Just fancy, my husband has been made manager of the Bank!

MRS. LINDE: Your husband? What good luck!

NORA: Yes, tremendous! A barrister's profession is such an uncertain thing, especially if he won't undertake unsavoury cases; and naturally Torvald has never 270 been willing to do that, and I quite agree with him. You may imagine how pleased we are! He is to take up his work in the Bank at the New Year, and then he will have a big salary and lots of commissions. For the future we can live quite differently—we can do 275 just as we like. I feel so relieved and so happy, Christine! It will be splendid to have heaps of money and not need to have any anxiety, won't it?

MRS. LINDE: Yes, anyhow I think it would be delightful to have what one needs.

280 **NORA:** No, not only what one needs, but heaps and heaps of money.

MRS. LINDE: (*smiling*) Nora, Nora, haven't you learnt sense yet? In our schooldays you were a great spendthrift.

285 **NORA:** (*laughing*) Yes, that is what Torvald says now. (*Wags her finger at her.*) But "Nora, Nora" is not so silly as you think. We have not been in a position for me to waste money. We have both had to work.

MRS. LINDE: You too?

290 **NORA:** Yes; odds and ends, needlework, crotchet-work, embroidery, and that kind of thing. (*Dropping her voice.*) And other things as well. You know Torvald left his office when we were married? There was no prospect of promotion there, and he had to try and 295 earn more than before. But during the first year he over-worked himself dreadfully. You see, he had to make money every way he could, and he worked early and late; but he couldn't stand it, and fell dreadfully ill, and the doctors said it was necessary 300 for him to go south.

MRS. LINDE: You spent a whole year in Italy, didn't you?

NORA: Yes. It was no easy matter to get away, I can tell you. It was just after Ivar was born; but naturally we had to go. It was a wonderfully beautiful journey, and it saved Torvald's life. But it cost a tremendous 305 lot of money, Christine.

MRS. LINDE: So I should think.

NORA: It cost about two hundred and fifty pounds. That's a lot, isn't it?

MRS. LINDE: Yes, and in emergencies like that it is 310 lucky to have the money.

NORA: I ought to tell you that we had it from papa.

MRS. LINDE: Oh, I see. It was just about that time that he died, wasn't it?

NORA: Yes; and, just think of it, I couldn't go and nurse 315 him. I was expecting little Ivar's birth every day and I had my poor sick Torvald to look after. My dear, kind father—I never saw him again, Christine. That was the saddest time I have known since our marriage. 320

MRS. LINDE: I know how fond you were of him. And then you went off to Italy?

NORA: Yes; you see we had money then, and the doctors insisted on our going, so we started a month later.

MRS. LINDE: And your husband came back quite well? 325

NORA: As sound as a bell!

MRS. LINDE: But—the doctor?

Nora (Juliet Stevenson) catches up with Mrs. Linde (Geraldine James) in the 1992 film directed by David Thacker.

NORA: What doctor?

MRS. LINDE: I thought your maid said the gentleman who arrived here just as I did, was the doctor?

NORA: Yes, that was Doctor Rank, but he doesn't come here professionally. He is our greatest friend, and comes in at least once every day. No, Torvald has not had an hour's illness since then, and our children are strong and healthy and so am I. (*Jumps up and claps her hands.*) Christine! Christine! it's good to be alive and happy!—But how horrid of me; I am talking of nothing but my own affairs. (*Sits on a stool near her, and rests her arms on her knees.*) You mustn't be angry with me. Tell me, is it really true that you did not love your husband? Why did you marry him?

MRS. LINDE: My mother was alive then, and was bedridden and helpless, and I had to provide for my two younger brothers; so I did not think I was justified in refusing his offer.

NORA: No, perhaps you were quite right. He was rich at that time, then?

MRS. LINDE: I believe he was quite well off. But his business was a precarious one; and, when he died, it all went to pieces and there was nothing left.

NORA: And then?—

MRS. LINDE: Well, I had to turn my hand to anything I could find—first a small shop, then a small school, and so on. The last three years have seemed like one long working-day, with no rest. Now it is at an end, Nora. My poor mother needs me no more, for she is gone; and the boys do not need me either; they have got situations and can shift for themselves.

NORA: What a relief you must feel it—

MRS. LINDE: No, indeed; I only feel my life unspeakably empty. No one to live for any more. (*Gets up restlessly.*) That was why I could not stand the life in my little backwater any longer. I hope it may be easier here to find something which will busy me and occupy my thoughts. If only I could have the good luck to get some regular work—office work of some kind—

NORA: But, Christine, that is so frightfully tiring, and you look tired out now. You had far better go away to some watering-place.

MRS. LINDE: (*walking to the window*) I have no father to give me money for a journey, Nora.

NORA: (*rising*) Oh, don't be angry with me.

MRS. LINDE: (*going up to her*) It is you that must not be angry with me, dear. The worst of a position like mine is that it makes one so bitter. No one to work for, and yet obliged to be always on the look-out for chances. One must live, and so one becomes selfish. When you told me of the happy turn your fortunes have taken—you will hardly believe it—I was delighted not so much on your account as on my own.

NORA: How do you mean?—Oh, I understand. You mean that perhaps Torvald could get you something to do.

MRS. LINDE: Yes, that was what I was thinking of.

NORA: He must, Christine. Just leave it to me; I will broach the subject very cleverly—I will think of something that will please him very much. It will make me so happy to be of some use to you.

MRS. LINDE: How kind you are, Nora, to be so anxious to help me! It is doubly kind in you, for you know so little of the burdens and troubles of life.

NORA: I—? I know so little of them?

MRS. LINDE: (*smiling*) My dear! Small household cares and that sort of thing!—You are a child, Nora.

NORA: (*tosses her head and crosses the stage*) You ought not to be so superior.

MRS. LINDE: No?

NORA: You are just like the others. They all think that I am incapable of anything really serious—

MRS. LINDE: Come, come—

NORA: —that I have gone through nothing in this world of cares.

MRS. LINDE: But, my dear Nora, you have just told me all your troubles.

NORA: Pooh!—those were trifles. (*Lowering her voice.*) I have not told you the important thing.

MRS. LINDE: The important thing? What do you mean?

NORA: You look down upon me altogether, Christine—but you ought not to. You are proud, aren't you, of having worked so hard and so long for your mother?

MRS. LINDE: Indeed, I don't look down on any one. But it is true that I am both proud and glad to think that I was privileged to make the end of my mother's life almost free from care.

NORA: And you are proud to think of what you have done for your brothers.

MRS. LINDE: I think I have the right to be.

NORA: I think so, too. But now listen to this; I too have something to be proud and glad of.

420 **MRS. LINDE:** I have no doubt you have. But what do you refer to?

NORA: Speak low. Suppose Torvald were to hear! He mustn't on any account—no one in the world must know, Christine, except you.

425 **MRS. LINDE:** But what is it?

NORA: Come here. (*Pulls her down on the sofa beside her.*) Now I will show you that I too have something to be proud and glad of. It was I who saved Torvald's life.

MRS. LINDE: "Saved"? How?

430 **NORA:** I told you about our trip to Italy. Torvald would never have recovered if he had not gone there—

MRS. LINDE: Yes, but your father gave you the necessary funds.

NORA: (*smiling*) Yes, that is what Torvald and all the
435 others think, but—

MRS. LINDE: But—

NORA: Papa didn't give us a shilling. It was I who procured the money.

MRS. LINDE: You? All that large sum?

440 **NORA:** Two hundred and fifty pounds. What do you think of that?

MRS. LINDE: But, Nora, how could you possibly do it? Did you win a prize in the Lottery?

NORA: (*contemptuously*) In the Lottery? There would
445 have been no credit in that.

MRS. LINDE: But where did you get it from, then?

NORA: (*humming and smiling with an air of mystery*) Hm, hm! Aha!

MRS. LINDE: Because you couldn't have borrowed it.

450 **NORA:** Couldn't I? Why not?

MRS. LINDE: No, a wife cannot borrow without her husband's consent.

NORA: (*tossing her head*) Oh, if it is a wife who has any head for business—a wife who has the wit to be a
455 little bit clever—

MRS. LINDE: I don't understand it at all, Nora.

NORA: There is no need you should. I never said I had borrowed the money. I may have got it some other

way. (*Lies back on the sofa.*) Perhaps I got it from some other admirer. When anyone is as attractive as I am— 460

MRS. LINDE: You are a mad creature.

NORA: Now, you know you're full of curiosity, Christine.

MRS. LINDE: Listen to me, Nora dear. Haven't you been a little bit imprudent?

NORA: (*sits up straight*) Is it imprudent to save your 465 husband's life?

MRS. LINDE: It seems to me imprudent, without his knowledge, to—

NORA: But it was absolutely necessary that he should not know! My goodness, can't you understand that? 470 It was necessary he should have no idea what a dangerous condition he was in. It was to me that the doctors came and said that his life was in danger, and that the only thing to save him was to live in the south. Do you suppose I didn't try, first of all, to get 475 what I wanted as if it were for myself? I told him how much I should love to travel abroad like other young wives; I tried tears and entreaties with him; I told him that he ought to remember the condition I was in, and that he ought to be kind and indulgent 480 to me; I even hinted that he might raise a loan. That nearly made him angry, Christine. He said I was thoughtless, and that it was his duty as my husband not to indulge me in my whims and caprices—as I believe he called them. Very well, I thought, you 485 must be saved—and that was how I came to devise a way out of the difficulty—

MRS. LINDE: And did your husband never get to know from your father that the money had not come from him? 490

NORA: No, never. Papa died just at that time. I had meant to let him into the secret and beg him never to reveal it. But he was so ill then—alas, there never was any need to tell him.

MRS. LINDE: And since then have you never told your 495 secret to your husband?

NORA: Good Heavens, no! How could you think so? A man who has such strong opinions about these things! And besides, how painful and humiliating it would be for Torvald, with his manly independence, 500 to know that he owed me anything! It would upset our mutual relations altogether; our beautiful happy home would no longer be what it is now.

MRS. LINDE: Do you mean never to tell him about it?

505 **NORA:** *(meditatively, and with a half smile)* Yes—some day, perhaps, after many years, when I am no longer as nice-looking as I am now. Don't laugh at me! I mean, of course, when Torvald is no longer as devoted to me as he is now; when my dancing and dressing-up
510 and reciting have palled on him; then it may be a good thing to have something in reserve— *(Breaking off.)* What nonsense! That time will never come. Now, what do you think of my great secret, Christine? Do you still think I am of no use? I can tell you, too, that
515 this affair has caused me a lot of worry. It has been by no means easy for me to meet my engagements punctually. I may tell you that there is something that is called, in business, quarterly interest, and another thing called payment in instalments, and it is
520 always so dreadfully difficult to manage them. I have had to save a little here and there, where I could, you understand. I have not been able to put aside much from my housekeeping money, for Torvald must have a good table. I couldn't let my children be shabbily
525 dressed; I have felt obliged to use up all he gave me for them, the sweet little darlings!

MRS. LINDE: So it has all had to come out of your own necessaries of life, poor Nora?

NORA: Of course. Besides, I was the one responsible for
530 it. Whenever Torvald has given me money for new dresses and such things, I have never spent more than half of it; I have always bought the simplest and cheapest things. Thank Heaven, any clothes look well on me, and so Torvald has never noticed it. But
535 it was often very hard on me, Christine—because it is delightful to be really well dressed, isn't it?

MRS. LINDE: Quite so.

NORA: Well, then I have found other ways of earning money. Last winter I was lucky enough to get a lot of
540 copying to do; so I locked myself up and sat writing every evening until quite late at night. Many a time I was desperately tired; but all the same it was a tremendous pleasure to sit there working and earning money. It was like being a man.

545 **MRS. LINDE:** How much have you been able to pay off in that way?

NORA: I can't tell you exactly. You see, it is very difficult to keep an account of a business matter of that kind. I only know that I have paid every penny that I
550 could scrape together. Many a time I was at my wit's end. *(Smiles.)* Then I used to sit here and imagine that a rich old gentleman had fallen in love with me—

MRS. LINDE: What! Who was it?

NORA: Be quiet!—that he had died; and that when his will was opened it contained, written in big letters,
555 the instruction: "The lovely Mrs. Nora Helmer is to have all I possess paid over to her at once in cash."

MRS. LINDE: But, my dear Nora—who could the man be?

NORA: Good gracious, can't you understand? There
560 was no old gentleman at all; it was only something that I used to sit here and imagine, when I couldn't think of any way of procuring money. But it's all the same now; the tiresome old person can stay where he is, as far as I am concerned; I don't care about
565 him or his will either, for I am free from care now. *(Jumps up.)* My goodness, it's delightful to think of, Christine! Free from care! To be able to be free from care, quite free from care; to be able to play and romp with the children; to be able to keep the house
570 beautifully and have everything just as Torvald likes it! And, think of it, soon the spring will come and the big blue sky! Perhaps we shall be able to take a little trip—perhaps I shall see the sea again! Oh, it's a wonderful thing to be alive and be happy. *(A bell is*
575 *heard in the hall.)*

MRS. LINDE: *(rising)* There is the bell; perhaps I had better go.

NORA: No, don't go; no one will come in here; it is sure to be for Torvald.
580

SERVANT: *(at the hall door)* Excuse me, ma'am—there is a gentleman to see the master, and as the doctor is with him—

NORA: Who is it?

Nora tells Mrs. Linde (Anna Massey) about her troubles.

585 **KROGSTAD:** *(at the door)* It is I, Mrs. Helmer. *(*MRS. LINDE *starts, trembles, and turns to the window.)*

NORA: *(takes a step towards him, and speaks in a strained, low voice)* You? What is it? What do you want to see my husband about?

590 **KROGSTAD:** Bank business—in a way. I have a small post in the Bank, and I hear your husband is to be our chief now—

NORA: Then it is—

KROGSTAD: Nothing but dry business matters, Mrs. Helmer; absolutely nothing else.

595 **NORA:** Be so good as to go into the study, then. *(She bows indifferently to him and shuts the door into the hall; then comes back and makes up the fire in the stove.)*

MRS. LINDE: Nora—who was that man?

NORA: A lawyer, of the name of Krogstad.

600 **MRS. LINDE:** Then it really was he.

NORA: Do you know the man?

MRS. LINDE: I used to—many years ago. At one time he was a solicitor's clerk in our town.

NORA: Yes, he was.

605 **MRS. LINDE:** He is greatly altered.

NORA: He made a very unhappy marriage.

MRS. LINDE: He is a widower now, isn't he?

NORA: With several children. There now, it is burning up. *(Shuts the door of the stove and moves the rocking-chair aside.)*

610

MRS. LINDE: They say he carries on various kinds of business.

NORA: Really! Perhaps he does; I don't know anything about it. But don't let us think of business; it is so tiresome.

615

DOCTOR RANK: *(comes out of* HELMER's *study. Before he shuts the door he calls to him)* No, my dear fellow, I won't disturb you; I would rather go in to your wife for a little while. *(Shuts the door and sees* MRS. LINDE.*)* I beg your pardon; I am afraid I am disturbing you too.

620

NORA: No, not at all. *(Introducing him.)* Doctor Rank, Mrs. Linde.

RANK: I have often heard Mrs. Linde's name mentioned here. I think I passed you on the stairs when I arrived, Mrs. Linde?

625

MRS. LINDE: Yes, I go up very slowly; I can't manage stairs well.

RANK: Ah! some slight internal weakness?

MRS. LINDE: No, the fact is I have been overworking myself. 630

RANK: Nothing more than that? Then I suppose you have come to town to amuse yourself with our entertainments?

MRS. LINDE: I have come to look for work. 635

RANK: Is that a good cure for overwork?

MRS. LINDE: One must live, Doctor Rank.

RANK: Yes, the general opinion seems to be that it is necessary.

NORA: Look here, Doctor Rank—you know you want to live. 640

RANK: Certainly. However wretched I may feel, I want to prolong the agony as long as possible. All my patients are like that. And so are those who are morally diseased; one of them, and a bad case too, is at this very moment with Helmer— 645

MRS. LINDE: *(sadly)* Ah!

NORA: Whom do you mean?

RANK: A lawyer of the name of Krogstad, a fellow you don't know at all. He suffers from a diseased moral character, Mrs. Helmer; but even he began talking of its being highly important that he should live. 650

NORA: Did he? What did he want to speak to Torvald about?

RANK: I have no idea; I only heard that it was something about the Bank. 655

NORA: I didn't know this—what's his name—Krogstad had anything to do with the Bank.

RANK: Yes, he has some sort of appointment there. *(To* MRS. LINDE.*)* I don't know whether you find also in your part of the world that there are certain people who go zealously snuffing about to smell out moral corruption, and, as soon as they have found some, put the person concerned into some lucrative position where they can keep their eye on him. Healthy natures are left out in the cold. 660
665

MRS. LINDE: Still I think the sick are those who most need taking care of.

RANK: *(shrugging his shoulders)* Yes, there you are. That is the sentiment that is turning Society into a sick-house. 670

Nora, Mrs. Linde, and Dr. Rank (Ralph Richardson) chat about Torvald and Krogstad.

(NORA, *who has been absorbed in her thoughts, breaks out into smothered laughter and claps her hands.*)

RANK: Why do you laugh at that? Have you any notion what Society really is?

675 **NORA:** What do I care about tiresome Society? I am laughing at something quite different, something extremely amusing. Tell me, Doctor Rank, are all the people who are employed in the Bank dependent on Torvald now?

RANK: Is that what you find so extremely amusing?

680 **NORA:** (*smiling and humming*) That's my affair! (*Walking about the room.*) It's perfectly glorious to think that we have—that Torvald has so much power over so many people. (*Takes the packet from her pocket.*) Doctor Rank, what do you say to a macaroon?

685 **RANK:** What, macaroons? I thought they were forbidden here.

NORA: Yes, but these are some Christine gave me.

MRS. LINDE: What! I?—

NORA: Oh, well, don't be alarmed! You couldn't know
690 that Torvald had forbidden them. I must tell you that he is afraid they will spoil my teeth. But, bah!—once in a way—That's so, isn't it, Doctor Rank? By your leave! (*Puts a macaroon into his mouth.*) You must have one too, Christine. And I shall have one, just a little
695 one—or at most two. (*Walking about.*) I am tremendously happy. There is just one thing in the world now that I should dearly love to do.

RANK: Well, what is that?

NORA: It's something I should dearly love to say, if
700 Torvald could hear me.

RANK: Well, why can't you say it?

NORA: No, I daren't; it's so shocking.

MRS. LINDE: Shocking?

RANK: Well, I should not advise you to say it. Still,
with us you might. What is it you would so much like 705
to say if Torvald could hear you?

NORA: I should just love to say—Well, I'm damned!

RANK: Are you mad?

MRS. LINDE: Nora, dear—!

RANK: Say it, here he is! 710

NORA: (*hiding the packet*) Hush! Hush! Hush! (HELMER
comes out of his room, with his coat over his arm and his hat in his hand.)

NORA: Well, Torvald dear, have you got rid of him?

HELMER: Yes, he has just gone. 715

NORA: Let me introduce you—this is Christine, who has come to town.

HELMER: Christine—? Excuse me, but I don't know—

NORA: Mrs. Linde, dear; Christine Linde.

HELMER: Of course. A school friend of my wife's, I 720
presume?

MRS. LINDE: Yes, we have known each other since then.

NORA: And just think, she has taken a long journey in order to see you.

HELMER: What do you mean? 725

MRS. LINDE: No, really, I—

NORA: Christine is tremendously clever at book-keeping, and she is frightfully anxious to work under some clever man, so as to perfect herself—

HELMER: Very sensible, Mrs. Linde. 730

NORA: And when she heard you had been appointed manager of the Bank—the news was telegraphed, you know—she travelled here as quick as she could. Torvald, I am sure you will be able to do something for Christine, for my sake, won't you? 735

HELMER: Well, it is not altogether impossible. I presume you are a widow, Mrs. Linde?

MRS. LINDE: Yes.

HELMER: And have had some experience of book-keeping? 740

MRS. LINDE: Yes, a fair amount.

HELMER: Ah! well, it's very likely I may be able to find something for you—

745 NORA: (*clapping her hands*) What did I tell you? What did I tell you?

HELMER: You have just come at a fortunate moment, Mrs. Linde.

MRS. LINDE: How am I to thank you?

HELMER: There is no need. (*Puts on his coat.*) But to-day
750 you must excuse me—

RANK: Wait a minute; I will come with you. (*Brings his fur coat from the hall and warms it at the fire.*)

NORA: Don't be long away, Torvald dear.

HELMER: About an hour, not more.

755 NORA: Are you going too, Christine?

MRS. LINDE: (*putting on her cloak*) Yes, I must go and look for a room.

HELMER: Oh, well then, we can walk down the street together.

760 NORA: (*helping her*) What a pity it is we are so short of space here; I am afraid it is impossible for us—

MRS. LINDE: Please don't think of it! Good-bye, Nora dear, and many thanks.

NORA: Good-bye for the present. Of course you will
765 come back this evening. And you too, Dr. Rank. What do you say? If you are well enough? Oh, you must be! Wrap yourself up well. (*They go to the door all talking together. Children's voices are heard on the staircase.*)

770 NORA: There they are! There they are! (*She runs to open the door. The NURSE comes in with the children.*) Come in! Come in! (*Stoops and kisses them.*) Oh, you sweet blessings! Look at them, Christine. Aren't they darlings?

RANK: Don't let us stand here in the draught.

775 HELMER: Come along, Mrs. Linde; the place will only be bearable for a mother now!

(*RANK, HELMER, and MRS. LINDE go downstairs. The NURSE comes forward with the children; NORA shuts the hall door.*)

NORA: How fresh and well you look! Such red cheeks!—like apples and roses. (*The children all talk at once while she speaks to them.*) Have you had great fun? That's

Torvald greets Mrs. Linde.

splendid! What, you pulled both Emmy and Bob 780
along on the sledge?—both at once?—that *was* good. You are a clever boy, Ivar. Let me take her for a little, Anne. My sweet little baby doll! (*Takes the baby from the MAID and dances it up and down.*) Yes, yes, mother will dance with Bob too. What? Have you been 785
snowballing? I wish I had been there too! No, no, I will take their things off, Anne; please let me do it, it is such fun. Go in now, you look half frozen. There is some hot coffee for you on the stove.

(*The NURSE goes into the room on the left. NORA takes off the children's things and throws them about, while they all talk to her at once.*)

NORA: Really? Did a big dog run after you? But it 790
didn't bite you? No, dogs don't bite nice little dolly children. You mustn't look at the parcels, Ivar. What are they? Ah, I daresay you would like to know. No, no—it's something nasty! Come, let us have a game! What shall we play at? Hide and Seek? Yes, we'll play 795
Hide and Seek. Bob shall hide first. Must I hide? Very well, I'll hide first. (*She and the children laugh and shout, and romp in and out of the room; at last NORA hides under the table, the children rush in and out for her, but do not see her; they hear her smothered laughter, run to 800
the table, lift up the cloth and find her. Shouts of laughter. She crawls forward and pretends to frighten them. Fresh laughter. Meanwhile there has been a knock at the hall door, but none of them has noticed it. The door is half opened, and KROGSTAD appears. He waits a little; the game goes on.*) 805

KROGSTAD: Excuse me, Mrs. Helmer.

NORA: (*with a stifled cry, turns round and gets up on to her knees*) Ah! what do you want?

KROGSTAD: Excuse me, the outer door was ajar; I suppose someone forgot to shut it. 810

NORA: *(rising)* My husband is out, Mr. Krogstad.

KROGSTAD: I know that.

NORA: What do you want here, then?

KROGSTAD: A word with you.

815 **NORA:** With me?— *(To the children, gently.)* Go in to nurse. What? No, the strange man won't do mother any harm. When he has gone we will have another game. *(She takes the children into the room on the left, and shuts the door after them.)* You want to speak to me?

820 **KROGSTAD:** Yes, I do.

NORA: To-day? It is not the first of the month yet.

KROGSTAD: No, it is Christmas Eve, and it will depend on yourself what sort of a Christmas you will spend.

825 **NORA:** What do you mean? To-day it is absolutely impossible for me—

KROGSTAD: We won't talk about that till later on. This is something different. I presume you can give me a moment?

830 **NORA:** Yes—yes, I can—although—

KROGSTAD: Good. I was in Olsen's Restaurant and saw your husband going down the street—

NORA: Yes?

KROGSTAD: With a lady.

835 **NORA:** What then?

KROGSTAD: May I make so bold as to ask if it was a Mrs. Linde?

NORA: It was.

KROGSTAD: Just arrived in town?

840 **NORA:** Yes, to-day.

KROGSTAD: She is a great friend of yours, isn't she?

NORA: She is. But I don't see—

KROGSTAD: I knew her too, once upon a time.

NORA: I am aware of that.

845 **KROGSTAD:** Are you? So you know all about it; I thought as much. Then I can ask you, without beating about the bush—is Mrs. Linde to have an appointment in the Bank?

NORA: What right have you to question me, Mr. 850 Krogstad?—You, one of my husband's subordinates!

But since you ask, you shall know. Yes, Mrs. Linde *is* to have an appointment. And it was I who pleaded her cause, Mr. Krogstad, let me tell you that.

KROGSTAD: I was right in what I thought, then.

855 **NORA:** *(walking up and down the stage)* Sometimes one has a tiny little bit of influence, I should hope. Because one is a woman, it does not necessarily follow that—. When anyone is in a subordinate position, Mr. Krogstad, they should really be careful to avoid offending anyone who—who— 860

KROGSTAD: Who has influence?

NORA: Exactly.

KROGSTAD: *(changing his tone)* Mrs. Helmer, you will be so good as to use your influence on my behalf.

NORA: What? What do you mean? 865

KROGSTAD: You will be so kind as to see that I am allowed to keep my subordinate position in the Bank.

NORA: What do you mean by that? Who proposes to take your post away from you?

KROGSTAD: Oh, there is no necessity to keep up the 870 pretence of ignorance. I can quite understand that your friend is not very anxious to expose herself to the chance of rubbing shoulders with me; and I quite understand, too, whom I have to thank for being turned off. 875

NORA: But I assure you—

KROGSTAD: Very likely; but, to come to the point, the time has come when I should advise you to use your influence to prevent that.

NORA: But, Mr. Krogstad, I *have* no influence. 880

KROGSTAD: Haven't you? I thought you said yourself just now—

NORA: Naturally I did not mean you to put that construction on it. I! What should make you think I have any influence of that kind with my husband? 885

KROGSTAD: Oh, I have known your husband from our student days. I don't suppose he is any more unassailable than other husbands.

NORA: If you speak slightingly of my husband, I shall turn you out of the house. 890

KROGSTAD: You are bold, Mrs. Helmer.

NORA: I am not afraid of you any longer. As soon as the New Year comes, I shall in a very short time be free of the whole thing.

895 **KROGSTAD:** (*controlling himself*)   Listen to me, Mrs. Helmer. If necessary, I am prepared to fight for my small post in the Bank as if I were fighting for my life.

NORA: So it seems.

900 **KROGSTAD:**   It is not only for the sake of the money; indeed, that weighs least with me in the matter. There is another reason—well, I may as well tell you. My position is this. I daresay you know, like everybody else, that once, many years ago, I was guilty of an indiscretion.

905 **NORA:**   I think I have heard something of the kind.

KROGSTAD: The matter never came into court; but every way seemed to be closed to me after that. So I took to the business that you know of. I had to do something; and, honestly, I don't think I've been one 910 of the worst. But now I must cut myself free from all that. My sons are growing up; for their sake I must try and win back as much respect as I can in the town. This post in the Bank was like the first step up for me—and now your husband is going to kick me 915 downstairs again into the mud.

NORA: But you must believe me, Mr. Krogstad; it is not in my power to help you at all.

KROGSTAD: Then it is because you haven't the will; but I have means to compel you.

920 **NORA:**   You don't mean that you will tell my husband that I owe you money?

KROGSTAD: Hm!—suppose I were to tell him?

Krogstad (David Calder) confronts Nora with the discrepancy in her father's signature.

NORA: It would be perfectly infamous of you. (*Sobbing.*) To think of his learning my secret, which has been my joy and pride, in such an ugly, clumsy way—that 925 he should learn it from you! And it would put me in a horribly disagreeable position—

KROGSTAD: Only disagreeable?

NORA: (*impetuously*)   Well, do it, then!—and it will be the worse for you. My husband will see for himself 930 what a blackguard you are, and you certainly won't keep your post then.

KROGSTAD: I asked you if it was only a disagreeable scene at home that you were afraid of?

NORA: If my husband does get to know of it, of course 935 he will at once pay you what is still owing, and we shall have nothing more to do with you.

KROGSTAD: (*coming a step nearer*)   Listen to me, Mrs. Helmer. Either you have a very bad memory or you know very little of business. I shall be obliged to 940 remind you of a few details.

NORA: What do you mean?

KROGSTAD: When your husband was ill, you came to me to borrow two hundred and fifty pounds.

NORA: I didn't know anyone else to go to. 945

KROGSTAD: I promised to get you that amount—

NORA: Yes, and you did so.

KROGSTAD: I promised to get you that amount, on certain conditions. Your mind was so taken up with your husband's illness, and you were so anxious to 950 get the money for your journey, that you seem to have paid no attention to the conditions of our bargain. Therefore it will not be amiss if I remind you of them. Now, I promised to get the money on the security of a bond which I drew up. 955

NORA: Yes, and which I signed.

KROGSTAD: Good. But below your signature there were a few lines constituting your father a surety for the money; those lines your father should have signed. 960

NORA: Should? He did sign them.

KROGSTAD: I had left the date blank; that is to say, your father should himself have inserted the date on which he signed the paper. Do you remember that?

NORA: Yes, I think I remember— 965

KROGSTAD: Then I gave you the bond to send by post to your father. Is that not so?

NORA: Yes.

KROGSTAD: And you naturally did so at once, because five or six days afterwards you brought me the bond with your father's signature. And then I gave you the money.

NORA: Well, haven't I been paying it off regularly?

KROGSTAD: Fairly so, yes. But—to come back to the matter in hand—that must have been a very trying time for you, Mrs. Helmer?

NORA: It was, indeed.

KROGSTAD: Your father was very ill, wasn't he?

NORA: He was very near his end.

KROGSTAD: He died soon afterwards?

NORA: Yes.

KROGSTAD: Tell me, Mrs. Helmer, can you by any chance remember what day your father died?—on what day of the month, I mean.

NORA: Papa died on the 29th of September.

KROGSTAD: That is correct; I have ascertained it for myself. And, as that is so, there is a discrepancy (*taking a paper from his pocket*) which I cannot account for.

NORA: What discrepancy? I don't know—

KROGSTAD: The discrepancy consists, Mrs. Helmer, in the fact that your father signed this bond three days after his death.

NORA: What do you mean? I don't understand—

KROGSTAD: Your father died on the 29th of September. But, look here; your father has dated his signature the 2nd of October. It is a discrepancy, isn't it? (*NORA is silent.*) Can you explain it to me? (*NORA is still silent.*) It is a remarkable thing, too, that the words "2nd of October" as well as the year, are not written in your father's handwriting but in one that I think I know. Well, of course it can be explained; your father may have forgotten to date his signature, and someone else may have dated it haphazard before they knew of his death. There is no harm in that. It all depends on the signature of the name; and *that* is genuine, I suppose, Mrs. Helmer? It was your father himself who signed his name here?

NORA: (*after a short pause, throws her head up and looks defiantly at him*) No, it was not. It was I that wrote papa's name.

KROGSTAD: Are you aware that is a dangerous confession?

NORA: In what way? You shall have your money soon.

KROGSTAD: Let me ask you a question; why did you not send the paper to your father?

NORA: It was impossible; papa was so ill. If I had asked him for his signature, I should have had to tell him what the money was to be used for; and when he was so ill himself I couldn't tell him that my husband's life was in danger—it was impossible.

KROGSTAD: It would have been better for you if you had given up your trip abroad.

NORA: No, that was impossible. That trip was to save my husband's life; I couldn't give that up.

KROGSTAD: But did it never occur to you that you were committing a fraud on me?

NORA: I couldn't take that into account; I didn't trouble myself about you at all. I couldn't bear you, because you put so many heartless difficulties in my way, although you knew what a dangerous condition my husband was in.

KROGSTAD: Mrs. Helmer, you evidently do not realise clearly what it is that you have been guilty of. But I can assure you that my one false step, which lost me all my reputation, was nothing more or nothing worse than what you have done.

NORA: You? Do you ask me to believe that you were brave enough to run a risk to save your wife's life?

KROGSTAD: The law cares nothing about motives.

NORA: Then it must be a very foolish law.

KROGSTAD: Foolish or not, it is the law by which you will be judged, if I produce this paper in court.

NORA: I don't believe it. Is a daughter not to be allowed to spare her dying father anxiety and care? Is a wife not to be allowed to save her husband's life? I don't know much about law; but I am certain that there must be laws permitting such things as that. Have you no knowledge of such laws—you who are a lawyer? You must be a very poor lawyer, Mr. Krogstad.

KROGSTAD: Maybe. But matters of business—such business as you and I have had together—do you think I don't understand that? Very well. Do as you please. But let me tell you this—if I lose my position a second time, you shall lose yours with me. (*He bows, and goes out through the hall.*)

NORA: (*appears buried in thought for a short time, then tosses her head*) Nonsense! Trying to frighten me like that!—I am not so silly as he thinks. (*Begins to busy* *herself putting the children's things in order.)* And yet—?

1060 No, it's impossible! I did it for love's sake.

THE CHILDREN: *(in the doorway on the left)* Mother, the stranger man has gone out through the gate.

NORA: Yes, dears, I know. But, don't tell anyone about the stranger man. Do you hear? Not even papa.

1065 **CHILDREN:** No, mother; but will you come and play again?

NORA: No, no,—not now.

CHILDREN: But, mother, you promised us.

NORA: Yes, but I can't now. Run away in; I have such a lot to do. Run away in, my sweet little darlings. *(She*
1070 *gets them into the room by degrees and shuts the door on them; then sits down on the sofa, takes up a piece of needle-work and sews a few stitches, but soon stops.)* No! *(Throws down the work, gets up, goes to the hall door and calls out.)* Helen! bring the Tree in. *(Goes to the table on the left,*
1075 *opens a drawer, and stops again.)* No, no! it is quite impossible!

MAID: *(coming in with the Tree)* Where shall I put it, ma'am?

NORA: Here, in the middle of the floor.

1080 **MAID:** Shall I get you anything else?

NORA: No, thank you. I have all I want.

(Exit MAID.*)*

NORA: *(begins dressing the tree)* A candle here—and flowers here—. The horrible man! It's all nonsense— there's nothing wrong. The Tree shall be splendid!
1085 I will do everything I can think of to please you, Torvald!—I will sing for you, dance for you— *(*HELMER *comes in with some papers under his arm.)* Oh! are you back already?

HELMER: Yes. Has any one been here?

1090 **NORA:** Here? No.

HELMER: That is strange. I saw Krogstad going out of the gate.

1095 **NORA:** Did you? Oh yes, I forgot, Krogstad was here for a moment.

HELMER: Nora, I can see from your manner that he has been here begging you to say a good word for him.

NORA: Yes.

1100 **HELMER:** And you were to appear to do it of your own accord; you were to conceal from me the fact of his having been here; didn't he beg that of you too?

NORA: Yes, Torvald, but—

HELMER: Nora, Nora, and you would be a party to that sort of thing? To have any talk with a man like 1105 that, and give him any sort of promise? And to tell me a lie into the bargain?

NORA: A lie—?

HELMER: Didn't you tell me no one had been here? *(Shakes his finger at her).* My little song-bird must never 1110 do that again. A song-bird must have a clean beak to chirp with—no false notes! *(Puts his arm round her waist.)* That is so, isn't it? Yes, I am sure it is. *(Lets her go.)* We will say no more about it. *(Sits down by the stove.)* How warm and snug it is here! *(Turns over his* 1115 *papers.)*

NORA: *(after a short pause, during which she busies herself with the Christmas Tree)* Torvald!

HELMER: Yes.

NORA: I am looking forward tremendously to the fancy- 1120 dress ball at the Stenborgs' the day after to-morrow.

HELMER: And I am tremendously curious to see what you are going to surprise me with.

NORA: It was very silly of me to want to do that.

HELMER: What do you mean? 1125

NORA: I can't hit upon anything that will do; every- thing I think of seems so silly and insignificant.

HELMER: Does my little Nora acknowledge that at last?

NORA: *(standing behind his chair with her arms on the back of it)* Are you very busy, Torvald? 1130

HELMER: Well—

NORA: What are all those papers?

HELMER: Bank business.

NORA: Already?

HELMER: I have got authority from the retiring man- 1135 ager to undertake the necessary changes in the staff and in the rearrangement of the work; and I must make use of the Christmas week for that, so as to have everything in order for the new year.

NORA: Then that was why this poor Krogstad— 1140

HELMER: Hm!

NORA: *(leans against the back of his chair and strokes his hair)* If you hadn't been so busy I should have asked you a tremendously big favour, Torvald.

HELMER: What is that? Tell me. 1145

Nora and Torvald (Trevor Eve) discuss Krogstad's visit.

NORA: There is no one has such good taste as you. And I do so want to look nice at the fancy-dress ball. Torvald, couldn't you take me in hand and decide what I shall go as, and what sort of a dress I shall wear?

1150 **HELMER:** Aha! so my obstinate little woman is obliged to get someone to come to her rescue?

NORA: Yes, Torvald, I can't get along a bit without your help.

HELMER: Very well, I will think it over, we shall man-
1155 age to hit upon something.

NORA: That is nice of you. (*Goes to the Christmas Tree. A short pause.*) How pretty the red flowers look—. But, tell me, was it really something very bad that this Krogstad was guilty of?

1160 **HELMER:** He forged someone's name. Have you any idea what that means?

NORA: Isn't it possible that he was driven to do it by necessity?

HELMER: Yes; or, as in so many cases, by imprudence.
1165 I am not so heartless as to condemn a man alto-gether because of a single false step of that kind.

NORA: No, you wouldn't, would you, Torvald!

HELMER: Many a man has been able to retrieve his character, if he has openly confessed his fault and
1170 taken his punishment.

NORA: Punishment—?

HELMER: But Krogstad did nothing of that sort; he got himself out of it by a cunning trick, and that is why he has gone under altogether.

NORA: But do you think it would—? 1175

HELMER: Just think how a guilty man like that has to lie and play the hypocrite with every one, how he has to wear a mask in the presence of those near and dear to him, even before his own wife and children. And about the children—that is the most terrible 1180 part of it all, Nora.

NORA: How?

HELMER: Because such an atmosphere of lies infects and poisons the whole life of a home. Each breath the children take in such a house is full of the germs 1185 of evil.

NORA: (*coming nearer him*) Are you sure of that?

HELMER: My dear, I have often seen it in the course of my life as a lawyer. Almost everyone who has gone to the bad early in life has had a deceitful mother. 1190

NORA: Why do you only say—mother?

HELMER: It seems most commonly to be the mother's influence, though naturally a bad father's would have the same result. Every lawyer is familiar with the fact. This Krogstad, now, has been persistently 1195 poisoning his own children with lies and dissimula-tion; that is why I say he has lost all moral character. (*Holds out his hands to her.*) That is why my sweet little Nora must promise me not to plead his cause. Give me your hand on it. Come, come, what is this? Give 1200 me your hand. There now, that's settled. I assure you it would be quite impossible for me to work with him; I literally feel physically ill when I am in the company of such people.

NORA: (*takes her hand out of his and goes to the opposite side of* 1205 *the Christmas Tree*) How hot it is in here; and I have such a lot to do.

HELMER: (*getting up and putting his papers in order*) Yes, and I must try and read through some of these be-fore dinner; and I must think about your costume, 1210 too. And it is just possible I may have something ready in gold paper to hang up on the Tree. (*Puts his hand on her head.*) My precious little singing-bird! (*He goes into his room and shuts the door after him.*)

NORA: (*after a pause, whispers*) No, no—it isn't true. It's 1215 impossible; it must be impossible.

(*The* NURSE *opens the door on the left.*)

NURSE: The little ones are begging so hard to be al-lowed to come in to mamma.

NORA: No, no, no! Don't let them come in to me! You stay with them, Anne. 1220

NURSE: Very well, ma'am. *(Shuts the door.)*

NORA: *(pale with terror)*   Deprave my little children? Poison my home? *(A short pause. Then she tosses her head.)* It's not true. It can't possibly be true.

ACT II

THE SAME SCENE: *The Christmas Tree is in the corner by the piano, stripped of its ornaments and with burnt-down candle-ends on its dishevelled branches.* NORA's *cloak and hat are lying on the sofa. She is alone in the room, walking about uneasily. She stops by the sofa and takes up her cloak.*

NORA: *(drops her cloak)*   Someone is coming now! *(Goes to the door and listens.)* No—it is no one. Of course, no one will come to-day, Christmas Day—nor to-morrow either. But, perhaps—*(opens the door and looks out).* No,
5 nothing in the letter-box; it is quite empty. *(Comes forward.)* What rubbish! of course he can't be in earnest about it. Such a thing couldn't happen; it is impossible—I have three little children.

(Enter the NURSE *from the room on the left, carrying a big cardboard box.)*

NURSE: At last I have found the box with the fancy
10 dress.

NORA: Thanks; put it on the table.

NURSE: *(doing so)*   But it is very much in want of mending.

NORA: I should like to tear it into a hundred thousand
15 pieces.

Nora confides in the nurse (Helen Blatch) her fears of being away from the children.

NURSE: What an idea! It can easily be put in order—just a little patience.

NORA: Yes, I will go and get Mrs. Linde to come and help me with it.

NURSE: What, out again? In this horrible weather?   20
You will catch cold, ma'am, and make yourself ill.

NORA: Well, worse than that might happen. How are the children?

NURSE: The poor little souls are playing with their
Christmas presents, but—   25

NORA: Do they ask much for me?

NURSE: You see, they are so accustomed to have their mamma with them.

NORA: Yes, but, nurse, I shall not be able to be so much with them now as I was before.   30

NURSE: Oh well, young children easily get accustomed to anything.

NORA: Do you think so? Do you think they would forget their mother if she went away altogether?

NURSE: Good heavens!—went away altogether?   35

NORA: Nurse, I want you to tell me something I have often wondered about—how could you have the heart to put your own child out among strangers?

NURSE: I was obliged to, if I wanted to be little Nora's nurse.   40

NORA: Yes, but how could you be willing to do it?

NURSE: What, when I was going to get such a good place by it? A poor girl who has got into trouble should be glad to. Besides, that wicked man didn't do a single thing for me.   45

NORA: But I suppose your daughter has quite forgotten you.

NURSE: No, indeed she hasn't. She wrote to me when she was confirmed, and when she was married.

NORA: *(putting her arms round her neck)*   Dear old Anne,   50
you were a good mother to me when I was little.

NURSE: Little Nora, poor dear, had no other mother but me.

NORA: And if my little ones had no other mother, I am sure you would— What nonsense I am talking!   55
(Opens the box.) Go in to them. Now I must—. You will see to-morrow how charming I shall look.

NURSE: I am sure there will be no one at the ball so charming as you, ma'am. *(Goes into the room on the left.)*

60

NORA: *(begins to unpack the box, but soon pushes it away from her)* If only I dared go out. If only no one would come. If only I could be sure nothing would happen here in the meantime. Stuff and nonsense! No one will come. Only I mustn't think about it. I will brush my muff. What lovely, lovely gloves! Out of my thoughts, out of my thoughts! One, two, three, four, five, six— *(Screams.)* Ah! there is someone coming—. *(Makes a movement towards the door, but stands irresolute.)*

65

(Enter MRS. LINDE *from the hall, where she has taken off her cloak and hat.)*

70 **NORA:** Oh, it's you, Christine. There is no one else out there, is there? How good of you to come!

MRS. LINDE: I heard you were up asking for me.

NORA: Yes, I was passing by. As a matter of fact, it is something you could help me with. Let us sit down here on the sofa. Look here. To-morrow evening there is to be a fancy-dress ball at the Stenborgs', who live above us; and Torvald wants me to go as a Neapolitan fisher-girl, and dance the Tarantella that I learnt at Capri.

75

80 **MRS. LINDE:** I see; you are going to keep up the character.

NORA: Yes, Torvald wants me to. Look, here is the dress; Torvald had it made for me there, but now it is all so torn, and I haven't any idea—

85 **MRS. LINDE:** We will easily put that right. It is only some of the trimming come unsewn here and there. Needle and thread? Now then, that's all we want.

NORA: It *is* nice of you.

MRS. LINDE: *(sewing)* So you are going to be dressed up to-morrow, Nora. I will tell you what—I shall come in for a moment and see you in your fine feathers. But I have completely forgotten to thank you for a delightful evening yesterday.

90

NORA: *(gets up, and crosses the stage)* Well, I don't think yesterday was as pleasant as usual. You ought to have come to town a little earlier, Christine. Certainly Torvald does understand how to make a house dainty and attractive.

95

100 **MRS. LINDE:** And so do you, it seems to me; you are not your father's daughter for nothing. But tell me, is Doctor Rank always as depressed as he was yesterday?

NORA: No; yesterday it was very noticeable. I must tell you that he suffers from a very dangerous disease. He has consumption of the spine, poor creature. His father was a horrible man who committed all sorts of excesses; and that is why his son was sickly from childhood, do you understand?

105

MRS. LINDE: *(dropping her sewing)* But, my dearest Nora, how do you know anything about such things?

NORA: *(walking about)* Pooh! When you have three children, you get visits now and then from—from married women, who know something of medical matters, and they talk about one thing and another.

110

MRS. LINDE: *(goes on sewing. A short silence)* Does Doctor Rank come here every day?

115

NORA: Every day regularly. He is Torvald's most intimate friend, and a great friend of mine too. He is just like one of the family.

MRS. LINDE: But tell me this—is he perfectly sincere? I mean, isn't he the kind of man that is very anxious to make himself agreeable?

120

NORA: Not in the least. What makes you think that?

MRS. LINDE: When you introduced him to me yesterday, he declared he had often heard my name mentioned in this house; but afterwards I noticed that your husband hadn't the slightest idea who I was. So how could Doctor Rank—?

125

NORA: That is quite right, Christine. Torvald is so absurdly fond of me that he wants me absolutely to himself, as he says. At first he used to seem almost jealous if I mentioned any of the dear folk at home, so naturally I gave up doing so. But I often talk about such things with Doctor Rank, because he likes hearing about them.

130

135

MRS. LINDE: Listen to me, Nora. You are still very like a child in many things, and I am older than you in many ways and have a little more experience. Let me tell you this—you ought to make an end of it with Doctor Rank.

140

NORA: What ought I to make an end of?

MRS. LINDE: Of two things, I think. Yesterday you talked some nonsense about a rich admirer who was to leave you money—

NORA: An admirer who doesn't exist, unfortunately! But what then?

145

MRS. LINDE: Is Doctor Rank a man of means?

NORA: Yes, he is.

MRS. LINDE: And has no one to provide for?

150 **NORA:** No, no one; but—

MRS. LINDE: And comes here every day?

NORA: Yes, I told you so.

MRS. LINDE: But how can this well-bred man be so tactless?

155 **NORA:** I don't understand you at all.

MRS. LINDE: Don't prevaricate, Nora. Do you suppose I don't guess who lent you the two hundred and fifty pounds?

NORA: Are you out of your senses? How can you think
160 of such a thing! A friend of ours, who comes here every day! Do you realise what a horribly painful position that would be?

MRS. LINDE: Then it really isn't he?

NORA: No, certainly not. It would never have en-
165 tered into my head for a moment. Besides, he had no money to lend then; he came into his money afterwards.

MRS. LINDE: Well, I think that was lucky for you, my dear Nora.

170 **NORA:** No, it would never have come into my head to ask Doctor Rank. Although I am quite sure that if I had asked him—

MRS. LINDE: But of course you won't.

NORA: Of course not. I have no reason to think it could
175 possibly be necessary. But I am quite sure that if I told Doctor Rank—

MRS. LINDE: Behind your husband's back?

NORA: I must make an end of it with the other one, and that will be behind his back too. I *must* make an
180 end of it with him.

MRS. LINDE: Yes, that is what I told you yesterday, but—

NORA: *(walking up and down)* A man can put a thing like that straight much easier than a woman—

185 **MRS. LINDE:** One's husband, yes.

NORA: Nonsense! *(Standing still.)* When you pay off a debt you get your bond back, don't you?

MRS. LINDE: Yes, as a matter of course.

NORA: And can tear it into a hundred thousand pieces,
190 and burn it up—the nasty dirty paper!

Nora and Mrs. Linde discuss Dr. Rank and the problem of Krogstad.

MRS. LINDE: *(looks hard at her, lays down her sewing and gets up slowly)* Nora, you are concealing something from me.

NORA: Do I look as if I were?

MRS. LINDE: Something has happened to you since 195
yesterday morning. Nora, what is it?

NORA: *(going nearer to her)* Christine! *(Listens.)* Hush! there's Torvald come home. Do you mind going in to the children for the present? Torvald can't bear to see dressmaking going on. Let Anne help you. 200

MRS. LINDE: *(gathering some of the things together)* Certainly—but I am not going away from here till we have had it out with one another. *(She goes into the room on the left, as* HELMER *comes in from the hall.)*

NORA: *(going up to* HELMER*)* I have wanted you so much, 205
Torvald dear.

HELMER: Was that the dressmaker?

NORA: No, it was Christine; she is helping me to put my dress in order. You will see I shall look quite smart.

HELMER: Wasn't that a happy thought of mine, now? 210

NORA: Splendid! But don't you think it is nice of me, too, to do as you wish?

HELMER: Nice?—because you do as your husband wishes? Well, well, you little rogue, I am sure you did not mean it in that way. But I am not going to 215
disturb you; you will want to be trying on your dress, I expect.

NORA: I suppose you are going to work.

HELMER: Yes. *(Shows her a bundle of papers.)* Look at that. I have just been into the bank. *(Turns to go into* 220
his room.)

NORA: Torvald.

HELMER: Yes.

NORA: If your little squirrel were to ask you for some-
225 thing very, very prettily—?

HELMER: What then?

NORA: Would you do it?

HELMER: I should like to hear what it is, first.

NORA: Your squirrel would run about and do all her
230 tricks if you would be nice, and do what she wants.

HELMER: Speak plainly.

NORA: Your skylark would chirp about in every room,
with her song rising and falling—

HELMER: Well, my skylark does that anyhow.

235 **NORA:**   I would play the fairy and dance for you in the
moonlight, Torvald.

HELMER: Nora—you surely don't mean that request
you made to me this morning?

NORA: (*going near him*) Yes, Torvald, I beg you so
240 earnestly—

HELMER: Have you really the courage to open up that
question again?

NORA: Yes, dear, you *must* do as I ask; you *must* let
Krogstad keep his post in the bank.

245 **HELMER:**   My dear Nora, it is his post that I have arranged Mrs. Linde shall have.

NORA: Yes, you have been awfully kind about that; but
you could just as well dismiss some other clerk instead of Krogstad.

250 **HELMER:**   This is simply incredible obstinacy! Because
you chose to give him a thoughtless promise that you
would speak for him, I am expected to—

NORA: That isn't the reason, Torvald. It is for your own
sake. This fellow writes in the most scurrilous news-
255 papers; you have told me so yourself. He can do you
an unspeakable amount of harm. I am frightened to
death of him—

HELMER: Ah, I understand; it is recollections of the
past that scare you.

260 **NORA:**   What do you mean?

HELMER: Naturally you are thinking of your father.

NORA: Yes—yes, of course. Just recall to your mind
what these malicious creatures wrote in the papers

about papa, and how horribly they slandered him. I
believe they would have procured his dismissal if the 265
Department had not sent you over to inquire into it,
and if you had not been so kindly disposed and helpful to him.

HELMER: My little Nora, there is an important difference between your father and me. Your father's repu- 270
tation as a public official was not above suspicion.
Mine is, and I hope it will continue to be so, as long
as I hold my office.

NORA: You never can tell what mischief these men
may contrive. We ought to be so well off, so snug 275
and happy here in our peaceful home, and have no
cares—you and I and the children, Torvald! That is
why I beg you so earnestly—

HELMER: And it is just by interceding for him that you
make it impossible for me to keep him. It is already 280
known at the Bank that I mean to dismiss Krogstad.
Is it to get about now that the new manager has
changed his mind at his wife's bidding—

NORA: And what if it did?

HELMER: Of course!—if only this obstinate little per- 285
son can get her way! Do you suppose I am going to
make myself ridiculous before my whole staff, to let
people think that I am a man to be swayed by all
sorts of outside influence? I should very soon feel the
consequences of it, I can tell you! And besides, there 290
is one thing that makes it quite impossible for me to
have Krogstad in the Bank as long as I am manager.

NORA: Whatever is that?

HELMER: His moral failings I might perhaps have
overlooked, if necessary— 295

NORA: Yes, you could—couldn't you?

HELMER: And I hear he is a good worker, too. But I
knew him when we were boys. It was one of those
rash friendships that so often prove an incubus in
after life. I may as well tell you plainly, we were once 300
on very intimate terms with one another. But this
tactless fellow lays no restraint on himself when
other people are present. On the contrary, he thinks
it gives him the right to adopt a familiar tone with
me, and every minute it is "I say, Helmer, old fellow!" 305
and that sort of thing. I assure you it is extremely
painful for me. He would make my position in the
Bank intolerable.

NORA: Torvald, I don't believe you mean that.

HELMER: Don't you? Why not? 310

NORA: Because it is such a narrow-minded way of looking at things.

HELMER: What are you saying? Narrow-minded? Do you think I am narrow-minded?

315   **NORA:**   No, just the opposite, dear—and it is exactly for that reason.

HELMER: It's the same thing. You say my point of view is narrow-minded, so I must be so too. Narrow-minded! Very well—I must put an end to this. *(Goes to the hall door and calls.)* Helen!

320

NORA: What are you going to do?

HELMER: *(looking among his papers)*   Settle it. *(Enter* MAID.*)* Look here; take this letter and go downstairs with it at once. Find a messenger and tell him to deliver it, and be quick. The address is on it, and here is the money.

325

MAID: Very well, sir. *(Exit with the letter.)*

HELMER: *(putting his papers together)*   Now then, little Miss Obstinate.

330   **NORA:** *(breathlessly)*   Torvald—what was that letter?

HELMER: Krogstad's dismissal.

NORA: Call her back, Torvald! There is still time. Oh, Torvald, call her back! Do it for my sake—for your own sake—for the children's sake! Do you hear me, Torvald? Call her back! You don't know what that letter can bring upon us.

335

HELMER: It's too late.

NORA: Yes, it's too late.

HELMER: My dear Nora, I can forgive the anxiety you are in, although really it is an insult to me. It is, indeed. Isn't it an insult to think that I should be afraid of a starving quill-driver's vengeance? But I forgive you nevertheless, because it is such eloquent witness to your great love for me. *(Takes her in his arms.)* And that is as it should be, my own darling Nora. Come what will, you may be sure I shall have both courage and strength if they be needed. You will see I am man enough to take everything upon myself.

340

345

NORA: *(in a horror-stricken voice)*   What do you mean by that?

350

HELMER: Everything, I say—

NORA: *(recovering herself)*   You will never have to do that.

HELMER: That's right. Well, we will share it, Nora, as man and wife should. That is how it shall be.

(Caressing her.) Are you content now? There! there!—not these frightened dove's eyes! The whole thing is only the wildest fancy!—Now, you must go and play through the Tarantella and practise with your tambourine. I shall go into the inner office and shut the door, and I shall hear nothing; you can make as much noise as you please. *(Turns back at the door.)* And when Rank comes, tell him where he will find me. *(Nods to her, takes his papers and goes into his room, and shuts the door after him.)*

355

360

NORA: *(bewildered with anxiety, stands as if rooted to the spot, and whispers)*   He was capable of doing it. He will do it. He will do it in spite of everything.—No, not that! Never, never! Anything rather than that! Oh, for some help, some way out of it! *(The door-bell rings.)* Doctor Rank! Anything rather than that—anything, whatever it is! *(She puts her hands over her face, pulls herself together, goes to the door and opens it.* RANK *is standing without, hanging up his coat. During the following dialogue it begins to grow dark.)*

365

370

NORA: Good-day, Doctor Rank. I knew your ring. But you mustn't go in to Torvald now; I think he is busy with something.

375

RANK: And you?

NORA: *(brings him in and shuts the door after him)*   Oh, you know very well I always have time for you.

380

RANK: Thank you. I shall make use of as much of it as I can.

NORA: What do you mean by that? As much of it as you can?

RANK: Well, does that alarm you?

385

NORA: It was such a strange way of putting it. Is anything likely to happen?

RANK: Nothing but what I have long been prepared for. But I certainly didn't expect it to happen so soon.

NORA: *(gripping him by the arm)*   What have you found out? Doctor Rank, you must tell me.

390

RANK: *(sitting down by the stove)*   It is all up with me. And it can't be helped.

NORA: *(with a sigh of relief)*   Is it about yourself?

RANK: Who else? It is no use lying to one's self. I am the most wretched of all my patients, Mrs. Helmer. Lately I have been taking stock of my internal economy. Bankrupt! Probably within a month I shall lie rotting in the churchyard.

395

NORA: What an ugly thing to say!

400

Dr. Rank (Patrick Malahide) makes his confession to Nora.

RANK: The thing itself is cursedly ugly, and the worst of it is that I shall have to face so much more that is ugly before that. I shall only make one more examination of myself; when I have done that, I shall know pretty certainly when it will be that the horrors of dissolution will begin. There is something I want to tell you. Helmer's refined nature gives him an unconquerable disgust at everything that is ugly; I won't have him in my sick-room.

NORA: Oh, but, Doctor Rank—

RANK: I won't have him there. Not on any account. I bar my door to him. As soon as I am quite certain that the worst has come, I shall send you my card with a black cross on it, and then you will know that the loathsome end has begun.

NORA: You are quite absurd to-day. And I wanted you so much to be in a really good humour.

RANK: With death stalking beside me?—To have to pay this penalty for another man's sin! Is there any justice in that? And in every single family, in one way or another, some such inexorable retribution is being exacted—

NORA: *(putting her hands over her ears)* Rubbish! Do talk of something cheerful.

RANK: Oh, it's a mere laughing matter, the whole thing. My poor innocent spine has to suffer for my father's youthful amusements.

NORA: *(sitting at the table on the left)* I suppose you mean that he was too partial to asparagus and pâté de foie gras, don't you?

RANK: Yes, and to truffles.

NORA: Truffles, yes. And oysters too, I suppose?

RANK: Oysters, of course, that goes without saying.

NORA: And heaps of port and champagne. It is sad that all these nice things should take their revenge on our bones.

RANK: Especially that they should revenge themselves on the unlucky bones of those who have not had the satisfaction of enjoying them.

NORA: Yes, that's the saddest part of it all.

RANK: *(with a searching look at her)* Hm!—

NORA: *(after a short pause)* Why did you smile?

RANK: No, it was you that laughed.

NORA: No, it was you that smiled, Doctor Rank!

RANK: *(rising)* You are a greater rascal than I thought.

NORA: I am in a silly mood to-day.

RANK: So it seems.

NORA: *(putting her hands on his shoulders)* Dear, dear Doctor Rank, death mustn't take you away from Torvald and me.

RANK: It is a loss you would easily recover from. Those who are gone are soon forgotten.

NORA: *(looking at him anxiously)* Do you believe that?

RANK: People form new ties, and then—

NORA: Who will form new ties?

RANK: Both you and Helmer, when I am gone. You yourself are already on the high road to it, I think. What did that Mrs. Linde want here last night?

NORA: Oho!—you don't mean to say you are jealous of poor Christine?

RANK: Yes, I am. She will be my successor in this house. When I am done for, this woman will—

NORA: Hush! don't speak so loud. She is in that room.

RANK: To-day again. There, you see.

NORA: She has only come to sew my dress for me. Bless my soul, how unreasonable you are! *(Sits down on the sofa.)* Be nice now, Doctor Rank, and to-morrow you will see how beautifully I shall dance, and you can imagine I am doing it all for you—and for Torvald too, of course. *(Takes various things out of the box.)* Doctor Rank, come and sit down here, and I will show you something.

RANK: *(sitting down)* What is it?

NORA: Just look at those!

RANK: Silk stockings.

NORA: Flesh-coloured. Aren't they lovely? It is so dark here now, but to-morrow—. No, no, no! you must only look at the feet. Oh well, you may have leave to look at the legs too.

480 **RANK:** Hm!—

NORA: Why are you looking so critical? Don't you think they will fit me?

RANK: I have no means of forming an opinion about that.

485 **NORA:** (*looks at him for a moment*) For shame! (*Hits him lightly on the ear with the stockings.*) That's to punish you. (*Folds them up again.*)

RANK: And what other nice things am I to be allowed to see?

490 **NORA:** Not a single thing more, for being so naughty. (*She looks among the things, humming to herself.*)

RANK: (*after a short silence*) When I am sitting here, talking to you as intimately as this, I cannot imagine for a moment what would have become of me if I
495 had never come into this house.

NORA: (*smiling*) I believe you do feel thoroughly at home with us.

RANK: (*in a lower voice, looking straight in front of him*) And to be obliged to leave it all—

500 **NORA:** Nonsense, you are not going to leave it.

RANK: (*as before*) And not be able to leave behind one the slightest token of one's gratitude, scarcely even a fleeting regret—nothing but an empty place which the first comer can fill as well as any other.

505 **NORA:** And if I asked you now for a—? No!

RANK: For what?

NORA: For a big proof of your friendship—

RANK: Yes, yes!

NORA: I mean a tremendously big favour—

510 **RANK:** Would you really make me so happy for once?

NORA: Ah, but you don't know what it is yet.

RANK: No—but tell me.

NORA: I really can't, Doctor Rank. It is something out of all reason; it means advice, and help, and a
515 favour—

RANK: The bigger a thing it is the better. I can't conceive what it is you mean. Do tell me. Haven't I your confidence?

NORA: More than any one else. I know you are my truest and best friend, and so I will tell you what it is. 520 Well, Doctor Rank, it is something you must help me to prevent. You know how devotedly, how inexpressibly deeply Torvald loves me; he would never for a moment hesitate to give his life for me.

RANK: (*leaning towards her*) Nora—do you think he is 525 the only one—?

NORA: (*with a slight start*) The only one—?

RANK: The only one who would gladly give his life for your sake.

NORA: (*sadly*) Is that it? 530

RANK: I was determined you should know it before I went away, and there will never be a better opportunity than this. Now you know it, Nora. And now you know, too, that you can trust me as you would trust no one else. 535

NORA: (*rises, deliberately and quietly*) Let me pass.

RANK: (*makes room for her to pass him, but sits still*) Nora!

NORA: (*at the hall door*) Helen, bring in the lamp. (*Goes over to the stove.*) Dear Doctor Rank, that was really horrid of you. 540

RANK: To have loved you as much as any one else does? Was that horrid?

NORA: No, but to go and tell me so. There was really no need—

RANK: What do you mean? Did you know—? (MAID 545 *enters with lamp, puts it down on the table, and goes out.*) Nora—Mrs. Helmer—tell me, had you any idea of this?

NORA: Oh, how do I know whether I had or whether I hadn't? I really can't tell you— To think you could 550 be so clumsy, Doctor Rank! We were getting on so nicely.

RANK: Well, at all events you know now that you can command me, body and soul. So won't you speak out?

NORA: (*looking at him*) After what happened? 555

RANK: I beg you to let me know what it is.

NORA: I can't tell you anything now.

RANK: Yes, yes. You mustn't punish me in that way. Let me have permission to do for you whatever a man may do. 560

NORA: You can do nothing for me now. Besides, I really don't need any help at all. You will find that the whole thing is merely fancy on my part. It really is so—of course it is! *(Sits down in the rocking-chair, and looks at him with a smile.)* You are a nice sort of man, Doctor Rank!—don't you feel ashamed of yourself, now the lamp has come?

RANK: Not a bit. But perhaps I had better go—for ever?

NORA: No, indeed, you shall not. Of course you must come here just as before. You know very well Torvald can't do without you.

RANK: Yes, but you?

NORA: Oh, I am always tremendously pleased when you come.

RANK: It is just that, that put me on the wrong track. You are a riddle to me. I have often thought that you would almost as soon be in my company as in Helmer's.

NORA: Yes—you see there are some people one loves best, and others whom one would almost always rather have as companions.

RANK: Yes, there is something in that.

NORA: When I was at home, of course I loved papa best. But I always thought it tremendous fun if I could steal down into the maids' room, because they never moralised at all, and talked to each other about such entertaining things.

RANK: I see—it is *their* place I have taken.

NORA: *(jumping up and going to him)* Oh, dear, nice Doctor Rank, I never meant that at all. But surely you can understand that being with Torvald is a little like being with papa—

(Enter MAID *from the hall.)*

MAID: If you please, ma'am. *(Whispers and hands her a card.)*

NORA: *(glancing at the card)* Oh! *(Puts it in her pocket.)*

RANK: Is there anything wrong?

NORA: No, no, not in the least. It is only something—it is my new dress—

RANK: What? Your dress is lying there.

NORA: Oh, yes, that one; but this is another. I ordered it. Torvald mustn't know about it—

RANK: Oho! Then that was the great secret.

NORA: Of course. Just go in to him; he is sitting in the inner room. Keep him as long as—

RANK: Make your mind easy; I won't let him escape. *(Goes into* HELMER's *room.)*

NORA: *(to the* MAID*)* And he is standing waiting in the kitchen?

MAID: Yes; he came up the back stairs.

NORA: But didn't you tell him no one was in?

MAID: Yes, but it was no good.

NORA: He won't go away?

MAID: No; he says he won't until he has seen you, ma'am.

NORA: Well, let him come in—but quietly. Helen, you mustn't say anything about it to any one. It is a surprise for my husband.

MAID: Yes, ma'am, I quite understand.   *(Exit.)*

NORA: This dreadful thing is going to happen! It will happen in spite of me! No, no, no, it can't happen—it shan't happen! *(She bolts the door of* HELMER's *room. The* MAID *opens the hall door for* KROGSTAD *and shuts it after him. He is wearing a fur coat, high boots and a fur cap.)*

NORA: *(advancing towards him)* Speak low—my husband is at home.

KROGSTAD: No matter about that.

NORA: What do you want of me?

KROGSTAD: An explanation of something.

NORA: Make haste then. What is it?

KROGSTAD: You know, I suppose, that I have got my dismissal.

Krogstad (Denholm Elliott) meets secretly with Nora to reveal his decision.

NORA: I couldn't prevent it, Mr. Krogstad. I fought as hard as I could on your side, but it was no good.

635 **KROGSTAD:** Does your husband love you so little, then? He knows what I can expose you to, and yet he ventures—

NORA: How can you suppose that he has any knowledge of the sort?

640 **KROGSTAD:** I didn't suppose so at all. It would not be the least like our dear Torvald Helmer to show so much courage—

NORA: Mr. Krogstad, a little respect for my husband, please.

645 **KROGSTAD:** Certainly—all the respect he deserves. But since you have kept the matter so carefully to yourself, I make bold to suppose that you have a little clearer idea, than you had yesterday, of what it actually is that you have done?

NORA: More than you could ever ever teach me.

650 **KROGSTAD:** Yes, such a bad lawyer as I am.

NORA: What is it you want of me?

KROGSTAD: Only to see how you were, Mrs. Helmer. I have been thinking about you all day long. A mere cashier, a quill-driver, a—well, a man like me—even 655 he has a little of what is called feeling, you know.

NORA: Show it, then; think of my little children.

KROGSTAD: Have you and your husband thought of mine? But never mind about that. I only wanted to tell you that you need not take this matter too seri-660 ously. In the first place there will be no accusation made on my part.

NORA: No, of course not; I was sure of that.

KROGSTAD: The whole thing can be arranged amicably; there is no reason why anyone should know 665 anything about it. It will remain a secret between us three.

NORA: My husband must never get to know anything about it.

KROGSTAD: How will you be able to prevent it? Am I 670 to understand that you can pay the balance that is owing?

NORA: No, not just at present.

KROGSTAD: Or perhaps that you have some expedient for raising the money soon?

675 **NORA:** No expedient that I mean to make use of.

KROGSTAD: Well, in any case, it would have been of no use to you now. If you stood there with ever so much money in your hand, I would never part with your bond.

NORA: Tell me what purpose you mean to put it to. 680

KROGSTAD: I shall only preserve it—keep it in my possession. No one who is not concerned in the matter shall have the slightest hint of it. So that if the thought of it has driven you to any desperate resolution— 685

NORA: It has.

KROGSTAD: If you had it in your mind to run away from your home—

NORA: I had.

KROGSTAD: Or even something worse— 690

NORA: How could you know that?

KROGSTAD: Give up the idea.

NORA: How did you know I had thought of *that*?

KROGSTAD: Most of us think of that at first. I did, too—but I hadn't the courage. 695

NORA: (*lifelessly*) No more had I.

KROGSTAD: (*in a tone of relief*) No, that's it, isn't it—you hadn't the courage either?

NORA: No, I haven't—I haven't.

KROGSTAD: Besides, it would have been a great piece 700 of folly. Once the first storm at home is over—. I have a letter for your husband in my pocket.

NORA: Telling him everything?

KROGSTAD: In as lenient a manner as I possibly could.

NORA: (*quickly*) He mustn't get the letter. Tear it up. I 705 will find some means of getting money.

KROGSTAD: Excuse me, Mrs. Helmer, but I think I told you just now—

NORA: I am not speaking of what I owe you. Tell me what sum you are asking my husband for, and I will 710 get the money.

KROGSTAD: I am not asking your husband for a penny.

NORA: What do you want, then?

KROGSTAD: I will tell you. I want to rehabilitate myself, Mrs. Helmer; I want to get on; and in that your 715 husband must help me. For the last year and a half

I have not had a hand in anything dishonourable, and all that time I have been struggling in most restricted circumstances. I was content to work my way up step by step. Now I am turned out, and I am not going to be satisfied with merely being taken into favour again. I want to get on, I tell you. I want to get into the Bank again, in a higher position. Your husband must make a place for me—

NORA: That he will never do!

KROGSTAD: He will; I know him; he dare not protest. And as soon as I am in there again with him, then you will see! Within a year I shall be the manager's right hand. It will be Nils Krogstad and not Torvald Helmer who manages the Bank.

NORA: That's a thing you will never see.

KROGSTAD: Do you mean that you will—?

NORA: I have courage enough for it now.

KROGSTAD: Oh, you can't frighten me. A fine, spoilt lady like you—

NORA: You will see, you will see.

KROGSTAD: Under the ice, perhaps? Down into the cold, coal-black water? And then, in the spring, to float up to the surface, all horrible and unrecognisable, with your hair fallen out—

NORA: You can't frighten me.

KROGSTAD: Nor you me. People don't do such things, Mrs. Helmer. Besides, what use would it be? I should have him completely in my power all the same.

NORA: Afterwards? When I am no longer—

KROGSTAD: Have you forgotten that it is I who have the keeping of your reputation? (NORA *stands speech-lessly looking at him.*) Well, now, I have warned you. Do not do anything foolish. When Helmer has had my letter, I shall expect a message from him. And be sure you remember that it is your husband himself who has forced me into such ways as this again. I will never forgive him for that. Good-bye, Mrs. Helmer. (*Exit through the hall.*)

NORA: (*goes to the hall door, opens it slightly and listens*) He is going. He is not putting the letter in the box. Oh no, no! that's impossible! (*Opens the door by degrees.*) What is that? He is standing outside. He is not going downstairs. Is he hesitating? Can he—? (*A letter drops into the box; then* KROGSTAD's *footsteps are heard, till they die away as he goes downstairs.* NORA *utters a stifled cry, and runs across the room to the table by the sofa. A short pause.*)

NORA: In the letter-box. (*Steals across to the hall door.*) There it lies—Torvald, Torvald, there is no hope for us now!

(MRS. LINDE *comes in from the room on the left, carrying the dress.*)

MRS. LINDE: There, I can't see anything more to mend now. Would you like to try it on—?

NORA: (*in a hoarse whisper*) Christine, come here.

MRS. LINDE: (*throwing the dress down on the sofa*) What is the matter with you? You look so agitated!

NORA: Come here. Do you see that letter? There, look—you can see it through the glass in the letter-box.

MRS. LINDE: Yes, I see it.

NORA: That letter is from Krogstad.

MRS. LINDE: Nora—it was Krogstad who lent you the money!

NORA: Yes, and now Torvald will know all about it.

MRS. LINDE: Believe me, Nora, that's the best thing for both of you.

NORA: You don't know all. I forged a name.

MRS. LINDE: Good heavens—!

NORA: I only want to say this to you, Christine—you must be my witness.

MRS. LINDE: Your witness? What do you mean? What am I to—?

NORA: If I should go out of my mind—it might easily happen—

MRS. LINDE: Nora!

Nora tries to pry open the letter box.

NORA: Or if anything else should happen to me—
anything, for instance, that might prevent my being

790   here—

MRS. LINDE: Nora! Nora! you are quite out of your
mind.

NORA: And if it should happen that there were some
one who wanted to take all the responsibility, all the

795   blame, you understand—

MRS. LINDE: Yes, yes—but how can you suppose—?

NORA: Then you must be my witness, that it is not
true, Christine. I am not out of my mind at all; I am
in my right senses now, and I tell you no one else

800   has known anything about it; I, and I alone, did the
whole thing. Remember that.

MRS. LINDE: I will, indeed. But I don't understand all
this.

NORA: How should you understand it? A wonderful

805   thing is going to happen!

MRS. LINDE: A wonderful thing?

NORA: Yes, a wonderful thing!—But it is so terrible,
Christine; it *mustn't* happen, not for all the world.

MRS. LINDE: I will go at once and see Krogstad.

810   NORA: Don't go to him; he will do you some harm.

MRS. LINDE: There was a time when he would gladly
do anything for my sake.

NORA: He?

MRS. LINDE: Where does he live?

815   NORA: How should I know—? Yes (*feeling in her pocket*),
here is his card. But the letter, the letter—!

HELMER: (*calls from his room, knocking at the door*)   Nora!

NORA: (*cries out anxiously*)   Oh, what's that? What do you
want?

820   HELMER: Don't be so frightened. We are not coming
in; you have locked the door. Are you trying on your
dress?

NORA: Yes, that's it. I look so nice, Torvald.

MRS. LINDE: (*who has read the card*)   I see he lives at the

825   corner here.

NORA: Yes, but it's no use. It is hopeless. The letter is
lying there in the box.

MRS. LINDE: And your husband keeps the key?

NORA: Yes, always.

Nora practices her dancing for Torvald.

MRS. LINDE: Krogstad must ask for his letter back   830
unread, he must find some pretence—

NORA: But it is just at this time that Torvald generally—

MRS. LINDE: You must delay him. Go in to him in the
meantime. I will come back as soon as I can. (*She goes
out hurriedly through the hall door.*)   835

NORA: (*goes to* HELMER's *door, opens it and peeps in*)
Torvald!

HELMER: (*from the inner room*)   Well? May I venture at
last to come into my own room again? Come along,
Rank, now you will see— (*Halting in the doorway.*) But   840
what is this?

NORA: What is what, dear?

HELMER: Rank led me to expect a splendid
transformation.

RANK: (*in the doorway*)   I understood so, but evidently I   845
was mistaken.

NORA: Yes, nobody is to have the chance of admiring
me in my dress until to-morrow.

HELMER: But, my dear Nora, you look so worn out.
Have you been practising too much?   850

NORA: No, I have not practised at all.

HELMER: But you will need to—

NORA: Yes, indeed I shall, Torvald. But I can't get on a
bit without you to help me; I have absolutely forgotten the whole thing.   855

HELMER: Oh, we will soon work it up again.

NORA: Yes, help me, Torvald. Promise that you will! I
am so nervous about it—all the people—. You must

give yourself up to me entirely this evening. Not the tiniest bit of business—you mustn't even take a pen in your hand. Will you promise, Torvald dear?

HELMER: I promise. This evening I will be wholly and absolutely at your service, you helpless little mortal. Ah, by the way, first of all I will just— *(Goes towards the hall door.)*

NORA: What are you going to do there?

HELMER: Only see if any letters have come.

NORA: No, no! don't do that, Torvald!

HELMER: Why not?

NORA: Torvald, please don't. There is nothing there.

HELMER: Well, let me look. *(Turns to go to the letter-box. NORA, at the piano, plays the first bars of the Tarantella. HELMER stops in the doorway.)* Aha!

NORA: I can't dance to-morrow if I don't practise with you.

HELMER: *(going up to her)* Are you really so afraid of it, dear?

NORA: Yes, so dreadfully afraid of it. Let me practise at once; there is time now, before we go to dinner. Sit down and play for me, Torvald dear; criticise me, and correct me as you play.

HELMER: With great pleasure, if you wish me to. *(Sits down at the piano.)*

NORA: *(takes out of the box a tambourine and a long variegated shawl. She hastily drapes the shawl round her. Then she springs to the front of the stage and calls out)* Now play for me! I am going to dance!

(HELMER plays and NORA dances. RANK stands by the piano behind HELMER, and looks on.)

HELMER: *(as he plays)* Slower, slower!

NORA: I can't do it any other way.

HELMER: Not so violently, Nora!

NORA: This is the way.

HELMER: *(stops playing)* No, no—that is not a bit right.

NORA: *(laughing and swinging the tambourine)* Didn't I tell you so?

RANK: Let me play for her.

HELMER: *(getting up)* Yes, do. I can correct her better then.

(RANK sits down at the piano and plays. NORA dances more and more wildly. HELMER has taken up a position beside the stove, and during her dance gives her frequent instructions. She does not seem to hear him; her hair comes down and falls over her shoulders; she pays no attention to it, but goes on dancing. Enter MRS. LINDE.)

MRS. LINDE: *(standing as if spell-bound in the doorway)* Oh!—

NORA: *(as she dances)* Such fun, Christine!

HELMER: My dear darling Nora, you are dancing as if your life depended on it.

NORA: So it does.

HELMER: Stop, Rank; this is sheer madness. Stop, I tell you! *(RANK stops playing, and NORA suddenly stands still. HELMER goes up to her.)* I could never have believed it. You have forgotten everything I taught you.

NORA: *(throwing away the tambourine)* There, you see.

HELMER: You will want a lot of coaching.

NORA: Yes, you see how much I need it. You must coach me up to the last minute. Promise me that, Torvald!

HELMER: You can depend on me.

NORA: You must not think of anything but me, either to-day or to-morrow; you mustn't open a single letter—not even open the letter-box—

HELMER: Ah, you are still afraid of that fellow—

NORA: Yes, indeed I am.

HELMER: Nora, I can tell from your looks that there is a letter from him lying there.

NORA: I don't know; I think there is; but you must not read anything of that kind now. Nothing horrid must come between us till this is all over.

RANK: *(whispers to HELMER)* You mustn't contradict her.

HELMER: *(taking her in his arms)* The child shall have her way. But to-morrow night, after you have danced—

NORA: Then you will be free. *(The MAID appears in the doorway to the right.)*

MAID: Dinner is served, ma'am.

NORA: We will have champagne, Helen.

MAID: Very good, ma'am. *(Exit)*

HELMER: Hullo!—are we going to have a banquet?

NORA: Yes, a champagne banquet till the small hours. (*Calls out.*) And a few macaroons, Helen—lots, just for once!

835   HELMER: Come, come, don't be so wild and nervous. Be my own little skylark, as you used.

NORA: Yes, dear, I will. But go in now and you too, Doctor Rank. Christine, you must help me to do up my hair.

840   RANK: (*whispers to* HELMER *as they go out*)   I suppose there is nothing—she is not expecting anything?

HELMER: Far from it, my dear fellow; it is simply nothing more than this childish nervousness I was telling you of.

(*They go into the right-hand room.*)

845   NORA: Well!

MRS. LINDE: Gone out of town.

NORA: I could tell from your face.

MRS. LINDE: He is coming home to-morrow evening. I wrote a note for him.

850   NORA: You should have let it alone; you must prevent nothing. After all, it is splendid to be waiting for a wonderful thing to happen.

MRS. LINDE: What is it that you are waiting for?

855   NORA: Oh, you wouldn't understand. Go in to them, I will come in a moment. (MRS. LINDE *goes into the dining-room.* NORA *stands still for a little while, as if to compose herself. Then she looks at her watch.*) Five o'clock.
860   Seven hours till midnight; and then four-and-twenty hours till the next midnight. Then the Tarantella will be over. Twenty-four and seven? Thirty-one hours to live.

HELMER: (*from the doorway on the right*)   Where's my little skylark?

NORA: (*going to him with her arms outstretched*)   Here she is!

ACT III

THE SAME SCENE: *The table has been placed in the middle of the stage, with chairs round it. A lamp is burning on the table. The door into the hall stands open. Dance music is heard from the room above.* MRS. LINDE *is sitting at the table idly turning over the leaves of a book; she tries to read, but does not seem able to collect her thoughts. Every now and then she listens intently for a sound at the outer door.*

MRS. LINDE: (*looking at her watch*)   Not yet—and the time is nearly up. If only he does not—. (*Listens again.*) Ah, there he is. (*Goes into the hall and opens the outer door carefully. Light footsteps are heard on the stairs. She whispers.*) Come in. There is no one here.   5

KROGSTAD: (*in the doorway*)   I found a note from you at home. What does this mean?

MRS. LINDE: It is absolutely necessary that I should have a talk with you.

KROGSTAD: Really? And is it absolutely necessary that it should be here?   10

MRS. LINDE: It is impossible where I live; there is no private entrance to my rooms. Come in; we are quite alone. The maid is asleep, and the Helmers are at the dance upstairs.   15

KROGSTAD: (*coming into the room*)   Are the Helmers really at a dance to-night?

MRS. LINDE: Yes, why not?

KROGSTAD: Certainly—why not?

MRS. LINDE: Now, Nils, let us have a talk.   20

KROGSTAD: Can we two have anything to talk about?

MRS. LINDE: We have a great deal to talk about.

KROGSTAD: I shouldn't have thought so.

MRS. LINDE: No, you have never properly understood me.   25

KROGSTAD: Was there anything else to understand except what was obvious to all the world—a heartless woman jilts a man when a more lucrative chance turns up?

MRS. LINDE: Do you believe I am as absolutely heartless as all that? And do you believe that I did it with a light heart?   30

KROGSTAD: Didn't you?

MRS. LINDE: Nils, did you really think that?

KROGSTAD: If it were as you say, why did you write to me as you did at the time?   35

MRS. LINDE: I could do nothing else. As I had to break with you, it was my duty also to put an end to all that you felt for me.

KROGSTAD: (*wringing his hands*)   So that was it. And all this—only for the sake of money!   40

Mrs. Linde calls on Krogstad with a plan of her own.

MRS. LINDE: You must not forget that I had a helpless mother and two little brothers. We couldn't wait for you, Nils; your prospects seemed hopeless then.

45 **KROGSTAD:** That may be so, but you had no right to throw me over for anyone else's sake.

MRS. LINDE: Indeed I don't know. Many a time did I ask myself if I had the right to do it.

KROGSTAD: *(more gently)* When I lost you, it was as if
50 all the solid ground went from under my feet. Look at me now—I am a shipwrecked man clinging to a bit of wreckage.

MRS. LINDE: But help may be near.

KROGSTAD: It *was* near; but then you came and stood
55 in my way.

MRS. LINDE: Unintentionally, Nils. It was only to-day that I learnt it was your place I was going to take in the Bank.

KROGSTAD: I believe you, if you say so. But now that
60 you know it, are you not going to give it up to me?

MRS. LINDE: No, because that would not benefit you in the least.

KROGSTAD: Oh, benefit, benefit—I would have done it whether or no.

65 **MRS. LINDE:** I have learnt to act prudently. Life, and hard, bitter necessity have taught me that.

KROGSTAD: And life has taught me not to believe in fine speeches.

MRS. LINDE: Then life has taught you something very
70 reasonable. But deeds you must believe in?

KROGSTAD: What do you mean by that?

MRS. LINDE: You said you were like a shipwrecked man clinging to some wreckage.

KROGSTAD: I had good reason to say so.

MRS. LINDE: Well, I am like a shipwrecked woman 75
clinging to some wreckage—no one to mourn for, no one to care for.

KROGSTAD: It was your own choice.

MRS. LINDE: There was no other choice—then.

KROGSTAD: Well, what now? 80

MRS. LINDE: Nils, how would it be if we two ship-wrecked people could join forces?

KROGSTAD: What are you saying?

MRS. LINDE: Two on the same piece of wreckage would stand a better chance than each on their own. 85

KROGSTAD: Christine!

MRS. LINDE: What do you suppose brought me to town?

KROGSTAD: Do you mean that you gave me a thought?

MRS. LINDE: I could not endure life without work. All 90
my life, as long as I can remember, I have worked, and it has been my greatest and only pleasure. But now I am quite alone in the world—my life is so dreadfully empty and I feel so forsaken. There is not the least pleasure in working for one's self. Nils, give 95
me someone and something to work for.

KROGSTAD: I don't trust that. It is nothing but a wom-an's overstrained sense of generosity that prompts you to make such an offer of yourself.

MRS. LINDE: Have you ever noticed anything of the 100
sort in me?

KROGSTAD: Could you really do it? Tell me—do you know all about my past life?

MRS. LINDE: Yes.

KROGSTAD: And do you know what they think of me 105
here?

MRS. LINDE: You seemed to me to imply that with me you might have been quite another man.

KROGSTAD: I am certain of it.

MRS. LINDE: Is it too late now? 110

KROGSTAD: Christine, are you saying this deliber-ately? Yes, I am sure you are. I see it in your face. Have you really the courage, then—?

MRS. LINDE: I want to be a mother to someone, and
115   your children need a mother. We two need each
other. Nils, I have faith in your real character—I can
dare anything together with you.

KROGSTAD: *(grasps her hands)*   Thanks, thanks, Christine! Now I shall find a way to clear myself in the
120   eyes of the world. Ah, but I forgot—

MRS. LINDE: *(listening)*   Hush! The Tarantella. Go, go!

KROGSTAD: Why? What is it?

MRS. LINDE: Do you hear them up there? When that is
over, we may expect them back.

125   KROGSTAD: Yes, yes—I will go. But it is all no use. Of
course you are not aware what steps I have taken in
the matter of the Helmers.

MRS. LINDE: Yes, I know all about that.

KROGSTAD: And in spite of that have you the cour-
130   age to—?

MRS. LINDE: I understand very well to what lengths
a man like you might be driven by despair.

KROGSTAD: If I could only undo what I have done!

MRS. LINDE: You cannot. Your letter is lying in the
135   letter-box now.

KROGSTAD: Are you sure of that?

MRS. LINDE: Quite sure, but—

KROGSTAD: *(with a searching look at her)*   Is that what it
all means?—that you want to save your friend at any
140   cost? Tell me frankly. Is that it?

MRS. LINDE: Nils, a woman who has once sold herself
for another's sake, doesn't do it a second time.

KROGSTAD: I will ask for my letter back.

MRS. LINDE: No, no.

145   KROGSTAD: Yes, of course I will. I will wait here till
Helmer comes; I will tell him he must give me my
letter back—that it only concerns my dismissal—that
he is not to read it—

MRS. LINDE: No, Nils, you must not recall your letter.

150   KROGSTAD: But, tell me, wasn't it for that very purpose that you asked me to meet you here?

MRS. LINDE: In my first moment of fright, it was. But
twenty-four hours have elapsed since then, and in
that time I have witnessed incredible things in this
155   house. Helmer must know all about it. This unhappy
secret must be disclosed; they must have a complete

understanding between them, which is impossible
with all this concealment and falsehood going on.

KROGSTAD: Very well, if you will take the responsibility. But there is one thing I can do in any case, and I   160
shall do it at once.

MRS. LINDE: *(listening)*   You must be quick and go! The
dance is over; we are not safe a moment longer.

KROGSTAD: I will wait for you below.

MRS. LINDE: Yes, do; You must see me back to my door.   165

KROGSTAD: I have never had such an amazing piece
of good fortune in my life! *(Goes out through the outer
door. The door between the room and the hall remains open.)*

MRS. LINDE: *(tidying up the room and laying her hat and
cloak ready)*   What a difference! what a difference!   170
Some one to work for and live for—a home to bring
comfort into. That I will do, indeed. I wish they
would be quick and come— *(Listens.)* Ah, there they
are now. I must put on my things. *(Takes up her hat
and cloak. HELMER's and NORA's voices are heard outside;*   175
*a key is turned, and HELMER brings NORA almost by force
into the hall. She is in an Italian costume with a large black
shawl round her; he is in evening dress, and a black domino
which is flying open.)*

NORA: *(hanging back in the doorway, and struggling with him)*   180
No, no, no!—don't take me in. I want to go upstairs
again; I don't want to leave so early.

HELMER: But, my dearest Nora—

NORA: Please, Torvald dear—please, *please*—only an
hour more.   185

HELMER: Not a single minute, my sweet Nora. You
know that was our agreement. Come along into
the room; you are catching cold standing there. *(He
brings her gently into the room, in spite of her resistance.)*

MRS. LINDE: Good-evening.   190

NORA: Christine!

HELMER: You here, so late, Mrs. Linde?

MRS. LINDE: Yes, you must excuse me; I was so anxious to see Nora in her dress.

NORA: Have you been sitting here waiting for me?   195

MRS. LINDE: Yes, unfortunately I came too late, you
had already gone upstairs; and I thought I couldn't
go away again without having seen you.

HELMER: *(taking off NORA's shawl)*   Yes, take a good
look at her. I think she is worth looking at. Isn't she   200
charming, Mrs. Linde?

MRS. LINDE: Yes, indeed she is.

HELMER: Doesn't she look remarkably pretty? Everyone thought so at the dance. But she is terribly self-willed, this sweet little person. What are we to do with her? You will hardly believe that I had almost to bring her away by force.

NORA: Torvald, you will repent not having let me stay, even if it were only for half an hour.

HELMER: Listen to her, Mrs. Linde! She had danced her Tarantella, and it had been a tremendous success, as it deserved—although possibly the performance was a trifle too realistic—a little more so, I mean, than was strictly compatible with the limitations of art. But never mind about that! The chief thing is, she had made a success—she had made a tremendous success. Do you think I was going to let her remain there after that, and spoil the effect? No, indeed! I took my charming little Capri maiden—my capricious little Capri maiden, I should say—on my arm; took one quick turn round the room; a curtsey on either side, and, as they say in novels, the beautiful apparition disappeared. An exit ought always to be effective, Mrs. Linde; but that is what I cannot make Nora understand. Pooh! this room is hot. *(Throws his domino on a chair, and opens the door of his room.)* Hullo! it's all dark in here. Oh, of course—excuse me—. *(He goes in, and lights some candles.)*

NORA: *(in a hurried and breathless whisper)* Well?

MRS. LINDE: *(in a low voice)* I have had a talk with him.

NORA: Yes, and—

MRS. LINDE: Nora, you must tell your husband all about it.

NORA: *(in an expressionless voice)* I knew it.

MRS. LINDE: You have nothing to be afraid of as far as Krogstad is concerned; but you must tell him.

NORA: I won't tell him.

MRS. LINDE: Then the letter will.

NORA: Thank you, Christine. Now I know what I must do. Hush—!

HELMER: *(coming in again)* Well, Mrs. Linde, have you admired her?

MRS. LINDE: Yes, and now I will say good-night.

HELMER: What, already? Is this yours, this knitting?

MRS. LINDE: *(taking it)* Yes, thank you, I had very nearly forgotten it.

HELMER: So you knit?

MRS. LINDE: Of course.

HELMER: Do you know, you ought to embroider.

MRS. LINDE: Really? Why?

HELMER: Yes, it's far more becoming. Let me show you. You hold the embroidery thus in your left hand, and use the needle with the right—like this—with a long, easy sweep. Do you see?

MRS. LINDE: Yes, perhaps—

HELMER: But in the case of knitting—that can never be anything but ungraceful; look here—the arms close together, the knitting-needles going up and down—it has a sort of Chinese effect—. That was really excellent champagne they gave us.

MRS. LINDE: Well,—good-night, Nora, and don't be self-willed anymore.

HELMER: That's right, Mrs. Linde.

MRS. LINDE: Good-night, Mr. Helmer.

HELMER: *(accompanying her to the door)* Good-night, good-night. I hope you will get home all right. I should be very happy to—but you haven't any great distance to go. Good-night, good-night. *(She goes out; he shuts the door after her, and comes in again.)* Ah!—at last we have got rid of her. She's a frightful bore, that woman.

NORA: Aren't you very tired, Torvald?

HELMER: No, not in the least.

NORA: Nor sleepy?

HELMER: Not a bit. On the contrary, I feel extraordinarily lively. And you?—you really look both tired and sleepy.

After Mrs. Linde leaves, Torvald has Nora to himself.

NORA: Yes, I am very tired. I want to go to sleep at once.

HELMER: There, you see it was quite right of me not to let you stay there any longer.

280 **NORA:** Everything you do is quite right, Torvald.

HELMER: (*kissing her on the forehead*) Now my little skylark is speaking reasonably. Did you notice what good spirits Rank was in this evening?

NORA: Really? Was he? I didn't speak to him at all.

285 **HELMER:** And I very little, but I have not for a long time seen him in such good form. (*Looks for a while at her and then goes nearer to her.*) It is delightful to be at home by ourselves again, to be all alone with you— you fascinating, charming little darling!

290 **NORA:** Don't look at me like that, Torvald.

HELMER: Why shouldn't I look at my dearest treasure?—at all the beauty that is mine, all my very own?

NORA: (*going to the other side of the table*) You mustn't say 295 things like that to me to-night.

HELMER: (*following her*) You have still got the Tarantella in your blood, I see. And it makes you more captivating than ever. Listen—the guests are beginning to go now. (*In a lower voice.*) Nora—soon the whole 300 house will be quiet.

NORA: Yes, I hope so.

HELMER: Yes, my own darling Nora. Do you know, when I am out at a party with you like this, why I speak so little to you, keep away from you, and 305 only send a stolen glance in your direction now and then?—do you know why I do that? It is because I make believe to myself that we are secretly in love, and you are my secretly promised bride, and that no one suspects there is anything between us.

NORA: Yes, yes—I know very well your thoughts are 310 with me all the time.

HELMER: And when we are leaving, and I am putting the shawl over your beautiful young shoulders—on your lovely neck—then I imagine that you are my young bride and that we have just come from the 315 wedding, and I am bringing you for the first time into our home—to be alone with you for the first time—quite alone with my shy little darling! All this evening I have longed for nothing but you. When I watched the seductive figures of the Tarantella, my 320 blood was on fire; I could endure it no longer, and that was why I brought you down so early—

NORA: Go away, Torvald! You must let me go. I won't—

HELMER: What's that? You're joking, my little Nora! You won't—you won't? Am I not your husband—? 325 (*A knock is heard at the outer door.*)

NORA: (*starting*) Did you hear—?

HELMER: (*going into the hall*) Who is it?

RANK: (*outside*) It is I. May I come in for a moment?

HELMER: (*in a fretful whisper*) Oh, what does he want 330 now? (*Aloud.*) Wait a minute! (*Unlocks the door.*) Come, that's kind of you not to pass by our door.

RANK: I thought I heard your voice, and felt as if I should like to look in. (*With a swift glance round.*) Ah, yes!—these dear familiar rooms. You are very happy 335 and cosy in here, you two.

HELMER: It seems to me that you looked after yourself pretty well upstairs too.

RANK: Excellently. Why shouldn't I? Why shouldn't one enjoy everything in this world?—at any rate as 340 much as one can, and as long as one can. The wine was capital—

HELMER: Especially the champagne.

RANK: So you noticed that too? It is almost incredible how much I managed to put away! 345

NORA: Torvald drank a great deal of champagne to-night too.

RANK: Did he?

NORA: Yes, and he is always in such good spirits afterwards. 350

Dr. Rank stops in to say good-bye to the Helmers.

RANK: Well, why should one not enjoy a merry evening after a well-spent day?

HELMER: Well spent? I am afraid I can't take credit for that.

355 RANK: *(clapping him on the back)*   But I can, you know!

NORA: Doctor Rank, you must have been occupied with some scientific investigation to-day.

RANK: Exactly.

HELMER: Just listen!—little Nora talking about scien-
360 tific investigations!

NORA: And may I congratulate you on the result?

RANK: Indeed you may.

NORA: Was it favourable, then?

RANK: The best possible, for both doctor and patient—
365 certainty.

NORA: *(quickly and searchingly)*   Certainty?

RANK: Absolute certainty. So wasn't I entitled to make a merry evening of it after that?

NORA: Yes, you certainly were, Doctor Rank.

370 HELMER: I think so too, so long as you don't have to pay for it in the morning.

RANK: Oh well, one can't have anything in this life without paying for it.

NORA: Doctor Rank—are you fond of fancy-dress balls?

375 RANK: Yes, if there is a fine lot of pretty costumes.

NORA: Tell me—what shall we two wear at the next?

HELMER: Little featherbrain!—are you thinking of the next already?

RANK: We two? Yes, I can tell you. You shall go as a
380 good fairy—

HELMER: Yes, but what do you suggest as an appropri-ate costume for that?

RANK: Let your wife go dressed just as she is in every-day life.

385 HELMER: That was really very prettily turned. But can't you tell us what you will be?

RANK: Yes, my dear friend, I have quite made up my mind about that.

HELMER: Well?

390 RANK: At the next fancy-dress ball I shall be invisible.

HELMER: That's a good joke!

RANK: There is a big black hat—have you never heard of hats that make you invisible? If you put one on, no one can see you.

395 HELMER: *(suppressing a smile)*   Yes, you are quite right.

RANK: But I am clean forgetting what I came for. Hel-mer, give me a cigar—one of the dark Havanas.

HELMER: With the greatest pleasure. *(Offers him his case.)*

RANK: *(takes a cigar and cuts off the end)*   Thanks.

400 NORA: *(striking a match)*   Let me give you a light.

RANK: Thank you. *(She holds the match for him to light his cigar.)* And now good-bye!

HELMER: Good-bye, good-bye, dear old man!

NORA: Sleep well, Doctor Rank.

405 RANK: Thank you for that wish.

NORA: Wish me the same.

RANK: You? Well, if you want me to sleep well! And thanks for the light. *(He nods to them both and goes out.)*

HELMER: *(in a subdued voice)*   He has drunk more than
410 he ought.

NORA: *(absently)*   Maybe. *(HELMER takes a bunch of keys out of his pocket and goes into the hall.)* Torvald! what are you going to do there?

HELMER: Empty the letter-box; it is quite full;
there will be no be room to put the newspaper in
415 to-morrow morning.

NORA: Are you going to work to-night?

HELMER: You know quite well I'm not. What is this? Someone has been at the lock.

420 NORA: At the lock—?

HELMER: Yes, someone has. What can it mean? I should never have thought the maid—. Here is a broken hairpin. Nora, it is one of yours.

NORA: *(quickly)*   Then it must have been the children—

425 HELMER: Then you must get them out of those ways. There, at last I have got it open. *(Takes out the contents of the letter-box, and calls to the kitchen.)* Helen!—Helen, put out the light over the front door. *(Goes back into the room and shuts the door into the hall. He holds out his hand full of letters.)* Look at that—look what a heap of them
430 there are. *(Turning them over.)* What on earth is that?

NORA: *(at the window)*   The letter—No! Torvald, no!

HELMER: Two cards—of Rank's.

NORA: Of Doctor Rank's?

435 HELMER: *(looking at them)*   Doctor Rank. They were on the top. He must have put them in when he went out.

NORA: Is there anything written on them?

HELMER: There is a black cross over the name. Look there—what an uncomfortable idea! It looks as if he 440 were announcing his own death.

NORA: It is just what he is doing.

HELMER: What? Do you know anything about it? Has he said anything to you?

NORA: Yes. He told me that when the cards came it 445 would be his leave-taking from us. He means to shut himself up and die.

HELMER: My poor old friend! Certainly I knew we should not have him very long with us. But so soon! And so he hides himself away like a wounded animal.

450 NORA: If it has to happen, it is best it should be without a word—don't you think so, Torvald?

HELMER: *(walking up and down)*   He had so grown into our lives. I can't think of him as having gone out of them. He, with his sufferings and his loneliness, was 455 like a cloudy background to our sunlit happiness. Well, perhaps it is best so. For him, anyway. *(Standing still.)* And perhaps for us too, Nora. We two are thrown quite upon each other now. *(Puts his arms round her.)* My darling wife, I don't feel as if I could 460 hold you tight enough. Do you know, Nora, I have often wished that you might be threatened by some great danger, so that I might risk my life's blood, and everything, for your sake.

NORA: *(disengages herself, and says firmly and decidedly)* 465 Now you must read your letters, Torvald.

HELMER: No, no; not to-night. I want to be with you, my darling wife.

NORA: With the thought of your friend's death—

HELMER: You are right, it has affected us both. Some-470 thing ugly has come between us—the thought of the horrors of death. We must try and rid our minds of that. Until then—we will each go to our own room.

NORA: *(hanging on his neck)*   Good-night, Torvald— Good-night!

475 HELMER: *(kissing her on the forehead)*   Good-night, my little singing-bird. Sleep sound, Nora. Now I will read my letters through. *(He takes his letters and goes into his room, shutting the door after him.)*

NORA: *(gropes distractedly about, seizes* HELMER's *domino, throws it round her, while she says in quick, hoarse, spas-* 480 *modic whispers)*   Never to see him again. Never! Never! *(Puts her shawl over her head.)* Never to see my children again either—never again. Never! Never!— Ah! the icy, black water—the unfathomable depths— If only it were over! He has got it now—now he is 485 reading it. Good-bye, Torvald and my children! *(She is about to rush out through the hall, when* HELMER *opens his door hurriedly and stands with an open letter in his hand.)*

HELMER: Nora! 490

NORA: Ah!—

HELMER: What is this? Do you know what is in this letter?

NORA: Yes, I know. Let me go! Let me get out!

HELMER: *(holding her back)*   Where are you going? 495

NORA: *(trying to get free)*   You shan't save me, Torvald!

HELMER: *(reeling)*   True? Is this true, that I read here? Horrible! No, no—it is impossible that it can be true.

NORA: It is true. I have loved you above everything else in the world. 500

HELMER: Oh, don't let us have any silly excuses.

NORA: *(taking a step towards him)*   Torvald—!

HELMER: Miserable creature—what have you done?

NORA: Let me go. You shall not suffer for my sake. You shall not take it upon yourself. 505

HELMER: No tragedy airs, please. *(Locks the hall door.)* Here you shall stay and give me an explanation. Do you understand what you have done? Answer me! Do you understand what you have done?

NORA: *(looks steadily at him and says with a growing look of* 510 *coldness in her face)*   Yes, now I am beginning to understand thoroughly.

HELMER: *(walking about the room)*   What a horrible awakening! All these eight years—she who was my joy and pride—a hypocrite, a liar—worse, worse— 515 a criminal! The unutterable ugliness of it all!—For shame! For shame! *(NORA is silent and looks steadily at him. He stops in front of her.)* I ought to have suspected that something of the sort would happen. I ought to have foreseen it. All your father's want of principle— 520 be silent!—all your father's want of principle has

Torvald, having read the letter, confronts Nora.

come out in you. No religion, no morality, no sense
of duty—. How I am punished for having winked at
what he did! I did it for your sake, and this is how
you repay me.

NORA: Yes, that's just it.

HELMER: Now you have destroyed all my happiness.
You have ruined all my future. It is horrible to think
of! I am in the power of an unscrupulous man; he
can do what he likes with me, ask anything he likes
of me, give me any orders he pleases—I dare not
refuse. And I must sink to such miserable depths
because of a thoughtless woman!

NORA: When I am out of the way, you will be free.

HELMER: No fine speeches, please. Your father had
always plenty of those ready, too. What good would
it be to me if you were out of the way, as you say? Not
the slightest. He can make the affair known everywhere; and if he does, I may be falsely suspected of
having been a party to your criminal action. Very
likely people will think I was behind it all—that it
was I who prompted you! And I have to thank you
for all this—you whom I have cherished during the
whole of our married life. Do you understand now
what it is you have done for me?

NORA: *(coldly and quietly)*   Yes.

HELMER: It is so incredible that I can't take it in. But
we must come to some understanding. Take off that
shawl. Take it off, I tell you. I must try and ap-
pease him some way or another. The matter must
be hushed up at any cost. And as for you and me, it
must appear as if everything between us were just as
before—but naturally only in the eyes of the world.

You will still remain in my house, that is a matter
of course. But I shall not allow you to bring up the
children; I dare not trust them to you. To think that
I should be obliged to say so to one whom I have
loved so dearly, and whom I still—. No, that is all
over. From this moment happiness is not the question; all that concerns us is to save the remains, the
fragments, the appearance—

(A ring is heard at the front-door bell.)

HELMER: *(with a start)*   What is that? So late! Can the
worst—? Can he—? Hide yourself, Nora. Say you
are ill.

*(NORA stands motionless. HELMER goes and unlocks the
hall door.)*

MAID: *(half dressed, comes to the door)*   A letter for the
mistress.

HELMER: Give it to me. *(Takes the letter, and shuts the
door.)* Yes, it is from him. You shall not have it; I will
read it myself.

NORA: Yes, read it.

HELMER: *(standing by the lamp)*   I scarcely have the courage to do it. It may mean ruin for both of us. No, I
must know. *(Tears open the letter, runs his eye over a few
lines, looks at a paper enclosed, and gives a shout of joy.)*
Nora! *(She looks at him questioningly.)* Nora!—No, I
must read it once again—. Yes, it is true! I am saved!
Nora, I am saved!

NORA: And I?

HELMER: You too, of course; we are both saved, both
you and I. Look, he sends you your bond back. He
says he regrets and repents—that a happy change
in his life—never mind what he says! We are saved,
Nora! No one can do anything to you. Oh, Nora,
Nora!—no, first I must destroy these hateful things.
Let me see—. *(Takes a look at the bond.)* No, no, I won't
look at it. The whole thing shall be nothing but a bad
dream to me. *(Tears up the bond and both letters, throws
them all into the stove, and watches them burn.)* There—
now it doesn't exist any longer. He says that since
Christmas Eve you—. These must have been three
dreadful days for you, Nora.

NORA: I have fought a hard fight these three days.

HELMER: And suffered agonies, and seen no way out
but—. No, we won't call any of the horrors to mind.
We will only shout with joy, and keep saying, "It's
all over! It's all over!" Listen to me, Nora. You don't
seem to realise that it is all over. What is this?—such

525

530

535

540

545

550

555

560

565

570

575

580

585

590

595

600 a cold, set face! My poor little Nora, I quite understand; you don't feel as if you could believe that I
have forgiven you. But it is true, Nora, I swear it; I
have forgiven you everything. I know that what you
did, you did out of love for me.

NORA: That is true.

605 HELMER: You have loved me as a wife ought to love
her husband. Only you had not sufficient knowledge
to judge of the means you used. But do you suppose
you are any the less dear to me, because you don't
understand how to act on your own responsibility?
610 No, no; only lean on me; I will advise you and direct
you. I should not be a man if this womanly helplessness did not just give you a double attractiveness
in my eyes. You must not think any more about the
hard things I said in my first moment of consterna-
tion, when I thought everything was going to over-
615 whelm me. I have forgiven you, Nora; I swear to you
I have forgiven you.

NORA: Thank you for your forgiveness. (*She goes out
through the door to the right.*)

HELMER: No, don't go—. (*Looks in.*) What are you doing
620 in there?

NORA: (*from within*) Taking off my fancy dress.

HELMER: (*standing at the open door*) Yes, do. Try and
calm yourself, and make your mind easy again, my
frightened little singing-bird. Be at rest, and feel
625 secure; I have broad wings to shelter you under.
(*Walks up and down by the door.*) How warm and cosy
our home is, Nora. Here is shelter for you; here I will
protect you like a hunted dove that I have saved from
a hawk's claws; I will bring peace to your poor beat-
630 ing heart. It will come, little by little, Nora, believe
me. To-morrow morning you will look upon it all
quite differently; soon everything will be just as it
was before. Very soon you won't need me to assure
you that I have forgiven you; you will yourself feel
635 the certainty that I have done so. Can you suppose I
should ever think of such a thing as repudiating you,
or even reproaching you? You have no idea what a
true man's heart is like, Nora. There is something so
indescribably sweet and satisfying, to a man, in the
640 knowledge that he has forgiven his wife—forgiven
her freely, and with all his heart. It seems as if that
had made her, as it were, doubly his own; he has
given her a new life, so to speak; and she has in a
way become both wife and child to him. So you shall
645 be for me after this, my little scared, helpless darling.
Have no anxiety about anything, Nora; only be frank

and open with me, and I will serve as will and conscience both to you—. What is this? Not gone to bed?
Have you changed your things?

650 NORA: (*in everyday dress*) Yes, Torvald, I have changed
my things now.

HELMER: But what for?—so late as this.

NORA: I shall not sleep to-night.

HELMER: But, my dear Nora—

655 NORA: (*looking at her watch*) It is not so very late. Sit
down here, Torvald. You and I have much to say to
one another. (*She sits down at one side of the table.*)

HELMER: Nora—what is this?—this cold, set face?

NORA: Sit down. It will take some time; I have a lot to
660 talk over with you.

HELMER: (*sits down at the opposite side of the table*) You
alarm me, Nora!—and I don't understand you.

NORA: No, that is just it. You don't understand me, and
I have never understood you either—before to-night.
665 No, you mustn't interrupt me. You must simply listen
to what I say. Torvald, this is a settling of accounts.

HELMER: What do you mean by that?

NORA: (*after a short silence*) Isn't there one thing that
strikes you as strange in our sitting here like this?

670 HELMER: What is that?

NORA: We have been married now eight years. Does
it not occur to you that this is the first time we two,
you and I, husband and wife, have had a serious
conversation?

675 HELMER: What do you mean by serious?

Torvald tries to comfort Nora after his tirade.

NORA: In all these eight years—longer than that—from the very beginning of our acquaintance, we have never exchanged a word on any serious subject.

680   **HELMER:**   Was it likely that I would be continually and for ever telling you about worries that you could not help me to bear?

NORA: I am not speaking about business matters. I say that we have never sat down in earnest together to try and get at the bottom of anything.

685   **HELMER:**   But, dearest Nora, would it have been any good to you?

NORA: That is just it; you have never understood me. I have been greatly wronged, Torvald—first by papa and then by you.

690   **HELMER:**   What! By us two—by us two, who have loved you better than anyone else in the world?

NORA: (shaking her head)   You have never loved me. You have only thought it pleasant to be in love with me.

HELMER: Nora, what do I hear you saying?

695   **NORA:**   It is perfectly true, Torvald. When I was at home with papa, he told me his opinion about everything, and so I had the same opinions; and if I differed from him I concealed the fact, because he would not have liked it. He called me his doll-child, and he played with me just as I used to play with my dolls. And when I came to live with you—

700

HELMER: What sort of an expression is that to use about our marriage?

NORA: (undisturbed)   I mean that I was simply trans-
705   ferred from papa's hands into yours. You arranged everything according to your own taste, and so I got the same tastes as you—or else I pretended to, I am really not quite sure which—I think sometimes the one and sometimes the other. When I look back on
710   it, it seems to me as if I had been living here like a poor woman—just from hand to mouth. I have existed merely to perform tricks for you, Torvald. But you would have it so. You and papa have committed a great sin against me. It is your fault that I have made
715   nothing of my life.

HELMER: How unreasonable and how ungrateful you are, Nora! Have you not been happy here?

NORA: No, I have never been happy. I thought I was, but it has never really been so.

720   **HELMER:**   Not—not happy!

NORA: No, only merry. And you have always been so kind to me. But our home has been nothing but a playroom. I have been your doll-wife, just as at home I was papa's doll-child; and here the children have been my dolls. I thought it great fun when you played   725
with me, just as they thought it great fun when I played with them. That is what our marriage has been, Torvald.

HELMER: There is some truth in what you say—exaggerated and strained as your view of it is. But   730
for the future it shall be different. Playtime shall be over, and lesson-time shall begin.

NORA: Whose lessons? Mine, or the children's?

HELMER: Both yours and the children's, my darling Nora.   735

NORA: Alas, Torvald, you are not the man to educate me into being a proper wife for you.

HELMER: And you can say that!

NORA: And I—how am I fitted to bring up the children?

HELMER: Nora!   740

NORA: Didn't you say so yourself a little while ago—that you dare not trust me to bring them up?

HELMER: In a moment of anger! Why do you pay any heed to that?

NORA: Indeed, you were perfectly right. I am not fit   745
for the task. There is another task I must undertake first. I must try and educate myself—you are not the man to help me in that. I must do that for myself. And that is why I am going to leave you now.

HELMER: (springing up)   What do you say?   750

NORA: I must stand quite alone, if I am to understand myself and everything about me. It is for that reason that I cannot remain with you any longer.

HELMER: Nora, Nora!

NORA: I am going away from here now, at once. I am   755
sure Christine will take me in for the night—

HELMER: You are out of your mind! I won't allow it! I forbid you!

NORA: It is no use forbidding me anything any longer. I will take with me what belongs to myself. I will   760
take nothing from you, either now or later.

HELMER: What sort of madness is this!

NORA: To-morrow I shall go home—I mean, to my old home. It will be easiest for me to find something to do there.

HELMER: You blind, foolish woman!

NORA: I must try and get some sense, Torvald.

HELMER: To desert your home, your husband and your children! And you don't consider what people will say!

NORA: I cannot consider that at all. I only know that it is necessary for me.

HELMER: It's shocking. This is how you would neglect your most sacred duties.

NORA: What do you consider my most sacred duties?

HELMER: Do I need to tell you that? Are they not your duties to your husband and your children?

NORA: I have other duties just as sacred.

HELMER: That you have not. What duties could those be?

NORA: Duties to myself.

HELMER: Before all else, you are a wife and a mother.

NORA: I don't believe in that any longer. I believe that before all else I am a reasonable human being, just as you are—or, at all events, that I must try and become one. I know quite well, Torvald, that most people would think you right; and that views of that kind are to be found in books; but I can no longer content myself with what most people say, or with what is found in books. I must think over things for myself and get to understand them.

HELMER: Can you not understand your place in your own home? Have you not a reliable guide in such matters as that?—have you no religion?

NORA: I am afraid, Torvald, I do not exactly know what religion is.

HELMER: What are you saying?

NORA: I know nothing but what the clergyman said, when I went to be confirmed. He told us that religion was this, and that, and the other. When I am away from all this, and am alone, I will look into that matter too. I will see if what the clergyman said is true, or at all events if it is true for me.

HELMER: This is unheard of in a girl of your age! But if religion cannot lead you aright, let me try and awaken your conscience. I suppose you have some moral sense? Or—answer me—am I to think you have none?

NORA: I assure you, Torvald, that is not an easy question to answer. I really don't know. The thing perplexes me altogether. I only know that you and I look at it in quite a different light. I am learning, too, that the law is quite another thing from what I supposed; but I find it impossible to convince myself that the law is right. According to it a woman has no right to spare her old dying father, or to save her husband's life. I can't believe that.

HELMER: You talk like a child. You don't understand the conditions of the world in which you live.

NORA: No, I don't. But now I am going to try. I am going to see if I can make out who is right, the world or I.

HELMER: You are ill, Nora; you are delirious; I almost think you are out of your mind.

NORA: I have never felt my mind so clear and certain as to-night.

HELMER: And is it with a clear and certain mind that you forsake your husband and your children?

NORA: Yes, it is.

HELMER: Then there is only one possible explanation.

NORA: What is that?

HELMER: You do not love me any more.

NORA: No, that is just it.

HELMER: Nora!—and you can say that?

NORA: It gives me great pain, Torvald, for you have always been so kind to me, but I cannot help it. I do not love you any more.

HELMER: *(regaining his composure)* Is that a clear and certain conviction too?

NORA: Yes, absolutely clear and certain. That is the reason why I will not stay here any longer.

HELMER: And can you tell me what I have done to forfeit your love?

NORA: Yes, indeed I can. It was to-night, when the wonderful thing did not happen; then I saw you were not the man I had thought you.

HELMER: Explain yourself better. I don't understand you.

NORA: I have waited so patiently for eight years; for, goodness knows, I knew very well that wonderful

855 things don't happen every day. Then this horrible misfortune came upon me; and then I felt quite certain that the wonderful thing was going to happen at last. When Krogstad's letter was lying out there, never for a moment did I imagine that you would consent to accept this man's conditions. I was so absolutely certain that you would say to him: Publish the thing to the whole world. And when that was done—

860 HELMER: Yes, what then?—when I had exposed my wife to shame and disgrace?

NORA: When that was done, I was so absolutely certain, you would come forward and take everything upon yourself, and say: I am the guilty one.

865 HELMER: Nora—!

NORA: You mean that I would never have accepted such a sacrifice on your part? No, of course not. But what would my assurances have been worth against yours? That was the wonderful thing which I hoped
870 for and feared; and it was to prevent that, that I wanted to kill myself.

HELMER: I would gladly work night and day for you, Nora—bear sorrow and want for your sake. But no man would sacrifice his honour for the one he loves.

875 NORA: It is a thing hundreds of thousands of women have done.

HELMER: Oh, you think and talk like a heedless child.

NORA: Maybe. But you neither think nor talk like the man I could bind myself to. As soon as your fear was
880 over—and it was not fear for what threatened me, but for what might happen to you—when the whole thing was past, as far as you were concerned it was exactly as if nothing at all had happened. Exactly as before, I was your little skylark, your doll, which you
885 would in future treat with doubly gentle care, because it was so brittle and fragile. (*Getting up.*) Torvald—it was then it dawned upon me that for eight years I had been living here with a strange man, and had borne him three children—. Oh, I can't bear to
890 think of it! I could tear myself into little bits!

HELMER: (*sadly*) I see, I see. An abyss has opened between us—there is no denying it. But, Nora, would it not be possible to fill it up?

NORA: As I am now, I am no wife for you.

895 HELMER: I have it in me to become a different man.

NORA: Perhaps—if your doll is taken away from you.

Nora, dressed for travel, explains her epiphany to Torvald.

HELMER: But to part!—to part from you! No, no, Nora, I can't understand that idea.

NORA: (*going out to the right*) That makes it all the more certain that it must be done. (*She comes back with her
900 cloak and hat and a small bag which she puts on a chair by the table.*)

HELMER: Nora, Nora, not now! Wait till to-morrow.

NORA: (*putting on her cloak*) I cannot spend the night in a strange man's room.
905

HELMER: But can't we live here like brother and sister—?

NORA: (*putting on her hat*) You know very well that would not last long. (*Puts the shawl round her.*) Goodbye, Torvald. I won't see the little ones. I know they are in better hands than mine. As I am now, I can
910 be of no use to them.

HELMER: But some day, Nora—some day?

NORA: How can I tell? I have no idea what is going to become of me.

HELMER: But you are my wife, whatever becomes of
915 you.

NORA: Listen, Torvald. I have heard that when a wife deserts her husband's house, as I am doing now, he is legally freed from all obligations towards her. In any case I set you free from all your obligations. You are
920 not to feel yourself bound in the slightest way, any more than I shall. There must be perfect freedom on both sides. See, here is your ring back. Give me mine.

HELMER: That too?

NORA: That too.
925

HELMER: Here it is.

Torvald, alone, gazes around the empty house.

NORA: That's right. Now it is all over. I have put the keys here. The maids know all about everything in the house—better than I do. To-morrow, after I have left her, Christine will come here and pack up my own things that I brought with me from home. I will have them sent after me.

930

HELMER: All over! All over!—Nora, shall you never think of me again?

935 **NORA:** I know I shall often think of you and the children and this house.

HELMER: May I write to you, Nora?

NORA: No—never. You must not to do that.

HELMER: But at least let me send you—

NORA: Nothing—nothing— 940

HELMER: Let me help you if you are in want.

NORA: No. I can receive nothing from a stranger.

HELMER: Nora—can I never be anything more than a stranger to you?

NORA: *(taking her bag)* Ah, Torvald, the most wonderful 945 thing of all would have to happen.

HELMER: Tell me what would that be!

NORA: Both you and I would have to be so changed that—. Oh, Torvald, I don't believe any longer in wonderful things happening. 950

HELMER: But I will believe in it. Tell me! So changed that—?

NORA: That our life together would be a real wedlock. Good-bye. *(She goes out through the hall.)*

HELMER: *(sinks down on a chair at the door and buries his* 955 *face in his hands)* Nora! Nora! *(Looks round, and rises.)* Empty. She is gone. *(A hope flashes across his mind.)* The most wonderful thing of all—?

(The sound of a door shutting is heard from below.)

Writing from Reading

Summarize

1 Some call this much-discussed and widely performed play the first feminist play. This script challenged and in some cases outraged contemporary audiences. In fact, the first German productions of *A Doll's House* in the 1880s had an altered ending at the request of the producers. Ibsen referred to this version as a "barbaric outrage" to be used only in emergencies. What other endings could you imagine that Ibsen might endorse?

Analyze Craft

2 Dr. Rank assumes the role of the wise, elder statesman—a familiar figure in such theater. In truth, however, he's someone who's ill and even rotting, not elevated. What does his desire for Nora suggest as to his character, and in what if any ways does Ibsen cast him in a sympathetic light?

3 When Nora, in Act III, tells Torvald that they must "sit down and discuss all this that has been happening between us," *A Doll's House* diverges from the final resolution of the well-made play. What do you imagine is the future of the marriage; who has changed, and how?

4 Nora's father is a major figure here, though always offstage. List his characteristics. How does Nora reveal how she feels about her father's characteristics? Does Nora want her husband to have more of her father's qualities, or qualities that are less similar?

Analyze Voice

5 Descriptive names for Nora include "little skylark," "fascinating, charming little darling," "my darling wife," "my little singing-bird," "little, scared darling," "blind, foolish woman," and "a heedless child." Which of these strikes you as most appropriate—or are they all true? How do they vary in the course of the play?

6 Nora often disguises the truth and—several times—lies in the course of the play. Are these white lies or genuine falsehoods? How do they increase or decrease our trust in her and why?

7 When Nora says that she requires Torvald to help her practice for the dance, what does she imply?

8 The first act takes place on Christmas Eve. Christmas is not, however, presented as a religious holiday and religion as a concept is questioned by Nora in Act III. In fact, it is discussed much more often as a material than a spiritual experience. Does Ibsen here endorse or disapprove of the centrality of material goods over personal connection; what solution does he propose?

9 What overall tone does the play project? In what way does the tone change over the course of the play?

Synthesize Summary and Analysis

10 The plot contrasts an old way of life with the glimmer of a new way to live. How would you explain this in terms of the struggle between illusion and reality as seen in Greek tragedy?

Interpret the Play

11 Ibsen believed that "a dramatist's business is not to answer questions, but only to ask them." Would you describe the play's conclusion as closer to comic or tragic in tone? In what ways is it happy or unhappy, and what questions has he asked?

THE REAL AND THE SURREAL

While Arthur Miller's *Death of a Salesman* represented on the American stage the realist tradition of Ibsen and its overt social criticism, other dramatic techniques came largely into view in the modern theater. **Expressionism,** particularly as practiced by the German playwright Frank Wedekind (1864–1918), whose *Spring Awakening* scandalized audiences with its exploration of sexuality and puberty, draws strongly and mainly on subjective emotions and attempts to find symbolic means to depict them onstage. **Symbolism,** represented by the late works of the Swede August Strindberg (1849–1912) and whose chief practitioner in English is W. B. Yeats (1865–1939), employed poetic techniques by using image, character, or action to suggest meaning beyond the everyday literal level. The deployment of **surrealism,** a technique that bloomed in the early part of the twentieth century in which, as French writer and poet André Breton (1896–1966) suggests in his 1924 "Surrealist Manifesto," the realism of conscious and of unconscious experience are fused together into "an absolute reality, a surreality," added to the ultimate dreamlike quality of the lives onstage. By contrast, Bertolt Brecht's (1898–1956) development of **Epic Theater** brought to the theater a spare and highly stylized set that celebrated ideas over emotions. **Theater of the Absurd** combined comedic elements with a sense of meaninglessness as practiced by Eugene Ionesco (1909–1994), Samuel Beckett (1906–1989), and Edward Albee (chapter 32).

"Someone like Tennessee Williams . . . wrote . . . with a sort of added measure of lyricism and poetry." Conversation with Edwin Wilson

In addition, the American theater's Tennessee Williams's heightened form of realism supplied a poetic overlay to the situation and language, even a kind of *surrealism* in the family dynamic. Williams moves from actual scene to imagined or remembered encounter, and we follow the events almost as though we hallucinate them; the logic of the action is close to the logic of dream.

As Williams—who was born Thomas Lanier Williams, but kept his college nickname "Tennessee"—wrote in *Production Notes to The Glass Menagerie*,

> *Being a memory play,* The Glass Menagerie *can be presented with unusual freedom of convention. Because of its considerably delicate or tenuous material, atmospheric touches and subtleties of direction play a particularly important part. Expressionism and all other unconventional techniques in drama have only one valid aim, and that is a closer approach to truth. When a play employs unconventional techniques, it is not, or certainly shouldn't be, trying to escape its responsibility of dealing with reality, or interpreting experience, but is actually or should be attempting to find a closer approach, a more penetrating and vivid expression of things as they are.*

Much of the rest of that essay—and much of Williams's subsequent work—insists on avoiding "The straight realistic play with its genuine Frigidaire and authentic ice cubes . . . " but his is a kind of lover's quarrel with the idea of realism; he heightens the language of everyday discourse and lowers the lighting so that "the stage is dim." Characters stand in spotlit shafts of light when, turn by turn, they speak, and often what

"Tennessee was splendid enough a mind to be able to write his women as women, and his men as men. I don't think he was hiding anything. . . . It was only the half-blind straight critics who decided [that if] Tennessee Williams was gay, he must have been lying when he wrote women, which strikes me as being the critical fallacy, as we love to call it." Conversation with Edward Albee

passes for dialogue is a kind of back-and-forth monologue. Nonetheless, the underlying assumption here is that the playwright must scrutinize the real world and portray actual behavior.

In *The Glass Menagerie*, the family is middle class—southern and shabby genteel. The mother with her insistence on manners and self-deluding remembrance of "gentlemen callers," the crippled daughter Laura and the tortured brother Tom—who attempts to both escape from and come to terms with his heritage—form a traditional family unit (with the father gone). But, as the play's title suggests, things are brittle, breakable, and this particular middle-class "menagerie" is just as much at risk as the Loman clan.

Tennessee Williams (1911–1983)

Born in Mississippi, Tennessee Williams lived in a small town with his mother and maternal grandparents. His father, a salesman, was frequently away. However, when his father moved the family to St. Louis, Williams grew unhappy—largely because of the taunts his father constantly directed toward him—and turned to writing as an escape. After drifting among three universities, Williams earned a B.A. from the University of Iowa and began a life of wandering and writing plays. He became one of the most important American playwrights of the century, writing masterpiece after masterpiece including *The Glass Menagerie* (1945), *A Streetcar Named Desire* (1947), *Cat on a Hot Tin Roof* (1954), and *Suddenly Last Summer* (1958). Symbolic and poetic, much of his work is set in the South, where his highly developed characters struggle with feelings of isolation. Williams himself struggled with such feelings, as his homosexuality excluded him from mainstream society. Although he won his second Pulitzer Prize in 1955, Williams experienced an artistic and personal decline from that point to the end of his life.

AS YOU READ Trace the intertwining threads of the starkly real and the lyrical element in the language.

The Glass Menagerie (1945)

nobody, not even the rain, has such small hands

—e. e. cummings

CHARACTERS

AMANDA WINGFIELD, *the mother. A little woman of great but confused vitality clinging frantically to another time and place. Her characterization must be carefully created, not copied from type. She is not paranoiac, but her life is paranoia. There is much to admire in Amanda, and as much to love and pity as there is to laugh at. Certainly she has endurance and a kind of heroism, and though her foolishness makes her unwittingly cruel at times, there is tenderness in her slight person.*

LAURA WINGFIELD, *her daughter. Amanda, having failed to establish contact with reality, continues to live vitally in her illusions, but Laura's situation is even graver. A childhood illness has left her crippled, one leg slightly shorter than the other, and held in a brace. This defect need not be more than suggested on the stage. Stemming from this, Laura's separation increases till she is like a piece of her own glass collection, too exquisitely fragile to move from the shelf.*

TOM WINGFIELD, *her son. And the narrator of the play. A poet with a job in a warehouse. His nature is not remorseless, but to escape from a trap he has to act without pity.*

JIM O'CONNOR, *the gentleman caller. A nice, ordinary, young man.*

SCENE: *An alley in St. Louis.*

PART I: *Preparation for a Gentleman Caller.*

PART II: *The Gentleman Calls.*

TIME: *Now and the Past.*

SCENE I

The Wingfield apartment is in the rear of the building, one of those vast hivelike conglomerations of cellular living-units that flower as warty growths in overcrowded urban centers of lower middle-class population and are symptomatic of the impulse of this largest and fundamentally enslaved section of American society to avoid fluidity and differentiation and to exist and function as one interfused mass of automatism.

The apartment faces an alley and is entered by a fire-escape, a structure whose name is a touch of accidental poetic truth, for all of these huge buildings are always burning with the slow and implacable fires of human desperation. The fire-escape is included in the set—that is, the landing of it and steps descending from it.

The scene is memory and is therefore nonrealistic. Memory takes a lot of poetic license. It omits some details; others are exaggerated, according to the emotional value of the articles it touches, for memory is seated predominantly in the heart. The interior is therefore rather dim and poetic.

At the rise of the curtain, the audience is faced with the dark, grim rear wall of the Wingfield tenement. This building, which runs parallel to the footlights, is flanked on both sides by dark, narrow alleys which run into murky canyons of tangled clotheslines, garbage cans, and the sinister lattice-work of neighboring fire-escapes. It is up and down these side alleys that exterior entrances and exits are made, during the play. At the end of TOM's *opening commentary, the dark tenement wall slowly reveals (by means of transparency) the interior of the ground floor Wingfield apartment.*

Downstage is the living room, which also serves as a sleeping room for LAURA, *the sofa unfolding to make her bed. Upstage, center, and divided by a wide arch or second proscenium with transparent faded portieres (or second curtain), is the dining room. In an old-fashioned what-not in the living room are seen scores of transparent glass animals. A blown-up photograph of the father hangs on the wall of the living room, facing the audience, to the left of the archway. It is the face of a very handsome young man in a doughboy's First World War cap. He is gallantly smiling, ineluctably smiling, as if to say, "I will be smiling forever."*

The audience hears and sees the opening scene in the dining room through both the transparent fourth wall of the building and the transparent gauze portieres of the dining-room arch. It is during this revealing scene that the fourth wall slowly ascends, out of sight. This transparent exterior wall is not brought down again until the very end of the play, during TOM's *final speech.*

The narrator is an undisguised convention of the play. He takes whatever license with dramatic convention as is convenient to his purposes.

TOM *enters dressed as a merchant sailor from alley, stage left, and strolls across the front of the stage to the fire-escape. There he stops and lights a cigarette. He addresses the audience.*

TOM: Yes, I have tricks in my pocket, I have things up my sleeve. But I am opposite of a stage magician. He gives you illusion that has the appearance of truth. I give you truth in the pleasant disguise of illusion. To begin with, I turn back time. I reverse it to that   5
quaint period, the thirties, when the huge middle class of America was matriculating in a school for the blind. Their eyes had failed them, or they had failed their eyes, and so they were having their fingers pressed forcibly down on the fiery Braille alphabet   10
of a dissolving economy. In Spain there was revolution. Here there was only shouting and confusion. In Spain there was Guernica. Here there were disturbances of labor, sometimes pretty violent, in otherwise peaceful cities such as Chicago, Cleveland, Saint   15
Louis. . . . This is the social background of the play.

(Music.)

The play is memory. Being a memory play, it is dimly lighted, it is sentimental, it is not realistic. In memory everything seems to happen to music. That explains

Tom (Sam Waterston) delivers the opening monologue in the 1973 film directed by Anthony Harvey.

20 the fiddle in the wings. I am the narrator of the play, and also a character in it. The other characters are my mother, Amanda, my sister, Laura, and a gentleman caller who appears in the final scenes. He is the

25 most realistic character in the play, being an emissary from a world of reality that we were somehow set apart from. But since I have a poet's weakness for symbols, I am using this character also as a symbol; he is the long delayed but always expected something that we live for. There is a fifth character in the play who doesn't appear except in this larger-than-life

30 photograph over the mantel. This is our father who left us a long time ago. He was a telephone man who fell in love with long distances; he gave up his job with the telephone company and skipped the light

35 fantastic out of town. . . . The last we heard of him was a picture post-card from Mazatlán, on the Pacific coast of Mexico, containing a message of two words— "Hello—Goodbye!" and no address. I think the rest of the play will explain itself. . . .

AMANDA's voice becomes audible through the portieres.

(Legend on screen: "Où sont les neiges.")
  He divides the portieres and enters the upstage area.
  AMANDA and LAURA are seated at a drop-leaf table.
  Eating is indicated by gestures without food or utensils.
  AMANDA faces the audience.
    TOM and LAURA are seated in profile.
  The interior has lit up softly and through the scrim we see AMANDA and LAURA seated at the table in the upstage area.

40 **AMANDA:** *(calling)* Tom?

TOM: Yes, Mother.

AMANDA: We can't say grace until you come to the table!

TOM: Coming, Mother. *(He bows slightly and withdraws,*
45 *reappearing a few moments later in his place at the table.)*

AMANDA: *(to her son)* Honey, don't *push* with your *fingers*. If you have to push with something, the thing to push with is a crust of bread. And chew—chew! Animals have sections in their stomachs which enable

50 them to digest food without mastication, but human beings are supposed to chew their food before they swallow it down. Eat food leisurely, son, and really enjoy it. A well-cooked meal has lots of delicate flavors that have to be held in the mouth for apprecia-

55 tion. So chew your food and give your salivary glands a chance to function!

TOM deliberately lays his imaginary fork down and pushes his chair back from the table.

TOM: I haven't enjoyed one bite of this dinner because of your constant directions on how to eat it. It's you that makes me rush through meals with your hawk-like attention to every bite I take. Sickening—spoils 60 my appetite—all this discussion of animals' secretion—salivary glands—mastication!

AMANDA: *(lightly)* Temperament like a Metropolitan star! *(He rises and crosses downstage.)* You're not excused from the table. 65

TOM: I am getting a cigarette.

AMANDA: You smoke too much.

LAURA rises.

LAURA: I'll bring in the blanc mange.

He remains standing with his cigarette by the portieres during the following.

AMANDA: *(rising)* No, sister, no, sister—you be the lady this time and I'll be the darky. 70

LAURA: I'm already up.

AMANDA: Resume your seat, little sister—I want you to stay fresh and pretty—for gentlemen callers!

LAURA: I'm not expecting any gentlemen callers.

AMANDA: *(crossing out to kitchenette. Airily)* Sometimes 75 they come when they are least expected! Why, I remember one Sunday afternoon in Blue Mountain— *(Enters kitchenette.)*

TOM: I know what's coming!

LAURA: Yes. But let her tell it. 80

TOM: Again?

LAURA: She loves to tell it.

AMANDA returns with a bowl of dessert.

AMANDA: One Sunday afternoon in Blue Mountain— your mother received—*seventeen!*—gentlemen callers! Why, sometimes there weren't chairs enough 85 to accommodate them all. We had to send the nigger over to bring in folding chairs from the parish house.

TOM: *(remaining at the portieres)* How did you entertain those gentlemen callers?

AMANDA: I understood the art of conversation! 90

TOM: I bet you could talk.

AMANDA: Girls in those days *knew* how to talk, I can tell you.

Amanda (Katharine Hepburn) clears the table.

TOM: Yes?

(Image: AMANDA as a girl on a porch greeting callers.)

95 **AMANDA:** They knew how to entertain their gentlemen callers. It wasn't enough for a girl to be possessed of a pretty face and a graceful figure—although I wasn't slighted in either respect. She also needed to have a nimble wit and a tongue to meet all occasions.

100 **TOM:** What did you talk about?

AMANDA: Things of importance going on in the world! Never anything coarse or common or vulgar. *(She addresses TOM as though he were seated in the vacant chair at the table though he remains by the portieres. He plays* 105 *this scene as though he held the book.)* My callers were gentlemen—all! Among my callers were some of the most prominent young planters of the Mississippi Delta—planters and sons of planters!

TOM *motions for music and a spot of light on* AMANDA. *Her eyes lift, her face glows, her voice becomes rich and elegiac.*
(Screen legend: "Où sont les neiges.")

There was young Champ Laughlin who later became 110 vice-president of the Delta Planters Bank. Hadley Stevenson who was drowned in Moon Lake and left his widow one hundred and fifty thousand in Government bonds. There were the Cutrere brothers, Wesley and Bates. Bates was one of my bright partic- 115 ular beaux! He got in a quarrel with that wild Wainwright boy. They shot it out on the floor of Moon Lake Casino. Bates was shot through the stomach. Died in the ambulance on his way to Memphis. His widow was also well-provided for, came into eight or

ten thousand acres, that's all. She married him on 120 the rebound—never loved her—carried my picture on him the night he died! And there was that boy that every girl in the Delta had set her cap for! That beautiful, brilliant young Fitzhugh boy from Greene County! 125

TOM: What did he leave his widow?

AMANDA: He never married! Gracious, you talk as though all of my old admirers had turned up their toes to the daisies!

TOM: Isn't this the first you mentioned that still 130 survives?

AMANDA: That Fitzhugh boy went North and made a fortune—came to be known as the Wolf of Wall Street! He had the Midas touch, whatever he touched turned to gold! And I could have been Mrs. Duncan 135 J. Fitzhugh, mind you! But—I picked your *father!*

LAURA: *(rising)* Mother, let me clear the table.

AMANDA: No dear, you go in front and study your typewriter chart. Or practice your shorthand a little. Stay fresh and pretty!—It's almost time for our 140 gentlemen callers to start arriving. *(She flounces girlishly toward the kitchenette.)* How many do you suppose we're going to entertain this afternoon?

TOM *throws down the paper and jumps up with a groan.*

LAURA: *(alone in the dining room)* I don't believe we're going to receive any, Mother. 145

AMANDA: *(reappearing, airily)* What? No one—not one? You must be joking! *(LAURA nervously echoes her laugh. She slips in a fugitive manner through the half-open portieres and draws them gently behind her. A shaft of very clear light is thrown on her face against the faded tapes-* 150 *try of the curtains.) (Music: "The Glass Menagerie" under faintly.) (Lightly.)* Not one gentleman caller? It can't be true! There must be a flood, there must have been a tornado!

LAURA: It isn't a flood, it's not a tornado, Mother. I'm 155 just not popular like you were in Blue Mountain. . . . *(TOM utters another groan. LAURA glances at him with a faint, apologetic smile. Her voice catching a little.)* Mother's afraid I'm going to be an old maid.

(The scene dims out with the "Glass Menagerie" music.)

SCENE II

"Laura, Haven't You Ever Liked Some Boy?"

On the dark stage the screen is lighted with the image of blue roses.

Gradually LAURA's *figure becomes apparent and the screen goes out.*

The music subsides.

LAURA *is seated in the delicate ivory chair at the small clawfoot table.*

She wears a dress of soft violet material for a kimono—her hair tied back from her forehead with a ribbon.

She is washing and polishing her collection of glass.

AMANDA *appears on the fire-escape steps. At the sound of her ascent,* LAURA *catches her breath, thrusts the bowl of ornaments away, and seats herself stiffly before the diagram of the typewriter keyboard as though it held her spellbound. Something has happened to* AMANDA. *It is written in her face as she climbs to the landing: a look that is grim and hopeless and a little absurd.*

She has on one of those cheap or imitation velvety-looking cloth coats with imitation fur collar. Her hat is five or six years old, one of those dreadful cloche hats that were worn in the late twenties, and she is clasping an enormous black patent-leather pocketbook with nickel clasp and initials. This is her full-dress outfit, the one she usually wears to the D.A.R.

Before entering she looks through the door.

She purses her lips, opens her eyes wide, rolls them upward, and shakes her head.

Then she slowly lets herself in the door. Seeing her mother's expression LAURA *touches her lips with a nervous gesture.*

LAURA: Hello, Mother, I was— (*She makes a nervous gesture toward the chart on the wall.* AMANDA *leans against the shut door and stares at* LAURA *with a martyred look.*)

AMANDA: Deception? Deception? (*She slowly removes*
5   *her hat and gloves, continuing the swift suffering stare. She lets the hat and gloves fall on the floor—a bit of acting.*)

Laura (Joanna Miles) gazes at her glass ornaments.

LAURA: (*shakily*) How was the D.A.R. meeting? (AMANDA *slowly opens her purse and removes a dainty white handkerchief, which she shakes out delicately and delicately touches to her lips and nostrils.*) Didn't you go   10 to the D.A.R. meeting, Mother?

AMANDA: (*faintly, almost inaudibly*) —No.—No. (*Then more forcibly.*) I did not have the strength—to go to the D.A.R. In fact, I did not have the courage! I wanted to find a hole in the ground and hide myself   15 in it forever! (*She crosses slowly to the wall and removes the diagram of the typewriter keyboard. She holds it in front of her for a second, staring at it sweetly and sorrowfully—then bites her lips and tears it in two pieces.*)

LAURA: (*faintly*) Why did you do that, Mother?   20 (AMANDA *repeats the same procedure with the chart of the Gregg Alphabet.*) Why are you—

AMANDA: Why? Why? How old are you, Laura?

LAURA: Mother, you know my age.

AMANDA: I thought that you were an adult; it seems   25 that I was mistaken. (*She crosses slowly to the sofa and sinks down and stares at* LAURA.)

LAURA: Please don't stare at me, Mother.

AMANDA *closes her eyes and lowers her head. Count ten.*

AMANDA: What are we going to do, what is going to become of us, what is the future?   30

Count ten.

LAURA: Has something happened, Mother? (AMANDA *draws a long breath and takes out the handkerchief again. Dabbing process.*) Mother, has—something happened?

AMANDA: I'll be all right in a minute. I'm just bewildered—(*count five*)—by life. . . .   35

LAURA: Mother, I wish that you would tell me what's happened.

AMANDA: As you know, I was supposed to be inducted into my office at the D.A.R. this afternoon. (*Image: A swarm of typewriters.*) But I stopped off at Rubicam's   40 Business College to speak to your teachers about your having a cold and ask them what progress they thought you were making down there.

LAURA: Oh. . . .

AMANDA: I went to the typing instructor and intro-   45 duced myself as your mother. She didn't know who you were. Wingfield, she said. We don't have any such student enrolled at the school! I assured her she

50 did, that you had been going to classes since early in January. "I wonder," she said, "if you could be talking about that terribly shy little girl who dropped out of school after only a few days' attendance?" "No," I said, "Laura, my daughter, has been going to school every day for the past six weeks!" "Excuse me," she

55 said. She took the attendance book out and there was your name, unmistakably printed, and all the dates you were absent until they decided that you had dropped out of school. I still said, "No, there must have been some mistake! There must have been

60 some mix-up in the records!" And she said, "No—I remember her perfectly now. Her hands shook so that she couldn't hit the right keys! The first time we gave a speed-test, she broke down completely—was sick at the stomach and almost had to be carried

65 into the wash-room! After that morning she never showed up any more. We phoned the house but never got any answer"—while I was working at Famous and Barr, I suppose, demonstrating those—Oh! I felt so weak I could barely keep on my feet. I had

70 to sit down while they got me a glass of water! Fifty dollars' tuition, all of our plans—my hopes and ambitions for you—just gone up the spout, just gone up the spout like that. (LAURA *draws a long breath and gets awkwardly to her feet. She crosses to the Victrola, and winds*

75 *it up.*) What are you doing?

LAURA: Oh! (*She releases the handle and returns to her seat.*)

AMANDA: Laura, where have been going when you've gone out pretending that you were going to business college?

80 LAURA: I've just been going out walking.

AMANDA: That's not true.

LAURA: It is. I just went walking.

AMANDA: Walking? Walking? In winter? Deliberately courting pneumonia in that light coat? Where did

85 you walk to, Laura?

LAURA: It was the lesser of two evils, Mother. (*Image: Winter scene in park.*) I couldn't go back up. I—threw up—on the floor!

AMANDA: From half past seven till after five every day

90 you mean to tell me you walked around in the park, because you wanted to make me think that you were still going to Rubicam's Business College?

LAURA: It wasn't as bad as it sounds. I went inside places to get warmed up.

95 AMANDA: Inside where?

LAURA: I went in the art museum and the bird-houses at the Zoo. I visited the penguins every day! Sometimes I did without lunch and went to the movies. Lately I've been spending most of my afternoons in the Jewel-box, that big glass house where they raise 100 the tropical flowers.

AMANDA: You did all this to deceive me, just for the deception? (LAURA *looks down.*) Why?

LAURA: Mother, when you're disappointed, you get that awful suffering look on your face, like the picture of Jesus' mother in the museum! 105

AMANDA: Hush!

LAURA: I couldn't face it.

Pause. A whisper of string.
(Legend: "The Crust of Humility.")

AMANDA: (*hopelessly fingering the huge pocketbook*) So what are we going to do the rest of our lives? Stay 110 home and watch the parades go by? Amuse ourselves with the glass menagerie, darling? Eternally play those worn-out phonograph records your father left as a painful reminder of him? We won't have a business career—we've given that up because it gave us 115 nervous indigestion! (*Laughs wearily.*) What is there left but dependency all our lives? I know so well what becomes of unmarried women who aren't prepared to occupy a position. I've seen such pitiful cases in the South—barely tolerated spinsters living upon the 120 grudging patronage of sister's husband or brother's wife!—stuck away in some little mousetrap of a room—encouraged by one in-law to visit another— little birdlike women without any nest—eating the crust of humility all their life! Is that the future that 125 we've mapped out for ourselves? I swear it's the only alternative I can think of! It isn't a very pleasant alternative, is it? Of course—some girls *do marry.* (LAURA *twists her hands nervously.*) Haven't you ever liked some boy? 130

LAURA: Yes. I liked one once. (*Rises.*) I came across his picture a while ago.

AMANDA: (*with some interest*) He gave you his picture?

LAURA: No, it's in the year-book.

AMANDA: (*disappointed*) Oh—a high-school boy. 135

(*Screen image:* JIM *as the high school hero bearing a silver cup.*)

LAURA: Yes. His name was Jim. (LAURA *lifts the heavy annual from the clawfoot table.*) Here he is in *The Pirates of Penzance.*

Laura and Amanda discuss the future.

AMANDA: *(absently)* The what?

140 **LAURA:** The operetta the senior class put on. He had a wonderful voice and we sat across the aisle from each other Mondays, Wednesdays, and Fridays in the Aud. Here he is with the silver cup for debating! See his grin?

145 **AMANDA:** *(absently)* He must have had a jolly disposition.

LAURA: He used to call me—Blue Roses.

(Image: Blue roses.)

AMANDA: Why did he call you such a name as that?

LAURA: When I had that attack of pleurosis—he asked
150 me what was the matter when I came back. I said pleurosis—he thought that I said Blue Roses! So that's what he always called me after that. Whenever he saw me, he'd holler, "Hello, Blue Roses!" I didn't care for the girl that he went out with. Emily Meisen-
155 bach. Emily was the best-dressed girl at Soldan. She never struck me, though, as being sincere. . . . It says in the Personal Section—they're engaged. That's—six years ago! They must be married by now.

AMANDA: Girls that aren't cut out for business careers
160 usually wind up married to some nice man. *(Gets up with a spark of revival.)* Sister, that's what you'll do!

LAURA utters a startled, doubtful laugh. She reaches quickly for a piece of glass.

LAURA: But, Mother—

AMANDA: Yes? *(Crossing to photograph.)*

LAURA: *(in a tone of frightened apology)* I'm—crippled!

(Image: Screen.)

165 **AMANDA:** Nonsense! Laura, I've told you never, never to use that word. Why, you're not crippled, you just

have a little defect—hardly noticeable, even! When people have some slight disadvantage like that, they cultivate other things to make up for it—develop charm—and vivacity—and—*charm!* That's all you 170 have to do! *(She turns again to the photograph.)* One thing your father had *plenty of*—was *charm!*

TOM motions to the fiddle in the wings.
(The scene fades out with music.)

SCENE III

(Legend on the screen: "After the Fiasco—")
 TOM speaks from the fire-escape landing.

TOM: After the fiasco at Rubicam's Business College, the idea of getting a gentleman caller for Laura began to play a more important part in Mother's calculations. It became an obsession. Like some archetype of the universal unconscious, the image 5 of the gentleman caller haunted our small apart-ment. . . . *(Image: Young man at door with flowers.)* An evening at home rarely passed without some allusion to this image, this specter, this hope. . . . Even when he wasn't mentioned, his presence hung in Mother's 10 preoccupied look and in my sister's frightened, apolo-getic manner—hung like a sentence passed upon the Wingfields! Mother was a woman of action as well as words. She began to take logical steps in the planned direction. Late that winter and in the early spring— 15 realizing that extra money would be needed to properly feather the nest and plume the bird—she conducted a vigorous campaign on the telephone, roping in subscribers to one of those magazines for matrons called *The Home-maker's Companion,* the 20 type of journal that features the serialized subli-mations of ladies of letters who think in terms of delicate cuplike breasts, slim, tapering waists, rich, creamy thighs, eyes like wood smoke in autumn, fingers that soothe and caress like strains of music, 25 bodies as powerful as Etruscan sculpture.

(Screen image: Glamour magazine cover.)
 AMANDA enters with phone on long extension cord. She is spotted in the dim stage.

AMANDA: Ida Scott? This is Amanda Wingfield! We *missed* you at the D.A.R. last Monday! I said to my-self: She's probably suffering with that sinus condi-tion! How is that sinus condition? Horrors! Heaven 30 have mercy!—You're a Christian martyr, yes, that's what you are, a Christian martyr! Well, I just now happened to notice that your subscription to the *Companion*'s about to expire! Yes, it expires with the next issue, honey!—just when that wonderful new 35 serial by Bessie Mae Hopper is getting off to such an exciting start. Oh, honey, it's something that you can't miss! You remember how *Gone with the Wind* took everybody by storm? You simply couldn't go out if you hadn't read it. All everybody *talked* was Scarlett O'Hara. Well, this is a book that critics already compare to *Gone with the Wind*. It's the *Gone with the Wind* of the post–World War generation!—What?—Burning?—Oh, honey, don't let them burn, go take a look in the oven and I'll hold the wire! Heavens—I think she's hung up!

(Dim out.)

(Legend on screen: "You think I'm in love with Continental Shoemakers?")

Before the stage is lighted, the violent voices of TOM *and* AMANDA *are heard. They are quarreling behind the portieres. In front of them stands* LAURA *with clenched hands and panicky expression.*

A clear pool of light on her figure throughout this scene.

TOM: What in Christ's name am I—

AMANDA: *(shrilly)* Don't you use that—

TOM: Supposed to do!

AMANDA: Expression! Not in my—

TOM: Ohhh!

AMANDA: Presence! Have you gone out of your senses?

TOM: I have, that's true, *driven* out!

AMANDA: What is the matter with you, you—big—big—IDIOT!

TOM: Look!—I've got *no thing*, no single thing—

AMANDA: Lower your voice!

Amanda scolds her son.

TOM: In my life here that I can call my own! Everything is—

AMANDA: Stop that shouting!

TOM: Yesterday you confiscated my books! You had the nerve to—

AMANDA: I took that horrible novel back to the library—yes! That hideous book by that insane Mr. Lawrence. *(TOM laughs wildly.)* I cannot control the output of diseased minds or people who cater to them—*(TOM laughs still more wildly.)* BUT I WON'T ALLOW SUCH FILTH BROUGHT INTO MY HOUSE! No, no, no, no, no!

TOM: House, house! Who pays rent on it, who makes a slave of himself to—

AMANDA: *(fairly screeching)* Don't you DARE to—

TOM: No, no, *I* mustn't say things! *I've* got to just—

AMANDA: Let me tell you—

TOM: I don't want to hear any more! *(He tears the portieres open. The upstage area is lit with a turgid smoky red glow.)*

AMANDA's *hair is in metal curlers and she wears a very old bathrobe, much too large for her slight figure, a relic of the faithless Mr. Wingfield.*

The upright typewriter and a wild disarray of manuscripts are on the drop-leaf table. The quarrel was probably precipitated by AMANDA's *interruption of his creative labor. A chair lying overthrown on the floor.*

Their gesticulating shadows are cast on the ceiling by the fiery glow.

AMANDA: You *will* hear more, you—

TOM: No, I won't hear more, I'm going out!

AMANDA: You come right back in—

TOM: Out, out, out! Because I'm—

AMANDA: Come back here, Tom Wingfield! I'm not through talking to you!

TOM: Oh, go—

LAURA: *(desperately)* Tom!

AMANDA: You're going to listen, and no more insolence from you! I'm at the end of my patience! *(He comes back toward her.)*

TOM: What do you think I'm at? Aren't I supposed to have any patience to reach the end of, Mother? I know, I know. It seems unimportant to you, what I'm *doing*—what I *want* to do—having a little *difference* between them! You don't think that—

AMANDA: I think you've been doing things that you're ashamed of. That's why you act like this. I don't be-
95   lieve that you go every night to the movies. Nobody goes to the movies night after night. Nobody in their right minds goes to the movies as often as you pretend to. People don't go to the movies at nearly mid-night, and movies don't let out at two A.M. Come in
100   stumbling. Muttering to yourself like a maniac! You get three hours' sleep and then go to work. Oh, I can picture the way you're doing down there. Moping, doping, because you're in no condition.

TOM: *(wildly)* No, I'm in no condition!

105   **AMANDA:** What right have you got to jeopardize your job? Jeopardize the security of us all? How do you think we'd manage if you were—

TOM: Listen! You think I'm crazy *about* the *warehouse!* *(He bends fiercely toward her slight figure.)* You think
110   I'm in love with the Continental Shoemakers? You think I want to spend fifty-five *years* down there in that—*celotex interior!* with—*fluorescent—tubes!* Look! I'd rather somebody picked up a crowbar and battered out my brains—than go back mornings! I
115   *go!* Every time you come in yelling that God damn *"Rise and Shine!" "Rise and Shine!"* I say to myself, "How *lucky dead* people are!" But I get up. I *go!* For sixty-five dollars a month I give up all that I dream of doing and being *ever!* And you say self—*self's* all I
120   ever think of. Why, listen, if self is what I thought of, Mother, I'd be where he is—! *(Pointing to father's picture.)* As far as the system of transportation reaches! *(He starts past her. She grabs his arm.)* Don't grab at me, Mother!

125   **AMANDA:** Where are you going?

TOM: I'm going to the *movies!*

AMANDA: I don't believe that lie!

TOM: *(crouching toward her, overtowering her tiny figure. She backs away, gasping)* I'm going to opium dens! Yes,
130   opium dens, dens of vice and criminals' hangouts, Mother. I've joined the Hogan gang, I'm a hired as-sassin, I carry a tommy-gun in a violin case! I run a string of cat-houses in the Valley! They call me Killer, Killer Wingfield, I'm leading a double-life, a
135   simple, honest warehouse worker by day, by night a dynamic *czar* of the *underworld, Mother.* I go to gambling casinos, I spin away fortunes on the rou-lette table! I wear a patch over one eye and a false mustache, sometimes I put on green whiskers. On
140   those occasions they call me—*El Diablo!* Oh, I could tell you many things to make you sleepless! My en-emies plan to dynamite this place. They're going to blow us all sky-high some night! I'll be glad, very

happy, and so will you! You'll go up, up on a broom-stick, over Blue Mountain with seventeen gentlemen   145
callers! You ugly—babbling old—*witch.* . . . *(He goes through a series of violent, clumsy movements, seizing his overcoat, lunging to the door, pulling it fiercely open. The women watch him, aghast. His arm catches in the sleeve of the coat as he struggles to pull it on. For a moment he is*   150
pinioned by the bulky garment. With an outraged groan he tears the coat off again, splitting the shoulders of it, and hurls it across the room. It strikes against the shelf of LAURA's *glass collection, there is a tinkle of shattering glass.* LAURA *cries out as if wounded.)*   155

(Music legend: "The Glass Menagerie.")

LAURA: *(shrilly)* My glass!—menagerie. . . . *(She covers her face and turns away.)*

But AMANDA *is still stunned and stupefied by the "ugly witch" so that she barely notices the occurrence. Now she recovers her speech.*

AMANDA: *(in an awful voice)* I won't speak to you—until you apologize! *(She crosses through the portieres and draws them together behind her.* TOM *is left with* LAURA.   160
LAURA *clings weakly to the mantel with her face averted.* TOM *stares at her stupidly for a moment. Then he crosses to shelf. Drops awkwardly to his knees to collect the fallen glass, glancing at* LAURA *as if he would speak but couldn't.)*

"The Glass Menagerie" music steals in as

(The scene dims out.)

SCENE IV

The interior is dark. Faint light in the alley.

A deep-voiced bell in a church is tolling the hour of five as the scene commences.

TOM *appears at the top of the alley. After each solemn boom of the bell in the tower, he shakes a little noise-maker or rattle as if to express the tiny spasm of man in contrast to the sustained power and dignity of the Almighty. This and the unsteadiness of his advance make it evident that he has been drinking.*

As he climbs the few steps to the fire-escape landing light steals up inside. LAURA *appears in night-dress, observing* TOM's *empty bed in the front room.*

TOM *fishes in his pockets for his door-key, removing a motley assortment of articles in the search, including a perfect shower of movie-ticket stubs and an empty bottle. At last he finds the key, but just as he is about to insert it, it slips from his fingers. He strikes a match and crouches below the door.*

TOM: *(bitterly)* One crack—and it falls through!

LAURA *opens the door.*

LAURA: Tom! Tom, what are you doing?

TOM: Looking for a door-key.

LAURA: Where have you been all this time?

5 **TOM:** I have been to the movies.

LAURA: All this time at the movies?

TOM: There was a very long program. There was a Garbo picture and a Mickey Mouse and a travelogue and a newsreel and a preview of coming attractions.
10 And there was an organ solo and a collection for the milk-fund—simultaneously—which ended up in a terrible fight between a fat lady and an usher!

LAURA: *(innocently)* Did you have to stay through everything?

15 **TOM:** Of course! And, oh, I forgot! There was a big stage show! The headliner on this stage show was Malvolio the Magician. He performed wonderful tricks, many of them, such as pouring water back and forth between pitchers. First it turned to wine
20 and then it turned to beer and then it turned to whisky. I know it was whiskey it finally turned into because he needed somebody to come up out of the audience to help him, and I came up—both shows! It was Kentucky Straight Bourbon. A very gener-
25 ous fellow, he gave souvenirs. *(He pulls from his back pocket a shimmering rainbow-colored scarf.)* He gave me this. This is his magic scarf. You can have it, Laura. You wave it over a canary cage and you get a bowl of gold-fish. You wave it over the gold-fish bowl and
30 they fly away canaries. . . . But the wonderfullest trick of all was the coffin trick. We nailed him into a coffin and he got out of the coffin without remov-ing one nail. *(He has come inside.)* There is a trick that would come in handy for me—get me out of this 2 by
35 4 situation! *(Flops onto bed and starts removing his shoes.)*

LAURA: Tom—Shhh!

TOM: What you shushing me for?

LAURA: You'll wake up Mother.

TOM: Goody, goody! Pay 'er back for all those "Rise an'
40 Shines." *(Lies down, groaning.)* You know it don't take much intelligence to get yourself into a nailed-up coffin, Laura. But who in hell ever got himself out of one without removing one nail?

As if in answer, the father's grinning photograph lights up. (Scene dims out.)
Immediately following: The church bell is heard striking six. At the sixth stroke the alarm clock goes off in AMANDA's *room, and after a few moments we hear her calling: "Rise*

Laura helps her brother into bed.

and Shine! Rise and Shine! Laura, go tell your brother to rise and shine!"

TOM: *(sitting up slowly)* I'll rise—but I won't shine.

The light increases.

AMANDA: Laura, tell your brother his coffee is ready. 45

LAURA *slips into front room.*

LAURA: Tom! It's nearly seven. Don't make Mother nervous. *(He stares at her stupidly. Beseechingly.)* Tom, speak to Mother this morning. Make up with her, apologize, speak to her!

TOM: She won't to me. It's her that started not speaking. 50

LAURA: If you just say you're sorry she'll start speaking.

TOM: Her not speaking—is that such a tragedy?

LAURA: Please—please!

AMANDA: *(calling from the kitchenette)* Laura, are you go-ing to do what I asked you to do, or do I have to get 55 dressed and go out myself?

LAURA: Going, going—soon as I get on my coat! *(She pulls on a shapeless felt hat with nervous, jerky movement, pleadingly glancing at* TOM. *Rushes awkwardly for coat. The coat is one of* AMANDA's, *inaccurately made-over, the* 60 *sleeves too short for* LAURA.*)* Butter and what else?

AMANDA: *(entering upstage)* Just butter. Tell them to charge it.

LAURA: Mother, they make such faces when I do that.

AMANDA: Sticks and stones may break my bones, but 65 the expression on Mr. Garfinkel's face won't harm us! Tell your brother his coffee is getting cold.

LAURA: *(at door)* Do what I asked you, will you, will you, Tom?

He looks sullenly away.

70 AMANDA: Laura, go now or just don't go at all!

LAURA: *(rushing out)*   Going—going! *(A second later she cries out.* TOM *springs up and crosses to the door.* AMANDA *rushes anxiously in.* TOM *opens the door.)*

TOM: Laura?

75 LAURA: I'm all right. I slipped, but I'm all right.

AMANDA: *(peering anxiously after her)*   If anyone breaks a leg on those fire-escape steps, the landlord ought to be sued for every cent he possesses! *(She shuts door. Remembers she isn't speaking and returns to other room.)*

As TOM *enters listlessly for his coffee, she turns her back to him and stands rigidly facing the window on the gloomy gray vault of the areaway. Its light on her face with its aged but childish features is cruelly sharp, satirical as a Daumier print.*
    (Music under: "Ave Maria.")
    TOM *glances sheepishly but sullenly at her averted figure and slumps at the table. The coffee is scalding hot; he sips it and gasps and spits it back in the cup. At his gasp,* AMANDA *catches her breath and half turns. Then she catches herself and turns back to window.*
    TOM *blows on his coffee, glancing sidewise at his mother. She clears her throat.* TOM *clears his. He starts to rise. Sinks back down again, scratches his head, clears his throat again.* AMANDA *coughs.* TOM *raises his cup in both hands to blow on it, his eyes staring over the rim of it at his mother for several moments. Then he slowly sets the cup down and awkwardly and hesitantly rises from the chair.*

80 TOM: *(hoarsely)*   Mother. I—I apologize. Mother. *(*AMANDA *draws a quick, shuddering breath. Her face works grotesquely. She breaks into childlike tears.)* I'm sorry for what I said, for everything that I said, I didn't mean it.

85 AMANDA: *(sobbingly)*   My devotion has made me a witch and so I make myself hateful to my children!

TOM: No, you *don't.*

AMANDA: I worry so much, don't sleep, it makes me nervous!

90 TOM: *(gently)*   I understand that.

AMANDA: I've had to put up a solitary battle all these years. But you're my right-hand bower! Don't fall down, don't fail!

TOM: *(gently)*   I try, Mother.

95 AMANDA: *(with great enthusiasm)*   Try and you will SUCCEED! *(The notion makes her breathless.)* Why, you—

you're just *full* of natural endowments! Both of my children—they're *unusual* children! Don't you think I know it? I'm so—*proud!* Happy and—feel I've—so much to be thankful for but—Promise me one thing, son!

100

TOM: What, Mother?

AMANDA: Promise, son, you'll—never be a drunkard!

TOM: *(turns to her grinning)*   I will never be a drunkard, Mother.

105

AMANDA: That's what frightened me so, that you'd be drinking! Eat a bowl of Purina!

TOM: Just coffee, Mother.

AMANDA: Shredded wheat biscuit?

TOM: No. No, Mother, just coffee.

110

AMANDA: You can't put in a day's work on an empty stomach. You've got ten minutes—don't gulp! Drinking too-hot liquids makes cancer of the stomach. . . . Put cream in.

TOM: No, thank you.

115

AMANDA: To cool it.

TOM: No! No, thank you, I want it black.

AMANDA: I know, but it's not good for you. We have to do all that we can to build ourselves up. In these trying times we live in, all that we have to cling to is—each other. . . . That's why it's so important to—Tom, I—I sent out your sister so I could discuss something with you. If you hadn't spoken I would have spoken to you. *(Sits down.)*

120

TOM: *(gently)*   What is it, Mother, that you want to discuss?

125

AMANDA: Laura!

TOM *puts his cup down slowly.*
    (Legend on screen: "Laura.")
    (Music: "The Glass Menagerie.")

TOM: —Oh.—Laura . . .

AMANDA: *(touching his sleeve)*   You know how Laura is. So quiet but—still water runs deep! She notices things and I think she—broods about them. *(*TOM *looks up.)* A few days ago I came in and she was crying.

130

TOM: What about?

AMANDA: You.

TOM: Me?

135

AMANDA: She has an idea that you're not happy here.

TOM: What gave her that idea?

AMANDA: What gives her any idea? However, you do
act strangely. I—I'm not criticizing, understand *that!*
140   I know your ambitions do not lie in the warehouse,
that like everybody in the whole wide world—you've
had to—make sacrifices, but—Tom—Tom—life's not
easy, it calls for—Spartan endurance! There's so
many things in my heart that I cannot describe to
145   you! I've never told you but I—*loved* your father. . . .

TOM: (*gently*) I know that, Mother.

AMANDA: And you—when I see you taking after his
ways! Staying out late—and—well, you *had* been
drinking the night you were in that—terrifying con-
150   dition! Laura says that you hate the apartment and
that you go out nights to get away from it! Is that
true, Tom?

TOM: No. You say there's so much in your heart that
you can't describe to me. That's true of me, too.
155   There's so much in my heart that I can't describe to
you! So let's respect each other's—

AMANDA: But, why—*why,* Tom—are you always so
restless? Where do you go to, nights?

TOM: I—go to the movies.

160 **AMANDA:** Why do you go to the movies so much, Tom?

TOM: I go to the movies because—I like adventure. Adventure is something I don't have much of at work, so
I go to the movies.

AMANDA: But, Tom, you go to the movies *entirely too*
165   *much!*

TOM: I like a lot of adventure.

    AMANDA *looks baffled, then hurt. As the familiar inquisition*
    resumes he becomes hard and impatient again. AMANDA
    slips back into her querulous attitude toward him.
    (*Image on screen: Sailing vessel with Jolly Roger.*)

AMANDA: Most young men find adventure in their
careers.

TOM: Then most young men are not employed in a
170   warehouse.

AMANDA: The world is full of young men employed in
warehouses and offices and factories.

TOM: Do all of them find adventure in their careers?

AMANDA: They do or they do without it! Not every-
175   body has a craze for adventure.

TOM: Man is by instinct a lover, a hunter, a fighter, and
none of those instincts are given much play at the
warehouse!

AMANDA: Man is by instinct! Don't quote instinct to
me! Instinct is something that people have got away   180
from! It belongs to animals! Christian adults don't
want it!

TOM: What do Christian adults want, then, Mother?

AMANDA: Superior things! Things of the mind and the
spirit! Only animals have to satisfy instincts! Surely   185
your aims are somewhat higher than theirs! Than
monkeys—pigs—

TOM: I reckon they're not.

AMANDA: You're joking. However, that isn't what I
wanted to discuss.   190

TOM: (*rising*) I haven't much time.

AMANDA: (*pushing his shoulders*) Sit down.

TOM: You want me to punch in red at the warehouse,
Mother?

AMANDA: You have five minutes. I want to talk about   195
Laura.

    (*Legend: "Plans and Provisions."*)

TOM: All right! What about Laura?

AMANDA: We have to be making some plans and provisions for her. She's older than you, two years, and
nothing has happened. She just drifts along doing   200
nothing. It frightens me terribly how she just drifts
along.

TOM: I guess she's the type that people call home girls.

AMANDA: There's no such type, and if there is, it's a
pity! That is unless the home is hers, with a husband!   205

TOM: What?

AMANDA: Oh, I can see the handwriting on the wall
as plain as I see the nose in front of my face! It's
terrifying! More and more you remind me of your
father! He was out all hours without explanation—   210
Then *left! Good-bye!* And me with the bag to hold.
I saw a letter you got from the Merchant Marine. I
know what you're dreaming of. I'm not standing here
blindfolded. Very well, then. Then *do* it! But not till
there's somebody to take your place.   215

TOM: What do you mean?

AMANDA: I mean that as soon as Laura has got somebody to take care of her, married, a home of her own,

220 independent—why, then you'll be free to go wherever you please, on land, on sea, whichever way the wind blows you! But until that time you've got to look out for your sister. I don't say me because I'm old and don't matter! I say for your sister because she's young 225 and dependent. I put her in business college—a dismal failure! Frightened her so it made her sick to her stomach. I took her over to the Young People's League at the church. Another fiasco. She spoke to nobody, nobody spoke to her. Now all she does is fool 230 with those pieces of glass and play those worn-out records. What kind of a life is that for a girl to lead!

TOM: What can I do about it?

AMANDA: Overcome selfishness! Self, self, self is all that you ever think of! *(TOM springs up and crosses to get his coat. It is ugly and bulky. He pulls on a cap with ear-* 235 *muffs.)* Where is your muffler? Put your wool muffler on! *(He snatches it angrily from the closet and tosses it around his neck and pulls both ends tight.)* Tom! I haven't said what I had in mind to ask you.

TOM: I'm too late to—

240 AMANDA: *(catching his arms—very importunately. Then shyly.)* Down at the warehouse, aren't there some—nice young men?

TOM: No!

AMANDA: There *must* be—*some.*

245 TOM: Mother—

    Gesture.

AMANDA: Find out one that's clean-living—doesn't drink and—ask him out for sister!

TOM: What?

AMANDA: For *sister!* To *meet!* Get *acquainted!*

250 TOM: *(stamping to the door)*   Oh, my *go-osh!*

AMANDA: Will you? *(He opens the door. Imploringly.)* Will you? *(He starts down.)* Will you? *Will* you, dear?

TOM: *(calling back)*   YES!

    AMANDA *closes the door hesitantly and with a troubled but faintly hopeful expression.*
        (Screen image: Glamour *magazine cover.)*
        Spot AMANDA *at phone.*

AMANDA: Ella Cartwright? This is Amanda Wing-255 field! How are you, honey? How is that kidney condition? *(Count five.) Horrors! (Count five.)* You're a Christian martyr, yes, honey, that's what you are, a Christian martyr! Well, I just happened to notice in

Amanda, now hopeful, places a sales call.

my little red book that your subscription to the *Companion* has just run out! I knew that you wouldn't 260 want to miss out on the wonderful serial starting in this new issue. It's by Bessie Mae Hopper, the first thing she's written since *Honeymoon for Three.* Wasn't that a strange and interesting story? Well, this one is even lovelier, I believe. It has a sophisti- 265 cated society background. It's all about the horsey set on Long Island!

(Fade out.)

SCENE V

(Legend on screen: "Annunciation.") Fade with music.
    It is early dusk of a spring evening. Supper has just been finished in the Wingfield apartment. AMANDA *and* LAURA *in light-colored dresses are removing dishes from the table, in the upstage area, which is shadowy, their movements formalized almost as a dance or ritual, their moving forms as pale and silent as moths.*
    TOM, *in white shirt and trousers, rises from the table and crosses toward the fire-escape.*

AMANDA: *(as he passes her)*   Son, will you do me a favor?

TOM: What?

AMANDA: Comb your hair! You look so pretty when your hair is combed! *(TOM slouches on the sofa with the evening paper. Enormous caption "Franco Triumphs.")* 5 There is only one respect in which I would like you to emulate your father.

TOM: What respect is that?

AMANDA: The care he always took of his appearance. He never allowed himself to look untidy. *(He throws* 10 *down the paper and crosses to fire-escape.)* Where are you going?

TOM: I'm going out to smoke.

AMANDA: You smoke too much. A pack a day at fifteen cents a pack. How much would that amount to in a month? Thirty times fifteen is how much, Tom? Figure it out and you will be astounded at what you could save. Enough to give you a night-school course in accounting at Washington U! Just think what a wonderful thing that would be for you, son!

TOM *is unmoved by the thought.*

TOM: I'd rather smoke. *(He steps out on landing, letting the screen door slam.)*

AMANDA: *(sharply)* I know! That's the tragedy of it.... *(Alone, she turns to look at her husband's picture.)*

(Dance music: "All the World Is Waiting for the Sunrise!")

TOM: *(to the audience)* Across the alley from us was the Paradise Dance Hall. On evenings in spring the windows and doors were open and the music came outdoors. Sometimes the lights were turned out except for a large glass sphere that hung from the ceiling. It would turn slowly about and filter the dusk with delicate rainbow colors. Then the orchestra played a waltz or a tango, something that had a slow and sensuous rhythm. Couples would come outside, to the relative privacy of the alley. You could see them kissing behind ash-pits and telephone poles. This was the compensation for lives that passed like mine, without any change or adventure. Adventure and change were imminent in this year. They were waiting around the corner for all these kids. Suspended in the mist over the Berchtesgaden, caught in the folds of Chamberlain's umbrella—In Spain there was Guernica! But here there was only hot swing music and liquor, dance halls, bars, and movies, and sex that hung in the gloom like a chandelier and flooded the world with brief, deceptive rainbows.... All the world was waiting for bombardments!

AMANDA *turns from the picture and comes outside.*

AMANDA: *(sighing)* A fire-escape landing's a poor excuse for a porch. *(She spreads a newspaper on a step and sits down, gracefully and demurely as if she were settling into a swing on a Mississippi veranda.)* What are you looking at?

TOM: The moon.

AMANDA: Is there a moon this evening?

TOM: It's rising over Garfinkel's Delicatessen.

AMANDA: So it is! A little silver slipper of a moon. Have you made a wish on it yet?

TOM: Um-hum.

AMANDA: What did you wish for?

TOM: That's a secret.

AMANDA: A secret, huh? Well, I won't tell mine either. I will be just as mysterious as you.

TOM: I bet I can guess what yours is.

AMANDA: Is my head so transparent?

TOM: You're not a sphinx.

AMANDA: No, I don't have secrets. I'll tell you what I wished for on the moon. Success and happiness for my precious children! I wish for that whenever there's a moon, and when there isn't a moon, I wish for it, too.

TOM: I thought perhaps you wished for a gentleman caller.

AMANDA: Why do you say that?

TOM: Don't you remember asking me to fetch one?

AMANDA: I remember suggesting that it would be nice for your sister if you brought home some nice young man from the warehouse. I think I've made that suggestion more than once.

TOM: Yes, you have made it repeatedly.

AMANDA: Well?

TOM: We are going to have one.

AMANDA: *What?*

TOM: A gentleman caller!

(The Annunciation is celebrated with music.)
AMANDA *rises.*
(Image on screen: Caller with bouquet.)

AMANDA: You mean you have asked some nice young man to come over?

TOM: Yep. I've asked him to dinner.

AMANDA: You really did?

TOM: I did!

AMANDA: You did, and did he—*accept?*

TOM: He did!

AMANDA: Well, well—well, well! That's—lovely!

TOM: I thought that you would be pleased.

AMANDA: It's definite, then?

TOM: Very definite.

AMANDA: Soon?

95 **TOM:** Very soon.

AMANDA: For heaven's sake, stop putting on and tell me some things, will you?

TOM: What things do you want me to tell you?

AMANDA: Naturally I would like to know when he's
100 *coming!*

TOM: He's coming tomorrow.

AMANDA: *Tomorrow?*

TOM: Yep. Tomorrow.

AMANDA: But, Tom!

105 **TOM:** Yes, Mother?

AMANDA: Tomorrow gives me no time!

TOM: Time for what?

AMANDA: Preparations! Why didn't you phone me at once, as soon as you asked him, the minute that he
110 accepted? Then, don't you see, I could have been getting ready!

TOM: You don't have to make any fuss.

AMANDA: Oh, Tom, Tom, Tom, of course I have to make a fuss! I want things nice, not sloppy! Not
115 thrown together. I'll certainly have to do some fast thinking, won't I?

TOM: I don't see why you have to think at all.

Tom tells Amanda about the man he's invited over to meet Laura.

AMANDA: You just don't know. We can't have a gentleman caller in a pig-sty! All my wedding silver has to be polished, the monogrammed table linen ought to 120 be laundered! The windows have to be washed and fresh curtains put up. And how about clothes? We have to *wear* something, don't we?

TOM: Mother, this boy is no one to make a fuss over!

AMANDA: Do you realize he's the first young man 125 we've introduced to your sister? It's terrible, dreadful, disgraceful that poor little sister has never received a single gentleman caller! Tom, come inside! *(She opens the screen door.)*

TOM: What for? 130

AMANDA: I want to ask you some things.

TOM: If you're going to make such a fuss, I'll call it off, I'll tell him not to come.

AMANDA: You certainly won't do anything of the kind. Nothing offends people worse than broken engage- 135 ments. It simply means I'll have to work like a Turk! We won't be brilliant, but we'll pass inspection. Come on inside. *(TOM follows, groaning.)* Sit down.

TOM: Any particular place you would like me to sit?

AMANDA: Thank heavens I've got that new sofa! I'm 140 also making payments on a floor lamp I'll have sent out! And put the chintz covers on, they'll brighten things up! Of course I'd hoped to have these walls repapered. . . . What is the young man's name?

TOM: His name is O'Connor. 145

AMANDA: That, of course, means fish—tomorrow is Friday! I'll have that salmon loaf—with Durkee's dressing! What does he do? He works at the warehouse?

TOM: Of course! How else would I—

AMANDA: Tom, he—doesn't drink? 150

TOM: Why do you ask me that?

AMANDA: Your father *did!*

TOM: Don't get started on that!

AMANDA: He *does* drink, then?

TOM: Not that I know of! 155

AMANDA: Make sure, be certain! The last thing I want for my daughter's a boy who drinks!

TOM: Aren't you being a little bit premature? Mr. O'Connor has not yet appeared on the scene!

160 AMANDA: But will tomorrow. To meet your sister, and what do I know about his character? Nothing! Old maids are better off than wives of drunkards!

TOM: Oh, my God!

AMANDA: Be still!

165 TOM: *(leaning forward to whisper)* Lots of fellows meet girls whom they don't marry!

AMANDA: Oh, talk sensibly, Tom—and don't be sarcastic! *(She has gotten a hairbrush.)*

TOM: What are you doing?

170 AMANDA: I'm brushing that cow-lick down! What is this young man's position at the warehouse?

TOM: *(submitting grimly to the brush and the interrogation)* This young man's position is that of a shipping clerk, Mother.

175 AMANDA: Sounds to me like a fairly responsible job, the sort of job *you* would be in if you just had more *get-up*. What is his salary? Have you any idea?

TOM: I would judge it to be approximately eighty-five dollars a month.

180 AMANDA: Well—not princely, but—

TOM: Twenty more than I make.

AMANDA: Yes, how well I know! But for a family man, eighty-five dollars a month is not much more than you can just get by on. . . .

185 TOM: Yes, but Mr. O'Connor is not a family man.

AMANDA: He might be, mightn't he? Some time in the future?

TOM: I see. Plans and provisions.

AMANDA: You are the only young man that I know
190 of who ignores the fact that the future becomes the present, the present the past, and the past turns into everlasting regret if you don't plan for it!

TOM: I will think that over and see what I can make of it.

195 AMANDA: Don't be supercilious with your mother! Tell me some more about this—what do you call him?

TOM: James D. O'Connor. The D. is for Delaney.

AMANDA: Irish on *both* sides! *Gracious!* And doesn't drink?

200 TOM: Shall I call him up and ask him right this minute?

AMANDA: The only way to find out about those things is to make discreet inquiries at the proper moment.

When I was a girl in Blue Mountain and it was suspected that a young man drank, the girl whose attentions he had been receiving, if any girl *was*, would 205 sometimes speak to the minister of his church, or rather her father would if her father was living, and sort of feel him out on the young man's character. That is the way such things are discreetly handled to keep a young woman from making a tragic mistake! 210

TOM: Then how did you happen to make a tragic mistake?

AMANDA: That innocent look of your father's had everyone fooled! He *smiled*—the world was *enchanted!* No girl can do worse than put herself at the mercy of 215 a handsome appearance! I hope that Mr. O'Connor is not too good-looking.

TOM: No, he's not too good-looking. He's covered with freckles and hasn't too much of a nose.

AMANDA: He's not right-down homely, though? 220

TOM: Not right-down homely. Just medium homely, I'd say.

AMANDA: Character's what to look for in a man.

TOM: That's what I've always said, Mother.

AMANDA: You've never said anything of the kind and I 225 suspect you would never give it a thought.

TOM: Don't be suspicious of me.

AMANDA: At least I hope he's the type that's up and coming.

TOM: I think he really goes in for self-improvement. 230

AMANDA: What reason have you to think so?

TOM: He goes to night school.

AMANDA: *(beaming)* Splendid! What does he do, I mean study?

TOM: Radio engineering and public speaking! 235

AMANDA: Then he has visions of being advanced in the world! Any young man who studies public speaking is aiming to have an executive job some day! And radio engineering? A thing for the future! Both of these facts are very illuminating. Those are the sort 240 of things that a mother should know concerning any young man who comes to call on her daughter. Seriously or—not.

TOM: One little warning. He doesn't know about Laura. I didn't let on that we had dark ulterior motives. I 245 just said, why don't you come have dinner with us? He said okay and that was the whole conversation.

AMANDA: I bet it was! You're eloquent as an oyster. However, he'll know about Laura when he gets here. When he sees how lovely and sweet and pretty she is, he'll thank his lucky stars he was asked to dinner.

TOM: Mother, you mustn't expect too much of Laura.

AMANDA: What do you mean?

TOM: Laura seems all those things to you and me because she's ours and we love her. We don't even notice she's crippled any more.

AMANDA: Don't say crippled! You know that I never allow that word to be used!

TOM: But face facts, Mother. She is and—that's not all—

AMANDA: What do you mean "not all"?

TOM: Laura is very different from other girls.

AMANDA: I think the difference is all to her advantage.

TOM: Not quite all—in the eyes of others—strangers—she's terribly shy and lives in a world of her own and those things make her seem a little peculiar to people outside the house.

AMANDA: Don't say peculiar.

TOM: Face the facts. She is.

(The dance-hall music changes to a tango that has a minor and somewhat ominous tone.)

AMANDA: In what way is she peculiar—may I ask?

TOM: *(gently)*   She lives in a world of her own—a world of—little glass ornaments, Mother. . . . *(Gets up.* AMANDA *remains holding brush, looking at him, troubled.)* She plays old phonograph records and—that's about all—*(He glances at himself in the mirror and crosses to door.)*

AMANDA: *(sharply)*   Where are you going?

TOM: I'm going to the movies. *(Out screen door.)*

AMANDA: Not to the movies, every night to the movies! *(Follows quickly to screen door.)* I don't believe you always go to the movies! *(He is gone.* AMANDA *looks worriedly after him for a moment. Then vitality and optimism return and she turns from the door. Crossing to portieres.)* Laura! Laura! *(*LAURA *answers from kitchenette.)*

LAURA: Yes, Mother.

AMANDA: Let those dishes go and come in front! *(*LAURA *appears with dish towel. Gaily.)* Laura, come here and make a wish on the moon!

LAURA: *(entering)*   Moon—moon?

AMANDA: A little silver slipper of a moon. Look over your left shoulder, Laura, and make a wish! *(*LAURA *looks faintly puzzled as if called out of sleep.* AMANDA *seizes her shoulders and turns her at angle by the door.)* Now! Now, darling, *wish!*

LAURA: What shall I wish for, Mother?

AMANDA: *(her voice trembling and her eyes suddenly filling with tears)*   Happiness! Good Fortune!

The violin rises and the stage dims out.

SCENE VI

(Image: High-school hero.)

TOM: And so the following evening I brought Jim home to dinner. I had known Jim slightly in high school. In high school Jim was a hero. He had tremendous Irish good nature and vitality with the scrubbed and polished look of white chinaware. He seemed to move in a continual spotlight. He was a star in basketball, captain of the debating club, president of the senior class and the glee club and he sang the male lead in the annual light operas. He was always running or bounding, never just walking. He seemed always at the point of defeating the law of gravity. He was shooting with such velocity through his adolescence that you would logically expect him to arrive at nothing short of the White House by the time he was thirty. But Jim apparently ran into more interference after his graduation from Soldan. His speed had definitely slowed. Six years after he left high school he was holding a job that wasn't much better than mine.

(Image: Clerk.)

Tom and Amanda discuss what kind of man he is bringing home for Laura.

20 He was the only one at the warehouse with whom I was on friendly terms. I was valuable to him as someone who could remember his former glory, who had seen him win basketball games and the silver cup in debating. He knew of my secret practice of
25 retiring to a cabinet of the washroom to work on poems when business was slack in the warehouse. He called me Shakespeare. And while the other boys in the warehouse regarded me with suspicious hostility, Jim took a humorous attitude toward me. Gradually
30 his attitude affected the others, their hostility wore off, and they also began to smile at me as people smile at an oddly fashioned dog who trots across their paths at some distance.

I knew that Jim and Laura had known each
35 other at Soldan, and I had heard Laura speak admiringly of his voice. I didn't know if Jim remembered her or not. In high school Laura had been as unobtrusive as Jim had been astonishing. If he did remember Laura, it was not as my sister, for when I
40 asked him to dinner, he grinned and said, "You know, Shakespeare, I never thought of you as having folks!"

He was about to discover that I did. . . .

(Light upstage.)

(Legend on screen: "The Accent of a Coming Foot.")

Friday evening. It is about five o'clock of a late spring evening which comes "scattering poems in the sky."

A delicate lemony light is in the Wingfield apartment.

AMANDA has worked like a Turk in preparation for the gentleman caller. The results are astonishing. The new floor lamp with its rose-silk shade is in place, a colored paper lantern conceals the broken light fixture in the ceiling, new billowing white curtains are at the windows, chintz covers are on chairs and sofa, a pair of new sofa pillows make their initial appearance.

Open boxes and tissue paper are scattered on the floor.

LAURA stands in the middle with lifted arms while AMANDA crouches before her, adjusting the hem of a new dress, devout and ritualistic. The dress is colored and designed by memory. The arrangement of LAURA's hair is changed; it is softer and more becoming. A fragile, unearthly prettiness has come out in LAURA: she is like a piece of translucent glass touched by light, given a momentary radiance, not actual, not lasting.

AMANDA: *(impatiently)* Why are you trembling?

LAURA: Mother, you've made me so nervous!

45 **AMANDA:** How have I made you nervous?

LAURA: By all this fuss! You make it seem so important!

AMANDA: I don't understand you, Laura. You couldn't be satisfied with just sitting home, and yet whenever I try to arrange something for you, you seem to resist it. *(She gets up.)* Now take a look at yourself. No, wait!
50 Wait just a moment—I have an idea!

LAURA: What is it now?

AMANDA produces two powder puffs which she wraps in handkerchiefs and stuffs in LAURA's bosom.

LAURA: Mother, what are you doing?

AMANDA: They call them "Gay Deceivers"!

55 **LAURA:** I won't wear them!

AMANDA: You will!

LAURA: Why should I?

AMANDA: Because, to be painfully honest, your chest is flat.

60 **LAURA:** You make it seem like we were setting a trap.

AMANDA: All pretty girls are a trap, a pretty trap, and men expect them to be. *(Legend: "A Pretty Trap.")* Now look at yourself, young lady. This is the prettiest you will ever be! I've got to fix myself now! You're going to be surprised by your mother's appearance! *(She*
65 *crosses through portieres, humming gaily.)*

LAURA moves slowly to the long mirror and stares solemnly at herself.

A wind blows the white curtains inward in a slow, graceful motion and with a faint, sorrowful sighing.

AMANDA: *(off stage)* It isn't dark enough yet. *(She turns slowly before the mirror with a troubled look.)*

(Legend on screen: "This Is My Sister: Celebrate Her with Strings!" Music.)

The women get ready for dinner.

AMANDA: *(laughing, off)* I'm going to show you some-
70 thing. I'm going to make a spectacular appearance!

LAURA: What is it, Mother?

AMANDA: Possess your soul in patience—you will see! Something I've resurrected from that old trunk! Styles haven't changed so terribly much after all. . . .
75 *(She parts the portieres.)* Now just look at your mother! *(She wears a girlish frock of yellowed voile with a blue silk sash. She carries a bunch of jonquils—the legend of her youth is nearly revived. Feverishly.)* This is the dress in which I led the cotillion. Won the cakewalk twice at
80 Sunset Hill, wore one spring to the Governor's ball in Jackson! See how I sashayed around the ball-room, Laura? *(She raises her skirt and does a mincing step around the room.)* I wore it on Sundays for my gentle-men callers! I had it on the day I met your father—I
85 had malaria fever all that spring. The change of cli-mate from East Tennessee to the Delta—weakened resistance—I had a little temperature all the time—not enough to be serious—just enough to make me restless and giddy! Invitations poured in—parties
90 all over the Delta! "Stay in bed," said Mother, "you have fever!"—but I just wouldn't.—I took quinine but kept on going, going!—Evenings, dances!—After-noons, long, long rides! Picnics—lovely!—So lovely, that country in May.—All lacy with dogwood, liter-
95 ally flooded with jonquils!—That was the spring I had the craze for jonquils. Jonquils became an abso-lute obsession. Mother said, "Honey, there's no more room for jonquils." And still I kept bringing in more jonquils. Whenever, wherever I saw them, I'd say,
100 "Stop! Stop! I see jonquils!" I made the young men help me gather the jonquils! It was a joke, Amanda and her jonquils. Finally there were no more vases to hold them, every available space was filled with jon-quils. No vases to hold them? All right, I'll hold them
105 myself! And then I—*(She stops in front of the picture.)* *(Music.)* met your father! Malaria fever and jonquils and then—this—boy. . . . *(She switches on the rose-colored lamp.)* I hope they get here before it starts to rain. *(She crosses upstage and places the jonquils in bowl on
110 table.)* I gave your brother a little extra change so he and Mr. O'Connor could take the service car home.

LAURA: *(with an altered look)* What did you say his name was?

115 **AMANDA:** O'Connor.

LAURA: What is his first name?

AMANDA: I don't remember. Oh, yes, I do. It was—Jim!

LAURA *sways slightly and catches hold of a chair.*
(Legend on screen: "Not Jim!")

LAURA: *(faintly)* Not—Jim!

AMANDA: Yes, that was it, it was Jim! I've never
120 known a Jim that wasn't nice!

(Music: Ominous.)

LAURA: Are you sure his name is Jim O'Connor?

AMANDA: Yes. Why?

LAURA: Is he the one that Tom used to know in high school?

125 **AMANDA:** He didn't say so. I think he just got to know him at the warehouse.

LAURA: There was a Jim O'Connor we both knew in high school—*(Then, with effort.)* If that is the one that Tom is bringing to dinner—you'll have to excuse me,
130 I won't come to the table.

AMANDA: What sort of nonsense is this?

LAURA: You asked me once if I'd ever liked a boy. Don't you remember I showed you this boy's picture?

AMANDA: You mean the boy you showed me in the
135 year-book?

LAURA: Yes, that boy.

AMANDA: Laura, Laura, were you in love with that boy?

LAURA: I don't know, Mother. All I know is I couldn't sit at the table if it was him!

140 **AMANDA:** It won't be him! It isn't the least bit likely. But whether it is or not, you will come to the table. You will not be excused.

LAURA: I'll have to be, Mother.

AMANDA: I don't intend to humor your silliness, Laura. I've had too much from you and your brother,
145 both! So just sit down and compose yourself till they come. Tom has forgotten his key so you'll have to let them in, when they arrive.

LAURA: *(panicky)* Oh, Mother—*you* answer the door!

AMANDA: *(lightly)* I'll be in the kitchen—busy!

150

LAURA: Oh, Mother, please answer the door, don't make me do it!

AMANDA: *(crossing into kitchenette)* I've got to fix the dressing for the salmon. Fuss, fuss—silliness!—over a gentleman caller!
155

(Door swings shut. LAURA is left alone.)
(Legend: "Terror!")

Amanda greets Jim O'Connor (Michael Moriarty).

She utters a low moan and turns off the lamp—sits stiffly on the edge of the sofa, knotting her fingers together.
(Legend on screen: "The Opening of a Door!")
TOM *and* JIM *appear on the fire-escape steps and climb to landing. Hearing their approach,* LAURA *rises with a panicky gesture. She retreats to the portieres.*
The doorbell. LAURA *catches her breath and touches her throat. Low drums.*

AMANDA: *(calling)*   Laura, sweetheart! The door!

LAURA *stares at it without moving.*

JIM: I think we just beat the rain.

TOM: Uh-huh. *(He rings again, nervously.* JIM *whistles and fishes for a cigarette.)*

160   **AMANDA:** *(very, very gaily)*   Laura, that is your brother and Mr. O'Connor! Will you let them in, darling?

LAURA *crosses toward kitchenette door.*

LAURA: *(breathlessly)*   Mother—you go to the door!

AMANDA *steps out of kitchenette and stares furiously at* LAURA. *She points imperiously at the door.*

LAURA: Please, please!

AMANDA: *(in a fierce whisper)*   What is the matter with
165   you, you silly thing?

LAURA: *(desperately)*   Please, you answer it, *please!*

AMANDA: I told you I wasn't going to humor you, Laura. Why have you chosen this moment to lose your mind?

170   **LAURA:**   Please, please, please, you go!

AMANDA: You'll have to go to the door because I can't!

LAURA: *(despairingly)*   I can't either!

AMANDA: *Why?*

LAURA: I'm *sick!*

AMANDA: I'm sick, too—of your nonsense! Why can't   175
you and your brother be normal people? Fantastic whims and behavior! *(TOM gives a long ring.)* Preposterous goings on! Can you give me one reason—*(Calls out lyrically.)* COMING! JUST ONE SECOND!—why you should be afraid to open a door? Now you answer it,   180
Laura!

LAURA: Oh, oh, oh . . . *(She returns through the portieres. Darts to the Victrola and winds it frantically and turns it on.)*

AMANDA: Laura Wingfield, you march right to that   185
door!

LAURA: Yes—yes, Mother!

A faraway, scratchy rendition of "Dardanella" softens the air and gives her strength to move through it. She slips to the door and draws it cautiously open.
TOM *enters with the caller,* JIM O'CONNOR.

TOM: Laura, this is Jim. Jim, this is my sister, Laura.

JIM: *(stepping inside)*   I didn't know that Shakespeare had a sister!   190

LAURA: *(retreating stiff and trembling from the door)*   How—how do you do?

JIM: *(heartily, extending his hand)*   Okay!

LAURA *touches it hesitantly with hers.*

JIM: Your hand's *cold,* Laura!

LAURA: Yes, well—I've been playing the Victrola . . .   195

JIM: Must have been playing classical music on it! You ought to play a little hot swing music to warm you up!

LAURA: Excuse me—I haven't finished playing the Victrola . . .

She turns awkwardly and hurries into the front room. She pauses a second by the Victrola. Then catches her breath and darts through the portieres like a frightened deer.

JIM: *(grinning)*   What was the matter?   200

TOM: Oh—with Laura? Laura is—terribly shy.

JIM: Shy, huh? It's unusual to meet a shy girl nowadays. I don't believe you ever mentioned you had a sister.

TOM: Well, now you know. I have one. Here is the *Post Dispatch.* You want a piece of it?   205

JIM: Uh-huh.

TOM: What piece? The comics?

JIM: Sports! *(Glances at it.)* Ole Dizzy Dean is on his bad behavior.

210 **TOM:** *(disinterest)* Yeah? *(Lights cigarette and crosses back to fire-escape door.)*

JIM: Where are *you* going?

TOM: I'm going out on the terrace.

JIM: *(goes after him)* You know, Shakespeare—I'm going 215 to sell you a bill of goods!

TOM: What goods?

JIM: A course I'm taking.

TOM: Huh?

JIM: In public speaking! You and me, we're not the 220 warehouse type.

TOM: Thanks—that's good news. But what has public speaking got to do with it?

JIM: It fits you for—executive positions!

TOM: Awww.

225 **JIM:** I tell you it's done a helluva lot for me.

(Image: Executive at desk.)

TOM: In what respect?

JIM: In every! Ask yourself what is the difference between you an' me and men in the office down front? Brains?—No!—Ability?—No! Then what? Just one 230 little thing—

TOM: What is that one little thing?

JIM: Primarily it amounts to—social poise! Being able to square up to people and hold your own on any social level!

235 **AMANDA:** *(off stage)* Tom?

TOM: Yes, Mother?

AMANDA: Is that you and Mr. O'Connor?

TOM: Yes, Mother.

AMANDA: Well, you just make yourselves comfortable 240 in there.

TOM: Yes, Mother.

AMANDA: Ask Mr. O'Connor if he would like to wash his hands.

JIM: Aw—no—no—thank you—I took care of that at the warehouse. Tom— 245

TOM: Yes?

JIM: Mr. Mendoza was speaking to me about you.

TOM: Favorably?

JIM: What do you think?

TOM: Well— 250

JIM: You're going to be out of a job if you don't wake up.

TOM: I am waking up—

JIM: You show no signs.

TOM: The signs are interior.

(Image on screen: The sailing vessel with Jolly Roger again.)

TOM: I'm planning to change. *(He leans over the rail speak-* 255 *ing with quiet exhilaration. The incandescent marquees and signs of the first-run movie houses light his face from across the alley. He looks like a voyager.)* I'm right at the point of committing myself to a future that doesn't include the warehouse and Mr. Mendoza or even a night- 260 school course in public speaking.

JIM: What are you gassing about?

TOM: I'm tired of the movies.

JIM: Movies!

TOM: Yes, movies! Look at them—*(A wave toward the mar-* 265 *vels of Grand Avenue.)* All of those glamorous people—having adventures—hogging it all, gobbling the whole thing up! You know what happens? People go to the *movies* instead of *moving!* Hollywood characters are supposed to have all the adventures for everybody in 270 America, while everybody in America sits in a dark room and watches them have them! Yes, until there's a war. That's when adventure becomes available to the masses! *Everyone's* dish, not only Gable's! Then the people in the dark room come out of the dark 275 room to have some adventures themselves—Goody, goody—It's our turn now, to go to the South Sea Island—to make a safari—to be exotic, far-off—But I'm not patient. I don't want to wait till then. I'm tired of the *movies* and I am *about* to *move!* 280

JIM: *(incredulously)* Move?

TOM: Yes.

JIM: When?

TOM: Soon!

JIM: Where? Where? 285

(Theme three: Music seems to answer the question, while TOM *thinks it over. He searches among his pockets.)*

TOM: I'm starting to boil inside. I know I seem dreamy, but inside—well, I'm boiling! Whenever I pick up a shoe, I shudder a little thinking how short life is and what I am doing!—Whatever that means. I know it doesn't mean shoes—except as something to wear on a traveler's feet! *(Finds paper.)* Look—

JIM: What?

TOM: I'm a member.

JIM: *(reading)* The Union of Merchant Seamen.

TOM: I paid my dues this month, instead of the light bill.

JIM: You will regret it when they turn the lights off.

TOM: I won't be here.

JIM: How about your mother?

TOM: I'm like my father. The bastard son of a bastard! See how he grins? And he's been absent going on sixteen years!

JIM: You're just talking, you drip. How does your mother feel about it?

TOM: Shhh—Here comes Mother! Mother is not acquainted with my plans!

AMANDA: *(enters portieres)* Where are you all?

TOM: On the terrace, Mother.

They start inside. She advances to them. TOM *is distinctly shocked at her appearance. Even* JIM *blinks a little. He is making his first contact with girlish Southern vivacity and in spite of the night-school course in public speaking is somewhat thrown off the beam by the unexpected outlay of social charm.*

Certain responses are attempted by JIM *but are swept aside by* AMANDA's *gay laughter and chatter.* TOM *is embarrassed but after the first shock* JIM *reacts very warmly. He grins and chuckles, is altogether won over.*

(Image: Amanda as a girl.)

AMANDA: *(coyly smiling, shaking her girlish ringlets)* Well, well, well, so this is Mr. O'Connor. Introductions entirely unnecessary. I've heard so much about you from my boy. I finally said to him, Tom—good gracious!—why don't you bring this paragon to supper? I'd like to meet this nice young man at the warehouse!—Instead of just hearing him sing your praises so much! I don't know why my son is so stand-offish—that's not Southern behavior! Let's sit down and—I think we could stand a little more air in here! Tom, leave the door open. I felt a nice fresh breeze a moment ago. Where has it gone? Mmm, so warm already! And not quite summer, even. We're going to burn up when summer really gets started. However, we're having—we're having a very light supper. I think light things are better fo' this time of year. The same as light clothes are. Light clothes an' light food are what warm weather calls fo'. You know our blood gets so thick during th' winter—it takes a while fo' us to *adjust* ou'selves!—when the season changes. . . . It's come so quick this year. I wasn't prepared. All of a sudden—heavens! Already summer!—I ran to the trunk an' pulled out this light dress—Terribly old! Historical almost! But feels so good—so good an' co-ol, y'know. . . .

TOM: Mother—

AMANDA: Yes, honey?

TOM: How about—supper?

AMANDA: Honey, you go ask Sister if supper is ready! You know that Sister is in full charge of supper! Tell her you hungry boys are waiting for it. *(To* JIM.*)* Have you met Laura?

JIM: She—

AMANDA: Let you in? Oh, good, you've met already! It's rare for a girl as sweet an' pretty as Laura to be domestic! But Laura is, thank heavens, not only pretty but also very domestic. I'm not at all. I never was a bit. I never could make a thing but angel-food cake. Well, in the South we had so many servants. Gone, gone, gone. All vestiges of gracious living! Gone completely! I wasn't prepared for what the future brought me. All of my gentlemen callers were sons of planters and so of course I assumed that I would be married to one and raise my family on a large piece of land with plenty of servants. But man proposes—and woman accepts the proposal!—To vary that old, old saying a little bit—I married no planter! I married a man who worked for the telephone company!—that gallantly smiling gentleman over there! *(Points to the picture.)* A telephone man who—fell in love with long-distance!—Now he travels and I don't even know where!—But what am I going on for about my—tribulations! Tell me yours—I hope you don't have any! Tom?

TOM: *(returning)* Yes, Mother?

AMANDA: Is supper nearly ready?

TOM: It looks to me like supper is on the table.

AMANDA: Let me look—*(She rises prettily and looks through portieres.)* Oh, lovely—But where is Sister?

TOM: Laura is not feeling well and she says that she thinks she'd better not come to the table.

AMANDA: What?—Nonsense!—Laura? Oh, Laura!

370 **LAURA:** (off stage, faintly) Yes, Mother.

AMANDA: You really must come to the table. We won't be seated until you come to the table! Come in, Mr. O'Connor. You sit over there, and I'll—Laura? Laura Wingfield! You're keeping us waiting, honey! We

375 can't say grace until you come to the table!

The back door is pushed weakly open and LAURA *comes in. She is obviously quite faint, her lips trembling, her eyes wide and staring. She moves unsteadily toward the table.*
    (Legend: "Terror!")
    Outside a summer storm is coming abruptly. The white curtains billow inward at the windows and there is a sorrowful murmur and deep blue dusk.
    LAURA *suddenly stumbles—She catches at a chair with a faint moan.*

TOM: Laura!

AMANDA: Laura! *(There is a clap of thunder.) (Legend: "Ah!") (Despairingly.)* Why, Laura, you *are* sick, darling! Tom, help your sister into the living room, dear!

380 Sit in the living room, Laura—rest on the sofa. Well! *(To the gentleman caller.)* Standing over the hot stove made her ill!—I told her that it was just too warm this evening, but—(TOM *comes back in.* LAURA *is on the sofa.)* Is Laura all right now?

385 **TOM:** Yes.

AMANDA: What *is* that? Rain? A nice cool rain has come up! *(She gives the gentleman caller a frightened look.)* I think we may—have grace—now. . . *(TOM looks at her stupidly.)* Tom, honey—you say grace!

390 **TOM:** Oh . . . "For these and all thy mercies—" *(They bow their heads,* AMANDA *stealing a nervous glance at* JIM. *In the living room* LAURA, *stretched on the sofa, clenches her hand to her lips, to hold back a shuddering sob.)* God's Holy Name be praised—

(The scene dims out.)

SCENE VII

A Souvenir

Half an hour later. Dinner is just being finished in the up-stage area, which is concealed by the drawn portieres.
    As the curtain rises LAURA *is still huddled upon the sofa, her feet drawn under her, her head resting on a pale blue pillow, her eyes wide and mysteriously watchful. The new floor lamp with its shade of rose-colored silk gives a*

soft, becoming light to her face, bringing out the fragile, unearthly prettiness which usually escapes attention. There is a steady murmur of rain, but it is slackening and stops soon after the scene begins; the air outside becomes pale and luminous as the moon breaks out.
    A moment after the curtain rises, the lights in both rooms flicker and go out.

JIM: Hey, there, Mr. Light Bulb!

AMANDA *laughs nervously.*
    (Legend: "Suspension of a Public Service.")

AMANDA: Where was Moses when the lights went out? Ha-ha. Do you know the answer to that one, Mr. O'Connor?

JIM: No, Ma'am, what's the answer? 5

AMANDA: In the dark! (JIM *laughs appreciatively.)* Everybody sit still. I'll light the candles. Isn't it lucky we have them on the table? Where's a match? Which of you gentlemen can provide a match?

JIM: Here. 10

AMANDA: Thank you, sir.

JIM: Not at all, Ma'am!

AMANDA: I guess the fuse has burnt out. Mr. O'Connor, can you tell a burnt-out fuse? I know I can't and Tom is a total loss when it comes to mechanics. *(Sound:* 15 *Getting up: Voices recede a little to kitchenette.)* Oh, be careful you don't bump into something. We don't want our gentleman caller to break his neck. Now wouldn't that be a fine howdy-do?

JIM: Ha-ha! Where is the fuse-box? 20

Amanda entertains Jim after the lights have gone out.

AMANDA: Right here next to the stove. Can you see anything?

JIM: Just a minute.

25 **AMANDA:** Isn't electricity a mysterious thing? Wasn't it Benjamin Franklin who tied a key to a kite? We live in such a mysterious universe, don't we? Some people say that science clears up all the mysteries for us. In my opinion it only creates more! Have you found it yet?

30 **JIM:** No, Ma'am. All these fuses look okay to me.

AMANDA: Tom!

TOM: Yes, Mother?

AMANDA: That light bill I gave you several days ago. The one I told you we got the notices about?

35 **TOM:** Oh.—Yeah.

(Legend: "Ha!")

AMANDA: You didn't neglect to pay it by any chance?

TOM: Why, I—

AMANDA: Didn't! I might have known it!

JIM: Shakespeare probably wrote a poem on that light
40 bill, Mrs. Wingfield.

AMANDA: I might have known better than to trust him with it! There's such a high price for negligence in this world!

JIM: Maybe the poem will win a ten-dollar prize.

45 **AMANDA:** We'll just have to spend the remainder of the evening in the nineteenth century, before Mr. Edison made the Mazda lamp!

JIM: Candlelight is my favorite kind of light.

AMANDA: That shows you're romantic! But that's no
50 excuse for Tom. Well, we got through dinner. Very considerate of them to let us get through dinner before they plunged us into everlasting darkness, wasn't it, Mr. O'Connor?

JIM: Ha-ha!

55 **AMANDA:** Tom, as a penalty for your carelessness you can help me with the dishes.

JIM: Let me give you a hand.

AMANDA: Indeed you will not!

JIM: I ought to be good for something.

AMANDA: Good for something? *(Her tone is rhapsodic.)* 60
You? Why, Mr. O'Connor, nobody, *nobody's* given me this much entertainment in years—as you have!

JIM: Aw, now, Mrs. Wingfield!

AMANDA: I'm not exaggerating, not one bit! But Sister is all by her lonesome. You go keep her company in 65 the parlor! I'll give you this lovely old candelabrum that used to be on the altar at the church of the Heavenly Rest. It was melted a little out of shape when the church burnt down. Lightning struck it one spring. Gypsy Jones was holding a revival at the 70 time and he intimated that the church was destroyed because the Episcopalians gave card parties.

JIM: Ha-ha.

AMANDA: And how about coaxing Sister to drink a little wine? I think it would be good for her! Can you 75 carry both at once?

JIM: Sure. I'm Superman!

AMANDA: Now, Thomas, get into this apron!

The door of kitchenette swings closed on AMANDA's gay laughter; the flickering light approaches the portieres.
        LAURA sits up nervously as he enters. Her speech at first is low and breathless from the almost intolerable strain of being alone with a stranger.
        (Legend: "I Don't Suppose You Remember Me at All!")
        In her first speeches in this scene, before JIM's warmth overcomes her paralyzing shyness, LAURA's voice is thin and breathless as though she has run up a steep flight of stairs.
        JIM's attitude is gently humorous. In playing this scene it should be stressed that while the incident is apparently unimportant, it is to LAURA the climax of her secret life.

JIM: Hello there, Laura.

LAURA: *(faintly)* Hello. *(She clears her throat.)* 80

JIM: How are you feeling now? Better?

LAURA: Yes. Yes, thank you.

JIM: This is for you. A little dandelion wine. *(He extends it toward her with extravagant gallantry.)*

LAURA: Thank you. 85

JIM: Drink it—but don't get drunk! *(He laughs heartily. LAURA takes the glass uncertainly; laughs shyly.)* Where shall I set the candles?

LAURA: Oh—oh, anywhere . . .

JIM: How about here on the floor? Any objections? 90

LAURA: No.

Jim brings the candelabrum closer to Laura.

JIM: I'll spread a newspaper under to catch the drippings. I like to sit on the floor. Mind if I do?

LAURA: Oh, no.

95 **JIM:** Give me a pillow?

LAURA: What?

JIM: A pillow!

LAURA: *Oh . . . (Hands him one quickly.)*

JIM: How about you? Don't you like to sit on the floor?

100 **LAURA:** Oh—yes.

JIM: Why don't you, then?

LAURA: I—will.

JIM: Take a pillow! *(LAURA does. Sits on the other side of the candelabrum. JIM crosses his legs and smiles engagingly at*
105 *her.)* I can't hardly see you sitting way over there.

LAURA: I can—see you.

JIM: I know, but that's not fair, I'm in the limelight. *(LAURA moves her pillow closer.)* Good! Now I can see you! Comfortable?

110 **LAURA:** Yes.

JIM: So am I. Comfortable as a cow. Will you have some gum?

LAURA: No, thank you.

JIM: I think that I will indulge, with your permission.
115 *(Musingly unwraps it and holds it up.)* Think of the fortune made by the guy that invented the first piece of chewing gum. Amazing, huh? The Wrigley Building is one of the sights of Chicago.—I saw it summer before last when I went up to the Century of Progress.
120 Did you take in the Century of Progress?

LAURA: No, I didn't.

JIM: Well, it was quite a wonderful exposition. What impressed me most was the Hall of Science. Gives you an idea of what the future will be in America, even more wonderful than the present time is! 125 *(Pause. Smiling at her.)* Your brother tells me you're shy. Is that right, Laura?

LAURA: I—don't know.

JIM: I judge you to be an old-fashioned type of girl. Well, I think that's a pretty good type to be. Hope 130 you don't think I'm being too personal—do you?

LAURA: *(hastily, out of embarrassment)* I believe I *will* take a piece of gum, if you—don't mind. *(Clearing her throat.)* Mr. O'Connor, have you—kept up with your singing? 135

JIM: Singing? Me?

LAURA: Yes. I remember what a beautiful voice you had.

JIM: When did you hear me sing?

(Voice offstage in the pause.)

VOICE: *(offstage)* O blow, ye winds, heigh-ho,
A-roving I will go! 140
I'm off to my love
With a boxing glove—
Ten thousand miles away!

JIM: You say you've heard me sing?

LAURA: Oh, yes! Yes, very often . . . I—don't suppose 145 you remember me—at all?

JIM: *(smiling doubtfully)* You know I have an idea I've seen you before. I had that idea soon as you opened the door. It seemed almost like I was about to remember your name. But the name I started to call 150 you—wasn't a name! And so I stopped myself before I said it.

LAURA: Wasn't it—Blue Roses?

JIM: *(springing up, grinning)* Blue Roses! My gosh, yes— Blue Roses! That's what I had on my tongue when 155 you opened the door! Isn't it funny what tricks your memory plays? I didn't connect you with the high school somehow or other. But that's where it was; it was high school. I didn't even know you were Shakespeare's sister! Gosh, I'm sorry. 160

LAURA: I didn't expect you to. You—barely knew me!

JIM: But we did have a speaking acquaintance, huh?

LAURA: Yes, we—spoke to each other.

JIM: When did you recognize me?

LAURA: Oh, right away! 165

JIM: Soon as I came in the door?

LAURA: When I heard your name I thought it was probably you. I knew that Tom used to know you a little in high school. So when you came in the door— Well, then I was—sure.

170

JIM: Why didn't you *say* something, then?

LAURA: *(breathlessly)* I didn't know what to say, I was— too surprised!

JIM: For goodness' sakes! You know, this sure is funny!

175 LAURA: Yes! Yes, isn't it, though . . .

JIM: Didn't we have a class in something together?

LAURA: Yes, we did.

JIM: What class was that?

LAURA: It was—singing—Chorus!

180 JIM: Aw!

LAURA: I sat across the aisle from you in the Aud.

JIM: Aw.

LAURA: Mondays, Wednesdays, and Fridays.

JIM: Now I remember—you always came in late.

185 LAURA: Yes, it was so hard for me, getting upstairs. I had that brace on my leg—it clumped so loud!

JIM: I never heard any clumping.

LAURA: *(wincing at the recollection)* To me it sounded like—thunder!

190 JIM: Well, well, well. I never even noticed.

LAURA: And everybody was seated before I came in. I had to walk in front of all those people. My seat was in the back row. I had to go clumping all the way up the aisle with everyone watching!

195 JIM: You shouldn't have been self-conscious.

LAURA: I know, but I was. It was always such a relief when the singing started.

JIM: Aw, yes, I've placed you now! I used to call you Blue Roses. How was it that I got started calling you that?

200

LAURA: I was out of school a little while with pleurosis. When I came back you asked me what was the matter. I said I had pleurosis—you thought I said Blue Roses. That's what you always called me after that!

205 JIM: I hope you didn't mind.

LAURA: Oh, no—I liked it. You see, I wasn't acquainted with many—people. . . .

Laura and Jim look at the old high school annual.

JIM: As I remember you sort of stuck by yourself.

LAURA: I—I—never have had much luck at—making friends.

210

JIM: I don't see why you wouldn't.

LAURA: Well, I—started out badly.

JIM: You mean being—

LAURA: Yes, it sort of—stood between me—

JIM: You shouldn't have let it!

215

LAURA: I know, but it did, and—

JIM: You were shy with people!

LAURA: I tried not to be but never could—

JIM: Overcome it?

LAURA: No, I—I never could!

220

JIM: I guess being shy is something you have to work out of kind of gradually.

LAURA: *(sorrowfully)* Yes—I guess it—

JIM: Takes time!

LAURA: Yes—

225

JIM: People are not so dreadful when you know them. That's what you have to remember! And everybody has problems, not just you, but practically everybody has got some problems. You think of yourself as having the only problems, as being the only one who is disappointed. But just look around you and you will see lots of people as disappointed as you are. For instance, I hoped when I was going to high school that I would be further along at this time, six years later, than I am now—You remember that wonderful write-up I had in *The Torch*?

230

235

LAURA: Yes! (*She rises and crosses to table.*)

JIM: It said I was bound to succeed in anything I went into! (*LAURA returns with the annual.*) Holy Jeez! *The* 240 *Torch!* (*He accepts it reverently. They smile across it with mutual wonder. LAURA crouches beside him and they begin to turn through it. LAURA's shyness is dissolving in his warmth.*)

LAURA: Here you are in *Pirates of Penzance*!

245 JIM: (*wistfully*) I sang the baritone lead in that operetta.

LAURA: (*rapidly*) So—*beautifully!*

JIM: (*protesting*) Aw—

LAURA: Yes, yes—beautifully—beautifully!

JIM: You heard me?

250 LAURA: All three times!

JIM: No!

LAURA: Yes!

JIM: All three performances?

LAURA: (*looking down*) Yes.

255 JIM: Why?

LAURA: I—wanted to ask you to—autograph my program.

JIM: Why didn't you ask me to?

LAURA: You were always surrounded by your own 260 friends so much that I never had a chance to.

JIM: You should have just—

LAURA: Well, I—thought you might think I was—

JIM: Thought I might think you was—what?

LAURA: Oh—

265 JIM: (*with reflective relish*) I was beleaguered by females in those days.

LAURA: You were terribly popular!

JIM: Yeah—

LAURA: You had such a—friendly way—

270 JIM: I was spoiled in high school.

LAURA: Everybody—liked you!

JIM: Including you?

LAURA: I—yes, I—I did, too—(*She gently closes the book in her lap.*)

JIM: Well, well, well!—Give me that program, Laura. 275 (*She hands it to him. He signs it with a flourish.*) There you are—better late than never!

LAURA: Oh, I—what a—surprise!

JIM: My signature isn't worth very much right now. But some day—maybe—it will increase in value! Be- 280 ing disappointed is one thing and being discouraged is something else. I am disappointed but I'm not discouraged. I'm twenty-three years old. How old are you?

LAURA: I'll be twenty-four in June. 285

JIM: That's not old age.

LAURA: No, but—

JIM: You finished high school?

LAURA: (*with difficulty*) I didn't go back.

JIM: You mean you dropped out? 290

LAURA: I made bad grades in my final examinations. (*She rises and replaces the book and the program. Her voice strained.*) How is—Emily Meisenbach getting along?

JIM: Oh, that kraut-head!

LAURA: Why do you call her that? 295

JIM: That's what she was.

LAURA: You're not still—going with her?

JIM: I never see her.

LAURA: It said in the Personal Section that you were— engaged! 300

JIM: I know, but I wasn't impressed by that— propaganda!

LAURA: It wasn't—the truth?

JIM: Only in Emily's optimistic opinion!

LAURA: Oh— 305

(*Legend: "What Have You Done since High School?"*)
JIM *lights a cigarette and leans indolently back on his elbows smiling at* LAURA *with a warmth and charm which light her inwardly with altar candles. She remains by the table and turns in her hands a piece of glass to cover her tumult.*)

JIM: (*after several reflective puffs on his cigarette*) What have you done since high school? (*She seems not to hear him.*) Huh? (*LAURA looks up.*) I said what have you done since high school, Laura?

LAURA: Nothing much. 310

JIM: You must have been doing something these six long years.

LAURA: Yes.

JIM: Well, then, such as what?

315 **LAURA:** I took a business course at business college—

JIM: How did that work out?

LAURA: Well, not very—well—I had to drop out, it gave me—indigestion—

JIM *laughs gently.*

JIM: What are you doing now?

320 **LAURA:** I don't do anything—much. Oh, please don't think I sit around doing nothing! My glass collection takes up a good deal of time. Glass is something you have to take good care of.

JIM: What did you say—about glass?

325 **LAURA:** Collection I said—I have one—*(She clears her throat and turns away again, acutely shy.)*

JIM: *(abruptly)* You know what I judge to be the trouble with you? Inferiority complex! Know what that is? That's what they call it when someone low-rates himself! I understand it because I had it, too. Although
330 my case was not so aggravated as yours seems to be. I had it until I took up public speaking, developed my voice, and learned that I had an aptitude for science. Before that time I never thought of myself as being outstanding in any way whatsoever! Now I've
335 never made a regular study of it, but I have a friend who says I can analyze people better than doctors that make a profession of it. I don't claim that to be necessarily true, but I can sure guess a person's psychology, Laura! *(Takes out his gum.)* Excuse me, Laura.
340 I always take it out when the flavor is gone. I'll use this scrap of paper to wrap it in. I know how it is to get it stuck on a shoe. Yep—that's what I judge to be your principal trouble. A lack of confidence in yourself as a person. You don't have the proper amount
345 of faith in yourself. I'm basing that fact on a number of your remarks and also on certain observations I've made. For instance that clumping you thought was so awful in high school. You say that you even dreaded to walk into class. You see what you did?
350 You dropped out of school, you gave up an education because of a clump, which as far as I know was practically nonexistent! A little physical defect is what you have. Hardly noticeable even! Magnified thousands of times by imagination! You know what my
355 strong advice to you is? Think of yourself as *superior* in some way!

LAURA: In what way would I think?

JIM: Why, man alive, Laura! Just look about you a little. What do you see? A world full of common 360 people! All of 'em born and all of 'em going to die! Which of them has one-tenth of your good points! Or mine! Or anyone else's, as far as that goes—Gosh! Everybody excels in some one thing. Some in many! *(Unconsciously glances at himself in the mirror.)* All you've 365 got to do is discover in *what!* Take me, for instance. *(He adjusts his tie at the mirror.)* My interest happened to lie in electrodynamics. I'm taking a course in radio engineering at night school, Laura, on top of a fairly responsible job at the warehouse. I'm taking 370 that course and studying public speaking.

LAURA: Ohhhh.

JIM: Because I believe in the future of television! *(Turning back to her.)* I wish to be ready to go up right along with it. Therefore I'm planning to get in on 375 the ground floor. In fact, I've already made the right connections and all that remains is for the industry itself to get under way! Full steam—*(His eyes are starry.) Knowledge—*Zzzzzp! *Money—*Zzzzzzp!— *Power!* That's the cycle democracy is built on! *(His 380 attitude is convincingly dynamic.* LAURA *stares at him, even her shyness eclipsed in her absolute wonder. He suddenly grins.)* I guess you think I think a lot of myself!

LAURA: No—o-o-o, I—

JIM: Now how about you? Isn't there something you 385 take more interest in than anything else?

LAURA: Well, I do—as I said—have my—glass collection—

A peal of girlish laughter from the kitchen.

JIM: I'm not right sure I know what you're talking about. What kind of glass is it? 390

LAURA: Little articles of it, they're ornaments mostly! Most of them are little animals made out of glass, the tiniest little animals in the world. Mother calls them a glass menagerie! Here's an example of one, if you'd like to see it! This one is one of the oldest. It's 395 nearly thirteen. *(He stretches out his hand.) (Music: "The Glass Menagerie.")* Oh, be careful—if you breathe, it breaks!

JIM: I'd better not take it. I'm pretty clumsy with things.

LAURA: Go on, I trust you with him! *(Places it in his 400 palm.)* There now—you're holding him gently! Hold him over the light, he loves the light! You see how the light shines through him?

JIM: It sure does shine!

405 **LAURA:** I shouldn't be partial, but he is my favorite one.

JIM: What kind of a thing is this one supposed to be?

LAURA: Haven't you noticed the single horn on his forehead?

JIM: A unicorn, huh?

410 **LAURA:** Mmm-hmmm!

JIM: Unicorns, aren't they extinct in the modern world?

LAURA: I know!

JIM: Poor little fellow, he must feel sort of lonesome.

415 **LAURA:** *(smiling)* Well, if he does he doesn't complain about it. He stays on a shelf with some horses that don't have horns and all of them seem to get along nicely together.

JIM: How do you know?

420 **LAURA:** *(lightly)* I haven't heard any arguments among them!

JIM: *(grinning)* No arguments, huh? Well, that's a pretty good sign! Where shall I set him?

LAURA: Put him on the table. They all like a change of scenery once in a while!

425 **JIM:** *(stretching)* Well, well, well, well—Look how big my shadow is when I stretch!

LAURA: Oh, oh, yes—it stretches across the ceiling!

JIM: *(crossing to door)* I think it's stopped raining. *(Opens fire-escape door.)* Where does the music come from?

430 **LAURA:** From the Paradise Dance Hall across the alley.

JIM: How about cutting the rug a little, Miss Wingfield?

LAURA: Oh, I—

JIM: Or is your program filled up? Let me have a look at it. *(Grasps imaginary card.)* Why, every dance is taken!
435 I'll have to scratch some out. *(Waltz music: "La Golondrina.")* Ahhh, a waltz! *(He executes some sweeping turns by himself then holds his arms toward* LAURA.*)*

LAURA: *(breathlessly)* I—can't dance!

JIM: There you go, that inferiority stuff!

440 **LAURA:** I've never danced in my life!

JIM: Come on, try!

LAURA: Oh, but I'd step on you!

Laura and Jim study the glass unicorn.

JIM: I'm not made out of glass.

LAURA: How—how—how do we start?

JIM: Just leave it to me. You hold your arms out a little.   445

LAURA: Like this?

JIM: A little bit higher. Right. Now don't tighten up, that's the main thing about it—relax.

LAURA: *(laughing breathlessly)* It's hard not to.

JIM: Okay.   450

LAURA: I'm afraid you can't budge me.

JIM: What do you bet I can't? *(He swings her into motion.)*

LAURA: Goodness, yes, you can!

JIM: Let yourself go, now, Laura, just let yourself go.

LAURA: I'm—   455

JIM: Come on!

LAURA: Trying.

JIM: Not so stiff—Easy does it!

LAURA: I know but I'm—

JIM: Loosen th' backbone! There now, that's a lot better.   460

LAURA: Am I?

JIM: Lots, lots better! *(He moves her about the room in a clumsy waltz.)*

LAURA: Oh, my!

JIM: Ha-ha!   465

LAURA: Goodness, yes you can!

Jim waltzes Laura around the room.

JIM: Ha-ha-ha! *(They suddenly bump into the table.* JIM *stops.)* What did we hit on?

LAURA: Table.

470 **JIM:** Did something fall off it? I think—

LAURA: Yes.

JIM: I hope that it wasn't the little glass horse with the horn!

LAURA: Yes.

475 **JIM:** Aw, aw, aw. Is it broken?

LAURA: Now it is just like all the other horses.

JIM: It's lost its—

LAURA: Horn! It doesn't matter. Maybe it's a blessing in disguise.

480 **JIM:** You'll never forgive me. I bet that was your favorite piece of glass.

LAURA: I don't have favorites much. It's no tragedy, Freckles. Glass breaks so easily. No matter how careful you are. The traffic jars the shelves and things fall
485 off them.

JIM: Still I'm awfully sorry that I was the cause.

LAURA: *(smiling)* I'll just imagine he had an operation. The horn was removed to make him feel less—freakish! *(They both laugh.)* Now he will feel more at
490 home with the other horses, the ones that don't have horns . . .

JIM: Ha-ha, that's very funny! *(Suddenly serious.)* I'm glad to see that you have a sense of humor. You

know—you're—well—very different! Surprisingly different from anyone else I know! *(His voice becomes* 495 *soft and hesitant with a genuine feeling.)* Do you mind me telling you that? *(*LAURA *is abashed beyond speech.)* You make me feel sort of—I don't know how to put it! I'm usually pretty good at expressing things, but—This is something that I don't know how to say! *(*LAURA 500 *touches her throat and clears it—turns the broken unicorn in her hands.) (Even softer.)* Has anyone ever told you that you were pretty?

Pause: Music.

*(*LAURA *looks up slowly, with wonder, and shakes her head.)* Well, you are! In a very different way from 505 anyone else. And all the nicer because of the difference, too. *(His voice becomes low and husky.* LAURA *turns away, nearly faint with the novelty of her emotions.)* I wish that you were my sister. I'd teach you to have some confidence in yourself. The different people are not 510 like other people, but being different is nothing to be ashamed of. Because other people are not such wonderful people. They're one hundred times one thousand. You're one times one! They walk all over the earth. You just stay here. They're common as— 515 weeds, but—you—well, you're—*Blue Roses!*

(Image on screen: Blue Roses.)
(Music changes.)

LAURA: But blue is wrong for—roses . . .

JIM: It's right for you—You're—pretty!

LAURA: In what respect am I pretty?

JIM: In all respects—believe me! Your eyes—your 520 hair—are pretty! Your hands are pretty! *(He catches hold of her hand.)* You think I'm making this up because I'm invited to dinner and have to be nice. Oh, I could do that! I could put on an act for you, Laura, and say lots of things without being very sincere. 525 But this time I am. I'm talking to you sincerely. I happened to notice you had this inferiority complex that keeps you from feeling comfortable with people. Somebody needs to build your confidence up and make you proud instead of shy and turning 530 away and—blushing—Somebody ought to—ought to—*kiss* you, Laura! *(His hand slips slowly up her arm to her shoulder.) (Music swells tumultuously.) (He suddenly turns her about and kisses her on the lips. When he releases her* LAURA *sinks on the sofa with a bright, dazed look.* JIM 535 *backs away and fishes in his pocket for a cigarette.) (Legend on screen: "Souvenir.")* Stumble-john! *(He lights the cigarette, avoiding her look. There is a peal of girlish laughter from* AMANDA *in the kitchenette.* LAURA *slowly raises and opens her hand. It still contains the little broken glass* 540 *animal. She looks at it with a tender, bewildered expression.)* Stumble-john! I shouldn't have done that—That was way off the beam. You don't smoke, do you? *(She looks up, smiling, not hearing the question. He sits beside her a little gingerly. She looks at him speechlessly—waiting. He coughs decorously and moves a little farther aside as he considers the situation and senses her feelings, dimly, with perturbation. Gently.)* Would you—care for a—mint? *(She doesn't seem to hear him but her look grows brighter even.)* Peppermint?—Life Saver? My pocket's a regular drug store—wherever I go . . . *(He pops a mint in his mouth. Then gulps and decides to make a clean breast of it. He speaks slowly and gingerly.)* Laura, you know, if I had a sister like you, I'd do the same thing as Tom. I'd bring out fellows—introduce her to them. The right type of boys of a type to—appreciate her. Only—well—he made a mistake about me. Maybe I've got no call to be saying this. That may not have been the idea in having me over. But what if it was? There's nothing wrong about that. The only trouble is that in my case—I'm not in a situation to—do the right thing. I can't take down your number and say I'll phone. I can't call up next week and—ask for a date. I thought I had better explain the situation in case you misunderstood it and—hurt your feelings. . . . *(Pause. Slowly, very slowly,* LAURA's *look changes, her eyes returning slowly from his to the ornament in her palm.)*

AMANDA *utters another gay laugh in the kitchenette.*

LAURA: *(faintly)* You—won't—call again?

JIM: No, Laura, I can't. *(He rises from the sofa.)* As I was just explaining, I've—got strings on me, Laura, I've—been going steady! I go out all the time with a girl named Betty. She's a home-girl like you, and Catholic, and Irish, and in a great many ways we—get along fine. I met her last summer on a moonlight boat trip up the river to Alton, on the *Majestic.* Well—right away from the start it was—love! *(Legend: Love!)* (LAURA *sways slightly forward and grips the arm of the sofa. He fails to notice, now enrapt in his own comfortable being.)* Being in love has made a new man of me! *(Leaning stiffly forward, clutching the arm of the sofa,* LAURA *struggles visibly with her storm. But* JIM *is oblivious, she is a long way off.)* The power of love is really pretty tremendous! Love is something that—changes the whole world, Laura! *(The storm abates a little and* LAURA *leans back. He notices her again.)* It happened that Betty's aunt took sick, she got a wire and had to go to Centralia. So Tom—when he asked me to dinner—I naturally just accepted the invitation, not knowing that you—that he—that I—*(He stops awkwardly.)* Huh—I'm a stumble-john! *(He flops back on the sofa. The holy candles in the altar of* LAURA's *face have been snuffled out! There is a look of almost infinite desolation.* JIM *glances at her uneasily.)* I wish that you would—say something. *(She bites her lip which was trembling and then bravely smiles. She opens her hand again on the broken glass ornament. Then she gently takes his hand and raises it level with her own. She carefully places the unicorn in the palm of his hand, then pushes his fingers closed upon it.)* What are you—doing that for? You want me to have him?—Laura? *(She nods.)* What for?

LAURA: A—souvenir . . .

She rises unsteadily and crouches beside the Victrola to wind it up.

(Legend on screen: "Things Have a Way of Turning Out So Badly.")

(Or image: "Gentleman caller waving good-bye!—Gaily.")

At this moment AMANDA *rushes brightly back in the front room. She bears a pitcher of fruit punch in an old-fashioned cut-glass pitcher and a plate of macaroons. The plate has a gold border and poppies painted on it.*

AMANDA: Well, well, well! Isn't the air delightful after the shower? I've made you children a little liquid refreshment. *(Turns gaily to the gentleman caller.)* Jim, do you know that song about lemonade?

"Lemonade, lemonade
Made in the shade and stirred with a spade—
Good enough for any old maid!"

JIM: *(uneasily)* Ha-ha! No—I never heard it.

AMANDA: Why, Laura! You look so serious!

JIM: We were having a serious conversation.

AMANDA: Good! Now you're better acquainted!

Jim and Laura kiss.

JIM: *(uncertainly)* Ha-ha! Yes.

615 AMANDA: You modern young people are much more serious-minded than my generation. I was so gay as a girl!

JIM: You haven't changed, Mrs. Wingfield.

AMANDA: Tonight I'm rejuvenated! The gaiety of the occasion, Mr. O'Connor! *(She tosses her head with a peal 620 of laughter. Spills lemonade.)* Oooo! I'm baptizing myself!

JIM: Here—let me—

AMANDA: *(setting the pitcher down)* There now. I discovered we had some maraschino cherries. I dumped them in, juice and all!

625 JIM: You shouldn't have gone to that trouble, Mrs. Wingfield.

AMANDA: Trouble, trouble? Why it was loads of fun! Didn't you hear me cutting up in the kitchen? I bet your ears were burning! I told Tom how outdone 630 with him I was for keeping you to himself so long a time! He should have brought you over much, much sooner! Well, now that you've found your way, I want you to be a very frequent caller! Not just occasional but all the time. Oh, we're going to have a lot of 635 gay times together! I see them coming! Mmm, just breathe that air! So fresh, and the moon's so pretty! I'll skip back out—I know where my place is when young folks are having a—serious conversation!

JIM: Oh, don't go out, Mrs. Wingfield. The fact of the 640 matter is I've got to be going.

AMANDA: Going, now? You're joking! Why, it's only the shank of the evening, Mr. O'Connor!

JIM: Well, you know how it is.

AMANDA: You mean you're a young workingman 645 and have to keep workingmen's hours. We'll let you off early tonight. But only on the condition that next time you stay later. What's the best night for you? Isn't Saturday night the best night for you workingmen?

650 JIM: I have a couple of time-clocks to punch, Mrs. Wingfield. One at morning, another one at night!

AMANDA: My, but you *are* ambitious! You work at night, too?

JIM: No, Ma'am, not work but—Betty! *(He crosses deliber-* 655 *ately to pick up his hat. The band at the Paradise Dance Hall goes into a tender waltz.)*

AMANDA: Betty? Betty? Who's—Betty! *(There is an ominous cracking sound in the sky.)*

JIM: Oh, just a girl. The girl I go steady with! *(He smiles charmingly. The sky falls.)* 660

(Legend: "The Sky Falls.")

AMANDA: *(a long-drawn exhalation)* Ohhhh . . . Is it a serious romance, Mr. O'Connor?

JIM: We're going to be married the second Sunday in June.

AMANDA: Ohhhh—how nice! Tom didn't mention that 665 you were engaged to be married.

JIM: The cat's not out of the bag at the warehouse yet. You know how they are. They call you Romeo and stuff like that. *(He stops at the oval mirror to put on his hat. He carefully shapes the brim and the crown to give a* 670 *discreetly dashing effect.)* It's been a wonderful evening, Mrs. Wingfield. I guess this is what they mean by Southern hospitality.

AMANDA: It really wasn't anything at all.

JIM: I hope it don't seem like I'm rushing off. But I 675 promised Betty I'd pick her up at the Wabash depot, an' by the time I get my jalopy down there her train'll be in. Some women are pretty upset if you keep 'em waiting.

AMANDA: Yes, I know—The tyranny of women! *(Ex-* 680 *tends her hand.)* Good-bye, Mr. O'Connor. I wish you luck—and happiness—and success! All three of them, and so does Laura—Don't you, Laura?

LAURA: Yes!

JIM: *(taking her hand)* Good-bye, Laura. I'm certainly 685 going to treasure that souvenir. And don't you forget the good advice I gave you. *(Raises his voice to a cheery shout.)* So long, Shakespeare! Thanks again, ladies— Good night!

He grins and ducks jauntily out.
   Still bravely grimacing, AMANDA *closes the door on the gentleman caller. Then she turns back to the room with a puzzled expression. She and* LAURA *don't dare to face each other.* LAURA *crouches beside the Victrola to wind it.*

AMANDA: *(faintly)* Things have a way of turning out so 690 badly. I don't believe that I would play the Victrola. Well, well—well—Our gentleman caller was engaged to be married! Tom!

TOM: *(from back)* Yes, Mother?

AMANDA: Come in here a minute. I want to tell you 695 something awfully funny.

TOM: *(enters with a macaroon and a glass of the lemonade)* Has the gentleman caller gotten away already?

AMANDA: The gentleman caller has made an early departure. What a wonderful joke you played on us!

TOM: How do you mean?

AMANDA: You didn't mention that he was engaged to be married.

TOM: Jim? Engaged?

AMANDA: That's what he just informed us.

TOM: I'll be jiggered! I didn't know about that.

AMANDA: That seems very peculiar.

TOM: What's peculiar about it?

AMANDA: Didn't you call him your best friend down at the warehouse?

TOM: He is, but how did I know?

AMANDA: It seems extremely peculiar that you wouldn't know your best friend is going to be married!

TOM: The warehouse is where I work, not where I know things about people!

AMANDA: You don't know things anywhere! You live in a dream; you manufacture illusions! *(He crosses to door.)* Where are you going?

TOM: I'm going to the movies.

AMANDA: That's right, now that you've had us make such fools of ourselves. The effort, the preparations, all the expense! The new floor lamp, the rug, the clothes for Laura! All for what? To entertain some other girl's fiancé! Go to the movies, go! Don't think about us, a mother deserted, an unmarried sister who's crippled and has no job! Don't let anything interfere with your selfish pleasure! Just go, go, go—to the movies!

TOM: All right, I will! The more you shout about my selfishness to me the quicker I'll go, and I won't go to the movies!

AMANDA: Go, then! Then go to the moon—you selfish dreamer!

TOM *smashes his glass on the floor. He plunges out on the fire-escape, slamming the door.* LAURA *screams—cut by door.*

Dance-hall music up. TOM *goes to the rail and grips it desperately, lifting his face in the chill white moonlight penetrating the narrow abyss of the alley.*

(Legend on screen: "And So Good-Bye . . .")

TOM'*s closing speech is timed with the interior pantomime. The interior scene is played as though viewed through sound-proof glass.* AMANDA *appears to be making a comforting speech to* LAURA *who is huddled upon the sofa. Now that we cannot hear the mother's speech, her silliness is gone and she has dignity and tragic beauty.* LAURA'*s dark hair hides her face until at the end of the speech she lifts it to smile at her mother.* AMANDA'*s gestures are slow and graceful, almost dancelike, as she comforts the daughter. At the end of her speech she glances a moment at the father's picture—then withdraws through the portieres. At close of* TOM'*s speech,* LAURA *blows out the candles, ending the play.*

TOM: I didn't go to the moon, I went much further—for time is the longest distance between two places—Not long after that I was fired for writing a poem on the lid of a shoe-box. I left Saint Louis. I descended the steps of this fire-escape for a last time and followed, from then on, in my father's footsteps, attempting to find in motion what was lost in space—I traveled around a great deal. The cities swept about me like dead leaves, leaves that were brightly colored but torn away from the branches. I would have stopped, but I was pursued by something. It always came upon me unawares, taking me altogether by surprise. Perhaps it was a familiar bit of music. Perhaps it was only a piece of transparent glass—Perhaps I am walking along a street at night, in some strange city, before I have found companions. I pass the lighted window of a shop where perfume is sold. The window is filled with pieces of colored glass, tiny transparent bottles in delicate colors, like bits of a shattered rainbow. Then all at once my sister touches my shoulder. I turn around and look into

Amanda berates Tom for his error.

755 her eyes. . . . Oh, Laura, Laura, I tried to leave you behind me, but I am more faithful than I intended to be! I reach for a cigarette, I cross the street, I run into the movies or a bar, I buy a drink, I speak to the nearest stranger—anything that can blow your can-

760 dles out! (LAURA *bends over the candles*)—for nowadays the world is lit by lightning! Blow out your candles, Laura—and so good-bye . . .

> *She blows the candles out.*
> *(The Scene Dissolves.)*

Laura and Amanda sit huddled alone in the dark.

Writing from Reading

Summarize

1 In this day, a small family, living on hopes, dreams, and illusions, seems destined to take a fall. Does the theme seem specific to the time and place, or does it have larger implications?

2 What are some of the central "problems" in this problem play? What would you describe as its themes?

Analyze Craft

3 In Tom Wingfield's first speech, he—and through him the play-wright—declares, " I am the opposite of a stage magician. He gives you illusion that has the appearance of truth. I give you truth in the pleasant disguise of illusion." How does this relate to the notion of realistic representation onstage?

4 In the stage direction, Williams writes of Tom, "His nature is not remorseless, but to escape from a trap he has to act without pity." In what ways does he do so, and how fully does he succeed?

5 The glass collection—with its fragility, its safe haven on the shelf—is of course Laura's, and it repre-sents her beauty as well as her predica-ment. In real life, Williams's sister was institutionalized for schizophrenia. How might this experience have contributed to the development of Laura's charac-ter, and how does Laura's fantasy life here feel real?

Analyze Voice

6 "And so good-bye. . ." is the play's final line as well as the "Legend on screen." Describe the nature of this farewell and the degree of finality. How does Amanda continue, and are things truly over for Laura and Tom? In what ways is this play an act of continuity as well as one of closure?

7 How would you describe the lan-guage of the play? What tone does the language create? Harsh? Lyrical? A mix of tones?

Synthesize Summary and Analysis

8 In what ways does the style of the play—the stage directions, the language, and the representation of in-ner and outer states of the characters—seem to have affinities with *Death of a Salesman*? In what ways does it differ?

Interpret the Play

9 Is there something particular to the fate of this family that ties its destiny to eternal illusion, or does the playwright infer that all families are alike in this regard?

THE BARD OF PITTSBURGH

August Wilson, one of the most widely praised dramatists of the late twentieth cen-tury in America, has had a large impact on a subsequent generation of actors and playwrights. We can make an analogy here with Shakespeare and suggest that in his

"August Wilson plays [are] very similar to Tennessee Williams plays [in that] there's somebody fighting for more. . . . The people that he is dealing with, they have been bourgeois . . . a whole way of life that's crumbling, and they're looking for somebody to save them. August Wilson's characters aren't crumbling; they're down, looking for a way to get up." Conversation with Ruben Santiago-Hudson

own way August Wilson is the Shakespeare of the twentieth-century black American experience. He does not, however, deal with kings, and no armies clash just offstage in his theater. Growing out of the realistic tradition, Wilson makes plays that give us a sense of ordinary life in an extraordinary way. His characters dig deeper into themselves than do most people we know, whether we are black or white or red or yellow, and whether in an actual theater or the theater of our minds. *Fences*, arguably his finest creation, is set in Pittsburgh during the 1950s.

August Wilson (1945–2005)

Raised in a two-room apartment above a garage in Pittsburgh, August Wilson grew up to become an American playwright with two Pulitzer Prizes, several Tony Award nominations, and numerous other awards and fellowships. He was raised by his African-American mother, who had been abandoned by Wilson's German father. When she remarried, the black family moved to a white neighborhood where they were the victims of racist comments and behavior. This, along with his love of the blues as a form of black expression, led Wilson to become a playwright whose central concern was the plight of blacks and the hope of finding healing in black communities. After founding a black theater company in Pittsburgh, Wilson's first major success came with his play *Ma Rainey's Black Bottom* (1984). Two of his plays, *Fences* (1985) and *Joe Turner's Come and Gone* (1986), ran simultaneously on Broadway—a rare achievement. Wilson's body of work functions as a history of black American life in the twentieth century.

AS YOU READ Scan the script for the details of the family's life. Find references to Troy Maxon's life at work and at home and with friends.

FOR INTERACTIVE READING . . . Mark the places in the script where you notice that scenes appear to begin and end.

Fences (1986)

For Lloyd Richards, who adds to whatever he touches

When the sins of our fathers visit us
We do not have to play host.
We can banish them with forgiveness
As God, in His Largeness and Laws.

—AUGUST WILSON

CHARACTERS

TROY MAXSON

JIM BONO, *Troy's friend*

ROSE, *Troy's wife*

LYONS, *Troy's oldest son by previous marriage*

GABRIEL, *Troy's brother*

CORY, *Troy and Rose's son*

RAYNELL, *Troy's daughter*

SETTING: *The setting is the yard which fronts the only entrance to the Maxson household, an ancient two-story brick house set back off a small alley in a big-city neighborhood. The entrance to the house is gained by two or three steps leading to a wooden porch badly in need of paint.*

A relatively recent addition to the house and running its full width, the porch lacks congruence. It is a sturdy porch with a flat roof. One or two chairs of dubious value sit at one end where the kitchen window opens onto the porch. An old-fashioned icebox stands silent guard at the opposite end.

The yard is a small dirt yard, partially fenced, except for the last scene, with a wooden saw horse, a pile of lumber, and other fence-building equipment set off to the side. Opposite is a tree from which hangs a ball made of rags. A baseball bat leans against the tree. Two oil drums serve as garbage receptacles and sit near the house at right to complete the setting.

THE PLAY: *Near the turn of the century, the destitute of Europe sprang on the city with tenacious claws and an honest and solid dream. The city devoured them. They swelled its belly until it burst into a thousand furnaces and sewing machines, a thousand butcher shops and bakers' ovens, a thousand churches and hospitals and funeral parlors and money-lenders. The city grew. It nourished itself and offered each man a partnership limited only by his talent, his guile, and his willingness and capacity for hard work. For the immigrants of Europe, a dream dared and won true.*

The descendants of African slaves were offered no such welcome or participation. They came from places called the Carolinas and the Virginias, Georgia, Alabama, Mississippi, and Tennessee. They came strong, eager, searching. The city rejected them and they fled and settled along the riverbanks and under bridges in shallow, ramshackle houses made of sticks and tarpaper. They collected rags and wood.

They sold the use of their muscles and their bodies. They cleaned houses and washed clothes, they shined shoes, and in quiet desperation and vengeful pride, they stole, and lived in pursuit of their own dream. That they could breathe free, finally, and stand to meet life with the force of dignity and whatever eloquence the heart could call upon.

By 1957, the hard-won victories of the European immigrants had solidified the industrial might of America. War had been confronted and won with new energies that used loyalty and patriotism as its fuel. Life was rich, full, and flourishing. The Milwaukee Braves won the World Series, and the hot winds of change that would make the sixties a turbulent, racing, dangerous, and provocative decade had not yet begun to blow full.

ACT I

SCENE I

It is 1957. TROY and BONO enter the yard, engaged in conversation. TROY is fifty-three years old, a large man with thick, heavy hands; it is this largeness that he strives to fill out and make an accommodation with. Together with his blackness, his largeness informs his sensibilities and the choices he has made in his life.

Of the two men, BONO is obviously the follower. His commitment to their friendship of thirty-odd years is rooted in his admiration of TROY's honesty, capacity for hard work, and his strength, which BONO seeks to emulate.

It is Friday night, payday, and the one night of the week the two men engage in a ritual of talk and drink. TROY is usually the most talkative and at times he can be crude and almost vulgar, though he is capable of rising to profound heights of expression. The men carry lunch buckets and wear or carry burlap aprons and are dressed in clothes suitable to their jobs as garbage collectors.

BONO: Troy, you ought to stop that lying!

TROY: I ain't lying! The nigger had a watermelon this big. *(He indicates with his hands.)* Talking about . . . "What watermelon, Mr. Rand?" I liked to fell out! 5 "What watermelon, Mr. Rand?" . . . And it sitting there big as life.

BONO: What did Mr. Rand say?

TROY: Ain't said nothing. Figure if the nigger too dumb to know he carrying a watermelon, he wasn't gonna 10 get much sense out of him. Trying to hide that great big old watermelon under his coat. Afraid to let the white man see him carry it home.

BONO: I'm like you . . . I ain't got no time for them kind of people.

TROY: Now what he look like getting mad cause he see 15 the man from the union talking to Mr. Rand?

BONO: He come to me talking about . . . "Maxson gonna get us fired." I told him to get away from me with that. He walked away from me calling you a troublemaker. What Mr. Rand say? 20

TROY: Ain't said nothing. He told me to go down the Commissioner's office next Friday. They called me down there to see them.

BONO: Well, as long as you got your complaint filed, they can't fire you. That's what one of them white 25 fellows tell me.

TROY: I ain't worried about them firing me. They gonna fire me cause I asked a question? That's all I did. I went to Mr. Rand and asked him, "Why? Why you got the white mens driving and the colored lift- 30 ing?" Told him, "what's the matter, don't I count? You think only white fellows got sense enough to drive a truck. That ain't no paper job! Hell, anybody can drive a truck. How come you got all whites driving and the colored lifting?" He told me "take it to 35 the union." Well, hell, that's what I done! Now they wanna come up with this pack of lies.

BONO: I told Brownie if the man come and ask him any questions . . . just tell the truth! It ain't nothing but something they done trumped up on you cause 40 you filed a complaint on them.

TROY: Brownie don't understand nothing. All I want them to do is change the job description. Give everybody a chance to drive the truck. Brownie can't see that. He ain't got that much sense. 45

BONO: How you figure he be making out with that gal be up at Taylors' all the time . . . that Alberta gal?

TROY: Same as you and me. Getting just as much as we is. Which is to say nothing.

BONO: It is, huh? I figure you doing a little better than 50 me . . . and I ain't saying what I'm doing.

TROY: Aw, nigger, look here . . . I know you. If you had got anywhere near that gal, twenty minutes later you be looking to tell somebody. And the first one you gonna tell . . . that you gonna want to brag to . . . is 55 gonna be me.

BONO: I ain't saying that. I see where you be eyeing her.

TROY: I eye all the women. I don't miss nothing. Don't never let nobody tell you Troy Maxson don't eye the women.

BONO: You been doing more than eyeing her. You done bought her a drink or two.

TROY: Hell yeah, I bought her a drink! What that mean? I bought you one, too. What that mean cause I buy her a drink? I'm just being polite.

BONO: It's alright to buy her one drink. That's what you call being polite. But when you wanna be buying two or three . . . that's what you call eyeing her.

TROY: Look here, as long as you known me . . . you ever known me to chase after women?

BONO: Hell yeah! Long as I done known you. You forgetting I knew you when.

TROY: Naw, I'm talking about since I been married to Rose?

BONO: Oh, not since you been married to Rose. Now, that's the truth, there. I can say that.

TROY: Alright then! Case closed.

BONO: I see you be walking up around Alberta's house. You supposed to be at Taylors' and you be walking up around there.

TROY: What you watching where I'm walking for? I ain't watching after you.

BONO: I seen you walking around there more than once.

TROY: Hell, you liable to see me walking anywhere! That don't mean nothing cause you see me walking around there.

BONO: Where she come from anyway? She just kinda showed up one day.

TROY: Tallahassee. You can look at her and tell she one of them Florida gals. They got some big healthy women down there. Grow them right up out the ground. Got a little bit of Indian in her. Most of them niggers down in Florida got some Indian in them.

BONO: I don't know about that Indian part. But she damn sure big and healthy. Woman wear some big stockings. Got them great big old legs and hips as wide as the Mississippi River.

TROY: Legs don't mean nothing. You don't do nothing but push them out of the way. But them hips cushion the ride!

BONO: Troy, you ain't got no sense.

TROY: It's the truth! Like you riding on Goodyears!

(ROSE *enters from the house. She is ten years younger than* TROY. *Her devotion to him stems from her recognition of the possibilities of her life without him: a succession of abusive men and their babies, a life of partying and running the streets, the Church, or aloneness with its attendant pain and frustration. She recognizes* TROY's *spirit as a fine and illuminating one and she either ignores or forgives his faults, only some of which she recognizes. Though she doesn't drink, her presence is an integral part of the Friday night rituals. She alternates between the porch and the kitchen, where supper preparations are under way.)*

ROSE: What you all out here getting into?

TROY: What you worried about what we getting into for? This is men talk, woman.

ROSE: What I care what you all talking about? Bono, you gonna stay for supper?

BONO: No, I thank you, Rose. But Lucille say she cooking up a pot of pigfeet.

TROY: Pigfeet! Hell, I'm going home with you! Might even stay the night if you got some pigfeet. You got something in there to top them pigfeet, Rose?

ROSE: I'm cooking up some chicken. I got some chicken and collard greens.

TROY: Well, go on back in the house and let me and Bono finish what we was talking about. This is men talk. I got some talk for you later. You know what kind of talk I mean. You go on and powder it up.

ROSE: Troy Maxson, don't you start that now!

TROY: *(Puts his arm around her.)* Aw, woman . . . come here. Look here, Bono . . . when I met this woman . . . I got out that place, say, "Hitch up my pony, saddle up my mare . . . there's a woman out there for me somewhere. I looked here. Looked there. Saw Rose and latched on to her." I latched on to her and told her—I'm gonna tell you the truth—I told her, "Baby, I don't wanna marry, I just wanna be your man." Rose told me . . . tell him what you told me, Rose.

ROSE: I told him if he wasn't the marrying kind, then move out the way so the marrying kind could find me.

TROY: That's what she told me. "Nigger, you in my way. You blocking the view! Move out the way so I can find me a husband." I thought it over two or three days. Come back—

ROSE: Ain't no two or three days nothing. You was back the same night.

TROY: Come back, told her . . . "Okay, baby . . . but I'm gonna buy me a banty rooster and put him out there in the backyard . . . and when he see a stranger come,
140 he'll flap his wings and crow . . . " Look here, Bono, I could watch the front door by myself . . . it was that back door I was worried about.

ROSE: Troy, you ought not talk like that. Troy ain't doing nothing but telling a lie.

145 **TROY:** Only thing is . . . when we first got married . . . forget the rooster . . . we ain't had no yard!

BONO: I hear you tell it. Me and Lucille was staying down there on Logan Street. Had two rooms with the outhouse in the back. I ain't mind the outhouse
150 none. But when that goddamn wind blow through there in the winter . . . that's what I'm talking about! To this day I wonder why in the hell I ever stayed down there for six long years. But see, I didn't know I could do no better. I thought only white folks had
155 inside toilets and things.

ROSE: There's a lot of people don't know they can do no better than they doing now. That's just something you got to learn. A lot of folks still shop at Bella's.

TROY: Ain't nothing wrong with shopping at Bella's.
160 She got fresh food.

ROSE: I ain't said nothing about if she got fresh food. I'm talking about what she charge. She charge ten cents more than the A&P.

TROY: The A&P ain't never done nothing for me. I
165 spends my money where I'm treated right. I go down to Bella, say, "I need a loaf of bread, I'll pay you Friday." She give it to me. What sense that make when I got money to go and spend it somewhere else and ignore the person who done right by me? That ain't
170 in the Bible.

ROSE: We ain't talking about what's in the Bible. What sense it make to shop there when she overcharge?

TROY: You shop where you want to. I'll do my shopping where the people been good to me.

175 **ROSE:** Well, I don't think it's right for her to overcharge. That's all I was saying.

BONO: Look here . . . I got to get on. Lucille going be raising all kind of hell.

TROY: Where you going, nigger? We ain't finished this
180 pint. Come here, finish this pint.

BONO: Well, hell, I am . . . if you ever turn the bottle loose.

TROY: (*Hands him the bottle.*) The only thing I say about the A&P is I'm glad Cory got that job down there. Help him take care of his school clothes and things.
185 Gabe done moved out and things getting tight around here. He got that job . . . He can start to look out for himself.

ROSE: Cory done went and got recruited by a college football team.
190

TROY: I told that boy about that football stuff. The white man ain't gonna let him get nowhere with that football. I told him when he first come to me with it. Now you come telling me he done went and got more tied up in it. He ought to go and get recruited in how
195 to fix cars or something where he can make a living.

ROSE: He ain't talking about making no living playing football. It's just something the boys in school do. They gonna send a recruiter by to talk to you. He'll tell you he ain't talking about making no living play-
200 ing football. It's a honor to be recruited.

TROY: It ain't gonna get him nowhere. Bono'll tell you that.

BONO: If he be like you in the sports . . . he's gonna be alright. Ain't but two men ever played baseball
205 as good as you. That's Babe Ruth and Josh Gibson. Them's the only two men ever hit more home runs than you.

TROY: What it ever get me? Ain't got a pot to piss in or a window to throw it out of.
210

ROSE: Times have changed since you was playing baseball, Troy. That was before the war. Times have changed a lot since then.

TROY: How in hell they done changed?

ROSE: They got lots of colored boys playing ball now.
215 Baseball and football.

BONO: You right about that, Rose. Times have changed, Troy. You just come along too early.

TROY: There ought not never have been no time called too early! Now you take that fellow . . . what's that
220 fellow they had playing right field for the Yankees back then? You know who I'm talking about, Bono. Used to play right field for the Yankees.

ROSE: Selkirk?

TROY: Selkirk! That's it! Man batting .269, under-
225 stand? .269. What kind of sense that make? I was hitting .432 with thirty-seven home runs! Man batting .269 and playing right field for the Yankees! I

230 saw Josh Gibson's daughter yesterday. She walking around with raggedy shoes on her feet. Now I bet you Selkirk's daughter ain't walking around with raggedy shoes on her feet! I bet you that!

ROSE: They got a lot of colored baseball players now. Jackie Robinson was the first. Folks had to wait for 235 Jackie Robinson.

TROY: I done seen a hundred niggers play baseball better than Jackie Robinson. Hell, I know some teams Jackie Robinson couldn't even make! What you talking about Jackie Robinson. Jackie Robinson 240 wasn't nobody. I'm talking about if you could play ball then they ought to have let you play. Don't care what color you were. Come telling me I come along too early. If you could play . . . then they ought to have let you play.

(TROY takes a long drink from the bottle.)

245 **ROSE:** You gonna drink yourself to death. You don't need to be drinking like that.

TROY: Death ain't nothing. I done seen him. Done wrassled with him. You can't tell me nothing about death. Death ain't nothing but a fastball on the 250 outside corner. And you know what I'll do to that! Lookee here, Bono . . . am I lying? You get one of them fastballs, about waist high, over the outside corner of the plate where you can get the meat of the bat on it . . . and good god! You can kiss it goodbye. 255 Now, am I lying?

BONO: Naw, you telling the truth there. I seen you do it.

TROY: If I'm lying . . . that 450 feet worth of lying! *(Pause.)* That's all death is to me. A fastball on the outside corner.

260 **ROSE:** I don't know why you want to get on talking about death.

TROY: Ain't nothing wrong with talking about death. That's part of life. Everybody gonna die. You gonna die, I'm gonna die. Bono's gonna die. Hell, we all 265 gonna die.

ROSE: But you ain't got to talk about it. I don't like to talk about it.

TROY: You the one brought it up. Me and Bono was talking about baseball . . . you tell me I'm gonna 270 drink myself to death. Ain't that right, Bono? You know I don't drink this but one night out of the week. That's Friday night. I'm gonna drink just enough to where I can handle it. Then I cuts it loose. I leave it alone. So don't you worry about me drinking myself

to death. 'Cause I ain't worried about Death. I done 275 seen him. I done wrestled with him.

Look here, Bono . . . I looked up one day and Death was marching straight at me. Like Soldiers on Parade! The Army of Death was marching straight at me. The middle of July, 1941. It got real cold just 280 like it be winter. It seem like Death himself reached out and touched me on the shoulder. He touch me just like I touch you. I got cold as ice and Death standing there grinning at me.

ROSE: Troy, why don't you hush that talk. 285

TROY: I say . . . what you want, Mr. Death? You be wanting me? You done brought your army to be getting me? I looked him dead in the eye. I wasn't fearing nothing. I was ready to tangle. Just like I'm ready to tangle now. The Bible say be ever vigilant. That's 290 why I don't get but so drunk. I got to keep watch.

ROSE: Troy was right down there in Mercy Hospital. You remember he had pneumonia? Laying there with a fever talking plumb out of his head.

TROY: Death standing there staring at me . . . carry- 295 ing that sickle in his hand. Finally he say, "You want bound over for another year?" See, just like that . . . "You want bound over for another year?" I told him, "Bound over hell! Let's settle this now!"

It seem like he kinda fell back when I said that, 300 and all the cold went out of me. I reached down and grabbed that sickle and threw it just as far as I could throw it . . . and me and him commenced to wrestling.

We wrestled for three days and three nights. I 305 can't say where I found the strength from. Every- time it seemed like he was gonna get the best of me, I'd reach way down deep inside myself and find the strength to do him one better.

ROSE: Everytime Troy tell that story he find different 310 ways to tell it. Different things to make up about it.

TROY: I ain't making up nothing. I'm telling you the facts of what happened. I wrestled with Death for three days and three nights and I'm standing here to tell you about it. *(Pause.)* Alright. At the end of the 315 third night we done weakened each other to where we can't hardly move. Death stood up, throwed on his robe . . . had him a white robe with a hood on it. He throwed on that robe and went off to look for his sickle. Say, "I'll be back." Just like that. "I'll be back." 320 I told him, say, "Yeah, but . . . you gonna have to find me!" I wasn't no fool. I wasn't going looking for him. Death ain't nothing to play with. And I know he's gonna get me. I know I got to join his army . . . his

325 camp followers. But as long as I keep my strength and see him coming . . . as long as I keep up my vigilance . . . he's gonna have to fight to get me. I ain't going easy.

BONO: Well, look here, since you got to keep up your
330 vigilance . . . let me have the bottle.

TROY: Aw hell, I shouldn't have told you that part. I should have left out that part.

ROSE: Troy be talking that stuff and half the time don't even know what he be talking about.

335 TROY: Bono know me better than that.

BONO: That's right. I know you. I know you got some Uncle Remus in your blood. You got more stories than the devil got sinners.

TROY: Aw hell, I done seen him too! Done talked with
340 the devil.

ROSE: Troy, don't nobody wanna be hearing all that stuff.

(LYONS *enters the yard from the street. Thirty-four years old,* TROY's *son by a previous marriage, he sports a neatly trimmed goatee, sport coat, white shirt, tieless and buttoned at the collar. Though he fancies himself a musician, he is more caught up in the rituals and "idea" of being a musician than in the actual practice of the music. He has come to borrow money from* TROY, *and while he knows he will be successful, he is uncertain as to what extent his lifestyle will be held up to scrutiny and ridicule.)*

LYONS: Hey, Pop.

TROY: What you come "Hey, Popping" me for?

345 LYONS: How you doing, Rose? (*He kisses her.*) Mr. Bono. How you doing?

BONO: Hey, Lyons . . . how you been?

TROY: He must have been doing alright. I ain't seen him around here last week.

350 ROSE: Troy, leave your boy alone. He come by to see you and you wanna start all that nonsense.

TROY: I ain't bothering Lyons. (*Offers him the bottle.*) Here . . . get you a drink. We got an understanding. I know why he come by to see me and he know I know.

355 LYONS: Come on, Pop . . . I just stopped by to say hi . . . see how you was doing.

TROY: You ain't stopped by yesterday.

ROSE: You gonna stay for supper, Lyons? I got some chicken cooking in the oven.

LYONS: No, Rose . . . thanks. I was just in the neighbor-
360 hood and thought I'd stop by for a minute.

TROY: You was in the neighborhood alright, nigger. You telling the truth there. You was in the neighborhood cause it's my payday.

LYONS: Well, hell, since you mentioned it . . . let me
365 have ten dollars.

TROY: I'll be damned! I'll die and go to hell and play blackjack with the devil before I give you ten dollars.

BONO: That's what I wanna know about . . . that devil
370 you done seen.

LYONS: What . . . Pop done seen the devil? You too much, Pops.

TROY: Yeah, I done seen him. Talked to him too!

ROSE: You ain't seen no devil. I done told you that man
375 ain't had nothing to do with the devil. Anything you can't understand, you want to call it the devil.

TROY: Look here, Bono . . . I went down to see Hertzberger about some furniture. Got three rooms for two-ninety-eight. That what it say on the radio.
380 "Three rooms . . . two-ninety-eight." Even made up a little song about it. Go down there . . . man tell me I can't get no credit. I'm working every day and can't get no credit. What to do? I got an empty house with some raggedy furniture in it. Cory ain't got no bed.
385 He's sleeping on a pile of rags on the floor. Working every day and can't get no credit. Come back here— Rose'll tell you—madder than hell. Sit down . . . try to figure what I'm gonna do. Come a knock on the door. Ain't been living here but three days. Who
390 know I'm here? Open the door . . . devil standing there bigger than life. White fellow . . . got on good clothes and everything. Standing there with a clipboard in his hand. I ain't had to say nothing. First words come out of his mouth was . . . "I understand
395 you need some furniture and can't get no credit." I liked to fell over. He say "I'll give you all the credit you want, but you got to pay the interest on it." I told him, "Give me three rooms worth and charge whatever you want." Next day a truck pulled up here
400 and two men unloaded them three rooms. Man what drove the truck give me a book. Say send ten dollars, first of every month to the address in the book and every thing will be alright. Say if I miss a payment the devil was coming back and it'll be hell to pay.
405 That was fifteen years ago. To this day . . . the first of the month I send my ten dollars, Rose'll tell you.

ROSE: Troy lying.

TROY: I ain't never seen that man since. Now you tell me who else that could have been but the devil? I ain't sold my soul or nothing like that, you understand. Naw, I wouldn't have truck with the devil about nothing like that. I got my furniture and pays my ten dollars the first of the month just like clockwork.

BONO: How long you say you been paying this ten dollars a month?

TROY: Fifteen years!

BONO: Hell, ain't you finished paying for it yet? How much the man done charged you?

TROY: Aw hell, I done paid for it. I done paid for it ten times over! The fact is I'm scared to stop paying it.

ROSE: Troy lying. We got that furniture from Mr. Glickman. He ain't paying no ten dollars a month to nobody.

TROY: Aw hell, woman. Bono know I ain't that big a fool.

LYONS: I was just getting ready to say . . . I know where there's a bridge for sale.

TROY: Look here, I'll tell you this . . . it don't matter to me if he was the devil. It don't matter if the devil give credit. Somebody has got to give it.

ROSE: It ought to matter. You going around talking about having truck with the devil . . . God's the one you gonna have to answer to. He's the one gonna be at the Judgment.

LYONS: Yeah, well, look here, Pop . . . Let me have that ten dollars. I'll give it back to you. Bonnie got a job working at the hospital.

TROY: What I tell you, Bono? The only time I see this nigger is when he wants something. That's the only time I see him.

LYONS: Come on, Pop, Mr. Bono don't want to hear all that. Let me have the ten dollars. I told you Bonnie working.

TROY: What that mean to me? "Bonnie working." I don't care if she working. Go ask her for the ten dollars if she working. Talking about "Bonnie working." Why ain't you working?

LYONS: Aw, Pop, you know I can't find no decent job. Where am I gonna get a job at? You know I can't get no job.

TROY: I told you I know some people down there. I can get you on the rubbish if you want to work. I told

you that the last time you came by here asking me for something.

LYONS: Naw, Pop . . . thanks. That ain't for me. I don't wanna be carrying nobody's rubbish. I don't wanna be punching nobody's time clock.

TROY: What's the matter, you too good to carry people's rubbish? Where you think that ten dollars you talking about come from? I'm just supposed to haul people's rubbish and give my money to you cause you too lazy to work. You too lazy to work and wanna know why you ain't got what I got.

ROSE: What hospital Bonnie working at? Mercy?

LYONS: She's down at Passavant working in the laundry.

TROY: I ain't got nothing as it is. I give you that ten dollars and I got to eat beans the rest of the week. Naw . . . you ain't getting no ten dollars here.

LYONS: You ain't got to be eating no beans. I don't know why you wanna say that.

TROY: I ain't got no extra money. Gabe done moved over to Miss Pearl's paying her the rent and things done got tight around here. I can't afford to be giving you every payday.

LYONS: I ain't asked you to give me nothing. I asked you to loan me ten dollars. I know you got ten dollars.

TROY: Yeah, I got it. You know why I got it? Cause I don't throw my money away out there in the streets. You living the fast life . . . wanna be a musician . . . running around in them clubs and things . . . then, you learn to take care of yourself. You ain't gonna find me going and asking nobody for nothing. I done spent too many years without.

LYONS: You and me is two different people, Pop.

TROY: I done learned my mistake and learned to do what's right by it. You still trying to get something for nothing. Life don't owe you nothing. You owe it to yourself. Ask Bono. He'll tell you I'm right.

LYONS: You got your way of dealing with the world . . . I got mine. The only thing that matters to me is the music.

TROY: Yeah, I can see that! It don't matter how you gonna eat . . . where your next dollar is coming from. You telling the truth there.

LYONS: I know I got to eat. But I got to live too. I need something that gonna help me to get out of the bed in the morning. Make me feel like I belong in the world. I don't bother nobody. I just stay with my music cause that's the only way I can find to live in the world. Otherwise there ain't no telling what I might do. Now I don't come criticizing you and how you live. I just come by to ask you for ten dollars. I don't wanna hear all that about how I live.

TROY: Boy, your mamma did a hell of a job raising you.

LYONS: You can't change me, Pop. I'm thirty-four years old. If you wanted to change me, you should have been there when I was growing up. I come by to see you . . . ask for ten dollars and you want to talk about how I was raised. You don't know nothing about how I was raised.

ROSE: Let the boy have ten dollars, Troy.

TROY: (*To* LYONS.) What the hell you looking at me for? I ain't got no ten dollars. You know what I do with my money. (*To* ROSE.) Give him ten dollars if you want him to have it.

ROSE: I will. Just as soon as you turn it loose.

TROY: (*Handing* ROSE *the money.*) There it is. Seventy-six dollars and forty-two cents. You see this, Bono? Now, I ain't gonna get but six of that back.

ROSE: You ought to stop telling that lie. Here, Lyons. (*She hands him the money.*)

LYONS: Thanks, Rose. Look . . . I got to run . . . I'll see you later.

TROY: Wait a minute. You gonna say, "thanks, Rose" and ain't gonna look to see where she got that ten dollars from? See how they do me, Bono?

LYONS: I know she got it from you, Pop. Thanks. I'll give it back to you.

TROY: There he go telling another lie. Time I see that ten dollars . . . he'll be owing me thirty more.

LYONS: See you, Mr. Bono.

BONO: Take care, Lyons!

LYONS: Thanks, Pop. I'll see you again.

(LYONS *exits the yard.*)

TROY: I don't know why he don't go and get him a decent job and take care of that woman he got.

BONO: He'll be alright, Troy. The boy is still young.

TROY: The *boy* is thirty-four years old.

ROSE: Let's not get off into all that.

BONO: Look here . . . I got to be going. I got to be getting on. Lucille gonna be waiting.

TROY: (*Puts his arm around* ROSE.) See this woman, Bono? I love this woman. I love this woman so much it hurts. I love her so much . . . I done run out of ways of loving her. So I got to go back to basics. Don't you come by my house Monday morning talking about time to go to work . . . 'cause I'm still gonna be stroking!

ROSE: Troy! Stop it now!

BONO: I ain't paying him no mind, Rose. That ain't nothing but gin-talk. Go on, Troy. I'll see you Monday.

TROY: Don't you come by my house, nigger! I done told you what I'm gonna be doing.

(*The lights go down to black.*)

SCENE II

The lights come up on ROSE *hanging up clothes. She hums and sings softly to herself. It is the following morning.*

ROSE: (*Sings.*)
Jesus, be a fence all around me every day
Jesus, I want you to protect me as I travel on
     my way.
Jesus, be a fence all around me every day.

(TROY *enters from the house.*)

Jesus, I want you to protect me
As I travel on my way.
(*To* TROY.) 'Morning. You ready for breakfast? I can fix it soon as I finish hanging up these clothes.

TROY: I got the coffee on. That'll be alright. I'll just drink some of that this morning.

ROSE: That 651 hit yesterday. That's the second time this month. Miss Pearl hit for a dollar . . . seem like those that need the least always get lucky. Poor folks can't get nothing.

TROY: Them numbers don't know anybody. I don't know why you fool with them. You and Lyons both.

ROSE: It's something to do.

TROY: You ain't doing nothing but throwing your money away.

ROSE: Troy, you know I don't play foolishly. I just play a nickel here and a nickel there.

TROY: That's two nickels you done thrown away.

ROSE: Now I hit sometimes . . . that makes up for it. It always comes in handy when I do hit. I don't hear you complaining then.

25 **TROY:** I ain't complaining now. I just say it's foolish. Trying to guess out of six hundred ways which way the number gonna come. If I had all the money niggers, these Negroes, throw away on numbers for one week—just one week—I'd be a rich man.

30 **ROSE:** Well, you wishing and calling it foolish ain't gonna stop folks from playing numbers. That's one thing for sure. Besides . . . some good things come from playing numbers. Look where Pope done bought him that restaurant off of numbers.

35 **TROY:** I can't stand niggers like that. Man ain't had two dimes to rub together. He walking around with his shoes all run over bumming money for cigarettes. Alright. Got lucky there and hit the numbers . . .

ROSE: Troy, I know all about it.

40 **TROY:** Had good sense, I'll say that for him. He ain't thrown his money away. I seen niggers hit the numbers and go through two thousand dollars in four days. Man bought him that restaurant down there . . . fixed it up real nice. . . . and then didn't want
45 nobody to come in it! A Negro go in there and can't get no kind of service. I seen a white fellow come in there and order a bowl of stew. Pope picked all the meat out of the pot for him. Man ain't had nothing but a bowl of meat! Negro come behind him and
50 ain't got nothing but the potatoes and carrots. Talking about what numbers do for people, you picked a wrong example. Ain't done nothing but make a worser fool out of him than he was before.

ROSE: Troy, you ought to stop worrying about what
55 happened at work yesterday.

TROY: I ain't worried. Just told me to be down there at the Commissioner's office on Friday. Everybody think they gonna fire me. I ain't worried about them firing me. You ain't got to worry about that. *(Pause.)*
60 Where's Cory? Cory in the house? *(Calls.)* Cory?

ROSE: He gone out.

TROY: Out, huh? He gone out 'cause he know I want him to help me with this fence. I know how he is. That boy scared of work.

(GABRIEL enters. He comes halfway down the alley and, hearing TROY's voice, stops.)

65 **TROY:** *(Continues.)* He ain't done a lick of work in his life.

ROSE: He had to go to football practice. Coach wanted them to get in a little extra practice before the season start.

TROY: I got his practice . . . running out of here before he get his chores done.
70

ROSE: Troy, what is wrong with you this morning? Don't nothing set right with you. Go on back in there and go to bed . . . get up on the other side.

TROY: Why something got to be wrong with me? I ain't said nothing wrong with me.
75

ROSE: You got something to say about everything. First it's the numbers . . . then it's the way the man runs his restaurant . . . then you done got on Cory. What's it gonna be next? Take a look up there and see if the weather suits you . . . or is it gonna be how you gonna
80 put up the fence with the clothes hanging in the yard?

TROY: You hit the nail on the head then.

ROSE: I know you like I know the back of my hand. Go on in there and get you some coffee . . . see if that straighten you up. 'Cause you ain't right this
85 morning.

(TROY starts into the house and sees GABRIEL. GABRIEL starts singing. TROY's brother, he is seven years younger than TROY. Injured in World War II, he has a metal plate in his head. He carries an old trumpet tied around his waist and believes with every fiber of his being that he is the Archangel Gabriel. He carries a chipped basket with an assortment of discarded fruits and vegetables he has picked up in the strip district and which he attempts to sell.)

GABRIEL: *(Singing.)*
    Yes, ma'am, I got plums
    You ask me how I sell them
    Oh ten cents apiece
    Three for a quarter
90
    Come and buy now
    'Cause I'm here today
    And tomorrow I'll be gone

(GABRIEL enters.)

Hey, Rose!

ROSE: How you doing, Gabe?
95

GABRIEL: There's Troy . . . Hey, Troy!

TROY: Hey, Gabe.

(Exit into kitchen.)

ROSE: *(To GABRIEL.)* What you got there?

GABRIEL: You know what I got, Rose. I got fruits and vegetables.
100

ROSE: *(Looking in basket.)* Where's all these plums you talking about?

GABRIEL: I ain't got no plums today, Rose. I was just singing that. Have some tomorrow. Put me in a big order for plums. Have enough plums tomorrow for St. Peter and everybody. [105]

(TROY *reenters from kitchen, crosses to steps.*)

(*To* ROSE.) Troy's mad at me.

TROY: I ain't mad at you. What I got to be mad at you about? You ain't done nothing to me.

GABRIEL: I just moved over to Miss Pearl's to keep out from in your way. I ain't mean no harm by it. [110]

TROY: Who said anything about that? I ain't said anything about that.

GABRIEL: You ain't mad at me, is you?

TROY: Naw . . . I ain't mad at you, Gabe. If I was mad at you I'd tell you about it. [115]

GABRIEL: Got me two rooms. In the basement. Got my own door too. Wanna see my key? (*He holds up a key.*) That's my own key! Ain't nobody else got a key like that. That's my key! My two rooms! [120]

TROY: Well, that's good, Gabe. You got your own key . . . that's good.

ROSE: You hungry, Gabe? I was just fixing to cook Troy his breakfast.

GABRIEL: I'll take some biscuits. You got some biscuits? Did you know when I was in heaven . . . every morning me and St. Peter would sit down by the gate and eat some big fat biscuits? Oh, yeah! We had us a good time. We'd sit there and eat us them biscuits and then St. Peter would go off to sleep and tell me to wake him up when it's time to open the gates for the judgment. [125] [130]

ROSE: Well, come on . . . I'll make up a batch of biscuits.

(ROSE *exits into the house.*)

GABRIEL: Troy . . . St. Peter got your name in the book. I seen it. It say . . . Troy Maxson. I say . . . I know him! He got the same name like what I got. That's my brother! [135]

TROY: How many times you gonna tell me that, Gabe?

GABRIEL: Ain't got my name in the book. Don't have to have my name. I done died and went to heaven. He got your name though. One morning St. Peter was looking at his book . . . marking it up for the judgment . . . and he let me see your name. Got it in there under M. Got Rose's name . . . I ain't seen it like I seen yours . . . but I know it's in there. He got a [140] [145]

great big book. Got everybody's name what was ever been born. That's what he told me. But I seen your name. Seen it with my own eyes.

TROY: Go on in the house there. Rose going to fix you something to eat. [150]

GABRIEL: Oh, I ain't hungry. I done had breakfast with Aunt Jemimah. She come by and cooked me up a whole mess of flapjacks. Remember how we used to eat them flapjacks?

TROY: Go on in the house and get you something to eat now. [155]

GABRIEL: I got to sell my plums. I done sold some tomatoes. Got me two quarters. Wanna see? (*He shows* TROY *his quarters.*) I'm gonna save them and buy me a new horn so St. Peter can hear me when it's time to open the gates. (GABRIEL *stops suddenly. Listens.*) Hear that? That's the hellhounds. I got to chase them out of here. Go on get out of here! Get out! [160]

(GABRIEL *exits singing.*)

> Better get ready for the judgment
> Better get ready for the judgment
> My Lord is coming down [165]

(ROSE *enters from the house.*)

TROY: He gone off somewhere.

GABRIEL: (*Offstage.*) Better get ready for the judgment
Better get ready for the judgment morning
Better get ready for the judgment [170]
My God is coming down

ROSE: He ain't eating right. Miss Pearl say she can't get him to eat nothing.

TROY: What you want me to do about it, Rose? I done did everything I can for the man. I can't make him get well. Man got half his head blown away . . . what you expect? [175]

ROSE: Seem like something ought to be done to help him.

TROY: Man don't bother nobody. He just mixed up from that metal plate he got in his head. Ain't no sense for him to go back into the hospital. [180]

ROSE: Least he be eating right. They can help him take care of himself.

TROY: Don't nobody wanna be locked up, Rose. What you wanna lock him up for? Man go over there and fight the war . . . messin' around with them Japs, get half his head blown off . . . and they give him a lousy [185]

190 three thousand dollars. And I had to swoop down on that.

ROSE: Is you fixing to go into that again?

TROY: That's the only way I got a roof over my head . . . cause of that metal plate.

195 **ROSE:** Ain't no sense you blaming yourself for nothing. Gabe wasn't in no condition to manage that money. You done what was right by him. Can't nobody say you ain't done what was right by him. Look how long you took care of him . . . till he wanted to have his own place and moved over there with Miss Pearl.

200 **TROY:** That ain't what I'm saying, woman! I'm just stating the facts. If my brother didn't have that metal plate in his head . . . I wouldn't have a pot to piss in or a window to throw it out of. And I'm fifty-three years old. Now see if you can understand that!

(TROY *gets up from the porch and starts to exit the yard.*)

205 **ROSE:** Where you going off to? You been running out of here every Saturday for weeks. I thought you was gonna work on this fence?

TROY: I'm gonna walk down to Taylors'. Listen to the ball game. I'll be back in a bit. I'll work on it when I
210 get back.

(*He exits the yard. The lights go to black.*)

SCENE III

The lights come up on the yard. It is four hours later. ROSE *is taking down the clothes from the line.* CORY *enters carrying his football equipment.*

ROSE: Your daddy like to had a fit with you running out of here this morning without doing your chores.

CORY: I told you I had to go to practice.

ROSE: He say you were supposed to help him with this
5 fence.

CORY: He been saying that the last four or five Saturdays, and then he don't never do nothing, but go down to Taylors'. Did you tell him about the recruiter?

ROSE: Yeah, I told him.

10 **CORY:** What he say?

ROSE: He ain't said nothing too much. You get in there and get started on your chores before he gets back. Go on and scrub down them steps before he gets back here hollering and carrying on.

CORY: I'm hungry. What you got to eat, Mama? 15

ROSE: Go on and get started on your chores. I got some meat loaf in there. Go on and make you a sandwich . . . and don't leave no mess in there.

(CORY *exits into the house.* ROSE *continues to take down the clothes.* TROY *enters the yard and sneaks up and grabs her from behind.*)

Troy! Go on, now. You liked to scared me to death. What was the score of the game? Lucille had me on 20 the phone and I couldn't keep up with it.

TROY: What I care about the game? Come here, woman. (*He tries to kiss her.*)

ROSE: I thought you went down Taylors' to listen to the game. Go on, Troy! You supposed to be putting 25 up this fence.

TROY: (*Attempting to kiss her again.*) I'll put it up when I finish with what is at hand.

ROSE: Go on, Troy. I ain't studying you.

TROY: (*Chasing after her.*) I'm studying you . . . fixing to 30 do my homework!

ROSE: Troy, you better leave me alone.

TROY: Where's Cory? That boy brought his butt home yet?

ROSE: He's in the house doing his chores. 35

TROY: (*Calling.*) Cory! Get your butt out here, boy!

(ROSE *exits into the house with the laundry.* TROY *goes over to the pile of wood, picks up a board, and starts sawing.* CORY *enters from the house.*)

TROY: You just now coming in here from leaving this morning?

CORY: Yeah, I had to go to football practice.

TROY: Yeah, what? 40

CORY: Yessir.

TROY: I ain't but two seconds off you noway. The garbage sitting in there overflowing . . . you ain't done none of your chores . . . and you come in here talking about "Yeah." 45

CORY: I was just getting ready to do my chores now, Pop . . .

TROY: Your first chore is to help me with this fence on Saturday. Everything else come after that. Now get that saw and cut them boards. 50

(CORY takes the saw and begins cutting the boards. TROY continues working. There is a long pause.)

CORY: Hey, Pop . . . why don't you buy a TV?

TROY: What I want with a TV? What I want one of them for?

CORY: Everybody got one. Earl, Ba Bra . . . Jesse!

55 **TROY:** I ain't asked you who had one. I say what I want with one?

CORY: So you can watch it. They got lots of things on TV. Baseball games and everything. We could watch the World Series.

60 **TROY:** Yeah . . . and how much this TV cost?

CORY: I don't know. They got them on sale for around two hundred dollars.

TROY: Two hundred dollars, huh?

CORY: That ain't that much, Pop.

65 **TROY:** Naw, it's just two hundred dollars. See that roof you got over your head at night? Let me tell you something about that roof. It's been over ten years since that roof was last tarred. See now . . . the snow come this winter and sit up there on that roof like
70 it is . . . and it's gonna seep inside. It's just gonna be a little bit . . . ain't gonna hardly notice it. Then the next thing you know, it's gonna be leaking all over the house. Then the wood rot from all that water and you gonna need a whole new roof. Now, how much
75 you think it cost to get that roof tarred?

CORY: I don't know.

TROY: Two hundred and sixty-four dollars . . . cash money. While you thinking about a TV, I got to be thinking about the roof . . . and whatever else go
80 wrong here. Now if you had two hundred dollars, what would you do . . . fix the roof or buy a TV?

CORY: I'd buy a TV. Then when the roof started to leak . . . when it needed fixing . . . I'd fix it.

TROY: Where you gonna get the money from? You done
85 spent it for a TV. You gonna sit up and watch the water run all over your brand new TV.

CORY: Aw, Pop. You got money. I know you do.

TROY: Where I got it at, huh?

CORY: You got it in the bank.

90 **TROY:** You wanna see my bankbook? You wanna see that seventy-three dollars and twenty-two cents I got sitting up in there?

CORY: You ain't got to pay for it all at one time. You can put a down payment on it and carry it on home with you. 95

TROY: Not me. I ain't gonna owe nobody nothing if I can help it. Miss a payment and they come and snatch it right out your house. Then what you got? Now, soon as I get two hundred dollars clear, then I'll buy a TV. Right now, as soon as I get two hun- 100 dred and sixty-four dollars, I'm gonna have this roof tarred.

CORY: Aw . . . Pop!

TROY: You go on and get you two hundred dollars and buy one if ya want it. I got better things to do with 105 my money.

CORY: I can't get no two hundred dollars. I ain't never seen two hundred dollars.

TROY: I'll tell you what . . . you get you a hundred dollars and I'll put the other hundred with it. 110

CORY: Alright, I'm gonna show you.

TROY: You gonna show me how you can cut them boards right now.

(CORY begins to cut the boards. There is a long pause.)

CORY: The Pirates won today. That makes five in a row.

TROY: I ain't thinking about the Pirates. Got an all- 115 white team. Got that boy . . . that Puerto Rican boy . . . Clemente. Don't even half-play him. That boy could be something if they give him a chance. Play him one day and sit him on the bench the next.

CORY: He gets a lot of chances to play. 120

TROY: I'm talking about playing regular. Playing every day so you can get your timing. That's what I'm talking about.

CORY: They got some white guys on the team that don't play every day. You can't play everybody at the 125 same time.

TROY: If they got a white fellow sitting on the bench . . . you can bet your last dollar he can't play! The colored guy got to be twice as good before he get on the team. That's why I don't want you to get all tied up in 130 them sports. Man on the team and what it get him? They got colored on the team and don't use them. Same as not having them. All them teams the same.

CORY: The Braves got Hank Aaron and Wes Covington. Hank Aaron hit two home runs today. That makes 135 forty-three.

TROY: Hank Aaron ain't nobody. That's what you supposed to do. That's how you supposed to play the
game. Ain't nothing to it. It's just a matter of tim-
140 ing . . . getting the right follow-through. Hell, I can
hit forty-three home runs right now!

CORY: Not off no major-league pitching, you couldn't.

TROY: We had better pitching in the Negro leagues.
I hit seven home runs off of Satchel Paige. You can't
145 get no better than that!

CORY: Sandy Koufax. He's leading the league in
strikeouts.

TROY: I ain't thinking of no Sandy Koufax.

CORY: You got Warren Spahn and Lew Burdette. I bet
150 you couldn't hit no home runs off of Warren Spahn.

TROY: I'm through with it now. You go on and cut them
boards. (*Pause.*) Your mama tell me you done got
recruited by a college football team? Is that right?

CORY: Yeah. Coach Zellman say the recruiter gonna be
155 coming by to talk to you. Get you to sign the permission papers.

TROY: I thought you supposed to be working down
there at the A&P. Ain't you suppose to be working
down there after school?

160 CORY: Mr. Stawicki say he gonna hold my job for me
until after the football season. Say starting next
week I can work weekends.

TROY: I thought we had an understanding about this
football stuff? You suppose to keep up with your
165 chores and hold that job down at the A&P. Ain't been
around here all day on a Saturday. Ain't none of your
chores done . . . and now you telling me you done
quit your job.

CORY: I'm going to be working weekends.

170 TROY: You damn right you are! And ain't no need for
nobody coming around here to talk to me about
signing nothing.

CORY: Hey, Pop . . . you can't do that. He's coming all
the way from North Carolina.

175 TROY: I don't care where he coming from. The white
man ain't gonna let you get nowhere with that football noway. You go on and get your book-learning so
you can work yourself up in that A&P or learn how
to fix cars or build houses or something, get you a
180 trade. That way you have something can't nobody
take away from you. You go on and learn how to

put your hands to some good use. Besides hauling
people's garbage.

CORY: I get good grades, Pop. That's why the recruiter
wants to talk with you. You got to keep up your 185
grades to get recruited. This way I'll be going to college. I'll get a chance . . .

TROY: First you gonna get your butt down there to the
A&P and get your job back.

CORY: Mr. Stawicki done already hired somebody else 190
'cause I told him I was playing football.

TROY: You a bigger fool than I thought . . . to let somebody take away your job so you can play some football. Where you gonna get your money to take out
your girlfriend and whatnot? What kind of foolish- 195
ness is that to let somebody take away your job?

CORY: I'm still gonna be working weekends.

TROY: Naw . . . naw. You getting your butt out of here
and finding you another job.

CORY: Come on, Pop! I got to practice. I can't work 200
after school and play football too. The team needs
me. That's what Coach Zellman say . . .

TROY: I don't care what nobody else say. I'm the boss . . .
you understand? I'm the boss around here. I do the
only saying what counts. 205

CORY: Come on, Pop!

TROY: I asked you . . . did you understand?

CORY: Yeah . . .

TROY: What?!

CORY: Yessir. 210

TROY: You go on down there to that A&P and see if you
can get your job back. If you can't do both . . . then
you quit the football team. You've got to take the
crookeds with the straights.

CORY: Yessir. (*Pause.*) Can I ask you a question? 215

TROY: What the hell you wanna ask me? Mr. Stawicki
the one you got the questions for.

CORY: How come you ain't never liked me?

TROY: Liked you? Who the hell say I got to like you?
What law is there say I got to like you? Wanna stand 220
up in my face and ask a damn fool-ass question like
that. Talking about liking somebody. Come here, boy,
when I talk to you.

(CORY *comes over to where* TROY *is working. He stands
slouched over and* TROY *shoves him on his shoulder.*)

Troy (Laurence Fishburne) reminds Cory (Bryan Clark) of the deal they made in this 2006 production directed by Sheldon Epps.

Straighten up, goddammit! I asked you a question . . . what law is there say I got to like you?

CORY: None.

TROY: Well, alright then! Don't you eat every day? *(Pause.)* Answer me when I talk to you! Don't you eat every day?

CORY: Yeah.

TROY: Nigger, as long as you in my house, you put that sir on the end of it when you talk to me.

CORY: Yes . . . sir.

TROY: You eat every day.

CORY: Yessir!

TROY: Got a roof over your head.

CORY: Yessir!

TROY: Got clothes on your back.

CORY: Yessir.

TROY: Why you think that is?

CORY: Cause of you.

TROY: Aw, hell I know it's 'cause of me . . . but why do you think that is?

CORY: *(Hesitant.)* Cause you like me.

TROY: Like you? I go out of here every morning . . . bust my butt . . . putting up with them crackers every day . . . cause I like you? You about the biggest fool I ever saw. *(Pause.)* It's my job. It's my responsibility! You understand that? A man got to take care of his family. You live in my house . . . sleep you behind on my bedclothes . . . fill you belly up with my food . . . cause you my son. You my flesh and blood. Not 'cause I like you! Cause it's my duty to take care of you. I owe a responsibility to you!

Let's get this straight right here . . . before it go along any further . . . I ain't got to like you. Mr. Rand don't give me my money come payday cause he likes me. He gives me cause he owe me. I done give you everything I had to give you. I gave you your life! Me and your mama worked that out between us. And liking your black ass wasn't part of the bargain. Don't you try and go through life worrying about if somebody like you or not. You best be making sure they doing right by you. You understand what I'm saying, boy?

CORY: Yessir.

TROY: Then get the hell out of my face, and get on down to that A&P.

(ROSE has been standing behind the screen door for much of the scene. She enters as CORY exits.)

ROSE: Why don't you let the boy go ahead and play football, Troy? Ain't no harm in that. He's just trying to be like you with the sports.

TROY: I don't want him to be like me! I want him to move as far away from my life as he can get. You the only decent thing that ever happened to me. I wish him that. But I don't wish him a thing else from my life. I decided seventeen years ago that boy wasn't getting involved in no sports. Not after what they did to me in the sports.

ROSE: Troy, why don't you admit you was too old to play in the major leagues? For once . . . why don't you admit that?

TROY: What do you mean too old? Don't come telling me I was too old. I just wasn't the right color. Hell, I'm fifty-three years old and can do better than Selkirk's .269 right now!

ROSE: How's was you gonna play ball when you were over forty? Sometimes I can't get no sense out of you.

TROY: I got good sense, woman. I got sense enough not to let my boy get hurt over playing no sports. You

290 been mothering that boy too much. Worried about if people like him.

ROSE: Everything that boy do . . . he do for you. He wants you to say "Good job, son." That's all.

TROY: Rose, I ain't got time for that. He's alive. He's
295 healthy. He's got to make his own way. I made mine. Ain't nobody gonna hold his hand when he get out there in that world.

ROSE: Times have changed from when you was young, Troy. People change. The world's changing around
300 you and you can't even see it.

TROY: (*Slow, methodical.*) Woman . . . I do the best I can do. I come in here every Friday. I carry a sack of potatoes and a bucket of lard. You all line up at the door with your hands out. I give you the lint from my
305 pockets. I give you my sweat and my blood. I ain't got no tears. I done spent them. We go upstairs in that room at night . . . and I fall down on you and try to blast a hole into forever. I get up Monday morning . . . find my lunch on the table. I go out. Make my way.
310 Find my strength to carry me through to the next Friday. (*Pause.*) That's all I got, Rose. That's all I got to give. I can't give nothing else.

(*TROY exits into the house. The lights go down to black.*)

SCENE IV

It is Friday. Two weeks later. CORY *starts out of the house with his football equipment. The phone rings.*

CORY: (*Calling.*) I got it! (*He answers the phone and stands in the screen door talking.*) Hello? Hey, Jesse. Naw . . . I was just getting ready to leave now.

ROSE: (*Calling.*) Cory!

5 **CORY:** I told you, man, them spikes is all tore up. You can use them if you want, but they ain't no good. Earl got some spikes.

ROSE: (*Calling.*) Cory!

CORY: (*Calling to* ROSE) Mam? I'm talking to Jesse.
10 (*Into phone.*) When she say that? (*Pause.*) Aw, you lying, man. I'm gonna tell her you said that.

ROSE: (*Calling.*) Cory, don't you go nowhere!

CORY: I got to go to the game, Ma! (*Into the phone.*) Yeah, hey, look, I'll talk to you later. Yeah, I'll meet
15 you over Earl's house. Later. Bye, Ma.

(*CORY exits the house and starts out the yard.*)

ROSE: Cory, where you going off to? You got that stuff all pulled out and thrown all over your room.

CORY: (*In the yard.*) I was looking for my spikes. Jesse wanted to borrow my spikes.

ROSE: Get up there and get that cleaned up before your 20 daddy get back in here.

CORY: I got to go to the game! I'll clean it up *when I get back.*

(CORY *exits.*)

ROSE: That's all he need to do is see that room all messed up. 25

(ROSE *exits into the house.* TROY *and* BONO *enter the yard.* TROY *is dressed in clothes other than his work clothes.*)

BONO: He told him the same thing he told you. Take it to the union.

TROY: Brownie ain't got that much sense. Man wasn't thinking about nothing. He wait until I confront them on it . . . then he wanna come crying seniority. 30 (*Calls.*) Hey, Rose!

BONO: I wish I could have seen Mr. Rand's face when he told you.

TROY: He couldn't get it out of his mouth! Liked to bit his tongue! When they called me down there to the 35 Commissioner's office . . . he thought they was gonna fire me. Like everybody else.

BONO: I didn't think they was gonna fire you. I thought they was gonna put you on the warning paper.

TROY: Hey, Rose! (*To* BONO.) Yeah, Mr. Rand like to bit 40 his tongue.

(TROY *breaks the seal on the bottle, takes a drink, and hands it to* BONO.)

BONO: I see you run right down to Taylors' and told that Alberta gal.

TROY: (*Calling.*) Hey Rose! (*To* BONO.) I told everybody. Hey, Rose! I went down there to cash my check. 45

ROSE: (*Entering from the house.*) Hush all that hollering, man! I know you out here. What they say down there at the Commissioner's office?

TROY: You supposed to come when I call you, woman. Bono'll tell you that. (*To* BONO.) Don't Lucille come 50 when you call her?

ROSE: Man, hush your mouth. I ain't no dog . . . talk about "come when you call me."

TROY: (*Puts his arm around* ROSE.) You hear this, Bono? I had me an old dog used to get uppity like that. You 55 say, "C'mere, Blue!" . . . and he just lay there and look at you. End up getting a stick and chasing him away trying to make him come.

ROSE: I ain't studying you and your dog. I remember you used to sing that old song.

TROY: (*He sings.*)
Hear it ring! Hear it ring!
I had a dog his name was Blue.

ROSE: Don't nobody wanna hear you sing that old song.

TROY: (*Sings.*)
You know Blue was mighty true.

ROSE: Used to have Cory running around here singing that song.

BONO: Hell, I remember that song myself.

TROY: (*Sings.*)
You know Blue was a good old dog.
Blue treed a possum in a hollow log.
That was my daddy's song. My daddy made up that song.

ROSE: I don't care who made it up. Don't nobody wanna hear you sing it.

TROY: (*Makes a song like calling a dog.*) Come here, woman.

ROSE: You come in here carrying on, I reckon they ain't fired you. What they say down there at the Commissioner's office?

TROY: Look here, Rose . . . Mr. Rand called me into his office today when I got back from talking to them people down there . . . it come from up top . . . he called me in and told me they was making me a driver.

ROSE: Troy, you kidding!

TROY: No I ain't. Ask Bono.

ROSE: Well, that's great, Troy. Now you don't have to hassle them people no more.

(*LYONS enters from the street.*)

TROY: Aw hell, I wasn't looking to see you today. I thought you was in jail. Got it all over the front page of the *Courier* about them raiding Sefus's place . . . where you be hanging out with all them thugs.

LYONS: Hey, Pop . . . that ain't got nothing to do with me. I don't go down there gambling. I go down there to sit in with the band. I ain't got nothing to do with the gambling part. They got some good music down there.

TROY: They got some rogues . . . is what they got.

LYONS: How you been, Mr. Bono? Hi, Rose.

BONO: I see where you playing down at the Crawford Grill tonight.

ROSE: How come you ain't brought Bonnie like I told you? You should have brought Bonnie with you, she ain't been over in a month of Sundays.

LYONS: I was just in the neighborhood . . . thought I'd stop by.

TROY: Here he come . . .

BONO: Your daddy got a promotion on the rubbish. He's gonna be the first colored driver. Ain't got to do nothing but sit up there and read the paper like them white fellows.

LYONS: Hey, Pop . . . if you knew how to read you'd be alright.

BONO: Naw . . . naw . . . you mean if the nigger knew how to *drive* he'd be alright. Been fighting with them people about driving and ain't even got a license. Mr. Rand know you ain't got no driver's license?

TROY: Driving ain't nothing. All you do is point the truck where you want it to go. Driving ain't nothing.

BONO: Do Mr. Rand know you ain't got no driver's license? That's what I'm talking about. I ain't asked if driving was easy. I asked if Mr. Rand know you ain't got no driver's license.

TROY: He ain't got to know. The man ain't got to know my business. Time he find out, I have two or three driver's licenses.

LYONS: (*Going into his pocket.*) Say, look here, Pop . . .

TROY: I knew it was coming. Didn't I tell you, Bono? I know what kind of "Look here, Pop" that was. The nigger fixing to ask me for some money. It's Friday night. It's my payday. All them rogues down there on the avenue . . . the ones that ain't in jail . . . and Lyons is hopping in his shoes to get down there with them.

LYONS: See, Pop . . . if you give somebody else a chance to talk sometime, you'd see that I was fixing to pay you back your ten dollars like I told you. Here . . . I told you I'd pay you when Bonnie got paid.

TROY: Naw . . . you go ahead and keep that ten dollars. Put in the bank. The next time you feel like you wanna come by here and ask me for something . . . you go on down there and get that.

LYONS: Here's your ten dollars, Pop. I told you I don't want you to give me nothing. I just wanted to borrow ten dollars.

TROY: Naw . . . you go on and keep that for the next time you want to ask me.

145 **LYONS:**   Come on, Pop . . . here go your ten dollars.

ROSE: Why don't you go on and let the boy pay you back, Troy?

LYONS: Here you go, Rose. If you don't take it I'm gonna have to hear about it for the next six months.
150 *(He hands her the money.)*

ROSE: You can hand yours over here too, Troy.

TROY: You see this, Bono. You see how they do me.

BONO: Yeah, Lucille do me the same way.

(GABRIEL is heard singing offstage. He enters.)

GABRIEL: Better get ready for the Judgment! Better
155 get ready for . . . Hey! . . . Hey! . . . There's Troy's boy!

LYONS: How are you doing, Uncle Gabe?

GABRIEL: Lyons . . . The King of the Jungle! Rose . . . hey, Rose. Got a flower for you. *(He takes a rose from his pocket.)* Picked it myself. That's the same rose like
160 you is!

ROSE: That's right nice of you, Gabe.

LYONS: What you been doing, Uncle Gabe?

GABRIEL: Oh, I been chasing hellhounds and waiting on the time to tell St. Peter to open the gates.

165 **LYONS:**   You been chasing hellhounds, huh? Well . . . you doing the right thing, Uncle Gabe. Somebody got to chase them.

GABRIEL: Oh, yeah . . . I know it. The devil's strong. The devil ain't no pushover. Hellhounds snipping at
170 everybody's heels. But I got my trumpet waiting on the judgment time.

LYONS: Waiting on the Battle of Armageddon, huh?

GABRIEL: Ain't gonna be too much of a battle when God get to waving that Judgment sword. But the
175 people's gonna have a hell of a time trying to get into heaven if them gates ain't open.

LYONS: *(Putting his arm around GABRIEL.)*   You hear this, Pop. Uncle Gabe, you alright!

GABRIEL: *(Laughing with LYONS.)*   Lyons! King of the
180 Jungle.

ROSE: You gonna stay for supper, Gabe? Want me to fix you a plate?

GABRIEL: I'll take a sandwich, Rose. Don't want no plate. Just wanna eat with my hands. I'll take a sandwich. 185

ROSE: How about you, Lyons? You staying? Got some short ribs cooking.

LYONS: Naw, I won't eat nothing till after we finished playing. *(Pause.)* You ought to come down and listen to me play, Pop. 190

TROY: I don't like that Chinese music. All that noise.

ROSE: Go on in the house and wash up, Gabe . . . I'll fix you a sandwich.

GABRIEL: *(To LYONS, as he exits.)*   Troy's mad at me.

LYONS: What you mad at Uncle Gabe for, Pop? 195

ROSE: He thinks Troy's mad at him cause he moved over to Miss Pearl's.

TROY: I ain't mad at the man. He can live where he want to live at.

LYONS: What he move over there for? Miss Pearl don't 200 like nobody.

ROSE: She don't mind him none. She treats him real nice. She just don't allow all that singing.

TROY: She don't mind that rent he be paying . . . that's what she don't mind. 205

ROSE: Troy, I ain't going through that with you no more. He's over there cause he want to have his own place. He can come and go as he please.

TROY: Hell, he could come and go as he please here. I wasn't stopping him. I ain't put no rules on him. 210

ROSE: It ain't the same thing, Troy. And you know it.

(GABRIEL comes to the door.)

Now, that's the last I wanna hear about that. I don't wanna hear nothing else about Gabe and Miss Pearl. And next week . . .

GABRIEL: I'm ready for my sandwich, Rose. 215

ROSE: And next week . . . when that recruiter come from that school . . . I want you to sign that paper and go on and let Cory play football. Then that'll be the last I have to hear about that.

TROY: *(To ROSE as she exits into the house.)*   I ain't thinking 220 about Cory nothing.

LYONS: What . . . Cory got recruited? What school he going to?

TROY: That boy walking around here smelling his piss . . . thinking he's grown. Thinking he's gonna do what he want, irrespective of what I say. Look here, Bono . . . I left the Commissioner's office and went down to the A&P . . . that boy ain't working down there. He lying to me. Telling me he got his job back . . . telling me he working weekends . . . telling me he working after school . . . Mr. Stawicki tell me he ain't working down there at all!

LYONS: Cory just growing up. He's just busting at the seams trying to fill out your shoes.

TROY: I don't care what he's doing. When he get to the point where he wanna disobey me . . . then it's time for him to move on. Bono'll tell you that. I bet he ain't never disobeyed his daddy without paying the consequences.

BONO: I ain't never had a chance. My daddy came on through . . . but I ain't never knew him to see him . . . or what he had on his mind or where he went. Just moving on through. Searching out the New Land. That's what the old folks used to call it. See a fellow moving around from place to place . . . woman to woman . . . called it searching out the New Land. I can't say if he ever found it. I come along, didn't want no kids. Didn't know if I was gonna be in one place long enough to fix on them right as their daddy. I figured I was going searching too. As it turned out I been hooked up with Lucille near about as long as your daddy been with Rose. Going on sixteen years.

TROY: Sometimes I wish I hadn't known my daddy. He ain't cared nothing about no kids. A kid to him wasn't nothing. All he wanted was for you to learn how to walk so he could start you to working. When it come time for eating . . . he ate first. If there was anything left over, that's what you got. Man would sit down and eat two chickens and give you the wing.

LYONS: You ought to stop that, Pop. Everybody feed their kids. No matter how hard times is . . . everybody care about their kids. Make sure they have something to eat.

TROY: The only thing my daddy cared about was getting them bales of cotton in to Mr. Lubin. That's the only thing that mattered to him. Sometimes I used to wonder why he was living. Wonder why the devil hadn't come and got him. "Get them bales of cotton in to Mr. Lubin" and find out he owe him money . . .

LYONS: He should have just went on and left when he saw he couldn't get nowhere. That's what I would have done.

TROY: How he gonna leave with eleven kids? And where he gonna go? He ain't knew how to do nothing but farm. No, he was trapped and I think he knew it. But I'll say this for him . . . he felt a responsibility toward us. Maybe he ain't treated us the way I felt he should have . . . but without that responsibility he could have walked off and left us . . . made his own way.

BONO: A lot of them did. Back in those days what you talking about . . . they walk out their front door and just take on down one road or another and keep on walking.

LYONS: There you go! That's what I'm talking about.

BONO: Just keep on walking till you come to something else. Ain't you never heard of nobody having the walking blues? Well, that's what you call it when you just take off like that.

TROY: My daddy ain't had them walking blues! What you talking about? He stayed right there with his family. But he was just as evil as he could be. My mama couldn't stand him. Couldn't stand that evilness. She run off when I was about eight. She sneaked off one night after he had gone to sleep. Told me she was coming back for me. I ain't never seen her no more. All his women run off and left him. He wasn't good for nobody.

When my turn come to head out, I was fourteen and got to sniffing around Joe Canewell's daughter. Had us an old mule we called Greyboy. My daddy sent me out to do some plowing and I tied up Greyboy and went to fooling around with Joe Canewell's daughter. We done found us a nice little spot, got real cozy with each other. She about thirteen and we done figured we was grown anyway . . . so we down there enjoying ourselves . . . ain't thinking about nothing. We didn't know Greyboy had got loose and wandered back to the house and my daddy was looking for me. We down there by the creek enjoying ourselves when my daddy come up on us. Surprised us. He had them leather straps off the mule and commenced to whupping me like there was no to-morrow. I jumped up, mad and embarrassed. I was scared of my daddy. When he commenced to whupping on me . . . quite naturally I run to get out of the way. (Pause.) Now I thought he was mad cause I ain't done my work. But I see where he was chasing me off so he could have the gal for himself. When I see what the matter of it was, I lost all fear of my daddy. Right there is where I become a man . . . at fourteen years of age. (Pause.) Now it was my turn to run him off. I picked up them same reins that he had used on me. I picked up them reins and commenced to whupping

325 on him. The gal jumped up and run off . . . and when my daddy turned to face me, I could see why the devil had never come to get him . . . cause he was the devil himself. I don't know what happened. When I 330 woke up, I was laying right there by the creek, and Blue . . . this old dog we had . . . was licking my face. I thought I was blind. I couldn't see nothing. Both my eyes were swollen shut. I layed there and cried. I didn't know what I was gonna do. The only thing I knew was the time had come for me to leave my daddy's house. And right there the world suddenly 335 got big. And it was a long time before I could cut it down to where I could handle it.

Part of that cutting down was when I got to the place where I could feel him kicking in my blood and knew that the only thing that separated us was the 340 matter of a few years.

(GABRIEL enters from the house with a sandwich.)

LYONS: What you got there, Uncle Gabe?

GABRIEL: Got me a ham sandwich. Rose gave me a ham sandwich.

TROY: I don't know what happened to him. I done lost 345 touch with everybody except Gabriel. But I hope he's dead. I hope he found some peace.

LYONS: That's a heavy story, Pop. I didn't know you left home when you was fourteen.

TROY: And didn't know nothing. The only part of the 350 world I knew was the forty-two acres of Mr. Lubin's land. That's all I knew about life.

LYONS: Fourteen's kinda young to be out on your own. *(Phone rings.)* I don't even think I was ready to be out on my own at fourteen. I don't know what I would 355 have done.

TROY: I got up from the creek and walked on down to Mobile. I was through with farming. Figured I could do better in the city. So I walked the two hundred miles to Mobile.

360 **LYONS:** Wait a minute . . . you ain't walked no two hundred miles, Pop. Ain't nobody gonna walk no two hundred miles. You talking about some walking there.

BONO: That's the only way you got anywhere back in them days.

365 **LYONS:** Shhh. Damn if I wouldn't have hitched a ride with somebody!

TROY: Who you gonna hitch it with? They ain't had no cars and things like they got now. We talking about 1918.

370 **ROSE:** *(Entering.)* What you all out here getting into?

TROY: *(To ROSE.)* I'm telling Lyons how good he got it. He don't know nothing about this I'm talking.

ROSE: Lyons, that was Bonnie on the phone. She say you supposed to pick her up.

375 **LYONS:** Yeah, okay, Rose.

TROY: I walked on down to Mobile and hitched up with some of them fellows that was heading this way. Got up here and found out . . . not only couldn't you get a job . . . you couldn't find no place to live. I thought I was in freedom. Shhh. Colored folks living down 380 there on the riverbanks in whatever kind of shelter they could find for themselves. Right down there under the Brady Street Bridge. Living in shacks made of sticks and tarpaper. Messed around there and went from bad to worse. Started stealing. First it was 385 food. Then I figured, hell, if I steal money I can buy me some food. Buy me some shoes too! One thing led to another. Met your mama. I was young and anxious to be a man. Met your mama and had you. What I do that for? Now I got to worry about feeding you 390 and her. Got to steal three times as much. Went out one day looking for somebody to rob . . . that's what I was, a robber. I'll tell you the truth. I'm ashamed of it today. But it's the truth. Went to rob this fellow . . . pulled out my knife . . . and he pulled out a gun. Shot 395 me in the chest. It felt just like somebody had taken a hot branding iron and laid it on me. When he shot me I jumped at him with my knife. They told me I killed him and they put me in the penitentiary and locked me up for fifteen years. That's where I met 400 Bono. That's where I learned how to play baseball. Got out that place and your mama had taken you and went on to make life without me. Fifteen years was a long time for her to wait. But that fifteen years cured me of that robbing stuff. Rose'll tell you. She 405 asked me when I met her if I had gotten all that foolishness out of my system. And I told her, "Baby, it's you and baseball all what count with me." You hear me, Bono? I meant it too. She say, "Which one comes first?" I told her, "Baby, ain't no doubt it's baseball 410 . . . but you stick and get old with me and we'll both outlive this baseball." Am I right, Rose? And it's true.

ROSE: Man, hush your mouth. You ain't said no such thing. Talking about, "Baby you know you'll always be number one with me." That's what you was 415 talking.

TROY: You hear that, Bono. That's why I love her.

BONO: Rose'll keep you straight. You get off the track, she'll straighten you up.

ROSE: Lyons, you better get on up and get Bonnie. She waiting on you.

LYONS: *(Gets up to go.)*   Hey, Pop, why don't you come on down to the Grill and hear me play?

TROY: I ain't going down there. I'm too old to be sitting around in them clubs.

BONO: You got to be good to play down at the Grill.

LYONS: Come on, Pop . . .

TROY: I got to get up in the morning.

LYONS: You ain't got to stay long.

TROY: Naw, I'm gonna get my supper and go on to bed.

LYONS: Well, I got to go. I'll see you again.

TROY: Don't you come around my house on my payday.

ROSE: Pick up the phone and let somebody know you coming. And bring Bonnie with you. You know I'm always glad to see her.

LYONS: Yeah, I'll do that, Rose. You take care now. See you, Pop. See you, Mr. Bono. See you, Uncle Gabe.

GABRIEL: Lyons! King of the Jungle!

(LYONS exits.)

TROY: Is supper ready, woman? Me and you got some business to take care of. I'm gonna tear it up too.

ROSE: Troy, I done told you now!

TROY: *(Puts his arm around BONO.)*   Aw hell, woman . . . this is Bono. Bono like family. I done known this nigger since . . . how long I done know you?

BONO: It's been a long time.

TROY: I done known this nigger since Skippy was a pup. Me and him done been through some times.

BONO: You sure right about that.

TROY: Hell, I done know him longer than I known you. And we still standing shoulder to shoulder. Hey, look here, Bono . . . a man can't ask for no more than that. *(Drinks to him.)* I love you, nigger.

BONO: Hell, I love you too . . . but I got to get home see my woman. You got yours in hand. I got to go get mine.

(BONO starts to exit as CORY enters the yard, dressed in his football uniform. He gives TROY a hard, uncompromising look.)

CORY: What you do that for, Pop?

(He throws his helmet down in the direction of TROY.)

ROSE: What's the matter? Cory . . . what's the matter?

CORY: Papa done went up to the school and told Coach Zellman I can't play football no more. Wouldn't even let me play the game. Told him to tell the recruiter not to come.

ROSE: Troy . . .

TROY: What you Troying me for. Yeah, I did it. And the boy know why I did it.

CORY: Why you wanna do that to me? That was the one chance I had.

ROSE: Ain't nothing wrong with Cory playing football, Troy.

TROY: The boy lied to me. I told the nigger if he wanna play football . . . to keep up his chores and hold down that job at the A&P. That was the conditions. Stopped down there to see Mr. Stawicki . . .

Rose (Angela Bassett) asks Troy why he got Cory kicked off the football team.

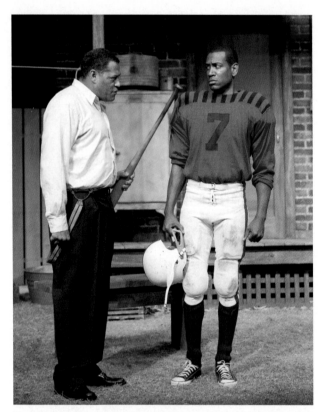

Troy tells Cory that he's committed strike one.

CORY: I can't work after school during the football season, Pop! I tried to tell you that Mr. Stawicki's hold-
475   ing my job for me. You don't never want to listen to nobody. And then you wanna go and do this to me!

TROY: I ain't done nothing to you. You done it to yourself.

CORY: Just cause you didn't have a chance! You just
480   scared I'm gonna be better than you, that's all.

TROY: Come here.

ROSE: Troy . . .

(CORY *reluctantly crosses over to* TROY.)

TROY: Alright! See. You done made a mistake.

CORY: I didn't even do nothing!

485 **TROY:** I'm gonna tell you what your mistake was. See . . . you swung at the ball and didn't hit it. That's strike one. See, you in the batter's box now. You swung and you missed. That's strike one. Don't you strike out!

(*Lights fade to black.*)

ACT II

SCENE I

The following morning. CORY *is at the tree hitting the ball with the bat. He tries to mimic* TROY, *but his swing is awkward, less sure.* ROSE *enters from the house.*

ROSE: Cory, I want you to help me with this cupboard.

CORY: I ain't quitting the team. I don't care what Poppa say.

ROSE: I'll talk to him when he gets back. He had to go see about your Uncle Gabe. The police done arrested   5
him. Say he was disturbing the peace. He'll be back directly. Come on in here and help me clean out the top of this cupboard.

(CORY *exits into the house.* ROSE *sees* TROY *and* BONO *coming down the alley.*)

Troy . . . what they say down there?

TROY: Ain't said nothing. I give them fifty dollars and   10
they let him go. I'll talk to you about it. Where's Cory?

ROSE: He's in there helping me clean out these cupboards.

TROY: Tell him to get his butt out here.

(TROY *and* BONO *go over to the pile of wood.* BONO *picks up the saw and begins sawing.*)

TROY: (*To* BONO.) All they want is the money. That   15
makes six or seven times I done went down there and got him. See me coming they stick out their *hands.*

BONO: Yeah. I know what you mean. That's all they care about . . . that money. They don't care about what's right. (*Pause.*) Nigger, why you got to go and   20
get some hard wood? You ain't doing nothing but building a little old fence. Get you some soft pine wood. That's all you need.

TROY: I know what I'm doing. This is outside wood. You put pine wood inside the house. Pine wood is   25
inside wood. This here is outside wood. Now you tell me where the fence is gonna be?

BONO: You don't need this wood. You can put it up with pine wood and it'll stand as long as you gonna be here looking at it.   30

TROY: How you know how long I'm gonna be here, nigger? Hell, I might just live forever. Live longer than old man Horsely.

BONO: That's what Magee used to say.

35 **TROY:** Magee's a damn fool. Now you tell me who you ever heard of gonna pull their own teeth with a pair of rusty pliers.

BONO: The old folks . . . my granddaddy used to pull his teeth with pliers. They ain't had no dentists for 40 the colored folks back then.

TROY: Get clean pliers! You understand? Clean pliers! Sterilize them! Besides we ain't living back then. All Magee had to do was walk over to Doc Goldblum's.

BONO: I see where you and that Tallahassee gal . . . that 45 Alberta . . . I see where you all done got tight.

TROY: What you mean "got tight"?

BONO: I see where you be laughing and joking with her all the time.

TROY: I laughs and jokes with all of them, Bono. You 50 know me.

BONO: That ain't the kind of laughing and joking I'm talking about.

(CORY enters from the house.)

CORY: How you doing, Mr. Bono?

TROY: Cory? Get that saw from Bono and cut some 55 wood. He talking about the wood's too hard to cut. Stand back there, Jim, and let that young boy show you how it's done.

BONO: He's sure welcome to it.

(CORY takes the saw and begins to cut the wood.)

Whew-e-e! Look at that. Big old strong boy. Look 60 like Joe Louis. Hell, must be getting old the way I'm watching that boy whip through that wood.

CORY: I don't see why Mama want a fence around the yard noways.

TROY: Damn if I know either. What the hell she keep-65 ing out with it? She ain't got nothing nobody want.

BONO: Some people build fences to keep people out . . . and other people build fences to keep people in. Rose wants to hold on to you all. She loves you.

TROY: Hell, nigger, I don't need nobody to tell me my 70 wife loves me. Cory . . . go on in the house and see if you can find that other saw.

CORY: Where's it at?

TROY: I said find it! Look for it till you find it!

(CORY exits into the house.)

What's that supposed to mean? Wanna keep us in?

BONO: Troy . . . I done known you seem like damn near 75 my whole life. You and Rose both. I done know both of you all for a long time. I remember when you met Rose. When you was hitting them baseball out the park. A lot of them old gals was after you then. You had the pick of the litter. When you picked Rose, I 80 was happy for you. That was the first time I knew you had any sense. I said . . . My man Troy knows what he's doing . . . I'm gonna follow this nigger . . . he might take me somewhere. I been following you too. I done learned a whole heap of things about life 85 watching you. I done learned how to tell where the shit lies. How to tell it from the alfalfa. You done learned me a lot of things. You showed me how to not make the same mistakes . . . to take life as it comes along and keep putting one foot in front of the other. 90 (Pause.) Rose a good woman, Troy.

TROY: Hell, nigger, I know she a good woman. I been married to her for eighteen years. What you got on your mind, Bono?

BONO: I just say she a good woman. Just like I say any-95 thing. I ain't got to have nothing on my mind.

TROY: You just gonna say she a good woman and leave it hanging out there like that? Why you telling me she a good woman?

BONO: She loves you, Troy. Rose loves you. 100

TROY: You saying I don't measure up. That's what you trying to say. I don't measure up cause I'm seeing this other gal. I know what you trying to say.

BONO: I know what Rose means to you, Troy. I'm just trying to say I don't want to see you mess up. 105

TROY: Yeah, I appreciate that, Bono. If you was messing around on Lucille I'd be telling you the same thing.

BONO: Well, that's all I got to say. I just say that because I love you both.

TROY: Hell, you know me . . . I wasn't out there look-110 ing for nothing. You can't find a better woman than Rose. I know that. But seems like this woman just stuck onto me where I can't shake her loose. I done wrestled with it, tried to throw her off me . . . but she just stuck on tighter. Now she's stuck on for 115 good.

BONO: You's in control . . . that's what you tell me all the time. You responsible for what you do.

TROY: I ain't ducking the responsibility of it. As long as it sets right in my heart . . . then I'm okay. Cause 120 that's all I listen to. It'll tell me right from wrong every time. And I ain't talking about doing Rose no bad turn. I love Rose. She done carried me a long ways and I love and respect her for that.

125   **BONO:**   I know you do. That's why I don't want to see you hurt her. But what you gonna do when she find out? What you got then? If you try and juggle both of them . . . sooner or later you gonna drop one of them. That's common sense.

130   **TROY:**   Yeah, I hear what you saying, Bono. I been trying to figure a way to work it out.

  BONO: Work it out right, Troy. I don't want to be getting all up between you and Rose's business . . . but work it so it come out right.

135   **TROY:**   Aw hell, I get all up between you and Lucille's business. When you gonna get that woman that refrigerator she been wanting? Don't tell me you ain't got no money now. I know who your banker is. Mellon don't need that money bad as Lucille want that 140 refrigerator. I'll tell you that.

  BONO: Tell you what I'll do . . . when you finish building this fence for Rose . . . I'll buy Lucille that refrigerator.

  TROY: You done stuck your foot in your mouth now!

(TROY grabs up a board and begins to saw. BONO starts to walk out the yard.)

Hey, nigger . . . where you going?

145   **BONO:**   I'm going home. I know you don't expect me to help you now. I'm protecting my money. I wanna see you put that fence up by yourself. That's what I want to see. You'll be here another six months without me.

  TROY: Nigger, you ain't right.

150   **BONO:**   When it comes to my money . . . I'm right as fireworks on the Fourth of July.

  TROY: Alright, we gonna see now. You better get out your bankbook.

(BONO exits, and TROY *continues to work.* ROSE *enters from the house.)*

  ROSE: What they say down there? What's happening 155 with Gabe?

  TROY: I went down there and got him out. Cost me fifty dollars. Say he was disturbing the peace. Judge set up a hearing for him in three weeks. Say to show cause why he shouldn't be recommitted.

160   **ROSE:**   What was he doing that cause them to arrest him?

  TROY: Some kids was teasing him and he run them off home. Say he was howling and carrying on. Some folks seen him and called the police. That's all it was.

  ROSE: Well, what's you say? What'd you tell the judge? 165

  TROY: Told him I'd look after him. It didn't make no sense to recommit the man. He stuck out his big greasy palm and told me to give him fifty dollars and take him on home.

  ROSE: Where's he at now? Where'd he go off to? 170

  TROY: He's gone on about his business. He don't need nobody to hold his hand.

  ROSE: Well, I don't know. Seem like that would be the best place for him if they did put him into the hospital. I know what you're gonna say. But that's what I 175 think would be best.

  TROY: The man done had his life ruined fighting for what? And they wanna take and lock him up. Let him be free. He don't bother nobody.

  ROSE: Well, everybody got their own way of looking at 180 it I guess. Come on and get your lunch. I got a bowl of lima beans and some cornbread in the oven. Come on get something to eat. Ain't no sense you fretting over Gabe.

(ROSE turns to go into the house.)

  TROY: Rose . . . got something to tell you. 185

  ROSE: Well, come on . . . wait till I get this food on the table.

  TROY: Rose!

(She stops and turns around.)

I don't know how to say this. *(Pause.)* I can't explain it none. It just sort of grows on you till it gets out of 190 hand. It starts out like a little bush . . . and the next thing you know it's a whole forest.

  ROSE: Troy . . . what is you talking about?

  TROY: I'm talking, woman, let me talk. I'm trying to find a way to tell you . . . I'm gonna be a daddy. I'm 195 gonna be somebody's daddy.

  ROSE: Troy . . . you're not telling me this? You're gonna be . . . what?

  TROY: Rose . . . now . . . see . . .

  ROSE: You telling me you gonna be somebody's daddy? 200 You telling your *wife* this?

(GABRIEL enters from the street. He carries a rose in his hand.)

GABRIEL: Hey, Troy! Hey, Rose!

ROSE: I have to wait eighteen years to hear something like this.

205 **GABRIEL:** Hey, Rose . . . I got a flower for you. (*He hands it to her.*) That's a rose. Same rose like you is.

ROSE: Thanks, Gabe.

GABRIEL: Troy, you ain't mad at me is you? Them bad mens come and put me away. You ain't mad at 210 me is you?

TROY: Naw, Gabe, I ain't mad at you.

ROSE: Eighteen years and you wanna come with this.

GABRIEL: (*Takes a quarter out of his pocket.*) See what I got? Got a brand new quarter.

215 **TROY:** Rose . . . it's just . . .

ROSE: Ain't nothing you can say, Troy. Ain't no way of explaining that.

GABRIEL: Fellow that give me this quarter had a whole mess of them. I'm gonna keep this quarter till it stop 220 shining.

ROSE: Gabe, go on in the house there. I got some watermelon in the Frigidaire. Go on and get you a piece.

GABRIEL: Say, Rose . . . you know I was chasing hellhounds and them bad mens come and get me and 225 take me away. Troy helped me. He come down there and told them they better let me go before he beat them up. Yeah, he did!

ROSE: You go on and get you a piece of watermelon, Gabe. Them bad mens is gone now.

230 **GABRIEL:** Okay, Rose . . . gonna get me some watermelon. The kind with the stripes on it.

(GABRIEL *exits into the house.*)

ROSE: Why, Troy? Why? After all these years to come dragging this in to me now. It don't make no sense at your age. I could have expected this ten or fifteen 235 years ago, but not now.

TROY: Age ain't got nothing to do with it, Rose.

ROSE: I done tried to be everything a wife should be. Everything a wife could be. Been married eighteen years and I got to live to see the day you tell me you 240 been seeing another woman and done fathered a child by her. And you know I ain't never wanted no half nothing in my family. My whole family is half. Everybody got different fathers and mothers . . . my two sisters and my brother. Can't hardly tell who's

who. Can't never sit down and talk about Papa and 245 Mama. It's your papa and your mama and my papa and my mama . . .

TROY: Rose . . . stop it now.

ROSE: I ain't never wanted that for none of my children. And now you wanna drag your behind in here 250 and tell me something like this.

TROY: You ought to know. It's time for you to know.

ROSE: Well, I don't want to know, goddamn it!

TROY: I can't just make it go away. It's done now. I can't wish the circumstance of the thing away. 255

ROSE: And you don't want to either. Maybe you want to wish me and my boy away. Maybe that's what you want? Well, you can't wish us away. I've got eighteen years of my life invested in you. You ought to have stayed upstairs in my bed where you belong. 260

TROY: Rose . . . now listen to me . . . we can get a handle on this thing. We can talk this out . . . come to an understanding.

ROSE: All of a sudden it's "we." Where was "we" at when you was down there rolling around with some god- 265 forsaken woman? "We" should have come to an understanding before you started making a damn fool of yourself. You're a day late and dollar short when it comes to an understanding with me.

TROY: It's just . . . She gives me a different idea . . . a 270 different understanding about myself. I can step out of this house and get away from the pressures and problems . . . be a different man. I ain't got to wonder how I'm gonna pay the bills or get the roof fixed. I can just be a part of myself that I ain't never been. 275

ROSE: What I want to know . . . is do you plan to continue seeing her. That's all you can say to me.

TROY: I can sit up in her house and laugh. Do you understand what I'm saying. I can laugh out loud . . . and it feels good. It reaches all the way down to the 280 bottom of my shoes. (*Pause.*) Rose, I can't give that up.

ROSE: Maybe you ought to go on and stay down there with her . . . if she's a better woman than me.

TROY: It ain't about nobody being a better woman or nothing. Rose, you ain't the blame. A man couldn't 285 ask for no woman to be a better wife than you've been. I'm responsible for it. I done locked myself into a pattern trying to take care of you all that I forgot about myself.

ROSE: What the hell was I there for? That was my job, 290 not somebody else's.

TROY: Rose, I done tried all my life to live decent . . . to live a clean . . . hard . . . useful life. I tried to be a good husband to you. In every way I knew how. Maybe I come into the world backwards, I don't know. But . . . you born with two strikes on you before you come to the plate. You got to guard it closely . . . always looking for the curve-ball on the inside corner. You can't afford to let none get past you. You can't afford a call strike. If you going down . . . you going down swinging. Everything lined up against you. What you gonna do. I fooled them, Rose. I bunted. When I found you and Cory and a halfway decent job . . . I was safe. Couldn't nothing touch me. I wasn't gonna strike out no more. I wasn't going back to the penitentiary. I wasn't gonna lay in the streets with a bottle of wine. I was safe. I had me a family. A job. I wasn't gonna get that last strike. I was on first looking for one of them boys to knock me in. To get me home.

ROSE: You should have stayed in my bed, Troy.

TROY: Then when I saw that gal . . . she firmed up my backbone. And I got to thinking that if I tried . . . I just might be able to steal second. Do you understand after eighteen years I wanted to steal second.

ROSE: You should have held me tight. You should have grabbed me and held on.

TROY: I stood on first base for eighteen years and I thought . . . well, goddamn it . . . go on for it!

ROSE: We're not talking about baseball! We're talking about you going off to lay in bed with another woman . . . and then bring it home to me. That's what we're talking about. We ain't talking about no baseball.

TROY: Rose, you're not listening to me. I'm trying the best I can to explain it to you. It's not easy for me to admit that I been standing in the same place for eighteen years.

ROSE: I been standing with you! I been right here with you, Troy. I got a life too. I gave eighteen years of my life to stand in the same spot with you. Don't you think I ever wanted other things? Don't you think I had dreams and hopes? What about my life? What about me. Don't you think it ever crossed my mind to want to know other men? That I wanted to lay up somewhere and forget about my responsibilities? That I wanted someone to make me laugh so I could feel good? You not the only one who's got wants and needs. But I held on to you, Troy. I took all my feelings, my wants and needs, my dreams . . . and I buried them inside you. I planted a seed and watched and prayed over it. I planted myself inside you and waited to bloom. And it didn't take me no eighteen years to find out the soil was hard and rocky and it wasn't never gonna bloom.

But I held on to you, Troy. I held you tighter. You was my husband. I owed you everything I had. Every part of me I could find to give you. And upstairs in that room . . . with the darkness falling in on me . . . I gave everything I had to try and erase the doubt that you wasn't the finest man in the world. And wherever you was going . . . I wanted to be there with you. Cause you was my husband. Cause that's the only way I was gonna survive as your wife. You always talking about what you give . . . and what you don't have to give. But you take too. You take . . . and don't even know nobody's giving!

(ROSE turns to exit into the house. TROY grabs her arm.)

TROY: You say I take and don't give!

ROSE: Troy! You're hurting me!

TROY: You say I take and don't give.

ROSE: Troy . . . you're hurting my arm! Let go!

TROY: I done give you everything I got. Don't you tell that lie on me.

ROSE: Troy!

TROY: Don't you tell that lie on me!

(CORY enters from the house.)

CORY: Mama!

ROSE: Troy. You're hurting me.

TROY: Don't you tell me about no taking and giving.

(CORY comes up behind TROY and grabs him. TROY, surprised, is thrown off balance just as CORY throws a glancing blow that catches him on the chest and knocks him down. TROY is stunned, as is CORY.)

ROSE: Troy. Troy. No!

(TROY gets to his feet and starts at CORY.)

Troy . . . no. Please! Troy!

(ROSE pulls on TROY to hold him back. TROY stops himself.)

TROY: *(To CORY.)* Alright. That's strike two. You stay away from around me, boy. Don't you strike out. You living with a full count. Don't you strike out.

(TROY exits out the yard as the lights go down.)

SCENE II

It is six months later, early afternoon. TROY *enters from the house and starts to exit the yard.* ROSE *enters from the house.*

ROSE: Troy, I want to talk to you.

TROY: All of a sudden, after all this time, you want to talk to me, huh? You ain't wanted to talk to me for months. You ain't wanted to talk to me last night. You ain't wanted no part of me then. What you wanna talk to me about now?

ROSE: Tomorrow's Friday.

TROY: I know what day tomorrow is. You think I don't know tomorrow's Friday? My whole life I ain't done nothing but look to see Friday coming and you got to tell me it's Friday.

ROSE: I want to know if you're coming home.

TROY: I always come home, Rose. You know that. There ain't never been a night I ain't come home.

ROSE: That ain't what I mean . . . and you know it. I want to know if you're coming straight home after work.

TROY: I figure I'd cash my check . . . hang out at Taylors' with the boys . . . maybe play a game of checkers . . .

ROSE: Troy, I can't live like this. I won't live like this. You livin' on borrowed time with me. It's been going on six months now you ain't been coming home.

TROY: I be here every night. Every night of the year. That's 365 days.

ROSE: I want you to come home tomorrow after work.

TROY: Rose . . . I don't mess up my pay. You know that now. I take my pay and I give it to you. I don't have no money but what you give me back. I just want to have a little time to myself . . . a little time to enjoy life.

ROSE: What about me? When's my time to enjoy life?

TROY: I don't know what to tell you, Rose. I'm doing the best I can.

ROSE: You ain't been home from work but time enough to change your clothes and run out . . . and you wanna call that the best you can do?

TROY: I'm going over to the hospital to see Alberta. She went into the hospital this afternoon. Look like she might have the baby early. I won't be gone long.

ROSE: Well, you ought to know. They went over to Miss Pearl's and got Gabe today. She said you told them to go ahead and lock him up.

TROY: I ain't said no such thing. Whoever told you that is telling a lie. Pearl ain't doing nothing but telling a big fat lie.

ROSE: She ain't had to tell me. I read it on the papers.

TROY: I ain't told them nothing of the kind.

ROSE: I saw it right there on the papers.

TROY: What it say, huh?

ROSE: It said you told them to take him.

TROY: Then they screwed that up, just the way they screw up everything. I ain't worried about what they got on the paper.

ROSE: Say the government send part of his check to the hospital and the other part to you.

TROY: I ain't got nothing to do with that if that's the way it works. I ain't made up the rules about how it work.

ROSE: You did Gabe just like you did Cory. You wouldn't sign the paper for Cory . . . but you signed for Gabe. You signed that paper.

(The telephone is heard ringing inside the house.)

TROY: I told you I ain't signed nothing, woman! The only thing I signed was the release form. Hell, I can't read, I don't know what they had on that paper! I ain't signed nothing about sending Gabe away.

ROSE: I said send him to the hospital . . . you said let him be free . . . now you done went down there and signed him to the hospital for half his money. You went back on yourself, Troy. You gonna have to answer for that.

TROY: See now . . . you been over there talking to Miss Pearl. She done got mad cause she ain't getting Gabe's rent money. That's all it is. She's liable to say anything.

ROSE: Troy, I seen where you signed the paper.

TROY: You ain't seen nothing I signed. What she doing got papers on my brother anyway? Miss Pearl telling a big fat lie. And I'm gonna tell her about it too! You ain't seen nothing I signed. Say . . . you ain't seen nothing I signed.

(ROSE exits into the house to answer the telephone. Presently she returns.)

ROSE: Troy . . . that was the hospital. Alberta had the baby.

TROY: What she have? What is it?

ROSE: It's a girl.

TROY: I better get on down to the hospital to see her.

ROSE: Troy . . .

85 **TROY:** Rose . . . I got to go see her now. That's only right . . . what's the matter . . . the baby's alright, ain't it?

ROSE: Alberta died having the baby.

TROY: Died . . . you say she's dead? Alberta's dead?

90 **ROSE:** They said they done all they could. They couldn't do nothing for her.

TROY: The baby? How's the baby?

ROSE: They say it's healthy. I wonder who's gonna bury her.

95 **TROY:** She had family, Rose. She wasn't living in the world by herself.

ROSE: I know she wasn't living in the world by herself.

TROY: Next thing you gonna want to know if she had any insurance.

100 **ROSE:** Troy, you ain't got to talk like that.

TROY: That's the first thing that jumped out your mouth. "Who's gonna bury her?" Like I'm fixing to take on that task for myself.

ROSE: I am your wife. Don't push me away.

105 **TROY:** I ain't pushing nobody away. Just give me some space. That's all. Just give me some room to breathe.

(ROSE exits into the house. TROY walks about the yard.)

TROY: *(With a quiet rage that threatens to consume him.)* Alright . . . Mr. Death. See now . . . I'm gonna tell you what I'm gonna do. I'm gonna take and build me a
110 fence around this yard. See? I'm gonna build me a fence around what belongs to me. And then I want you to stay on the other side. See? You stay over there until you're ready for me. Then you come on. Bring your army. Bring your sickle. Bring your wrestling
115 clothes. I ain't gonna fall down on my vigilance this time. You ain't gonna sneak up on me no more. When you ready for me . . . when the top of your list say Troy Maxson . . . that's when you come around here. You come up and knock on the front door.
120 Ain't nobody else got nothing to do with this. This is between you and me. Man to man. You stay on the other side of that fence until you ready for me. Then you come up and knock on the front door. Anytime you want. I'll be ready for you.

(The lights go down to black.)

SCENE III

The lights come up on the porch. It is late evening three days later. ROSE *sits listening to the ball game waiting for* TROY. *The final out of the game is made and* ROSE *switches off the radio.* TROY *enters the yard carrying an infant wrapped in blankets. He stands back from the house and calls.*

ROSE *enters and stands on the porch. There is a long, awkward silence, the weight of which grows heavier with each passing second.*

TROY: Rose . . . I'm standing here with my daughter in my arms. She ain't but a wee bittie little old thing. She don't know nothing about grownups' business. She innocent . . . and she ain't got no mama.

ROSE: What you telling me for, Troy? 5

(She turns and exits into the house.)

TROY: Well . . . I guess we'll just sit out here on the porch.

(He sits down on the porch. There is an awkward indelicateness about the way he handles the baby. His largeness engulfs and seems to swallow it. He speaks loud enough for ROSE *to hear.)*

A man's got to do what's right for him. I ain't sorry for nothing I done. It felt right in my heart. *(To the baby.)* What you smiling at? Your daddy's a big man. 10 Got these great big old hands. But sometimes he's scared. And right now your daddy's scared cause we sitting out here and ain't got no home. Oh, I been homeless before. I ain't had no little baby with me. But I been homeless. You just be out on the road by 15 your lonesome and you see one of them trains coming and you just kinda go like this . . .

(He sings as a lullaby.)

> Please, Mr. Engineer let a man ride the line
> Please, Mr. Engineer let a man ride the line
> I ain't got no ticket please let me ride the blinds 20

(ROSE enters from the house. TROY, *hearing her steps behind him, stands and faces her.)*

She's my daughter, Rose. My own flesh and blood. I can't deny her no more than I can deny them boys. *(Pause.)* You and them boys is my family. You and them and this child is all I got in the world. So I guess what I'm saying is . . . I'd appreciate it if you'd 25 help me take care of her.

ROSE: Okay, Troy . . . you're right. I'll take care of your baby for you . . . cause . . . like you say . . . she's innocent . . . and you can't visit the sins of the father upon the child. A motherless child has got a hard time. 30

(She takes the baby from him.) From right now . . . this child got a mother. But you a womanless man.

(ROSE turns and exits into the house with the baby. Lights go down to black.)

SCENE IV

It is two months later. LYONS enters from the street. He knocks on the door and calls.

LYONS: Hey, Rose! *(Pause.)* Rose!

ROSE: *(From inside the house.)* Stop that yelling. You gonna wake up Raynell. I just got her to sleep.

LYONS: I just stopped by to pay Papa this twenty dollars I owe him. Where's Papa at?

ROSE: He should be here in a minute. I'm getting ready to go down to the church. Sit down and wait on him.

LYONS: I got to go pick up Bonnie over her mother's house.

ROSE: Well, sit it down there on the table. He'll get it.

LYONS: *(Enters the house and sets the money on the table.)* Tell Papa I said thanks. I'll see you again.

ROSE: Alright, Lyons. We'll see you.

(LYONS starts to exit as CORY enters.)

CORY: Hey, Lyons.

LYONS: What's happening, Cory? Say man, I'm sorry I missed your graduation. You know I had a gig and couldn't get away. Otherwise, I would have been there, man. So what you doing?

CORY: I'm trying to find a job.

LYONS: Yeah I know how that go, man. It's rough out here. Jobs are scarce.

CORY: Yeah, I know.

LYONS: Look here, I got to run. Talk to Papa . . . he know some people. He'll be able to help get you a job. Talk to him . . . see what he say.

CORY: Yeah . . . alright, Lyons.

LYONS: You take care. I'll talk to you soon. We'll find some time to talk.

(LYONS exits the yard. CORY wanders over to the tree, picks up the bat, and assumes a batting stance. He studies an imaginary pitcher and swings. Dissatisfied with the result, he tries again. TROY enters. They eye each other for a beat. CORY puts the bat down and exits the yard. TROY starts into the house as ROSE exits with RAYNELL. She is carrying a cake.)

TROY: I'm coming in and everybody's going out.

ROSE: I'm taking the cake down to the church for the bake sale. Lyons was by to see you. He stopped by to pay you your twenty dollars. It's laying in there on the table.

TROY: *(Going into his pocket.)* Well . . . here go this money.

ROSE: Put it in there on the table, Troy. I'll get it.

TROY: What time you coming back?

ROSE: Ain't no use in you studying me. It don't matter what time I come back.

TROY: I just asked you a question, woman. What's the matter . . . can't I ask you a question?

ROSE: Troy, I don't want to go into it. Your dinner's in there on the stove. All you got to do is heat it up. And don't you be eating the rest of them cakes in there. I'm coming back for them. We having a bake sale at the church tomorrow.

(ROSE exits the yard. TROY sits down on the steps, takes a pint bottle from his pocket, opens it, and drinks. He begins to sing.)

TROY:

Hear it ring! Hear it ring!
Had an old dog his name was Blue
You know Blue was mighty true
You know Blue was a good old dog
Blue trees a possum in a hollow log
You know from that he was a good old dog

(BONO enters the yard.)

BONO: Hey, Troy.

TROY: Hey, what's happening, Bono?

BONO: I just thought I'd stop by to see you.

TROY: What you stop by and see me for? You ain't stopped by in a month of Sundays. Hell, I must owe you money or something.

BONO: Since you got your promotion I can't keep up with you. Used to see you every day. Now I don't even know what route you working.

TROY: They keep switching me around. Got me out in Greentree now . . . hauling white folks' garbage.

BONO: Greentree, huh? You lucky, at least you ain't got to be lifting them barrels. Damn if they ain't getting heavier. I'm gonna put in my two years and call it quits.

TROY: I'm thinking about retiring myself.

BONO: You got it easy. You can *drive* for another five years.

70 **TROY:** It ain't the same, Bono. It ain't like working the back of the truck. Ain't got nobody to talk to . . . feel like you working by yourself. Naw, I'm thinking about retiring. How's Lucille?

75 **BONO:** She alright. Her arthritis get to acting up on her sometime. Saw Rose on my way in. She going down to the church, huh?

TROY: Yeah, she took up going down there. All them preachers looking for somebody to fatten their pockets. *(Pause.)* Got some gin here.

80 **BONO:** Naw, thanks. I just stopped by to say hello.

TROY: Hell, nigger . . . you can take a drink. I ain't never known you to say no to a drink. You ain't got to work tomorrow.

85 **BONO:** I just stopped by. I'm fixing to go over to Skinner's. We got us a domino game going over his house every Friday.

TROY: Nigger, you can't play no dominoes. I used to whup you four games out of five.

BONO: Well, that learned me. I'm getting better.

90 **TROY:** Yeah? Well, that's alright.

BONO: Look here . . . I got to be getting on. Stop by sometime, huh?

TROY: Yeah, I'll do that, Bono. Lucille told Rose you bought her a new refrigerator.

95 **BONO:** Yeah, Rose told Lucille you had finally built your fence . . . so I figured we'd call it even.

TROY: I knew you would.

BONO: Yeah . . . okay. I'll be talking to you.

TROY: Yeah, take care, Bono. Good to see you. I'm gonna stop over.

100

BONO: Yeah. Okay, Troy.

(BONO exits. TROY drinks from the bottle.)

TROY:
> Old Blue died and I dug his grave
> Let him down with a golden chain
> Every night when I hear old Blue bark
105 > I know Blue treed a possum in Noah's Ark.
> Hear it ring! Hear it ring!

(CORY enters the yard. They eye each other for a beat. TROY is sitting in the middle of the steps. CORY walks over.)

CORY: I got to get by.

TROY: Say what? What's you say?

CORY: You in my way. I got to get by.

TROY: You got to get by where? This is my house. 110 Bought and paid for. In full. Took me fifteen years. And if you wanna go in my house and I'm sitting on the steps . . . you say excuse me. Like your mama taught you.

CORY: Come on, Pop . . . I got to get by. 115

(CORY starts to maneuver his way past TROY. TROY grabs his leg and shoves him back.)

TROY: You just gonna walk over top of me?

CORY: I live here too!

TROY: *(Advancing toward him.)* You just gonna walk over top of me in my own house?

CORY: I ain't scared of you. 120

TROY: I ain't asked if you was scared of me. I asked you if you was fixing to walk over top of me in my own house? That's the question. You ain't gonna say excuse me? You just gonna walk over top of me?

CORY: If you wanna put it like that. 125

TROY: How else am I gonna put it?

CORY: I was walking by you to go into the house cause you sitting on the steps drunk, singing to yourself. You can put it like that.

TROY: Without saying excuse me??? 130

(CORY doesn't respond.)

I asked you a question. Without saying excuse me???

CORY: I ain't got to say excuse me to you. You don't count around here no more.

TROY: Oh, I see . . . I don't count around here no more. You ain't got to say excuse me to your daddy. All of a 135 sudden you done got so grown that your daddy don't count around here no more . . . Around here in his own house and yard that he done paid for with the sweat of his brow. You done got so grown to where you gonna take over. You gonna take over my house. 140 Is that right? You gonna wear my pants. You gonna go in there and stretch out on my bed. You ain't got to say excuse me cause I don't count around here no more. Is that right?

CORY: That's right. You always talking this dumb stuff. 145 Now, why don't you just get out my way?

TROY: I guess you got someplace to sleep and something to put in your belly. You got that, huh? You got that? That's what you need. You got that, huh?

150 CORY: You don't know what I got. You ain't got to worry about what I got.

TROY: You right! You one hundred percent right! I done spent the last seventeen years worrying about what you got. Now it's your turn, see? I'll tell you
155 what to do. You grown . . . we done established that. You a man. Now, let's see you act like one. Turn your behind around and walk out this yard. And when you get out there in the alley . . . you can forget about this house. See? Cause this is my house. You go on
160 and be a man and get your own house. You can forget about this. Cause this is mine. You go on and get yours cause I'm through with doing for you.

CORY: You talking about what you did for me . . . what'd you ever give me?

165 TROY: Them feet and bones! That pumping heart, nigger! I give you more than anybody else is ever gonna give you.

CORY: You ain't never gave me nothing! You ain't never done nothing but hold me back. Afraid I was gonna
170 be better than you. All you ever did was try and make me scared of you. I used to tremble every time you called my name. Every time I heard your footsteps in the house. Wondering all the time . . . what's Papa gonna say if I do this? . . . What's he gonna say
175 if I do that? . . . What's Papa gonna say if I turn on the radio? And Mama, too . . . she tries . . . but she's scared of you.

TROY: You leave your mama out of this. She ain't got nothing to do with this.

180 CORY: I don't know how she stand you . . . after what you did to her.

TROY: I told you to leave your mama out of this!

(He advances toward CORY.)

CORY: What you gonna do . . . give me a whupping? You can't whup me no more. You're too old. You just
185 an old man.

TROY: (Shoves him on his shoulder.) Nigger! That's what you are. You just another nigger on the street to me!

CORY: You crazy! You know that?

TROY: Go on now! You got the devil in you. Get on
190 away from me!

CORY: You just a crazy old man . . . talking about I got the devil in me.

TROY: Yeah, I'm crazy! If you don't get on the other side of that yard . . . I'm gonna show you how crazy I am! Go on . . . get the hell out of my yard. 195

CORY: It ain't your yard! You took Uncle Gabe's money he got from the army to buy this house and then you put him out.

TROY: (Advances on CORY.) Get your black ass out of my yard! 200

(TROY's advance backs CORY up against the tree. CORY grabs up the bat.)

CORY: I ain't going nowhere! Come on . . . put me out! I ain't scared of you.

TROY: That's my bat!

CORY: Come on!

TROY: Put my bat down! 205

CORY: Come on, put me out.

(CORY swings at TROY, who backs across the yard.)

What's the matter? You so bad . . . put me out!

(TROY advances toward CORY.)

CORY: (Backing up.) Come on! Come on!

TROY: You're gonna have to use it! You wanna draw that bat back on me . . . you're gonna have to use it. 210

CORY: Come on! . . . Come on!

(CORY swings the bat at TROY a second time. He misses. TROY continues to advance toward him.)

TROY: You're gonna have to kill me! You wanna draw that bat back on me. You're gonna have to kill me.

(CORY, backed up against the tree, can go no farther. TROY taunts him. He sticks out his head and offers him a target.)

Come on! Come on!

(CORY is unable to swing the bat. TROY grabs it.)

TROY: Then I'll show you. 215

(CORY and TROY struggle over the bat. The struggle is fierce and fully engaged. TROY ultimately is the stronger, and takes the bat from CORY and stands over him ready to swing. He stops himself.)

Go on and get away from around my house.

(CORY, stung by his defeat, picks himself up, walks slowly out of the yard and up the alley.)

CORY: Tell Mama I'll be back for my things.

TROY: They'll be on the other side of that fence.

(CORY *exits.*)

220 **TROY:**   I can't taste nothing. Helluljah! I can't taste nothing no more. (TROY *assumes a batting posture and begins to taunt Death, the fastball on the outside corner.*) Come on! It's between you and me now! Come on! Anytime you want! Come on! I be ready for you . . . but I ain't gonna be easy.

(*The lights go down on the scene.*)

SCENE V

The time is 1965. The lights come up in the yard. It is the morning of TROY's *funeral. A funeral plaque with a light hangs beside the door. There is a small garden plot off to the side. There is noise and activity in the house as* ROSE, LYONS, *and* BONO *have gathered. The door opens and* RAYNELL, *seven years old, enters dressed in a flannel nightgown. She crosses to the garden and pokes around with a stick.* ROSE *calls from the house.*

ROSE: Raynell!

RAYNELL: Mam?

ROSE: What you doing out there?

RAYNELL: Nothing.

(ROSE *comes to the door.*)

5 **ROSE:**   Girl, get in here and get dressed. What you doing?

RAYNELL: Seeing if my garden growed.

ROSE: I told you it ain't gonna grow overnight. You got to wait.

RAYNELL: It don't look like it never gonna grow. Dag!

10 **ROSE:**   I told you a watched pot never boils. Get in here and get dressed.

RAYNELL: This ain't even no pot, Mama.

ROSE: You just have to give it a chance. It'll grow. Now you come on and do what I told you. We got to be getting ready. This ain't no morning to be playing around. You hear me?

15

RAYNELL: Yes, Mam.

(ROSE *exits into the house.* RAYNELL *continues to poke at her garden with a stick.* CORY *enters. He is dressed in a Marine corporal's uniform, and carries a duffel-bag. His posture is that of a military man, and his speech has a clipped sternness.*)

CORY: (*To* RAYNELL.)   Hi. (*Pause.*) I bet your name is Raynell.

RAYNELL: Uh huh.   20

CORY: Is your mama home?

(RAYNELL *runs up on the porch and calls through the screen door.*)

RAYNELL: Mama . . . there's some man out here. Mama?

(ROSE *comes to the door.*)

ROSE: Cory? Lord have mercy! Look here, you all!

(ROSE *and* CORY *embrace in a tearful reunion as* BONO *and* LYONS *enter from the house dressed in funeral clothes.*)

BONO: Aw, looka here . . .   25

ROSE: Done got all grown up!

CORY: Don't cry, Mama. What you crying about?

ROSE: I'm just so glad you made it.

CORY: Hey Lyons. How you doing, Mr. Bono.

(LYONS *goes to embrace* CORY.)

LYONS: Look at you, man. Look at you. Don't he look   30 good, Rose. Got them Corporal stripes.

ROSE: What took you so long?

CORY: You know how the Marines are, Mama. They got to get all their paperwork straight before they let you do anything.   35

ROSE: Well, I'm sure glad you made it. They let Lyons come. Your Uncle Gabe's still in the hospital. They don't know if they gonna let him out or not. I just talked to them a little while ago.

LYONS: A Corporal in the United States Marines.   40

BONO: Your daddy knew you had it in you. He used to tell me all the time.

LYONS: Don't he look good, Mr. Bono?

BONO: Yeah, he remind me of Troy when I first met him. (*Pause.*) Say, Rose, Lucille's down at the church   45 with the choir. I'm gonna go down and get the pall-bearers lined up. I'll be back to get you all.

ROSE: Thanks, Jim.

CORY: See you, Mr. Bono.

LYONS: (*With his arm around* RAYNELL.)   Cory . . . look at   50 Raynell. Ain't she precious? She gonna break a whole lot of hearts.

Cory greets Rose on the day of Troy's funeral.

ROSE: Raynell, come and say hello to your brother. This is your brother, Cory. You remember Cory.

55 **RAYNELL:**   No, Mam.

CORY: She don't remember me, Mama.

ROSE: Well, we talk about you. She heard us talk about you. *(To* RAYNELL.*)* This is your brother, Cory. Come on and say hello.

60 **RAYNELL:**   Hi.

CORY: Hi. So you're Raynell. Mama told me a lot about you.

ROSE: You all come on into the house and let me fix you some breakfast. Keep up your strength.

65 **CORY:**   I ain't hungry, Mama.

LYONS: You can fix me something, Rose. I'll be in there in a minute.

ROSE: Cory, you sure you don't want nothing? I know they ain't feeding you right.

70 **CORY:**   No, Mama . . . thanks. I don't feel like eating. I'll get something later.

ROSE: Raynell . . . get on upstairs and get that dress on like I told you.

*(*ROSE *and* RAYNELL *exit into the house.)*

LYONS: So . . . I hear you thinking about getting married.   75

CORY: Yeah, I done found the right one, Lyons. It's about time.

LYONS: Me and Bonnie been split up about four years now. About the time Papa retired. I guess she just got tired of all them changes I was putting her   80 through. *(Pause.)* I always knew you was gonna make something out yourself. Your head was always in the right direction. So . . . you gonna stay in . . . make it a career . . . put in your twenty years?

CORY: I don't know. I got six already, I think that's   85 enough.

LYONS: Stick with Uncle Sam and retire early. Ain't nothing out here. I guess Rose told you what happened with me. They got me down the workhouse. I thought I was being slick cashing other people's   90 checks.

CORY: How much time you doing?

LYONS: They give me three years. I got that beat now. I ain't got but nine more months. It ain't so bad. You learn to deal with it like anything else. You   95 got to take the crookeds with the straights. That's what Papa used to say. He used to say that when he struck out. I seen him strike out three times in a row . . . and the next time up he hit the ball over the grandstand. Right out there in Homestead Field.   100 He wasn't satisfied hitting in the seats . . . he want to hit it over everything! After the game he had two hundred people standing around waiting to shake his hand. You got to take the crookeds with the straights. Yeah, Papa was something else.   105

CORY: You still playing?

LYONS: Cory . . . you know I'm gonna do that. There's some fellows down there we got us a band . . . we gonna try and stay together when we get out . . . but yeah, I'm still playing. It still helps me to get out of   110 bed in the morning. As long as it do that I'm gonna be right there playing and trying to make some sense out of it.

ROSE: *(Calling.)*   Lyons, I got these eggs in the pan.

LYONS: Let me go on and get these eggs, man. Get   115 ready to go bury Papa. *(Pause.)* How you doing? You doing alright?

(CORY nods. LYONS touches him on the shoulder and they share a moment of silent grief. LYONS exits into the house. CORY wanders about the yard. RAYNELL enters.)

RAYNELL: Hi.

CORY: Hi.

120 **RAYNELL:** Did you used to sleep in my room?

CORY: Yeah . . . that used to be my room.

RAYNELL: That's what Papa call it. "Cory's room." It got your football in the closet.

(ROSE comes to the door.)

ROSE: Raynell, get in there and get them good shoes on.

125 **RAYNELL:** Mama, can't I wear these? Them other one hurt my feet.

ROSE: Well, they just gonna have to hurt your feet for a while. You ain't said they hurt your feet when you went down to the store and got them.

130 **RAYNELL:** They didn't hurt then. My feet done got bigger.

ROSE: Don't you give me no backtalk now. You get in there and get them shoes on.

(RAYNELL exits into the house.)

135 Ain't too much changed. He still got that piece of rag tied to that tree. He was out here swinging that bat. I was just ready to go back in the house. He swung that bat and then he just fell over. Seem like he swung it and stood there with this grin on his face . . . and then he just fell over. They carried him
140 on down to the hospital, but I knew there wasn't no need . . . why don't you come on in the house?

CORY: Mama . . . I got something to tell you. I don't know how to tell you this . . . but I've got to tell you . . . I'm not going to Papa's funeral.

145 **ROSE:** Boy, hush your mouth. That's your daddy you talking about. I don't want hear that kind of talk this morning. I done raised you to come to this? You standing there all healthy and grown talking about you ain't going to your daddy's funeral?

150 **CORY:** Mama . . . listen . . .

ROSE: I don't want to hear it, Cory. You just get that thought out of your head.

CORY: I can't drag Papa with me everywhere I go. I've got to say no to him. One time in my life I've got to
155 say no.

ROSE: Don't nobody have to listen to nothing like that. I know you and your daddy ain't seen eye to eye, but I ain't got to listen to that kind of talk this morning. Whatever was between you and your daddy . . . the time has come to put it aside. Just take it and set it
160 over there on the shelf and forget about it. Disrespecting your daddy ain't gonna make you a man, Cory. You got to find a way to come to that on your own. Not going to your daddy's funeral ain't gonna
165 make you a man.

CORY: The whole time I was growing up . . . living in his house . . . Papa was like a shadow that followed you everywhere. It weighed on you and sunk into your flesh. It would wrap around you and lay there
170 until you couldn't tell which one was you anymore. That shadow digging in your flesh. Trying to crawl in. Trying to live through you. Everywhere I looked, Troy Maxson was staring back at me . . . hiding under the bed . . . in the closet. I'm just saying I've got
175 to find a way to get rid of that shadow, Mama.

ROSE: You just like him. You got him in you good.

CORY: Don't tell me that, Mama.

ROSE: You Troy Maxson all over again.

CORY: I don't want to be Troy Maxson. I want to be me.

180 **ROSE:** You can't be nobody but who you are, Cory. That shadow wasn't nothing but you growing into yourself. You either got to grow into it or cut it down to fit you. But that's all you got to make life with. That's all you got to measure yourself against that world out
185 there. Your daddy wanted you to be everything he wasn't . . . and at the same time he tried to make you into everything he was. I don't know if he was right or wrong . . . but I do know he meant to do more good than he meant to do harm. He wasn't always
190 right. Sometimes when he touched he bruised. And sometimes when he took me in his arms he cut.

When I first met your daddy I thought . . . Here is a man I can lay down with and make a baby. That's the first thing I thought when I seen him. I was
195 thirty years old and had done seen my share of men. But when he walked up to me and said, "I can dance a waltz that'll make you dizzy," I thought, Rose Lee, here is a man that you can open yourself up to and be filled to bursting. Here is a man that can fill all them
200 empty spaces you been tipping around the edges of. One of them empty spaces was being somebody's mother.

I married your daddy and settled down to cooking his supper and keeping clean sheets on the bed.
205 When your daddy walked through the house he was

so big he filled it up. That was my first mistake. Not to make him leave some room for me. For my part in the matter. But at that time I wanted that. I wanted a house that I could sing in. And that's what your daddy gave me. I didn't know to keep up his strength I had to give up little pieces of mine. I did that. I took on his life as mine and mixed up the pieces so that you couldn't hardly tell which was which anymore. It was my choice. It was my life and I didn't have to live it like that. But that's what life offered me in the way of being a woman and I took it. I grabbed hold of it with both hands.

    By the time Raynell came into the house, me and your daddy had done lost touch with one another. I didn't want to make my blessing off of nobody's misfortune . . . but I took on to Raynell like she was all them babies I had wanted and never had.

(The phone rings.)

Like I'd been blessed to relive a part of my life. And if the Lord see fit to keep up my strength . . . I'm gonna do her just like your daddy did you . . . I'm gonna give her the best of what's in me.

RAYNELL: *(Entering, still with her old shoes.)* Mama . . . Reverend Tollivier on the phone.

(ROSE exits into the house.)

RAYNELL: Hi.

CORY: Hi.

RAYNELL: You in the Army or the Marines?

CORY: Marines.

RAYNELL: Papa said it was the Army. Did you know Blue?

CORY: Blue? Who's Blue?

RAYNELL: Papa's dog what he sing about all the time.

CORY: *(Singing.)*
    Hear it ring! Hear it ring!
    I had a dog his name was Blue
    You know Blue was mighty true
    You know Blue was a good old dog
    Blue treed a possum in a hollow log
    You know from that he was a good old dog.
    Hear it ring! Hear it ring!

(RAYNELL joins in singing.)

CORY AND RAYNELL:
    Blue treed a possum out on a limb
    Blue looked at me and I looked at him
    Grabbed that possum and put him in a sack

    Blue stayed there till I came back
    Old Blue's feets was big and round
    Never allowed a possum to touch the ground.

    Old Blue died and I dug his grave
    I dug his grave with a silver spade
    Let him down with a golden chain
    And every night I call his name
    Go on Blue, you good dog you
    Go on Blue, you good dog you.

RAYNELL:
    Blue laid down and died like a man
    Blue laid down and died . . .

BOTH:
    Blue laid down and died like a man
    Now he's treeing possums in the Promised Land
    I'm gonna tell you this to let you know
    Blue's gone where the good dogs go
    When I hear old Blue bark
    When I hear old Blue bark
    Blue treed a possum in Noah's Ark
    Blue treed a possum in Noah's Ark.

(ROSE comes to the screen door.)

ROSE: Cory, we gonna be ready to go in a minute.

CORY: *(To RAYNELL.)* You go on in the house and change them shoes like Mama told you so we can go to Papa's funeral.

RAYNELL: Okay, I'll be back.

(RAYNELL exits into the house. CORY gets up and crosses over to the tree. ROSE stands in the screen door watching him. GABRIEL enters from the alley.)

GABRIEL: *(Calling.)* Hey, Rose!

ROSE: Gabe?

GABRIEL: I'm here, Rose. Hey, Rose, I'm here!

(ROSE enters from the house.)

ROSE: Lord . . . Look here, Lyons!

LYONS: See, I told you, Rose . . . I told you they'd let him come.

CORY: How you doing, Uncle Gabe?

LYONS: How you doing, Uncle Gabe?

GABRIEL: Hey, Rose. It's time. It's time to tell St. Peter to open the gates. Troy, you ready? You ready, Troy. I'm gonna tell St. Peter to open the gates. You get ready now.

The family looks up into the wide-open gates of heaven.

(GABRIEL, *with great fanfare, braces himself to blow. The trumpet is without a mouthpiece. He puts the end of it into his mouth and blows with great force, like a man who has been waiting some twenty-odd years for this single moment. No sound comes out of the trumpet. He braces himself and blows again with the same result. A third time he blows. There is a weight of impossible description that falls away and leaves him bare and exposed to a frightful realization. It is a trauma that a sane and normal mind would be unable to withstand. He begins to dance. A slow, strange dance, eerie and life-giving. A dance of atavistic signature and ritual.* LYONS *attempts to embrace him.* GABRIEL *pushes* LYONS *away. He begins to howl in what is an attempt at song, or perhaps a song turning back into itself in an attempt at speech. He finishes his dance and the gates of heaven stand open as wide as God's closet.*)

That's the way that go!

BLACKOUT

Writing from Reading

Summarize

1 Which family relationships does the play emphasize; which does it downplay?

Analyze Craft

2 Explain the importance of the title and how it relates to the play's theme or themes. Of all the elements in the play—dialogue, character, plot, setting, language—which do you think might have the most impact on the audience, and why?

3 Which character goes through the most dramatic change in the course of the play? What evidence do you see of this change?

Analyze Voice

4 Identify an exchange of dialogue that you found particularly powerful and explain why. How does it promote or portray the conflict and theme of the play?

Synthesize Summary and Analysis

5 How successful is August Wilson in elevating his working-class characters to the level of the tragic hero portrayed in Greek drama?

6 Throughout the play, stage directions indicate that lines are to be sung. How does the incorporation of song bring the African-American tradition of the blues into the tone of the play? Compare the use of song in *Fences* with the blues poems of Langston Hughes (see chapter 26 in Poetry). How do both use the blues to comment on the African-American experience?

Interpret the Play

7 Discuss the theme of power and powerlessness as raised in this play.

"August's plays are the blues. Listen to the blues . . . Lightnin' Hopkins . . . Bessie Smith . . . Big Maybell. Listen to these things, listen to the words because they're poetry and they're plays. They're whole dramas told in one song."

Conversation with Ruben Santiago-Hudson

AN ACTOR'S PERSPECTIVE ON MODERN THEATER AND AUGUST WILSON

As Ruben Santiago-Hudson makes clear in his interview, his mentor and guiding light in the theater was August Wilson. Now that you have read the play, you will begin to see why, among other things, it called out to a young writer and actor like Santiago-Hudson. First performed in 1985, the play has entered the American repertory. Because of its subject matter it has drawn a new audience to theaters and, as the example of Santiago-Hudson suggests, has opened a path for new playwrights and actors to follow.

"I have a sense that—our literature is more and more filled with socially relevant work than it was years back. . . . The escapist notion is always where people want to get out of their troubles. . . . But there's been a lot of literature in the last years that I think is relevant." Conversation with Arthur Miller

A Glimpse at the Work of Ruben Santiago-Hudson

As Santiago-Hudson suggests, whether in Shakespeare's day or our own, the constant factor is the actor, wrestling with a role, preparing to take the stage. If you happen to watch a DVD of the movie *Lackawanna Blues* (there is currently no publicly available script), you immediately feel a sense of deep emotion, as the movie opens with a telephone call in the middle of the night and a man awakes to pick up the instrument and listen for a moment before announcing that he is on his way. He's going to the upstate New York hospital where the woman who raised him, the owner of a Lackawanna boarding house for black people in the still-segregated mid-1950s, lies dying. The audience is on its way, too, because within seconds we're seeing images from the hospital and then flash back to the '50s to witness, in a dazzling series of cross-cuts, a raucous and joyful Friday night fish fry dance and the birth of the boy the woman will raise to manhood.

"I was raised in a rooming house, pretty much abandoned by my mother. See the film *Lackawanna Blues*. That's my life."

Conversation with Ruben Santiago-Hudson

Theater can transcend anything.

Q&A

A Conversation on Writing

Ruben Santiago-Hudson

You need to feed your soul.

Theater Makes a Person Whole

I choose to do plays first and foremost because I love them. . . . I can't get that love out of me—and I don't want to get it out of me. . . . I have to balance the theater with my film and TV, which is sustenance . . . but theater is the place where I am whole as a human being. . . . The reason I choose theater foremost is not only desire, but need. I need to feel whole because I'm in a business where they don't see you as whole. If you're good at one thing, if you're a good gangster, you're going to be a gangster in twenty films. If you're a good teacher, that's what you're going to be. If you're a good back man, you'll be in the back. . . . In theater, we're all even. Even if somebody's name's above the title, all roles are good roles. . . . So those possibilities are there in theater that I don't find in film.

August Wilson Speaks Straight into My Heart

My favorite playwright is August Wilson, simply because he speaks to me straight into my heart. But something that's very clear in August Wilson's writing is that he loves the characters. August loves these people. . . . It's the simplicity of his work, the poetry of his work—no matter what their lot in life is. Whether somebody's an elevator operator or somebody is selling refrigerators, we don't know where the refrigerators come from, but he's selling the refrigerators. . . . Some people walk around with the Daily Word; I walk around with August Wilson, because he speaks to me.

To view the whole interview and hear Ruben Santiago-Hudson read from August Wilson's *Fences,* go to **www.mhhe.delbanco1e**.

RESEARCH ASSIGNMENT: When Ruben Santiago-Hudson says, "I can't hide" and then is identified as the actor in *Shaft* by a boy at the basketball game, what is the moral of the story and what does the actor tell us about the importance of race?

Ruben Santiago-Hudson (b. 1956)

Born in Lackawanna, New York, Ruben Santiago-Hudson wrote the autobiographical play *Lackawanna Blues* about his youth in a segregated American steel town. His father, Ruben Santiago, was a Puerto Rican railroad worker. His mother, Alean Hudson, was African American. In *Lackawanna Blues,* Santiago-Hudson portrays his abandonment by his mother, then the community of music and love that embraced him as he was raised by a woman who ran a local boarding house for African Americans. He played over twenty characters in the production of *Lackawanna Blues* and was awarded an Obie. His script was made into an HBO movie directed by George C. Wolfe (2005)—for which Wolfe won the Director's Guild Award for Outstanding Movies for Television—and starring S. Epatha Merkerson, who won an Emmy. Santiago-Hudson graduated from the University of Binghamton and went on to study Shakespeare and classical theater at the Hilberry Classical Repertory Theater. He now lives in New York and has acted in over sixty films and TV movies, including *Devil's Advocate, Blown Away,* and *Shaft,* and the TV miniseries based on Zora Neale Hurston's novel *Their Eyes Were Watching God.* But for writer, director, and actor Santiago-Hudson, who has played opposite Gregory Hines in *Jelly's Last Jam* (also directed by George C. Wolfe) and won a Tony for his performance in August Wilson's *Seven Guitars,* theater remains his first love.

Lackawanna Blues (2005)

Adapted from the stage for film by Ruben Santiago-Hudson

Director: George C. Wolfe

An ensemble cast, starring S. Epatha Merkerson and including Marcus Carl Franklin, Mos Def, Carmen Ejogo, Louis Gossett Jr., Macy Gray, Rosie Perez, Ruben Santiago-Hudson, Liev Schreiber, Jimmy Smits, Lily Santiago, and Trey Santiago.

Freddie Cobbs (Ruben Santiago-Hudson), a boarder, talks to young Ruben (Marcus Carl Franklin) in the doorway of the boarding house. Why do you think Santiago-Hudson chose to juxtapose his real self with the child acting out his past? How might your interpretation of this scene be affected by your knowledge that the grown man playing Cobbs is the adult version of the boy in the movie?

Rachel "Nanny" Crosby (S. Epatha Merkerson) jokes around with the men gambling at the boarding house fish fry. What do you notice about the men in this image? Do the people in this photo fit your conception of the common man as Santiago-Hudson describes him in his interview?

Young Ruben and Nanny Crosby converse in the restaurant of the boarding house. Consider that *Lackawanna Blues* was written as a one-man performance. How do you imagine such an interaction as staged by only one actor?

An aged and ailing Nanny Crosby is surprised by old friends with donations to fund her medical care. To what extent is this celebration of heroic deeds by a common woman characteristic of modern theater? In what ways? Would you consider Nanny Crosby an "everyman"? Why or why not?

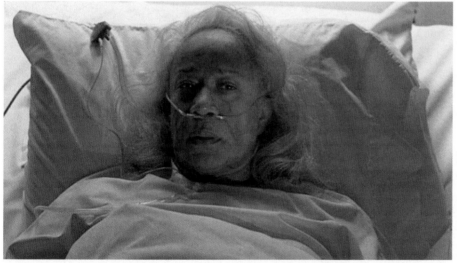

Nanny Crosby, now old and ill, lies in a hospital bed. Would you describe Nanny's death as tragic in the sense of Greek tragedy, or as naturalistic?

Reading Modern Drama

When reading or viewing modern drama . . .

Consider how the play is staged.	Modern drama commonly is written for the **proscenium stage,** which features an arch through which the main set is visible (and can be separated by a curtain). • Is the set dressing detailed and realistic, as though you are glimpsing the action in a room through the missing **fourth wall**? • Is the set dressing minimal, inviting surrealistic interpretation and imagination?
Identify the structure and aim of the play.	• **Well-made plays** take place in a three-act sequence: The first act *poses* a problem, the next *complicates* the problem, and the third *resolves* the problem. • **Problem plays** confront a social issue with no clear-cut resolution, often in order to raise awareness of that issue.
Note the conventions of naturalistic theater, which shines a light on the painful realities of life.	• Is the protagonist an **antihero**—one who is not elevated socially or morally and does not exhibit common heroic characteristics like bravery or morality? • Is the protagonist an **everyman,** a character whose station in life is not unlike that of the audience? The everymen of modern drama are generally ordinary middle-class people struggling with life.
Recognize the difference between realism and surrealism.	• **Realism** describes acting that features realistic language and physical gestures enacted by characters who are familiar in a setting that resembles the audience's real life. • **Surrealism** describes staging and events that represent an overlap of the conscious and the unconscious experience—often depicting dreams and internal struggles.
Identify instances of symbolism in the play.	• **Symbolism** occurs when an object, image, character, or action suggests meaning beyond the everyday literal interpretation. • **Expressionist** plays use scenes and onstage cues as **symbols** for characters' subjective emotions.

Suggestions for Writing about Modern Drama

1. Taking the long view, choose a modern play that you believe has something approaching the stature and sweep of a classical Greek tragedy and compare and contrast the two theater pieces. Can you make an exact match with respect to questions of tragedy? How do the traditional and modern characters differ in the way they behave? How does the social background of the plays appear to differ? Does it seem possible, given the belief systems of modern life, that a modern play can become truly tragic?

2. What is the role of modern drama in relation to society at large? How does this contrast, if it does contrast, with plays at the origins of Western theater? Does modern drama respond in the fullest possible fashion to the questions of modern psychology and modern life? What to your mind are the greatest problems and questions that arise in our lives today? How do modern plays rise to the level of these problems?

3. Some highly educated and sophisticated critics and instructors might argue that movies are the greatest dramatic creation of the modern age. Do you agree or disagree? Why? What aspects of the film might appear to trump those of the stage play? Which seem to suffer by comparison?

36 Contemporary Theater

AS we have seen, the origins of theater are as old as Western culture; of the literature we've studied in *Craft and Voice*, drama is the ancient and enduring mode. That we can speak of *Oedipus the King* and *Death of a Salesman* in, in effect, the same sentence should demonstrate how much is constant and how much has changed. Actors were walking out on stage long before the novel was "born" or came into fashion as a genre; they will do so, possibly, long after the sonnet and narrative poem are "dead." We put these words in quotes because it's obvious—or should be by now—that we believe in the ongoing life of poetry and fiction and expect both of those genres to thrive. But as *Literature: Craft and Voice* draws to a close, it may be worth repeating that drama is a supple form, with many incarnations, and it has been a part of human discourse from the start.

Our contemporary world is an eclectic place, a world made up out of individual elements from a variety of sources, systems, and styles. Science, religion, art, business—we draw from all of these realms and more to figure out how to get through working days and dream-filled nights. Technology has altered the speed of communication, and contemporary theater reflects the way we live today. The brevity of television plays and situation comedies (in which scenes are in-

"How do you begin writing plays? . . . You write some lines, some people get together, they read the lines, they do it in any room. Just somebody reads stage direction, they say it's night, it's cold, it's snowing. Okay. I got it. You know? I don't need, you know, nobody has to say where we gonna get the snowflakes? We'll believe it. And it's fun."

Conversation on Writing with Arthur Kopit, available online at www.mhhe/delbanco1e

SOUND OF WIND

LIGHTS CHANGE INTO A COOL AND AIRY BLUE. SENSE OF WEIGHTLESSNESS, SERENITY.

IN ANOTHER REALM NOW.

> *Yes, out there walking not holding even danger ever-present*
> *How I loved it love it still no doubt will again hear them*
> *Cheering wisht or waltz away to some place like Rumania . . .*

THE WIND DISAPPEARS.

Nothing . . .

THE SERENE BLUE LIGHT BEGINS TO FADE AWAY.
SOME PLACE ELSE NOW THAT SHE IS GOING . . .

—from Wings *by Arthur Kopit*

terspersed with commercials), the various possibilities of camera angles in films, the availability of cell-phone cameras, emails, YouTube, Facebook, and the rest, all these have had a transforming effect on the nature of communication and performance. It's not so much a question of information overload as of more rapid transmission; whereas the ancient Greeks might dedicate a day to the production of a trilogy and satyr play, we expect our sound bites to be brief.

Most contemporary playwrights create multi-scene and multi-act plays. But one-act plays have recently emerged as an important part of theatrical discourse. In some sense they bear the same relation to full-length plays as the short story does to the novel; they are necessarily more focused and contained. (In part this has to do with economic reality; one-act plays—with a small cast—are, of course, less expensive to produce.) One playwright who has put his mark on contemporary theater—both in the multi-act and the one-act form—is Arthur Kopit. In his arresting theater piece *Wings,* this New York-born, Harvard-educated playwright evokes the chaos of a stroke patient's perception by breaking with realistic stage setting. *Wings* was first produced as a radio play (available online at *www.mhhe* *.com/delbanco1e*), and then for television.

Other one-act plays that you will find in this chapter display a remarkable diversity, even as they focus on themes and motifs important to contemporary audiences—family and social relations, and the swift passage of time. Each illuminates the lives we lead together now.

You've got to be very careful not to censor yourself.

Q & A

The task for the playwright is to find your own play.

A Conversation on Writing
Arthur Kopit

On Doing My Research for *Wings*

The play had been inspired or spurred on by my having observed my father in a stroke, in a massive stroke. He had hardly any speech and I wanted to find some way for myself to see what could it be like. And it was an alien world, clearly. . . . I had done research so that I could be accurate . . . and that included interviewing people that'd had strokes . . . trying to get the speech right, speaking to neurologists, psychiatrists, speech-pathologists, and everything I had observed with my father.

Wings and the Order of Chaos

There really is a sequence. . . . You would have images, which said mostly it's whiteness, dazzling, blinding. . . . Mirrors, of course . . . nothing seen that is not a fragment. At the same time we're hearing sounds . . . Simultaneously with these images . . . the sounds outside of herself, and then Mrs. Stilson's voice.

How to Read a Play

Some plays don't read very well. . . . You have to see it to realize the impact, because the writing itself is awfully clumsy. . . . A play is written to be performed, but it is also literature. It is also a text. And I think what's crucial for someone reading plays in the course is to also know how would this play on a stage? What is the effect of this? There isn't only one answer.

To listen to this entire interview and hear the author read from *Wings,* go to **www.mhhe/delbanco1e.**

RESEARCH ASSIGNMENT   In his interview, Kopit talks about writing coming from a "mysterious place" and admonishes writers to write "about what you didn't know you knew." What does he mean by this and how would this compare with your own writing?

Arthur Kopit (b. 1937)

Born in New York City, Arthur Kopit grew up on Long Island never dreaming of becoming a playwright. However, while a student on scholarship at Harvard, Kopit began to write plays, and his *Oh Dad, Poor Dad, Mama's Hung You in the Closet and I'm Feelin' So Sad* (1960) won a playwriting contest. Soon, Kopit's work was being performed internationally as well as on Broadway, and—though he earned a degree in engineering—he has made his living as a playwright ever since. Kopit's works, though sporadic (at times there has been a nine-year gap between plays, at others, a single year), have been successful because of their special blend of humor, wackiness, innovation, satire, and seriousness. Two of his plays—*Indians* (1969) and *Wings* (1978)—as well as his script for the musical *Nine* (1983) have received Tony Award nominations. He has received prestigious awards and fellowships, including the National Institute of Arts and Letters Award, a Guggenheim, and a Rockefeller grant. Married since 1968, he and his wife, the writer Leslie Garis, have three children

AS YOU READ This play was first produced for the radio. Try to imagine hearing it for the first time, with the images described and the confusion that images, sounds, and Mrs. Stilson's voice would create when going on simultaneously. Imagine yourself coping with the kind of confusion into which Mrs. Stilson awakes.

Wings (1978)

CHARACTERS

EMILY STILSON

AMY

DOCTORS

NURSES

BILLY

MR. BROWNSTEIN

MRS. TIMMINS

The play takes place over a period of two years; it should be performed without an intermission.

I weave in and out of the strange clouds, hidden in my tiny cockpit, submerged, alone, on the magnitude of this weird, unhuman space, venturing where man has never been, perhaps never meant to go. Am I myself a living, breathing, earth-bound body, or is this a dream of death I'm passing through? Am I alive, or am I really dead, a spirit in a spirit world. Am I actually in a plane, or have I crashed on some worldly mountain, and is this the afterlife?

—Charles Lindbergh, *The Spirit of St. Louis.*

NOTES ON THE PRODUCTION OF THIS PLAY

The stage as a void.

System of black scrim panels that can move silently and easily, creating the impression of featureless, labyrinthine corridors.

Some panels mirrored so they can fracture light, create the impression of endlessness, even airiness, multiply and confound images, confound one's sense of space.

Sound both live and pre-recorded, amplified; speakers all around the theater.

No attempt should be made to create a literal representation of MRS. STILSON's *world, especially since* MRS. STILSONs' *world is no longer in any way literal.*

The scenes should blend. No clear boundaries or domains in time or space for MRS. STILSON *any more.*

It is posited by this play that the woman we see in the center of the void is the intact inner self of MRS. STILSON. *This inner self does not need to move physically when her external body (which we cannot see) moves. Thus, we infer movement from the context; from whatever clues we can obtain. It is the same for her, of course. She learns as best she can.*

And yet, sometimes, the conditions change; then the woman we observe is MRS. STILSON *as others see her. We thus infer who it is we are seeing from the context, too. Sometimes we see both the inner and outer self at once.*

Nothing about her world is predictable or consistent. This fact is its essence.

The progression of the play is from fragmentation to integration. By the end, boundaries have become somewhat clearer. But she remains always in another realm from us.

PRELUDE

AS AUDIENCE ENTERS, A COZY ARMCHAIR VISIBLE DOWNSTAGE IN A POOL OF LIGHT, DARKNESS SURROUNDING IT.

A CLOCK HEARD TICKING IN THE DARK.

LIGHTS TO BLACK.

HOLD.

WHEN THE LIGHTS COME BACK, EMILY STILSON, A WOMAN WELL INTO HER SEVENTIES, IS SITTING IN THE ARMCHAIR READING A BOOK. SOME DISTANCE AWAY, A FLOOR LAMP GLOWS DIMLY. ON THE OTHER SIDE OF HER CHAIR, ALSO SOME DISTANCE AWAY, A SMALL TABLE WITH A CLOCK. THE CHAIR, THE LAMP, AND THE TABLE WITH THE CLOCK ALL SIT ISOLATED IN NARROW POOLS OF LIGHT, DARKNESS BETWEEN AND AROUND THEM.

THE CLOCK SEEMS TO BE TICKING A TRIFLE LOUDER THAN NORMAL.

MRS. STILSON, ENJOYING HER BOOK AND THE PLEASANT EVENING, READS ON SERENELY.

AND THEN SHE LOOKS UP.

THE LAMP DISAPPEARS INTO THE DARKNESS.

BUT SHE TURNS BACK TO HER BOOK AS IF NOTHING ODD HAS HAPPENED; RESUMES READING.

AND THEN, A MOMENT LATER, SHE LOOKS UP AGAIN, AN EXPRESSION OF SLIGHT PERPLEXITY ON HER FACE. FOR NO DISCERNIBLE REASON, SHE TURNS TOWARD THE CLOCK.

THE CLOCK AND THE TABLE IT IS SITTING ON DISAPPEAR INTO THE DARKNESS.

SHE TURNS FRONT. STARES OUT INTO SPACE.

THEN SHE TURNS BACK TO HER BOOK. RESUMES READING. BUT THE READING SEEMS AN EFFORT; HER MIND IS ON OTHER THINGS.

THE CLOCK SKIPS A BEAT.

ONLY AFTER THE CLOCK HAS RESUMED ITS NORMAL RHYTHM DOES SHE LOOK UP. IT IS AS IF THE SKIPPED BEAT HAS ONLY JUST THEN REGISTERED. FOR THE FIRST TIME, SHE DISPLAYS WHAT ONE MIGHT CALL CONCERN.

AND THEN THE CLOCK STOPS AGAIN. THIS TIME THE INTERVAL LASTS LONGER.

THE BOOK SLIPS OUT OF MRS. STILSON'S HANDS; SHE STARES OUT IN TERROR.

BLACKOUT.

NOISE.

The moment of a stroke, even a relatively minor one, and its immediate aftermath, are an experience in chaos. Nothing at all makes sense. Nothing except perhaps this overwhelming disorientation will be remembered by the victim. The stroke usually happens suddenly. It is a catastrophe.

It is my intention that the audience recognize that some real event is occurring; that real information is being received by the victim, but that it is coming in too scrambled and too fast to be properly decoded. Systems overload.

And so this section must not seem like utter "noise," though certainly it must be more noisy than intelligible. I do not believe there is any way to be true to this material if it is not finally "composed" in rehearsal, on stage, by "feel." Theoretically, any sound or image herein described can occur anywhere in this section. The victim cannot process. Her familiar world has been rearranged. The puzzle is in pieces. All at once, and with no time to prepare, she has been picked up and dropped into another realm.

In order that this section may be put together in rehearsal (there being no one true "final order" to the images and sounds she perceives), I have divided this section into three discrete parts with the understanding that in performance these parts will blend together to form one cohesive whole.

The first group consists of the visual images MRS. STILSON *perceives.*

The second group consists of those sounds emanating outside herself. Since these sounds are all filtered by her mind, and since her mind has been drastically altered, the question of whether we in the audience are hearing what is

actually occurring or only hearing what she believes is occurring is unanswerable.

The third group contains MRS. STILSON's *words: the words she thinks and the words she speaks. Since we are perceiving the world through* MRS. STILSON's *senses, there is no sure way for us to know whether she is actually saying any of these words aloud.*

Since the experience we are exploring is not of logic but its opposite, there is no logical reason for these groupings to occur in the order in which I have presented them. These are but components, building blocks, and can therefore be repeated, spliced, reversed, filtered, speeded up or slowed down. What should determine their final sequence and juxtaposition, tempi, intensity, is the "musical" sense of this section as a whole; it must pulse and build. An explosion quite literally is occurring in her brain, or rather, a series of explosions: the victim's mind, her sense of time and place, her sense of self, all are being shattered if not annihilated. Fortunately, finally, she will pass out. Were her head a pinball game it would register TILT—*game over—stop. Silence. And resume again. Only now the victim is in yet another realm. The Catastrophe section is the journey or the fall into this strange and dreadful realm.*

In the world into which MRS. STILSON *has been so violently and suddenly transposed, time and place are without definition. The distance from her old familiar world is immense. For all she knows, she could as well be on another planet.*

In this new world, she moves from one space or thought or concept to another without willing or sometimes even knowing it. Indeed, when she moves in this maze-like place, it is as if the world around her and not she were doing all the moving. To her, there is nothing any more that is commonplace or predictable. Nothing is as it was. Everything comes as a surprise. Something has relieved her of command. Something beyond her comprehension has her in its grip.

In the staging of this play, the sense should therefore be conveyed of physical and emotional separation (by the use, for example, of the dark transparent screens through which her surrounding world can be only dimly and partly seen, or by alteration of external sound) and of total immersion in strangeness.

Because our focus is on MRS. STILSON's *inner self, it is important that she exhibit no particular overt physical disabilities. Furthermore, we should never see her in a wheelchair, even though, were we able to observe her through the doctors' eyes, a wheelchair is probably what she would, more often than not, be in.*

One further note: because MRS. STILSON *now processes information at a different rate from us, there is no reason that what we see going on around her has to be the visual equivalent of what we hear.*

CATASTROPHE

IMAGES	SOUNDS OUTSIDE HERSELF	MRS. STILSON'S VOICE
	(SOUNDS live or on tape, altered or unadorned)	*(VOICE live or on tape, unaltered or unadorned)*
	Of wind.	*Oh my God oh my God oh my God—*
Mostly, it is whiteness, dazzling, blinding.	Of someone breathing with effort, unevenly.	
	Of something ripping, like a sheet.	*—trees clouds houses mostly planes flashing past, images without words, utter disarray disbelief, never seen this kind of thing before!* 5
Occasionally, there are brief rounds of color, explosions of color, the color red being dominant.	Of something flapping, the sound suggestive of an old screen door perhaps, or a sheet or sail in the wind. It is a rapid fibrillation. And it is used mostly to mark transitions. It can seem ominous or not.	*Where am I? How'd I get here?*
The mirrors, of course, reflect infinitely. Sense of endless space, endless corridors.	Of a woman's scream (though this sound should be altered by filters so it resembles other things, such as sirens).	*My leg (What's my leg?) feels wet arms . . . wet too, belly same chin nose everything (Where are they taking me?) something sticky (What* 10 *has happened to my plane?) feel something sticky.*
	Of random noises recorded in a busy city hospital, then altered so as to be only minimally recognizable.	
Nothing seen that is not a fragment. Every aspect of her world has been shattered.	Of a car's engine at full speed.	*Doors! Too many doors!*
	Of a siren (altered to resemble a woman screaming).	*Must have . . . fallen cannot . . . move at all sky . . . (Gliding!) dark cannot* 15 *. . . talk (Feel as if I'm gliding!).*
	Of an airplane coming closer, thundering overhead, then zooming off into silence.	*Yes, feels cool, nice . . . Yes, this is the life all right!*
Utter isolation.	Of random crowd noises, the crowd greatly agitated. In the crowd, people can be heard calling for help, a doctor, an ambulance. But all the sounds are garbled.	*My plane! What has happened to my plane!* 20
In this vast whiteness, like apparitions, partial glimpses of doctors and nurses can be seen. They appear and disappear like a pulse. They are never in one place for long. The mirrors multiply their incomprehensibility.	Of people whispering.	*Help . . .*

IMAGES	SOUNDS OUTSIDE HERSELF	MRS. STILSON'S VOICE
Sometimes the dark panels are opaque, sometimes transparent. Always, they convey a sense of layers, multiplicity, separation. Sense constantly of doors opening, closing, opening, closing.	Of many people asking questions simultaneously, no question comprehensible. Of doors opening, closing, opening, closing. Of someone breathing oxygen through a mask.	*—all around faces of which nothing known no sense ever all wiped out blank like ice I think saw it once flying over something some place all was white sky and sea clouds ice almost crashed couldn't tell where I was heading right side up topsy-turvy under over I was flying actually if I can I do yes do recall was upside down can you believe it almost scraped my head on the ice caps couldn't tell which way was up wasn't even dizzy strange things happen to me that they do!*

Line numbers: 25, 30, 35 appear alongside Mrs. Stilson's voice text.

VOICES: *(garbled)* Just relax. / No one's going to hurt you. / Can you hear us? / Be careful. / You're hurting her! / No, we're not. / Don't lift her, leave her where she is! / Someone call an ambulance! / I don't think she can hear.

MALE VOICE: Have you any idea—

OTHER VOICES: *(garbled)* Do you know your name? / Do you know where you are? / What year is this? / If I say the tiger has been killed by the lion, which animal is dead?

A hospital paging system heard.

Equipment being moved through stone corridors, vast vaulting space. Endless echoing.

MRS. STILSON's movements seem random. She is a person wandering through space, lost.

Finally, MRS. STILSON is led by attendants downstage, to a chair. Then left alone.

What's my name? I don't know my name!

Where's my arm? I don't have an arm!

What's an arm? 40

AB-ABC-ABC123DE451212 what? 123—12345678972357 better yes no problem I'm okay soon be out soon be over storm . . . will pass I'm sure. Always has. 45

AWAKENING

In performance, the end of the Catastrophe section should blend, without interruption, into the beginning of this.

MRS. STILSON DOWNSTAGE ON A CHAIR IN A POOL OF LIGHT, DARKNESS ALL AROUND HER. IN THE DISTANCE BEHIND HER, MUFFLED SOUNDS OF A HOSPITAL. VAGUE IMAGES OF DOCTORS, NURSES ATTENDING TO SOMEONE WE CANNOT SEE. ONE OF THE DOCTORS CALLS MRS. STILSON'S NAME. DOWNSTAGE, MRS. STILSON SHOWS NO TRACE OF RECOGNITION. THE DOCTOR CALLS HER NAME AGAIN. AGAIN NO RESPONSE. ONE OF THE DOCTORS SAYS, "IT'S POSSIBLE SHE MAY HEAR US BUT BE UNABLE TO RESPOND."

ONE OF THE NURSES TRIES CALLING OUT HER NAME. STILL NO RESPONSE. THE DOCTOR LEAVES. THE REMAINING DOCTORS AND NURSES FADE INTO THE DARKNESS.

ONLY MRS. STILSON CAN BE SEEN.

PAUSE.

MRS. STILSON: *Still . . . sun moon too or . . . three times happened maybe globbidged rubbidged uff and firded-forded me to nothing there try again* [WE HEAR A WINDOW BEING RAISED SOMEWHERE BEHIND HER] *window! up and heard* [SOUNDS OF BIRDS] *known them know I know* 5 *them once upon a birds! that's it better getting better soon be out of this.*

PAUSE.

Out of . . . what?

PAUSE.

10 *Dark . . . space vast of . . . in I am or so it seems feels no real clues to speak of.* [BEHIND HER, BRIEF IMAGE OF A DOCTOR PASSING] *Something tells me I am not alone. Once! Lost it. No here back thanks work fast now, yes empty vast reach of space* 15 *desert think they call it I'll come back to that anyhow down I . . . something what* [BRIEF IMAGE OF A NURSE] *it's SOMETHING ELSE IS ENTERING MY!—no wait got it crashing OH MY GOD! CRASHING! deadstick dead-of-night thought the stars were* 20 *airport lights upside down was I what a way to land glad no one there to see it, anyhow tubbish blaxed and vinkled I commenshed to uh-oh where's it gone to somewhere flubbished what? with* [BRIEF IMAGES OF HOSPITAL STAFF ON THE MOVE] 25 *images are SOMETHING ODD IS! . . . yes, then there I thank you crawling sands and knees still can feel it hear the wind all alone somehow wasn't scared why a mystery, vast dark track of space, we've all got to die that I know, anyhow then day came light came* 30 *with it so with this you'd think you'd hope just hold on they will find me I am . . . still intact.*

PAUSE.

In here.

LONG SILENCE.

Seem to be the word removed.

LONG SILENCE.

How long have I been here? . . . And wrapped in dark.

PAUSE.

35 *Can remember nothing.*

OUTSIDE SOUNDS BEGIN TO IMPINGE; SAME FOR IMAGES. IN THE DISTANCE, AN ATTENDANT DIMLY SEEN PUSHING A FLOOR POLISHER. ITS NOISE RESEMBLES AN ANIMAL'S GROWL.

[TRYING HARD TO BE CHEERY]: *No, definitely I am not alone!*

THE SOUND OF THE POLISHER GROWS LOUDER, SEEMS MORE BESTIAL, VORACIOUS; IT OVERWHELMS EVERYTHING. EXPLOSION! SHE GASPS.

[RAPIDLY AND IN PANIC, SENSE OF GREAT COMMOTION BEHIND HER. A CRISIS HAS OCCURRED] *There I go there I go hallway now it's* 40 *screaming crowded pokes me then the coolbreeze needle scent of sweetness can see palms flowers flummers couldn't fix the leaking sprouting everywhere to save me help me CUTS UP THROUGH to something movement I am something moving without* 45 *movement!*

SOUND OF A WOMAN'S MUFFLED SCREAM FROM BEHIND HER. THE SCREAM GROWS LOUDER.

[WITH DELIGHT] *What a strange adventure I am having!*

LIGHTS TO BLACK ON EVERYTHING.

IN THE DARK, A PAUSE.

WHEN HER VOICE IS HEARD AGAIN, IT IS HEARD FIRST FROM ALL THE SPEAKERS. HER VOICE SOUNDS GROGGY, SLURRED. NO LONGER ANY SENSE OF PANIC DISCERNIBLE. A FEW MOMENTS AFTER HER VOICE IS HEARD, THE LIGHTS COME UP SLOWLY ON HER. SOON, ONLY SHE IS SPEAKING; THE VOICE FROM THE SPEAKERS HAS DISAPPEARED.

Hapst aporkshop fleetish yes of course it's yes the good ol' times when we would mollis I mean collis all 50 *around still what my son's name is cannot for the life of me yet face gleams smiles as he tells them what I did but what his name is cannot see it pleasant anyway yes palms now ocean sea breeze wafting floating up and lifting holding weightless and goes swoooop-* 55 *ing down with me least I . . . think it's me.*

SOUND OF SOMETHING FLAPPING RAPIDLY OPEN AND CLOSED, OPEN AND CLOSED.

SOUND OF WIND.

LIGHTS CHANGE INTO A COOL AND AIRY BLUE. SENSE OF WEIGHTLESSNESS, SERENITY.

IN ANOTHER REALM NOW.

Yes, out there walking not holding even danger ever-present how I loved it love it still no doubt will again hear them cheering wisht or waltz away to some place like Rumania . . . 60

THE WIND DISAPPEARS.

Nothing . . .

THE SERENE BLUE LIGHT BEGINS TO FADE AWAY. SOME PLACE ELSE NOW THAT SHE IS GOING.

Of course beyond that yet 1, 2 came before the yeast rose bubbled and MY CHUTE DIDN'T OPEN PROPERLY! Still for a girl did wonders getting down and it was Charles! no Charlie, who is Charlie? see him smiling as they tell him what I—

OUTSIDE WORLD BEGINS TO IMPINGE. LIGHTS ARE CHANGING, GROWING BRIGHTER, SOMETHING ODD IS HAPPENING. SENSE OF IMMINENCE. SHE NOTICES.

[BREATHLESS WITH EXCITEMENT]: *Stop hold cut stop wait stop come-out-break-out light can see it ready heart can yes can feel it pounding something underway here light is getting brighter lids I think the word is that's it lifting of their own but slowly knew I should be patient should be what? wait hold on steady now it's spreading no no question something underway here spreading brighter rising lifting light almost yes can almost there a little more now yes can almost see this . . . place I'm . . . in and . . .*

LOOK OF HORROR.

Oh my God! Now I understand! THEY'VE GOT ME!

FOR THE FIRST TIME DOCTORS, NURSES, HOSPITAL EQUIPMENT ALL CLEARLY VISIBLE BEHIND HER. ALL ARE GATHERED AROUND SOMEONE WE CANNOT SEE. FROM THE WAY THEY ARE ALL BENDING OVER, WE SURMISE THIS PERSON WE CANNOT SEE IS LYING IN A BED.

LIGHTS DROP ON MRS. STILSON, DOWNSTAGE.

NURSE: [TALKING TO THE PERSON UPSTAGE WE CANNOT SEE] Mrs. Stilson, can you open up your eyes?

PAUSE.

MRS. STILSON: [SEPARATED FROM HER QUESTIONERS BY GREAT DISTANCE] *Don't know how.*

DOCTOR: Mrs. Stilson, you just opened up your eyes. We saw you. Can you open them again?

NO RESPONSE.

Mrs. Stilson . . . ?

MRS. STILSON: [PROUDLY, TRIUMPHANTLY] *My name then—Mrs. Stilson!*

VOICE ON A P.A. SYSTEM: Mrs. Howard, call on three! Mrs. Howard . . . !

MRS. STILSON: *My name then—Mrs. Howard?*

LIGHTS FADE TO BLACK ON HOSPITAL STAFF.

SOUND OF WIND, SENSE OF TIME PASSING.

LIGHTS COME UP ON MRS. STILSON. THE WIND DISAPPEARS.

The room that I am in is large, square. What does large mean?

PAUSE.

The way I'm turned I can see a window. When I'm on my back the window isn't there.

DOCTOR: [IN THE DISTANCE, AT BEST ONLY DIMLY SEEN] Mrs. Stilson, can you hear me?

MRS. STILSON: *Yes.*

SECOND DOCTOR: Mrs. Stilson, can you hear me?

MRS. STILSON: *Yes! I said yes! What's wrong with you?*

FIRST DOCTOR: Mrs. Stilson, CAN YOU HEAR ME!

MRS. STILSON: *Don't believe this—I've been put in with the deaf!*

SECOND DOCTOR: Mrs. Stilson, if you can hear us, nod your head.

MRS. STILSON: *All right, fine, that's how you want to play it—there!*

SHE NODS.

THE DOCTORS EXCHANGE GLANCES.

FIRST DOCTOR: Mrs. Stilson, if you can hear us, NOD YOUR HEAD!

MRS. STILSON: *Oh my God, this is grotesque!*

CACOPHONY OF SOUNDS HEARD FROM ALL AROUND, BOTH LIVE AND FROM THE SPEAKERS. IMAGES SUGGESTING SENSATION OF ASSAULT AS WELL.

IMPLICATION OF ALL THESE SOUNDS AND IMAGES IS THAT MRS. STILSON IS BEING MOVED THROUGH THE HOSPITAL FOR PURPOSES OF EXAMINATION, PERHAPS EVEN TORTURE. THE INFORMATION WE RECEIVE COMES IN TOO FAST AND DISTORTED FOR RATIONAL COMPREHENSION. THE REALM SHE IS IN IS TERRIFYING. FORTUNATELY, SHE IS NOT IN IT LONG.

AS LONG AS SHE IS, HOWEVER, THE SENSE SHOULD BE CONVEYED THAT HER WORLD MOVES AROUND HER MORE THAN SHE THROUGH IT.

WHAT WE HEAR (THE COMPONENTS):   Are we moving you too fast? / Mustlian potid or blastigrate, no not that way this, that's fletchit gottit careful now. / Now put your nose here on this line, would you? That's it, thank you, well done, well done. / How are the wickets today? / [SOUND OF A COUGH] / Now close your— / Is my finger going up or— / Can you feel this? / Can you feel this? / Name something that grows on trees. / Who fixes teeth? What room do you cook in? What year is this? / How long have you been here? / Are we being too rippled shotgun? / Would you like a cup of tea? / What is Jim short for? / Point to your shoulder. / No, your shoulder. / What do you do with a book? / Don't worry, the water's warm. We're holding you, don't worry. In we go, that's a girl!

AND THEN, AS SUDDENLY AS THE ASSAULT BEGAN, IT IS OVER.

ONCE AGAIN, MRS. STILSON ALL ALONE ON STAGE, DARKNESS ALL AROUND HER, NO SENSE OF WALLS OR FURNITURE. UTTER ISOLATION.

MRS. STILSON: [TRYING HARD TO KEEP SMILING] *Yes, all in all I'd say while things could be better could be worse, far worse, how? Not quite sure. Just a sense I have. The sort of sense that only great experience can mallees or rake, plake I mean, flake . . . Drake! That's it.*

SHE STARES INTO SPACE.

SILENCE.

IN THE DISTANCE BEHIND HER, TWO DOCTORS APPEAR.

FIRST DOCTOR: Mrs. Stilson, who was the first President of the United States?

MRS. STILSON: *Washington.*

PAUSE.

SECOND DOCTOR: [SPEAKING MORE SLOWLY THAN THE FIRST DOCTOR DID; PERHAPS SHE SIMPLY DIDN'T HEAR THE QUESTION]   Mrs. Stilson, who was the first President of the United States?

MRS. STILSON: *Washington!*

SECOND DOCTOR: [TO FIRST]   I don't think she hears herself.

FIRST DOCTOR: No, I don't think she hears herself.

THE TWO DOCTORS EMERGE FROM THE SHADOWS, APPROACH MRS. STILSON. SHE LOOKS UP IN TERROR. THIS SHOULD BE THE FIRST TIME THAT THE WOMAN ON STAGE HAS BEEN DIRECTLY FACED OR CONFRONTED BY THE HOSPITAL STAFF. HER INNER AND OUTER WORLDS ARE BEGINNING TO COME TOGETHER.

FIRST DOCTOR: Mrs. Stilson, makey your naming powers?

MRS. STILSON: What?

SECOND DOCTOR: Canju spokeme?

MRS. STILSON: Can I what?

FIRST DOCTOR: Can do peeperear?

MRS. STILSON: *Don't believe what's going on!*

SECOND DOCTOR: Ahwill.

FIRST DOCTOR: Pollycadjis.

SECOND DOCTOR: Sewyladda?

FIRST DOCTOR: [WITH A NOD]   Hm-hm.

EXIT DOCTORS.

MRS. STILSON: [ALONE AGAIN]   *How it came to pass that I was captured!* [SHE PONDERS] *Hard to say really. I'll come back to that.*

PAUSE.

The room that I've been put in this time is quite small, square, what does square mean? . . . Means . . .

SENSE OF TIME PASSING. THE LIGHTS SHIFT. THE SPACE SHE IS IN BEGINS TO CHANGE ITS SHAPE.

Of course morning comes I think . . . [SHE PONDERS] *Yes, and night of course comes . . .* [PONDERS MORE] *Though sometimes . . .*

MRS. STILSON SOME PLACE ELSE NOW. AND SHE IS AWARE OF IT.

Yes, the way the walls choose to move around me . . . Yes, I've noticed that, I'm no fool!

A NURSE APPEARS CARRYING A DAZZLING BOUQUET OF FLOWERS. THIS BOUQUET IS THE FIRST REAL COLOR WE HAVE SEEN.

NURSE: Good morning! Look what somebody's just sent you! [SHE SETS THEM ON A TABLE] Wish I had as many admirers as you.

EXIT NURSE, SMILING WARMLY.

MRS. STILSON'S EYES ARE DRAWN TO THE FLOWERS. AND SOMETHING ABOUT THEM APPARENTLY RENDERS IT IMPOSSIBLE FOR HER TO SHIFT HER GAZE AWAY. SOMETHING ABOUT THESE FLOWERS HAS HER IN THEIR THRALL.

WHAT IT IS IS THEIR COLOR.

IT IS AS IF SHE HAS NEVER EXPERIENCED COLOR BEFORE. AND THE EXPERIENCE IS SO OVERWHELMING, BOTH PHYSIOLOGICALLY AND PSYCHOLOGICALLY, THAT HER BRAIN CANNOT PROCESS ALL THE INFORMATION. HER CIRCUITRY IS OVERLOADED. IT IS TOO MUCH SENSORY INPUT FOR HER TO HANDLE. AN EXPLOSION IS IMMINENT. IF SOMETHING DOES NOT INTERVENE TO DIVERT HER ATTENTION, MRS. STILSON WILL VERY LIKELY FAINT, PERHAPS EVEN SUFFER A SEIZURE.

A NARROW BEAM OF LIGHT, GROWING STEADILY IN INTENSITY, FALLS UPON THE BOUQUET OF FLOWERS, CAUSING THEIR COLORS TO TAKE ON AN INTENSITY THEMSELVES THAT THEY OTHERWISE WOULD LACK. AT THE SAME TIME, A SINGLE MUSICAL TONE IS HEARD, VOLUME INCREASING.

A NURSE ENTERS THE ROOM.

170 NURSE: May I get you something?

MRS. STILSON: [ABSTRACTED, EYES REMAINING ON THE FLOWERS] Yes, a sweater.

NURSE: Yes, of course. Think we have one here. [THE NURSE OPENS A DRAWER, TAKES OUT A PILLOW, HANDS THE PILLOW TO MRS. STILSON]
175 Here.

MRS. STILSON ACCEPTS THE PILLOW UNQUESTIONINGLY, EYES NEVER LEAVING THE FLOWERS. SHE LAYS THE PILLOW ON HER LAP, PROMPTLY FORGETS ABOUT IT. THE MUSICAL TONE AND THE BEAM OF LIGHT CONTINUE RELENTLESSLY TOWARD THEIR PEAK.

THE NURSE, OBLIVIOUS OF ANY CRISIS, EXITS.

THE SINGLE TONE AND THE BEAM OF LIGHT CREST TOGETHER.

SILENCE FOLLOWS. THE BEAM DISAPPEARS. THE FLOWERS SEEM NORMAL. THE LIGHTS AROUND MRS. STILSON RETURN TO THE WAY THEY WERE BEFORE THE GIFT OF FLOWERS WAS BROUGHT IN.

MRS. STILSON: [SHAKEN] *This is not a hospital of course, and I know it! What it is is a farmhouse made up to look like a hospital. Why? I'll come back to that.* 180

ENTER ANOTHER NURSE.

NURSE: Hi! Haven't seen you in a while. Have you missed me?

MRS. STILSON: [NO HINT OF RECOGNITION VISIBLE] What?

NURSE: [WARMLY] They say you didn't touch your dinner. Would you like some pudding? 185

MRS. STILSON: No.

NURSE: Good, I'll go get you some.

EXIT NURSE, VERY CHEERFULLY.

MRS. STILSON: *Yes no question they have got me I've been what that word was captured is it? No it's—Yes,* 190 *it's captured how? Near as it can figure. I was in my prane and crashed, not unusual, still in all not too common. Neither is it very grub. Plexit rather or I'd say propopic. Well that's that, jungdaball! Anyhow to resume, what I had for lunch? That's not* 195 *it, good books I have read, good what, done what? Whaaaaat? Do the busy here! Get inside this, rubbidge all around let the vontul do some yes off or it of above semilacrum pwooosh! What with noddygobbit nip-n-crashing inside outside witsit watchit funnel* 200 *vortex sucking into backlash watchit get-out caughtin spinning ring-grab grobbit help woooosh! cannot stoppit on its own has me where it wants* [AND SUDDENLY SHE IS IN ANOTHER REALM. LIGHTS TRANSFORMED INTO WEIGHTLESS 205 BLUE. SENSE OF EASE AND SERENITY] *Plane! See it thanks, okay, onto back we were and here it is. Slow down easy now. Captured. After crashing, that is what we said or was about to, think it so, cannot tell for sure, slow it slow it, okay here we* 210 *go . . .* [SPEAKING SLOWER NOW] *captured after crashing by the enemy and brought here to this farm masquerading as a hospital. Why? For I would say offhand information. Of what sort though hard to*

215 *tell. For example, questions such as can I raise my*
fingers, what's an overcoat, how many nickels in a
rhyme, questions such as these. To what use can they
be to the enemy? Hard to tell from here. Nonetheless,
I would say must be certain information I possess
220 *that they want well I won't give it I'll escape! Strange*
things happen to me that they do! Good thing I'm all
right! Must be in Rumania. Just a hunch of course.
[THE SERENE BLUE LIGHT STARTS TO FADE]
Ssssh, someone's coming.

A NURSE HAS ENTERED. THE NURSE GUIDES
MRS. STILSON TO A DOCTOR. THE BLUE
LIGHT IS GONE. THE NURSE LEAVES.

THE SPACE MRS. STILSON NOW IS IN APPEARS
MUCH MORE "REAL" AND LESS FRAGMEN-
TARY THAN WHAT WE HAVE SO FAR BEEN
OBSERVING. WE SEE MRS. STILSON HERE AS
OTHERS SEE HER.

225 **DOCTOR:** Mrs. Stilson, if you don't mind, I'd like to ask
you some questions. Some will be easy, some will be
hard. Is that all right?

MRS. STILSON: Oh yes I'd say oh well yes that's the
twither of it.

230 **DOCTOR:** Good. Okay. Where were you born?

MRS. STILSON: Never. Not at all. Here the match
wundles up you know and drats flames fires I keep
careful always—

DOCTOR: Right . . . [SPEAKING VERY SLOWLY,
235 PRECISE ENUNCIATION] Where were you born?

MRS. STILSON: Well now well now that's a good thing
knowing yushof course wouldn't call it such as I did
andinjurations or aplovia could it? No I wouldn't
think so. Next?

PAUSE.

240 **DOCTOR:** Mrs. Stilson, are there seven days in a week?

MRS. STILSON: . . . Seven . . . Yes.

DOCTOR: Are there five days in a week?

PAUSE.

MRS. STILSON: [AFTER MUCH PONDERING] No.

DOCTOR: Can a stone float on water?

LONG PAUSE.

245 **MRS. STILSON:** No.

DOCTOR: Mrs. Stilson, can you cough?

MRS. STILSON: Somewhat.

DOCTOR: Well, would you show me how you cough?

MRS. STILSON: Well now well now not so easy what
you cromplie is to put these bushes open and— 250

DOCTOR: No no Mrs. Stilson, I'm sorry—I would like
to hear you cough.

MRS. STILSON: Well I'm not bort you know with
plajits or we'd see it wencherday she brings its pillow
with the fistils-opening I'd say outward always out- 255
ward never stopping it.

LONG SILENCE.

DOCTOR: Mrs. Stilson, I have some objects here. [HE
TAKES A COMB, A TOOTHBRUSH, A PACK OF
MATCHES, AND A KEY FROM HIS POCKET,
SETS THEM DOWN WHERE SHE CAN SEE] 260
Could you point to the object you would use for
cleaning your teeth?

VERY LONG SILENCE.

FINALLY SHE PICKS UP THE COMB AND
SHOWS IT TO HIM. THEN SHE PUTS IT DOWN.
WAITS.

Mrs. Stilson, here, take this object in your hand.
[HE HANDS HER THE TOOTHBRUSH] Do you
know what this object is called? 265

MRS. STILSON: [WITH GREAT DIFFICULTY]
Tooooooooovvvv . . . bbrum?

DOCTOR: Very good. Now put it down.

SHE PUTS IT DOWN.

Now, pretend you have it in your hand. Show me
what you'd do with it. 270

SHE DOES NOTHING.

What does one do with an object such as that, Mrs.
Stilson?

NO RESPONSE.

Mrs. Stilson, what is the name of the object you are
looking at?

MRS. STILSON: Well it's . . . wombly and not at all . . . 275
rigged or tuned like we might twunter or toring to
work the clambness out of it or—

DOCTOR: Pick it up.

MRS. STILSON: [AS SOON AS SHE'S PICKED IT UP]
Tooovebram, tooove-britch bratch brush bridge, 280
two-bridge.

DOCTOR: Show me what you do with it.

FOR SEVERAL MOMENTS SHE DOES
NOTHING.

THEN SHE PUTS IT TO HER LIPS, HOLDS IT
THERE MOTIONLESS.

Very good. Thank you.

SHE SIGHS HEAVILY, PUTS IT DOWN.

THE DOCTOR GATHERS UP HIS OBJECTS,
LEAVES.

ONCE AGAIN MRS. STILSON ALL ALONE.

SHE STARES INTO SPACE.

THEN HER VOICE IS HEARD COMING FROM
ALL AROUND; SHE HERSELF DOES NOT
SPEAK.

HER VOICE: *Dark now again out the window on my*
285   *side lying here all alone . . .*

VERY LONG SILENCE.

MRS. STILSON: *Yesterday my children came to see me.*

PAUSE.

*Or at least, I was told they were my children. Never
saw them before in my life.*

SHE STARES OUT, MOTIONLESS. NO
EXPRESSION.

THEN AFTER A WHILE SHE LOOKS AROUND.
STUDIES THE DARK FOR CLUES.

Time has become peculiar.

AND SHE CONTINUES THIS SCRUTINY OF
THE DARK.

BUT IF THIS ACTIVITY STEMS FROM CURIOS-
ITY, IT IS A MILD CURIOSITY AT MOST. NO
LONGER DOES SHE CONVEY OR PROBABLY
EVEN EXPERIENCE THE EXTREME, DISORI-
ENTED DREAD WE SAW EARLIER WHEN
SHE FIRST ARRIVED IN THIS NEW REALM.
HER SENSE OF URGENCY IS GONE. INDEED,
WERE WE ABLE TO OBSERVE MRS. STILSON
CONSTANTLY, WE WOULD INEVITABLY CON-
CLUDE THAT HER CURIOSITY IS NOW ONLY
MINIMALLY PURPOSEFUL; THAT, IN FACT,
MORE LIKELY HER INVESTIGATIONS ARE
THE ACTIONS, POSSIBLY MERELY THE RE-
FLEX ACTIONS, OF SOMEONE WITH LITTLE
OR NOTHING ELSE TO DO.

THIS IS NOT TO DENY THAT SHE IS DESPER-
ATELY TRYING TO PIECE HER SHATTERED
WORLD TOGETHER. UNDOUBTEDLY, IT IS
THE DOMINANT MOTIF IN HER MIND. BUT IT
IS A MOTIF PROBABLY MORE ABSENT FROM
HER CONSCIOUSNESS THAN PRESENT, AND
THE QUEST IT INSPIRES IS INTERMITTENT
AT BEST. HER MENTAL ABILITIES HAVE NOT
ONLY BEEN SEVERELY ALTERED, THEY HAVE
BEEN DIMINISHED: THAT IS THE TERRIBLE
FACT ONE CANNOT DENY.

AND THEN SUDDENLY SHE IS AGITATED.

Mother! . . . didn't say as she usually . . .   290

PAUSE.

*And I thought late enough or early rather first light
coming so when didn't move I poked her then with
shoving but she didn't even eyes or giggle when I
tickled.*

PAUSE.

What it was was not a trick as I at first had—   295

PAUSE.

*Well I couldn't figure, he had never lied, tried to get
her hold me couldn't it was useless. Then his face
was, I had never known a face could . . . It was like
a mask then like sirens it was bursting open it was
him then I too joining it was useless. Can still feel*   300
what it was like when she held me.

PAUSE.

*So then well I was on my own. He was all destroyed,
had I think they say no strength for this.*

THEN SHE'S SILENT. NO EXPRESSION.
STARES INTO SPACE.

ENTER A DOCTOR AND A NURSE.

DOCTOR: [WARMLY]   Hello Mrs. Stilson.

HE COMES OVER NEXT TO HER. WE CAN-
NOT TELL IF SHE NOTICES HIM OR NOT. THE
NURSE, CHART IN HAND, STANDS A SLIGHT
DISTANCE AWAY.

You're looking much, much better. [HE SMILES   305
AND SITS DOWN NEXT TO HER. HE WATCHES
HER FOR SEVERAL MOMENTS, SEARCHING
FOR SIGNS OF RECOGNITION] Mrs. Stilson, do
you know why you're here?

310　MRS. STILSON:　Well now well now . . .

SHE GIVES IT UP.

SILENCE.

DOCTOR:　You have had an accident—

MRS. STILSON: [HER WORDS OVERPOWERING HIS]	DOCTOR: [TO ALL INTENTS AND PURPOSES, WHAT HE SAYS IS LOST]
I don't trust him, don't *trust anyone. Must get* *word out, send a message* 315　*where I am. Like a wall* *between me and others.* *No one ever gets it right* *even though I tell them* *right. They are playing* 320　*tricks on me, two sides,* *both not my friends,* *goes in goes out too fast* *too fast hurts do the* *busy I'm all right I talk* 325　*right why acting all* *these others like I don't,* *what's he marking,* *what's he writing?*	At home. Not in an airplane. It's called a stroke. This means that your brain has been injured and brain tissue destroyed, though we are not certain of the cause. You could get better, and you're certainly making progress. But it's still too soon to give any sort of exact prognosis. [HE STUDIES HER. THEN HE RISES AND MARKS SOMETHING ON HIS CLIPBOARD]

EXIT DOCTOR AND NURSE.

MRS. STILSON:　*I am doing well of course!*

PAUSE.

330　[SECRETIVE TONE] *They still pretend they do not*
understand me. I believe they may be mad.

PAUSE.

No they're not mad, I am mad. Today I heard it.
Everything I speak is wronged. SOMETHING HAS
BEEN DONE TO ME!

335　DOCTOR:　[BARELY VISIBLE IN THE DISTANCE]
Mrs. Stilson, can you repeat this phrase: "We live
across the street from the school."

SHE PONDERS.

MRS. STILSON:　"Malacats on the forturay are the
kesterfats of the romancers."

LOOK OF HORROR COMES ACROSS HER FACE;
THE DOCTOR VANISHES.

THROUGH THE SCREENS, UPSTAGE, WE SEE
A NURSE BRINGING ON A TRAY OF FOOD.

NURSE: [BRIGHTLY]　Okay ups-a-girl, ups-a-baby,　340
dinnertime! Open wide now, mustn't go dribble-
dribble—at's-a-way!

MRS. STILSON SCREAMS, SWINGING HER
ARMS IN FURY. IN THE DISTANCE, UPSTAGE,
THE TRAY OF FOOD GOES FLYING.

MRS. STILSON: [SCREAMING]　Out! Get out! Take
this shit away! I don't want it! Someone get me out
of here!　345

NURSE: [WHILE MRS. STILSON CONTINUES
SHOUTING]　Help, someone, come quick! She's
talking! Good as you or me! It's a miracle! Help!
Somebody! Come quick!

WHILE MRS. STILSON CONTINUES TO
SCREAM AND FLAIL HER ARMS, NURSES
AND DOCTORS RUSH ON UPSTAGE AND SUR-
ROUND THE PATIENT WE NEVER SEE.

AND ALTHOUGH MRS. STILSON CONTINUES
TO SCREAM COHERENTLY, IN FACT SHE ISN'T
ANY BETTER, NO MIRACLE HAS OCCURRED.
HER ABILITY TO ARTICULATE WITH APPAR-
ENT NORMALCY HAS BEEN BROUGHT ON
BY EXTREME AGITATION AND IN NO WAY
IMPLIES THAT SHE COULD PRODUCE THESE
SOUNDS AGAIN "IF SHE ONLY WANTED";
WILL POWER HAS NOTHING TO DO WITH
WHAT WE HEAR.

HER LANGUAGE, AS IT MUST, SOON SLIPS
BACK INTO JARGON. SHE CONTINUES TO
FLAIL HER ARMS. IN THE BACKGROUND,
WE CAN SEE A NURSE PREPARING A
HYPODERMIC.

MRS. STILSON:—[STRUGGLING] flubdgy please　350
no-mommy-callming holdmeplease to sleeEEEEP
SHOOOOP shop shnoper CRROOOOOCK
SNANNNNG wuduitcoldly should I gobbin flutter
truly HELP ME yessisnofun, snofun, wishes awhin
dahd killminsilf if . . . could [IN THE DISTANCE,　355
WE SEE THE NEEDLE GIVEN] OW! . . . would
I but . . . [SHE'S BECOMING DROWSY] . . .
awful to me him as well moas of all no cantduit . . .
jusscantduit . . .

HEAD DROPS.

INTO SLEEP SHE GOES.

EXIT DOCTORS, NURSES.

SOUND OF A GENTLE WIND IS HEARD.

LIGHTS FADE TO BLACK ON MRS. STILSON.

DARKNESS EVERYWHERE; THE SOUND OF THE WIND FADES AWAY.

SILENCE.

LIGHTS UP ON AMY, DOWNSTAGE RIGHT.

THEN LIGHTS UP ON MRS. STILSON STARING INTO SPACE.

360 **AMY:**   Mrs. Stilson?

MRS. STILSON TURNS TOWARD THE SOUND, SEES AMY.

You have had what's called a stroke.

CHANGE OF LIGHTS AND PANELS OPEN. SENSE OF TERRIBLE ENCLOSURE GONE. BIRDS HEARD. WE ARE OUTSIDE NOW. AMY PUTS A SHAWL AROUND MRS. STILSON'S SHOULDERS.

AMY: Are you sure that will be enough?

MRS. STILSON: Oh yes . . . thhhankyou.

SHE TUCKS THE SHAWL AROUND HERSELF.

THEN AMY GUIDES HER THROUGH THE PANELS AS IF THROUGH CORRIDORS; NO RUSH, SLOW GENTLE STROLL.

THEY EMERGE OTHER SIDE OF STAGE. WARM LIGHT. AMY TAKES IN THE VIEW. MRS. STIL- SON APPEARS INDIFFERENT.

AMY: Nice to be outside, isn't it? . . . Nice view.

365 **MRS. STILSON:** [STILL WITH INDIFFERENCE] Yes indeed.

THERE ARE TWO CHAIRS NEARBY, AND THEY SIT.

SILENCE FOR A TIME.

AMY: Are you feeling any better today?

BUT SHE GETS NO RESPONSE.

THEN A MOMENT LATER, MRS. STILSON TURNS TO AMY; IT IS AS IF AMY'S QUESTION HAS NOT EVEN BEEN HEARD.

MRS. STILSON: The thing is . . .

BUT THE STATEMENT TRAILS OFF INTO NOTHINGNESS.

SHE STARES OUT, NO EXPRESSION.

AMY: Yes? What?

LONG SILENCE.

MRS. STILSON: I can't make it do it like it used to.   370

AMY: Yes, I know. That's because of the accident.

MRS. STILSON: [SEEMINGLY OBLIVIOUS OF AMY'S WORDS]   The words, they go in sometimes then out they go, I can't stop them here inside or make maybe globbidge to the tubberway or—   375

AMY: Emily. Emily!

MRS. STILSON: [SHAKEN OUT OF HERSELF] . . . What?

AMY: Did you hear what you just said?

MRS. STILSON: . . . Why?   380

AMY: [SPEAKING SLOWLY]   You must listen to what you're saying.

MRS. STILSON: Did I . . . do . . .

AMY: [NODDING, SMILING; CLEARLY NO RE- PROACH INTENDED]   Slow down. Listen to what   385 you're saying.

SILENCE.

MRS. STILSON: [SLOWER]   The thing is . . . doing all this busy in here gets, you know with the talk- ing it's like . . . sometimes when I hear here [SHE TOUCHES HER HEAD] . . . but when I start   390 to . . . kind more what kind of voice should . . . it's like pfffft! [SHE MAKES A GESTURE WITH HER HAND OF SOMETHING FLYING AWAY]

AMY: [SMILING]   Yes, I know. It's hard to find the words for what you're thinking of.   395

MRS. STILSON: Well yes.

LONG PAUSE.

And then these people, they keep waiting . . . And I see they're smiling and . . . they keep . . . waiting . . . [FAINT SMILE, HELPLESS GESTURE. SHE STARES OFF]   400

LONG SILENCE.

AMY: Emily.

MRS. STILSON LOOKS UP.

Can you remember anything about your life . . . be- fore the accident?

MRS. STILSON: Not sometimes, some days it goes bet- ter if I see a thing or smell . . . it . . . remembers me   405 back, you see? And I see things that maybe they were me and maybe they were just some things you know that happens in the night when you . . . [STRUG-GLING VISIBLY] have your things closed, eyes.

410 **AMY:** A dream you mean.

MRS. STILSON: [WITH RELIEF] Yes. So I don't know for sure.

PAUSE.

If it was really me.

LONG SILENCE.

AMY: Your son is bringing a picture of you when you
415   were younger. We thought you might like that.

NO VISIBLE RESPONSE. LONG SILENCE.

You used to fly, didn't you?

MRS. STILSON: [BRIGHTLY] Oh yes indeed! Very much! I walked . . . out . . .

PAUSE.

[SOFTLY, PROUDLY] I walked out on wings.

LIGHTS FADE ON AMY. MRS. STILSON ALONE AGAIN.

420   *Sitting here on my bed I can close my eyes shut out all that I can't do with, hearing my own talking, others, names that used to well just be there when I wanted now all somewhere else. No control. Close my eyes then, go to—*

SOUND OF SOMETHING FLAPPING RAPIDLY.

A FIBRILLATION.

LIGHTS BECOME BLUE. SENSE OF WEIGHT-LESSNESS. SERENITY.

425   *Here I go. No one talks here. Images coming I seem feel it feels better this way here is how it goes: this time I am still in the middle Stilson in the middle going out walking out wind feels good hold the wires feel the hum down below far there they are now we
430   turn it bank it now we spin! Looks more bad than really is, still needs good balance and those nerves and that thing that courage thing don't fall off! . . . And now I'm out . . . and back and . . .* [WITH SUR-PRISE] *there's the window.*

LIGHTS HAVE RETURNED TO NORMAL. SHE IS BACK WHERE SHE STARTED.

AMY ENTERS.

435 **AMY:** Hello, Emily.

MRS. STILSON: Oh, Amy! . . . Didn't hear what you was . . . coming here to . . . Oh!

AMY: What is it?

MRS. STILSON: Something . . . wet.

AMY: Do you know what it is?   440

MRS. STILSON: Don't . . . can't say find it word.

AMY: Try. You can find it.

MRS. STILSON: Wet . . . thing, many, both sides yes.

AMY: Can you name them? What they are? You do know what they are.   445

PAUSE.

MRS. STILSON: . . . Tears?

AMY: That's right, very good. Those are tears. And do you know what that means?

MRS. STILSON: . . . Sad?

AMY: Yes, right, well done, it means . . . that you are   450
sad.

EXPLORATIONS

STAGE DARK.

IN THE DARK, A PIANO HEARD: SOMEONE FOOLING AROUND ON THE KEYBOARD, BRIEF HALTING SNATCHES OF OLD SONGS EMERGING AS THE PRODUCT; WOULD CON-STITUTE A MEDLEY WERE THE SEGMENTS ONLY LONGER, MORE COHESIVE. AS IT IS, SUSPICION AROUSED THAT WHAT WE HEAR IS ALL THE PIANIST CAN REMEMBER.

SOUND OF GENERAL LAUGHTER, HUBBUB.

LIGHTS RISE.

WHAT WE SEE IS A REC ROOM, IN SOME PLACES CLEARLY, IN OTHERS NOT (THE ROOM BEING OBSERVED PARTLY THROUGH THE DARK SCRIM PANELS).

UPSTAGE RIGHT, AN UPRIGHT PIANO, PLAY-ERS AND FRIENDS GATHERED ROUND. DOC-TORS, THERAPISTS, NURSES, ATTENDANTS, PATIENTS, VISITORS CERTAINLY ARE NOT ALL SEEN, BUT THOSE WE DO SEE COME FROM SUCH A GROUP. WE ARE IN THE REC ROOM OF A REHABILITATION CENTER. SOME PATIENTS IN WHEELCHAIRS.

THE ROOM ITSELF HAS BRIGHT COMFORT-ABLE CHAIRS, PERHAPS A CARD TABLE, MAG-

AZINE RACK, CERTAINLY A TV SET. SOMEONE NOW TURNS ON THE TV.

WHAT EMERGES IS THE SOUND OF ELLA FITZGERALD IN LIVE PERFORMANCE. SHE SINGS SCAT: MELLOW, UPBEAT.

THE PATIENTS AND STAFF PERSUADE THE PIANIST TO CEASE. ELLA'S RIFFS OF SCAT CAST SOMETHING LIKE A SPELL.

MRS. STILSON WANDERS THROUGH THE SPACE.

THE REC ROOM, IT SHOULD BE STRESSED, SHOWS MORE DETAIL AND COLOR THAN ANY SPACE WE'VE SO FAR SEEN. PERHAPS A VASE OF FLOWERS HELPS TO SIGNAL THAT MRS. STILSON'S WORLD IS BECOMING FULLER, MORE INTEGRATED.

MOVEMENTS TOO SEEM NORMAL, SAME FOR CONVERSATIONS THAT GO ON DURING ALL OF THIS, THOUGH TOO SOFTLY FOR US TO COMPREHEND.

THE MUSIC OF COURSE SETS THE TONE. ALL WHO LISTEN ARE IN ITS THRALL.

NEW TIME SENSE HERE, A LANGUOR AL-MOST. THE DREAD MRS. STILSON FELT HAS BEEN REPLACED BY AN ACKNOWLEDG-MENT OF HER CONDITION, THOUGH NOT AN UNDERSTANDING.

IN THIS TIME BEFORE SHE SPEAKS, AND IN FACT DURING, WE OBSERVE THE LIFE OF THE REC ROOM BEHIND AND AROUND HER. THIS IS NOT A HOSPITAL ANY MORE, AND A KIND OF NORMALCY PREVAILS.

THE SENSE SHOULD BE CONVEYED OF COR-RIDORS LEADING TO AND FROM THIS ROOM.

THEN THE MUSIC AND THE REC ROOM SOUNDS GROW DIM; MRS. STILSON COMES FORWARD, LOST IN THE DRIFTS OF A THOUGHT.

MRS. STILSON: [RELAXED, MELLOW] *Wonder... what's inside of it...?*

PAUSE.

I mean, how does it work? What's inside that... makes it work?

LONG PAUSE. SHE PONDERS.

5   *I mean when you... think about it all...*

PAUSE.

And when you think that it could... ever have been... possible to... be another way...

SHE PONDERS.

BUT IT'S HARD FOR HER TO KEEP IN MIND WHAT SHE'S BEEN THINKING OF, AND SHE HAS TO FIGHT THE NOISE OF THE REC ROOM, ITS INTRUSIVE PRESENCE. LIKE A NOVICE JUGGLER, MRS. STILSON IS UNABLE TO KEEP OUTSIDE IMAGES AND INNER THOUGHTS GOING SIMULTANEOUSLY. WHEN SHE'S WITH HER THOUGHTS, THE OUTSIDE WORLD FADES AWAY. WHEN THE OUTSIDE WORLD IS WITH HER, HER THOUGHTS FADE AWAY.

BUT SHE FIGHTS HER WAY THROUGH IT, AND KEEPS THE THOUGHT IN MIND.

THE REC ROOM, WHOSE NOISE HAS JUST INCREASED, GROWS QUIET.

Maybe... if somehow I could—[SHE SEARCHES FOR THE WORDS THAT MATCH HER CONCEPT]*—get inside...*   10

PAUSE.

SOUNDS OF THE REC ROOM PULSE LOUDER. SHE FIGHTS AGAINST IT. THE REC ROOM SOUNDS DIMINISH.

Prob'ly... very dark inside... [SHE PONDERS; TRIES TO PICTURE WHAT SHE'S THINKING] *Yes... twisting kind of place I bet...* [PONDERS MORE] *With lots of...* [SHE SEARCHES FOR THE PROPER WORD; FINDS IT] *...passageways*   15 *that... lead to...* [AGAIN, SHE SEARCHES FOR THE WORD]

THE OUTSIDE WORLD RUSHES IN.

PATIENT IN A WHEELCHAIR: [ONLY BARELY AU-DIBLE] My foot feels sour.

AN ATTENDANT PUTS A LAP RUG OVER THE PATIENT'S LIMBS. THEN THE REC ROOM, ONCE AGAIN, FADES AWAY.

MRS. STILSON: [FIGHTING ON] *...lead to... some-*   20 *thing... Door! Yes... closed off now I... guess possib... ly for good I mean... forever, what does that mean?* [SHE PONDERS]

ATTENDANT: Would you like some candy?

MRS. STILSON: No.   25

ATTENDANT: Billy made it.

MRS. STILSON: No!

THE ATTENDANT MOVES BACK INTO THE
SHADOWS.

Where was I? [SHE LOOKS AROUND] *Why can't
they just . . . let me . . . be when I'm . . .*

LIGHTS START TO CHANGE. HER WORLD
SUDDENLY IN FLUX. THE REC ROOM FADES
FROM VIEW. SOUNDS OF BIRDS HEARD,
DIMLY AT FIRST.

30   [AWARE OF THE CHANGE AS IT IS OCCUR-
RING] *. . . okay. Slipping out of . . . it and . . .*

MRS. STILSON IN A DIFFERENT PLACE.

Outside now! How . . . did I do that?

AMY: [EMERGING FROM THE SHADOWS]   Do you
like this new place better?

35   MRS. STILSON: Oh well oh well yes, much, all . . .
nice flowers here, people seem . . . more like me.
Thank you.

AMY MOVES BACK TOWARD THE SHADOWS.

And then I see it happen once again . . .

AMY GONE FROM SIGHT.

Amy kisses me. Puts her—what thing is it, arm! yes,
40   *arm, puts her arm around my . . .*

PAUSE.

. . . shoulder, turns her head away so I can't . . .

PAUSE.

*Well, it knows what she's doing. May not get much
better even though I'm here. No, I know that. I know
that. No real need for her to . . .*

LONG PAUSE.

45   *Then she kisses me again.*

PAUSE.

Walks away . . .

PAUSE.

LIGHTS CHANGE AGAIN, WORLD AGAIN IN
FLUX. NOISES OF THE BUILDING'S INTERIOR
CAN BE HEARD LIKE A BABEL, ONLY FLEET-
INGLY COHERENT. THE REC ROOM SEEN
DISSOLVING.

MRS. STILSON: *Where am I?*

SHE BEGINS TO WANDER THROUGH A MAZE
OF PASSAGEWAYS. THE MIRRORS MUL-
TIPLY HER IMAGE, CREATE A SENSE OF
ENDLESSNESS.

*[Note. The following blocks of sound, which accompany her
expedition, are meant to blend and overlap in performance
and, to that end, can be used in any order and combined
in any way desired, except for the last five blocks, numbers
12–16, which must be performed in their given sequence and
in a way that is comprehensible. The sounds themselves
may be live or pre-recorded; those which are pre-recorded
should emanate from all parts of the theater and in no
predictable pattern. The effect should be exhilarating and
disorienting. An adventure. With terrifying aspects to be
sure. But the sense of mystery and adventure must never be
so overwhelmed by the terror that it is either lost altogether
or submerged to the point of insignificance.*

MRS. STILSON *may be frightened here, but the fear does not
prevent her from exploring.*

*She wanders through the labyrinth of dark panels as if
they were so many doors, each door leading into yet another
realm.]*

BLOCK 1:   It was but a few years later that Fritsch and
Hitzig stimulated the cortex of a dog with an electric
current. Here at last was dramatic and indisputable   50
evidence that—

BLOCK 2:   Would you like me to change the channel?

BLOCK 3:   . . . presented, I would say, essentially similar
conclusions on the behavioral correlates of each
cerebral convolution.   55

BLOCK 4: [BEING THE DEEP MALE VOICE, SPEAK-
ING SLOWLY, ENUNCIATING CAREFULLY,
THAT ONE HEARS ON THE SPEECH-THERAPY
MACHINE KNOWN AS "THE LANGUAGE MAS-
TER"]   Mother led Bud to the bed.   60

BLOCK 5:   . . . In the laboratory then, through electrical
stimulation of neural centers or excisions of areas of
the brain, scientists acquired information about the
organization of mental activities in the monkey, the
dog, the cat, and the rat. The discovery of certain   65
peculiar clinical pictures, reminiscent of bizarre human syndromes, proved of special interest.

BLOCK 6:   Can you tell me what this object's called?

BLOCK 7:   ELLA'S RIFFS OF SCAT, AS IF WE WERE
STILL IN THE REC ROOM AFTER ALL.   70

BLOCK 8:   One has only to glance through the writings
of this period to sense the heightened excitement attendant upon these discoveries!

BLOCK 9: Possibly some diaschisis, which would of course help account for the apparent mirroring. And then, of course, we must not overlook the fact that she's left-handed.

BLOCK 10: Of course, you understand, these theories may all be wrong! [SOUND OF LAUGHTER FROM AN AUDIENCE] Any other questions? Yes, over there, in the corner.

BLOCK 11: Mrs. Stilson, this is Dr. Rogans. Dr. Rogans, this is Emily Stilson.

BLOCK 12: MALE VOICE: —definite possibility I would say of a tiny subclinical infarct in Penfield's area. Yes? FEMALE VOICE: Are you sure there is a Penfield's area? MALE VOICE: No. [LAUGHTER FROM HIS AUDIENCE] MALE VOICE AGAIN [ITSELF ON THE VERGE OF LAUGHTER]: But *something* is wrong with her! [RAUCOUS LAUGHTER FROM HIS AUDIENCE]

[*Note. Emerging out of the laughter in Block 12, a single musical TONE. This tone increases in intensity. It should carry through Block 16 and into* MRS. STILSON's *emergence from the maze of panels, helping to propel her into the realm and the memory to which this expedition has been leading.*]

BLOCK 13: The controversy, of course, is that some feel it's language without thought, and others, thought without language . . .

BLOCK 14: What it is, of course, is the symbol system. Their symbol system's shot. They can't make analogies.

BLOCK 15: You see, it's all so unpredictable. There are no fixed posts, no clear boundaries. The victim, you could say, has been cut adrift . . .

BLOCK 16: Ah, now you're really flying blind there!

MRS. STILSON EMERGES FROM THE MAZE OF CORRIDORS. SOUND PERHAPS OF WIND, OR BELLS. LIGHTS BLUE, SENSE AGAIN OF WEIGHTLESSNESS, AIRINESS.

MRS. STILSON: [IN AWE AND ECSTASY] *As I see it now, the plane was flying BACKWARDS! Really, wind that strong, didn't know it could be! Yet the sky was clear, not a cloud, crystal blue, gorgeous, angels could've lived in sky like that . . . I think the cyclone must've blown in on the Andes from the sea . . .*

BLUE LIGHT FADES. WIND GONE, BELLS GONE, MUSICAL TONE IS GONE.

[COMING OUT OF IT] Yes . . . [SHE LOOKS AROUND; GETS HER BEARINGS] *Yes, no ques-tion, this . . . place better.* [AND NOW SHE'S LANDED] *All these people just . . . like me, I guess.*

SHE TAKES IN WHERE SHE IS, SEEMS SLIGHTLY STUNNED TO BE BACK WHERE SHE STARTED. SENSE OF WONDERMENT APPARENT.

AN ATTENDANT APPROACHES.

ATTENDANT: Mrs. Stilson?

MRS. STILSON: [STARTLED] Oh!

ATTENDANT: Sorry to—

MRS. STILSON: Is it . . . ?

ATTENDANT: Yes.

MRS. STILSON: Did I . . . ?

ATTENDANT: No, no need to worry. Here, I'll take you.

THE ATTENDANT GUIDES MRS. STILSON TO A THERAPY ROOM, THOUGH, IN FACT, MORE LIKELY (ON THE STAGE) THE ROOM ASSEMBLES AROUND HER. IN THE ROOM ARE AMY, BILLY (A MAN IN HIS MIDDLE THIRTIES), MRS. TIMMINS (ELDERLY, IN A WHEELCHAIR), AND MR. BROWNSTEIN (ALSO ELDERLY AND IN A WHEELCHAIR).

THE ATTENDANT LEAVES.

AMY: Well! Now that we're all here on this lovely afternoon, I thought that maybe—

BILLY: She looks really good.

AMY: What?

BILLY: This new lady here, can't remember what her name is, no bother, anyhow, she looks really nice all dressed like this, an' I jus' wanna extent a nice welcome here on behalf o' all of us.

THE OTHER PATIENTS MUMBLE THEIR ASSENT.

AMY: Well, that is very nice, Billy, very nice. Can any of the rest of you remember this woman's name?

BILLY: I seen her I think when it is, yesterday, how's that?

AMY: Very good, that's right, you met her for the first time yesterday. Now, can any of you remember her name?

BILLY: Dolores.

AMY: [LAUGHING SLIGHTLY] No, not Dolores.

MR. BROWNSTEIN: She vas, I caught sight ya know, jussaminute, flahtied or vhat, vhere, midda [HE HUMS A NOTE]—

AMY: Music.

140 **MR. BROWNSTEIN:** Yeah right goodgirlie right she vas lissning, I caught slight, saw her vooding bockstond tipping-n-topping de foot vas jussnow like dis. [HE STARTS TO STAMP HIS FOOT]

AMY: Mrs. Stilson, were you inside listening to some
145 music just now?

MRS. STILSON: Well . . .

PAUSE.

[VERY FAST] Well now I was yes in the what in-the-in-the where the—

AMY: [CHEERFULLY] Ssssslllow dowwwwn.

THE OTHER PATIENTS LAUGH; MRS. TIMMINS SOFTLY ECHOES THE PHRASE "SLOW DOWN."

150 [SPEAKING VERY SLOWLY] Listen to yourself talking.

MRS. STILSON: [SPEAKING SLOWLY] Well yes, I was . . . listening and it was it was going in . . . good I

think, I'd say, very good yes I liked it very nice it made it very nice inside. 155

AMY: Well, good.

MRS. TIMMINS: Applawdgia!

AMY: Ah, Mrs. Timmins! You heard the music, too?

MRS. TIMMINS: [WITH A LAUGH] Ohshorrrrrn.
Yossssso, TV. 160

AMY: Well, good for you! Anyway, I'd like you all to know that this new person in our group is named Mrs. Stilson.

MR. BROWNSTEIN: Ssssssstaa-illllllsssim.

AMY: Right! Well done. Mr. Brownstein! 165

MR. BROWNSTEIN: [LAUGHING PROUDLY] It's vurktiddiDINGobitch!

AMY: That's right it's working. I told you it would.

BILLY: Hey! Wait, hold on here—jus' remembered!

AMY: What's that, Billy? 170

BILLY: You've been holdin' out pay up where is it?

AMY: Where . . . is what?

March 2008 production by the Bas Blue Theatre Company in Fort Collins, CO.

BILLY: Where is for all what I did all that time labor which you—don't kid me, I see you grinning back there ate up [HE MAKES MUNCHING SOUNDS] so where is it, where's the loot?

175

AMY: For the cheesecake.

BILLY: That's right you know it for the cheesecape, own recipe, extra-special, pay up.

180 **AMY:** [TO MRS. STILSON]   Billy is a terrific cook.

MRS. STILSON: [DELIGHTED]   Oh!

BILLY: Well used t' be, not now much what they say, anyhow, hah-hah! See? look, laughing, giggles, tries t' hide it, she knows she knows, scoundrel, thief, 185 can't sleep nights can you, people give their arms whatnots recipe like that one is. Cheapskate. Come on fork over hand it over, don't be chief.

AMY: . . . What?

BILLY: Don't be chief.

PAUSE.

190 You know, when someone don' pay, you say he's chief.

AMY: [WARMLY, NEARLY LAUGHING]   Billy, you're not listening.

BILLY: Okay not the word not the right word what's the word? I'll take any help you can give me. [HE 195 LAUGHS]

AMY: Cheap.

BILLY: That's it that's the word that's what you are, from now on I'm gonna sell my recipes somewheres else.

AMY: Billy, say cheap.

HE SIGHS MIGHTILY.

200 **BILLY:**   . . . Chief.

HER EXPRESSION TELLS HIM EVERYTHING.

Not right okay, try again this thing we can, what's its, lessee okay here we go CHARF! Nope. Not right. Ya know really, this could take all day.

AMY: Well then, the sooner you do it, the sooner we can 205 go on to what I've planned.

BILLY: You've got somethin' planned? You've never got somethin' planned.

AMY: I've *always* got something planned.

BILLY: Oh come on don' gimme that, you're jus' tryin' 210 to impress this new lady, really nice new lady, Mrs. . . .

AMY: Stilson.

BILLY: Yeah her, you're jus' tryin'—what's that word again?

AMY: Cheap.

BILLY: Cheap right okay lessee now— 215

AMY: Billy! You just said it!

BILLY: Did I? Good. Then maybe we can go on to somethin' else, such as when you're gonna fork over for the cheesecake, I could be a rich man now.

AMY: Billy, I never made the cheesecake. 220

BILLY: I'll bet you've gone sold the recipe to all the stores the whatnot everywhere fancy bigdeal places made a fortune, gonna retire any day t' your farm in New Jersey.

AMY: I don't have a farm in New Jersey, *you* have a 225 farm in New Jersey!

BILLY: Oh? Then what were you doin' on my farm then?

AMY: I wasn't on your farm, Billy, I've been here!

[BILLY STARTS ARGUING ABOUT SOMETHING INCOMPREHENSIBLE AND SEEMINGLY UN-RELATED TO FARM LIFE, THE ARGUMENT CONSISTING MOSTLY OF THE RECITATION OF A CONVOLUTED STRING OF NUMBERS; AMY CUTS HIM SHORT BEFORE HE GOES TOO FAR ASTRAY]

Billy, cheap, say cheap!

LONG SILENCE.

BILLY: [SIMPLY AND WITHOUT EFFORT]   Cheap. 230

AMY CHEERS.

[OVERJOYED] Cheap!— Cheap-cheap-cheap-cheap-cheap!

MR. BROWNSTEIN: I vas hoping you could polsya and git vid mustard all dis out of dis you gottit right good I say hutchit and congratulupsy! 235

AMY: Congratu*lations*.

MR. BROWNSTEIN: Yeah right dassit goodgirlie, phhhhew! fin'lly!

LIGHTS FADE TO BLACK ALL AROUND MRS. STILSON. NOTHING SEEN BUT HER.

SILENCE FOR A TIME.

MRS. STILSON: *What it was . . . how I heard it how I said it not the same, you would think so but it's not.* 240 *Sometimes . . . well it just goes in so fast, in-and-out all the sounds. I know they mean—*

PAUSE.

I mean I know they're . . . well like with me, helping, as their at their in their best way knowing how I guess they practice all the time so I'd say must be good or even better, helps me get the dark out just by going you know sssslowww and thinking smiling . . . it's not easy.

PAUSE.

Sometimes . . . how can . . . well it's just I think these death things, end it, stuff like sort of may be better not to listen anything no more at all or trying even talking cause what good's it, I'm so far away! Well it's crazy I don't mean it I don't think, still it's just like clouds that you can't push through. Still you do it, still you try to. I can't hear things same as others say them.

PAUSE.

So the death thing, it comes in, I don't ask it, it just comes in, plays around in there, I can't get it out till it's ready, goes out on its own. Same I guess for coming. I don't open up the door.

SILENCE.

LIGHTS UP ON A CHAIR, SMALL TABLE.

ON THE TABLE, A CASSETTE RECORDER.

MRS. STILSON GOES TO THE CHAIR. SITS. STARES AT THE RECORDER.

A FEW MOMENTS LATER, BILLY AND A DOCTOR ENTER.

BILLY: Oh, I'm sorry, I didn't know you was in . . . here or . . .

MRS. STILSON: Dr. Freedman said I could . . . use room and his . . . this . . . [SHE GESTURES TOWARD THE RECORDER]

DOCTOR: No problem, we'll use another room.

HE SMILES. EXIT BILLY AND DOCTOR.

MRS. STILSON TURNS BACK TO THE MACHINE. STARES AT IT. THEN SHE REACHES OUT, PRESSES A BUTTON.

DOCTOR'S VOICE: [FROM CASSETTE RECORDER] All right, essentially, a stroke occurs when there's a stoppage . . . When blood flow ceases in one part of the brain . . . And that brain can no longer get oxygen . . . And subsequently dies. Okay? Now, depending upon which part of the brain is affected by the stroke, you'll see differences in symptoms. Now what

you've had is a left cerebral infarction. Oh, by the way, you're doing much, much better. We were very worried when you first arrived . . .

SILENCE.

SHE CLICKS OFF THE RECORDING MACHINE. DOES NOTHING, STARES AT NOTHING. THEN SHE REACHES OUT AND PUSHES THE REWIND BUTTON. THE MACHINE REWINDS TO START OF TAPE. STOPS AUTOMATICALLY. SHE STARES AT THE MACHINE. DEEP BREATH. REACHES OUT AGAIN. PRESSES THE PLAYBACK BUTTON.

DOCTOR'S VOICE: All right, essentially, a stroke occurs when there's a stoppage . . . When blood flow ceases in one part of the brain . . . And that brain can no long—

SHE SHUTS IT OFF.

STARES INTO SPACE.

SILENCE.

———

MRS. STILSON WITH AMY SITTING NEXT TO HER ON ANOTHER CHAIR.

MRS. STILSON: [STILL STARING INTO SPACE] "Memory" . . .

PAUSE.

AMY: Yes, come on, "memory" . . .

NO RESPONSE.

Anything.

STILL NO RESPONSE.

[WARMLY]: Oh, come on, I bet there are lots of things you can talk about . . . You've been going out a lot lately . . . With your son . . . With your niece . . .

PAUSE.

What about Rhinebeck? Tell me about Rhinebeck.

PAUSE.

MRS. STILSON: On . . . Saturday . . . [SHE PONDERS] On . . . Sunday my . . . son . . . [PONDERS AGAIN] On Saturday my son . . . took me to see them out at Rhinebeck.

AMY: See what?

MRS. STILSON: What I used to . . . fly in.

AMY: Can you think of the word?

MRS. STILSON: . . . What word?

AMY: For what you used to fly in.

LONG PAUSE.

MRS. STILSON: Planes!

AMY: Very good!

300 MRS. STILSON: Old . . . planes.

AMY: That is very good. Really!

MRS. STILSON: I sat . . . inside one of them. He said
it was like the kind I used to . . . fly in and walk . . .
out on wings in. I couldn't believe I could have ever
305 done this.

PAUSE.

But he said I did, I had. He was very . . . proud.

PAUSE.

Then . . . I saw my hand was pushing on this . . .
stick . . . Then my hand was . . . pulling. Well I hadn't
you know asked my hand to do this, it just went and
310 did it on its own. So I said okay Emily, if this is how
it wants to do it you just sit back here and watch . . .
But . . . my head, it was really . . . hurting bad. And
I was up here both . . . sides, you know . . .

AMY: Crying.

315 MRS. STILSON: [WITH EFFORT] Yeah.

LONG PAUSE.

And then all at once—it remembered everything!

LONG PAUSE.

But now it doesn't.

SILENCE.

————

FAINT SOUND OF WIND. HINT OF BELLS.

THE SCREENS OPEN.

WE ARE OUTSIDE. SENSE OF DISTANCE
OPENNESS. ALL FEELING OF CONSTRAINT
IS GONE. AMY HELPS MRS. STILSON INTO
AN OVERCOAT; AMY IS IN AN OVERCOAT
ALREADY.

AMY: Are you sure you'll be warm enough?

MRS. STILSON: Oh yes . . .

AND THEY START TO WALK—A LEISURELY
STROLL THROUGH A PARK OR MEADOW,
SENSE OF WHITENESS EVERYWHERE. THEY

HEAD TOWARD A BENCH WITH SNOW ON
ITS SLATS. THE SOUND OF WIND GROWS
STRONGER.

FAINT SOUND OF AN AIRPLANE OVERHEAD,
THE SOUND QUICKLY DISAPPEARING.

MRS. STILSON: This is winter, isn't it?   320

AMY: Yes.

MRS. STILSON: That was just a guess, you know.

AMY: [WITH A WARM, EASY LAUGH] Well, it was a
good one, keep it up!

MRS. STILSON LAUGHS.

AMY STOPS BY THE BENCH.

Do you know what this is called?   325

MRS. STILSON: Bench!

AMY: Very good! No, I mean what's on top of it.

NO RESPONSE.

What I'm brushing off . . .

STILL NO RESPONSE.

What's falling from the sky . . .

LONG SILENCE.

MRS. STILSON: Where do you get names from?   330

AMY: I? From in here, same as you.

MRS. STILSON: Do you know how you do it?

AMY: No.

MRS. STILSON: Then how am I supposed . . . to learn?

AMY: [SOFTLY] I don't really know.   335

MRS. STILSON STARES AT AMY. THEN SHE
POINTS AT HER AND LAUGHS.

AT FIRST, AMY DOESN'T UNDERSTAND.

THEN SHE DOES.

AND THEN BOTH OF THEM ARE LAUGHING.

MRS. STILSON: Look. You see? [SHE SCOOPS SOME
SNOW OFF THE BENCH] If I pick this . . . stuff up
in my hand, then . . . I know its name. I didn't have
to pick it up to know . . . what it *was*.

AMY: No . . .   340

MRS. STILSON: But to find its name . . . [SHE
STARES AT WHAT IS IN HER HAND] I had to
pick it up.

AMY: What's its name?

345   MRS. STILSON: Snow. It's really nuts, isn't it!

AMY: It's peculiar!

THEY LAUGH.

THEN, LAUGHTER GONE, THEY SIT; STARE OUT.

SILENCE FOR A TIME.

MRS. STILSON: A strange thing happened to me . . .

PAUSE.

I think last night.

AMY: Can you remember it?

350   MRS. STILSON: Perfectly.

AMY: Ah!

MRS. STILSON: I think it may have been . . . you know, when you sleep . . .

AMY: A dream.

355   MRS. STILSON: Yes, one of those, but I'm not . . . sure that it was . . . that.

PAUSE. THEN SHE NOTICES THE SNOW IN HER HAND.

Is it all right if I . . . eat this?

AMY: Yes! We used to make a ball of it, then pour maple syrup on top. Did you ever do that?

360   MRS. STILSON: I don't know.

PAUSE.

No, I remember—I did!

SHE TASTES THE SNOW. SMILES

AFTER A TIME, THE SMILE VANISHES.

SHE TURNS BACK TO AMY.

Who was that man yesterday?

AMY: What man?

MRS. STILSON: In our group. He seemed all right.

365   AMY: Oh, that was last week.

MRS. STILSON: I thought for sure he was all right! I thought he was maybe, you know, a doctor.

AMY: Yes, I know.

MRS. STILSON: [SEARCHING HER MEMORY]   And
370   you asked him to show you where his . . . hand was.

AMY: And he knew.

MRS. STILSON: That's right, he raised his hand, he knew. So I thought, why is Amy joking?

SHE PONDERS.

Then you asked him . . . [SHE TRIES TO REMEMBER] . . . where . . . [SHE TURNS TO AMY]   375

AMY: His elbow was.

MRS. STILSON: Yes! And he . . . [SHE STRUGGLES TO FIND THE WORD]

AMY: [HELPING]   Pointed—

MRS. STILSON: [AT THE SAME TIME]   Pointed!   380
to . . . [BUT THE STRUGGLE'S GETTING HARDER]

AMY: The corner of the room.

MRS. STILSON: Yes.

PAUSE.

[SOFTLY] That was very . . . scary.   385

AMY: Yes.

MRS. STILSON STARES INTO SPACE.

SILENCE.

What is it that happened to you last night?

MRS. STILSON: Oh yes! Well, this . . . *person* . . . came into my room I couldn't tell if it was a man or woman or . . . young or old. I was in my bed and it came.   390
Didn't seem to have to walk just . . . came over to my . . . bed and . . . smiled at where I was.

PAUSE.

And then it said . . . [IN A WHISPER] "Emily . . . we're glad you changed your mind."

PAUSE.

And then . . . it turned and left.   395

AMY: Was it a doctor? [MRS. STILSON SHAKES HER HEAD] One of the staff? [MRS. STILSON SHAKES HER HEAD] How do you know?

MRS. STILSON: I just know.

PAUSE.

Then . . . I left my body.   400

AMY: *What?*

MRS. STILSON: [WITH GREAT EXCITEMENT]   I was on the . . . what's the name over me—

AMY: Ceiling?

405 MRS. STILSON: Yes! I was floating like a . . .

AMY: Cloud?

MRS. STILSON SHAKES HER HEAD.

Bird?

MRS. STILSON: Yes, up there at the—[SHE SEARCHES FOR THE WORD; FINDS IT]—ceiling, and I
410 looked down and I was still there in my bed! Wasn't even scared, which you'd think I would be . . . And I thought, wow! this is the life isn't it?

SOUND OF WIND.

LIGHTS BEGIN TO CHANGE.

AMY RECEDES INTO THE DARKNESS.

It comes now without my asking . . . Amy is still
beside me but I am somewhere else. I'm not scared.
415 *It has taken me, and it's clear again. Something is*
about to happen.

PAUSE.

AMY NOW COMPLETELY GONE.

MRS. STILSON IN A NARROW SPOT OF LIGHT, DARKNESS ALL AROUND.

I am in a plane, a Curtiss Jenny, and it's night.
Winter. Snow is falling. Feel the tremble of the wings!
How I used to walk out on them! Could I have really
420 *done— . . . Yes. What I'd do, I'd strap myself with a*
tether to the stays, couldn't see the tether from below,
then out I'd climb! Oh my, but it was wonderful! I
could feel the wind! shut my eyes, all alone—FEEL
THE SOARING!

THE WIND GROWS STRONGER.

THEN THE WIND DIES AWAY.

SILENCE.

SHE NOTICES THE CHANGE.

425 MRS. STILSON: *But this is in another time. Where*
I've been also . . . It is night and no one else is in the
plane. Is it . . . remembering?

PAUSE.

No . . . No, I'm simply there again!

PAUSE.

And I'm lost . . . I am lost, completely lost, have to get
430 *to . . . somewhere, Omaha I think. The radio is out,*
or rather for some reason picks up only Bucharest.

Clouds all around, no stars only snow, don't possess
a clue to where I am, flying blind, soon be out of gas
. . . And then the clouds open up a bit, just a bit, and
lights appear below, faint, a hint, like torches. Down 435
I drop! heart pounding with relief, with joy, hop-
ing for a landing place. I'll take anything—a field,
a street, and down I drop! No place to land . . . It's a
town but the smallest—one tiny street is all, three
street lamps, no one on the street, all deserted . . . just 440
a street and some faint light in the middle of dark-
ness. Nothing. Still, down I go! Maybe I can find a
name on a railroad station, find out where I am! . . .
But I see nothing I can read . . . So I begin to circle,
though I know I'm wasting fuel and I'll crash if I 445
keep this up! But somehow, I just can't tear myself
away! Though I know I should pull back on the stick,
get the nose up, head north into darkness—Omaha
must be north! But no, I keep circling this one small
silly street in this one small town . . . I'm scared to 450
leave it, that's what, as if I guess once away from it
I'll be inside something empty, black, and endless . . .

PAUSE.

So I keep circling—madness!—but I love it, what I
see below! And I just can't bring myself to give it up,
it's that simple—just can't bring myself to give it up! 455

PAUSE.

Then I know I have to. It's a luxury I can't afford.
Fuel is running low, almost gone, may be too late
anyway, so—

PAUSE.

I pull the nose up, kick the rudder, bank, and head
out into darkness all in terror! GOD, BUT IT TAKES 460
EFFORT! JUST DON'T WANT TO DO IT! . . . But
I do.

PAUSE.

[SUDDENLY CALM] *Actually, odd thing, once I*
did, broke free, got into the dark, found I wasn't even
scared . . . Or was I? [SLIGHT LAUGH] Can't re- 465
member . . . Wonder where that town was . . . ?

PAUSE.

Got to Omaha all right.

PAUSE.

Was it Omaha . . . ?

PAUSE.

Yes, I think so . . . Yes, Topeka, that was it!

PAUSE.

470 *God, but it was wonderful!* [SLIGHT LAUGH] *Awful scary sometimes, though!*

AMY SEEN IN THE DISTANCE.

AMY: Emily! Emily, are you all right!

SUDDEN, SHARP, TERRIFYING FLAPPING SOUND.

MRS. STILSON GASPS.

AMY DISAPPEARS.

MRS. STILSON: [RAPIDLY] *Around! There here spins saw it rumple chumps and jumps outgoes inside up*
475 *and . . . takes it, gives it, okay . . .*

PAUSE.

[EASIER] *Touch her for me, would you?*

PAUSE.

[EVEN EASIER] *Oh my, yes, and here it goes then out . . . there I think on . . . wings? Yes . . .*

PAUSE.

[SOFTLY, FAINT SMILE] *Thank you.*

NO TRACE OF TERROR.

MUSIC. HINT OF BELLS.

LIGHTS TO BLACK.

SILENCE.

Writing from Reading

Summarize

1 Mrs. Stilson has a number of problems with perception. List them.

2 In this play a woman suffers a stroke and seeming chaos follows. How does the play's structure mark her progress?

Analyze Craft

3 The playwright chooses to portray the chaos of what he calls Mrs. Stilson's "catastrophe" by a mix of image, sound, and physical action. If you were directing the play, what would the effect be if you follow his stage directions to the letter? What other choices might you make?

4 What elements of the play do you find familiar? Which do you find innovative?

5 How might Mrs. Stilson's perception problems manifest themselves on stage?

6 How is the author's research into the realm of medicine and neuroscience evident in his presentation of the action? What effect does it have on your reception of the play?

Analyze Voice

7 Try reading the first few pages and the last few pages aloud. How is speech presented? How does that affect your understanding of the text?

Synthesize Summary and Analysis

8 Research and insight into character come together on stage for this presentation of one woman's plight. Does the end strike you as a satisfying resolution to the problem?

Interpret the Play

9 How much does the play speak to your understanding of your own perception of the world?

"People go into the theater now hoping that they'll get out of it and go into movies. . . . The idea of developing actors, writers, who want to be actors and writers for the theater is, I think, diminished. . . . Can we continue to create new plays and new productions and new actors?" Conversation with Arthur Miller

Experimental Theater

For many theatergoers, contemporary theater has its roots in a slightly earlier period of experimental theater, that variety of post World War II European play that modifies the traditional assumptions and, often, the actual forms of classic theater. The influence of Bertolt Brecht's notions of Epic Theater (in which the playwright favors characters who represent certain ideas as opposed to characters from life) and the Theater of the Absurd (in which the playwright presents life as random seeming and, often, darkly comical) as practiced by Eugene Ionesco, and the so-called Theater of Cruelty of Antonin Artaud (in which the playwright employs shock value in order to jar the audience into a recognition of harsh reality) have all had an impact on contemporary playwrights. Nobel Laureate Samuel Beckett, with such plays as *Waiting for Godot*, *Endgame*, and *Krapp's Last Tape*, was a transformative presence on the stage and page. The influence of such playwrights can be felt in the work of Edward Albee (chapter 31) and Arthur Kopit, among other American playwrights, and in the work of

> "For a young playwright it doesn't cost anything for anybody to put your play on . . . the way you wrote it. But if it's going to cost a lot of money they get scared and they want to make the play safe." Conversation with Edward Albee

New York City's Living Theater, headed by Julian Beck and Judith Malina. Their productions of Jack Gelber's improvised *The Connection* and Kenneth Brown's *The Brig* had a major impact on the contemporary theater scene, as did Richard Schechner's production of *Dionysus in '69*. Work by such playwrights as Maria Irena Fornes and Liz Swados also enlivened the theater scene.

Joan Ackermann (b. 1950)

Joan Ackermann is a contemporary playwright whose plays have been produced off-Broadway and in theater venues across the nation. In addition to plays like *Zara Spook and Other Lures* (1993), *The Batting Cage* (1999), *Marcus Is Walking* (1999), *Staying Afloat* (2006), *The Big Picture,* and *The Taster,* Ackermann has written the music and lyrics for a musical—*Isabella: A Young Physician's Primer on the Perils of Love.* She also adapted one of her plays into the screenplay for the film *Off the Map,* which premiered at the Sundance Film Festival in 2003. Beyond her works for the stage, Ackermann is a journalist and has been a special contributor to *Sports Illustrated.* Her articles have also appeared in *The Atlantic Monthly* and *Time,* among other magazines. Ackermann makes her home in the Berkshires of Massachusetts, not far from the Mixed Company Theatre, a company which she cofounded and for which she serves as artistic director. It has been in existence for more than twenty-five years.

AS YOU READ Recall a struggle or competition similar to the one in the audition that you yourself might have experienced.

The Second Beam (2004)

CHARACTERS

GEORGIA

JENNIFER

MEG

CASTING AGENT

PATTI SCHARER

PLACE: An audition waiting room.

In an audition waiting room, three women— GEORGIA, JENNIFER, *and* MEG—*sit on folded chairs and study pages from a script. They are all dressed in lab coats as scientists. After a moment, a casting agent opens a door and sticks her head in.*

CASTING AGENT: Georgia? *[*GEORGIA *smiles up at her, grabs her stuff and exits. The other two smile at her as she exits into the audition room, closing the door behind her.* MEG *is the older of the two, more mature, grounded.* JENNI-
5 FER *is soft-spoken, sweet.]*

JENNIFER: *[Approaching* MEG.*]* Pardon me . . . Do you have a tissue? *[*MEG *opens her bag and gives her one. Goes back to studying.* JENNIFER *sits down with the tissue and very discreetly wipes under both her armpits.]* You were
10 at *The Flannerys.* *[*MEG *looks at her blankly.]* You read for the sister. Of the boxer, with the bad hand. The malpractice suit.

MEG: *[Remembering.]* Oh. Right.

JENNIFER: I heard that show didn't get picked up. You
15 were at *Mind of a Married Man,* too. The jockey's wife. *[Concerned.]* Are you memorizing that?

MEG: *[Friendly.]* No. No, just studying. *[Pause.]*

JENNIFER: Do you happen to know who got the part?

MEG: Which part. The sister, of the boxer?

20 **JENNIFER:** No. Yes.

MEG: Or the jockey's wife.

JENNIFER: Either. Both.

MEG: Well, the same actress got them both.

JENNIFER: Patti Scharer?

MEG: Patti Scharer.   25

JENNIFER: I knew it. Patti Scharer. Patti Scharer. Every part my agent sends me out on, every single part it seems, Patti Scharer gets. Care for a mint? *[*MEG *shakes her head no, takes out a lipstick and puts some on, looking at herself in a small compact mirror.]* Are you   30
doing an accent?

MEG: Accent?

JENNIFER: For the scientist.

MEG: What kind of accent?

JENNIFER: Foreign.   35

MEG: I think she's American. *[Pause.]*

JENNIFER: *[Concerned.]* So you're not doing an accent? *[*MEG *shakes her head, goes back to studying the pages.]* I was going to do a French accent. Madame Curie. The scientist. You don't think I should?   40

MEG: If you've worked on it that way. It's a choice.

JENNIFER: Yes, it is. It's a choice. *[Pause.]* I never know about choices. My agent always says they like it when you make a choice, but I'm not so sure. I've been making choices, strong choices, but . . . they haven't   45
really been panning out for me. *[She discreetly picks something out from between her teeth.]* I really need the work. I really, really, really need the work. I'm sorry, I'll let you concentrate. *[Pause.]* Have you read for

50   him before? *[MEG looks at her.]* Ethan Schroeder. The director. Have you read for him? *[MEG nods. Goes back to her pages, concentrating.]* My friend Annette says he's a monster. She read for him for a movie of the week and he ate his lunch the entire time.

55   **MEG:**   He can be a jerk.

JENNIFER: That's all I need. *[She sighs, smooths her skirt.]* Can I just ask you . . . is this lipstick, the color of my lipstick, all right? I've never worn this shade before.

60   **MEG:**   It looks good on you. It's a good color for you.

JENNIFER: You think so? Really?

MEG: I do. *[Smiling.]* It's a good "choice."

JENNIFER: Thanks. I don't know. It felt like a scientist choice. I don't know why. Sometimes you just have to
65   go with your gut. *[MEG nods, goes back to her pages.]*

JENNIFER: *[Worrying.]* Patti Scharer. Do you get the light thing? They won't expect us to understand that, do you think? Stopping light? They won't grill us about that.

70   **MEG:**   Probably not.

JENNIFER: I don't know. I read for the part of a veterinarian and they acted like they expected me to know everything about a dog's digestive system. I just winged it, talked about heartworm. I've seen them.
75   In a jar. *[MEG doesn't respond.]* It's not just about the money. Truth be known, I'm feeling kind of stuck. *[Pause.]* If he's eating in there, stuffing his mouth with California pizza, Koo-koo-charoo chicken . . . You said you've read for him?

80   **MEG:**   I used to go out with him.

JENNIFER: *[Stunned.]* You went out with him? You went out with Ethan Schroeder? *[MEG nods.]*

JENNIFER: Ohmygod, I'm so sorry. What I said . . . I didn't mean to call him a monster. Maybe he
85   was just . . . hungry when my friend read for him. Maybe he's perfectly—

MEG: It's okay. A lot of people think he's an asshole.

JENNIFER: They do. You're not going out with him any more? *[MEG shakes her head.]* You're still friends?
90   I mean, you're okay reading for him?

MEG: I really like this part.

JENNIFER: *[Not really like it.]* You do?

MEG: I do. How often does that happen?

JENNIFER: Yeah. Really. You must like this part.

MEG: I find the subject fascinating. I've read quite a bit   95
about it.

JENNIFER: Oh. So . . . Light travels a hundred and eighty thousand miles an hour . . .

MEG: A second.

JENNIFER: And . . . *[JENNIFER waits for MEG to ex-*   100
plain it.] Then they stop it in a jar. *[Thinking . . .]* Like heartworm. Preserve it in formaldehyde.

MEG: Chilled sodium gas, actually.

JENNIFER: It just hangs in there? Frozen?

MEG: Well, the light goes out. It gets fainter and fainter   105
as it slows down. The most amazing part to me—it's all amazing—they can revive the light any time by flashing a second beam of light through the gas.

JENNIFER: Oh.

MEG: They can bring a beam of light to a full stop, hold   110
it, and then send it on its way with a second beam. *[Pause.]*

JENNIFER: I like scenes best . . . when I can go deep. Cry. I like emotion. My background is theatre.

MEG: Not a lot of emotion in these scenes, not   115
ostensibly.

JENNIFER: No. That's why I was thinking the French . . .

MEG: Go for the accent.

120 **JENNIFER:** You think so? [*Another actress enters. She is very appealing, made-up, a knock-out. She takes a seat. Exudes confidence. Both* MEG *and* JENNIFER *look at her, silently, as she takes out many pages and starts going through them.*]

125 **PATTI:** [*To* JENNIFER, *all business.*] Excuse me, are your pages with the reporter dated May eleventh or May fifteenth? [JENNIFER *looks at her pages . . .*]

JENNIFER: The reporter? I don't have . . . [JENNIFER *flips through, looking . . .*]

130 **PATTI:** Never mind. [*Noticing . . .*] Meg.

MEG: Hi, Patti.

PATTI: How *are* you? [MEG *nods, friendly, a little guarded.*]

PATTI: It's so great to see you, are you here now?

MEG: I'm here.

135 **PATTI:** You know I'd heard that. I ran into Carolyn, she was stage managing *Vanya* at the Taper, she told me you'd moved back.

MEG: I did.

PATTI: That's great. And you're reading for Ethan?

140 **MEG:** I am.

PATTI: Wow. Wow. [PATTI *studies* MEG, *waiting for some kind of response, which is not forthcoming.*]

MEG: How's Olivia?

145 **PATTI:** Olivia is three, God help me. Meg, can I borrow your lipstick, I actually forgot mine.

MEG: I'm sorry. I actually left all my makeup in the car.

PATTI: Really? What were you thinking? [PATTI *maintains her charming smile, miffed underneath.* JENNIFER *stares at* PATTI *in a mixed stupor of defeat and envy.*]

150 **JENNIFER:** [*Stirring.*] I have some lipstick. You can borrow.

PATTI: [*Brightly.*] Great. Thanks. [JENNIFER *reaches down into her purse and takes out her lipstick, takes off the cap, and offers it to* PATTI. PATTI, *looking at* JENNIFER's 155 *lips:*] Oh. Is it the color you're wearing?

JENNIFER: Uh-huh.

PATTI: That's okay. That color . . . I can't wear that color. But, thanks. [*Mortified,* JENNIFER *looks down at the color, gradually retreats her hand, puts the cover back on and sticks the lipstick back in her purse. Pause as all study* 160 *the script.*]

PATTI: [*To* MEG.] I admire you, Meg. I really do. Reading for Ethan. That takes guts.

MEG: Not really.

165 **PATTI:** The way he treated you. You know Carolyn's first A. D. [MEG *nods.*] You know they're an item. Ethan and Carolyn. She's pregnant. That's ironic, huh? [MEG *did not know this. She flinches slightly. The door opens and* GEORGIA *enters with the casting agent* 170 *behind her.* GEORGIA *grabs a sweater she left on a chair, waves to the* CASTING AGENT, *exiting.*]

CASTING AGENT: Thanks, Georgia. Patti. You made it.

PATTI: I'm so sorry I'm late. The 405 was a nightmare.

175 **CASTING AGENT:** You want to come in? Or do you want to take a minute. Jennifer . . . ? [JENNIFER, *discombobulated, jumps up, dropping all her pages as* PATTI *grabs her purse, coat, stands up.*]

180 **PATTI:** I'm fine. [PATTI *heads smoothly into the audition room. The* CASTING AGENT *smiles at* MEG, *looks down at the pages* JENNIFER *has dropped, and exits into the audition room.*]

JENNIFER: [*Crying, wiping her nose on her sleeve.*] I'm sorry. Do you have another tissue? [MEG *hands her another tissue which* JENNIFER *uses to wipe her nose and wipe* 185 *away tears.* JENNIFER *grabs her stuff and hurries out.*]

JENNIFER: [*Not looking at* MEG.] It was very nice meeting you.

MEG: Where are you going?

190 **JENNIFER:** [*Crying, halfway out the door.*] I don't know. Bye.

MEG: Wait! [JENNIFER *turns and looks at her.*] You can get this part. [JENNIFER *is sobbing.*]

JENNIFER: I can't get this part.

MEG: You can.

195 **JENNIFER:** I can't. I can't even audition for this part.

MEG: Sit down.

JENNIFER: What?

MEG: Pull yourself together. Sit down.

JENNIFER: [*Weepy, discombobulated.*] Where?

MEG: On the chair. Go ahead. Sit! *[JENNIFER sits back down on her chair, sniffling.]* Here. Put these on. *[MEG takes the pair of tortoise-shell glasses she is wearing and gives them to JENNIFER.]* Put them on. *[JENNIFER does.]*

JENNIFER: Why does she want this part? It's not even very big.

MEG: Patti Scharer is not going to get this part.

JENNIFER: Yes, she is.

MEG: No she's not.

JENNIFER: *[Crying.]* She's already got it. She's already in there. With the part.

MEG: Ethan can't stand Patti Scharer. He's not going to give her this part. He's going to give you this part, because it's your part. *[JENNIFER, pauses crying to look at her.]*

JENNIFER: He can't stand her?

MEG: Jennifer, listen to me. Light . . . is emotion. *[JENNIFER, somewhat calmer but still a mess, response to the intensity of MEG's voice. Listens . . .]* Think of light, a beam of light . . . as a story, a story with its own past, its own history. The light has been who knows where, has illuminated who knows what. Maybe it's been traveling for a long, long time—decades, centuries. And somewhere along its journey, it starts to slow down . . . Take a pause, fold into itself . . . *[The lights on them start to dim . . .]* Okay, so . . . Now, I want you to imagine you're at the theatre. You're sitting in the audience, and you're watching a play. You say you love theatre?

JENNIFER: *[Blowing her nose.]* I do. Why are you doing this?

MEG: So the curtain has just opened, and there are three people on stage, and they're still, not moving. *[Lights keep dimming.]* Who are these people, these characters? What is their past? Their history? We don't know. At the beginning of the play, we don't know anything about them at all. Their pasts are frozen. Suspended. *[The lights stop dimming, and MEG and JENNIFER are still for a few moments, frozen in close to dark.]* Then the play begins . . . *[Lights start to slowly fade up.]* . . . and we start to learn things about them. Information unfolds. One character leaves. Facts are revealed. We learn that this character really needs something, or this character has a dream, a passion, or maybe this one's been hurt . . . *[A spotlight lights her dimly and gets brighter slowly during the following . . .]* . . . been hurt really, really badly and we don't know how. Within minutes we can learn so much about them. In less than ten minutes, we can see the DNA of their whole lives. Even though there are mysteries, we feel we know them, quite well. Then, there comes that moment, that inevitable pivotal moment in a scene when things turn. The epiphany. The revelation. Something is illuminated. *[The spotlight on her is very bright now. Other lights are up to half full.]*

JENNIFER: I think . . . you're probably saying something but I'm not sure what it is. *[MEG looks at her. Takes the barrette out of her hair.]*

MEG: I think you should put your hair back. Here, take my barrette. *[MEG hands her barrette to JENNIFER, who puts her hair back.]* That's good. You look . . . like a scientist.

JENNIFER: What did Ethan Schroeder do to you that was so bad? *[MEG takes a moment to answer.]*

MEG: Nothing terribly original. *[MEG goes to get her things to leave.]*

JENNIFER: You're not going to read for this part?

MEG: No.

JENNIFER: One thing . . . I do feel emotional, right now. *[A spotlight on JENNIFER starts to come up, as all other lights start to fade, including the spotlight on MEG.]* For you, mainly.

MEG: Use it. Hold it inside. And, I would suggest you drop the accent.

JENNIFER: Really?

MEG: You don't need it. Another thing . . . when you go in there, tell Ethan he looks like a young Richard Burton.

JENNIFER: Okay. I can do that. I can do that.

MEG: This is your part. *[All lights are out now except the spotlight on JENNIFER.]*

JENNIFER: *[Confidently, seriously looking like a scientist.]* I know. This is my part. This is my part. *[The spotlight on JENNIFER is up to full. Then it fades out.]*

Writing from Reading

Summarize

1 In this play a trio of actresses shows up at an audition, with unexpected results. Describe the temperaments of each of the actresses.

Analyze Craft

2 How would you characterize the relationships between the two actresses as the scene opens? Does the mood change? If so, what prompts the change? How does the entrance of the third actress affect the situation?

Analyze Voice

3 How would you describe the overall tone of the play? How is this tone achieved?

Synthesize Summary and Analysis

4 How does the playwright integrate science—the experiment with the beam of light—into the action of the play?

Interpret the Play

5 How does the motif of illusion versus reality unfold in this play?

6 Would a male playwright have treated the scene differently, and in what ways?

David Henry Hwang (b. 1957)

Born in a suburb of Los Angeles, David Henry Hwang has become one of the most prominent Asian-American voices in contemporary drama. His parents, Chinese by birth, met and married in the United States, raising Hwang under his mother's fundamentalist Christian influence. Although Hwang later abandoned fundamentalism, it continues to be an element in his plays. Hwang began writing plays while an undergraduate at Stanford, and his first, *F.O.B*, which stands for "fresh off the boat" in reference to Chinese immigrants, met with great success. His biggest success came with *M. Butterfly,* a play that was performed on Broadway and that brought Hwang a Tony Award and a Pulitzer Prize nomination. Hwang's other projects include collaborations with the composer Phillip Glass on a science-fiction production and on an opera about Christopher Columbus. He also collaborated on the script for the Disney rock musical version of *Aida* and for the screen adaptation of A.S. Byatt's novel *Possession*. Although his work shows great range and variety, it most often concerns itself with the Asian-American identity.

AS YOU READ Think of the work on the railroad performed by all the Chinese laborers who never appear in the play. What is the "dance" the two actors perform against that unseen backdrop of labor.

The Dance and the Railroad (1982)

CHARACTERS

LONE, *twenty years old, ChinaMan railroad worker.*

MA, *eighteen years old, ChinaMan railroad worker.*

PLACE A mountaintop near the transcontinental railroad.

TIME June, 1867.

SYNOPSIS OF SCENES
Scene 1. Afternoon
Scene 2. Afternoon, a day later.
Scene 3. Late afternoon, four days later.
Scene 4. Late that night.
Scene 5. Just before the following dawn.

SCENE 1

A mountaintop. LONE is practicing opera steps. He swings his pigtail around like a fan. MA enters, cautiously, watches from a hidden spot. MA approaches LONE.

LONE: So, there are insects hiding in the bushes.

MA: Hey, listen, we haven't met, but—

LONE: I don't spend time with insects.

[LONE whips his hair into MA's face; MA backs off; LONE pursues him, swiping at MA with his hair.]

MA: What the—? Cut it out!

[MA pushes LONE away.]

5 **LONE:** Don't push me.

MA: What was that for?

LONE: Don't ever push me again.

MA: You mess like that, you're gonna get pushed.

LONE: Don't push me.

MA: You started it. I just wanted to watch.   10

LONE: You "just wanted to watch." Did you ask my permission?

MA: What?

LONE: Did you?

MA: C'mon.   15

LONE: You can't expect to get in for free.

MA: Listen. I got some stuff you'll wanna hear.

LONE: You think so?

MA: Yeah. Some advice.

LONE: Advice? How old are you, anyway?   20

MA: Eighteen.

LONE: A child.

MA: Yeah. Right. A child. But listen—

LONE: A child who tries to advise a grown man—

MA: Listen, you got this kind of attitude.   25

LONE: —is a child who will never grow up.

MA: You know, the ChinaMen down at camp, they can't stand it.

LONE: Oh?

MA: Yeah. You gotta watch yourself. You know what   30
they say? They call you "Prince of the Mountain." Like you're too good to spend time with them.

LONE: Perceptive of them.

MA: After all, you never sing songs, never tell stories.
35   They say you act like your spit is too clean for them,
        and they got ways to fix that.

LONE: Is that so?

MA: Like they're gonna bury you in the shit buckets, so
        you'll have more to clean than your nails.

40 **LONE:**   But I don't shit.

MA: Or they're gonna cut out your tongue, since you
        never speak to them.

LONE: There's no one here worth talking to.

MA: Cut it out, Lone. Look, I'm trying to help you, all
45   right? I got a solution.

LONE: So young yet so clever.

MA: That stuff you're doing—it's beautiful. Why don't
        you do it for the guys at camp? Help us celebrate?

LONE: What will "this stuff" help celebrate?

50 **MA:**   C'mon. The strike, of course. Guys on a railroad
        gang, we gotta stick together, you know.

LONE: This is something to celebrate?

MA: Yeah. Yesterday, the weak-kneed ChinaMen, they
        were running around like chickens without a head:
55   "The white devils are sending their soldiers! Shoot us
        all!" But now, look—day four, see? Still in one piece.
        Those soldiers—we've never seen a gun or a bullet.

LONE: So you're all warrior-spirits, huh?

MA: They're scared of us, Lone—that's what it means.

60 **LONE:**   I appreciate your advice. Tell you what—you go
        down—

MA: Yeah?

LONE: Down to the camp—

MA: Okay.

65 **LONE:**   To where the men are—

MA: Yeah?

LONE: Sit there—

MA: Yeah?

LONE: And wait for me.

70 **MA:**   Okay.

[Pause.]

That's it? What do you think I am?

LONE: I think you're an insect interrupting my prac-
        tice. So fly away. Go home.

MA: Look, I didn't come here to get laughed at.

LONE: No, I suppose you didn't.   75

MA: So just stay up here. By yourself. You deserve it.

LONE: I do.

MA: And don't expect any more help from me.

LONE: I haven't gotten any yet.

MA: If one day, you wake up and your head is buried in 80
        the shit can—

LONE: Yes?

MA: You can't find your body, your tongue is cut out—

LONE: Yes.

MA: Don't worry, 'cuz I'll be there.   85

LONE: Oh.

MA: To make sure your mother's head is sitting right
        next to yours.

[MA exits.]

LONE: His head is too big for this mountain. *[Returns to
        practicing]*   90

SCENE 2

Mountaintop. Next day. LONE is practicing. MA enters.

MA: Hey.

LONE: You? Again?

MA: I forgive you.

LONE: You . . . what?

MA: For making fun of me yesterday. I forgive you.   5

LONE: You can't—

MA: No. Don't thank me.

LONE: You can't forgive me.

MA: No. Don't mention it.

LONE: You—! I never asked for your forgiveness.   10

MA: I know. That's just the kinda guy I am.

LONE: This is ridiculous. Why don't you leave? Go
        down to your friends and play soldiers, sing songs,
        tell stories.

15   **MA:**   Ah! See? That's just it. I got other ways I wanna spend my time. Will you teach me the opera?

LONE: What?

MA: I wanna learn it. I dreamt about it all last night.

LONE: No.

20   **MA:**   The dance, the opera—I can do it.

LONE: You think so?

MA: Yeah. When I get outa here, I wanna go back to China and perform.

LONE: You want to become an actor?

25   **MA:**   Well, I wanna perform.

LONE: Don't you remember the story about the three sons whose parents send them away to learn a trade? After three years, they return. The first one says, "I have become a coppersmith." The parents say, "Good.
30   Second son, what have you become?" "I've become a silversmith." "Good—and youngest son, what about you?" "I have become an actor." When the parents hear that their son has become only an actor, they are very sad. The mother beats her head against the
35   ground until the ground, out of pity, opens up and swallows her. The father is so angry he can't even speak, and the anger builds up inside him until it blows his body to pieces—little bits of his skin are found hanging from trees days later. You don't know
40   how you endanger your relatives by becoming an actor.

MA: Well, I don't wanna become an "actor." That sounds terrible. I just wanna perform. Look, I'll be rich by the time I get out of here, right?

45   **LONE:**   Oh?

MA: Sure. By the time I go back to China, I'll ride in gold sedan chairs, with twenty wives fanning me all around.

LONE: Twenty wives? This boy is ambitious.

50   **MA:**   I'll give out pigs on New Year's and keep a stable of small birds to give to any woman who pleases me. And in my spare time, I'll perform.

LONE: Between your twenty wives and your birds, where will you find a free moment?

55   **MA:**   I'll play Gwan Gung and tell stories of what life was like on the Gold Mountain.

LONE: Ma, just how long have you been in "America"?

MA: Huh? About four weeks.

LONE: You are a big dreamer.

MA: Well, all us ChinaMen here are—right? Men with 60 little dreams—have little brains to match. They walk with their eyes down, trying to find extra grains of rice on the ground.

LONE: So, you know all about "America"? Tell me, what kind of stories will you tell? 65

MA: I'll say, "We laid tracks like soldiers. Mountains? We hung from cliffs in baskets and the winds blew us like birds. Snow? We lived underground like moles for days at a time. Deserts? We—"

LONE: Wait. Wait. How do you know these things after 70 only four weeks?

MA: They told me—the other ChinaMen on the gang. We've been telling stories ever since the strike began.

LONE: They make it sound like it's very enjoyable.

MA: They said it is. 75

LONE: Oh? And you believe them?

MA: They're my friends. Living underground in winter—sounds exciting, huh?

LONE: Did they say anything about the cold?

MA: Oh, I already know about that. They told me about 80 the mild winters and the warm snow.

LONE: Warm snow?

MA: When I go home, I'll bring some back to show my brothers.

LONE: Bring some—? On the boat? 85

MA: They'll be shocked—they never seen American snow before.

LONE: You can't. By the time you get snow to the boat, it'll have melted, evaporated, and returned as rain already. 90

MA: No.

LONE: No?

MA: Stupid.

LONE: Me?

MA: You been here awhile, haven't you? 95

LONE: Yes. Two years.

MA: Then how come you're so stupid? This is the Gold Mountain. The snow here doesn't melt. It's not wet.

LONE: That's what they told you?

100   **MA:**   Yeah. It's true.

LONE: Did anyone show you any of this snow?

MA: No. It's not winter.

LONE: So where does it go?

MA: Huh?

105   **LONE:**   Where does it go, if it doesn't melt? What happens to it?

MA: The snow? I dunno. I guess it just stays around.

LONE: So where is it? Do you see any?

MA: Here? Well, no, but . . . *[Pause]* This is probably
110   one of those places where it doesn't snow—even in winter.

LONE: Oh.

MA: Anyway, what's the use of me telling you what you
already know? Hey, c'mon—teach me some of that
115   stuff. Look—I've been practicing the walk—how's
this? *[Demonstrates]*

LONE: You look like a duck in heat.

MA: Hey—it's a start, isn't it?

LONE: Tell you what—you want to play some *die siu*?

120   **MA:**   *Die siu?* Sure.

LONE: You know, I'm pretty good.

MA: Hey, I play with the guys at camp. You can't be any
better than Lee—he's really got it down.

[LONE pulls out a case with two dice.]

LONE: I used to play till morning.

125   **MA:**   Hey, us too. We see the sun start to rise, and say,
"Hey, if we go to sleep now, we'll never get up for
work." So we just keep playing.

LONE: *[Holding out dice]* *Die* or *siu*?

MA: *Siu.*

130   **LONE:**   You sure?

MA: Yeah!

LONE: All right. *[He rolls.]* *Die!*

MA: *Siu!*

[They see the result.]

MA: Not bad.

*[They continue taking turns rolling through the following
section; MA always loses.]*

LONE: I haven't touched these in two years.   135

MA: I gotta practice more.

LONE: Have you lost much money?

MA: Huh? So what?

LONE: Oh, you have gold hidden in all your shirt
linings, huh?   140

MA: Here in "America"—losing is no problem. You
know—End of the Year Bonus?

LONE: Oh, right.

MA: After I get that, I'll laugh at what I lost.

LONE: Lee told you there was a bonus, right?   145

MA: How'd you know?

LONE: When I arrived here, Lee told me there was a
bonus, too.

MA: Lee teach you how to play?

LONE: Him? He talked to me a lot.   150

MA: Look, why don't you come down and start playing
with the guys again?

LONE: "The guys."

MA: Before we start playing, Lee uses a stick to write
"Kill!" in the dirt.   155

LONE: You seem to live for your nights with "the guys."

MA: What's life without friends, huh?

LONE: Well, why do *you* think I stopped playing?

MA: Hey, maybe you were the one getting killed, huh?

LONE: What?   160

MA: Hey just kidding.

LONE: Who's getting killed here?

MA: Just a joke.

LONE: That's not a joke, it's blasphemy.

MA: Look, obviously you stopped playing 'cause you   165
wanted to practice the opera.

LONE: Do you understand that discipline?

MA: But, I mean, you don't have to overdo it either. You
don't have to treat 'em like dirt. I mean, who are you
trying to impress?   170

[Pause. LONE throws dice into the bushes.]

LONE: Oooops. Better go see who won.

MA: Hey! C'mon! Help me look!

LONE: If you find them, they are yours.

MA: You serious?

175 LONE: Yes.

MA: Here. *[Finds the dice]*

LONE: Who won?

MA: I didn't check.

LONE: Well, no matter. Keep the dice. Take them and
180 go play with your friends.

MA: Here. *[He offers them to* LONE.] A present.

LONE: A present? This isn't a present!

MA: They're mine, aren't they? You gave them to me,
right?

185 LONE: Well, yes, but—

MA: So now I'm giving them to you.

LONE: You can't give me a present. I don't want them.

MA: You wanted them enough to keep them two years.

LONE: I'd forgotten I had them.

190 MA: See, I know, Lone. You wanna get rid of me. But
you can't. I'm paying for lessons.

LONE: With my dice.

MA: Mine now. *[He offers them again.]* Here.

[Pause. LONE *runs* MA's *hand across his forehead.]*

LONE: Feel this.

195 MA: Hey!

LONE: Pretty wet, huh?

MA: Big deal.

LONE: Well, it's not from playing *die siu*.

MA: I know how to sweat. I wouldn't be here if I didn't.

200 LONE: Yes, but are you willing to sweat after you've
finished sweating? Are you willing to come up after
you've spent the whole day chipping half an inch off a
rock, and punish your body some more?

MA: Yeah. Even after work, I still—

205 LONE: No, you don't. You want to gamble, and tell
dirty stories, and dress up like women to do shows.

MA: Hey, I never did that.

LONE: You've only been here a month. *[Pause.]* And
what about "the guys"? They're not going to treat
you so well once you stop playing with them. Are you 210
willing to work all day listening to them whisper,
"That one—let's put spiders in his soup"?

MA: They won't do that to me. With you, it's different.

LONE: Is it?

MA: You don't have to act that way. 215

LONE: What way?

MA: Like you're so much better than them.

LONE: No. You haven't even begun to understand. To
practice every day, you must have a fear to force you
up here. 220

MA: A fear? No—it's 'cause what you're doing is
beautiful.

LONE: No.

MA: I've seen it.

LONE: It's ugly to practice when the mountain has 225
turned your muscles to ice. When my body hurts too
much to come here, I look at the other ChinaMen
and think, "They are dead. Their muscles work only
because the white man forces them. I live because
I can still force my muscles to work for me." Say it. 230
"They are dead."

MA: No. They're my friends.

LONE: Well, then, take your dice down to your friends.

MA: But I want to learn—

LONE: This is your first lesson. 235

MA: Look, it shouldn't matter—

LONE: It does.

MA: It shouldn't matter what I think.

LONE: Attitude is everything.

MA: But as long as I come up, do the exercises— 240

LONE: I'm not going to waste time on a quitter.

MA: I'm not!

LONE: Then say it—"They are dead men."

MA: I can't.

LONE: Then you will never have the dedication. 245

MA: That doesn't prove anything.

LONE: I will not teach a dead man.

MA: What?

LONE: If you can't see it, then you're dead too.

250   MA: Don't start pinning—

LONE: Say it!

MA: All right.

LONE: What?

MA: All right. I'm one of them. I'm a dead man too.

  [Pause.]

255   LONE: I thought as much. So, go. You have your friends.

MA: But I don't have a teacher.

LONE: I don't think you need both.

MA: Are you sure?

LONE: I'm being questioned by a child.

  [LONE returns to practicing. Silence.]

260   MA: Look, Lone, I'll come up here every night—after work—I'll spend my time practicing, okay? *[Pause]* But I'm not gonna say that they're dead. Look at them. They're on strike; dead men don't go on strike, Lone. The white devils—they try and stick us with a 265 ten-hour day. We want a return to eight hours and also a fourteen-dollar-a-month raise. I learned the demon English—listen: "Eight hour a day good for white man, alla same good for ChinaMan." These are the demands of live ChinaMen, Lone. Dead men 270 don't complain.

LONE: All right, this is something new. But no one can judge the ChinaMen till after the strike.

MA: They say we'll hold out for months if we have to. The smart men will live on what we've hoarded.

275   LONE: A ChinaMan's mouth can swallow the earth. *[He takes the dice.]* While the strike is on, I'll teach you.

MA: And afterwards?

LONE: Afterwards—we'll decide then whether these are dead or live men.

280   MA: When can we start?

LONE: We've already begun. Give me your hand.

SCENE 3

  LONE *and* MA *are doing physical exercises.*

MA: How long will it be before I can play Gwan Gung?

LONE: How long before a dog can play the violin?

MA: Old Ah Hong—have you heard him play the violin?

LONE: Yes. Now, he should take his violin and give it to a dog.   5

MA: I think he sounds okay.

LONE: I think he caused that avalanche last winter.

MA: He used to play for weddings back home.

LONE: Ah Hong?

MA: That's what he said.   10

LONE: You probably heard wrong.

MA: No.

LONE: He probably said he played for funerals.

MA: He's been playing for the guys down at camp.

LONE: He should play for the white devils—that will   15 end this stupid strike.

MA: Yang told me for sure—it'll be over by tomorrow.

LONE: Eight days already. And Yang doesn't know anything.

MA: He said they're already down to an eight-hour day   20 and five dollar raise at the bargaining sessions.

LONE: Yang eats too much opium.

MA: That's doesn't mean he's wrong about this.

LONE: You can't trust him. One time—last year—he went around camp looking in everybody's eyes and   25 saying, "Your nails are too long. They're hurting my eyes." This went on for a week. Finally, all the men clipped their nails, made a big pile, which they wrapped in leaves and gave to him. Yang used the nails to season his food—he put it in his soup,   30 sprinkled it on his rice, and never said a word about it again. Now tell me—are you going to trust a man who eats other men's fingernails?

MA: Well, all I know is we won't go back to work until they meet all our demands. Listen, teach me some   35 Gwan Gung steps.

LONE: I should have expected this. A boy who wants to have twenty wives is the type who demands more than he can handle.

MA: Just a few.   40

LONE: It takes years before an actor can play Gwan Gung.

MA: I can do it. I spend a lot of time watching the opera when it comes around. Every time I see Gwan Gung, I say, "Yeah. That's me. The god of fighters. The god of adventurers. We have the same kind of spirit."

LONE: I tell you, if you work very hard, when you return to China, you can perhaps be the Second Clown.

MA: Second Clown?

LONE: If you work hard.

MA: What's the Second Clown?

LONE: You can play the *p'i p'a*, and dance and jump all over.

MA: I'll buy them.

LONE: Excuse me?

MA: I'm going to be rich, remember? I'll buy a troupe and force them to let me play Gwan Gung.

LONE: I hope you have enough money, then, to pay audiences to sit through your show.

MA: You mean, I'm going to have to practice here every night—and in return, all I can play is the Second Clown?

LONE: If you work hard.

MA: Am I that bad? Maybe I shouldn't even try to do this. Maybe I should just go down.

LONE: It's not you. Everyone must earn the right to play Gwan Gung. I entered opera school when I was ten years old. My parents decided to sell me for ten years to this opera company. I lived with eighty other boys and we slept in bunks four beds high and hid our candy and rice cakes from each other. After eight years, I was studying to play Gwan Gung.

MA: Eight years?

LONE: I was one of the best in my class. One day, I was summoned by my master, who told me I was to go home for two days, because my mother had fallen very ill and was dying. When I arrived home, Mother was standing at the door waiting, not sick at all. Her first words to me, the son away for eight years, were, "You've been playing while your village has starved. You must go to the Gold Mountain and work."

MA: And you never returned to school?

LONE: I went from a room with eighty boys to a ship with three hundred men. So, you see, it does not come easily to play Gwan Gung.

MA: Did you want to play Gwan Gung?

LONE: What a foolish question!

MA: Well, you're better off this way.

LONE: What?

MA: Actors—they don't make much money. Here, you make a bundle, then go back and be an actor again. Best of both worlds.

LONE: "Best of both worlds."

MA: Yeah!

[LONE *drops to the ground, begins imitating a duck, waddling and quacking.*]

MA: What are you doing?

[LONE *quacks.*]

You're a duck?

[LONE *quacks.*]

I can see that.

[LONE *quacks.*]

Is this an exercise? Am I supposed to do this?

[LONE *quacks.*]

This is dumb. I never seen Gwan Gung waddle.

[LONE *quacks.*]

Okay. All right. I'll do it.

[MA *and* LONE *quack and waddle.*]

You know, I never realized before how uncomfortable a duck's life is. And you have to listen to yourself quacking all day. Go crazy!

[LONE *stands up straight.*]

Now, what was that all about?

LONE: No, no. Stay down there, duck.

MA: What's the—

LONE: [*Prompting*] Quack, quack, quack

MA: I don't—

LONE: Act your species!

MA: I'm not a duck!

LONE: Nothing worse than a duck that doesn't know his place.

MA: All right. [*Mechanically*] Quack, quack.

LONE: More.

115   MA: Quack.

LONE: More!

MA: Quack, quack, quack!

[MA *now continues quacking, as* LONE *gives commands.*]

LONE: Louder! It's your mating call! Think of your
twenty duck wives! Good! Louder! Project! More!
120   Don't slow down! Put your tail feathers into it! They
can't hear you!

[MA *is now quacking up a storm.* LONE *exits, unnoticed
by* MA.]

MA: Quack! Quack! Quack! Quack. Quack . . . quack.

[*He looks around.*]

Quack . . . quack . . . Lone? . . . Lone?

[*He waddles around the stage looking.*]

Lone, where are you? Where'd you go?

[*He stops, scratches his left leg with his right foot.*]

125   C'mon—stop playing around. What is this?

[LONE *enters as a tiger, unseen by* MA.]

Look, let's call it a day, okay? I'm getting hungry.

[MA *turns around, notices* LONE *right before* LONE *is to
bite him.*]

Aaaaah! Quack, quack, quack!

[*They face off, in character as animals. Duck—*MA *is
terrified.*]

LONE: Grrrr!

MA: [*As a cry for help*] Quack, quack, quack!

[LONE *pounces on* MA. *They struggle, in character.* MA
is quacking madly, eyes tightly closed. LONE *stands up
straight.* MA *continues to quack.*]

130   LONE: Stand up.

MA: [*Eyes still closed.*] Quack, quack, quack!

LONE: [*Louder*] Stand up!

MA: [*Opening his eyes*] Oh.

LONE: What are you?

135   MA: Huh?

LONE: A ChinaMan or a duck?

MA: Huh? Gimme a second to remember.

LONE: You like being a duck?

MA: My feet fell asleep.

LONE: You change forms so easily.   140

MA: You said to.

LONE: What else could you turn into?

MA: Well, you scared me—sneaking up like that.

LONE: Perhaps a rock. That would be useful. When the
men need to rest, they can sit on you.   145

MA: I got carried away.

LONE: Let's try . . . a locust. Can you become a locust?

MA: No. Let's cut this, okay?

LONE: Here. It's easy. You just have to know how to hop.

MA: You're not gonna get me—   150

LONE: Like this. [*He demonstrates.*]

MA: Forget it, Lone.

LONE: I'm a locust. [*He begins jumping toward* MA.]

MA: Hey! Get away!

LONE: I devour whole fields.   155

MA: Stop it.

LONE: I starve babies before they are born.

MA: Hey, look, stop it!

LONE: I cause famines and destroy villages.

MA: I'm warning you! Get away!   160

LONE: What are you going to do? You can't kill a
locust.

MA: You're not a locust.

LONE: You kill one, and another sits on your hand.

MA: Stop following me.   165

LONE: Locusts always trouble people. If not, we'd feel
useless. Now, if you became a locust, too . . .

MA: I'm not going to become a locust.

LONE: Just stick your teeth out!

MA: I'm not gonna be a bug! It's stupid!   170

LONE: No man who's just been a duck has the right to
call anything stupid.

MA: I thought you were trying to teach me something.

LONE: I am. Go ahead.

175 MA: All right. There. That look right?

LONE: Your legs should be a little lower. Lower! There. That's adequate. So, how does it feel to be a locust? [*LONE gets up.*]

MA: I dunno. How long do I have to do this?

180 LONE: Could you do it for three years?

MA: Three years? Don't be—

LONE: You couldn't, could you? Could you be a duck for that long?

MA: Look, I wasn't born to be either of those.

185 LONE: Exactly. Well, I wasn't born to work on a railroad, either. "Best of both worlds." How can you be such an insect!

[*Pause.*]

MA: Lone . . .

LONE: Stay down there! Don't move! I've never told
190 anyone my story—the story of my parents' kidnapping me from school. All the time we were crossing the ocean, the last two years here—I've kept my mouth shut. To you, I finally tell it. And all you can say is, "Best of both worlds." You're a bug to me, a
195 locust. You think you understand the dedication one must have to be in the opera? You think it's the same as working on the railroad.

MA: Lone, all I was saying is that you'll go back too, and—

200 LONE: You're no longer a student of mine.

MA: What?

LONE: You have no dedication.

MA: Lone, I'm sorry.

LONE: Get up.

205 MA: I'm honored that you told me that.

LONE: Get up.

MA: No.

LONE: No?

MA: I don't want to. I want to talk.

210 LONE: Well, I've learned from the past. You're stubborn. You don't go. All right. Stay there. If you want to prove to me that you're dedicated, be a locust till morning. I'll go.

MA: Lone, I'm really honored that you told me.

LONE: I'll return in the morning. [*Exits.*] 215

MA: Lone? Lone, that's ridiculous. You think I'm gonna stay like this? If you do, you're crazy. Lone? Come back here.

SCENE 4

Night. MA, *alone, as a locust.*

MA: Locusts travel in huge swarms, so large that when they cross the sky, they block out the sun, like a storm. Second Uncle—back home—when he was a young man, his whole crop got wiped out by locusts one year. In the famine that followed, Second Uncle 5 lost his eldest son and his second wife—the one he married for love. Even to this day, we look around before saying the word "locust," to make sure Second Uncle is out of hearing range. About eight years ago, my brother and I discovered Second Uncle's cave in 10 back of the stream near our house. We saw him come out of it one day around noon. Later, just before the sun went down, we sneaked in. We only looked once. Inside, there must have been hundreds—maybe five hundred or more—grasshoppers in huge bamboo 15 cages—and around them—stacks of grasshopper legs, grasshopper heads, grasshopper antennae, grasshoppers with one leg, still trying to hop but toppling like trees coughing, grasshoppers wrapped around sharp branches rolling from side to side, 20 grasshopper legs cut off grasshopper bodies, then tied around grasshoppers and tightened till grasshoppers died. Every conceivable kind of grasshopper in every conceivable stage of life and death, subject to every conceivable grasshopper torture. We ran out 25 quickly, my brother and I—we know an evil place by the thickness of the air. Now, I think of Second Uncle. How sad that the locusts forced him to take out his agony on innocent grasshoppers. What if Second Uncle could see me now? Would he cut off my legs? 30 He might as well. I can barely feel them. But then again, Second Uncle never tortured actual locusts, just weak grasshoppers.

SCENE 5

Night. MA *still as a locust.*

LONE: [*Off, singing.*]
Hit your hardest
Pound out your tears
The more you try
The more you'll cry
At how little I've moved 5
And how large I loom
By the time the sun goes down

MA: You look rested.

LONE: Me?

10 **MA:** Well, you sound rested.

LONE: No, not at all.

MA: Maybe I'm just comparing you to me.

LONE: I didn't even close my eyes all last night.

MA: Aw, Lone, you didn't have to stay up for me. You
15 coulda just come up here and—

LONE: For you?

MA: —apologized and everything woulda been—

LONE: I didn't stay up for you.

MA: Huh? You didn't?

20 **LONE:** No.

MA: Oh. You sure?

LONE: Positive. I was thinking, that's all.

MA: About me?

LONE: Well . . .

25 **MA:** Even a little?

LONE: I was thinking about the ChinaMen—and you.
Get up, Ma.

MA: Aw, do I have to? I've gotten to know these grasshoppers real well.

30 **LONE:** Get up. I have a lot to tell you.

MA: What'll they think? They take me in, even though
I'm a little large, then they find out I'm a human being. I stepped on their kids. No trust. Gimme a hand,
will you? *[LONE helps MA up, but MA's legs can't support
35 him.]* Aw, shit. My legs are coming off. *[He lies down
and tries to straighten them out.]*

LONE: I have many surprises. First, you will play Gwan
Gung.

MA: My legs will be sent home without me. What'll my
40 family think? Come to port to meet me and all they
get is two legs.

LONE: Did you hear me?

MA: Hold on. I can't be in agony and listen to Chinese
at the same time.

45 **LONE:** Did you hear my first surprise?

MA: No. I'm too busy screaming.

LONE: I said, you'll play Gwan Gung.

MA: Gwan Gung?

LONE: Yes.

MA: Me? 50

LONE: Yes.

MA: Without legs?

LONE: What?

MA: That might be good.

LONE: Stop that! 55

MA: I'll become a legend. Like the blind man who de-
fended Amoy.

LONE: Did you hear?

MA: "The legless man who played Gwan Gung."

LONE: Isn't this what you want? To play Gwan Gung? 60

MA: No, I just wanna sleep.

LONE: No, you don't. Look. Here. I brought you
something.

MA: Food?

LONE: Here. Some rice. 65

MA: Thanks, Lone. And duck?

LONE: Just a little.

MA: Where'd you get the duck?

LONE: Just bones and skin.

MA: We don't have duck. And the white devils have 70
been blockading the food.

LONE: Sing—he had some left over.

MA: Sing? That thief?

LONE: And something to go with it.

MA: What? Lone, where did you find whiskey? 75

LONE: You know, Sing—he has almost anything.

MA: Yeah. For a price.

LONE: Once, even some thousand-day-old eggs.

MA: He's a thief. That's what they told me.

LONE: Not if you're his friend. 80

MA: Sing don't have any real friends. Everyone talks
about him bein' tied in to the head of the klan in San
Francisco. Lone, you didn't have to do this. Here
Have some.

ON THE CENTRAL PACIFIC RAILROAD.

85 **LONE:** I had plenty.

MA: Don't gimme that. This cost you plenty, Lone.

LONE: Well, I thought if we were going to celebrate, we should do it as well as we would at home.

MA: Celebrate? What for? Wait.

90 **LONE:** Ma, the strike is over.

MA: Shit, I knew it. And we won, right?

LONE: Yes, the ChinaMen have won. They can do more than just talk.

MA: I told you. Didn't I tell you?

95 **LONE:** Yes. Yes, you did.

MA: Yang told me it was gonna be done. He said—

LONE: Yes, I remember.

MA: Didn't I tell you? Huh?

LONE: Ma, eat your duck.

MA: Nine days. In nine days we civilized the white devils. I knew it. I knew we'd hold out till theirs ears started twitching. So that's where you got the duck, right? At the celebration? 100

LONE: No, there wasn't a celebration.

MA: Huh? You sure? ChinaMen—they look for any excuse to party. 105

LONE: But I thought *we* should celebrate.

MA: Well, that's for sure.

LONE: So you will play Gwan Gung.

MA: God, nine days. Shit, it's finally done. Well, we'll show them how to party. Make noise. Jump off rocks. Make the mountain shake. 110

LONE: We'll wash your body, to prepare you for the role.

MA: What role?

LONE: Gwan Gung. I've been telling you. 115

MA: I don't wanna play Gwan Gung.

LONE: You've shown the dedication required to become my student, so—

120 MA: Lone, you think I stayed up last night 'cause I wanted to play Gwan Gung?

LONE: You said you were like him.

MA: I am. Gwan Gung stayed up all night once to prove his loyalty. Well, now I have too. Lone, I'm honored that you told me your story.

125 LONE: Yes . . . That is like Gwan Gung.

MA: Good. So let's do an opera about *me.*

LONE: What?

MA: You wanna party or what?

LONE: About you?

130 MA: You said I was like Gwan Gung, didn't you?

LONE: Yes, but—

MA: Well, look at the operas he's got? I ain't even got one.

LONE: Still, you can't—

135 MA: You tell me, is that fair?

LONE: You can't do an opera about yourself.

MA: I just won a victory, didn't I? I deserve an opera in my honor.

LONE: But it's not traditional.

140 MA: Traditional? Lone, you gotta figure any way I could do Gwan Gung wasn't gonna be traditional anyway. I may be as good a guy as him, but he's a better dancer. *[Sings]*

145
Old Gwan Gung, just sits about
Till the dime-store fighters have had it out
Then he pitches his peach pit
Combs his beard
Draws his sword
And they scatter in fear

150 LONE: What are you talking about?

MA: I just won a great victory. I get—whatcha call it?—poetic license. C'mon. Hit the gongs. I'll immortalize my story.

LONE: I refuse. This goes against all my training. I try and give you your wish and—

155

MA: Do it. Gimme my wish. Hit the gongs.

LONE: I never—I can't.

MA: Can't what? Don't think I'm worth an opera? No, I guess not. I forgot—you think I'm just one of those dead men.   160

[Silence. LONE *pulls out a gong.* MA *gets into position.* LONE *hits the gong. They do the following in a mock-Chinese-opera style.]*

MA: I am Ma. Yesterday I was kicked out of my house by my three elder brothers, calling me the lazy dreamer of the family. I am sitting here in front of the temple trying to decide how I will avenge this indignity. Here comes the poorest beggar in this   165 village. *[He cues* LONE.*]* He is called Fleaman because his body is the most popular meeting place for fleas from around the province.

LONE: *[Singing]*

Fleas in love,
Find your happiness   170
In the gray scraps of my suit

MA: Hello, Flea—

LONE: *[Continuing]*

Fleas in need,
Shield your families
In the gray hairs of my beard   175

MA: Hello, Flea—

*[*LONE *cuts* MA *off, continues an extended improvised aria.]*

MA: Hello, Fleaman.

LONE: Hello, Ma. Are you interested in providing a home for these fleas?

MA: No!   180

LONE: This couple here—seeking to start a new home. Housing today is so hard to find. How about your left arm?

MA: I may have plenty of my own fleas in time. I have been thrown out by my elder brothers.   185

LONE: Are you seeking revenge? A flea epidemic on your house? *[To a flea]* Get back there. You should be asleep. Your mother will worry.

MA: Nothing would make my brothers angrier than seeing me rich.   190

LONE: Rich? After the bad crops of the last three years, even the fleas are thinking of moving north.

MA: I heard a white devil talk yesterday.

LONE: Oh—with hair the color of a sick chicken and
195   eyes round as eggs? The fleas and I call him Chicken-
        Laying-an-Egg.

MA: He said we can make our fortunes on the Gold
      Mountain, where work is play and the sun scares off
      snow.

200 LONE: Don't listen to chicken-brains.

MA: Why not? He said gold grows like weeds.

LONE: I have heard that it is slavery.

MA: Slavery? What do you know, Fleaman? Who told
      you? The fleas? Yes, I will go to Gold Mountain.

        [Gongs. MA strikes a submissive pose to LONE.]

205 LONE: "The one hundred twenty-five dollars passage
        money is to be paid to the said head of said Hong,
        who will make arrangements with the coolies,
        that their wages shall be deducted until the debt is
        absorbed."

        [MA bows to LONE. Gongs. They pick up fighting sticks and
        do a water-crossing dance. Dance ends. They stoop next to
        each other and rock.]

210 MA: I have been in the bottom of this boat for thirty-six
        days now. Tang, how many have died?

LONE: Not me. I'll live through this ride.

MA: I didn't ask you how you are.

LONE: But why's the Gold Mountain so far?

215 MA: We left with three hundred and three.

LONE: My family's depending on me.

MA: So tell me, how many have died?

LONE: I'll be the last one alive.

MA: That's not what I wanted to know.

220 LONE: I'll find some fresh air in this hole.

MA: I asked, how many have died.

LONE: Is that a crack in the side?

MA: Are you listening to me?

LONE: If I had some air—

225 MA: I asked, don't you see—?

LONE: The crack—over there—

MA: Will you answer me, please?

LONE: I need to get out.

MA: The rest here agree—

LONE: I can't stand the smell.   230

MA: That a hundred eighty—

LONE: I can't see the air—

MA: Of us will not see—

LONE: And I can't die.

MA: Our Gold Mountain dream.   235

        [LONE/TANG dies; MA throws his body overboard. The boat
        docks. MA exits, walks through the streets. He picks up one of
        the fighting sticks, while LONE becomes the mountain.]

MA: I have been given my pickax. Now I will attack the
      mountain.

        [MA does a dance of labor. LONE sings.]

LONE:
        Hit your hardest
        Pound out your tears
        The more you try   240
        The more you'll cry
        At how little I've moved
        And how large I loom
        By the time the sun goes down

        [Dance stops.]

LONE: This mountain is clever. Buy why shouldn't it   245
        be? It's fighting for its life, like we fight for ours.

        [The MOUNTAIN picks up a stick. MA and the MOUNTAIN
        do a battle dance. Dance ends.]

MA: This mountain not only defends itself—it also at-
      tacks. It turns our strength against us.

        [LONE does MA's labor dance, while MA plants explosives in
        midair. Dance ends.]

MA: This mountain has survived for millions of years.   250
      Its wisdom is immense.

        [LONE and MA begin a second battle dance. This one ends
        with them working the battle sticks together. LONE breaks
        away, does a warrior strut.]

LONE: I am a white devil! Listen to my stupid lan-
        guage: "Wha che doo doo blah blah." Look at my
        wide eyes—like I have drunk seventy-two pots of
        tea. Look at my funny hair—twisting, turning, like   255
        a snake telling lies. [To MA] Bla bla doo doo tee tee.

MA: We don't understand English.

LONE: [Angry] Bla bla doo doo tee tee!

MA: [With Chinese accent] Please you-ah speak-ah
      Chinese?   260

LONE: Oh. Work—uh—one—two—more—work—two—

MA: Two hours more? Stupid demons. As confused as your hair. We will strike!

[*Gongs.* MA *is on strike.*]

265 MA: [*In broken English*] Eights hours day good for white man, alla same good for ChinaMan.

LONE: The strike is over! We've won!

MA: I knew we would.

LONE: We forced the white devil to act civilized.

MA: Tamed the barbarians!

270 LONE: Did you think—

MA: Who woulda thought?

LONE: —it could be done?

MA: Who?

LONE: But who?

275 MA: Who could tame them?

MA *and* LONE: Only a ChinaMan! [*They laugh.*]

LONE: Well, c'mon.

MA: Let's celebrate!

LONE: We have.

280 MA: Oh.

LONE: Back to work.

MA: But we've won the strike.

LONE: I know. Congratulations! And now—

MA: —back to work?

285 LONE: Right.

MA: No.

LONE: But the strike is over.

[LONE *tosses* MA *a stick. They resume their stick battle as before, but* MA *is heard over* LONE'S *singing.*]

LONE:	MA:
Hit your hardest	Wait.
Pound out your tears	I'm tired of this!
290 The more you try	How do we end it?
The more you'll cry	Let's stop now, all right?
At how little I've moved	Look, I said enough!
And how large I loom	
By the time the sun goes	
295 down	

[MA *tosses his stick away, but* LONE *is already aiming a blow toward it, so that* LONE *hits* MA *instead and knocks him down.*]

MA: Oh! Shit . . .

LONE: I'm sorry! Are you all right?

MA: Yeah. I guess.

LONE: Why'd you let go? You can't just do that.

MA: I'm bleeding.   300

LONE: That was stupid—where?

MA: Here.

LONE: No.

MA: Ow!

LONE: There will probably be a bump.   305

MA: I dunno.

LONE: What?

MA: I dunno why I let go.

LONE: It was stupid.

MA: But how were we going to end the opera?   310

LONE: Here. [*He applies whiskey to* MA's *bruise.*] I don't know.

MA: Why didn't we just end it with the celebration? Ow! Careful.

LONE: Sorry. But Ma, the celebration's not the end.   315
We're returning to work. Today. At dawn.

MA: What?

LONE: We've already lost nine days of work. But we got eight hours.

MA: Today? That's terrible.   320

LONE: What do you think we're here for? But they listened to our demands. We're getting a raise.

MA: Right. Fourteen dollars.

LONE: No. Eight.

MA: What?   325

LONE: We had to compromise. We got an eight-dollar raise.

MA: But we wanted fourteen. Why didn't we get fourteen?

LONE: It was the best deal they could get.   330
Congratulations.

MA: Congratulations? Look, Lone, I'm sick of you making fun of the ChinaMen.

335 LONE: Ma, I'm not. For the first time. I was wrong. We got eight dollars.

MA: We wanted fourteen.

LONE: But we got eight hours.

MA: We'll go back on strike.

LONE: Why?

340 MA: We could hold out for months.

LONE: And lose all that work?

MA: But we just gave in.

LONE: You're being ridiculous. We got eight hours. Besides, it's already been decided.

345 MA: I didn't decide. I wasn't there. You made me stay up here.

LONE: The heads of the gangs decide.

MA: And that's it?

LONE: It's done.

350 MA: Back to work? That's what they decided? Lone, I don't want to go back to work.

LONE: Who does?

MA: I forgot what it's like.

LONE: You'll pick up the technique again soon enough.

355 MA: I mean, what it's like to have them telling you what to do all the time. Using up your strength.

LONE: I thought you said even after work, you still feel good.

MA: Some days. But others . . . *[Pause]* I get so frus-
360 trated sometimes. At the rock. The rock doesn't give in. It's not human. I wanna claw it with my fingers, but that would just rip them up. I want to throw myself head first onto it, but it'd just knock my skull open. The rock would knock my skull open, then just
365 sit there, still, like nothing had happened, like a faceless Buddha. *[Pause]* Lone, when do I get out of here?

LONE: Well, the railroad may get finished—

MA: It'll never get finished.

LONE: —or you may get rich.

370 MA: Rich. Right. This is the Gold Mountain. *[Pause]* Lone, has anyone gone home rich from here?

LONE: Yes. Some.

MA: But most?

LONE: Most . . . do go home.

375 MA: Do you still have the fear?

LONE: The fear?

MA: That you'll become like them—dead men?

LONE: Maybe I was wrong about them.

380 MA: Well, I do. You wanted me to say it before. I can say it now: "They are dead men." Their greatest accomplishment was to win a strike that's gotten us nothing.

LONE: They're sending money home.

MA: No.

385 LONE: It's not much, I know, but it's something.

MA: Lone, I'm not even doing that. If I don't get rich here, I might as well die here. Let my brothers laugh in peace.

390 LONE: Ma, you're too soft to get rich here, naïve—you believed the snow was warm?

MA: I've got to change myself. Toughen up. Take no shit. Count my change. Learn to gamble. Learn to win. Learn to stare. Learn to deny. Learn to look at men with opaque eyes.

395 LONE: You want to do that?

MA: I will. 'Cause I've got the fear. You've given it to me.

[Pause.]

LONE: Will I see you here tonight?

MA: Tonight?

LONE: I just thought I'd ask.

400 MA: I'm sorry, Lone. I haven't got time to be the Second Clown.

LONE: I thought you might not.

MA: Sorry.

LONE: You could have been a . . . fair actor.

405 MA: You coming down? I gotta get ready for work. This is gonna be a terrible day. My legs are sore and my arms are outa practice.

LONE: You go first. I'm going to practice some before work. There's still time.

410   **MA:**   Practice? But you said your lost your fear. And you said that's what brings you up here.

    LONE: I guess I was wrong about that, too. Today, I am dancing for no reason at all.

    MA: Do whatever you want. See you down at camp.

415   **LONE:**   Could you do me a favor?

    MA: A favor?

    LONE: Could you take this down so I don't have to take it all?

[LONE points to a pile of props.]

  MA: Well, okay. *[Pause]* But this is the last time.

  LONE: Of course, Ma. *[MA exits.]* See you soon. The last time. I suppose so.   420

[LONE resumes practicing. He twirls his hair around as in the beginning of the play. The sun begins to rise. It continues rising until LONE is moving and seen only in shadow.]

CURTAIN

Writing From Reading

Summarize

1 Out of historical material, the playwright weaves a fantasylike creation about the relationship between two immigrant laborers. Describe the work situation from which they emerge.

Analyze Craft

2 How does the playwright make these two characters stand out from the crowd of workers?

3 How do history, myth, and individual desire intersect in the text?

Analyze Voice

4 Does the dialogue seem real to you? How does its shape and texture differ from what you have heard before?

Synthesize Summary and Analysis

5 What is the role of Chinese myth and theater in *The Dance and the Railroad*? How do the activities of work and performance come together here?

Interpret the Play

6 How might this play affect someone's understanding of the making of the American West?

David Ives (b. 1951)

David Ives was born in Chicago and received his college degree from Northwestern University. While there, he began writing plays. After three years of editing the magazine *Foreign Affairs,* Ives earned an M.F.A. in playwriting from Yale. He is best known for his one-act comedies, such as those collected in *All in the Timing,* the collection that brought him the John Gassner Playwriting Award. In addition to his plays, Ives has contributed articles to magazines including *The New Yorker* and *New York* magazine, and he has also published two children's books. He lives in New York City and has taught at Columbia University.

AS YOU READ   Consider how slang and stylized language contribute to the comedy.

Moby Dude, OR: The Three-Minute Whale (2004)

SFX: sound of waves and gulls. Distant ship's bell.

Our Narrator is a stoned-out surfer of seventeen.

OUR NARRATOR: *Call me Ishmael,* dude. Yes, Mrs. Podgorski, I *did* read *Moby-Dick* over the summer like I was supposed to. It was bohdacious. Actually, y'know, it's "Moby-*hyphen*-Dick." The title's got
5 a little hyphen before the "Dick." And what is the meaning of this dash before the "Dick"? *WHOAAA!* Another mystery in this awesome American masterpiece, a peerless allegorical saga of mortal courage, metaphysical ambiguity and maniacal obsession!
10 *What*, Mrs. Podgorski? You don't believe I really *read* Herman Melville's *Moby-Dick Or The Whale*? Five hundred sixty-two pages, fourteen ounces, published 1851, totally tanked its first weekend, re-released in the 1920s as one of the world's gnarliest works of
15 Art? You think I copped all this like off the back of the tome or by watching the crappy 1956 film starring Gregory Peck? Mrs. P., you been chasing my tail since middle school, do *I* get all testy? Do *I* say, what is the plot in under two minutes—besides a whale
20 and a hyphen? *Moby-Dick* in two minutes, huh? Okay, kyool. Let's rip.

(SFX: ship's bell, close up and sharp, to signal the start and a ticking watch, underneath. Very fast.)

Fade in the boonies of Massachusetts, eighteen-something. Young dude possibly named Ishmael, like the Bible, meets-cute with, TAA-DAA!, *Queequeg*,
25 a South Sea cannibal with a heart of gold.

(SFX: cutesy voice going "Awwww.")

Maybe they're gay.

(SFX: tongue slurp.)

Or maybe they represent some east-west, pagan-Christian duality action. Anyway, the two newfound bros go to Mass and hear a sermon about Jonah . . .

(SFX: one second of church organ.)

30 Biblical tie-in, then ship out on Christmas Day (*could be symbolical!*) aboard the USS *Pequod* with its mysterious wacko Captain Ahab . . .

(SFX: madman laughter.)

. . . who—*backstory*—is goofyfoot because the equally mysterious momboosaloid white whale Moby-like-the-singer Dick bit his leg off.
35

(SFX: chomp.)

Freudian castration action. I mean he's big and he's got sperm and his last name is "Dick," right? Moby is also a metaphor for God, Nature, Truth, obsessisical love, the world, the past, and white people. Check out Pip the Negro cabin boy who by a *fluke* . . .
40

(SFX: rimshot.)

. . . goes wacko too. Ahab says,

(SFX: echo effect.)

"Bring me the head of the Great White Whale and you win this prize!"

(SFX: echo effect out, cash register sound.)

The crew is stoked, by *NOT* first-mate like-the-coffee-Starbuck. Ahab wants the big one, Starbuck
45 wants the whale juice. Idealism versus capitalism.

(SFX: an impressed "Whoo.")

Radical. Queequeg tells the carpenter to build him a coffin shaped like a canoe.

(SFX: theremin.)

Foreshadowing! Then lots of chapters everybody skips about the scientology of whales.
50

(SFX: yawn.)

Cut to . . .

(SFX: trumpet fanfare.)

Page 523, the Pacific Ocean. *"Surf's up!"* Ahab sights the Dick. He's totally amped. The boards hit the waves, the crew snakes the Dick for three whole days, bottom of the third Ahab is ten-toes-on-the-
55 nose, he's aggro, Moby goes aerial, Ahab's in the zone, he fires his choicest harpoon, the rope does a 360 round his neck, Ahab crushes out, Moby totals

60 the *Pequod*, everybody eats it 'cept our faithful narrator Ishmael who boogies to safety on Queequeg's coffin . . .

(*SFX: resounding echo effect, deeper voice.*)

"AND I ONLY AM ESCAPED ALONE TO TELL THEE!"

(*Resume normal voice.*)

Roll final credits. The End.

(*SFX: ship's bell to signal end of fight. End ticking watch.*)

65 So what do you say, Mrs. Podgorski? You want to like hang and catch a cup of Starbucks sometime . . . ?— *Tubular!*

End of play

Writing from Reading

Summarize

1 A student attempts to summarize Herman Melville's massive masterpiece *Moby-Dick* in under three minutes. Why would that seem appropriate given the life of the average student today?

Analyze Craft

2 How does the brevity contribute to the comic effect?

Analyze Voice

3 Make a list of surfer terminology. Make a list of mock-serious critical terms. How do these contributes to the voice of the *narrator*?

Synthesize Summary and Analysis

4 Take a look at a description of the Herman Melville novel, *Moby-Dick*.

In what ways does the play take liberties with the original material? In what ways does it keep the integrity of the material?

Interpret the Play

5 The playwright intends to amuse us. What commentary on reading and education does Ives make in the play?

Denise Chavez (b. 1948)

The American playwright and novelist Denise Chavez has lived in her native New Mexico most of her life. She attended New Mexico State University and received her Masters degree in Dramatic Arts from Trinity University in Texas. After graduation she worked at the Dallas Theater Center and eventually earned an M.F.A. degree from the University of New Mexico . She published her first collection of short stories, called *The Last of the Menu Girls*, in 1986 and since then has gone on to publish novels, more short stories, and plays. She is the founder of the Border Book Festival that is held every year in her hometown of Las Cruces, New Mexico, and devoted to the cause of literature in her native community.

Guadalupe × 3 (2009)

CHARACTERS

LA MUJER / THE WOMAN (LUPITA, LUPE, MAMA LUPITA)

SCENE ONE: EARLY MORNING

We see the Guadalupe at different ages: seventeen, thirty and seventy-two.

At Rise: Early morning around six thirty A.M. LUPITA, age seventeen, is climbing Tortugas Peak for the Feast Day of Our Lady of Guadalupe, December 12. Dressed in jeans, or black pants, with a sweat shirt with a pull-over headpiece, LUPITA wears a jean jacket and tennis shoes or black hiking shoes. She carries a heavy backpack on her shoulders. She leans on a walking stick and rests from time to time on her climb.

LUPITA: *(Talking to a girlfriend who is climbing with her)*

You've never climbed Tortugas Peak before? Híjole, where have you been? I climb every year with my Granma. She tells me, Lupita Gonzales, this is our tradition and our culture. I've been climbing ever since I was a little girl and I'm sixteen now.

(looking into a compact and then at the sky)

So, are you ready? Let's check out our backpacks to see if we have everything we'll need.

(Opening up the backpack and checking off items inside)

A candle/veladora de Nuestra Señora de Guadalupe to take up to the altar on the Cerrito. Check. Knife to cut quiotes, the yucca and stool staffs. Check. Colored string to decorate quiote. Check. Bottle of water. Check. Burritos from the Go Burger. Check. Rosary. Check. Cheetoes. Check.

(looking at the sky)

It looks like it might snow this year. That's Las Cruces for you.

(Now at the base of Tortugas Peak)

Let's go up the middle path. Not the one on the right, that's a goat path and slippery. And not the wild path on the left.

(Talking to herself)

Take it slow.

(Stepping to the side to greet other pilgrims)

Hello. Good morning.

(Picking up pace again)

We're getting higher. Soon you'll be able to see all of Las Cruces and the entire Mesilla Valley. It's real pretty from here.

(A little tired)

Rest. Don't go so fast. Pace yourself. That's what my Granma says. Now that she's old, she does the velorio in the church, staying up all night praying the day before the climb because she can't climb anymore. Everyone does what they can, she says, when they can. Whatever you do, do it out of love for La Virgencita.

(Taking water out of the backpack)

So you've never come on the climb before? How come? You heard of the climb on December eleventh but you thought it would be too hard? Well, it is and it isn't. You just take it slow and you go down the middle path.

(Stopping to rest)

My Granma says that the Guadalupe is the Mother of All the Americas. She's our Mother who is with us always. La Guadalupe es el madre de toda la gente de las Americas. y tenemos que recordar que es nuestra Madre que está con nosotros, siempre. That's what my Granma says in Spanish. The Guadalupe is the Mother of all the Americas and we have to remember that she is with us always.

(Pausing)

Chee, my hair is getting all messed up. I don't want nobody to see me flat-headed. Especially Johnny Flores. He's all you know and I'll be all you know. You know. He used to be an esquintle chapito lleno de espinillas with these you know roñas on his arms, anyway, but that was then. Ahora el vato's all you know. I got to have hair, girlfriend!

(Checking compact and putting on black lipstick)

So what if he don't like me. I don't care. I'm not climbing for Johnny Flores. I'm climbing for my family and for my manda, my promise to La Virgencita.

(Stopping to rest)

What? You don't know the story of La Virgencita? And here you living in Las Cruces and the climb every year in your backyard. Where you been, huh? My abuelita told me the story a long time ago, when I was a little girl . . .

(Stopping and taking off backpack, sitting on rock, looking out)

There was this Nativo, this Indio called Juan Diego. He lived in México in 1531, what my Granma calls El Año del Oso, very long ago. One day he was going to early Mass. It was on December 9. Suddenly he heard the most incredible music. Out of a cloud on top of the Cerrito appeared the most beautiful young woman. She wore a blue dress full of stars. Juan Diego knew she was a noblewoman because of her fur-trimmed robe. He knew by her black sash that she was carrying a child. She had a cross around her neck, the symbol of life and death. And the beautiful woman was dark-skinned, like him.

(Telling the story and becoming the Guadalupe)

Juanito, Juan Diegüito, the lady called him like a mother would. Where are you going? I am the Mother of the True God, by whom we all live. I want you to go to Bishop Zumárraga, to ask him to build a church for me on this spot so I can care for my children. Juan Diego excused himself from the Beautiful Lady and made his way to the Bishop's house. But he couldn't get in. He returned, very disappointed, to the Beautiful Lady.

(Getting up)

Hey, we better start climbing again, it's getting cold. Got to keep moving. I'll tell you the rest of the story as we go along.

(Pointing out to landscape)

That's where I live, and over there, that's where my Granma lives, and over there . . .

(Giggling)

That's where Johnny Flores lives . . .

(Making the sign of the cross and then fluffing her hair)

Que Viva La Virgencita, que Viva!

SCENE TWO: LATER THAT MORNING

(LUPE, a thirty-five year old woman, looks out to the landscape for a long time. A sigh of tiredness. She looks unhappy. Looks to the sky. Then out again. She ties her shoelaces. She wears an old pair of jeans, an old black sweatshirt with a scarf of Our Lady of Guadalupe pinned on it. She carries an old resilient Mexican shopping bag full of things.)

LUPE: Long live our Lady of Guadalupe! Que Viva La Virgencita, que Viva!

(Crossing herself and moving on. She talks to herself as people pass her. She is not in a hurry)

Got to keep moving! You'd think after all these years of climbing, the walk would get easier.

(Adjusting her shopping bag)

Yes, I married Johnny Flores. So now I'm Lupe Gonzales Flores, age thirty-five and counting. Me and Johnny have three kids, el Junior, la Jennifer, y la Vicki.

(Stopping to rest and look out)

Poor Johnny! He's a victim of the Gulf War. That stuff they used. He's not right in the head. He drinks a lot. His father died and he don't climb with me anymore like he used to. They think he has a brain tumor. But we don't know. La Jennifer is pregnant from her boyfriend, Manny. La Vicki is driving me

the climb, my Granma wouldn't have allowed it, no   35
Señorita.

(To a group of young people)

Be careful, mi'ja. Giggle. Giggle. The girls, they're
so silly. Have you noticed? All they do is talk about
boys. Boys!

(Calling out to the young people)

Be careful! Cuidado!   40

(Tucking her hair under her hat)

I'm still climbing, Virgencita, after all these years!

(Stopping to rest on her staff)

Too many years. Too many stories, too many sorrows, too many too many's! I wish I could take all
those kids aside and tell them to wait. Wait! Espe-
rense! Don't be all ready to get married. Just because   45
your honey has a tattoo del Sagrado Corazón aqui en
el brazo y otro tattoo aca con el nombre de su Mamá,
con la Virgencita all splayed out on his back doesn't
mean he's going to be a good provider. I can only talk
for myself.   50

(An accounting)

Estoy cansada, Virgencita. I'm tired, Virgencita.
Very tired. Bien cansada. Like my Granma used to
say, "All of me hurts. Toda la mujer duele."

(Talking to her Granma)

I remember how you told me the story of Juan Diego, that story of wonder and majesty. Juan Diego   55
returned to tell the Beautiful Lady that the Bishop
had refused to see him. Once again she repeated her
request. He left her with the promise that he would
return the next day to see the Bishop. The next day,
with great difficulty, Juan Diego was admitted to   60
Bishop Zumárraga's chambers. The Bishop did not
believe what he had to say and requested proof of the
Lady's existence. Juan Diego returned to the Beautiful Lady. She told him to return the following day
and that she would give him a sign for the Bishop.   65
But when he returned home, Juan Diego was greeted
with the news that his Uncle, Juan Bernardino, was
dying. The day came and went and Juan Diego forgot to return to the Beautiful Lady. The next day,
Juan Diego was sent to get a priest to give his Uncle   70
the Last Rites. Only then did he remember he had
promised the Guadalupe he would go see the Bishop
with a sign. And just in case he would run into her,
he took another route. Sure enough, La Virgencita
met him on the path.   75

15   crazy with her texting this texting that, ya me trae
con ese teléfono and Junior is in rehab because of the
drugs. Yeah, and I'm still working at the K-Mart. In
charge of households. Not too many people I know
have anything to do with La Martha Stewart. You
20   tell me how many Méxicanos love plaid. And we're
not a typical Chicano family. We're going up, up and
we're all going to make it. I'm climbing this year for
the kids. And Johnny. And for my Granma. It's been
sixteen years.

(Irritated)

25   Someone almost fell back there. You have to be very
careful or you're going to fall. You know, it makes
me happy to see all the kids out here today. So many
teenagers and babies, people of all ages! The way
they dress! Con esos tattoos y con los arêtes en las
30   cejas o en el ombligo and that cow thing in the nose.
Fuchee! What has the world come to? When I was
young all we had was black eye liner como la Cleopatra and white lipstick or those textured hose and
short skirts. Not that we would have worn them on

(In the Guadalupe's Voice)

The smallest of my children, el más pequeño de mis hijos, where are you going? she asked. Juan Diego told her about his uncle. Do not let your heart be troubled. . . Am I not here who am your Mother?
80 The Virgencita instructed him to climb the hill and bring her the flowers he would find there. Juan Diego had never seen such exquisite roses. Roses in the wintertime! He took them back to her and the Guadalupe arranged them in his tilma, his poncho made
85 of maguey, and sent him on his way . . .

(Watching people go by)

And here I am feeling sorry for myself, Virgencita. There goes a young boy with crutches going up the hill, one crutch forward like an oar and then another . . . One crutch and then another . . . And
90 there's an old woman, descalza, barefooted, without shoes, walking carefully on the rocks, with bloody feet, doing her mand . . . her promise. . . .

(Getting up and prodding herself)

I'm over halfway up the mountain, I can see the top of the crest there, and from here it's not so far. I'll
95 get up there and have some water. Then I'll leave our candle up there on the Cerrito, on the altar, out of the wind, near the back, and my prayers will rise high, over Las Cruces, all the way to the Heavens, all the way to God.

(With reverence)

100 Long Live Our Lady of Guadalupe! Que Viva La Virgencita, que Viva!

SCENE THREE: LATER IN THE MORNING

(MAMA LUPITA, age seventy-three.)
(She is waiting by the side of the road at the foot of the mountain, leaning on her walking stick.)

I'm waiting for the truck to pick me up. Me, Lupita Gonzales Torres. Too old to walk up the mountain anymore. Not since two years ago when I almost fainted. Casi me desmayé. And what good is an old
5 woman that fainted on the side of the road like a costal of chile, a sack of chile? Now I'm going up in style, with the Mayordomo, the Chief of Tortugas Pueblo. They treat me like a queen. La Reina de Las Cruces! That's me. You can call me Mamá Lupita.
10 That's what my kids and grankids all call me.

(Looking around)

My grankids started climbing with me last year. That's more than I can say for my kids. La Vicki. La Jennifer. El Junior. Uuuuuque, el Johnny Jr., if he ever gets out of his chair for anything it has to be for a cold beer. And whose fault is it? Mine, Virgencita, 15
for giving in to his father, may he rest in peace. Pobrecito Johnny. I'm climbing for them. And for the soul of my husband, Johnny, may you rest in peace.

(With her hand on her walking stick)

I still have my old walking stick. It's served me well all these years. Me ha servido. I've walked this path 20
for more years than you can say mi'ijo. . . .

(Talking to someone along the path)

Come on, get in the truck, there's plenty of room. I didn't mean to get in between you and el compadre. Compadre, don't get jealous. No te pongas celosa.

(Getting comfortable)

When we get up to the Cerrito, you help me and 25
I'll help you. Me ayudas a caminar, y yo te ayudo a tí. We'll go get the humo, the sacred smoke, we'll cleanse ourselves in the sacred chaparral, and then we'll talk down to our favorite spot, facing the Organ Mountains, and just look at God's wonder. I've 30
brought a little blanket and some food . . .

(Takes things out of her mochila—a large Guadalupe bag)

Only the best . . . Kentucky Fried Chicken . . . Extra crispy . . . Que burritos ni que burritos, compadre. No traje burritos este año, porque you know . . . A mi edad me afectan los frijoles . . . when you get older 35
the beans, you know. . . .

(Resting in the sun)

We'll sit in the sun like lizards. We'll stay that way un rato, a little while, and then we'll make our quiotes like we do every year. Our wooden yucca staffs will be beautiful like they always are. 40

(Looking out)

Look, there's my house. My neighborhood. The Bank. My Granma grew up there and me and el Johnny and then my kids. And there's Jennifer's house up in Telshor. There's the hospital. And the Bank. You know what they call it. OR rather what the President, Mr. Papen, called it. Papen's Last Erection. 45

(Laughing to herself and then crossing herself)

I can't help myself Madrecita, that's what it's called.

(Sighing)

Ay! We'll pray for everybody, eh? Familia—what else is there? Qué más hay, compadre? Remember that you are connected to everyone on this living earth, human, animal, plant, and mineral.

(Crossing herself again)

We made it, Bendito sea Dios, otro año de gracia. Y de humildad. Just like the moment el Obispo, Bishop Zumárraga opened Juan Diego's tilma and out tumbled the beautiful rosas de Casilla. It was in the wintertime. Oh, what a miracle! Juan Diego never gave up and finally the miracle took place that last visit to the Bishop. There, on his robe was imprinted the image of La Virgencita de Guadalupe.

(With reverence)

I want to think about where I've been and where I'm going. And I want to give thanks to God and Our Lady of Guadalupe for another year of love and many blessings. Y quiero darle las gracias a Mi Diosito, y especialmente a La Virgencita, por otro año lleno de amor tantas bendiciones.

(Getting up a little stiff, but still spry)
　(Looking out)

Long Live Our Lady of Guadalupe! Que Viva La Virgencita, que Viva!

Writing from Reading

Summarize

1 List, and describe, the three stages of Lupita's life.

Analyze Craft

2 How does the playwright reshape the literal time of Lupita's life?

3 What role does the setting play in the evolution of character?

4 What roles do church rituals play?

Analyze Voice

5 How much of Lupita's language is high speech; how much is low? Give examples. What is the effect of this voice on the play?

Synthesize Summary and Analysis

6 What is the function of the story (of the Virgin of Guadalupe) in the story of the play?

Interpret the Play

7 Three pilgrimages up to the top of a New Mexico peak make up a woman's lifetime. In what way is this celebratory, in what way a description of life's difficulties?

8 How representative of the lives of Chicana women is Lupita's particular life? Can you see similar patterns in the lives of women in your own family, whether Chicana or otherwise?

"Theater is thriving now—it's thriving all over the world . . . You've got these large theaters that produce Broadway-type shows; but you've got hundreds of smaller theaters and theaters like college and university theaters, community theaters, resident theaters. These theaters are producing things and people are going to see them." Conversation with Edwin Wilson

Getting Started: A Research Project

Research is a skill that will carry you through your college career. To help acquaint you with the research process, the materials you need for this project are made available on our website (www.mhhe.com/delbanco1e). Other ideas for research projects and sources appear at the end of this chapter.

A theater critic is someone who watches a production and then gives a summary of it, including his or her critique of various aspects of the play. Since we can't ask you to go see a live production of Arthur Kopit's *Wings,* we have provided you with excerpts of the original radio version as performed on NPR's *Earplay,* available at our website, www.mhhe.com/delbanco1e. The following assignments will give you the chance to play the critic, using the script printed in this chapter along with the radio clips as sources. You may also consult other resources, including the interview with Arthur Kopit, as directed below.

1. In his interview, Kopit talks about his realization that his research notes on file cards were the start of actually writing the play. "It was the juxtaposition of notes and scenes. I hadn't worked linearly." He also discusses order and sequence, saying that the play's images can appear "in any sequence, although there is a sequence, but just allowing it to be mixed up put the audience in the right way." Compare the reader's sense of time reading the script and the listener's sense of time in the radio play. Are they similar? Different? Give your critical opinion of which techniques related to time are the most or least effective.

2. Some critics explain the end of the play as Mrs. Stilson's tragic death; others, hesitant to say whether she dies, see her possible death as her last, brave act. Form your own critical opinion—or interpretation—of the ending, based on both the ra-

dio play and the script. Do you get a different idea from one version than the other? Be sure to support your opinion with quotes from each adaptation. You might also go a step further and, as a critic would do, make an evaluation of which is more successful.

3. "Plays are idiosyncratic," Kopit says in his interview. "They're all idiosyncratic if they're any good." Listen to the excerpt of his interview in which he talks about the playwright's voice. Then, considering both the script and the radio play, write a critical review in which you give an opinion as to how idiosyncratic you believe *Wings* is. Support your opinion with specific examples from either version. Hint: You might first want to explain idiosyncratic in relation to plays, using the dictionary and what Kopit says as tools in forming your definition.

Suggestions for Writing about Contemporary Theater

1. Read one of the plays as a first-night reviewer might. Write a review of the play based on your immediate reactions to it (see chapter 31 for an example of a play review). Comment on the characters and the plot, describe the setting, the language, and so forth. Make a recommendation for others to read this play or not.

2. Do you find there is a sharp line drawn between what we have called modern theater and experimental theater or do you see experimental theater as a continuation of the modern play? Explain.

A Handbook
for Writing
from Reading

Handbook Contents

1 Critical Approaches to Literature

1a APPROACH CRITICISM AS AN ONGOING CONVERSATION

Literary theorist Kenneth Burke famously described literary criticism as an ongoing conversation, one that began before we arrived and will continue after we leave. If the thought of engaging in literary criticism intimidates you, think of it instead as adding your voice to those of others who have read the same work of literature and want to talk about it. You need not interpret the work as if you've been the first to read it, and you certainly don't have to feel as though you must deliver the final response. You need only contribute to the conversation.

Whenever we discuss literature, whether we acknowledge our appreciation or disdain for a text, interpret its meanings and mysteries, or cite it as an example of a larger trend in culture, we engage in an act of **literary criticism.** Such responsiveness is all around us and probably has its origins in the genesis of literature itself. The classical philosophers Plato and Aristotle laid the foundations for studying the creation, interpretation, and impact of the written and spoken word—in a sense, they began the conversation we now join.

1b USE A CRITICAL APPROACH AS A LENS FOR EXAMINATION

While these classical theories are still relevant, approaches to literature have changed with new developments in human thought. Literary critics and theorists are almost inevitably influenced by major shifts in philosophy, politics, history, science, technology, and economics. For example, the advent of Freud's theories of psychology opened up a way of examining literature by applying psychoanalytic concepts to characters and authors. Later in the century, the feminist movement led critics to apply ideas about gender roles to literary criticism. These borrowings from other fields are particularly influential for twentieth-century theory and criticism, as our discussion of the major approaches to criticism will show.

It may be helpful to think of each of the critical approaches described here as a *lens* through which a piece of literature can be examined. Any work can be looked at from several different points of view, but the lens itself cannot do the interpreting—a reader must do that. Still, the lens provides the reader with a set of guiding principles with which to limit all of the possible questions the reader might ask. For students engaging in literary criticism for the first time, these lenses can be enormously helpful because they narrow down the overwhelming array of possibilities, providing specific approaches to take and questions to ask. Studying and understanding the work of readers who have come before us can make the task of coming up with our own ideas less daunting.

1c   CONSIDER MULTIPLE APPROACHES

Many of the critical schools described here initially defined themselves in opposition to the dominant theories of their times. It is important to keep in mind, though, that in current practice many critics are comfortable adopting methods from several critical approaches. For example, a reader who considers herself a Marxist critic may draw on historical and deconstructionist theories to help her analyze a work. Each approach described here has its own merits and shortcomings, proponents, and skeptics. These approaches are not necessarily mutually exclusive, and it is possible for critics to choose the most useful strategies from several approaches in their own writing. Though we will refer to "feminist critics" and "formalist critics" in the descriptions below, there are very few scholars who confine themselves solely to one theory without sometimes turning to other approaches.

What follows is an overview of different major critical methods.

Formalist Criticism

Formalist criticism emerged in Russia in the early twentieth century in the work of critics like Boris Eikhenbaum, Viktor Shklovsky, and Mikhail Bakhtin. Their ideas were adopted and further developed in the United States and Great Britain under the heading of **new criticism** by critics such as John Crowe Ransom, Allen Tate, Robert Penn Warren, I. A. Richards, William Wimsatt, T. S. Eliot, and Cleanth Brooks.

Formalists/new critics consider a successful text to be a complete, independent, unified artifact whose meaning and value can be understood purely by analyzing the interaction of its formal and technical components, such as plot, imagery, structure, style, symbol, and tone. Rather than drawing their textual interpretations from *extrinsic* factors such as the historical, political, or biographical context of the work, formalist critics focus on the text's *intrinsic* formal elements. As Cleanth Brooks explains in his article, "The Formalist Critic," published in 1951 in the *Kenyon Review*,

> . . . *the formalist critic is concerned primarily with the work itself. Speculation on the mental processes of the author takes the critic away from the work into biography and psychology. There is no reason, of course, why he should not turn away into biography and psychology. Such explorations are very much worth making. But they should not be confused with an account of the work.*

Formalist criticism relies heavily on **close reading** or explication of the text in order to analyze the ways in which distinct formal elements combine to create a unified artistic experience for the reader. A major tenet of formalism is the notion that form and content are so intertwined that in a successful work of art they cannot be dissevered or separated out.

For formalist or new critics the study and interpretation of literature is an intrinsically valuable intellectual activity rather than a means to advance moral, religious, or political ideologies. There are those who consider this approach to be a limited one—they have argued that formalism can be elitist, willfully dismissive of historical and biographical factors in the work. *All* study of literature has to include at least a component of close reading; the question other critics raise is whether it suffices as a way to approach a text.

Boris Eikhenbaum (1886–1959)
The Theory of the Formal Method (1926)

The organization of the Formal method was governed by the principle that the study of literature should be made specific and concrete. All efforts were directed toward terminating the earlier state of affairs, in which literature, as A. Veselovskij observed, was *res nullius.*[1] That was what made the Formalists so intolerant of other "methods" and of eclectics. In rejecting these "other" methods, the Formalists actually were rejecting (and still reject) not methods but the gratuitous mixing of different scientific disciplines and different scientific problems. Their basic point was, and still is, that the object of literary science, as literary science, ought to be the investigation of the specific properties of literary material, of the properties that distinguish such material from material of any other kind, notwithstanding the fact that its secondary and oblique features make that material properly and legitimately exploitable, as auxiliary material, by other disciplines. The point was consummately formulated by Roman Jakobson:

> The object of study in literary science is not literature but "literariness," that is, what makes a given work a *literary* work. Meanwhile, the situation has been that historians of literature act like nothing so much as policemen, who, out to arrest a certain culprit, take into custody (just in case) everything and everyone they find at the scene as well as any passers-by for good measure. The historians of literature have helped themselves to everything—environment, psychology, politics, philosophy. Instead of a science of literature, they have worked up a concoction of home-made disciplines. They seem to have forgotten that those subjects pertain to their own fields of study—to the history of philosophy, the history of culture, psychology, and so on, and that those fields of study certainly may utilize literary monuments as documents of a defective and second-class variety among other materials.

To establish this principle of specificity without resorting to speculative aesthetics required the juxtaposing of the literary order of facts with another such order. For this purpose one order had to be selected from among existent orders, which, while contiguous with the literary order, would contrast with it in terms of functions. It was just such a methodological procedure that produced the opposition between "poetic" language and "practical" language. This opposition [. . .] served as the activating principle for the Formalists' treatment of the fundamental problems of poetics. Thus, instead of an orientation toward a

---

[1] A legal term describing something that has no ownership.

history of culture or of social life, towards psychology, or aesthetics, and so on, as had been customary for literary scholars, the Formalists came up with their own characteristic orientation toward linguistics, a discipline contiguous with poetics in regard to the material under investigation, but one approaching that material from a different angle and with different kinds of problems to solve.

from *The Theory of the Formal Method*

Biographical Criticism

Biographical criticism emphasizes the belief that literature is created by authors whose unique experiences shape their writing and therefore can inform our reading of their work. Biographical critics research and use an author's biography to interpret the text as well as the author's stated *intentions* or comments on the process of composition itself. These critics often consult the author's memoirs to uncover connections between the author's life and the author's work. They may also study the author's rough drafts to trace the evolution of a given text or examine the author's library to discern potential influences on the author's work.

Knowledge of an author's biography can surely help readers interpret or understand a text. For example, awareness of Flannery O'Connor's devout Catholicism will make the religious elements of her stories and novels more meaningful to readers. However, as we have just seen, formalist critics reject biographical criticism, arguing that any essential meaning in a text should be discernable to readers purely through close reading. They reject the notion that an author's thought processes and stated *intentions* for a text necessarily define the work's meaning. They call this emphasis on discerning or trusting an author's own stated purpose the **intentional fallacy** and believe a text's meaning must be contained in and communicated only by the text as such.

While biographical criticism was once quite common, in recent decades it is more often used as *part* of a larger critical approach than as the primary critical strategy.

Gary Lee Stonum (b. 1947)
Dickinson's Literary Background (1998)

Books and reading were [Emily] Dickinson's primary access to a world beyond Amherst. We can thus at least be reasonably confident that the cultural contexts of Dickinson's writing are primarily literary, particularly if that term is defined inclusively. Her surviving letters are filled with references to favorite authors, and some of the poems allude in one way or another to recognizable elements of her reading (Pollak, "Allusions"). To be sure, she is by no means a learned poet in the vein of Milton or Pope, writers who can hardly be appreciated without understanding their allusions and allegiances. Yet she is also surely not the unlettered author Richard Chase once unguardedly deemed her, uninfluenced by literary sources in either style or thought.

A few cautions need to be kept in mind as we examine various claims about Dickinson's literary milieu. First, we know very little about how or even whether Dickinson imagined her work as participating in any public enterprise. By contrast to Keats, who dreamed of being among the English poets after his death, or a James Joyce, who schemed tirelessly to shape his own reputation, Dickinson hardly trafficked in any cultural arena. We do possess information about the books she read or admired, and we know from the persistent testimony of her letters and poems that she regarded poetry as an exalted calling. Yet, although we can reasonably infer from this a certain broad ambition, we simply do not know if Dickinson regarded her vocation as entailing some sense of a role in literary history or as obliging her to bargain in the cultural marketplace. We do not, for example, know whether or in what respect she regarded herself as a woman poet, in spite of a number of lively arguments supposing that she did.

[. . .] At the writerly end of the spectrum lie the sources Dickinson drew upon or referred to as she wrote, which are of varying importance. Dickinson's regard for Elizabeth Barrett Browning makes it likely that her "Vision of Poets" is a source of "I died for Beauty," as well as or even rather than Keats's now more famous "Ode on a Grecian Urn." On the other hand, the identification is by no means crucial to an understanding of the poem.

The more interesting cases are those in which the source is disputed and identification would make some difference to our reading. Dickinson was notably fond of exotic place-names, most of which she must have come upon in her reading and some of which may carry thematic associations. The reference to "Chimborazo" in "Love—thou are high" may well derive incidentally from Edward Hitchcock's *Elementary Geology*, where it stands among a list of the world's tallest mountains, or it may originate from similarly casual uses in Barrett Browning and Emerson. On the other hand, if we heed Judith Farr's investigations into the influence of contemporary painting, then we might recall that Frederic Church's mammoth painting of Chimborazo was one of the most celebrated luminist canvases of the day. If the poem is read in the latter context, then the "Love" addressed by the poem as like the mountain would function more insistently as a figure of sublime theophany. (The poem also clearly alludes to Exodus 33, the chief biblical commonplace for such an event.)

[. . .] Many of the references in Dickinson's writings are discussed in Jack Capps's indispensable *Emily Dickinson's Reading*, which includes a detailed index of the books and authors she mentions in poems or letters. Capps also surveys the contents of the family library, much of which is now at Harvard. Unfortunately, the usefulness of the library "is limited by the fact that books from the Austin Dickinson and Edward Dickinson household have been mixed and, in most cases, dates of acquisition and individual ownership are uncertain." Likewise, although these volumes include inscriptions, marginalia, and other evidence of use, few of the markings can be confidently traced to the poet herself.

from *Dickinson's Literary Background*

Historical Criticism

Historical criticism emphasizes the relationship between a text and its historical context. When interpreting a text, historical critics highlight the cultural, philosophical, and political movements and ideologies prevalent during the text's creation and reception. Such critics may also use literary texts as a means of studying or promoting a particular movement in history—cultural , political, or otherwise.

Historical critics do extensive research to uncover the social and intellectual trends that influenced the life and work of the author and his or her original audience. This research brings to light allusions, concepts, and vocabulary or word usage that would have been easily understood by the author or the original audience but may elude contemporary readers. Historical critics also study the ways in which the meanings of a given text change over time, looking, for example, at the ways in which Victorians staged or responded to Shakespeare's *A Midsummer Night's Dream*.

One frequent objection to historical criticism is that these methods can reveal more about the context surrounding a text than about the meaning or value of the text itself. Another objection is that historical criticism sometimes views literature simply as an expression of the historical trends of a given era, rather than viewing texts as autonomous, idiosyncratic expressions of a particular author's views. Historical criticism, some argue, oversimplifies the relationship between a text and the prevailing or dominant cultural context, overlooking the possibility that the text may have a subversive, distorted, distanced, or anachronistic relationship to the dominant culture of the author's time.

Carl Van Doren (1885–1950)
Mark Twain (1921)

Of the major American novelists Mark Twain derived least from any literary, or at any rate from any bookish, tradition. Hawthorne had the example of Irving, and Cooper had that of Scott, when they began to write; Howells and Henry James instinctively fell into step with the classics. Mark Twain came up into literature from the popular ranks, trained in the school of newspaper fun-making and humorous lecturing, only gradually instructed in the more orthodox arts of the literary profession. He seems to most eyes, however, less indebted to predecessors than he actually was, for the reason that his provenance has faded out with the passage of time and the increase of his particular fame. Yet he had predecessors and a provenance. As a printer he learned the mechanical technique of his trade of letters; as a jocose writer for the newspapers of the Middle West and the Far West at a period when a well established mode of burlesque and caricature and dialect prevailed there, he adapted himself to a definite convention; as a raconteur he not only tried his methods on the most diverse auditors but consciously studied those of Artemus Ward, then the American master of the craft; Bret Harte, according to Mark Twain, "trimmed and trained and schooled me"; and thereafter, when the "Wild Humorist of the Pacific Slope," as it did not at first seem violent to call him, came into contact with professed men of letters, especially Howells, he had already a mastership of his own, though in a second rank.

To be a "humorist" in the United States of the sixties and seventies was to belong to an understood and accepted class. It meant, as Orpheus C. Kerr and John Phœnix and Josh Billings and Petroleum V. Nasby and Artemus Ward had recently and typically been showing, to make fun as fantastically as one liked but never to rise to beauty; to be intensely shrewd but never profound; to touch pathos at intervals but never tragedy. The humorist assumed a name not his own, as Mark Twain did, and also generally a character—that of some rustic sage or adventurous eccentric who discussed the topics of the moment keenly and drolly. Under his assumed character, of which he ordinarily made fun, he claimed a wide license of speech, which did not, however, extend to indecency or to any very serious satire. His fun was the ebullience of a strenuous society, the laughter of escape from difficult conditions. It was rooted fast in that optimism which Americans have had the habit of considering a moral obligation. It loved to ridicule those things which to the general public seemed obstacles to the victorious progress of an average democracy; it laughed about equally at idlers and idealists, at fools and poets, at unsuccessful sinners and unsuccessful saints. It could take this attitude toward minorities because it was so confident of having the great American majority at its back, hearty, kindly, fair-intentioned, but self-satisfied and unspeculative. In time Mark Twain partly outgrew this type of fun—or rather, had frequent intervals of a different type and also of a fierce seriousness—but the origins of his art lie there. So do the origins of his ideas lie among the populace, much as he eventually outgrew the evangelical orthodoxy and national complacency and personal hopefulness with which he had first been burdened.

from *The American Novel*

Psychological or Psychoanalytic Criticism

Psychoanalytic criticism originally stemmed, like psychoanalysis itself, from the work of Sigmund Freud. That revolutionary thinker sought to analyze the conscious and subconscious mental workings of his patients by listening to them discuss their dreams, their erotic urges, and their childhoods. Psychoanalytical critics in a sense study characters and authors as they would patients, looking in the text for evidence of childhood trauma, repressed sexual impulses, preoccupation with death, and so on. Through the lens of psychology they attempt to explain the motivations and meanings behind characters' actions. Such critics have, for example, noted Hamlet's Oedipus complex, his desire to kill his (step)father and possess his mother.

At the same time, psychological critics use textual and biographical evidence as a means to better understand the *author's* psychology. They may attribute the somber tone of a group of poems to the poet's contemporaneous loss of a spouse, or may look for patterns in several texts to identify an author's subconscious preoccupations, fears, or motivations. Psychological critics have, for example, attributed sexist tendencies to Hemingway by arguing that women rarely play major roles in his fiction and are often manipulative or emasculating when they do. Others disagree, noting that Hemingway's female characters, while not dominant, frequently offer the story's wisest, most lucid perspectives through what are often the story's most memorable lines of dialogue. To relate these issues to Hemingway's conflicted love for his mother is to consider the work in psychological as well as biographical terms.

Finally, psychoanalytical critics also examine the process and nature of literary creation, studying the ways in which texts create an emotional and intellectual effect for readers and authors. Here too the strategy is most effective when inclusive as opposed to exclusive; this is a useful tool for reading when it's not the *only* approach to a text.

Kenneth Burke (1897–1993)
The Poetic Process (1925)

If we wish to indicate a gradual rise to a crisis, and speak of this as a climax, or a crescendo, we are talking in intellectualistic terms of a mechanism which can often be highly emotive. There is in reality no such general thing as a crescendo. What does exist is a multiplicity of individual artworks each of which may be arranged as a whole, or in some parts, in a manner which we distinguish as climactic. And there is also in the human brain the potentiality for reacting favorably to such a climactic arrangement. Over and over again in the history of art, different material has been arranged to embody the principle of the crescendo; and this must be so because we "think" in a crescendo, because it parallels certain psychic and physical processes which are at the roots of our experience. The accelerated motion of a falling body, the cycle of a storm, the procedure of the sexual act, the ripening of crops—growth here is not merely a linear progression, but a fruition. Indeed, natural processes are, inevitably, "formally" correct, and by merely recording the symptoms of some physical development we can obtain an artistic development. Thomas Mann's work has many such natural forms converted into art forms, as, in *Death in Venice,* his charting of a sunrise and of the progressive stages in a cholera epidemic. And surely, we may say without much fear of startling anyone, that the work of art utilizes climactic arrangement because the human brain has a pronounced potentiality for being arrested, or entertained, by such an arrangement.

[. . .] Whereupon, returning to the Poetic Process, let us suppose that while a person is sleeping some disorder of the digestion takes place, and he is physically depressed. Such depression in the sleeper immediately calls forth a corresponding psychic depression, while this psychic depression in turn translates itself into the invention of details which will more or less adequately symbolize this depression. If the sleeper has had some set of experiences strongly marked by the feeling of depression, his mind may summon details from this experience to symbolize his depression. If he fears financial ruin, his depression may very reasonably seize upon the cluster of facts associated with this fear in which to individuate itself. On the other hand, if there is no strong set of associations in his mind clustered about the mood of depression, he may invent details which, on waking, seem inadequate to the mood. This fact accounts for the incommunicable wonder of a dream, as when at times we look back on the dream and are mystified at the seemingly unwarranted emotional responses which the details "aroused" in us. Trying to convey to others the emotional overtones of this dream, we laboriously recite the details, and are compelled at every turn to put in such confessions of defeat as "There was something strange about the room," or "For some reason or other I was afraid of this boat, although there doesn't seem to be any good reason now." But the details were not the cause of the emotion; the emotion, rather, dictated the selection of the details. Especially when the emotion was one of marvel or mystery, the invented details seem inadequate—the dream becoming, from the standpoint of communication, a flat failure, since the emotion failed to individuate itself into adequate symbols. And the sleeper himself, approaching his dream from the side of consciousness after the mood is gone, feels how inadequate are the details for conveying the emotion that caused them, and is aware that even for him the wonder of the dream exists only in so far as he still remembers the quality pervading it. Similarly, a dreamer may awaken himself with his own hilarious laughter, and be forthwith humbled as he recalls the witty saying of his dream. For the delight in the witty saying came first (was causally prior) and the witty saying itself was merely the externalization, or individuation, of this delight. Of a similar nature are the reminiscences of old men, who recite the facts of their childhood, not to force upon us the trivialities and minutiae of these experiences, but in the forlorn hope of conveying to us the "overtones" of their childhood, overtones which, unfortunately, are beyond reach of the details which they see in such an incommunicable light, looking back as they do upon a past which is at once themselves and another.

> The analogy between these instances and the procedure of the poet is apparent. In this way the poet's moods dictate the selection of details and thus individuate themselves into one specific work of art.
>
> from *The Poetic Process*

Archetypal, Mythic, or Mythological Criticism

Archetypal or **mythological criticism** focuses on the patterns or features that recur through much of literature, regardless of its time period or cultural origins. The archetypal approach to criticism stems from the work of Carl Jung, a Swiss psychoanalyst (and contemporary of Freud) who argued that humans share in a **collective unconscious,** or a set of characters, plots, symbols, and images that each evoke a universal response. Jung calls these recurring elements **archetypes** and likens them to *instincts*—knowledge or associations with which humans are born. Some examples of archetypes are the quest story, the story of rebirth, or the initiation story; others are the good mother, the evil stepmother, the wise old man, the notion that a desert symbolizes emptiness or hopelessness, or that a garden symbolizes fertility or paradise.

Archetypal or mythological critics analyze the ways in which such archetypes function in literature and attempt to explain the power that literature has over us or the reasons why certain texts continue to hold power over audiences many centuries after their creation.

Northrop Frye (1912–1991)
The Archetypes of Literature (1951)

We say that every poet has his own peculiar formation of images. But when so many poets use so many of the same images, surely there are much bigger critical problems involved than biographical ones. As Mr. Auden's brilliant essay *The Enchafèd Flood* shows, an important symbol like the sea cannot remain within the poetry of Shelley or Keats or Coleridge: it is bound to expand over many poets into an archetypal symbol of literature. And if the genre has a historical origin, why does the genre of drama emerge from medieval religion in a way so strikingly similar to the way it emerged from Greek religion centuries before? This is a problem of structure rather than origin, and suggests that there may be archetypes of genres as well as of images.

It is clear that criticism cannot be systematic unless there is a quality in literature which enables it to be so, an order of words corresponding to the order of nature in the natural sciences. An archetype should be not only a unifying category of criticism, but itself a part of a total form, and it leads us at once to the question of what sort of total form criticism can see in literature. [. . .] the search for archetypes is a kind of literary anthropology, concerned with the way that literature is informed by pre-literary categories such as ritual, myth and folk tale. We next realize that the relation between these categories and literature is by no means purely one of descent, as we find them reappearing in the greatest classics—in fact there seems to be a general tendency on the part of great classics to revert to them.

[. . .] In the solar cycle of the day, the seasonal cycle of the year, and the organic cycle of human life, there is a single pattern of significance, out of which myth constructs a central narrative around a figure who is partly the sun, partly vegetative fertility and partly a god or archetypal human being. [. . .] I supply the following table of its phases:

1. The dawn, spring and birth phase. Myths of the birth of the hero, of revival and resurrection, of creation and (because the four phases are a cycle) of the defeat of the powers of darkness, winter and death. Subordinate characters: the father and the mother. The archetype of romance and of most dithyrambic and rhapsodic poetry.

2. The zenith, summer, and marriage or triumph phase. Myths of apotheosis, of the sacred marriage, and of entering into Paradise. Subordinate characters: the companion and the bride. The archetype of comedy, pastoral and idyll.

3. The sunset, autumn and death phase. Myths of fall, of the dying god, of violent death and sacrifice and of the isolation of the hero. Subordinate characters: the traitor and that siren. The archetype of tragedy and elegy.

4. The darkness, winter and dissolution phase. Myths of the triumph of these powers; myths of floods and the return of chaos, of the defeat of the hero[. . .] Subordinate characters: the ogre and the witch. The archetype of satire (see, for instance, the conclusion of *The Dunciad*).

from *The Archetypes of Literature*

Marxist Criticism

Marxist criticism is one of the most significant types of **sociological criticism.** Sociological criticism is the study of literary texts as products of the cultural, political, and economic context of the author's time and place. Critics using this approach examine practical factors such as the ways in which economics and politics influence the publishing and distribution of texts, shaping the audience's reception of a text and therefore its potential to influence society. Such factors, of course, may also affect the author's motives or options while writing the text. Sociological critics also identify and analyze the sociological content of literature, or the ways in which authors or audiences may use texts directly or indirectly to promote or critique certain sociological views or values.

Marxist or **economic determinist criticism** is based on the writings of Karl Marx, who argued that economic concerns shape lives more than anything else, and that society is essentially a struggle between the working classes and the dominant capitalist classes. Rather than assuming that culture evolves naturally or autonomously out of individual human experience, Marxist critics maintain that culture—including literature—is shaped by the interests of the dominant or most powerful social class.

Although Marxist critics do not ignore the artistic construction of a literary text, they tend to focus more on the ideological and sociological content of literary texts—such as the ways in which a character's poverty or powerlessness limits his or her choice of actions in a story, making his or her efforts futile or doomed to failure. These critics use literary analysis to raise awareness about the complex and powerful relationship between class and culture. At the same time, some Marxist critics also promote literature or interpretations of literature that can *change* the balance of power between social classes, often by subverting the values of the dominant class, or by inspiring the working classes to heroic or communal rebellion. As Marx wrote, "The philosophers have only *interpreted* the world in various ways; the point is to *change* it."

Leon Trotsky (1879–1940)
Literature and Revolution (1924)

The form of art is, to a certain and very large degree, independent, but the artist who creates this form, and the spectator who is enjoying it are not empty machines, one for creating form and the other for appreciating it. They are living people, with a crystallized psychology representing a certain unity, even if not entirely harmonious. This psychology is the result of social conditions. The creation and perception of art forms is one of the functions of this psychology. And no matter how wise the Formalists try to be, their whole conception is simply based upon the fact that they ignore the psychological unity of the social man, who creates and who consumes what has been created.

The proletariat has to have in art the expression of the new spiritual point of view which is just beginning to be formulated within him, and to which art must help him give form. This is not a state order, but an historic demand. Its strength lies in the objectivity of historic necessity. You cannot pass this by, nor escape its force. [. . .] It is unquestionably true that the need for art is not created by economic conditions. But neither is the need for food created by economics. On the contrary, the need for food and warmth creates economics. It is very true that one cannot always go by the principles of Marxism in deciding whether to reject or to accept a work of art. A work of art should, in the first place, be judged by its own law, that is, by the law of art. But Marxism alone can explain why and how a given tendency in art has originated in a given period of history; in other words, who it was who made a demand for such an artistic form and not for another, and why.

It would be childish to think that every class can entirely and fully create its own art from within itself, and, particularly, that the proletariat is capable of creating a new art by means of closed art guilds or circles, or by the Organization for Proletarian Culture, etc. Generally speaking, the artistic work of man is continuous. Each new rising class places itself on the shoulders of its preceding one. But this continuity is dialectic, that is, it finds itself by means of internal repulsions and breaks. New artistic needs or demands for new literary and artistic points of view are stimulated by economics, through the development of a new class, and minor stimuli are supplied by changes in the position of the class, under the influence of the growth of its wealth and cultural power. Artistic creation is always a complicated turning inside out of old forms, under the influence of new stimuli which originate outside of art. In this sense of the word, art is a handmaiden. It is not a disembodied element feeding on itself, but a function of social man indissolubly tied to his life and environment.

from *Literature and Revolution*

Structuralist Criticism

Structuralism emerged in France in the 1950s, largely in the work of scholars like Claude Levi-Strauss and Roland Barthes. They were indebted in part to the earlier work of the Swiss linguist Ferdinand de Saussure, who emphasized that the meanings of words or signs are shaped by the overarching structure of the language or system to which they belong. Similarly, structuralist literary critics work from the belief that a given work of literature can be fully understood only when a reader considers the system of conventions, or the *genre* to which it belongs or responds.

Structuralist critics therefore define and study systematic patterns or structures exhibited by many texts in a given genre. A classic example of this type of study is Vladimir Propp's *Morphology of the Folktale,* in which the critic identifies several key patterns in the plots of folk tales (the hero leaves home, the hero is tested, the hero gains use of a magic agent, etc.). Structuralists thus study the relationship between a given literary text and the larger system of meanings and expectations in the genre or culture from which that text emerges. They also look to literature to study the ways in which meaning is created across culture by means of a system of signs—for example, the pattern of associations that has developed around the images of light (purity, good) and darkness (evil, somber). Here the study of **semiotics** is germane; the way a thing looks to the individual reader or how and what a word *signifies* can change our understanding of a text.

The structuralist approach has been used more frequently and successfully in the study of fiction than poetry. Because of its emphasis on the commonalities within a genre, the structuralist approach has also been helpful to critics attempting to compare works from different time periods or cultures.

Vladimir Propp (1895–1970)
Fairy Tale Transformations (1928)

The study of the fairy tale may be compared in many respects to that of organic formation in nature. Both the naturalist and the folklorist deal with species and varieties which are essentially the same. The Darwinian problem of the origin of species arises in folklore as well. The similarity of phenomena both in nature and in our field resists any direct explanation which would be both objective and convincing. It is a problem in its own right. Both fields allow two possible points of view: either the internal similarity of two externally dissimilar phenomena does not derive from a common genetic root—the theory of spontaneous generation—or else this morphological similarity does indeed result from a known genetic tie—the theory of differentiation owing to subsequent metamorphoses or transformations of varying cause and occurrence.

In order to resolve this problem, we need a clear understanding of what is meant by similarity in fairy tales. Similarity has so far been invariably defined in terms of a plot and its variants. We find such an approach acceptable only if based upon the idea of the spontaneous generation of species. Adherents to this method do not compare plots; they feel such comparison to be impossible or, at the very least, erroneous. Without our denying the value of studying individual plots and comparing them solely from the standpoint of their similarity, another method, another basis for comparison may be proposed. Fairy tales can be compared from the standpoint of their composition or structure; their similarity then appears in a new light.

We observe that the actors in the fairy tale perform essentially the same actions as the tale progresses, no matter how different from one another in shape, size, sex, and occupation, in nomenclature and other static attributes.

This determines the relationship of the constant factors to the variables. The functions of the actors are constant; everything else is a variable. For example:

1. The king sends Ivan after the princess; Ivan departs.
2. The king sends Ivan after some marvel; Ivan departs.
3. The sister sends her brother for medicine; he departs.
4. The stepmother sends her stepdaughter for fire; she departs.
5. The smith sends his apprentice for a cow; he departs.

The dispatch and departure on a quest are constants. The dispatching and departing actors, the motivations behind the dispatch, and so forth, are variables. In later stages of the quest, obstacles impede the hero's progress; they, too, are essentially the same, but differ in the form of imagery.

The functions of the actors may be singled out. Fairy tales exhibit thirty-one functions, not all of which may be found in any one fairy tale; however, the absence of certain functions does not interfere with the order of appearance of the others. Their aggregate constitutes one system, one composition. This system has proved to be extremely stable and widespread. The investigator, for example, can determine very accurately that both the ancient Egyptian fairy tale of the two brothers and the tale of the firebird, the tale of *Morozka*, the tale of the fisherman and the fish, as well as a number of myths follow the same general pattern. An analysis of the details bears this out.

from *Fairy Tale Transformations*

New Historicism

Both **new historicism** and structuralism owe a debt to the work of the influential French philosopher Michel Foucault. Among other things, Foucault studied the ways in which power dynamics affect human society and, more important, the acquisition and spread of knowledge. Individuals and institutions in positions of power have greater potential to shape the discourse in their field and thus to influence human knowledge and shape the "truth." New historicists look in literary history for "sites of struggle"—developments or texts that illustrate or seek to shift the balance of power.

New historicism emerged as a reaction to new criticism's disregard of historical context, but also in response to the perceived shortcomings of older methods of historical criticism. Rather than focusing on canonical texts as representations of the most powerful or dominant historical movements, new historicists give equal or more attention to marginal texts and non-literary texts (newspapers, pamphlets, legal documents, medical documents, etc.). New historicists attempt to highlight overlooked or suppressed texts, particularly those that express deviation from the dominant culture of the time. In this way, new historicists study not just the historical context of a major literary text, but the complex relationship between texts and culture, or the ways in which literature can challenge as well as support a given culture.

A weakness of this method is implicit in its strength. Those who disagree with Foucault and his followers would stress that the plays of William Shakespeare are more important documents than laundry lists or tax rolls from Elizabethan and Jacobean England—that a work of individual excellence can tell us more about a period than does its census or burial records. Again, it's useful here to remember that critical approaches need not be exclusive, and a sophisticated critic will likely use more than a single strategy when dealing with a text.

Stephen Greenblatt (b. 1943)
The Power of Forms in the English Renaissance (1982)

The earlier historicism tends to be monological; that is, it is concerned with discovering a single political vision, usually identical to that said to be held by the entire literate class or indeed the entire population ("In the eyes of the later middle ages," writes Dover Wilson, Richard II "represented the type and exemplar of royal martyrdom" [p. 50]). This vision, most often presumed to be internally coherent and consistent, though occasionally analyzed as the function of two or more elements, has the status of an historical fact. It is not thought to be the product of the historian's interpretation, nor even of the particular interests of a given social group in conflict with other groups. Protected then from interpretation and conflict, this vision can serve as a stable point of reference, beyond contingency, to which literary interpretation can securely refer. Literature is conceived to mirror the period's beliefs, but to mirror them, as it were, from a safe distance.

The new historicism erodes the firm ground of both criticism and literature. It tends to ask questions about its own methodological assumptions and those of others [. . .].

Moreover, recent criticism has been less concerned to establish the organic unity of literary works and more open to such works as fields of force, places of dissension and shifting interests, occasions for the jostling of orthodox and subversive impulses. [. . .] The critical practice represented in this volume challenges the assumptions that guarantee a secure distinction between "literary foreground" and "political background" or, more generally, between artistic production and other kinds of social production. Such distinctions do in fact exist, but they are not intrinsic to the texts; rather they are made up and constantly redrawn by artists, audiences, and readers. These collective social constructions on the one hand define the range of aesthetic possibilities within a given representational mode and, on the other, link that mode to the complex network of institutions, practices, and beliefs that constitute the culture as a whole. In this light, the study of genre is an exploration of the poetics of culture.

from *The Power of Forms in the English Renaissance*

Gender Criticism

Feminist criticism also focuses on sociological determinants in literature, particularly the ways in which much of the world's canonical literature presents a patriarchal or male-dominated perspective. Feminist critics highlight the ways in which female characters are viewed with prejudice, are subjugated to male interests, or are simply overlooked in literature. They highlight these injustices to women and seek to reinterpret texts with special attention to the presentation of women. Feminist critics also study the ways in which women *authors* have been subjected to prejudice, disregard, or unfair interpretation. They attempt to recover and champion little-known or little-valued texts by women authors—who have been marginalized by the male establishment since the formal study of literature began.

Gay and lesbian studies are, if not directly related to feminist criticism, similar in operational strategy. Interpretation of recognized classics may bring a new vantage to bear and cast a new light on old writings; a discussion of "cross-dressing in Shakespeare" or "male bonding in Melville" would belong to this mode of analysis. Here the critic focuses on submerged or hidden aspects of a text, as well as more overt referents; here too a part of the project is to recover lost or little known works of art from earlier generations.

While the focus on overt prejudice is the easiest feature of feminist criticism to recognize, the approach as a whole actually involves much more subtle and nuanced interpretations of texts. As the passage below from Judith Fetterley indicates, feminist critics in some cases find the more subtle traces of male dominance in literature to be the most insidious, because they so easily can go overlooked and pass for the universal or true experience. This puts female readers in the awkward position of doubting the very validity of a female perspective.

Queer theory emerged from **gay and lesbian criticism** partly in response to the AIDS epidemic and owes much to Michel Foucault's work on power and discourse and how language itself shapes our sense of who we are. He argues that the idea of being a "homosexual" would have been impossible without psychoanalytic institutions and discourse that created the category of homosexuality. Sexuality is looked upon as straight (or *normative*) or queer (or *non-normative*) and as a social construction rather than an essential component of one's identity. Some believe this undermines a critique of oppression and prejudice toward gays and lesbians.

Judith Fetterley (b. 1938)
On the Politics of Literature (1978)

Literature is political. It is painful to have to insist on this fact, but the necessity of such insistence indicates the dimensions of the problem. John Keats once objected to poetry "that has a palpable design upon us." The major works of American fiction constitute a series of designs on the female reader, all the more potent in their effect because they are "impalpable." One of the main things that keep the design of our literature unavailable to the consciousness of the woman reader, and hence impalpable, is the very posture of the apolitical, the pretense that literature speaks universal truths through forms from which all the merely personal, the purely subjective, has been burned away or at least transformed through the medium of art into the representative. When only one reality is encouraged, legitimized, and transmitted and when that limited vision endlessly insists on its comprehensiveness, then we have the conditions necessary for that confusion of consciousness in which impalpability flourishes. It is the purpose of this book to give voice to a different reality and different vision, to bring a different subjectivity to bear on the old "universality." To examine American fictions in light of how attitudes toward women shape their form and content is to make available to consciousness that which has been largely left unconscious and thus to change our understanding of these fictions, our relation to them, and their effect on us. It is to make palpable their designs.

American literature is male. To read the canon of what is currently considered classic American literature is perforce to identify as male. Though exceptions to this generalization can be found here and there—a Dickinson poem, a Wharton novel—these exceptions usually function to obscure the argument and confuse the issue: American literature is male. Our literature neither leaves women alone nor allows them to participate. It insists on its universality at the same time that it defines that universality in specifically male terms. "Rip Van Winkle" is paradigmatic of this phenomenon. While the desire to avoid work, escape authority, and sleep through the major decisions of one's life is obviously applicable to both men and women, in Irving's story this "universal" desire is made specifically male. Work, authority, and decision making are symbolized by Dame Van Winkle, and the longing for flight is defined against her. She is what one must escape from, and the "one" is necessarily male. In Mailer's *An American Dream*, the fantasy of eliminating all one's ills through the ritual of scapegoating is equally male: the sacrificial scapegoat is the woman/wife and the cleansed survivor is the husband/male. In such fictions the female reader is co-opted into participation in an experience from which she is explicitly excluded; she is asked to identify with a selfhood that defines itself in opposition to her; she is required to identify against herself.

from *On the Politics of Literature*

Ethnic Studies and Postcolonialism

Ethnic studies emerged after the Civil Rights movement in the United States, but you can find its roots in the pioneering work of W.E.B. DuBois and others of the black arts movement and the Harlem Renaissance. Ethnic studies employs a cross-curricular analysis that is concerned with the social, economic, and cultural aspects of ethnic groups and an approach to literature that includes artistic and cultural traditions that are often pushed to the margins or considered only in relation to a dominant culture. Asian American, Native American, Afro-Caribbean, Italian American, and Latinos are a few of many examples of groups that ethnic studies might explore. Ethnic studies seeks to give voice to literature that has previously been overlooked in the traditionally Eurocentric worldview by reclaiming literary traditions and taking on subjects that explore identity outside the Eurocentric mainstream. But even works that are not written by ethnic writers lend themselves to ethnic studies. For example, a critic wishing to analyze William Faulkner's work from an ethnic studies perspective might focus on his portrayal of African Americans.

Ethnic studies has helped open the American literary **canon**—works deemed essential milestones in a literary tradition—to works by authors outside the white majority. Another far-reaching effect of ethnic studies is that it questions applying traditional modes of literary inquiry (such as feminist and Marxist approaches) to all literature. It suggests that we might be able to learn something more if we approach a text by examining the cultural and social conventions and realities out of which it was created. With the publication in the 1950s of work by Caribbean poet and legislator Aimée Césaire and North African writer Frantz Fanon, the discipline of **postcolonialism** found its beginnings, offering views of relations between the colonizing West and colonized nations and regions that differed sharply from the conventional Western perspectives. The field's modern American academic roots go back to the 1978 publication of *Orientalism* by the late Columbia University scholar Edward Said, a Palestinian by birth, who posits that the concept of the Orient was a projection of the West's ideas of the "other." Many of today's major writers have come out of the old British colonies, from Chinua Achebe to V.S. Naipal to Salman Rushdie, to name a few.

One of the major practitioners of this mode of criticism, Harvard scholar Henry Louis Gates, places such variety of study in a cultural context in which the urgency of the matter becomes plain to hear.

Henry Louis Gates (b. 1950)
Loose Canons: Notes on the Culture Wars (1992)

There's no denying that the multicultural initiative arose, in part, because of the fragmentation of American society by ethnicity, class, and gender. To make it the culprit for this fragmentation is to mistake effect for cause. [. . .] Perhaps we should try to think of American culture as a conversation among different voices—even if it's a conversation that some of us weren't able to join until recently. Perhaps we should think about education, as the conservative philosopher Michael Oakeshott proposed, as "an invitation into the art of this conversation in which we learn to recognize the voices," each conditioned, as he says, by a different perception of the world. Common sense says that you don't bracket 90 percent of the world's cultural heritage if you really want to learn about the world.

To insist that we "master our own culture" before learning others only defers the vexed question: What gets to count as "our" culture? What makes knowledge worth knowing? Unfortunately, as history has taught us, an Anglo-American regional culture has too often masked itself as universal, passing itself off as our "common culture," and depicting different cultural traditions as "tribal" or "parochial." So it's only when we're free to explore the complexities of our hyphenated American culture that we can discover what a genuinely common American culture might actually look like. Common sense . . . reminds us that we're all ethnics, and the challenge of transcending ethnic chauvinism is one we all face.

Granted, multiculturalism is no magic panacea for our social ills. We're worried when Johnny can't read. We're worried when Johnny can't add. But shouldn't we be worried, too, when Johnny tramples gravestones in a Jewish cemetery or scrawls racial epithets on a dormitory wall? It's a fact about this country that we've entrusted our schools with the fashioning and refashioning of a democratic policy; that's why the schooling of America has always been a matter of political judgment. But in America, a nation that has theorized itself as plural from its inception, our schools have a very special task.

The society we have made simply won't survive without the values of tolerance. And cultural tolerance comes to nothing without cultural understanding. In short, the challenge facing Americans in the next century will be the shaping, at long last, of a truly common public culture, one responsive to the long-silenced cultures of color. If we relinquish the ideal of America as a plural nation, we've abandoned the very experiment that America represents.

From *Loose Canons: Notes on the Cultural Wars*

Reader-Response Criticism

The **reader-response** approach emphasizes the role of the reader in the writer-text-reader transaction. Reader-response critics believe a literary work is not complete until someone reads and interprets it. Such critics acknowledge that each reader has a different set of experiences and views; therefore, each reader's response to a text may be different. (Moreover, a single reader may have several and contradictory responses to a work of art depending on the reading-context: a good dinner, a bad breakfast, a single flickering fluorescent bulb—all these affect the way we look at and absorb a page.) This plurality of interpretations is acceptable, even inevitable, since readers are not interpreting a fixed, completed text, but rather *creating* the text as they read it. Reader-response critics do stress that texts limit the possibilities of interpretation; it is not correct for readers to derive an interpretation that textual evidence does not support. So, for instance, it's inappropriate to claim that the character in a story is a vampire because she only ever appears during nighttime scenes in the story—but it's appropriate to compare the housewife in Susan Glaspell's play *Trifles* (chapter 30), to a "caged" bird once we understand the nature of her plight.

Reader-response criticism, moreover, acknowledges the subjectivity of interpretation and aims to discover the ways in which cultural values affect readers' interpretations. Rather than only emphasizing values embodied in an author or literary work, this approach examines the values embodied in the *reader*.

Wolfgang Iser (1926–2007)
Interplay between Text and Reader (1978)

Textual models designate only one aspect of the communicatory process. Hence textual repertoires and strategies simply offer a frame within which the reader must construct for himself the aesthetic object. Textual structures and structured acts of comprehension are therefore the two poles in the act of communication, whose success will depend on the degree in which the text establishes itself as a correlative in the reader's consciousness. This "transfer" of text to reader is often regarded as being brought about solely by the text. Any successful transfer however—though initiated by the text—depends on the extent to which this text can activate the individual reader's faculties of perceiving and processing. Although the text may well incorporate the social norms and values of its possible readers, its function is not merely to *present* such data, but, in fact, to use them in order to secure its uptake. In other words, it offers guidance as to what is to be produced, and therefore cannot itself be the product. This fact is worth emphasizing, because there are many current theories which give the impression that texts automatically imprint themselves on the reader's mind of their own accord. This applies not only to linguistic theories but also to Marxist theories, as evinced by the term "Rezeptionsvorgabe"[1] (structured

---

[1] See Manfred Naumann et al., *Gesellschaft—Literatur—Lesen. Literaturrezeption in theoretischer Sicht* (Aufbau-Verlag, Berlin and Weimar, 1973), p. 35.

prefigurement) recently coined by East German critics. Of course, the text is a "structured prefigurement," but that which is given has to be received, and the *way* in which it is received depends as much on the reader as on the text. Reading is not a direct "internalization," because it is not a one-way process, and our concern will be to find means of describing the reading process as a dynamic *interaction* between text and reader. We may take as a starting-point the fact that the linguistic signs and structures of the text exhaust their function in triggering developing acts of comprehension. This is tantamount to saying that these acts, though set in motion by the text, defy total control by the text itself, and, indeed, it is the very lack of control that forms the basis of the creative side of reading.

This concept of reading is by no means new. In the eighteenth century, Laurence Sterne was already writing in *Tristram Shandy*: ". . . no author, who understands the just boundaries of decorum and good-breeding, would presume to think all: The truest respect which you can pay to the reader's understanding, is to halve this matter amicably, and leave him something to imagine, in his turn, as well as yourself. For my own part, I am eternally paying him compliments of this kind, and do all that lies in my power to keep his imagination as busy as my own."[2] Thus author and reader are to share the game of the imagination, and, indeed, the game will not work if the text sets out to be anything more than a set of governing rules. The reader's enjoyment begins when he himself becomes productive, i.e., when the text allows him to bring his own faculties into play. There are, of course, limits to the reader's willingness to participate, and these will be exceeded if the text makes things too clear or, on the other hand, too obscure: boredom and overstrain represent the two poles of tolerance, and in either case the reader is likely to opt out of the game.

from *Interplay Between Text and Reader (1978)*

Poststructuralism and Deconstruction

The poststructuralist approach (**poststructuralism**) was primarily developed in France in the late 1960s by Roland Barthes and Jacques Derrida. Poststructuralists believe that texts do not have a single, stable meaning or interpretation, in part because language itself is filled with ambiguity, multiple meanings, and meanings that can change with time or context. Even a simple dictionary definition reveals several multiple uses for each word, and we know that context and tone can expand the number of possible meanings. Moreover, within any work of literature, authors intentionally and unintentionally create even more multiple meanings through sound sense, connotation, or patterns of usage. Poststructuralists revel in the possibility of so many interpretations not just for words but for every element of a text's construction.

Like formalists, poststructuralists use the technique of close reading to focus very precisely on the language and construction of a text. Yet whereas formalists do this in order to develop a sense of the text as a unified artistic whole, poststructuralists "deconstruct" the text, deliberately seeking to reveal the inevitable *inconsistency* or *lack of unity* in even the most successful and revered texts (**deconstruction**). Poststructuralists do not believe that interpretation can reconstruct an author's intentions; they do not even privilege an author's intentions, believing that the text stands apart from the author and may well contain meanings unintended by its maker. These meanings are, in the eyes of poststructuralists, as valid as any other, if textual evidence supports them.

---

[2]Laurence Sterne, *Tristram Shandy II*, 11 (Everyman's Library; London, 1956), p. 79.

Poststructuralists thus reject the notion of "privileged" or standard interpretations and embrace what might sometimes seem like a chaotic approach to literary interpretation. In his book *The Pleasure of the Text,* for example, Roland Barthes presents his random observations on narrative *in alphabetical order,* rather than in the form of a methodically unified argument, since the notion of textual unity is, in his eyes, an illusion.

Roland Barthes (1915–1980)
The Death of the Author (1967)

In his story *Sarrasine,* Balzac, describing a castrato disguised as a woman, writes the following sentence: "This was woman herself, with her sudden fears, her irrational whims, her instinctive worries, her impetuous boldness, her fussings, and her delicious sensibility." Who is speaking thus? Is it the hero of the story bent on remaining ignorant of the castrato hidden beneath the woman? Is it Balzac the individual, furnished by his personal experience with a philosophy of Woman? Is it Balzac the author professing "literary" ideas on femininity? Is it universal wisdom? Romantic psychology? We shall never know, for the good reason that writing is the destruction of every voice, of every point of origin. Writing is that neutral, composite, oblique space where our subject slips away, the negative where all identity is lost, starting with the very identity of the body of writing.

No doubt it has always been that way. As soon as a fact is *narrated* no longer with a view to acting directly on reality but intransitively, that is to say, finally outside of any function other than that of the very practice of the symbol itself, this disconnection occurs, the voice loses its origin, the author enters into his own death, writing begins. [. . .] The *author* still reigns in histories of literature, biographies of writers, interviews, magazines, as in the very consciousness of men of letters anxious to unite their person and their work through diaries and memoirs. The image of literature to be found in ordinary culture is tyrannically centered on the author, his person, his life, his tastes, his passions [. . .] The *explanation* of a work is always sought in the man or woman who produced it, as if it were always in the end, through the more or less transparent allegory of the fiction, the voice of a single person, the *author* "confiding" in us.

[. . .] We know now that a text is not a line of words releasing a single "theological" meaning (the "message" of the Author-God) but a multi-dimensional space in which a variety of writings, none of them original, blend and clash. The text is a tissue of quotations drawn from the innumerable centres of culture. [. . .] the writer can only imitate a gesture that is always anterior, never original. His only power is to mix writings, to counter the ones with the others, in such a way as never to rest on any one of them. Did he wish to *express himself,* he ought at least to know that the inner "thing" he thinks to "translate" is itself only a ready-formed dictionary, its words only explainable through other words, and so on indefinitely [. . .]. Succeeding the Author, the scriptor no longer bears within him passions, humours, feelings, impressions, but rather this immense dictionary from which he draws a writing that can know no halt: life never does more than imitate the book, and the book itself is only a tissue of signs, an imitation that is lost, infinitely deferred.

Once the Author is removed, the claim to decipher a text becomes quite futile. To give a text an Author is to impose a limit on the text, to furnish it with a final signified, to close the writing. Such a conception suits criticism very well, the latter then allotting itself the important task of discovering the Author (or its hypostases: society, history, psyche, liberty) beneath the work: when the Author has been found, the text is "explained"—victory to the critic. Hence there is no surprise in the fact that, historically, the reign of the Author has also been that of the Critic, nor again in the fact that criticism (be it new) is today undermined along with the author. In the multiplicity of writing, everything is to be *disentangled*, nothing *deciphered;* the structure can be followed, "run" (like the thread of a stocking) at every point and at every level, but there is nothing beneath: the space of writing is to be ranged over, not pierced; writing ceaselessly posits meaning ceaselessly to evaporate it, carrying out a systematic exemption of meaning. In precisely this way literature (it would be better from now on to say *writing*), by refusing to assign a "secret," an ultimate meaning, to the text (and to the world as texts), liberates what may be called an anti-theological activity, an activity that is truly revolutionary since to refuse to fix meaning is, in the end, to refuse God and his hypostases—reason, science, law.

from *The Death of the Author*

Cultural Studies

The critical perspective usually referred to as **cultural studies** developed mainly in England in the sixties by such New Left writers and sociologists as Raymond Williams, Richard Hoggart, and Stuart Hall. These critics took a sociological approach to literature and their views were colored by the philosophical leftism of such social philosophers as the Italian Antonio Gramsci. The movement grew mainly out of the desire to view social life and social movements from an analytical perspective somewhat akin to the analysis of film and literature.

The American academic branch of this form of criticism also incorporated (mainly in translation) the formal philosophical and critical approaches of a number of French academics including Foucault and other so-called deconstructionists. (Novelist Saul Bellow, affronted by this method, called these writings "Stale chocolates, imported from France. . . ."). Whatever good the English approach might have produced was muted, if not negated, by the French influence, which emphasized viewing society as comprised of various "texts" and imbuing everything from literature to the placement of traffic lights with equal value.

Twentieth-century sociological criticism has been a productive and interesting variety of criticism, as in, for example, studies of the relation of the literacy rate and the rise of the English novel or the effects of the rise of the dime novel in nineteenth-century America or the elevation of film studies to a high place within the university curriculum. Cultural criticism cheerfully blurs the boundaries among the disciplines and acts with a vengeance to blur the lines between high art and popular culture.

Vincent B. Leitch (b. 1944)
Poststructuralist Cultural Critique (1992)

Whereas a major goal of New Criticism and much other modern formalistic criticism is aesthetic evaluation of freestanding texts, a primary objective of cultural criticism is cultural critique, which entails investigation and assessment of ruling and oppositional beliefs, categories, practices, and representations, inquiring into the causes, constitutions, and consequences as well as the modes of circulation and consumption of linguistic, social, economic, political, historical, ethical, religious, legal, scientific, philosophical, educational, familial, and aesthetic discourses and institutions. In rendering a judgment on an aesthetic artifact, a New Critic privileges such key things as textual coherence and unity, intricacy and complexity, ambiguity and irony, tension and balance, economy and autonomy, literariness and spatial form. In mounting a critique of a cultural "text," an advocate of poststructuralist cultural criticism evaluates such things as degrees of exclusion and inclusion, of complicity and resistance, of domination and letting-be, of abstraction and situatedness, of violence and tolerance, or monologue and polylogue, of quietism and activism, of sameness and otherness, of oppression and emancipation, or centralization and decentralization. Just as the aforementioned system of evaluative criteria underlies the exegetical and judgmental labor of New Criticism, so too does the above named set of commitments undergird the work of poststructuralist cultural critique.

Given its commitments, poststructuralist cultural criticism is, as I have suggested, suspicious of literary formalism. Specifically, the trouble with New Criticism is its inclination to advocate a combination of quietism and asceticism, connoisseurship and exclusiveness, aestheticism and apoliticism. [. . .] The monotonous practical effect of New Critical reading is to illustrate the subservience of each textual element to a higher, overarching, economical poetic structure without remainders. What should be evident here is that the project of poststructuralist cultural criticism possesses a set of commitments and criteria that enable it to engage in the enterprise of cultural critique. It should also be evident that the cultural ethicopolitics of this politics is best characterized, using current terminology, as "liberal" or "leftist," meaning congruent with certain socialist, anarchist, and libertarian ideals, none of which, incidentally, are necessarily Marxian. Such congruence, derived from extrapolating a generalized stance for poststructuralism, constitutes neither a party platform nor an observable course of practical action; avowed tendencies often account for little in the unfolding of practical engagements.

from *Cultural Criticism, Literary Theory, Poststructuralism*

2 Writing from Reading

2a CONSIDER THE VALUE OF READING IN A DIGITAL AGE

If you want to savor a cup of coffee or a good meal, you will have to linger over it; you can't just gulp it down. In this supercharged world of instant access and the Internet, reading literature helps you slow down long enough to feel, almost firsthand, the experience of characters from nations, cultures, religions, genders, social classes, and temperaments different from your own. Complexity involves consciously sensing multiple aspects of an experience at one time, and reading literature is a training ground for understanding complex situations. In an era when the global economy makes the world smaller every day, this experience can enhance your ability to work with diverse groups of people—both in college and in your career—by helping you see others' points of view clearly. It will also help prepare you for most of the writing you will do in college, where understanding a variety of viewpoints is fundamental to academic thinking.

2b MASTER WRITING FROM READING FOR COLLEGE SUCCESS

Not only will you have required reading for almost all courses in college, you will likely be required to write about what you read. Your success will depend on how well you can turn your reading into writing. College writing assignments have a variety of specific purposes, but one of their main benefits is that when you write about what you read you become a better reader as well as a better writer. Your personal reaction causes you to be more attentive to the text, and this focused response contributes to your ability to remember what you've read, clarify your observations, and explore complex relationships. In this chapter you will find a step-by-step approach to any text-based writing assignment, from a short response to a research paper. In the handbook chapter 4, you will find several sample papers for a variety of common writing assignments.

2c   USE READING STRATEGIES THAT SUPPORT WRITING

Critical reading is a process of digesting and understanding a text so you can appreciate not just the ideas it presents or the story it tells but how it presents those ideas, why it presents them, and the way those ideas exist in a certain context. Below are the three steps for successful critical reading.

1. Preview the text.   The process of gathering information about a piece of literature before you read it is called *previewing*. When you **preview,** look for information that will help you know how to approach the text. This information can be found in or on the book itself and includes:

- *Date of publication.* Check the copyright page—or, for older classics, you may need to consult the book's introduction or the author's biographical note—to find out when the book or story was published. This will help you determine whether the author was writing about his or her own time, or about a historical period. It might surprise you, for example, to find that Tolstoy wrote *War and Peace* more than fifty years after the time in which the story takes place.

- *Genre.* Sometimes you can tell genre simply from the cover. If it shows a shirtless man gazing at the attractive woman he holds in his arms, you can bet you're in for a romance novel. Knowing whether what you are about to read is fiction or nonfiction, and if it is science fiction, crime, literary, or another form of fiction will help you focus your expectations of your reading experience.

- *The foreword, preface, or other introductory material.* Read the introductory notices to help prepare for your reading. If the selection is part of an anthology or textbook, the surrounding text and questions will be especially helpful in giving your reading direction.

- *The epigraph,* if there is one. An epigraph is a quotation that the author selects and places at the beginning of a work, and it usually alerts you to an important theme.

Previewing Non-Literary Works

If you are reading something that is not a piece of literature, say for another of your college courses or for research on a piece of literature, previewing is still an important step. For non-literary works,

- Try to identify the purpose of a work and the audience for which it was intended. This information can be found, often in great detail, in the foreword or introduction.

- Also, read the author's biographical note to see if you can identify a bias or school of thought, if the author has one.

- Finally, take note of the context of the work. Scan the copyright page to see where a work was published and by whom. Note how many editions the text has had and if the one you have is current.

2. Interact with the text: Annotate, keep a journal, take notes.   Reading closely is the first step to writing about literature. A careful reading and simple markup leads to observations that can form the basis of a written response. Annotating a text is a very basic process of noting impressions as they occur throughout a reading. Annotation should be as simple as circling repeated words, underlining interesting phrases, and jotting down brief sets of words. Remember that annotation is a process of *observation;* deeper analysis and interpretation will come later.

Look back at the student's annotation of Jamaica Kincaid's story "Girl" in chapter 3, and notice that this student does not come up with any actual *ideas* in his annotation. Instead, he makes *observations* about what he noticed as he read the story. This is an important distinction. For example, our student, Andrew, noticed that the narrator repeats certain phrases in the story, but he doesn't yet ask why. In fact, by comparing Andrew's original annotation to his final draft, you can see that most of his observations did not make their way into the final paper. He first had to notice many details about the story's tone, patterns, words, and his own reactions before he could start narrowing down the details that would be helpful in firming up his interpretation.

Annotation is a skill that improves with practice like any other. The skill of annotating is best described as learning to *notice what you notice.* Everyone has had the experience of reading a story, poem, or play for the first time and coming across something odd or jarring. Maybe while reading John Updike's "A&P" (chapter 1) you were surprised or even offended by the narrator's comparison of the female mind to a "little buzz like a bee in a glass jar." Students new to reading literature are often tempted to ignore that feeling of surprise, blaming themselves for the disruption. "I must not get what the author is trying to do," they tell themselves, or, "I just don't understand literature." In fact, those feelings are useful, the beginnings of your ideas. Don't ignore them. Even feeling bored by what you read is worth noticing.

Interactive Readings

Annotated selections can be found in the following chapters:
- Anton Chekhov's story "Rapture" (chapter 2)
- Jamaica Kincaid's story "Girl" (chapter 3)
- Carolyn Forché's poem "The Museum of Stones" (chapter 15)
- William Shakespeare's poem "My mistress' eyes are nothing like the sun" (chapter 16)
- Li-Young Lee's poem "Eating Alone" (chapter 17)
- Susan Glaspell's play *Trifles* (chapter 30)
- Edward Albee's play *Zoo Story* (chapter 31)

Keeping a reading journal is a great way to develop all kinds of skills—your observational skills, your writing skills, and even your skill for appreciating literature. Often, instructors will ask you to keep a journal and give you prompts to which you will respond. But whether or not you have that kind of guidance, you can keep your own journal in which you record what you have read, what you thought about it, and what you felt about it. There is no one right way to keep a journal; you may choose to fill it with personal reactions to literature, with ideas for paper topics, or with quotes that you liked and a description of what that quote means to you.

For samples of journal entries as part of the entire writing process, see chapter 3 (Writing about Fiction), chapter 17 (Writing about Poetry), and chapter 32 (Writing about Drama). Our student models from chapters 3 and 17 used their journals as a place to write a slightly more formal and focused response. Their strategy is worth emulating: By focusing their ideas in their journals, each student will be able to look back later in the semester if he or she has an exam—or later in their college career when they want to revisit literature that they enjoyed—and will immediately have a springboard into remembering the Jamaica Kincaid story or the Li-Young Lee poem and what makes it effective.

3. Read the text again for craft and context.   Reading a good piece of literature is like getting to know somebody new: Your first impression is meaningful, but your second and third impressions can reveal to you entirely different aspects of the work. For a second reading, take into account how the elements of craft work together to create the selection you are reading, and for a third reading, put the selection into context. When was it written? What does its theme say about the perspective of the author on issues or circumstances of the day? It is important to make note of these impressions as well, because they will become the body of information you draw from when you write your responses. The practice of annotation and note taking will not only produce a fuller, more informed response, but will also save you time later.

2d   MOVE FROM SUMMARY TO INTERPRETATION

When you start to write down your thoughts about a piece of literature, first make sure you understand the basics: What has happened in the selection, who is the main character or speaker, and whose point of view is at stake? This is a summary. Building on summary, you will want to think about the tone and style of the work, to analyze how the story, poem, or play is told. As you analyze, look for the role of the setting (particularly if you're reading a story), or important symbols, repeated words or sounds (which is critical when reading a poem), and the way dialogue pushes the plot forward (a central element in analyzing a play). Your analysis should take special note of who is telling the story; in a poem, identifying the speaker allows you to get underneath the hood of the "machine of words."

When you look at what was said (summary) and how it was said (analysis), you can put these together, bring in the context in which a work was written, and synthesize the work of literature to find themes and subthemes that the substance and style mutually support. You are now prepared to interpret the selection and support your interpretation with points taken from the selection itself. You may take a particular approach (see the preceding chapter on Critical Approaches to Literature) or point of view, and this framework can be useful as you interpret anything you read, whether it is literature or basic prose. Whether or not you take a particular point of view, this approach to reading will set you up to express your thoughts on what is important and meaningful to you in a literary work.

1. Summarize.   After a first reading, solidify your understanding of the text by *summarizing* what you have read. **Summary** involves condensing a story, poem, or play into your own words, making sure to capture the text's main points. In the case of prose, a summary is much shorter than the original source and is often no more than a paragraph or two in length. For poetry, it may take a line-by-line paraphrase to result in the information you need to condense into the summary of a poem. Before summarizing, you might reread your annotations and notes with an eye toward picking out important points to include.

Remember that summary should be *objective*—focused more on what you saw happen in the work than on how you reacted to it. It should also not get bogged down with details and examples, but should focus on capturing the main events of the story or the main idea if it is a poem or an article.

One easy approach to summarizing is outlined below:

- *Pinpoint the main idea and write it in a sentence.* For a scholarly article, a main idea usually emerges in the thesis or is stated concisely in the conclusion. When you are summarizing a story, the main idea is often contained in the broad trajectory of the main character. For example: "In Alice Munro's *An Ounce of Cure*, the main character embarrasses herself while babysitting by getting drunk to ease her heartache."

- *Break the text into its sections.* Some scholarly sources might already have headings that divide the text for you. In a story or poem, identify the places where shifts occur—scene changes, a change in tone, or other points where the work takes a new direction.

- *Summarize each section's main idea.* As you did in the first step, write a sentence describing the key point the author makes in each section—or for a piece of literature, the key action or idea of the section. Think of this step as writing a topic sentence for each section. For example, the student who wrote the paper on Albee's *Zoo Story,* which appears in chapter 32, summarizes the beginning of Peter and Jerry's conversation and makes a point about the significance of animals in the play. In her discussion, she includes the following summary to support her point that Peter is associated with domesticated animals:

  > *After learning that Peter has a wife and two daughters, Jerry is eager to know what type of pets Peter owns. The animals he guesses are typical house pets: dogs and cats.*

Summaries are sometimes their own goal. See the chapter on Common Writing Assignments for help if your assignment is to write a **summary paper** or a **précis.** For that assignment, your professor is looking for a short paper that represents the main ideas of the text as the writer has presented it—*not* your own ideas or interpretation.

2. Analyze craft and voice.   Summary helps you understand *what* happened in the text, and you will likely use your summary to support a point. The next step is to **analyze** the text by determining *how* the author created the work. When you analyze, you take the text apart and examine its elements: the different writing devices the author uses (such as point of view, plot, and imagery) and the voice the author brings to the piece (tone, word choice).

3. Synthesize summary and analysis.   The goal of **synthesis** is to bring together the ideas and observations you've generated in your reading and analysis in order to make a concrete statement about the work you've read. The secret ingredients to synthesis are your own personal opinions and perspectives. (In a research paper, you will want to include the opinions and perspectives from academic sources as well.) Thus, synthesis takes the *what* happened from summary and the *how* it was accomplished from analysis and shapes them into an argument or statement.

4. Interpret the text.   By *analyzing* a text and *synthesizing* your thoughts into a statement on the text, you will set yourself up to **interpret** a particular element of a work by suggesting what that element means. **Interpretation** means striving to increase understanding of some aspect of a work to illuminate its meaning. Interpretation does not mean identifying one correct answer, one key to unlock a text. Rather, it means taking an argument or statement you've generated through synthesis and using it as an angle from which to enter a work and explore some new, insightful aspect. It is important to remember that an interpretation must have a strong foundation of evidence from the text itself.

Other Strategies for Exploring Ideas

A walkthrough of the entire writing process from exploring ideas to writing the final draft can be found in chapter 3 (Writing about Fiction), chapter 17 (Writing about Poetry), and chapter 32 (Writing about Drama). When you're stuck, here are some additional strategies that might get you going again.

Freewriting

1 It is all right to start with obvious impressions. Try to answer some of the questions that you asked yourself while annotating the text. Don't worry about finding the "right" answer, and don't limit yourself to just one—there are probably many possible interpretations. *Freewriting* is private writing, just for you. You need not worry about proper spelling or grammar, or even proper sentences and paragraphs.

Talking

2 Try explaining a story, poem, or play to someone who has never read it before, and encourage that person to ask you questions. If this sounds odd to you, consider what you do after seeing a new movie you had looked forward to seeing.

Brainstorming

3 If you find it simpler to think in diagrams, your freewrite might take the shape of a web or cluster of related or unrelated impressions. Start with a central idea, literary device, or character that you wish to explore and place that in the center. Then, draw lines to the elements or characteristics associated with your central term.

Charting

4 Another way to draw connections between your observations is by charting them. This is an especially helpful method if you have identified opposites of some sort in the text, whether it be a hero and a villain, rainy weather and fair weather, or light images and dark images.

2e   DEVELOP AN ARGUMENT

A literary analysis builds a complex argument around a particular aspect of a work of literature. Summarizing, analyzing, and synthesizing might help you come up with an interpretation that could be your paper's topic, but when you're looking for a topic for a paper, you probably wonder: Where do ideas come from? For all of us, coming up with ideas—and developing those ideas into claims worth writing about—is a challenge.

Claim: An argument is based on a claim that requires a defense. It isn't an opinion ("I liked the characters in this story"), and it isn't a fact or a generally recognized truth ("Langston Hughes is one of the most important American poets"). Your essay's claim will be reflected in your thesis (see the following section for guidance on creating a defendable thesis).

Persuasion: Aristotle, the same great philosopher who defined tragedy in ancient Greek theater (chapter 33) also defined logic and the art of persuasion. What we call *logic* today Aristotle would have called *analytics*, as in *to analyze*. When we refer to an academic argument, therefore, we are not referring to a fight but rather to a well-reasoned, logical analysis that is based on evidence.

Evidence: For literature, the text itself is your most convincing evidence; other kinds of evidence might be statistics, expert opinions, and anecdotes.

Different Kinds of Source-Based Evidence
Summary vs. Paraphrase vs. Quotation

Reference to a source is a form of evidence, and it can take many forms.

Summary: A boiled down analysis of the line of action or thought in a passage or full text, a summary is used not only to represent your understanding of a text but also as a point of reference that provides context for your argument. See the summary paper in the next chapter on Common Writing Assignments.

Paraphrase: Using your own words, a paraphrase is a restatement ("in other words") of someone else's language that makes a point more clearly than could be made by using the quotation itself. A paraphrase, therefore, may blend your own view with the words of the source. A paraphrase can help you understand a passage, particularly in poetry. Make sure you mention the source when you paraphrase. Use phrases like "According to," "As said in," "We know from."

Quotation: When the meaning of what was said would be distorted or changed in any other words, a quotation needs to be used to make your point. Do not avoid making a point by overusing quotations. A quotation is your evidence out of which you should build a point, using the quotation as a springboard for your own ideas.

You will need to show details, patterns, and ideas from the text when you present your evidence. The tips that follow are possible ways of developing or refining your ideas and then finding the evidence to support them. Together with the critical approaches outlined in the preceding chapter, they offer ways to generate new possibilities to develop an effective argument.

1. Follow your interests and expertise whenever possible.   If you are a psychology major and the family's interactions in *Death of a Salesman* (chapter 35) remind you of a theory you have just studied in a psychology seminar, don't be afraid to use that knowledge to aid in your interpretation. If you are an avid sailor and that makes you especially interested in analyzing the "open boat" scenes in Stephen Crane's short story (chapter 9), take advantage of your knowledge in creating your argument.

2. Acknowledge your gut reactions, but then analyze them.   If you found a given text or page extremely frustrating to read, it is absolutely legitimate to admit this to yourself and others. But don't stop there. Ask yourself,

- *What was it that frustrated me so much about this passage?*
- *Was it the slow pace of the action?*
- *Was it my own lack of familiarity with the language used at the time the piece was written?*
- *Was it the fact that the character I most identified with died in the previous scene?*
- *Was it the wordy prose style?*
- *What might have motivated the author to use such convoluted language?*
- *Are there any benefits to it?*

Certainly some works of art will appeal to you more than others; elements of taste and personal preference affect every reading. It is legitimate to say, "I hated that story," and intelligent analysis can come from that reaction if you analyze the ways in which the text creates specific impressions on readers.

Similarly, if you enjoy a text and feel a deep personal connection with it, keep in mind that you will have to ask yourself questions similar to those above to make sure you are being specific in examining the attributes you admire. You need not try to develop negative observations, but make sure that your affection isn't clouding your ability to see all aspects of the work clearly.

3. Choose a single aspect of the genre to examine.   For instance, look at meter in poetry, voice in fiction, or stage directions in drama. Reread the text closely, looking only at that one aspect. It may be counterintuitive, but it can be especially useful to choose an aspect of the genre that is *not* the most noticeable in the particular text. For instance, most readers notice right away that Elizabeth Bishop's poem "One Art" (chapter 23) is a villanelle, a tricky form that requires a complex rhyme scheme and repetition. It would be easy to comment on her use of the form, but it might be more fruitful, and certainly more original, to think about something less obvious, like the poem's use of images or its rhythm.

4. Pay attention to detail.   It is a convention of literary criticism to assume that *every* element of a text is potentially significant, no matter how small it seems. Whether or not the author specifically intended everything we notice, once it is written down, everything is fair game for interpretation. When a literary argument does go too far, it is generally *not* because the argument depended on minor details for its support but because it failed to present sufficient evidence or to form a coherent, logical argument. Some of the most insightful interpretations sound as though they are "reading too deeply" into the text until we hear all the supporting evidence and analysis.

Of course, this does not mean that we can arbitrarily assign meaning to any single detail in a text. It is not convincing, for instance, to argue that "Bartleby" (chapter 14) is Melville's rallying cry for Marxism, since there is little evidence for that interpretation in Melville's biography or his other works. The details, however, that might lead to this conclusion—Bartleby's escalating refusal to make copies, his boss's obliviousness to his condition, and the depressing metaphor of Bartleby staring at the brick wall—*could* work together to support a more subtle, complex claim about work and social class in the story. Each of these details on its own does not necessarily carry meaning, but a good paper will *note* them *and put them together* to form a meaningful interpretation.

So, do not be nervous about "reading too deeply" into a text. No claim is too outlandish, no detail too random or seemingly insignificant, no conclusion too far-fetched or implausibly small if your literary argument provides sufficient evidence. "Did Herman Melville *really* mean to use the brick wall as a symbol of class struggle?" you might ask. "Is every tiny detail really so important?" Keep in mind that some interpretations that seemed to be reading too much into the text when they first appeared later became widely accepted. Today's audacious argument might be tomorrow's commonplace one, so don't be afraid to add to the conversation.

5. Compare the text with other things you have read.   Even if your assignment does not require or allow you to discuss more than one work of art, you may still find it helpful to compare your text to others while in the process of developing your topic. Comparing the spare, straightforward prose of Ernest Hemingway (chapter 7) with the more elaborate prose style of James Joyce (chapter 4), for example, may lead you to useful conclusions about the ways each of these authors uses language. It often helps to look at texts in juxtaposition or opposition; the differences are as important as the similarities.

6. Pay attention to the things a text does *not* contain. Thinking about what an author decides to leave out of a text is as revealing as considering what he or she includes. Painters talk about the blank space surrounding an object in a composition, and literary critics often do the same. Looking at the blank space, or what *isn't there,* will cast our subject in relief, enabling us to see it more clearly. Consider which events a play summarizes through dialogue rather than staging; consider whose points of view are left out of a short story; consider why a poet writes without using rhyme. What are the possible motivations for and consequences of those decisions?

7. Try lumping ideas together. Sometimes two (or more) minor ideas can combine into one strong one. Let's say your freewrite about Thomas Lynch's poem "Liberty" (chapter 29) turns up an interesting observation: the appearance of the "ex-wife" in line ten tells us that she and the speaker are divorced, which makes the light argument between them suddenly seem more serious. Much later in your freewrite, you notice that it was the great-great-grandfather who bought the plant, but it was "the missus" who planted it.

Neither of these ideas on its own is enough to generate much more, but what if you try putting them together? The ex-wife and the great-great-grandmother are the only two women in a poem about men taking the "liberty" of urinating outside. You find it interesting that the two women seem so different, and they might represent two different responses to male "nature," one American and one Irish. By *lumping* your two separate observations together, you stumble upon a complex and specific idea for an essay.

8. Or try splitting ideas apart. You might *split* an unwieldy idea into two or more by narrowing or qualifying it. Narrow a broad observation to just one character, scene, or metaphor. For example, in Flannery O'Connor's "A Good Man Is Hard to Find" (chapter 12) you might notice that every scene in the story contains a moment of foreshadowing that the family will encounter the Misfit. This is a useful observation, but too broad for a short essay. If you instead concentrate on how descriptions of objects foreshadow the end (the car that looks like a hearse, for example), you will find it more manageable to gather evidence and make a clear argument.

9. Look for patterns. If an author repeats an image, word, metaphor, gesture, or setting, make note of it. A poem might use words with "sh" sounds in many lines, a story might include images of animals repeatedly, or a play might have two important scenes set in kitchens. Notice these patterns and ask yourself how they are working—is the pattern emphasizing something, providing a sense of comfort, showing the ineffectuality of characters' attempts to change things? Repetition often works together with other aspects of the work and can serve as evidence that the author wanted to emphasize a point.

10. Look for breaks in the pattern. Once an author establishes a given pattern, he or she may also disrupt that pattern in a way that compels a reader's attention. If there is a part that seems quite different from the rest of the text, don't ignore it! You can safely assume that such a passage merits special consideration. If a poem is in perfect sonnet form, conforming exactly to the traditional meter and rhyme scheme *except for one line,* it is likely the author wanted this line to disrupt the pattern and create a sense of surprise. If two characters seem alike in almost every regard, look more closely to discover what *distinguishes* them. If a play contains two scenes in the same setting, with nearly the same action, pay attention to the *differences* in these scenes.

Developing an Argument for Robert Pinsky's "Shirt" (chapter 23)

Follow your interests and expertise whenever possible.	Maybe your Gender Studies course has been discussing the treatment of women who work in sweatshops; a research paper could combine information about how clothes are made now with Pinsky's description of garment workers in the twentieth century. Or: Let's say your Journalism course has been studying newspaper stories from the turn of the twentieth century. You could use your new knowledge about how stories were written to compare and contrast the *New York Times* coverage of the Triangle Factory fire with the description of the fire in Pinsky's poem.
Acknowledge your gut reactions, but then analyze them.	This poem at first seems like a mishmash of depressing situations: the sweatshop workers, the girls jumping to their deaths in the Triangle fire, Scottish workers tricked into believing in a fake heritage, slaves growing cotton. All of this is disturbing when combined with the speaker's satisfaction with his new shirt—in the face of the workers' suffering, that satisfaction seems shallow. But these histories are not just tragic, because many of the people in the stories are behaving nobly (like the man who helped girls jump out of the burning building). Maybe Pinsky is saying that every object we own has this kind of tragic history or that our belongings' histories are also positive, because people like Irma are proud of doing good work even if they are exploited.
Choose a single aspect of the genre to examine.	Some of the more obvious aspects of this poem to write about are Pinsky's use of lists and his inclusion of stories and images from history. Those might lead to good essay topics, but it might be more interesting to look at a less obvious aspect of the poem, such as Pinsky's use of sound. For example, compare the hard, iambic words in the lists of objects with the longer, softer sounds of words in the stories.
Pay attention to detail.	The speaker's comparison of the matching pattern to "a strict rhyme" makes it seem as though he finds rhyme pleasing—but this poem does not rhyme, which would seem to suggest that its own speaker wouldn't like it. It would be going too far to argue that the speaker of "Shirt" dislikes the poem and is presenting it ironically, based on this one word. However, the observation of the word *rhyme* in an unrhymed poem is intriguing—maybe it could lead to looking for other kinds of rhyme, for instance combinations such as "the back, the yoke" and "sizing and facing."
Compare the text with other things you have read.	It might be useful to compare this poem to other poems by Robert Pinsky ("To Television," chapter 21) other poems about work ("The Fisherman," chapter 21), or to other poems that closely examine a single object ("The Red Wheelbarrow," chapter 20 and "Anecdote of the Jar," chapter 20).
Pay attention to the things a text does *not* contain.	You might notice that the poem doesn't contain any information about the speaker except that he has a new shirt. The poem offers no name, no history of the speaker, and no other people in the poem except those he imagines sewing shirts. You might come up with some ideas about what effect this anonymity has on the poem—how would it be different if we knew the speaker's name, his occupation, his tastes and preferences, etc.?
Try lumping and splitting your ideas.	Let's say you noticed the repeated use of jargon (vocabulary specialized to a specific profession)—terms like *yoke* and *navvy* that most readers will not be familiar with. You are also struck by the detail about Scottish workers being tricked into believing a false story about their heritage. Neither of these observations on its own is very useful, so you try *lumping* them: both the jargon and the lies about heritage are instances of people being left out of some important knowledge because of language.

continued

	Or you noticed that all the workers in the poem seem to be somehow exploited. Your first idea is to write a research paper exploring the situations of garment workers Pinsky mentions—Koreans and Malaysians, labor unions, the Triangle Factory, Scottish workers, and slaves in the American South. Then you realize this is too much even for a long essay and decide to *split* these possibilities and focus on only one, the Triangle Factory workers' union.
Look for patterns.	You might notice that most of the poem is made up of sentences that are not grammatically complete but just noun phrases—even some long sentences, like the second one (48 words) are just noun phrases, even though they span multiple stanzas.
Look for breaks in the pattern.	The pattern breaks in the fourth stanza with "One hundred and forty-six died in the flames . . ." The verb "died" jumps out and seems even more disturbing because it's the first verb in the poem.

2f FORM A DEFENDABLE THESIS

A thesis is not the topic of the paper or the topic sentence to the entire paper. Unlike a topic sentence, a thesis must be more than just a statement of fact. A **thesis** is the writer's argument about the topic of the paper, the controlling idea that he or she will show and develop in the body of the essay. Your interpretation will need to be set forth in a strong arguable thesis. Two strategies may be useful in developing your thesis:

- **Do a focused freewrite.** For example, if you are interested in how Shakespeare uses the seasons symbolically, you might want to highlight all the lines in the sonnets you are addressing that have to do with spring, summer, fall, or winter. It would also be a good idea to write a few sentences about your initial impressions of his handling of the seasons: Does he mention more than one season in a given poem, or does he limit it to one? What details of the season does he incorporate? Is the season mentioned a principal subject of the poem or a subpoint?

- **Write an observation as a sentence.** Then ask yourself which part of the observation you made is arguable. Try to imagine the opposite of your statement. If there is an opposite, you are well on your way to having a thesis. If not, you might try writing another of your observations as a statement, and then see if there is an opposite or argument in your new sentence.

Often, you may find it difficult to know exactly what your argument is until you have made it in the course of writing the paper. That's perfectly fine. Although you want to give yourself the best start possible with a well-planned thesis, don't worry too much about getting your thesis right the first time. Instead, look at the thesis in your first draft as a *working thesis*, one that serves as a diving board to launch you into a draft of your paper. At the end of the paper, chances are you'll have come to a more nuanced understanding of your topic. At that point, you'll want to revise your thesis so that it accurately reflects what you ended up saying in the paper itself. The defendable thesis that follows is arguable, supportable, complex, and purpose-driven.

1. A thesis must be arguable. A thesis is not just a statement of fact. Rather, a thesis is your argument, or to put it another way, a meaning you see in the story that not every other reader will necessarily see. Since your idea is not readily apparent to every reader, it is your job over the course of the paper to show why and how you have formed your interpretation. A good way to test whether you have a thesis statement or simply a statement of fact is to ask, "What is the opposite side of this statement? Is that opposite equally arguable?" If it is, you have a good thesis. If not, you either have a statement of fact or a weak argument, one that is widely accepted as true without needing to be explored in a paper.

INEFFECTIVE THESIS:

Some of Langston Hughes's poetry was inspired by jazz.

➡ *The statement is a widely accepted fact. Although this particular sentence may function as a good topic sentence or a sentence in the introduction to the paper, it is not an effective thesis statement because there is nothing about it that the writer has to defend.*

ARGUABLE THESIS:

Beyond being a jazz poet, Hughes understood the significance of jazz—even

as it was being created—and used only those aspects of jazz that express the

African-American experience.

➡ *As you will see this arguable thesis is also supportable, complex, and purpose driven. This statement takes a widely accepted fact—that Hughes is a jazz poet—and offers a particular and original interpretation of the significance of jazz in Hughes's poetry. Notice that the sentence is arguable: one could say that Hughes's interest in jazz was for another reason altogether—perhaps that it served the type of free verse he wanted to write or that it gave a popular appeal to his poetry. This thesis promises to show how race is the prominent factor in determining Hughes's use of jazz, and in so doing, it also promises a nuanced discussion of the elements of jazz present in Hughes's poetry.*

2. A thesis must be supported by the text.   In a good thesis, the writer puts forth a statement that is arguable, or, in other words, a statement of the writer's opinion. It may seem, then, that the writer can say whatever he or she wants in a thesis, but on the contrary, a thesis must be supportable. This support will come primarily from the text itself. You don't want to take your idea and quote the text in a way that misrepresents it, simply to make your idea work. Instead, your thesis should be a reflection of your broad and open reading of the text in question. Although you must ultimately settle on an opinion in your thesis, you must reach that opinion through observation, not through fabrication.

INEFFECTIVE THESIS:

Beyond being a jazz poet, Hughes understood the significance of jazz—even

as it was being created—and deliberately used very specific elements of jazz to

exclude non-musical audiences.

SUPPORTABLE THESIS:

> Beyond being a jazz poet, Hughes understood the significance of jazz—even
>
> as it was being created—and used only those aspects of jazz that express the
>
> African-American experience.

➡ *You may choose to support this with poems that come from Hughes's* Montage of a Dream Deferred *collection, which Hughes identified as being "like be-bop." Also, since the thesis has to do with all of Hughes's jazz poetry, you would want to choose support from poems written at different times in Hughes's career. Whichever poems you choose, you will need to explicate sections of those poems to show how their elements are primarily influenced by race.*

3. A thesis must be complex, yet focused. You may not perfect this aspect of your thesis until a later draft, but your goal is to write a thesis that points you toward a topic with enough material to fill a paper. However, it should also be refined enough that the scope of your topic is manageable—that is, in a paper about Shakespeare's sonnets, you need not address the entire evolution of the sonnet form, just one aspect that interests you, such as Shakespeare's symbolic use of the seasons.

INEFFECTIVE THESIS:

> Beyond being a jazz poet, Hughes understood the significance of jazz—even as
>
> it was being created—and aspects of the jazz form can be found in every one of
>
> his poems.

COMPLEX, YET FOCUSED THESIS:

> Beyond being a jazz poet, Hughes understood the significance of jazz—even
>
> as it was being created—and used only those aspects of jazz that express the
>
> African-American experience.

➡ *This thesis has plenty of potential for a long paper. The author can easily limit the scope, however, by choosing a few key poems to use in his or her discussion.*

4. A thesis must be purpose-driven and significant. If your thesis is doing its job well, it should lead the reader to answer the question "So what?" As the writer of the paper, you'll want to answer this question yourself over the course of the paper and perhaps more explicitly in your conclusion. But the seed of the answer to "So what?" or "Why is this significant?" lies in the thesis. A good thesis leads the writer (and the reader) to a particular perspective of an aspect of the text, or the writers' oeuvre, or literature in general.

INEFFECTIVE THESIS:

> Beyond being a jazz poet, Langston Huges was also a big fan of listening to jazz music.

PURPOSE-DRIVEN THESIS:

> Beyond being a jazz poet, Hughes understood the significance of jazz—even as it was being created—and used only those aspects of jazz that express the African-American experience.

➡ *The purpose of this thesis is to better understand the role of race and jazz in Hughes's poems—an endeavor that may lead to a greater appreciation of Hughes's achievement and a deeper understanding of how to read his poems.*

2g   CREATE A PLAN

If you have ever printed road directions from websites like MapQuest or Google Maps, you know that they provide step-by-step instructions for how to get from point A to point B. Some students may have such a finely tuned sense of direction that they are able to dive directly into writing a first draft. Or maybe a lucky few simply prefer to see where their writing takes them. Most, however, need some kind of a road map for their paper. An outline provides you with step-by-step instructions on how to get from your introduction (Point A) to your conclusion (Point B). It might help to sketch out an informal plan.

- introduction (includes your thesis and why the thesis is important to you and why you want to explore it in your paper)
- body (indicates the points you will use to support your thesis in a series of paragraphs)
- conclusion (adds a final comment that connects your thesis to a larger issue or places your thesis in a larger context that will make it more meaningful to the person who reads your paper)

Outlines can be very brief and simple or longer and in-depth. You might just write a **scratch outline,** or a list of topics you want to cover. If you're writing a shorter paper that analyzes one work, a **topic outline** might be enough. Topic outlines simply provide the order in which you plan to talk about your broad topics. Look at the student outline in chapter 17, Emma Baldwin's paper on Li-Young Lee's "Eating Alone."

    I. Introduction
        A. confusing because last lines contradict
        B. thesis: A close reading shows the entire poem is created out of contradictory elements. Through contrasts of imagery, tone, and the literal events of the poem, Lee uses paradox to give full expression to the grief his speaker feels about his father's death.

II. Imagery
    A. imagery that suggests life
    B. imagery that suggests death
III. Tone
    A. plain language
    B. syntax is not complicated . . .
    C. . . . but subject matter is. This = understatement
IV. Time/Literal Events
    A. present, past "years back," past "this morning"
    B. talk about contrast in time
V. Conclusion
    A. address contrast in last lines
    B. we can understand them in context of poem

Notice how the major headers following the Roman numerals are the topics Emma plans to address: imagery, tone, and events. Supporting ideas can be listed with the alphabet (*A, B, C*). Evidence (quotations, for example) could be numbered in a third level as *1., 2., 3.*

I. Topic
    A. Supporting Idea
        1. Evidence
        2. More Evidence
    B. Second Supporting Idea

Instead of single words or phrases, you might find it more helpful to state every idea in a complete sentence, giving you a **sentence outline** to work from.

Until you have written many papers and learned more about the way your own writing process works best for you, an outline can help you to organize your thoughts and to understand where your paper is headed. Generally, the longer or more complex your paper, the more useful a detailed outline will be. For example, before writing a research paper, you may want to make an outline so detailed that it includes the quotes you plan to integrate. In fact, you may find a full formal outline absolutely necessary.

A more detailed outline example follows for a research paper on Langston Hughes and jazz. The final draft is found in the chapter on Writing the Research Paper. Compare this slice of outline with the third and fourth paragraphs of that paper. Notice how the outline is so detailed that the author had only to flesh out the outline points into complete sentences when writing the actual paper.

II. Blues in the Jazz Age
    A. "The Dream Keeper" and the Jazz Age
        1. Hughes's *The Weary Blues* published in 1925
            a. 1925 was middle of Jazz Age
                1. Marked by energy and optimism
                2. Jazz connoted rebellion
        2. "The Dream Keeper" influenced by blues, not jazz
            b. Part of *The Weary Blues* collection
                1. "The Dream Keeper" reads like abbreviated blues lyrics
                2. Compound words "cloud-cloth" and "too-rough" slow pacing to slow blues pace
    B. The Jazz Age and African-American experience
        1. Jazz Age and the blues have contrasting relationship
            a. Blues related to jazz; jazz grew out of blues roots
            b. Jazz exuberant, blues melancholy

2. Historical context is key
    a. Jazz Age "unprecedented prosperity" ("Roaring Twenties" article) for whites
    b. Great Migration—10% of blacks moved from South to North
        (1) low wages, poor housing conditions
        (2) disease

2h DRAFT YOUR PAPER

The word *draft* is used here to help keep the pressure down. Don't worry about spelling and grammar at this stage. Get your thoughts out on paper. *Draft* connotes that what you are writing is not final, that it is a work-in-progress. You will likely revise your first draft, so you will want to save your drafts early and often. Label your drafts so that you can retrace your steps (*draft 1, draft 2* . . . or use specific dates to show what the most current draft is). Print the original. Having a hard copy may free you up to tinker and explore.

Introductions, Conclusions, and Body Paragraphs.   You may find you want to write your introduction last or right before your conclusion but after you've developed the supporting points of the paper. If you do, these two framing paragraphs can speak to each other more obviously, with the introduction stating your thesis and why it matters to you and the conclusion bringing in your thesis and why it might matter to your reader.

Drafting Body Paragraphs

- Focus each paragraph on one idea.
- State the main idea of each paragraph in a topic sentence.
- Connect the information clearly in each paragraph to support the topic.
- Make sure the paragraph clearly supports your thesis.

2i REVISE YOUR DRAFT

Once you've finished a draft you feel is complete, take a break from your paper—distance can sometimes help you see if your ideas flow as naturally as you thought when you first wrote them. Distance can also help you catch editing mistakes you miss in the heat of developing your ideas. It is also good to get some feedback from a fellow student in your class or a friend. When you come back to your paper, annotate the issues you find. (It is great if you can get your peer to annotate your paper as well.) As you write and revise your paper you have a chance to re-envision how to make your argument clearer and to support it more effectively. In the chapter on Writing the Research Paper you will find the entire final paper for the paragraphs that follow.

Draft Introductory Paragraph

Jazz poetry, according to the American Academy of Poets website, is "a literary genre defined as poetry necessarily informed by jazz music—that is, poetry in which the poet responds to and writes about jazz." By this definition, Langston Hughes was a jazz poet. Many critics point to specific techniques that Hughes employs to create the effect of jazz. Although the observations are true, such technical readings fail to show the full extent of Hughes's achievement in jazz poetry. More than just a jazz poet, Hughes understood the significance of jazz as it was being created, and he used only the aspects of jazz that expressed the African-American experience.

In what way? Back up this assertion.

Which critics? What techniques? May be a good place for an outside source.

Used how? Maybe back this up. Is there an existing critical argument my claim could respond to in order to create a stronger thesis?

Revised Introductory Paragraph

Jazz poetry, according to the American Academy of Poets website, is "a literary genre defined as poetry necessarily informed by jazz music—that is, poetry in which the poet responds to and writes about jazz." Langston Hughes was a jazz poet in that his poetry often captured jazz in a literary form. Many critics point to specific techniques that Hughes employs to create the effect of jazz. One such critic is Lionel Davidas, who writes:

> Langston Hughes, in his collection of poems, lavishly uses such characteristics of jazz as repetitions, choruses, riffs, scats, and nonsensical onomatopoeia to achieve musical success as well as audience participation. It is also significant to note that Hughes's poems are often marked by dissonance, discordance, and line irregularity, which all contribute to the representation of the jazz spirit in verse forms. (268)

Although these observations are true, readings like Davidas's fail to show the full extent of Hughes's achievement in jazz poetry. Beyond being a jazz poet, Hughes understood the significance of jazz—even as it was being created—and used only those aspects of jazz that express the African-American experience.

Draft Supporting Paragraph (Body)

Maybe need some more here—how did jazz, just a music form, connote rebellion?

The discussion here is a little unfounded . . . maybe I need a researched source.

"The Dream Keeper" was published in 1925. At that time, America was in the midst of the "Jazz Age," the period from 1920-1930 marked by energy and optimism. Jazz itself was popular and connoted rebellion. However, Hughes's collection *The Weary Blues* was influenced more by (obviously) the blues than by this new form of jazz. While "The Dream Keeper" doesn't have as obvious a connection to the blues as Hughes's poems that copy blues lyrics directly—such as "Po' Boy Blues"—the repetition early in the poem bears echoes of the repetition characteristic of the blues. Consider the repetition of "Bring me all of your" in the first three lines; typical blues lyrics follow a pattern where the first couplet repeats before a third couplet resolves it, and here half the couplet is repeated and half resolved in both instances. Since Hughes was writing in the "Jazz Age," it may seem surprising that so many of his poems in *The Weary Blues* reflect the blues (lines 1, 3). His decision may in part have been informed by the fact that jazz grew out of the blues, and they were closely related enough that Hughes could use blues and be safe in the jazz realm. But whereas blues are "blue" and melancholy, jazz is "jazzy." The solution to this puzzle is in the historical context. The Roaring Twenties brought "unprecedented prosperity" to the United States ("Roaring Twenties") but it was also the era of the Great Migration, when many African Americans left the south and moved north. Times were difficult for blacks, who faced low wages and poor housing conditions (Marks). So, at the time that Hughes was writing these poems, jazz had two forms: the exuberant, new jazz, and the blues roots it came from. Hughes chose the form—the blues—that best reflected the state of the common black man at the time.

This is too informal! Need to keep an eye out for these.

This explanation is cluttered and a bit confusing; illustrate or clarify.

Reads like a topic sentence. Break the paragraph here?

Cute, but is it meaningful?

Are these common knowledge? Maybe include a brief description.

Didn't I see a good image for this when I was researching online? That might help engage the reader here and enrich the discussion of historical context.

Maybe I need more research here, since understanding historical context is so important to my argument.

Could this point have its own paragraph?

Revised Supporting Paragraphs (Body)

Hughes first published "The Dream Keeper" in 1925 and included it in his collection *The Weary Blues* the following year (Rampersad 617). At that time, America was in the midst of the "Jazz Age," the period from 1920–1930 marked by energy and optimism. Jazz itself was popular and connoted rebellion as it was associated with nightclubs, sex, and drinking (Tucker, screen 4). But Hughes's collection was clearly influenced more by the blues than by this new form of jazz. The title of the collection suggests the blues takes center stage in these poems, and indeed, "The Dream Keeper" is no exception. While it does not have as overt a connection to the blues as Hughes's poems that replicate blues lyrics directly—such as "Po Boy Blues"—the repetition early in the poem bears echoes of the repetition characteristic of the blues. "Bring me all of your" is repeated twice within the first three lines; the object the addressee is told to bring, however, varies (lines 1, 3). In a way, lines one through three are a compounded version of blues lyrics. Typical blues lyrics follow a pattern where the first couplet repeats before a third couplet resolves it. Here, half the couplet is repeated and half resolved in both instances. Blues also has a hand in the pace of the poem. Compound phrases like "cloud-cloth" and "too-rough" slow the pace of reading, as does the high number of line breaks compared to the small number of words (6, 7).

Draft Concluding Paragraph

Too familiar, not the right tone for a research paper.

As you can see, "The Dream Keeper" and "Harlem [2]" demonstrate how Hughes effectively incorporated new forms of jazz as they arose. While he does successfully use technical elements of jazz music, to end a reading there would be to miss Hughes's larger achievement. He did not simply adopt jazz technique; he selected only

Embellish conclusion to include new arguments based on content. Remember to restate the argument.

the trends that reflected the African-American experience. He leaves

out the "white" sounds of swing and opts instead for the forms of blues

and bebop. In so doing, Hughes's poetry captures both the music, as it

evolved from blues to bebop, and the African-American experience.

Elaborate or change wording; doesn't sound right.

Tie in history and time period with this, since it's the basis for the argument.

Revised Concluding Paragraph

As "The Dream Keeper" and "Harlem [2]" demonstrate, Hughes effectively incorporated new forms of jazz as they arose. While he does successfully use formal elements of jazz music, to end a reading there would be to miss Hughes's larger achievement. Hughes did not simply adopt jazz technique; he selected only those trends in jazz that reflected the African-American experience of the time in which he wrote. There is no room in his poetry for the smooth sounds of swing at the hands of whites; instead, he used the true African-American forms of blues and bebop. In so doing, Hughes's poetry captures both the music, as it evolved from blues to bebop, and the African-American experience, as it moved from the blues of the Great Migration to the bitter conflict of continued discrimination.

Revising

- *Rethink your introduction:* Have you drawn your readers in by explaining how the topic of your paper is meaningful to you?
- *Rethink your thesis:* Have you changed your mind? Can you make your thesis clearer?
- *Rethink your structure:* Do you have a beginning, a middle, and an end? Do they flow naturally and logically into each other, with each paragraph focusing on an idea that supports your thesis? Are your transitions between ideas and paragraphs effective?
- *Rethink your argument:* Do you have sufficient and convincing evidence to prove your thesis? Does the evidence build logically to your conclusion?
- *Rethink your conclusion:* Have you made your case? Have you connected your thesis to a larger issue that gives it more meaning for your reader?

2i EDIT AND FORMAT YOUR PAPER

After you have looked at your paper as a whole, take one more look at its sentence structure, spelling, and formatting. These simple matters, if not done correctly, can interfere with your instructor's good opinion of a well thought-out paper. You may have been making small corrections all along, but consider this last edit your dress rehearsal for making your paper public.

Questions to Guide Editing

1. Are my sentences wordy?
2. Have I dropped a word out of a sentence?
3. Is my point of view consistent?
4. Does each sentence make sense?
5. Do I have any sentence fragments?
6. Are my commas in the right places?
7. Do my subjects and verbs agree—*single to single/plural to plural?*
8. Are my apostrophe's used correctly—**'s** for singular possession (this *critic's* opinion; Hughes's work); **s'** for plural possession when the word ends in **s** (the *singers'* music)?
9. Do my quotation marks represent the exact words of the writer?
10. Have I paraphrased without giving credit to the source?

In addition to formatting your paper with a heading and a title, you will need to follow the formatting guidelines your professor prefers, particularly as you cite sources in your papers:

- *The Modern Language Association* (MLA) provides guidelines for formatting papers and citing sources for courses in the humanities (see handbook chapter 6, MLA Documentation Style Guide).

- *The Chicago Manual of Style* (Chicago or Turabian) is sometimes required for humanities courses where an instructor requires that footnotes be used.

- *The American Psychological Association* (APA) has a different set of formatting guidelines for citing sources in the social sciences.

- *The Council of Science Editors* (CSE) have put together guidelines for papers in mathematics, engineering, computer sciences, and the natural sciences.

Whatever form your instructor wishes you to follow, pay close attention to the conventions for quoting and citing sources that are provided. Mistakes can be misconstrued as plagiarism, and following the correct form will have the added benefit of making your paper consistent and clear. This is the effect you want your paper's design to convey. Variety is the spice of life but not the spice you need for your paper. Be consistent with the features of your design, and make your paper look clean, clear, and serious.

Formatting

1. Include a heading on the left with your name, the professor's name, your class, and the date.
2. Center your title (it can be larger than the rest of the type in your paper).
3. Headings within the paper should be the same style and typeface each time.
4. Make your margins wide enough to make the paper easy to read and not so wide as to make your professor suspect you are stretching out thin content.
5. Make your type big enough to be read easily (12-point type is fairly standard) and not so big your professor suspects you are stretching out thin content.
6. Select a common typeface that is easy to read (Times New Roman, for example).
7. Include a caption with any visual in the paper.
8. Double-space your paper.
9. Number the pages.
10. Print on standard 8½ by 11 paper with an ink-jet or laser printer.

3 Common Writing Assignments across the Curriculum

3a CONNECT WRITING IN COLLEGE TO WRITING BEYOND COLLEGE

In our digital age, we actually write more than ever, and our writing is quite public—on Facebook pages, blogs, or email. Writing after college becomes even more public. Writing for success—especially in the business world—must be succinct, logical, and persuasive. Most professions demand excellent writing skills, even if the job does not seem to depend on writing. According to a recent survey, more than half of major corporations say they take writing skills into consideration when hiring salaried employees—and exceptional writing skills are required for advancement. While it is unlikely you will be asked to write an essay on Coleridge's "Kubla Khan" or Shakespeare's *Hamlet* after graduation, you will very likely be asked to articulate an argument that reveals a better understanding of a complex situation and a complex text or set of texts. Writing about literature is a training ground in dealing with complexity and expressing yourself with clarity

3b WRITE TO LEARN ACROSS THE CURRICULUM

The ability to summarize, analyze, synthesize, and critique information is also essential for college writing. In almost all your college courses, you will be asked to respond to something you have read, whether it be a piece of literature, a textbook, a critical article or book, a primary source, a blog, or a website. You may find these sources in a library, in your bookstore, or on the Internet, but whatever the particular assignment, you will have to *show that you understand* the text and *explain* it clearly, and you will have to *develop your own ideas* about how it works and *persuade* your reader that your interpretation is correct.

As you interpret a work of literature, you will use critical thinking skills—from summary to analysis, synthesis, and critique—that require you to look more carefully at how the text has been put together and whether the text effectively accomplishes its purpose. You will use your critical thinking skills in a summary to determine what details to leave out and which ones to keep or in a research paper when you synthesize your research into your presentation. The interpretations that you create in writing about literature employ a number of strategic skills that will prepare you to write throughout your college career:

- Summary
- Analysis
- Synthesis
- Critique

3c USE SUMMARY TO DISTILL A TEXT

Summary is used across the curriculum. It is used to condense a whole passage or text and may be a specific part of another paper (where a summary is a necessary reference point for your readers to understand your analysis) or the purpose of your paper as a whole. A summary is useful whenever you need to communicate the content of a text and represent the ideas behind any article or complex essay accurately. Summary is a mainstay of academic writing and is used in a variety of ways in all your courses, including some of the following:

- To summarize a source in order to critique it (as you would in a book review)
- To summarize several sources to reveal the body of knowledge on a particular topic (as in a report)
- To summarize the evidence you have compiled in an argument
- To summarize a critical perspective you are using to analyze a work

The goal of a summary paper (or précis or abstract) is to boil down into a few of your own words a whole text, without using your opinion or commentary. While you do have to decide what to include and what to leave out, your presentation should strive to be fair-minded and neutral. The summary paper is a way for you and your instructor to make sure you understand the main trajectory of action or thought in a reading.

Throughout this text, summary has been invoked to enhance learning, to help you make sure you have understood what has happened in a reading. The summary, therefore, needs to show that you have understood the overarching idea of what you've read. Begin by distilling the text to its single most compelling issue. Unlike a paraphrase, which is something said in another way (see the box on Summary vs. Paraphrase vs. Quotation in the handbook chapter 2 on Writing from Reading), a summary begins with a sentence that is a general condensation of all the *somethings* that were said and done in a text.

Your *interaction* with the text—the notes and annotations you have made while reading—will guide you as you identify how the story, play, or poem unfolds. You may find it useful to break the text into parts and write down each part's main idea. Use your notes or annotations to help you understand the text's twists and turns, its patterns and its allusions, and to explain comprehensively, concisely, and coherently how the main idea is supported by the entire reading.

Writing a Summary: Just the Facts

- Be neutral; don't include your opinion.
- Begin with a summary sentence of the whole text.
- Be concise; do not paraphrase the whole text.
- Explain how the elements in the reading work with the main idea.
- Look for repetitions and variations that provide insight into the main idea of the text.
- Check the text's context: When was it written? What form does it use?

Sample Student Summary

Solis 1

Lily Solis

Professor Bennett

Composition 102

30 September 2009

Précis of "Bartleby, the Scrivener"

Herman Melville's short story "Bartleby, the Scrivener" presents a businessman narrator who hires an unusual employee named Bartleby, and who consequently struggles with what to do about Bartleby's behavior. The first-person narrator introduces himself as an elderly gentleman who owns a law office. His three employees, Turkey, Nippers, and Ginger Nut, are so temperamental that the narrator is forced to hire a fourth man to fill in the gaps of their work. He hires Bartleby, who at first works industriously. However, when the narrator asks him to fulfill tasks beyond copying, Bartleby consistently replies "I would prefer not to." This pattern continues, with the narrator becoming more annoyed at Bartleby's refusals and yet feeling unwilling to turn him out. When the narrator discovers that Bartleby is living at the office, he makes an attempt at befriending Bartleby, which Bartleby evades with his usual "prefer not to" responses. Soon, Bartleby stops working entirely, due to damaged eyesight, but even when his eyes improve, Bartleby does nothing but stand all day in the office. The narrator gives Bartleby a friendly ultimatum that he must leave in six days. However, at the end of six days, Bartleby is still there, and the narrator—out of Christian charity—decides to let him remain. Still, Bartleby's presence is a nuisance, and the narrator at last decides to move his offices to another building. He receives complaints from the new tenants, asking him to remove the man he left behind. The narrator

Begins with a neutral statement that presents the basis for all plot elements in the story.

Important element identified specifically.

Concise statements introduce major characters and define their roles in the story.

Concise, neutral statements explain the sequence of action

Solis 2

returns to the old building and offers to Bartleby that he come to the narrator's private home and live there, but Bartleby refuses. A short time later, the narrator learns that Bartleby has been taken to prison as a vagrant. Although the narrator makes provisions for Bartleby to be well-fed in prison, Bartleby refuses to eat, and the narrator visits one day to find him dead. The narrator concludes the story by offering a rumor that Bartleby previously worked in a Dead Letter Office.

Gives story's resolution without offering reader's interpretation.

Work Cited

Melville, Herman. "Bartleby, the Scrivener." *Literature: Craft & Voice*. Eds. Nicholas Delbanco and Alan Cheuse. Vol. 1. New York: McGraw-Hill, 2009. 553–572. Print.

3d USE ANALYSIS TO EXAMINE HOW THE PARTS CONTRIBUTE TO THE WHOLE

Like summary, analysis is critical to college writing. In an analysis, you break the selection down into its parts and examine how the parts of a work contribute to the whole. Whether you are writing about irony in Flannery O'Connor or the impact of gunpowder on warfare, your analysis will look at how your source has put together its case, and you will use the source itself as evidence for your analysis. Your thesis will point specifically to the scope of your analysis. Possible analyses include:

- An explication of several aspects of how language is used—most often line by line—to point out the connotations and denotations of words as well as the reinforcing images that are used (see the following paper on William Blake's "The Garden of Love").
- An analysis of one aspect of a specific text, like dialect in Gish Jen's "Who's Irish?" or parallelism in The Museum of Stones by Carolyn Forché (see the Interactive Reading in chapter 15).
- A card report on the various elements of a story, generally only what you can fit on a 5" x 8" index card (see the sample card report at the end of this section).

1. Explication. An explication is a kind of analysis that shows how words, images, or other textual elements relate to each other and how these relationships make the meaning of the text clearer. Outside literature, an explication is a close reading of any text where the goal is to logically analyze details within the text itself to uncover deeper meanings or contradictions. According to *Merriam-Webster*, the definition of explicate is "to give a detailed explanation of" or "to develop the implications of; analyze logically." An explication paper does both of these things, as it *gives a detailed* *explanation of* the devices present in order to *analyze logically* the work in question. In other words, the goal of an explication is to unpack the elements of a poem, short passage of fiction or drama, or other text. The thesis statement in an explication is usually a summary of the central idea that all the devices combine to create.

Many explications take a line-by-line or sentence-by-sentence approach. Others organize the paper according to a few elements of craft that seem most meaningful to the work. However you decide to tailor your paper, remember that an explication should touch on more than one element. When explicating fiction or drama, pay attention to character, diction, and tone, and how those connect with larger thematic concerns. In the following paper on a poem, you will see an explanation of the significance of elements like rhyme, meter, diction, simile, metaphor, symbol, imagery, tone, and allusion. Although the author doesn't exactly move line by line through the poem, she does start where the poem starts and walks through it to the end. She organizes her paper in light of the shift she identifies in the poem, which she addresses in the introduction. Notice, too, that her thesis states the sum total of the devices explicated: an overall shift from an innocent state to a repressed state.

Sample Student Explication

Brown 1

Deborah Brown

Dr. Cranford

English 200

16 September 2007

Title introduces the poem and poet.

Repression and the Church: Understanding Blake's "The Garden of Love"

William Blake's "The Garden of Love" is seemingly appropriate for either *Songs of Innocence* or *Songs of Experience,* for it contains elements of both states. In publishing the poem under the latter, however, Blake suggests that beneath the singsong, child-like quality is a serious message. While the poem begins with colorful imagery and nursery-rhyme rhythm, there is a marked shift as it progresses with an increasingly dark setting and disrupted meter. This shift is triggered by the appearance of a chapel. It is only when considering how this shift occurs that we can fully appreciate how "The Garden of Love" inverts the idea of the church as good, aligning it instead with oppression.

Thesis statement that gives the central idea conveyed by the elements to be explicated.

At the beginning of the poem, several poetic factors work together to create the impression of youthfulness, and therefore a sense of innocence. The meter consists of an iamb followed by two anapestic feet, which makes a beat reminiscent of a nursery rhyme recitation. This nursery rhyme quality is supported by the rhyme scheme which, until the last stanza, follows a regular pattern of abcb. In addition to the structure of the poem, Blake's diction contributes to the child-like voice of the speaker, for he selects

Brown 2

Discuses how each poetic device—meter, rhyme, diction, simile, and imagery— contributes to theme of innocence.

simple words that are, for the most part, monosyllabic. At the most, the words contain two syllables, the longest being "garden" (lines 1, 7), "chapel" (3, 5), and "tombstones" (10). Furthermore, the syntax follows in accord with the simplicity of the diction, as the words are organized in a straightforward, sentence-like manner. The tone comes across as particularly child-like when we consider that seven of the twelve lines in this poem begin with "And," creating the effect of a child who is incapable of forming complex sentences and so advances his story by adding onto the same sentence time and again. The absence of simile and metaphor also lends a lack of complexity to the speaker (although this is certainly not to say that there is a lack of complexity in the poem). In fact, the seeming simplicity of the poem is furthered by the way in which the speaker offers observations rather than reflections. This is set up in the second line when the speaker says, "And saw what I never had seen." The rest of the poem, then, is merely a description of the scene without offering any interpretation. The innocence of the speaker is also established through the imagery at the beginning of the poem. Blake describes the Garden of Love as full of "so many sweet flowers" (8), and he also mentions "the green" (4). These images suggest growth and spring, both of which connote youth. Green especially holds connotations with innocence or a lack of maturity, since both wood that is not yet mature and un-ripened fruit are green.

Specific support from the poem.

Topic sentences identify the shift in the poem.

All of these elements that are associated with childhood and innocence are found at the beginning of the poem. In the second stanza, there is a change in meter with the line, "And the gates of the Chapel were shut" (5). Here, just before the first hint of repression found in the word "shut," Blake has omitted the iamb and included three anapests instead of two. Although still predominantly anapestic, Blake continues to vary the meter, such as in lines 11 and 12 in which he alternates an iamb with an anapest and further deviates from his original form by changing from the abcb end rhyme scheme to internal rhyme—"And binding with *briars* my joys & *desires*" (emphasis added, 12). This altered structure is significant because it indicates that something has changed from the beginning of the poem. To understand this shift, we must first note where the disruptions occur.

Discusses how meter contributes to shift identified in topic sentence.

Specific support from the poem.

The first major disruption of meter comes when Blake writes, "And 'Thou shalt not' writ over the door" (6). Because there are so many monosyllabic words, it is ambiguous where the stresses should lie, yet it is clearly impossible to read this as

Brown 3

strictly anapestic. The result is that "thou shalt not" is emphasized, a message that contrasts the carefree state of "play" (4) in the first stanza. Blake again disrupts the meter when he writes, "And I saw it was filled with graves" (9), which draws attention to the word "graves." Here, too, Blake creates a stark contrast between the image of a garden full of life and the image of a garden filled with graves. Furthermore, the change in the color of Blake's imagery from the first stanza to the last represents a loss of the vibrant nature of youth. What began as a green is now filled with the bleak, monochromatic image of "tombstones where flowers should be" (10) while the priests add to the gloom of the scene by wearing "black gowns" (11). While all these changes are important to note, the key to understanding this poem can be found in the source that sparked this change of setting: a Chapel.

Discusses symbol.

The Chapel in the poem acts as a symbol, a metonymical device that can be taken as a representative of the church as an institution. The shut doors and the phrase "thou shalt not" written over them suggest that the Chapel represents repression. Blake writes that, "A Chapel was built [in the garden's] midst, / Where I used to play on the green" (3, 4), furthering the Chapel—a symbol of religion—as a repressive force by implying that it impedes playing and all the carefree ways that accompany playing. The Priests, who enter the scene with the Chapel, enforce the repression dictated by the church, for they are the ones who end up "binding with briars [the speaker's] joys & desires" (12). Blake's choice of the word "binding" is significant because it implies passivity and restraint; the same qualities are evoked in the idea of routine found in the image of the priests "walking their rounds" (11).

Topic sentence moves discussion towards the thesis.

Further explication of symbol.

In addition to the Chapel and the Priests, there are several religious elements that suggest that this poem is making a statement about the church. To begin with, the Garden of Love is in many ways reminiscent of the Garden of Eden. Both house abundant growth and are originally places of innocence. However, they each contain something forbidden which brings a loss of innocence and death. In Eden, it was the forbidden fruit from the Tree of Knowledge that led to sin and ultimately death. The forbidden part in the Garden of Love is the implication of "thou shalt not." The appearance of this forbidding message—a statement of repression—is accompanied by an appearance of graves (representative of death) instead of flowers (representative of growth/life). A second religious element in the poem is the phrase "thou shalt not"

Identifies allusion.

Brown 4

itself, which alludes to the Bible, and more specifically, the Ten Commandments. These commandments are statements of what man should not do; thus the phrase automatically echoes with connotations of restraint and repression. Another element reminiscent of religion is Blake's use of capitalization. Just as "He" is capitalized as a sign of respect when used in reference to God, so too does Blake capitalize only those words which are related to religion: Garden of Love, Chapel, and Priests. The poem becomes ironic when one considers that it is the Chapel and the Priests, the very objects that the capitalization suggests we should revere, that bring about the change from a place of life and play to a place of restraint and death. It is through these religious allusions that Blake allows the reader to connect the repressive, restrictive setting wrought by the appearance of a Chapel to the church at large as an institution.

Explains significance of Biblical allusions; ties elements previously discussed to thesis.

The diction, imagery, symbols, and allusions used in "The Garden of Love" work together to create a contrast between the energy and youthfulness of innocence found in the first stanza and the repression and death that is increasingly present after the chapel's appearance. In this way, Blake shows that the church turns happy innocence into dark forbidding, creating in a mere twelve lines of poetry a statement against the repressive nature of the church in his time.

Reviews key points of the discussion; re-statement and refinement of thesis.

Work Cited

Blake, William. "The Garden of Love." *Literature: Craft & Voice.* Eds. Nicholas Delbanco and Alan Cheuse. Vol. 2. New York: McGraw-Hill, 2009. 396. Print.

2. Card report.   A card report asks you to represent in a condensed space the various elements of a story. Most instructors require that your report not exceed the amount of information you can fit on a 5" x 8" inch note card, and therefore you must make every word count. As you take apart the pieces of the story, you will naturally forge a deeper understanding of it, and likely a new opinion of the work as a whole. Card reports are a great way to keep track of what you have read and can be an invaluable tool in preparing for exams.

In the following card report, our student, Tessa Harville, was instructed to include the list of information that appears below:

1.   Title of the story and date of publication

2. Author's name, dates of birth and death, and the nationality or region (if applicable) with which he/she is associated

3. The name and a brief description of the main character, especially important personality traits

4. Additional characters who play important roles and their major traits

5. The setting, including time and place

6. The type of narration or point of view

7. A summary of the story's major events in the order in which they occur

8. The tone or voice in which the author relates the story

9. The overall style of the work, including (if space allows) short quotes that exemplify the style

10. A brief analysis of irony in the story

11. The theme of the story

12. The major symbols in the story and a brief explanation of what you think each means

13. A critique of the story in which you give your evaluation or opinion of the story in question

As you look at the following model, note the amount of thought and effort to refine language that the student put into the "Critique" portion. Although it is brief, your critique should reflect the amount of thought you might put into a three-page paper.

Sample Student Card Report

Front of Card

Tessa Harville

English 101, Section 2

Title: "A Good Man Is Hard to Find" (1955)

Author: Flannery O'Connor, 1925-1964, American, Southern writer

Main Character: The grandmother, who lives with her son's family and refuses to be ignored. She considers herself a lady, but is stubborn, talkative, and insists on her own way.

Other Characters: Bailey, the father of the family, who is grumpy and sullen; Bailey's unnamed wife, who quietly tends the children and is ineffectual; John Wesley and June Star, Bailey's son and daughter who are typical children that bluntly speak their minds and are excited by adventure; and The Misfit, an escaped murderer who philosophizes with the grandmother.

Setting: Georgia, presumably around the 1950s, when the story was written. Much of the story recounts a car trip so the scenery changes.

Narration: Third-person omniscient; primarily follows grandmother.

Summary: 1. The grandmother tries to convince Bailey to take the family to Tennessee for vacation, rather than Florida, and uses the newspaper article she reads about The Misfit as a reason not to travel toward Florida. 2. The family leaves for Florida. The car trip is full of bickering and a restaurant stop where the grandmother talks with the owners about how bad people have become. 3. Back on the road, the grandmother convinces Bailey to take a detour so she can see a plantation she visited years ago. 4. The grandmother's cat, which she snuck into the car, causes an accident while they are on a deserted road looking for the plantation. 5. Three men arrive to help the family. The grandmother recognizes one as The Misfit, and as a result, he has his men shoot the family, one by one. The grandmother is shot last, after a moment of connection with The Misfit in which she sees him as "one of [her] own children" (437).

Tone/Voice: The tone is deadpan, with no comments from the narrator. This makes for a reportorial voice with the precision of an acute observer.

Back of Card

Style: The sentences are straightforward and often declarative: "The grandmother didn't want to go to Florida" (429). The description is vivid but concise: "The car raced roughly along in a swirl of pink dust" (433).

Irony: Becomes most apparent after reading the story and looking back, making it dramatic irony. The family does not know to heed the grandmother's preposterous warning about The Misfit before taking the vacation, but the reader knows she is right. The dramatic irony is aided by the large amount of foreshadowing, such as the grandma's remembering the plantation outside of "Toombsboro" (432). The grandmother's behavior is at times ironic—she is concerned with being a lady, but talks too much; she says people should be more respectful, but then uses biased language as she ogles a "pickaninny" (430). The way she causes her own trouble is ironic.

Theme: A feeling of connection can transcend the shocking reality of life's brutality.

Symbols: The grandmother could symbolize the South: her vanity and pretense to being a lady cause a violent downfall. The family burial ground with "five or six graves" seen from the car is both a foreshadowing tool and symbolic of the family's impending death (431).

Critique: Although the story relies on wild coincidence, elements including highly believable characters, perfectly placed description, and economic movement of the plot make this story gripping and a representation of life with all its vanity, surprises, and connections.

3e USE A SYNTHESIS TO SHOW RELATIONSHIPS

Synthesis requires two or more sources and shows significant relationships among those sources. The classic synthesis in college writing is the research project, which asks you to look at a topic in depth and from multiple perspectives. The next chapter will follow closely a research paper on the poetry of Langston Hughes, from finding a topic to selecting sources. Here we will look at how that research project is an argument. Another synthesis across the curriculum could be a report on a body of information (on, for example, the effect of AIDS on Africa). The comparison-contrast paper, like the research project, is found in almost every area of college study.

1. Argument. The primary goal of an argument paper is to take a position on an issue or form an opinion about a piece of literature and defend that position/opinion using evidence. In a single-source paper (such as the critique of Chekhov's "Rapture" discussed under critique in this chapter), your evidence will be examples and quotations from the text itself. Most of the time, however, an argument paper will be an assignment that involves outside or secondary sources. Secondary sources, such as literary criticism, report, describe, comment on, or analyze a written work other than itself. You can use secondary sources to see what people have learned and written about a topic or an existing work of literature.

Nearly every sample paper cited in this chapter is an argument paper in some sense—a thesis statement in most papers is a type of argument because it posits an opinion that the writer must then support. The best examples of argument papers are the Chekhov student paper, which appears in chapter 2, and the model research project, which appears in the next chapter. In the Chekhov paper, the student argues that the story is incomplete and unsatisfying. Because the student responds to a single source, he supports his argument by citing Chekhov's text directly.

In the research paper on Langston Hughes in the next chapter, the student argues that Langston Hughes uses only those aspects of jazz that reflect the African-American experience. In that paper, the student uses multiple sources to make her argument. To support her points about jazz, she uses secondary sources that provide historical context. To support her reading of jazz devices in Hughes's poems, she relies on quotes taken directly from two of Hughes's poems.

2. Comparison and contrast. A compare/contrast paper asks you to consider two works side-by-side and highlight the similarities and differences between them in order to make a point about one or both texts. When you are selecting texts to compare, you must make sure that there is some basis for the comparison—perhaps the works share a common theme; or, they may be vastly different but both products of the same region.

Let's break that definition down a little bit, using the example of comparing *Beowulf* the epic poem with *Beowulf* the 2007 movie version (see chapter 13, Fiction and the Visual Arts, for these two works). The basis for comparison of these sources is self-evident: they are two versions of the same story. After reading the epic and watching the movie, you would ask yourself what the major similarities are and list them. In this case, you might make a list of the characters that the two have in common or the scenes that are common to both text and movie. Then, you should do the same for differences. In the *Beowulf* example, you might note the major plot change that Grendel's mother seduces King Hrothgar and Beowulf, so that they are the fathers of monsters.

As you make your lists, you might further think if some of the items you listed under similarities might in fact hold small differences when examined closely. Continuing with the *Beowulf* example, you might first have noted that Grendel appears in both versions and is a monster in both versions. But as you think about the movie, you might see that, in fact, he seems more distressed than evil.

The following student paper grew out of just such a comparison. Our author, Anthony Melmott, used the similarities and particularly the differences he saw in the two versions of Grendel to make a point about the role of the villain in today's world. Notice how he moves through the paper: after an introduction and an overview of the characters' similarities, Anthony delves into a detailed analysis of how the two differ. He then ties his entire discussion together in the concluding paragraph, and impressively broadens it to make a statement about contemporary society.

Sample Student Comparison/Contrast Paper

Melmott 1

Anthony Melmott

Professor Wallace

English 150

30 November 2008

Visions of the Villain:

The Role of Grendel in *Beowulf* the Epic and the Movie

In the movie version of *Beowulf,* directed by Robert Zemeckis and released in 2007, there are obvious deviations from the plot of the original epic. Most viewers who are familiar with the epic will readily recognize a major change: Beowulf does not kill Grendel's mother but is instead seduced by her. Clearly, Beowulf in the movie

Opening sentence establishes the works that will be compared.

Melmott 2

Thesis state-
ment. Also,
the mention
of three points
sets up the
organization of
the paper.

version is no longer the hero that he was in the original epic. But what many viewers might miss is that the movie changes more than the hero. Grendel, too, is no longer the evil villain he was in the original epic. Whereas the poem leaves no question that Grendel is a demon with evil intent, the movie portrays him as a tortured, childish soul through differences in his motivation, his power status, and his lineage.

Discussion of
similarities.

The reason that many *Beowulf* movie viewers might miss the change to Grendel's character is that in many respects, he is similar to the original Grendel. In both versions, Grendel is a monster who eats and kills men. His overall trajectory does not change from the epic to the movie: in each, he attacks Hereot's hall and gets away with it until Beowulf comes and tears off his arm, thereby killing him. Even certain details of Grendel's portrayal in the movie echo the original epic. For example, the epic introduces Grendel by calling him an inhabitant of "the abode of monster kind" (14). The movie visually represents him as a monster by making him tall and hideous: his body—which drips with slime—looks as if it is turned inside out. As in the original epic, Grendel appears at night, thus aligning him with darkness in both versions. In these ways, he is meant to be seen as a terrible being in each.

Transition into
discussion of
differences.

But a little digging suggests otherwise. A major difference between the epic and the movie is that Grendel does not speak in the epic but does speak in the movie. Since Grendel does not speak, and since he is portrayed through narrative rather than visual effect, the epic uses a variety of language to describe Grendel. He is called a "fiend of hell"; "wrathful spirit"; "mighty stalker of the marches" (14); "creature of destruction, fierce and greedy, wild and furious" (15); and a "terrible monster, like a dark shadow of death" (17). All of this language reinforces Grendel's evilness and angry mode of existence. Grendel's fearsome appearance in the movie might lead a viewer to imagine him as the above list describes. However, the movie version allows Grendel to speak, and when he does, we hear a different story. Grendel speaks in Old English, even though the other characters speak in contemporary English, so his lines are difficult to understand. But listening closely reveals that when Beowulf says to Grendel, whose arm is caught in the door, "Your bloodletting days are finished, demon," Grendel replies, "I am not a demon."

Textual
support.

Support from
the movie.

On its own, this example could be explained as Grendel lacking the self-awareness that he is a demon. But other details corroborate Grendel's statement. Both of Grendel's attacks are triggered by the loud rollicking of the men in Hereot. As the scene pans from the meadhall to Grendel's underground lair, the noise of the chanting sounds as if it has been submerged. The effect is that we are hearing the men as Grendel hears them—a constant, throbbing, bass line that makes Grendel's membranous ears quiver. When Grendel bursts into full view, his screams are more like cries of anguish than roars meant to frighten. The attention given to Grendel's sensitive ears, his clutching at his head as he screams, and his posture all suggest that he is in physical agony from the parties at Heorot, and thus bursts in to put a stop to it. This is a far less demoniac motivation than that cited in the epic.

In the original, Grendel's first attack reads, "The creature of destruction, fierce and greedy, wild and furious, was ready straight. He seized thirty thanes upon their bed" (15). Nothing in this suggests any sort of pain or anguish that Grendel experiences, as he appears to in the movie. Further, while the movie shows him as provoked, the epic clearly states after that first attack, "It was no longer than a single night ere he wrought more deeds of murder; he recked not of the feud and the crime—he was too fixed in them!" (16). According to the *Oxford English Dictionary,* "reck" means "To take heed or have a care of some thing (or person), so as to be alarmed or troubled thereby, or to modify one's conduct or purpose on that account." In other words, this quote shows that Grendel's killings do not bother him or give him pause because he is so set in his evil ways. Hence, even if Grendel could speak in the original epic, he certainly wouldn't say "I am no demon" and even if he did, we would know by his actions that this was not true. On the contrary, when Grendel utters that line in the movie, we have seen that, indeed, his motivation is not naturally demonic but provocation.

Consistent with the change in motivation is the change in Grendel's power status from the epic to the movie. In the epic, Grendel holds a reign of terror. Although it is difficult to analyze language in a translation, it is safe to say that the text refers to Grendel in several places as a ruling authority of sorts. One example follows Grendel's

Defines unknown word to add textual support.

Transition sentence that leads into the second point of the thesis.

Textual support.

Melmott 4

first series of attacks in which the poem reads, "Thus he tyrannized over them" (16). In another translation, that of Seamus Heaney, the same line reads "So Grendel ruled" (35). Both "rule" and "tyranny" are ways of describing an all-powerful governing body. Later, when he fights Beowulf, Grendel is described as the "master of evils" (43), and in the Heaney translation as "the captain of evil" (47). "Master" and "captain" both refer to someone in charge, someone with power, and both are applied to Grendel in the original epic.

Yet for all the power the epic accords to Grendel, the movie portrays Grendel as child-like. While Grendel has a mother in both versions, only the movie shows Grendel interact with her like a child. After his first attack in the movie, he returns to his lair and speaks with his mother. Throughout their dialogue, he lays on the floor of the cave in a position reminiscent of a fetus. The words he speaks are likewise childish; at one point, he cries out, "The men screamed! The men bellowed and screamed! The men hurt me, hurt my ear." Not only do his simple, repetitive sentences suggest a child's voice, but his fear of and dismay at the men show him to be the opposite of their tyrant, ruler, master, or captain.

The reduction of Grendel's evilness and power can perhaps be traced to the biggest difference between the epic and the movie's Grendel: that of Grendel's lineage. As mentioned in the introduction, the movie portrays Grendel's mother as a seductress, with the premise that she once seduced King Hrothgar, making Grendel the offspring of Hrothgar and the mother. On the other hand, the original epic is very clear—and frequently emphasizes—that Grendel is a descendent of Cain, who committed the first murder. Referring to Cain, the epic reads, "From him there woke to life all the evil broods, monsters and elves and sea-beasts, and giants too, who long time strove with God" (14–15). There is no room for a human in this description, and certainly not Hrothgar, whom the epic praises as being a "good king." By changing Grendel's parentage, the movie shifts the root of evil from Grendel to Hrothgar. It is because of Hrothgar's past weakness that his kingdom is plagued by the fruit of that very weakness. Grendel, then, is a by-product, a mere pawn in the struggle between Hrothgar's kingdom and the mother's corrupting ways. The mother uses Grendel's

Support from the movie.

Transition sentence that leads into the third point of the thesis.

Melmott 5

death as a way to further corrupt the kingdom through her seduction of Beowulf—and Beowulf succumbs.

In the retelling of an existing story—whether that retelling be in the form of a story, a poem, or a movie—there will always be similarities and differences. But the difference in the role of the villain between an epic written in 1000 and a movie filmed in 2007 tells us something about our contemporary society. As we noted briefly in the introduction, Beowulf's seduction makes him less heroic; likewise, we have seen that the movie makes Grendel less villainous in motivation, in power, and in lineage. We might ask ourselves: What does it mean to live in an age where we see heroes as fallible and villains as innocent? The difference between the epic Grendel and the movie Grendel offers an answer: the original villain has been turned into a product of human vice, suggesting that true villainy lies in human behavior. Or, to put it another way, in a world where human deeds are monstrous, there isn't much room for a monster.

Brief reit-eration of the three points made in the paper.

Conclusion broadens significance to our own society.

Conclusion explains the implication of the thesis; answers the "so what?" question.

Works Cited

Beowulf. Dir. Robert Zemeckis. Perf. Crispin Glover, Anthony Hopkins, Angelina Jolie, and Ray Winstone. Paramount Pictures, 2007. Film.

Beowulf. Trans. Seamus Heaney. *The Norton Anthology of English Literature.* 7th ed. Ed. M.H. Abrams and Stephen Greenblatt. New York: W.W. Norton, 2000. 32–99. Print.

Beowulf. Trans. Chauncey Brewster Tinker. New York: Newson & Co., 1902. Print.

"Reck." Def. 1b. *The Oxford English Dictionary.* 2nd ed. 1989. Print.

3f USE CRITIQUE TO BRING IN YOUR OWN EVALUATION

We define a critique as a summary with your own reasonable opinion. Whether you are asked to critique a reading for an essay exam, the accuracy of a website as a source, or respond to an argument, in most of your courses, you will be required to evaluate the presentation of information.

- What is the work (or performance) trying to accomplish?
- Does it achieve its purpose?
- Do you agree or disagree with the piece, like or dislike it?
- How has the piece created this reaction in you?

Review. A critique is a formal evaluation of a text, and one of the most common forms of critique in literature is the review. In a review, you—as the reviewer—get to evaluate the text or, in the case of live theatre, a performance. For an example of a review, see the response to Anton Chekhov's early story "Rapture" in chapter 2. After a few general, opening sentences, the discussion becomes more specific as the student asserts that the main character's lack of change makes the story unsatisfying. The student continues by analyzing the various parts of the story. As your review progresses and you begin to make evaluative statements—such as *The story begins on a strong note but deteriorates; The casting was so well-done that it carries the play from start to finish; The poem's sonnet form is perfect for its content*—you will also need to analyze why you are reacting to the text in that particular way. Particularly strong is his division of the story into three parts:

> *Part one: the clerk runs in, announcing himself, disrupting the household, waking his brothers. Part two: Mitya takes out the newspaper and urges his father to read it aloud. In the closing sequence, a reader may expect something to happen as a result of Mitya's "rapture" that he has become famous because his name is in the paper and on the police record. However, as the ancient philosopher and critic Aristotle might put it, what is the dramatic purpose here? . . . His parents and his siblings humor him instead of contradicting or berating him; thus making change less likely for Mitya. The reader is left to wonder what the point is, and without that concluding action, the dramatic purpose is unclear, and the story is incomplete and ultimately unsatisfying.*

Notice here that the author is not afraid to make bold claims: that the story is incomplete and unsatisfying. You may feel a little intimidated the first time you write a review, especially if the author is well known. Take the Chekhov paper to heart; the validity of an evaluation rests not on how highly you are ranking a noted author but on how your analysis of the story supports your evaluation. In this case, the student has analyzed the structure of the story, and found that in a story set up for a three-part movement, the third part is missing. Therefore, when he claims that the story is incomplete and unsatisfying, we see the author's point.

Guidelines for Writing Reviews

Introduce What You Are Evaluating

- Include the title and author.

- For a live performance, include who performed, when, and under what circumstances (a full house? an outdoor amphitheater?).

- Be clear about what you are evaluating.

Set Up Your Review with a Summary

- Your summary is to be used as a reference point for your discussion; you may not want to give the ending away, however.

Put the Piece into Context

- What type of work is it? A comedy? A tragedy?

- When was it written?

- If it is a well-known play such as Shakespeare, include any unusual information on the "take" of the director (what's the director's purpose in staging Shakespeare's "Hamlet" in Pakistan, for example).

Analyze the Text

- For a play, note the staging, lighting, and costuming as well as the acting.

- Note how the work is structured.

- Look at the individual elements: plot, character, dialogue.

- Determine the purpose of the work.

Include Your Reasoned Opinion: This Is Your Evaluation

- Did the work achieve its purpose?

- What is your response to the selection and why?

- Agree or disagree with the presentation of information (whether or not it achieved its purpose).

- Base your agreement or disagreement on evidence.

End with a Balanced Conclusion

- Recap the pros and cons of the piece.

- Give your overall reaction.

3g FIND AN EFFECTIVE APPROACH TO THE ESSAY EXAM

Timed writing on an exam may seem like an intimidating prospect. Reviewing the tips below will help you learn an effective approach to essay exams, whether you are taking one for a class in English, political science, or psychology.

1. Prepare.   If you have been diligent in annotating the texts you read and keeping a journal or freewriting exercises, be sure to review these materials before the day of your exam. Jog your memory about each story, poem, novel, or play you have read for the class by reviewing major characters and events of the work, as well as any important information about the authors.

2. Pace yourself.   When you receive the exam, glance through it to see approximately how much time you should spend on each section. Remember that if an essay is worth, say, 70 percent of the grade, you want to make it a priority to spend sufficient time on it.

3. Read the assignment carefully.   When you arrive at the essay question, circle key words as you read the assignment. Pay particular attention to the verbs your instructor uses: common choices are *explain, discuss, analyze, compare, contrast, interpret,* and *argue.* Your understanding of the different types of assignments addressed in this chapter can help you here.

Understanding Essay Exam Assignments

The words explain *or* discuss *ask you to engage in a detailed way, much like an explication or a close reading.*

Analyze *should remind you of what you know about an analysis paper—that your job is to explore one element of the text and show how it contributes to the overall work.*

Compare *and* contrast *asks you to find similarities and differences between two items and to suggest what those similarities or differences emphasize or illuminate.*

Argue *is a way of asking you to take a position about an issue, or in the case of a literary text, to defend what you see in the work that may not be readily apparent to others.*

4. Form a thesis.   In an essay exam, your thesis will likely be a simpler statement than the type of complex argument you would form in a longer research paper or analysis. Look at the phrasing of the question itself to help you shape your thesis.

EXAMPLE OF AN ESSAY EXAM ASSIGNMENT

➡ *Analyze Frost's use of imagery in "Stopping By Woods on a Snowy Evening."*

EXAMPLE OF A THESIS THAT RESPONDS TO THE ASSIGNMENT

Frost uses idyllic, New England imagery to disguise a more serious statement about death.

5. Outline briefly.   Even if you don't typically work from an outline when writing a paper, take a few moments to jot down a brief outline. In an essay exam, even a brief outline will keep you from freezing up entirely. And, if you find you are spending too much time on the first paragraph, you can quickly wrap it up to move on to the next point in your outline. In short, an outline can help you budget time and space in your essay while eliminating the stressful feeling of not knowing where to go next.

6. Check your work.   Try your best to allow a little extra time in which to read over what you have written. Time constraints often make even the best students leave out words or write sentences that make no sense. Rereading your work will allow you to fix these problems.

Follow our model student, Renee Knox, as she completes the following essay assignment on a timed exam.

Notes for a Sample Student Essay Exam

Renee identifies key words in the prompt. Already, she knows her paper must focus on the significance of the imagery.

Renee underlines the imagery in the poem and highlights phrases she finds significant.

Assignment: Analyze Frost's use of imagery in "Stopping By Woods on a Snowy Evening," reproduced below.

Stopping By Woods On A Snowy Evening

Whose woods these are I think I know.	1
His house is in the village though;	2
He will not see me stopping here	3
To watch his woods fill up with snow.	4
My little horse must think it queer	5
To stop without a farmhouse near	6
Between the woods and frozen lake	7
The darkest evening of the year.	8
He gives his harness bells a shake	9
To ask if there is some mistake.	10
The only other sound's the sweep	11
Of easy wind and downy flake.	12
The woods are lovely, dark and deep.	13
But I have promises to keep,	14
And miles to go before I sleep,	15
And miles to go before I sleep.	16

Renee numbers the lines for easy reference when she quotes in the essay.

Renee notes that many of her underlined phrases bring to mind a farm-like, New England setting. Then she separates out the other images and names their connotations.

Important images: woods, snow, horse, house, village, dark, wind, snowflakes, dark

woods, snow, horse, farmhouse, village=New England; ideal Christmas scene

no farmhouse near, dark, deep, winter=cold, alone, death??

sleep=death?

Thesis: Frost uses pretty New England imagery to disguise a more serious statement about death.

Renee formulates a thesis based on her observations.

Renee generates a brief outline to follow. In constructing her essay, she will use a 5 paragraph structure.

I.   Introduction and thesis
II.   Set up "pretty" imagery
      A. Mention horse
      B. Mention farmhouse
      C. Mention woods
      D. Mention snow
      E. Adds up to ideal Christmas village scene
III. Set up dark imagery and cold effect
      A. Snow
      B. Woods
      C. Wind
      D. Solitary
IV.   Discuss symbolic significance of images
      A. Snow=winter=death
      B. Woods=wild, easily lose your way
      C. Sleep=form of death
V.   Conclusion—why would Frost do this?

Sample Student Essay Exam

Renee Knox

Professor Giordano

ENGL 1203

5 November 2008

Imagery in Frost's "Stopping By Woods on a Snowy Evening"

Many times in literature, as in life, something appears to be one thing but is actually another. One need only think of tales like "Little Red Riding Hood" in which the woman who appears to be her grandmother turns out to be a wolf. In a similar way, Robert Frost's "Stopping By Woods on a Snowy Evening" appears to be a simple and charming experience. Instead, Frost uses idyllic New England imagery to disguise a more serious statement about death.

Even in the poem's title, Frost is already using imagery, for the title presents woods, snow, and evening. We can picture an evening scene in which snow is softly falling on woods. And indeed, the speaker is there with his "little horse" (line 5) that wears "harness bells" (9). The mention of a village (2) and a farmhouse (6), even though the speaker is not near them, suggests that villages and farmhouses dot the landscape in which the speaker moves. Put all together—snow, a horse with harness bells, a village, and a farmhouse—Frost's imagery conjures a New England scene that is so quaint, it is exactly the type of scene many people replicate with porcelain villages at Christmas time—it is that perfect.

However, if we look at the nature imagery, we get a much darker picture. While evening might connote a soothing time of leisure after the day's work is done, it is also the time of oncoming dark, as Frost's imagery indicates when he describes it as "the darkest evening of the year" (8). In fact, Frost calls attention to the fact that it is the darkest evening by placing that description in line 8, the exact center of the 16-line poem. Furthermore, he repeats "dark" again when he describes the woods as "dark and deep" (13), adding emphasis to the imagery of dark through repetition. We also know that the evening is cold, and although snow is a part of an idyllic New England Christmas scene, it is equally an unpleasant feeling with bleak connotations. If the world is cold, it means that it is not treating you well. Beyond this kind of cold, there

---

Margin notes:

Renee uses a simple but complete title, in order not to spend too much time on it.

Renee stays on topic by following her outline.

Renee helps her paper flow by using "however" to signal her transition to her next point.

Thesis statement. When Renee reread her essay, she changed "pretty" to "idyllic" for more sophisticated diction.

Knox 2

is the sensory imagery of the only sound being "the sweep / of easy wind and downy flake" (11-12). In other words, the narrator is not only out in the cold, but he is so alone that he actually hears the snowflakes falling in the wind. When put together with the dark, this is a bleak and lonely scene.

Beyond the sensory unpleasantness of dark and cold, these images have symbolic meaning when placed in the context of other literature. Frost's imagery clearly places this moment in winter, which traditionally symbolizes death, much as spring symbolizes rebirth. Moreover, even though the woods are "lovely," they are also "dark and deep," a place where in much of literature, like Shakespeare's "A Midsummer Night's Dream," characters easily lose themselves or succumb to supernatural forces. Perhaps the woods are "lovely" because their darkness tantalizes the narrator to lose himself, but if you followed such an idea through, the speaker would end up lost and frozen in the dark woods. The last lines reinforce the idea that he is being tempted by death. When recalling himself from gazing into the cold, dark woods, the speaker gives his reason as having "miles to go before I sleep" (15). Sleep, like winter, is another way of suggesting death, for much of literature speaks of death as a type of eternal sleep.

Thus, while the scene's first impression is one of a quaint New England night—an impression built through imagery of horse, village, farmhouse, and snow—the cold and dark nature imagery tells another story of death and the temptation to remain in the presence of death. By bringing these two types of imagery together in one poem, Frost perhaps suggests that death is always near, even when we think we are looking at a vivid scene of comfort. Or, to put a more optimistic spin on things, since some of the images overlap (snowy woods are both beautiful and dangerous), Frost might be trying to tell us that death is nothing to fear, that even on the darkest evening, there is still loveliness in the dark of the woods and the sweep of the flake.

Renee further analyzes the imagery she set up in the previous paragraph to ensure she sufficiently answers the prompt.

Renee supports her point with specific examples from the text.

Renee transitions to a brief but insightful conclusion.

In reading Renee's essay, you may have noticed that there were places that sounded a little rough or colloquial and other spots that weren't perfectly explained, such as the end of the fourth paragraph. However, her main ideas are clear and her conclusion compelling. She also used specific support and stayed exactly on topic with what the assignment asked her to do. For these reasons, Renee's essay is well done because the constraints of a timed setting often force the writer to leave a few rough spots. If you have time, do your best to revise, but remember that a timed essay will almost never have the same polished quality as a paper you have had time to think about, draft, and revise.

4 Quoting, Paraphrasing, Summarizing, and Avoiding Plagiarism

4a KNOW WHAT INFORMATION REQUIRES DOCUMENTATION

When writing from sources—whether a single source, as when you respond to a story, poem, or play you have just read, or multiple sources, as when you include research—you will need to effectively use quotation, paraphrase, and summary in your paper. Quotation, paraphrase, and summary are the evidence you use for your interpretation of a work, and it is common for all three to be employed in the same paper. **Plagiarism** occurs when this material isn't presented accurately. In this chapter, you will find information on how to keep track of the author, title, or URL for any source you have consulted (see also Writing the Research Paper, Avoiding Plagiarism, and Documenting Sources). Keeping track of sources is critical, because how you present your evidence determines more than just how convincing your paper is; it keeps your paper honest by giving your readers

- A framework (who, what, when, where, and how) for your response.
- The specifics in the source that led you to your observations, thoughts, and connections.

Marginal annotations, underlined and highlighted passages, or notes in a reading journal help you trace your response back to specific source material. Your interaction with one text or many provides the basis of your interpretation and the thesis of your paper. Whether you base your paper on a single source or you work with multiple sources, you will likely need to summarize a work to provide your reader with a framework for your analysis. When working with multiple sources, you may also need to summarize a number of critical opinions. It is likely you will paraphrase a short passage to give your reader context for your assessment or the point of view of a scholarly work. Should you be writing about drama, you'll likely quote from the play; should you be discussing a poem, it's almost inevitable that several lines of poetry will be included in your discussion. The guidelines provided here will keep you from plagiarizing when you have summarized, paraphrased, or quoted sources. You will always want to document in your paper where you found the kinds of information listed in the following box.

Information Requiring Documentation

- Lines from a story, poem, or play
- Opinions, observations, interpretations by writers, critics, and scholars
- Information from expert and/or sponsored sites
- Visual materials, including tables, charts, or graphs
- Footnotes from printed sources
- Statements that are open to debate
- Historical information that is not commonly known
- Statistics, or surveys, census or poll results if you use them

SAMPLES OF TYPES OF INFORMATION REQUIRING DOCUMENTATION

The whaling industry in nineteenth-century America collapsed when flexible steel hoops replaced whalebone in women's corsets.

A twenty-year Swiss study of organic farming found that organic farms yielded more produce per unit of energy consumed than farms that did not use organic farming methods.

Smoking kills over 418,000 people every year in the United States.

The easiest way to avoid plagiarism is to remember that you must tell your reader the sources of all facts, ideas, and opinions that are taken from others that are not considered common knowledge. If a number of sources contain the same information and that information is widely considered to be true, it is considered common knowledge. For example, in biology, the structure of DNA and the process of cell division or photosynthesis are considered common knowledge. A recent scientific discovery about genetics, however, would not be common knowledge, so you would need to cite the source of this information. When in doubt cite your source; citing is never incorrect.

COMMON KNOWLEDGE (DOCUMENTATION NOT REQUIRED)

Millions of soldiers died in the trenches of the Western front in World War I.

Mohandas K. Gandhi was assassinated in 1948.

The cheetah is the fastest-moving land animal.

Tip for Avoiding Plagiarism and the Web.   What you find on the Web requires extra precaution to make sure you document correctly where you got your information. Do not assume that what you find on the Web is common knowledge. Write in your notes the URL as well as *the date* that you accessed the site. Websites are notoriously prone to change, so this helps you keep your source clear. In your notes, put quotation marks around anything that is a direct quotation (wherever you found the information, print or online) so that you can easily see when you are using another's words. It is easy to cut whole passages from the Internet and paste them into your paper, or to think you have paraphrased when you have quoted if your notes aren't effective. This is plagiarism. Diligence is needed to avoid cobbling together a patchwork of sources without complete and accurate source information.

4b   USE SOURCES TO SUPPORT YOUR COMMENTARY

Your paper is your own independent thought. A quotation, paraphrase, or summary should be used only if you are going to comment on it in your paper. You can expand upon a quotation, paraphrase, or summary. You can interpret it. You can indicate what you believe the work implies. You can refer to a quotation, paraphrase, or a summary. You can even disagree. Your instructor is looking at your work to make sure you have understood a selection and to see what you have discovered for yourself. So, do not worry that you don't have anything original to say. Few do, even among professionals. *How* you say what you have to say is original to you. Don't apologize by suggesting this is only your opinion ("it seems to me" or "in my opinion"). Make your case. Be confident that, if you have discovered something that is interesting to you, it will also be interesting to your reader.

- A paper with too few references to sources does not provide the evidence you need to support your case.
- A paper with too many references to sources prevents you from making your case because it is overshadowed by the ideas of others.

Use Quotation, Summary, Paraphrase

- To support a point
- To present your source's point of view
- To disagree with your source
- To generalize from examples
- To reason through examples
- To make comparisons
- To distinguish fact from opinion
- To provide context

1. Quotation: *A word-for-word copy from an original source.* Direct quotation is especially useful when you are writing about literature because the way a writer uses words is central to an understanding of the text You will use quotations as examples of the way a writer uses language. However, you can also use a quotation from another source if a technical term is used that is not easily rephrased or if rephrasing it would change its meaning. You may want to use a quotation when the ideas are so vividly and beautifully expressed that you prefer to avoid paraphrase. Even if you do, a direct quotation is not to be used as a conclusion or summation of your main point in your work. It doesn't stand on its own. You must expand upon any quotation—or paraphrase or summary—that you include in your paper.

Tip on Avoiding Plagiarism in a Quotation: Using quotation marks around information from a source while changing or omitting information from that source is a serious error. Use *brackets* **[ ]** around a word or words you insert in a quotation. Use three periods in succession (**ellipses**) **. . .** to show that you have omitted something that was in the original quotation: "He turned green **. . .** but he went on [to steer the ship]."

ORIGINAL SOURCE (from page 7 of *The Metaphysical Club* by Louis Menand).

> We think of the Civil War as a war to save the union and to abolish slavery, but before the fighting began most people regarded these as incompatible ideals. Northerners who wanted to preserve the union did not wish to see slavery extended into the territories; some of them hoped it would wither away in the states where it persisted. But many Northern businessmen believed that losing the South would mean economic catastrophe, and many of their employees believed that freeing the slaves would mean lower wages. They feared secession far more than they disliked slavery, and they were unwilling to risk the former by trying to pressure the South into giving up the latter.

➡ *For more practice with quotation, paraphrase, and summary using this example and many others, visit www.mhhe.com/delbancole.*

SERIOUS ERROR

> Menand notes that "many Northern businessmen and many of their employees feared secession far more than they disliked slavery, and they were unwilling to risk the former by trying to pressure the South into giving up the latter" (7).

➡ *This sentence is unacceptable because the writer has not used ellipses to indicate where words have been omitted from the quotation.*

CORRECT QUOTATION

> Menand notes that "many Northern businessmen . . . and many of their employees . . . feared secession far more than they disliked slavery, and they were unwilling to risk the former by trying to pressure the South into giving up the latter" (7).

2. Paraphrase: *Someone else's ideas in your own words.* When writing about literature, you may paraphrase some of the story line in order to get to the point you want to make. In research, paraphrase is most often used when you are referring to the work of critics and scholars. If you find that the language you are trying to put into your words is already broken down to its most simple form, or that the language is too perfectly worded to change, you may want to use a quotation instead of a paraphrase. Don't paraphrase if you are not entirely sure you understand the original or you risk misrepresenting its original meaning. One test of a good paraphrase is if you can restate what you are trying to paraphrase without looking at the source.

Tip on Avoiding Plagiarism in a Paraphrase: A true paraphrase is not just a few different words, even if you feel the scholar has said something better than you could have said it yourself. *Your words* are the words that matter to your instructor. Just changing a few words—*even when you indicate the source of the paraphrase*—is still plagiarism. In a true paraphrase, the sentence structure is your own. It doesn't sound like the original; it sounds like you.

PLAGIARISM

> Menand observes that before the Civil War, many Northerners feared secession far more than they disliked slavery, and they were unwilling to risk the former by trying to pressure the South into giving up the latter (7).

➡ *This quotation is plagiarized because it uses the exact words of the source—most of a sentence—without quotation marks.*

CORRECT PARAPHRASE

> Menand observes that before the Civil War, many Northerners were afraid that secession would be worse for the country than slavery, and they were not willing to try and force the South to give up slavery for fear that a disastrous Southern secession would follow (7).

3. Summary: *A condensation of the main idea or action that includes only the supporting details related directly to that main idea.* Unlike a paraphrase, where a concept or action from a brief passage is explained in your own words, a summary lays out a long passage (such as an act in a play or a whole poem, story, play, or other work). When writing about literature, a plot summary is not enough. A summary sets the stage for an analysis, providing your readers with enough information for them to understand your commentary. In a research paper, summary can also be used to provide examples of a variety of points of view on your topic. Make comparisons between two points of view, then summarize several sources to build upon for your conclusion. (See the chapter on Common Writing Assignments for a discussion of the summary paper.)

Tip on Avoiding Plagiarism in a Summary: When you summarize information, you must include information on the source or it will appear as if you are using someone else's ideas as your own. Omitting information in a summary that alters the source's meaning is also unacceptable. Offering an inaccurate interpretation of your source in a summary is not satisfactory either. If the source's words or meaning do not support your argument as fully as you might like, find another source that does.

PLAGIARISM

> People believed that the Civil War was a war to save the union and to abolish slavery, but before the fighting began most people regarded these as incompatible ideals.

➡ *The sentence does not acknowledge that the idea comes from a source and is, therefore, an example of plagiarism. Ideas and words from a source cannot be included as if they are your own. You must give credit to the original writer.*

CORRECT SUMMARY

> According to Menand, during the Civil War people did not believe both that slavery could be abolished and the union could be saved (7).

4c ACKNOWLEDGE YOUR SOURCES

In the case of paraphrases, summaries, and direct quotations, your paper itself must include information about your source (an in-text citation), including an introductory phrase with the author and title, and the page number(s), URL, or line numbers (for a poem or play) placed immediately following the cited material and usually preceding any punctuation marks that divide or end the sentence. (See block quotation later in the next section, p. H-79.)

IN-TEXT CITATION

According to Louis Menand in his book on the Civil War, *The Metaphysical Club,* people believed that "the Civil War was a war to save the union and to abolish slavery, but before the fighting began most people regarded these as incompatible ideals" (7).

Professional organizations (such as the Modern Language Association or the American Psychological Association) provide guidelines for how sources should be acknowledged in a paper. MLA guidelines are commonly used in writing for the humanities, and those guidelines are followed here. For more information on how to properly cite electronic and print sources using the MLA documentation styles, see the chapters on Writing the Research Paper and MLA Documentation.

Keep a running list of your sources. The more accurate and complete the information on your sources, the easier it will be to present that source accurately and completely in your paper. In addition to in-text citation, you must also provide a complete and accurate list of all the texts you have consulted in a list at the end of your paper called a **bibliography.** Anything you have cited in your paper must be included in the final bibliography for that paper. Other works, not referenced in your paper, can be included as well. The best way to prevent plagiarism is to make sure you keep precise records of the sources you consult while preparing your paper in a **working bibliography**—a list of all the sources you've used, as well as all the information you'll use to cite them later. For your working bibliography, make sure to include this information:

- The names of all the authors, editors, and/or translators of the piece
- The complete title of the work and relevant chapter title or heading; for Web pages, the name of the site and the page on which the information appears
- The publisher, copyright date, edition, and place of publication should be recorded for sources from books.
- The date, volume, issue, and page number should be included for all sources from periodicals or journals (including those you have pulled up from an online database).
- The URL (complete web address), the date the page was updated, and the date you viewed the page should be recorded for all sources from the Internet.

Plagiarism can be intentional or unintentional. Professors are adept at recognizing papers obtained via the Web—they've likely seen them before! However, unintentional plagiarism carries the same penalties. This chapter should help you avoid plagiarizing unintentionally, and you will soon be found out if your plagiarism is of the other kind.

Two Kinds of Plagiarism

Intentional plagiarism	Intentional plagiarism occurs when you buy someone else's work or copy something from a source, usually word for word, and use it without quotation marks or acknowledgment of the source, as if it were your own words.
Unintentional plagiarism	Unintentional plagiarism can result from careless note taking, such as forgetting to put quotation marks around material you copy, cutting and pasting from the web, and using material you have summarized or paraphrased and forgetting to tell readers the source of that material.

4d FORMAT QUOTATIONS TO AVOID PLAGIARISM

When you integrate your ideas with those of your sources, you will want to format your quotations so that they flow naturally into your sentences and build toward your conclusion. Where possible, keep your quotation brief, four or fewer lines for prose and no more than three for poetry or drama, since you will comment on the entire quotation in your paper. If you include a long quotation (five lines or more for prose or four or more for poetry or drama) make sure you include the entire quotation for your interpretation or analysis. Otherwise, the quotation overshadows your argument instead of supporting it. Introducing a direct quotation into a text can happen in two ways depending on whether it is short or long; each is formatted differently.

- A short quotation within a sentence is identified by quotation marks.
- A long quotation formatted in an indented block of text separated out from a sentence does not use quotation marks.

1. Refer to your source in an introductory phrase.   Whether your quotation is short or long, however, you will need to introduce it with an introductory (*signal*) phrase. You need to identify the source and the author *before* the quotation. An in-text citation requires that you include the author's full name (without Mr., Miss, Mrs., or Ms.) the first time you quote from the source. Unless there is a long lapse between references to the source, the second time you quote from the same source you should use only the author's last name. Treat women and men equally when you cite them as authors, using the last name only for the second citation and no *Miss, Mrs.,* or *Ms.* Avoid the repetition of *the author says*.

Verbs to Use in an Introductory Phrase

according to	considers	notes
adds		
admits	declares	observes
aknowledges	denies	
agrees	describes	points out
asks	disagrees	proposes
asserts		proves
argues	emphasizes	
	establishes	refutes
believes	explains	rejects
	expresses	remarks
charges		reports
claims	finds	responds
comments		
compares	holds	shows
complains		states
concedes	implies	speculates
concludes	insists	suggests
contends	interprets	
continues		warns
	maintains	

2. Integrate a short quotation in a sentence and always use quotation marks. Always put a short quotation into quotation marks. Not to do so constitutes plagiarism. Keep your quotations to the point. The source material you quote as a reference should provide backup for the argument you have made. Avoid the temptation to use sources to make your arguments for you, however well the source is worded. References from outside sources, whether they are paraphrased or quoted, are *evidence* or *support* for your own arguments.

You should not use outside sources to make arguments for you.

- Use an introductory phrase to identify the source.
- If the quotation flows into the natural wording of the sentence, begin the quotation with a lowercase letter whether or not the original is capitalized.
- If your introductory phrase ends with a comma, use a capital letter.
- Use quotation marks.
- When quoting poetry in a sentence, use the format of the lines in the poem and break the lines exactly as they appear in the poem with a slash / mark.
- Place periods and commas inside the quotation marks.
- Semicolons, colons, and dashes are placed outside the quotation marks.
- Question marks and exclamation points are sometimes placed inside the quotation marks and sometimes placed outside. If the quotation is itself a question or exclamation, the question mark/exclamation point goes inside the quotation marks.
- Include page numbers for prose, line numbers for poems, act, scene, and line numbers for plays written in verse and page numbers for plays written in prose.

A SHORT QUOTATION FROM A POEM

In Robert Frost's "Stopping by Woods on a Snowy Evening," the hypnotic rhythm of the poem is reinforced through the repetition of the speaker's last lines, "And I have miles to go before I sleep / And I have miles to go before I sleep" (lines 15-16).

INTEGRATING A QUOTATION WITH A LOWERCASE LETTER

Even certain details of Grendel's portrayal in the movie echo the original epic. For example, the epic introduces him by calling him an inhabitant of "the abode of monster kind" (line 14).

PERIOD INSIDE QUOTATION MARK

Blake again disrupts the meter when he writes, "And I saw it was filled with graves" (line 9), which draws attention to the word "graves."

> —from the student paper on William Blake's "The Garden of Love" in Common Assignments across the Curriculum.

SEMICOLON OUTSIDE QUOTATION MARKS

> He is called a "fiend of hell"; "wrathful spirit"; "mighty stalker of the marches"
> (line 14); "creature of destruction, fierce and greedy, wild and furious" (15); and
> a "terrible monster, like a dark shadow of death" (17).
>
> > —from the student paper on the role of Grendel in *Beowulf,* the epic and
> > the movie, in Common Assignments across the Curriculum.

3. Set off a long quotation in a block, and don't use quotation marks.   Quotations in block format should be used sparingly because they break up your discussion and can be distracting. If you find that you do not need to refer back to a long quote in several instances, consider using a paraphrase or more precise direct quotation to present the information. If you use a long quotation to support your point, you must set the quote apart:

- Use an introductory phrase to identify the source.
- Punctuate the end of an introductory phrase with a comma or a colon.
- Leave a line of space before and after the long quotation.
- Do not use quotation marks.
- Indent each line of the quotation by ten spaces from the left margin (right margin is not indented).
- Capitalize the first word whether or not it is capitalized in the original unless quoting poetry.
- When quoting poetry, follow the line format exactly as it appears in the poem.
- Double-space.
- Include a page number (or line numbers for a poem) in parentheses after the final punctuation in the quotation.

BLOCK QUOTATION

> As her spirit wanes, our heroine in Charlotte Perkins Gilman's "Yellow
> Wallpaper" gives her soliloquy:
>
> > I lie down ever so much now. John says it is good for me, and to sleep
> > all I can. Indeed he started the habit by making me lie down for an hour
> > after each meal. It is a very bad habit, I am convinced, for you see, I don't
> > sleep. And that cultivates deceit, for I don't tell them I'm awake—oh, no!
> > The fact is I'm getting a little afraid of John. (226)

4e FORMAT A PARAPHRASE TO AVOID PLAGIARISM

Using paraphrase in your paper is similar to using quotation, but there are some areas that require extra care. Make sure you have understood the text you are paraphrasing; your paraphrase must be true to the original meaning of the text. Don't guess at the meaning of a text by changing a few words and letting it stand for your own idea. This is plagiarism. Even if one part of the text can be construed to support your argument, don't use it if that part doesn't represent the whole source accurately. Make it clear where your ideas end and the ideas of others begin. In addition to giving credit to others for their ideas, a clear transition from your own work to your source materials gives your writing credibility.

- Keep your paraphrase brief.
- Refer to the source in an introductory phrase.
- Include the page number in parentheses after the paraphrase.
- A period, question mark, or exclamation point goes after the page number when the page number is at the end of a sentence.

ORIGINAL SOURCE MATERIAL

Although Emily Dickinson was a noted wit in her circle of friends and family, and although her poetry is surely clever, frequently downright funny, and as we shall argue, throughout possessed of a significant comic vision, criticism has paid little attention to her humor. Dickinson's profound scrutiny of life-and-death matters has usually taken precedence in the analysis and evaluation of her work. Yet comedy is a part of that profundity.

—from "Comedy and Audience in Emily Dickinson's Poetry" by Suzanne Juhasz, Cristanne Miller, and Martha Nell Smith (See the McGraw-Hill website for the full text of this article that accompanies the Frost/Dickinson case studies.)

PARAPHRASE

Because Emily Dickinson's poetry concerns itself with serious issues like mortality, critics have long overlooked the comedy that aids her poems' success. Those who knew Dickinson personally recognized her smart humor, which shines through her poems but has since gone unnoticed. The authors of the article wish to reverse this trend of neglect, as Dickinson's witty touches are important to understanding her oeuvre.

4f FORMAT SUMMARY TO AVOID PLAGIARISM

Summary and paraphrase are certainly related, but they are not the same thing. In general, paraphrase is used for a smaller portion of the original source, and your goal is to capture the spirit of the passage you are paraphrasing, without exactly copying the sentence structure or word choice. Summary is useful for relating a larger idea that you gained from a longer passage of text, as the above example shows.

Paraphrase	Summary
• a relatively short passage	• a passage of any length
• covers every point in the passage	• condenses main idea and support
• takes up points consecutively	• changes order when necessary
• includes no interpretation	• explains point of passage

When you write a summary, introduce your source and identify the main ideas of the text. Break the discussion of those ideas into sections, and then write a sentence or two in your own words that captures each section.

ORIGINAL SOURCE

A figure who played a major role in popularizing swing in the mid-1930s was Benny Goodman. Like Whiteman earlier and Elvis Presley a few decades later, Goodman was a white musician who could successfully mediate between a black American musical tradition and the large base of white listeners making up the majority population in the USA. Wearing glasses and conservative suits—"looking like a high school science teacher," according to one observer (Stowe 45)—Goodman appeared to be an ordinary, respectable white American. Musically he was anything but ordinary: a virtuoso clarinetist, a skilled improviser who could solo "hot" on up tempo numbers and "sweet" on ballads, and a disciplined bandleader who demanded excellence from his players. [. . .]

In the guise of swing, jazz became domesticated in the 1930s. Earlier, jazz had been associated with gin mills and smoky cabarets, illegal substances (alcohol and drugs) and illicit sex. Swing generally enjoyed a more wholesome reputation, although some preached of the dangers it posed to the morals of young people. This exuberant, extroverted music performed by well-dressed ensembles and their clean-cut leaders entered middle-class households through everyday appliances like the living-room Victrola and the kitchen radio. It reached a wider populace as musicians transported it from large urban centers into small towns and rural areas. Criss-crossing North America by bus, car, and train, big bands played single night engagements in dance halls, ballrooms, theatres, hotels, night clubs, country clubs, military bases, and outdoor pavilions. They attracted hordes of teenagers who came to hear the popular songs of the day and dance the jitterbug, lindy hop and Susie Q. The strenuous touring schedule of big bands was far from glamorous. Nevertheless, musicians who played in these ensembles could symbolize achievement and prove inspirational, as the writer Ralph Ellison recalled from his early years growing up in Oklahoma City. . . .

Mark Tucker and Travis A. Jackson. "Jazz." *Grove Music Online.* Oxford UP. Web. 11 May 2008.

EXAMPLE OF SUMMARY

Swing, which became the popular dance music in more reputable venues than just bars and clubs, was usually performed by big bands under the direction of white leaders like Benny Goodman and Glenn Miller. Thus, jazz became mainstream and middle class, unlike the "hot jazz" of the twenties.

5 Writing the Research Paper, Avoiding Plagiarism, and Documenting Sources

5a UNDERSTAND RESEARCH TODAY

Research today often makes its first stop at the World Wide Web. You might even access the library through your computer. Navigating the research process, therefore, requires critical skills not asked of your predecessors for one of the most common assignments across the curriculum. While the Web makes it more convenient to do your research at three o'clock in the morning if you like, it also brings with it a new set of challenges. Today you don't just find sources, you have to manage the thousands of hits you might get when you google a topic. The Web also makes it more difficult to see what is credible and valid when every site looks largely the same on the computer screen. Plus, the Web makes it easy to create a patchwork cut-and-paste of sources that can lead to unintentional plagiarism. Plagiarism occurs when a source is not properly acknowledged, and whenever you conduct research from outside sources, you run the risk of taking credit for another person's ideas. For more information on acknowledging sources, see our chapter on Quoting, Paraphrasing, Summarizing, and Avoiding Plagiarism.

This chapter will get you started on your research project and also provide guidelines for documentation that keep you from unintentionally plagiarizing someone else's work. How you take notes is more important than ever if you are to distinguish your own work from the work you have found online (or in print). In literature, your instructor is likely to want a variety of sources, not just online references. There are three basic kinds of sources with which you will be working:

- Books
- Print magazines, newspapers, or scholarly journals
- Non-print online sources

The type of source you want to use depends on the type of project you are working on. If you are approaching a piece of literature from a particular critical perspective—like the feminist, Marxist, or psychoanalytical schools of thought discussed in our chapter on Critical Approaches to Literature—your research will likely involve reading literary criticism. If you are embarking on historical criticism or biographical criticism, you will need to gear your research to sources that inform you about a time period or your author's life. This chapter provides a step-by-step walkthrough of the research process. Read the student research paper on Langston Hughes at the end of this chapter to see how these steps look in action.

5b CHOOSE A TOPIC

Often, your instructor will assign a topic or provide some guidance. Or, you can find several research topics in this textbook, especially at the end of each case study. We have provided not only the topics, but also a list of good sources to get you started. In addition, there are many relevant secondary sources that you can find for each case study on our website at www.mhhe.com/delbanco1e. Research projects require a considerable amount of reading and a good deal of thinking. Your job is to make your process and the research project fun. Explore a topic that interests you, and discover new ideas that will help inform your own idea. Break the topic down so that you can manage your research and create a project that teaches you about a subject you enjoy.

1. Identify what interests you.   Choose your topic, or choose how you want to address your assigned topic, by considering what strikes you as important or interesting in the work of literature you are researching.

> **Example:** Our student author, Christine Keenan, was assigned to write a research paper on Langston Hughes. To find a topic, she thought of what she knew about Hughes that interested her. Since Christine loves music, she decided she would like to know more about how jazz influenced Langston Hughes.

2. Form a question.   Once you have a topic in mind, explore how that aspect of the work is meaningful to you. Do some of the brainstorming exercises that students used to get started in chapter 3, Writing about Fiction, chapter 17, Writing about Poetry, and chapter 32, Writing about Drama. Turn this aspect into a question. Christine made a list of words that she associated with jazz.

> *improvisation, be-bop, Duke Ellington, and nightclubs*

She also considered that jazz has several forms including blues, swing, be-bop, and cool jazz. Based on this, she formed the question.

> **Example:** "What elements of jazz influenced Langston Hughes when he wrote his poems?"

3. Narrow your topic. She then decided to narrow her question further by picking two poems influenced by jazz, an early poem, "The Dream Keeper," and a later poem, "Harlem [2]."

5c   FIND AND MANAGE PRINT AND ONLINE SOURCES

The sources you cite in your research should be *reliable* and *relevant*—significant in the context of your current discussion. Refining your keyword search can help prevent information overload and find sources that are pertinent to your topic. Your instructor may have some recommendations for good sources on a topic, and there are also sources listed in this textbook as good starting places. The Web does not offer any guarantees about the accuracy of its content. However, some websites and search engines are better than others for trustworthiness. If your website ends in *.org, .edu,* or *.gov,* it's like having a good character reference for the content on the site. If your search engine has preselected source material (such as GoogleScholar) or if you have accessed a library database, you will have saved yourself the painful weeding through of hits that cannot help you. Some tips for finding reliable and relevant sources include:

- *Title.* In a scholarly article or book, the title and subtitle will usually be designed to convey the topic of the piece as specifically as possible. If the title doesn't seem relevant to your topic, that author or piece of work might not be the best source for your discussion.

- *Date of publication.* For print sources, this will often be found on the copyright page of the book. Note not just the copyright of the current edition, but the original copyright. Journals will have dates printed with their issue numbers and often on individual articles themselves to inform the reader when the article's research was originally conducted. A reliable web page will usually print the date last modified at the bottom of the page. Bear in mind that "relevant" doesn't always mean "current." A classic source is one that is a hallmark in the field. If you see a source cited when you're reading sources elsewhere, you've likely come upon a classic work. A current source is just what the word suggests, something written about a topic within the past five years.

- *Abstract.* Most research papers in journals will have **abstracts,** or summaries, that explain the research done, briefly detail the findings, and state the conclusion of the research.

- *Chapter titles or headings.* A perusal of a print source's detailed table of contents can help you determine if the source will contain information useful and relevant to your research. If you are searching for an interpretation of Shakespeare's *Romeo & Juliet* and the index of the book indicates that all mentions of that play occur in a chapter called "Shakespeare: The Fraud," that text might be biased toward a perspective beyond the scope of your paper.

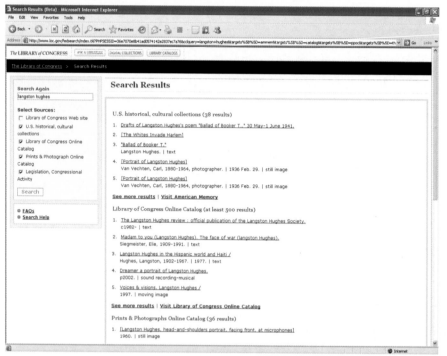

(Library of Congress search for "Langston Hughes")

1. Refine your keyword search. Whether you are searching one of your library's databases or the Web, refine your key words by grouping words together, e.g. "Harlem Renaissance." Use *and* or + to bring up sites that have both topics together. Use *or* when you list sites that are for either topic. Two words are better than one to help you narrow the number of sites that come up; use quotation marks around titles or parentheses around key phrases to manage the number of hits as well. To find information on Web pages and avoid the information flood, a good key word search is essential. Experiment with the phrasing of your keyword.

2. Use more than one search engine. The Internet brings the world to your door, but don't just google. Use at least three general search engines to locate the sources you need. In addition to Google, you may want to try Yahoo! (http://www.yahoo.com) or WebCrawler (http://www.webcrawler.com). Some sites search several different search engines at once: Library of Congress (http://www.loc.gov) or the Librarian's Index to the Internet (http://www.lii.org). You even have search sites that have already been vetted by experts, such as GoogleScholar (http://scholar.google.com), About.com (http://www.about.com), and Looksmart (http://www.looksmart.com).

3. Use the library, on campus and online. Check out your library's website. Talk to your librarian. The library is not just a collection of printed texts anymore. Your librarian can help you find the library's computerized catalog of books and discipline-specific encyclopedias, bibliographies, and almanacs, such as the *MLA International Bibliography of Books and Articles on Modern Language and Literature* (also available online) or the *Oxford History of English Literature*. In addition, the librarian can help you locate the library's database of scholarly journals and other electronic resources.

(Google Scholar Advanced Search Page)

Databases, Online Periodicals

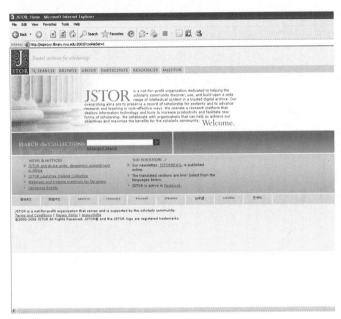

(*JSTOR Online Database*)

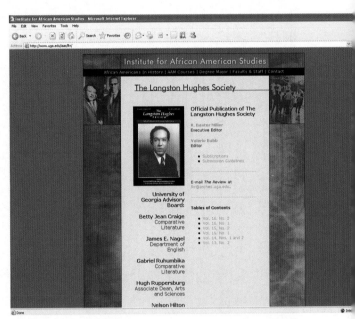

(*Langston Hughes Society online Periodical*)

Library searches can help you find the kinds of sources your professor wants to see on your topic.

Example: Christine used a database through her university's library to do keyword searches using the words "Langston Hughes" and "jazz." She skimmed the results and picked a few that seemed most related to her topic.

Searching the Internet

When you go online for help, you may feel all the information is the same. It only looks that way. The Internet serves up information in a couple of ways that it is important for you to differentiate.

- A *general search* from the entire World Wide Web includes everything that anyone has posted on your topic, from very personal blogs to news groups. You will need to carefully evaluate anything you find in a general search to determine if it is providing information that is reliable.

- An *online database* from your library searches through a collection of reliable published articles and electronic journals. The results of a database search will include only publications and will connect you to abstracts, summaries, or full text (that is, the entire article).

These film shots illustrate portrayals of the Grendel monster and the Beowulf hero in the movie Beowulf *(top) and the movie* The 13th Warrior *(bottom).*

5d EVALUATE VISUAL SOURCES

A picture is worth a thousand words, or so the old proverb goes. We live in a visual world and visual data is now as easy as a cut-and-paste job off GoogleImage. Like all source information, however, it must be relevant and reliable. Visuals must serve a specific purpose in your paper. A graph or chart can be a useful snapshot of quantitative data. A diagram is a useful flowchart to explain a process. A picture is qualitative evidence that is used to strengthen or amplify your point. If you have taken your visual from the Web or another source, it must be documented in your bibliography and identified in your paper with a caption. The example here is evidence for a paper on adapting the *Beowulf* epic.

5e EVALUATE TEXT SOURCES

Sources can be popular or scholarly. A popular source is something you could buy easily at a store, such as *Time* magazine. It will likely have advertisements in it or be advertised to the general public (such as a self-help book like *Rich Dad, Poor Dad*). A scholarly source is generally found through a library rather than a store. The writers focus on discipline-specific rather than broad, general topics and are usually affiliated with a university. These books are likely to have footnotes or include citations to sources and bibliographies. When considering whether a print publication is popular or scholarly, follow these guidelines:

- *Note the publisher of the book, magazine, or journal.* A commercial publisher will probably suggest a popular aim, whereas an academic publisher such as a university press will suggest a scholarly aim.

- *Consider the authors of the articles.* Take note of both the authors' names and their affiliations (generally universities for scholarly articles), and consider how their titles match up with the topic of their article. For instance, Alton Brown might be a name you recognize as an authority from The Food Network, but he would not be a trustworthy expert to cite in a paper on comparative politics.

- *Notice the range of topics in the publication.* A popular publication will usually cover a range of topics to appeal to a wide readership, whereas a scholarly publication will focus on various aspects of one topic.

- *Observe the visual presentation of the publication.* Is it flashy and full of ads and cartoons? Or is it mostly text-based, with fewer but higher quality captioned images?

- *Evaluate the articles themselves.* Academic articles will often be preceded by abstracts that summarize their findings and followed by bibliographies or listings of works cited. Popular articles, on the other hand, may lead in with a catchy line that leaves an unanswered question and will seldom list references.

- *Ask whether the source is refereed or peer reviewed.* A publication may or may not specify this, but most trustworthy scholarly publications accept articles only after they have been reviewed, debated, and accepted by a body of experts in the field. Some research databases will allow you to filter for peer-reviewed publications; or, when in doubt, you can ask your librarian whether a publication has been refereed.

You may find it difficult when using the Web to tell the difference not only between a popular and a scholarly site, but also between a reliable site and one that is biased. The Library of Congress website can be counted on, as can its search engine, so don't just google. Find search engines that will save you the time by leading you to reliable sites. Many of the same guidelines you use for evaluating print sources can apply to evaluating an online publication as well. Some other things you can pay attention to when considering whether an electronic source like a website is reliable include

- *The Web address.* As mentioned earlier, often reliable content will be found on websites with the domains *.org* (non-profit organization), *.edu* (educational institution), *.mil* (military), or *.gov* (United States government). Keep in mind that not all information on a *.org* or *.edu* (or sometimes *.gov* or *.mil*) is reliable. Information on these pages may be biased; or, sometimes, the information might be from a personal page hosted by that specific domain. In this case, you will often notice a tilde (~) followed by a name or personalized "handle" (such as your school ID or AIM screen name) in the Web address.

- *The host of the page.* Is the Web page hosted by a university or academic association? Is it an article of an online encyclopedia? Be careful of sites like Wikipedia, which can claim to be "encyclopedias" or "dictionaries" but may not be accurate. Do not use Wikipedia as a citation in a college paper. You will need to verify the content you find on Wikipedia through another source, and if it is common knowledge (a birth date, for example), it won't need a citation.

- *The visual presentation.* As with print sources, you can tell a lot about a Web page's content and intended audience just by looking at how it is presented. Flashy ads, pop-up windows, intricate backgrounds, complex layouts, and funky colors are all indications that a website might not contain reliable content. A reliable Web page, created by an academic for academic use, will be laid out functionally, without intricate designs or distracting colors.

• *The tone of the information.* Tone is a major indicator of scholarliness and bias. Avoid Web pages that use poor grammar or punctuation or employ colloquial Internet shorthand. Scholarly information will seldom be presented so informally. Also take note of aggravated tone of voice, or hyperbolic claims, or a failure to consider more than one point of view. These are indicators of bias—which might support your point of view, but will detract from the legitimacy of the source as support.

Whenever you are conducting research, if an opinion or piece of information seems fishy or flimsy, you should double-check. If you find that information or point of view in only one place, there's a good chance it is unsupported or not widely agreed upon by the academic community. Many databases now provide information on where an article or book has been cited by other academics in their research; this can be a valuable resource in confirming the reliability of a research source.

5f   RECOGNIZE UNRELIABLE WEBSITE WARNING SIGNS

The following example shows two websites containing the text of Langston Hughes's poem "Harlem," one unreliable and one reliable. Note the striking differences between the two. Likely your eye will go first to the unreliable site; whereas the reliable site by the Poetry Foundation is designed as a resource, the unreliable site hosted by PoemHunter.com is designed to attract attention and amass visits to the page.

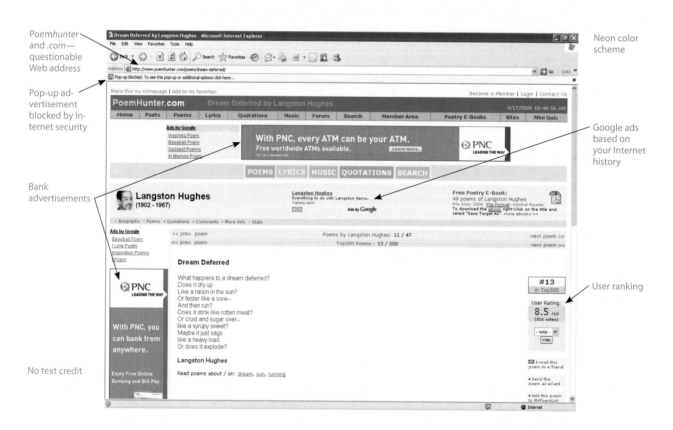

Poem*hunter* and *.com*— questionable Web address

Pop-up advertisement blocked by Internet security

Bank advertisements

No text credit

Neon color scheme

Google ads based on your Internet history

User ranking

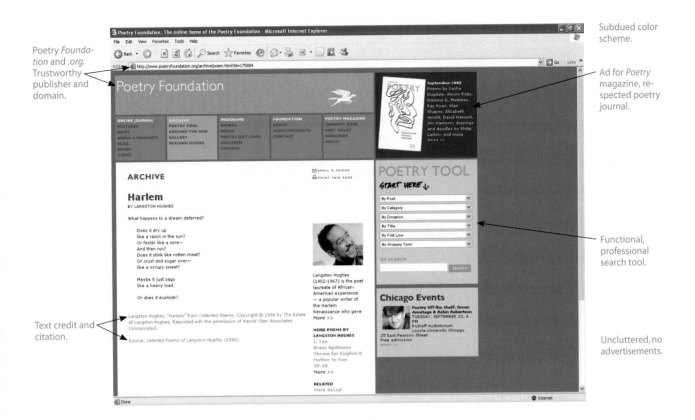

Poetry *Foundation* and *.org.* Trustworthy publisher and domain.

Subdued color scheme.

Ad for *Poetry* magazine, respected poetry journal.

Functional, professional search tool.

Text credit and citation.

Uncluttered, no advertisements.

Besides flashy colors and design, there are other major differences between the two. Whereas PoemHunter.com has bank ads (don't ignore that blocked pop-up ad, it's a major clue to unreliability), the Poetry Foundation website advertises only its own publication, *Poetry* magazine, a well-known and respected journal of poetry. Notice also the references that follow the poem text: PoemHunter.com does attribute the author of the poem but does not cite any permission or original publication information.

It will save you time if you can quickly recognize the difference between reliable and unreliable sites. A google search for Langston Hughes's "Harlem" will list PoemHunter.com before the Poetry Foundation, so strong searching skills and judgment are your keys to efficient, effective Web research.

5g WORK WITH SOURCES TO AVOID PLAGIARISM

As you collect your sources for your papers, your source notes will protect you from plagiarism. Take careful notes as you read your sources. You may want to use sticky notes to flag specific quotes or passages that you find interesting or of particular relevance to your topic. A necessary part of writing a research paper is the inclusion and citation of outside sources, usually scholarly works from books, journals, and trustworthy Web pages. Because of the risk of plagiarism (taking credit for another's words or ideas), it is important to know the several appropriate ways to include outside information.

There are two different approaches to including outside information into your own research paper, and both require **in-text parenthetical citation** and documentation in the **Works Cited** (or **Bibliography,** depending on the documentation style you are working within) at the end of your paper. Always be sure to copy the bibliographical information of the source so you can easily return to it when writing your paper and properly cite it (for more on this, see the MLA Documentation Style Guide that follows this chapter). All works that have been included in your paper with in-text parenthetical citations must be included in your Works Cited page. Some general tips to avoid plagiarism during research are:

- **Take notes on your sources.** First, when taking notes, make sure to underline or put into quotation marks all direct quotations you copy from books or journals. Record the page numbers and other source information that you'll need for your in-text parenthetical citation. This will help you distinguish your own impressions and conclusions from those that you copied directly and to avoid plagiarism by correctly citing your sources.

- **Do not copy and paste directly into your paper.** Next, when working with Web sources, try not to copy and paste directly into the body of your work; consider instead pasting into a separate document and printing it out to consult alongside your other notes. It's much easier to catch yourself retyping whole passages from another source.

- **Keep bibliographical information.** Finally, choose a documentation style (MLA, APA) early and stick to it as you create the body of your work. Usually your instructor will have assigned you a style for the assignment. If you cannot cite as you write, make sure to note "citation needed" in appropriate places, such as after paraphrases, figures, or direct quotations.

5h REFERENCE CITATIONS WITHIN THE PAPER IN THE END-OF-PAPER WORKS CITED PAGE

When you use sources in an MLA -style paper, you must include a parenthetical reference in the body of your paper (for more information, see our chapter on Quoting, Paraphrasing, Summarizing, and Avoiding Plagiarism) and a corresponding entry in a Works Cited page at the end of your paper. The idea is simple: full information about the books, journals, or websites you used in writing your paper appears in a list (the Works Cited page) at the end of your paper. Including all that information in the body of your paper would bog down both you and your reader. Instead, insert a brief reference in parentheses after the word or idea you have borrowed from an outside source. This parenthetical citation does two jobs: (1) It shows your reader exactly which sentences of your paper include ideas that are not your own, and (2) It points the reader to the original source by corresponding with the full citation that occurs in the Works Cited page.

1. In-text parenthetical reference.   Here, the parenthetical citation tells the reader that the student author has summarized or paraphrased an idea that she found on pages 61 and 62 of a source with an author whose last name is Borshuk.

SENTENCE FROM STUDENT PAPER:

Also, the traditionally African-American art form had now been taken over and turned into a commercial success largely by whites, with a few exceptions like Duke Ellington and Count Basie (Borshuk 61-62).

2. Corresponding entry from works cited page.   Turning to the Works Cited page at the end of the paper, the reader can find the entry beginning with "Borshuk" and know that the information following it is the source from which it came. In this case, the source is a book called *Swinging the Vernacular* by Michael Borshuk. The parenthetical citation and the works cited entry have worked together to inform the reader of the original source of the idea.

Borshuk, Michael. <u>Swinging the Vernacular.</u> New York: Routledge, 2006.

5i ORGANIZE YOUR RESEARCH AND DEVELOP A THESIS

1. Connect your interpretation of a text to various sources.   Consider what each source tells you about your topic. Particularly if you are reading literary criticism, decide whether or not you agree with the critic. If you agree, you may want to use what that critic says to corroborate your reading. If you disagree, use that critic's perspective as a springboard into talking about your own perspective.

Example: Christine read the following quote in one of her sources:

Langston Hughes, in his collection of poems, lavishly uses such characteristics of jazz as repetitions, choruses, riffs, scats, and nonsensical onomatopoeia, to achieve musical success as well as audience participation. It is also significant to note that Hughes's poems are often marked by dissonance, discordance, and line irregularity, which all contribute to the representation of the jazz spirit in verse forms.

Although this quote directly related to her topic, Christine found that she was dissatisfied with the vague way in which most sources—like this one—talked about the jazz elements in Hughes's poems. She began to consider the historical reasons why Hughes might have chosen these specific elements.

2. Form a working thesis.   Once you have gathered your own ideas and taken notes on your sources, try to state your overall idea in a sentence or two. Most likely, your thesis will have the kernel of the idea that you started with, but it will have become more nu-anced by your research. (See more on thesis in our chapter on Writing from Reading.)

> **Example:** Christine's original idea was to talk about jazz elements in Hughes's poems. Her research showed her that most critics approach his jazz poetry from a general angle. As a result, she formed the following thesis, which shows a very specific interpretation of why Hughes chose certain jazz elements.
>
> **Working thesis:** Hughes used jazz in a significant way. More than simply feeling jazz's influence generally, Hughes felt the influence of African-American jazz specifically.

3. Choose your best support. Review the notes you took on your sources and on the primary text. Select a few quotes that best illustrate a point you want to make. Note ideas that you will want to paraphrase or summarize in your paper, and remember that these are important forms of support as well. For examples of successful summary, paraphrase, and direct quotation refer to our chapter on Quoting, Paraphrasing, Summarizing, and Avoiding Plagiarism and the sample research paper in this chapter.

5j DRAFT AND REVISE YOUR DRAFT

Now that you have conducted your research and developed a thesis, you are ready to draft your paper. This is just a first draft, so leave yourself time to revise.

- **Introduction.** Your introduction sets up the rest of your paper.
- **Body.** The body of your paper presents your supporting evidence.
- **Conclusion.** Your conclusion relates your paper to a larger issue.

You may want to share your first draft with a friend or classmate. Then put your draft away and return to it fresh. You may see things you hadn't seen before. When you think through your thesis and look at the supporting evidence for your thesis, you may even find that you've changed your mind. Your thesis can be refined in response to your writing. To see revisions of the introduction, body, and conclusion in the paper on Langston Hughes, go to our Chapter on Writing from Reading. There you will find more on the drafting and revising process.

You can see in-text references and a properly formatted Works Cited page by looking at the student research paper that follows. Other student papers, like the ex-plication of William Blake's "The Garden of Love," which appear in Common Writing Assignments, can also serve as models for in-text references. In that particular paper, note the proper parenthetical citation of lines of poetry rather than page numbers.

Remember, too, that even if you respond to a single source, you should still cite that work. This is especially important when many versions of the same text exist—for example, if you are reading Charlotte Bronte's classic *Jane Eyre* from a Penguin Clas-sics edition, the pagination will be different from the *Jane Eyre* edition published by Oxford World's Classics. Only a full citation in a Works Cited page will tell your reader from which version you are reading. For an example of a single source, see the final draft of the student paper in chapter 3 on Jamaica Kincaid's "Girl."

Sample Student Research Paper

Christine Keenan

Professor Jackson

English 200

15 May 2008

From Dream Keeper to Dream Deferred:

Langston Hughes and Jazz Poetry

Jazz poetry, according to the American Academy of Poets website, is "a literary genre defined as poetry necessarily informed by jazz music—that is, poetry in which the poet responds to and writes about jazz" ("A Brief Guide to Jazz Poetry"). Langston Hughes was a jazz poet in that his poetry often captured jazz in a literary form. Many critics point to specific techniques that Hughes employs to create the effect of jazz. One such critic is Lionel Davidas, who writes:

> Langston Hughes, in his collection of poems, lavishly uses such
> characteristics of jazz as repetitions, choruses, riffs, scats, and nonsensical
> onomatopoeia, to achieve musical success as well as audience
> participation. It is also significant to note that Hughes's poems are often
> marked by dissonance, discordance, and line irregularity, which all
> contribute to the representation of the jazz spirit in verse forms. (268)

Although these observations are true, readings like Davidas's fail to show the full extent of Hughes's achievement in jazz poetry. Beyond being a jazz poet, Hughes understood the significance of jazz—even as it was being created—and used only those aspects of jazz that express the African-American experience.

Two of Hughes's collections that have an overt connection to music are *The Weary Blues,* published in 1926, and *Montage of a Dream Deferred,* published in 1951. In the twenty-five years between their publications, jazz music changed dramatically. Two poems, "The Dream Keeper" from *The Weary Blues* and "Harlem [2]" from *Montage of a Dream Deferred,* show how Hughes effectively responded to the current trends in jazz from an African-American perspective.

Topic sentence
introduces first
poem to be
analyzed.

Hughes first published "The Dream Keeper" in 1925 and included it in his collection *The Weary Blues* the following year (Rampersad 617). At that time, America was in the midst of the "Jazz Age," the period from 1920-1930 marked by energy and optimism. Jazz itself was popular and connoted rebellion as it was associated with nightclubs, sex, and drinking (Tucker, screen 4). But Hughes's collection was clearly influenced more by the blues than by this new form of jazz. The title of the collection suggests the blues takes center stage in these poems, and indeed, "The Dream Keeper" is no exception. While it does not have as overt a connection to the blues as Hughes's poems that replicate blues lyrics directly—such as "Po Boy Blues"—the repetition early in the poem bears echoes of the repetition characteristic of the blues. "Bring me all of your" is repeated twice within the first three lines; the object the addressee is told to bring, however, varies (lines 1, 3). In a way, lines one through three are a compounded version of blues lyrics. Typical blues lyrics follow a pattern where the first couplet repeats before a third couplet resolves it. Here, half the couplet is repeated and half resolved in both instances. Blues also has a hand in the pace of the poem. Compound phrases like "cloud-cloth" and "too-rough" slow the pace of reading, as does the high number of line breaks compared to the small number of words (6, 7).

Example of
paraphrase.

Student's own
analysis.

Since Hughes was writing in the Jazz Age, it may seem surprising that so many of his poems in *The Weary Blues* reflect the blues. In part, his decision may have been informed by the fact that jazz grew out of the blues, and the close relationship of the two forms of music allowed Hughes to use blues and still be in the realm of jazz. But blues is marked by a "blue" or melancholy frame of mind (Oliver, screen 1), not the exuberance of the Jazz Age. Examining the historical context offers an answer for why Hughes chose blues over jazz. While the Roaring Twenties brought "unprecedented prosperity" to the United States ("Roaring Twenties"), it was also the era of the Great Migration, the movement in which ten percent of African Americans left the South and moved North. These were difficult times for blacks, as they faced low wages, poor housing conditions, and disease in the northern cities to which they relocated (Marks). Also, while positive advances did occur in the African-American community, such as the Harlem Renaissance, Emily Bernard has noted that most blacks were not affected

Example of
summary.

by the Renaissance—only a so-called talented tenth participated, leaving most blacks to face everyday problems (Bernard xvi-xvii).

To put it simply, jazz at the time that Hughes was writing poems for *The Weary Blues* had two forms: the exuberant new jazz and the blues roots from which it came. Hughes chose the form of music—the blues—that best reflected the state of the common black man. By the time Hughes was writing the poems for *Montage of a Dream Deferred,* however, jazz had changed and once again offered two new forms.

The 1930s and 40s brought a change to jazz: ensembles of about twelve players began to change the rhythms of jazz into swing. Swing, which became the popular dance music in more reputable venues than just bars and clubs, was usually performed by big bands under the direction of white leaders like Benny Goodman and Glenn Miller.[1] Thus, jazz became mainstream and middle class, unlike the "hot jazz" of the 20s (Tucker, screen 5). Also, the traditionally African-American art form had now been taken over and turned into a commercial success largely by whites, with a few exceptions like Duke Ellington and Count Basie (Borshuk 61-62).

Margin notes:

Transition paragraph. The first two sentences conclude the blues discussion. The last sentence segues into discussion of the second poem.

Example of summary.

Example of paraphrase.

Fig. 1 The Glenn Miller Orchestra Source: Photo Gallery. Glenn Miller Orchestra Online. Glenn Miller Productions, Inc. Web. 12 May 2008.

Jazz underwent another major change in the 1940s. Young African-American musicians in Harlem met in informal jam sessions where they began to experiment with nearly every aspect of the music—melody, harmony, and rhythm.[2] Musicians such as Dizzy Gillespie, Thelonious Monk, and Charlie Parker increasingly championed improvisation and creativity over the organized big band aesthetic. Their innovations included "rapid tempo, irregular phrase groups . . . sudden, sharp drum accents, [and] chromatically altered notes" (Tucker, screen 7). This new form of jazz became known as bebop, a form of music that many critics see as "the revolt of young black musicians of the ghetto against the commercialization of 'swing music' of the time" (Lenz 274). In other words, bebop made jazz into a predominantly African-American art once more.

Citation of both para-phrase and direct quote.

Fig. 2 Tommy Potter, Charlie Parker, Dizzy Gillespie, and John Coltrane—leaders of the bebop movement—pictured at the famous jazz club Birdland, c. 1951. Source: "Charlie Parker, Uptown and Down." *New York Times on the Web. The New York Times.* Web. 12 May 2008.

When Langston Hughes penned "Harlem [2]," two types of jazz existed: the mellow, organized sound of swing and the creative, frantic sound of bebop. For *Montage of a Dream Deferred,* Hughes chose to use the latter jazz form, as his preface to the collection suggests:

> In terms of current Afro-American popular music and the sources from which it has progressed—jazz, ragtime, swing, blues, boogie-woogie, and be-bop—this poem on contemporary Harlem, like be-bop, is marked by conflicting changes, sudden nuances, sharp and impudent interjections, broken rhythms, and passages sometimes in the manner of the jam session, sometimes the popular song, punctuated by the riffs, runs, breaks, and disc-tortions [sic] of the music of a community in transition.
> (Rampersad 387)

Indeed, these bebop-like traits are present in "Harlem [2]": "conflicting changes" and "sudden nuance" can be seen in the series of images Hughes selects; "sharp and impudent interjections" occur in the form of the last line, *"Or does it explode?"* (line 11); and "broken rhythms" are created by the space after the first line and the space before the last line. Hughes, then, successfully reflects bebop technique in his poetry, and in so doing, uses the form of jazz aligned with African Americans, rather than the form of mainstream, middle-class whites.

More significant than the blues and bebop form, however, is Hughes's use of blues and bebop content. "The Dream Keeper" and "Harlem [2]" share the theme of dreams, yet each reflects the mindset of the music that influenced it—music that in turn was influenced by the historical events of its day. "The Dream Keeper" is itself dreamy in its imagery of "blue cloud-cloth" and the diction of phrases like "heart melodies" (6, 7). Despite these whimsical elements, the act of tucking away one's dreams so the world will not harm them is a sad one. In fact, the tone of the poem is melancholy, or "blue." Even the one color mentioned in the poem is "blue," which

Margin notes:

Topic sentence introduces the second poem to be analyzed.

Example of paraphrase.

Conclusion that shows significance of student's preceding analysis.

Citation of line in poem.

Topic sentence that introduces a new thread of discussion and analysis.

Reiteration that citation is to poetic line. Avoids confusion with source page numbers found in other citations.

Student's analysis.

Example of summary.

guides the reader toward blue (i.e., sad) feelings (6). This laying aside of dreams is more than the material of blues music; it was also, for many blacks, the reality of the Great Migration. Reading "The Dream Keeper" with the Great Migration in mind makes the poem seem as if it is directly about the blues created by the migration. Blacks were motivated to migrate by the promise of opportunity and freedom from the South's discrimination; once in the North, however, blacks often found limited advancement possibilities in their jobs and continued to suffer from segregation (Marks). In a sense, then, African Americans of the Great Migration often had to lay aside their dreams from the "too-rough fingers" of reality (7).

Similarly, "Harlem [2]" captures the mindset and historical context that gave rise to bebop. Although the dream theme is the same as in "The Dream Keeper," its imagery of "fester[ing] like a sore" and "stink[ing] like rotten meat" suggests an uglier, bitterer side of dreams than anything that appears in "The Dream Keeper" (4, 6). John Lowney's characterization of Harlem is helpful in understanding this shift; he writes, "By the 1940s, Harlem was of course no longer the center of refuge and hope associated with the New Negro Renaissance. Although still a major destination for poor migrant blacks during the Great Depression, Harlem had become better known nationally as an explosive site of urban racial conflict, first in 1935 and then in 1943" (362). Those years saw race riots in Harlem, and racial tension continued to grow as blacks faced discrimination even in the World War II era (362). Lowney notes that "the agitated sound of *Montage* struck many of [Hughes's] contemporaries as a radical departure from the more straightforward 'populist' rhetoric of his best-known work" (369). Indeed, in reflecting bebop's dramatic change from swing, Hughes's poetry also takes a dramatic shift from earlier modes. This shift shows the rising frustration of

Student's synthesis of poem and historical context.

Student's analysis.

Example of direct quotation.

Student's synthesis of poem and historical context.

African Americans whose dreams were no longer the root of melancholy from being tucked away, but were now the product of dreams that continued to be deferred, nearly halfway into the twentieth century.

As "The Dream Keeper" and "Harlem [2]" demonstrate, Hughes effectively incorporated new forms of jazz as they arose. While he does successfully use formal elements of jazz music, to end a reading there would be to miss Hughes's larger achievement. Hughes did not simply adopt jazz technique; he selected only those trends in jazz that reflected the African-American experience of the time in which he wrote. There is no room in his poetry for the smooth sounds of swing at the hands of whites; instead, he used the true African-American forms of blues and bebop. In so doing, Hughes's poetry captures both the music, as it evolved from blues to bebop, and the African-American experience, as it moved from the blues of the Great Migration to the bitter conflict of continued discrimination.

Notes

[1]Fig. 1 shows Glenn Miller's orchestra, which exemplifies the white, mainstream big band associated with swing of the 1930s and 1940s.

[2] Fig. 2 represents the smaller, black ensembles associated with bebop in the early 1940s. Comparing the two figures gives a visual representation of the stark difference between the two forms of jazz.

Reiteration of thesis and broadening to encompass Hughes's overall achievement.

Topic sentence that signals conclusion.

Broadens thesis to include historical discussion presented in the body of the paper

Properly formatted "Notes" section for additional information.

Works Cited

Introduction to a book. → Bernard, Emily. Introduction. *Remember Me to Harlem: The Letters of Langston Hughes and Carl Van Vechten, 1925-1964*. Ed. Bernard. New York: Knopf, 2001. Print.

Book. → Borshuk, Michael. *Swinging the Vernacular*. New York: Routledge, 2006. Print.

"A Brief Guide to Jazz Poetry." *Poets.org*. The American Academy of Poets. Web. 8 May 2008. ← Article on a website.

Visual from Web. → "Charlie Parker, Uptown and Down." *New York Times on the Web*. The New York Times. Web. 12 May 2008.

Davidas, Lionel. " 'I, Too, Sing America': Jazz and Blues Techniques and Effects in Some of Langston Hughes's Selected Poems." *Dialectical Anthropology* 26 (2001): 267-272. Print. ← Print periodical.

Book. → Hughes, Langston. *Montage of a Dream Deferred*. New York: Henry Holt, 1951. Print.

Hughes, Langston. *The Weary Blues*. New York: Knopf, 1926. Print. ← Book.

Article from a database. → Lenz, Gunter. "The Riffs, Runs, Breaks, and Distortions of the Music of a Community in Transition." *The Massachusetts Review* 44.1-2 (Spring 2003): 269-282. *ProQuest*. Web. 11 May 2008.

Lowney, John. "Langston Hughes and the 'Nonsense' of Bebop." *American Literature Online*. Duke University. Web. 11 May 2008. ← Online periodical.

Article on a scholarly website. → Marks, Carole. "The Great Migration: African Americans Searching for the Promised Land, 1916-1930." *In Motion: The African-American Migration Experience*. Ed. Howard Dodson and Sylviane A. Diouf. Schomburg Center for Research in Black Culture. Web. 11 May 2008.

Oliver, Paul. "Blues." *Grove Music Online*. Oxford UP. Web. 11 May 2008. ← Online music dictionary.

Visual from web. → Photo Gallery. *Glenn Miller Orchestra Online*. Glenn Miller Productions, Inc. Web. 12 May 2008.

Rampersad, Arnold, ed. *The Collected Poems of Langston Hughes*. New York: Knopf, 1995. Print. ← Book, emphasis on editor.

Article on a website. → "Roaring Twenties." *JAZZ: A Film by Ken Burns*. PBS. Web. 11 May 2008.

Tucker, Mark and Travis A. Jackson. "Jazz." *Grove Music Online*. Oxford UP. Web. 11 May 2008. ← Online music dictionary.

6 MLA Documentation Style Guide

6a DOCUMENT SOURCES CONSISTENTLY IN APPROPRIATE STYLE

Anytime you use a direct quotation, paraphrase, or summary from a source—in other words, any text or idea that is not your own—you must indicate the author and work from which it came. This is called citing your sources. Different fields of study follow different guidelines for how to format citation. Psychology, for example, requires APA style, while anthropology typically uses the *Chicago Manual of Style*. English and most humanities, however, use MLA style, a format developed and maintained by the Modern Language Association. (For more on documentation styles, see p. H-108.)

This chapter will provide a quick overview and an abbreviated guide to MLA style. For a full description of how to properly cite works, you will want to consult the *MLA Handbook for Writers of Research Papers* (often referred to as simply the *MLA Handbook*), which is the authoritative guide to MLA style. Be sure to consult the 6th edition, which is the most current, as the rules vary slightly from edition to edition.

6b DOCUMENT IN-TEXT CITATIONS, MLA STYLE

1. Author Named in Parenthesis

A parenthetical reference in MLA consists of the author's last name and the page number from which you are quoting, summarizing, or paraphrasing. The reference comes at the end of the sentence *before* the period. Do *not* insert a comma, hyphen, or other punctuation between the last name and the page number.

> **Example:** While documenting sources may take extra time, it is worth it because
>
> "your reader might want to see the source for his or her own research" (Smith
>
> 42-43).

When you need to cite a page range, simply put a hyphen between the start and end pages, as in the example above. When citing two different pages, separate them with a comma.

> **Example:** (Smith 42, 51)

2. Author Named in Sentence

If you mention the author's name in the text surrounding the sentence, you need insert only the page number in parentheses.

> **Example:** As John Smith points out, "Your reader might want to see the source
>
> for his or her own research" (42).

3. Two or More Works by the Same Author

If you use two books or articles by John Smith in your paper, you must let your reader know which source you are using by inserting the title of the work into your sentence *or* by abbreviating the title and inserting it in the parenthetical reference as shown below.

> **Example:** As John Smith points out in his article "Using Sources," "Your reader might want to see the source for his or her own research" (42).

> **Example:** While documenting sources may take extra time, it is worth it because "your reader might want to see the source for his or her own research" (Smith, "Sources" 42).

*For parenthetical references for works with two, three, or more authors, see p. H-108.

4. Source of a Long Quotation

When citing a block quotation—one that is four lines or longer in poetry or five lines or longer in prose—indent by one inch and do not include quotation marks. The citation comes *after* the period.

> **Example:** Many critics point to specific techniques that Hughes employs to create the effect of jazz. One such critic is Lionel Davidas, who writes:
>
> > Langston Hughes, in his collection of poems, lavishly uses such characteristics of jazz as repetitions, choruses, riffs, scats, and nonsensical onomatopoeia to achieve musical success as well as audience participation. It is also significant to note that Hughes's poems are often marked by dissonance, discordance, and line irregularity, which all contribute to the representation of the jazz spirit in verse forms. (268)

6c   DOCUMENT LIST OF WORKS CITED, MLA STYLE

To properly format a Works Cited page:

- Begin on a new page, following the end of your paper. If your paper ends on page 5, your Works Cited page will begin on page 6.
- Just like your paper itself, a Works Cited page should be double spaced with one-inch margins.

- At the top of the page, type "Works Cited" and center it. Do not include quotation marks around the words "Works Cited."
- Do not skip spaces. Drop down one double-spaced line, and align your entry to the left.
- If an entry runs longer than one line, indent every line one-half inch (or five spaces) after the first line.
- Put a period at the end of each entry.
- Alphabetize your Works Cited list by the first word of the entry. In most cases, this will be the author's last name.

For an example of a Works Cited page, see the model research paper in the previous chapter on Writing the Research Paper.

Common Formatting Errors

- Single spacing a Works Cited page
- Adding extra spaces between entries
- Numbering entries

What goes in an entry on a Works Cited page? First determine what type of source it is—a book, a periodical, an online resource. Then follow the instructions in the appropriate section, as follows:

Citing Book Sources

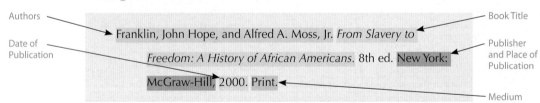

Authors · Date of Publication · Book Title · Publisher and Place of Publication · Medium

Franklin, John Hope, and Alfred A. Moss, Jr. *From Slavery to Freedom: A History of African Americans*. 8th ed. New York: McGraw-Hill, 2000. Print.

1. Book with One Author. Reverse the author's name for alphabetizing, adding a comma after the last name and a period after the first name. The book title follows in italics, followed by a period. Then list the city of publication, followed by a colon. Then the publisher, followed by a comma, then the year, followed by a period. Then list the medium. For how to abbreviate the publisher's name, see Additional Tips, p. H-111.

Borshuk, Michael. *Swinging the Vernacular*. New York: Routledge, 2006. Print.

Elements in Works Cited Entry: Books

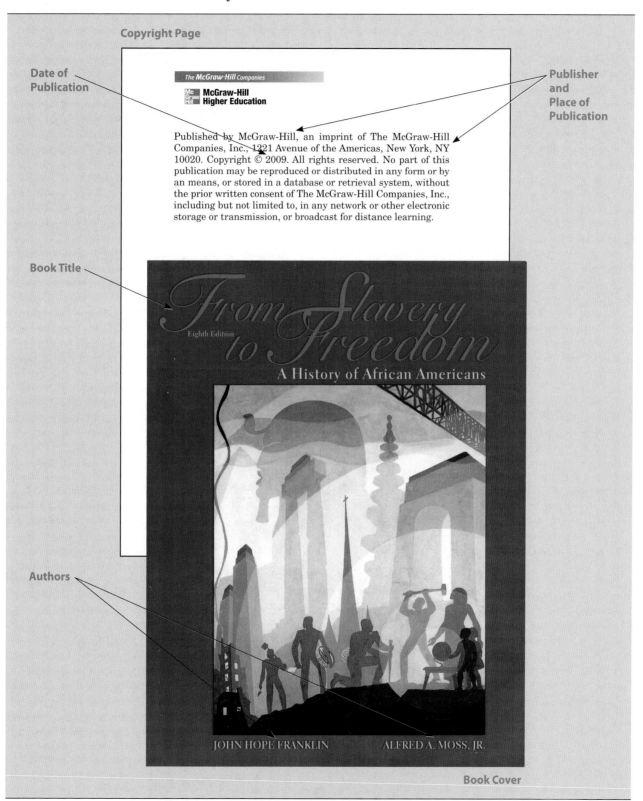

Copyright Page

Date of Publication

Publisher and Place of Publication

Published by McGraw-Hill, an imprint of The McGraw-Hill Companies, Inc., 1221 Avenue of the Americas, New York, NY 10020. Copyright © 2009. All rights reserved. No part of this publication may be reproduced or distributed in any form or by an means, or stored in a database or retrieval system, without the prior written consent of The McGraw-Hill Companies, Inc., including but not limited to, in any network or other electronic storage or transmission, or broadcast for distance learning.

Book Title

Eighth Edition

From Slavery to Freedom
A History of African Americans

Authors

JOHN HOPE FRANKLIN   ALFRED A. MOSS, JR.

Book Cover

2. Book with Two or Three Authors. This entry follows the same formula as a book with a single author *except* that you will name the authors in the order listed on the title page. Reverse only the name of the first author. Then add a comma and list additional authors by first name followed by last name. Separate each author's complete name from the next author by a comma.

> Gilbert, Sandra M., and Susan Gubar. *The Madwoman in the Attic: The Woman Writer and the Nineteenth-Century Literary Imagination.* New Haven: Yale UP, 2000. Print.

*A parenthetical reference for **two** authors should look like this:

> (Gilbert and Gubar 34)

*A parenthetical reference for **three** authors should look like this:

> (Gilbert, Gilbert, and Gubar 34)

3. Book with Four or More Authors. Indicate the name of the first author appearing on the title page, followed by "et al." (the Latin abbreviation for "and others"). As an alternative, however, you may list the names of all the authors *if convenient.*

> Jordan, Frank, et al. *The English Romantic Poets: A Review of Research and Criticism.* New York: MLA, 1985. Print.

*A parenthetical reference for **four or more** authors would look like this:

> (Gilbert et al. 34)

4. Two or More Books by the Same Author. Follow the same formula as the single book entry, but in this case, you need not repeat the author's name. Instead, indicate the same author with three hyphens and a period.

> Bloom, Harold. *The Art of Reading Poetry.* New York: Perennial, 2005. Print.
>
> ——. *How to Read and Why.* New York: Scribner, 2000. Print.

5. Book with an Editor. In place of an author's name, put the editor's name, followed by a comma and the abbreviation "ed." If there is more than one editor, follow the format for "Book with more than one author" but place a comma and the abbreviation "eds." after the final editor's name listed.

> Rampersad, Arnold, ed. *The Collected Poems of Langston Hughes*. New York:
>
> Knopf, 1995. Print.

6. Book with Two Editors.   Use the abbreviation "eds." after the names of the editors.

> Opie, Iona, and Peter Opie, eds. *The Oxford Book of Children's Verse*. New
>
> York: Oxford, 1973. Print.

7. Book with an Author and an Editor.   Start with the name of the author, followed by the book title and a period. Then write "Ed." followed by the editor's name in normal order.

> Twain, Mark. *Adventures of Huckleberry Finn*. Ed. Henry Nash Smith. Boston:
>
> Houghton, 1958. Print.

8. Book by an Unknown Author.   Begin with the title of the book, followed by the translator or editor (if appropriate). Follow with the publication information. Remember to alphabetize such a book in your Works Cited list by the first major word in the title, *not* by an article (*a, an,* or *the*).

> *The Bhagavad Gita*. Trans. Eknath Easwaran. Berkeley: Blue Mountain Center for
>
> Meditation, 2007. Print.

9. Work in an Anthology or Chapter in an Edited Book.   Selection author's last name, first name. "Selection or Chapter Title." *Book Title*. Editor's name. City: Publisher, Year. Page numbers of selection. Medium.

> Fox, Paula. "The Broad Estates of Death." *The O. Henry Prize Stories*. Ed. Laura
>
> Furman. New York: Anchor, 2006. 46-58. Print.

10. Translation of a Text.   Author's last name, first name. *Title of Book*. Abbreviation "Trans." for "translator." City of publication; publisher, year. Medium.

> Alighieri, Dante. *The Divine Comedy*. Trans. John Ciardi. New York: Norton,
>
> 1970. Print.

11. Introduction/Preface/Foreword/Afterword to a Text   If the introduction, preface, foreword, or afterword was written by *someone other than the book's author*, start with the writer and the title of *this* part. Then, indicate the book's title, followed by the word "By" and the name of the book's author in normal order. In the following example, Anita Brookner wrote the introduction to Edith Wharton's novel *The House of Mirth*.

> Brookner, Anita. Introduction. *The House of Mirth*. By Edith Wharton. New York:
>
> Scribner, 1977. ii- ix. Print.

If the introduction, preface, foreword, or afterword *was written by the author*, use **only** his or her last name preceded by the word "By." In the following example, Thomas Hardy wrote both the book itself and the introduction.

> Hardy, Thomas. Introduction. *Tess of the D'Urbervilles*. By Hardy. New York:
>
> Barnes and Noble, 1993. Print.

12. Multivolume Work   If you have taken information from only one of the work's volumes, indicate the number of that volume and abbreviate to "Vol" (no period after "Vol").

> Poe, Edgar Allan. *The Collected Works of Edgar Allan Poe*. Ed. Thomas Ollive
>
> Mabboth. Vol 2. Cambridge: Harvard UP, 1969. Print.

If you have taken information from more than one volume, indicate the total number of volumes used, abbreviate to "vols" and follow with a period.

> Poe, Edgar Allan. *The Collected Works of Edgar Allan Poe*. Ed. Thomas Ollive
>
> Mabboth. 2 vols. Cambridge: Harvard UP, 1969. Print.

13. Book in a Series   Place the name of the series after the medium. Indicate the book's number in the series if available.

> Franchere, Hoyt C., ed. *Edwin Arlington Robinson*. New York: Twayne, 1968.
>
> Print. Twaynes's United States Authors Series 137.

14. Encyclopedia Article

Signed A signed article is one that is attributed to an author.

Invert author's name. "Title of the Article." *Title of the Encyclopedia.* Editor(s). Volume number (if appropriate). City of publication; publisher, year. Page number(s). Medium.

> Merlan, Philip. "Athenian School." *The Encyclopedia of Philosophy.* Ed. Paul
>
> Edwards. Vol. 1. New York: Macmillan, 1967. 192-93. Print.

Unsigned An unsigned article is not attributed to an author. Start with the title of the article. Then proceed as above.

> "Pericles." *The Columbia Concise Encyclopedia.* Eds. Judith S. Levey and Agnes
>
> Greenhall. New York: Columbia UP, 1983. 655. Print.

15. Dictionary Definition   "Title of Entry." *Title of Dictionary.* Edition. Year of publication. Medium.

> "Fresco." *Merriam-Webster's Collegiate Dictionary.* 11th ed. 2003. Print.

Additional Tips

When a book lists multiple cities in which the publisher exists, choose the closest one geographically to put in your citation. For W. W. Norton & Company, which lists New York and London, you would use New York as the city for publication. Also, if the city is relatively unknown, or if there is more than one U.S. city with the same name, indicate the state in addition to the city, as in the following examples:

> Durham, NC: Duke UP
>
> Springfield, IL: Charles C Thomas

You will want to abbreviate or condense the publisher's name. Anytime you see "University Press," you can abbreviate it as "UP." For Southern Methodist University Press, write Southern Methodist UP. Alfred A. Knopf can be condensed to simply "Knopf."

If a book has multiple years on the copyright page, put only the most recent year in your Works Cited entry.

Citing Periodical Sources

Author · Article Title · Journal Title · Date · Volume number · Pages · Medium

Davidas, Lionel. "'I, Too, Sing America': Jazz and Blues Techniques and Effects in Some of Langston Hughes's Selected Poems." *Dialectical Anthropology* 26 (2001): 267-272. Web.

Journal Title · Volume · Article Title · Author · Author Affiliation · Page numbers · Date of Publication · Starting page number

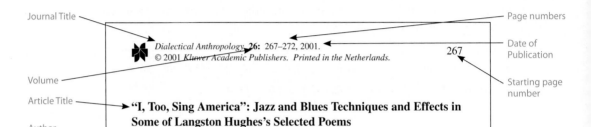

Dialectical Anthropology **26:** 267–272, 2001.
© 2001 *Kluwer Academic Publishers. Printed in the Netherlands.*

267

"I, Too, Sing America": Jazz and Blues Techniques and Effects in Some of Langston Hughes's Selected Poems

LIONEL DAVIDAS
Université des Antilles et de la Guyane, Martinique, West Indies

It is commonly accepted that oral poetry has been greatly influenced by jazz and blues, a phenomenon that developed mainly in the USA. In light of this, we may infer that such poems should logically be considered as mere scores to be deciphered and performed, or records that should be heard rather than read, and that have many of the dynamics of "the music" about them.[1] In point of fact, a significant number of jazz techniques are to be found within the framework of poetry and combine with it to produce a highly personalized mode of free expression, which is the essence and spirit of of jazz creation. As it appears, Langston Hughes's outstanding collection of poems exemplifies the greatest of those qualities of jazz and blues, and his talent truly makes these poems come alive in the same way that jazz and blues music comes alive for the audience as well as for the musicians.

To those who are familiar with such music, it is quite clear that *Selected Poems of Langston Hughes*, a book which reveals the author's personal choice, unquestionably includes blues poetry, as evidenced by the many characteristics of blues music that pervade most of the selected pieces. To start with, it is significant to note that Hughes's poems are not at all static. They are pervaded with lively and active repetitions, and we notice a series of variations within each poem which closely resemble the variations present in a blues song. Many of Hughes's poems exhibit a slow tempo and rhythm which is a common trait to most styles of blues. What is more, there exists some degree of internal variation in breath rhythm that contributes to the blues effect. In addition, those poems definitely seek the interaction of call-and-response, making the reader feel an active participant in the "concert" provided by the poet as musician, as performer.

Periodicals include scholarly journals, magazines, and newspapers. For print periodicals (as opposed to online periodicals), use the following citation formulas.

1. Article in a Scholarly Journal Author's last name, first name. "Article Title." *Journal Title* Volume. Issue (Year): Page numbers of article. Medium.

> Davidas, Lionel. "'I, Too, Sing America': Jazz and Blues Techniques and Effects
>
> in Some of Langston Hughes's Selected Poems." *Dialectical Anthropology*
>
> 26 (2001): 267-272. Print.

Note that not all journals have an issue number, as in the example above. If that is the case, simply include the volume and the year.

2. Article in a Magazine Author's last name, first name. "Article Title." *Magazine Title* Day Month Year: Page numbers of article. Medium.

> Lehrer, Jonah. "The Eureka Hunt." *The New Yorker* 28 July 2008: 40-45. Print.

Note that monthly magazines will not have a day with the month; in that case, simply list the month. Also, abbreviate months except for May, June, and July.

3. Article in a Newspaper Author's last name, first name. "Article Headline." *Newspaper's Name* Day Month Year: Section letter Page number +. Medium.

> Svrluga, Barry. "Phelps Earns Eighth Gold." *The Washington Post* 17 Aug. 2008:
>
> A1+. Print.

Use the plus sign after the page number only if the article is continued on nonconsecutive pages.

4. Book Review Start with the reviewer's name, followed by the title of the review (if it has one) in quotation marks. Follow with "Rev. of" (the abbreviation for "review of"), the title of the book, and the name of the book's author preceded by the word "by." The author's name should be in normal order.

In the following example, the reviewer is Robert Kelly; the author of the book is Umberto Eco.

> Kelly, Robert. "Castaway." Rev. of *The Island of the Day Before,* by Umberto Eco.
>
> *New York Times* 22 Oct. 1995: BR7. Print.

Citing Online Resources

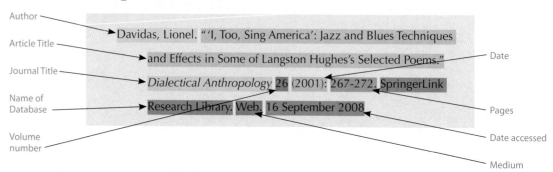

Author —
Article Title —
Journal Title —
Name of Database —
Volume number —

Davidas, Lionel. "'I, Too, Sing America': Jazz and Blues Techniques and Effects in Some of Langston Hughes's Selected Poems." *Dialectical Anthropology* 26 (2001): 267-272. SpringerLink Research Library. Web. 16 September 2008

— Date
— Pages
— Date accessed
— Medium

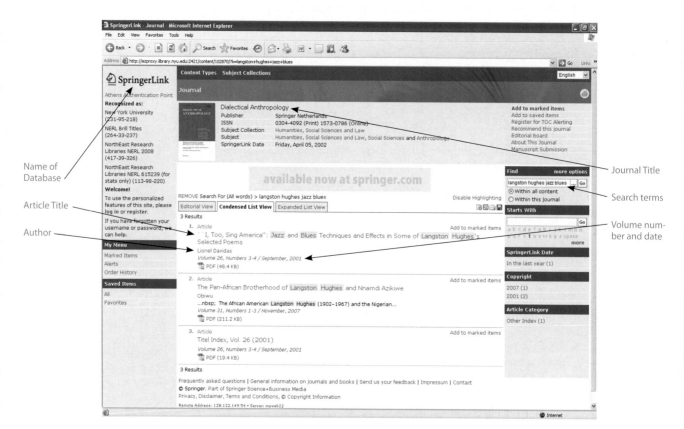

1. Web Site. The amount of source information provided varies from Web site to Web site. Include as much of the information below as you can. Remember, too, to choose your online resources wisely. If there is little or no information on the person or institution that created it, you may want to reconsider using it in your paper.

Last name of person responsible for site, first name. *Name of Web site.* Name of publisher, date of publication or last update. Medium. Day you accessed site—Month Year. Note: If no publisher is listed, use the abbreviation "n.p."

> Souther, Randy. *Celestial Timepiece: A Joyce Carol Oates Homepage.* N.p., Web.
>
> 8 Oct. 2007.

2. Article on a Web Site/Part of an Online Scholarly Project. Segment author's last name, first name. "Title of the Part of the Project." Ed. Name of person responsible for project. Date of publication or update. Name of sponsoring institution. Medium. Date you accessed site.

> "Roaring Twenties." *JAZZ: A Film by Ken Burns.* PBS. Web. 11 May 2008.

*Note that in the above example, the date of the Web site's publication was not available, so the student simply put the date she accessed the site.

3. Article in an Online Periodical. Article author's last name, first name. "Article Title." *Periodical's Web site.* Web site sponsor (if available). Day Month Year of publication. Medium. Date you accessed site.

> Lowney, John. "Langston Hughes and the 'Nonsense' of Bebop." *American*
>
> *Literature Online.* June 2000. Web. 11 May 2008.

4. Article from a Database. Cite the article as you normally would for a print article, but at the end of your entry add the following information:

Database Name. Medium. Date of access.

> Lenz, Gunter. "The Riffs, Runs, Breaks, and Distortions of the Music of a
>
> Community in Transition." *The Massachusetts Review* 44.1-2 (Spring
>
> 2003): 269-282. *ProQuest.* Web. 11 May 2008.

5. Online Book.

The entire online book. Start with the information you would include for any printed book. Follow with the name of the database, project, or other entity in which you found the book. Then, indicate the medium and the date you accessed the book.

> Hardy, Thomas. *Wessex Poems and Other Verses.* New York: Harper, 1898.
>
> *Bartleby.com.* Web. 30 Sept. 2008.

Part of an online book. Start with the name of the author, followed by the title of the part of the book you have cited. Then, proceed as above. The following example is an entry for Thomas Hardy's poem "Neutral Tones," which appears in an online book entitled *Wessex Poems and Other Verses*.

> Hardy, Thomas. "Neutral Tones." *Wessex Poems and Other Verses*. New York:
>
> Harper, 1898. *Bartleby.com*. Web. 30 Sept. 2008.

6. Online Posting.   Treat an online posting as you would a Web site.

> Brantley, Ben. "London Theater Journal: Hitting Bottom." *Artsbeat. New York*
>
> *Times*. 17 July 2008. Web. 29 Sept. 2008.

Citing Other Media

1. Audio Recording.   Start with the name of the composer, performer, or conductor—depending on whom you have discussed in your paper. Then, indicate the title of the recording, followed by the name(s) of the composer (s), performer(s), and/or conductor (if they were not mentioned earlier). Follow this with the distributor, the date, and the medium.

> Chopin. Frederic. *Chopin: Etudes*. Maurizio Pollini. Deutsche Grammaphon,
>
> 1972. CD.

2. Film.   Begin with the title of the film. Then, write the name of the director preceded by "Dir." (the abbreviation for "director"). Next indicate the name(s) of the principal performer(s) preceded by "Perf." (the abbreviation for "performers"). Follow this with the distributor, the date, and the medium.

> *Cinema Paradiso*. Dir. Giuseppe Tornatore. Perf. Phillipe Noiret, Jacques Perrin,
>
> Antonella Attilli, Pupella Maggio, and Salvatore Cascio. Miramar, 1988.
>
> Film.

3. Television Program.   Start with the title of the episode in quotation marks. Then, list the title of the program. Follow with the name of the network or channel, the city, the date you viewed the program, and the medium.

> "Noah: Myth or Fact." *Into the Unknown with Josh Bernstein*. Discovery
>
> Channel, Silver Springs, MD. 15 Aug. 2008. Television.

Glossary of Literary Terms

Abstract   A short **summary** at the beginning of a scholarly article that states the **thesis,** the major points of **evidence,** and the **conclusion** of the article.

Abstract Diction   Language referring to a general or conceptual thing or quality, such as *progress,* or *justice.*

Accent   The vocal emphasis on a syllable in a word. Often used interchangeably with **stress,** which sometimes refers to emphasis within a line of poetry, rather than a single word.

Accentual Meter   A kind of **meter** or verse measure that uses a fixed number of stressed syllables in each line, although based on a number of unstressed syllables may vary. Accentual meters often can be heard in rap music and children's rhymes.

Accentual-Syllabic Verse   A verse form that uses a fixed number of **stresses** and syllables per line. This is the most common verse form in English poetry, and includes, for example, **iambic pentameter,** where each line has five **stressed** syllables and five unstressed syllables.

Act   A subdivision of the action of a play, similar to a chapter in a book. Acts generally occur during a change in **scenery,** cast of **characters,** or mood, and the end of an act usually suggests the advancement of time in the play. Acts are often divided into subunits called **scenes.**

Allegory   A story in which major elements such as **characters** and settings represent universal truths or moral lessons in a one-to-one correspondence.

Alliteration   The repetition of the initial consonant sounds of a sequence of words.

Allusion   A reference to another work of art or literature, or to a person, place, or event outside the text.

Amphibrach   A syllable pattern characterized by three syllables in the order *unstressed, stressed, unstressed.*

Amphitheater   A stage surrounded on all sides by the audience, who watch the action from above.

Anagnorisis   In **tragedy,** a change from ignorance to knowledge, producing love or hate between the persons destined by the poet for good or bad fortune.

Anagram   A word or phrase created using the letters that spell a different word or phrase. For example, *dirty room* is an anagram for *dormitory.*

Analyze   To take a text apart and examine its elements: the different written devices the author uses (such as **point of view, plot,** and imagery) and the **voice** the author brings to the piece (**tone,** word choice).

Anapestic Meter   A **meter** using feet with two unstressed syllables followed by a **stressed** syllable.

Anecdote   A personal remembrance or brief story.

Antagonist   A **character** in **conflict** with the **protagonist.** A story's **plot** often hinges on a protagonist's conflict with an antagonist.

Anticlimax   The opposite of a **climax;** a point in a narrative that is striking for its *lack* of excitement, intensity, or emphasis. An anticlimax generally occurs at a point of high action where a true climax is expected to occur.

Antihero   A main **character** who acts outside the usual lines of heroic behavior (brave, honest, true).

Apostrophe   A **figure of speech** in which a writer directly addresses an unseen person, force, or personified idea. The term *apostrophe* derives from the Greek term meaning *turning away* and often marks a digression.

Approximate Rhyme   *See* **Slant Rhyme.**

Archetypal Criticism   *See* **Mythological Criticism.**

Archetype   An **image** or **symbol** with a universal meaning that evokes a common emotional reaction in readers.

Arena Theater   Also called *Theater in the Round,* an arena stage is surrounded on all sides by the audience, with all the action taking place on a stage in the center.

Argument   A position or perspective based on a **claim** that can be supported with **evidence.**

Aside   In drama, a remark made by an actor to the audience, which the other **characters** do not hear. This convention is sometimes discernable in fiction writing, when a self-conscious **narrator** breaks the flow of the narrative to make a remark directly to the reader.

Assonance   A repetition of vowel sounds or patterns in neighboring words.

Auditory Imagery **Images** that appeal to a reader's sense of hearing.

Augustan Age A distinct period in early-eighteenth-century neoclassical English literature characterized by formal structure and diction. This Augustan Age is named after the great period of Roman literature during Emperor Augustus's reign, when Ovid, Horace, and Virgil were writing. Famous writers of the English Augustan Age were Alexander Pope, Thomas Gray, and Jonathan Swift.

Authorial Intrusion *See* **Editorial Omniscience.**

Ballad Stanza A **quatrain** in which the first and third lines possess four stresses, while the second and fourth have three stresses. The **rhyme scheme** is often *abcb*.

Ballad A song or poem that tells a lively or tragic story in simple language using rhyming four-line **stanzas** and a set **meter.**

Bathos An error that occurs when a writer attempts elevated language but is accidentally trite or ridiculous; a sort of **anticlimax.**

Beat Generation A group of writers in the 1950s and '60s who represented the counterculture to 1950s American prosperity. The word "beat" comes from the slang for being down and worn out, suggesting their weariness with mainstream culture and their adoption of a freespirited attitude. Jack Kerouac's *On the Road* and Allen Ginsberg's poem "Howl" are major works of the Beat Generation.

Bibliography A list of the works consulted in the preparation of a paper, containing adequate information for readers to locate the source materials themselves.

Bildungsroman A **coming of age story** that details the growth or maturity of a youth, usually an adolescent. The term is German, meaning "**novel** of formation."

Biographical Criticism **Literary criticism** that emphasizes the belief that literature is created by authors whose unique experiences shape their writing and therefore can inform our reading of their work. Biographical critics research and use an author's biography to interpret the text as well as the author's stated intentions or comments on the process of composition itself. These critics often consult the author's memoirs to uncover connections between the author's life and the author's work. They may also study the author's rough drafts to trace the evolution of a given text or examine the author's library to discern potential influences on the author's work.

Biography The factual account of a person's life.

Blank Verse Unrhymed **iambic pentameter,** often used in Shakespeare's plays or for epic subject matter, as in Milton's *Paradise Lost.*

Blues A form of music that originated in the Deep South. Descended from African-American spirituals and work songs, the blues reflects the hardships of life and love in its lyrics. Most blues songs follow a form made of three phrases equal in length: a first phrase, a second that repeats the first phrase, and a third phrase different from the first two that concludes the verse.

Box Set *See* **Proscenium Stage.**

Brainstorming A process of generating and collecting ideas on a topic.

Burlesque A work of drama or literature that ridicules its subject matter through exaggerated mockery and broad **comedy.**

Cacophony Harsh-sounding, grating, or even hard-to-pronounce language.

Caesura A pause, usually in the middle of a line, that marks a kind of rhythmic division.

Canon In a literary context, the group of works considered by academics and scholars to be essential to and representative of the body of respected literature.

Carpe diem Latin for *seize the day.* A phrase used commonly in poetry that emphasizes the brevity of life and the importance of living in the moment.

Catharsis The purging of emotions which the audience experiences as a result of the powerful **climax** of a classical **tragedy**; the sense of relief and renewal experienced through art.

Central Intelligence Henry James's term for the **narrator** of a story—distinct from the author—whose impressions and ideas shape the telling of the story and determine the details revealed.

Character The depiction of human beings (and nonhumans) within a story.

Characters The actors (human and nonhuman) in a story.

Characteristics The physical and mental attributes of a **character,** established through **characterization.**

Characterization The way a writer crafts and defines a **character**'s personality to give an insight into that character's thoughts and actions.

Charting A technique for generating ideas that involves placing related concepts and themes in a chart to view their relationships.

Chorus A group of amateurs and trained actors who participated in traditional Greek plays. The chorus represents a group of citizens with worries and questions, expressed in poetry and music and dance movement.

Claim An idea or stance on a particular subject; a defendable claim is necessary for a strong **thesis.**

Classifications of Drama These four categories are generally assigned to Shakespeare's theater, but are commonly used in reference to the works of other **playwrights. Histories** focus on the reign of kings from the past, from Julius

Caesar to Henry V. Because histories naturally contain very astute and sometimes troubling political commentaries, playwrights had to limit their subjects to rulers of the distant past. **Comedies** are plays for entertainment, and as a convention end in the marriage of two main **characters.** A comedic **plot** generally begins with a complication or misunderstanding between two lovers, which is complicated by further scheming and misunderstandings until finally a **resolution** is attained and the two are wed. **Tragedies** are darker plays, with more complex **characters** and more dire consequences, usually dramatizing the fall from a high state of life of a royal or special **character. Romances** (from the French *roman,* which means an "extended narrative") involve lovers whose potential happiness is complicated by misunderstandings, mistaken identities, and any number of other difficulties. Although similar in plot to a **comedy,** a romance play does not guarantee a happy ending.

Cliché   A **figure of speech** that has been used so commonly that it has become trite. The use of cliché may suggest an ironic tone.

Climax   The narrative's turning point in a struggle between opposing forces. The point of highest **conflict** in a story.

Close Reading   The **explication** of a text in order to **analyze** the ways in which distinct formal elements interact to create a unified artistic experience for the reader.

Closed Couplet   A pair of rhymed lines that capture one complete idea. If the couplet is **end-stopped** and in **iambic pentameter,** it is called a **heroic couplet.**

Closed Denouement   A **resolution** to a story that leaves no loose ends.

Closed Form   *See* **Fixed Form.**

Closet Drama   A piece of literature written as though for the stage, but intended only to be read.

Collective Unconscious   A set of **characters, plots, symbols,** and **images** that each evoke a universal response.

Colloquial Speech   Familiar and conversational speech.

Comedy   A type of drama that deals with light or humorous subject matter and usually includes a happy ending. The opposite of **tragedy.** *See* **Classifications of Drama.**

Comedy of Manners   A work of **satire** that pokes fun at human behavior in particular social circles. Since a comedy of manners concerns itself with social interactions, it tends to reveal the **characters'** foibles or follies as they try to appear or act in a certain way.

Comic Relief   A **character** or situation that provides humor in the midst of a work that is predominantly serious. A classic example is the bumbling Falstaff, a character in Shakesepeare's *Henry IV* who makes the audience laugh, even as England's fate hangs in the balance.

Coming of Age Story   A story that follows a **character's** physical, emotional, or spiritual maturation, often from youth into adulthood. *See* ***Bildungsroman.***

Common Measure   A variation on **ballad** meter that uses **iambic quatrains** with the first and third lines containing four feet (**tetrameter**) and the second and fourth containing three feet (**trimeter**). The rhyme scheme is often *abab* rhyme. Common measure, also called *common meter,* is the **meter** most associated with hymns.

Comparison   Looking at two or more texts, **characters,** authors, or other items side by side to draw similarities between them.

Conceit   A complex comparison or **metaphor** that extends throughout a poem

Conclusion   The final idea and **resolution** of a text. In a good essay,

the conclusion not only reiterates the **thesis** but offers a reason for its significance or a reflection that pushes it toward a broader meaning beyond the essay itself. In a story or play, the conclusion refers to the resolution or **dénouement.**

Concrete Diction   Language referring to a specific, definite thing or quality, such as *lawn mower* or *street light.*

Concrete Poetry   Also called *visual poetry.* Poetry written in the shape of something it describes.

Confessional Poetry   Poetry that includes pieces of a poet's autobiography or personal experience. This mode of poetry was prevalent in the mid-twentieth century with poets like Sylvia Plath, Anne Sexton, and Robert Lowell.

Conflict   The central problem in a story. The source of tension between the **protagonist** and **antagonist.**

Connotation   The associations a word carries beyond its literal meaning. Connotations are formed by the context of the word's popular usage; for example, *green,* aside from being a color, connotes money. The opposite of **denotation.**

Consonance   A repetition of consonant sounds or similar patterns in neighboring words.

Context   The literary, historical, biographical, or poetical situation that influences the writing of a work of literature.

Contextual Reading   Reading and interpreting a story while mindful of its author, the time and place it was written, the traditions of its form, and the criticism it explicitly or implicitly responds to.

Contrast   Looking at two or more texts, **characters,** authors, or other items side by side to highlight the differences between them.

Convention   In literature, a feature or element of a **genre** that is commonly used and therefore widely accepted—and expected—

by readers and writers alike. For example, it is a convention of Shakespearean **comedy** to end with a marriage.

Conventional Symbols **Symbols** that have accrued a widely accepted **interpretation** through their repeated use in literature and the broader culture. For example, spring and winter are conventional symbols of birth and death, as they appear with that meaning in Shakespeare's works through Frost's poetry. Colors, too, can be used as conventional symbols; in contemporary society, a pink ribbon is a conventional symbol of breast cancer awareness.

Cosmic Irony A literary convention where forces beyond the control of **characters**—such as God or fate or the supernatural—foil plans or expectations.

Couplet Two lines of poetry forming one unit of meaning. Couplets are often **rhymed,** strung together without a break, and share the same **meter.**

Cothurni Tall boots, worn by actors in the Ancient Greek theater, which served both to elevate an actor and make him more visible to the massive crowds, and also to make the **character**s seem larger than life.

Craft As a noun, craft refers to the elements that comprise a story; as a verb, craft refers to the process of making or fashioning a story out of those elements.

Cretic Also called *Amphimacer.* A syllable pattern characterized by three syllables in the order *stressed, unstressed, stressed.*

Crisis *See* **Climax.**

Critical Reading A process of digesting and understanding a text so you can appreciate not just the ideas it presents or the story it tells, but how it presents those ideas, why it presents them, and how those ideas exist in a certain context. Critical reading involves **summary, analysis, synthesis,** and **interpretation.**

Critique A **summary** accompanied by one's own personal opinion and perspectives.

Cultural Studies This critical perspective was developed mainly in England in the sixties by New Left writers, social philosophers, and sociologists. Cultural studies incorporates the techniques of literary analysis to **analyze** social life and social movements as though they were written texts.

Dactylic Meter A **meter** in which the foot contains a stressed syllable followed by two unstressed syllables.

Deconstruction A critical approach to analyzing literature based on the idea that texts do not have a single, stable meaning or **interpretation.** Deconstructionists seek to break down literature to reveal the inevitable inconsistency or lack of unity in even the most successful and revered texts, believing that the author's intentions have no bearing on the meaning of the text to the reader.

Decorum A certain level of propriety appropriate to a given text. As well as demanding a certain level of **diction,** decorum can also have bearing on the **characters, setting,** and **plot** events of a piece of literature.

Denotation The literal meaning of a word. The opposite of **connotation.**

Denouement The period after the story's **climax** when **conflicts** are addressed and/or resolved. Includes the **falling action** and **resolution** of a story.

Deus ex machina Latin for *God from the machine;* a literary device, often seen in drama, where a **conflict** is resolved by unforeseen and often far-fetched means.

Dialect **Dialogue** written to phonetically or grammatically replicate a particular **sound,** cadence, **rhythm,** or emphasis in a **character's** speech.

Dialogue Spoken interaction between two or more **characters.** A **characterization** technique that can signal class, education, intelligence, ethnicity, and attitude in the characters involved.

Diction An author's or **character's** distinctive choice of words and style of expression.

Didactic Literature Literature, such as a fable or **allegory,** written to instruct or teach a moral.

Dimeter A poetic **meter** comprised of two poetic feet.

Dirge A funeral song.

Doggerel An obviously patterned piece of **rhyme,** often lunging or twisting word order in order to get a rhyme. Doggerel can sometimes seem almost childish and, when extensive, boring.

Drama A term that comes from the Greek word for doing or acting and refers to a literary work that is represented through performance.

Dramatic Irony A situation in which an author or **narrator** lets the reader know more about a situation than a **character** does.

Dramatic Monologue A poem in which a **character** addresses another character or the reader. Dramatic monologues are offshoots of the epic form.

Dramatic Poetry Poetry in which the speaker of the poem is not the poet. Dramatic poetry often tells a story.

Dramatic Point of View A **third-person point of view** in which the **narrator** presents only bare details and the **dialogue** of other **characters.**

Dramatic Question The overarching challenge or issue in a piece of drama—the complication which the events of a play work to resolve.

Dynamic Character A **character** whose personality and behavior alter over the course of the action in response to challenges and changing circumstances.

Dramatis Personae "People of the play"; a list of the **characters** in a play, usually one of the first elements of a script.

Echo Verse Poetry in which words at the ends of lines or **stanzas** are repeated, mimicking an echo.

Economic Determinist Criticism *See* **Marxist Criticism.**

Editorial Omniscience A **narrator** inserts his or her own commentary about **characters** or events into the narrative.

Electra Complex The female version of the **Oedipus Complex,** the Electra Complex suggests that female children are hostile toward their mothers because of subconscious sexual attraction to their fathers.

Elegy A poem of lamentation memorializing the dead or contemplating some nuance of life's melancholy. Early Greek elegies employed a fixed form of **dactylic hexameter** and **iambic pentameter couplets.**

Elision The omission of a vowel or consonant sound within or between words, such as "ne'er" for "never" and "o'er" for "over." Elision dramatizes language and allows for flexibility within a poem's **meter.**

Ellipses Three periods placed in succession (. . .) to illustrate that something has been omitted.

End Rhyme **Rhyme** that occurs at the end of two or more lines of poetry. An example of end rhyme can be found in "The Love Song of J. Alfred Prufrock": "Let us go through certain half-deserted streets, / The muttering retreats."

End-stopped Line A line that ends with a full stop or period.

Endnote Information placed at the end of a text in an explanatory note. In a research paper, endnotes are used to comment on sources or provide additional analysis that is slightly tangential to the focus of your paper. An endnote is indicated by a superscript number ([1]) in the text itself, which corresponds to a numbered explanatory note at the end.

English Sonnet *See* **Shakespearean Sonnet.**

Enjambment The running over of a phrase from one line into another so that closely related words belong to different lines.

Envoi The final **stanza** of a **sestina,** which summarizes the entire poem. Envoi is French for *farewell.*

Epic A long **narrative poem,** traditionally recited publicly, whose subject matter reflects the values of the culture from which it came by portraying important legends or heroes. Classical epics include the *Odyssey* and the *Aeneid,* while English epics include *Beowulf* and *Paradise Lost.*

Epigram A short, often satirical observation on a single subject.

Epigraph A quotation or brief passage from another source, included at the beginning of a piece of literature. Writers use epigraphs to suggest a major theme or idea in their work.

Epiphany A sudden realization or new understanding achieved by a **character** or speaker. In many short stories, the character's epiphany is the **climax** of the story.

Episode A unified event or incident within a longer narrative.

Episodia The scenes of a Greek tragedy, divided by *stasimon* from the **Chorus.**

Epistolary Novel A novel written in the form of letters between two or more **characters,** or in the form of diary entries. Epistolary novels were particularly popular in the eighteenth century.

Ethnic Studies A critical approach to literature that seeks to give voice to literature that has previously been overlooked in the traditionally Euro-centric worldview—not simply by including ethnically diverse literature in the **canon,** but by attention to historically underrepresented groups, like African Americans and Native Americans.

Euphony Musically pleasing poetic language.

Evidence Reliable information, such as statistics, expert opinions, and anecdotes, used to support a **claim** in an **argument.**

Exact Rhyme A rhyme in which the final vowel and consonant sounds are identical, regardless of spelling. Also called *pure rhyme, perfect rhyme,* and *true rhyme.*

Exodos The concluding scene of a Greek **tragedy.**

Explication a **close reading** of any text where the goal is to logically **analyze** details within the text itself to uncover deeper meanings or contradictions.

Exposition: The narrative presentation of necessary information about the **character, setting,** or character's history provided to make the reader care what happens to the characters in the story.

Expressionism A mode of theater in which the playwright attempts to portray his or her subjective emotions in a symbolic way on stage.

Extended Metaphor A figurative analogy that is woven through a poem.

Eye Rhyme Words that share similar spellings but—when spoken—have different sounds. For example, *lint* and *pint.* Also called *Sight Rhyme.*

Fables A short narrative in which the **characters** (often animals or inanimate things) illustrate a lesson. The characters in fables are *actors* rather than **symbols.**

Fairy Tale A story, usually for children, that involves magical creatures or circumstances and usually has a happy ending.

Falling Action The events following the **climax** and leading up to the **resolution.** These events reveal how the **protagonist** has been impacted by and dealt with the preceding **conflicts** of the story.

Falling Meter A **meter** comprised of feet that begin with a stressed syllable, followed by an unstressed syllable or syllables. **Trochaic** and **dactylic** feet both create falling meter, which is named for the effect of *falling* from the initial stressed syllable to the unstressed.

Fantasy A literary **genre** that uses magical **characters** or circumstances.

Farce A work of drama or literature that uses broad, often physical **comedy,** exaggerated **characters,** absurd situations, and improbable **plot** twists to evoke laughter without intending social criticism.

Feminine Rhyme Rhymes between multisyllable words in which the final syllable is unstressed, such as *bother* and *father*. Also called *falling rhyme*.

Feminist Criticism An approach to literary criticism that highlights literature written by women and the exploration of the experience of female **characters**; also a critical examination of the ways in which female characters are viewed with prejudice, are subjugated to male interests, or are simply overlooked in literature.

Fiction A genre of literature that describes events and **characters** invented by the author.

Figurative Language Language that describes one thing by relating it to something else.

Figure of Speech A technique of using language to describe one thing in terms of another, often comparing two unlike objects, such as *the sun* and *the face of the beloved*, to condense and heighten the effect of language, particularly the effect of **imagery** or **symbolism** in a poem.

First-Person Narrator The story is narrated by a **character** in the story, identified by use of the pronoun *I* or the plural first-person, *we*.

Fixed Form An arrangement of text that requires a poet to obey set written combinations, including line length, **meter, stanza** structure, and **rhyme scheme.** Also called *closed form.*

Flashback The device of moving back in time to a point before the primary action of the story.

Flat Character A **character** with a narrow range of speech or action. Flat characters are predictable and do not develop over the course of the **plot.**

Foil A **character** who contrasts with the central character, often with the purpose of emphasizing some trait in the central character. For example, a cruel sister emphasizes the other sister's kindness.

Folklore A traditional **canon** of stories, sayings, and **characters.**

Folktale A short, often fantastic tale passed down over time.

Foot The smallest unit of measure in poetic **meter.** A foot usually contains a stressed syllable and one or two unstressed syllables. **Meter** is formed when the same foot repeats more than once. For example, in **iambic pentameter,** *iambic* refers to the type of foot (an unstressed syllable followed by a stressed syllable), while *pentameter* tells us that there are five (pent) iambic feet in each line.

Footnote Like an **endnote,** a way to include commentary on sources or other information tangential to the focus of a text. A footnote occurs at the bottom of the page on which the subject is most closely addressed. To create a footnote, a superscript number ([1]) is placed in the text itself and corresponds to the number of the explanatory note at the bottom of the page.

Foreshadowing A hint about **plot** elements to come, both to advance the plot and build **suspense.**

Form The shape, structure, and style of a poem, as distinguishable from, but integral to, the content or substance of the poem.

Formal Diction Complex, grammatically proper, and often polysyllabic language in writing. It sounds grandiloquent—a *formal* word—and tends not to resemble the sort of talk heard in daily life.

Formalist Criticism An approach to literary criticism that considers a successful text to be a complete, independent, unified artifact whose meaning and value can be understood purely by analyzing the interaction of its formal and technical components, such as **plot, imagery,** structure, style, **symbol,** and **tone.** Rather than drawing their textual interpretations from *extrinsic* factors such as the historical, political, or biographical context of the work, formalist critics focus on the text's *intrinsic* formal elements.

Found Poem A poem created from already existing text that the poet reshapes and presents in poetic form. Text may come from advertisements, labels on household items, newspapers, magazines, or any other printed source not intended originally as poetry. A poet may piece together several sources like a collage, or he/she might take a short text exactly as it is and insert line breaks.

Fourth Wall The *invisible wall* of the stage, through which the audience views the action.

Free Verse Poetry in which the poet does not adhere to a preset metrical or **rhyme scheme.** Free verse has become increasingly prevalent since the nineteenth century, when it was first used. *See* **Open Form.**

Freewrite Writing continuously to generate ideas, without worrying about mistakes.

Gay and Lesbian Criticism A critical approach that is similar to **feminist criticism** in its quest to uncover previously overlooked undertones and themes in literature. Gay and lesbian criticism seeks to identify underlying homosexual themes in literature.

Gender Criticism   A critical approach to literature that seeks to understand how gender and sexual identity reflect upon the interpretation of literary works. Feminist criticism and gay and lesbian criticism are derivatives of gender criticism.

Genre   A literary category or form, such as the short story or novel, or a specific type of fiction, such as science fiction or mystery.

Groundlings   "Standing room only" spectators in the Elizabethan theater who paid a penny to stand on the ground surrounding the stage.

Haiku   A poetic form containing seventeen syllables in three lines of five, seven, and five syllables each. Haiku traditionally contain a natural-world reference or central **image.**

Hamartia   A tragic flaw or weakness in a tragic **character** that leads to his or her downfall. **Hubris** is a type of *hamartia.*

Heptameter   A poetic **meter** that consists of seven feet in each line.

Hero/Heroine   The **protagonist** of a story, often possessing positive traits such as courage or honesty.

Heroic Couplet   Two successive rhyming lines in **iambic pentameter.**

Hexameter   A poetic **meter** that consists of six feet in each line. If the six feet are **iambic,** the line is known as an alexandrine, which was the preferred line of French epic poetry.

High Comedy   **Comedy,** often a satire of upper-class society, that relies on sophisticated wit and **irony.**

Hip Hop   An intensely rhythmical form of popular music developed by African-Americans and Latinos in the 1970s in which vocalists deploy rhyme—known as rap—over the rhythm.

Historical Criticism   An approach to **literary criticism** that em-

phasizes the relationship between a text and its historical context. When interpreting a text, historical critics highlight the cultural, philosophical, and political movements and ideologies prevalent during the text's creation and reception.

Historical Fiction   A type of fiction writing wherein the author bases his or her **characters, plot,** or **setting** on actual people, events, or places.

Histories   *See* **Classifications of Drama.**

Hubris   Excessive arrogance or pride. In classical literature, the hero's tragic flaw was often hubris, which caused his downfall in the tragedy.

Hyperbole   A type of figurative speech that uses verbal exaggeration to make a point. Hyperbole is sometimes called *overstatement.*

Iamb   A poetic **foot** consisting of an unstressed syllable followed by a stressed syllable.

Iambic Meter   A poetic **meter** created when each line contains more than one **iamb** (a unit with an unstressed syllable followed by a stressed syllable).

Iambic Pentameter   A poetic **meter** in which each line contains five feet, predominantly iambs. Iambic pentameter is the most commonly used meter in English poetry, comprising **sonnets,** much of Shakespeare's plays, Milton's *Paradise Lost,* Wordsworth's *The Prelude* and Wallace Stevens' "Sunday Morning."

Iconography   **Symbols** that commonly engender a certain meaning. For example, a skull equals *death,* and a dove equals *peace.*

Image   A sensory impression created by language. Not all images are visual pictures; an image can appeal to any of the five senses, emotions, or the intellect.

Imagism   A poetic practice wherein the *thing itself*—the object seen and not discussed or **analyzed**—

becomes the poet's focus and the poem's primary concern. Imagism is associated with poets like Ezra Pound and William Carlos Williams.

Impartial Omniscience   A **narrator** who remains neutral, relating events and **characters'** thoughts without passing judgment or offering an opinion.

Implied Metaphor   A suggested comparison that is never stated plainly.

Impressionism   In literature, a style of writing that focuses on a **protagonist**'s reactions to external events rather than the events themselves.

Indirect Discourse   A **narrator**'s description of an action or event as experienced by a **character** in the story.

Informal Diction   An author's use of words that are conversational or easily understood, as opposed to elevated or formal language. For example, using *you* instead of *thou.*

Initial Alliteration   The repetition of consonant or vowel sounds in the middle of a line of poetry.

Initiation Story   *See* **Coming of Age Story** and *Bildungsroman.*

In medias res   Latin for *in the middle of things.* A term applied when a story begins with relevant story events already having occurred.

Innocent Narrator   *See* **Naïve Narrator.**

Intentional Fallacy   The practice by **formalist** critics of discerning or trusting an author's own stated purpose for the meaning of a text.

Interior Monologue   A **character**'s conscious or unconscious thought processes, narrated as they occur, with only minimal-seeming guidance from the **narrator.**

Internal Alliteration   The repetition of consonant or vowel sounds in the middle of a line of poetry.

Internal Refrain   The repetition of words or phrases within the lines of a poem.

Internal Rhyme **Rhyme** that occurs within a line. The placement of internal rhyme can vary; for example, a word in the middle of the line might rhyme with the word at the end of that same line, or both rhyming words might occur in the middle of two consecutive lines.

Interpret The act of **interpretation.**

Interpretation The process of contributing to the overall understanding of some aspect of a work in order to illuminate its meaning.

In-Text Parenthetical Citation A reference within the body of a paper that links a **quotation, paraphrase,** or **summary** from another source to its full citation in the list of **works cited.**

In the Round *See* **Arena Theater.**

Inverted Syntax A reversal of expected or traditional word order, often used to aid a poem's sounds, **rhyme,** and/or **meter.**

Ironic Point of View Describes a **narrator** who does not understand the significance of the events of a story.

Irony A **tone** characterized by a distance between what occurs and what is expected to occur, or between what is said and what is meant.

Italian Sonnet *See* **Petrarchan Sonnet.**

Jargon Words used with specific meaning for a particular group of people. For example, *starboard* in nautical jargon refers to the right side of a ship.

Journal Entry A writing exercise that expands **freewriting** into a more focused discussion that reflects a growing understanding of a topic.

Language, Tone, and Style The elements that conjure a story's particular flavor and **voice,** as achieved by means of the words the author chooses and the **rhythm** with which he or she puts the words together

Language The words of a story, including **syntax** (how words or other elements of the sentence are arranged) and **diction** (what words the author chooses).

Levels of Diction Refers to the three major categories of diction: high, middle, and low diction. The level of diction a writer uses determines whether the words in the work will be formal or informal, poetic or conversational, etc.

Limerick A light, often humorous verse form consisting of five **anapestic** (two short syllables followed by one long one) lines, with a rhyme scheme of *aabba.* The first, second, and fifth lines consist of three feet, while lines three and four consist of two feet.

Limited Omniscient Narrator A **third-person narrator** who enters into the mind of only one **character** at a time. This narrator serves more as an interpreter than a source of the main **character's** thoughts.

Line A row of words containing phrases and/or sentences. The line is a defining feature of poetry, in which there are often set amounts of syllables or poetic feet in each line.

Literary Ballad A story told in **ballad** form.

Literary Criticism The acts of analyzing, interpreting, and commenting on literature.

Literary Epic *See* **Epic.**

Literary Theory The body of criticism and schools of thought (such as **Feminist, Deconstructionist,** or **Biographical** Criticism) that govern how we study literature.

Low Comedy An informal brand of **comedy** that uses crude humor and **slapstick.**

Lyric A short poem with a central pictorial **image** written in an uninflected (direct and personal) **voice.**

Madrigal A variety of contrapuntal song that originated in 16th-century Italy. Madrigal features secular verse sung by two or more voices without instrumental accompaniment.

Magic Realism A type of fiction in which something "magical" happens in an otherwise realistic world. The form is particularly associated with Latin American writers like Gabriel García Márquez. Unlike **fantasy** or science fiction, magic realism generally has only one fantastical element and the rest relies on realistic **characters** and settings. Notable examples in this book are Franz Kafka's *The Metamorphosis* and Aimee Bender's "The Rememberer."

Marxist Criticism Marxist or Economic Determinist Criticism is based on the writings of Karl Marx, who argued that economic concerns shape lives more than anything else, and that society is essentially a struggle between the working classes and the dominant capitalist classes. Rather than assuming that culture evolves naturally or autonomously out of individual human experience, Marxist critics maintain that culture— including literature—is shaped by the interests of the dominant or most powerful social class.

Masculine Rhyme The **end rhymes** of multisyllable words with a stressed final syllable, such as *remove* and *approve.* Also called rising rhyme.

Melodrama A literary work, mainly a stage play, movie, or television play or show in which **characters** display exaggerated emotions and the **plot** takes sensational turns, sometimes accompanied by music intended to lead the audience's feelings.

Melody The linear succession of various musical pitches recognized as a unit.

Metafiction A work of fiction that self-consciously draws attention to itself as a work of fiction. Rather than upholding the standard pretense, prevalent in realist fiction, that a story creates or refers to a "real world" beyond the text, metafiction self-consciously reveals the fact and sometimes the manner of its own construction. Metafiction is often associated with **postmodernism,** but examples of metafiction also occur in many other literary movements.

Metaphor A close comparison of two dissimilar things that creates a fusion of identity between the things that are compared. A metaphor joins two dissimilar things *without* using words such as *like* or *as*. While a **simile** suggests that X is *like* Y a metaphor states that X *is* Y.

Meter A measure of verse, based on regular patterns of sound.

Metonymy A **figure of speech** that uses an identifying emblem or closely associated object to represent another object. For example, the phrase *the power of the purse* makes little sense literally (there is no purse that has power), but in the metonymical sense, *purse* stands for money.

Middle Diction Poetic language characterized by sophisticated word usage and grammatical accuracy. Middle diction reads as educated, cultured language but is not extravagant like **poetic diction.**

Mime The act of performing a play without words.

Miracle Plays During the tenth century, when drama was suppressed by the church, these anonymous plays were acted out as religious instruction for the benefit of spectators who could not read the Bible.

Mixed Metaphor A failed comparison that results when a writer uses at least two separate, mismatched comparisons in one statement—to confusing, and sometimes comical effect. For example, *The early bird strikes when the iron's hot!*

Monologue A single **character's** discourse, without interaction or interruption by other **characters.**

Monometer A poetic **meter** comprised of one poetic foot.

Monosyllabic A word with one syllable.

Moral The lesson taught by a piece of **didactic literature** such as a fable. A moral is often phrased simply and memorably.

Morality Play A form of drama in which the figures on stage taught right and proper behavior—morality—to those who watched.

Motif A pattern of **imagery** or a concept that recurs throughout a work of literature.

Motivation A **character's** reason for doing something.

Mystery Play A play that enacted stories of the Bible, such as the Creation or the Crucifixion. These plays appeared during the tenth century, when drama was suppressed in England.

Myth The pre-Classical Greek word for sacred story or religious narrative, which by the Classical period had come to mean **plot,** as used in Aristotle's *Poetics*.

Mythological Criticism Also called the *archetypal approach,* mythological criticism stems from the work of Carl Jung, a Swiss psychoanalyst (and contemporary of Freud) who argued that humans share in a **collective unconscious,** or a set of **characters,** plots, symbols, and **images** that each evoke a universal response. Jung calls these recurring elements **archetypes,** and likens them to *instincts*—knowledge or associations with which humans are born. Mythological critics **analyze** the ways in which such archetypes function in literature and attempt to explain the power that literature has over us or the reasons why certain texts continue to hold power over audiences many centuries after their creation.

Naïve Narrator An unreliable **narrator** who remains unaware of the full complexity of events in the story being told, often due to youth, innocence, or lack of cultural awareness.

Narrative Poem A poem that tells a story. Examples include Tennyson's "The Charge of the Light Brigade," Longfellow's "The Midnight Ride of Paul Revere," and most ballads.

Narrator The **character** or consciousness that tells a story. For specific types of narrators, see **First-Person Narrator, Second-Person Narrator, Third-Person narrator, Omniscient Narrator, Limited Omniscient Narrator, Impartial Omniscience, Editorial Omniscience, Naïve Narrator,** and **Unreliable Narrator.**

Naturalistic Theater Drama that shines a light on the painful realities and problems of everyday life.

Near Rhyme *See* **Slant Rhyme.**

New Criticism *See* **Formalist Criticism.**

New Historicism A critical approach that emerged as a reaction to **new criticism**'s disregard of historical context, but also in response to the perceived shortcomings of older methods of **historical criticism.** Rather than focusing on texts in the **canon** as representations of the most powerful or dominant historical movements, new historicists give equal or greater attention to less dominant texts and non-literary texts (newspapers, pamphlets, legal documents, medical documents, etc.). New historicists attempt to highlight overlooked or suppressed texts, particularly those that express deviation from the dominant culture of the time. In this way, new historicists study not just the historical context of a major literary text, but the complex relationship between texts and culture, or the ways in which literature can challenge as well as support a given culture.

Nonfiction Novel   A presentation of real events using the craft and technique of a fiction novel.

Novel   A long fictional work. Because of their greater length, novels are typically complex and may follow more than one **character** or **plot.**

Novella   A short novel, which generally means it has more complexity than a short story but without the usual length of a novel.

Objective Point of View   The story is told by an observer who relates only facts, providing neither commentary nor insight into the **character's** thoughts or actions.

Observer   A **first-person narrator** who does not participate in the action of the story.

Octameter   A poetic **meter** that consists of eight feet in each line.

Octave   Eight lines of poetry grouped together in a **stanza** or a unit of thought, as in the **Petrarchan sonnet** where the octave sets up a thought or feeling that the following **sestet** resolves.

Ode   An elevated, formal **lyric** poem often written in ceremony to someone or to an abstract subject. In Greek **tragedy,** a song and dance performed by the **Chorus** between *episodia.*

Oedipus Complex: Sigmund Freud's theory of behavior (derived from the **plot** of Sophocles's *Oedipus the King*) which holds that male children are jealous of the father because of their sexual attraction to the mother. In *Oedipus the King,* Oedipus kills his father and sleeps with his mother.

Off Rhyme   *See* **Slant Rhyme.**

O. Henry Ending   A short story ending that consists of a sudden surprise, often ironic or coincidental in nature, named for the short story writer O. Henry, who frequently ended his stories in this way. A classic example is O. Henry's "The Gift of the Magi" in which a husband and wife

each give something precious of theirs to purchase a gift for the other; the ending reveals that each has sacrificed the very thing that would have allowed him or her to enjoy the gift received from their spouse.

Omniscient Narrator   A **third-person narrator** who observes the thoughts and describes the actions of multiple **characters** in the story. The omniscient narrator can see beyond the physical actions and **dialogue** of **characters** and is able to reveal the inner thoughts and emotions of anyone in the story.

One-Act Play   A play that consists of a single act that contains the entire action of the play. One-act plays usually portray a single **scene** with an exchange among a smaller number of **characters**; for example, Edward Albee's *The Zoo Story.*

Onomatopoeia   The use of words that imitate the sounds they refer to, such as *buzz* or *pop.*

Open Denouement   A **resolution** to a story that leaves loose ends and does not completely resolve the overarching **conflict.**

Open Form   Poetry ungoverned by metrical or rhyme schemes. Also called free verse.

Orchestra   The open area in front of the stage (or *skene*) in the Greek **amphitheater.**

Overstatement   *See* **Hyperbole.**

Oxymoron   A version of **paradox** that combines contradictory words into a compact, often two-word term, such as *jumbo shrimp* or *definitely maybe.*

Paean   The final choral **ode** of a Greek **tragedy.**

Pantoum   A variation on the **villanelle,** consisting of an unspecified number of **quatrains** with the rhyme scheme *abab.* The first line of each quatrain repeats the second line of the preceding quatrain, and the third line repeats

the final line of the preceding quatrain. In the final quatrain, the second line repeats the third line of the first quatrain, and the last line of the poem repeats the first line of the poem.

Parable   A short narrative that illustrates a lesson using comparison to familiar **characters** and events. The characters and events in parables often have obvious significance as **symbols** and **allegories.**

Parados   The **Chorus'** first **ode** in a Greek **tragedy.**

Paradox   Seemingly contradictory statements that, when closely examined, have a deeper, sometimes complicated, meaning.

Parallelism   The arrangement of words or phrases in a grammatically similar way.

Paraphrase   Condensing a passage or idea from an existing text into your own words. Paraphrase does not mean simply changing the words from the original; rather, it should re-present the original in a way that demonstrates your understanding of it.

Parody   Mimicking another author or work of literature in such a way as to make fun of the original, often by exaggerating its characteristic aspects.

Participant narrator   A **first-person narrator** who takes part in the action of the story.

Pastoral Poetry   A variety of poem in which life in the countryside, mainly among shepherds, is glorified and idealized.

Pentameter   A poetic **meter** that consists of five feet in each line.

Peripeteia   An element of Greek **tragedy,** *peripeteia* occurs when an action has the opposite result of what was intended. In a **tragedy,** this generally occurs at a turning point for the **hero** and signals his downfall.

Persona   A poem's speaker, which may or may not use the **voice** of the poet.

Personae Masks, often representative of certain **iconography** and familiar **characters,** worn by actors in the Ancient Greek theater to enable one actor to perform as many **characters.** *Personae* often were designed to project an actor's voice to the far rows of the **amphitheater.**

Personification A **figure of speech** in which a writer ascribes human traits or behavior to something inhuman.

Persuasion The process of using **analysis** and logical **argument** to prove the validity of a certain **interpretation** or **point of view.**

Petrarchan (Italian) Sonnet A sonnet consisting of an **octave** and a **sestet,** all in **iambic pentameter,** with the rhyme scheme *abbaabba cdecde* or *abbaabba cdcdcd.* The **volta,** or turn, typically occurs between the octave and sestet, around line nine of the poem.

Plagiarism The act of taking credit for another's work or ideas.

Play A work of drama, usually performed before an audience.

Players Traveling actors, men and boys, who spoke their lines for pay.

Play Review The critique of a play.

Playwright The author of a dramatic work.

Plot The artful arrangement of incidents in a story, with each incident building on the next in a series of causes and effects.

Poetic Diction Lofty and elevated language, used traditionally in poetry written before the nineteenth century to separate poetic speech from common speech.

Point of View The perspective from which the story is told to the reader.

Polysyllabic A word that has many syllables.

Portmanteau Word A word invented by combining two other words to achieve the effect of both. Lewis Carroll's poem "Jabberwocky" is comprised largely of portmanteau

words such as *slithy,* which means *slimy* and *lithe.*

Postcolonialism A critical approach to **literary criticism** that seeks to offer views of relations between the colonizing West and colonized nations and regions that differed sharply from the conventional Western perspectives.

Poststructuralist Criticism Criticism based on the belief that texts do not have a single, stable meaning or **interpretation,** in part because language itself is filled with ambiguity, multiple meanings, and meanings that can change with time or context.

Precís *See* **Summary Paper.**

Preview The process of gathering information about a piece of literature before you read it.

Problem Play A play about a social problem, written with an aim to create awareness of the problem.

Prologue The introduction to a literary work.

Proscenium Stage A realistic **setting** with three flat walls (two flat sides, and a ceiling) that simulates a room; the audience views the action through the missing **fourth wall.**

Prose Poem A poem that uses the devices and **imagery** characteristic of traditionally lined poetry, but in compact units without clearly defined line breaks.

Prosody The analysis of a poem's rhythm and metrical structures.

Protagonist The main figure (or principal actor) in a work of literature. A story's **plot** hinges equally on the protagonist's efforts to realize his or her desires and to cope with failure if and when plans are thwarted and desires left unfulfilled.

Psalm A sacred song, usually written to or in honor of a deity.

Psychoanalytic Criticism Also called *psychological criticism,* this approach in a sense studies **characters** and authors as one would patients, looking in the text for

evidence of childhood trauma, repressed sexual impulses, preoccupation with death, and so on. Through the lens of psychology critics attempt to explain the motivations and meanings behind characters' actions. Psychological critics also use textual and biographical evidence as a means to better understand the author's psychology, as well as examine the process and nature of literary creation, studying the ways in which texts create an emotional and intellectual effect for their readers and authors.

Pun A play on words that reveals different meanings in words that are similar or even identical.

Pyrrhic A poetic foot characterized by two unstressed syllables.

Quantitative Meter A type of poetry that counts the length of syllables, rather than the emphasis they receive (as in **accentual meter** and syllabic verse). Quantitative meter primarily appears in Greek and Latin poetry and is rarely used in English since English vowel lengths are not clearly quantified.

Quatrain A four-line **stanza.** Quatrains are the most popular stanzaic form in English poetry because they are easily varied in **meter,** line length, and **rhyme scheme.**

Queer Theory The idea that power is reflected in language and that discourse itself shapes our sense of who we are and how we define ourselves sexually.

Rap An oral form of poetry that is akin to spoken word, but distinguished by musical qualities and choral repetitions. *See* **Hip Hop.**

Reader-Response Criticism The reader-response approach emphasizes that the reader is central to the writer-text-reader interaction. Reader-response critics believe a literary work is not complete until someone reads and **interprets** it.

Such critics acknowledge that because each reader has a different set of experiences and views, each reader's response to a text may be different.

Realism A mode of literature in which the author depicts **characters** and scenarios that could occur in real life. Unlike **fantasy** or **surrealism,** realism seeks to represent the world as it is.

Recognition The moment in a **tragedy** when the **hero** comes to recognize the actuality of events and is no longer under illusion.

Refrain A line or **stanza** that is repeated at regular intervals in a poem or song.

Resolution The end of the story, where the **conflict** is ultimately resolved and the effects of the story's events on the **protagonist** become evident.

Restoration Comedy A bawdy play about fallen virtue and infidelity that became popular after the Puritans were displaced in England in the mid-seventeenth century.

Retrospect *See* **Flashback.**

Reversal *See Peripeteia.*

Rhyme The echoing repetition of sounds in the end syllables of words, often (though not always) at the end of a line of poetry.

Rhyme Scheme The pattern of **rhyme** throughout a particular poem.

Rhythm The sequence of stressed and unstressed sounds in a poem.

Rising Action Story events that increase tension and move the plot toward the climax.

Rising Meter A **meter** comprised of feet that begin with an unstressed syllable, followed by a stressed syllable or syllables. **Iambic** and **anapestic** feet both create rising meter, which is named for the effect of *rising* from the initial unstressed syllable to the stressed.

Romance *See* **Classifications of Drama.**

Romantic Comedy A type of **comedy** in which two would-be/ should-be lovers find each other after a series of misunderstandings and false starts.

Round Character A **character** with complex, multifaceted characteristics. Round characters behave as real people. For example, a round **hero** may suffer temptation, and a round **villain** may show compassion.

Run-On Line A line of poetry that, when read, does not come to a natural conclusion where the line breaks. *See* **Enjambment.**

Sarcasm Verbal irony that is intended in a mean-spirited, malicious, or critical way.

Satire An artistic critique, sometimes heated, on some aspect of human immorality or absurdity.

Satiric Comedy A derisive and dark **comedy** in which there is no promise that good will prevail.

Satyr Play An often obscene satirical fourth play, provided after a trilogy of tragedies, meant to provide **comic relief.**

Scansion The process of determining the metrical pattern of a line of poetry by marking its stresses and feet.

Scene A defined moment of action or interaction in a story usually confined to a single **setting.** Scenes are the building blocks of a story's **plot.**

Scenery The set pieces and stage decorations onstage during the performance of a play.

Scratch Outline A multi-tiered, ordered list of topics that should be covered in a paper. A scratch outline goes into deeper detail than a topic outline.

Screenplay A script that is specifically tailored and structured for television or film rather than the stage.

Script The written text of a play, which may include set descriptions and actor cues.

Second-Person Narrator A **narrator** who addresses the character as *you,* often involving the reader by association.

Semiotics The study of how meaning is attached to and communicated by symbols.

Sentence Outline An outline that uses complete sentences instead of brief words or phrases.

Sestet Six lines of poetry grouped together in a stanza or a unit of thought, as in the **Petrarchan sonnet** where the last six lines of the poem resolve the idea or question set up by the initial **octave.**

Sestina A poem of six six-line **stanzas** and a three-line **envoi,** usually unrhymed, in which each stanza repeats the end words of the lines of the first stanza, but in different order, the envoi using the six words again, three in the middle of the lines and three at the end.

Setting The time and place where the story occurs. Setting creates expectations for the types of **characters** and situations encountered in the story.

Shakespearean (English) Sonnet A **sonnet** form composed of three quatrains and a final couplet, all in **iambic pentameter** and rhymed *abab cdcd efef gg.* The **volta,** or turn, occurs in the final **couplet** of the poem.

Short Story A brief fictional narrative that attempts to dramatize or illustrate the effect or meaning of a single incident or small group of incidents in the life of a single **character** or small group of characters.

Simile A direct comparison of two dissimilar things using the words *like* or *as.*

Situational Irony A situation portrayed in a poem when what occurs is the opposite or very different from what's expected to occur.

Skene The stage in the Greek **amphitheater.**

Slam Poetry in a variety of styles, performed competitively in clubs and halls.

Slant Rhyme A case in which vowel or consonant sounds are similar but not exactly the same, such as *heap* and *rap* and *tape*. Also called *near rhyme, imperfect rhyme* and *off rhyme*.

Slapstick A type of low **comedy** characterized by unexpected, often physical humor. A classic example of slapstick is the man walking along who accidentally slips on a banana peel.

Social Environment A study of **setting** that considers era and location as well as a **character's** living and working conditions.

Sociological Criticism The study of literary texts as products of the cultural, political, and economic context of the author's time and place.

Soliloquy A **monologue** delivered by a **character** in a play who is alone onstage. Soliloquies generally have a **character** revealing his or her thoughts to the audience.

Sonnet A poem of fourteen lines of **iambic pentameter** in a recognizable pattern of **rhyme.** Sonnets contain a **volta,** or turn, in which the last lines resolve or change direction from the controlling idea of the preceding lines.

Sound The rhythmic structure of the lines of a poem, which draws the reader in, often utilizing **rhyme** and created through word choice and word order.

Spoken Word Poetry Poetry that derives from the **Beat** poets, characterized by emphasis of the *performance* of a poem over the written form. Spoken word often employs improvisation.

Spondee A poetic foot characterized by two stressed syllables.

Stage Directions Cues, included by the playwright in the script of a play, which inform the actions of the actors during the play.

Stanza A unit of two or more lines, set off by a space, often sharing the same **rhythm** and **meter.**

Stasimon In Greek **tragedy,** an ode performed by the **Chorus** which interprets and responds to the preceding scene.

Static Character A **character,** often flat, who does not change over the course of the story.

Stock Character A **character** who represents a concept or type of behavior, such as a "mean teacher" or "mischievous student," and offers readers the comfort of repetition and reliability.

Stream of Consciousness: A **character's** thoughts are presented flowing by in free association, and the literary convention that rules is that there is no writer mediating the consciousness of the subject.

Stress The vocal emphasis on a syllable in a line of verse, largely a matter of pitch.

Structuralism Structuralist literary critics work from the belief that a given work of literature can be fully understood only when a reader considers the system of conventions, or the *genre* to which it belongs or responds.

Style The characteristic way in which any writer uses language.

Subplot A **plot** that is not the central plot of the work, but nonetheless appears in the same work. Longer works, like **novels** and plays, tend to have subplots that might follow side **characters** or somehow affect the action of the main plot.

Summary Restating concisely the main ideas of a text without adding opinion or commentary. The best approach to summary is to divide the text into its major sections and then write a sentence for each section stating its main idea.

Summary Paper A short paper that represents the main ideas of the text as the author has presented them, excluding any subjective ideas or interpretations.

Surrealism A technique of the modern theater in which the realms of conscious and unconscious experience are fused together to create a total reality. In this way the fiction writer, poet, and **playwright,** tap into the resources of the unconscious mind and the imagination and portray in story on the page or on the modern stage the stuff of human desire, hope, and dreams.

Suspense A sense of anticipation or excitement about what will happen and how the **characters** will deal with their newfound predicament.

Syllabic verse A verse form that uses a fixed number of syllables per line or stanza, regardless of the number of stressed or unstressed syllables.

Symbol Any object, **image, character,** or action that suggests meaning beyond the everyday literal level.

Symbolic Act A gesture or action beyond the everyday practical definition.

Synecdoche A **figure of speech** that uses a piece or part of a thing to represent the thing in its entirety. For example, in the Biblical saying that man does not live by bread alone, *bread* stands for the larger concept of food or physical sustenance.

Synopsis A **summary** or **précis** of a work.

Syntax The meaningful arrangement of words and phrases. Syntax can refer to word placement and order, as well as the overall length and shape of a sentence.

Synthesis The act of bringing together the ideas and observations generated by reading and analysis in order to make a concrete statement about a work.

Tactile Imagery Imagery that appeals to a reader's sense of touch.

Tercet A group of three lines of poetry, sometimes called a **triplet** when all three lines rhyme.

Terminal Refrain Repeated lines which appear at the end of each **stanza** in a poem.

Terza Rima A **tercet** fixed form featuring the interlocking rhyme scheme *aba, bcb, cdc, ded*, etc.

Tetrameter A poetic **meter** that contains four feet in each line.

Theme The central or underlying meanings of a literary work.

Thesis Statement A sentence, usually but not always included in a paper's introductory paragraph, that defines a paper's purpose and argument.

Thesis A paper's purpose and **argument,** defined by the **thesis statement** and proved by the paper's **conclusion.**

Third-Person Narrator A **narrator** who is outside the story. The narrator refers to all the **characters** in the story with the pronouns *he, she,* or *they.*

Tiring House In the Elizabethan theater, a room, adjoined to the stage, in which actors changed their costumes.

Tone The author's attitude toward his or her **characters** or subject matter.

Topic Outline A multi-tiered organization of a paper's topics and **arguments,** used to structure a paper.

Tragedy A dramatic form in which **characters** face serious and important challenges that end in disastrous failure or defeat for the **protagonist.** *See* **Classifications of Drama.**

Tragic Flaw In classical literature, the hero's weakness that causes his downfall.

Tragic Hero A heroic **protagonist** who from the beginning, due to some innate flaw in his **character** or some unforeseeable mistake (*see* **Tragic Flaw**), is doomed. The inevitability of a tragic hero's demise inspires sympathy in the audience.

Tragic Irony The situation in a **tragedy** where the audience is aware of the **tragic hero's** fate although the **character** has not yet become aware.

Tragicomedy A play with the elements of **tragedy** that ends happily.

Transferred Epithet A description that pairs an adjective with a noun that does not logically follow, such as *silver sounds.*

Trimeter A poetic **meter** that contains three feet in each line.

Triplet A **tercet** of three rhymed lines.

Trochaic Meter: A poetic **meter** created when each line contains more than one **trochee** (a unit with a stressed syllable followed by an unstressed syllable). Trochaic meter is a type of **falling meter.**

Trochee A poetic **foot** consisting of a stressed syllable followed by an unstressed syllable. The opposite of an **iamb,** and so sometimes called an "inverted foot," often beginning a line of **iambic pentameter.**

Understatement A purposeful underestimation of something, used to emphasize its actual magnitude.

Unreliable Narrator A **narrator** who cannot be trusted to present an undistorted account of the action because of inexperience, ignorance, personal bias, intentional deceptiveness, or even insanity.

Verbal Irony A statement in which the stated meaning is very different (sometimes opposite) from the implied meaning.

Verisimilitude How alike an imitation is to its original. The goal of literature, especially when written in the mode of realism, is to provide a likeness, or a verisimilitude, of real life.

Verse A broad term to describe poetic lines.

Vers libre See **Free Verse.**

Villanelle A poem consisting of five **tercets** and a concluding **quatrain.** Each tercet rhymes *aba* and the final quatrain rhymes *abaa.* The poem's opening line repeats as the final line of the second and fourth stanzas, and in the second-to-last line of the poem. The last line of the first **stanza** repeats as the final line of the third and fifth stanzas and is also the final line of the poem overall.

Visual imagery **Imagery** and descriptions that appeal to a reader's sense of sight.

Voice The unique sound of an author's writing, created by elements such as **diction, tone,** and sentence construction.

Volta In a sonnet, the turn where a shift in thought or emotion occurs. In the **Petrarchan sonnet,** the **volta** occurs between the **octave** and the **sestet;** in the **Shakespearean sonnet,** the ending couplet provides the volta.

Vulgate A term to describe the common people, often used in reference to a level of speech or **diction.**

Well-made Play A type of theater popularized in France. Well-made plays feature a three-act sequence that *poses* a problem, *complicates* and then *resolves* it; usually that **resolution** comes when a **character's** past is revealed. The first act offers *exposition,* the second a *situation,* the third an unraveling or *completion.* Meticulous plotting and **suspense** are components of this mode of theater.

Working Bibliography A list of all the sources consulted in preparing a paper, as well as all the information necessary to cite them in the final list of works cited.

Works Cited A list of all the primary and secondary sources consulted in the creation of a paper.

Credits

Photo Credits

Index

Note: Page references in **boldface** refer to literary works included in their entirety.